THE AMERICAN JOURNEY

A History of the United States

Brief Edition

COMBINED VOLUME

DAVID GOLDFIELD

CARL ABBOTT

VIRGINIA DeJOHN ANDERSON

JO ANN E. ARGERSINGER

PETER H. ARGERSINGER

WILLIAM L. BARNEY

ROBERT M. WEIR

Prentice Hall, Upper Saddle River, New Jersey 07458

Library of Congress Cataloging-in-Publication Data

The American journey: a history of the United States / David Goldfield . . .
[et al.]—Brief combined ed.
  p.   cm.
Includes bibliographical references and index.
ISBN 0-13-656653-7
1. United States—History. I. Goldfield David R., (date)
E178.1.A4925 1998a
973—dc21   97-49900
                                                          CIP

Editorial director: Charlyce Jones Owen
Director of production and manufacturing:
  Barbara Kittle
Editorial/production supervision: Judith Winthrop
  and Barbara DeVries
Development editors: David Chodoff and Gerald
  Lombardi
Development of Brief Edition: Sarah Lewis and
  Rekha Packer
Marketing manager: Sheryl Adams
Executive manager, new media: Alison Pendergast

Editorial assistant: Holly Brown
Copy editor: Bruce Emmer
Creative director: Leslie Osher
Design director: Carole Anson
Interior and cover designer: Carole Anson
Photo editor: Lorinda Morris-Nantz
Photo researcher: Kathy Ringrose
Fact checker: Ann Hofstra Grogg
Manufacturing manager: Nick Sklitsis
Manufacturing buyer: Lynn Pearlman
Line art coordinator: Michele Giusti

Cartographer: CARTO-GRAPHICS with shaded relief from
  Mountain High Maps®, Digital Wisdom, Inc.
Cover art: William Hahn, American, 1829–1887, "Sacramento
  Railroad Station," 1874. Oil on canvas, Mounted on board, 53¾ x
  87¾ in. Signed lower right: Wm. Hahn. (Copyright) The Fine Arts
  Museums of San Francisco. Gift of the M. H. de Young
  Endowment Fund, 54936.

This book was set in 10.5/12 New Baskerville Roman by
  HSS in-house formatting and production services group
  and was printed and bound by Von Hoffman Press, Inc.
  The cover was printed by The Lehigh Press, Inc.

 © 1998 by Prentice-Hall, Inc.
Simon & Schuster/A Viacom Company
Upper Saddle River, NJ 07458

Printed in the United States of America
10 9 8 7 6 5 4 3 2

ISBN 0-13-656653-7

Prentice Hall International (UK) Limited, *London*
Prentice-Hall of Australia Pty. Limited, *Sydney*
Prentice-Hall Canada Inc., *Toronto*
Prentice-Hall Hispanoamericana, S.A., *Mexico*

Prentice-Hall of India Private Limited, *New Delhi*
Prentice-Hall of Japan, Inc., *Tokyo*
Simon & Schuster Asia Pte. Ltd., *Singapore*
Editora Prentice-Hall do Brasil, Ltda., *Rio de Janeiro*

FOR OUR STUDENTS, WHO HELPED US WRITE THIS BOOK.

CONTENTS

5

IMPERIAL BREAKDOWN,
1763-1774   78

6

THE WAR FOR INDEPENDENCE,
1774-1783   94

7

THE FIRST REPUBLIC,
1776-1789 116

WE THE PEOPLE 1789 136

8

A NEW REPUBLIC
AND THE RISE OF PARTIES,
1789-1800 138

9

THE TRIUMPH AND COLLAPSE
OF JEFFERSONIAN REPUBLICANISM,
1800-1824 154

10
THE JACKSONIAN ERA,
1824-1845   172

11
INDUSTRIAL CHANGE AND URBANIZATION,
1820-1850   190

12
THE WAY WEST   208

13
SLAVERY AND THE OLD SOUTH,
1800-1860   227

14

REFORMING ANTEBELLUM SOCIETY, 1815-1850   245

15

THE POLITICS OF SECTIONALISM, 1846-1861   264

16

BATTLE CRIES AND FREEDOM SONGS THE CIVIL WAR, 1861-1863   283

17
THE UNION PRESERVED
THE CIVIL WAR, 1863-1865   303

WE THE PEOPLE 1789-1865   318

18
RECONSTRUCTION, 1865-1877   321

19
A NEW SOUTH, 1877-1900   337

20

INDUSTRY, IMMIGRANTS, AND CITIES, 1870-1900   357

21

TRANSFORMING THE WEST, 1865-1890   381

22

POLITICS AND GOVERNMENT, 1877-1900   398

23

THE PROGRESSIVE ERA, 1900-1917   416

24

CREATING AN EMPIRE, 1865-1917   438

25

AMERICA AND THE GREAT WAR, 1914-1920   456

26
Toward a Modern America: The 1920s   476

27
The Great Depression and the New Deal, 1929-1939   495

28

WORLD WAR II, 1939-1945　514

29

THE COLD WAR AT HOME AND ABROAD, 1946-1952　534

30

THE CONFIDENT YEARS, 1953-1964　552

31
SHAKEN TO THE ROOTS,
1965-1980   570

32
SHAPING A NEW AMERICA,
1965-1995   586

FIGURES AND TABLES

Summary Tables

MAPS

American Views

PREFACE

The personal journeys that led each of us to *The American Journey* began in the classroom with our students. We wrote this book for them. Responding to the many American history textbooks we have subjected them to over the years, they have let us know what they liked and disliked, what they found difficult and what they grasped easily, what they skipped and what they devoured, what stories resonated with their own experiences and what seemed unconnected to them and their world.

But if we wrote this book to appeal to our students, we also wrote it to engage their minds. We wanted to avoid academic trendiness, particularly the restricting categories that have divided the discipline of history over the last twenty years or so. We believe that the distinctions involved in the debates about multiculturalism and identity, between social and political history, between the history of the common people and the history of the elite, are unnecessarily confusing.

What we seek is integration—to combine political and social history, to fit the experience of particular groups into the broader perspective of the American past, to give voice to minor and major players alike because of their role in the story we have to tell.

What is that story? A principal theme of *The American Journey* is the emergence of distinctively American ideals and the way the conflict between those ideals and reality has shaped the nation's development. At best, that conflict has broadened the understanding and application of American ideals to more and more formerly excluded people. This is not to say that American history is a heroic tale of constant improvement. Many conflicts over the meaning of our ideals have been resolved, if at all, only after great struggle. The United States is a diverse nation not always comfortable with its diversity but confronted—in the words of its founding documents, particularly the Declaration of Independence—with ideals that set a higher standard than its people might otherwise set for themselves. We remind the readers, our students, in "We the People" essays placed at strategic junctures in the text, what those ideals are and how and why we are or are not making progress in fulfilling them. You might call the essays the "reality checks" for this text, a taking stock of where we are at crucial periods in our history.

APPROACH

In telling our story, we had some definite ideas about what we might include and emphasize that other texts do not—information we felt that the current and next generations of students will need to know about our past to function best in a new society. We wanted to present that information in a clear, engaging style in such a way that it would stick with students after the course is over.

CHRONOLOGICAL ORGANIZATION: A strong chronological backbone supports the book. We have found that the jumping back and forth in time characteristic of some American history textbooks confuses students. They abhor dates but need to know the sequence of events in history. A chronological presentation is the best way to be sure they do.

GEOGRAPHICAL LITERACY: We also want students to be geographically literate. We expect them not only to know what happened in American history, but where it happened as well, for physical locations and spatial relationships were often important in shaping historical events. *The American Journey* has more than 70 maps, all numbered and called out in the text. They are an integral part of our story.

COVERAGE OF THE SOUTH AND WEST: The South and the West play significant roles in this text. American history is too often written from a Northeastern perspective, at least when it comes to discussing cities, economic development, and reform. But not only were the South and West developing in their own ways throughout American history, they were and remain important keys to the emerging character of the nation as a whole.

POINT OF VIEW: *The American Journey* presents a balanced overview of the American past. But "balanced" does not mean bland. We do not shy away from definite positions on controversial issues. If students and instructors disagree, that's great; discussion and dissent are important catalysts for understanding and learning.

RELIGION: Nor do we shy away from some topics that play relatively minor roles in other texts, like religion. Historians are often uncomfortable writing about religion and tend to slight its influence. This text stresses the importance of religion in American society both as a source of strength and as a reflection of some its more troubling aspects.

Historians write mostly for each other. That's too bad. We need to reach out and expand our audience. An American history text is a good place to start. Our students are not only our future historians but, more important, the future of the country. Let their American journey begin!

THE BRIEF EDITION

We prepared the brief version of our text, *The American Journey*, in response to the demand for abridged textbooks in the field, by instructors who wanted to use readings, computer simulations, or a variety of other sources of information as well as a textbook in their courses.

The Brief Edition of *The American Journey* is about 60 percent as long as the complete version. We cut 25 percent of the text, and made up the rest of the cuts by eliminating some of the photographs and maps. In cutting the text, deletions were made on a line-by-line basis, mostly by cutting extra details and examples. Painful as that process was, we are pleased that we were able to keep all of the topics covered in the big book, the narrative chronology, and many of the revealing quotes. All of the pedagogical features are still there—the key topics at the beginning of the chapter, the chronologies, summary tables, and primary source documents in the body of the chapter, and the review questions at the end of the chapter.

FEATURES OF THE TEXT

The American Journey includes an array of features and pedagogical tools designed to make American history accessible to students.

- ❖ The **Student Tool Kit** that follows this preface helps students get the most out of the text and its features. It introduces students to key conventions of historical writing, and it explains how to read maps, graphs, and tables.
- ❖ An **outline** and **key topics** list give students a succinct overview of each chapter.
- ❖ Each chapter begins with an engaging **opening story** that highlights important themes.
- ❖ The **American Views** box in each chapter contains a relevant primary source document. Taken from letters, diaries, newspapers, government papers, and other sources, these bring the people of the past and their concerns vividly alive. An *introduction* and *prereading questions* relate the documents to the text and direct students' attention to important issues.

- ❖ **Summary tables** in each chapter provide an overview of complex issues.
- ❖ Chapter **chronologies** help students build a framework of key events.
- ❖ **Key terms** are highlighted within each chapter and defined in an end-of-book **glossary.**
- ❖ Chapter **review questions** help students review the material in a chapter and relate it to broader themes.
- ❖ Lists of **key readings** and **additional sources** at the end of each chapter directs interested students to further information about the subject of the chapter.
- ❖ **Where To Learn More** sections describe important historical sites students can visit to gain a deeper understanding of the events discussed in the chapter.
- ❖ Four **We the People essays** focus on the relationship between American ideals and American reality at critical junctures in the nation's history—after the ratification of the Constitution, after the Civil War, after World War I, and at the present.

SUPPLEMENTARY INSTRUCTIONAL MATERIALS

The American Journey comes with an extensive package of supplementary print and multimedia materials for both instructors and students.

Print Supplements
Instructor's Resource Manual
Test Item File
Prentice Hall Custom Test,
Transparency Pack
Study Guide (Volumes I and II)
The American Journey: Documents in U.S. History (Vols. I and II)
Reading Critically about History
Understanding and Answering Essay Questions
Themes of the Times
Retrieving the American Past: A Customized U.S. History Reader

Multimedia Supplements
History on the Internet
The American Journey, Interactive Edition
The American Journey World Wide Web
Companion Study Guide
Powerpoint U.S. History

STUDENT TOOL KIT

In writing history, historians use various tools such as maps, tables, and chronologies to help their readers understand the past. This book contains many of these tools. What follows is a simple explanation of how to use the historians' tools that are in this book.

TEXT

The text itself, whether a biography of George Washington, an article on the Civil War, or a survey of American history such as this one, is the historian's basic tool for discussing the past. Historians write about the past in two ways, narration and analysis, and this book contains both types of writing. Narration is the story line of history. It tells what happened in the past, who did it, and where and when it occurred. Most of the text of this book is narration. Narration is also used to describe how people in the past lived, how they spent their daily lives, and even, when the historical evidence allows, what they thought, felt, feared, or desired. Analysis tells you *why* historians think events in the past happened the way they did. Analysis offers an explanation for the narrative, for the story of history. In this book, you will find narration and analysis interwoven in each chapter.

This book also contains a number of features that are designed to help you study history. Each chapter begins with a short list of *Key Topics* that high-

lights the most important points that will be made in the chapter. Each chapter ends with a brief *Conclusion* section that puts the subject of the chapter in the broader perspective of U.S. history. Both the *Key Topics* and the *Conclusion* are study aids. You can

Map 5-1 Colonial Settlement and the Proclamation line of 1763
This map depicts the regions claimed and settled by the major groups competing for territory in eastern North America. With the Proclamation Line of 1763, positioned along the crest of the Appalachian Mountains, the British government tried to stop the westward migration of settlers under its jurisdiction, and thereby limit conflict with the Indians. The result, however, was frustration and anger on the part of land-hungry settlers.

use them to help you review your understanding of the text itself.

MAPS

Most of the chapters in this book contain maps. Maps are important historical tools. They show how geography has affected history and can concisely summarize complex relationships and events. You need to know how to "read" a map to absorb the information it has to offer. To help you understand how to do this, let's look at an example, Map 5-1 from Chapter 5. The map shows the British colonies on the eastern seaboard of North America in 1763, about twelve years before the American Revolution. It has three features to help you read it: a caption, a legend, and a scale. The caption is a paragraph of text that explains the historical significance of the map, that is, the point it is designed to make. Here the caption tells us that in 1763, the British government attempted to restrict colonial settlement to the eastern side of the Appalachian Mountains so that the colonists would not come into conflict with the Indian tribes who lived west of the mountains or had earlier been pushed there. Colonial frustration with this policy contributed to the outbreak of the American Revolution.

The legend and the scale appear at the lower right of the map. The legend tells you what the symbols on the map mean. Using it, we see that the solid line stretching along the Appalachian Mountains from Maine to Georgia represents the Proclamation Line of 1763—the line meant to restrict colonial settlement. Colonial capitals are marked with a dot in a circle, and forts with a black square. Spanish territory west of the Mississippi River is colored orange; territory settled by Europeans is colored green. The map also shows the lands inhabited by Indian tribes—Algonquins, Mohegans, Delawares, Creeks, and others. Note that these territories are not bounded by the solid lines the way the colonies are. The tribal lands of Native Americans did not have formal boundaries mapped out by surveyors. The scale tells us that 7/8 inch on the map represents 300 miles (about 480 kilometers) on the ground. You can use this information to estimate the distance between points on the map.

The map also shows us the topography of the region—its mountains, rivers, and lakes. This helps us understand how geography influenced history in this case. You can see, for example, that the Appalachian Mountains divide the eastern seaboard from the rest of the continent. The mountains obstructed colonial migration to the west for a long time. By running the Proclamation Line along the Appalachians, the British hoped to use this natural barrier to separate Indians and colonists. Note how small the green areas, the areas of European settlement, are, relative to the immense size of North America. Note also how the map shows that the Europeans tended to settle near the coasts and along rivers and across plains.

SUMMARY TABLES

Tables summarize information by organizing it into columns and rows. The *Summary Tables* in this text are a special feature designed to help you understand some important aspect of a chapter. The Summary Table on page 73 in Chapter 4, for example, summarizes information about the various colonial wars that were fought in North America between 1689 and 1763. Besides listing the wars by name, it allows you to compare how long each war lasted and what the results of each war were.

CHRONOLOGIES

Each chapter has a *Chronology*, a list of the key events discussed in the chapter arranged in chronological order, that is, according to the date on which they happened. The word *chronology* comes from the ancient Greek word for "time," *chronos*. A chronology is like a historical calendar, giving the dates of important events. The chronology in Chapter 2 on page 24 lists the dates of key events in the colonization of North America from 1603 to 1681. Chronologies can help you understand when important events occurred and their relationship to one another.

PRIMARY SOURCE DOCUMENTS

Our knowledge of the past comes from many sources. These include artworks like paintings, drawings, and sculptures as well as material artifacts like buildings and tools. Historians find most of their information, however, in written records, original documents that have survived from the past. These include government publications, letters, diaries, newspapers—whatever people wrote or printed, including many private documents never intended for publication. Each chapter in the book contains a feature called *American Views* with a selection from a primary source document. Each begins with a brief introduction followed by several questions to help you think about the selection. Within the documents themselves—as well as in other quoted material throughout the text—you will often encounter two types of punctuation with which you may not be familiar: ellipsis points and brackets. Points of ellipsis—three dots . . . —indicate that words have been edited out to save space or remove irrelevant material. This is often done when reprinting original documents. Brackets [ ] are printed around words or sentences that the authors of this book have added to the documents to clarify or improve your understanding. Brackets tell you that the words within them have been added, just as ellipsis points tell you that words have been left out.

RECOMMENDED READING AND WHERE TO LEARN MORE

At the end of each chapter is a list of books that you can read to deepen your knowledge of what was discussed in the chapter. *Recommended Reading* is annotated—that is, the authors of this text explain what is important about each of these books. The section called *Where to Learn More* lists historical sites and museums where you can go to gain a deeper understanding of the events discussed in the chapter.

GLOSSARY

Significant historical terms are emphasized with **heavy type** throughout the text. These are listed alphabetically and defined in the *glossary* at the end of the book.

PHOTO CREDITS

1 WORLDS APART

KEY TOPICS

❖ Native American, West African, and European society on the eve of contact
❖ The reasons for Europe's impulse to global exploration
❖ The Spanish, French, and English experiences in America in the sixteenth century
❖ Consequences of contact between the Old and New Worlds

By October 11, 1492, the three tiny ships had been sailing westward for more than five weeks. Over 3,000 miles of empty ocean separated them from their last landfall, in the Canary Islands off the coast of North Africa. Several times sailors had claimed to see land, but their sightings proved only mirages. Officers and crew threatened mutiny unless they turned back for Spain. The admiral, Christopher Columbus, still confident that he could reach Asia and its riches by sailing west across the Atlantic, asked for two or three more days. His men agreed. Scouring sea and sky for signs, they saw floating branches and flying birds but still no land. Surely tomorrow night they would turn around.

Then on October 12, in the pale light of dawn, a sliver of white sand beach appeared. As the ships drew closer, the men thought they could smell the rich spices of the Orient. They searched the horizon for the golden-roofed temples about which they had heard so much. What they did not know was that this land was not the Orient.

Many historians believe Columbus landed on an island in the Bahamas now called Watling Island. Remarking on their nakedness and few possessions, Columbus judged the island inhabitants—part of a group called the Tainos— "a people very poor in everything," although he noticed that a few of them wore gold nose ornaments. What the Tainos thought of Columbus and his men will never be known.

Thus began one of the most momentous encounters in human history. Columbus claimed the island as a possession of the monarchs of Spain and, grateful for his safe arrival, renamed it San Salvador (Holy Savior). Still convinced that he was near Asia, he did not realize he had found what was soon to be called the New World. At first, of course, it was new only to Europeans ignorant of its existence, not to the people whose ancestors had lived there for thousands of years. Columbus's voyage would ultimately bring together people who had previously lived in worlds apart—Native American, African, and European—to forge a world that was new in fact as well as name.

Different Worlds

The New World that emerged after 1492 reflected the experience of the people who built it. Spain, Portugal, France, and England, competing for political, economic, and religious domination within Europe, carried their conflict over into the Americas. Native Americans drew upon their familiarity with the land and its resources, their long-established patterns of political and religious authority, and their well-developed systems of trade and warfare to deal with the European newcomers. And when faced with a need for labor in the New World, Europeans turned to the West African slave market they had already known for half a century.

Native American Societies before 1492

Convinced that he had landed in the East Indies, Columbus called the people he met *indios.* His error is preserved in the word *Indian,* used by Europeans to identify the original inhabitants of the two American continents.

By 1492, the continents of North and South America had been inhabited for a very long time—estimates range from 15,000 to 50,000 years. The human population of the two continents may have been as high as 70 million—nearly equal to the population of Europe at that time—with only 7 million or so living north of the Rio Grande in what is now the United States and Canada. These people belonged to hundreds of groups, each with its own language or dialect, history, and way of life.

The first Americans were nomadic hunters from Siberia who probably came in three waves across a land bridge that once connected Siberia and Alaska. They gradually ranged southward and eastward. Within a few thousand years, their descendants had spread throughout North and South America.

These early hunters, whom archaeologists call **Paleo-Indians,** traveled in small bands, tracking and killing mammoths, bison, and other large game. But Paleo-Indians were also resourceful hunters who crafted sharp stone points for their spears. Their efficiency may in fact have led to overhunting. The world's climate also began to grow warmer, turning grasslands into deserts and reducing the animals' food supply, hastening the animals' disappearance. By around 9000 B.C., mammoths, mastodons, and other large animals had become extinct in the Americas. This meant that humans too had to find other food sources.

With a warmer climate, melting glaciers raised the sea level, created coastal marshes, and filled the Great Lakes and inland rivers. Forests with many varieties of trees and bushes replaced grasslands and stands of evergreens. The largest animals had disappeared, but many smaller creatures roamed the land and swam in rivers and lakes. Deserts appeared in much of the West, with sparser plant and animal life.

Between roughly 8000 B.C. and 1500 B.C.—what archaeologists call the **Archaic** period—Indians adapted to regional environments, learning to use local resources efficiently. Along North America's northeast coast, for instance, they became proficient fishermen who took small boats out onto the North Atlantic to catch swordfish and perhaps even whales. In the Southwest, people hunted desert-dwelling mammals and birds and gathered various nuts, seeds, and roots.

More efficient food collection led to other changes in the Archaic period. Populations grew, and people began living in larger villages with recognized leaders. Men did most of the hunting and fishing. Women remained closer to home, gathering and preparing wild plant foods and caring for children. Each group probably made the tools it used, with men carving fishhooks and arrowheads and women making such items as bone needles and baskets.

Archaic Indians also collected local nonfood resources, including rocks, shells, and bones. They fashioned goods from these materials and traded them with other peoples, sometimes hundreds of miles away. At Indian Knoll, in western Kentucky, archaeologists have found copper from the Great Lakes area and shells from as far away as the Gulf of Mexico. Ideas as well as goods circulated among Archaic Indian peoples. Across the continent, human burials became more elaborate, suggesting that ideas about death and the afterlife passed between groups. Bodies might be wrapped in woven mats or cloths, and the deceased's personal possessions were often placed in the grave.

Near the end of the Archaic period, some groups began farming. Around 5000 B.C., the people

CHRONOLOGY

c. 50,000–15,000 B.C.	Ancestors of Native Americans cross Bering land bridge.
c. 10,000–9000 B.C.	Paleo-Indians expand through the Americas.
c. 9000 B.C.	Extinction of large land mammals in North America.
c. 8000–1500 B.C.	Archaic Indian era.
c. 5000 B.C.	Beginnings of agriculture in Mesoamerica.
c. 1500 B.C.	Earliest mound-building culture begins.
c. 500 B.C.–A.D. 400	Adena-Hopewell mound-building culture.
c. A.D. 700–1600	Rise of West African empires.
c. 900	First mounds built at Cahokia. Anasazi expansion.
c. 1000	Spread of Islam in West Africa.
c. 1000–1500	Last mound-building culture, the Mississippian.
c. 1290s	Anasazi dispersal into smaller pueblos.
1400–1600	Renaissance in Europe.
1430s	Beginnings of Portuguese slave trade in West Africa.

1492	Christopher Columbus's first voyage. End of *reconquista* in Spain.
1494	Treaty of Tordesillas.
1497	John Cabot visits Nova Scotia and Newfoundland.
1497–1499	Vasco da Gama sails around Africa to reach India.
1517	Protestant Reformation begins in Germany.
1519–1521	Hernán Cortés conquers the Aztec empire.
1532–1533	Francisco Pizarro conquers the Inca empire.
1534–1542	Jacques Cartier explores eastern Canada for France.
1542–1543	Roberval's failed colony in Canada.
1540–1542	Coronado explores southwestern North America.
1558	Elizabeth I becomes queen of England.
1565	Spanish establish outpost at St. Augustine in Florida.
1560s–1580s	English renew attempts to conquer Ireland.
1587	Founding of "Lost Colony" of Roanoke.
1598	Spanish found colony at New Mexico.

of southern Mexico started raising an ancient type of maize, or corn. At first, farming supplemented a diet still largely dependent on hunting and gathering. But agriculture gradually became more widespread. In addition to maize, the main crop in both South and North America, farmers in Mexico, Central America, and the Peruvian Andes learned to cultivate manioc, peppers, beans, pumpkins, squash, avocados, sweet and white potatoes (native to the Peruvian highlands), and tomatoes. Mexican farmers also grew cotton. Maize and bean cultivation spread from Mexico in a wide arc to the north and east. Peoples in what is now the southwestern United States began farming between 1500 and 500 B.C., and by A.D. 200, farmers tilled the soil in present-day Georgia and Florida.

Wherever agriculture took hold, populations grew, since farming produced a more secure food supply than hunting and gathering. Permanent villages appeared as farmers settled near their fields.

In places such as central Mexico, agriculture eventually sustained the populations of large cities. Trade in agricultural surpluses flowed through existing exchange networks and may have created new links. In many Indian societies, women's status improved because of their role as the principal farmers. Specialized craft workers made technological and artistic advances in producing pottery and baskets to store harvested grains. Even religious beliefs and practices reflected the centrality of farming. In describing the origins of their people, Pueblo Indians of the Southwest compared their emergence from the underworld to a maize plant sprouting from the earth.

Despite their diversity, certain generalizations can be made about societies that developed within broad regions, or **culture areas** (see Map 1-1). Throughout the North and West, Indians did not adopt agriculture. In the challenging environment

Map 1-1   North American Culture Areas, c. 1500
Over the course of centuries, Indian peoples in North America developed distinctive cultures suited to the environments in which they lived. Inhabitants of each culture area shared basic patterns of subsistence, craft work, and social organization. Most, but not all, Indian peoples combined farming with hunting and gathering.

of the Arctic and Subarctic, small nomadic bands moved seasonally to fish, follow game, and, in the brief summers, gather wild berries. Far to the north, Eskimos and Aleuts hunted whales, walruses, seals, and other sea mammals. Further inland, the Crees and other peoples followed migrating herds of caribou and moose. Northern peoples fashioned tools and weapons of bone and ivory, clothing and boats from animal skins, and houses of whalebones and hides or blocks of sod or snow.

Along the Northwest Coast and Columbia River Plateau, people developed a settled way of life without agriculture. With rivers teeming with salmon and other fish and forests full of game and edible plants, these were some of the most densely populated areas of North America. Among groups like the Kwakiutls and Chinooks, extended families lived in large communal houses constructed of cedar planks. These were often located in villages of several hundred people, where chiefs ruled over lower-ranking individuals.

Farther south, in present-day California, hunter-gatherers lived in smaller villages of perhaps one hundred people. A single chief often led several villages. These settlements usually adjoined oak groves, where Indians gathered acorns. To protect their access to this important food, chiefs and villagers vigorously defended their territorial claims to the oak groves.

Small nomadic bands in the Great Basin, where the climate was warm and dry, lived in caves and rock shelters. Shoshone hunters captured antelope in corrals and trapped small game, such as groundhogs, squirrels, and rabbits. In present-day Utah and western Colorado, Utes hunted elk, bison, and mountain sheep and fished in mountain streams. Women gathered pinyon nuts, seeds, and wild berries. In hard times, people ate rattlesnakes, horned toads, and insects. They celebrated whenever food was plentiful and urged religious leaders to seek supernatural help when starvation loomed.

Mesoamerica, the birthplace of agriculture in North America, extends from central Mexico into Central America. A series of complex, literate, urban cultures emerged in this region, beginning around 1200 B.C. with the Olmecs, who flourished on Mexico's Gulf Coast until 400 B.C. The Olmecs and other early Mesoamerican peoples built cities featuring large pyramids, developed religious practices that included human sacrifice, and devised calendars and writing systems.

Mayan civilization followed, reaching its greatest glory between about A.D. 150 and 900 in the southern Yucatán, creating Mesoamerica's most advanced writing and calendrical systems and developing a sophisticated mathematics that included the concept of zero. The Mayans of the southern Yucatán suffered a decline after 900, but there were still many thriving Mayan centers in the northern Yucatán in 1492. The great city of Teotihuacán dominated central Mexico from the first century to the eighth century A.D. and influenced much of the rest of Mesoamerica through trade and conquest.

Some two hundred years after the fall of Teotihuacán, the Toltecs, a warrior people, rose to prominence, dominating central Mexico from about 900 to

1100. In the wake of the Toltec collapse, the Aztecs, another warrior people, migrated from the north into the Valley of Mexico and built a great empire that soon controlled much of Mesoamerica. The Aztec capital, Tenochtitlán, was a city of great plazas, broad avenues, magnificent temples and palaces, ball courts, busy marketplaces, and residential neighborhoods. Built on islands in the middle of Lake Texcoco, it was connected to the mainland by four broad causeways. In 1492, Tenochtitlán was home to some 200,000 people, one of the largest cities in the world at the time.

In the great pyramid in Tenochtitlán, Aztec priests sacrificed human victims—by cutting open their chests and removing their still-beating hearts—to offer to the gods to prevent them from destroying the earth. Hundreds, even thousands, of victims died in ceremonies that sometimes lasted for days.

Aztec culture expanded through continuous military conquest, driven by a quest for sacrificial victims and for wealth in the form of tribute payments of gold, food, and handcrafted goods. Neighboring peoples hated the Aztecs and submitted to them out of fear. With a powerful ally to lead them, they would readily turn on their overlords and bring the empire down.

Native societies emerging north of Mexico shared certain characteristics with those of Mesoamerica. The introduction of a drought-resistant type of maize (probably from Mexico) into the desert Southwest in 400 B.C. enabled a series of cultures to develop. Beginning about 300 B.C., the Hohokams settled in southern Arizona, eventually building permanent villages of several hundred people. Substantial harvests of beans, corn, and squash, watered by a complex system of canals, fed Hohokam villagers. In large communities, inhabitants built ball courts similar to those found in Mexico. Artisans wove cotton cloth and made goods reflecting Mesoamerican artistic styles out of shell, turquoise, and clay. Extensive trade networks linked the Hohokams to peoples as far away as California and Mexico. Their culture endured for over a thousand years, then disappeared mysteriously by 1450.

Beginning about A.D. 1, the Anasazis (their name is Navajo for "ancient alien ones") settled where the borders of present-day Colorado, Utah, Arizona, and New Mexico meet. They gradually adopted agriculture, adding first maize and later beans and squash to a diet of wild foods. Scarce rainfall, routed through dams and hillside terraces, watered the crops. By 900, Anasazi villagers lived in distinctive multistoried stone houses, often perched high on mesas or carved into steep canyon walls. They included special rooms, or **kivas,** for religious ceremonies. The largest communal dwelling, Pueblo Bonito in New Mexico's Chaco

Canyon, covered 3 acres and contained 650 to 800 rooms to house about 1,200 people.

Anasazi culture reached its peak around the eleventh century. Unusually plentiful rainfall encouraged population growth and village expansion. Networks of roads carried people and goods between villages. By the late 1200s, however, Anasazi culture collapsed, probably due to drought and invasion.

The Pueblo peoples of the Southwest, including the Hopis and Zunis, are the descendants of the Anasazis. In 1492, many lived in large communal dwellings in permanent villages (*pueblo* is the Spanish word for "village"). Pueblo men did most of the farming. Regular public ceremonies reinforced a sense of village identity. Religious rituals directed prayers to the gods for enough rain for the all-important harvest.

The Great Plains of the continent's interior were much less densely settled than the desert Southwest. Scattered villages of Mandans, Pawnees, and other groups clung to tree-lined rivers. Women raised crops and gathered wild plants for food and medicine. Men hunted bison, whose skin and bones were used for clothing, shelter, and tools. Plains Indians moved frequently, seeking more fertile land or better hunting.

The introduction of agriculture transformed native societies in the Eastern Woodlands, a vast territory extending from the Mississippi Valley to the Atlantic seaboard. As early as 2500 B.C., Indians in present-day Missouri and Kentucky grew pumpkins to supplement game and wild plant foods. Peoples in the Ohio Valley were growing corn by 300 B.C. Agriculture did not dominate Woodlands Indian subsistence, however, until about A.D. 700.

As agriculture spread, several "mound-building" societies—named for the large earthworks their members constructed—developed in the Ohio and Mississippi Valleys. The oldest flourished in Louisiana between 1500 and 700 B.C. By 1000 B.C., its main city of five thousand residents served as the center of an extensive trade in quartz, copper, crystal, and other valuable materials. Another mound-building culture, the Adena-Hopewell, appeared in the Ohio Valley between 500 B.C. and A.D. 400. Its members built hundreds of mounds, often in the shapes of humans, birds, and serpents. Most were grave sites, where people were buried with valuable goods, many obtained through long-distance trade.

The last mound-building culture, the Mississippian, emerged between 1000 and 1500 in the Mississippi Valley. One of the largest cities was Cahokia, located on the Mississippi River across from present-day St. Louis. By 1250, Cahokia, the largest city north of Mexico, had perhaps thirty thousand residents,

British Museum, London.

In 1585, the Englishman John White sketched this composite picture of the Algonquian village of Secoton, located in the Eastern Woodlands region of North America in what is now North Carolina. Its details reveal many features of Eastern Woodlands life, including cornfields at different stages of ripeness, easily assembled bark dwellings, an outdoor place of worship (the "place of solemne prayer"), ceremonial dancing, and a tomb for the dead ("the Tombe of their Herounds").

making it about the same size as medieval London. Its central feature was a 100-foot-high mound, the world's largest earthwork.

Cahokia dominated the Mississippian culture, but numerous other Mississippian towns, some with hundreds or thousands of residents, dotted the Woodlands region, linked by extensive trade networks. Artisans crafted pottery and sculpture, often for use in religious ceremonies conducted in large temples built atop platform mounds. Powerful chiefs, thought to be related to the sun, dominated these communities.

Mississippian culture began to decline in the thirteenth century. Food shortages and warfare drove people from the great cities into the countryside. Elements of Mississippian culture survived among dispersed Woodlands people, particularly methods of maize and bean agriculture. By 1492, although the large cities of the Mississippian era had disappeared, Woodlands Indians maintained long-distance trade links throughout the region, with such precious goods as copper, shell beads, and pearls passing among groups.

The Caribbean islanders whom Columbus first encountered descended from ancient cultures. Ancestors of the Tainos probably came from what is now Venezuela. The Guanahatabeys of western Cuba originated in Florida, and the Caribs of the easternmost islands moved from Brazil's Orinoco Valley. Island peoples began farming perhaps in the first century A.D. on clearings made in the tropical forests. Canoes carried trade goods throughout the Caribbean, as well as to Mesoamerica and coastal South America.

By 1492, as many as 4 million people may have inhabited the Caribbean islands. Powerful chiefs ruled over villages, conducted war and diplomacy, and distributed food and other goods obtained as tribute from villagers, who were divided into several social ranks. Elite islanders were easily recognized by their fine clothing, bright feather headdresses, and golden ear and nose ornaments—items that eventually attracted European visitors' attention.

Long before 1492, North America had witnessed centuries of dynamic change. Populations grew and spread across thousands of miles of territory. Farmers developed new varieties of essential food plants. Empires rose and fell. Large cities flourished and disappeared. People formed alliances with trading partners and warred with groups who refused to trade. Because their histories have been preserved in oral traditions and archaeological evidence rather than written documents, they are less distinct, but no less real, than the Europeans whom they would soon meet.

Cultural Perceptions and Misperceptions

Misunderstandings inevitably arose between Indians and Europeans when such dissimilar peoples encountered each other for the first time. Even simple transactions had unexpected results. When Columbus showed swords to the Tainos, for example, "they took them by the edge and through ignorance cut themselves" because they had never seen metal weapons. Similarly, French explorers choked when they tried to smoke unfamiliar Iroquois tobacco, which tasted, one of them reported, like "powdered pepper."

Many misunderstandings, however, had far graver consequences for the outcome of the encounter. Each group struggled to understand the strange behavior and customs of the other. Europeans usually decided that native practices were not just different from their own but inferior. Indians doubtless felt the same, but their opinions about European practices were rarely recorded.

Religious differences were the hardest to reconcile. Seeing no churches or recognizable religious practices among the Tainos, Columbus wrote, "I do not detect in them any religion." His comment derived from his own Christian background. Christian Europeans worshiped one God in an organized church led by trained priests. They preserved their religious traditions in a written bible. Most Indians, however, believed in a variety of gods. They considered nature itself to be sacred and understood certain beings, including plants, animals, and stars, to possess spiritual powers. Indians living north of Mexico preserved religious beliefs through oral traditions, not in writing. Their religious leaders performed ceremonies that mediated between the human and spiritual worlds. Europeans, however, thought that these men were magicians or even witches. They assumed that Indians worshiped the devil and insisted that they adopt Christianity. In the face of this demand, many native peoples doubtless shared the opinion voiced by some Iroquois: "We do not know that God, we have never seen him, we know not who he is."

Europeans also disapproved of the relative equality of men and women they observed among some Native American peoples. Europeans believed that men were naturally superior to women and should dominate them. But in North America they encountered female rulers among the Wampanoags and Powhatans and learned that among groups such as the Hurons, women helped select chiefs. They found that many Indian societies, including the Pueblos, Hurons, and Iroquois, were **matrilineal;** that is, they traced descent through the mother's family line instead of the father's, as Europeans did.

In most Indian societies, women were the principal farmers. Men cleared the fields, but women planted and harvested the crops. They also prepared food, cared for children, made clothing and baskets, carried burdens, and, in some regions, broke down, transported, and reassembled shelters when villages changed location. Europeans, who came from a society in which men did most agricultural work, thought that Indian women lived "a most slavish life." Misjudging the importance of Indian men's role as hunters and warriors, Europeans scorned them as lazy husbands who wasted their time "gambling, sleeping, singing, dancing, smoking or going to feasts." When European women arrived in Massachusetts, Indians in turn ridiculed English husbands "for spoiling good working creatures" because they did not send their wives into the fields.

The ultimate source of conflict between Indians and Europeans was the intention of the Europeans to dominate the land. Within three days of his arrival in America, Columbus announced his intention "not to pass by any island of which I did not take possession" and soon speculated on the possibility of enslaving Indians. Native peoples everywhere would challenge European claims to possession of their lands and resist European attempts at domination.

West African Societies

Many Europeans followed Columbus's lead in exploring what they soon realized was not Asia after all. Yet in the three centuries after 1492, fully six out of seven people who crossed the Atlantic to the Americas were not Europeans but Africans, the vast majority of whom arrived as slaves. Most came from West Africa, and like the inhabitants of North America or Europe, they belonged to many different ethnic groups, each with its own language and culture (see Map 1-2).

In 1492, Timbuktu, with a population of perhaps seventy thousand, was one of the greatest cities in West Africa. Located on the Niger River, the flourishing commercial metropolis was the seat of the powerful Songhai empire ruled by Sunni Ali. The city was a center of trade as well as government. A visitor in 1526 described Timbuktu's busy streets lined with "shops of artificers and merchants, and especially of such as weave linen and cotton cloth," and reported—with some exaggeration—that the inhabitants "are exceeding rich."

The Songhai empire was only the latest in a series of powerful states to develop in the western Sudan, the vast plain that lies south of the arid Sahara. This large and wealthy empire emerged around 1450, dominating the Sudan until it fell to a Moroccan invasion in 1591. Large empires did not appear in coastal West Africa, although the Asante, Dahomey, Oyo, and Bini kingdoms there grew to be quite powerful. Other coastal peoples, such as the Mendes and Ibos, were decentralized, living in autonomous villages where all adult males participated in making decisions.

In the vast grasslands of the Sudan, people raised cattle and cultivated millet and sorghum. In the 1500s, European visitors introduced varieties of Asian rice, which soon became another important crop. On the coast—where rain falls nearly every day—people grew yams, bananas, and various kinds of beans and peas in forest clearings. They also kept sheep, goats, and poultry.

West Africans were skilled artisans and particularly fine metalworkers. Smiths produced intricate bronze sculptures, designed distinctive miniature gold weights, and forged weapons.

Complex trade networks linked inland and coastal states, and long-distance commercial connections tied West Africa to southern Europe and the Middle East. For centuries, mines in the area of present-day Guinea and Mali produced tons of gold each year, which was exchanged for North African salt, a rare commodity in West Africa. North African merchants also bought pepper, leather, and ivory. The wealth generated by this trans-Saharan trade contributed to the rise of the Songhai and earlier empires.

Most West Africans, however, were farmers, not merchants. West African men and women shared agricultural tasks, with children also contributing their labor. Men generally prepared fields for planting, while women cultivated the crops, harvested them, and dried grain for storage. Men also hunted and, in the grassland regions, herded cattle. Women in the coastal areas owned and cared for other kinds of livestock, including goats and sheep. West African women regularly traded goods, including their crops, in local markets.

Family connections helped define each person's place in society. West Africans emphasized not only ties between parents and children but also those linking aunts, uncles, cousins, and grandparents. Groups of families often formed clans that further extended an individual's kin ties. Most clans were **patrilineal**—tracing descent through the father's line—but some (including the Akans and Ibos) were matrilineal.

Religious beliefs magnified the powerful influence of family on African life. Africans believed that their ancestors acted as mediators between the worlds of the living and the dead. Families held elaborate funerals, which helped keep the memory of ancestors alive for younger generations.

West Africans worshiped a supreme being and several subordinate deities. West Africans, like Native Americans, believed that the gods often sent spirits to speak to people. And like Native American priests who mediated between the human and spirit worlds, West African medicine men and women provided protection against evil spirits and sorcerers. Religious

Ibos Tribes

Kingdoms

Sahel

Trans-Saharan trade routes

Venice-India trade route

Boundaries of the Holy Roman Empire

ICELAND

SWEDEN

NORTH SEA

BALTIC SEA

RUSSIA

SCOTLAND

DENMARK

IRELAND

NETHERLANDS

PRUSSIA

POLAND

Dublin

ENGLAND

London

Amsterdam

GERMAN STATES

HOLY ROMAN EMPIRE

HUNGARY

Paris

FRANCE

SWITZ.

Gonova

Genoa

Venice

ITALIAN STATES

Rome

BLACK SEA

OTTOMAN EMPIRE

Constantinople

ATLANTIC OCEAN

PORTUGAL

SPAIN

ARAGON

CACTILE

Granada

Palos

MEDITERRANEAN SEA

Azores

Ceuta

ALGIERS

NORTH

Fez

Alexandria

Cairo

Madeira

MOROCCO

Sijilmassa

Warzla

Ghadames

AFRICA

EGYPT

Canary Islands

SAHARA

Murzuk

Nile River

Tuat

Ghat

Terhazza

Tamanrasset

To India

Arguin

Bilma

NILOTIC SUDAN

Suakin

Cape Verde Islands

SONGHAI

Timbuktu

CENTRAL SUDAN

Agades

SENEGAMBIA

GHANA

MALI

Gao

Katsina

Lake Chad

Sennar

Wolofs

WESTERN SUDAN

HAUSA STATES

Kano

BORNU

WADAI

DARFUR

FUNJ

TEKRUR

SEGU

Djenné

Niger River

MOSSI STATES

NUPE

Windward Coast

GUINEA COAST

Mendes

ASANTE

DAHOMEY

Yorubas

OYO

BENIN

Ibos

Grain Coast

AKAN

Elmina

Benin

Ivory Coast

Gold Coast

Slave Coast

Sao Tomé

0 250 500 750 1,000 Miles

0 500 1,000 Kilometers

Map 1-2   West Africa and Europe in 1492

Before Columbus's voyage, Europeans knew little about the world beyond the Mediterranean basin and the coast of West Africa. Muslim merchants from North Africa largely controlled European traders' access to African gold and other materials.

Located in Djenné, Mali, this massive mosque, made of sun-hardened mud, dates from the fourteenth century. At that time, Djenné prospered as a center of trade and Islamic learning.

ceremonies took place in sacred places—often near water—but not in buildings that Europeans recognized as churches. And like the Indians, West Africans preserved their faith through oral traditions.

Islam began to take root in West Africa around the eleventh century, probably introduced by Muslim traders from North Africa. By the fifteenth century, the cities of Timbuktu and Djenné had become centers of Islamic learning. Even so, most West Africans probably retained traditional religious beliefs and practices.

Before the fifteenth century, Europeans knew little about Africa beyond its Mediterranean coast. Spain, much of which had been subject to Islamic rule before 1492, had stronger ties to North Africa than most of Europe. But Christian merchants from other European lands had also traded for centuries with North Africans. When stories of West African gold reached the ears of European traders, they tried to move deeper into the continent. But they encountered powerful Muslim merchants intent on monopolizing the gold trade.

The kingdom of Portugal, eager to expand its trade, sought in the early fifteenth century to circumvent this Muslim monopoly. In 1415, Portuguese forces conquered Ceuta in Morocco and gained a foothold on the continent. Portuguese mariners gradually explored the West African coast, establishing trading posts along the way to exchange horses, clothing, wine, lead, iron, and steel for African gold, grain, animal skins, cotton, pepper, and camels.

By the 1430s, the Portuguese had discovered perhaps the greatest source of wealth they could extract from Africa—slaves. Slavery had long been a part of West African society. African law made land

available to anyone willing to cultivate it—provided that no one else was using the same plot—and the possession of a large labor force to work the land became the principal means to wealth. Some people became slaves as punishment for crime, but the majority of slaves were captured in raids into neighboring territories, a regular feature of African life.

Most slaves worked at a variety of tasks for their owners. Many labored more or less independently as farmers, producing surplus crops for their masters. Some rulers acquired female slaves to serve as wives or concubines but also as workers. Powerful Sudanese rulers employed large numbers of slaves as bureaucrats and soldiers, rewarding them for loyal service with good treatment and, occasionally, freedom.

Europeans who observed African slaves' relative freedom and variety of employment often concluded that slaves in Africa were "slaves in name only." Slavery in Africa was not necessarily a permanent status and did not automatically apply to the slaves' children. European purchasers of African slaves generally treated them much more harshly. Slavery became even more oppressive as it developed in the Americas.

Western Europe on the Eve of Discovery

When Columbus sailed from the Spanish port of Palos in 1492, he left a continent recovering from the devastating disease and warfare of the fourteenth century and about to embark on the devastating religious conflicts of the sixteenth. Between 1337 and 1453, England and France had exhausted each other in a series of conflicts known as the Hundred Years' War. And between 1347 and 1351, an epidemic known as the **Black Death** (probably the pneumonic form of bubonic plague) killed perhaps a third of all Europeans, with results that were felt for more than a century.

The plague left Europe with far fewer workers, but the survivors learned to be more efficient, adopting labor-saving techniques to increase productivity. Metalworkers, for instance, built larger furnaces with huge bellows driven by water power. Shipbuilders redesigned vessels with steering mechanisms that could be managed by smaller crews. Innovations in banking, accounting, and insurance also fostered economic recovery.

By 1500, Europe had a stronger, more productive economy than ever before, but not everyone prospered equally. In parts of England, France, Sweden, and the German states, peasants and workers rebelled against the propertied classes. Protests grew from the workers' desire to protect their improving economic fortunes. They did not want to see their rising wages eaten up by higher rents and taxes.

In some parts of Europe, economic improvement encouraged an extraordinary cultural movement known as the **Renaissance**—a "rebirth" of interest in the classical civilizations of ancient Greece and Rome. The Renaissance originated in the city-states of Italy, where a prosperous and educated urban class promoted learning and artistic expression. Wealthy townspeople joined princes in becoming patrons of the arts, offering financial support to numerous painters, sculptors, architects, writers, and musicians.

European states were hierarchical, with their populations divided into fairly rigid classes. Monarchs stood at the top of society. Just below were the aristocrats, who, along with the royal family, dominated government and owned most of the land. Next came prosperous gentry families, independent landowners, and, at the bottom, landless peasants and laborers.

Most of Europe's people were peasant farmers. Peasant men did most of the heavy field work, while women helped at planting and harvest time and cared for children, livestock, and the household. The economic recovery after the Black Death brought prosperity to some families, but crop failures and disease could often cause great suffering in villages and towns.

European society was **patriarchal,** with men dominating political and economic life. Men also controlled the Catholic Church. Inheritance was patrilineal, and only men could own property.

By the end of the fifteenth century, after more than a hundred years of incessant conflict, a measure of stability had returned to Western Europe. Ferdinand and Isabella of Spain, Louis XI of France, and Henry VII of England successfully asserted royal authority over their previously fragmented realms, creating strong state bureaucracies to control political rivals. They gave special trading privileges to merchants to gain their support, creating links that would later prove important in financing overseas expeditions.

The consolidation of military power went hand in hand with the strengthening of political authority. Portugal developed a strong navy to defend its seaborne merchants. Louis XI of France commanded a standing army, and Ferdinand of Spain created a palace guard to use against potential opponents. Before overseas expansion began, European monarchs exerted military force to extend their authority closer to home. Louis XI and his successors used warfare and intermarriage with ruling families of nearby provinces to expand French influence. In the early sixteenth century, England's Henry VIII sent soldiers to conquer Ireland. And the Spain of 1492 was forged from the successful conclusion of the *reconquista* ("reconquest") of territory from Muslim control.

Even as these rulers sought to unify their realms, religious conflicts began to tear Europe apart. For more than a thousand years, Catholic Christianity had united western Europeans in one faith. By the sixteenth century, the Catholic Church had accumulated enormous wealth and power. The pope wielded influence not only as a spiritual leader but also as the political ruler of parts of Italy. The church owned considerable property throughout Europe. Many Christians, especially in northern Europe, began to criticize the worldliness of the popes and the church itself for corruption, abuse of power, and betrayal of the legacy of Christ.

In 1517, a German monk, Martin Luther, invited open debate on these issues, asserting that the church had become too insistent on the performance of good works, such as charitable donations or other actions intended to please God. He called for a return to what he understood to be the purer practices and beliefs of the early church, emphasizing that salvation came not by good deeds but only by faith in God. With the help of the newly invented printing press, his ideas spread widely, inspiring a challenge to the Catholic Church that has come to be called the **Reformation.**

When the church refused to compromise, Luther and other critics withdrew to form their own religious organizations, emphasizing the relationship between God and the individual believer. He urged people to take responsibility for their own spiritual growth by reading the Bible, which he translated for the first time into German. What started as a religious movement, however, quickly acquired an important political dimension.

Sixteenth-century Germany was a fragmented region of small kingdoms and principalities that were officially part of the **Holy Roman Empire.** Many German princes supported Luther for both spiritual and secular reasons. When the Holy Roman Empire under Charles V (who was also king of Spain) tried to silence them, the reformist princes protested. From that point on, these princes—and all Europeans who supported religious reform—became known as "Protestants."

The Protestant movement took a more radical turn under the influence of the French reformer John Calvin, who emphasized the doctrine of **predestination.** Calvin maintained that an all-powerful and all-knowing God chose at the moment of creation which humans would be saved and which would be damned. Each person's fate is thus foreordained, or predestined, by God, although we cannot know our fate during our lifetimes. Good Calvinists, however, struggled to behave as God's chosen, continually searching their souls for evidence of divine grace.

Calvin founded a religious community consistent with his principles at Geneva, a Swiss city-state near the French border. From Germany and Geneva the Protestant Reformation spread to France, the Netherlands, England, and Hungary. In succeeding years, other Protestant groups formed, split, and split again, increasing Europe's religious fragmentation. The new religious ideas particularly interested literate city-dwellers, while peasants adopted the new ideas more slowly.

The Reformation addressed spiritual needs that the Catholic Church had left unfulfilled, but it also fractured the religious unity of western Europe and spawned a century of warfare unprecedented in its bloody destructiveness. Protestants fought Catholics in France and the German states. Popes initiated a "Counter-Reformation," intending to strengthen the Catholic Church. Europe thus fragmented into warring camps just at the moment when Europeans were coming to terms with their discovery of America.

Contact

Portugal, Spain, France, and England competed to establish footholds on other continents in an intense scramble for riches and dominance. The success of these early endeavors was a reflection of Europe's prosperity and a series of technological breakthroughs that enabled its mariners to navigate beyond familiar waters. By the end of the sixteenth century, Spain had emerged as the apparent winner among the European competitors for New World dominance. Its astonishingly wealthy empire included vast territories in Central and South America.

The Lure of Discovery

Most Europeans, busy making a living, cared little about distant lands. But certain princes and merchants anticipated spiritual and material benefits from voyages of discovery. The spiritual advantages included making new Christian converts and blocking Islam's expansion. On the material side, the voyages would contribute to Europe's prosperity by increasing trade.

Merchants especially sought access to the lucrative Asian trade in spices like pepper, cinnamon, ginger, and nutmeg that added interest to an otherwise monotonous diet and helped preserve certain foods. But the overland spice trade—and the trade in other luxury goods such as silk and furs—spanned thousands of miles, involved many middlemen, and was controlled at key points by Muslim merchants. One critical center was Constantinople, the bastion of Christianity in the eastern Mediterranean. When it fell to the Ottomans—the Muslim rulers of Turkey—in 1453, Europeans feared that caravan routes to Asia would be disrupted. This encouraged merchants to turn westward and seek alternate routes. Mariners ventured farther into ocean waters, hoping to sail around Africa and chart a sea route to Asia.

Ocean voyages required sturdier ships and more reliable navigational tools. In the early fifteenth century, Prince Henry of Portugal, excited by the idea of overseas discovery, sponsored the efforts of shipbuilders, mapmakers, and other workers to solve these practical problems. Iberian shipbuilders perfected the caravel, a ship whose narrow shape and steering rudder suited it for ocean travel. Ship designers combined square sails (good for speed) with triangular "lateen" sails, which increased maneuverability. Two Arab inventions—the magnetic compass and the astrolabe (which allowed mariners to determine their position in relation to a star's known location in the sky)—gained popularity among European navigators. As sailors acquired practical experience on the high seas, mapmakers recorded their observations of landfalls, wind patterns, and ocean currents.

After Portugal's conquest of the Moroccan city of Ceuta in 1415, its mariners slowly worked their way along Africa's western coast, establishing trading posts where they exchanged European goods for gold, ivory, and slaves. Bartolomeu Días reached the southern tip of Africa in 1488. Eleven years later, Vasco da Gama brought a Portuguese fleet around Africa to India, opening a sea route to Asia. These initiatives gave Portugal a virtual monopoly on Far Eastern trade for some time.

The new trade routes gave strategic importance to the islands that lie in the Atlantic off the west coast of Africa and Europe. Spain and Portugal vied for control of the Canary Islands, located 800 miles southwest of the Iberian peninsula. Spain eventually prevailed in 1496 by defeating the islands' inhabitants. Portugal acquired Madeira and the Cape Verde Islands, along with a set of tiny islands off Africa's Guinea Coast.

Sugar, like Asian spices, commanded high prices in Europe, so the conquerors of the Atlantic islands began to cultivate sugar cane on them, on large plantations worked by slave labor. In the Canaries, the Spanish first enslaved the native inhabitants. When disease and exhaustion reduced their numbers, the Spanish brought in African slaves, often purchased from Portuguese traders.

These island societies, in which a small European master class dominated a much larger population of native peoples or imported African slaves, were to provide a model for Spain's and Portugal's later exploitation of their American colonies. Even as early as 1494, Christopher Columbus wrote to Ferdinand and Isabella of Spain to suggest that Caribbean islanders could be sold as slaves in order to cover the costs of exploration.

Christopher Columbus

Columbus was not the first European to believe that he could reach Asia by sailing westward. The idea developed logically during the fifteenth century as mariners gained knowledge and experience from their exploits in the Atlantic and around Africa. Columbus himself may have gained valuable experience on a voyage to Iceland. He also read widely in geographical treatises and paid close attention to the stories and rumors that circulated among mariners.

Most Europeans knew that the world was round, but most also scoffed at the idea of a westward voyage to Asia, believing that it would take so long, it would exhaust any ship's supplies. Columbus's confidence that he could make the voyage grew from a mistaken calculation of the earth's circumference as 18,000 (rather than 24,000) miles, which led him to conclude that Asia lay just 3,500 miles west of the Canary Islands. Columbus first sought financial support from the king of Portugal,

whose advisers warned him that he would starve at sea before reaching Asia. Undaunted, he turned to Portugal's rival, Spain.

Columbus tried to convince Ferdinand and Isabella that his plan suited Spain's national goals: Spain could grow rich from Asian trade, send Christian missionaries to Asia (a goal in keeping with the religious ideals of the *reconquista*), and perhaps enlist the Great Khan of China as an ally in the long struggle with Islam. If he failed, the "enterprise of the Indies" would cost little. The Spanish monarchs nonetheless kept Columbus waiting nearly seven years—until 1492, when the last Muslim stronghold at Granada fell to Spanish forces—before they gave him their support.

After thirty-three days at sea, Columbus and his men mad landfall and were puzzled not to find the fabled cities of China or Japan, but still believed that they had reached Asia. Three more voyages, between 1493 and 1504, however, failed to yield clear evidence of an Asian landfall or substantiate Columbus's reports of "great mines of gold and other metals" and spices in abundance.

Obsessed with the wealth he had promised himself and others, Columbus and his men turned violent, sacking the villages of Tainos and Caribs and demanding tribute in gold. The Spanish forced native gangs to pan rivers for the precious nuggets. Dissatisfied with the meager results, Columbus sought to enslave islanders, a desperate attempt to show that the Indies could yield a profit. Queen Isabella initially opposed the enslavement of people she considered to be new Spanish subjects. Within thirty years of Columbus's first voyage, however, Spanish exploitation of native labor had brought the populations of many Caribbean islands close to extinction.

Columbus died in Spain in 1506, still convinced he had found Asia. What he had done was to set in motion a process that would transform both sides of the Atlantic. It would eventually bring wealth to many Europeans and immense suffering to Native Americans and Africans.

Spanish Conquest and Colonization

Of all European nations, Spain was best suited to take advantage of Columbus's discovery. Its experience with the *reconquista* gave it both a religious justification for conquest (bringing Christianity to nonbelievers) and an army of seasoned soldiers—**conquistadores.** In addition, during the *reconquista* and the conquest of the Canary Islands, Spain's rulers had

Map 1-3   *Spanish, English, and French Settlements in North America in the Sixteenth Century*
By the end of the sixteenth century, only Spain had established permanent settlements in North America. French outposts in Canada and at Fort Caroline, as well as the English settlement at Roanoke, failed to thrive. European rivalries for North America, however, would intensify after 1600.

developed efficient techniques for controlling newly conquered lands that could be applied to New World colonies.

The Spanish first established outposts on Cuba, Puerto Rico, and Jamaica (see Map 1-3). The conquistadores, who were more interested in finding gold and slaves than in creating permanent settlements, attacked Taino and Carib villages and killed or captured the inhabitants. By 1524, the Tainos had

all but died out; the Caribs survived on more isolated islands until the eighteenth century. Spanish soldiers then ventured to the mainland. Juan Ponce de León led an expedition to Florida in 1513. In that same year, Vasco Núñez de Balboa arrived in Central America, crossing the isthmus of Panama to the Pacific Ocean.

In 1519, Hernán Cortés led a force of six hundred men to the coast of Mexico. "I and my companions," he declared, "suffer from a disease of the heart which can be cured only with gold." By 1521, Cortés and his men had conquered the powerful Aztec empire. The Spanish soldiers also discovered riches beyond their wildest dreams. They "picked up the gold and fingered it like monkeys," reported one Aztec witness. They were "transported by joy, as if their hearts were illumined and made new."

The swift, decisive Spanish victory over a more numerous enemy depended on several factors. Spanish guns and horses often enabled them to overwhelm larger groups of Aztec foot soldiers armed with spears and wooden swords edged with obsidian.

Cortés benefited from divisions within the Aztec empire, acquiring indispensable allies among subject Indians who resented Aztec domination. Cortés led only six hundred Spanish soldiers but eventually gained 200,000 Indian allies eager to throw off Aztec rule.

An even more significant contribution to this quick victory was the fact that Indians lacked resistance to European diseases. One of Cortés's men was infected with smallpox, which soon devastated the native population. Nearly 40 percent of the inhabitants of central Mexico died of smallpox within a year. Other diseases followed, including typhus, measles, and influenza. By 1600, the population of Mexico may have declined from over 15 million to less than a million people.

Aztec society and culture collapsed in the face of appalling mortality. One survivor recalled, "The sick were so utterly helpless that they could only lie on their beds like corpses, unable to move their limbs or even their heads. . . . If they did move their bodies, they screamed with pain." Early in their bid to gain control of the Aztec empire, the Spanish seized Moctezuma, the Aztec king, and eventually put him to death. His successor died of disease less than three months after gaining the throne.

In 1532, Francisco Pizarro and 180 men discovered the Inca empire high in the Peruvian Andes. Taking advantage of a civil war within the empire following its ruler's death, the Spaniards then captured Cuzco, the Inca capital, and established a new one at Lima.

By 1550, Spain's New World empire extended from the Caribbean through Mexico to Peru. It was administered from Spain by the Council of the Indies. The council aimed to project royal authority into every village in New Spain in order to maintain political control and extract as much wealth as possible from the land and its people.

For more than a century, Spanish ships crossed the Atlantic carrying seemingly limitless treasure from the colonies. The colonial rulers subjected the native inhabitants of New Spain to compulsory tribute payments and forced labor. Tens of thousands of Indians toiled in silver mines in Peru and Bolivia and on sugar plantations in the Caribbean. When necessary, Spaniards imported African slaves to supplement a native labor force ravaged by disease and exhaustion.

The desire for gold eventually lured Spaniards farther into North America. In 1528, an expedition to Florida ended in the deaths of nearly all Spanish intruders when they provoked an attack by Apalachee Indians. In 1539, Hernán de Soto led an expedition from Florida to the Mississippi River. Along the way, the Spaniards harassed Creeks, Cherokees, Choctaws, and other groups. They demanded provisions, burned villages, and captured native women to be servants and concubines. They also exposed the Indians to deadly European diseases. The expedition kept up its rampage for three years, turning toward Mexico only after de Soto died in 1542. In these same years, Francisco Vásquez de Coronado led three hundred troops on an equally destructive expedition through present-day Arizona, New Mexico, and Colorado on a futile search for gold and precious stones.

The failure to find gold and silver halted the Spanish attempt to extend their empire to the north. By the end of the sixteenth century, they maintained just two precarious footholds north of Mexico. One was at St. Augustine, on Florida's Atlantic coast. Founded in 1565, this fortified outpost served as a naval base to defend Spanish treasure fleets from raids by English and French privateers. The other settlement was located far to the west in what is now New Mexico. Juan de Oñate, on a futile search for silver mines, claimed the region for Spain in 1598. He and his men occupied a Pueblo village, and proceeded to antagonize the area's inhabitants. Having earned the enmity of the Pueblo people—astonishing even his own superiors with his brutality—Oñate barely managed to keep his tiny colony together.

The conquistadores' bloody tactics aroused some protest back in Spain. The Indians' most eloquent advocate was Bartolomé de Las Casas, a Dominican priest shamed by his own role (as a layman) in the conquest of Hispaniola. Las Casas wrote *In Defense of the Indians,* including graphic descriptions of native sufferings. Instead of eliciting Spanish reforms, however, his work inspired Protestant Europeans to create the "Black Legend," an exaggerated story according to which a fanatical Catholic Spain sought to spread its control at any cost (see "American Views: The Debate between Bartolomé de Las Casas and Juan Ginés de Sepúlveda" on page 18).

Meanwhile, between 1500 and 1650, an estimated 181 tons of gold and 16,000 tons of silver were shipped from the New World to Spain, making it the richest and most powerful state in Europe. But this influx of American treasure had unforeseen consequences that would soon undermine Spanish predominance.

In 1492, the Spanish crown expelled from Spain all Jews who refused to become Christians. The refugees included many leading merchants who had contributed significantly to Spain's economy. The remaining Christian merchants, now awash in American riches, saw no reason to invest in new trade or productive enterprises that might have sustained the economy once the flow of New World treasure diminished. As a result, Spain's economy eventually stagnated.

The flood of American gold and silver also inflated prices throughout Europe, hurting workers, whose wages failed to rise as fast, and aristocrats, dependent on fixed rents from their estates. Most damaging, Spain's monarchs wasted their American wealth fighting expensive wars in Europe that ultimately only weakened the nation. By 1600, some disillusioned Spaniards were arguing that the conquest had brought more problems than benefits to their country.

The Columbian Exchange

Spain's long-term economic decline was just one of many consequences of the conquest of the New World. In the long run, the biological consequences of contact—what one historian has called the **Columbian exchange**—proved to be the most momentous (see the summary table "The Columbian Exchange").

The most catastrophic result of the exchange was the exposure of Native Americans to Old World diseases. Epidemics of smallpox, measles, typhus, and influenza struck Native Americans with great force, killing half, and sometimes as much as 90 percent, of the people in communities exposed to them. The only American disease to infect the Old World was syphilis, which appeared in Spain just after Columbus returned from his first voyage.

The Columbian exchange also introduced Old World livestock to the New World. Columbus brought horses, sheep, cattle, pigs, and goats with him on his second voyage in 1493. Native Americans had few domesticated animals and initially marveled at these large beasts. However, with few natural predators to limit their numbers, livestock populations boomed in the New World, competing with native mammals, such as bison, for good grazing. The use of horses also often gave European soldiers a decisive military advantage in conflicts with Indians.

But the introduction of European livestock created opportunities for Yaquis, Pueblos, and other peoples in the American Southwest, who began to raise cattle and sheep. By the eighteenth century, Plains Indians, including the Arapahos, Sioux, Nez Percé, and Comanches, had not only adopted horses but also become exceptionally skilled riders. The men found it much easier to hunt buffalo on horseback than on foot, and the women valued horses as beasts of burden.

European ships carried unintentional passengers as well, including the black rat and honeybees, both previously unknown in the New World. Ships also brought weeds such as thistles and dandelions, whose seeds were often embedded in hay for animal fodder.

Europeans brought a variety of seeds and plant cuttings in order to grow familiar foods. Columbus's men planted wheat, chickpeas, melons, onions, and fruit trees on Caribbean islands. European plants did not always fare well, at least not everywhere in the New World, so Europeans learned to cultivate native foods, such as corn, tomatoes, squash, beans, and potatoes, as well as nonfood plants such as tobacco and cotton. They carried many of these plants back to Europe, enriching Old World diets with new foods.

Competition for a Continent

In 1494, the pope resolved the conflicting claims of Portugal and Spain for New World territory with the **Treaty of Tordesillas.** The treaty drew a north-south line approximately 1,100 miles west of the Cape Verde Islands. Spain received all lands west of the line, while Portugal held sway to the east. This limited Portugal's New World empire to Brazil, where settlers followed the precedent of the Atlantic island colonies and established sugar plantations worked by slave labor. But the treaty also protected Portugal's claims in Africa and Asia, which lay east of the line.

France and England, of course, rejected the papal grant of the Western Hemisphere to Spain and Portugal. Initially, domestic troubles—largely sparked by the Protestant Reformation—distracted the two countries from the pursuit of empire. By the close of

SUMMARY

THE COLUMBIAN EXCHANGE

	From Old World to New World	From New World to Old World
Diseases	Smallpox, measles, plague, typhus, influenza, yellow fever, diphtheria, scarlet fever	Syphilis
Animals	Horses, cattle, pigs, sheep, goats, donkeys, mules, black rats, honeybees, cockroaches	Turkeys
Plants	Wheat, sugar, barley, coffee, rice, dandelion and other weeds	Maize, beans, peanut, potato, sweet potato, manioc, squash, papaya, guava, tomato, avocado, pineapple, chili pepper, cocoa

Source: *Adapted from Alfred Crosby Jr.,* The Columbian Exchange: Biological and Cultural Consequences of 1492 *(1972).*

the sixteenth century, both France and England insisted on their rights to New World lands, but neither had created a permanent settlement to support its claim.

Early French Efforts in North America

France was a relative latecomer to New World exploration. Preoccupied with European affairs, France's rulers paid little attention to America until news of Cortés's exploits in Mexico arrived in the 1520s.

In 1524, King Francis I sponsored a voyage by Giovanni da Verrazano, an Italian navigator, who mapped the North American coast from present-day South Carolina to Maine. During the 1530s and 1540s, the French mariner Jacques Cartier made three voyages in search of rich mines to rival those of Mexico and Peru. He explored the St. Lawrence River up to what is now Montreal, hoping to discover a water route through the continent to Asia (what came to be called the Northwest Passage). On his second voyage, in 1535, he and his crew almost froze to death and suffered from scurvy, a disease caused by a lack of vitamin C. Some of the men survived because the Iroquois showed them how to make a vitamin-rich concoction of boiled white cedar needles and bark.

On his third voyage, in 1541, Cartier was to serve under the command of a nobleman, Jean-François de la Rocque, sieur de Roberval, who was commissioned by the king to establish a permanent settlement in Canada. Unable to recruit colonists, he finally set sail in 1542, taking convicts as settlers. Cartier had sailed ahead, gathered samples of what he thought were gold and diamonds, and returned to France without Roberval's permission.

Roberval's expedition was poorly organized, and his cruel treatment of the convicts provoked several uprisings. The Iroquois, suspicious of repeated French intrusions on their lands, saw no reason to help them. A year after they arrived in Canada, Roberval and the surviving colonists were back in France. Their return coincided with news that the gold brought back by Cartier was iron pyrite (fool's gold) and the diamonds were quartz crystals.

Disappointed with their Canadian expeditions, the French made a few brief forays to the south, establishing outposts in what is now South Carolina in 1562 and Florida in 1564. They soon abandoned the Carolina colony (though not before the starving settlers resorted to cannibalism), and Spanish forces captured the Florida fort. Then, back in France, a prolonged civil war broke out between Catholics and Protestants. Renewed interest in colonization would have to await the return of peace at home.

English Attempts in the New World

The English were quicker than the French to stake a claim to the New World but no more successful at colonization. In 1497, King Henry VII sent John Cabot, an Italian mariner, to explore eastern Canada on England's behalf. But neither Henry nor his

American Views

THE DEBATE BETWEEN BARTOLOMÉ DE LAS CASAS AND JUAN GINÉS DE SEPÚLVEDA

In 1550, in response to criticism of Spanish colonial tactics, the Spanish king called a special council to decide if it was lawful to wage war on Indians before preaching to them, in order to make them more submissive converts to Christianity. The council summoned Juan Ginés de Sepúlveda and Bartolomé de Las Casas to debate the issue. Sepúlveda, a noted classical scholar who had never visited America, argued that warfare was indeed just and that Indians were fit only to be Spanish slaves. Las Casas, the well-known defender of the Indians, insisted that the Indians' humanity demanded gentler treatment from the Spanish. In the end, this debate only polarized the issue even more. The council members began arguing among themselves and reached no decision. These extracts illustrate the two sides of the argument.

❖ **What are the main points of disagreement?**

❖ **Do the views of Sepúlveda and Las Casas share any common elements?**

❖ **What, according to the Spanish, were essential features of civilized society?**

❖ **Why were the Spanish so intent on converting the Indians?**

Sepúlveda's position

In prudence, talent, virtue, and humanity they are as inferior to the Spaniards as children to adults, women to men, as the wild and cruel to the most meek, as the prodigiously intemperate to the continent and temperate, that I have almost said, as monkeys to men.

[The Indians] not only lack culture but do not even know how to write, [they] keep no records of their history except certain obscure and vague reminiscences of some things put down in certain pictures, and [they] do not have written laws but only barbarous institutions and customs. . . . And don't think that before the arrival of the Chris-

---

wealthier subjects would invest the funds necessary to follow up on Cabot's discoveries.

The lapse in English activity in the New World stemmed from religious troubles at home. Between 1534 and 1558, England changed its official religion several times. King Henry VIII took up the Protestant cause when the pope refused to annul his marriage to Catherine of Aragon. In 1534, Henry declared himself the head of a separate Church of England and seized the Catholic Church's English property. But in 1553, Mary—daughter of the spurned Catherine of Aragon—became queen and tried to bring England back to Catholicism. She had nearly three hundred Protestants burned at the stake for their beliefs (earning her the nickname "Bloody Mary"), and many others went into exile in Europe.

After Mary's death in 1558, her half-sister Elizabeth, a committed Protestant, became queen, restoring Protestantism as the state religion, bringing stability to the nation, and renewing England's interest in the New World. She and her subjects saw colonization not only as a way to gain wealth and political advantage but also as a Protestant crusade against Catholic domination.

England's first target for colonization, however, was not America but Ireland. Located less than 60 miles west of England and populated by Catholics, Ireland threatened to become a base from which Spain or another Catholic power might invade England. Elizabeth launched a series of brutal expeditions that destroyed Irish villages and slaughtered the inhabitants. Several veterans of these campaigns tians they were living in quiet. . . . On the contrary they were making war continuously and ferociously against each other with such rage that they considered their victory worthless if they did not satisfy their monstrous hunger with the flesh of their enemies. . . . [Yet] these Indians are so cowardly and timid, that they scarcely withstand the appearance of our soldiers and often many thousands of them have given ground, fleeing like women before a very few Spaniards, who did not even number a hundred.

Las Casas's position

From the fact that the Indians are barbarians it does not necessarily follow that they are incapable of government and have to be ruled by others, except to be taught about the Catholic faith and to be admitted to the holy sacraments. They are not ignorant, inhuman, or bestial. Rather, long before they had heard the word Spaniard, they had properly organized states, wisely ordered by excellent laws, religion, and custom. They cultivated friendship and, bound together in common fellowship, lived in populous cities in which they wisely administered the affairs of both peace and war justly and equitably, truly governed by laws which at very many points surpass ours. . . .

The Indians are our brothers, and Christ has given his life for them. Why, then, do we persecute them with such inhuman savagery when they do not deserve such treatment? . . . [They] will embrace the teaching of the gospel, as I well know, for they are not stupid or barbarous but have a native sincerity and are simple, moderate, and meek, and, finally, such that I do not know whether there is any people readier to receive the gospel.

Source: *Lewis Hanke*, All Mankind Is One: A Study of the Disputation between Bartolomé de Las Casas and Juan Ginés de Sepúlveda in 1550 on the Intellectual and Religious Capacity of the American Indians (1974), pp. 84, 85, 76.

later took part in New World colonization and drew on their Irish experience for guidance.

The English transferred their assumptions about Irish "savages" to native Americans. Englishmen in America frequently observed similarities between Indians and the Irish. "The natives of New England," noted one Englishman, "are accustomed to build their houses much like the wild Irish." When Indians resisted conquest, the English recalled the Irish example, claiming that native "savagery" required brutal suppression.

The Irish experience also influenced English ideas about colonial settlement. English conquerors set up "plantations" surrounded by palisades on seized Irish lands, importing Protestant tenants from England and Scotland to farm the land. Native Irish people were excluded. English colonists in America followed this precedent when they established plantations that separated English and native peoples.

Sir Humphrey Gilbert, a notoriously cruel veteran of the Irish campaigns, composed a treatise to convince Queen Elizabeth to support New World colonization. The queen authorized several exploratory voyages, including Martin Frobisher's three trips in 1576–1578 in search of the Northwest Passage to Asia. Frobisher failed to find the elusive passage and sent back shiploads of glittering ore that proved to be fool's gold. Elizabeth had better luck in allowing privateers, such as John Hawkins and Francis Drake, to raid Spanish ships and New World ports for gold and silver.

Meanwhile, Gilbert continued to promote New World settlement, arguing that it would increase

England's trade and provide a place for the nation's unemployed people. Like many of his contemporaries, Gilbert believed that England's "surplus" population threatened social order. The population was indeed growing, and economic changes often made it difficult for people to support themselves. Gilbert suggested offering free land in America to English families willing to emigrate.

In 1578, Gilbert received permission to set up a colony anywhere along the North American coast. It took him five years to organize an expedition to Newfoundland, which he claimed for England. After sailing southward seeking a more favorable site for a colony, Gilbert headed home, only to be lost at sea during an Atlantic storm. His half-brother, Sir Walter Raleigh (another veteran of the Irish wars), immediately took up the cause of English colonization.

In 1585 Raleigh sent men to build a settlement on Roanoke Island off the Carolina coast. Most colonists were soldiers fresh from Ireland who refused to grow their own food, insisting that the Roanoke Indians should feed them. When the local chief, Wingina, organized native resistance, they killed him. Eventually, the colonists, disappointed not to have found gold or precious stones and exhausted by a harsh winter, returned to England in 1586.

Two members of these early expeditions, however, left a more positive legacy. Thomas Hariot studied the Roanoke and Croatoan Indians and identified plants and animals in the area, hoping that some might prove to be profitable commodities. John White drew maps and painted a series of watercolors depicting the natives and the coastal landscape. When Raleigh tried once more, in 1587, to found a colony, he chose White to be its leader.

This attempt also failed. The ship captain dumped the settlers—who, for the first time, included women and children—on Roanoke Island so that he could pursue Spanish treasure ships. White waited until his granddaughter, Virginia Dare (the first English child born in America), was safely born and then sailed to England for supplies. But the outbreak of war with Spain delayed his return for three years. Spain had gathered an immense fleet to invade England, and all English ships were needed for defense. Although England defeated the Armada in 1588, White could not obtain a relief ship for Roanoke until 1590.

White found the colony deserted. Digging through the ruins of the village, he found "my books torn from the covers, the frames of some of my pictures and Maps rotten and spoiled with rain." He also saw the word CROATOAN carved on a post and assumed that the colonists had moved to nearby Croatoan Island. But bad weather prevented him from searching there. For years, English and Spanish mariners reported seeing white people along the coast of Chesapeake Bay. But no Roanoke colonists were ever found.

England's interest in colonization did not wane. In 1584, Richard Hakluyt had aroused enthusiasm for America by writing the "Discourse of Western Planting" for the queen and her advisers. He argued that England would prosper from the expansion of trade and the sale of New World commodities. Once the Indians were civilized, Hakluyt added, they would eagerly purchase English goods. Equally important, England could plant "sincere religion" (that is, Protestant Christianity) in the New World and prevent the power of "the Spanish king from flowing over all the face . . . of America."

Hakluyt's arguments fired the imaginations of many people, and the defeat of the Spanish Armada emboldened England to challenge Spain's New World dominance. The experience of Roanoke should have tempered that enthusiasm. The colony's fate underscored the need for adequate funding, the unsuitability of soldiers as colonists, and the need to maintain good relations with the Indians. But the English were slow to learn these lessons. As it was, the sixteenth century ended with no permanent English settlement in the New World.

Conclusion

After Columbus's first voyage, Europeans, eager for wealth and power, came by the thousands to a continent that just a hundred years earlier they had not dreamed existed. Africans came in even greater numbers to the Caribbean, Mexico, and Brazil, forced to labor for white masters in unfamiliar lands. In many parts of the Americas, native peoples encountered white and black strangers whose presence often destroyed their accustomed ways of life.

In 1600 only Spain had established North American colonies. Though its New World dominance seemed secure, even Spain had struggled to expand north of Mexico. Virtually the entire continent north of the Rio Grande remained firmly in Indian hands. Except in Mexico and the Caribbean, Europeans had merely touched the continent's shores. In 1600, native peoples still greatly outnumbered European and African immigrants. The next century, however, brought powerful challenges both to native control and to the Spanish monopoly of settlement.

Review Questions

1. Compare men's and women's roles in Native American, West African, and European societies. What were the similarities and differences? How did differences between European and Native American gender roles lead to misunderstandings?

2. Many of the first European colonizers in North America were military veterans. What impact did this have on their relations with Indian peoples?

3. Why did Spain so quickly become the dominant colonial power in North America? What advantages did it enjoy over France and England?

4. What role did religion play in early European efforts at overseas colonization? Did religious factors always encourage colonization, or did they occasionally interfere with European expansion?

Recommended Reading

Hassig, Ross. *Mexico and the Spanish Conquest* (1994). A brief account of Cortés's expedition, focusing on the military aspects of the Spanish conquest.

Josephy, Alvin M., Jr. *America in 1492: The World of the Indian Peoples before the Arrival of Columbus* (1991). A collection of essays describing the wide variety of Indian cultures in North America prior to contact with Europeans.

Leon-Portillo, Miguel. *The Broken Spears: The Aztec Account of the Conquest of Mexico* (1962). Reprints of translated Indian chronicles, providing a moving account of the Aztec experience of the Spanish conquest.

Parry, J. H. *The Age of Reconnaissance* (1963). A comprehensive account of European exploration and the rise of overseas empires.

Phillips, William D., Jr., and Phillips, Carla Rahn. *The Worlds of Christopher Columbus* (1992). A judicious biography of Columbus that places him firmly in the context of fifteenth-century European culture.

Thornton, John. *Africa and Africans in the Making of the Atlantic World, 1400–1680* (1992). A thorough examination of the causes and consequences of the movement of Africans throughout the Atlantic world and the rise of the slave trade.

Where to Learn More

❖ **Chillicothe, Ohio.** The Mound City Group National Monument: This site preserves a prehistoric Indian burial site. The holdings in the museum include excavated grave goods from burial mounds dating from 200 B.C. to A.D. 500. There is also a library with research materials on prehistoric Native American culture.

❖ **Washington, Connecticut.** American Indian Archaeological Institute: With both a museum and library materials, the institute preserves artifacts of Eastern Woodlands Indians and has a special collection of Algonquin baskets.

❖ **Acoma Pueblo, New Mexico.** Adobe pueblo built on a 350-foot-high mesa; site of early contact between Pueblo Indians and Spanish soldiers. Contains San Estevan del Rey Mission, built 1629–1642. Site mainly used for ceremonial purposes, and travelers should obtain permission before visiting.

❖ **St. Augustine, Florida.** Founded in 1565, St. Augustine is the site of the first permanent Spanish settlement in North America. Today the restored community resembles a Spanish colonial town, with narrow, winding streets and seventeenth- and eighteenth-century buildings. The site also contains the restored Castillo de San Marcos, now a national park. The Historic St. Augustine Preservation Board owns and administers several historic house museums and offers programs in living history and craft exhibits.

2 TRANSPLANTATION, 1600–1685

KEY TOPICS

❖ Development of New France
❖ Diversity of English colonies in the seventeenth century
❖ Growth of staple crop economies in the southern and Caribbean colonies
❖ Role of religion in the founding of colonies
❖ Creation of biracial slave societies in the West Indies and Carolina

Captain John Smith wrote his brief book, *A Description of New England,* under difficult circumstances. It was the summer of 1615, and he was being held captive aboard a French pirate ship. Smith had left England with a crew of thirty sailors, bound for the northeast coast of North America, where they planned to set up a colony. They had not gone far before being seized by the pirates, who justified their action by accusing Smith of participating in an earlier English raid on a French settlement in Maine. When Smith boarded the pirate ship to bargain for their release, his crew escaped, leaving the captain stranded. With little else to occupy him during months of captivity, Smith composed his book promoting colonization of the region he named "New England" as a challenge to rival colonies in New Spain and New France.

Smith eventually made it back to England and published his book in 1616. By then, England and France had joined Spain as founders of New World colonies. Smith's work testified to the intensifying rivalry among European nations for control of North America. He emphasized the vast wealth of Spain's empire and scolded Protestant Englishmen for allowing Spanish Catholics to spread their faith among the natives. The Spanish king, Smith declared, scarcely knew "one halfe Quarter of those Territories" he claimed, and so the English "neede not greatly feare his furie" if they expanded their own settlements.

John Smith's name is usually associated with the founding of Virginia, England's first permanent colony in North America, in 1607. After a brief stint as Virginia's leader, Smith was ousted in 1609 by disgruntled colonists. Back in England, he developed a plan to set up a rival colony in New England. But he never returned to America after his ill-fated voyage of 1615, and New England settlement began in 1620 without him. England eventually founded at least two dozen colonies on the North American mainland and in the Caribbean before 1700.

The French in North America

The English raid on the French settlement in Maine—for which the French pirates held John Smith accountable—virtually wiped out the tiny outpost, but it left French influence in the area scarcely diminished. The economic base of France's New World empire, known as New France, was the fur trade, which depended more on the control of waterways and alliances with Indians than on the occupation of land.

The focus of the French colony was the St. Lawrence River, which provided access to a vast interior populated by an abundance of beavers and by Indian peoples eager for trade. Because of its emphasis on the fur trade rather than extensive settlement, New France's population grew slowly in the seventeenth century. Its few, scattered villages were linked as closely to their Indian neighbors as to each other.

The Development of New France

As we saw in Chapter 1, French efforts to found American colonies in the late sixteenth century ended in failure. But French fishermen continued to visit the Newfoundland coast. Setting up frames onshore to dry their catch, they met Indians with furs to trade for European goods. The already strong market for furs in Europe soon expanded dramatically as broad-brimmed beaver fur hats became fashionable.

Once it was clear that a profit could be made in Canada, France's interest revived. French kings sold exclusive trading rights to merchants willing to set up outposts in Canada. But to succeed, the merchants needed to bring farmers to New France to produce food and other supplies for the traders.

Quebec, organized in 1608 by Samuel de Champlain, was the first permanent French settlement in Canada (see Map 2-1). It was inhabited for

its first two decades by only a few dozen settlers dependent on France for supplies. Thereafter, efforts to recruit colonists to New France intensified, and French Jesuits—members of a Catholic religious order founded during the Counter-Reformation—sent missionaries to convert the Indians. In 1642, Montreal was founded as a religious and commercial center.

By 1700, New France had about fifteen thousand settlers. One observer reported that "if they are the least inclined to work," immigrants could prosper in Canada. Colonists generally lived in sturdier houses, enjoyed a better diet, and paid lower taxes than their relatives back home. They could acquire land to pass on to their children with an ease that French peasants could only envy. However, few French people moved to North America, and two-thirds of those who did eventually returned to France. Canada's fifteen thousand settlers in 1700 amounted to less than 7 percent of the number of English colonists in mainland North America that same year.

Accounting for this reluctance to emigrate was Canada's reputation as a distant and inhospitable place. Rumors about frigid winters and surprise Indian attacks circulated among French peasants and villagers. In addition, the government required

Map 2-1 New France, c. 1650
By 1650, New France contained a number of thinly populated settlements along the St. Lawrence River Valley and the eastern shore of Lake Huron. Most colonists lived in Quebec and Montreal; other sites served mainly as fur-trading posts and Jesuit missions to the Huron Indians.

prospective settlers to be Catholic, reducing the pool from which they could be drawn.

Most settlers were sponsored by the government or by employers who paid their passage in return for three years of labor. Those who completed their terms of service received land. Most settlers were young men eager to marry and raise children to help them farm. But as late as 1666, only one out of three French settlers was female. Some young Frenchmen married Indian women. Others found brides from among the female orphans that the French government paid to send to Canada in an attempt to remedy the sexual imbalance. Most young men, however, chose to go home to France.

The Fur Trade

Fur traders, not settlers, determined the colony's success. Furs were an ideal commodity—light, easy to transport, and very profitable. For the French, at least, the fur trade was also not very hard work. It was Indians who trapped the beavers, prepared the skins, and carried them from the interior to French trading posts. French traders paid for the pelts with such goods as axes, knives, metal pots, and glass beads.

The Indians understood trade as part of a broader process of alliance that involved the exchange of gifts and mutual military assistance. When Champlain approached the Hurons for trade, they insisted that the French agree to help them fight the Iroquois. By becoming Huron allies, the French acquired Iroquois enemies. Thereafter the security of the colony depended on the ability of its governors to handle delicate diplomatic relations with the Indians.

Beginning in 1663, the colony was placed under the rule of a governor and *intendant*, royal appointees who in turn appointed several lesser officials. New France's settlers never developed institutions of self-government as English colonists did. The king also insisted on a strong military force to protect the colony from attack by Indian enemies or European rivals. He ordered the construction of forts and sent several companies of professional soldiers.

Yet colonial officials disobeyed orders from France when it suited them. Even though instructions from Paris prohibited westward expansion, the *intendant* in Quebec allowed explorers to move inland. By the 1670s, French traders and missionaries had

Chronology

1603–1625	James I reigns as king of England.	**1635–1636**	Roger Williams banished from Massachusetts, founds Providence, Rhode Island.
1607	Founding of English colonies at Jamestown and Sagadahoc.	**1637**	Anne Hutchinson banished from Massachusetts.
1608	Establishment of French colony at Quebec.		Pequot War.
1619	Virginia's House of Burgesses meets for the first time.	**1638**	New Haven colony founded.
1620	Founding of Plymouth Colony in New England.	**1640s**	Sugar cultivation and slavery established in West Indies.
	Mayflower Compact signed.	**1642–1660**	English Civil War and Interregnum.
1620s	Tobacco boom in Virginia.	**1649**	Maryland's Act for Religious Toleration.
1624	Dutch found colony of New Netherlands.	**1660**	Charles II restored to English throne; reigns until 1685.
1625	Virginia becomes a royal colony.	**1663**	Founding of Carolina colony.
	Fort Amsterdam founded.	**1664**	New Netherlands conquered by the English, becomes New York.
1625–1649	Charles I reigns as king of England.		New Jersey established.
1627	English colony at Barbados founded.	**1673**	French explorers reach the Mississippi River.
1630	Massachusetts Bay Colony founded.	**1681**	Founding of Pennsylvania.
1630–1642	Great Migration to New England.		
1634	Lord Baltimore (Cecilius Calvert) founds proprietary colony of Maryland.		

reached the Mississippi River, and in 1681–1682, Robert, sieur de La Salle, followed it to the Gulf of Mexico, claiming the entire river valley (which he named Louisiana in honor of King Louis XIV) for France. Scores of independent fur traders, known as *coureurs de bois* ("woods runners"), roamed the forests, living and trading among the Indians there.

English Settlement in the Chesapeake

When the English again attempted to settle in America in 1607, they chose the lower Chesapeake Bay region. The new settlement, Jamestown, eventually developed into the prosperous colony of Virginia. The reason for Virginia's success was an American plant—tobacco—that commanded good prices from European consumers. Tobacco also underlay the economy of a neighboring colony, Maryland, and had a profound influence on the development of Chesapeake society.

The Ordeal of Early Virginia

In 1606, a group of English merchants, convinced that they could succeed where others had failed, petitioned King James I for a charter incorporating two companies, the **Virginia Company** and the **Plymouth Company**, to attempt New World settlement. James I agreed to issue a charter granting the companies two tracts of land along the mid-Atlantic coast. These **joint-stock companies** sold shares to investors (who expected a profit in return) to raise money for colonization.

On a peninsula about 50 miles up a river they named the James, in honor of their king, 104 colonists, all men, built a fortified settlement they called Jamestown (see Map 2-2). They immediately began searching for gold and exploring the James in search of the Northwest Passage to Asia. All they found was disappointment and suffering. The swampy land around the settlement was a perfect breeding area for malarial mosquitoes and parasites carrying other diseases. The settlers neglected to plant crops, and their food supplies dwindled. By January 1608, only thirty-eight of them were still alive.

The colony's governing council then turned to Captain John Smith for leadership. Just 28 years old, Smith had fought against Spain in the Netherlands and the Ottomans in Hungary. He imposed military discipline on Jamestown's settlers, forming them into work gangs and decreeing that "he that will not worke shall not eate." His high-handed

Map 2-2 **English and Dutch Mainland Colonies in North America, c. 1655**
Early English colonies clustered in two areas of the Atlantic seaboard—New England and the Chesapeake Bay. Between them lay Dutch New Netherlands, with settlements stretching up the Hudson River. The Dutch also acquired territory at the mouth of the Delaware River in 1655 when they seized a short-lived Swedish colony located there.

methods revived the colony but antagonized certain settlers. When a gunpowder explosion wounded Smith in 1609 and forced him to return to England, his enemies had him replaced as leader.

Once again, the colony nearly disintegrated. New settlers arrived, only to die of disease and starvation. Of the five hundred people in Jamestown in the autumn of 1609, just sixty remained alive by the spring of 1610—some of whom survived only by eating their dead companions. Facing financial ruin, company officials back in England tried to conceal the state of the colony. They reorganized the company twice and sent more settlers, including glassmakers, winegrowers, and silkmakers in a desperate effort to find a marketable colonial product. They experimented with harsh military discipline, with a legal code—the *Lawes Divine, Morall and Martiall*—that prescribed the death penalty for offenses as trivial as swearing or killing a chicken. When it became clear that such severity discouraged immigration, the company tried more positive inducements.

The first settlers had been expected to work together in return for food and other necessities. With no profits forthcoming, governors began assigning small plots of land to colonists who finished their terms of service to the company. In 1616, the company instituted the **headright system**, giving 50 acres to anyone who paid his own way to Virginia and an additional 50 for each person (or "head") he brought with him.

In 1619, three other important developments occurred. The company began transporting women to Virginia to become wives for planters and induce them to stay in the colony. It also sent over the first African slaves to Virginia. And the company created the first legislative body in English America, the **House of Burgesses**, setting a precedent for the establishment of self-government in other English colonies. Landowners elected representatives to the House of Burgesses, which, subject to the approval of the company, made laws for Virginia.

The settlers were still unable to earn the company a profit. To make things worse, the headright system expanded English settlement beyond Jamestown, straining the already tense relations between the Indians and the intruding English.

The English settlement was in the heart of territory ruled by the Indian leader Powhatan, then at the peak of his power and chief of a confederacy of about thirty tribes with some fourteen thousand people. After an initial skirmish with English soldiers, he sent gifts of food, assuming that by accepting the gifts, the colonists acknowledged their dependence on him. Further action against the settlers seemed unnecessary, since they seemed fully capable of destroying themselves.

However, armed colonists began to seize corn from Indian villages whenever the natives refused to supply it. During one raid in 1609, John Smith held a pistol to the chest of Opechancanough, Powhatan's younger brother, until the Indians ransomed him with loads of corn. Protesting that the English came "to invade my people and possesse my Country," Powhatan laid siege to Jamestown and tried to starve the colony to extinction. The colony was saved only by reinforcements from England. War with the Indians continued until 1614, when colonist John Rolfe married Pocahontas, Powhatan's daughter. Pocahontas had briefly been held captive by the English during the war and had been instructed in English manners and religion by Rolfe. Sent to negotiate with Powhatan in the spring of 1614, Rolfe asked the chief for his daughter's hand. Powhatan gave his consent, and Pocahontas—baptized in the Church of England and renamed Rebecca—became Rolfe's wife.

Pocahontas died on a trip to England in 1617, severing the tie between her family and the English.

POWHATAN
Held this state & fashion when Capt. Smith was delivered to him prisoner

Powhatan's first meeting with John Smith followed the rules of Indian formality. Smith was conducted down a long building made of bark and saplings. Powhatan sat at the far end, bedecked with "many Chaynes of great Pearles about his neck" and covered with raccoon skins. Several of Powhatan's wives and councilors sat before him, and "40 or 50 of the tallest men his Country doth afford" stood guard outside.

Powhatan died in 1618, and Opechancanough succeeded him as chief. Still harboring intense resentment against the English, the new chief made plans to retaliate against them. Early in the morning on March 22, 1622, hundreds of Indian men traveled to the scattered English settlements, as if they meant to visit or trade. Instead they attacked the unsuspecting colonists, killing 347 by the end of the day—more than one-fourth of the English population.

The English gathered to plot revenge. English forces struck at native villages, killing the inhabitants and burning cornfields. During peace talks held in April 1623, the English served poisoned wine to their enemies, killing two hundred more. During nine years of war, the English treated the Indians with a ferocity that recalled their earlier subjugation of the Irish.

Economic activity ceased as settlers retreated to fortified garrisons. The Virginia company went bankrupt. A royal commission investigating the 1622 surprise attack was shocked to discover that nearly ten times more colonists had died from starvation and disease than at the hands of Indians. King James had little choice but to dissolve the company in 1624 and Virginia became a royal colony the following year. Now the king chose the colony's governor and council, and royal advisers monitored its affairs.

Tobacco Colony

In their search for a marketable product, some settlers had begun growing tobacco after 1610. Initially expensive, it had become popular among wealthy European consumers. The first cargo of Virginia-grown tobacco arrived in England in 1617 and sold at a highly profitable 3 shillings per pound.

Settlers immediately planted tobacco everywhere—even in the streets of Jamestown. Company officials, unwilling to base the colony's economy on a single crop, especially one that many people (including King James) considered unhealthy, tried to restrict annual production. After company rule ended, tobacco planting surged.

Between 1627 and 1669, tobacco exports climbed from 250,000 pounds to more than 15 million pounds. As the supply grew, the price plunged from 13 pence in 1624 to a mere penny in the late 1660s, where it remained for the next half century. The only way colonists could compensate for falling prices was to grow even more, pushing exports to England to more than 20 million pounds by the late 1670s.

Tobacco shaped nearly every aspect of Virginia society, from patterns of settlement to the recruitment of colonists. Planters scrambled to claim lands near navigable rivers so that ships could easily reach their plantations and carry their crops to market. As a result, the colonists dispersed across the countryside instead of gathering in towns. People settled, one governor wrote, wherever "a choice veine of rich ground invited them, and further from neighbours the better." Colonists competed to produce the biggest and best crop and get it to market the fastest, hoping to enjoy even a small price advantage over everyone else.

The key to success was to control a large labor force. Tobacco kept workers busy nine months of the year. Planters sowed seeds in the early spring, transplanted seedlings a few weeks later, and spent the summer pinching off the tops of the plants (so they would produce larger leaves) and removing worms. After the harvest, the leaves were "cured"—dried in ventilated sheds—and packed in large barrels. During the winter, planters cleared and fenced more land and made barrels for next year's crop. Working on his own, one planter could tend two thousand plants, which yielded about 500 pounds of cured tobacco.

To make a profit, planters needed help. They turned to England, importing thousands of **indentured servants**, or contract workers, who agreed to a fixed term of labor, usually four to seven years, in exchange for free passage to Virginia. The master provided food, shelter, clothing, and, at the end of the term of service, "freedom dues" paid in corn and clothing. Between 1625 and 1640, an estimated one thousand or more indentured servants arrived each year. Some were orphans; others were condemned criminals given a choice between execution and transportation to Virginia. Most, however, came from the ranks of England's unemployed, who emigrated in hopes of "bettering their condition in a Growing Country."

Most found such hopes quickly dashed. Many servants died from disease, and some servants died from mistreatment. Richard Price beat his servant, Endymion Inleherne, for "being a common runaway and one that did use to feign himself sick" so severely that the young man died. A jury refused to charge Price with murder, reasoning that Inleherne deserved punishment and Price had not intended to kill him. The courts (administered by masters) usually favored masters' authority over servants' rights.

For every ex-servant who made it into the ranks of Virginia landholders, dozens died in poverty. Many ex-servants could find farms only in parts of the colony that were less suitable for tobacco cultivation and more vulnerable to Indian attack.

Because of their labor needs, masters favored young men in their teens and twenties as indentured servants, importing three or four times as many of them as women. As a result, Virginia's population in the seventeenth century was overwhelmingly young and male. Many free male servants found that marriage was as remote a possibility as landownership. John Rolfe's union with Pocahontas was one of only three English-Indian marriages recorded in seventeenth-century Virginia.

Population growth was further slowed because servants could not marry until their indentures were completed. Many men were already in their thirties when they married, usually to women in their early twenties. Older couples had fewer children than younger couples would have had. Few colonists lived past 50, and many of their offspring died young. Children who survived had usually lost one or both parents by the time they reached adulthood.

Surviving spouses often remarried a widow or widower with children, creating complex households with stepparents and half-brothers and half-sisters. Widows controlled property left to them by their husbands, assuming the normally male responsibility of managing estates for their children's benefit. A widow tried to choose a new spouse wisely, for he would generally take over management of the property that the children of her first marriage would inherit.

The number of settlers rose from about 2,500 in 1630 to 21,000 in 1660, thanks to the demand for indentured servants. When Opechancanough launched another raid in 1644 that killed nearly five hundred colonists, it had a far less devastating effect than his attack of 1622 because the settler population had grown so much and now outnumbered the Indians.

Some settlers acquired large estates and grew wealthy from the labor of indentured servants tilling their tobacco fields. Others, cultivating small landholdings or renting plots from more successful colonists, grew just enough food to survive and as much tobacco as they could manage. But even the most successful settlers, investing every penny of profit in labor and land, lived under quite primitive conditions.

Early colonial dwellings were often no larger than 16 by 20 feet, with one or two rooms. The poorest settlers slept on the floor on straw mattresses and had few other furnishings. Even among middling planters, amenities were few. Rich planters owned more goods, though often of poor quality. In 1655, for instance, William Brocas, a prominent colonial official, owned "a parcell of old hangings, very thin and much worn"; seven chairs, "most of them unusefull"; and seven guns, "most unfixt."

Maryland

Encouraged by Virginia's success, King Charles I in 1632 granted 10 million acres of land north of Chesapeake Bay to the nobleman George Calvert, Lord Baltimore. Unlike Virginia, which was founded by a joint-stock company, Maryland was a **proprietary colony**—the sole possession of Calvert and his heirs. They owned all the land, which they could divide up as they pleased, and had the right to set up the colony's government.

Calvert, who was Catholic, intended Maryland to be a refuge for others of his faith. English Catholics were a disadvantaged minority. They paid double taxes, could not worship in public or hold political office, and could not send their children to universities. In Maryland, Calvert wanted Catholic colonists to enjoy economic and political power. He intended to divide the land into manors—large private estates like those of medieval England—and distribute them to wealthy Catholic friends. These manor lords would live on rents collected from tenant farmers, hold the most important governmental offices, and run their own law courts.

Calvert died before settlement began, and his plans unraveled. The majority of colonists, who began arriving in 1634, were Protestants who despised Catholics. Refusing to live as tenants on Catholic estates, they claimed land of their own—a process that accelerated after 1640, when Maryland adopted a headright system like Virginia's as a way to recruit settlers.

Maryland's problems intensified when civil war broke out in England in 1642. Charles I, who became king in 1625, clashed with Protestants who called for further reform of the Church of England. He also antagonized many government leaders by dissolving Parliament in 1629 and ruling on his own for eleven years. Needing funds to suppress a rebellion in Scotland in 1640, however, Charles was forced to recall Parliament, which quickly turned against him. Both king and Parliament recruited armies and went to war in 1642. Parliamentary forces triumphed, and in 1649, they executed Charles. For the next decade, Oliver Cromwell, a general, ruled until his death in 1658. His son, Richard, proved an inept successor, and in 1660 a group of army officers invited Charles's exiled son to accept the throne.

During the 1640s and 1650s, Maryland Protestants took advantage of the upheaval in England, contesting the Calverts' control of the colony. To pacify them, Calvert's son Cecilius established a legislature, assuming that Protestants would dominate the elective lower house while he could appoint Catholics to the upper house, or council. In 1649, Calvert also approved the **Act for Religious Toleration**, the first law in America to call for freedom of worship for all Christians, but the Protestant majority continued to resist Catholic political influence, at one point passing a law that prohibited Catholics from voting.

Instead of the peaceful Catholic refuge Calvert intended, Maryland soon resembled neighboring Virginia. Its settlers raised tobacco and imported as many indentured servants as possible. Because Maryland initially provided former servants with 50 acres of land, more of them than in Virginia made it into the ranks of landholders. As in Virginia, however, economic opportunity diminished after 1660 when the price of tobacco dropped. Maryland's settlers enjoyed more peaceful relations with the

Indians among whom they settled than Virginians had, but they fought intensely among themselves.

The Founding of New England

The first English attempt to settle the northeastern coast of North America was a miserable failure. In 1607, the Plymouth Company sent a group of settlers who abandoned their settlement in present-day Maine the next summer. But English explorers and fishermen continued to visit New England, among them John Smith, who in 1616, published his book extolling its virtues as a site for colonization.

Six colonies appeared in the region between 1620 and 1640, settled by thousands of people troubled by religious, political, and economic upheavals in England. The society these settlers created differed markedly from the one developing in the Chesapeake—not least of all in the absence of significant Indian opposition. Between 1616 and 1618 a terrible epidemic swept through coastal New England, killing up to 90 percent of the Indians living there. The devastated survivors were unable to prevent the encroaching English from building towns where their villages had once stood.

The Pilgrims and Plymouth Colony

Plymouth Colony, the first of the New England settlements, was founded in 1620. Its origins lay in religious disputes that had plagued England since the late sixteenth century. Most of Queen Elizabeth's subjects approved of her efforts to keep England a Protestant nation, but some believed that she had not sufficiently rid the Church of England of Catholic practices. The enemies of these reformers, ridiculing them for wanting to purify the Church of England (or **Anglican** Church) of all corruption, called them **Puritans**.

Following the doctrine of predestination taught by John Calvin, English Puritans believed in an all-powerful God who, at the moment of Creation, had determined which humans would be saved and which would be damned. The centerpiece of their spiritual life was conversion: the transforming experience that occurred when individuals felt the stirrings of grace in their souls and began to hope that they were among the saved. Those who experienced conversion were considered **saints** and acquired new strength to live godly lives.

Puritans rejected the Book of Common Prayer, which regulated Anglican worship, insisting that ministers should pray from the heart and preach from the Bible. They objected when Anglican clergy wore rich vestments that set them apart from ordinary Christians. And they objected to any church organization above the level of individual congregations, seeing no need for bishops and archbishops. But what they hated most of all about the Anglican Church was that anyone could be a member. Puritans believed that everyone should attend church services, but they wanted church membership—which conferred the right to partake in the Lord's Supper, or communion—to be limited to saints.

Puritans thus insisted on further reform. Elizabeth and the rulers who followed her disagreed and tried to silence them. Some Puritans, known as **separatists**, were convinced that the Church of England would never change and left it to form their own congregations.

One such group, mainly artisans and middling farmers from the village of Scrooby, in Nottinghamshire, left England in 1607–1608, settling for more than a decade in Holland. There they worshiped in peace, but many of them struggled to make a living and feared that their children were being tempted by the worldly pleasures of Dutch city life. Some of the Scrooby separatists gained the backing of the Plymouth Company for a move to America. Called **Pilgrims** because they thought of themselves as spiritual wanderers, they were joined by other separatists and by nonseparatist "strangers" hired to help get the colony started. In all, 102 men, women, and children set sail on the *Mayflower* in September 1620.

After a long and miserable voyage, they landed near Massachusetts Bay. Since this was about 200 miles north of the land their charter permitted them to settle, some of the "strangers" claimed that they were no longer legally bound to obey the expedition's separatist leaders. The leaders responded by drafting the **Mayflower Compact**, which became the first document to establish self-government in any North American colony, and urging all adult males to sign it.

The Pilgrims settled at Plymouth, the site of a Wampanoag village recently depopulated by disease, where they found abandoned cornfields, Indian graves, and baskets of corn buried underground. Even with this corn, nearly half of the Pilgrims died of starvation and disease that first winter.

Two English speaking natives, Squanto and Samoset, emerged from the woods the next spring and approached the Pilgrims on behalf of Massasoit, the Wampanoag leader. The Wampanoags thought the Pilgrims might be useful allies against Wampanoag enemies, such as the Narragansetts, who had escaped the recent epidemics.

In 1621, the Wampanoags and the Pilgrims signed a treaty of alliance. The Pilgrims assumed that Massasoit had submitted to the superior authority of King James, whereas Massasoit assumed that the agreement treated himself and the English king as equal partners. Despite frequent disputes caused by English assertion of authority over the Wampanoags, the two groups enjoyed relatively peaceful relations for nearly half a century.

The Indians taught the English how to plant corn and traded corn with them for manufactured goods. The Pilgrims also exchanged corn with other Indians to the north for furs, which they shipped back to England to help pay off their debts to English investors. In the autumn of 1621, Indians and Pilgrims gathered for a feast celebrating the settlers' first harvest—an event Americans still commemorate as the first Thanksgiving.

Plymouth remained small, poor, and weak. It never grew to more than seven thousand settlers and never produced more than small shipments of furs, fish, and timber to sell in England. It took the Pilgrims more than twenty years to repay their English creditors. Yet because of the idealistic visions of the founders of Plymouth Colony, who saw in the New World a chance to escape religious persecution and create peaceful communities and pure churches, it has become an important symbol in American history.

Massachusetts Bay Colony and Its Offshoots

The Puritans who settled Massachusetts shared many of the Pilgrims' beliefs. But they insisted that the Anglican Church *could* be reformed and so were not separatists. They went to New England to create godly churches to serve as models for English reform. And England, they believed, was in more desperate need of reformation than ever.

Charles I, who became king in 1625, opposed Puritans more forcefully than his father had and supported changes in Anglican worship that recalled Catholic practices. England at the time was also suffering from economic troubles that many Puritans saw as signs of God's displeasure with their country.

In 1629, a group of Puritan merchants received a royal charter for a joint-stock enterprise, the Massachusetts Bay Company, to set up a colony north of Plymouth. They chose John Winthrop, a prosperous Puritan lawyer, as their leader. In the spring of 1630, a fleet of eleven ships carried about a thousand men, women, and children across the Atlantic.

Before Winthrop's ship landed, he preached a lay sermon, called "A Model of Christian Charity," to his fellow passengers, reminding them of their goal "to do more service to the Lord." They should "love one another with a pure heart" and place the good of all above private ambitions. Winthrop argued that the Lord had made them his chosen people, and that as a result, "we shall be as a city upon a hill, the eyes of all people are upon us." If they failed to live up to God's expectations, he would punish them. With this mingled encouragement and threat, the emigrants soon landed and founded Boston and six adjoining towns.

Winthrop described the settlers' mission in New England as a **covenant**, or contract, with God, binding them to meet their religious obligations in return for God's favor. The settlers also created covenants when they founded towns and churches, agreeing to live together in peace. The desire for peace and purity could breed intolerance. Settlers closely scrutinized their neighbors for signs of unacceptable behavior. But the insistence on covenants and conformity also created a remarkably stable society, far more peaceable than Virginia's.

That stability was enhanced by the development of representative government. The **General Court**, which initially included only the shareholders of the joint-stock company, was transformed into a two-house legislature. Freemen—adult males who held property and were church members—had the right to elect representatives (two per town) to the lower house, as well as eighteen members (called "assistants") to the upper house. They also chose a governor and a deputy governor.

Between 1630 and 1642, at least thirteen thousand settlers came to New England and established dozens of towns. The progress of settlement was generally untroubled in coastal Massachusetts, but when colonists moved into the distant Connecticut River Valley, tensions with Indians grew rapidly. These erupted in 1637 in the brief, tragic conflict called the **Pequot War.**

English settlers from Massachusetts first arrived in the Connecticut Valley in the mid-1630s. Dutch traders already in the region had been dealing exclusively with the Pequot Indians as partners. In 1633, however, they invited other Indian groups to trade with them. The Pequots, suffering terribly from a recent smallpox epidemic, resented losing their special trading rights and began fighting the Dutch. Initially, they saw the new English settlers as potential allies against the Dutch. But when the settlers demanded Pequot submission to English authority as the price of an alliance, they turned against them too.

American Views

MIANTONOMO'S PLEA FOR INDIAN UNITY (1642)

Until European colonization began to force a change in outlook, the native inhabitants of North America never thought of themselves as one people, any more than Europe's residents considered themselves "Europeans." Miantonomo, a Narragansett living in Rhode Island, was one of the first native leaders to call for a unified response to English intrusion. With the gruesome lessons of the Pequot War fresh in his mind, he urged the Montauks of Long Island to put aside their differences with the Narragansetts and join them in opposing the settlers. His appeal, recorded by Lion Gardiner, an English officer during the Pequot War, was uttered in vain. Captured by the English and tried and convicted of the murder of an Indian, Miantonomo was turned over to a Mohegan rival for execution.

❖ **How did Miantonomo describe Indian life before the arrival of the English?**

❖ **What changes occurred as a result of their settlement?**

Brothers, we must be as one as the English are, or we shall all be destroyed. You know our fathers had plenty of deer and skins and our plains were full of game and turkeys, and our coves and rivers were full of fish.

But, brothers, since these Englishmen have seized our country, they have cut down the grass with scythes, and the trees with axes. Their cows and horses eat up the grass, and their hogs spoil our bed of clams; and finally we shall all starve to death; therefore, stand not in your own light, I ask you, but resolve to act like men. All the sachems both to the east and the west have joined with us, and we are resolved to fall upon them at a day appointed, and therefore I come secretly to you, [be]cause you can persuade your Indians to do what you will.

Source: *Steven Mintz, ed.*, Native American Voices: A History and Anthology (*1995*), *pp. 84–85.*

The English settlers formed alliances with the Narragansetts and Mohegans, who were both rivals of the Pequots. In May 1637, English forces surrounded a Pequot village inhabited mainly by women and children, located on the Mystic River. They set it ablaze and shot anyone who tried to escape. Between three hundred and seven hundred Pequots died, a toll that shocked the settlers' Indian allies, who protested that English-style warfare was "too furious, and slays too many men" (see "American Views: Miantonomo's Plea for Indian Unity"). After the surviving Pequots had fled or been sold into slavery, many more settlers moved to Connecticut, which soon declared itself a separate colony. In 1639, the settlers adopted the **Fundamental Orders**, creating a government similar to that of Massachusetts, and the English government granted them a royal charter in 1662.

Massachusetts spun off other colonies as its population expanded in the 1630s and dissenters ran afoul of its intolerant government. Puritan leaders tried to suppress unorthodox religious opinions whenever they emerged, for fear that God would interpret their failure to do so as a breach of their covenant with him. Some dissenting colonists, however, refused to be silenced.

Roger Williams was one such irrepressible dissenter. Williams was a separatist minister who declared that because Massachusetts churches had not rejected the Church of England, they shared its corruption. He argued for the separation of church and state, and also attacked the Massachusetts charter, insisting that the king had no right to grant Indian lands to English settlers.

Williams was an immensely likable man—even Governor Winthrop remained on friendly terms with him. But the General Court sentenced him to banishment, intending to ship him back to England. In the winter of 1635, Williams slipped away with a few followers and found refuge among the Narragansett Indians, from whom he purchased land for the village of Providence, founded in 1636. More towns soon sprang up nearby when a new religious crisis, provoked by a woman named Anne Hutchinson, sent additional refugees to Rhode Island from Massachusetts.

Anne Hutchinson arrived in Boston from England with her husband and seven children in 1634. Welcomed by the town's women for her talents as a midwife, she also began to hold religious meetings in her house, where she denounced several ministers.

Many people, including prominent Boston merchants, flocked to Hutchinson's meetings. But her critics believed her to be a dangerous **antinomian** (someone who claimed to be free from obedience to moral law) because she seemed to maintain that saints were accountable only to God and not to any worldly authority. Her opponents also objected to her teaching of mixed groups of men and women, a breach of normal gender roles. Colony magistrates arrested her and tried her for sedition—that is, for advocating the overthrow of the government.

During her trial, Hutchinson mounted a lively defense. In the end, however, the court found her guilty and banished her from the colony. With many of her followers, she moved to Rhode Island, where Roger Williams had proclaimed a policy of religious toleration.

At the height of the Hutchinson controversy, a group of zealous Puritan emigrants led by the Reverend John Davenport departed Boston to found New Haven in 1638. Davenport's efforts to impose perfect Puritan conformity in his colony made Massachusetts seem easygoing in comparison. But New Haven failed to thrive, and in 1662, the poor, intolerant, and isolated colony was absorbed into Connecticut.

The Growth of New England

"This plantation and that of Virginia went not forth upon the same reasons," declared one of Massachusetts's founders. Virginians came "for profit," whereas New Englanders emigrated to bear witness to their Puritan faith. Unlike the unmarried young men who moved in great numbers to Virginia, most New Englanders settled with their families.

The average family in early New England had seven or eight children. Because women and men arrived in nearly equal numbers, young adults easily found spouses and produced more children. Thus the population continued to grow rapidly even when immigration slowed after 1642, so that by 1660, New England's settlers numbered more than 33,000.

New Englanders were largely spared from the diseases that ravaged Virginia's settlers and devastated Indian populations. It seemed a "marvelous providence of God" to Plymouth's Governor Bradford that many settlers made it to their seventies and eighties when few of England's adults lived past 60. Longevity strengthened economic security as well as emotional ties. Fathers lived long enough to build prosperous farms to pass along to their sons. And they accumulated herds of livestock and stores of household goods to give to their daughters when they married.

Unlike Chesapeake colonists, who spread out on tobacco lands near navigable rivers, New Englanders clustered in towns. The Massachusetts government strongly encouraged town formation by granting land to groups of families who promised to settle together. The families divided the land among themselves, allotting each family a farm of sufficient size to support all its members. People who had had higher social standing in England received larger farms than those of lower standing. Land that the original families could not yet farm was held "in common" to be distributed to their children as they grew up. Settlers and their children generally remained in their chosen towns for the rest of their lives.

Towns—usually made up of fifty to a hundred families—provided the context for religious, political, and economic activity. The importance Puritans placed on worship with fellow Christians helped promote community feeling. Every Sunday, townspeople gathered at the meetinghouse, usually located near the town center, to listen to the minister preach God's word. At other times, the meetinghouse served as a town hall, where men assembled to discuss matters ranging from local taxes to making sure that everyone's fences were mended. Townsmen tried to reach decisions by consensus in order to preserve harmony. To oversee day-to-day local affairs, men chose five to seven of their most trusted neighbors to serve as **selectmen**.

Economic life likewise centered on the town. New England's stony soil and short growing season offered few ways to get rich, but even "the poorest person . . . hath a house and land of his own, and bread of his own growing." Farmers grew corn and other foods and raised livestock. Their goal was to achieve what they called **competency**—the possession of enough property to ensure their families' economic independence.

Maintaining competency was a family affair. New England farmers relied on their wives and children for labor. Women cared for children, cleaned, cooked, sewed and mended, milked cows, and tended poultry. Many farmwives made butter and cheese, brewed beer, preserved fruits and vegetables, salted meat, spun yarn, and wove cloth. Although they generally did not perform heavy agricultural work, women helped with planting and harvesting crops and tended gardens near their houses. If their husbands worked as merchants or craftsmen, wives might also help out in the shop.

Children began work shortly after their fifth birthday. Older siblings cared for younger ones, fetched tools, and minded cattle. Around age 10, girls began learning more complicated housekeeping skills from their mothers, and boys received instruction from their fathers in such tasks as plowing, cutting hay and wood, and caring for livestock. Many children in their early teens performed tasks little different from adult duties.

No family could produce all the goods that it needed, so New Englanders regularly traded with their neighbors. A skilled carpenter might erect a house in return for barrels of salted beef. Men with several sons sent them to help neighbors whose children were too young to work. Midwives delivered babies in return for cheese or eggs. Women nursed sick neighbors, whom they might one day call on for similar help. These sorts of transactions allowed most New Englanders to enjoy a fairly comfortable life.

Without a staple crop like tobacco, New England prospered by exploiting a variety of resources, developing a diversified economy that was less vulnerable to depression than Virginia's. Farmers sent livestock and meat to merchants to be marketed abroad. Fishermen caught thousands of pounds of cod, haddock, and other fish to be sold in Europe. Some of the region's timber found its way abroad, but most of it ended up in shipyards. New Englanders became such skilled shipbuilders and seafaring merchants that by the 1670s, London merchants complained about competition from them. England itself had little use for the dried fish, livestock, salted meat, and wood products that New England vessels carried, but enterprising merchants found exactly the market they needed in the West Indies.

The English in the Caribbean

The Spanish claimed all Caribbean islands by right of Columbus's discovery, but during the early seventeenth century, French, Dutch, and English adventurers defied them. By the 1640s, the English occupied Antigua, Barbados, Montserrat, Nevis, and St. Christopher; in 1655, they conquered the Spanish-held island of Jamaica. The West Indies soon became the jewel of England's empire, producing vast wealth from the cultivation of sugar. Caribbean planters created a society totally unlike any of the mainland colonies—not least of all because their prosperity depended on the exploitation of African slaves.

Sugar and Slaves

The first English colonists who came to the West Indies in the 1630s raised tobacco and imported indentured servants to work their fields. By that time, however, tobacco fetched low prices. Moreover, the disease environment of the West Indies proved even harsher than that of the Chesapeake, and settlers died in great numbers.

But by the 1640s, a Barbados planter boasted of "a great change on this island of late from the worse to the better, praised be God." That change was a shift from tobacco to sugar cane. Many sugar planters grew wealthy. In 1646, a 500-acre plantation on Barbados sold for £16,000—more than the whole island had been worth just a few years before. On average, the estate of a Caribbean sugar planter was worth four times as much as a prosperous Chesapeake plantation.

Sugar rapidly transformed the West Indies. Planters deforested whole islands to raise sugar cane. They stopped planting food crops and raising livestock—thereby creating a demand for lumber and provisions that boosted New England's economy.

The sugar boom also led to a scramble for labor. Planters continued to import white indentured servants, including some kidnapped English and Irish youths, but soon turned to African slaves. Africans were already used to agricultural work in a tropical climate. And the English would not have to enslave any Africans themselves; they could simply import people who had already been enslaved by other Africans and sold to Dutch or Portuguese

Authentic portraits of West Indian slaves are extremely rare. These sketches of Jamaican slaves show them going about the mundane tasks of daily life.

Buddy.Qua

traders. The planters' choice has been called an "unthinking decision," but it had an enormous impact on English colonial life, first in the islands and then on the mainland.

A Biracial Society

The West Indies had the first biracial plantation society in the English colonial world. By 1700, more than 250,000 slaves had been imported into the region, quickly becoming the most numerous segment of its population. Slaves lived in wretched conditions, underfed, poorly dressed, and housed in rough huts. They labored six days a week from sunrise to sunset—except at harvest time, when they toiled seven days a week in round-the-clock shifts. Masters considered them property, often branding them like livestock and hunting them with bloodhounds when they ran away.

Laws declared slavery to be a lifelong condition that passed from slave parents to their children. Slaves had no legal rights and were under the complete control of their masters. Only rarely would masters who killed slaves face prosecution, and those who did and were found guilty were subject only to fines. Slaves, in contrast, could be whipped, branded, or maimed for stealing food or harboring a runaway compatriot. Serious crimes such as murder or arson brought execution without trial. Slaves who rebelled were burned to death.

When masters began to import African women as well as men—hoping to create a self-reproducing labor force—slaves began to form families and preserve at least some African traditions.

They gave their children African names (although masters often gave them English names as well). They celebrated with African music and worked to the rhythm of familiar songs. They performed West African funeral rituals, often burying their dead with food and other goods to accompany them on the journey to the happier afterlife.

Some planters, profiting handsomely from their slaves' toil, lived better than many English gentlemen, dwelling in large houses, with fine furnishings. But sugar production required a heavy investment in land, slaves, mills, and equipment. As great planters took vast amounts of land for themselves, freed servants and small farmers struggled to survive. After 1650, some poorer white colonists headed for the mainland. They were soon joined by planters looking for a place to expand their operations once most of the good land on the islands had been brought under cultivation.

The Proprietary Colonies

The initial burst of English colonization ended in 1640 when England tottered on the brink of civil war. With the accession of Charles II to the English throne in 1660, however, interest in North American colonies revived. Charles II rewarded the supporters who had remained loyal to him during his long exile in France with huge tracts of American land. Four new colonies—Carolina, Pennsylvania, New Jersey, and New York—resulted from such grants during his reign (1660–1685) (see Map 2-3). All were propri-

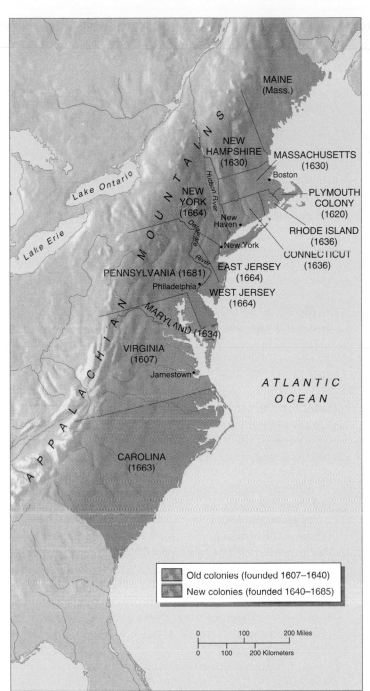

Map 2-3   *English North American Colonies, c. 1685*
After the restoration of Charles II in 1660, several large proprietary colonies joined earlier English settlements in New England and the Chesapeake. By 1685, a growing number of English settlers solidified England's claim to the Atlantic coast from Maine (then part of Massachusetts Bay Colony) to the southern edge of Carolina.

etary colonies, essentially the private property of the people to whom they had been given. Carolina and Pennsylvania, like the earlier proprietary colony of Maryland, provided their owners the chance to test idealistic social visions. The origins of New York and

New Jersey as English colonies, in contrast, lay not in proprietary visions of social harmony but in the stern reality of military conquest (see the summary table "English Colonies in the Seventeenth Century").

Early Carolina

In 1663, Charles II granted a group of supporters an enormous tract of land stretching from southern Virginia to northern Florida. The proprietors, who included several Barbados planters, called their colony Carolina, after the Latin form (Carolus) of the king's name. They envisioned it growing into a prosperous, orderly society.

One of the proprietors, Anthony Ashley Cooper, working closely with his secretary, John Locke, devised the **Fundamental Constitutions of Carolina**, a plan to ensure the stability of the colony by balancing property ownership and political rights. It called for the creation of a colonial aristocracy, with three kinds of nobles, who would own two-fifths of the land and wield extensive political power. Below them, a large class of freeholders would own small farms and elect representatives to an assembly. At the bottom of the social order would be slaves.

This plan never went into effect. People moved in from Virginia and the West Indies and settled where they pleased. They even voted in the assembly to reject the Fundamental Constitutions. When English traders first appeared, eager to buy deerskins, many Indians had welcomed them. But they grew hostile when some traders began selling guns to some tribes in exchange for captives from rival tribes who were sold as slaves to the West Indies. Resentments deepened as settlers moved onto native lands.

The colonists at first raised livestock to be sold to the West Indies. But the introduction of rice in Carolina in the 1690s transformed the settlers' economy, making it, as one planter noted, "as much their staple Commodity, as Sugar is to Barbadoes and Jamaica, or Tobacco to Virginia and Maryland." West African slaves probably introduced rice cultivation in Carolina. Ironically, the profits earned from rice persuaded Carolina planters to invest even more heavily in slave labor.

By 1708, there were more black slaves than white settlers in the colony, and two decades after that, blacks outnumbered whites by two to one. Rice farming required a substantial investment in land, labor, and equipment, including dikes and dams for flooding fields. Those who could afford such an investment set themselves up as planters in Carolina's coastal rice district, acquiring large estates and forcing poorer settlers to move elsewhere.

Some of these dislocated men went to the northern part of Carolina, where the land and climate were unsuited to rice. There they raised tobacco and produced pitch, tar, and timber products from the region's pine forests. So different were the two regions that the colony formally split into two provinces—North and South Carolina—in 1729.

South Carolina rice planters became some of the wealthiest colonists on the mainland. But their luxurious style of life came at a price. As Carolina began to look "more like a negro country than like a country settled by white people," planters came to dread the prospect of slave rebellion. To avert this nightmare, they enacted slave codes as harsh as those of the sugar islands. Carolina would not become the harmonious colony that John Locke and Cooper had envisioned. It evolved instead into a racially divided society founded on the oppression of a black majority and permeated by fear.

Pennsylvania

William Penn put his own utopian plans into action in 1681, when Charles II granted him a huge tract of land north of Maryland as payment for a royal debt owed to Penn's father. Penn intended his colony to be a model of justice and peace, as well as a refuge for members of the Society of Friends, or **Quakers**, a persecuted religious sect to which Penn himself belonged.

Like the separatists, Quakers abandoned the Church of England as hopelessly corrupt. But they went even further in their beliefs. Rejecting predestination, they maintained that every soul had a spark of grace and that salvation was possible for all who heeded that "Inner Light." They rejected trained clergy and elaborate church rituals. Instead of formal religious services, Quakers held meetings in silence until someone, inspired by the Inner Light, rose to speak.

Quaker beliefs had disturbing social and political implications. Quakers granted women spiritual equality with men, allowing them to preach, hold separate prayer meetings, and exercise authority over "women's matters." Arguing that social distinctions were not the work of God, Quakers refused to remove their hats in the presence of those of higher social class. And instead of the formal *you,* Quakers addressed superiors with the informal *thee* and *thou.* Because their faith required them to renounce the use of force, Quakers also refused to perform military service.

When English authorities began harassing Quakers, William Penn (who was himself jailed briefly) conceived his plan for a New World "holy experiment," a harmonious society governed by brotherly love. Using his father's connection with the king, he acquired the land that became Pennsylvania ("Penn's Woods") and recruited settlers from among Europe's oppressed peoples and persecuted religious sects. By 1700, eighteen thousand emigrants had left England, Wales, Scotland, Ireland, and various German provinces for the new colony.

Many came in families and settled in an area occupied by the Delaware Indians, whose numbers had recently been reduced by disease and warfare. The "holy experiment" required colonists to live "as Neighbours and friends" with the Indians as well as with one another. Penn paid Indians for land and regulated trade. As long as he remained in control of the colony, relations between the settlers and the Indians were generally peaceful—so much so that refugee Indians from nearby colonies moved into Pennsylvania. Relations between Penn and the settlers, however, were less cordial.

In the **Frame of Government**, his constitution for Pennsylvania, Penn remained true to his Quaker principles with a provision allowing for religious freedom. But true to his aristocratic origins, he designed a legislature with limited powers and reserved considerable authority for himself. When Penn returned to England after a brief stay in the colony (1682–1684), the governor and council—both appointed by Penn—fought with elected members of the assembly. Penn's opponents—many of whom were fellow Quakers—objected to his proprietary privileges, including his control of foreign trade and his collection of fees from landholders. Settlers on the lower Delaware River gained autonomy for themselves with their own legislature, in effect creating an unofficial colony that later became Delaware.

Settlers continued to fight among themselves, and with Penn's heirs, after his death. A flood of increasingly aggressive immigrants undermined peaceful relations with the Indians, forcing many natives to abandon their homelands and move west.

By 1720, Pennsylvania's ethnically and religiously diverse population numbered more than thirty thousand. The colony had some of the richest farmland along the Atlantic coast and was soon widely known as the "best poor man's country in the world." Growing wheat and other crops, the settlers lived mostly on scattered farms rather than in towns. From the thriving port of Philadelphia, ships carried much of the harvest to markets in the West Indies and southern Europe. Penn's "holy experiment" in

SUMMARY

ENGLISH COLONIES IN THE SEVENTEENTH CENTURY

Colony	Date of Founding	Established Religion	Economy	Government
Virginia	1607	Anglican	Tobacco	Royal (after 1625)
Plymouth	1620	Puritan	Mixed farming	Corporate
St. Christopher	1624	Anglican	Sugar	Royal
Barbados	1627	Anglican	Sugar	Royal
Nevis	1628	Anglican	Sugar	Royal
Massachusetts (including present-day Maine)	1630	Puritan	Mixed farming, fishing, shipbuilding	Corporate
New Hampshire	1630 (first settlement, annexed to Mass. 1643–1679; royal colony after 1679)	Puritan	Mixed farming	Corporate (royal after 1679)
Antigua	1632	Anglican	Sugar	Royal
Monserrat	1632	Anglican	Sugar	Royal
Maryland	1634	None (Anglican after 1692)	Tobacco	Proprietary
Rhode Island	1636	None	Mixed farming	Corporate
Connecticut	1636	Puritan	Mixed farming	Corporate
New Haven	1638	Puritan	Mixed farming	Corporate
Jamaica	1655 (captured from Spanish)	Anglican	Sugar	Royal
Carolina	1663	Anglican	Rice	Proprietary
New York	1664 (captured from Dutch)	None	Mixed farming, furs	Proprietary (royal after 1685)
New Jersey	1664	None	Mixed farming	Proprietary
Pennsylvania	1681	None	Wheat, mixed farming	Proprietary

social harmony may have failed, but as a thriving colony, Pennsylvania succeeded handsomely.

New Netherlands Becomes New York

The proprietary colonies of New York and New Jersey originated as the Dutch colony of New Netherlands. By the early seventeenth century, the Dutch Republic had become the most powerful trading nation in Europe, with thousands of ships plying the world's oceans.

The first Dutch colonists arrived in North America in 1624 to set up a permanent settlement at Fort Orange (Albany) in the as yet unclaimed region between New France and English Virginia. The heart of the colony was the Hudson River Valley from New Amsterdam (founded 1625) on Manhattan Island up to Fort Orange. The Dutch established a profitable trade with the Iroquois, who were eager to exchange furs for European tools and weapons.

The **Dutch West India Company**, the trading enterprise that established and governed New Netherlands, offered large landed estates (called **patroonships**), located mainly along the Hudson River, to wealthy Dutchmen willing to sponsor new emigrants. Few such estates were created, however, because most would-be patroons would not agree to company-imposed limits on their rights. In addition, few Dutchmen wanted to emigrate only to rent land from patroon landlords. At its maximum, the settler population of New Netherlands reached perhaps ten thousand.

Ethnic differences prevented the colonists from developing a sense of community. Among the colony's Dutch, German, French, English, Swedish, Portuguese, and African settlers were Calvinists, Lutherans, Quakers, Catholics, Jews, Muslims, and people of other faiths. Scattered in villages from Albany to the Atlantic, the colonists often lived isolated and insecure lives.

The Dutch West India Company dispatched a series of inept but aggressive governors who often provoked conflict with Indians. Although New Netherlands generally maintained good relations with its Iroquois trading partners at Fort Orange (Albany) on the upper Hudson River, it had far less friendly dealings with other Indian peoples along the lower Hudson, around New Amsterdam (New York City). In 1645, Governor Willem Kieft ordered a massacre at an encampment of Indians who had refused to pay tribute. A horrified Dutch witness described Indian children being "thrown into the river, and when the fathers and mothers endeavoured to save them, the soldiers would not let them come on land, but made both parents and children drown." He saw victims "with their hands, some with their legs cut off, and some holding their entrails in their arms." Ten years later, Governor Peter Stuyvesant antagonized Susquehannock Indians along the Delaware River by leading Dutch forces in the seizure of a small Swedish colony where the Susquehannocks had traded.

Though profitable, the fur trade did not match the riches to be found in other parts of the Dutch empire. When an English fleet appeared off the coast in 1664 Governor Stuyvesant, in command of just 150 soldiers, surrendered without firing a shot. Charles II made his brother James, duke of York, proprietor of this new English possession, which was now renamed New York. James immediately created another colony, New Jersey, when he granted some of the land to a group of his supporters.

New York was the most valuable part of the former Dutch colony. It included the port of New York City (the former New Amsterdam) and the Hudson Valley fur trade. James, who succeeded his brother to the English throne in 1685, encouraged Dutch colonists to remain and promoted immigration from England. By 1700, the settlers numbered twenty thousand.

For nearly twenty years after its takeover by the English, New York lacked something all other English colonies had—a representative assembly. After neighboring New Jersey and Pennsylvania created their own assemblies, however, New Yorkers pressed James to follow suit. Only in 1683, when it became clear that New York might lose population to Pennsylvania, did James relent and create the assembly that brought New York into line with the other English colonies.

Conclusion

During the seventeenth century, France and England joined Spain as colonial powers in North America. New France's small and scattered settlements clung to the St. Lawrence River Valley. The profits from the fur trade encouraged the French to maintain friendly relations with their Indian allies and ensured that French kings would monitor the colony's affairs and invest in its defense. English kings granted charters—sometimes to joint-stock companies (Virginia, Plymouth, Massachusetts), sometimes to proprietors (Maryland, Carolina, New York, New Jersey, Pennsylvania)—and let the colonies develop more or less on their own.

English settlers adjusted to different environments, developed different economies and labor systems, and worshiped in different churches. In many places—South Carolina, New York, Pennsylvania, the West Indies—the majority of settlers were not even of English origin. What held these colonies together was an overlay of common English institutions of government. By the mid-1680s, all the colonies had legislatures that provided for self-government, and had developed laws and judicial institutions based on English models.

The planting of French and English colonies not only ended Spain's monopoly of settlement in North America but also challenged the Indians' hold on the continent. Native peoples were forced to deal with a rising tide of settlers and often to choose sides between European antagonists. Transplanted Europeans adapted too, not only in their dealings with native peoples but also in finding sufficient labor to make their colonies prosper. For English colonists in the south, this meant the adoption of slavery. For millions of Africans, the result was forced migration to the New World.

Review Questions

1. The early settlers of New France and Virginia included few women. What effects did this have on the development of each colony?

2. Which English settlements were proprietary colonies? Did they share any common characteristics? What plans did the various proprietors have for their colonies, and to what extent were those plans put into effect?

3. When Virginia's settlers first arrived, they encountered a numerous and powerful confederation of Powhatan Indians. New England's colonists, in contrast, began settlement after epidemics had drastically reduced the local native population. In what ways did the presence or absence of Indians affect each region's early history?

4. In both Massachusetts and Pennsylvania, religion figured prominently as a motive for settlement. What were the religious beliefs of the settlers in each colony, and how did those beliefs help shape each colony's development?

5. Three colonial regions—the Chesapeake, the West Indies, and Carolina—developed economies dependent on staple crops. What were those crops? In what ways did staple crop agriculture shape society in each region?

Recommended Reading

Anderson, Virginia DeJohn. *New England's Generation: The Great Migration and the Formation of Society and Culture in the Seventeenth Century* (1991). Examines the experiences of nearly seven hundred emigrants to New England and explores the ways in which the composition of the settler population shaped early New England society.

Dunn, Richard S. *Sugar and Slaves: The Rise of the Planter Class in the English West Indies, 1624–1713* (1972). The authoritative account of British settlement in the West Indies and the development of the slave labor system.

Eccles, W. J. *The Canadian Frontier, 1534–1760* (rev. ed., 1983). Provides a comprehensive overview of French settlement in Canada.

Morgan, Edmund S. *American Slavery, American Freedom: The Ordeal of Colonial Virginia* (1975). This vividly written account of the founding of Virginia and the development of an unfree labor system remains the best study of an early American colony.

Wood, Peter H. *Black Majority: Negroes in Colonial South Carolina from 1670 through the Stono Rebellion* (1974). This study of the founding of South Carolina emphasizes the contributions of the black slaves who eventually comprised a majority of the colony's settlers.

Where to Learn More

❖ **Jamestown Festival Park, Williamsburg, Virginia.** A museum here contains indoor and outdoor exhibits on the site of the first permanent English colony in North America. The library holds some material on early settlers and Virginia Indians; in addition, there are films and videotapes about early Virginia.

❖ **St. Mary's City, Maryland.** Visitors to this site of the first permanent settlement under the Calvert family may tour the area and view exhibits and living history programs that describe life in early Maryland.

❖ **Plimoth Plantation, Plymouth, Massachusetts.** A living history museum, Plimoth Plantation re-creates colony life in the year 1627. There are reproductions of the English village and a Wampanoag settlement. Visitors may also see a replica of the *Mayflower.*

❖ **Pennsbury Manor, Morrisville, Pennsylvania.** Here is a reconstruction of William Penn's seventeenth-century plantation. The site includes furnished buildings and restored gardens. There are also interpreters to inform visitors about agricultural life in early Pennsylvania.

3 THE CREATION OF NEW WORLDS

KEY TOPICS

❖ Patterns of contact between Native Americans
  and French, Spanish, and English colonists
❖ The development of slavery and other unfree
  labor systems in early America
❖ The formation of African-American communities
❖ Causes and consequences of European
  immigration to America

Sometime before the spring of 1712, a Carolina slave named Harry took a terrible chance. His master, fed up with Harry's "roguery," had sold him to a new master in Virginia. But before he could be sent there, Harry ran away. Harry then sought refuge among the Tuscarora Indians, who might have killed him or returned him to his master for a reward.

But Harry was lucky, for he knew how to design and construct forts and helped the Indians build a stronghold to protect themselves. From this structure, the Tuscaroras could attack the white colonists under whose oppression they too had suffered.

For years, Europeans had occupied the Tuscaroras' land, cheated them in trade, and kidnapped and enslaved them. When Swiss and German settlers marched across Tuscarora territory late in 1711, the Indians raided frontier towns and killed or captured their inhabitants. The Carolina government recruited a volunteer force of colonists and Yamasees and other Indian allies and ordered it to search out and destroy Tuscarora settlements.

When these soldiers came near Harry's fort, their commander spied it "with a prospective glass and found it strong as well by situation on the river's bank as [by] Workmanship." Under Harry's direction, the Indians had dug a deep trench around the fort and surrounded the high earthworks with "large limbs of trees [that] lay confusedly about" to make entrance difficult. They also arranged "large reeds and canes to run into people's legs" as they attacked the walls. The commander had never seen "such subtill contrivances for Defence."

Although the fort withstood a siege of nearly two months, the colonial forces ultimately prevailed. Most of the surviving Tuscaroras fled north to join the powerful Iroquois nations. Others "scattered as the wind scatters the smoke." Harry's fate is unknown.

This episode reveals three important features of the new society that was developing in England's Carolina colony. First, it had a diverse population that included such Native American peoples as the Tuscaroras, Yamasees, Creeks, and Catawbas; Africans brought directly from Gambia, Guinea, and Angola or by way of the West Indies; and Europeans from England, Scotland, Ireland, Barbados, German provinces, and Swiss cantons. Second, the interactions among these peoples ranged from cooperation to outright violence. And third, what governed their interactions was a struggle for the control of resources, including trade goods, land, and labor. For slaves like Harry, the struggle was over the most fundamental resource, control of one's own life—freedom.

In many ways, the history of North America in the seventeenth and eighteenth centuries is the history of early Carolina writ large. From the southwestern deserts to the Canadian forests to the Atlantic coastal plain, diverse peoples met to trade, work, feast, worship, and fight. Their interactions, which varied from place to place and over time, created not one but many New Worlds.

Indians and Europeans

Between 1650 and 1750, a rising tide of immigrants—European and African, willing and unwilling—irrevocably altered the lives of North America's native population. By 1750, Indians had become a minority north of the Rio Grande. But despite their growing numbers, the colonists were concentrated in certain areas. Indians living along the northern Pacific coast, for instance, met their first white men—Russian fur traders—only in the 1740s. In contrast, the Pueblos of the Southwest, the Hurons of Canada, and the Algonquians of the Atlantic seaboard had by this time dealt with European colonists for a century or more.

The character of the relationship between Indians and Europeans depended on more than relative population size and the length of time they had been in contact. It was also shaped by the intentions of the newcomers—whether they came to trade, to settle, or to gain converts—and the responses of particular Native American groups as each struggled to preserve its own culture.

The Web of Trade

Europeans eager to trade with Indians had to prove their friendship by offering gifts and military aid as well as trading goods. French traders in Canada brought gifts and prepared feasts for their native partners, obliging the Indians to offer the furs that the French wanted. One seventeenth-century observer described the French governor giving the Hurons barrels of hatchets and arrowheads, in part "to waft their canoes gently homewards, [in] part to draw them to us next year." The Indians also got iron tools, kettles, cloth, beads, and—eventually—guns.

Trading with Europeans would lead gradually to the destruction of the Indians' way of life. Contact with traders exposed Indians to deadly European diseases. The Huron population declined by half in just six years between 1634 and 1640. Indians trading with the Dutch in New Netherlands in the 1650s insisted "their population had been melted down" by smallpox.

Trade also undermined self-sufficiency. Before the French arrived, for instance, the Micmacs in easternmost Canada supported themselves mainly by fishing. After becoming partners of the French around 1610, they trapped beaver year round, relying on the French and New England Indians for food. After they had trapped virtually all the beavers on their lands, they were abandoned by the French, who turned instead to the Hurons. The once prosperous Micmacs barely survived.

Other groups would suffer a similar fate. "The Cloaths we wear, we cannot make ourselves," a Carolina Cherokee used to woolen garments observed in 1753. "We cannot make our Guns. . . . Every necessary Thing in Life we must have from the white People."

Before European contact, most Indian bands living north of the Rio Grande made war to seek revenge for violent acts committed against their own people. But after the Europeans arrived, Indians began to fight each other for economic advantage, and the hostilities became far more deadly. Rivalries among French, English, and Dutch traders led to conflicts among their Indian partners. The **Beaver Wars**, one such struggle between the Hurons and the Iroquois, began in the 1640s.

Because the French already traded with the Hurons, Dutch merchants in the Hudson River Valley seeking to break into the fur trade turned to the **Iroquois League**. Composed of five separate Indian nations—the Mohawks, Oneidas, Onondagas, Cayu-

CHRONOLOGY

1440s	Portuguese enter slave trade in West Africa.		**1680s**	Second phase of Beaver Wars begins.
c. 1450	League of the Iroquois formed.		**1690s**	Shift from white indentured servants to black slaves as principal labor force in the Chesapeake.
1610–1614	First war between English settlers and Powhatan Indians.		**1701**	Iroquois adopt policy of neutrality toward French and English.
1619	First Africans arrive in Virginia.		**1711–1713**	Tuscarora War in Carolina.
1622–1632	Second war between English settlers and Powhatan Indians.		**1713**	Beginnings of substantial Scottish, Scots-Irish, and German immigration to colonies.
1637	Pequot War in New England.		**1715–1716**	Yamasee War in Carolina.
1640s	Slave labor begins to dominate in the West Indies. First phase of the Beaver Wars.		**1720s**	Black population begins to increase naturally in English mainland colonies.
1651	First "praying town" established at Natick, Massachusetts.		**1732**	Georgia established.
1661	Maryland law defines slavery as lifelong, inheritable status.		**1739**	Stono Rebellion in South Carolina.
1670	Virginia law defines status of slaves.		**1741**	Slave conspiracy discovered in New York City.
1675–1676	King Philip's War in New England.		**1750**	Slavery legalized in Georgia.
1676	Bacon's Rebellion in Virginia.		**1760–1775**	Peak of European and African immigration to English colonies.
1680	Pueblo Revolt in New Mexico.			

gas, and Senecas—it functioned as a religious organization to preserve peace among the five nations and strengthen them in their conflicts with other Indian peoples. The Iroquois agreed to supply the Dutch with furs in return for trade goods.

By the 1630s, the Hurons and Iroquois had killed nearly all the beavers on their own lands and began to look elsewhere for furs. The Hurons traded corn for furs with Indians living north of the Great Lakes. The Iroquois began to raid Huron trading parties and then to attack Huron villages.

The Iroquois triumphed in the resulting conflict largely because the Dutch readily supplied them with guns while the French did not arm the Hurons. In the end, the Hurons were destroyed. A French traveler reported seeing no Hurons in "districts which, not ten years ago, I reckoned to contain eight or ten thousand men."

The cycle of warfare did not end with the destruction of the Hurons. The Iroquois went on to challenge Indian nations near the Great Lakes and in the Ohio Valley. Seeking iron kettles more durable than earthenware pots, cloth that was lighter and more colorful than animal skins, and guns that were deadlier than bows and arrows, Indians who traded with Europeans changed their lives in ways that suited European needs as much as their own.

Occupying the Land

Trading colonies relied on Indian partners to supply them with furs and so maintained friendly relations with them out of self-interest. The European population of the trading colonies also stayed fairly low. Even after the devastation of disease, Indians outnumbered Europeans in New France and New Netherlands. As late as 1650, there were just 657 French people in Canada (compared to perhaps ten thousand Hurons) and only three thousand Europeans in New Netherlands. The English, in contrast, came mainly to settle. By 1650 there were more than fifty thousand Europeans and two thousand Africans in England's North American colonies.

The influx of settlers into the English colonies, as always, exposed native peoples to European diseases. So swift was the decline in native populations—and so rapid the influx of Europeans—that in coastal Massachusetts and eastern Virginia, colonists outnumbered Indians by 1650.

Largely because of the colonists' desire for land, violence between Europeans and Indians occurred with greater regularity in the English colonies than in New France or New Netherlands. Coming from an England where all good farming land had been cultivated for centuries, colonists thrilled at the sight of what they saw as vast unoccupied territory. One New England settler declared that the natives "do but run over the grass, as do also the foxes and wild beasts" and that therefore the "spacious and void" land was free for the taking.

The settlers misunderstood how Indians used their territory. Eastern Algonquian peoples cleared areas for villages and planting fields, which native women farmed until the soil grew less fertile. Then they moved to a new location, allowing the former village site to return to forest. In ten to twenty years, they or their descendants might return to that site to clear and farm it again. Indians often built villages near the seacoast or rivers so they could fish and use reeds and grasses for weaving. In the winter, village communities broke up into small bands to hunt in the forest for deer and other animals.

Thus what the colonists considered "vacant" lands were either being used for nonfarming activities or recovering from human occupation in order to be farmed in years to come. Settlers who built towns on abandoned Indian village sites deprived the Indians of these future planting fields. Competition from the rapidly increasing settlers threatened Indian survival.

Disputes between Europeans and Indians frequently arose from misunderstandings about land ownership and property rights. Indian villages claimed collective sovereignty over a certain territory to be used for farming, fishing, hunting, and gathering. For Europeans, ownership conferred on an individual the exclusive right to use or sell a piece of land.

When Indians transferred land to settlers, the settlers assumed that they had obtained complete rights to the land, whereas the Indians assumed that they had given the settlers not the land itself but only the *right to use it*. Often they thought they had given only the right to share the land and that they themselves would not have to leave. It was the English understanding that ultimately prevailed, enforced in the settlers' courts under the settlers' laws.

Settlers' agricultural practices also strained their relations with the Indians. When settlers cut down forests, they destroyed Indian hunting lands. When they dammed rivers, they disrupted Indian fishing. When they surrounded fields with log fences

and stone walls, they made trespassers of natives who crossed them. Yet the colonists felt free to let their cattle and pigs loose to graze in the woods and meadows, where they could wander into unfenced Indian cornfields and damage the crops.

The settlers gradually displaced Indian inhabitants, acquiring their lands in various ways. Some colonial leaders, such as Roger Williams in Rhode Island and William Penn of Pennsylvania, insisted on buying it. But sometimes settlers bought collectively owned land from individual Indians who had no right to sell it. Indians frequently misunderstood the terms of sale recorded in English. Even Indian groups that had willingly sold land grew resentful as colonists approached them repeatedly for more. Finally, native peoples were often forced to sell land to settle debts they had run up with English creditors.

Increasingly, colonists simply settled on Indian lands without permission and appealed to colonial governments for help when the Indians objected. Land speculators amplified this kind of unrest as they sought to acquire land as cheaply as possible and sell it for as much as they could.

Finally, the settlers often seized Indian lands in the aftermath of war. The Pequots in Connecticut in 1637, the Tuscaroras in 1713 and the Yamasees in Carolina in 1715, all lost their lands as their people were killed, captured, and dispersed by colonial forces. Sometimes colonial leaders contrived for some Indian groups to help them displace others. During the Pequot War, Narragansetts had aided Connecticut settlers' efforts to oust the Pequots. Carolina colonists enlisted the help of the Yamasees against the Tuscaroras and then turned to the Cherokees to help them against the Yamasees.

The English viewed the Indians, as they had the Irish, as savages with whom it would be better not to mix. Colonists built communities on lands bought or taken from natives and then discouraged them from living there. In New France and New Spain, Europeans and Indians mingled more freely and even intermarried, but in the English colonies, separation prevailed.

Priests and Preachers

In early colonial North America, the three major New World empires—those of Spain, France, and England—competed for Indians' souls as well as their lands and riches.

Catholic missionaries—mainly Franciscan priests—were the driving force behind Spain's efforts to assert control over its colonies of New Mexico and Florida. Spain's bases in Florida helped protect Spanish ships bearing treasure from the mines of Mexico and Peru and discouraged the southward spread of English settlement. New Mexico similarly served as a buffer between the silver mines of northern Mexico and roaming Plains Indians. Neither colony attracted many settlers, however, because neither appeared to offer much opportunity for wealth. When Franciscan missionaries proposed to move into New Mexico and Florida in order to convert their inhabitants to Christianity, Spanish officials agreed and even provided financial support.

The priests wore their finest vestments and displayed religious paintings and statues, trying to impress the Indians with European goods and Catholic ceremonies. They gave away bells, knives, scissors, cloth, and food. According to one Franciscan in New Mexico, these gifts brought Indians to the missions "like fish to the fish hook." The natives believed that accepting these gifts obliged them to listen to the priests' Christian message and help them build houses and churches.

After brief religious instruction, the missionaries convinced many Indians to accept baptism into the Catholic Church and with it the promise of salvation and a heavenly afterlife. Such conversions often followed epidemics that devastated native villages but spared the Spanish, leading many Indians to wonder if the Christian God might indeed be more powerful than their own gods. In New Mexico, the Spanish offered Pueblo converts protection against raids from their Apache rivals and access to Franciscan storehouses in times of famine.

Many Indians did not understand that baptism would commit them to abandoning native beliefs and adopting Spanish food, clothing, and work routines. Priests in New Mexico, objecting to the ease with which Pueblo marriages could be dissolved, tried to enforce lifelong unions. Punishments for violating the new code were severe and in rare cases led to their victims' deaths.

By the mid-seventeenth century, Spanish missionaries claimed to have baptized tens of thousands of Indians. But many converts blended Christianity with native religion, adding Jesus, Mary, and the Catholic saints to the list of Indian gods and accepting missionaries as counterparts to native priests. Many converts were **mestizos**—people of mixed Indian and Spanish descent—who often practiced native rituals in secret. Some groups, such as the Zuni and Hopi peoples, rejected Christianity altogether. In the end, the spread of Christianity in the Spanish borderlands was not as complete as the Franciscans claimed.

French priests in Canada also tried to convert Indians to Catholicism. Like the Franciscans,

they tried to impress potential converts with the rituals and material objects of their religion. Priests also amazed Indians with clocks, magnets, and their ability to predict eclipses and to read and write. "All this serves to gain their affections, and to render them more docile when we introduce the admirable and incomprehensible mysteries of our Faith," explained one priest.

French missionaries also resorted to economic pressure, convincing merchants to sell guns only to converted Indians and to offer them other trade goods at a discount. The Jesuits were generally more tolerant than the Franciscans of native ways. "One must be careful before condemning a thousand things among their customs," warned one priest, because to do so would "greatly offend minds brought up and nourished in another world."

The Protestant English were less successful than the Catholic Spanish and French at attracting Native American converts. Puritans frowned on the rituals and religious objects that drew Indian converts to Catholicism. And with its emphasis on the direct study of scripture, Protestantism required that potential converts learn to read.

Beginning in the 1650s, Puritan ministers in New England, such as John Eliot, established several **praying towns**, communities where Indians lived apart from settlers to learn Protestant Christianity and English ways. The few residents attracted to these towns, however, were mostly the remnants of groups otherwise destroyed by disease. Efforts at conversion in the Anglican southern colonies were even less successful. English settlers preferred to isolate Indians rather than convert them.

After the First Hundred Years

After nearly a century of European settlement, violent confrontations between colonists and Indians erupted in all three North American empires, in **King Philip's War** in New England, **Bacon's Rebellion** in Virginia, the **Pueblo Revolt** in New Mexico, and the resumption and conclusion of the Beaver Wars in New France.

King Philip's War, which broke out in 1675, was sparked by the growing frustration of the Wampanoags—the Indians who had befriended the Pilgrims more than half a century before—with the land-hungry settlers whose towns now surrounded them. Massasoit's younger son, Metacom—called King Philip by the English—now led the Wampanoags and was struggling to preserve their independence. He had little reason to trust the colonists. His older brother had died mysteriously while being questioned by colonial officials about rumors of an

Nearly a century after King Philip's War, Paul Revere engraved this portrait of the Wampanoag leader to accompany a new edition of a history of that conflict. Note that Philip is shown in European-style dress and has the weapons of war—a gun and a tomahawk—nearby. Behind him are angry warriors. These bellicose images suggest that the antagonism produced by New England's fiercest war lingered among the colonists for generations.

One out of every sixteen male colonists of military age was killed, making this the deadliest conflict in American history in terms of the proportion of casualties to total population. The Indians succeeded in forcing back the line of settlement but lost what remained of their independence in New England. Philip died in an ambush in August 1676, and the war ended soon after. The victorious English sold many native survivors, including Philip's wife and young son, into slavery in the West Indies. Philip's head, impaled on a stake, was left for decades on the outskirts of Plymouth as a grisly warning of the price to be paid for resisting colonial expansion.

A bloody conflict erupted in Virginia that had a similarly devastating effect on that colony's remaining native population. Frustrated by shrinking economic opportunities in eastern Virginia, many settlers moved to Virginia's western frontier. In the summer of 1675, a group of frontier settlers attacked the Susquehannocks in order to seize their lands. The Indians struck back the next winter, prompting Nathaniel Bacon, a young, wealthy planter who had only recently arrived in Virginia, to lead the settlers in a violent campaign against all Indians, even those at peace with the colonial government. Governor William Berkeley ordered Bacon and his men to stop their attacks. They defied him and marched on Jamestown, turning a war between settlers and Indians into a rebellion of settlers against the colonial authorities.

The rebels believed that Berkeley and the colonial government represented only the interests of established tobacco planters. Desperate because of the low price of tobacco, the rebels demanded lower taxes and easier access to land. They also wanted help exterminating the Indians. Rebels captured and burned the colonial capital at Jamestown, forcing Berkeley to flee. They burned Indian villages and massacred or enslaved the inhabitants. Trying to appease the rebels, the House of Burgesses passed measures allowing them to seize lands belonging to Indians and legalizing the enslavement of Indians.

By the time troops arrived from England to put down the rebellion, Bacon had died of a fever and most of his men had drifted home. Berkeley hanged twenty-three rebels, but the real victims of the rebellion were Virginia's Indians. The remnants of the once powerful Powhatans lost their remaining lands and either moved west or lived in poverty on the edges of English settlement. Hatred of Indians became a permanent feature of frontier life in Virginia.

In 1680 the Pueblo Revolt erupted against Spain's colony of New Mexico. Nearly twenty thousand Pueblo Indians in New Mexico had grown restless under the harsh rule of only 2,500 Spaniards.

Indian conspiracy. Philip himself had been accused of plotting against the settlers and then forced to sign a treaty submitting to English authority.

In the spring of 1675, a colonial court found three Wampanoags guilty of murdering a Christian Indian who had warned the English of Wampanoag preparations for war. The court sentenced the men to be hanged. The Wampanoags decided to strike back against the English. Only "a small part of the dominion of my ancestors remains," declared Philip. "I am determined not to live until I have no country."

At least a thousand colonists and perhaps three thousand Indians died in King Philip's War.

During a prolonged drought that began in the 1660s, many people starved. The Apaches, who had once traded with the Pueblos for corn, now raided their storehouses instead, and Spanish soldiers could not stop them.

The spark that ignited the revolt, however, was an act of religious persecution. Spanish officials unwisely chose this troubled time to stamp out Pueblo religion. In 1675, the governor arrested forty-seven native religious leaders on charges of sorcery. The court ordered most of them to be publicly whipped and released but sentenced four of them to death.

Spanish soldiers marched into Pueblo villages and destroyed kivas, the underground chambers that Indians used for religious ceremonies. Led by Popé, one of the freed leaders, the outraged Pueblos organized a network of rebels. By the summer of 1680, Popé had at his command seventeen thousand rebels drawn from twenty Pueblo villages. On August 10, the rebels attacked the Spanish settlements. Popé urged them to "break up and burn the images of the holy Christ, the Virgin Mary and the other saints, the crosses, and everything pertaining to Christianity." Within a few weeks, the rebels had destroyed or damaged every Spanish building and killed more than four hundred Spaniards, including twenty-one of the colony's thirty-three missionaries. By October, all Spaniards had fled New Mexico.

They did not return for thirteen years. By then, internal rivalries had split the victorious Pueblo coalition. Even so, the Spanish understood the folly of pushing the Indians too far. Officials reduced demands for tribute, and the Franciscans eased their attacks on Pueblo religion.

In the last phase of the Beaver Wars, what began as a struggle between the Iroquois and western native peoples for control of the fur trade blossomed into a larger conflict as it was absorbed into the imperial rivalry between England and France.

Looking for new trading partners, the French turned in the 1680s to the Ottawas, Wyandots, and other Indian peoples living near the Great Lakes. But the Iroquois had begun to raid these same peoples for furs and captives, much as they had attacked the Hurons in the first phase of the Beaver Wars in the 1640s. They exchanged the furs with their English allies. The Iroquois objected to French traders' attempt to "have all the Bevers" for themselves.

The French attacked the Iroquois to prevent them and their English allies from extending their influence in the west. In June 1687, a combined force of French and Christian Indian soldiers invaded the lands of the Senecas, the westernmost of the five nations of the Iroquois League. The soldiers burned villages and cornfields and looted Seneca cemeteries. The Iroquois retaliated by besieging a French garrison at Niagara, where nearly two hundred soldiers starved to death, and killing hundreds of colonists in attacks on French villages along the St. Lawrence River.

In 1689, France and England went to war in Europe, and the struggle between them and their Indian allies for control of the fur trade in North America became part of a larger imperial contest between the two countries. The European powers made peace in 1697, but calm did not immediately return to the Great Lakes region.

The conflict was devastating for the Iroquois. Perhaps a quarter of their population died from disease and warfare by 1689. The devastation encouraged Iroquois diplomats to find a way to extricate themselves from future English-French conflicts. In 1701, a pair of treaties, negotiated separately with Albany and Montreal, recognized Iroquois neutrality and, at least for a few decades, prevented either the English or the French from dominating the western lands.

English settlers fought with Wampanoags, Powhatans, and Susquehannocks for control of land, and the losers were the outnumbered Indians. Spanish colonists clashed with Pueblos over religion, and the more numerous natives won a temporary victory and a long-run accommodation with the Spanish Catholic minority. French soldiers battled with the Iroquois over control of the fur trade until both sides agreed to an uneasy truce. In each case, nearly a century of contact culminated in a struggle that revealed how difficult, if not impossible, it was to reconcile European and native interests.

Africans and Europeans

Many more Africans than Europeans came to the New World during the colonial period. Virtually all of them arrived as slaves; thus the history of African experience in America is inseparable from the history of slavery and the slave trade.

The Evolution of Slavery in the New World

Europeans in the New World thrilled to find that land was abundant and quite cheap by European standards. They were perplexed, however, by the unexpectedly high cost of labor. In Europe, the reverse had been true. There land was expensive but labor cheap because competition for jobs among large numbers of workers pushed wages down.

Colonial workers commanded high wages because there were so few of them compared to the supply of land waiting to be developed. Moreover, few settlers wanted to work for others when they could get farms of their own. The scarcity and high cost of labor led some colonial employers to turn to enslaved Africans as a solution.

Europeans had owned slaves (both white and black) long before the beginning of American colonization. But by 1500 slavery had all but disappeared in northern Europe. It persisted longer in southern Europe and the Middle East. Because neither Christians nor Muslims would hold as slaves members of their own faiths, Arab traders turned to sub-Saharan Africa to find slaves who did not belong to either religion. Eventually the Arabic word for slave—`abd`—became a synonym for "black man." By the fifteenth century, a durable link between slave status and black skin had been forged in European minds.

When Spanish and Portuguese adventurers needed workers to develop newly colonized Atlantic islands and New World lands, they turned to slavery. Masters exercised complete control over slaves and paid them no wages. English colonists later adopted slavery in America even though it was unknown as a system of labor at home.

It was Indians, however, not Africans, whom the Europeans first forced into slavery in the Americas. Spaniards held native slaves in all their New World colonies and English colonists condemned Indian enemies captured in wartime to slavery. In early Carolina, English traders encouraged Indians "to make War amongst themselves to get Slaves" whom the traders could buy and then resell to West Indian and local planters.

Native American slaves, however, could not fill the settlers' labor needs. Disease and harsh working conditions reduced their numbers. Enslaved Indian men refused to perform agricultural labor, which they considered women's work. Because they knew the land better than the colonists, Indians could easily escape and make their way back to their own people. By 1700 the Indian slave trade had given way to a much larger traffic in Africans.

The Spanish and Portuguese were first to bring Africans to the Americas to supplement the dwindling numbers of Indian slaves toiling in silver mines and on sugar plantations. English colonists adopted slavery more slowly. West Indian planters were the first to do so on a large scale in the 1640s, following the Portuguese example in using black slaves to grow sugar.

Black slaves first arrived in Virginia in 1619 when a Dutch trader sold "20. and odd Negroes" in Jamestown. But they did not form a significant portion of the colony's population until the end of the century. For decades, tobacco planters saw no reason to switch from white indentured servants to slaves. Servants were cheap, available, and familiar; slaves were expensive, difficult to obtain, and exotic.

Beginning in the 1680s, planters in the Chesapeake colonies of Virginia and Maryland began to shift from servants to slaves. White indentured servants became harder to find. Fewer young English men and women chose to emigrate as servants after 1660 because an improving economy in England provided more jobs for them at home. And Virginia's white population tripled between 1650 and 1700, rapidly increasing the competition for a shrinking supply of laborers. Chesapeake planters also faced competition from newer colonies.

As white servants grew scarcer, African slaves became more available, largely due to changes in the slave trade. After 1698, England's Royal African Company lost its special trading rights and many English merchants—and New Englanders—entered the fiercely competitive trade.

Chesapeake planters eventually came to prefer slaves to servants. Although more expensive than servants, slaves were a better long-term investment. Buying both men and women gave planters a self-reproducing labor force. Runaway black slaves were more easily recaptured than escaped servants, who blended into the white population. And unlike indentured servants, slaves were slaves for life and would not someday compete as planters with their former masters.

Chesapeake planters' view of white servants as possessions, whose labor could be bought and sold like any other commodity, eased the gradual transition in the 1680s and 1690s to the much harsher system of slavery. In Carolina, slaves had arrived right from the start, brought in the 1670s by colony founders accustomed to slavery in Barbados. By 1720, one-third of Virginia's settlers—and nearly three-quarters of South Carolina's—were black.

Slavery grew rapidly in the South because it answered the labor needs of planters engaged in the commercial production of tobacco and rice. When James Oglethorpe founded Georgia in 1732, however, he intended to keep slavery out. Oglethorpe's idea was to send English debtors to Georgia to produce exotic goods like silk and wine. But when only rice turned a profit in Georgia, its founders reluctantly legalized slavery. By 1770, slaves made up nearly half of the colony's settlers.

In the northern colonies, slaves were too expensive for farmers who mainly produced food for their families, not export crops. The relatively few northern slaves generally worked as domestic servants, craftsmen, and day laborers, often in cities such as New York and Boston.

Race relations in the mainland colonies were less rigid in the seventeenth century than they would later become. In the few Chesapeake households that had slaves, whites and blacks lived and worked in close contact. Black slaves and white servants cooperated during Bacon's Rebellion. In some areas, free blacks—often slaves who had bought their own freedom—prospered in an atmosphere of racial tolerance that would be unthinkable by the eighteenth century.

The career of an ambitious black Virginian named Anthony Johnson, for example, resembled that of many white settlers—a remarkable achievement given that he arrived in the colony as a slave in 1621. Once freed (by unknown means), Johnson married and, with his wife, Mary, raised at least four children. By 1651, he had acquired a large plantation and even bought a slave. But historical records preserve no trace of his descendants after 1706. By then slavery had become the dominant labor system in the Chesapeake. Tobacco planters no longer welcomed free blacks, fearing that they might encourage slaves to escape. In 1699, Virginia's assembly had passed a law requiring newly freed blacks to leave the colony.

Even in the seventeenth century, few whites, if any, claimed blacks as their equals. After 1700, laws defined slavery as lifelong and hereditary according to the condition of the mother and identified slave status with black skin. Other measures deprived black persons, slave or free, of basic civil rights. They could not vote, testify in court against whites, hold property, congregate in public places, or travel without permission. Interracial marriages, never common, were now prohibited as "shameful Matches."

Colonists resorted to these **slave codes**—which reduced human beings to the status of property—largely because of fears generated by a rising black population. In 1720, a South Carolina planter predicted that slaves would soon rise up against their masters because blacks were "too numerous in proportion to the White Men there." The changing composition of the slave labor force also created tensions.

Most seventeenth-century slaves came to the southern colonies by way of the West Indies or New Netherlands, where they had acquired some familiarity with Europeans and perhaps a few words of English. But after 1700, slave traders brought cargoes of what colonists called "outlandish" slaves directly from Africa.

The Shock of Enslavement

European traders relied on other Africans to capture slaves for them, tapping into a preexisting African slave trade and helping to expand it. Europeans built forts and trading posts (called "factories") on the West African coast and bought slaves from African traders (see Map 3-1). Attracted by European cloth, iron, liquor, guns, and other goods, West Africans fought increasingly among themselves to secure captives and began to send raiding parties to kidnap individuals from the interior.

People of all social ranks ended up on the slave ships. Some had already lived as slaves in Africa; others had been prominent members of their villages. Even members of African royal families ended up in shackles as slavery reduced all Africans, regardless of their social origins, to the same degraded status.

Once captured, slaves marched in chains to the coast, to be confined in cages called "barracoons" until there were enough to fill a ship. Captains examined them to ensure their fitness and branded them like cattle with a hot iron. The slaves then boarded canoes to be ferried to the ships.

Slaves suffered through a horrendous six- to eight-week-long ocean voyage known as the **Middle Passage**. Captains wedged men below decks into spaces about 6 feet long, 16 inches wide, and 30 inches high. Women and children were packed even tighter. They occasionally came up on deck for fresh air, where in a ceremony called "dancing the slaves," sailors, with whips in hand, commanded them (often shackled in irons) to dance and sing for exercise. Most of the time, slaves remained below decks, where the hot and humid air grew foul from the vomit, blood, and excrement in which the terrified victims lay. Sailors sometimes heard a "howling melancholy noise" coming from below. Some slaves tried to commit suicide by jumping overboard or starving themselves. Between 5 and 20 percent of the slaves perished from disease, but captains had usually packed the ships tightly enough to make a profit selling the rest.

Survivors of the dreadful voyage endured the fear and humiliation of sale. Sometimes buyers rushed aboard ship in a scramble to choose slaves. Ship captains also sold slaves at public auctions, where eager purchasers poked them, looking for

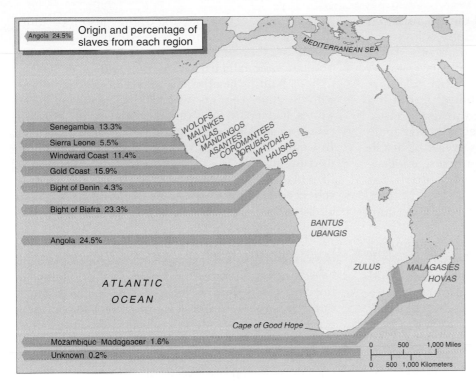

Map 3-1 *African Origins of North American Slaves, 1690–1807*
Nearly all slaves in English North America were West Africans. Most had been captured or purchased by African slave traders, who then sold them to European merchants.
Source: *After Philip Curtin,* The Atlantic Slave Trade: A Census *(1969), tab. 45, p. 157.*

signs of disease. The terrified Africans often thought they were about to be eaten.

African-American Families and Communities

The vast majority of all Africans brought to the New World went to New Spain, Brazil, or the West Indies. Black communities developed slowly in English America. In the northern colonies, most slaves lived alone or in pairs with their master's family. Only in the cities, where slaves were more numerous, could they have regular contact with other blacks. In the South, until the eighteenth century, slaves were dispersed among a much larger white population. Slave numbers grew after 1700, but much of the increase consisted of African immigrants. These people thought of themselves and their fellows not as Africans but as Ibos and Fulas, Yorubas and Wolofs, with different languages, religions, and customs.

By about 1750, more slaves in the southern colonies were **creoles** (American-born) than African natives. Creoles lived longer than African immigrants, and creole women usually bore twice as many children as African-born mothers. The mainland slave population therefore began to grow by natural increase.

Creole slaves grew up without personal memories of Africa, so African ethnic differences seemed less important to them. Most creoles knew some English and spoke dialects they had created by mixing English and African words and speech patterns. The ability to communicate helped them develop a new identity as African-Americans that mingled aspects of their African heritage and a common experience of slavery.

Kinship ties, crucial to West Africans' sense of identity, remained important to American slaves. But slave families were fragile units, subject to the whims of masters who could break up families by sale at any time, and who could take slave women as sexual partners at will. Even so, slaves managed to form families that preserved and modified African traditions.

Households headed by mothers reappeared in America. Slave fathers often belonged to different masters than their wives and children and had to live apart from their families. Some slave husbands, like West African men, took more than one wife (a practice masters allowed because it led to more slave children). Slave parents gave their children African names, often secretly adding them to the "official" names given by masters.

Carolina slaves followed West African practice by building their houses of "tabby," a mixture of lime and seashells, and constructing houses on a circular plan. Potters and basketmakers used African designs in their work. Slaves raised African food plants (millet, yams, sesame seeds) in their gardens.

They also made music, performed dances, and told folk tales derived from African models.

Labor, however, consumed most of a slave's waking hours. On tobacco plantations, slaves toiled in gangs supervised by overseers. Rice planters allowed their workers more flexibility, permitting them free time after they finished assigned tasks. On large plantations, masters selected a few male slaves to be trained as shoemakers, weavers, or tailors. Only a few slave women—nurses, cooks—avoided the drudgery of field work. And after a day in the fields, slave women had to take care of their families, doing the cooking, child care, washing, and housework.

The growth of slave family and community ties made it much more difficult for slaves to risk escape or contemplate rebellion. The master could use his power to break up families as a tool to ensure compliant behavior. In effect, every slave child was his hostage.

Resistance and Rebellion

Slaves on ships anchored off the Guinea Coast waiting to leave for America sometimes mutinied, but rarely succeeded. The powerful desire for freedom and the spirit of resistance remained strong among Africans and their descendants in America.

Hundreds of slaves ran away from masters. Deciding where else to go posed a problem as slavery was legal in every colony. Some runaways went to Florida, where Spanish officials promised them freedom. Others tried to survive on their own in the woods or join the Indians. But South Carolina planters paid Indians to catch escaped slaves, causing distrust between the two peoples. Running away also carried the high emotional cost of separation from loved ones as well as physical danger. Many slaves chose other ways to resist their bondage.

Landon Carter of Virginia, who complained that his slaves "seem to be quite dead hearted and either cannot or will not work," was the target of another form of resistance. Slaves worked slowly, broke tools, and pretended to be ill in order to conserve strength and exert some control over their working lives. When provoked, they also took more direct action, damaging crops, stealing goods, and setting fire to their masters' barns, houses, and fields. Some occasionally tried to poison whites.

South Carolinians and coastal Virginians, who lived in regions where blacks outnumbered whites, had a particular dread of slave revolt. No slave rebellion succeeded in the British colonies, however. In Charleston, South Carolina, rumors of a planned uprising in 1740 led to the torture and execution of fifty blacks. The following year, thirty-five accused rebels (including four whites—one a tavernkeeper and another allegedly a Spanish priest) were executed in New York City.

Two slave revolts did occur in the colonial period, and instilled lasting fear in whites. In 1712 in New York City, about twenty slaves set a building on fire and killed nine white men who came to put it out. The revolt was quickly suppressed. The court sentenced twenty-four alleged rebels to death: thirteen were hanged, three burned at the stake, one starved to death, and one was broken on the wheel. Six committed suicide before execution.

The **Stono Rebellion**, colonial America's largest slave uprising, occurred in South Carolina in 1739. About twenty slaves—including several recently arrived Angolans—broke into a store and armed themselves with stolen guns. As the rebels marched southward along the Stono River, their ranks grew to

This eighteenth-century painting from South Carolina records the preservation of certain African traditions in American slave communities. The dance may be Yoruba in origin, while the stringed instrument and drum were probably modeled on African instruments.

perhaps a hundred. Heading for freedom in Spanish Florida, they boldly attacked white settlements along the way. White troops (with Indian help) defeated the rebels within a week, but tensions remained high for months. The death toll, in the end, was about two dozen whites and perhaps twice as many blacks.

In the wake of the Stono Rebellion, South Carolina's assembly passed a comprehensive Negro Act, requiring stricter supervision of slave activities. Other measures encouraged more white immigration to offset the colony's black majority. But the colony continued to consider slavery indispensable to economic survival and would not end it.

Nonslave Labor in Early America

Slavery was one of several responses to the scarcity of labor in the New World. It took hold mainly in areas where the profits from growing export crops such as sugar, rice, and tobacco offset the high purchase price of slaves and where a warm climate permitted year-round work. Elsewhere, Europeans found other means to acquire and manage laborers.

Indian Workers in New France and the Spanish Borderlands

The French and Spanish colonies relied more heavily on native laborers than the English did. French officials promised military support and French merchants extended credit in order to get native hunters to trap beavers and bring them furs. By supplying Indians with trade goods in advance, merchants obligated them to bring in furs as payment. If unsuccessful hunters tried to ignore or postpone payment, merchants refused to give them any more of the trade goods on which they had come to depend.

The Spanish used more direct means to control Indian labor, employing three main methods. **Encomiendas**, granted to influential Spaniards in New Mexico, gave them the right to collect tribute—usually in the form of corn, blankets, and animal hides—from a specific group of natives. The tribute was not supposed to include forced labor but often Spaniards required native men to work on their farms and ranches and native women to become domestic servants.

In New Mexico and Florida, the **repartimiento**—a mandatory draft of native labor for public projects—set Indians to work building forts, bridges, and roads. The Spanish often ignored limits on

length of service, and sometimes forced Indians to work on their private estates. Spaniards also acquired laborers by ransoming captives that Indian tribes seized from one another, a practice called **rescate** ("ransom"). These "freed" Indians usually became servants in Spanish households, often for years.

These methods of labor control depended on the existence of sizable Indian communities and Spanish military force. Native villages provided plenty of workers as well as structures of government that the Spanish could use to collect tribute and organize gangs of workers. Spanish soldiers ensured that the Indians—who outnumbered the colonists—obeyed orders.

Laborers in the English Colonies

Most colonial laborers were, in some measure, unfree. One-half to two-thirds of all white emigrants to the English colonies arrived as indentured servants. Servants were most common in the Chesapeake, and to a lesser extent in Pennsylvania, where they produced export crops valuable enough to enable their masters to feed, clothe, and shelter them—and still make a profit.

Slaves gradually replaced white indentured servants in Chesapeake tobacco fields. By the middle of the eighteenth century, white servitude was in decline as a dominant labor system throughout the colonies.

Eighteenth-century Chesapeake planters availed themselves of another unfree labor source: transported English convicts, serious criminals who might otherwise have been executed. Between 1718 and 1775, nearly fifty thousand convicts were sent to the colonies, 80 percent of whom ended up in the Chesapeake. Labor-hungry planters eagerly bought them for seven-year terms at relatively low prices and exploited them ruthlessly. A few convicts eventually prospered in America, but most faced lives as miserable as those they had known in England.

The **redemptioner** system brought many German families to the colonies in the eighteenth century. Instead of negotiating contracts for service before leaving Europe, as indentured servants did, redemptioners promised to redeem, or pay, the costs of passage on arrival in America. They often paid part of the fare themselves before sailing. If they could not raise the rest soon after landing, the ship captain who brought them sold them into servitude. The length of their service depended on how much they still owed. Most Germans went to Pennsylvania, where they hoped to find friends or relatives willing to help them pay off their debt quickly.

Purchasing slaves, servants, or convicts did not make sense for everyone. Colonists who owned unde-

American Views

JOB BECOMES A SLAVE (1730)

Job ben Solomon was no ordinary slave. Born in Senegal to a family of Muslim clerics, he was captured by a rival African tribe, sold to an English slaver, and set to work on a Maryland plantation. He tried and failed to escape but astonished his jailers by writing a letter in Arabic describing his plight. The letter made its way to James Oglethorpe, an official of the Royal African Company as well as founder of Georgia, who bought Job and brought him to England. Englishmen marveled at Job's learning, which he demonstrated by writing the entire Koran from memory. Job was entertained all over London and even presented to King George, but he begged to go home. In 1734, he finally returned to Africa—an unprecedented accomplishment for an American slave. Thomas Bluett, a Maryland colonist who met Job while he was in jail, wrote and published an account of Job's experiences.

❖ **How did Job come to be captured in Africa?**

❖ **What humiliations did he suffer as a result of his enslavement?**

❖ **Does this account demonstrate any evidence of bias on the part of its English author?**

In February, 1730, Job's father hearing of an English ship at Gambia River, sent him, with two servants to attend him, to sell two Negroes, and to buy paper, and some other necessaries; but desired him not to venture over the river, because the country of the Mandingoes, who are enemies to the people of Futa, lies on the other side. Job . . . intended to go farther. Accordingly having agreed with another man, named Loumein Yoas, who understood the Mandingoe language, to go with him as his interpreter, he crossed the River Gambia, and disposed of his Negroes for some cows. As he was returning

veloped land faced many tasks—cutting trees, clearing fields, building fences and barns—that brought no immediate profit. These landowners, many of whom lived in Pennsylvania, New Jersey, and New York, rented undeveloped tracts to propertyless families. Both tenants and landlords benefited from this arrangement. Tenants enjoyed greater independence than servants and could save toward the purchase of their own farms. The landlord secured the necessary labor to transform his property into a working farm, which increased the land's value. He also received an annual rent payment, usually a portion of the tenant's crop, and eventually profited from selling the land— often to the tenant family that had rented it. Tenancy worked best in Pennsylvania, New Jersey, and the Hudson and Connecticut River Valleys, where farmers raised wheat and other grains for the market.

Merchants eager to develop New England's fisheries devised other means to fill their labor needs.

Because it was fairly easy to get a farm, few New Englanders cared to take on the difficult and risky job of fishing. Moreover, few could afford the necessary equipment. New England fish merchants advanced credit to coastal villagers so they could outfit their own boats and become fishermen. To pay off the debt, the fishermen were legally bound to bring their catch to the merchant, who then sold it to Europe and the West Indies.

In the northern colonies, the cost of servants or slaves exceeded whatever small profit could be made on farms that produced no export crops and could not be worked during cold winter months. So northern farmers turned to the cheapest and most dependable workers they could find—their children.

Children as young as 5 or 6 years old began with simple tasks and moved on to more complex work as they grew older. By the time they were in their late teens, girls knew how to run households home, he stopped for some refreshment at the house of an old acquaintance; and the weather being hot, he hung up his arms in the house, while he refreshed himself. . . . It happened that a company of the Mandingoes, who live upon plunder, passing by at that time, and observing him unarmed, rushed in, to the number of seven or eight at once, at a back door, and pinioned Job, before he could get to his arms, together with his interpreter, who is a slave in Maryland still. They then shaved their heads and beards, which Job and his man resented as the highest indignity; tho' the Mandingoes meant no more by it, than to make them appear like Slaves taken in war. On the 27th of February, 1730, they carried them to Captain Pike at Gambia, who purchased them; and on the first of March they were put on board. . . .

[Job was sold to a Maryland planter] who put him to work in making tobacco; but he was soon convinced that Job had never been used to such labour. He every day showed more and more uneasiness under this exercise, and at last grew sick, being no way able to bear it; so that his master was obliged to find easier work for him, and therefore put him to tend the cattle. Job would often leave the cattle, and withdraw into the woods to pray; but a white boy frequently watched him, and whilst he was at his devotion would mock him, and throw dirt in his face. This very much disturbed Job, and added considerably to his other misfortunes; all which were increased by his ignorance of the English language, which prevented his complaining, or telling his case to any person about him.

Source: *Philip D. Curtin, ed.*, Africa Remembered: Narratives by West Africans from the Era of the Slave Trade *(1967), pp. 39–41.*

and boys knew how to farm. Fathers used their ownership of property to prolong the time their sons worked for them. Young men in New England could not marry and set up their own households until they could support a wife and family. Often sons did not actually own any land until their fathers died and left it to them in their wills.

Thus New England's labor shortage produced strong ties of dependency between generations. Fathers kept their sons working for them as long as possible; sons accepted this arrangement as a way to become independent farmers, eventually employing their own children in the same way.

Property owners in all the English colonies found different ways to control laborers. But where property owners saw problems—high wages (often twice what workers in England received) and abundant land (which deterred colonists from working for others when they could have their own farms)—

others saw opportunities. For tens of thousands of Europeans, the chance to own or rent a farm or to find steady employment made North America an irresistible magnet, promising a prosperity that was beyond their reach at home.

Transplanted Europeans

European immigrants flooded into America in the seventeenth and eighteenth centuries. By 1773, the tremendous outflow of Britons—Protestant Scots-Irish, Scots, and Irish Catholics—to America sparked debate in England over whether emigration should be prohibited lest the British Isles be left empty. Continental Europe contributed another stream of emigrants, mostly from the German states. Perhaps 100,000 Protestants left the Rhine Valley, where war, economic hardship, and religious persecution had brought misery. French Protestants (known as Huguenots) began emigrating after 1685, when their

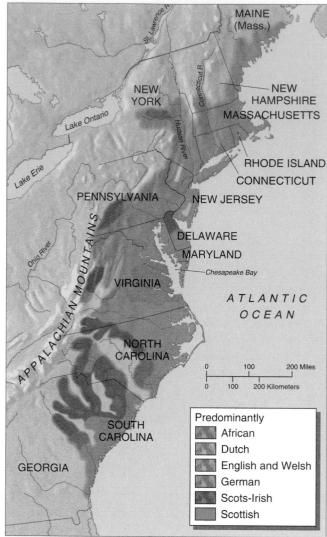

Map 3-2   Ethnic Distribution of Settler Population in British Mainland Colonies, c. 1755
Settlers of different ethnic backgrounds tended to concentrate in certain areas. Only New Englanders were predominantly English, while Africans dominated in the Chesapeake tidewater and South Carolina. German, Scottish, and Scots-Irish immigrants often settled in the backcountry.

faith was made illegal in France. Swiss Protestants likewise fled religious persecution. Even a few Poles, Greeks, Italians, and Jews reached the colonies in the eighteenth century.

Streams of emigrants flowed to places where land was cheap and labor most in demand (see Map 3-2). Few went to New England, where descendants of the first settlers already occupied the best land. They also avoided areas where slavery predominated—the Chesapeake tidewater region and lowland South Carolina—in favor of the foothills of the Appalachian Mountains from western Pennsylvania to the Carolinas.

Not all emigrants realized their dreams of becoming independent landowners. The scarcity of labor in the colonies led as easily to the exploitation of white workers as of slaves and Indians. Even so, for many people facing bleak prospects in Europe, the chance that emigration might bring prosperity was too tempting to ignore.

Conclusion

By the middle of the eighteenth century, America offered a strikingly diverse mosaic of peoples and communities. Along the St. Lawrence River, for instance, lay Kahnawake, a village of Mohawks and Abenakis who had adopted Catholicism and French ways under Jesuit instruction. In Andover, Massachusetts, New Englanders tilled fields that their Puritan grandparents had cleared. German immigrants who had forsaken the world in search of spiritual perfection populated the isolated Pennsylvania settlement of Ephrata. The hundred or so slaves on Robert Carter's Virginia plantation at Nomini Hall gathered on Sunday evenings to nurture ties of community with songs and dances, while the master cultivated his very different sense of community with neighboring planters. Near St. Augustine, runaway slaves farmed and gathered shellfish under the protection of Spanish soldiers. Far to the west, the Spanish, mestizo, and Pueblo residents of Santa Fe warily reestablished ties broken during the Pueblo Revolt.

In these and many other communities, peoples from three continents changed in fundamental ways as they adapted to one another and to American conditions. Indians struggled with the consequences of disease, trade, religious conversion, settlement, and warfare resulting from European immigration. Africans exchanged their traditional ethnic connections for a new identity as African-Americans. English settlers became landowners in unprecedented numbers, and adopted new ways to control laborers, reinventing slavery, unknown in England for centuries. No European settlement in America fully reproduced Old World patterns, and no native village fully preserved the precontact Indian way of life.

Review Questions

1. English colonists experienced more frequent, and more violent, conflicts with Indians than the

settlers of New France did. Why was this so? What factors affected Indian-white relations in the two colonial regions?

2. Why were Catholic missionaries more successful than Protestants in converting Indians to Christianity in early America?

3. When did Chesapeake planters switch from servants to slaves? What factors contributed to their decision to make this change?

4. By about 1750, more slaves in the mainland British colonies were creoles (American-born) than African-born. What effects did this have on the formation of an African-American community in America?

5. Different labor systems predominated in various regions of British America. How did the economy of each region help determine its labor system?

6. Tens of thousands of European immigrants came to America in the eighteenth century, but they tended to settle only in certain colonial regions. What destinations did they favor and why?

Recommended Reading

Cronon, William. *Changes in the Land: Indians, Colonists, and the Ecology of New England* (1983). This pathbreaking study examines the ecological consequences of Indian settlement in New England and of the displacement of Indians by English colonists.

Delage, Denys. *Bitter Feast: Amerindians and Europeans in Northeastern North America, 1600–64* (English ed., 1993). Offering a comprehensive analysis of French, Dutch, and English colonization in northeastern North America, this study focuses on European strategies for trade and economic development and their impact on native peoples.

Jordan, Winthrop. *White over Black: American Attitudes toward the Negro, 1550–1812* (1968). This prizewinning book traces white attitudes toward black people over nearly three centuries of contact, exploring the way in which racial stereotypes contributed to the development of slavery. It is available in an abridged edition as *The White Man's Burden: Historical Origins of Racism in the United States* (1974).

Moore, Brian. *Black Robe* (1985). This powerful novel explores the experiences of a Jesuit missionary among the Indians in seventeenth-century New France.

Nash, Gary B. *Red, White, and Black: The Peoples of Early America* (3d ed., 1991). This important synthesis treats the history of early America as the complex story of interactions between peoples from three major cultures—Native American, European, and African.

Vickers, Daniel. *Farmers and Fishermen: Two Centuries of Work in Essex County, Massachusetts, 1630–1830* (1994). This beautifully written and sophisticated analysis explores the way in which settlers adapted their English experiences to deal with the shortages of labor and capital in New England.

Where to Learn More

❖ **Ste. Marie among the Hurons, near Midland, Ontario, Canada.** This site contains a reconstructed Jesuit mission from the seventeenth century. There is a museum with information about seventeenth-century France as well as life among the Huron Indians.

❖ **Taos Pueblo, Taos, New Mexico.** Still a residence for Pueblo Indians, portions of this multi-storied pueblo date from the fifteenth century. This was the site from which Popé directed the beginnings of the Pueblo Revolt in 1680.

❖ **Ephrata Cloister, Ephrata, Pennsylvania.** Founded by German immigrants in the eighteenth century, the Ephrata community attracted religious pietists. The site now contains a museum, buildings that reflect medieval German architectural styles, and a collection of decorative art objects.

❖ **Six Nations Indian Museum, Onchiota, New York.** This museum preserves a rich collection of artifacts relating to Iroquois history and culture. Open to the public in the summer.

❖ **Rhode Island Black Heritage Society, Providence, Rhode Island.** This organization has assembled an archive and museum collection with information about the state's black residents from the colonial period to the present.

CONVERGENCE AND CONFLICT, 1660s–1763

KEY TOPICS

❖ Development of closer connections between Britain and the colonies
❖ Rising aspirations of the colonial elite
❖ Religious life in eighteenth-century America
❖ Political developments in England and the colonies
❖ Renewed competition among Britain, France, and Spain in North America
❖ Impact of imperial warfare in North America

The young man came to Williamsburg in the spring of 1763 to take his seat in Virginia's House of Burgesses. When not engaged in government business, his main concern was to arrange for the shipment of tobacco from his plantation to England. But he also found time to write to his tailor, Charles Lawrence of London. "Be pleased to send me," he wrote, "a genteel suit of Clothes made of superfine broad Cloth handsomely chosen," cut to fit a man "Six feet high & proportionably made; if any thing rather Slender than thick for a Person of that height with pretty long arms & thighs." The colonist then wrote to his financial agent requesting that he send "4 Yards of Silk . . . according to the Inclosed pattern" for a dress for his wife. If the Virginian meant to impress his neighbors with his new suit, it was only fitting that his wife also display her latest London finery.

At the age of 31, this planter, George Washington, had joined the ranks of Virginia's leaders. His father had died when Washington was only 11 years old, and most of the family property had gone to his older brother. Because he could not expect to inherit wealth, Washington learned surveying—a useful skill in a colony where land was constantly being divided into new farms. His maps of territory west of the Blue Ridge Mountains helped open up the region, and he became an expert at locating prime lands to buy and resell to the settlers who flooded into the area. When tensions between England and France over rival claims to those western lands flared into war, Washington took up arms to defend England's right. Military service brought him to the attention of Virginia's leaders, even as his economic fortunes improved. His older brother died and left him the family plantation at Mount Vernon, and in 1759, at age 27, Washington married a wealthy widow, Martha Custis. He thus became one of the richest men in northern Virginia.

By 1763, Washington had spent his whole adult life trying to live, look, and behave like an English country gentleman. Throughout British America, colonists who had achieved wealth and power tried, like Washington, to imitate the habits and manners of the English gentry. Their aspirations testified to important developments in the eighteenth century. Prosperity and the demand of a growing population for English manufactures tied the colonies ever more tightly into a trade network centered on the imperial metropolis, London. No longer a collection of rough outposts clinging to the Atlantic seaboard, British America was growing in size and sophistication.

These developments in Britain's American colonies brought them to the attention of European statesmen, who increasingly factored North America into their political, diplomatic, and military calculations. Spain and France viewed the growth of British North America as a threat to their own colonial possessions, and they responded aggressively by expanding their territorial claims. With expansion came conflict, and with conflict, war: a series of four imperial wars, which themselves became powerful engines of change in the New World.

Economic Development and Imperial Trade in the British Colonies

The greatest assets that Great Britain could call on in its competition with other European nations were a dynamic economy and a sophisticated financial system that put commerce at the service of the state. In the century after 1690, England became the most advanced economic power in Europe.

England's leaders came to see colonies as indispensable to the nation's economic welfare. Colonies supplied raw materials unavailable in the mother country, and settlers provided a healthy market for English manufactures. As the eighteenth century progressed, colonial economies grew in

tandem with England's. Parliament knitted the colonies into an empire with commercial legislation, while British merchants traded with and extended credit to growing numbers of colonial merchants and planters.

The Regulation of Trade

England, the Netherlands, and France competed vigorously in the transatlantic trade. Between 1651 and 1733, Parliament passed laws that regulated trade in order to ensure that more wealth flowed into England's treasury than out of it (see the summary table "British Imperial Trade Regulations, 1651–1733"). This governmental intervention in the economy for the purpose of increasing national wealth—called **mercantilism**—aimed to draw the colonies into a mutually beneficial relationship with England.

Parliament enacted four types of mercantilist regulations. The first dealt with ships and their owners and aimed at ending Dutch dominance in England's overseas trade. Beginning with the **Navigation Act of 1651**, all trade in the empire had to be conducted in English or colonial ships, with crews that were at least half Englishmen or colonists. The act stimulated rapid growth in both England's merchant marine and New England's shipping industry. Indeed, shipbuilding and earnings from what was called the "carrying trade" soon became the most profitable sector of New England's economy.

The second type of legislation channeled certain colonial goods, called **"enumerated products,"** through England or another English colony. These raw materials initially included tobacco, sugar, indigo, and cotton. Pitch, tar, hemp, rice, molasses, and furs were added later. European goods also had to pass through England before they could be shipped to the colonies. When these goods entered English ports, they were taxed, which made them more expensive and encouraged colonists to buy English-made items.

With the third and fourth sorts of regulation Parliament subsidized certain goods, including linen, gunpowder, and silks, to allow manufacturers to undersell European competitors in the colonies. Other laws protected English manufacturers from colonial competition by prohibiting colonists from manufacturing wool, felt hats, and iron on a large scale.

The colonies prospered under mercantilist legislation. Between 1650 and 1770, the colonial economy grew twice as fast as England's did. Because the trade laws allowed colonial merchants to operate on equal terms with English traders, they could take full advantage of commercial opportunities within the empire.

CHRONOLOGY

1651–1733	Parliament passes series of Navigation Acts to regulate imperial trade.
1660	Charles II becomes king of England.
1662	Halfway Covenant adopted by Massachusetts clergy.
1685	James II becomes king of England.
1686–1689	Dominion of New England.
1688	Glorious Revolution in England; James II loses the throne.
1689	William and Mary become English monarchs; Leisler's Rebellion begins in New York.
1689–1697	King William's War in America.
1691–1692	Witchcraft trials in Salem, Massachusetts.
1698	First French settlements near mouth of Mississippi River.
1701	Iroquois adopt policy of neutrality toward France and Britain.
1702–1713	Queen Anne's War in America.
1718	Establishment of San Antonio, Texas; New Orleans founded.
1734–1735	Jonathan Edwards leads religious revival in Northampton, Massachusetts.
1739	Great Awakening begins in Middle Colonies with George Whitefield's arrival.
1744–1748	King George's War in America.
1754–1763	Seven Years' War in America.
1760s	Spanish begin establishing missions in California.

The Colonial Export Trade and the Spirit of Enterprise

By the mid-eighteenth century, the Atlantic had become a busy thoroughfare of international commerce (see Map 4-1). Between 1700 and 1770, the number of British merchant ships nearly tripled, from 3,300 to 9,400. At the heart of Anglo-American trade lay the highly profitable commerce in staple crops, most of which were produced by slave labor.

West Indian sugar was the most important colonial product. By the late 1760s, the value of sugar and sugar by-product exports reached almost £4 million per year—*nearly 50 percent more than the total value of exports from all the other British American colonies combined.* Many West Indian planters joined with the English merchants who marketed their sugar to lobby Parliament for favorable treatment. The "sugar interest" convinced Parliament in 1733 to pass the **Molasses Act,** which taxed sugar products from foreign sources, especially the French West Indies. (Although the act aimed to encourage mainland colonists to buy British sugar and molasses, it in fact only stimulated the ingenuity of New England smugglers, who evaded British customs officials.) Parliament removed sugar from the list of enumerated items in 1739, allowing merchants to ship it directly from the islands to southern Europe.

Tobacco from the Chesapeake colonies was the second most valuable staple crop. Exports worth about £750,000 arrived each year in England during the late 1760s. Nearly 90 percent of the crop was later reexported to continental Europe. But persistent low prices led many tobacco planters, after 1750, to sow some of their land with wheat.

Exports of rice and indigo helped make South Carolina planters some of the richest mainland colonists. Most of the rice went to England and the West Indies. Parliament subsidized indigo production as well as colonial production of naval stores—such as tar, pitch, and turpentine—in order to reduce England's dependence on Swedish suppliers for materials essential to its navy. The export of these items made up a small but important part of the North and South Carolina economies.

Wheat exports from the Middle Colonies boomed after 1750, when a combination of poor harvests and warfare in Europe created strong overseas demand. Ships traveling from Philadelphia or New York to English ports also carried a variety of goods, including unrefined iron, potash (used in making soap and glass), salted meats, and wood products—naval stores, wooden shingles, and barrel staves.

New England had no staple crop and produced little for export to Great Britain except whale products, such as oil. The region's merchants nevertheless developed a thriving transatlantic trade, eventually dominating shipping within the empire. By 1770, New England's earnings from shipping fees,

Map 4-1   Anglo-American Transatlantic Commerce
By the eighteenth century, Great Britain and its colonies were enmeshed in a complex web of trade. Britain exchanged manufactured goods for colonial raw materials, while Africa provided the enslaved laborers who produced the most valuable colonial crops.

freight charges, and insurance exceeded the total value of its exports.

New England merchants also strengthened trade links to the West Indies. By the mid-eighteenth century, more than half of all New England exports went to the islands: salted meat for planters' dinners, salted fish for slaves, wood for sugar barrels and other equipment. Merchants accepted molasses and other sugar by-products in payment, bringing them back to New England to be distilled into cheap rum. Enterprising traders then carried rum to Africa to exchange for slaves. Because New Englanders trafficked in slaves and provisioned the West Indies, their commercial economy depended on the institution of slavery, even though few slaves lived in the region.

The Import Trade and Ties of Credit

By the late 1760s, the colonists imported goods worth nearly £4 million each year, almost all of which came from Great Britain. Most imports consisted of man-

ufactured goods, which could not be produced in America. Some of these goods—ironware, salt, sugar, hats, linen cloth—were made of materials that had come from the colonies in the first place.

In terms of value, colonists in fact imported more goods than they exported. Earnings from shipping fees, as well as payments from the British government for colonial military expenses, made up most of the difference between imports and exports. The colonial economy may have run an annual deficit of £40,000 by the late 1760s, but that amounted to only about 1 percent of a transatlantic trade worth over £4 million a year.

Great tobacco planters like Washington virtually lived on the easy credit that British merchants provided. These merchants marketed the planters' tobacco and supplied them with English goods, charging the costs of purchase and transportation against the profits they expected the next year's crop to bring.

SUMMARY

BRITISH IMPERIAL TRADE REGULATIONS, 1651–1733

Name of Act	Key Features
Navigation Act of 1651	• Aimed to eliminate Dutch competition in overseas trade • Required most goods to be carried in English or colonial ships • Required crews to be at least half English
Navigation Act of 1660	• Required all colonial trade to be carried in English ships • Required master and three-quarters of crew to be English • Created list of enumerated goods, such as tobacco and sugar, that could be shipped only to England or another English colony
Staple Act of 1663	• Required products from Europe, Asia, and Africa to be landed in England before being shipped to the colonies
Plantation Duty Act of 1673	• Attempted to reduce smuggling • Required captains of colonial ships to post bond that they would deliver enumerated goods to England or pay the "plantation duty" that would be owed in England
Navigation Act of 1696	• Plugged loopholes in earlier laws • Created vice-admiralty courts in colonies to enforce trade regulations
Woolens Act of 1699	• Forbade export of woolen cloth made in the colonies, to prevent competition with English producers
Hat Act of 1732	• Prohibited export of colonial-made hats
Molasses Act of 1733	• Placed high tax on French West Indian and other foreign molasses imported into colonies to encourage importation of British West Indian molasses

Gradually, planters sank into debt. A Virginian noted in 1766 that no planter would have dared run up a debt of £1,000 in the 1740s, but now "Ten times that sum is . . . spoke of with Indifference." When tobacco prices dropped or an international crisis made overseas trading risky, creditors called in the debts owed to them. At such times, colonial debtors realized how much they (like Indians involved in European trade) depended on goods and credit supplied by distant merchants.

Becoming More Like England

By 1770, Philadelphia's population had reached 30,000, New York's 25,000, Boston's 16,000, and Charleston's 12,000. A fifth city, Baltimore, was rapidly developing as the best harbor on Chesapeake Bay. Only about 5 percent of all mainland colonists lived in cities, but the influence of urban centers far outweighed their size.

An English visitor declared in 1759 that Philadelphia "must certainly be the object of every one's wonder and admiration." Less than eighty years old, it already boasted three thousand houses, impressive public buildings, "handsomely built" streets, two libraries, eight or ten churches, and a college (chartered as the College of Philadelphia in 1755, now the University of Pennsylvania). This same visitor judged Boston to be a "most flourishing" place with "much the air of some of our best country towns in England."

All colonial cities (like England's major ones) were seaports. Indeed, in their bustle and cos-

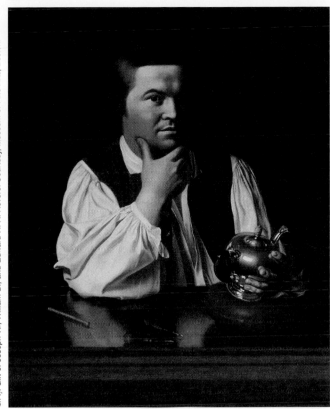

John Singleton Copley's portrait of the silversmith Paul Revere, painted about 1769, depicts one of Boston's most prominent artisans. As colonists grew wealthier, some commissioned portraits for their homes to serve as emblems of their rising social aspirations. Even so, Copley despaired that America would ever provide a suitable market for his artistic talents and he eventually moved to England.

mopolitan atmosphere, colonial cities resembled English provincial cities more than they did the villages and farms of the American countryside. Cities provided all sorts of amenities, including inns, taverns, coffeehouses, theaters, and social clubs. Their populations were much more diverse in ethnic origin and religion.

Perhaps two out of three adult white males living in cities worked at a craft. Many of them—shipbuilders, ropemakers, sailmakers—labored at trades directly related to overseas commerce. Others produced pottery, furniture, paper, glassware, iron tools, and various household items. Talented colonists such as the Boston silversmith Paul Revere and the Philadelphia furniture maker John Folwell fashioned goods that would have been prized possessions in any English gentleman's home.

Colonial manufacturing took place in workshops often attached to artisans' houses. Artisans managed a work force consisting of their wives and children, along with apprentices, usually teenage boys, who contracted to work for a master for four to seven years in order to learn the craft. Like indentured servants, they worked for food, clothing, shelter, and a small payment at the end of their service. Once an apprentice finished his training, he became a journeyman, working for a master but now earning wages and saving until he could afford to set up his own shop.

Many artisans flourished in colonial cities. Adino Paddock moved from the countryside to Boston in 1736 to learn how to make the light carriages known as chaises. By 1758, he had his own shop, and as his business prospered, Bostonians elected him to important local offices. As a gesture of public spirit, Paddock arranged for the transplanting of elm trees on Boston Common, to beautify the city where he had made his fortune, which by 1775 amounted to more than £3,000.

Craft work also offered economic opportunities to city women that were generally unavailable to rural women. Mary Wallace and Clementia Ferguson stitched fashionable hats and dresses for New York customers. Nonetheless, even in cities, women's options were limited. Many employed women were widows striving to maintain a family business until sons grew old enough to take over.

Workers at less skilled crafts often earned only a bare living, and ordinary laborers faced seasonal unemployment. The gap between rich and poor widened during the eighteenth century. In 1687, the richest 10 percent of Boston residents owned 46 percent of the taxable property in the town; by 1771, the top tenth held 63 percent of taxable wealth. Similar changes occurred in Philadelphia, South Carolina, and the Chesapeake, wherever colonists engaged heavily in commerce. Over time, it became extremely difficult for newcomers to enter the ranks of the elite.

Most cities built workhouses and other shelters for people who could not take care of themselves. Towns collected funds for poor relief in greater amounts than ever before. Even so, poverty had not yet become an entrenched problem. Temporary downturns in the economy were more often than not the result of dislocations caused by war.

Even in the worst of times, no more than one out of ten white colonists (mainly city-dwellers) depended on public assistance. As much as one-third of England's population regularly received relief, and the numbers swelled during hard times. So long as land was available—even if one had to move to the edges of settlement to get it—colonists could at least eke out a bare subsistence, and many did much better.

The growth of colonial cities mirrored British urban development. The widening gap between rich and poor convinced many colonists that their society had at last matured from its crude beginnings. Eighteenth-century Britons on both sides of the Atlantic believed that societies ought to be organized hierarchically, with people arranged in ranks from rich to poor according to their abilities and God's design. The more America resembled Britain, many colonists assumed, the more stable and prosperous it would be.

The Transformation of Culture

Despite the convergence of English and colonial society, many influential settlers worried that America remained culturally inferior to Great Britain. Just as Washington trusted a London tailor he had never met to make him a fashionable suit, other colonial gentlemen tended to see American architecture, fashion, manners, and intellectual life as poor imitations of British models. Some colonial gentlemen even reshaped their religious beliefs to reflect European notions that God played only an indirect role in human affairs.

Most colonists, however, had little interest in copying the manners of the English elite, and very few altered their spiritual beliefs to fit European patterns. Indeed, religion flourished in eighteenth-century America and, when a tremendous revival swept through the colonies beginning in the 1730s, it occupied center stage in American life.

Goods and Houses

Eighteenth-century Americans imported more manufactures from England with every passing year. In the less secure economic climate of the seventeenth century, colonists had limited their purchases of goods, investing instead in land to pass on to their children. But by the eighteenth century, prosperous colonists felt secure enough to buy goods to make their lives more comfortable.

Benjamin Franklin described such changes in his own household. Accustomed to eating his breakfast of bread and milk with a pewter spoon from an earthenware bowl, he found it one morning "in a China Bowl with a Spoon of Silver" that had cost "the enormous Sum of three and twenty Shillings." His wife, Deborah, justified the purchase by declaring "that she thought *her* Husband deserved a Silver Spoon & China Bowl as well as any of his

Neighbors." Many colonists likewise acquired such goods to advertise their refined style of life.

By the 1760s, nearly every item that George Washington ordered from his London agent could have been purchased in Philadelphia. But Washington and many other colonists wanted to get the latest English styles. One visitor to Maryland declared that he was "almost inclined to believe that a new fashion is adopted earlier by the polished and affluent American than by many opulent persons" in London.

Prosperous colonists built grand houses where they lived in greater comfort than ever before. In the seventeenth century, Virginia's governor lived in a four-room dwelling. His eighteenth-century counterpart, however, resided in Williamsburg in the Governor's Palace, an elegant two-storied mansion designed after British architectural styles. Washington extensively remodeled Mount Vernon, adding a second story and extra wings. In the northern colonies, merchants built the most impressive houses, often following architectural pattern books imported from England.

These houses were different in design from the homes of less affluent colonists. Most settlers cooked, ate, and slept in the same chamber. But the owners of great houses could devote rooms to specialized uses. Cooking and other domestic work took place in back or in separate outbuildings. Private bedrooms were located upstairs. The most distinctive feature of these grand homes was the parlor, an elaborately decorated room used for receiving guests. Prosperous colonists built such homes to emulate the English gentry in their country estates and London townhouses.

Shaping Minds and Manners

Colonists knew that the manners of English gentlefolk set them apart from ordinary people. Many Americans imported "courtesy books," which contained the rules of polite behavior. The young George Washington studied such books carefully. At age 13, he copied 110 rules from *Youth's Behaviour, or Decency in Conversation among Men*, including such advice as "In the Presence of Others Sing not to yourself with a humming Noise, nor Drum with your Fingers or Feet" and "In Company of those of Higher Quality than yourself Speak not till you are ask'd a Question then Stand upright put of[f] your Hat and Answer in few words."

In Charleston, South Carolina, dozens of girls' boarding schools advertised instruction in "the different branches of Polite Education." Female pupils studied reading, writing, and arithmetic but also learned French, music, dancing, and fancy needlework. This curriculum prepared them for married lives as mistresses of great houses, mothers of future gentlemen and ladies, and hostesses of grand entertainments. Invitations to balls, dances, musical performances, and tea parties circulated among well-bred neighbors. Such occasions excluded ordinary settlers and reinforced elite colonists' sense of themselves as a separate—and better—class of people.

Prominent colonists, intent on developing America's intellectual life, began to participate in a transatlantic world of ideas. Literacy rates among white colonists were quite high by eighteenth-century standards. In New England, where settlers placed great emphasis on Bible study, about 70 percent of men and 45 percent of women could read and write. Farther south, literacy rates were lower, but still higher than in England, where only a third of all men and even fewer women could read and write.

Elite colonists, however, were more consumers of British and European ideas than producers of an American intellectual tradition. They imported thousands of books, subscribed to British journals, and established libraries in Philadelphia, Charleston, and New York where borrowing privileges could be purchased for a modest fee. Students at Harvard in Cambridge (founded in 1636) modeled their college newspaper on an English periodical, the *Spectator*. In Virginia, William Byrd—the son of an Indian trader who had risen to the rank of gentleman—composed verse in the style of contemporary English poets, and Thomas Jefferson copied out passages from the English novel *Tristram Shandy*. Benjamin Franklin honed his writing skills by rewriting essays from the *Spectator* and comparing his versions to the originals.

Educated colonists were especially interested in the new ideas that characterized what has been called the **Age of Enlightenment**. A group of European thinkers drew inspiration from recent advances in science—such as the English scientist Isaac Newton's explanation of the laws of gravity—that suggested that the universe operated according to natural laws that human reason could discover. They also drew on the work of the English philosopher John Locke, who maintained that God did not dictate human knowledge but rather gave us the power to acquire knowledge through experience and understanding. The hallmark of Enlightenment thought was thus a belief in the power of human reason to improve the human condition.

Enlightenment thinkers rejected earlier ideas about God's unknowable will and continued intervention in human and natural events. They instead assigned God a less active role as the creator of the universe, who had set the world running according to predictable laws, and then let nature—and human beings—shape events.

Colonial intellectuals sought membership in a growing international community of scholars. A few of them—the Reverend Cotton Mather of Massachusetts, William Byrd, Benjamin Franklin—gained election to the Royal Society of London, the most prestigious learned society in the empire. Most of their scholarly contributions were unimpressive, but Benjamin Franklin achieved genuine intellectual prominence. His experiments with a kite proved that lightning was electricity and gained him an international reputation. Franklin also invented the lightning rod (which prevented fires in wooden buildings by channeling the electrical charge of a lightning bolt into the ground), bifocal spectacles, the iron "Franklin stove" (in which wood burned more efficiently than in fireplaces), and the glass harmonica.

Very few prosperous and educated colonists could afford to pursue their interest in the world of ideas. Only after retiring from business at age 42 could Franklin purchase the equipment for his electrical discoveries and begin his scientific work, devoting the "leisure during the rest of my life for philosophical studies and amusements." Most colonists remained ignorant of scientific advances and Enlightenment ideas. They had little leisure to devote to literature and polite conversation.

Colonial Religion and the Great Awakening

Church steeples dominated the skylines of colonial cities. Often the largest and finest buildings in town, they bore witness to the thriving—and diverse—condition of religion in America.

In all New England colonies except Rhode Island, the Puritan (or Congregationalist) faith was the established religion. The many Congregational churches in the region, headed by ministers trained at Harvard College and Yale (founded 1701), served the majority of the colonists and received financial support from their taxes. Ministers and believers adapted in important ways to changing social and religious conditions.

The principal adaptation consisted of a move away from strict requirements for church membership. New England's founders had required prospective members to give convincing evidence that they had experienced a spiritual conversion. Only members could receive communion and have their children baptized. By the 1660s, however, fewer colonists sought admission under such strict standards, which left them and their unbaptized children outside of the church. In 1662 the clergy adopted the **Halfway Covenant**, which allowed adults who had been baptized (because their parents were church members), but who had not themselves experienced conversion, to have their own children baptized. By the 1680s, some ministers made church admission even easier, requiring members only to demonstrate knowledge of the Christian faith and to live godly lives.

The Congregational Church also had gradually to permit a measure of religious toleration in New England. In 1691, Massachusetts received a royal charter granting "liberty of Conscience" to all Protestants, bringing the colony into line with England's religious policy. Anglicans and Baptists eventually won exemptions from paying taxes to support the Congregational Church. At the same time, some Congregationalist preachers began emphasizing personal piety and good works in their sermons, ideas usually associated with Anglicanism.

In the South, the established Church of England consolidated its authority in the early eighteenth century but never succeeded in exerting effective control over spiritual life. Parishes often lacked trained clergy, and those who did emigrate encountered unexpected obstacles.

Anglican clergymen in the southern colonies served parishes that were vast and sparsely settled. One South Carolina parish, for example, contained 10,400 square miles—and only seven hundred white residents. Aware that the planters' taxes paid their salaries, many ministers found it easiest simply to preach and behave in ways that offered the least offense. In frontier regions, dissenting religious groups, such as Presbyterians, Quakers, and Baptists, gained followers among people neglected by the Anglican establishment.

No established church dominated in the Middle Colonies of New York, New Jersey, and Pennsylvania. The region's ethnically diverse population and William Penn's policy of religious toleration guaranteed that a multitude of groups would compete for followers. By the mid-eighteenth century, the region had more congregations per capita than even New England.

Groups such as the Quakers and the Mennonites, who did not believe in having specially trained ministers, easily formed new congregations in response to local demand. Lutheran and German Reformed churches, however, required European-educated clergy, who were always scarce. So pious laymen held worship services in their homes. When more Lutheran and Reformed clergy arrived in the 1740s and 1750s, they sometimes discovered that laymen balked at relinquishing control of the churches. Because so many other religious alternatives were available, these ministers had to compete for their parishioners' allegiance.

Bewildering spiritual diversity, relentless religious competition, and a comparatively weak Anglican Church all distinguished the colonies from England. Yet in one important way, religious developments during the middle third of the eighteenth century drew the colonies closer to England. A transatlantic religious revival, the **Great Awakening**, originated in Scotland and England, and first touched the Middle Colonies in the 1730s.

By 1730, Presbyterians in Pennsylvania had split into factions. One group was led by an immigrant Scottish evangelist, William Tennent Sr., and his four sons. In the 1730s, Tennent set up the Log College in Neshaminy, Pennsylvania, to train his sons and other young men to be evangelical ministers. His challenge to the Presbyterian establishment gained momentum in late 1739, when one of the most charismatic evangelists of the century, George Whitefield, arrived in the colonies from England.

Whitefield, an Anglican priest, had experienced an intense religious conversion while he was still a university student. Famous in Britain as a preacher of great emotional intensity, he embarked on a tour of the colonies. In Pennsylvania and New Jersey, Whitefield's powerful preaching on the experience of conversion lent support to the Presbyterian faction led by the Tennents and sparked local revivals. Whitefield then moved on to New England, where some communities had already experienced small, local awakenings.

Whitefield exhorted his audiences to examine their souls for evidence of the "indwelling of Christ" that would indicate that they were saved. He criticized most ministers for emphasizing good works and "head-knowledge" instead of the emotional side of religion.

Whitefield's sermons scarcely resembled the colonists' structured church services. His sermons were highly dramatic performances. He preached outdoors to thousands of strangers, jostling in crowds that often outnumbered the populations of several villages put together.

In the wake of Whitefield's visits, Benjamin Franklin noted, "it seem'd as if all the World were growing Religious." Revivals and mass conversions often followed his appearances, to the happy astonishment of local clergy. But their approval evaporated

George Whitefield (who, contemporaries noted, was cross-eyed) enjoyed a remarkable career as a powerful preacher on both sides of the Atlantic. This portrait shows him preaching indoors to a rapt audience. During his tour of the colonies, Whitefield reportedly had a similar effect on crowds of thousands who gathered outdoors to hear his sermons.

when disputes between individuals converted in the revivals—called "**New Lights**"—and those who were not ("Old Lights") split churches. "Formerly the People could bear with each other in Charity when they differ'd in Opinion," lamented one colonist, "but they now break Fellowship and Communion with one another on that Account."

The Awakening came late to the southern colonies, but it was there, in the 1760s, that it produced perhaps its greatest controversy. Many southern converts became Baptists, combining their religious criticism of the Anglicans with a general condemnation of the wealthy planters' way of life. Planters, in turn, viewed Baptists as dangerous people who could not "meet a man upon the road, but they must ram a text of Scripture down his throat." Most of all, they hated the Baptists for their willingness to preach to slaves.

The Great Awakening had a lasting impact on colonial society, forging new links between Great Britain and the colonies. Evangelical ministers on both sides of the Atlantic exchanged correspondence. Periodicals such as *The Christian History*

informed British and American subscribers of advances in true religion throughout the empire.

In the colonies, the Awakening led to the founding of new colleges. Middle Colony evangelicals founded the College of New Jersey (now Princeton University) in 1746. In the 1760s, New England Baptists established the College of Rhode Island (now Brown University). An evangelical wing of the Dutch Reformed Church founded Queens College (now Rutgers University) in 1766.

Everywhere, the New Light challenge to established ministers and churches undermined habits of deference to authority. Revivalists urged colonists to think for themselves in choosing which church to join and which minister to follow, not just conform to what the rest of the community did. As their churches fractured, Americans—particularly New Englanders—faced more choices than ever before in their religious lives.

The exercise of religious choice also influenced political behavior. Voters took note of whether candidates for office were New or Old Lights and cast their ballots for men on their own side. Tactics first used to mobilize religious groups—organizing committees, writing petitions and letters—proved useful for political activities as well.

The Colonial Political World

The political legacy of the Great Awakening—particularly the emphasis on individual choice and resistance to authority—corresponded to developments in the colonial political world. For most of the seventeenth century, ties within the empire developed from trade rather than governance. But as America grew in wealth and population, king and Parliament sought to manage colonial affairs more directly than ever before.

The Dominion of New England and the Limits of British Control

When Charles II became king in 1660, he initially showed little interest in the colonies except as sources of land and government offices with which he could reward his supporters. With the passage of mercantile regulations governing colonial trade, for example, Parliament required customs officers to administer the imperial trading system and thus created a certain number of jobs.

Charles's brother James, the duke of York, envisioned a more tightly controlled empire. He encouraged Charles to appoint military officers, with strong ties of loyalty to him, as royal governors in America. In 1675, James convinced Charles to create the **Lords of Trade**, a committee of the Privy Council (the group of nobles who served as royal advisers), to oversee colonial affairs.

When James became king in 1685, the whole character of the empire abruptly changed. James set out to reorganize it along the lines of Spain's empire, combining the colonies into three or four large provinces. He appointed powerful governors to carry out policies that he himself would formulate.

James began in the north, creating the **Dominion of New England** out of eight previously separate colonies stretching from New Hampshire to New Jersey. He chose Sir Edmund Andros, a former army officer, to govern the vast region with an appointive council but no elective assembly. Andros moved to Boston and antagonized New Englanders by rigidly enforcing the Navigation Acts, limiting towns to just one annual meeting, remodeling the law courts, challenging property titles, and levying taxes without the colonists' consent. He even compelled Boston Puritans to share a meetinghouse with Anglicans.

Events in England ultimately sealed the fate of the Dominion. For years, English Protestants had worried about James's absolutist governing style and his conversion to Catholicism. But their fears increased when in 1688, the queen bore a son to carry on a Catholic line of succession. Parliament's leaders invited James's Protestant daughter, Mary, and her husband, William of Orange, the Stadtholder of the Netherlands, to take over the throne. In November 1688, William landed in England and gained the support of most of the English army. In December, James fled to France, ending a bloodless coup known as the **Glorious Revolution**.

Bostonians overthrew and imprisoned Andros the following April, even before they knew for sure that William was king. In 1691, Massachusetts received a new charter. Massachusetts now included within its borders what had formerly been Plymouth Colony as well as Maine. Its colonists no longer elected their governor, who would instead be appointed by the English monarch. Voters no longer had to be church members, and religious toleration was extended to all Protestants.

The new charter ended exclusive Puritan control in Massachusetts but also restored political stability. During the three years between Andros's imprisonment and the arrival of a royal governor in 1692, the colony lacked a legally established government. In this atmosphere of uncertainty, a local

outbreak of accusations of witchcraft in Salem grew to unprecedented proportions. In the winter of 1691–1692, when several young girls of Salem experienced fits and other strange behavior, hundreds of settlers were accused of witchcraft, and nineteen were hanged. Salem's crisis gathered momentum because the courts, which would normally have intervened to settle matters, were unable to function.

The impact of the Glorious Revolution in other colonies likewise reflected distinctive local conditions. In New York, Jacob Leisler, a rich merchant and militia captain, gained power and ruled in an increasingly dictatorial fashion. Too slow in relinquishing command to the newly arrived royal governor in 1691, Leisler was arrested for treason and executed. In Maryland, Protestants used the occasion of William and Mary's accession to challenge the Catholic proprietorship. The Calvert family lost its governing powers but retained rights to vast quantities of land. The Anglican Church became the established faith, and Catholics were barred from public office.

The colonists' support of the Glorious Revolution largely reflected powerful anti-Catholic sentiment. William's firm Protestantism reassured them. But the Glorious Revolution in England and the demise of the Dominion had long-lasting effects that shaped political life in England and America for years to come.

The Legacy of the Glorious Revolution

In England, the Glorious Revolution signaled a return to political stability after years of upheaval. In 1689, Parliament passed the Bill of Rights, which justified James's ouster and bound future monarchs to abide by the rule of law. They could not suspend parliamentary laws, collect taxes or engage in foreign wars without Parliament's consent, or maintain a standing army in peacetime. Parliamentary elections and meetings would follow a regular schedule without royal interference. In sum, Parliament claimed to be the crown's equal partner in governing England.

Colonists believed that their successful resistance to Andros confirmed that their membership in the empire was founded on voluntary allegiance and not forced submission to the mother country. Observing the similarity between Parliament and the colonial assemblies, they concluded that their own legislatures had a critical role in governance and in the protection of their rights. Parliament, however, claimed full authority over the colonies and did not recognize their assemblies as its equal.

William and his immediate successors lacked James's compulsion to control the colonies. In 1696,

William replaced the Lords of Trade with the **Board of Trade**, which gathered information from the colonies and recommended policy changes but itself had no executive role. William also approved the **Navigation Act of 1696**, which closed loopholes in earlier laws and created **vice-admiralty courts** in the colonies similar to those of England. Admiralty judges settled maritime disputes and smuggling cases without using juries.

The mild imperial rule of the early eighteenth century, later called the era of "salutary neglect," allowed the colonies to grow in wealth, population, and self-government. It also encouraged colonial self-confidence, leading Americans to assume equality with the English as members of the empire.

Diverging Politics in the Colonies and Great Britain

English people on both sides of the Atlantic believed that politics ought to reflect social organization. They often compared the state to a family. Just as fathers headed families, adult men led societies. In particular, adult male property holders, who enjoyed economic independence, claimed the right to vote and hold office. Women (who generally could not own property), propertyless men, and blacks had no political role because they, like children, were subordinate to the authority of others, which rendered them incapable of exercising freedom of choice.

English people believed that rulers ought to govern with the same fairness and benevolence that fathers presumably exercised within their families. When George II became king in 1727, he reassured Parliament of his "constant care" to "secure to All My subjects, the full Enjoyment of their religious and civil Rights." In return for protection, the people owed their rulers the same obedience that children accorded their parents. The House of Commons responded to George II's assurance of goodwill in 1727 with its own promise of "the highest Returns of Duty, Zeal and Affection to Your Majesty's Person and Government."

Eighteenth-century people also believed that government should reflect society's hierarchical organization. In England, the crown represented the interests of the royal family. Parliament represented society's two main divisions: the aristocracy in the **House of Lords** and the common people in the **House of Commons**. Americans shared the view that government should mirror social hierarchies but found it much more difficult to put the idea into practice.

American social and political structure never fully mirrored that of England. One of the most obvious differences was that America lacked an aristocracy. In England, the members of this tiny privileged minority were easily recognizable by their great wealth, prestigious family lines, leisured lives, and official titles of nobility. British America had elites—mainly rich planters and merchants—but no aristocracy.

In both England and America, land ownership was the prerequisite for political participation. By the mid-eighteenth century, only one-tenth of all English heads of households owned all the country's land, and just four hundred great landlords held nearly a quarter of it. Thus only a tiny portion of adult English men—perhaps 15 percent—could vote. In America, however, a large majority of white male farmers owned the land they tilled. In most colonies, 50 to 75 percent of white men were eligible to vote.

In England, electoral districts for Parliament often reflected their status in past centuries. Dunwich retained its right to elect a parliamentary representative long after the city itself had washed into the North Sea. Meanwhile, rapidly growing cities, such as Manchester, lacked any representative. Most of the English accepted the idea of **virtual representation**, which held that representatives served the interests of the nation as a whole, not just the locality from which they came. They also assumed that since the colonists held interests in common with English people at home, they were virtually represented in Parliament—just like Manchester's residents.

Since the founding of their colonies, however, Americans had experienced **actual representation** and believed that elected representatives should be directly responsive to local interests. They were accustomed to instructing their legislators about how to vote on important issues. Colonial representatives, unlike members of Parliament, resided in their districts. The Americans' experience with actual representation made them extremely skeptical of Parliament's claims to virtual representation.

The most direct political confrontations between England and the colonies focused on the role of colonial governors. In every colony except Connecticut and Rhode Island, either the king or proprietors appointed the governors. Their interests thus lay with their English patrons and not the colonies. Governors exercised greater powers over the colonial assemblies than the king (after the Glorious Revolution) did over Parliament. Governors could veto laws enacted by the assemblies and initiate legislation in consultation with councilors whom they appointed. They could delay legislative sessions,

American Views

BOSTON CELEBRATES A NEW KING (AUGUST 1727)

The first colonial newspaper, the *Boston News-Letter*, appeared in that city in 1704. By the 1720s, Bostonians could choose from three newspapers, and New York and Philadelphia each had one. Published weekly, these papers mainly reported on English and European affairs and often reprinted essays by prominent English political writers. Their pages carried little local news, on the assumption that colonists could learn it by word of mouth. But when truly extraordinary events occurred, such as the accession of a new British monarch, colonial newspapers reported on the local response. The following extract describes Bostonians' reaction to news that George II had become Britain's new king.

❖ **How did Bostonians commemorate the new king's accession?**

❖ **What does this reveal about their attitudes toward George II and British government in general?**

❖ **Who was invited to the "splendid Entertainment," and what does this tell us about the structure of Boston society?**

On Wednesday Morning by order of His Honour William Dummer, Esq., our Lieut. Governour & Commander in chief[,] three Regiments of the Militia and five Troops of horse were under arms in the great street before the State-house, making a very fine appearance. The number of Spectators exceeded the Men in Arms, covering the houses on every side. As

---

dissolve the assemblies at will, and nominate and dismiss colonial judges as they wished.

Several conditions hampered governors' efforts to exercise their legal authority. Many arrived with detailed instructions on how to govern, which limited their ability to negotiate with colonists over sensitive issues. Governors controlled few offices or other prizes with which to buy the allegiance of their opponents. They struggled to dominate assemblies that grew in size as the colonial population expanded. And in several colonies, including Massachusetts and New York, governors relied on the assemblies to appropriate the money for their salaries—a financial dependence that restrained even the most autocratic executive.

In response to the perceived threat of powerful governors, colonial assemblies asserted themselves as never before. They sent agents (including such prominent figures as Benjamin Franklin) to England to lobby on behalf of colonial interests. Local factions fought for election to the increasingly important legislature, leading to some of the most contentious politics in the British Empire.

Decades of struggles with governors led colonists to exalt the assemblies' role as the guarantors of their liberties. Most colonists, however, believed that so long as Parliament treated the Americans as partners in empire and refrained from ruling by coercion, colonists could celebrate British government as "the most perfect combination of human powers in society . . . for the preservation of liberty and the production of happiness."

Expanding Empires

During the first half of the eighteenth century, England, Spain, and France all increased their North American holdings. England's empire continued to expand as a result of the unrelenting growth of its colonial population. Spain and France still relied on missionaries, soldiers, and traders to stake their soon as the Herauld had said his Amen to God Save the King, the loud and joyful Huzza's of so great a multitude rent the skies, the Regiments made a tripple discharge, the Castle Forts & Ships fir'd their cannon; and a splendid Entertainment follow'd for the Lieut. Governour and his Majesty's Council, Officers, Justices, and the Rev[eren]d Ministers present; with suitable provisions for the Regiments and Troops. The bells rung all the day, and in the Evening the Rejoycing was continued with Fireworks and Bonfires, and the whole Town illuminated in an extraordinary manner, the Windows of each story of the Houses in the principal streets having three or four rows of candles in them. The streets were fill'd all the Evening with the Gentry of both Sexes, who appear'd with much decency and gravity, and with gayety and chearfulness. At nine of the clock a welcome rain, after a time of much heat and drought, put an end to the Ceremony. . . . We pray God, by whom Kings reign, that the royal smiles of His Majesty King George the Second, and the happy influences of his wise and just Government, may ever be falling on all his Majesty's Dominions, and on this loyal and dutiful Province in particular. . . .

Source: New England Weekly Journal (*August 21, 1727*).

claims to American territory. In the eighteenth century as in the seventeenth, English settlement generally displaced native peoples. Newly established Spanish and French colonies, however, contained small numbers of Europeans amid much larger populations of Indians. Over time, these empires came into closer contact with one another, intensifying the competition for land, trade, resources, and Indian allies.

The English in the Backcountry

Black and white settlers in the mainland colonies numbered 265,000 in 1700; by 1770, they had increased to 2.3 million. Benjamin Franklin predicted in 1750 that if the colonial population continued to grow at this rate, within two hundred years "the greatest Number of Englishmen will be on this Side" of the Atlantic Ocean.

Much of this growth stemmed from natural increase. White families, particularly in the northern colonies, had large numbers of children, most of whom survived to produce many more offspring. Most women married in their early twenties (a younger age, on average, than European women) and often bore between five and ten children. When 80-year-old Judith Coffin, the matriarch of an unusually large Massachusetts family, died in 1705, she had a total of 177 children and grandchildren. By the mid-eighteenth century, even the slave population began to reproduce itself, although more slowly than the white population.

Immigration also boosted the population. Thousands of Scots-Irish and German settlers—and many involuntary African immigrants—increased the population of the Lower South at nearly twice the rate of New England, which attracted few immigrants (and therefore remained the most thoroughly English of all colonial regions). By 1770, Pennsylvania had 240,000 settlers—ten times the number it had in 1710. Indeed, extensive German immigration worried Pennsylvania leaders. Like Benjamin Franklin, they feared that the newcomers would "never adopt our

Language or Customs" and would soon "be so numerous as to Germanize us."

Most of the coast from Maine to Georgia was settled by 1760, forcing many immigrants and descendants of earlier settlers to move inland. The most dramatic expansion occurred in the foothills and valleys of the Appalachian Mountains from Pennsylvania to Georgia, a region known as the **backcountry**. Between 1730 and 1770, nearly a quarter of a million German, Scots-Irish, and English colonists entered the backcountry. They mainly raised crops and livestock for subsistence on small, isolated farms. Community life developed slowly, in part because backcountry settlers often moved frequently. In addition, a surplus of men among the first settlers delayed the formation of families.

Contemporary observers derided the crudeness of frontier life. William Byrd, a wealthy planter from Virginia's Tidewater, scornfully described one backcountry house as a "castle containing of one dirty room with a dragging door to it that will neither open or shut." Charles Woodmason, an English-born Anglican missionary, was appalled by the sight of settlers who "Live in Logg Cabbins like Hogs" in western Carolina. Genteel observers offered what they considered the most damaging insult by referring to such settlers as "white Indians."

Yet many coastal planters—including William Byrd and George Washington—acquired vast tracts of western land with the intent to sell it to these "crude" settlers. During the 1740s and 1750s, scores of Virginia planters, northern merchants, and London investors formed companies whose purpose was to profit from this kind of land speculation. Their interests collided with those of settlers—squatters—who occupied the land without acquiring legal title in the hope that their labor in clearing farms would establish their property rights.

Backcountry settlers often complained that rich eastern planters, who dominated the colonial legislatures, ignored western demands for adequate representation. Many western settlers argued that the crudeness of frontier life was only temporary and that they, too, would soon be producing tobacco and other cash crops. Perhaps the best measure of their desire to resemble eastern planters was the spread of slaveholding. In one western Virginia county in 1750, only one-fifth of the household heads owned slaves. Just nineteen years later, more than half of them did.

Colonists who moved to the backcountry often displaced native groups. Indians moving to avoid friction with whites, however, frequently encroached on lands claimed by other tribes—particularly those of the Iroquois Confederacy—leading to conflict among native peoples.

Even where English settlers had not yet appeared, English and Scottish traders could often be found, aggressively pursuing trade with the Indians. Spanish and French observers feared this commercial expansion even more than the movement of settlers. Knowing that the Indians viewed trade as a counterpart to military alliance, the Spanish and French expanded their own territorial claims and tried to strengthen relations with Indian peoples.

The Spanish in Texas and California

Spanish Florida had become the target of English raiders from South Carolina. Years of religious persecution and forced labor under Spanish rule encouraged Florida's Indians to oppose the Spanish, but the natives also liked English trade goods and guns. Spain held on to coastal bases at St. Augustine, San Marcos de Apalachee, and Pensacola. By the mid-eighteenth century, however, control of Florida's interior effectively passed to Indian bands allied with the English.

In 1700, Franciscan priests in New Mexico, fearful of sparking another native revolt, eased their labor demands and avoided outright religious persecution, allowing the Pueblos to retain many of their customs and religious practices. New Mexican officials worried about news brought by Apache hunters that Frenchmen who might contest Spanish control had been seen on the plains.

To create a buffer zone around their existing colonies, the Spanish moved into Texas and California. Franciscan priests established several missions in east Texas between 1690 and 1720. San Antonio, founded in 1718, served as a way station between the Rio Grande and east Texas missions; its fortified chapel, San Antonio de Valero, later became famous as the Alamo. The Spanish advance into Texas, however, met with resistance from the French (who also had outposts on the Gulf Coast) and from the Caddos and other Indians armed with French guns. With only 1,800 settlers there as late as 1742, Spain exerted a weak hold on Texas.

Largely through the efforts of two men—José de Gálvez, a royal official, and Junípero Serra, a Franciscan priest—the Spanish constructed a string of forts and missions in California from San Diego north to San Francisco between 1769 and 1776. They initially encountered little opposition from California's Indians, who lived in small, scattered villages and lacked experience with organized warfare. With no European rivals nearby to compete with them, the Spanish erected an extensive mission

This panel of an eighteenth-century painting by an unknown Mexican artist is representative of a genre of portraits illustrating the categories Spanish colonists developed to designate the offspring of various kinds of mixed marriage. This one, labeled "Español, con India, Mestizo," depicts a Spanish father, an Indian mother, and their mestizo child. The scarcity of European women made mixed marriage common in Spanish colonies. Such unions were exceedingly rare in the English colonies, where cultural preferences and the relative abundance of European women discouraged intermarriage.

system designed to convert and educate Indians and set them to work. Thousands of native laborers farmed irrigated fields and tended horses, sheep, and cattle.

The Spanish worked the Indians hard and maintained them in overcrowded, unsanitary dwellings. Native women suffered from sexual exploitation by Spanish soldiers. Epidemics of European diseases reduced the Indian population from 300,000 in 1769 to about 200,000 fifty years later. Signs of native resistance met with quick and cruel punishment—including whipping, burning, and execution—so that the Indians would not (as one official later wrote) "come to know their power" over the vastly outnumbered Spanish. (As late as 1790, California had only 990 Spanish residents.) Despite the gruesome consequences, natives staged several revolts during the eighteenth century, but Spanish soldiers usually suppressed them quickly.

Spain's empire grew, even as it weakened, during the eighteenth century. From the beginning, Spain's vision of empire had rested not on extensive settlement but on expansive territorial claims backed up by soldiers and missionaries who subjugated native peoples in order to control their labor for Spanish profit. After 1700, however, the Spanish simply could not compete with the vigorous commercial empires of France and England.

The French along the Mississippi

French expansion followed major waterways—the St. Lawrence River, the Great Lakes, the Mississippi—into the heart of North America. Explorers reached the Mississippi Valley in the 1670s. Within twenty years, French outposts appeared along the Gulf Coast. New Orleans, the capital and main port of French Louisiana, was founded in 1718. Soon forts, trading posts, and villages began to spring up in the continent's interior—a chain of way stations between Canada and the Gulf of Mexico. Defying official regulators, French colonists settled in six villages along the Mississippi in a place they called the *Pays des Illinois.*

The first Illinois settlers were independent fur traders (*coureurs de bois*, or "woods runners") unwilling to return to Canada after the French government tried to prohibit their direct trade with Indians. Many found Christian Indian wives and began farming the rich lands along the river. The settlers and other Canadian emigrants, using the labor of their families and of black and Indian slaves, produced profitable surpluses of wheat, corn, and livestock to feed the growing population of New Orleans and the lower Mississippi Valley.

French Louisiana contained a diverse population of Indian peoples, French soldiers and settlers, German immigrants, and African slaves who, by the 1730s, outnumbered European colonists. Louisiana's economy depended mainly on the combined efforts of Indians, settlers, and slaves, who farmed, herded, fished, and traded deerskins. Due to the lack of profits, however, substantial European emigration to Louisiana essentially ceased after the 1720s.

But the French approach to empire—in Louisiana as in Canada —had always depended more on Indian alliances than on settlement. Louisiana's principal allies, the Choctaws, and other natives offered trade and military assistance in return for guns, trade goods, French help in fighting English raiders seeking Indian slaves, and occasional French mediation of Indian disputes.

French expansion along the Mississippi Valley drove a wedge between Florida and Spain's other mainland colonies; it also blocked the westward movement of English settlers. But France's enlarged empire was only as strong as the Indian alliances on which it rested. The fear of losing Indian favor preoccupied officials because France's empire in America consisted of two disconnected pieces: New France, centered in the St. Lawrence Valley and the Great Lakes basin, and Louisiana, stretching from New Orleans to the *Pays de Illinois*. Between them lay 1,000 miles of wilderness through which only one thoroughfare passed—the Ohio River. For decades, communication between the two parts of France's North American empire posed no problem because Indians in the Ohio Valley allowed the French free passage through their lands. If that policy ended, however, France's New World empire would be dangerously divided.

A Century of Warfare

From the time of the Glorious Revolution, English foreign policy aimed at limiting the expansion of French influence. This resulted in a series of four wars, which increasingly involved French and English colonies as well as Spain and its colonies. The conclusion of the final conflict signaled a dramatic shift in North American history (see the summary table "The Colonial Wars, 1689–1763").

Imperial Conflict and the Establishment of an American Balance of Power, 1689–1738

When he became king of England in 1688, the Dutch Protestant William of Orange was already fighting the **War of the League of Augsburg** against France's Catholic king, Louis XIV. William brought England into the conflict as a Dutch ally. The war lasted until 1697 and ended—as most eighteenth-century European wars did—in a negotiated peace that reestablished the balance of power. Little territory actually changed hands, either in this war or in the **War of the Spanish Succession** (1702–1713), which followed it.

In America, these two wars—known to British colonists as **King William's War** and **Queen Anne's War**, after the monarchs on the throne at the time—ended with equal indecisiveness. New France's Indian allies attacked New England's northern frontier with devastating success. New Englanders struck back at the exposed settlements of Acadia, which ultimately entered the British Empire as Nova Scotia, and tried unsuccessfully to seize Quebec. Neither war caused more than marginal changes for the colonies in North America. Both had profound effects, however, on the English state and on the Iroquois League.

All European states of the eighteenth century financed their wars by borrowing. But the English were the first to realize that wartime debts did not necessarily have to be repaid during the following peace. The government instead created a **funded debt**. Having borrowed heavily from large joint-stock corporations, the government agreed to use tax revenues to pay interest on those loans but not to pay off the loans themselves. The corporations agreed because the interest payments amounted to a steady form of income that over the long run could amount to more than the original loans. In this way, England became the first European country to harness its national economy efficiently to military ends.

As the debt grew ever larger, more taxes were necessary to pay interest on it and for a powerful navy and a standing army. When the treasury created a larger and more efficient bureaucracy to collect taxes, many Englishmen's anxiety emerged as a strain of thought known as **Country**, or "**Real Whig**," **ideology**, which stressed the threats that a standing army and a powerful state posed to personal liberty. It also emphasized the dangers of taxation to property rights and the need for property holders to retain their right to consent to taxation. Real Whig politicians publicized their fears but could not stop the growth of the state. In every successive war, the claims of national interest and patriotism—and the prospect of profit for parties rich enough to lend money to the government—overrode the objections of those who feared the expansion of state power.

In America, the first two imperial wars transformed the role of the Iroquois League. By 1700, the League had suffered such horrendous losses—perhaps a quarter of the population had died from causes related to King William's War—that its leaders created the **Grand Settlement of 1701**, a policy of neutrality with regard to the French and British Empires. Their goal was to refrain from alliances with either European power and instead maneuver between them. The Iroquois' strategic location between New France and the English colonies allowed them to serve as a geographical and diplomatic buffer between the two. This neutralist policy ensured that for nearly fifty years neither England nor France could gain ascendancy in North America.

Iroquois neutrality offered benefits to the Europeans as well as the Indians. To smooth relations with the English, the Iroquois sold them land formerly occupied by Delawares and Susquehannocks. This simultaneously helped satisfy the colonists' land hunger and enrich the Iroquois League. Meanwhile,

SUMMARY

THE COLONIAL WARS, 1689–1763

Name in the Colonies	European Name and Dates	Dates in America	Results for Britain
King William's War	War of the League of Augsburg, 1688–1697	1689–1697	• Reestablished balance of power between England and France
Queen Anne's War	War of Spanish Succession, 1702–1714	1702–1713	• Britain acquired Nova Scotia
King George's War	War of Austrian Succession, 1739–1748	1744–1748	• Britain returned Louisbourg to France • British settlers began moving westward • Weakening of Iroquois neutrality
French and Indian War	Seven Years' War, 1756–1763	1754–1763	• Britain acquired Canada and all French territory east of Mississippi • Britain gained Florida from Spain

a neutral Iroquois League claiming control over the Ohio Valley and blocking English access across the Appalachian Mountains helped the French protect the strategic corridor of the Ohio and Mississippi Valleys that linked Canada and Louisiana.

If the English ever established a permanent presence on this strategic corridor, however, the Iroquois would cease to be of use to the French. The Iroquois remained reasonably effective at keeping the British out of the Ohio Valley until the late 1740s. The next European war, however, altered these circumstances.

King George's War Shifts the Balance, 1739–1754

What became the third confrontation between Britain and France in Europe, the **War of the Austrian Succession** (**King George's War** to the British colonists) began as a small war between Britain and Spain in 1739. Its immediate cause was British attempts to poach on trade to Spain's Caribbean colonies. But in 1744, France joined in the war against Britain and conflict erupted in North America.

New Englanders tried once again to attack Canada. This time, their target was the great fortress of Louisbourg on Cape Breton Island, a naval base that dominated the Gulf of St. Lawrence. An expedition from Massachusetts and Connecticut, supported by a squadron of Royal Navy warships, captured Louisbourg in 1745, and cut Canada off from French reinforcement and resupply. English forces should now have been able to conquer New France.

Instead, politically influential merchants in Albany, New York, continued to trade with the enemy via Lake Champlain, enabling Canada to hold out until the end of the war. When the peace treaty was signed in 1748, Britain, which had fared badly in the European fighting, agreed to return Louisbourg to France. This diplomatic adjustment, routine by European standards, shocked New Englanders. New York's illegal trade with the enemy, unremarkable by previous colonial standards, appalled British administrators.

Even before the war's end, aggressive English traders from Pennsylvania began moving west to buy furs from Indians who had once traded with the French. The movements of these traders, along with the appearance of Virginians in the Ohio Valley after 1748, gravely concerned the French.

In 1749, the governor general of New France set out to assert direct control over the region by building a set of forts from Lake Erie to the Forks of the Ohio. This signaled the end of France's commitment to Iroquois neutrality. The chiefs of the Iroquois League now found themselves trapped between empires edging closer to confrontation in the Ohio Valley.

The appearance of English traders in the valley offering goods on better terms than the French or the Iroquois had ever provided undermined Iroquois dominance. The Ohio Valley Indians increasingly ignored Iroquois claims of control and pursued their own independent course.

One spur to their disaffection from the Iroquois was the 1744 **Treaty of Lancaster**, by which Iroquois chiefs had sold a group of Virginia land speculators rights to trade at the Forks of the Ohio. The Virginians assumed that these trading rights included the right to acquire land for eventual sale to settlers. The Ohio Valley Indians found this intolerable, as did the French. When in 1754 the government of Virginia sent out a small body of soldiers under Lieutenant Colonel George Washington to protect Virginia's claims to the Forks of the Ohio, the French struck decisively to stop them.

Decision: The French and Indian War, 1754–1760

In April 1754, French soldiers overwhelmed a group of Virginians who had been trying to build a small fort at the Forks of the Ohio. They then erected a much larger fort of their own on the spot, Fort Duquesne. The French intended to follow up by similarly ousting Washington's weak, untrained troops, who had encamped further up the Monongahela River. However, at the end of May, Washington's men killed or captured all but one of the members of a small French reconnaissance party. The French decided to teach the Virginians a lesson. On July 3, they attacked Washington at his encampment, Fort Necessity. The next day, with a quarter of his troops killed or wounded, Washington surrendered.

British imperial officials worried that the Iroquois might abandon their neutrality for a French alliance. Britain ordered New York's governor to convene an intercolonial meeting in Albany—known as the **Albany Congress**—to discuss matters with the Iroquois. Several prominent colonists, including Governor William Shirley of Massachusetts and Benjamin Franklin, took advantage of the occasion to put forward the **Albany Plan of Union**, which called for an intercolonial union to coordinate colonial defense,

levy taxes, and regulate Indian affairs. But the colonies, too suspicious of one another to see their common interests, rejected the Albany Plan.

Meanwhile, the French expulsion of the Virginians left the Indians of the region, Delawares and Shawnees, with no choice but to ally with the French in what came to be called the **French and Indian War**. Soon French and Indian attacks fell like hammer blows on backcountry settlements from Pennsylvania to the Carolinas. Iroquois neutrality no longer mattered. Europeans were at last contending directly for control of the Ohio Country.

The French and Indian War blazed in America for two years before it erupted as a fourth Anglo-French war in Europe in 1756. Known in Europe as the **Seven Years' War** (1756–1763), it involved fighting in the Caribbean, Africa, India, and the Philippine Islands as well as in Europe and North America. It was unlike any other eighteenth-century conflict not only in its immense scope and expense but also in its decisive outcome.

During the first phase of the war, the French enjoyed a string of successes as they followed what had been a proven strategy in previous conflicts, guerrilla war. Relying on Indian allies and Canadian soldiers, the French raided English frontier settlements, killing and capturing hundreds of civilians and forcing tens of thousands more to flee. Then they attacked fortified outposts whenever the opportunity appeared. This style of warfare allowed the Canadians' Indian allies—who came from all over the Northeast and the upper Midwest—to act independently in choosing targets and tactics.

In 1755, Britain dispatched troops to attack Fort Duquesne. Major General Edward Braddock marched to within 10 miles of Fort Duquesne, only to have his 1,450-man force surrounded by Indians and Canadian militiamen and destroyed. Braddock's defeat set the tone for virtually every military engagement of the next three years and opened a period of demoralization and internal conflict in the British colonies.

Britain responded by sending a new commander in chief, Lord Loudoun, to set colonial military affairs on a professional footing. He insisted on managing every aspect of the war effort, not only directing the campaigns but also dictating the amount of support, in men and money, that each colony would provide. The colonists grew increasingly stubborn in response to Loudoun's high-handed style. Colonial soldiers objected to Loudoun's command and colonial assemblies refused to cooperate.

Britain's aim had been to "rationalize" the war by making it conform to European professional military standards. This approach to warfare required soldiers to advance in formation in the face of massed musket fire without breaking rank. Such iron discipline was enforced—as in the British army—by savage punishments, including hundreds of lashes at the whipping post. Few colonial volunteers met professional standards, and few colonists thought them necessary. British officers assumed that colonial soldiers were simply lazy cowards. Colonial volunteers, appalled to see men lashed "till the blood came out at the knee" of their breeches, saw British officers as brutal task-masters. They resisted all efforts to impose such discipline on their own units, even to the point of desertion and mutiny.

In 1756, the marquis de Montcalm, a strong proponent of European professional standards of military conduct, assumed command of French forces. In his first battle, the successful siege of Fort Oswego, New York, Montcalm was horrified by the behavior of his Indian allies, which included killing wounded prisoners, taking personal captives, and collecting scalps as trophies. As a result, he came to regard the Indians—so essential to the defense of New France—as mere savages.

Following his next victory, the capture of Fort William Henry, New York, Montcalm conformed to European practice by agreeing that the defeated garrison could go home in return for the promise not to fight again. Montcalm's Indian allies—a thousand or more strong—were not to take prisoners, trophies, or plunder. The tragic result came to be known as the Massacre of Fort William Henry. Feeling betrayed by their French allies, the Indians took captives and trophies anyway, killing as many as 185 defenders and taking about 300 captive. Ironically, Montcalm's efforts to limit the war's violence prepared the way for the British army and its colonial auxiliaries to win an unlimited victory.

At the same time that the Europeanization of the war was weakening the French, the British moderated their policies and reached accommodation with the colonists. William Pitt, who as secretary of state directed the British war effort from late 1757 through 1761, realized that friction between the colonists and the commander in chief arose from the colonists' sense that they were bearing all the financial burdens of the war without having any say in how the war was fought. Pitt's ingenious solutions were to promise reimbursements to the colonies in proportion to their contribution to the war effort, to deemphasize the power of the commander in chief, and to replace the arrogant Loudoun with a less objectionable officer.

Pitt's money and measures restored colonial morale. He sent thousands of British soldiers to America to fight alongside tens of thousands of colonial troops. The Anglo-American forces operated more successfully, seizing Louisbourg again in 1758. Once more, Canada experienced crippling shortages of supplies, weapons, and trade goods. British emissaries persuaded the Delawares and Shawnees to abandon their French alliance, and late in 1758, an Anglo-American force again marched on Fort Duquesne. In command of its lead battalion was Colonel George Washington. The French defenders, abandoned by their native allies and confronted by overwhelming force, blew up the fort and retreated to the Great Lakes.

From this point on, the Anglo-Americans suffered no setbacks and the French won no victories. Montcalm, forced back to Quebec, decided to risk everything in a European-style, open-field battle against a British force led by General James Wolfe. At the Battle of Quebec (September 13, 1759), Montcalm lost the gamble—and his life (as did the victorious General Wolfe).

What finally decided the outcome of the war in America was the Battle of Quiberon Bay in France (November 20, 1759), which cost the French navy its ability to operate on the Atlantic, preventing it from carrying reinforcements and supplies to Canada. The Iroquois decision to enter the war on the side of the Anglo-Americans tipped the balance irrevocably against the French. The last ragged, hungry defenders of Canada, surrounded at Montreal by a vastly superior Anglo-American-Iroquoian force, surrendered on September 8, 1760.

The Triumph of the British Empire, 1763

The war pitting Britain against France and Spain (which had entered the fighting as a French ally in 1762) concluded with an uninterrupted series of British victories. In the Caribbean, every valuable sugar island the French owned eventually came under British control. Britain's capture of the Philippine capital of Manila on October 5 literally carried British power around the world.

Hostilities ended formally on February 10, 1763, with the conclusion of the **Treaty of Paris**. France regained its West Indian sugar islands—its most valuable colonial possessions—but lost the rest of its North American empire. France ceded to Britain all its claims to lands east of the Mississippi River (except the city of New Orleans) and compensated Spain for the losses it had sustained as an ally by handing over all claims to the Trans-Mississippi West and the port of New Orleans (see Map 4-2). Britain returned Cuba and the Philippines to Spain and in compensation received Florida. Now Great Britain owned everything east of the Mississippi, from the Gulf of Mexico to Hudson's Bay. With France and Spain both humbled and on the verge of financial collapse, Britain seemed preeminent in Europe and ready to dominate in the New World. Never before had Americans felt more pride in being British.

Conclusion

The George Washington who ordered a suit in 1763 was not a revolutionary; on the contrary, he was a man who longed to be part of the elite of the great British Empire. For Washington, as for virtually all other colonial leaders, 1763 was a moment of great promise and patriotic devotion to the British Empire. It was a time to rejoice in the fundamental British identity and liberty and rights that seemed to ensure that life in the colonies would be better and more prosperous than ever.

Review Questions

1. In what ways did economic ties between Britain and the colonies grow closer in the century after 1660?

2. What did elite colonists think about American society and culture in the eighteenth century? What changes did they want to introduce?

3. What was the Great Awakening, and what impact did it have on colonial society?

Map 4-2   European Empires in North America, 1750–1763
Great Britain's victory in the French and Indian War transformed the map of North America. France lost its mainland colonies, England claimed all lands east of the Mississippi, and Spain gained nominal control over the Trans-Mississippi West.

4. In what ways were colonial and British political ideas and practices similar? In what ways were they different?

5. Why did England, Spain, and France renew their competition for North America in the eighteenth century?

6. What role did warfare play in North America in the eighteenth century? How would you characterize the role of the Iroquois in these conflicts?

Recommended Reading

Anderson, Fred. *A People's Army: Massachusetts Soldiers and Society in the Seven Years' War* (1984). A sensitive exploration of the wartime experiences of Massachusetts provincial soldiers and their relations with the British army.

Bushman, Richard L. *The Refinement of America: Persons, Houses, Cities* (1992). A sophisticated exploration of the quest for gentility in early America.

Franklin, Benjamin. *Autobiography* (numerous editions). The classic account of Franklin's rise from poor beginnings to prominence in colonial Philadelphia.

Lambert, Frank. *"Pedlar in Divinity": George Whitefield and the Transatlantic Revivals, 1737–1770* (1994). An intriguing study of Whitefield's career as preacher and commercializer of religion in England and America.

McCusker, John J., and Menard, Russell R. *The Economy of British America, 1607–1789* rev. ed.

(1991). The most comprehensive study of the economies of each colonial region.

Where to Learn More

❖ **Mission Parkway, San Antonio, Texas.** Three Spanish missions (Mission Nuestra Señora de la Purisma Concepción, Mission San Francisco de la Espada, Mission San Juan Capestrano) founded in the early eighteenth century are located along this road. Their architecture indicates that they were intended to be fortifications as well as churches.

❖ **Ste. Genevieve Historic District, Ste. Genevieve, Missouri.** This restored site of an early-eighteenth-century French settlement in the *Pays des Illinois* contains many historic buildings open for tours.

❖ **Colonial Williamsburg, Williamsburg, Virginia.** A reconstruction of the capital of eighteenth-century Virginia, this site covers 173 acres and contains many restored and rebuilt structures, including houses, churches, the House of Burgesses, and the Governor's Palace. Many educational and cultural programs are available. Historical interpreters, dressed in period costume, provide information about eighteenth-century Chesapeake life.

❖ **Historical Society of Pennsylvania, Philadelphia, Pennsylvania.** The society preserves many documents and material objects relating to early American, and particularly Philadelphia, history. Its collections include exhibits of paintings, furniture, silver, and costumes.

5 IMPERIAL BREAKDOWN, 1763–1774

CHAPTER OUTLINE

KEY TOPICS

- ❖ British problems and policies in North America after the French and Indian War
- ❖ Native Americans' changing strategic position and their wars with the colonists
- ❖ The American reaction to British attempts to tax the colonies
- ❖ Social tensions and the Regulator movements in North and South Carolina
- ❖ Intercolonial union and resistance to British measures

In 1774, Christopher Gadsden, a leader of the American opposition to British taxation, impetuously urged an attack on British troops in Boston, declaring that were his wife and children to perish there by the sword, it would not alter his support for American liberty. A native of Charleston, South Carolina, he and others like him continued until the eve of Independence in 1776 to feel immense pride to be a British subject and part of Britain's increasingly powerful empire. But over the course of the eighteenth century, largely governing themselves through their own legislatures, they also developed a sense of their identity as Americans. In the wake of the French and Indian War, the British authorities, under pressure from burdensome debt and a vastly increased territory to administer, imposed direct taxes on the colonies for the first time and set in motion developments that would ultimately cause a rebellion against the Crown. Why Gadsden and other Americans felt compelled to take this drastic step is the subject of this chapter.

Imperial Reorganization

At the close of the French and Indian War, British officials adopted a new and ultimately disastrous course in dealing with America. Lacking experience, they panicked at the magnitude of the problems confronting them, and led by a young and somewhat naive monarch (George III, who ascended to the English throne in 1760), they tried to fix a relationship between England and the colonies that most Americans would have said was not broken. They did this by adopting measures that worked mostly to the disadvantage of the colonies. As one contemporary critic observed, "A great Empire and little minds go ill together."

British Problems

Britain's empire in 1763 was indeed a great one, and the problems its rulers faced were correspondingly large. Its territories in North America stretched from Hudson's Bay in the north to the Caribbean Sea in the south and from the Atlantic Ocean west to the Mississippi River. (While French territory on the North American mainland had been reduced to two tiny islands in the Gulf of St. Lawrence. But France would be eager for revenge, and French inhabitants in the recently acquired territories might prove disloyal.)

Spain was less powerful militarily than France but a more significant presence on the North American mainland. In the territorial settlement at the end of the French and Indian War, it surrendered East and West Florida to Britain but got back its possessions in Cuba and the Philippines and acquired Louisiana from France. Shocked by their inability to defend Cuba and the Philippines, Spanish officials stepped up the pace of reforms that they had begun making earlier in the century. They appointed new officials—who were generally Spaniards rather than colonials—to ensure better tax collection. Spain also expelled the Jesuit order from its dominions because Jesuit priests were too independent of royal control to suit Spanish officials. Spain further strengthened its military forces in much of the empire, and began to settle in California and Louisiana.

Protecting and controlling the old and new territories in North America as inexpensively as possible presented British officials with difficult questions. How should they administer the new territories? How should they deal with Indians likely to resist further encroachments on their lands? And perhaps most vexing, how could they rein in the seemingly out-of-control colonists in the old territories?

Permitting most of the new areas to have their own assemblies appeared inadvisable and indeed, for quite some time British authorities had wanted to roll back the power of the old colonial assemblies. Britain had needed the cooperation of the assemblies during the years of war with France. But now, with France vanquished, imperial officials felt they could crack down on the local governments. Some British statesmen, however, realized that with France gone from the continent, Americans would be less dependent on Britain for protection and therefore more inclined to resist unpopular restrictions.

Resentment against American conduct during the war colored British thinking. Some of the colonies failed to enlist their quota of recruits, and for this the British blamed the local assemblies. Worse yet, some Americans continued to smuggle goods to and from the enemy in the French West Indies during the war. Smuggling was so common in New England that it cost Britain more to operate the customs service in America than it collected in duties.

England emerged from the war with what was then an immense national debt of approximately £130 million. Interest payments alone accounted for half the government's annual expenditures after the war. Alarmed by the unprecedented debt, many Britons concluded that Americans should bear more of the financial burden of running the empire. The colonists certainly appeared prosperous to British soldiers who had served in America. Compared to the English, who paid on average perhaps a third of their income in taxes, many Americans normally rendered no more than 5 percent.

Dealing with the New Territories

In 1763, the British government took several important steps to deal with the new territories, protect the old colonies, and maintain peace with the Indians. One was to keep a substantial body of troops stationed in America even in peacetime. Another, accomplished in the **Proclamation of 1763**, was to temporarily forbid white settlement west of the Appalachian Mountains. The purpose of the **Proclamation Line** restricting white settlement was presumably twofold: to keep whites and Indians apart, preventing fighting between them, and to keep the colonists closer to the coast where they would be easier to control (see Map 5-1).

Neither the Proclamation Line nor the stationing of troops in America was particularly wise. The Proclamation Line provoked resentment be-

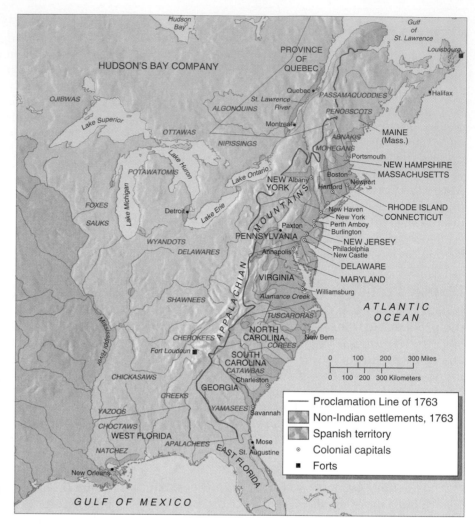

Map 5-1   Colonial Settlement and the Proclamation Line of 1763
This map depicts the regions claimed and settled by the major groups competing for territory in eastern North America. With the Proclamation Line of 1763, positioned along the crest of the Appalachian Mountains, the British government tried to stop the westward migration of settlers under its jurisdiction, and thereby limit conflict with the Indians. The result, however, was frustration and anger on the part of land-hungry settlers.

cause it threatened to deprive settlers and speculators in the rapidly developing colonies of the land they coveted, and was often ignored. As for the troops, the British government further provoked American resentment with passage of **Quartering Acts** that required colonial assemblies to provide barracks and certain supplies for the troops.

The presence of troops in peacetime alarmed Americans. Imbued with a traditionally English distrust of standing armies, they wondered whether the soldiers were there to coerce rather than protect them. Given their wariness, Americans would doubtless have objected to the troops and the taxes necessary to support them even if the troops had done an exemplary job of protecting the frontiers. But conflicts with Indians cast doubt on their ability to do even that.

Indian Affairs

From a Native American standpoint, the problems Britain confronted in America were nothing compared to their own troubles in dealing with the British. Colonial settlers and livestock were displacing Indians from their ancient lands. Free-flowing rum and rampant cheating among traders were making the fur and deerskin trades increasingly violent. Regulation of the Indian traders by the colonists was uncoordinated and generally ineffective.

The British victory over the French and the westward expansion of British territory undermined the Indians' traditional strategies and alignments. British officials no longer found Native American neutrality or military help as important as they once had. Increasingly superfluous as allies and unable to play the European powers off against each other, Native Americans lost much of their former ability to protect themselves by any means short of military resistance. The British took advantage of this increasing vulnerability: traders exploited the Indians, and settlers encroached on their lands.

Two major Indian wars—one breaking out in the late 1750s during the closing years of the French and Indian War and the other erupting in its aftermath in the early 1760s—challenged British policy

CHRONOLOGY

1759–1761 Cherokee War.	**1766** Stamp Act repealed; Declaratory Act passed.
1760 George III becomes king.	New York Assembly refuses to comply with the Quartering Act.
1761–1762 Writs of Assistance case in Massachusetts.	**1767** Townshend duties imposed.
1763 Peace of Paris ends French and Indian War.	Regulator movements [see page 84] in North and South Carolina.
Spanish accelerate imperial reforms.	**1770** Boston Massacre.
British troops remain in America.	Tea duty retained, other Townshend duties repealed.
Proclamation Line of 1763 limits western expansion of colonial settlement.	**1771** North Carolina Regulator movement defeated.
Pontiac's Rebellion begins.	**1772** *Gaspee* burned.
Paxton Boys murder peaceful Indians.	Committees of Correspondence formed.
Virginia Court decides Parson's Cause.	**1773** Boston Tea Party.
1764 Sugar Act passed.	**1774** Coercive Acts passed.
Currency Act passed.	Quebec Act passed.
1765 Quartering Act passed.	First Continental Congress meets and agrees to boycott British imports.
Stamp Act passed.	
Stamp Act Congress meets in New York.	

toward Native Americans. The first conflict, the **Cherokee War**, took place in the southern Appalachian highlands and resulted in a treaty in 1761 in which the Cherokees agreed to surrender land in the Carolinas and Virginia to the colonists. The second major conflict, **Pontiac's Rebellion**, represented a united effort to resist the British and revitalize Indian cultures. The spiritual catalyst for this movement was a Delaware leader named Neolin, also known as the Delaware Prophet, who began urging Native Americans to reject European goods and ways. The Pontiac Rebellion itself, named for an Ottawa chief who was one of its principal leaders, began when at least eight major groups joined in attacking British forces and American settlers from the Great Lakes to Virginia in 1763. Pontiac's Rebellion raged until 1766. The British eventually forced the Indians to give up portions of their territory in return for compensation and guarantees that traditional hunting grounds in the Ohio Valley would remain theirs.

At one point during the war, a British commander used germ warfare against the Indians, sending them blankets that smallpox victims had used. Settlers in Paxton township (near modern Harrisburg, Pennsylvania) were equally indiscriminate. Angered by the Pennsylvania Assembly's lack of aggressive action against the Indians, the settlers lashed out at convenient targets, massacring their peaceful neighbors, the Conestogas. Facing arrest and trial for this outrage, the so-called **Paxton Boys** marched toward Philadelphia, threatening the Pennsylvania Assembly. Benjamin Franklin convinced them to disperse. Despite the government's efforts, the Paxton Boys were never effectively prosecuted.

Pontiac's Rebellion was costly for both sides, claiming the lives of hundreds of Indians and whites. Hoping to prevent such outbreaks, British officials began experimenting with centralized control of Indian affairs during the 1760s. Following the recommendations of the Albany Congress in 1754 (see Chapter 4), they had already created two districts, northern and southern, for the administration of Indian affairs, each with its own superintendent. The Proclamation of 1763, and the line it established restricting further white settlement, gave these superintendents increased responsibility for protecting the Indians against the encroachments of settlers. But they faced daunting obstacles in their efforts to mediate between Indians and colonists and in 1768 Britain returned supervision of the Indian traders to the individual colonies.

Curbing the Assemblies

As an episode in Virginia known as the **Parson's Cause** illustrates, British authorities took advantage of opportunities to curb the American legislatures as early as the 1750s. Anglican ministers in Virginia drew tax-supported salaries computed in pounds of tobacco. As a result, when a drought in the mid-1750s caused a sharp rise in tobacco prices, they expected a windfall. The Virginia House of Burgesses, however, restricted their payment to two pennies a pound, below the market value of the tobacco that backed their salaries. Lobbying by the clergy convinced the king to disallow the Two Penny Act, and some Virginia clergymen sued for the unpaid portion of their salaries.

In the most famous of these cases, the Virginia government was defended by Patrick Henry, a previously obscure young lawyer who looked like "a Presbyterian clergyman, used to haranguing the people." Henry gained instant notoriety when he declared that a king who vetoed beneficial acts became a tyrant and thereby forfeited "all right to his subjects' obedience." Given Henry's eloquence, the juries found in favor of the suing minister but awarded him only one penny in damages. This pittance reflected the hostility many Virginians of all denominations felt toward the pretensions of the Anglican clergy.

British authorities also sought to restrict the power of colonial legislatures to issue **legal tender** currency, paper notes that could be used to settle debts. These notes frequently depreciated to only a fraction of their face value in British money. Not surprisingly, British merchants who had to accept them felt cheated and complained. Parliament had responded in 1751 by forbidding further issues of legal tender paper money in New England. In the **Currency Act** of 1764, Parliament extended this restriction to the rest of the colonies, prohibiting all of them from printing their own legal tender paper money. Because the new restrictions came when most colonies were in an economic recession, Americans considered this step an especially burdensome attempt to curtail the assemblies' powers. To deprive them of their paper money was, in the words of one American, "downright Robbery." Worse, however, was yet to come.

The Sugar and Stamp Acts

In 1764, the British prime minister, George Grenville, convinced Parliament—it was not a difficult task—to pass the **American Revenue Act**, commonly known as the **Sugar Act** "for improving the revenue of this kingdom." To generate funds, the Sugar Act and its accompanying legislation combined new and revised duties on colonial imports with strict provisions for collecting those duties. To prevent trade with other countries the Sugar Act legislation also lengthened the list of enumerated products—goods that could be sent only to England or within the empire—and required that ships carry elaborate new documents certifying the legality of their cargoes. A ship's captain could have his entire cargo seized if any of the complicated documents were out of order.

To enforce these cumbersome regulations, the British government continued to use the Royal Navy to seize smugglers' ships, a practice begun during the French and Indian War. It also ordered colonial customs collectors to discharge their duties personally, rather than through the use of easily bribed deputies. Responsibility for trying violations would (3 years later) eventually rest in vice-admiralty courts in Boston, Philadelphia, and Charleston, which normally operated without a jury and were more likely to enforce trade restrictions.

In the spring of 1765, Parliament enacted another tax on Americans, the **Stamp Act**. This required that all valid legal documents, as well as newspapers, playing cards, and various other papers, bear a government-issued stamp for which there was a charge. The Sugar Act, though intended to raise revenue, appeared to fall within Britain's accepted authority to regulate commerce; the Stamp Act, by contrast, was the first internal tax (as opposed to an external trade duty) that Parliament had imposed on the colonies. Grenville, a lawyer, realized that it raised a constitutional issue: Did Parliament have the right to impose direct taxes on Americans when Americans had no elected representatives in Parliament? Following the principle of virtual representation—that members of Parliament served the interests of the nation as a whole, not just the locality from which they came—Grenville maintained that it did. Americans, he would find, vigorously disagreed. Nor were they without at least some support in Parliament. Colonel Isaac Barré, a member who had served in the colonies, spoke out against the Stamp Act. In one speech he referred to Americans as "Sons of Liberty," a label Americans soon would adopt for themselves.

American Reactions

The measures Britain took to solve its financial and administrative problems first puzzled, then shocked, and eventually outraged Americans. The colonists had emerged from the French and Indian War believing that they had done their fair share and more toward making Great Britain ruler of the greatest empire in the world and expected to be respected for their efforts. They were certain that as British-Americans they shared in the glory and enjoyed all the rights of

Englishmen in England. The new restrictions and taxes accordingly hit them like a slap in the face.

Constitutional Issues

To Americans, it was self-evident that the British measures were unfair. It was difficult to contend, however, that the British authorities had no right to impose them. Then as now, the **British Constitution** was not a single written document. It consisted, rather, of the accumulated body of English law and custom, including acts of Parliament. How, then, could the colonists claim that an act of Parliament was unconstitutional?

Constitutional conflict surfaced early in Massachusetts over the issue of **writs of assistance**. These general search warrants, which gave customs officials in America the power to inspect virtually any building suspected of holding smuggled goods, had to be formally renewed at the accession of a new monarch. When George III became king in 1760, Massachusetts merchants—perhaps out of a fondness for smuggling as well as for liberty—sought to block the reissuance of the writs. Their attorney, James Otis Jr., arguing before the Massachusetts superior court, called the writs "instruments of slavery." The court, however, did not believe that it could legally agree with him. Otis lost, but "then and there," a future president of the United States, John Adams, would later write, "the child independence was born."

Taxation and the Political Culture

The constitutional issue that most strained the bond between the colonies and the empire was taxation. British measures on other issues annoyed and disturbed Americans, but it was outrage over taxation—the most fundamental issue—that would be the midwife of American independence. Because Parliament had customarily refrained from taxing them, Americans assumed that it could not. To deprive them of the right to be taxed only by their own elected representatives was to deny them one of the most basic rights of Englishmen. If taxes were imposed "without our having a legal Representation where they are laid," one American asked, "are we not reduced from the Character of free Subjects to the miserable State of tributary Slaves?"

American views on taxation and the role of government reflected the influence of country ideology. As mentioned in Chapter 4, this opposition political philosophy emerged in England in the late seventeenth and early eighteenth centuries. Country ideology held that government power, no matter how necessary or to whom entrusted, is inherently aggressive and expansive. According to the English political philosopher John Locke, rulers have the authority to enforce law "only for the public good." When government exceeds this proper function, the people have the right to change it. But only in the last resort does this right justify revolution.

Country ideology stressed that in the English system of government, it was the duty of Parliament, in particular the House of Commons (which represented the people as a whole), to check the executive power of the Crown. The House of Commons' control of taxation enabled it to curb tyrannical rulers. When the Crown did its job properly, the Commons appropriated the necessary funds; when rulers infringed on the liberty of the people, the Commons restrained them by withholding taxes.

Such important responsibilities required that the people's representatives be men of sufficient property and judgment to make independent decisions. A representative should be "virtuous" (meaning public-spirited), and avoid political partisanship. A representative of the appropriate social status who exhibited the proper behavior, many assumed, was more qualified to understand and manage public affairs than his constituents and should accordingly be followed. But if he did not measure up, the people should be able to vote him out.

Country ideology appealed to Americans for a number of reasons. In part, colonists were drawn to it as they were to other English fashions. The works of Alexander Pope, the most widely read English poet of the eighteenth century and a proponent of a version of country ideology, appeared in many colonial libraries. So also did the works of two readable and prolific country ideology publicists, John Trenchard and Thomas Gordon, who collaborated in writing *Cato's Letters* (1720–1724) and the *Independent Whig* (1721). More important, country ideology's suspicion of those in power suited American politics on the local level, where rivalries and factionalism fostered distrust between those with and without power. And it emboldened the many Americans who feared they had no voice in the decisions of the government in London. Finally, with its insistence on the important political role of the propertied elite, country ideology appealed to America's local gentry. These ideas have had an enduring influence on American politics, surfacing even today in the suspicion of Washington and "big government," and they helped inspire the American Revolution.

Protesting the Taxes

Given this ideological background, the initial American response to the Sugar Act was surprisingly mild. This was because not every colonist was equally affected by it. The speaker of the legislature in one southern colony commented that it was "much divided" over the effects of the act and would probably not petition against it. In New England, in contrast, the Sugar Act threatened to cut into the profits of the lucrative smuggling trade with the French West Indies. As a result, people there and in other northern colonies were quicker to recognize the act's implications. The legislative body that imposed it—Parliament—and whose constituents in England stood to gain from it, was not accountable to the people on whom it was imposed, the colonists. As one alarmed colonist noted, if his fellow Americans submitted to any tax imposed by Parliament, they were dumb and docile donkeys.

The size of the burden was less important than the principle involved. To Americans steeped in country ideology, direct taxation by London threatened to undercut the elected representatives' power of the purse and thereby remove the traditional first line of defense against a tyrannical executive. Eventually all the assemblies passed resolutions flatly maintaining that any parliamentary tax on America, including the Sugar Act, was unconstitutional. By the end of 1764, New York merchants had joined the artisans and merchants of Boston in a **nonimportation** movement, an organized boycott of British manufactured goods.

Unlike the Sugar Act, the Stamp Act had an equal impact throughout the colonies, and the response to it was swift and vociferous. Newspapers and pamphlets were filled with denunciations of the supposedly unconstitutional measure, and in taverns everywhere outraged patrons roundly condemned it. "The minds of the freeholders," wrote one observer, "were inflamed . . . by many a hearty damn of the Stamp Act over bottles, bowls and glasses." Parliament, Americans were convinced, did not represent them. The colonial legislatures were also quick to condemn the new measure. Virginia's lower house was the first to act, approving Patrick Henry's strong resolutions against the Stamp Act.

Shared outrage at the Stamp Act inspired the colonies to join in unified political action. The **Sons of Liberty**, a collection of loosely organized protest groups, put pressure on stamp distributors and British authorities. In August 1765, a Boston crowd led by shoemaker Ebenezer MacIntosh demolished property belonging to a revenue agent, and another mob sacked Lieutenant Governor Thomas Hutchinson's house. Later disturbances organized by the Sons of Liberty in other cities were kept more peaceful with tighter discipline.

Members of the Sons of Liberty included people from all ranks of society. The leaders, however,

Samuel Adams, the leader of the Boston radicals, as he appeared to John Singleton Copley in the early 1770s. In this famous picture, thought to be commissioned by another revolutionary leader, John Hancock, Adams points to legal documents guaranteeing American rights.

among them Christopher Gadsden, came mostly from the middle and upper classes. Some of them doubtless joined to control a movement that might threaten their own interests. Indeed, in Charleston, slaves alarmed their masters and other whites when they paraded through the streets crying, "Liberty!"

Movement leaders were also concerned that disorderly behavior could discredit the American cause. Even the fiery Samuel Adams, one of the leading organizers of the protest in Boston, would later claim, "I am no friend to *Riots*." Still, he added, "when the People are oppressed," they will be "discontented, and they are not to be blamed."

Partly as a result of the growing unrest, leaders throughout the colonies determined to meet and agree on a unified response to Britain. As Gadsden observed at the time, "There ought to be no New England men, no New Yorker, etc. known on the Continent, but all of us Americans." Nine colonies eventually sent delegates to the **Stamp Act Congress**, which met in New York City in October 1765. A humorist in the South Carolina legislature, who had opposed sending anyone, observed that the gathering would produce a most unpalatable combination: New England would throw in fish and onions; the middle provinces, flax-seed and flour; Virginia and Maryland, tobacco; North Carolina, pitch, turpentine, and tar; South Carolina, indigo and rice—and Georgia would sprinkle the whole with sawdust. "Such an absurd jumble will you make if you attempt to form [a] union among such discordant materials as the thirteen British provinces," he concluded. A quick-witted member of the assembly shot back that he would not choose his colleague for a cook but that the congress would prepare a dish fit for any king.

It did indeed. The congress adopted the **Declaration of Rights and Grievances**, which denied Parliament's right to tax the colonies, and petitioned unsuccessfully both king and Parliament to repeal the Stamp and Sugar acts. As protests spread, the stamp distributors got the message and resigned, "for the welfare of the people." In some areas, Americans went about their business as usual without using stamped paper. In other places, they avoided activities that required taxed items. They also stepped up the boycott of British goods that had begun in response to the Sugar Act. British merchants, hurt by this economic pressure, petitioned Parliament for repeal of the Stamp Act, and a new ministry obliged them by rescinding it in March 1766.

The Aftermath of Crisis

At this point, Americans were in no mood to accept any tax imposed by Parliament, and they misunderstood the **Declaratory Act** that accompanied the repeal of the Stamp Act. Intended to make Parliament's retreat more acceptable to its members, this act stated that Parliament had the right to "legislate for the colonies in all cases whatsoever." Americans assumed the Declaratory Act was a mere face-saving gesture. Unfortunately, it was more than that. As one colonist later observed, it created a "platform for the Invincible Reasoning from the Mouths of four and twenty pounders [cannons]."

A Strained Relationship

The aftermath of the Stamp Crisis was growing strain between Parliament and the colonies. Most members of Parliament continued to believe that they represented everyone in the empire and that they could therefore tax people in the colonies as well as in England. Americans believed just as strongly that "in taxing ourselves and making Laws for our own internal government . . . we can by no means allow our Provincial legislatures to be subordinate to any legislative power on earth."

An exchange between British merchants and their American correspondents in the wake of the Stamp Act's repeal illustrates how far apart Englishmen and Americans had become. The British merchants lectured the Americans, enjoining them "to express filial duty and gratitude to your parent country." To which one Virginia planter tartly replied, "We rarely see anything from your side of the water free from the authoritative style of a master to a schoolboy." This, he observed, was more than "a little ridiculous."

Events likewise testified to enduring tensions between the two sides. When British authorities required Massachusetts to compensate those who had suffered damage in the Stamp Act rioting, the legislature complied but pardoned the rioters. In 1767, an irritated Parliament then passed an act suspending the New York legislature because it had not complied with the Quartering Act of 1765. New York finally complied with the act just before the suspending act went into effect.

Regulator Movements

Growing strain was also evident on the local level with the emergence in 1766 of vigilante groups calling themselves **Regulators** in response to official corruption in North Carolina and lawlessness in South Carolina. North Carolina's western farmers were oppressed by high taxes, court costs and debt resulting from the limited supply of money in circulation after the Currency Act. In South Carolina, outlaws roamed the back country stealing livestock and raiding isolated houses. In neither colony did representation in the assemblies reflect the growing back-country population and its pressing needs. As a result, the regulators did by extralegal action what they couldn't do through legal channels—in North Carolina they closed courts and intimidated tax officials and in South Carolina they pursued outlaws and whipped people suspected of harboring them.

The activities of the Regulators brought them into conflict with the local elites and the assemblies in North and South Carolina, which were slow in redressing regulator grievances. British officials made matters worse by doing the opposite of what was required. Instead of encouraging the assemblies to increase their western representation, they tried to limit their power by forbidding them to increase their size. As for the shortage of currency, they callously dismissed "any possible local inconvenience" that might result.

Thanks to such help from London and their own mistakes, local authorities faced an increasingly serious situation. In South Carolina, bloodshed was narrowly averted when the assembly belatedly reapportioned itself and established courts for the backcountry. But in North Carolina, peace was restored only after fighting between the local militia and the Regulators killed 29 men and wounded more than 150 on both sides. The rise of the Regulators proved that colonial leaders had to understand and be able to deal with local conditions and further highlighted the lack of wisdom and flexibility in Britain's response. Worse yet, London was once again trying to tax Americans.

The Townshend Crisis

After an unsuccessful attempt by the British to introduce a new collection of taxes, the Townshend duties, in 1767, a relatively quiet period followed until Britain made yet another attempt to enforce compliance with the one duty still on the books, the duty on tea.

Townshend's Plan

Charles Townshend became the leading figure in Britain's government in 1767. The **Townshend Duty Act** was based on Townshend's mistaken assumption that the colonists were willing to accept new duties or external taxes, but no direct, or internal, taxes like the Stamp Tax. The duties covered a number of items the colonists regularly imported—tea, paper, paint, lead, and glass. To make sure that the duties were collected, British authorities added a new board of customs commissioners for America and located its headquarters in Boston, the presumed home of many smugglers. To the alarm of the Americans, the new customs officials were far more diligent than their predecessors, going after wealthy Boston merchants like John Hancock, perhaps because he was so openly contemptuous of them. The officials seized Hancock's appropriately named vessel *Liberty* and accused him of smuggling. Hancock may indeed have violated the acts of trade at times, but in this case the accusations were apparently false. The incident sparked a riot in Boston during which a crowd on the waterfront roughed up members of the customs service. British authorities responded in 1768 by sending troops to Boston, and maintaining them there for the next year and a half.

American Boycott

The Townshend duties, like the stamp tax, provoked resistance throughout the colonies. Rejecting the argument that duties were somehow different from taxes, John Dickinson, a wealthy lawyer who wrote under the pen name "A Farmer in Pennsylvania," reminded everyone that a tax was a tax, whatever its form.

There was no equivalent to the Stamp Act Congress in response to the Townshend Act because British officials (acting through the colonial governors) barred the assemblies from sending delegates to such a meeting. Even so, Americans gradually organized an effective nonimportation movement. Many Americans signed subscription lists binding them, with the other signers, to buy only goods made in the colonies and nothing made in Great Britain. Handbills, like one urging "the Sons and Daughters of *LIBERTY*" to shun a particular Boston merchant, brought pressure to bear on uncooperative importers. To avoid imported English textiles, American women spun more thread and wove more cloth at home. Wearing homespun became a moral virtue, a sign of self-reliance, personal independence, and the rejection of "corrupting" English luxuries (see "American Views: Social Status and the Enforcement of the Nonimportation Movement").

The nonimportation movement forged a sense of common purpose among all who participated in it—men and women, southern planters and northern artisans alike—giving them the sense of belonging to a larger community of fellow Americans. Although it was at this point more an imagined community than a political community, it was real enough and large enough to reduce imports from Britain by 40 percent after only one year.

By 1770, Britain was prepared to concede that the Townshend duties had been counterproductive because they interfered with British trade. When Parliament eventually repealed most of the Townshend articles it left the duty on tea. This symbolic equivalent of the Declaratory Act served to assert Parliament's continuing right to tax the colonies.

The Boston Massacre

Ironically, on the same day that the proposal to rescind most of the Townshend duties was introduced to Parliament —March 5, 1770—British troops fired on American civilians in Boston. This incident, which came to be known as the **Boston Massacre**, resulted from months of increasing friction between townspeople and the British troops stationed in the city. The townspeople complained that the soldiers insulted them, leered at women, and competed for scarce jobs. Samuel Adams recounted these real and imagined misdeeds in a column called "A Journal of the Times" that he circulated to other American cities. The hostility was so great, complained a British officer, that "twenty" soldiers could be "knocked down in the Streets" and nothing be heard of it, but if a Bostonian "meets with no more than just a Kick for an Insult to a Soldier, the Town is immediately in an Alarm."

The Boston Massacre occurred when angry and frightened British soldiers fired on a crowd that

The Boston Massacre, March 5, 1770, in an engraving by Paul Revere. Copied from an earlier print, Revere's widely circulated version shows—somewhat inaccurately—well organized soldiers firing on helpless civilians; the names of the dead, including Crispus Attucks, appear below.

was pelting them with sticks and stones. Five men died, including Crispus Attucks—"that half Indian, half negro and altogether rowdy," as someone once called him—who has since become the most celebrated casualty of the incident. To preserve order, the troops withdrew from the city. But the damage had been done.

The "Quiet Period"

Chastened a bit, both British authorities and American patriots pulled back from the brink with the repeal of the Townshend duties. In the so-called **Quiet Period** that followed, no general grievance united all Americans. But in almost every colony, issues continued to simmer. Local circumstances produced the most spectacular confrontation in Rhode Island. The crew of a British revenue schooner, the *Gaspee*, had been patrolling Narragansett Bay, seizing smugglers and, it was said, stealing livestock and cutting down farmers' fruit trees for firewood. Thus when the *Gaspee* ran aground while chasing some American ships, Rhode Islanders got even. Led by John Brown, a local merchant, they boarded the vessel, shot its captain in the buttocks, putting him

and his crew ashore, and burned the ship. The British government offered a reward for information about the incident, but learned nothing. The British attempt to stamp out smuggling in the colonies was so heavy-handed that it offended the innocent more than it frightened the guilty.

Such incidents, and in particular the British threat to send Americans to England for trial, led American leaders to resolve to keep one another informed about British actions. Twelve colonies established **committees of correspondence** for this purpose. and Boston soon became the scene of a showdown between imperial authority and colonial resistance.

The Boston Tea Party

During the Quiet Period, Americans drank smuggled (and therefore untaxed) Dutch tea and contributed to the financial problems of The British East India Company, which had the exclusive right to distribute tea in the British Empire and stood on the verge of bankruptcy. With the **Tea Act of 1773**, Lord North, the prime minister, came to the company's aid. The act permitted the company to ship tea from its warehouses in Britain without paying the duty normally collected there. The idea was to make its tea more competitive in price with the Dutch product and thereby to induce Americans to buy it and at the same time to pay the old Townshend duty.

When the colonists heard of this plan, their response surprised British officials. What outraged most Americans was the attempt to seduce them into paying the tax on tea. Thousands decided not to touch the tea. Newspapers discussed its dangers to the body as well as to the body politic and offered recipes for substitutes. Many women rejected the tea and put pressure on others to do likewise, and schoolboys collected and burned tea leaves.

Thomas Hutchinson, who had been lieutenant governor of Massachusetts during the Stamp Act riots, was now the colony's royal governor. In most other cities, threats from the Sons of Liberty had convinced the captains of the tea ships to return to England without landing their cargo. Hutchinson, however, was determined to have the tea landed in Boston, and he barred the tea ships there from leaving. As a result, violence once again erupted in the city.

When the Sons of Liberty realized they could not force the ships to leave, they decided on dramatic action. On December 16, 1773, Samuel Adams reportedly told a large gathering at Old South Meeting House that it "could do nothing more to preserve the liberties of America." This remark was apparently a prearranged signal for what came to be known as the

American Views

SOCIAL STATUS AND THE ENFORCEMENT OF THE NONIMPORTATION MOVEMENT

Many Americans enthusiastically supported the nonimportation movement called in response to the Townshend Duty Act crisis of the late 1760s. A few, however, openly opposed it. Among these was William Henry Drayton of South Carolina, who objected to the composition of the committee that had been chosen to enforce the nonimportation agreement in his region. The committee included artisans and shopkeepers, men whom Drayton claimed should have no role in public affairs. Their education prepared them only "to cut up a beast in the market to the best advantage, to cobble an old shoe in the neatest manner, or to build a necessary house [outhouse]," not to make public policy. As the following document makes clear, they emphatically disagreed with him. Drayton was later to reverse himself and actively support the Continental Association's ban on importing British goods in 1775. "The people" wanted it, he would later explain, and "it was our duty, to satisfy our constituents; as we were only servants of the public [at large]."

❖ **Who makes policy in the United States today?**

❖ **What qualifications do you think they should have?**

❖ **How do your answers to these questions differ from Drayton's? From the "Mechanics"?**

❖ **How would you explain Drayton's later switch?**

The Mechanics of the General Committee to William Henry Drayton

The gracious Giver of all good things, has been pleased to bestow a certain principle on mankind, which properly may be called *common sense.* . . . yet, to the misfortune of society, many persons fall short of this most necessary gift of God; the want of which cannot be compensated by all the learning of the schools.

The *Mechanicks* pretend to nothing more, than having a claim from nature, to their share in this inestimable favour, in common with *Emperors and Kings*, and, were it safe to carry the comparison still higher, they would say with William-Henry Drayton himself; who, in his great condescention, has been pleased to allow us a place amongst human beings: But whether it might have happened from an ill construction of his sensory, or his upper works being damaged by some rough treatment of the person who conducted his birth, we know not; however so it is, that, to us, he seems highly defective in this point, whatever exalted notions he may entertain of his own abilities.

By attending to the dictates of *common sense*, the *Mechanicks* have been able to distinguish between RIGHT and WRONG; in doing which

Boston Tea Party. War whoops immediately answered him from the street outside, and a well-organized band of men disguised as Indians raced aboard the tea ship *Dartmouth,* broke open 342 chests of tea, and systematically heaved the contents in the harbor.

The Intolerable Acts

The destruction of property in the Boston Tea Party shocked many Americans. British officials reacted even more strongly. The response in Parliament was to pass a series of repressive measures known as the **Coercive Acts**. The first of these, effective June 1, 1774, was the **Boston Port Act**, which closed the port of Boston to all incoming and outgoing traffic until the East India Company and the crown received payment for the dumped tea and its duties. The **Administration of Justice Act**, which followed, declared that an official who killed a colonist while indeed no great merit is claimed, because every man's own feelings will direct him thereto, unless he obstinately, or from a pertinacious opinion of his own superior knowledge, shuts his eyes, and stoickally submits to all the illegal encroachments that may be made on his property, by an ill-designing and badly-informed ministry.

Mr. Drayton may value himself as much as he pleases, on his having had a liberal education bestowed on him, tho' the good fruits thereof have not hitherto been conspicuous either in his public or private life: He ought however to know, that this is not so absolutely necessary to these, who move in the low sphere of *mechanical* employments. But still, though he pretends to view them with so contemptuous and oblique an eye, these men hope, that they are in some degree useful to society, without presuming to make any comparisons between themselves and him, except with regard to *love for their country;* for he has amply shewn, that an attachment of this sort is not *one* of his *ruling* passions. Nor does he appear in the least to have regarded the peace and good order of that community of which he is a member; otherwise he would not wilfully, and without any cause, have knocked his head against ninety-nine out of every hundred of the people. . . .

After an avowal of principles, incompatible with the essential rights of freemen under the English constitution, surely, no parish in this province, will ever think it prudent, to trust their interests in such hands, for the time to come? Besides, who can say he ever shewed any capacity for business, when he was honoured with a seat in the House of Assembly? . . .

Mr. Drayton may be assured, that so far from being ashamed of our trades, we are in the highest degree thankful to our friends, who put us in the way of being instructed in them; and that we bless God for giving us strength and *judgment* to pursue them, in order to maintain our families, with a decency suitable to their stations in life. Every man is not so lucky as to have a fortune ready provided to his hand, either by his own or his wife's parents, as has been his lot; nor ought it to be so with all men; and Providence accordingly hath wisely ordained otherwise, by appointing the greatest part of mankind, to provide for their support by manual labour; and we will be bold to say, that such are the most useful people in a community. . . .

We are, Yours, &c.
MECHANICKS of the COMMITTEE.
October 3d, 1769.

Source: South Carolina Gazette, *October 5, 1769; reprinted in* The Letters of Freeman, etc.: Essays on the Nonimportation Movement in South Carolina Collected by William Henry Drayton, *ed. Robert M. Weir (1977), pp. 111–114.*

performing his duties could be tried in England (where he would almost certainly receive sympathetic treatment) rather than in Massachusetts. The third measure, the **Massachusetts Government Act**, drastically modified that colony's charter of 1691, providing that the crown would appoint members to the governor's council and limiting the number of town meetings that could be held without the governor's prior approval. A new Quartering Act declared that the troops under the governor's command could be lodged in virtually any uninhabited building.

On the same day that Parliament enacted these measures, it also passed the **Quebec Act**, which enlarged the boundaries of Quebec south to the Ohio River, provided for trial of civil cases without a jury, and recognized the Catholic Church, giving it the privileges it had enjoyed under the French. The colonists labeled the Quebec and Coercive Acts together as the **Intolerable Acts**.

The Road to Revolution

American Response to the Intolerable Acts

Americans found the territorial, administrative, and religious provisions of the Quebec Act deeply disturbing. By giving Canada jurisdiction over lands north of the Ohio River that were claimed by Virginia, Connecticut, and Massachusetts, the Quebec Act deprived settlers of their hoped-for homesteads and speculators of their hoped-for profits, angering both. The religious provisions of the Quebec Act were ominous reminders of an attempt by Anglican clergymen during the 1760s to have a bishop appointed for America.

The Quebec Act accordingly "gave a General Alarm to all Protestants," whose ministers throughout the continent warned their congregations that they might be "bound by Popish chains."

The Boston Port Act arbitrarily punished innocent and guilty Bostonians alike. The Administration of Justice Act—which some with vivid imaginations dubbed the "Murder Act"—seemed to declare an open season on colonists, allowing crown officials to kill them without fear of punishment. The Massachusetts Government Act raised the more realistic fear that no colonial charter was safe. A Parliament that had stripped the Massachusetts legislature of an important power might equally decide to abolish the lower houses of all the colonies.

Nightmarish scenarios filled the colonial newspapers. One clergyman observed that the terms of the Coercive Acts were such that if someone were to "make water" on the door of the royal customs house, an entire colonial city "might be laid in Ashes." He undoubtedly knew that he exaggerated, but his words embodied real fear and anger. Trying to make an example of Boston, British authorities had taken steps that united Americans as nothing had ever done before (see the summary table "New Restraints and Burdens on Americans, 1759–1774").

The First Continental Congress

Leaders in most colonies wanted to organize a coordinated response and called for another meeting like the Stamp Act Congress. The colonies accordingly agreed to send delegates to a meeting in Philadelphia that came to be called the First Continental Congress, and in the end, all the colonies except Georgia were represented.

The First Continental Congress met at Carpenter's Hall in Philadelphia from September 5 to October 26, 1774, with fifty-five delegates present at one time or another. All were leading figures in their home colonies, but only a few knew members from elsewhere. Each colony had one vote, irrespective of the size of its delegation. Those who favored strong measures—like Samuel Adams and his cousin John, Patrick Henry, and Christopher Gadsden—prevailed. They persuaded most of their colleagues to endorse the **Suffolk Resolves**, which had been passed at a meeting held in Suffolk County (the site of Boston). These resolves denounced the Coercive Acts as unconstitutional, advised the people to arm, and called for general economic sanctions against Britain. The wording was so forceful that one British official told an American, "If these Resolves of your people are to be depended on, they have declared War against us . . . "

The Continental Association

The Congress created the **Continental Association** to organize and enforce sanctions against the British. As a first step, the Association pledged Americans to cut off imports from Britain after December 1, 1774. If the dispute with Britain was not resolved by September 1775, the Association called for barring most exports to Britain and the West Indies. All who violated the terms of the association were to be considered "enemies of American liberty" and ostracized.

Congress also issued a declaration of rights and grievances summarizing its position. The declaration condemned most of the steps taken by British authorities since 1763 but "cheerfully" consented to trade regulations for the good of the whole empire. The Congress sent addresses to the people of America, to the inhabitants of Great Britain, and to the king. The address to the king asked him to use his "royal authority and interposition" to protect his loyal subjects in America.

The proceedings of the First Continental Congress revealed division as well as agreement among its delegates. All of the delegates believed that the Coercive Acts were unconstitutional, but they differed over how to resist them. Only a minority was prepared to take up arms against Britain. Most representatives tried to protect the interests of their own colonies. Some South Carolina delegates, in an early example of the sectional stubbornness that would culminate nearly a century later in the U.S. Civil War, threatened to walk out of the meet-

SUMMARY

NEW RESTRAINTS AND BURDENS ON AMERICANS, 1759–1774

	Restraints on Legislative Action	Restraints on Territorial Expansion	Restraints on Colonial Trade	Imposition of New Taxes
1759	Royal instructions restrict the ability of the Virginia assembly to pass timely legislation.			
1762			Writs of assistance issued.	
1763		Proclamation Line keeps white settlement east of the Appalachians.	Peacetime use of the navy and new customs officials to enforce Navigation Acts.	
1764	Currency Act limits the colonial legislatures' ability to issue paper money.		Vice-admiralty courts strengthened for Sugar Act.	Sugar Act imposes taxes for revenue (modified 1766).
1765				Quartering Act requires assemblies to provide facilities for royal troops. Stamp Act imposes internal taxes on legal documents, newspapers, and other items, 1765 (repealed 1766).
1767	Royal instructions limit the size of colonial assemblies.		Vice-admiralty courts strengthened for Townshend duties. American Customs Service established in Boston.	Townshend duties imposed on some imported goods in order to pay colonial officials. (All but tax on tea repealed, 1770.)
1773				Tea Act reduces duty and prompts Boston Tea Party.
1774 (Intolerable Acts)	Massachusetts Government Act limits town meetings, changes legislature, and violates Massachusetts charter.	Quebec Act enlarges Quebec at expense of colonies with claims in the Ohio River Valley.	Boston Port Act closes harbor until East India Company's tea is paid for.	Quartering Act of 1774 declares that troops could be lodged in virtually any uninhabited building in Boston.

ing unless the nonexportation agreement omitted rice, most of which went to northern Europe by way of Britain. To placate the Carolinians, northerners agreed to the exemption. Gadsden was disgusted, feeling that these actions betrayed the spirit of united purpose that Patrick Henry had spoken of so stirringly earlier in the Congress: "The distinctions between Virginians, Pennsylvanians, New Yorkers and New Englanders are no more. I am not a Virginian, but an American."

Political Divisions

In the wake of the First Continental Congress, Americans were forced to take sides for and against the Continental Association. But even such well-known radicals as Adams and Gadsden were far from advocating independence for the colonies. Throughout the pre-Revolutionary period, most colonists hoped and expected that imperial authorities would change their policy toward America. English history, Americans believed, was full of instances in which the resolute opposition of a free people forced oppressive ministries and tyrannical kings to back down. They were confident that it could happen again.

What Americans were divided over was the extent of Parliament's authority over them and the degree to which they could legitimately challenge its power. As British officials failed, with the passing of time, to accommodate American views of their rights, Americans began in increasing numbers to challenge London's power over them. The experience of James Wilson, a Pennsylvania lawyer, illustrates this shift. In *Considerations on the Nature and Extent of the Legislative Authority of the British Parliament* (published in 1774), Wilson writes that he set out to find a reasonable dividing line between those areas in which Parliament had legitimate authority over the colonies and those in which it did not. But the more he thought, the more he became convinced "that such a line does not exist" and that there can be "no medium between acknowledging and denying that power in all cases." Wilson therefore concluded that Parliament had no authority at all over the colonies.

During 1774 and early 1775, as the British-American confrontation grew more heated, lively debates raged in newspapers and pamphlets, and the colonists became increasingly polarized. In the last months before the outbreak of the American Revolution, the advocates of colonial rights began to call themselves **Whigs** and condemned their opponents as **Tories**. These traditional English party labels dated from the accession of the Catholic James II to England's throne in the late seventeenth century. The Tories had supported his accession; the Whigs had opposed it. By calling themselves Whigs and their opponents Tories (**loyalist** was a more accurate label), the advocates of colonial rights cast themselves as champions of liberty and their enemies as defenders of religious intolerance and royal absolutism.

Conclusion

All Americans, Whigs and Tories alike, had considered themselves good British subjects. But Americans were a more diverse and more democratic people than the English. A considerably larger percentage of them could participate in government, and for all practical purposes, had been governing themselves for a long time.

Perhaps because they came from a more rigid and aristocratic society, British officials first realized the different character of American society. Their perception of this difference led them to fear Americans rejection of British controls. But the steps they took to prevent this from happening had the opposite effect.

From Britain's perspective, the measures it took in the wake of the French and Indian War were a reasonable response to its administrative and financial problems in the colonies. Taken one by one from the colonists' perspective, however, they were a rain of blows that finally impelled them to rebel. No wonder that Americans, whose political ideology had already made them wary of governmental power, believed that they were the victims of a conspiracy in London to deprive them of their liberty. That Parliament should be a party to this presumed conspiracy particularly shocked and offended them.

Yet Americans probably should not have been surprised at Parliament's role. Indeed, both Parliament and the colonial assemblies were doing what similar bodies throughout Europe were also doing at roughly the same time—asserting their powers and defending their liberties against encroachments from above and below.

The attempts to protect their accustomed autonomy first brought the colonial assemblies into conflict with Parliament. Asserting their rights led the individual colonies to cooperate more among themselves. This in turn led to increasingly widespread resistance, then to rebellion, and finally to revolution. Moving imperceptibly from one stage to the next, Americans grew conscious of their common interests and their differences from the English. They became aware, as Benjamin Franklin would later write, of the need to break "through the bounds, in which a dependent people had been accustomed to think, and act" so that they might "properly comprehend the character they had assumed."

Review Questions

1. How did the British victory and French withdrawal from North America after the French and Indian War affect the relations between Native Americans and whites? Between British authorities and Americans?

2. What was the relationship between the French and Indian War and changes in British policy toward America? What problems were British officials trying to solve in 1763? What difficulties confronted Americans in 1763? How did the expectations of American and British authorities differ in 1763? Why were the new policies offensive to Americans?

3. How was stationing British troops in America related to British taxation of the colonists? Why did the colonists consider taxation by Parliament an especially serious threat to their freedom as well as to their pocketbooks?

4. How did Americans oppose the new measures? Who participated in the various forms of resistance? How effective were the different kinds of resistance? What were the effects of American resistance to British measures on their own sense of identity as Americans? What were the effects on their own internal politics?

5. What led to the meeting of the First Continental Congress? What steps did the Congress take? What did it expect to achieve? What were the differences between Whigs and Tories?

Recommended Reading

Bernard Bailyn, *The Ideological Origins of the American Revolution*, 2nd ed. (1992). A clear and illuminating account of how the colonists' ideas about politics prepared them to resist British measures.

Edward Countryman, *The American Revolution* (1985). A brief, readable general history of the Revolutionary period that focuses on the involvement of the common people.

Robert A. Gross, *The Minutemen and Their World* (1976). An example of "history from the bottom up," this book provides a close look at the Minutemen of Concord from the late colonial period through the Revolution.

Edmund S. Morgan and Helen M. Morgan, *The Stamp Act Crisis: Prologue to Revolution* (1963, 1995). The classic account of the most important pre-Revolutionary crisis, beautifully written.

Samuel Eliot Morison, ed., *Sources and Documents Illustrating the American Revolution, 1764–1788, and the Formation of the Federal Constitution* (1965). The most readily available and conveniently used collection of documents (mostly official) from the era of the American Revolution.

Where to Learn More

❖ **Charleston, South Carolina.**   Many buildings date from the eighteenth century. Local officials stored tea in one of them—the Exchange—to prevent a local version of the Boston Tea Party.

❖ **Philadelphia, Pennsylvania.**   Numerous buildings and sites date from the eighteenth century. Independence National Historical Park, between Second and Sixth streets on Walnut and Chestnut streets, contains Carpenter's Hall, where the First Continental Congress met, and the Pennsylvania State House (now known as Independence Hall), where the Declaration of Independence was adopted.

❖ **Boston, Massachusetts.**   Many important buildings and sites in this area date from the seventeenth and eighteenth centuries. They include Faneuil Hall (Dock Square), where many public meetings took place prior to the Revolution, and the Old State House (Washington and State streets), which overlooks the site of the Boston Massacre.

❖ **Fort Michilimackinac National Historic Landmark, Mackinaw City, Michigan.**   Near the south end of the Mackinac Bridge, the present structure is a modern restoration of the fort as it was when Pontiac's Rebellion took a heavy toll of its garrison.

6

THE WAR
FOR INDEPENDENCE
1774–1783

KEY TOPICS

❖ Mounting tensions between Britain and America
and the outbreak of fighting
❖ Organizing for war and declaring independence
❖ The contending forces
❖ The major military campaigns of the Revolution
❖ The alliance with France and the transformation
of the Revolution into a worldwide conflict
❖ The peace settlement
❖ The effect of the war on American society

It was May 1780, during some of the darkest days
for the American Revolution. Charleston, South
Carolina, was soon to fall to an advancing British
army. A German officer—a professional mercenary soldier—serving with the British army saw a wounded American sergeant who had been shot and captured after ven-
turing far in front of his unit. Asked why he had been so
foolhardy, the American replied that he had been
promised an officer's commission if he would successfully
scout the enemy lines. His captors told him that he was
mortally wounded. "He quietly lay down like a brave man,"
wrote the German officer, and managed to say, "Well, then,
I die for my country and for its just cause." Someone
handed him a glass of wine, which he "drank . . . down
with relish," and he died.

American independence would be won by the
dogged courage of ordinary soldiers like this nameless
man. Like him, many fought in hopes of an immediate
reward. And also like him, they risked death because they
believed in their country's cause.

Between 1774 and 1783, the thinking of those
Americans who challenged British authority changed dramatically. As late as 1774, they were still seeking self-government within the British Empire. After 1776, they were
struggling for full independence from their once-revered
mother country. To be sure, however, most of them, asked
what was their country, would have named their home
state, and asked what was their cause, would have replied,
simply, "Liberty."

American political identity emerged in part from
a new ideology of republicanism that combined a New

Whig distrust of central authority with a belief in a government rooted in the public spirit of a virtuous citizenry. Clinging fervently to this ideology, Americans relied at the outset of the war on the efficacy of a zealous citizens' militia to defeat the British army. But as the war grew fiercer, they learned that they could prevail only by developing an equally professional fighting force of their own. With vital French assistance, the new American army overcame the enemy. But eight long years of warfare strained and in some ways profoundly altered the fabric of American society.

The Outbreak of War and the Declaration of Independence, 1774–1776

Mounting Tensions

After the Boston Tea Party, both the British and the Americans knew they were approaching a crisis. In 1774, after General Thomas Gage, the commander in chief of the British army in America, and governor of Massachusetts dissolved the legislature it defied him by assembling anyway. Calling itself the **Provincial Congress**, the legislature in October 1774 appointed an emergency executive body, the **Committee of Safety**, headed by John Hancock, which began stockpiling weapons and organizing militia volunteers. Some localities had already provided for the formation of special companies of **Minute Men**, who were to be ready at "a minutes warning in Case of an alarm."

Local committees assaulted suspected loyalists and destroyed their property. The increasingly polarized atmosphere, combined with the drift toward military confrontation, drove a growing wedge between American loyalists and the **patriot** anti-British American Whigs.

The Loyalists' Dilemma

Loyalists and Whigs began to part company in earnest during the fall and winter of 1774–1775 as the threat of war mounted. Most Loyalists were farmers, officeholders and professionals, and many were recent immigrants to the colonies, who felt more secure under the protection of the crown than with more established Americans. Including those who did not actually fight, the loyalists numbered close to half a million men and women—some 20 percent of the colonies' free population.

British Coercion and Conciliation

The British parliamentary elections in the fall of 1774 strengthened Prime Minister Lord North's hand and enabled Parliament to prohibit the New England (and later other) colonies from trading outside the British Empire or sending their ships to the North Atlantic fishing grounds. Meanwhile, in a gesture of appeasement, Parliament endorsed Lord North's **Conciliatory Proposition** pledging not to tax the colonies if they would voluntarily contribute to the defense of the empire. Had it specified a maximum colonial contribution and had it been offered ten years earlier, the colonists might have found the Conciliatory Proposition acceptable. Now it was too late. North's government, in any case, had already sent orders to General Gage to take decisive action against the Massachusetts rebels. These orders triggered the first clash between British and American forces.

The Battles of Lexington and Concord

Gage received his orders on April 14, 1775. On the night of April 18, he assembled seven hundred men on the Boston Common and marched them toward the little towns of Lexington and Concord, some 20 miles away (see Map 6-1). Their mission was to arrest rebel leaders Samuel Adams and John Hancock (then staying in Lexington) and to destroy the military supplies the Committee of Safety had assembled at Concord. Patriots in Boston got wind of the troop movements and sent out riders—one of them the silversmith Paul Revere—to warn their fellows. Adams and Hancock escaped.

When the British soldiers reached Lexington at dawn, they found about seventy armed militiamen drawn up in formation on the village green. Their precise intentions are not clear. Outnumbered ten to one, they probably did not plan to begin a fight. More likely, they were there in a show of defiance.

Months of mounting tension exploded on the Lexington green. A British major ordered the militia to disperse. They were starting to obey when a shot cracked through the dawn stillness. No one now knows who fired. The British responded with a volley that killed or wounded eighteen Americans.

Map 6-1   *The Battles of Lexington and Concord*
This map shows the area around Boston, Massachusetts, where in April 1775 British and American forces fought the first military engagements of the Revolution.

established a post office, and authorized the printing of paper **continental dollars** to meet its expenses. Denying Parliament's claim to govern the colonies but not yet ready to declare themselves independent, the delegates sought to preserve their ties to Britain by expressing loyalty to the crown. In the **Olive Branch Petition**, addressed to George III on July 5, they asked the king to protect his American subjects from the military actions ordered by Parliament. The following day, Congress approved the **Declaration of the Causes and Necessity of Taking Up Arms**, asserting the resolve of American patriots "to die freemen, rather than to live slaves."

The British troops pressed on to Concord and burned what few supplies the Americans had not been able to hide. When their rear guard came under patriot fire at Concord's North Bridge, the British panicked. As they retreated to Boston, patriot Minute Men and other militia harried them from both sides of the road. By the time the column reached safety, 273 British soldiers were either dead, wounded, or missing. The four thousand Americans who had shot at them along the way suffered nearly 100 dead, wounded, and missing.

The speed with which distant colonies heard about the outbreak of fighting at the Battle of Lexington and Concord suggests both the importance Americans attached to it and the extraordinary efforts patriots made to spread word of it. Everywhere, news of Lexington and Concord spurred Whigs into action. The shots fired that April morning would, in the words of the nineteenth-century Concord philosopher and poet Ralph Waldo Emerson, be "heard round the world." They signaled the start of the American Revolution.

The Second Continental Congress, 1775–1776

By the time the Second Continental Congress convened in Philadelphia on May 10, 1775, it had a war on its hands. Assuming leadership of the rebellion, Congress in the succeeding months became, in effect, a national government. It called for the patchwork of local forces to be organized into the **Continental Army**, authorized the formation of a navy,

Commander in Chief George Washington

To take command of the patriot forces around Boston—the newly named Continental Army—Congress turned to George Washington. John Adams, a Whig leader from Massachusetts, selected the Virginian. Realizing that this would help transform a local quarrel in New England into a continental conflict, Adams also expected Washington's leadership to help attract recruits from Virginia, which was then the most populous colony.

He was the ideal person for the job. Some of his contemporaries had quicker minds and broader educations; Washington, however, was blessed with good judgment, a profound understanding of both the uses and the limitations of power, and a quiet air of authority. In short, he had the gift of command. He soon also realized that the fate of the patriot cause depended on the survival of the army. The troops revered him. In a crisis, wrote a man who served under him, "his likeness was worth more . . . than the British would have given for his person"—presumably a great deal.

Early Fighting

General Gage, finding himself besieged in Boston after the fighting at Lexington and Concord, decided to seize and fortify territory south of Boston, where his cannons could command the harbor. But the Americans seized high ground first, entrenching themselves on Breeds Hill north of

This engraving of Washington and his family, including two of his wife's grandchildren from her first marriage and a waiting-man, dates from the 1790s, but the artist, Edward Savage, presented Washington in his uniform as Commander of the Continental Army. Note the authoritative manner in which Martha Washington points to the map. The African-American was probably William Lee, who would be singled out in Washington's last will and testament for his loyalty and "faithful services during the Revolution."

town. On June 17, 1775, Gage sent 2,200 well-trained soldiers to drive the 1,700 patriot men and boys from their new position. The British succeeded, but at great cost. In three assaults, they suffered more than a thousand casualties. The Americans, who retreated when they ran short of gunpowder, lost just under four hundred dead or wounded. One glum British officer observed afterward that another such victory "would have ruined us." Misnamed for another hill nearby, this encounter has gone down in history as the **Battle of Bunker Hill** (see Map 6-2).

During the winter of 1775–1776, the Americans dragged some sixty cannons 300 miles through snow and over mountains from Fort Ticonderoga to Boston, mounting them overlooking Boston harbor, and putting the British in an indefensible position. The British then evacuated Boston and moved their troops to Halifax, Nova Scotia. New England was for the moment secure for the patriots. Initial fighting in the South also went well for the patriots, who defeated Loyalist forces at Great Bridge, near Norfolk, and Moore's Creek Bridge in North Carolina. In June 1776, patriot forces also successfully repulsed a large British expedition sent to capture Charleston, South Carolina.

In contrast, an attempt to win Canada to the Whig side met with disaster. Two American armies attacked in late 1775. One quickly captured Montreal. The other, under Benedict Arnold, approached Quebec through the Maine wilderness in the face of great hardships. Linking up outside heavily fortified Quebec, the American commanders attacked the city on December 31. The assault, followed by the **Siege of Quebec**, failed. Canada remained a British province.

Independence

The stunning American successes in New England and the South in late 1775 and early 1776 bolstered the patriots' confidence.

In August 1775, King George III rejected Congress's Olive Branch Petition. Instead, he issued a proclamation declaring the colonies in rebellion and denying them his protection. In December, Parliament barred all exports from the American colonies. These aggressive actions, especially the king's, persuaded many colonists to abandon their loyalty to the crown. More and more, Whigs began to think seriously of declaring full independence from Britain.

At this critical moment, a ne'er-do-well Englishman, recently arrived on American soil, gave the cause of independence a powerful boost. Thomas Paine was by trade a corsetmaker—and twice a fired tax collector. Also a man of radical ideas that he expressed forcefully in the everyday English of ordinary people, he became a powerful polemicist for the American cause. In his pamphlet **Common Sense**, published in Philadelphia in January 1776, Paine denounced King George and made the case for independence. He ridiculed the absurdity of "supposing a continent to be perpetually governed by an island," and described the King as "the Royal Brute" whose tyranny should be thrown off. Simple common sense, Paine concluded, dictated that "'TIS TIME TO PART."

Common Sense, which promptly sold more than 100,000 copies throughout the colonies, helped predispose Americans toward independence. Tactical considerations also led patriot leaders toward a formal separation from Great Britain. Such a move would make it easier for America to gain desperately needed aid from foreign coun-

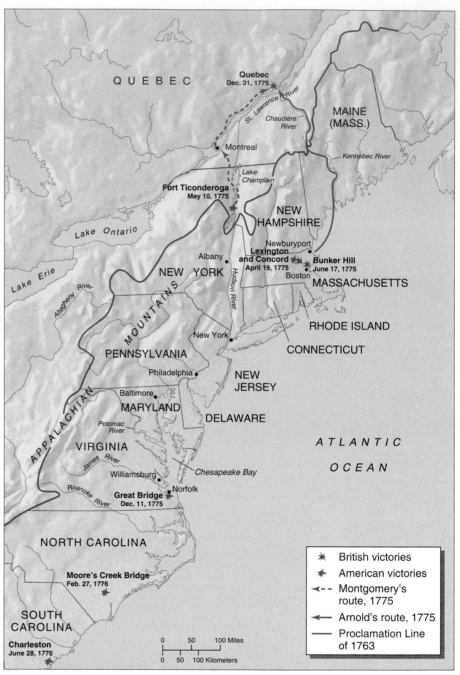

Map 6-2   Early Fighting, 1775–1776
As this map clearly reveals, even the earliest fighting occurred in widely scattered areas, thereby complicating Britain's efforts to subdue the Americans.

tries, especially from England's ancient enemy, France. Declaring independence would also give the local political elites leading the resistance to British rule a solid legal basis for their newly claimed authority.

On June 7, 1776, Virginian Richard Henry Lee introduced in Congress a resolution stating that the united colonies "are, and of right ought to be, free and independent States." Postponing a vote on

The Battle of Bunker Hill, June 17, 1775. Painted by John Trumbull, who witnessed the battle from the other side of Boston harbor, this dramatic depiction of the fighting in which Major General Joseph Warren of the Massachusetts militia lies dying was completed a decade after the events. The African-American who appears on the far right was the servant of a lieutenant from Connecticut; another African-American not clearly shown, Peter Salem, was reported to have fired one of the shots that killed Major John Pitcairn, who had led the British troops at the battle of Lexington.

Jefferson's prose, however, transformed what might have been a bland statement into one of history's great assertions of human rights.

The Declaration of Independence consists of a magnificently stated opening assumption, two premises, and a powerful conclusion. The opening assumption is that all men are created equal, that they therefore have equal rights, and that they can neither give up these rights nor allow them to be taken away. The first premise—that people establish governments to protect their fundamental rights to life, liberty, and property—is a restatement of contract theory. (With a wonderful flourish reflecting the Enlightenment's optimism about human potential, Jefferson changed "property" to "the pursuit of happiness.") The second premise is a long list of charges meant to justify the Americans' rejection of their hitherto legitimate ruler. Then follows the dramatic conclusion: that Americans can rightfully overthrow King George's rule and replace it with something more satisfactory.

Historians have spilled oceans of ink debating Jefferson's use of the expression "all men." Almost certainly he was thinking in the abstract and meant "humanity in general." In practice, of course, many people were excluded from full participation in eighteenth-century American society. Women, propertyless white, and free black men had no formal political rights and limited legal rights, and slaves enjoyed no rights at all. (Although himself a slave-owner, Jefferson was deeply troubled by American slavery. He had wanted to include a denunciation of the slave trade among the charges against George III in the Declaration of Independence, but Congress took it out, believing that to blame the king for this inhumane business would appear hypocritical.) But if the words "all men are created equal" had limited practical meaning in 1776, they have ever since confronted Americans with a moral challenge.

the issue, Congress appointed a committee to draw up a declaration of independence. The committee turned to a young Virginian named Thomas Jefferson to compose the first draft. "You can write ten times better than I," John Adams told Jefferson. When the committee presented the document to Congress and it became clear that the majority favored independence, the Pennsylvania and South Carolina delegations switched sides in favor of it, and the New York delegation decided to abstain. Thus when Congress voted on the resolution for independence on July 2, 1776, it was approved unanimously by all voting delegations. After further tinkering with the wording, Congress officially approved the **Declaration of Independence** on July 4, 1776.

Congress intended the declaration to be a justification for America's secession from the British Empire. Jefferson later maintained that he did not write any more than what everyone was thinking. The political theory that lies behind the declaration is known as the **contract theory of government**. Developed by the late seventeenth-century English philosopher John Locke and others, the contract theory maintains that legitimate government rests on an agreement between the people and their rulers. The people are bound to obey their rulers only so long as the rulers offer them protection.

Republicanism

Americans reacted to news of the Declaration of Independence with mixed emotions. There was rejoicing as orators read the declaration to great

CHRONOLOGY

1775 **April 19:** Battles of Lexington and Concord.

May 10: Second Continental Congress meets.

June 17: Battle of Bunker Hill.

December 31: American attack on Quebec.

1776 **January 9:** Thomas Paine's *Common Sense.*

July 4: Declaration of Independence.

September 15: British take New York City.

December 26: Battle of Trenton.

1777 **January 3:** Battle of Princeton.

September 11: Battle of Brandywine Creek.

October 17: American victory at Saratoga.

Runaway inflation begins.

Continental Army winters at Valley Forge.

1778 **February 6:** France and the United States sign an alliance.

June 17: Congress refuses to negotiate with British peace commissioners.

July 4: George Rogers Clark captures British post in the Mississippi Valley.

December 29: British capture Savannah.

1779 **June 21:** Spain declares war on Britain.

Americans devastate the Iroquois country.

September 23: John Paul Jones captures the British ship *Serapis.*

1780 **May 12:** Fall of Charleston, South Carolina.

October 7: Americans win Battle of Kings Mountain.

Nathanael Greene takes command in the South.

1781 **January 17:** Americans defeat British at Battle of Cowpens.

March 15: Battle of Guilford Court House.

October 19: Cornwallis surrenders at Yorktown.

1783 **March 15:** Washington quells the Newburgh "Conspiracy."

September 3: Peace of Paris signed.

November 21: British begin evacuating New York.

---

crowds. But even many who favored independence worried how Americans would govern themselves. Most Whigs, animated by the political ideology known as **republicanism**, thought a republican government was best suited to American society.

Republicanism held that self-government—either directly by the citizens of a country or indirectly by their elected representatives—provided a more reliable foundation for the good society and individual freedom than rule by kings. Thus drawing on contract theory, as in the Declaration of Independence, republicanism called for government by consent of the governed. Drawing on country ideology, it was suspicious of excessively centralized government and insistent on the need for virtuous, public-spirited citizenry. Republicanism therefore helped give the American Revolution a moral dimension.

But other than a state that was not ruled by a hereditary king, what was a republic?

Americans had at hand a recent example of a republic in the English Civil War of the mid-seventeenth century, in which English Puritans had for a time replaced the monarchy with a republican "Commonwealth," dedicated to advancing the "common weal," or common good. Some New Englanders, spiritual descendants of the Puritans, considered the Commonwealth to have been a noble experiment and regarded the American Revolution as another chance to establish a republic of the godly. "When the mere Politician weighs the Danger or Safety of his Country," warned one clergyman, "he computes them in Proportion to its Fortresses, Arms, Money, Provisions, Numbers of Fighting Men, and its Enemies." But, the clergyman continued, the "Christian Patriot" calculates them "by its Numbers of Sinful or praying People, and its Degrees of Holiness or Vice." Such language recalled the Great Awakening; it reached beyond the upper classes who had been directing resistance to the British and mobilized ordinary people for what their ministers repeatedly assured them was a just war against sin and despotism.

The Combatants

Republican theory mistrusted professional armies as the instruments of tyrants. A free people, republicans insisted, relied for defense on their own patriotism. When individual or community rights were in danger, free men should grab their muskets from over the fireplace, assemble as the local militia, take care of the problem, and go home. But militiamen, as one American general observed, had trouble coping with "the shocking scenes of war" because they were not "steeled by habit or fortified by military pride." In real battles, they often proved unreliable. Americans therefore faced a hard choice: develop a professional army or lose the war. In the end, they did what they had to do. While state militias continued to offer support, it was the disciplined forces of the Continental Army that won the crucial battles.

Professional Soldiers

Washington tightened things up in the new Continental Army. Eventually, he prevailed on Congress to adopt stricter regulations and to require enlistments for three years or the duration of the war. His consistent aim was to turn the Continental Army into a disciplined force that could defeat the British in the large engagements of massed troops characteristic of eighteenth-century European warfare. Guerrilla fighters shooting from behind trees like "savages" had their place in the American war effort, but they could never win a decisive, formal battle. And only such a "civilized" victory would impress the other European powers and establish the legitimacy of the United States.

Many soldiers of fortune, as well as a few idealists, offered their services to American representatives in Europe. France's 19-year-old Marquis de Lafayette was one of the youngest, wealthiest, and most idealistic. Two Poles, Tadeusz Kosciuszko, an engineer, and Kazimierz Pulaski, a cavalry commander mortally wounded at the Battle of Savannah in 1779, also rendered good service. Most useful of all, probably, was "Baron" von Steuben. His title was bogus, but he had genuine experience in the Prussian army, continental Europe's best. He knew how to get along with American soldiers by explaining the reasons for his orders. He became the Continental Army's drillmaster, and thanks partly to him, Washington's troops increasingly came to resemble their disciplined European counterparts.

The enemy British troopers—and the nearly thirty thousand German mercenaries (Americans called them "Hessians") whom the British government also employed—offered Americans the clearest model of a professional army. Most enlisted men did come from the lower classes and from economically depressed areas, but many also had skills. Most British troops carried the "Brown Bess" musket. With bayonet attached, it was almost 6 feet long and weighed over 16 pounds. In battle, soldiers usually stood close together in lines or squares. They were expected to withstand bombardment without flinching, fire on command in volleys, charge with the bayonet, and use their heavy musket stock (the wooden end) to crush the skulls of any wounded enemy they strode over.

Military life was tough. On the march, seasoned troops carrying 60-pound packs, normally covered about 15 miles a day but could go 30 miles in a "forced" march. In all weather conditions, they wore heavy woolen uniforms dyed bright red for visibility on smoke-filled battlefields (hence their nickname "Redcoats"). They were frequently undernourished, however, and many more died of disease than of injury in battle. Medical care was, by modern standards, primitive: Treatments for illness included bleeding and purging (induced vomiting and diarrhea). Serious arm or leg wounds usually meant amputation, without antiseptics or anesthetics, and often proved fatal.

Severe discipline held soldiers in line. Striking an officer or deserting could bring death; lesser offenses usually incurred a beating. Several hundred lashes, "well laid on" with the notorious cat-o'-nine-tails (a whip with multiple cords, each ending in a nasty little knot or a metal ball), were not uncommon.

Soldiers amused themselves with gambling (despite regulations against it) and drinking. Perhaps two-thirds of the Redcoats were illiterate, and they all suffered from loneliness and boredom. Camaraderie and a legendary loyalty to their regiments sustained them.

After the winter of 1777–1778, conditions in the Continental Army came to resemble those of the British army. Like British regulars, American recruits tended to be low on the social scale. The chances for talented enlisted men to win an officer's commission were greater in the Continental Army than the British army. And despite their ragged uniforms, they carried themselves like soldiers. Indeed, Continental soldiers frequently had little more than "their ragged shirt flaps to cover their nakedness," and more than once their bare marching feet left bloody tracks in the snow.

Both British and American authorities had trouble supplying their troops. Both sides suffered from bureaucratic inefficiencies, but the fundamental problems of each were different. The British had plenty of hard-coin money with a stable value, which many American merchants and farmers were happy to take in payment for supplies. But the British had to rely mostly on supplies shipped to them from the British Isles. The Continental Army, in contrast, had to pay for supplies in paper money, both continental dollars and state-issued currency, whose value sank steadily as the war progressed.

Feeling themselves outcasts from an uncaring society, the professional soldiers of the Continental Army developed a community of their own. The soldiers were "as strict a band of brotherhood as Masons," one later wrote, and their spirit kept them together in the face of misery. Attempts at mutiny in Washington's camp were few and largely unsuccessful.

Occasionally, American officers let their disgruntlement get out of hand. The most notorious such case was that of Benedict Arnold, a general who compiled a distinguished record during the first three years of the war but then came to feel himself shabbily treated by Congress and his superiors. Seeking better rewards for his abilities, he offered to surrender the strategic fort at West Point (which he commanded) to the enemy; before he could act, however, his plot was discovered, and he fled to the British, serving with them until the end of the war. Among Americans, his name became a synonym for *traitor*.

What was perhaps the most serious expression of army discontent—one that threatened the future of republican institutions and civilian government in the United Sates—occurred near Newburgh, New York, in March 1783, after the fighting was over. During the war, Congress had promised officers a pension of half pay for life (the custom in Great Britain), but now many veterans demanded instead full pay for six years. When Congress failed to grant real assurances that *any* pay would be forthcoming, hotheaded young officers called a meeting that could have led to an armed uprising and military coup. General Washington, in a dramatic speech, subtly warned the men of all that they might lose by insubordination. A military coup would "open the flood Gates of Civil discord" and "deluge" the nation in blood; loyalty now, he said, would be "one more distinguished proof" of their patriotism. With the fate of the Revolution and the honor of the army hanging apparently in the balance, the movement collapsed. The officers and politicians behind the "conspiracy" were only bluffing, using the threat of a discontented army to frighten the states into granting Congress the power (which it then lacked) to levy taxes so it would have the funds to pay the army.

Women in the Contending Armies

Women accompanied many units on both sides, as was common in eighteenth-century warfare. A few were prostitutes. Most were the married or common-law consorts of ordinary soldiers. These women "camp followers" cooked and washed for the troops, occasionally helped load artillery, and provided most of the nursing care. A certain number in a company were subject to military orders and were authorized to draw rations and pay. The role of these women found its way into American folklore in the legend of Molly Pitcher (probably Mary Ludwig Hays, the wife of a Continental artillery sergeant), who heroically carried water to gunners to cool them and their overheated guns at the Battle of Monmouth Court House in 1778.

Black and Native American Participation in the War

On June 30, 1779, the British commander in chief, Sir Henry Clinton, promised to allow slaves who fled from rebel owners to join the royal troops to "follow . . . any Occupation" they wished. Hedged as this promise of freedom was, news of it spread quickly among the slave communities, and late in the war enough blacks flocked to the British army in South Carolina and Georgia to make feeding and housing them a serious problem. The British shared the racial prejudices of many Americans, however, and despite their efforts to recruit African-Americans, were reluctant to arm them. Instead, the British put most of the ex-slaves to work as agricultural or construction workers (many of the free and enslaved blacks accompanying American troops were similarly employed). A few relatively well equipped black British dragoons (mounted troops), however, saw some combat in South Carolina, much to the horror of local Whigs.

Approximately five thousand African-Americans fought against the British and for American independence, hundreds of them in the Continental Army. Many were freemen from Massachusetts and Rhode Island (see "American Views: An African-American Veteran of the Revolutionary War Petitions for His Pension"). Several free blacks served among the defenders at Bunker Hill, and at least one distinguished himself sufficiently for his commander to commend him as "an experienced officer as well as an excellent soldier." But the idea of arming African-Americans was not well received in the South.

Many Indians also favored the British. To Native Americans, the key issue of the American Revolution, as well as in most disputes with whites, was about their land. Many Indian peoples, including the Cherokees, decided that it was in their interest to back the British. Their aid mainly took the form of attacks on white frontier settlements. Usually they did not tell the British in advance what they were planning to do. Thus in one notorious incident, an

Indian attack in the Hudson River Valley resulted in the mistaken scalping of Jane McCrae, the fiancée of a British officer. Whig propagandists exploited this tragedy to the fullest. Because they could not control the Indians, the British regarded their native allies as a liability as well as an asset and seldom made unrestricted use of them. Other Native Americans, such as the Oneidas and the Tuscaroras, however, joined the Americans.

The War in the North, 1776–1777

The Revolutionary War can be divided into three phases. In the first, from the outbreak of fighting in 1775 to 1778, most of the important battles took place in New England, New York, New Jersey, and Pennsylvania. During these years, the Americans faced the British alone. But in 1778, France entered the war on the American side, opening the second phase of the war. Fighting in the second phase would rage from 1778 to 1781 mainly in the South, at sea, and on the western frontier. The third phase of the war, from late 1781 to 1783, saw little actual fighting. With American victory assured, attention shifted to the diplomatic maneuvering leading up to the Treaty of Paris (1783), which ended the war and recognized American independence.

The British Army Hesitates

During the first phase of the war, the British concentrated on subduing New England, the hotbed of what they saw as "rebellious principles." Replacing General Gage, the government appointed Sir William Howe as commander in chief of British forces and his brother, Richard Howe, as admiral of the naval forces in North American waters. New York City had been the headquarters of the British army during the late colonial period, and the Howes decided to make it their base of operations. In August 1776, the Howes landed troops on Long Island and in the **Battle of Brooklyn Heights** quickly drove the American forces deployed there from Brooklyn Heights and back to Manhattan Island (see Map 6-3).

In the ensuing weeks, British forces overwhelmed Washington's forces, driving them out of Manhattan and then, moving north, clearing them from the area around the city at the **Battle of White Plains**. But the Howes were hesitant to deal a crushing blow, and the Americans were able to retreat across New Jersey into Pennsylvania. The American cause seemed lost, however; Congress fled from Philadelphia to Baltimore, and the Continental Army almost melted away.

On Christmas Eve, Washington led his forces back across the icy Delaware from Pennsylvania and, in the **Battle of Trenton**, launched an unorthodox surprise attack on a garrison of Hessian mercenaries at Trenton, New Jersey, on the morning of December 26. Still in the midst of their Christmas celebrations, the Hessians quickly surrendered. A week later, in the **Battle of Princeton**, Washington overwhelmed a British force at Princeton, New Jersey. Thereafter, Washington withdrew to winter quarters in Morristown, New Jersey, and the Howes made no further effort to pursue him. Both sides suspended operations until the spring.

The victories at Trenton and Princeton boosted morale and saved the American cause. But why did the Howes not annihilate the Continental Army while they had the chance? Clearly, they wanted to regain loyal subjects, not alienate them. But if they had inflicted a crushing defeat on the Americans, they would have risked making them permanent enemies of British rule. By the time it later became apparent that this cautious strategy was not working and the Howes were replaced with more aggressive commanders, the British had lost their best chance to win the war.

The Year of the Hangman

Contemporaries called 1777 the Year of the Hangman because the triple sevens suggested a row of gallows. Living up to its ominous name, it was indeed a crucial year for the American cause.

The British began the year by mounting a major effort to end the rebellion. Their strategy was to send a force south from Canada down the Hudson River to link up with the Howes in New York City, separate New England from the rest of the states, and then crush the rebellion in that most recalcitrant region. Unfortunately, there was no effort to coordinate strategy between the forces advancing from Canada and the forces under the command of the Howes in New York. Thus in the end, poorly planned, poorly executed, and unsupported from the South, the campaign ended in disaster for the British.

Some five thousand Redcoats and three thousand German mercenaries assembled in Canada during the winter of 1776–1777 under the command of the jaunty, high-living, and popular "Gentleman Johnny" Burgoyne. The army finally set off in June with 1,500 horses hauling its heavy artillery and ponderous supply train. Crossing Lake Champlain, Bur-

American Views

AN AFRICAN-AMERICAN VETERAN OF THE REVOLUTIONARY WAR PETITIONS FOR HIS PENSION

Rhode Island made a greater effort to recruit African-American soldiers than any other state. Indeed, three-quarters of the Rhode Island regiment that helped defeat Cornwallis at Yorktown was African-American, and a French officer who saw the Continental troops pass in review reported that it was "the most neatly dressed, the best under arms, and the most precise in its maneuvers." In theory at least, African-Americans were supposed to receive all the benefits to which other soldiers were entitled, including pensions. Thus when in 1832 Congress passed the first general pension act authorizing yearly payments to anyone who had served six months or more in any military unit, a number of African-Americans were eligible. Jehu Grant was one of them. Like many others who applied, he sought to document his military service by a narrative of his activities during the war. Few such accounts are as poignant as Grant's, whose letter inquiring about the fate of his application is reproduced here. Because he signed with his mark, one can infer that the original document was not in his own handwriting.

❖ **How did Grant enter the army, and what did he do while in it?**

❖ **How did he obtain his freedom, and what did he do later in life?**

❖ **Do you see any connection between the war service of men like Grant and the decision of the Rhode Island legislature to end slavery in 1784?**

Hon. J. L. Edwards, Commissioner of Pensions:

Your servant begs leave to state that he forwarded to the War Department a declaration founded on the Pension Act of June 1832 praying to be allowed a pension (if his memory serves him) for ten months' service in the American army of the Revolutionary War. That he enlisted as a soldier but was put to the service of a teamster in the summer and a waiter in the winter. In April 1834 I received a writing from Your Honour, informing me that my "services while a fugitive from my master's service was not embraced in said Act," and that my "papers were placed on file." In my said declaration, I just mentioned the cause of leaving my master, as may be seen by a reference thereunto, and I now pray that I may be permitted to express my feelings more fully on that part of my said declaration.

goyne's army on July 5, recaptured Fort Ticonderoga, but success eluded him after that.

Trouble began as the troops started moving overland through the woods at the southern end of the lake. Forced to clear away huge trees in its path felled by American axmen, the army crawled along at only 2 or 3 miles a day. Promised reinforcements never arrived, and a Whig militia force wiped out a

force of eight hundred men that Burgoyne had sent into Vermont to round up badly needed horses. By October 1777, Burgoyne's army was down to less than six thousand men and facing disaster. A force of nearly three thousand Continentals and nine thousand militia, commanded by General Horatio Gates, had now assembled to confront the British. Unable to break through the American lines, Burgoyne

I was then grown to manhood, in the full vigor and strength of life, and heard much about the cruel and arbitrary things done by the British. Their ships lay within a few miles of my master's house, which stood near the shore, and I was confident that my master traded with them, and I suffered much from fear that I should be sent aboard a ship of war. This I disliked. But when I saw liberty poles and the people all engaged for the support of freedom, I could not but like and be pleased with such [a] thing (God forgive me if I sinned in so feeling). And living on the borders of Rhode Island, where whole companies of colored people enlisted, it added to my fears and dread of being sold to the British. These considerations induced me to enlist into the American army, where I served faithful about ten months, when my master found and took me home. Had I been taught to read or understand the precepts of the Gospel, "Servants obey your masters," I might had done otherwise, notwithstanding the songs of liberty that saluted my ear, [and] thrilled through my heart. But feeling conscious that I have since compensated my master for the injury he sustained by my enlisting, and that God has forgiven me for so doing, and that I served my country faithfully, and that they having enjoyed the benefits of my service to an equal degree for the length [of] time I served with those generally who are receiving the liberalities of the government, I cannot but feel it becoming me to pray Your Honor to review my declaration on file and the papers herewith amended.

A few years after the war, Joshua Swan, Esq., of Stonington purchased me of my master and agreed that after I had served him a length of time named faithfully, I should be free. I served to his satisfaction and so obtained my freedom. He moved into the town of Milton, where I now reside, about forty-eight years ago. After my time expired with Esq. Swan, I married a wife. We have raised six children. Five are still living. I must be upward of eighty years of age and have been blind for many years, and, notwithstanding the aid I received from the honest industry of my children, we are still very needy and in part are supported from the benevolence of our friends. With these statements and the testimony of my character herewith presented, I humbly set my claim upon the well-known liberality of government.

Most respectfully your humble servant

Jehu Grant

his mark

Source: *John C. Dann, ed.*, The Revolution Remembered: Eyewitness Accounts of the War for Independence, *pp. 27–28.*

surrendered to Gates following the **Battle of Saratoga** on October 17, 1777. A stunning reversal for the British, Burgoyne's defeat would help convince the French to join the fighting on the American side.

While Burgoyne was meeting disaster, William Howe, rather than moving north to support him, was making plans to destroy Washington's army and capture Philadelphia. In July 1777, Howe's troops sailed from New York to Chesapeake Bay and from there marched on Philadelphia from the south. They met Washington's army on the banks of **Brandywine Creek**, near the Pennsylvania-Delaware border. The Americans put up a good fight before giving way with a loss of 1,200 killed or captured (twice as many as the British).

Map 6-3   The War in the North, 1776–1777
Most of the fighting between the British and Americans during the first part of the war occurred in the North, partly because British authorities assumed that the New England colonies were the most rebellious.

Howe occupied Philadelphia, and his men settled down in comfortable winter quarters. Congress fled to York, Pennsylvania, and the Continental Army established its own winter camp outside Philadelphia, at **Valley Forge**. Here Washington was joined by his wife, Martha, in a small stone farmhouse, surrounded by the log huts that his men built for themselves. The Continental Army's miserable winter at Valley Forge has become legendary in American history. Suffering from cold, disease, and starvation, as many as 2,500 soldiers died. Yet the troops managed to transform themselves into a disciplined professional army by drilling endlessly under the watchful eye of General von Steuben, and with the coming of spring, American prospects improved dramatically.

The War Widens, 1778–1781

The United States Gains an Ally

Since late 1776, Benjamin Franklin and a team of American diplomats had been in Paris negotiating French support for the patriot cause. In the winter of 1777–1778, aware that a Franco-American alliance was close, Parliament belatedly tried to end the rebellion by granting the former colonies full autonomy, including the exclusive right to tax themselves, in return for a resumption of allegiance to the crown. But France and the United States concluded an alliance on February 6, 1778, and news of it reached America before the British commission arrived. Seeing independence within reach, Congress refused to negotiate.

Foreign intervention would transform the American Revolution into a virtual world war, engaging British forces in heavy fighting not only in North America but also in the West Indies and India. In the end, had it not been for French assistance, the American side probably would not have won the clear cut victory it did.

The agreements the United States signed with France included both a commercial treaty and a military alliance. Both sides promised to fight together until Britain recognized the independence of the United States, and France pledged not to seek the return of lands in North America. In turn, France persuaded Spain to declare war on Britain in June 1779. The Spanish fleet augmented the naval power of the countries arrayed against Great Britain.

Meanwhile, Catherine the Great of Russia suggested that European powers form a **League of Armed Neutrality** to protect their trade with the United States and other warring countries against British interference. Denmark and Sweden soon joined; Austria, the Netherlands, Portugal, Prussia, and Sicily eventually followed. Britain, however, quickly went to war with Holland, ostensibly over another issue (to avoid war with the League), but really to cut off Dutch trade with the United States.

Great Britain thus found itself nearly completely isolated and even, briefly, threatened with invasion. Accordingly, as early in the spring of 1778, the British replaced the Howes with a tough new commander, Sir Henry Clinton, instructing him to detach some of his troops to attack the French West Indies. Knowing he now faced a serious French threat, Clinton began consolidating his forces. He evacuated Philadelphia and pulled his troops slowly back across New Jersey to New York.

On June 28, 1778, Washington caught up with the British and engaged them at the **Battle of Monmouth Court House**. The day was hot and the battle hard-fought. For a while, it looked as if the now well-trained Americans might win, but a mix-up in orders cost Washington the victory. This inconclusive battle proved to be the last major engagement in the North for the rest of the war. Clinton withdrew to New York, and Continental troops occupied the hills along the Hudson Valley north of the city. The war shifted to other fronts.

Fighting on the Frontier and at Sea

Native Americans called Kentucky "a dark and bloody ground," a designation that took on added meaning when Indians began raiding the territory in 1777 on British instructions. The nerve center for coordinating these attacks was the British post of Detroit, and the Americans accordingly made plans to capture it. After two unsuccessful expeditions, a third, under Virginian George Rogers Clark (see Map 6-4), captured three key British settlements in the Mississippi Valley (**Kaskaskia**, Cahokia, and Vincennes) in July 1778. These successes may have strengthened American claims to the West at the end of the war.

Blood also ran on the Pennsylvania and upstate New York frontiers with British and Indian raids on settlers in Pennsylvania's **Wyoming Valley** and New York's **Cherry Valley**. Both raids became the stuff of legends and stimulated equally savage reprisals against the Iroquois, destroying forty-one Indian villages in the New York Finger Lakes region.

Anglo-American clashes at sea had begun in 1775, shortly after the Battles of Lexington and Concord, and would continue until the end of the war as Americans struggled to break the British navy's blockade. Great Britain was the preeminent sea power of the age, and the United States never came close to matching it, in either the number or the size of its ships. But Congress did its best to challenge the British at sea, and the Americans engaged in what

Map 6-4 *The War on the Frontier, 1778–1779*
Significant battles in the Mississippi Valley and the frontiers of the seaboard states added to the ferocity of the fighting and strengthened some American claims to western lands.

was essentially a guerrilla naval war. Their naval flag, appropriately, pictured a rattlesnake and bore the motto "Don't Tread on Me."

The country's first naval hero, Scottish-born John Paul Jones, was primarily a hit-and-run raider. In the colonies by chance when the war broke out, this adventurer offered his services to Congress. Benjamin Franklin helped secure Jones an old French merchant ship, which he outfitted for war and renamed the *Bon Homme Richard*. After capturing seventeen enemy vessels, he encountered the formidable H.M.S. *Serapis* in the North Sea on September 23, 1779. Completely outgunned, Jones brought the *Bon Homme Richard* close enough to make his small arms fire more effective. Asked by the British if he was surrendering, Jones gave the legendary reply, "I have not yet begun to fight." More than four hours later, the *Serapis* surrendered. Jones's crew took possession of the British vessel and left the crippled *Bon Homme Richard* to sink.

Congress and the individual states supplemented America's naval forces by commissioning individual sea captains to outfit their merchant vessels with guns and act as privateers. Some two thousand American privateers captured more than six hundred British ships and forced the British navy to spread itself thin doing convoy duty.

The Land War Moves South

During the first three years of the war, the British had made little effort to mobilize what they believed to be considerable loyalist strength in the South. In 1778, however, facing a threat from France and with their forces in the North concentrated and inactive, they gave southern loyalists a key role in a new strategy for subduing the rebellion. The British southern strategy began to unfold in November 1778, when General Clinton dispatched 3,500 troops to take control of Georgia (see Map 6-5). Meeting only light resistance, they quickly seized **Savannah** and Augusta.

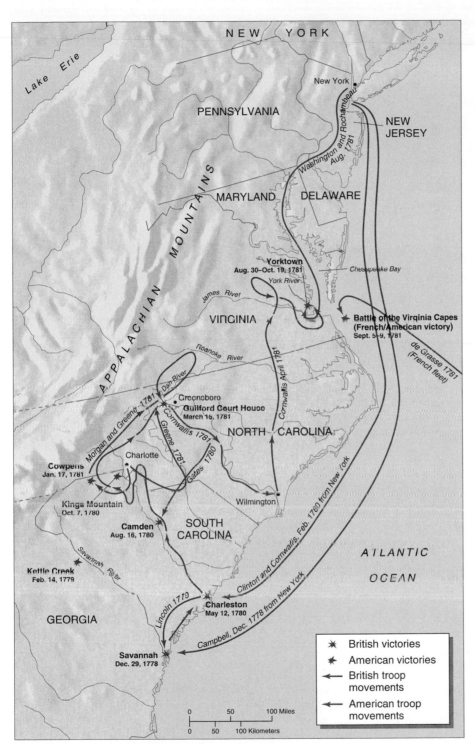

Map 6-5 *The War in the South, 1778–1781*
During the latter part of the war, most of the major engagements occurred in the South. British forces won most of the early ones, but could not control the immense territory involved and eventually surrendered at Yorktown.

cess, however, the British did suffer some serious setbacks. The Spanish entered the war and seized British outposts on the Mississippi and Mobile Rivers. And in February 1779, at the **Battle of Kettle Creek**, South Carolina's Whig militia decimated a loyalist militia contingent.

But the Americans could not beat the British army. In late September and early October 1779, a combined force of 5,500 American and French troops, supported by French warships, unsuccessfully attacked Savannah. The way was now open for the British to attack Charleston, the military key to the Lower South. In December 1779, Clinton sailed through storm-battered seas from New York to the Carolina coast with about nine thousand troops. In the **Battle of Charleston**, he encircled the city, trapping the patriot forces inside. On May 12, 1780, more than five thousand Continentals and militia laid down their arms—the worst American defeat of the war and the largest single loss of United States troops to a foreign army until the surrender of American forces in the Philippines to Japan in 1942.

The British were now poised to sweep all the South before them. So complete did the British success seem that Clinton tried to force the American troops whom he had taken prisoner to resume their duties as British subjects and join the loyalist militia. Thinking that matters were now well in hand, Clinton sailed back to New York, leaving the southern troops under the command of Lord Cornwallis.

Clinton's confidence that the South had returned securely to the loyalist camp was premature. Atrocities like Colonel Banastre Tarleton's slaughter of 350 Virginian Continentals who had already offered to surrender inflamed anti-British

Indeed, enough inhabitants seemed happy to have the British back that the old colonial government was restored under civilian control. After their initial suc-

SUMMARY

IMPORTANT BATTLES OF THE REVOLUTIONARY WAR

	Battle	Date	Outcome
Early Fighting	Lexington and Concord, Massachusetts	Apr. 19, 1775	Contested
	Fort Ticonderoga, New York	May 10, 1775	American victory
	Breeds Hill ("Bunker Hill"), Boston, Massachusetts	June 17, 1775	Contested
	Great Bridge, Virginia	Dec. 9, 1775	American victory
	Quebec, Canada	Dec. 31, 1775	British repulse American assault
	Moore's Creek Bridge, North Carolina	Feb. 27. 1776	American victory
The War in the North	Brooklyn Heights, New York	Aug. 27, 1776	British victory
	White Plains, New York	Oct. 28, 1776	British victory
	Trenton, New Jersey	Dec. 26, 1776	American victory
	Princeton, New Jersey	Jan. 3, 1777	American victory
	Brandywine Creek, Pennsylvania	Sept. 11, 1777	British victory (opened way for British to take Philadelphia)
	Saratoga, New York	Sept. 19 and Oct. 17, 1777	American victory (helped persuade France to form an alliance with United States)
	Monmouth Court House, New Jersey	June 28, 1778	Contested
The War on the Frontier	Wyoming Valley, Pennsylvania	June and July 1778	British victory
	Kaskaskia and Cahokia, Illinois; Vincennes, Indiana	July 4, 1778– Feb. 23, 1779	American victories strengthen claims to Mississippi Valley
	Cherry Valley, New York	Nov. 11, 1778	British victory
The War in the South	Savannah, Georgia	Dec. 29, 1778	British victory (took control of Georgia)
	Kettle Creek, Georgia	Feb. 14, 1779	American victory
	Savannah, Georgia	Sept. 3– Oct. 28, 1779	British victory opened way for British to take Charleston
	Charleston, South Carolina	Feb. 11– May 12, 1780	British victory
	Camden, South Carolina	Aug. 16, 1780	British victory
	Kings Mountain, South Carolina	Oct. 7, 1780	American victory
	Cowpens, South Carolina	Jan. 17, 1781	American victory
	Guilford Court House, North Carolina	Mar. 15, 1781	Contested
	Yorktown, Virginia	Aug. 30– Oct. 19, 1781	American victory (persuaded Britain to end the war)

feelings. And Clinton's decision to force former rebels into the loyalist militia backfired, infuriating real loyalists—who saw their enemies getting off lightly—as well as Whigs. Atrocities and reprisals mounted on both sides.

American Counterattacks

In 1780, after a complete rout of General Horatio Gates's forces near Camden, South Carolina. American morale revived when "over mountain men" (militia) from Virginia, western North and South Carolina, and what is today eastern Tennessee inflicted a defeat on the British at **Kings Mountain**, South Carolina, and Nathanael Greene replaced the discredited Gates, bringing competent leadership to the Continentals in the South. The resourceful Greene realized he would need an unorthodox strategy to defeat Cornwallis's larger army of seasoned professional troops. He divided his forces, keeping roughly half with him in northeastern South Carolina and sending the other half westward under General Daniel Morgan. At the **Battle of Cowpens** on January 17, 1781, Morgan cleverly posted his least reliable troops, the militia, in the front line, telling them to run after firing two volleys. When Tarleton attacked, the militia fired and withdrew. Thinking that the American ranks had broken, the Redcoats charged—straight into devastating fire from Morgan's Continentals. Tarleton escaped, but his reputation for invincibility had been destroyed.

Cornwallis now badly needed a battlefield victory. Burning his army's excess baggage, he set off in hot pursuit of Greene and Morgan, who had rejoined forces. The Continentals had the advantage of knowing the country, which was laced with rain-swollen rivers. Finally, on February 13, 1781, Greene's tired men crossed the Dan River into Virginia, and Cornwallis gave up the chase, marching his equally exhausted Redcoats southward. To his surprise, Cornwallis now found himself pursued—though cautiously, to be sure—by Greene. On March 15, the opposing forces met at **Guilford Court House** (near present-day Greensboro, North Carolina) in one of the war's bloodiest battles.

By the late summer of 1781, British fortunes were waning in the Lower South. The Redcoats held only the larger towns and the immediately surrounding countryside. With their superior staying power, they won most major engagements, but these victories brought them no lasting gain. As General Greene observed of the Americans, "We fight, get beat, and rise and fight again." Patriot guerrilla forces, led by such colorful figures as "Swamp Fox" Francis Marion, disrupted British communications between their Charleston headquarters and outlying garrisons. The loyalist militias that the British had hoped would pacify the countryside proved unequal to the task. Although Greene never whipped the Redcoats outright, his campaign was a strategic success. The British could not hold what they had taken; the Americans had time on their side. Frustrated, Cornwallis decided to conquer Virginia to cut off Greene's supplies and marched north to Yorktown, Virginia, during the summer of 1781.

The final military showdown of the war was at hand at Yorktown, Virginia. By now, five thousand French soldiers were in America ready to fight alongside the Continentals, and a large French fleet in the West Indies had orders to support an attack on the British in North America. Faking preparations for an assault on British-occupied New York, the Continentals (commanded by Washington) and the French headed for the Chesapeake. Cornwallis and his six thousand Redcoats soon found themselves besieged behind their fortifications at **Yorktown** by 8,800 Americans and 7,800 French. A French naval victory gave the allies temporary command of the waters around Yorktown. Cornwallis had nowhere to go, and Clinton—still in New York—could not reinforce him quickly enough. On October 19, 1781, the British army surrendered.

The American Victory, 1782–1783

The British surrender at Yorktown marked the end of major fighting in North America, though skirmishes continued for another year. But the majority in Parliament now felt that enough men and money had been wasted trying to keep the Americans within the empire. In March 1782, the king accepted Lord North's resignation and appointed Lord Rockingham as prime minister, with a mandate to make peace.

The Peace of Paris

The peace negotiations, which took place in Paris, were lengthy. The Americans demanded independence, handsome territorial concessions—Franklin, the senior American negotiator, asked for all of Canada—and access to the rich, British-controlled fishing grounds in the North Atlantic. The new British prime minister, Lord Shelburne (Rockingham had died in 1782), was inclined to be conciliatory, hoping to help British merchants recover their lost colonial trade.

The American negotiators, Franklin, John Adams, and John Jay, masterfully threaded their way

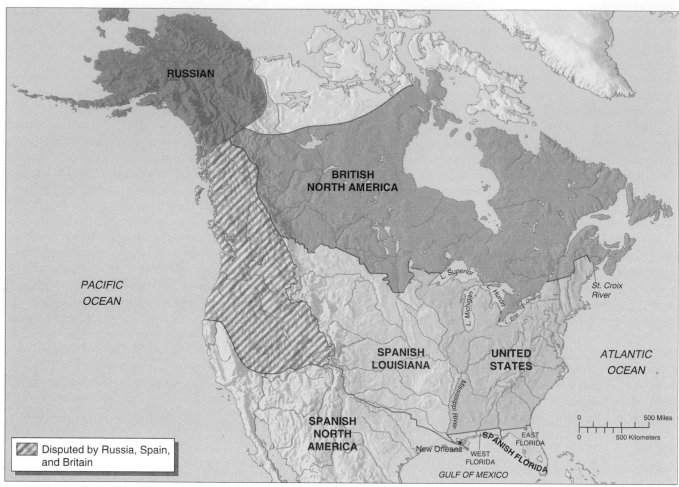

Map 6-6   North America after the Peace of Paris, 1783
The results of the American Revolution redrew the map of North America, confining Britain to Canada and giving the United States most of the area east of the Mississippi River, though Spain controlled its mouth for most of the next twenty years.

among the conflicting interests of the Americans, British, French, and Spanish. With good reason, they feared that the French and Spanish would strike a bargain with the British at the expense of the United States. As a result, the Americans disregarded Congress's instructions to avoid making peace unilaterally. Instead, they secretly worked out their own arrangements with the British that would meet Shelburne's objective of restoring Anglo-American commercial ties. On November 30, 1782, the negotiators signed a preliminary Anglo-American treaty of peace. Its terms were embodied in the final **Peace of Paris**, signed by all the belligerents on September 3, 1783.

The Peace of Paris gave the United States nearly everything it sought except Canada (which was never really a serious issue). Great Britain acknowledged that the United States was "free, sovereign and independent." The northern boundary of the new

nation extended west from the St. Croix River (which separated Maine from Nova Scotia) past the Great Lakes to what were thought to be the headwaters of the Mississippi River (see Map 6-6). The Mississippi itself—down to just north of New Orleans—formed the western border. Spain acquired the provinces of East and West Florida from Britain. This territory included a substantial chunk of present-day Louisiana, Mississippi, Alabama, and Georgia. It blocked the United States from access to the Gulf of Mexico and would be a source of diplomatic friction for years.

Several provisions of the treaty addressed important economic issues. Adams, on behalf of his fellow New Englanders, insisted on a provision granting American fishermen access to the waters off eastern Canada. The treaty also required that British forces, on quitting American soil, were to leave behind all American-owned property, including slaves. Another provision declared existing debts between citizens of Britain and the United States still valid, giving British merchants hope of collecting on their American accounts. Congress was to "recommend" that the states restore rights and property taken from loyalists during the war. Nothing was said about the slave trade, which Jay had hoped to ban.

The Components of Success

The War for Independence was over. In December 1783, the last British transports put to sea with troops evacuated from New York. Despite the provisions of the peace treaty and the objections of southern planters, about three thousand African-Americans went with them. Washington's Continental Army had already disbanded in the summer of 1783 (but not, as we have seen, before a dispute over pay came close to provoking a military coup). The American commander said an emotional farewell to his officers at New York City's Fraunces Tavern, resigned his commission to Congress, and like the legendary citizen-soldier Cincinnatus, who after defending the ancient Roman Republic gave up his power and went back to plowing his land, went home to Mount Vernon.

Washington's leadership was only one of the reasons why the Americans won the Revolutionary War. French assistance played a crucial role. Some historians even contend that without the massive infusion of French men and money in 1781, the Revolution would have failed. The British also contributed heavily to their own downfall. Their fatal mistakes included bureaucratic inefficiency, hesitant command, and, worst of all, overconfidence.

Yet it took 175,000 to 200,000 soldiers—Continentals and militia troops—to prevent Great Britain from recovering the colonies. Of these, some 7,000—like the nameless soldier recalled at the beginning of this chapter—died in battle for their "country and for its just cause." Those who served in the Continental Army, probably more than half of all who fought, served the longest and saw the most action. Their casualty rate—30 to 40 percent—may have been the highest of any war in which the United States has been engaged.

War and Society, 1775–1783

Regular combatants were not the only ones to suffer during the struggle for independence. Eight years of warfare also produced profound dislocations throughout American society. Military service wrenched families apart, and everyone endured economic disruptions. As a forge of nationhood, the Revolution tested all Americans, whatever their standing as citizens.

The Women's War

Everywhere women had to see their husbands, sons, brothers, and fiancés go off to fight and die. Like Mary Silliman in Connecticut, they waited, trying to stay calm until they knew "what tidings God" had for them. At first, with spirits still running high, Mary's letters to her husband, Selleck, reveal an affectionate lightheartedness. Later the couple's letters grew less playful. Then her husband was captured. The daily round of domestic duties helped to keep her going, but his extended absence increased her burdens and enlarged her responsibilities. Such circumstances elevated women's domestic status. Women also assumed new public roles during the conflict. Some nursed the wounded. More wove cloth for uniforms. The Ladies' Association of Philadelphia was established in 1780 to demonstrate women's patriotism and raise money to buy shirts for the army. Similar associations formed in other states.

Despite their increasing private responsibilities and new public activities, it did not occur to most women to encroach very far on traditional male prerogatives. When John Adams's wife, Abigail, urged him and the Second Continental Congress to "Remember the Ladies," she was not expecting equal political rights. What she wanted, rather, was some legal protections for women and recognition of their value and need for autonomy in the domestic sphere.

Republican ideology, responding to the changing status of women, assigned them a role that was at once exalted and subordinate. It was their job to nurture wise, virtuous, and public-spirited men. It would be this view of women that would prevail in the post-Revolutionary era.

Effect of the War on African-Americans and Native Americans

In the northern states, where slavery was already economically marginal and where blacks were welcome as volunteers in the Continental Army, the Revolutionary War helped bring an end to slavery, although it remained legal there for some time (see Chapter 7). In the South, however, slavery was integral to the economy, and white planters viewed it as crucial to their postwar recovery, so the war ultimately strengthened the institution, especially in the Carolinas and Georgia. Of the African-Americans who left with the British at the end of the war, many, both slave and free, went to the West Indies. Others settled in Canada, and some eventually went back to Africa, where Britain established the colony of Sierra Leone for them.

Survivors among the approximately thirteen thousand Native Americans who fought for the British did not have the option of leaving with them at the end of the war. How many died during the war is not known, but certainly many did. Their families and their communities also paid a high price. The Americans repeatedly invaded the Cherokees' homeland in the southern Appalachian Mountains and ravaged the Iroquois country in western New York.

With the peace treaty of 1783, Britain surrendered its territory east of the Mississippi, shocking and infuriating the Native Americans living there. They had not surrendered, and none of them had been at the negotiations in Paris. With the Americans now claiming their country by conquest, the Revolutionary War was a disaster for most Native Americans.

Economic Disruption

The British and American armies both needed enormous quantities of supplies. This heavy demand disrupted the normal distribution of goods and drove up real prices seven- or eightfold. The widespread use of depreciating paper money by the American side amplified this rise in prices and triggered severe inflation. By March 1780, Congress was forced to admit officially that the continental was worthless. (The popular expression "not worth a continental" suggests that the public had long since reached this conclusion.)

Necessity, not folly, drove Congress and the states to rely on the printing press. Rather than alienate citizens by immediately raising taxes to pay for the war, the states printed paper money supposedly redeemable by future tax revenues. Because the quantity of this paper money rose faster than the supply of goods and services, prices skyrocketed and the value of the money plunged. Savvy people tried to spend money before its value could drop further, whereas those who had salable commodities like grain tended to hoard them in the hope that the price would go even higher. The rampant inflation was demoralizing and divisive. Lucky speculators and unscrupulous profiteers grew rich while ordinary and patriotic people suffered. These conditions sparked more than thirty protest demonstrations. As usual, war and its deprivations brought out both the best and the worst in human nature.

The successful outcome of the war and the stable peace that followed suggest that most Americans somehow managed to cope. But during the last years of the conflict, their economic and psychological reserves ran low. The total real wealth of private individuals declined by an average of 0.5 percent annually from 1774 to 1805, even with the returning prosperity of the 1790s. Such statistics suggest the true economic cost of the War for Independence. And the atrocities committed on both sides provide nearly as accurate an indicator of the conflict's psychological cost.

Conclusion

Despite the devastation and divisiveness of the war, many people in Europe and the United States were convinced that it represented something momentous. The *Annual Register,* an influential British magazine reflecting respectable opinion, commented accurately in 1783 that the American Revolution

has already overturned those favourite systems of policy and commerce, both in the old and in the new world, which the wisdom of the ages, and the power of the greatest nations, had in vain endeavored to render permanent; and it seems to have laid the seeds of still greater revolutions in the history and mutual relations of mankind.

Americans, indeed, had fired a shot heard round the world. Thanks in part to its heavy investment in the American Revolution, France suffered a grave financial crisis in the late 1780s. This in turn ushered in the political crisis that culminated in the French Revolution of 1789.

Once prosperous but distant provinces of a far-flung empire, the North American states had become an independent confederation, a grand experiment in republicanism whose fate mattered to enlightened men and women throughout the Western world. In his written farewell to the rank and file of his troops at the end of October 1783, Washington maintained that "the enlarged prospects of happiness, opened by the confirmation of our independence and sovereignty, almost exceed the power of description." He urged those who had fought with him to maintain their "strong attachments to the union" and "prove themselves not less virtuous and useful as citizens, than they have been persevering and victorious as soldiers." The work of securing the promise of the American Revolution, Washington knew, would now shift from the battlefield to the political arena.

Review Questions

1. Who were the loyalists, and how many of them were there? What attempts did the British and Americans make in 1775 to avert war? Why did these steps fail?

2. What actions did the Second Continental Congress take in 1775 and 1776? Why did it choose George Washington as the commander of its army? Why was he a good choice?

3. Why did Congress declare independence in July 1776? How did Americans justify their claim to independence?

4. What was republicanism, and why was the enthusiasm that it inspired insufficient to win the war?

5. What were the chief characteristics of the British and American armies?

6. Why were most of the early battles fought in the northern states? Why did the British not crush the Americans immediately? Why did France decide to enter the war as an ally of the United States? What effect did French entry into the war have on British strategy?

7. Why did the initial British victories in the South not win the war for them? Why did the United States ultimately win? What did it obtain by winning?

8. What were the effects of the war on American society? What impact did it have on the status of women? On the lives of African-Americans? Native Americans? What was the price of victory—for the victors and for the vanquished? What were the immediate results of the American victory?

Recommended Reading

Joy D. Buel and Richard Buel Jr., *The Way of Duty: A Woman and Her Family in Revolutionary America* (1984). This is a readable and unusually full biography of Mary Fish of Connecticut, who lived from 1736 to 1818. Her experiences during the Revolutionary War while her husband, Selleck Silliman, was a prisoner of the British have become the subject of a good movie, *Mary Silliman's War* (1993).

John C. Dann, ed., *The Revolution Remembered: Eyewitness Accounts of the War for Independence* (1980). This collection of seventy-nine narratives by veterans seeking pensions for their Revolutionary War service is sometimes poignant and frequently illuminating.

John S. Pancake, *1777, the Year of the Hangman* (1977). This lively account of Britain's blunders in a crucial year of the war is full of good anecdotes even if it cannot always explain the behavior of decision makers.

Russell F. Weigley, *The Partisan War: The South Carolina Campaign of 1780–1782* (1970). This short, stimulating account of the American recovery of the Lower South takes "the perspective of our recent insights into unconventional war" and the communist victory in Vietnam.

Where to Learn More

❖ **Independence National Historical Park, Philadelphia, Pennsylvania.** Independence Hall, where Congress adopted the Declaration of Independence, is the most historic building in Philadelphia.

❖ **Kings Mountain National Military Park and Cowpens National Battlefield, South Carolina.** Situated approximately 20 miles apart, these were the sites of two battles in October 1780 and January 1781 that turned the tide of the war in the South. Both have museums and exhibits.

❖ **Minute Man National Historical Park, Lexington and Concord, Massachusetts.** There are visitors' centers at both Lexington and Concord with explanatory displays. Visitors may also follow the self-guided Battle Road Automobile Tour.

❖ **Saratoga National Historical Park, New York.** The park preserves and commemorates the American victory that led to French entry into the war. There is a museum with artifacts from the battlefield. Both the explanatory displays and the topography of the area make this an especially illuminating site.

❖ **Valley Forge National Historical Park, Valley Forge, Pennsylvania.** Reconstructed huts convey a sense of life in the Continental Army camp at Valley Forge during the hard winter of 1777–1778.

❖ **Yorktown Battlefield, Colonial National Historical Park, Yorktown, Virginia.** The park commemorates the great American victory here. Innovative exhibits enable visitors to follow the course of the war from a multicultural perspective.

7 THE FIRST REPUBLIC
1776–1789

KEY TOPICS

❖ Republicanism and the political philosophy of the new state constitutions
❖ Internal problems in the United States under the Articles of Confederation
❖ Efforts of Britain and Spain to exploit the weaknesses of the United States after the Revolution
❖ The movement for a stronger national government
❖ The drafting and ratification of the United States Constitution

"*I*nstead of a due reverence to authority, and submission to government . . . have you not endeavored . . . to overturn all government and order, to shake off all restraints, human and divine, to give up yourselves wholly to the power of the most restless, malevolent, destructive, tormenting passion?" With these harsh words, Chief Justice William Cushing of Massachusetts denounced the debt-ridden farmers who had taken up arms against the state government—and the merchants and creditors who controlled it.

Daniel Shays, a former captain in the Continental Army, led the rebels. **Shays's Rebellion** was a protest against legislative policies that had saddled them with high taxes, the possible loss of their farms when they couldn't pay their taxes or other debts, and blocked of an increase in currency that would have provided economic relief. State forces stamped out Shays's Rebellion early in 1787, but it sparked similar protest in other states, convincing many Americans that the republic stood on the brink of lawlessness.

Shays's Rebellion dramatized the ideological, social, and economic ferment of America's first republic. The rebellion underscored the difference in the meanings that newly independent Americans attributed to the concept of liberty. Conservatives—mainly large landowners, wealthy merchants and lawyers, and men of high social standing—equated liberty with the right of the individual to amass wealth and property. They sought a society founded on the rule of law and contract that would provide a stable foundation for an expanding economy. Ordinary farmers, artisans, and small producers, in contrast, defined liberty more in terms of the traditional right of communities to defend their interests against the threat of elite groups. Denounced as radicals by their opponents, the Shaysites viewed themselves as the true conservatives, the preservers of republican liberties won in the Revolution.

During the Revolutionary War, the states had engaged in an unprecedented period of constitution writing. In 1781, they ratified the Articles of Confederation, the first attempt at a political union of the states. The years that followed were a period of trial and error marked by a running debate over the meaning of liberty and the extent of power that could safely be entrusted to a national government. Regional conflicts and economic problems like those that sparked Shays's Rebellion emerged, and the nation found itself caught between the need for more central power and the desire of states to protect their sovereignty. By the end of the 1780s, influential leaders favoring a strong national government had lost confidence in the Articles of Confederation and began working to replace them. They succeeded with the enactment and ratification of the Constitution of the United States in 1788, bringing an end to America's first republic under the Confederation government.

The New Order of Republicanism

As royal authority collapsed during the Revolution, various provincial congresses and committees assumed power in each of the former colonies. The Continental Congress, seeking to build support for the war effort, was concerned that these new institutions should have a firm legal and popular foundation. In May 1776, the Congress called on the colonies to form new state governments "under the authority of the people."

This call reflected the political philosophy of republicanism that animated the Revolution (see Chapter 6). To Americans, republicanism meant that legitimate political authority derives from the people. The people are sovereign and should elect the officials who govern them; those officials should represent the people's interests. Another key aspect of republicanism was the revolutionary idea that the people could define and limit governmental power through written constitutions.

Defining the People

When news of the peace treaty with Britain reached New Bern, North Carolina, in June 1783, the citizens held a grand celebration. As reported by Francisco de Miranda, a visiting Spanish officer, "There was a barbecue [a roast pig] and a barrel of rum, from which the leading officials and citizens of the region promiscuously drank with the meanest and lowest kind of people, holding hands and drinking from the same cup.

For Miranda, this boisterous mingling of all citizens as seeming equals confirmed the republican belief that the people were sovereign. But republicanism also taught that political rights should be limited to property owners, as informed political judgment required economic self-sufficiency. This precept restricted political participation to propertied white men. Virtually everyone else—propertyless white men, servants legally bound to others, women, blacks (most free blacks and all slaves), and Native Americans—was denied political rights during the Revolutionary era.

Some 60 to 85 percent of adult white men owned property and could participate in politics—a far higher proportion than elsewhere in the world of the eighteenth century. The greatest concentration of the remaining 25 percent or so shut out of the political process were unskilled laborers and mariners living in port cities. In Philadelphia, for example, half the population of taxable adult men and women in the 1780s reported no taxable property. The city's working poor still included indentured servants, bound by contract to give personal service for a fixed time, as well as the walking poor—vagrants and transients.

The Revolution did little to change the traditional patriarchal assumption that politics and public life should be the exclusive domain of men. Women, according to republican beliefs, were dependent under the control of their husbands and fathers. Under common law (the customary, largely unwritten law that Americans had inherited from Britain), women surrendered their property rights at marriage. Legally and economically, husbands had complete control over their wives. As a result, argued Theophilus Parsons of Massachusetts in 1778, women were, as a matter of course, "so situated as to have no wills of their own."

CHRONOLOGY

1776 States begin writing the first constitutions.

1777 Articles of Confederation proposed.

1781 Articles ratified.

1783 Americans celebrate independence and the peace treaty with Britain.

1784 Onset of the postwar depression.
Spain closes the Mississippi.
Separatist plots in the West.
Treaty of Fort Stanwix.

1785 Land Ordinance of 1785.
States begin to issue more paper money.
Treaty of Fort McIntosh.

1786 Shays's Rebellion breaks out.
Jay-Gardoqui Treaty defeated.
Annapolis Convention.

1787 Constitutional Convention at Philadelphia.
Northwest Ordinance.

1788 Constitution ratified and goes into effect.
Publication of *The Federalist*.

To be sure, some women saw in the political and social enthusiasm of the Revolution an opportunity to protest the most oppressive features of their subordination. "I won't have it thought that because we are the weaker sex as to bodily strength we are capable of nothing more than domestic concerns," wrote Eliza Wilkinson of South Carolina. Men, she lamented, "won't even allow us liberty of thought and that is all I want." But most women accepted the view that their proper place was in the home with their families. Only the New Jersey constitution of 1776 defined **suffrage**—the right to vote—in gender-free terms, extending it to all propertied adults "worth fifty pounds," until 1807, when the state legislature changed its constitution.

The Revolution had a more immediate impact on the lives of many African-Americans. Revolutionary principles of liberty and equality and evangelical notions of human fellowship convinced many whites for the first time to challenge black slavery. In 1784, Virginia Methodists condemned slavery as "contrary to the Golden Law of God on which hang all the Laws and Prophets, and the unalienable Rights of Mankind, as well as every Principle of Revolution." Blacks seized opportunities for freedom that emerged from some whites' rejection of slavery, the disruptions of the war, and the needs of both sides for military manpower. As the number of free blacks increased from a few thousand at mid-century to 100,000 by 1800, African-American communities and cultures also expanded and developed.

Upwards of fifty thousand slaves, or one in ten of those in bondage, gained their freedom as a result of the war. One route was through military service, which generally carried a promise of freedom.

When the British began raising black troops, the Americans followed suit. All of the states except Georgia and South Carolina recruited black regiments. Some five thousand blacks served in the Continental armies, and they, like their counterparts in British units, were mostly slaves. Most slaves who gained freedom during the war, however, were those who fled their owners and made their way to the port cities of the North.

By making slave property generally less secure, the Revolution encouraged many masters to free their slaves. Once freed, blacks tried to break all the bonds of their former servitude. As the number of free blacks increased, those still enslaved grew bolder in their efforts to gain freedom. "Henny," warned a Maryland slaveowner in 1783, "will try to pass for a free woman as several have lately been set free in this neighbourhood."

If the control mechanisms of slavery experienced some strain in the South during the Revolution, in the North, where slaves were only a small percentage of the population, they crumbled. Most northern states ended slavery between 1777 and 1784. New York followed in 1799 and New Jersey in 1804. Although a majority of northern whites now agreed that slavery was incompatible with the Revolution's commitment to **natural rights** (the inherent human rights to life and liberty), they refused to sanction an immediate emancipation. The laws ending slavery in most of the northern states called only for the children of slaves to be freed, and only when they reached adulthood.

Although black males were allowed to vote if they met the property qualifications, most were poor and held little property. They faced discrimination

Sweeping chimneys, a dirty, dangerous job, was one of the few employment opportunities open to northern free blacks in the early republic.

in jobs and housing, were barred from juries, and were denied a fair share of funds for schools. With the help of the small class of property holders among them, they began establishing their own churches and self-help associations.

The impact of the Revolution on Native Americans was almost entirely negative (see Chapter 6). Most stayed neutral during the war or fought for the British. Just as the Americans sought to shake off British control, so the Indians—especially the western tribes and most of the Iroquois Confederation—sought to free themselves from American dominance. Thus British defeat deprived the Indians of a valuable ally and exposed them to the wrath of the victorious patriots. "The minds of these people appear as much agitated as those of the unhappy Loyalists," observed a British officer late in the war of the pro-British southern Indians; "they have very seriously proposed to abandon their country and accompany us [in an evacuation], having made all the world their enemies by their attachment to us."

After the Revolution, the state governments, and the Confederation Congress, now treated Indian lands as a prize of war to be distributed to white settlers. Even the few tribes that had furnished troops for the American cause lost control over most of their homelands. White Americans did not consider Native Americans to be part of their republican society. With the exception of Massachusetts, the states denied voting and legal rights to the Indians.

The State Constitutions

"Oppose everything that leans to aristocracy, of power in the hands of the rich and chief men exer-

cised to the oppression of the poor." So the voters of Mecklenburg County, North Carolina, instructed their delegates to the state's constitutional convention in 1776.

New state constitutions, ten of which were in place by 1777, were written documents, a striking departure from the English practice of treating a constitution as a collection of customary rights and practices that had evolved over time. In the American view, a constitution was a codification of the powers of government and the rights of citizenship that functioned as a fundamental law to which all public authority was held accountable. Annual elections were now the norm for governors, who were also made subject to **impeachment**—charges of misconduct, resolved at a public trial—and limited in the number of terms they could serve. Most important, for it struck at what patriots felt was the main source of executive domination and corruption, governors lost control over **patronage**, the power to appoint executive and judicial officials.

As the new constitutions curbed the power of governors, they increased that of the legislatures, making them the focal point of government. Colonial assemblies had been in the forefront of popular opposition to British authority; and the state legislatures that succeeded them were now seen as the most trustworthy defenders of individual liberty. The new constitutions expanded the power of the legislatures to appoint officials and to oversee military and financial matters. To make the legislatures more expressive of the popular will, the new constitutions included provisions that lowered property requirements for voting and officeholding, mandated annual elections,

American Views

A FRENCH OBSERVER DESCRIBES A NEW SOCIETY

In 1782, J. Hector St. John Crèvecoeur, a Frenchman who had lived and traveled in British North America, published his impressions of America. The following selection from his *Letters from an American Farmer* captures the striking optimism and sense of newness that he found. More so than any other literary work, the *Letters* stamped the new American republic, especially in the minds of Europeans, as the home of the world's freest and most equal people.

❖ **What is Crèvecoeur's image of America? Do you believe it was overly optimistic?**

❖ **Why does Crèvecoeur put such emphasis on the absence of titles and great disparities of wealth?**

❖ **Just what was so *new* about America to Crèvecoeur?**

❖ **Why did Crèvecoeur ignore African slaves in his definition of the American? What happened to Native Americans in his account of the making of the American?**

I wish I could be acquainted with the feelings and thoughts which must agitate the heart and present themselves to the mind of an enlightened Englishman when he first lands on this continent. . . . He is arrived on a new continent; a modern society offers itself to his contemplation, different from what he had hitherto seen. It is not composed, as in Europe, of great lords who possess everything and of a herd of people who have nothing. Here are no aristocratical families, no courts, no kings, no bishops, no ecclesiastical dominion, no invisible power giving to a few a very visible one, no great manufactures employing thousands, no great refinements of luxury. The rich and the poor are not so far removed from each other as they are in Europe. Some few towns excepted, we are all tillers of the earth, from Nova Scotia to West Florida. We are a people of cultivators scattered over an immense territory, communicating with each other by means of good roads and navigable rivers, united by the silken bands of mild government, all respecting the laws without dread-

---

increased the number of seats in the legislatures, and made representation more proportional to the geographical distribution of population. Upper houses were made independent of the executive office and opened to popular election as opposed to the colonial practice of having their members appointed by the governor.

Americans knew that legislatures, too, could act tyrannically. So in a final check on arbitrary power, each state constitution eventually included some form of a **bill of rights** that set explicit limits on the power of government to interfere in the lives of citizens. The Virginia Declaration of Rights, written by the planter George Mason and adopted in June 1776, set the precedent for this notable republican feature. By 1784, the constitutions of all thirteen states had provisions guaranteeing religious liberty, freedom of the press, and a citizen's right to such fair legal practices as trial by jury.

The new constitutions weakened but did not always sever the traditional tie between church and state for the support of religion. Many Americans held, as the Massachusetts Constitution of 1780 put it, that "the happiness of a people, and the good order and preservation of civil government, essentially depend upon piety, religion, and morality." Many states, notably in New England, levied taxes for the support of religion. The states of New England ing their power, because they are equitable. We are all animated with the spirit of an industry which is unfettered and unrestrained, because each person works for himself. . . . A pleasing uniformity of decent competence appears throughout our habitations. The meanest of our log-houses is a dry and comfortable habitation. Lawyer and merchant are the fairest titles our towns afford; that of a farmer is the only appellation of the rural inhabitants of our country. It must take some time ere he can reconcile himself to our dictionary, which is but short in words of dignity and names of honour. . . . We have no princes for whom we toil, starve, and bleed; we are the most perfect society now existing in the world. Here man is free as he ought to be, nor is this pleasing equality so transitory as many others are. Many ages will not see the shores of our great lakes replenished with inland nations, nor the unknown bounds of North America entirely peopled. . . .

The next wish of this traveller will be to know whence came all these people. They are a mixture of English, Scotch, Irish, French, Dutch, Germans, and Swedes. From this promiscuous breed, that race now called Americans have arisen. . . .

What, then, is the American, this new man? He is either an European or the descendant of an European; hence that strange mixture of blood, which you will find in no other country. . . . *He* is an American, who, leaving behind him all his ancient prejudices and manners, receives new ones from the new mode of life he has embraced, the new government he obeys, and the new rank he holds. He becomes an American by being received in the broad lap of our Alma Mater. Here individuals of all nations are melted into a new race of men, whose labours and posterity will one day cause great changes in the world.

Source: J. Hector St. John Crèvecoeur, *Letters from an American Farmer and Sketches of Eighteenth-Century America*, ed. Albert E. Stone (1986), pp. 66–70.

also continued to maintain Congregationalism as the state-supported religion while allowing dissenting Baptists and Methodists to use funds from the compulsory religious taxes.

The mid-Atlantic states lacked the religious uniformity of New England. The region had several prominent denominations—Quaker, Episcopalian, Presbyterian, Dutch Reformed, and Lutheran—and none was able to dominate the others. This pluralism checked legislative efforts to impose religious taxes or designate any denomination as the **established church.** In the South, where many Anglican (or Episcopalian) clergymen had been Tories, the Anglican Church lost its former established status.

Although in general the executive lost power and the legislative gained power under the new state constitutions, the actual structure of each state government reflected the outcome of political struggles between radical and conservative republicans. The radicals wanted to open government to all male citizens. The conservatives, though they agreed that government had to be derived from the people, feared "mob rule" and wanted to limit government to an educated elite of substantial property holders. Most conservatives, like Jeremy Belknap of New Hampshire, thought that the people had to be "taught . . . that they are not able to govern themselves."

In South Carolina, where conservative planters gained the upper hand, the constitution mandated property qualifications that barred 90 percent of the state's white males from holding elective public office. In contrast, Pennsylvania's Scots-Irish farmers and Philadelphia artisans took charge and gave the vote to all free males who paid taxes and eliminated property qualifications for officeholding. In addition, the constitution concentrated power in a **unicameral** (single-house) **legislature,** eliminating both the office of governor and the more elite upper legislative house. The constitution's framers also required legislators to stand for election annually and barred them from serving more than four years out of seven.

The constitutions of the other states, although not as bold in their democratic reforms as Pennsylvania's, typically enhanced the political influence of ordinary citizens more than the constitution of South Carolina did. Unlike the colonial assemblies, the new **bicameral** (two-house) **legislatures** included many artisans and small farmers. This growing political equality was accompanied by demands that those in government be more responsive to the people. Summing up the prevailing American view, William Hooper of North Carolina wrote in 1776, "Rulers must be conceived as the creatures of the people, made for their use, accountable to them, and subject to removal as soon as they act inconsistent with the purposes for which they were formed."

The Articles of Confederation

Once the Continental Congress decided on independence in 1776, it needed to create a legal basis for a permanent union of the states. According to the key provision of the **Articles of Confederation** that Congress submitted to the states in November 1777, "Each State retains its sovereignty, freedom and independence, and every power, jurisdiction and right, which is not by this confederation expressly delegated to the United States, in Congress assembled." The effect was to create a loose confederation of autonomous states.

The powers the Articles of Confederation delegated to the central government were extremely limited. There were no provisions for a national judiciary or a separate executive branch of government. The Articles made Congress the sole instrument of national authority but restricted it with a series of constitutional safeguards that virtually eliminated any possibility that it could ever threaten the interests of the states. Each state had one vote in Congress, making each politically equal regardless of size

or population. State legislatures were to choose congressional delegations in annual elections, and delegates could serve only three years out of six. Delegates were to follow the instructions of their state legislatures and could be recalled at any time. Important measures, such as those dealing with finances or war and peace, required approval from a majority of nine state delegations. Amendments to the Articles of Confederation, including the levying of national taxes, required the unanimous consent of the states.

Congress had authority primarily in the areas of foreign policy and national defense. It could declare war, make peace, conduct foreign affairs, negotiate with Native Americans, and settle disputes between states. But it had no authority to raise troops or impose taxes. It could only ask the states to supply troops and money.

The central principle behind the Articles was the fear of oppressive, centralized power. Edward Rutledge, a delegate from South Carolina to the Continental Congress, argued that the new Confederation Congress was vested "with no more Power than is absolutely necessary." Residents of West Springfield, Massachusetts, in instructions to their congressional representatives in 1778 resolved: "It is *freedom,* & not a choice of the *forms of servitude* for which we contend."

Most states quickly ratified the Articles of Confederation. But because they needed the approval of all thirteen states, it was not until Maryland ratified the articles in 1781 that they officially took effect. What caused the delay was the demand of some states to give Congress a power not included in the Articles submitted for ratification in 1777.

The issue here concerned the unsettled lands in the West between the Appalachian Mountains and the Mississippi River. Some states claimed these lands by virtue of their colonial charter rights. The so-called landless states—those with no claim to the West—insisted that it be set aside as a reserve of public land. Land speculators, many of them leading politicians, who had purchased huge blocs of land from the Indians before the Revolution sided with the landless states. They expected Congress would be more likely to honor their land titles than the individual states.

The British threat to the Chesapeake area in early 1781 finally broke the impasse that had delayed final approval of the Articles. Though retaining control of Kentucky, Virginia gave up its claim in the west to a vast area extending north of the Ohio River. In turn, Maryland, now desperate for military aid from Congress, agreed to ratify the Articles.

Problems at Home

Neither prosperity nor political stability accompanied the return of peace in 1783. The national government struggled to avoid bankruptcy, and in 1784, an economic depression struck the country. As fiscal problems deepened over the next few years, creditor and debtor groups clashed angrily in state legislatures. The only solid accomplishment of the Confederation Congress during this troubled period was to formulate an orderly and democratic plan for the settlement of the West under national controls.

The Fiscal Crisis

The Continental Congress and the states incurred heavy debts to finance the Revolutionary War. Unable to impose and collect sufficient taxes to cover the debts and without reserves of gold or silver, they had little choice but to borrow funds and issue certificates or bonds pledging repayment. Congress had the largest responsibility for war debts. To do so it printed close to $250 million in paper notes backed only by its good faith. By the end of the war in 1781, these Continental dollars were nearly worthless, and the national debt stood at $11 million. As Congress issued new securities to settle claims by soldiers and civilians, this sum rose to $28 million in just a few years.

Congress never did put its tottering finances on a sound footing. Its fiscal problems ultimately discredited the Articles of Confederation to the **nationalists,** a loose bloc of congressmen, army officers, and public creditors who wanted to strengthen the Confederation at the expense of the states. The nationalists first began to organize in the dark days of 1780 and 1781 when inflation was rampant, the army was going unpaid, Congress had ceased paying interest on the public debt, and the war effort itself seemed in danger of collapsing. Galvanized by this crisis, the nationalists rallied behind Robert Morris, a Philadelphia merchant appointed as superintendent of finance for the Confederation government.

Morris sought to enhance national authority through a bold program of financial and political reform. He began by securing a charter from Congress in 1781 for the Bank of North America, the nation's first commercial bank. Morris wanted it to serve as a national institution, and he used it to hold government funds, make loans to the government, and issue bank notes—paper money that could be used to settle debts and pay taxes owed to the United States.

Morris temporarily brought order and economy to the nation's finances. Nonetheless, he was blocked in his efforts to gain the taxing power needed to restore the shattered credit of the Confederation government.

Morris's central nationalist objective was to create a "bond of union" by having Congress assume payment of the entire national debt. Once paid back, the people who had financed the war would identify their economic self-interest with the effective exercise of power by the national government.

To achieve this political goal, Morris had to gain for Congress what it had always lacked: the power to tax. In 1781, he proposed a national impost, or tariff, of 5 percent on imported goods. Because this was a national tax, it required an amendment to the Articles of Confederation and the consent of all thirteen states. Rhode Island—critically dependent on its own import duties to finance its war debt—was the only state to reject it. When a revised impost plan was considered two years later, New York blocked its passage. These failures doomed Morris's financial reforms. He left office in 1784.

The failure of the impost tax was one of many setbacks that put the nationalists temporarily on the defensive. With the conclusion of peace in 1783, confidence in state government returned. The states continued to balk at paying Congress and denied it even limited authority to regulate foreign commerce. Most ominously for the nationalist cause, the states began to assume responsibility for part of the national debt. By 1786, New Jersey, Pennsylvania, Maryland, and New York had absorbed one-third of the debt by issuing state bonds to their citizens in exchange for national securities. As Morris had warned in 1781, such a policy entailed "a principle of disunion . . . which must be ruinous."

Without the power to tax, Congress was a hostage to the sovereignty of the individual states with no real authority over the nation's economic affairs. When the economy plunged into a severe depression in 1784, it could only look on helplessly.

Economic Depression

During the Revolutionary War, Britain closed its markets to American goods. After the war, the British continued this policy, hoping to keep the United States weak and dependent. In the summer of 1783, they excluded Americans from the lucrative trade with the British West Indies. Before the Revolution, this trade in foodstuffs and timber with the sugar islands had been the primary means by which the colonists had built up the credits they needed to offset their British imports.

Meanwhile, British merchants were happy to satisfy America's pent-up demand for consumer goods after the war. A flood of cheap British imports inundated the American market, and coastal merchants sold them to inland traders and shopkeepers by extending easy credit terms. In turn, these local businessmen sold the goods to farmers and artisans in the interior. Ultimately, however, the British merchants required payment in hard currency, gold and silver coins. By now, America's only source of hard currency was foreign loans obtained by Congress and what money the French army had spent during the war. This was soon exhausted as America's **trade deficit** with Britain—the excess of imports over exports—ballooned in the early 1780s to £5 million.

The result was an immense bubble of credit that finally burst in 1784, triggering a depression that would linger for most of the rest of the decade. As merchants began to press debtors for immediate payment, prices collapsed (they fell more than 25 percent between 1784 and 1786), and debtors were unable to pay. The best most could hope for was to avoid bankruptcy.

Small farmers everywhere had trouble paying their taxes. In 1786, James Swan of Massachusetts wrote of farmers in his state: "There is no family that does not want some money for some purposes, and the little which the farmer carries home from market, must be applied to other uses, besides paying off the [tax] collector's bills." Rural shopkeepers often could not move goods unless they agreed to barter them for farm produce. Western Massachusetts storeowner Abigail Dwight reported in 1785 that "most of these People sell on credit for To-Morrow at large—for very little Cash stirring this way—to be pay'd for in old Horses—cows some Boards—cabbages—turnips—Potatoes etc."

Wages fell 25 percent between 1785 and 1789, and workers began to organize. They called for tariffs on British imports and for legislative measures to promote American manufacturers. Farmers faced a wave of lawsuits for the collection of debts and the dread possibility of losing their land. "To be *tenants* to *landlords,* we know not who," protested the farmers of Conway, Massachusetts, "and pay rent for lands, *purchased with our money,* and converted from howling *wilderness,* into fruitful fields, by the *sweat of our brows,* seems . . . truly shocking."

With insufficient money in circulation to raise prices and reverse the downturn, the depression fed on itself. Congress was powerless to raise cash and was unable to pay off its old debts, including what it owed to the Revolutionary soldiers. Many

state governments made things worse by imposing heavy taxes payable in the paper money they had issued during the Revolution. The result was further to reduce the amount of money in circulation, which increased deflationary pressures, forcing prices still lower.

No longer protected under the old Navigation Acts as British vessels, American ships were now barred from most ports in the British Empire. Cargoes from the West Indies to the regions fell off sharply, and the market for whale oil and fish, two of New England's major exports, dried up.

The economy of the mid-Atlantic region was stronger, but even there the loss of the provisioning trade to the British West Indies in grains, livestock, and dairy products cut into the income of merchants and farmers and forced layoffs among artisans who serviced the shipping trade.

In the southern states, British policies compounded the problem of recovering from the physical damage and labor disruptions inflicted by the war. Some 10 percent of the region's slaves had fled during the war, and production levels on plantations fell in the 1780s. Chesapeake planters needed a full decade to restore the prewar output of tobacco, and a collapse in tobacco prices in 1785 left most of them in the same chronic state of indebtedness that had plagued them on the eve of the Revolution.

Farther south, in the Carolina lowcountry, the plantation economy was crippled throughout the 1780s. Planters piled up debts to purchase additional slaves and repair their war-damaged plantations and dikes. In spite of these investments, rice production was slow to recover. Burdened by new British duties on American rice, planters saw their rice exports fall by 50 percent. Small farmers in the pine barrens of North Carolina likewise lost their formerly protected British market for naval stores—tar, pitch, and turpentine.

By the late 1780s, an economic upturn was under way in the mid-Atlantic states. Food exports to continental Europe were on the rise, and American merchants were developing new trading ties with India and China. Commercial treaties with the Dutch, Swedes, and Prussians also opened up markets that had been closed to the colonists. Nonetheless, a full recovery had to await the 1790s.

A stagnant economy and burdensome debt combined with a growing population (there were 50 percent more Americans in 1787 than there had been in 1775) to reduce living standards. With more losers than winners, economic conflict dominated the politics of the states during the Confederation period.

The Economic Policies of the States

Britain was an obvious target of popular anger over the economic depression. Merchants poorly positioned to adjust to the postwar dislocations of trade led a campaign to retaliate with duties on British ships and special taxes on their goods. Artisans and workers, especially in the North, pushed for tariffs on British goods to encourage domestic manufacturing and protect jobs and wages. Most northern states imposed anti-British measures. But these varied from state to state, limiting their impact and producing squabbles when goods imported in one state were shipped to another.

Shippers evaded high tariffs by bringing their cargoes in through states with no tariffs or less restrictive ones. States without ports, like New Jersey and North Carolina, complained of economic discrimination. When they purchased foreign goods from a neighboring shipping state, they were forced to pay part of the tariff cost, but all the revenue from the tariff accrued only to the importing state. James Madison neatly summarized the plight of these states: "New Jersey, placed between Philadelphia and New York, was likened to a cask tapped at both ends; And North Carolina, between Virginia and South Carolina, to a patient bleeding at both Arms."

Tariff policies also undermined efforts to confer on Congress the power to regulate commerce. The agrarian states of the South had different interests from the states of the North. With the exception of Virginia, they favored free trade policies that encouraged British imports. Southern planters took advantage of the low rates charged by British ships for transporting their crops to Europe, putting pressure on northern shippers to reduce their rates.

The bitterest divisions, however, were between debtors and creditors within states. As the value of debt securities dropped during the Revolutionary War, speculators bought them up for a fraction of their face value and then put pressure on the states to raise taxes and repay the debts in full in hard currency. Wealthy landowners and merchants likewise supported higher taxes and the rapid repayment of debts in hard currency. Arrayed against these creditor groups by the mid-1780s was a broad coalition of debtors comprised of middling farmers, small shopkeepers, artisans, laborers, and people who had overextended themselves speculating in western land. The debtors wanted the states to issue paper money that they could use instead of hard money—gold and silver—to pay their debts. The paper money would have an inflationary effect, raising wages and the prices of farm commodities and reducing the value of debts contracted in gold and silver.

This was the economic context in which Shays's Rebellion exploded in the fall of 1786. Farm foreclosures and imprisonments for failure to pay debts increased sharply in western Massachusetts. Farmers petitioned the state legislators for economic relief. They demanded legislation that would temporarily prohibit creditors from seizing farms and processing suits for debt. When the creditor and seaboard interests in the legislature refused to pass any relief measures, some two thousand farmers took up arms against the state government. They shut down the courts and hence the legal machinery for collecting debts in three counties in western Massachusetts. When they marched on the state arsenal in Springfield, alarmed state officials raised troops to crush the uprising.

Outside of western Massachusetts, discontented debtors generally were successful in changing the monetary policy of their states. In 1785 and 1786, seven states enacted laws for new paper money issues. In most cases, combined with laws that prevented or delayed creditors from seizing property from debtors to satisfy debts, the currency issues helped keep a lid on popular discontent.

Rhode Island was an exception to this pattern of fiscal responsibility. A rural party that gained control of the Rhode Island legislature in 1786 pushed through a currency law that flooded the state with paper money that could be used to pay all debts. Creditors who balked at accepting the new money at face value were subject to heavy penalties. Shocked, they went into hiding or left the state entirely, and merchants denounced the law as outright fraud.

The actions of the debtor party in Rhode Island alarmed conservatives everywhere. Now they were convinced that state legislatures dominated by farmers and artisans were dangerous. One South Carolina conservative declared that he could see nothing but an "open and outrageous . . . violation of every principle of justice" in paper money and debt relief laws. Conservatives, creditors, and nationalists alike now spoke of a democratic tyranny that would have to be checked if the republic were to survive and protect its property holders.

Congress and the West

The Treaty of Paris and the surrender of charter claims by the states gave Congress control of a magnificent expanse of land between the Appalachian Mountains and the Mississippi River. Congress set forth a series of effective provisions for the settlement and governance of this first American West and eventual absorption into the Union.

Asserting for the national government the right to formulate Indian policy, Congress negotiated a series of treaties with the Indians beginning in 1784 for the abandonment of their land claims in the West. By threatening to use military force, congressional commissioners in 1784 coerced the Iroquois Confederation of New York to cede half of its territory to the United States in the Treaty of Fort Stanwix. Similar tactics in 1785 resulted in the Treaty of Fort McIntosh in which the northwestern tribes ceded much of their land in Ohio. In opposition to states intent on grabbing Indian lands for themselves, Congress resolved in 1787 that its treaties were binding on all the states. Anxious for revenue, Congress insisted on payment from squatters who had filtered into the West before provisions for the land sales.

The most pressing political challenge was to secure the loyalty of the West to the new and fragile Union. To satisfy the demands of settlers for self-government, Congress resolved as early as 1779 that new states would be carved out of the western domain with all the rights of the original states. In the **Ordinance of 1784,** Thomas Jefferson proposed to create ten districts or territories, each of which could apply for admission as a state when its population equaled that of the free inhabitants in the least populous of the existing states. Jefferson also proposed that settlers be permitted to choose their own officials, and he called for the prohibition of slavery in the West after 1800. Shorn of its no-slavery features, the ordinance passed Congress but was never put into practice.

If it couldn't regulate land sales and pass on clear titles, Congress would, in effect, have surrendered its claim to govern. Congress had to act on national land policy, warned a western Pennsylvanian, or else "lose the only opportunity they ever will have of extending their power and influence over this new region." One way or another, settlers were going to get their land, but a pell-mell process of private acquisitions in widely scattered settlements threatened to touch off costly Indian wars, deprive the national government of vitally needed revenue, and encourage separatist movements.

Congress responded with the **Land Ordinance of 1785.** The crucial feature of this seminal legislation was its stipulation that public lands be surveyed in a rectangular grid pattern before being offered for sale (see Figure 7-1). By requiring that land first be plotted into townships of thirty-six uniform sections of 640 acres each, the ordinance adopted the New England system of land settlement, an approach that promoted compact settlements and produced undisputed land titles.

Congress offered the plots of 640 acres at the then hefty sum of no less than $640, or $1 per acre, payable in hard currency or its equivalent. The goal here was to keep out the shiftless poor and reserve the West for enterprising and presumably law-abiding farm families who could afford the entry cost. Congress also set aside the income from the sale of the sixteenth section in each township for the support of public schools. Support for education, as a congressional report of 1783 put it, would help provide for "security against the increase of feeble, disorderly and dispersed settlements in those remote and extended territories [and] against the depravity of manners which they have a tendency to produce."

Before any land sales occurred under the Ordinance of 1785, impatient settlers continued to push north of the Ohio River and claim homesteads as squatters. They clashed both with local Indian tribes and the troops sent by Congress to evict them. Impatient itself with the slow process of surveying, Congress sold off a million and a half acres to a group of New England speculators organized as the Ohio Company. The speculators bought the land with greatly depreciated loan office certificates that had been issued to Revolutionary War veterans, and their cost per acre averaged less than 10 cents in hard money. They now pressed their allies in Congress to establish a governmental structure for the West that would protect their investment by bringing the unruly elements in the West under control. The **Northwest Ordinance of 1787,** the most significant legislative act of the Confederation Congress, filled this need, creating a political structure for the territories and a phased process for achieving statehood that neatly blended public and private interests.

According to the ordinance, controls on a new territory were to be strictest in the early stage of settlement, when Congress would appoint a territorial government consisting of a governor, a secretary, and three judges. When a territory reached a population of five thousand adult males, those with 50 acres of land or more could elect a legislature. The actions of the legislature, however, were subject to an absolute veto by the governor. Once a territory had a population of sixty thousand, the settlers could draft a constitution and apply for statehood "on an

Figure 7-1   *Land Ordinance of 1785*
The precise uniformity of the surveying system initiated in the Land Ordinance of 1785 created a
rectangular grid pattern that was the model for all future land surveyed in the public domain.

equal footing with the original states in all respects
whatsoever."

The Northwest Ordinance of 1787 stipu-
lated that only three to five states were to be formed
out of the Northwest. This was because the admission of new states would weaken the original thirteen states' control over Congress. Although less
democratic in many respects than Jefferson's plan
in mandating a period of outside control by Congress, the 1787 ordinance did provide greater protection for property rights as well as a bill of rights
guaranteeing individual freedoms. Most significant,
it prohibited slavery.

Southern congressmen agreed to the slavery
ban in part because they feared that planters in the

new states would compete with them in the production of slave-produced staples such as tobacco. More
important, however, they expected slavery to be permitted in the region south of the Ohio River that was
still under the administrative authority of Virginia,
North Carolina, and Georgia in the 1780s. Indeed,
slavery was allowed in this region when the **Southwest
Ordinance of 1790** brought it under national control,
a decision that would have grave consequences in the
future sectionalization of the United States.

Although the Northwest Ordinance applied
only to the national domain north of the Ohio River,
it provided the organizational blueprint by which all
future territory was brought into the Union. It went
into effect immediately and set the original Union

on a course of dynamic expansion through the addition of new states.

Diplomatic Weaknesses

In the international arena of the 1780s, the United States was a weak and often ridiculed nation. Under the Articles of Confederation, Congress had the authority to negotiate foreign treaties but no economic or military power to enforce their terms. Unable to regulate commerce or set tariffs, it had no leverage with which to pry open the restricted trading empires of France, Spain, and most important, Britain.

France and the United States remained on friendly terms. The United States even had a favorable trade balance with France, selling more there than it bought. Both Britain and Spain, however, sought to block American expansion into the trans-Appalachian West. And a dispute with Spain over the West produced the most serious diplomatic crisis of the period, one that spilled over into domestic politics, increasing tensions between northern and southern states and jeopardizing the country's chances of survival.

Impasse with Britain

Key among those issues that poisoned Anglo-American relations in the 1780s were provisions in the peace treaty of 1783 that concerned prewar American debts to the British and the treatment of Loyalists by the patriots. To justify its own violations of the treaty, Britain claimed that America had failed to satisfy those provisions. The result was a diplomatic deadlock that hurt American interests in the West and in foreign trade.

Article 4 of the peace treaty called for the payment of all prewar debts at their "full value in sterling money"—that is, in hard currency. Many tobacco planters in the Chesapeake region of Virginia and Maryland had outstanding debts to British creditors. During the Revolution, the British army had carried off and freed many of the region's slaves without compensating the planters. Still angry, the planters were in no mood to repay their debts and agreed only to pay the face value of their debts to their state treasuries in state or Continental paper money, which was practically worthless.

During the Revolution, all the states had passed anti-Loyalist legislation. Many state governments had seized Loyalists' lands and goods, selling them to raise revenue for the war effort. Upwards of 100,000 Loyalists fled to Canada and England, and their property losses ran into millions of dollars. Articles 5 and 6 of the peace treaty pledged Congress to "recommend" to the states that they stop persecuting Loyalists and restore Loyalist property. But wartime animosities remained high, ebbing only gradually as the 1780s wore on. Despite the pleadings of John Jay, the secretary for foreign affairs in the Confederation government, the states were slow to rescind their punitive legislation or allow the recovery of confiscated property.

Unpaid debts and the continued failure of the states to make restitution to the Loyalists gave the British a convenient pretext to hold on to the forts in the West that they had promised to give up in the Treaty of Paris. Refusal to abandon the forts, from Lake Champlain in upstate New York and westward along the Great Lakes was part of a strategy to keep the United States weak, divided, and small. The continued British presence in the region shut Americans out of the fur trade with the Indians, insulted the sovereignty of the United States, and threatened the security of its northern frontier. In 1784, exasperated New Yorkers warned Congress that unless the British were forced to leave, New York would "be compelled to consider herself as left to pursue her own Councils, destitute of the Protection of the United States." Spurred on by Canadian officials, the British also encouraged secessionist movements in the Northwest and sought out Indian allies to fight for a possible buffer state south of the Great Lakes that would keep Americans hemmed in along the Atlantic seaboard.

In Vermont, politician brothers Ethan, Ira, and Levi Allen offered the British a treaty of friendship in exchange for recognition of Vermont's independence and trading privileges within the British Empire. The British declined for fear of unduly antagonizing the United States. In 1791, Vermont joined the Union as the fourteenth state.

American officials viewed Britain's retaliatory trade policies as the gravest threat to American security and prosperity. John Adams, the American minister to London, sought in vain to counter Britain's anti-American economic policies. "I may reason till I die to no purpose," Adams reported to Jay in June 1785, and he complained that he was treated as a complete "cypher."

Adams soon concluded that the British would never lift their trading and shipping restrictions until forced to do so by a uniform American system of discriminatory duties on British goods. However a uniform policy was impossible to achieve under the Articles of Confederation.

Spain and the Mississippi River

At the close of the Revolutionary War, Spain reimposed barriers on American commerce within its empire. Spain also refused to recognize the southern and western boundaries of the United States as specified in the treaty with Britain in 1783, holding out instead for a more northerly border. And of greatest consequence, it denied the claim of the United States to free navigation of the entire length of the Mississippi River. Only with access to the Mississippi and the commercial right of deposit at New Orleans—that is, the right to transfer cargoes to oceangoing vessels—could the region's farmers, then mostly in what would become Tennessee and Kentucky, profitably reach national and international markets.

In the wake of the Revolution, the settlers of Kentucky, which was still part of Virginia, and Tennessee, which was still part of North Carolina, flirted with the idea of secession. Spain sought to trade on the divided loyalties of American speculators and frontier settlers to its advantage, employing some of them as spies and informers. Spain likewise sought to exploit divisions among Indian groups.

Spain stepped up pressure on the West in the summer of 1784 when it closed the Mississippi River within Spanish territory to American trade. Hoping now to benefit from American weakness, Spain also opened negotiations for a long-term settlement with the United States. The Spanish negotiator, Don Diego de Gardoqui, offered John Jay, negotiating for the Americans, a deal that cleverly played the interests of the North against those of the South and West. In exchange for an American agreement to surrender claims to navigate the Mississippi for thirty years, Gardoqui proposed to grant the United States significant trading concessions in the Spanish Empire that would benefit the financially pressed merchants of the northeastern states. Jay reluctantly accepted the offer.

When Jay released the terms of the proposed treaty with Spain in 1786, Congress erupted in angry debate. Southerners, who had taken the lead in the settlement of the West, accused Jay of selling out their interests. The treaty threatened the agrarian alliance they hoped to forge with the West, and increased the odds that the West would break from the East and go its own way. Vowing that they would not surrender the West, southern congressmen united to defeat the treaty nine votes (states) to seven.

The regional antagonisms exposed by the Jay-Gardoqui talks heightened the alarm over the future of the republic provoked by Shays's Rebellion earlier in 1786. The Union had never appeared more fragile or Congress under the Articles of Confedera-

This portrait, sketched in about 1790 by John Trumbull, is the only known likeness of Alexander McGillivray, a Creek leader who effectively played off Spanish and American interests in the Southeast to gain a measure of independence for the Creeks in the 1780s.

tion so powerless to resolve its differences. As the sense of crisis deepened in 1786, the nationalists, led by Alexander Hamilton of New York and James Madison of Virginia, grew in influence and numbers.

Toward a New Union

In June 1786, a worried John Jay wrote to General George Washington that he was "uneasy and apprehensive; more so than during the war. Then we had a fixed object. . . . The case is now altered; we are going and doing wrong, and therefore I look forward to evils and calamities, but without being able to guess at the instrument, nature, or measure of them." Other nationalists fully shared Jay's pessimism. Everywhere they saw unsolved problems and portents of disaster: unpaid debts, social unrest, squabbling states, sectional hostilities, the uncertain status of the West, blocked channels of trade, foreign intrigues, and a paralyzing lack of centralized authority and purpose. They feared that the republic's very survival was now at stake.

In September 1786, delegates from several states met at the **Annapolis Convention,** in Annapolis, Maryland, seeking to devise a uniform system of commercial regulation for the country. While there, a group of nationalist leaders called on all the states to send delegates to a convention at Philadelphia "to devise such further provisions as shall appear to them necessary to render the constitution of the Federal Government adequate to the exigencies of the Union." The leaders who met at the **Constitutional Convention** in Philadelphia forged an entirely new framework of governance, the **Constitution of the United States,** that called for a federal republic with a powerful and effective national government. In 1788, after a close struggle in state ratifying conventions, the Constitution was adopted.

The Road to Philadelphia

The timing of the call for the Philadelphia Convention could not have been better. During the fall and winter of 1786, the agrarian protests unleashed by Shays's Rebellion in Massachusetts spilled over into other states. Coupled with talk of a dismemberment of the Union in the wake of the Jay-Gardoqui negotiations, the agrarian unrest strengthened the case of the nationalists for more centralized authority.

All the states except Rhode Island sent delegates to Philadelphia. The fifty-five men who attended the convention were chiefly lawyers by training or profession, most of them had served in the Confederation Congress, and more than one-third had fought in the Revolution. The delegates were members of an intellectual and political elite and were far wealthier than the average American. Most had investments in land and the public securities of the United States. At least nineteen owned slaves. Their greatest asset as a working body was their common commitment to a nationalist solution to the crisis of confidence they saw gripping the republic. Strong supporters of the Articles of Confederation mostly refused to attend, perhaps because, as Patrick Henry of Virginia remarked, they "smelt a rat."

The Convention at Work

Congress authorized only a revision of the Articles of Confederation. Almost from the start, however, the delegates at the Philadelphia Convention set about replacing the Articles altogether. Their first action was to elect George Washington unanimously as the convention's presiding officer, gaining credibility for their deliberations from his prestige. The most ardent nationalists then immediately seized the initiative by presenting the **Virginia Plan.** Drafted by James Madison, this plan replaced the Confederation Congress with a truly national government organized like most state governments, with a bicameral legislature, an executive, and a judiciary.

Two features of the Virginia Plan stood out. First, it granted the national Congress power to legislate "in all cases in which the separate states are incompetent" and to nullify any state laws that in its judgment were contrary to the "articles of Union." Second, it made representation in both houses of Congress proportional to population. This meant that the most populous states would have more votes in Congress than the less populous states, giving them effective control of the government. In short, Madison sought to all but eliminate the independent authority of the states while also forcing the smaller states to defer to the more populous ones in national affairs.

Delegates from the small states countered with the **New Jersey Plan,** introduced on June 15 by William Paterson. This plan kept intact the basic structure of the Confederation Congress—one state, one vote—but otherwise amended the Articles by giving the national government the explicit power to tax and to regulate domestic and foreign commerce. In addition, it gave acts of Congress precedence over state legislation.

The New Jersey Plan was quickly voted down, and the convention remained deadlocked for another month. The issue was finally resolved on July 16 with the so-called **Great Compromise.** Based on a proposal by Roger Sherman of Connecticut, the compromise split the differences between the small and large states. Small states were given equal footing with large states in the Senate, or upper house, where each would have two votes. In the lower house, the House of Representatives, the number of seats was made proportional to population, giving larger states the advantage. The Great Compromise also settled a sectional dispute over representation between the free (or about to be free) states and slave states. The southern states wanted slaves counted for apportioning representation in the House but excluded from direct tax assessments. The northern states wanted slaves counted for tax assessments but excluded for apportioning representation. The Great Compromise settled on an expedient, if morally troubling, formula: Free residents were to be counted precisely; to that count would be added three-fifths "of all other persons," excluding Indians not taxed. Thus the slave states gained additional political representation while the states in the North received assurances that the owners of nonvoting slaves would have to bear part of the cost of any direct taxes levied by the new government.

Next the convention debated the specific powers to be delegated to the new government. It was at this point that the sectional cleavage between North and South came to a head. As Madison had warned in late June, "the great division of interests" in the United States would arise from the effect of states "having or not having slaves."

The sectional clash first erupted over the power of Congress to regulate commerce. To prevent a northern majority from passing navigation acts favoring northern shippers, delegates from the Lower South demanded that a two-thirds majority be required to enact trade legislation. Suddenly, the central plank in the nationalists' program—the unified power to force trading concessions from Britain—was endangered. A frustrated Madison urged his fellow southerners to remember that "as we are laying the foundation of a great empire, we ought to take a permanent view of the subject."

In the end, Madison had his way; the delegates agreed that enacting trade legislation would require only a simple majority. In return, however, southerners exacted concessions on the slavery issue. The convention abandoned a proposal to ban the foreign slave trade. Instead, antislavery New Englanders reached a compromise with the delegates from the Lower South: Congress would be barred from acting against the slave trade for twenty years. In addition, bowing to the fears of planters that Congress could use its taxing power to undermine slavery, the convention denied Congress the right to tax exports from any state. And to alleviate southern concerns that slaves might escape to freedom in the North, the new Constitution included an explicit provision calling on any state to return "persons held to Service or Labour" in another.

After settling the slavery question in late August, the convention had one last significant hurdle to clear: the question of the national executive. But in early September, close to exhaustion after working through a long, hot summer, the delegates moved quickly to fashion a chief executive office with broad discretionary powers. The prerogatives of the president included the rank of commander in chief of the armed forces, the authority to conduct foreign affairs and negotiate treaties, the right to appoint diplomatic and judicial officers, and the power to veto congressional legislation. The president's term of office was set at four years, with no limits on how often an individual could be reelected. Nearly everyone expected Washington to be the first president.

The delegates envisioned a forceful, energetic, and independent executive insulated from the whims of an uninformed public and the intrigues of the legislature. They rejected both popular election and election by Congress. The solution they hit upon was the convoluted system of an "electoral college." Each state was left free to determine how it would choose presidential electors equal to the number of its representatives and senators. These electors would then cast votes to select a president. If no candidate received a majority of the electoral votes, the election would be turned over to the House of Representatives, where each state would have one vote.

After a style committee polished the wording in the final draft of the Constitution, thirty-nine of the forty-two delegates still in attendance signed the document on September 17. The Preamble, which originally began with a list of the states, was reworded at the last minute to begin simply: "We the people of the United States, in order to form a more perfect Union. . . ." This subtle change had significant implications. By identifying the people, and not a collection of states, as the source of authority, it emphasized the national vision of the framers and their desire to create a government quite different from a confederation of states.

Overview of the Constitution

The central government outlined in the Constitution was to have far more powers than those entrusted to Congress under the Articles of Confederation (see the summary table "The Articles of Confederation and the Constitution Compared.") The Constitution's provision for a strong, single-person executive had no precedent in the Articles. Nor did the provision for a Supreme Court. The Constitution vested this Court, as well as the lower courts that Congress was empowered to establish, with the judicial power of the United States. In addition, the Constitution specifically delegated to Congress the powers to tax, borrow and coin money, regulate commerce, and raise armed forces that the Confederation government had lacked.

Most of the economic powers of Congress came at the expense of the states, which were prohibited from passing tariffs, issuing money, or—in an obvious reference to the debtor relief legislation in the 1780s—enacting any law that infringed on the contractual rights of creditors to collect money from debtors. Also included was a clause stipulating that the Constitution and all national legislation and treaties were to be "the supreme law of the land," in effect giving the central government the power to declare state laws unconstitutional

The Constitution's underlying political philosophy was that, in Madison's wonderful phrase, "ambition must be made to counter ambition." Madi-

SUMMARY

THE ARTICLES OF CONFEDERATION AND THE CONSTITUTION COMPARED

	Articles	Constitution
Sovereign power of the central government	No power to tax or raise armies	Power granted on taxes and armed forces
Source of power	Individual states	Shared through federalism between states and the national government
Representation in Congress	Equal representation of states in a unicameral Congress	A bicameral legislature with equal representation of the states in the Senate and proportional representation in the House
Amendment process	Unanimous consent of the states	Consent of three-fourths of the states
Executive	None provided for	Office of the president
National judiciary	None provided for	Established the Supreme Court

son and the other members of the national elite who met at Philadelphia were convinced that self-interest motivated political behavior. Accepting interest group politics as inevitable and seeking to prevent a tyrannical majority from forming at the national level, the architects of the Constitution designed a central government in which competing blocs of power counterbalanced one another.

The Constitution placed both internal and external restraints on the powers granted to the central government. The functional division of the government into executive, legislative, and judicial branches, each with ways to keep the others from exercising excessive power, created an internal system of checks and balances. For example, the president commanded the armed forces, but only Congress could declare war. The president could veto congressional legislation, but Congress could override that veto with a two-thirds vote. To pass in the first place, legislation had to be approved by both the House of Representatives, which, with its membership propor-

tional to population, represented the interests of the people at large, and the Senate, which represented the interests of the states. As an ultimate check against executive abuse of power, Congress could indict, convict, and remove from office a president who tried to set himself above the law.

Although the Constitution did not explicitly grant it, the Supreme Court soon claimed the right to invalidate acts of Congress and the president that it found to be unconstitutional. This power of **judicial review** provided another check against legislative and executive authority. To guard against an arbitrary federal judiciary, the Constitution empowered Congress to determine the size of the Supreme Court and to indict and remove federal judges appointed by the president.

The external restraints on the central government were to be found in the nature of its relationship to the state governments. This relationship was based on **federalism,** the division of power between local and central authorities. By listing specific powers for Congress, the Constitution implied that all other powers were to be retained by the states. Thus while strengthening the national government, the Constitution did not obliterate the sovereign rights of the states, leaving them free to curb the potential power of the national government in the ambiguous areas between national and state sovereignty.

This ambiguity in the federalism of the Constitution was both its greatest strength and its greatest weakness. It allowed both nationalists and advocates of states' rights to support the Constitution. But the issue of slavery, left unresolved in the gray area between state and national sovereignty, would continue to fester, sparking sectional conflict over the extent of national sovereignty that would plunge the republic into civil war three-quarters of a century later.

The Struggle over Ratification

The Philadelphia delegates knew that they had exceeded their instructions by proposing an entirely new government, not an amended version of the Articles. Also aware that the Articles' requirement of unanimous consent by the state legislatures to any amendment would result in certain defeat, the delegates boldly bypassed both Congress and the state legislatures.

The last article of the Constitution stipulated that it would go into effect when it had been ratified by at least nine of the states acting through specially elected popular conventions. Influenced by the nationalist sentiments of many of its members, one-third of whom had attended the Philadelphia Convention, and perhaps weary of its own impotence, Congress accepted this drastic and not clearly legal procedure, submitting the Constitution to the states in late September 1787.

The publication of the text of the Constitution touched off a great political debate. Those who favored the Constitution now referred to themselves as **Federalists,** a term that helped deflect charges that they favored an excessive centralization of political authority. By default, the opponents of the Constitution were known as **Antifederalists,** a negative-sounding label that obscured their support of the state-centered sovereignty that most Americans associated with federalism. Initially outmaneuvered in this way, the Antifederalists never did mount an effective campaign to counter the Federalists' output of pamphlets, speeches, and newspaper editorials (see the summary table "Federalists versus the Antifederalists").

The Antifederalists did attract some men of wealth and social standing. Three of them—Elbridge Gerry of Massachusetts and George Mason and Edmund Randolph of Virginia—had been delegates at Philadelphia. But most Antifederalists were back-country farmers, men with mud on their boots who lived far from centers of communication and market outlets for their produce. They argued that a large republic, such as the one framed by the Constitution, would inevitably become tyrannical because it was too distant and removed from the interests of common citizen-farmers.

The Antifederalists were no political match for the Federalists. They lacked the social connections, access to newspapers, and self-confidence of the more cosmopolitan and better-educated Federalists. In addition, the Federalists could more easily mobilize their supporters, who were concentrated in the port cities and commercial farming areas along the coast.

The Federalists skillfully built on the momentum for change that had developed out of the crisis atmosphere of 1786. They successfully portrayed the Constitution as the best opportunity to erect a governing structure capable of preserving and extending the gains of the Revolution.

Conservatives shaken by Shays's Rebellion lined up behind the Constitution. So too did groups—creditors, merchants, manufacturers, urban artisans, commercial farmers—whose interests would be promoted by economic development. The enhanced powers of the national government held out the promise of protecting the home market from British imports, enlarging foreign markets for American exports, promoting a stable and uniform currency, and raising revenues to pay off the Revolutionary War debt.

In the early stages, the Federalists scored a string of easy victories. Delaware ratified the Constitution on December 7, 1787, and within a month, so too had Pennsylvania, New Jersey, Georgia, and Connecticut. Except for Pennsylvania, these were small, sparsely populated states that stood to benefit economically or militarily from a stronger central government. The Constitution carried in the larger state of Pennsylvania because of the Federalists' strength in the commercial center of Philadelphia.

The Federalists faced their toughest challenge in the large states that had generally been more successful in going it alone during the 1780s. One of the most telling arguments of the Antifederalists in these and other states was the absence of a bill of rights in the Constitution. The framers had felt it unnecessary to include such an explicit protection of individual rights in a document intended to specify the powers of a national government and had barely discussed a bill of rights in Philadelphia. Realizing the importance of the issue, and citing Article 5 of the Constitution, which provided for an amendment process, the Federalists promised to recommend amending the Constitution with a bill of rights once it was ratified. By doing so, they split the ranks of the Antifederalists in Massachusetts. After the Federalists gained the support of two venerable heroes of the Revolution, John Hancock and Sam Adams, the Massachusetts convention approved the Constitution by a close vote in February 1788.

The major hurdles remaining for the Federalists were Virginia, the most populous state, and the strategically located New York. Technically, the Constitution could have gone into effect without them once Maryland, South Carolina, and New Hampshire had ratified it, bringing the total number of states to ratify to the required nine. But without Virginia and New York, the new Union would have been weak and the Federalist victory far from assured.

To eke out victory in these crucial states, the Federalists drew on their pragmatism and persua-

SUMMARY

FEDERALISTS VERSUS THE ANTIFEDERALISTS

	Federalists	Antifederalists
Position on the Constitution	Favored the Constitution	Opposed the Constitution
Position on the Articles of Confederation	Felt the Articles had to be abandoned	Felt the Articles needed only to be amended
Position on the power of the states	Sought to curb the power of the states with a new central government	Felt the power of the states should be paramount
Position on the need for a bill of rights	Initially saw no need for a bill of rights in the Constitution	Saw the absence of a bill of rights in the proposed Constitution as a threat to individual liberties
Position on the optimum size of the republic	Believed a large republic could best safeguard personal freedoms	Believed only a small republic formed on common interests could protect individual rights
Source of support	Commercial farmers, merchants, shippers, artisans, holders of the national debt	State-centered politicians, most backcountry farmers

argument Madison had developed a political rationale by which Americans could have both an empire and personal freedom.

New York ratified on June 25, and Virginia followed the next day. North Carolina and Rhode Island did not ratify until after the new government was functioning. North Carolina joined the Union in 1789 once Congress submitted the amendments that comprised the Bill of Rights. The obstinate Rhode Islanders stayed out until 1790, when Congress forced them in with a threat of commercial reprisal.

Conclusion

Between 1776 and 1780, Americans developed a unique system of constitutionalism. They proclaimed the supremacy of constitutions over ordinary legislation; detailed the powers of government in a written document; provided protection for individual freedoms in bills of rights; and fashioned a process for framing governments through the election of delegates to a special constitutional convention and the popular ratification of the work of that convention. In all of these areas, Americans were pioneers in demonstrating how common citizens could create their own governments.

siveness. As in Massachusetts, they were helped by their promise of a bill of rights. And for the New York campaign, Madison, Jay, and Hamilton wrote an eloquent series of eighty-five essays known collectively as *The Federalist* to allay fears that the Constitution would so consolidate national power as to menace individual liberties. In the two most original and brilliant essays in *The Federalist,* essays 10 and 51, Madison turned traditional republican doctrine on its head. A large, diverse republic like the one envisaged by the Constitution, he reasoned, not a small and homogeneous one, offered the best hope for safeguarding the rights of all citizens. This was because a large republic would include a multitude of contending interest groups, making it difficult for any combination of them to coalesce into a tyrannical majority that could oppose minority rights. With this

The curbs on centralized power that characterized the state constitutions also applied to what amounted to the first national constitution, the Articles of Confederation. Indeed, the inability of the Confederation Congress to exercise effective power in the areas of taxation and foreign trade was a crippling flaw that thoroughly discredited the Articles in the eyes of the nationalist-minded leaders who had emerged during the Revolution. These leaders overthrew the Articles at the Constitutional Convention in 1787 and engineered a peaceful revolution in securing the ratification of the Constitution. Their victory in creating a new central government with real national powers was built on the foundation of constitutional concepts and mechanisms that Americans had laid down in their states The new Constitution did rest on the consent of the governed, and it endured because it could be amended to reflect shifts in popular will and to widen the circle of Americans granted the rights of political citizenship.

Accepting as a given that self-interest drove political action, the framers of the Constitution designed the new national government to turn ambition against itself. They created rival centers of power that forced selfish factions to compete in a constant struggle to form a workable majority. The Constitution thus set the stage for an entirely new kind of national politics.

Review Questions

1. How would you define republicanism? Do you believe that Americans today still believe in the basic tenets of republicanism?

2. What was so unprecedented about the new state constitutions, and what principles of government did they embody?

3. What were the problems of the economy in the 1780s, and why did clashes between debtors and creditors become so divisive? Do you think that an economic recovery could have been achieved under the Articles of Confederation?

4. Do you feel that the diplomatic weaknesses of the United States under the Articles were as serious as its internal problems? What were the sources of those weaknesses, and what threat did they pose for national unity?

5. What sorts of men drafted the Constitution in 1787, and how representative were they of all Americans? What explains the differences between the Federalists and Antifederalists? Do you think they shared the same vision of what they wanted America to become? How widespread was the popular backing for the Constitution, and what accounts for its ratification?

Recommended Readings

J. Hector St. John Crèvecoeur, *Letters from an American Farmer and Sketches of Eighteenth-Century Amer-* *ica,* ed. Albert E. Stone (1986). This modern reprint of Crèvecoeur's work provides an accessible account of Americans and their living conditions in the late eighteenth century.

Merrill Jensen, *The New Nation: A History of the United States during the Confederation, 1781–1787* (1948). This work makes the strongest case for the Articles as a tentative success that was overturned in a conservative reaction that exaggerated threats to social order.

Richard B. Morris, *The Forging of the Union, 1781–1789* (1987). The best-balanced synthesis of the 1780s, this book documents the creative statesmanship of the leaders of the Constitutional Convention.

Gordon Wood, *The Creation of the American Republic, 1776–1787* (1969). This masterful study is indispensable for understanding the transformation in American republicanism between the winning of independence and the ratification of the Constitution.

Where to Learn More

❖ **South Street Seaport Museum, New York City, New York** Maritime commerce was the lifeblood of the postrevolutionary economy. The artifacts and the exhibits here offer a fine introduction to the seafaring world of the port city that became the nation's first capital in the new federal Union.

❖ **Independence National Historical Park, Philadelphia, Pennsylvania** Walks and guided tours through this historic district enable one to grasp much of the physical setting in which the delegates to the Constitutional Convention met.

❖ **Northern Indiana Center for History, South Bend, Indiana** The permanent exhibition on the St. Joseph River valley of northern Indiana and southern Michigan explains the material world of this region and how it changed as first Europeans and then Americans mingled and clashed with the Native American population.

WE THE PEOPLE

1789

*B*y the 1780s, Americans were a separate, independent people. Having freed themselves from British rule, they built on what they believed was their birthright of English liberties to create the world's largest republic of self-governing citizens. They saw themselves as the inheritors of both the British republican tradition and Britain's North American empire. As George Washington said in 1783, when independence had been secured, Americans were now "the lords and proprietors of a vast tract of continent." But who did Washington and the nation's other founders have in mind when they spoke of "Americans"? And if Americans were the lords, who were the subjects?

The language the founders of the United States had used to justify their revolution against Britain and to define their new republican society was expansive and universalistic. It spoke of human equality and the people's right to consent to their government. "All men are created equal," wrote Jefferson in the Declaration of Independence. And the framers of the Constitution emphasized the need for a government based on the consent of the governed when they wrote in the Preamble, "We the people of the United States, in order to form a more perfect Union . . . and secure the blessings of liberty . . . do ordain and establish this Constitution."

But initially at least, the beneficiaries of these ideals were almost exclusively white male propertyholders of English or European descent. Other Americans— including African-Americans, Native Americans, women, and propertyless white men —were mostly excluded from the rights and privileges of citizenship in the new American republic.

When the Constitution was written, nine out of ten African-Americans were enslaved. Most whites accepted black slavery. As John Jay reported to an English abolitionist, "Very few among them even doubted the propriety and rectitude of it." Whites didn't consider granting rights to slaves as part of the American political order, and they treated the small minority of free blacks as second-class citizens with no claim to equality. The racial character of slavery in North America implicitly linked a white skin to freedom and a black skin to bondage and servitude.

As for Native Americans, they were the subjects Washington had in mind when he spoke of Americans as "lords" of the North American continent. Except as isolated individuals willing to accept white notions of private property, Indians were not allowed an equitable part in the new republic. The state and federal governments vied with one another to dispossess them of their land and push them farther west.

Women, despite their contribution to patriot victory, remained outside the political sphere of republican citizenship. The ingrained legal and cultural assumptions that kept them dependent on their husbands and fathers survived the Revolution largely intact. Republican ideology granted them only the indirect political responsibility of raising their children to be virtuous citizens.

The ideals of freedom and equality that emerged from the American Revolution, however, transcended the barriers of race and gender that kept all but propertyholding white males from enjoying full political rights in 1789. The ideals remained a kind of moral imperative, a reminder of the unfulfilled promise of the Revolution. In succeeding generations, more and more excluded groups would turn to those ideals in their struggle to be included to make "We the people" stand for all Americans.

8 A NEW REPUBLIC AND THE RISE OF PARTIES
1789–1800

KEY TOPICS

❖ Regional diversity of the United States in 1789
❖ Laying the foundations of American government during Washington's first term
❖ Hamilton's financial policies
❖ The emergence of parties during Washington's second term
❖ The Adams administration and the election of 1800

When George Washington arrived in New York on April 23, 1789, for his inauguration as the first president of the United States, he struck many people as anything but presidential. As he took the oath of office a week later, he seemed to one observer "to have forgot half of what he was to say for he made a dead pause and stood for some time, to appearance, in a vacant mood." During his address to the assembled dignitaries he appeared "agitated and embarrassed more than he ever was by the leveled Cannon or pointed Musket."

The president's shakiness reflected the shaky start of the country's new government. Two states, North Carolina and Rhode Island, had not yet ratified the Constitution and were still outside the federal Union. The newly elected members of Congress felt no urgency to assume their duties. They had been scheduled to meet in New York on March 4, 1789, to count the ballots of the electoral college and officially confirm Washington's election, but only one-quarter of them had arrived by then. A month would go by before the minimum needed to count the ballots could be mustered. Washington, his dignity ruffled by this show of congressional indifference, dallied at Mount Vernon until formally notified of his election.

He had every reason to dread taking on the burden of the presidency. As head of the new national government, he would put at risk the legendary status he had achieved during the Revolution. Most Americans intensely feared centralized authority, which is why the framers deliberately left the word *national* out of the Constitution. Washington somehow had to establish loyalty to a new government whose main virtue in the eyes of many was the very vagueness of its defined powers.

The Constitution had created the framework for a national government, but pressing problems demanded the fleshing out of that framework. The government urgently needed revenue to begin paying off the immense debt incurred during the Revolution. It also had to address unstable conditions in the West, the territories between the Appalachians and the Mississippi, where western settlers wavered in their loyalties. The government would have to tie those people to the Union more tightly. Ultimately, the key to solving these and other problems was to establish the new republic's legitimacy. Washington and his supporters had to inspire popular backing for the government's right to exercise authority.

The realities of governing would soon shatter the nonpartisan ideal that had prevailed among the backers of the Constitution. By the end of Washington's first term, two political parties had begun to emerge. The **Federalist party** (not to be confused with the Federalists in the ratification debate), which included Washington and his successor, John Adams, favored a strong central government. The opposition party, the **Jeffersonian Republicans**, took shape as a result of differences over financial policy and the response to the French Revolution. Led by Thomas Jefferson, the Republicans were distrustful of excessive central power.

The Federalists, who governed through 1800, succeeded in showing a doubting world that the American experiment in republican government could work. But as inheritors of a political tradition that equated parties with factions—temporary coalitions of selfish private interests—the Federalists doubted the loyalty of the Republicans. When the Federalists under President Adams attempted to suppress the Republicans, the stage was set for the critical election of 1800. Jefferson's victory in that election ended both Federalist rule and the republic's first major internal crisis.

Washington's America

Who were the Americans whom Washington was called on to lead? There is no easy answer. In 1789, as now, Americans identified and grouped themselves according to many factors, including race, sex, class, ethnicity, religion, and degree of personal freedom. Variations in climate and soil further divided them into regions and sections. The resulting hodgepodge sorely tested the assumption that a single national government could govern Americans as a whole.

The Uniformity of New England

The national census of 1790 counted nearly 4 million Americans, one in four of whom lived in New England. It alone of the nation's formative regions had largely shut itself off from outsiders. New England's poor soils and long, cold winters made it an impractical place to cultivate cash crops like the tobacco and rice of the South. As a result, New England farmers had little need of imported white indentured servants or black slaves. Puritan values and a harsh environment thus combined to make New England the most religiously and ethnically uniform region in the United States. Most of the people living there were descended from English immigrants who had arrived in the seventeenth century. Small pockets of Quakers, Baptists, and Catholics had gained the legal right of worship by the 1720s, but Congregationalism remained the official, state-supported religion in Connecticut and Massachusetts. Blacks and Indians together barely constituted 3 percent of New England's population. The few remaining Indians lived on reservations of inferior land, which they usually left only to find work as servants or day laborers.

New Englanders found slavery incompatible with the natural rights philosophy that had emerged during the Revolution and abolished it in the 1780s. Slavery had, in any case, always been marginal in its economy. Women outnumbered men in parts of New England in 1789. This pattern—not found in other parts of the country—was the result of the pressure of an expanding population and the practice of dividing family farms among male heirs that left young men to migrate west in search of cheap, arable land. Thus by 1789, women formed a slight majority in Connecticut, Massachusetts, and Rhode Island. Yet despite their superior numbers, women in New England, as elsewhere, remained subordinate to men. Republican ideology, emphasizing the need of women to be intellectually prepared to raise virtuous, public-spirited children, led reformers in New England to seek equal access for women to education. In 1789, Massachusetts became the first state to allocate funds specifically for girls' elementary education. Liberalized divorce laws in New England also allowed a woman to seek legal separation from an abusive or unfaithful spouse.

CHRONOLOGY

1789 Inauguration of Washington.

Congress establishes the first federal departments.

French Revolution begins.

1790 Hamilton submits the first of his financial reports to Congress.

1791 Bill of Rights ratified.

Congress charters the Bank of the United States.

1792 St. Clair's defeat along the Wabash.

Reelection of Washington.

1793 France goes to war against Britain, Spain, and Holland.

Genêt Mission.

Washington issues Proclamation of Neutrality.

1794 Ohio is opened with the victory of General Anthony Wayne at the Battle of Fallen Timbers.

Suppression of the Whiskey Rebellion in western Pennsylvania.

1795 Jay's Treaty with Britain ratified.

Treaty of Greenville with Ohio Indians.

1796 Pinckney's Treaty with Spain ratified.

Washington's Farewell Address.

John Adams elected president.

1797 Beginning of the Quasi-War with France.

1798 XYZ Affair.

Alien and Sedition Acts.

Provisional army and direct tax.

Virginia and Kentucky Resolutions.

1799 Fries's Rebellion in Pennsylvania.

1800 Franco-American Accord.

Thomas Jefferson elected president.

In other respects, politics in New England remained rooted in the Puritan past. Age, property, and reputation determined one's standing in a culture that valued a clearly defined social order. The moral code that governed town life promoted curbs on individual behavior for the benefit of the community as a whole. With their notions of collective liberty, New Englanders subscribed to a version of republicanism that favored strong government, setting themselves apart from most other Americans, who embraced a more individualistic idea of liberty and a republicanism suspicious of government power.

The Pluralism of the Mid-Atlantic Region

The states of the mid-Atlantic region—New York, New Jersey, and Pennsylvania—were the most ethnically and religiously diverse in the nation. People of English descent comprised somewhat less than 40 percent of the population. Other major ethnic groups included the Dutch and Scots-Irish in New York and Germans and Scots-Irish in New Jersey and Pennsylvania. With ethnic diversity came religious diversity. In contrast to Puritan New England, the Middle Colonies had offered freedom of worship to attract settlers. In addition, economic opportunities

for newcomers were much greater than in New England. The soil was better, the climate was milder, and market outlets for agricultural products were more abundant. These conditions made the mid-Atlantic region the nation's first breadbasket.

The demand for labor had also been met by importing African slaves. But despite its considerable strength in the port cities and adjacent rural areas, slavery was never an economically vital institution in most of the mid-Atlantic region. The region's major cash crop, wheat, required seasonal labor, which did not warrant tying up capital in slaves.

Consequently, Pennsylvania in 1780, New York in 1799, and New Jersey in 1804 each passed laws of gradual emancipation. These laws did not free adult slaves but provided that children born of a slave mother were to be freed at ages ranging between 18 and 28. Nevertheless, African-Americans had to confront enduring white racism. The comments of one white New Yorker suggest what they were up against. "We may sincerely advocate the freedom of black men," he wrote, "and yet assert their moral and physical inferiority."

The diversity of the mid-Atlantic region created a complex political environment. Some mid-Atlantic groups, including mercantile and financial leaders and commercial farmers, favored a strong central government to foster economic development and maintain traditional authority. Others, coming principally from the middle and lower classes, wanted to keep government weak so as to foster a republican equality that would promote individual freedom.

The Slave South and Its Backcountry

In the South—the region from Maryland and Delaware to Georgia—climate and soil conditions favored the production of cash staples for world markets. Cultivating these crops required back-breaking labor and Southern planters relied on the coerced labor of African slaves, whose numbers made the South the most populous region in the country. Just under 40 percent of all Southerners were slaves, but their concentration varied within each region.

The free black population in the South had grown rapidly during the 1780s. Thousands of slaves fled behind British lines to win their freedom, and patriots freed others as a reward for enlisting in their forces. The Revolutionary values of liberty and equality also led many slave owners to question the morality of slavery. Legislatures in the Upper South passed laws making it financially easier than before for masters to manumit (free) their slaves. In Virginia alone, ten thousand slaves were manumitted in the 1780s. Slavery remained the foundation of the southern economy, however, and whites feared competition from freed blacks. As a result, no southern state embarked on a general program of emancipation, and slavery in the region survived the turbulence of the Revolutionary era.

Economic conditions in the South, where the raw poverty of the backcountry offset the great wealth of the lowcountry, stamped the region's politics and culture. Tidewater planters were predominantly Anglican and of English descent. Piedmont farmers were more likely to be Scots-Irish Presbyterians and Baptists. More evangelical in their religion, and with simpler habits and tastes, the backcountry Baptists denounced the lowcountry planters for their luxury and arrogance.

Planters understood liberty to mean the power of white males, unchecked by any outside authority, to rule over others. The only acknowledged check on this power was the planter's sense of duty, his obligation to adhere to an idealized code of conduct befitting a gentleman and a man of honor. Backcountry farmers also jealously guarded their liberties.

The Growing West

Between the Appalachian Mountains and the Mississippi River stretched the most rapidly growing region of the new nation, the West. During the 1780s, the white population of the West exploded from less than 10,000 to 200,000. The region's Native American population was, in contrast, about 150,000.

Although Indians and whites struck many friendships and mutually advantageous ties, their relations were more generally marked by tension and sporadic violence. For example, when James Boone, the eldest son of the fabled Daniel Boone, who had blazed the first trail for whites into Kentucky, was cap-

A frontier log cabin, such as this, was a squalid, rough-hewn structure that could be built in a day with the help of neighbors.

tured, tortured, and killed by a band of Indians, a group of whites sought vengeance. They lured some Mingo Indians into their camp, got them drunk, and then killed and scalped them. According to one account, they strung up a pregnant Mingo woman, "sliced open her belly with a tomahawk, and impaled her unborn child on a stake." Indians had every reason to oppose the white intrusion, and they strongly resisted white claims on their lands.

Most white migrants in Kentucky and Tennessee were the young, rural poor from the seaboard slave states. The West offered them the opportunity to claim their own farms and gain economic independence free from the dominance of planters and the economic competition of slave labor. But planters also saw the West as a land of opportunity, speculating in vast tracts of western land.

Life in the western settlements was harsh and often cruel. Mortality was high, especially among infants. Travelers from the East described settlers living in crudely built log cabins with squalid, filthy interiors infested with fleas and lice. Many were **squatters**, occupying land in the hopes of someday gaining title to it. Easterners also found an appallingly casual acceptance of violence in the West. Men commonly settled disputes in knife-slashing, eye-gouging brawls.

In Kentucky, squatters, aligned with a small class of middling landowners, spearheaded the movement for political separation from Virginia that gained statehood for the territory in 1792. But despite the statehood movement, the ultimate political allegiance of the West was uncertain in 1790. Westerners wanted the freedom to control their own affairs and outlets for their crops. Apparently, they were willing to strike a deal with any outside power including the British and the Spanish offering to meet these needs.

Forging a New Government

The Congress that assembled in New York from 1789 to 1791 faced a challenge scarcely less daunting than that of the Constitutional Convention of 1787. It had to give form and substance to the framework of the new national government outlined in the Constitution. Executive departments had to be established, a federal judiciary organized, sources of revenue found, terms of international trade and foreign policy worked out, and a commitment to add a bill of rights to the Constitution honored.

Staunch supporters of the new government had easily carried the first national elections in 1788 and enjoyed large majorities in both houses of Congress. These people brought superb administrative talents to the task of governing. Many, however, were clumsy politicians and unsympathetic to the egalitarian sensibilities of the electorate. By 1792, they faced growing political opposition.

"Mr. President" and the Bill of Rights

The first problem for Washington and Congress was to decide just how the chief executive of the new republic should be addressed. In a debate that tied up Congress for a month, the more democratically inclined members of the House argued that a title like "His Highness" smacked of a longing for monarchical rule; Adams and the others grudgingly agreed to accept "Mr. President." Whatever his title, Washington was intent on surrounding the presidency in a halo of respectability and he set down guidelines for Presidential etiquette. He established strict rules for his interactions with the public. He met with visitors twice a week for an hour and bowed with republican deference to the people but refused to shake hands. He traveled outside New York in a luxurious coach pulled by six horses, and at all times he carried himself with stern reserve.

Meanwhile Congress got down to business. James Madison, now a representative from Virginia, early emerged as the most forceful leader in the House. To allay the fears of Antifederalists that the Constitution granted too much power to the national government, the Federalists had promised to consider amendments that protected both individual rights and liberties and the rights of states. But Madison, concerned not to have the new government immediately hobbled by concessions to states, astutely kept the focus of the amendments on personal liberties. He submitted nineteen amendments, and Congress soon settled on twelve. Ten of these amendments, known collectively as the Bill of Rights, were ratified by the states and became part of the Constitution as of December 15, 1791.

The Bill of Rights has been one of the most enduring legacies of the first Congress. The first eight amendments are concerned mostly with individual rights. They guarantee religious freedom, freedom of expression, and the safeguarding of individuals and their property against arbitrary legal proceedings. Only three amendments speak of state interests. Citing the necessity of a "well regulated militia" for "the security of a free State," the Second Amendment guarantees "the right of the people to keep and bear Arms." The Ninth and Tenth Amendments stipulate that the powers not granted to the national government in the Constitution are retained by the people and the states.

The Bill of Rights broadened the government's base of popular support. Once Congress submitted the amendments to the states for ratification, North Carolina (1789) and Rhode Island (1790) overcame their lingering objections and joined the Union. The Bill of Rights also assured Americans that the central government would not try to impose on them a uniform national culture.

Departments and Courts

In the summer of 1789, Congress authorized the first executive departments: the State Department for foreign affairs, the Treasury for finances, and the War Department for the nation's defense. These departments already existed under the Articles of Confederation, and the only debate about them concerned the extent of presidential control over the officials who would head them. The Constitution was silent on whether or not the president could dismiss an official without the Senate's consent. Congress decided that the president could do so, setting an important precedent that bolstered presidential power. Department heads would now be closely bound to the president. As a group, they would evolve into the **cabinet**, the president's chief advisory body.

Greater controversy attended the creation of the federal judiciary. The Constitution called for "one Supreme Court" but left it up to Congress to authorize lower federal courts. The framers were deliberately vague about the federal judiciary because Antifederalists and proponents of states' rights did not want national courts enforcing a uniform judicial system.

The **Judiciary Act of 1789** represented an artful compromise that balanced the concerns of the Antifederalists and states' rights advocates with the concerns of nationalists who strongly opposed leaving matters of national law up to state courts. It created a hierarchical national judiciary based on thirteen federal district courts, one for each state. Appeals from these courts were to be heard in one of three circuit courts, and the Supreme Court was to have the final say in contested cases. In a major concession to the Antifederalists, however, the act limited jurisdiction in federal courts to legal issues stemming from the Constitution and the laws and treaties of the national government. The distinctive legal systems and customs of the states remained intact. State courts would continue to hear and rule on the vast majority of civil and criminal cases.

Revenue and Trade

The government's most pressing need was for revenue and Madison acted to put the finances of the new federal government on a firm footing. Nearly everyone agreed that the government's chief source of income should be a tariff on imported goods and tonnage duties (fees based on cargo capacity) on ships entering American ports. The United States imported most of its manufactured goods, as well as many raw materials, and foreign-owned ships accounted for nearly half of entering tonnage.

The **Tariff Act of 1789** levied a duty of 5 percent on most imported goods but imposed tariffs as high as 50 percent on a limited number of items such as steel, salt, cloth, and tobacco. The debate on the Tariff Act provoked some sectional sparring. In general, manufacturers, who were concentrated in the North, wanted high tariffs for protection against foreign competition. In contrast, farmers and southern planters wanted low tariffs to keep down the cost of the manufactured goods they purchased.

Madison originally hoped to use tonnage duties not only to raise revenue but also to strike at foreign nations like Great Britain that had not signed a commercial treaty with the United States. The duties Madison would impose on British ships entering American ports were in effect a declaration of economic warfare against Britain, and they failed to pass Congress, defeated by an unlikely coalition of sectional interests. Southerners voted against them because they feared their result would be to give New England merchants a monopoly on the carrying trade and raise the cost of shipping tobacco to Europe. Northern merchants, presumably the beneficiaries of the duties, also opposed them, leery of disrupting their profitable trade with Britain, especially with the economic slump of the 1780s abating. The **Tonnage Act of 1789**, as finally passed, treated all foreign ships equally.

Hamilton and the Public Credit

The Treasury was the largest and most important new department. To its head, Alexander Hamilton of New York, fell the task of bringing order out of the nation's ramshackle finances. The basic problem was the huge debt left over from the Revolution. With interest going unpaid, the debt was growing, and by 1789, it had reached $52 million.

More than any other individual, Hamilton imparted energy and purpose to the Washington administration. Coming from humble beginnings, he was ambitious, egotistical, and overbearing. When he spoke of the people, he usually did so with a sneer. But he also had a brilliant financial mind and a sweeping vision of national greatness. He was convinced that the economic self-interests of the wealthy and well-born offered the only sound foundation for the success of the new government.

At the request of Congress, Hamilton prepared a series of four reports on the nation's finances and economic condition. In the first, issued in January 1790, Hamilton proposed a bold plan to address the Revolutionary War debt. The federal government, he maintained, should fund the national debt at full face value. To do this, he proposed exchanging the old debt, including accrued interest, for new government bonds bearing interest at about 4 percent. In addition, Hamilton maintained that the federal government should assume the remaining war debt of the state governments. The intent of this plan was to give the nation's creditors an economic stake in the stability of the new nation.

In his second report, Hamilton called for an excise tax (a tax on the production, sale, or consumption of a commodity) on distilled whiskey produced within the United States to raise additional revenue for interest payments on the national debt and establish the government's authority to levy internal taxes on its citizens.

The third report recommended the chartering of a national bank, the Bank of the United States. Hamilton patterned his proposed bank after the Bank of England and intended it to meet a variety of needs. Jointly owned by the federal government and private investors, it would serve as the fiscal (financial) and depository agent of the government and make loans to businesses. Through a provision that permitted up to three-fourths of the value of bank stock to be purchased with government bonds, the bank would create a market for public securities and hence raise their value. Most important, the bank would provide the nation with a stable currency.

Hamilton's final report, issued in December 1791, recommended government actions to promote industry. Looking, as always, to the British model of economic development, he argued that the United States would never become a great power as long as it imported most of its manufactured goods. Hamilton advocated aid in the form of **protective tariffs** (high tariffs meant to make imported goods more expensive than domestic goods) for such industries as iron, steel, and shoemaking—which had already begun to establish themselves—and direct subsidies to assist with start-up costs for other industries. He believed that such "patronage," as he called it, would ultimately foster interregional economic dependence.

Reaction and Opposition

The breadth and boldness of Hamilton's program invited opposition. About half of the members of Congress owned some of the nation's debt, and nearly all of them agreed with Hamilton that it

should be paid off. Some opponents, however, were concerned that Hamilton's plan was unfair. Hard times had forced most of the original holders of the debt—by and large, ordinary citizens—to sell their certificates to speculators at a fraction of their face value. Others objected on republican grounds that Hamilton had no intention of actually eliminating the government's debt. He envisioned instead a permanent debt, with the government making regular interest payments as they came due. The debt, in the form of government securities, would serve as a vital prop for the support of moneyed groups.

Opposition to Hamilton's proposal to have the federal government assume state debts reflected sectional differences. With the exception of South Carolina, the southern states had already paid back a good share of their war debts. Thus Hamilton's plan stood to benefit the northern states disproportionately.

A compromise was reached in July. Southerners agreed to accept funding in its original form because, as Hamilton correctly noted, it would be impractical, if not impossible, to distinguish between the original and current holders of the national debt. Assumption passed after Hamilton cut a deal with Virginians James Madison and Thomas Jefferson. In exchange for southern support of assumption, Hamilton agreed to line up northern votes for locating the nation's permanent capital on the banks of the Potomac River, where it would be surrounded by the slave states of Maryland and Virginia.

The bank bill passed Congress on a vote that divided on sectional lines. Madison objected that the Constitution did not explicitly authorize Congress to charter a bank or any other corporation. Washington sought the cabinet's opinion, provoking the first great debate over how the Constitution should be interpreted. Thomas Jefferson, the secretary of state, sided with Madison and for the first time openly clashed with Hamilton. Taking a **strict constructionist** position, he argued that all powers the Constitution had not expressly delegated to the national government were reserved to the states under the Tenth Amendment. Hamilton, in a brilliant rejoinder, argued that Article 1, Section 8 of the Constitution, which declares that Congress has the right to "to make all laws which shall be necessary and proper" to exercise its powers and those of the federal government, gives Congress implicit authority beyond its explicitly enumerated powers. With this **broad constructionist** position, he won Washington to his side.

With Washington's signature on the bill, Hamilton's bank was chartered for twenty years and a hefty 25% tax on distilled liquor was also passed.

Little, however, of Hamilton's plan to promote manufacturing survived.

The Emergence of Parties

By the end of Washington's first term, Americans were dividing into two camps. On one side stood those who still called themselves Federalists. These were the supporters of Hamilton's program—speculators, creditors, merchants, manufacturers, and commercial farmers. They were the Americans most fully integrated into the market economy and were concentrated in the North. In both economic and cultural terms, the Federalists were drawn from the more privileged segments of society.

Jefferson and Madison shrewdly gave the name *Republican* to the party that formed in opposition to the Federalists, thus identifying it with individual liberties and the heritage of the Revolution. The Republicans accused Hamilton and the Federalists of attempting to impose a British system of economic privilege and social exploitation. The Republicans were committed to an agrarian America in which power remained in the hands of farmers and planters.

In 1792, parties were still in a formative stage. Washington remained aloof from the political infighting and was still seen as a great unifier. Unopposed, he was reelected in 1792. However, a series of crises in his second term deepened and broadened the incipient party divisions. By 1796, rival parties were contesting the presidency and vying for the support of an increasingly politically organized electorate.

The French Revolution

The French Revolution began in 1789, and in its early phase, most Americans applauded it. By 1792, however, the Revolution had turned violent and radical. Its supporters confiscated the property of aris-

SUMMARY

FEDERALIST PARTY VERSUS REPUBLICAN PARTY

Federalists	Republicans
Favored strong central government	Wanted to limit the role of the national government
Supported Hamilton's economic program	Opposed Hamilton's economic program
Opposed the French Revolution	Generally supported the French Revolution
Supported Jay's Treaty and closer ties to Britain	Opposed Jay's Treaty and favored closer ties to France
In response to the threat of war with France, proposed and passed the Direct Tax of 1798, the Alien and Sedition Acts, and legislation to enlarge the size of the army	Opposed the Alien and Sedition Acts and the enlarged army as threats to individual liberties
Drew strongest support from New England; lost support in the mid-Atlantic region after 1798	Drew strongest support from the South and West

tocrats and the church, slaughtered suspected enemies, and executed the king, Louis XVI.

These excesses touched off a bitter debate in America. Federalists drew back in horror arguing in the Federalist *Gazette of the United States* that: "The American Revolution, it ought to be repeated, was not accomplished as the French has been, by massacres, assassinations, or proscriptions." For the Republicans, the French remained the standard-bearers of the cause of liberty for common people everywhere. Jefferson admitted that the French Revolution was tarnished by the loss of innocent lives, but was convinced that its cause was just.

When the new French ambassador, Edmond Genêt arrived in the United States in April 1793—just as the debate in America over the French Revolution was heating up—Franco-American relations reached a turning point. Genêt, it soon became clear, hoped to embroil the United States in the French war against the British. He commissioned

American Views

THE GRASS-ROOTS POLITICS OF A DEMOCRATIC-REPUBLICAN ORGANIZATION

The Democratic-Republican societies that sprang up in sympathy with the French Revolution modeled themselves after the U.S. Revolutionary committees of the 1770s. Their members drew up constitutions, elected officers, issued resolutions and memorials, and drank toast after toast to the memory of the patriots who secured American independence. Above all, they insisted on the need for the constant vigilance of an informed citizenry to protect republican liberties against government encroachment. The following selection is from the constitution of the Democratic Society in Addison County, Vermont.

❖ **What moral principles does the society associate with republican government? What duties of citizenship does it outline? What does the society mean by a "strictly republican government"?**

❖ **What explains the society's suspicion of public officials? Why does it stress the need for an informed citizenry? How does the society hope to safeguard popular liberties? How practical do you feel this program would be in the United States today?**

❖ **Why did the Federalists oppose these ideas on popular government? How would they construe the nature of liberty and republican government differently?**

We, the undersigned, compact and associate ourselves into a Society . . . to promote the political ends expressed in the following articles, which shall be considered constitutional of our Society.

We make no apology for thus associating ourselves . . . to consider . . . and publish our sentiments, on the political interests, constitution and government of our country; this is a right, the disputation of which reflects on political freedom, and wears an appearance peculiarly absurd, proceeding from the tongue or pen of an American.

We declare the following . . . to be some of our political sentiments, and principles of government, . . .—That all men are naturally free, and possess equal rights. —That all legitimate government originates in the voluntary and social compact of the people. —That no rights of the people are surrendered to their rulers, as a price of protection and government. —That the constitution and laws of a country are the expressions of the general will of the body of the people or nation, that all officers of government are the ministers & servants of the people, and, as such, are amenable

American privateers to attack British shipping and tried to enlist an army of frontiersmen to attack Spanish possessions in Louisiana and Florida.

The president feared that Genêt would stampede Americans into the European war, with disastrous results for the nation's finances. The bulk of America's foreign trade was with the British, and tariff duties on British imports were the main source of revenue to pay for Hamilton's assumption and funding programs. Hamilton urged Washington to declare American neutrality in the European war,

maintaining that the president could commit the nation to neutrality on his own authority when Congress, as was then the case, was not in session. Jefferson, although he too wanted to avoid war, disputed Washington's power to act on his own, maintaining that the warmaking powers of Congress reserved for it alone the right to issue a declaration of neutrality.

Washington accepted Hamilton's argument on his authority to declare neutrality and issued a proclamation on April 22, 1793, stating that the to them, for all their conduct in office. —That it is the right, and becomes the duty of a people, as a necessary means of the security and preservation of their rights, and the future peace and political happiness of the nation, to exercise watchfullness and inspection, upon the conduct of all their public officers; to approve, if they find their conduct worthy of their high and important trusts— and to reprove and censure, if it be found otherwise. That frequent elections, directly from the body of the people, of persons, to important offices of trust, have an immediate tendency to secure the public power; that compensations for public service ought to be reasonable (and even moderate, when the debts and exigencies of a nation require it) and a reward only for actual service; that a public debt (and a financial funding system to continue the same) is a burthen upon a nation, and ought . . . to be reduced and discharged; that an increase of public officers, dependent on the executive power, [is] a foolish copying of ancient corrupt and foreign governments and courts, where the equal rights of men are trampled under the feet of kings and lords; and a standing army—are all highly dangerous to liberty; and that the constitution, laws, and government of a country are always of right, liable to amendation and improvement.

We are concerned that the present political state of our country calls for the rational, wise and vigilant attention of its citizens. . . . It shall be the objects . . . of this society to study the Constitution, to avail ourselves of the journals, debates, and laws of Congress and such other publications as may be judged necessary to give information as to the proceedings of Congress and the departments of government and also of the conduct of individual officers in the discharge of their trusts. . . . And on information, we will speak; and upon deliberation, we will write and publish our sentiments. A steady zeal and firmness for the liberties of our country, and a strictly republican government, in pursuing our enquiries, & in passing our resolutions, shall be severely guided by the reason and temperance, which a sense of moral obligation, and the dread of ignorant popular convulsions, demand. . . .

Source: *Philip S. Foner*, ed., The Democratic-Republican Societies, 1790–1800: A Documentary Sourcebook of Constitutions, Declarations, Addresses, Resolutions, and Toasts *(1976)*.

United States would be "friendly and impartial toward the belligerent powers."

After Genêt's visit, American politics became more open and aggressive. Pro-French enthusiasm lived on in a host of grass-roots political organizations known as the Democratic-Republican societies. As their name suggests, these societies reflected a belief that democracy and republicanism were one and the same. This was a new concept in American politics. As a letter writer to the Newark *Gazette* put it:

It must be the mechanics and farmers, or the poorer class of people (as they are generally called), that must support the freedom which they and their fathers purchased with their blood—the nobility will never do it—they will be always striving to get the reins of government into their own hands, and then they can ride the people at pleasure.

The Democratic-Republican societies attacked the Washington administration for failing to assist France, and they expressed the popular feeling that

This painting by an officer on General Wayne's staff shows Little Turtle, a Miami chief, speaking through an interpreter to General Wayne (with one hand behind his back) during the negotiations that led to the Treaty of Greenville.

Hamilton's program favored the rich over the poor. For the first time, Washington himself was personally assailed in the press.

Securing the Frontier

Control of the West remained an elusive goal throughout Washington's first term. Indian resistance in the Northwest Territory prevented whites from pushing north of the Ohio River. The powerful Miami Confederacy routed two ill-trained American armies in 1790 and 1791, the worst defeat an American army ever suffered in frontier fighting.

By 1793, many western settlers felt abandoned by the national government. They believed that the government had broken a promise to protect them against Indians and foreigners. Much of the popularity of the Democratic-Republican societies in the West fed off these frustrations. Westerners also demanded free and open navigation on the Mississippi River.

The Federalists, on the other hand, wanted submission to national authority from both the Indians and the western settlers. The War Department was reorganized, and it sent into the Ohio region a force built around veterans from the regular (or professional) army under General Anthony Wayne, a savvy, battle-hardened war hero.

On August 4, 1794, at the **Battle of Fallen Timbers**, near present-day Toledo, Wayne's army dealt a decisive blow to the Ohio Indians. In the

Treaty of Greenville, signed in August 1795, twelve tribes ceded most of the present state of Ohio to the U.S. government in return for an annual payment of $9,500. The Ohio country was now open to white settlement.

The Whiskey Rebellion

Within a few months of Wayne's victory at Fallen Timbers, another American army was on the move. The target this time was the so-called whiskey rebels of western Pennsylvania, who were openly resisting Hamilton's excise tax on whiskey. Hamilton was determined to enforce the tax and assert the supremacy of national laws. Although resistance to the tax was widespread, he singled out the Pennsylvania rebels. Washington was convinced that the Democratic-Republican societies of western Pennsylvania were behind the defiance of federal authority there and welcomed the opportunity to chastise these organizations, which he identified with the dangerous doctrines of the French Revolution.

Washington called on the governors of the mid-Atlantic states to supply militia forces to crush the **Whiskey Rebellion**. The 13,000-man army that assembled at Harrisburg and marched into western Pennsylvania in October 1794 was larger than any Washington had commanded during the Revolution. But the rebellion, as Jefferson sardonically noted, "could never be found." The army met no resistance and expended considerable effort rounding up twenty prisoners. Still, the Federalists had made their point: When its authority was openly challenged, this national government was prepared to use military force to compel obedience.

The Whiskey Rebellion starkly revealed the conflicting visions of local liberty and national order that divided Americans of the early republic. The non-English majority on the Pennsylvania frontier— Irish, Scots-Irish, German, and Welsh—justified resistance to the whiskey tax with the same republican ideology that had fueled the American Revolution. In putting down the Pennsylvania rebels, Washington and Hamilton acted on behalf of more English and cosmopolitan groups in the East who valued central power as a check on any local resistance movement that might begin unraveling the still fragile republic.

Treaties with Britain and Spain

Much of the unrest in the West stemmed from the menacing presence of the British and Spanish on the nation's borders. Washington's government had the resources to suppress Indians and frontier dissidents but lacked sufficient armed might to push Spain and especially Britain out of the West. Caught in the middle of mounting hostilities between Britain and France, and desperate to avert a war, Washington sent John Jay, the chief justice of the United States, to London to negotiate an accord.

From the American point of view, the resulting agreement, known as **Jay's Treaty**, was flawed but acceptable. Jay had to abandon the right of the United States to continue trading with France without British harassment. He also had to grant Britain "most favored nation" status, giving up the American right to discriminate against British shipping and merchandise. And he had to reconfirm the American commitment that pre-Revolutionary debts owed by Americans to the British would be repaid in full. In return for these major concessions, Britain pledged to compensate American merchants for the ships and cargoes it had seized in 1793 and 1794, to abandon the six forts it still held in the American Northwest, and to grant the United States limited trading rights in India and the British West Indies. Signed in November 1794, Jay's Treaty caused an uproar in the United States when its terms became known in March 1795. Southerners saw in it another sellout of their interests. The Senate ratified the treaty in June 1795, but only because Washington backed it.

Jay's Treaty helped convince Spain to adopt a more conciliatory attitude toward the United States. In the **Treaty of San Lorenzo** (also known as **Pinck-**ney's Treaty) of 1795, Spain accepted the American position on the 31st parallel as the northern boundary of Spanish Florida and granted American farmers the right of free transit through the port of New Orleans.

The First Partisan Election

Two terms in office were more than enough for Washington. The partisan politics that emerged during his second term—and its expression in an increasingly partisan press—disgusted him. He announced his decision to retire from public life in his Farewell Address of September 1796, less than two months before the presidential election. He intentionally delayed the announcement to minimize the time the Republicans would have to prepare for the campaign. Washington devoted most of his address to a denunciation of partisanship. He invoked the republican ideal of disinterested, independent statesmanship as the only sure and virtuous guide for the nation. He warned against any permanent foreign alliances and cautioned that the Union itself would be endangered if parties continued to be characterized "by geographical discriminations— *Northern* and *Southern*, *Atlantic* and *Western*."

Confirming Washington's fears, the election of 1796 was the first openly partisan election in American history. John Adams was the Federalist candidate and Thomas Jefferson the Republican candidate. Each was selected at a **party caucus**, a meeting of party leaders.

Adams won despite Alexander Hamilton's interference, which inadvertently almost threw the election to Jefferson. Now a private citizen in New York, Hamilton wanted to be the power behind the throne in any new Federalist administration. Uncomfortable with Adams, he connived to have Thomas Pinckney of South Carolina, the other Federalist running with Adams, win the election. The Constitution did not originally call for electors to cast separate ballots for president and vice president. The Constitution was written with absolutely no thought of organized partisan competition for the presidency. Taking advantage of this weakness, Hamilton convinced some of the South Carolina electors to drop Adams from their ballots. He expected that with the solid support of the New England electors for both Adams and Pinckney, Pinkney would be elected president and Adams vice president. But the scheme backfired. When New Englanders learned of it, they refused to vote for Pinckney. As a result, Adams came in first with seventy-one votes, but Jefferson came in second with sixty-eight. Thanks to Hamilton, Adams entered office with his chief rival as vice president and a politically divided administration. Adams received all the northern electoral votes, with the exception of Pennsylvania's. Jefferson was the overwhelming favorite in the South.

The Last Federalist Administration

The Adams administration got off to a rocky start from which it never recovered. Adams had been a lawyer before the Revolution; he was a veteran of both Continental Congresses, had been a diplomat in Europe for a decade, and had served as Washington's vice president for eight years. But despite this extraordinarily rich background in public affairs, he was politically naive. Scrupulously honest but quick to take offense, he lacked the politician's touch for inspiring personal loyalty and crafting compromises based on a realistic recognition of mutual self-interest. But putting the interests of the country before those of his party, he almost single-handedly prevented a nearly certain war with France and a possible civil war at home. The price he paid was a badly split Federalist party that refused to unite behind him when he sought reelection in 1800.

The French Crisis and the XYZ Affair

An aggressive coalition known as the Directory gained control of revolutionary France in 1795 and denounced the Jay treaty as evidence of an Anglo-American alliance against France. The French annulled the commercial treaty of 1778 with the United States, ordered the seizure of American ships carrying goods to the British, and declared that any American sailors found on British ships, including those forcibly pressed into service, would be summarily executed.

In the fall of 1797, Adams sent three commissioners to Paris in an effort to avoid war. The French treated the three with contempt. Having just conquered the Netherlands and detached Spain from its British alliance, France was in no mood to compromise. Through three intermediaries—identified by Adams only as X, Y, and Z when he informed Congress of the negotiations—the French foreign minister demanded a large bribe to initiate talks and an American loan of $12 million.

In April 1798, the Senate published a full account of the insulting behavior of the French in what came to be called the **XYZ Affair**. The public was indignant, and war fever swept the country. By the fall of 1798, American ships were waging an undeclared war against the French in Caribbean waters, a conflict that came to be known as the **Quasi-War**. The Federalists, who had always warned against the French, enjoyed greater popularity than they ever had or ever would again. Congress acted to upgrade the navy and the army dramatically, and adopted Washington's suggestion that Hamilton be appointed second in command.

To pay for both the expanded army and the naval rearmament, the Federalists pushed through the **Direct Tax of 1798**, a levy on the value of land, slaves, and dwellings.

Crisis at Home

The thought of Hamilton in charge of a huge army convinced many Republicans that their worst nightmares were about to materialize. The Federalists then passed four laws in the summer of 1798, known collectively as the **Alien and Sedition Acts**, that confirmed the Republicans' fears. The most dangerous of the four acts in the minds of Republicans was the **Sedition Act**, a measure that made it a federal crime to engage in any combination or conspiracy against the government or to utter or print anything "false, scandalous and malicious" against the government. Federalist judges were blatantly partisan in their enforcement of the Sedition Act. Twenty-five individuals, mostly Republican editors, were indicted under the act, and ten were convicted.

Facing a Congress and a Supreme Court dominated by the Federalists, Jefferson and Madison turned to the safely Republican legislatures of Kentucky and Virginia for a forum from which to attack the constitutionality of the Alien and Sedition Acts, and they produced the first significant articulation of the southern stand on **states' rights**. The resolutions—adopted in the fall of 1798—proposed a compact theory of the Constitution. They asserted that the states had delegated specific powers to the national government for their common benefit. It followed that the states reserved the right to rule whether the national government had unconstitutionally assumed power not granted to it. If a state decided that the national government had exceeded its powers, it could "interpose" its authority to shield its citizens from a tyrannical law. In a second set of resolutions, the Kentucky legislature introduced the doctrine of **nullification**, the right of a state to render null and void a national law it deemed unconstitutional.

Jefferson and Madison hoped that these resolutions would rally voters to the Republican party as the defender of threatened American liberties. Yet not a single additional state seconded them. In the end, what aroused popular rage against the Federalists was not legislation directed against aliens and subversives but the high cost of Federalist taxes.

The Direct Tax of 1798 fell on all owners of land, dwellings, or slaves and provoked widespread resentment. Enforcing it required an army of bureaucrats—more than five hundred for the state of Pennsylvania alone. In February 1799, in the heavily German southeastern counties of Pennsylvania, a group of men led by an auctioneer named John Fries released tax evaders from prison in Bethlehem. President Adams responded to **Fries's Rebellion** with a show of force, but the fiercest resistance the soldiers he sent to Pennsylvania encountered was from irate farm wives, who doused them with hot water. The Federalists had now lost much of their support in Pennsylvania.

The End of the Federalists

The events in Pennsylvania reflected an air of menace that gripped the country as the campaign of 1800 approached. The army was chasing private citizens whose only crime in the eyes of many was that they were honoring their Revolutionary heritage by resisting hateful taxes. Federal soldiers also roughed up Republican voters at polling places. Southern Republicans talked in private of the possible need to resist Federalist tyranny by force and, failing in that, to secede from the Union. Hamilton and his backers, known as the High Federalists, saw in the Kentucky and Virginia resolutions "a regular conspiracy to overturn the government."

No one did more to defuse this charged atmosphere than President Adams. The Federalists depended for their popular support on the expectation of a war with France, which as late as 1798 had swept them to victory in the congressional elections. Still, Adams refrained from asking for a declaration of war. Adams recognized that war with France could trigger a civil war at home. Hamilton and the High Federalists, he realized, would use war as an excuse to crush the Republican opposition in Virginia. Fearful of Hamilton's intentions and unwilling to run the risk of militarizing the government, Adams broke with his party and decided to reopen negotiations with France in February 1799.

The **Franco-American Accord of 1800** that resulted from Adams's initiative released the United States from its 1778 alliance with France and in return the United States surrendered all claims against the French for damages done to American shipping. The prospect of peace with France deprived the Hamilton Federalists of their trump card in the election. The Republicans could no

Short and pudgy, Adams had little of Hamilton's physical presence as a natural leader. But he had a first-rate mind and the political courage to place the nation's needs above those of his Federalist party when he peacefully ended the Quasi-War with France.

longer be branded as the traitorous friends of an enemy state. The enlarged army, with no foe to fight, became a political embarrassment, and the Federalists dismantled it. Although rumors of possible violence continued to circulate, the Republicans grew increasingly confident that they could peacefully gain control of the government.

The Federalists, hampered by party disunity, could not counter the Republicans' aggressive organizational tactics. They found it distasteful to appeal to common people. Wherever the Republicans organized, they attacked the Federalists as monarchists plotting to undo the gains of the Revolution. The Federalists responded with emotional appeals that depicted Jefferson as a godless revolutionary whose election would usher in a reign of terror. "The effect," intoned the Reverend William Linn, "would be to destroy religion, introduce immorality, and loosen all bonds of society."

Attacks like Linn's reflected the fears of Calvinist preachers that a tide of disbelief was about to submerge Christianity in the United States. **Deism,** an Enlightenment religious philosophy popular among the leaders of the Revolutionary era, was making inroads among common citizens as well. Deists viewed God as a kind of master clockmaker who created the laws by which the universe runs but otherwise leaves it alone. They rejected revelation for reason, maintaining that the workings of nature alone reveal God's design. These developments convinced Calvinist ministers, nearly all of them Federalists, that the atheism of the French Revolution was infecting American republicanism.

The Republicans won the election by mobilizing voters through strong party organizations. Voter turnout in 1800 was twice what it had been in the early 1790s, and most of the new voters were Republicans. The Direct Tax of 1798 cost the Federalists the support of commercial farmers in the mid-Atlantic states. Artisans in port cities had already switched to the Republicans in protest over Jay's Treaty, which they feared left them exposed to a flood of cheap British imports. Adams carried New England and had a smattering of support elsewhere. With New York added to their solid base in the South and the backcountry, the Jeffersonians gained an electoral majority (see Map 8-1).

Party unity among Republican electors was so strong that Jefferson and Burr each received seventy-three electoral votes. Consequently the election was thrown into the House of Representatives, which, until the newly elected Congress was seated, was still dominated by Federalists. Hoping to deny Jefferson the presidency, the Federalists in the House backed Burr. The result was a deadlock that persisted into the early months of 1801 when the Federalists yielded. Informed through intermediaries that Jefferson would not dismantle Hamilton's fiscal system, enough Federalists cast blank ballots to give Jefferson the majority he needed for election. The Twelfth Amendment to the Constitution, ratified in 1804, prevented a similar impasse from arising again by requiring electors to cast separate ballots for president and vice president.

Conclusion

In 1789, the American republic was little more than an experiment in self-government. The Federalists provided a firm foundation for that experiment. Hamilton's financial program, neutrality in the wars of the French Revolution, and the diplomatic settlement with Britain in Jay's Treaty bequeathed the young nation a decade of peace and prosperity.

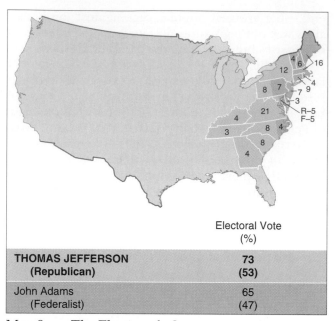

	Electoral Vote (%)
THOMAS JEFFERSON (Republican)	**73** **(53)**
John Adams (Federalist)	65 (47)

Map 8-1   The Election of 1800
The sharp erosion of Federalist strength in New York and Pennsylvania after 1798 swung the election of 1800 to the Republicans.

Federalist policies, however, provoked strong opposition rooted in conflicting economic interests and contrasting regional views over the meaning of liberty and government in the new republic. The Federalist coalition split during Washington's second term when southern planters joined urban artisans and backcountry Scots-Irish farmers in opposing Jay's Treaty and the commercially oriented program of the Federalists. When Quaker and German farmers in the mid-Atlantic states defected from the Federalists over the tax legislation of 1798, three of the four regions in Washington's America now lined up behind the Republicans in the belief that measures such as expansion of the army and passage of the Alien and Sedition Acts threatened individual liberty and regional autonomy.

The openly partisan politics of the 1790s surprised the country's founders, who equated parties with the evils of factionalism. They had not foreseen that parties would forge a necessary link between the rulers and the ruled and create a mechanism by which group values and regional interests could be given a political voice. To the credit of the Federalists, they relinquished control of the national government peacefully. The importance of this precedent can scarcely be exaggerated. It marked the first time in modern political history that a party in power handed over the government to its opposition.

Review Questions

1. What was distinctive about the four regions of the United States in 1790? What were the common values and goals that brought white Americans together?

2. What were the major problems confronting the Washington administration, and how effectively were they resolved?

3. Who were the Federalists and the Republicans, and how did they differ over the meaning of liberty and the power of the national government? What were the major steps in the formation of two distinct parties in the early United States?

4. Why did regional differences tend to pit the North against the South by the late 1790s?

5. How did the XYZ Affair lead to a political crisis in the United States? Why did the Federalists believe that they would benefit from a war against France?

6. Jefferson called his election in 1800 the "revolution of 1800." What do you think he meant? Would you agree with him?

Recommended Reading

Stanley Elkins and Eric McKitrick, *The Age of Federalism* (1993). A magisterial work of narrative history that includes brilliant sketches of the major political actors in the 1790s.

James T. Flexner, *George Washington and the New Nation, 1783–1793* (1969) and *George Washington: Anguish and Farewell, 1793–1799* (1972). These two volumes stand out for their readable and informative account of Washington's political career after the Revolution.

Richard Hofstadter, *The Idea of a Party System, 1780–1840* (1969). This book combines political and intellectual history in a graceful account of how Americans gradually came to accept political parties as a legitimate expression of the popular will.

Seymour Lipset, *The First New Nation: The United States in Historical and Comparative Perspective* (1963). This work draws on insights from political sociology to show what was unique and enduring in America's pioneering role as a new nation with a written constitution.

John C. Miller, *The Federalist Era, 1789–1801* (1960). This older work is still of great value for its relatively brief and well-balanced overview of the Washington and Adams administrations.

Where to Learn More

❖ **Cincinnati Historical Society, Cincinnati, Ohio.** Collections include written and visual materials on the history of the Old Northwest Territory.

❖ **Federal Hall National Memorial, New York, New York.** This museum and historic site holds artifacts relating to President Washington's inauguration.

❖ **Hamilton Grange National Memorial, New York, New York.** The home of Alexander Hamilton contains materials on his life.

❖ **Adams National Historic Site, Quincy, Massachusetts.** This site preserves buildings and manuscripts associated with four generations of the Adams family.

9 THE TRIUMPH AND COLLAPSE OF JEFFERSONIAN REPUBLICANISM, 1800–1824

KEY TOPICS

❖ The domination of the Republicans and the collapse of the Federalist party
❖ The territorial expansion of the United States to the west and the south
❖ The growth of nationalism and of sectional rivalry
❖ The first national crisis over slavery
❖ The collapse of the Republican party

"I have nothing more to offer than what George Washington would have had he been taken by the British officers and put to trial. I have ventured my life in endeavoring to obtain the liberty of my countrymen, and am a willing sacrifice to their cause." The condemned prisoner who uttered these words was a slave, one of twenty-seven who were executed by Virginia authorities for their suspected role in Gabriel's Rebellion of 1800. Gabriel Prosser, a slave blacksmith, had organized one thousand slaves for an attack on Richmond. By seizing arms and capturing key points in the city, Gabriel hoped to spark a general uprising of slaves and whites sympathetic to their cause. Planned for the night of August 30, 1800, the rebellion was eventually betrayed by slave informers.

Gabriel's Rebellion exposed the contradictory and potentially explosive nature of the Revolution's heritage of liberty and equality. As a Virginia Federalist remarked of the rebellion: "A doctrine [of liberty] which, however intelligible and admissible, in a land of freemen, is not only unintelligible and inadmissible, but dangerous and extremely wicked in this country, where every white man is a master, and every black man a slave." Ironically, where Gabriel Prosser erred was in not grasping that nearly all whites were determined to apply the libertarian principles of the Revolution only to themselves. The Jeffersonian democracy that Gabriel wanted to fuse into black Revolutionary activity was emphatically for whites only. Jefferson believed that only whites could achieve the propertied independence and sturdy self-sufficiency necessary to value the public good over private gain. His republic would escape the social hierarchy of corrupt Europe by filling North America with farm families of white yeomen, Who could improve their standard of living by exchanging agricultural surpluses for imported manufactured goods. Westward expansion and free and open trade with the outside world were the keys to Jefferson's empire of liberty.

To an extraordinary extent, Jefferson and his Republican successors, James Madison and James Monroe, succeeded in promoting the growth and independence of the United States in the first quarter of the nineteenth century. Expansionist policies to the south and west more than doubled the size of the republic and fueled the westward spread of slavery. A war against Britain in 1812–1814, if less than a military success, nonetheless freed Americans to look inward for economic development.

At the height of Republican success during the Era of Good Feelings just after the War of 1812, the Federalist party collapsed. Without an organized opposition to enforce party discipline among themselves, the Republicans soon followed the Federalists into political oblivion. By the mid-1820s, a new party system was emerging.

Jefferson's Presidency

Thomas Jefferson believed that a true revolution had occurred in 1800, a peaceful overthrow of the Federalist party and its hated principles of government consolidation and military force. In his eyes, the defeat of the monarchical Federalists reconfirmed the true political legacy of the Revolution by restoring the republican majority to its rightful control of the government.

Unlike the Hamiltonian Federalists, whose commercial vision of America accepted social and economic inequalities as inevitable, the Jeffersonians wanted a predominantly agrarian republic based on widespread economic equality for white yeomen families to counter any threat posed by the privileged few to the people's liberties. Jefferson's first administration was a solid success. A unified Republican party reduced the size and scope of the federal government, allowed the Alien and Sedition Acts to lapse, and celebrated the Louisiana Purchase. His second term, however, was a bitter disappointment,

marked by the failure of his unpopular embargo on American foreign trade. As a result, Jefferson left his successor, James Madison, a divided party, a temporarily revived Federalism, and an unresolved crisis in foreign affairs.

Reform at Home

Jefferson set the style and tone of his administration from the beginning. He was the first president to be inaugurated in Washington, D.C., and his inauguration was as unpretentious as the raw and primitive capital city itself. He walked from his lodgings to the Capitol building to be sworn in. His dress was neat but shorn of gentlemanly refinements such as a wig. After giving notice that an unadorned style of republican egalitarianism would now replace the aristocratic formalities of the Federalists, Jefferson emphasized in his inaugural address the overwhelming commitment of Americans to the "republican form" of government and affirmed his own support of civil liberties as an American principle.

A poor public speaker, Jefferson sent written messages to Congress to avoid having to read them in person. This change from Federalist policy both eliminated the impression of a monarch addressing his subjects and played to Jefferson's formidable skills as a writer. He replaced the stiff formalism and aristocratic etiquette of receptions for presidential visitors with more relaxed weekly meetings around a circular table at which fine food and wine were nevertheless served.

The cornerstone of Republican domestic policy was retrenchment, a return to the frugal, simple federal establishment the Jeffersonians believed was the original intent of the Constitution. The Republicans began with fiscal policy. Jefferson's secretary of the treasury was Albert Gallatin, who convinced Jefferson that the Bank of the United States was essential for financial stability and yet succeeded in reducing the national debt from $83 million in 1800 to $57 million by 1809. Gallatin's conservative fiscal policies shrank both the spending and taxes of the national government. The Republicans eliminated all internal taxes, including the despised tax on whiskey. Slashes in the military budget enabled government expenditures to stay below the level of 1800. The cuts in military spending combined with soaring revenues from customs collections left Gallatin with a surplus in the budget that he could devote to debt repayment.

Jeffersonian reform targeted the political character, as well as the size, of the national government. He moved to break the Federalist stranglehold on federal offices and appoint officials with sound

CHRONOLOGY

1801 Thomas Jefferson is inaugurated, the first Republican president.

John Marshall becomes chief justice.

1802 Congress repeals the Judiciary Act of 1801.

1803 *Marbury* v. *Madison* sets the precedent of judicial review by the Supreme Court.

Louisiana Purchase.

1804 Vice President Aaron Burr kills Alexander Hamilton in a duel.

Judges John Pickering and Samuel Chase impeached by Republicans.

Jefferson is reelected.

1806 Britain and France issue orders restricting neutral shipping.

Betrayal of the Burr conspiracy.

1807 *Chesapeake* affair.

Congress passes the Embargo Act.

1808 Congress prohibits the African slave trade.

James Madison elected president.

1809 Repeal of the Embargo Act.

Passage of the Nonintercourse Act.

1810 Macon's Bill No. 2 reopens trade with Britain and France.

United States annexes part of West Florida.

Georgia state law invalidated by the Supreme Court in *Fletcher* v. *Peck*.

1811 Battle of Tippecanoe and defeat of the Indian confederation.

Charter of the Bank of the United States expires.

1812 Congress declares war on Britain.

American loss of Detroit.

Madison reelected.

1813 Perry's victory at Battle of Put-in-Bay.

Battle of the Thames and death of Tecumseh.

1814 Jackson crushes the Creeks at the Battle of Horseshoe Bend.

British burn Washington, D.C., and attack Baltimore.

Macdonough's naval victory on Lake Champlain turns back a British invasion.

Hartford Convention meets.

Treaty of Ghent signed.

1815 Jackson routs British at the Battle of New Orleans.

1816 Congress charters the Second Bank of the United States and passes a protective tariff.

James Monroe elected president.

1817 Rush-Bagot Treaty demilitarizes the Great Lakes.

1818 Anglo-American Accords on trade and boundaries.

Jackson's border campaign in Spanish East Florida.

1819 Trans-Continental Treaty between United States and Spain.

Beginning of the Missouri controversy.

Financial panic sends economy into a depression.

Dartmouth College v. *Woodward* upholds the charter rights of corporations.

McCulloch v. *Maryland* upholds constitutionality of the Bank of the United States.

1820 Missouri Compromise on slavery in the Louisiana Purchase.

Monroe reelected.

1823 Monroe Doctrine proclaims Western Hemisphere closed to further European colonization.

1825 John Quincy Adams elected president by the House of Representatives.

Republican principles, replacing those deemed guilty of misusing their offices for political gain. By the time Jefferson left the presidency in 1809, Republicans held nearly all the appointive offices.

Jefferson moved most aggressively against the Federalists in the judiciary. Just days before they relinquished power, the Federalists enraged the Jeffersonians by passing the **Judiciary Act of 1801**, legislation that both enlarged the judiciary and packed it with more Federalists appointed by Adams, the outgoing president.

The Republicans fought back. Now dominant in Congress, they quickly repealed the Judiciary Act of 1801. Frustrated Federalists now turned to John Marshall, a staunch Federalist appointed chief justice of the United States by President Adams in 1801, in the hope that he would rule that Congress had acted unconstitutionally in removing the recently appointed federal judges. Marshall moved carefully, aware that the Republicans contended that Congress and the president had at least a coequal right with the Supreme Court to decide constitutional questions.

The issue came to a head in the case of ***Marbury* v. *Madison*** (1803), which centered on Secretary of State James Madison's refusal to deliver a commission to William Marbury, one of Adams's "midnight appointments." Marshall held that although Marbury had a legal right to his commission, the Court had no jurisdiction in the case. The Court ruled that the section of the Judiciary Act of 1789 granting it the power to order the delivery of Marbury's commission was unconstitutional because it conferred on the Court a power not specified in Article 3 of the Constitution on cases of original jurisdiction. Marshall created the precedent of judicial review, the power of the Supreme Court to rule on the constitutionality of federal law. This doctrine was of pivotal importance for the future of the Court. Marshall had brilliantly turned a threatening situation into a success for the judiciary.

The Louisiana Purchase

In foreign affairs, fortune smiled on Jefferson during his first term. The European war that had almost sucked in the United States in the 1790s subsided.

Dolly Madison, the engaging young wife of James Madison, Jefferson's secretary of state, served as the unofficial social hostess in the White House during the administration of Jefferson, a widower.

Jefferson, despite his distaste for a strong navy, ordered a show of force in the Mediterranean to punish the Barbary pirates who were preying on American shipping.

For years, the North African states of Morocco, Algeria, Tunis, and Tripoli had demanded cash tribute from foreigners as the price for allowing trade in the Mediterranean. Jefferson stopped the payments in 1801, and when the attacks on American shipping resumed, he retaliated by sending warships to the Mediterranean. The tribute system continued until 1815, but on much more favorable terms for the United States.

The Anglo-French peace was a mixed blessing for the United States. Although it removed any immediate threat of war, the return of peace also enabled Spain and France to reclaim their colonial trade in the Western Hemisphere. The new military ruler of France, Napoleon Bonaparte, in a secret treaty with Spain in 1800, reacquired for France the Louisiana Territory, a vast, vaguely defined area stretching between the Mississippi River and the Rocky Mountains. Sketchy, unconfirmed reports of the treaty in the spring of 1801 alarmed Jefferson. France, for its part, was a formidable opponent whose control of the Mississippi Valley, combined with the British presence in Canada, threatened to hem in the United States. Jefferson was prepared to reverse the traditional foreign policy of his party and opened exploratory talks with the British on an Anglo-American alliance to drive the French out of Louisiana. He also strengthened American forces in the Mississippi Valley and secured congressional approval for the Lewis and Clark expedition through upper Louisiana, which was initially intended to be more of a military than a scientific mission.

Jefferson then sought to acquire New Orleans and control the mouth of the Mississippi River, outlet to world markets. He persuaded Congress to pass resolutions threatening an attack on New Orleans (see Map 9-1).

Meanwhile, Napoleon had envisioned the rich sugar island of St. Domingue (today divided between Haiti and the Dominican Republic) as the jewel of his new empire and he intended to use the Louisiana Territory as a granary to supply the island. But he failed to recover St. Domingue from the slaves on the island, led by Touissant L'Ouverture, who had captured it in a bloody and successful bid for independence. Without firm French control of St. Domingue, Louisiana was of little use to Napoleon and a renewed war against Britain was looming. To Jefferson's surprise, Napoleon sold Louisiana to the United States for $15 million (the

Map 9-1 The Louisiana Purchase and the Lewis and Clark Expedition
The vast expanse of the Louisiana Purchase was virtually unknown territory to Americans before the Lewis and Clark expedition gathered a mass of scientific information about it.

cost to the United States was about 3½ cents per acre). Jefferson, the strict constructionist, now turned pragmatist. Despite the lack of any specific authorization in the Constitution for the acquisition of foreign territory, he accepted Napoleon's deal and doubled the size of the United States with the **Louisiana Purchase**. Jefferson was willing, as the Federalists had been when they were in power, to stretch the Constitution to support his definition of the national good. Ironically, it was now the Federalists, fearful of a further decline in their political power, who relied on a narrow reading of the Constitution.

Florida and Western Schemes

The magnificent prize of Louisiana did not satisfy Republican territorial ambitions. Still to be gained were river outlets on the Gulf Coast essential for the development of plantation agriculture in Alabama and Mississippi. The boundaries of the Louisiana

Purchase were so vague that Jefferson felt justified in claiming Spanish-held Texas and the Gulf Coast eastward from New Orleans to Mobile Bay, including the Spanish province of West Florida. This provoked the first challenge to his leadership of the party.

Once it was clear that Spain did not want to sell West Florida to the United States, Jefferson covertly accepted Napoleon's offer to act as a middleman in the acquisition. Former Republican stalwarts in Congress staged a party revolt against the president's devious tactics.

Jefferson's failed bid for West Florida emboldened Westerners to demand that Americans seize the territory by force. In 1804, Aaron Burr, Jefferson's first vice president, concocted a plan for a northern conspiracy. Burr had been suspect in the party since his dalliance with the Federalists in 1800 when he had sought the presidency. A minority of die-hard Federalists, fearing that incorporation of the vast territory of the Louisiana Purchase into the United States would reduce New England's power, backed Burr in the New York gubernatorial race of 1804. Burr lost, largely because Hamilton denounced his character. The enmity between the two men reached a tragic climax in July 1804, when Burr killed Hamilton in a duel. Facing murder charges, Burr fled to the West and lined up followers for a separatist plot.

The Burr conspiracy remains mysterious. Burr may have been thinking of carving out a separate western confederacy in the lower Mississippi Valley. Whatever he had in mind, he blundered in relying on General James Wilkinson as a coconspirator. Wilkinson, the military governor of the Louisiana Territory and also a double agent for Spain, betrayed Burr. Jefferson made extraordinary efforts to secure a conviction, but Burr was acquitted when the government failed to prove its case for treason in 1807.

Embargo and a Crippled Presidency

Concern about a possible war against Britain in 1807 soon quieted the uproar over Burr's trial. After Britain and France resumed their war in 1803, the United States became enmeshed in the same thicket of neutral rights, blockades, ship seizures, and impressment of American sailors that had almost dragged the country into war in the 1790s. Caught in the middle, but eager to supply both sides, was the American merchant marine, the world's largest carrier of neutral goods. American merchants and shippers had taken full advantage of the magnificent opportunities opened up by the European war. The flush years from 1793 to 1807 witnessed a tripling of American ship tonnage, and the value of exports soared five times over. American merchants dominated trade not only between Britain and the United States but also between the European continent and the French and Spanish colonies in the West Indies.

The *Chesapeake* incident in June 1807 nearly triggered an Anglo-American war. When the commander of the U.S. frigate *Chesapeake* refused to submit to a British search in coastal waters off Norfolk, the British ship *Leopard* opened fire, and three Americans were killed. Jefferson resisted the popular outcry for revenge. Instead, he barred American ports to British warships and called for monetary compensation and an end to impressment, not only because the country was woefully unprepared for war but also because he passionately believed that international law should resolve disputes between nations. In a last burst of the idealism that had animated the republicanism of the Revolution, Jefferson resorted to a trade embargo as a substitute for war. The **Embargo Act of 1807** prohibited American

ships from clearing port to any nation until Britain and France repealed their trading restrictions on neutral shippers.

The basic premise of the embargo, that Europe was completely dependent on American-supplied foodstuffs and raw materials, was not so much wrong as unrealistic. The embargo did hurt Europe, but the people who first felt the pain were British textile workers and slaves in the colonies, hardly those who wielded the levers of power. Meanwhile, the American export trade and its profits dried up, and nearly all economic groups suffered. Especially hard hit were New England shippers and merchants, who accused the Republicans of near-criminal irresponsibility for forcing a depression on the country. Jefferson responded with a series of enforcement acts that consolidated executive powers far beyond what the Federalists themselves had been able to achieve while in power. As the embargo tightened and the 1808 election approached, Federalism revived. The Federalist Charles C. Pinckney of South Carolina tripled his electoral vote over that of 1804, but Secretary of State Madison carried the South and the West, the heartland of Republican support. Before Madison took office, the Republicans abandoned Jefferson's embargo in 1809, replacing it with the **Nonintercourse Act**, a measure that prohibited American trade only with Britain and France.

Madison and the Coming of War

Frail-looking and short, Madison struck most contemporaries as an indecisive and weaker version of Jefferson. Yet in intellectual toughness and resourcefulness he was at least Jefferson's equal. He failed because of an inherited foreign policy that was partly of his own making as Jefferson's secretary of state. The Republicans' idealistic stand on neutral rights was ultimately untenable unless backed up by military and political force. Madison concluded as much when he decided on war against Britain in the spring of 1812. Thus did the Republicans push for a war they were eager to fight but unprepared to wage.

The Failure of Economic Sanctions

Early in his administration, Madison became convinced that the impasse in Anglo-American relations was about to be broken. Britain benefited from the Nonintercourse Act at the expense of France. Once at sea, American ships were kept away from France and steered to England by the strong British navy. Perhaps in recognition of this unintended consequence of the new American policy, the British began to relax their restrictions on neutral shipping, known as the **Orders in Council**, in favor of U.S. commerce. At the same time, the British minister in Washington, David Erskine, reached an agreement with Madison that called for completely rescinding the Orders in Council as they applied to the United States. Unfortunately, Erskine had exceeded his instructions, and the Madison-Erskine agreement was later disavowed in London. Although Madison reimposed sanctions on Britain in August, he was left looking the fool.

Congress stepped in with its own policy in 1810. **Macon's Bill No. 2** threw open American trade to everyone but stipulated that if either France or England lifted its restrictions, the president would resume trading sanctions against the other. Madison now looked even more foolish when he accepted Napoleon's duplicitous promises in 1810 to withdraw his decrees against American shipping on the condition that if Britain did not follow suit, Madison would force the British to respect American rights. French seizures of American ships continued, and by the time Napoleon's duplicity became clear, he had already succeeded in worsening Anglo-American tensions to the point that in November 1810, Madison reimposed nonintercourse against Britain, putting the two nations on a collision course.

The Frontier and Indian Resistance

Mounting frustrations in the South and West also pushed Madison toward a war against Britain. Farm prices, including those for the southern staples of cotton and tobacco, plunged when Jefferson's embargo shut off exports and stayed low after the embargo was lifted. Blame for the persistent agricultural depression focused on the British and their stranglehold on overseas trade after 1808.

Western settlers blamed the British for inspiring Indian attempts to resist them. However, it was the unceasing demand of Americans for ever more Indian land, not any British incitements, that triggered the **pan-Indian resistance movement** that so frightened western settlers on the eve of the War of 1812. Many Native Americans were also determined to lash back at such white attitudes as those expressed about the Miami Indians by an Ohioan in 1810: "We never permit them to be troublesome, for if any of them displease us, we take them out of doors and kick them a little, for they are like dogs, and so will love you the better for it."

In the Treaty of Greenville (1795), the American government had promised that any future acquisitions of Indian land would have to be approved by all native peoples in the region. Nonetheless, government agents continued their former tactics of playing one group against another and of dividing groups from within. By such means, William Henry Harrison, the governor of the Indiana Territory, procured most of southern Indiana in the **Treaty of Vincennes** of 1804. Two extraordinary leaders, the Shawnee chief Tecumseh and his brother, the Prophet Tenkswatawa, channeled Indian outrage over this treaty into a movement to unify tribes throughout the West for a stand against the white invaders. As preached by Tecumseh and the Prophet, Indian land could be saved and self-respect regained only through racial solidarity and a spiritual rebirth. With the assistance of Tecumseh, Tenkswatawa established the Prophet's Town in 1808, at the confluence of the Wabash and Tippecanoe Rivers in north-central Indiana, as headquarters of an intertribal confederation. As he tried to explain to the worried Governor Harrison, his goals were peaceful. He admonished his followers, "[Do] not take up the tomahawk, . . . do not meddle with any thing that does not belong to you, but mind your own business, and cultivate the ground, that your women and your children have enough to live on."

That ground, of course, was the very reason the Indians could not live in peace and dignity. The whites wanted it and would do anything to get it. In November 1811, Harrison marched an army to Prophet's Town and provoked the **Battle of Tippecanoe**. While Tecumseh was absent on a recruiting mission among the southern tribes, impetuous young braves attacked Harrison's army. Harrison's victory came at a high cost, for Tecumseh now joined forces with the British.

While Harrison's aggressiveness was converting fears of a British-Indian alliance into a self-fulfilling prophecy, expansionist-minded Southerners struck at Britain through Spain, now its ally against Napoleon. With the covert support of President Madison, American adventurers staged a bloodless revolt in Spanish West Florida extending to the Pearl River, the present Gulf Coast boundary between Louisiana and Mississippi. Hatred of Native Americans, expansionist pressures, the lingering agricultural depression, and impatience with the administration's policy of economic coercion all pointed in the same direction—a war against Britain coupled with an American takeover of British Canada and Spanish Florida. This was the rallying cry of the **War Hawks**, the forty or so prowar congressmen swept into office in 1810. Generally younger men from the South and West, the War Hawks were led by Henry Clay of Kentucky. Along with other outspoken nationalists such as John C. Calhoun of South Carolina, Clay played a key role in building congressional support for Madison's growing aggressiveness on the British issue.

Decision for War

In July 1811, deceived by Napoleon and dismissed by the British as the head of a second-rate power, Madison had run out of diplomatic options and was losing control of his party. When Congress met in November, Madison tried to lay the groundwork for war. But the Republican-controlled Congress balked at strenghtening the military or raising taxes to pay for a war that seemed ever more likely, citing their party's traditional view of high taxes and a strong military as the tools of despots. Madison secretly asked Congress on April 1 for a sixty day embargo, a move designed to give American merchant ships time to return safely to their home ports. On June 1, he sent a war message to Congress in which he laid out the stark alternative of submission or resistance to the British control of American commerce (see "American Views: Madison's War Message of June 1, 1812"). For Madison and most other Republicans, the impending conflict was a second war for independence. Free and open access to world markets was certainly at stake, but so was national pride. The arrogant British policy of impressment was a humiliating affront to American honor and headed the list of grievances in Madison's war message.

A divided Congress declared war on Britain. Support for the war was strongest in regions, like the South and the West, whose economies had been damaged the most by the British blockades and control of Atlantic commerce. The votes that carried the war declaration came from northern Republicans, who saw the impending struggle as a defense of America's experiment in self-government. Nine-tenths of the congressional Republicans voted for war, but not a single Federalist did so. For the Federalists, the real enemy was France, which had actually seized more American ships than the British. The Federalists' anger increased when they learned that the British had been prepared to revoke for one year the Orders in Council against the United States. A poor harvest and the ongoing economic pressure exerted by Madison had finally caused hard times in England and produced a policy reversal of placating the Americans. This concession, however, did not address impressment or monetary compensation, and news of it reached America too late to avert a war.

The War of 1812

The Republicans led the nation into a war it was unprepared to fight (see Map 9-2 on page 164). The bungled American invasions verged on tragicomedy, and for much of the war, Britain was preoccupied with Napoleon in Europe. When free to concentrate on the American sideshow in 1814, the British failed to secure naval control of the Great Lakes, their minimal strategic objective. By the fall of 1814, both sides were eager for an end to the military stalemate.

Internal dissent endangered the Union almost as much as the British. The war exacerbated Federalist disenchantment with southern dominance of national affairs. A minority of Federalists, convinced that New England could never regain its rightful place in shaping national policy, prepared to lead a secession movement. Although blocked by party moderates at the **Hartford Convention** in 1814, the secessionists tarred Federalism with the brush of treason. Consequently, the Republicans, the party that brought the country to the brink of a military disaster, emerged from the war more powerful than ever.

Setbacks in Canada

The outbreak of the **War of 1812** unleashed deep emotions that often divided along religious lines, with Federalists Congregationalists (mostly) opposing the war and the Baptists and Methodists favoring the war to be "just, necessary, and indispensable." Fiercely loyal to Madison, who had championed religious freedom in Virginia, these Methodists and Baptists harbored old grudges against the established churches of both Britain and New England for suppressing their religious rights.

Madison hoped to channel this Christian, anti-British patriotism into the conquest of Canada. Assuming the Canadians would welcome the U.S. Army with open arms Madison expected American militia troops to overpower the small British force of 5,000 soldiers that was initially stationed in Canada.

By seizing Canada, Madison also hoped to weaken Britain's navy and undercut its navigation system by cutting off American foodstuffs and provisions from the British West Indies.

Madison's strategic vision was clear, but its execution was pathetic. Three offensives against Canada in 1812 were embarrassing failures. In the

American Views

MADISON'S WAR MESSAGE OF JUNE 1, 1812

Mounting tensions between the United States and Britain during the Jefferson and Madison administrations climaxed in the War of 1812. Madison's war message to Congress summarized the Republican case for a declaration of war and cited a number of grievances. Central to the thinking of the Republicans was the belief that Americans could establish their own identity and independence only by standing up to British aggressions and escaping the status of a British dependency.

❖ **What factors did Madison stress in asking for a declaration of war?**

❖ **What influence of the War Hawks can you find in the war message?**

❖ **How did Madison argue that the goal of the British was to gain a monopoly on trade and injure the commercial interests of the United States?**

❖ **Why did many Americans view the War of 1812 as a second war for American independence?**

Without going back beyond the renewal in 1803 of the war in which Great Britain is engaged, and omitting unrepaired wrongs of inferior magnitude, the conduct of her Government presents a series of acts hostile to the United States as an independent and neutral nation.

British cruisers have been in the continued practice of violating the American flag on the great highway of nations, and of seizing and carrying off persons sailing under it, not in the exercise of a belligerent right founded on the law of nations against an enemy, but of a municipal prerogative over British subjects. . . .

Thousands of American citizens, under the safeguard of public law and of their national flag, have been torn from their country and from everything dear to them; have been dragged on board ships of war of a foreign nation and exposed, under the severities of their discipline, to be exiled to the most distant and deadly climes, to risk their lives in battles of their oppressors, and to be the melancholy instruments of taking away those of their own brethren.

Against this crying enormity, which Great Britain would be so prompt to avenge if committed against herself, the United States have in vain exhausted remonstrances and expostulations. . . .

British cruisers have been in the practice

---

first, in July, General William Hull surrendered to a smaller British-Indian force.

The loss of Detroit and the abandonment of Fort Dearborn (present-day Chicago) exposed western settlements to the full fury of frontier warfare. Americans in the Indiana Territory fled outlying areas for the safety of forts in the interior. By the end of the year, the British controlled half of the Old Northwest.

Farther east, the Americans botched two offensives in 1812. In October, an American thrust across the Niagara River was defeated when a New York state militia refused to cross the river to join the regular army troops on the Canadian side. This left the isolated forces under General Stephen Van Rensselaer an easy prey for the British at the **Battle of Queenston Heights**. Then the long-delayed third offensive aimed at Montreal, the center of British operations in Canada, ending in a bloodless fiasco.

All the Republicans had to show for the first year of the war were morale-boosting but otherwise insignificant naval victories. The small American navy acquitted itself superbly in individual ship-to-ship combat.

also of violating the rights and peace of our coasts. They hover over and harass our entering and departing commerce. . . .

Under pretended blockades, without the presence of an adequate force and sometimes without the practicability of applying one, our commerce has been plundered in every sea, the great staples of our country have been cut off from their legitimate markets, and a destructive blow aimed at our agricultural and maritime interests. . . .

It has become, indeed, sufficiently certain that the commerce of the United States is to be sacrificed, not as interfering with the belligerent rights of Great Britain, not as supplying the wants of her enemies, which she herself supplies; but as interfering with the monopoly which she covets for her commerce and navigation. She carries on a war against the lawful commerce of a friend that she may the better carry on a commerce with an enemy. . . .

In reviewing the conduct of Great Britain toward the United States our attention is necessarily drawn to the warfare just renewed by the savages on one of our extensive frontiers—a warfare which is known to spare neither age nor sex and to be distinguished by features peculiarly shocking to humanity. It is difficult to account for the activity and combinations which have for some time been developing themselves among tribes in constant intercourse with British traders and garrisons without connecting their hostility with that influence and without recollecting the authenticated examples of such interpositions heretofore furnished by the officers and agents of the Government. . . .

We behold, in fine, on the side of Great Britain a state of war against the United States, and on the side of the United States a state of peace toward Great Britain.

Whether the United States shall continue passive under these progressive usurpations and these accumulating wrongs, or, opposing force to force in defense of their national rights, shall commit a just cause into the hands of the Almighty Disposer of Events . . . is a solemn question which the Constitution wisely confides to the legislative department of the Government. . . .

Source: William Appleman Williams, ed., *The Shaping of American Diplomacy: Readings and Documents in American Foreign Relations* (1956).

Military setbacks and antiwar feelings in much of the Northeast hurt the Republicans in the election of 1812. Madison won only narrowly. The now familiar regional pattern in voting repeated itself with Madison sweeping the electoral vote of the South and West. He ran poorly in the Northeast and won only because his party held on to Pennsylvania.

Western Victories and British Offensives

American forces fared better in 1813. In September, the navy won a major engagement on Lake Erie that opened up a supply line in the western theater. Commodore Oliver Hazard Perry attacked the British fleet in the **Battle of Put-in-Bay**, on the southwestern shore of the lake, and forced the surrender of all six British ships.

With the loss of Lake Erie, the British were forced to abandon Detroit. Demonstrating bold leadership and relying on battle-tested western militias, General William Henry Harrison won a decisive victory on the banks of the Thames River in Ontario. Tecumseh, the most visionary of the Indian warriors, was killed, and the backbone of the Indian resistance

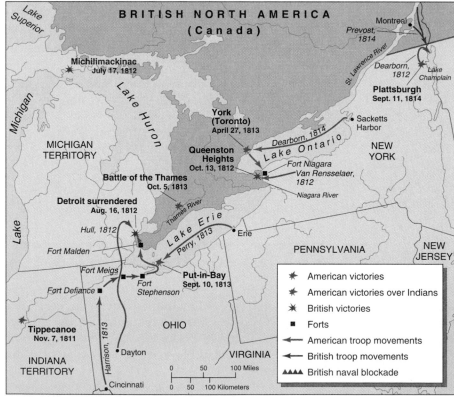

Map 9-2 The War of 1812
Most of the battles of the War of 1812 were fought along the Canadian-American border, where American armies repeatedly tried to invade Canada. Despite the effectiveness of the British naval blockade, the American navy was successful in denying the British strategic control of the Great Lakes. Andrew Jackson's smashing victory at the Battle of New Orleans convinced Americans that they had won the war.

broken. The Old Northwest was again safe for American settlement.

A coalition of European powers forced Napoleon to abdicate in April 1814, thus freeing Britain to focus on the American war. British strategy in 1814 called for two major offensives, an invasion south from Montreal down Lake Champlain in upstate New York and an attack on Louisiana aimed at seizing New Orleans with a task force out of Jamaica. The overall objective was nothing less than a reversal of America's post-1783 expansion.

The British attacks could hardly have come at a worse time for the Madison administration. The Treasury was nearly bankrupt. Against the wishes of Treasury Secretary Gallatin, Congress had refused to preserve the Bank of the United States when its charter expired in 1811. Lacking both a centralized means of directing wartime finances and any significant increase in taxes, the Treasury was forced to rely on makeshift loans. As the country's finances tottered toward collapse, political dissent in New England was reaching a climax.

The darkest hour came in August 1814. A British amphibious force occupied and torched Washington, D.C. in retaliation for an American raid on York (now Toronto), the capital of Upper Canada. The defense of Washington was slipshod at best. Baltimore's defenses held, stirring Francis Scott Key, a young lawyer who viewed the bombardment from a British prisoner-of-war ship, to write "The Star Spangled Banner." Fittingly in this strange war, the future national anthem was set to the tune of a British drinking song.

The Chesapeake campaign was designed to divert American attention from the major offensive General George Prevost was leading down the shores of Lake Champlain. Prevost commanded the largest and best-equipped army the British had yet assembled, but on September 11 he was defeated by Commodore Thomas Macdonough at the **Battle of Plattsburgh**. The British were now ready for peace, but one of their trump cards had yet to be played—the southern offensive against New Orleans.

The Treaty of Ghent and the Battle of New Orleans

Although the British signed the **Treaty of Ghent** in December 1814, they were not irrevocably committed to the as yet non-ratified peace settlement. The showdown between British and American forces at the **Battle of New Orleans** in January 1815 had immense strategic significance for the United States. The hero of New Orleans, in song and legend, was Andrew Jackson. A planter politician from Tennessee, Jackson rose to prominence during the war as a ferocious Indian fighter. As a general in the Tennessee militia, Jackson crushed Indian resistance in the Old Southwest at the Battle of Horseshoe Bend in March 1814 and forced the vanquished Creeks to cede two-thirds of their territory to the United States. After his Indian conquests, Jackson was promoted to general in the regular army and given command of the defense of the Gulf Coast. In November 1814, he seized Pensacola in Spanish Florida and then hurried to defend New Orleans. The overconfident British frontally attacked Jackson's lines on January 8, 1815. The result was a massacre. More than two thousand British soldiers were killed or wounded while American casualties totaled twenty-one.

Strategically, Jackson's smashing victory at New Orleans ended any possibility of a British sphere of influence in Louisiana. Politically, it was a deathblow to Federalism. As Americans were rejoicing with revived nationalism over the Treaty of Ghent and Jackson's routing of the British, the Federalists now seemed to be parochial sulkers who put regional interests above the national good.

The Era of Good Feelings

In 1817, on the occasion of a presidential visit by James Monroe, a Boston newspaper proclaimed the **Era of Good Feelings**, an expression that nicely captured the spirit of political harmony and sectional unity that washed over the republic in the immediate postwar years. National pride surged with the humbling of the British at New Orleans, the demise of the Federalists lessened political tensions, and the economy boomed. The Republicans had been vindicated, and for a short time they enjoyed de facto status as the only governing party.

In 1819, however, an economic depression and a bitter controversy over slavery shattered the harmony, and the Republicans divided on sectional and economic issues.

Economic Nationalism

The War of 1812 had taught the Republicans to appreciate old Federalist doctrines on centralized national power. For Henry Clay and John Calhoun, leaders of a new generation of young nationalist Republicans, the first order of business was creating a new national bank. Introduced by Calhoun, the Bank bill passed Congress in 1816. Modeled after Hamilton's original Bank and also headquartered in Philadelphia, the **Second Bank of the United States** was capitalized at $35 million, making it by far the nation's largest bank. Its sheer size, when combined with its official status as the depository and dispenser of the government's funds, gave the Bank tremendous power over the economy.

After moving to repair the fiscal damage of the war, the Republicans then acted to protect what the war had fostered. In 1815 and again in 1816, the British inundated the American market with cheap imports, a tactic openly designed to strangle American industry in its infancy. This challenge to the nation's economic independence united most Republicans against their traditional antagonist in foreign affairs. In retaliation, they passed the **Tariff of 1816**, the first protective tariff in American history. The act levied duties of 20 to 25 percent on manufactured goods that could be produced in the United States.

Revenue from the tariff and $1.5 million from the Bank of the United States were earmarked for internal improvements (roads and canals). The push for federal subsidies for transportation projects came from the War Department and the West. In early 1817, an internal improvements bill passed Congress. Despite the soaring rhetoric of John Calhoun, the bill's sponsor, seeking to "bind the republic together with a perfect system of roads and canals," President Madison remained unmoved. Though in agreement with the bill's objectives, he was convinced that the Constitution did not permit federal financing of primarily local projects. He vetoed the bill just before he left office.

Congressional passage of Calhoun's internal improvements bill marked the pinnacle of the Republicans' economic nationalism. Frightened by the sectional disunity of the war years, Republicans jettisoned many of the ideological trappings of Jefferson's original agrarian party. Their program was a call for economic, and therefore political, unity. Such unity was to be achieved through a generous program of national subsidies consisting of tariffs for manufacturers in the Northeast and transportation funds for planters and farmers in the South and West.

SUMMARY		
TERRITORIAL EXPANSION UNDER THE REPUBLICANS		
Benchmark	**Year**	**Land Area of United States and Its Territories (square miles)**
Republicans gain power	1801	864,746
Louisiana Purchase	1803	1,681,828
Trans-Continental Treaty	1819	1,749,462

Support for this program was strongest in the Mid-Atlantic and western states, the regions that stood to gain the most economically. Opposition centered in the Southeast and took on an increasingly hard edge in the South as the Supreme Court outlined an ever more nationalist interpretation of the Constitution.

Judicial Nationalism

The nationalist perspective championed by Republicans after the war had long been upheld in the Supreme Court under Chief Justice John Marshall, who dominated the Court throughout his tenure (1801–1835) by his forceful personality and the logical power of his nationalist convictions. The defining principles of Marshall's jurisprudence were the authority of the Supreme Court in all matters of constitutional interpretation and the sanctity of contractual property rights. In *Fletcher v. Peck* (1810), the Court overturned a Georgia law by ruling that it violated the prohibition in the federal Constitution against any state "impairing the obligation of contracts."

In *Dartmouth College v. Woodward*, the Court ruled that Dartmouth's original royal charter of 1769 was a contract protected by the Constitution and prohibited states from interfering with the rights and privileges they had bestowed on private corporations.

In *McCulloch v. Maryland*, a unanimous Court, in language similar to but even more sweeping than that used by Alexander Hamilton in the 1790s, upheld the constitutional authority of Congress to charter a national bank and thereby regulate the nation's currency and finances. As long as the end was legitimate "within the scope of the Constitution," Congress had full power to use any means not expressly forbidden by the Constitution to achieve that end. Here was the boldest statement to date of the loose or "implied powers" interpretation of the Constitution.

Toward a Continental Empire

Marshall's legal nationalism paralleled the diplomatic nationalism of John Quincy Adams, secretary of state from 1817 to 1825. A former Federalist and the son of the second president, Adams broke with the Federalist party over its refusal to support an expansionist policy. Adams made few friends as a negotiator but he was an effective diplomat, using whatever tactics were necessary to realize his vision of an America that stretched from the Atlantic to the Pacific.

Adams shrewdly exploited the British desire for friendly and profitable relations after the War of 1812. The **Rush-Bagot Agreement** of 1817 signaled the new pattern of Anglo-American cooperation. The agreement strictly limited naval armaments on the Great Lakes, thus effectively demilitarizing the border. The **Anglo-American Accords** of the following year resolved a number of issues left hanging after the war. Of great importance to New England, the British once again recognized American fishing rights off Labrador and Newfoundland. The boundary of the Louisiana Territory abutting Canada was set at the 49th parallel.

Having secured the northern flank of the United States, Adams was now free to deal with the South and West. Adams wanted all of Florida and an undisputed American window on the Pacific. The adversary here was Spain. In March 1818, Jackson led his troops across the border into Spanish Florida in

Map 9-3   *The Missouri Compromise of 1820 and Territorial Treaties with Britain and Spain, 1818–1819*
Treaties with Britain and Spain in 1818 and 1819 clarified and expanded the nation's boundaries. Britain accepted the 49th parallel as the boundary between Canada and the United States in the Trans-Mississippi West to the Oregon Country; Spain ceded Florida to the United States and agreed to a boundary stretching to the Pacific between the Louisiana Purchase territory and Spanish possessions in the Southwest. Sectional disputes over slavery led to the drawing of the Missouri Compromise line of 1820 that prohibited slavery in the Louisiana Territory north of 36°30′.

an attempt to stop Indian raids in the Alabama-Georgia frontier. He destroyed the encampments of the Seminole Indians, seized two Spanish forts, and executed two British subjects. Despite later protestations to the contrary, Jackson had probably exceeded his orders. But Adams took the offensive by lecturing Spain that Jackson was acting in the defense of American interests and warning that he might be unleashed again.

Spain yielded to the American threat in the **Trans-Continental Treaty of 1819** (see Map 9-3). The United States annexed East Florida, and Spain

recognized the prior American seizures of West Florida in 1810 and 1813. Adams secured an American hold on the Pacific Coast by drawing a boundary between the Louisiana Purchase and the Spanish Southwest.

Adams' success in the Spanish negotiations turned on the British refusal to threaten war or assist Spain in the wake of Jackson's highhanded actions in Florida. Spanish possessions and the lives of two British subjects were worth little when weighed against the economic advantages of retaining close trading ties with the United States. Moreover, Britain had a vested interest in the Latin American market opened by the loss of Spain's monopoly.

Adams was confident that within a generation, the United States would acquire California, Texas, and perhaps Cuba as well. He wanted to maintain the maximum freedom of action for future U.S. policy and avoid any impression that America was beholden to Britain. Thus originated the most famous diplomatic statement in early American history, the **Monroe Doctrine**. In his annual message to Congress in December 1823, Monroe declared that the Americas "are henceforth not to be considered as subjects for future colonization by any European power." In turn, Monroe pledged that the United States would not interfere in the internal affairs of European states.

The Breakdown of Unity

For all the intensity with which he pursued his continental vision, John Quincy Adams worried, as he confided to a congressman in early 1819, that "the greatest danger of this union was in the overgrown extent of its territory, combining with the slavery question." His words were prophetic. A sectional crisis flared up in 1819 over slavery and its expansion when the territory of Missouri sought admission to the Union as a slave state. Simultaneously, a financial panic ended postwar prosperity and crystallized regional discontent over banking and tariff policies. Party unity cracked under these pressures, and each region backed its own presidential candidate in the wide-open election of 1824.

The Panic of 1819

From 1815 to 1818, Americans enjoyed a wave of postwar prosperity. European markets were starved for American goods after a generation of war and trade restrictions, and farmers and planters met that demand by expanding production and bringing new land into cultivation. Before the bubble burst, cotton prices doubled to 30 cents a pound, real estate values became wildly inflated, and Westerners owed the federal government $21 million for the payment of public lands, a debt greater than the value of all western farm goods.

European markets for American cotton and food supplies returned to normal by late 1818. In January 1819, cotton prices sank in England, and the **Panic of 1819** was on. The fall in cotton prices triggered a credit contraction that soon engulfed the overextended American economy. A sudden shift in

policy by the Bank of the United States virtually guaranteed that the economic downturn would settle into a depression as the Bank stopped all loans, called in all debts, and refused to honor drafts drawn on its branches in the South and West. Hardest hit by these policies were farmers and businessmen in the West, who had mortgaged their economic futures. Bankruptcies mushroomed as creditors forced the liquidation of farms and real estate.

In addition to resenting the hard times brought on by low cotton prices, Southerners saw an ominous pattern of unchecked and unconstitutional federal power emerging in the form of high tariffs, the judicial nationalism of the Supreme Court, and northern efforts to interfere with slavery in Missouri. If Northerners, they asked, could stretch the Constitution to incorporate a bank or impose a protective tariff, what could prevent them from emancipating the slaves?

The Missouri Compromise

Until 1819, slavery had not been a major divisive issue in American politics. The Northwest Ordinance of 1787, which banned slavery in federal territories north of the Ohio River, and the Southwest Ordinance of 1790, which permitted slavery south of the Ohio, represented a compromise that had allowed slavery in areas where climate and soil conditions favored slave-based agriculture. What was unforeseen in the 1780s, however, was the explosive demand for slave-produced cotton generated by the English textile industry in the early nineteenth century. By 1819, Kentucky, Tennessee, Louisiana, Mississippi, and Alabama had all been added to the Union as slave states. Florida was expected to be another slave state, and even Missouri, a portion of the Louisiana Purchase, had fallen under the political control of slaveholders.

The Missouri issue pushed northern resentment over the spread of slavery and the southern dominance of national affairs under the Virginia presidents beyond the boiling point. In February 1819, James Tallmadge, a Republican congressman from New York, introduced an amendment in the House mandating a ban on future slave importations and a program of gradual emancipation as preconditions for the admission of Missouri as a state. Missourians, as well as Southerners in general, rejected the **Tallmadge Amendment** as completely unacceptable, arguing that any attempt by Congress to set conditions for statehood was unconstitutional. Without a two-party system in which each of the parties had to compromise to protect its intersectional interests, voting followed sectional lines. The northern-controlled House passed the amendment, but it was repeatedly blocked in the Senate, where there were eleven free and eleven slave states.

The stalemate persisted into the next session of Congress. Finally, Speaker of the House Henry Clay engineered a compromise in March 1820. Congress put no restrictions on slavery in Missouri, and the admission of Missouri as a slave state was balanced by admitting Maine (formerly part of Massachusetts) as a free state. In return for their concession on Missouri, northern congressmen obtained a prohibition on slavery in the remainder of the Louisiana Purchase north of the 36°30′ parallel, the southern boundary of Missouri (see Map 9-3 on page 167).

The compromise almost unraveled when Missouri submitted a constitution the next November that required the state legislature to bar the entry of free blacks. This mandate violated the guarantee in the U.S. Constitution that "the citizens of each State shall be entitled to all privileges and immunities of citizens in the several States." The nearly universal belief of whites that blacks were second-class citizens made it possible for Clay to pull off a baldfaced dodge. Missouri's constitution was accepted with the proviso that it "shall never be construed" to discriminate against citizens in other states. In short, with meaningless words that begged the issue of Missouri's defiance of the federal Constitution, the **Missouri Compromise** was salvaged. At the cost of ignoring the claims of free blacks for equal treatment as citizens, the Union survived its first great sectional crisis over slavery.

The Missouri crisis made southern whites realize that they were now a distinct political minority within the Union. More rapid population growth in the North had reduced southern representation in the House to just over 40 percent. Of greater concern was the crystallization in Congress of a northern majority arraigned against the expansion of slavery.

The Election of 1824

The election of 1820 made Monroe, like both his Republican predecessors, a two-term president. Voters had no choice in 1820, and without two-party competition, no outlets existed for expressing popular dissatisfaction with the Republicans. Instead, the Republicans split into factions as they began jockeying almost immediately for the election of 1824 (see Map 9-4).

The politics of personality dominated Monroe's second administration. Monroe had no

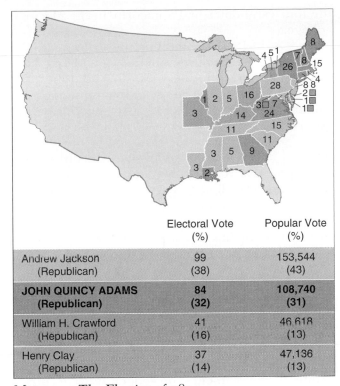

	Electoral Vote (%)	Popular Vote (%)
Andrew Jackson (Republican)	99 (38)	153,544 (43)
JOHN QUINCY ADAMS (Republican)	**84 (32)**	**108,740 (31)**
William H. Crawford (Republican)	41 (16)	46,618 (13)
Henry Clay (Republican)	37 (14)	47,136 (13)

Map 9-4 *The Election of 1824*
The regional appeal of each of the four presidential candidates in the election of 1824 prevented any candidate from receiving a majority of the electoral vote. Consequently, and as set forth in the Constitution, the House of Representatives now had to choose the president from the three leading candidates. Its choice was John Quincy Adams.

obvious successor, and five candidates competed to replace him. All of them (Secretary of War Calhoun, Secretary of the Treasury William Crawford, Secretary of State John Quincy Adams, Henry Clay and Andrew Jackson) were nominal Republicans, and three were members of his cabinet.

None of the candidates ran on a platform, but Crawford was identified with states' rights and Clay and Adams with centralized government. Clay in particular was associated with the national bank, protective tariffs, and federally funded internal improvements, a package of federal subsidies he called the **American System**. Jackson took no stand on any of the issues.

Jackson's noncommittal stance turned out to be a great asset. It helped him project the image of a military hero fresh from the people who was unsullied by any connection with Washington politicians, whom the public associated with hard times and sectional controversies. He was the highest vote getter (43 percent of the popular vote), but none of the four candidates had a majority in the electoral college.

As in 1800, the election was thrown into the House of Representatives. Anxious to undercut Jackson, his chief rival in the West, Clay used his influence as speaker of the House to line up support for Adams, a fellow advocate of a strong centralized government.

Adams won the election, and he immediately named Clay as his secretary of state, the office traditionally viewed as a steppingstone to the presidency. Jackson and his followers were outraged. They smelled a "corrupt bargain" in which Clay had bargained away the presidency to the highest bidder. Vowing revenge, they began building a new party that would usher in a more democratic era of mass-based politics.

Conclusion

In 1800, the Republicans were an untested party whose coming to power frightened many Federalists into predicting the end of the Union and constitutional government. The Federalists were correct in sensing that their days of power had passed, but they underestimated the ideological flexibility the Republicans would reveal once in office and the imaginative ways in which Jefferson and his successors would wield executive power to expand the size of the original Union. Far from being anarchists and demagogues, the Republicans were shrewd empire builders astute enough to add to their base of political support in the South and West. They also paved the way for the nation to evolve as a democratic republic rather than the more aristocratic republic preferred by the Federalists.

By the mid-1820s, with no Federalist threat to enforce party discipline, the Republicans lost their organizational strength. Embracing economic nationalism after the war made the party's original focus on states' rights all but meaningless. But the party left as its most enduring legacy the foundations of a continental empire.

Review Questions

1. What changes did the Republicans bring to the federal government? How did their policies differ from those of their Federalist predecessors?

2. Why were the Republicans so intent on expanding the boundaries of the United States, and why did the Federalists oppose an expansionist program?

3. What factors accounted for the Federalists' inability to regain national power after they lost the election of 1800?

4. What external and internal factors drew the United States into war against Britain? Could this war have been avoided?

5. What accounted for the difficulties of the United States in waging the War of 1812, and why was the war widely viewed as a great American victory? How did the war lead to an increasing pattern of diplomatic cooperation between the United States and Britain?

6. What explains the upsurge of nationalism that underlay the Era of Good Feelings? Why were the Republicans unable to maintain their party unity after 1819?

Recommended Reading

George Dangerfield, *The Era of Good Feelings* (1952). This masterful account of America in the years just after the War of 1812 is particularly strong on the reasons behind and the consequences of the new Anglo-American cooperation in foreign policy.

Donald R. Hickey, *The War of 1812: A Forgotten Conflict* (1989). This book breaks no new ground but presents a complete and very readable account of all aspects of the war.

Drew R. McCoy, *The Elusive Republic: Political Economy in Jeffersonian America* (1980). This gracefully written study examines how attitudes on economic development influenced Jeffersonian notions of republicanism and were central to the Republicans' stand on free trade.

Peter S. Onuf, ed., *Jeffersonian Legacies* (1993). This collection of essays presents the latest thinking on the extraordinary range of Jefferson's activities.

Marshall Smelser, *The Democratic Republic, 1801–1815* (1968). This book gives a sound overview of the Jefferson and Madison administrations. Smelser portrays Jefferson as a political moderate adept in wielding power and offers a spirited defense of Madison's record as a war president.

Gore Vidal, *Burr* (1973). This superbly, entertaining novel satirically brings to life the leading personalities of Jefferson's America.

William Earl Weeks, *John Quincy Adams and American Global Empire* (1992). Weeks presents Adams as a cynical, tough-minded negotiator utterly driven by his vision of an American continental empire. Though questioning his tactics, Weeks confirms Adams' reputation as America's greatest secretary of state.

Where to Learn More

❖ **Fort McHenry National Monument, Baltimore, Maryland.** This historic site preserves the fort that was the focal point of the British attack on Baltimore and contains a museum with materials on the battle and the writing of "The Star-Spangled Banner."

❖ **Tippecanoe Battlefield Museum, Battle Ground, Indiana.** This museum includes artifacts from the Indian and white settlement of Indiana and visual materials on the Battle of Tippecanoe of 1811.

❖ **Monticello, Charlottesville, Virginia.** The architecturally unique home of Thomas Jefferson and the headquarters for his plantation serves as a museum that provides insights into Jefferson's varied interests.

❖ **Montpelier, Montpelier Station, Virginia.** The museum here was the home of James Madison, and it includes material on his life as a politician and planter.

❖ **Perry's Victory and International Peace Memorial, Put-in-Bay, Ohio.** At the site of Perry's decisive victory on Lake Erie in 1813 now stands a museum that depicts the role of the Old Northwest in the War of 1812.

10 THE JACKSONIAN ERA, 1824–1845

KEY TOPICS

❖ The rise of new political parties: Jacksonian Democrats and Whigs
❖ The disfranchisement of free blacks and women
❖ Birth of Whig party
❖ The Second Great Awakening
❖ The Bank War
❖ The growing conflict over slavery

"*P*olitics at the present time are the all-engrossing topic of discourse" observed a New Englander in the fall of 1828. "In the ballroom, or at the dinner table, in the Stagecoach & in the tavern; even the social chitchat of the tea table must yield to the everlasting subject." The republic had seen spirited presidential elections before, notably the Jefferson-Adams contest of 1800, but something was clearly new in 1828. This election marked the entrance of ordinary Americans onto the political stage.

As Jefferson lamented shortly before his death in 1826, he and the other founders of the republic were "left alone midst a new gener[ation] whom we know not, and who know not us." This "new generation" impatiently pushed for greater political and social equality. Professional politicians realized that party success now depended on reaching and organizing the enlarged electorate. Trumpeting Andrew Jackson as the friend of the common man and the foe of aristocratic privilege, "Jacksonian Democrats" won a landslide victory in 1828 and held national power through the 1830s. The Jacksonians promised to protect farmers and workers from the monied elite, whom they portrayed as the enemies of equality and the corruptors of public morality.

By the mid-1830s, the Whig party had formed in opposition to the Jacksonians, offering an ordered vision of American progress and liberty, anchored in the use of governmental power to expand economic opportunities and promote morality. The Whigs captured the presidency in 1840. Their triumph heralded a new party system, one based on massive voter turnouts and two-party competition in every state.

The Egalitarian Impulse

Political democracy, defined as the majority rule of white males, was far from complete in early-nineteenth-century America. Legal barriers prevented the full expression of majority sentiments. Property requirements for voting and officeholding, the prevalence of appointed over elected offices, and the overrepresentation of older and wealthier regions in state legislatures came under increasing attack after 1800 and were all but eliminated by the 1820s.

As politics opened to mass participation, popular styles of religious leadership and worship erupted in a broad reaction against the formalism and elitism of the dominant Protestant churches. The same egalitarian impulse drove these twin democratic revolutions, and both movements represented an empowerment of the common man. (Women would have to wait longer.)

The Extension of White Male Democracy

In 1816, Congress voted itself a hefty pay raise, which seemed prudent and justified. The public thought otherwise. The citizens of Saratoga, New York, resolved that Congress was guilty of "wanton extravagance" and "a daring and profligate trespass against . . . the *morals* of the *Republic*."

So sharp was the reaction against the Salary Act of 1816 that 70 percent of the members of Congress were turned out of office at the next election. Congress quickly repealed the salary increase, but not before John C. Calhoun spoke for many in Congress when he plaintively asked, "Are we bound in all cases to do what is popular?" The answer was apparently yes. As Richard M. Johnson of Kentucky noted, "The presumption is, that the people are always right." The uproar over the Salary Act marked a turning point in the transition from the deferential politics of the Federalist-Republican period to the egalitarianism of the Jacksonian era. The public would no longer passively accept decisions handed down by local elites or established national figures.

Individual states, not the federal government, defined who could vote. Six states—Indiana, Mississippi, Illinois, Alabama, Missouri, and Maine—entered the Union between 1816 and 1821, and none of them required white male voters to own property. Constitutional conventions in Connecticut in 1818 and Massachusetts and New York in 1821 eliminated longstanding property requirements for voting. By the end of the 1820s, universal white male suffrage was the norm everywhere except Rhode Island, Virginia, and Louisiana.

Representation in most state legislatures was made more equal by giving more seats to newer, rapidly growing regions in the backcountry. States removed or reduced property qualifications for

John L. Krimmel, painting, 1815. Oil paint, canvas. H. 16⅜, W. 25⅝. Courtesy, Winterthur Museum.

This early nineteenth-century painting of a polling place in Philadelphia illustrates the growing involvement of common Americans in politics. As suffrage broadened and more Americans came out to vote, elections became more heated and emotional.

CHRONOLOGY

1826 Disappearance of William Morgan.

1827 Emergence of the Anti-Masons, the first third party.

1828 Andrew Jackson elected president.

John Calhoun writes *The South Carolina Exposition and Protest.*

1830 Congress passes the Indian Removal Act.

1831 William Lloyd Garrison starts publication of *The Liberator.*

Nat Turner leads a slave uprising in Virginia.

1832 Jackson vetoes bill for rechartering the Second Bank of the United States; Bank War begins.

South Carolina nullifies the Tariffs of 1828 and 1832.

Jackson reelected.

1833 Congress passes the Force Act and the Compromise Tariff.

American Anti-Slavery Society established.

1834 Whig party begins to organize.

1836 Texas War of Independence and establishment of the Republic of Texas.

Congress passes first gag rule on abolitionist petitions.

Van Buren elected president.

1837 Panic of 1837 sets off a depression.

1840 Independent Treasury Act passes.

William Henry Harrison elected as first Whig president.

1841 John Tyler succeeds to presidency on death of Harrison.

1842 United States and Britain sign the Webster-Ashburton Treaty.

1844 Polk elected president.

Gag rule repealed.

1845 Texas admitted to the Union.

officeholding. The selection of local officials and, in many cases, judges was taken out of the hands of governors and executive councils and given to the voters in popular elections. With the end of oral or "stand-up" voting, the act of casting a ballot became more private and freer from the intimidation of influential neighbors. Written ballots were the norm by the 1820s. Most significant for national politics, voters acquired the power to choose presidential electors. In 1800, only two states had provided for a statewide popular vote in presidential elections; by 1832 only South Carolina still clung to the practice of having the state legislature choose the electors.

Several currents swelled the movement for democratic reform. Limiting voting rights to those who owned landed property seemed increasingly elitist when economic changes were producing new classes—workers, clerks, and small tradesmen—whose livelihoods were not tied directly to the land. Propertyless laborers in Richmond argued in an 1829 petition that "virtue [and] intelligence are not among the products of the soil. Attachment to property, often a sordid sentiment, is not to be confounded with the sacred flame of patriotism."

Of greatest importance, however, was the incessant demand that all white men be treated equally. Seth Luther, an advocate for workers' rights, insisted that "we wish nothing, but those equal rights, which were designed for us all." This demand for equality was the logical extension of the ideology of the American Revolution. Only the will of the majority could be the measure of a republican government.

As political opportunities expanded for white males, they shrank for women and free blacks. New Jersey's constitution of 1776 was exceptional in also granting the suffrage to single women and widows who owned property. By the early 1800s, race and gender began to replace wealth and status as the basis for defining the limits of political participation. Thus when New Jersey's new constitution in 1807 broadened suffrage by requiring only a simple taxpaying qualification to vote, it specifically denied the ballot to women and free blacks. None of the ten states that entered the Union from 1821 to 1861 allowed black suffrage. African-Americans protested in vain. "Foreigners and aliens to the government and laws," complained New York blacks in 1837, "strangers to our institutions, are permitted to flock to this land and in a few years are endowed with all the privileges of citizens; but we *native* born Americans . . . are most of us shut out." By the 1850s, blacks could vote only in certain New England states.

Advocates of greater democratization explicitly argued that only white males had the rational intelligence and love of liberty necessary to be entrusted with political rights. Women were too weak and emotional, blacks too lazy and lascivious. (For the political role that women and blacks did create for themselves, see Chapter 14.) The white egalitarians simultaneously erected new distinctions based on race and sex that were supposedly natural and hence immutable. Thus personal liberties were now to be guarded by all white men, whose equality ultimately rested on assumptions of their shared political superiority over women and nonwhites.

The Popular Religious Revolt

In a blaze of fervor known as the **Second Great Awakening**, evangelical sects led by the Methodists and Baptists radically transformed the religious landscape between 1800 and 1840. A more popularly rooted Christianity moved outward and downward as it spread across frontier areas and converted marginalized and common folk. By 1850, one in three Americans was a regular churchgoer, a dramatic increase since 1800.

The Baptists and Methodists were the largest religious denominations by the 1820s. The key to their success was their ability to give a religious expression to the same popular impulse behind democratic reform. Especially in the backcountry of the South and West, where the first revivals occurred, itinerant preachers reshaped religion to fit the needs and values of ordinary Americans.

Evangelical Christianity emphasized personal, heartfelt experience that would produce a spiritual rebirth. Preaching became a form of theater in which scenes of damnation and salvation were acted out by both preacher and audience. "The scene that then presented itself to my mind was indescribable," recalled James Finley of the camp meeting at Cane Ridge, Kentucky, in 1801. "At one time I saw at least five hundred swept down in a moment, as if a battery of a thousand guns had been opened upon them, and then immediately followed shrieks and shouts that rent the very heavens."

Salvation no longer passively depended on an implacable God as taught by the Calvinist doctrine of individual predestination. Ordinary people could now actively choose salvation, and this possibility was exhilarating. "Why, then, I can be saved!" exclaimed Jesse Lee upon hearing a Methodist preacher in Massachusetts. "I have been taught that only a part of the race could be saved, but if this man's singing be true, all may be saved." Evangelical churches bound the faithful into tightly knit communities that expressed and enforced local values and standards of conduct. Their hymns borrowed melodies from popular music and were accompanied by fiddles and other folk instruments.

The revivals converted about twice as many women as men. Church membership offered them, as the wife of a Connecticut minister explained, a welcome release from "being treated like beasts of burden [and] drudges of domineering masters." In the first flush of evangelical excitement, female itinerant preachers spread the gospel up and down the East Coast. Other women organized their own institutions within denominations still formally controlled by men. Women activists founded and largely directed hundreds of church-affiliated charitable societies and missionary associations.

Evangelicalism also empowered black Americans. Baptists and Methodists welcomed slaves at their revivals, encouraged preaching by blacks, and, above all else, advocated secular and spiritual equality. Many of the early Baptist and Methodist preachers directly challenged slavery. In converting to Methodism, one slave stated that "from the sermon I heard, I felt that God had made all men free and equal, and that I ought not be a slave."

But evangelicalism was eventually bound by limits of race and gender in much the same way as the democratic reform movement. Denied positions of authority in white-dominated churches and resentful of white opposition to integrated worship, free blacks in the North founded their own independent churches. Southern evangelical attacks on slavery were replaced by a full-blown religious defense of it. Just as southern Protestant ministers rested their proslavery case on the biblical sanctioning of human bondage, they also used the Old Testament patriarchs to shore up the position of fathers as the unquestioned authority figures in their households, the masters of slaves, women, and children. Many popular religious sects in the North also used a particular reading of the Bible in the same way.

In religion as well as politics, white men still held the power in Jacksonian America. Still, the Second Great Awakening removed a major intellectual barrier to political democracy. Traditional Protestant theology—whether Calvinist, Anglican, or Lutheran—viewed the mass of humanity as sinners predestined to damnation. In rejecting this theology, ordinary Americans made a fundamental breakthrough in intellectual thought. "Salvation open to all" powerfully reinforced the legitimacy of "one man, one vote."

The Rise of the Jacksonians

At the core of the Jacksonian appeal was the same rejection of established authority that was the hall-

Thomas Sully, *General Andrew Jackson*, 1845. Oil on canvas. In the Collection of The Corcoran Gallery of Art, Washington, D.C. Gift of William Wilson Corcoran.

This 1845 painting captures the heroic, forceful side of Andrew Jackson that made him so appealing to many voters.

mark of the secular and religious populists. By tapping into the hopes and fears of ordinary Americans the Jacksonians built the first mass-based party in American history.

In Andrew Jackson the new **Democratic party** that formed between 1824 and 1828 had the perfect candidate for the increasingly democratic temperament of the 1820s. Born of Scots-Irish ancestry on the Carolina frontier in 1767, Jackson was a self-made product of the southern backcountry. Lacking any formal education, family connections, or inherited wealth to ease his way, he relied on his own wits and raw courage to carve out a career as a frontier lawyer and planter in Tennessee. He won fame as the military savior of the republic with his victory at the Battle of New Orleans. Conqueror of the British, the Spanish, and the Indians, all of whom had blocked frontier expansion, he achieved incredible popularity in his native South. His strengths and prejudices

were those most valued by the restless, mobile Americans to whom he became a folk hero.

Jackson lost the election of 1824, but his defeat turned out to be a blessing in disguise. The wheeling and dealing in Congress that gave the presidency to John Quincy Adams enveloped that administration in a cloud of suspicion from the start. It also enhanced Jackson's appeal as the honest tribune of the people. His supporters now claimed that the people, as well as Jackson, had been swindled by the "corrupt bargain" between Adams and Clay.

The ill-fated Adams presidency virtually destroyed itself. Though the same age as Jackson, Adams seemed frozen in an eighteenth-century past in which gentlemanly statesmen were aloof from the people.

Adams revealed how out of touch he was when he delivered his first annual message to Congress in 1825. He presented a bold vision of an activist federal government promoting economic growth, social advancement, and scientific progress. The Jacksonians charged that an administration born in corruption now wanted to waste the people's money by promoting more corruption and greed. They also pounced on Adams's political gaffe of urging Americans not to "proclaim to the world that we are palsied by the will of our constituents." Besides being depicted as the tool of the northeastern monied interests, Adams was attacked as an arrogant aristocrat contemptuous of the common man.

Little of Adams's program passed Congress, and his nationalist vision drove his opponents into the Jackson camp. Southern planters jumped onto the Jackson bandwagon out of fear that Adams might use federal power against slavery; more Westerners joined because Adams revived their suspicions of the East. The most important addition came from New York, where Martin Van Buren had built the **Albany Regency**, a tightly disciplined state political machine.

Van Buren was a new breed of politician. The son of a tavern keeper, he became a professional who made a business out of politics. The discipline and regularity of strict party organization gave him a winning edge in competition against his social betters. In battling against the system of family-centered wealth and prestige on which politics had previously been based, Van Buren redefined parties as indispensable instruments for the successful expression of the popular will against the dominance of elites.

State leaders such as Van Buren organized the first national campaign that relied extensively on new techniques of mass mobilization. In rallying support for Jackson against Adams in 1828, they put together chains of party-subsidized newspapers and coordinated a frantic schedule of meetings and rallies. Grass-roots Jackson committees reached out to the voters by knocking on their doors, pressing party literature into their hands, dispensing mass-produced medals and buttons with a likeness of Jackson, and lavishly entertaining all who would give them a hearing.

The election of 1828 centered on personalities, not issues. This in itself was a victory for Jackson's campaign managers, who proved far more skillful in image making.

Jackson carried every state south and west of Pennsylvania in 1828 and polled 56 percent of the popular vote. Voter turnout shot up to 55 percent from the apathetic 25 percent of 1824. Adams ran well only in New England and in commercialized areas producing goods for outside markets. Aside from the South, where he was virtually untouchable, Jackson's appeal was strongest among ordinary Americans who valued their local independence and felt threatened by outside centers of power beyond their control. He rolled up heavy majorities from Scots-Irish farmers in the Baptist-Methodist evangelical belt of the backcountry and unskilled workers with an Irish Catholic background.

Jackson's Presidency

Once in office, Jackson tolerated no interference from his subordinates. At one time or another, his administration angered southern planters, frightened eastern bankers and commercial interests, and outraged New England reformers. Nonetheless, Jackson remained popular because he portrayed himself as the embodiment of the people's will.

The Jacksonians had no particular program in 1828. Two political struggles that came to a head in 1832–1833—the **Bank War** and the **nullification crisis**—stamped the Jacksonians with a lasting party identity. By destroying the Second Bank of the United States and rejecting the attempt of South Carolina to nullify (or annul) a national tariff, Jackson firmly established the Democrats as the enemy of special privilege, the friend of the common man, and the defender of the Union.

The Jacksonian Appeal

Jackson's inauguration struck many conservatives as ushering in a vulgar new order in national affairs. A vast crowd poured into Washington to applaud their hero. They cheered loudly when Jackson took his oath of office and then rushed to the White House for a postinauguration reception. Bowls of liquor-laced punch went flying, and glass and china crashed to the floor as a seeming mob surged through the White House. "But it was the People's day," reported one conservative onlooker, "and the People's President and the People would rule. God grant that one day or other, the People do not put down all rule and rulers."

Jackson proclaimed his task as one of restoring the federal government to the ideal of Jeffersonian republicanism, in which farmers and artisans could pursue their individual liberty free of any government intervention that favored the rich and powerful. Jackson began his assault on special privilege by proclaiming a reform of the appointment process for federal officeholders. Accusing his predecessors, especially Adams, of having created a social elite of self-serving bureaucrats, he vowed to make government service more responsive to the popular will. He insisted that federal jobs required no special expertise or training and proposed to rotate honest, hard-working citizens in and out of the civil service.

In reality, Jackson removed only about one-fifth of the officeholders he inherited, and most of his appointees came from the same relatively high status groups as the Adams people. But he opened the way for future presidents to move more aggressively against incumbents by providing a democratic rationale for government service. Thus emerged the **spoils system**, in which the victorious party gave government jobs to its supporters and removed the appointees of the defeated party, tying party loyalty to the reward of a federal appointment.

When Jackson railed against economic privilege, he had in mind Henry Clay's American System, which called for a protective tariff, a national bank, and federal subsidies for internal improvements. Clay's goal was to bind Americans together in an integrated national market. To the Democrats, Clay's system represented government favoritism at its worst, a set of costly benefits at the public's expense for special-interest groups. In 1830, Jackson struck a blow for the Democratic conception of the limited federal role in economic development. He vetoed the Maysville Road Bill, which would have provided federal money for a road to be built entirely within Kentucky. He declared the bill unconstitutional on the grounds that it benefited only the citizens of Kentucky. Moreover, since the Maysville project was within Clay's congressional district, Jackson also embarrassed his most prominent political enemy.

Jackson's Maysville veto did not rule out congressional appropriations for projects deemed beneficial to the general public. This pragmatic loophole allowed Democrats to pass more internal improvement projects during Jackson's presidency than during all of the previous administrations together.

Jackson's strongest base of support was in the West and South. By driving Native Americans from these regions, he enhanced his appeal as the friend of the common (white) man.

Indian Removal

Some 125,000 Indians lived east of the Mississippi when Jackson became president. Five Indian confederations—the Cherokees, Creeks, Choctaws, Chickasaws, and Seminoles—controlled millions of acres of land in the Southeast that whites coveted for their own economic gain.

Pressure from the states to remove the Indians had been building since the end of the War of 1812. It was most intense in Georgia. In early 1825, Georgia authorities finalized a fraudulent treaty that ceded most of the Creek Indians' land to the state. When Adams tried to obtain fairer terms for the Creeks in a new treaty, he was brazenly denounced in Georgia. Not willing to risk an armed confrontation between federal and state authorities, Adams backed down.

In 1828, Georgia moved against the Cherokees. By now a prosperous society of small farmers with their own written alphabet and schools for their children, the Cherokees wanted to avoid the fate of their Creek neighbors. In 1827, they adopted a constitution declaring themselves an independent nation with complete sovereignty over their land. The Georgia legislature reacted by placing the Cherokees directly under state law, annulling Cherokee laws and even their right to make laws, and legally defining the Cherokees as tenants on land belonging to the state of Georgia. By also prohibiting Indian testimony in cases against whites, the legislature stripped the Cherokees of any legal rights. They were now easy prey for whites, who scrambled onto Cherokee land after gold was discovered in northern Georgia in 1829. Alabama and Mississippi followed Georgia's lead in denying Indians legal rights.

The stage was set for what Jackson always considered the most important measure of his first administration, the **Indian Removal Act**. Jackson allowed state officials to override federal protection of Native Americans. In his first annual message, Jackson sided with state authorities in the South and advised the Indians "to emigrate beyond the Mississippi or submit to the laws of those States." This advice enabled Jackson to pose as the friend of the Indians, the wise father who would lead them out of harm's way and save them from rapacious whites.

Congress acted on Jackson's recommendation in the Indian Removal Act of 1830. The act appropriated $500,000 for the negotiation of new treaties under which the southern Indians would surrender their territory and be removed to land in the trans-Mississippi area (primarily present-day Oklahoma). Although force was not authorized and Jackson stressed that removal should be voluntary, no federal protection was provided for Indians harassed into leaving by land-hungry whites. Ultimately, Jackson did deploy the U.S. Army, but only to round up and push out Indians who refused to comply with the new removal treaties.

And so most of the Indians were forced out of the eastern United States—the Choctaws in 1830, the Creeks and Chickasaws in 1832, and the Cherokees in 1838 (see Map 10-1). The private groups who won the federal contracts for transporting and provisioning the Indians were a shady lot interested only in making a quick buck. Thousands of Indians, perhaps as many as one-fourth of those who started the trek, died on the way to Oklahoma, the victims of cold, hunger, disease, and the general callousness of whites they met along the way. "It is impossible to conceive the frightful sufferings that attend these forced migrations," noted a Frenchman who observed the Choctaw removal. It was indeed, as recalled in the collective memory of the Cherokees, a **Trail of Tears**.

Federal troops joined local militias in 1832 in suppressing the Sauk and Fox Indians of Illinois and Wisconsin in what was called **Black Hawk's War**. This affair ended in the slaughter of five hundred Indian men, women, and children by the white troops and their Sioux allies. The Seminoles held out in the swamps of Florida for seven years between 1835 and 1842 in what became the longest Indian war in American history. Their resistance continued even after their leader, Osceola, was captured while negotiating under a flag of truce.

Aligned with conservatives concerned by Jackson's cavalier disregard of federal treaty obligations, eastern reformers and Protestant missionaries came within three votes of defeating the removal bill in the House of Representatives. Jackson ignored their protests (see "American Views: Memorial and Protest of the Cherokee Nation, 1836") as well as the legal rulings of the Supreme Court. In *Cherokee Nation* v. *Georgia* (1831) and *Worcester* v. *Georgia* (1832), the Court ruled that Georgia had violated the U.S. Constitution in extending its jurisdiction over the Cherokees. Chief Justice Marshall defined Indian tribes as "dependent domestic nations" subject only to the authority of the federal government. But Marshall

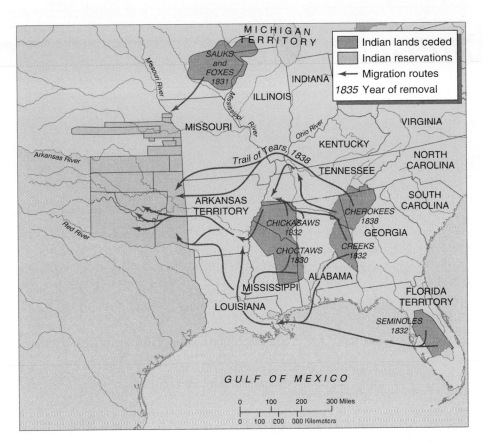

Map 10-1   *Indian Removals*
The fixed policy of the Jackson administration and pressure from the states forced Native Americans in the 1830s to migrate from their eastern homelands to a special Indian reserve west of the Mississippi River.

was powerless to enforce his decisions without Jackson's cooperation. Jackson ignored the Supreme Court rulings and pushed Indian removal to its tragic conclusion.

The Nullification Crisis

Jackson's stand on Indian removal confirmed the impression of many of his followers that on issues of centralized power, Jackson could be trusted to take the states' rights position. The most sensitive issue involving the power of the national government concerned tariffs. States' rights forces in South Carolina directly challenged Jackson in the early 1830s over tariff policy. After the first protective tariff in 1816, rates increased further in 1824 and then jumped to 50 percent in 1828 in what was denounced as the "Tariff of Abominations." Southerners were especially angry over the last tariff because it had been contrived by northern Democrats to win additional northern support for Jackson's presidential campaign. What fueled antitariff sentiment was not just the economic argument that high tariffs worsened the agricultural depression in the state. Protective tariffs were also denounced as an unconstitutional extension of national power over the states; many southern planters feared that it was only a prelude to forced emancipation.

South Carolina was the only state where African-Americans made up the majority of the population. In the marshes and tidal flats south of Charleston, South Carolina, the lowcountry district of huge rice plantations, blacks outnumbered whites ten to one in the summer months. Rice planters dreaded the possibility of a massive slave uprising, and they were convinced that slave unrest was being fed by the growing agitation over slavery in the North and in England. In the summer of 1831, the **Nat Turner slave revolt** in Virginia seemed to confirm their worst fears. Fifty-five whites were slain before the uprising was crushed. The revolt and renewed talk of emancipation would be "nothing to what we shall see," warned the South Carolina planter James Hamilton Jr., "if we do not stand manfully at the Safety Valve of Nullification."

Led by the lowcountry planters, the antitariff forces in South Carolina controlled state politics by 1832. They called themselves the nullifiers, a name derived from the constitutional theory developed by Calhoun in an anonymous tract of 1828 titled *The South Carolina Exposition and Protest.* Calhoun argued that a state, acting through a popularly elected convention, had the sovereign power to declare an act of the national government null and inoperative. Once a state nullified a law, it was to

American Views

MEMORIAL AND PROTEST OF THE CHEROKEE NATION, 1836

Of the major tribes in the Southeast, the Cherokees fought longest and hardest against the Jacksonian policy of Indian removal. Led by their principal chief, John Ross, the son of a Scot and a mixed-blood Cherokee woman, they submitted the following protest to Congress against the fraudulent 1835 Treaty of New Echota forced on them by the state of Georgia. Although clearly opposed by an overwhelming majority of the Cherokees, this treaty provided the legal basis for the forced removal of the Cherokee people from Georgia to the Indian Territory.

❖ **On what legal grounds did the Cherokees base their protest? What pledges had been made to them by the United States government?**

❖ **What did the Cherokees mean when they said they had been "taught to think and feel as the American citizen"? If the Cherokees had become "civilized" by white standards, why did most whites still insist on their removal?**

❖ **Why would President Jackson have allowed white intruders to remain on land reserved by treaties for the Cherokees?**

❖ **Do you feel that the Cherokees were justified in believing that they had been betrayed by the American government?**

The undersigned representatives of the Cherokee nation, east of the river Mississippi, impelled by duty, would respectfully submit . . . the following statement of facts: It will be seen, from the numerous treaties between the Cherokee nation and the United States, that from the earliest existence of this government, the United States, in Congress assembled, received the Cherokees and their nation into favor and protection; and that the chiefs and warriors, for themselves and all parts of the Cherokee nation, acknowledged themselves and the said Cherokee nation to be under the protection of the United States of America, and of no other sovereign whatsoever: they also stipulated,

---

remain unenforceable within that state's borders unless three-fourths of all the states approved a constitutional amendment delegating to the national government the power that was challenged. If such an amendment passed, the nullifying state had the right to leave the Union.

Calhoun, who had been elected Jackson's vice president in 1828, openly embraced nullification only after he had broken with the president. Jackson felt betrayed by Calhoun and vowed political revenge. With Calhoun's approval, a South Carolina convention in November 1832 nullified the tariffs of 1828 and 1832 and decreed that customs duties were not to be collected in South Carolina after February 1, 1833.

Calhoun always insisted that nullification was not secession. He defended his doctrine as a constitutional means of protecting minority rights within a Union dominated by a tyrannical national majority. Jackson rejected such reasoning as the talk of a scheming disunionist and vowed to crush any attempt to block the enforcement of federal laws. He told a congressman from South Carolina that "if a single drop of blood shall be shed there in opposition to the laws of the United States, I will hang the first man I can lay my hand on engaged in such that the said Cherokee nation will not hold any treaty with any foreign power, individual State, or with individuals of any State: that for, and in consideration of, valuable concessions made by the Cherokee nation, the United States solemnly guaranteed to said nation all their lands not ceded, and pledged the faith of the government, that "all white people who have intruded, or may hereafter intrude, on the lands reserved for the Cherokees, shall be removed by the United States, and proceeded against, according to the provisions of the act, passed 30th March, 1802," entitled "An act to regulate trade and intercourse with the Indian tribes, and to preserve peace on the frontiers." It would be useless to recapitulate the numerous provisions for the security and protection of the rights of the Cherokees, to be found in the various treaties between their nation and the United States. The Cherokees were happy and prosperous under a scrupulous observance of treaty stipulations by the government of the United States, and from the fostering hand extended over them, they made rapid advances in civilization, morals, and in the arts and sciences. Little did they anticipate, that when taught to think and feel as the American citizen, and to have with him a common interest, they were to be *despoiled by their guardian,* to become strangers and wanderers in the land of their fathers, forced to return to the savage life, and to seek a new home in the wilds of the far west, and that without their consent. An instrument purporting to be a treaty with the Cherokee people, has recently been made public by the President of the United States, that will have such an operation, if carried into effect. This instrument, the delegation aver before the civilized world, and in the presence of Almighty God, is fraudulent, false upon its face, made by unauthorized individuals, without the sanction, and against the wishes, of the great body of the Cherokee people. Upwards of fifteen thousand of those people have protested against it, solemnly declaring they will never acquiesce. . . .

Source: *U.S. Congress, Executive Documents (1836).*

treasonable conduct, upon the first tree I can reach."

In January 1833, Jackson received full Congressional authorization in the Force Act to put down nullification by military force. Simultaneously, he worked to defuse nullification by supporting a new tariff that would cut duties by half within two years. Because Jackson's opponents in Congress did not want him to get political credit for brokering a compromise, they pushed through their own tariff measure. The Compromise Tariff of 1833 lowered duties to 20 percent but extended the reductions over a ten-year period. Up against this combination of the carrot and the stick, the nullifiers backed down. In a final act of defiance, they nullified the Force Act.

Jackson's stand established the principle of national supremacy grounded in the will of the majority. Despite his victory, however, states' rights doctrines remained popular both in the South and among many northern Democrats. Many Southerners, and especially slaveholders, agreed that the powers of the national government had to be strictly limited. By dramatically affirming his right to use force against a state in defense of the Union, Jackson drove many planters out of the Democratic party. In the shock waves set off by the nullification crisis, a new anti-Jackson coalition began to form in the South.

The Bank War

What amounted to a war declared by Jackson against the Bank of the United States became the centerpiece of his presidency and a defining moment in the shaping of the Democratic party. Like most Westerners, Jackson distrusted banks. As a result of the scarcity of gold and silver coins and the absence of any paper currency issued and regulated by the national government, money consisted primarily of notes issued as loans by private and state banks. These bank notes fluctuated in value in accordance with the reputation and creditworthiness of the issuing banks. In the credit-starved West, many banks were "wildcat" operations that made a quick profit by issuing notes without the specie (gold or silver reserves) to redeem them and then skipping town when they were on the verge of being found out. Even when issued by honest bankers, notes often could not be redeemed at face value because of market conditions. All of this struck many Americans, and especially farmers and workers, as inherently dishonest. They wanted to be paid in "real" money, gold or silver coin, and they viewed bankers suspiciously.

The largest and most powerful bank was the Bank of the United States, and citizens who were wiped out or forced to retrench drastically by the Panic of 1819 never forgave the Bank for saving itself at the expense of its debtors. Still, prosperous times had returned, and the Bank underwrote the economic expansion with its healthy credit reserves and stable banknotes.

Beginning with his first annual message, Jackson had been making noise about not rechartering the Bank. In the presidential campaign of 1832, Clay then forced Jackson's hand and convinced Bank president Nicholas Biddle to apply to Congress for a new charter. Clay reasoned that he had Jackson trapped. If Jackson went along with the new charter, Clay could take credit for the measure. If he vetoed it, Clay could attack Jackson as the enemy of a sound banking system.

Clay's clever strategy backfired. Jackson turned on Clay and the Bank with a vengeance. As he told his heir apparent, "The bank, Mr. Van Buren, is trying to kill me, *but I will kill it!*" On July 10, 1832, Jackson vetoed the rechartering bill for the Bank in a message that appealed both to state bankers and to foes of all banks. He took a ringing "stand against all new grants of monopolies and exclusive privileges, against any prostitution of our Government to the advancement of the few at the expense of the many."

The business community and eastern elites in general lashed out at Jackson's veto as the demagogic ravings of an economic fool. For Biddle, the veto message had "all the fury of a chained panther, biting the bars of his cage." But Jackson won the political battle, and he went to the people in the election of 1832 as their champion against the banking aristocracy. Although his support was no stronger than in 1828, he easily defeated Clay, the candidate of the short-lived **National Republican party** that had also backed Adams in 1828.

Having blocked the rechartering of the Bank when Congress failed to override his veto, Jackson then set out to destroy it. He claimed that the people had given him a mandate to do so by reelecting him in 1832. He finally found a secretary of the treasury (his first two choices refused) who agreed to sign the order removing federal deposits from the Bank in 1833. The government's monies were deposited in "pet banks," state banks controlled by loyal Democrats.

Jackson won the Bank War, but he left the impression that the Democrats had played fast and loose with the nation's credit system. In his second term, high commodity prices and abundant credit, both at home and abroad, propelled a buying frenzy of western lands. Prices soared, and inevitably the speculative bubble had to burst. Jackson was out of office when the **Panic of 1837** hit; Van Buren, his successor, paid the political price for Jackson's economic policies.

Van Buren and Hard Times

Like John Adams and James Madison, Martin Van Buren followed a forceful president who commanded a strong popular following. Where Jackson forged ahead regardless of consequences, Van Buren tended to hang back, carefully calculating all the political angles. Facing a sharp economic downturn, Van Buren appeared indecisive and unwilling to advance a bold program. When the rise of a radical abolitionist movement in the North revived sectional tensions over slavery, he awkwardly straddled the middle of the divisive issue. In the end, he undermined himself by failing to offer a compelling vision of just what he wanted his presidency to be.

The Panic of 1837

Van Buren was barely settled into the White House when the nation was rocked by a financial panic. For over a decade, the economy had benefited from easy credit and the availability of western territories opened up by Jackson's Indian removal policy. Government land sales ballooned from under 4 million acres in 1833 to 20 million acres by 1836. As in 1817 and 1818, Americans piled up debt. A banking crisis in 1837 painfully reintroduced economic reality.

Even as it expanded, the American economy had remained vulnerable to disruptions in the supply of foreign capital and the sale of agricultural exports. The key foreign nation was Britain, a major source of credit and demand for exports. In late 1836, the Bank of England tightened its credit policies. Concerned with the large outflow of specie to the United States, it raised interest rates and reduced the credit lines of British merchants heavily involved in the American trade. Consequently, the British demand for cotton fell and with it the price of cotton. Because cotton, as the leading export, was the main security for most loans issued by American banks and mercantile firms, its drop in value set off a chain reaction of contracting credit and falling prices. When panic-stricken investors rushed to the banks to redeem their notes in specie, the hard-pressed banks suspended specie payments.

The shock waves hit New Orleans in March 1837 and spread to the major New York banks by May. What began as a bank panic soon dragged down the entire economy. Bankruptcies multiplied, investment capital dried up, and business stagnated. State governments slashed their budgets and halted all construction projects. Nine states in the South and West defaulted (stopped making payments) on their bonds. Workers in the shoe, textile, mining, and construction industries suddenly found themselves without jobs. "Workmen thrown out of employ by the hundreds daily," nervously noted a wealthy merchant in New York City in May 1837. He half expected that "we shall have a revolution here."

After a brief recovery in 1838, another round of credit contraction drove the economy into a depression that did not bottom out until 1843. In the manufacturing and commercial centers of the Northeast, unemployment reached an unheard-of 20 percent. The persistence of depressed agricultural prices meant that farmers and planters who had incurred debts in the 1830s faced the constant threat of losing their land or their slaves. Many fled west to avoid their creditors.

The Independent Treasury

Although the Democrats bore no direct responsibility for the economic downturn, their political opponents, now coalescing as the **Whig party**, pinned the blame on Jackson's destruction of the Bank of the United States. In their view, Jackson had then compounded his error by trying to force a hard-money policy on the state banks that had received federal deposits.

Jackson had taken his boldest step against paper money when he issued the **Specie Circular** of 1836, which stipulated that henceforth large blocks of public land could be bought only with specie. The Specie Circular likely contributed to the Panic of 1837 by requiring the transfer of specie to the West for land transactions just when eastern banks were strapped for specie reserves to meet demands on their own bank notes. Bankers and speculators denounced Jackson for unwarranted government interference with the natural workings of the economy and blundering into a monetary disaster.

By dramatically politicizing the banking issue and removing federal monies from the national bank, the Democrats had in effect assumed the burden of protecting the people from the paper aristocrats in the banking and business community. Once they shifted treasury receipts to selected state banks, they had to try to regulate these banks. But even the "pet banks" joined in the general suspension of specie payments when the Panic of 1837 hit. Thus the banks favored by the Democrats proved themselves unworthy of the people's trust.

Van Buren reestablished the Democrats' tarnished image as the party of limited government when he came out for the **Independent Treasury System**. Under this plan, the government would dispense with banks entirely. The Treasury would conduct its business only in gold and silver coin and would store its specie in regional vaults or subtreasuries.

The Independent Treasury System passed Congress in 1840 and restored the ideological purity of the Democrats as the friends of honest money. But it prolonged the depression. Specie locked up in government vaults was unavailable for loans in the private banking system that could expand the credit needed to revive the economy. The end result was to reduce the money supply and put even more downward pressure on prices.

Uproar over Slavery

In 1831, the year that Nat Turner led a slave uprising in Virginia, William Lloyd Garrison of Boston inaugurated a radical new phase in northern attacks on slavery with the publication of his abolitionist paper *The Liberator*. The abolitionists embraced the doctrine of *immediatism*, an immediate moral commitment to begin the work of emancipation. Inspired by the wave of religious revivals sweeping the North in the late 1820s, they called upon all Americans to recognize their Christian duty of ending a system of human bondage that deprived the enslaved of their God-given right to be free moral beings. (For more on the abolitionists, see Chapter 14.)

Most southern whites ignored the abolitionists until 1835, the year that the abolitionists produced over a million pieces of antislavery literature, much of which was sent to the South through the U.S. mails. Alarmed whites vilified the abolitionists as fanatics intent on enticing the slaves to revolt. Abolitionist tracts were burned, and, with the open approval of Jackson, southern postmasters violated federal law by censoring the mails to keep out antislavery materials.

Beginning in 1836 and continuing through Van Buren's presidency, hundreds of thousands of antislavery petitions, some of them with thousands of signatures, flooded into Congress. Most of them called for the abolition of slavery in the District of Columbia. Southern congressmen responded by demanding that free speech be repressed with the **gag rule**, a procedural device whereby antislavery petitions were automatically tabled with no discussion.

The gag rule first passed in 1836. With Van Buren's reluctant support, it became a Democratic party measure, and it identified the Democrats as a prosouthern party in the minds of many Northerners. Ironically, while Van Buren was attacked in the North as a lackey of the slave interests, he was damned in the South as a nonslaveholder from the North. Van Buren was to be cast as a vacillating president fully trusted by neither section.

The Rise of the Whig Party

The Bank War and Jackson's reaction to nullification shook loose pro-Bank Democrats and many southern states' righters from the original Jacksonian coalition, and these groups joined the opposition to Jackson. By 1834, the anti-Jacksonians started to call themselves Whigs, a name associated with the eighteenth-

SUMMARY

THE SECOND PARTY SYSTEM

	Democrats	Whigs
Ideology	Favor limited role of federal government in economic affairs and in matters of individual conscience; support territorial expansion	Favor government support for economic development and controls over individual morality; opposed or indifferent to expansion
Voter support	Mainly subsistence farmers, unskilled workers, and Catholic immigrants	Mainly manufacturers, commercial farmers, skilled workers, and northern evangelicals
Regional strength	South and West	New England and Upper Midwest

century American and British opponents of monarchical tyranny.

By 1840, the Whigs had mastered the techniques of political organization and mobilization pioneered by the Democrats in the late 1820s. They ran William Henry Harrison, their own version of a military hero, and swept to victory. The **second party system** of intense national competition between Whigs and Democrats was now in place (see the summary table "The Second Party System"). It would dominate politics until the rise of the antislavery Republican party in the 1850s.

The Party Taking Shape

The Whig party was born in the congressional reaction to Jackson's Bank veto and his subsequent attacks on the national bank. Led by the unlikely trio of Henry Clay and Daniel Webster, nationalists from the West and New England, and John C. Calhoun, a states' righter from the South, the congressional opposition accused Jackson of demagogic appeals to the poor against the rich. What upset them was the way Jackson wielded his executive power like a bludgeon. Whereas all earlier presidents together had used the veto only ten times, Jackson did so a dozen times. He openly defied the Supreme Court and Congress. To his opponents, Jackson was threatening to undermine the constitutional system of checks and balances.

Local and state coalitions of the Whigs sent an anti-Jackson majority to the House of Representatives in 1835. The most powerful of these coalitions was in New York, where a third party, the **Anti-Masons**, joined the Whigs. The party had originated in western New York in the late 1820s as a grass-roots response to the sudden disappearance and presumed murder of William Morgan, an itinerant artisan who threatened to expose the secrets of the Order of Freemasons. An all-male order steeped in ritual and ceremony, the Masons united urban and small-town elites into a tightly knit brotherhood of personal contacts and mutual aid. Rumors spread that the Masons constituted a vast conspiracy that conferred special privileges and legal protection on its exclusive members. Farmers and townspeople flocked to the new Anti-Masonic party, seeking, in the words of an 1831 Anti-Masonic address, "equal rights and equal privileges among the freemen of the country."

Despite spreading into New England and the neighboring mid-Atlantic states, the Anti-Masons were unable to sustain themselves as a separate party. Shrewd politicians, led by Thurlow Weed and William Seward of New York, took up the movement and absorbed most of it into the anti-Jackson coalition. They thus broadened the Whigs' mass base and added an egalitarian message to their appeal.

By 1836, the Whigs were strong enough to mount a serious challenge for the presidency. They ran three candidates—Webster of Massachusetts, William Henry Harrison of Ohio, and Hugh Lawson White of Tennessee—and some Whigs hoped that the regional popularity of these candidates would siphon off enough votes from Van Buren to throw the election into the House of Representatives. But Van Buren won an electoral majority by holding on to the populous mid-Atlantic states and improving on Jackson's showing in New England. Still, the Whigs were encouraged by the results. Compared to Jackson, Van Buren did poorly in what had been the overwhelmingly Democratic South, which was now open to further Whig inroads.

Whig Persuasion

The Whigs, like the Democrats, based their mass appeal on the claim that they could best defend the republican liberties of the people. They attributed the threat to those liberties to the expansive powers of the presidency as wielded by Jackson and in the party organization that put Jackson and Van Buren into office. In 1836, the Whigs called for the election of "a president of the *nation*, not a president of party." Underlying this call was the persistent Whig belief that parties fostered and rewarded the selfish interests of the party faithful. The Whigs always insisted that Congress should be the locus of power in the federal system.

The Whigs were quicker than the Democrats to embrace economic change in the form of banks and manufacturing corporations. Most Whigs viewed governmental power as a positive force to promote economic development. They favored encouraging the spread of banking and paper money, chartering corporations, passing protective tariffs to support American manufacturers, and opening up new markets for farmers through government-subsidized transportation projects.

The Whigs drew heavily from commercial and planting interests in the South. They were also the party of bankers, manufacturers, small-town entrepreneurs, farmers prospering from the market outlets of canals and railroads, and skilled workers who valued a high tariff as protection from the competition of goods produced by cheap foreign labor. These Whig groups also tended to be native-born Protestants of New England or Yankee ancestry, particularly those caught up in the religious revivals of the 1820s and 1830s. The strongest Whig constituencies comprised an arc of Yankee settlement stretching from rural New England through central New York and around the southern shores of the Great Lakes.

Whigs believed in promoting social progress and harmony through an interventionist government. The Whigs favored such social reforms as prohibiting the consumption of alcohol; preserving the sanctity of the Protestant Sabbath through bans on business activities on Sundays; caring for orphans, the physically handicapped, and the mentally ill in state-run asylums and hospitals; and teaching virtuous behavior and basic knowledge through a centralized system of public education.

Much of the Whigs' reform impulse was directed against non-English and Catholic immigrants, those Americans whom the Whigs believed most needed to be taught the virtues of self-control and disciplined work habits. Not coincidentally, these groups—the Scots-Irish in the backcountry, the Reformed Dutch, and Irish and German Catholics—were the most loyal Democrats. They resented the aggressive moralism of the Whigs. These Democrats were typically subsistence farmers on the periphery of market change or unskilled workers who equated an activist government with special privileges for the economically and culturally powerful and identified with the Democrats' demand for keeping the government out of the economy and individual religious practices.

The Election of 1840

Aside from the Independent Treasury Act and legislation establishing a ten-hour workday for federal employees, the Van Buren administration had no program to combat the Whig charge of helplessness in the face of economic adversity. The natural choice for the Whigs against Van Buren in 1840 was seemingly Henry Clay running on his American System to revive the economy with governmental aid. Yet the party dumped Clay for their version of a military hero popular with the people, William Henry Harrison of Ohio.

Harrison had run surprisingly well as one of the Whigs' regional candidates in 1836 and had revealed a common touch with the voters that the Whigs generally lacked. Unlike Clay, he was untainted by any association with the Bank of the United States, the Masonic Order, or slaveholding. As the victor at the Battle of Tippecanoe and a military hero in the War of 1812, he enabled Whigs to cast him in Jackson's former role as the honest, patriotic soldier worthy of the people's trust. In a decision that came back to haunt them the Whigs geographically balanced their ticket by selecting John Tyler, a planter from Virginia, as Harrison's running mate. Tyler was an advocate of states' rights and a former Democrat who had broken with Jackson over the Force Bill.

When a Democratic editor wisecracked that "Old Granny" Harrison (he was 67) was such a simpleton that he would like nothing better than to retire to a log cabin with a government pension and a barrel of hard cider, the Whigs created a Harrison who never was—a yeoman farmer of humble origins and homespun tastes whose rise to prominence was a democratic model of success for other Americans to follow. Thus Harrison, who was descended from the Virginia slaveholding aristocracy, became a Whig symbol of the common man. Indeed, the Whigs pinned the label of the dandified and elitist aristocrat on Van Buren whom they called "Martin Van Ruin."

The Whigs beat the Democrats at their own game of mass politics in 1840. They reversed the roles and symbolism of the Jackson-Adams election of 1828 and seized the high ground as the party of the people. In a further adaptation of earlier Democratic initiatives, Whig politics became a carnival in which voters were shamelessly wooed with food, drink, and music in huge rallies complete with live animals and gigantic buckskin balls that were triumphantly rolled from one rally to another.

The Whigs gained control of both Congress and the presidency in 1840. Harrison won 53 percent of the popular vote, and for the first time the Whigs carried the South (see Map 10-2). Voter turnout surged to an unprecedented 78 percent, a whopping increase over the average of 55 percent in the three preceding presidential elections (see Figure 10-1). As the new majority party, they finally had the opportunity, or so they thought, to implement their economic program.

The Whigs in Power

The Whigs expected that Clay would move quickly on Whig economic policies by marshaling his forces in Congress and trying to dominate a pliant Harrison. Harrison's death from pneumonia in April 1841, barely a month after his inauguration, ruined Clay's plans.

Harrison and Tyler

As president, Harrison fumed that "I am *bothered almost* to death with visitors. I have not time to attend to my person, *not even to change my shirt,* much less to attend to the *public* business." He had pledged to follow the dictates of party leaders in Congress and defer to the judgment of his cabinet. Bowing to Clay's demands, he agreed to call Congress into special session to act on Whig party measures. Thus his death was a real blow to Whig hopes of establishing the credibility of their party as an effective agent for positive change.

The first vice president to succeed on the death of a president Tyler was cut from quite different cloth than Harrison. This stiff, unbending planter subscribed to a states' rights agrarian philosophy that put him at odds with the urban and commercial elements of the Whig party even in his home state of Virginia. Clay's economic nationalism struck him as a program of rank corruption that surrendered the constitutional rights of the South to power-hungry politicians and manufacturers in the North. Clay forged ahead with the party agenda—the repeal of the Independent Treasury System and its replacement by a new national bank, a protective tariff, and the distribution of the proceeds of the government's public land sales to the states as funds for internal improvements.

Tyler used the negative power of presidential vetoes to stymie the Whig program. He twice vetoed bills to reestablish a national bank. The second veto led to the resignation of the cabinet he had inherited from Harrison, save for Secretary of State Daniel Webster, who was in the midst of negotiations with the British. Enraged congressional Whigs then expelled Tyler from the party.

A now desperate Clay sought to salvage what was left of his American System. He lined up southern votes for the distribution of federal funds to the states by agreeing to a ceiling of 20 percent on tariff rates. Westerners were won over by Clay's support for the Preemption Act of 1841, a measure that allowed squatters—settlers on public land that had not yet been surveyed and put on the market—to purchase with noncompetitive bids up to 160 acres of land at the minimum government price of $1.25 per acre.

Clay's legislative wizardry got him nowhere. When the Whigs passed a higher tariff in 1842 with a provision for distribution, Tyler vetoed it and forced them to settle for a protective tariff with no distribution. In the end, Clay had no national bank, no funds for internal improvements, and only a slightly higher tariff. Although Clay's leadership of the Whigs was strengthened, Tyler had deprived that leadership of meaning by denying the Whigs the legislature fruits of their victory in 1840.

The Texas Issue

In 1842, Webster wrapped up his negotiations with the British. The **Webster-Ashburton Treaty** of that year settled a long-standing dispute over the boundary between British Canada and Maine and parts of the Upper Midwest. An agreement was also reached to cooperate in suppressing the African slave trade. Webster now resigned from the cabinet to join his

Figure 10-1 *Voter Turnout in Presidential Elections, 1824–1840*
The creation of mass-based political parties dramatically increased voter turnout in presidential elections. Voting surged in 1828 with the emergence of the Jacksonian Democratic Party, and again in 1840 when the Whig Party learned to appeal to the mass electorate.

Source: Richard P. McCormick, "New Perspectives on Jacksonian Politics" in The Nature of Jacksonian America, ed. Douglas T. Miller (1972), p. 103

fellow Whigs, allowing Tyler to follow a prosouthern policy of expansion that he hoped would gain him the Democratic nomination for the presidency in 1844. His goal was the annexation of Texas.

Texas had been a slaveholding republic since 1836, when rebellious Americans, joined by some *tejanos* (Texans of Mexican descent), declared their independence from Mexico. Jackson extended diplomatic recognition before leaving office, but he refused the new nation's request to be annexed to the United States out of fear of provoking a war with Mexico. But he was also aware that the addition of Texas, a potentially huge area for the expansion of plantation slavery, would inflame sectional tensions and endanger Van Buren's chances in the upcoming presidential election. In private, however, he urged Texans to seize harbors on the Pacific Coast from Mexican control and thus make annexation more attractive to the commercial interests of the Northeast.

Party leaders sidestepped the Texas issue after 1836. Spurned by the Whigs and anxious to return to the Democrats, Tyler renewed the issue in 1843 to curry favor among southern and western Democrats. He replaced Webster as secretary of state with a proannexationist Virginian, Abel P. Upshur, and secretly opened negotiations with the Texans. After Upshur's death, Calhoun, his successor, com-

Map 10-2 *The Election of 1840*
Building upon their strength in the commercializing North, the Whigs attracted enough rural voters in the South and West to win the election of 1840.

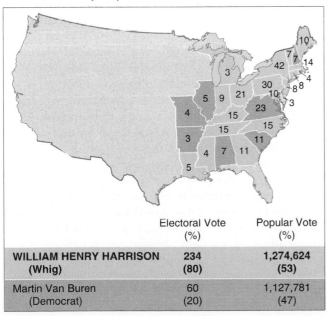

	Electoral Vote (%)	Popular Vote (%)
WILLIAM HENRY HARRISON (Whig)	**234 (80)**	**1,274,624 (53)**
Martin Van Buren (Democrat)	60 (20)	1,127,781 (47)

pleted the negotiations and, dramatically politicized the slavery issue. Calhoun made public his correspondence with Richard Pakenham, the British minister in Washington, accusing the British of seeking to force emancipation on Texas to block American expansion and destroy slavery in the South. Calhoun concluded that the security and preservation of the Union demanded the annexation of Texas.

The Pakenham letter hit the Senate like a bombshell, and antislavery Northerners were now convinced that the annexation of Texas was a slaveholders' conspiracy to extend slavery and swell the political power of the South. In June 1844, the Senate rejected Calhoun's treaty of annexation by a two-to-one margin. Still, the issue was hardly dead.

The Election of 1844

The Whig and Democratic National Conventions met in the spring of 1844. Both Clay, who had the Whig nomination locked up, and Van Buren, who was the strong favorite for the Democratic one, came out against immediate annexation. Clay's stand was consistent with Whig fears that territorial expansion would disrupt the party's plans for ordered economic development by leading to a breakdown of political and cultural controls. But Van Buren's anti-Texas stand cost him his party's nomination. In a carefully devised strategy, western and southern Democrats united to deny him the necessary two-thirds vote of convention delegates. A deadlocked convention turned to James K. Polk of Tennessee, a confirmed expansionist who had received the blessing of Jackson, the party's patriarch.

To counter the charge that they were a prosouthern party, the Democrats ran in 1844 on a platform that linked Oregon to Texas as territorial objectives. Glowing reports from Protestant missionaries of the boundless fertility of Oregon's Willamette Valley triggered a migration by midwestern farm families still reeling from the Panic of 1837. The report of a naval expedition sent to explore the Pacific aroused the interest of New England merchants in using Oregon for expanded trade with China.

Some six thousand Americans were in Oregon by the mid-1840s, and demands mounted, especially from northern Democrats, that the United States abandon its 1818 agreement of joint occupation with the British and lay exclusive claim to Oregon far to the north of the area of American settlement. The Polk Democrats seemed to endorse them when they asserted an American claim "to the whole of the Territory of Oregon."

Polk's expansionist program united the Democrats and enabled them to campaign with much more enthusiasm than in 1840. Acquiring Texas and Oregon not only held out the economic hope of cheap, abundant land to debt-burdened farmers in the North and planters in the South but also played on the anti-British sentiments of many voters. In contrast, the Whig campaign was out of focus. Clay began to waver on the issue of annexation of Texas but he failed to stem the defection of proslavery southern Whigs to the Democrats and lost support among antislavery Whigs in the North. Clay lost to Polk by less than 2 percent of the popular vote.

Tyler claimed Polk's victory as a mandate for the immediate annexation of Texas. He knew that it would still be impossible to gain the two-thirds majority in the Senate necessary for the approval of a treaty. Thus he resorted to the constitutionally unprecedented expedient of a joint resolution in Congress inviting Texas to join the Union. By the narrow margin of twenty-seven to twenty-five, the Senate concurred with the House in favor of annexation. Tyler signed the joint resolution on March 1, 1845.

Although Tyler had failed to secure the Democratic nomination in 1844, he had gained Texas. He also had the satisfaction of getting revenge against the Whigs, the party that had disowned him. Texas, more than any other issue, defeated Clay and the Whigs in 1844.

Conclusion

The Jacksonian era ushered in a revolution in American political life. Politicians learned how to appeal to a mass electorate and to build disciplined parties that channeled popular desires into distinctive party positions. Voter participation in national elections tripled, and Democrats and Whigs competed on nearly equal terms in every region.

Politics did not fully enter the mainstream of American life until the rise of the second party system of Democrats and Whigs. The election of 1824 revived interest in presidential politics, and Jackson's forceful style of leadership highlighted the presidency as the focal point of American politics. Voters in favor of government aid for economic development and a social order based on Protestant moral controls turned to the Whigs' program of an economically and morally activist government. Conversely, the Democratic position, stressing personal liberty, appealed to individuals who saw an activist government as a threat to their economic and cultural equality.

The national issues around which the Democrats and Whigs organized and battled down to 1844 were primarily economic. Slavery in the form of the Texas question replaced the economy as the decisive issue in the election of 1844. Once this shift occurred and party appeals began to focus on the place of slavery in American society, an escalating politics of sectionalization was set into motion.

Review Questions

1. Explain the democratic movements of the early nineteenth century. What role did race and gender play in these movements?

2. What distinguished Jackson's presidency from those of his predecessors? How did he redefine the role of the president?

3. How was the Bank War central to the development of the Democratic and Whig parties? Why did the political debates of the 1830s focus on financial issues?

4. In terms of ideology and voter appeal, how did the Democrats and Whigs differ? How did each party represent a distinctive response to economic and social change?

5. How would you describe the changes in American politics between 1824 and 1840, and what accounted for these changes?

6. How did the annexation of Texas emerge as a political issue in the early 1840s? Why were the Democrats more in favor of territorial expansion than the Whigs?

Recommended Reading

Lee Benson, *The Concept of Jacksonian Democracy: New York as a Test Case* (1964). This study challenges the traditional linkage of the Jacksonian Democrats and reform and argues that ethnicity and religion were the most important factors influencing voter preferences.

Daniel Feller, *The Jacksonian Promise: America, 1815–1840* (1995). This up-to-date survey emphasizes the optimism and innovation of the Jacksonian era.

Marvin Meyers, *The Jacksonian Persuasion* (1960). This gracefully written work explores the beliefs of the Jacksonians and concludes that their agrarian values made them fearful of economic change.

Edward Pessen, *Jacksonian America* (1985). This revisionist work argues that Democrats and Whigs, for all their talk of democratic change, were driven primarily by the goal of acquiring office as an end in itself.

Robert V. Remini, *The Life of Andrew Jackson* (1988). This lively account of Jackson's career was written by his most noted biographer.

Arthur Schlesinger Jr., *The Age of Jackson* (1945). This remains the enduring statement of the democratic impulse behind the Jackson movement.

Charles Sellers, *The Market Revolution: Jacksonian America, 1815–1846* (1991). This boldly conceived work places responses to market change at the center of the era's political development.

Alexis de Tocqueville, *Democracy in America*, ed. Phillips Bradley, 2 vols. (1945). This often-quoted work is a classic still popular for its first-hand depiction of Jacksonian society and institutions.

Harry Watson, *Liberty and Power: The Politics of Jacksonian America* (1990). Watson has produced a very readable and concise synthesis of Jacksonian politics.

Where to Learn More

❖ **Rice Museum, Georgetown, South Carolina.** Rice planters were the leaders of the nullification movement, and the interpretive materials here on the history of rice cultivation help one understand how slave labor was employed to produce their great wealth.

❖ **The Hermitage, Hermitage, Tennessee.** This was the plantation home of Andrew Jackson. The site includes a museum with artifacts of Jackson's life.

❖ **Martin Van Buren National Historic Site, Kinderhook, New York.** The site preserves Lindenwald, Van Buren's home after he left the presidency, and includes a library with materials on Van Buren and his political era.

❖ **The Alamo, San Antonio, Texas.** Originally a Franciscan mission, the Alamo was converted into a fort during the Texas War of Independence. The massacre of its defenders in 1836 by Santa Anna's army gave birth to the rallying cry for Texas independence, "Remember the Alamo."

11 INDUSTRIAL CHANGE AND URBANIZATION, 1820–1850

CHAPTER OUTLINE

KEY TOPICS

❖ The increasing industrialization of the U.S. economy between 1815 and 1850
❖ The effect of the transportation revolution on the pattern and direction of American commerce
❖ The growth of cities and the emergence of both a new middle-class society and a lower class of working poor
❖ Massive immigration starting in the 1840s, mainly from Ireland and Germany, providing a new labor force essential to industrialization
❖ New wealth and the increasing inequalities among the rich, the middle class, and the working classes
❖ The emergence of poorly paid, unskilled labor and the decline of the old artisan-mechanic class

"Oh, that I had wings!" wished Lucy Larcom as she leaned out a window in the factory at Lowell, Massachusetts, on a warm June afternoon in the 1830s. Like thousands of other young women from New England's farms, she had gone to work in the new textile mills and had become part of the nation's first large industrial work force. Larcom entered the mill when she was 11, glad to be able to relieve her widowed mother of the cost of her upkeep, and now she enjoyed the independence that came with earning her own wages. But Larcom "never cared much for machinery" and hated its noisy clatter, and she resented "being shut in to daily toil so early" in the morning. She recalled that "sometimes the confinement of the mill became very wearisome," and her "whole stifled being would cry out" for freedom. Still, she was there of her own choosing, and she conceded that the discipline of the mill had taught her self-control. "Perhaps," she mused, "I could have brought myself into the limitations of order and method in no other way."

Factories were new institutions with authoritarian work rules that deprived workers of their accustomed freedoms and radically altered the self-directed rhythm of farm and artisan work. Cities grew rapidly now—indeed, at the fastest relative rate in American history. Urbanization also brought new production patterns and increasingly separated one's home from one's place of work. New middle and working classes evolved in response to such changes, changes most pronounced in the Northeast.

The Transportation Revolution

In 1820, four in five people worked in agriculture, and manufacturing played a minor role in overall economic activity. Over the next three decades, however, America joined England as a world leader in industrialization. By 1850, manufacturing accounted for one third of total commodity output, and nonfarm employment had more than doubled to 45 percent of the labor force.

The most direct cause of this rapid and sustained surge in manufacturing was the increasing consumption within the United States of the goods the country was producing. The **transportation revolution** dramatically reduced transportation costs and shipping times, opened up new markets for farmers and manufacturers alike, and provided an ongoing incentive for expanding production (see Table 11-1). As agricultural and manufactured goods were exchanged more efficiently, a growing home market continually stimulated the development of American manufacturing.

Canals and Steamboats

The nation had no system of transportation in 1820. The states had chartered turnpike companies to build improved roads, graded with crushed stone, for overland transportation. Some 4,000 miles of these toll roads had been built by 1820, mostly in the Northeast, but their economic impact was marginal. It cost just as much to haul heavy goods by horse-drawn wagons 30 miles into the interior as to ship them 3,000 miles across the Atlantic Ocean. West of the Appalachian Mountains, where the need for improved transportation was the greatest, roads were mostly stump-strewn, muddy trails through forests and swamps.

Water transportation was much cheaper, but it was limited to the coast or navigable rivers. Only farmers located near a city or a river grew surplus crops for sale in an outside market. The southerly flow of the Ohio and Mississippi river systems directed western farm surpluses down toward New Orleans. Flatboats (rafts with a deck and a steering device) could carry heavy loads with the current but were useless for upriver traffic. Although keelboats could be poled upstream, they were slow and expensive.

Steamboats provided the first transportation breakthrough. In 1807, Robert Fulton demonstrated their commercial practicality when he sent the *Clare mont* 150 miles up the Hudson River from New York City to Albany. In 1815, the *Enterprise* carried a cargo upriver from New Orleans to Pittsburgh.

By the 1820s, steamboats had reduced the cost and the time of upriver shipments by 90 percent. By the 1840s, more than five hundred steamboats were plying western waters. More and more farmers could now reap the economic benefits of exporting corn, pork, and other regional foodstuffs.

Western trade did not start to flow eastward until the completion of the Erie Canal in 1825, the first and most successful of the artificial waterways designed to link eastern seaboard cities with western markets (see Map 11-1).

TABLE 11.1	IMPACT OF THE TRANSPORTATION REVOLUTION ON TRAVELING TIME		
Route	**1800**	**1830**	**1860**
New York to Philadelphia	2 days	1 day	Less than 1 day
New York to Charleston	More than 1 week	5 days	2 days
New York to Chicago	6 weeks	3 weeks	2 days
New York to New Orleans	4 weeks	2 weeks	6 days

Map 11-1   The Transportation Revolution

By 1830, a network of roads, canals, and navigable rivers was spurring economic growth in the first phase of the Transportation Revolution. By 1850, railroads, the key development in the second phase of the Transportation Revolution, were opening up additional areas to commercial activity.

CHRONOLOGY

1790 Samuel Slater opens the first permanent cotton mill in Rhode Island.

1793 Eli Whitney patents the first cotton gin.

1807 Robert Fulton's steamboat, the *Clermont*, makes its pioneering voyage up the Hudson River.

1811 Construction begins on the federally financed National Road at Cumberland, Maryland.

1814 The Boston Associates opens its Waltham mill, the first textile factory to mechanize all phases of production.

1817 Construction on the Erie Canal begins.

1819–1829 Economic depression.

1824 In *Gibbons* v. *Ogden*, the Supreme Court strikes down a state monopoly over steamboat navigation.

1825 Erie Canal is completed.

1828 The Baltimore and Ohio, the most important of the early railroads, is chartered.

1834 Female workers at the Lowell Mills stage their first strike.

National Trades Union is formed.

1837 In *Charles River Bridge* v. *Warren Bridge*, the Supreme Court encourages economic competition by ruling that presumed rights of monopolistic privileges could not be used to block new economic enterprises.

1839–1843 Economic depression.

1842 Massachusetts Supreme Court in *Commonwealth* v. *Hunt* strengthens the legal right of workers to organize trade unions.

1845 Potato famine in Ireland sets off a mass migration of Irish to the United States.

1847 Cyrus McCormick opens his main reaper factory in Chicago.

New York City merchants wanted to reach the agricultural markets of the Old Northwest. Prodded by Governor DeWitt Clinton, the New York legislature agreed to fund the Erie Canal in 1817. The United States had barely 100 miles of canals at this time, none longer than 28 miles. The Erie Canal was to stretch 364 miles from Albany to Buffalo, a small port on Lake Erie. Its construction—the excavation of massive amounts of earth, the building of locks to raise and lower the water level for boats, and the clearing and grading of towpaths for the horses and mules that pulled boats along the 40-foot-wide band of water—was the greatest engineering feat of its era.

The completion of the Erie depended on the backbreaking labor of Irish immigrants, who comprised the bulk of its work gangs. They worked for less than $10 a month, part of which (at their insistence) was paid in whiskey in a daily ration of 12 to 20 ounces. The workers lived in camps built by the canal contractors. One thousand workers contracted a fever in the marshes around Syracuse in the summer of 1819, and many of them died. Conditions for workers on the Erie promoted a violent culture of brawling and drinking that fed ethnic stereotypes of the Irish as drunken brutes. The stereotypes stuck,

and when New York City celebrated the completion of the canal in 1825, the Irish were excluded from the festivities.

The Erie was an immediate success. It reduced the cost of sending freight from Buffalo to New York City by more than 90 percent. As early as 1827, New York City leapfrogged Philadelphia and Baltimore as the leading exporter of flour, and by the mid-1840s, the Erie was pulling in more western trade than was being sent south to New Orleans on the Mississippi River. Profits from the Erie were so high that the construction cost of $7 million was paid off in just 12 years.

The Erie's success touched off a boom in canal building. Pennsylvania and Maryland launched plans for competing canals to the West, and other states soon joined them. More than 3,000 miles of canals were in place by 1840. The Erie ran through the only natural break in the Appalachian Mountains, the Mohawk Valley of central New York, and no other canal could overcome the tremendous advantage of the Erie's head start in fixing trading patterns along its route.

The Panic of 1837 abruptly ended the canal boom as financing dried up. Still, the canal boom had greatly accelerated economic growth. Three broad networks of canals existed by 1840. One set linked seaboard cities on the Atlantic with their agricultural hinterlands, another connected the mid-Atlantic states with the Ohio River Valley, and a third funneled western grain to ports on the Great Lakes. A unified national market was starting to take shape.

Railroads

Railroads were the last and ultimately the most important link in the transportation improvements that spurred economic development in Jacksonian America. Railroads struck Americans as a radically new technology that overturned traditional notions of time and space. "I cannot describe the strange sensation produced on seeing the train of cars come up. And when I started in them ... it seemed like a dream," exclaimed Christopher Columbus Baldwin of Massachusetts when he saw his first railroad car in 1835.

Moving at 15 to 20 miles per hour—four times as fast as a canal boat and twice the speed of a stagecoach—the railroads of the 1830s seemed to annihilate distance. After riding on the Western Railroad in Massachusetts, Caroline Fitch of Boston described her trip as a "lightning flash." The hissing of steam engines, squealing of iron wheels on iron rails, and gusts of air rushing into open rail cars made early rail travel an adventure.

In 1825, the same year the Erie Canal was completed, the world's first general-purpose steam-powered railroad, the Stockton and Darlington, opened in England. Businesspeople in the eastern cities of the United States, fearful that the canal would give New York a monopoly on the western trade, were quick to see the commercial promise of rail transport.

The construction of the first American railroads began in the late 1820s, and they all pushed outward from seaboard cities eager to connect to the western market. The Baltimore and Ohio was to cross the Appalachians and connect Baltimore with Wheeling, Virginia, on the Ohio River. Boston merchants saw the Boston and Worcester Railroad as a link between New England and the eastern terminus of the Erie Canal at Albany. By 1841, Boston had a rail connection to Albany. The Charleston enterprise sought to divert the lucrative cotton trade of the Carolina interior away from Savannah, Georgia. At its completion in 1833, the Charleston and Hamburg, with 136 miles of track, was the world's longest railroad.

By 1840, U.S. rail mileage had drawn even with that of canals and was twice as extensive as the total for all of Europe. Competition from the railroads soon overshadowed canals, which suffered from freezing in winter and low water in summer. The railroads were faster and more dependable and had more flexible schedules. They could serve land-locked areas beyond the reach of river and canal networks. As early as 1840, a railroad could move four times as much freight as a canal for the same cost in labor and capital.

The railroads became the most dynamic booster of interregional trade. Whereas the canal network stopped expanding after 1840, the railroads tripled their mileage in the 1840s. Revenues from freight traffic exceeded those from passenger travel for the first time in 1849. By then, trunk lines built westward from Atlantic Coast cities had reached the Great Lakes and the Ohio Valley and were about to enter the Mississippi Valley. Short lines were being consolidated into larger systems. New York and Pennsylvania took the lead in developing trunk lines to the west.

The rail network in place by midcentury was already altering the North-South sectional balance. Before the coming of canals and railroads, the bulk of western trade went downriver to New Orleans. By the early 1850s, this traditional trading pattern had been reversed, and most western produce went east. Moving in the opposite direction were northern-born settlers, manufactured goods, and cultural values that increasingly unified the free states east of the Mississippi into a common economic and cultural unit. The Northeast and the Old Northwest were becoming just the North. Significantly, no direct rail connection linked the North and the South.

Government and the Economy

Both national and state government played an active part in the economy. Congress twice voted funds for a network of roads and canals. However, the constitutional objections and vetoes of Presidents Madison and Monroe prevented the federal government from developing a national system of transportation. Still, it was widely accepted that government should promote and regulate economic growth for the benefit of its citizens.

State governments provided some 70 percent of the funding for canals. High construction costs made private investors leery of risking their scarce capital in such long-term transportation projects. The popular fear, as expressed by John Sergeant of Pennsylvania, was that the private owners of canals would "monopolize their benefits in perpetuity" and thereby deprive the people of part of their sovereign power. Similar arguments also induced the states to invest in the early railroads. About half of all railroad capital before the Civil War came from the state governments.

SUMMARY

CHANGES PROMOTING GROWTH IN THE TRANSFORMED ECONOMY

Sector	1815	1850
Travel and transportation	By foot and horse-drawn wagon	Cheaper and faster with canals, steamboats, and railroads opening up new markets
Population	Overwhelmingly native-born, rural, and concentrated east of the Appalachian Mountains	Four times larger as a result of natural increase and surge of immigration after 1840; settlement of West and growth of cities
Wage labor	Native-born, primarily women and children in manufacturing	Expanding as rural poor and immigrants enter the manufacturing work force
Power	Water-driven mills	Steam-driven engines
Farming	Subsistence-oriented; surplus sold in localized markets	Commercialized agriculture spreading in response to improvements in transportation
Manufacturing	Small-scale production in household units and artisan shops	Large-scale production in eastern cities and factories

The federal government provided engineers for railroad surveys, lowered tariff duties on iron used in rail construction, and granted public land that totaled 20 million acres by 1860. Such federal subsidies through grants of public land were the chief means for financing the transcontinental railroads after the Civil War.

State courts and legislatures after the War of 1812 began to confer new rights and powers on private enterprises that had incorporated as transportation companies. Investors in these corporations received the protection of limited liability. If the corporation went bankrupt, the investors' personal assets were safe from creditors; their potential loss was limited to their direct financial stake in the company. Second, these corporations acquired the power of eminent domain, the legal right to purchase whatever land they needed for their rights-of-way. State courts upheld these enhanced legal powers. The courts ruled that a greater good—the development of the economy through transportation improvements—took precedence over the private property rights of an individual.

By the 1830s, the states were making it easier for businesses to incorporate. The older view of the corporation as a privileged quasi-public institution entrusted with a communal responsibility gave way to the modern notion of the corporation was that of a private business that should receive no special government favors. Incorporation was increasingly seen as a democratic right of business enterprise that no longer required a special act of the legislature. The number of corporations grew rapidly under these new laws, and two-thirds of them were in transportation.

Artisans whose livelihoods were threatened by the spread of factories objected that incorporation "puts means into the hands of inexperienced capitalists to take from us the profits of our art which cost us so many years of labour to obtain." When railroads brought in outside goods that undersold local producers, farmers and artisans in Massachusetts accused the corporations of having delivered "the business and profits of general transportation into the hands of the capitalists." Their fears were well founded: "Scores of deserted villages in various sections of the Commonwealth bear witness to the wasting and blasting effects of this growing monopoly."

Two decisions of the Supreme Court helped open up the economy to competition. In **Gibbons** v. **Ogden** (1824), the Court overturned a New York law that had given Aaron Ogden a monopoly on steamboat service between New York and New Jersey. Thomas Gibbons, Ogden's competitor, had a federal license for the coastal trade. The right to compete under the national license, the Court ruled, took legal precedence over Ogden's monopoly. The decision affirmed the supremacy of the national government to regulate interstate commerce.

A new Court, presided over by Chief Justice Roger B. Taney, Jackson's former secretary of the treasury (John Marshall had died in 1835), struck a bolder blow against monopoly in the landmark case of **Charles River Bridge** v. **Warren Bridge** in 1837. Taney ruled in favor of the Warren Bridge Company by deciding that the older Charles River Bridge Company had not received a monopoly from Massachusetts to collect tolls across the Charles River. Any uncertainties in the charter rights of corporations, reasoned Taney, should be resolved in favor of the broader community interests that would be served by free and open competition.

The Rise of Cities

At midcentury, more than one in seven Americans was a city-dweller, and the nation had ten cities whose population exceeded fifty thousand. The transportation revolution triggered this surge in urban growth. The cities that prospered and grew were those with access to the expanding network of cheap transport on steamboats, canals, and railroads. This network opened up the rural interior for the purchase of farm commodities by city merchants and the sale of finished goods by urban importers and manufacturers. A huge influx of immigrants after the mid-1840s and simultaneous advances in steam engines provided the cheap labor and sources of power that increasingly made cities focal points of manufacturing production.

The Port Cities

America's largest cities in the early nineteenth century were its Atlantic ports: New York, Philadelphia, Baltimore, and Boston. As late as the 1820s, these four cities held more than half the total urban population and packed together merchants, artisans, and laborers near the waterfronts that were their economic lifeblood. "The carters were driving in every direction," an Englishman wrote of the New York City waterfront in 1806, "and the sailors and labourers upon the wharfs, and on board the vessels, were moving their ponderous burthens from place to place. The merchants and their clerks were busily engaged in their counting-houses, or upon the piers. . . . Everything was in motion; all was life, bustle, and activity."

These Atlantic seaports all benefited from the transportation revolution, but only New York experienced phenomenal growth. By 1810, New York had become the largest American city, and its population exceeded eight hundred thousand by the 1850s. One-third of the nation's exports and more than three-fifths of its imports passed through New York between 1820 and 1860. No wonder poet Walt Whitman trumpeted this metropolis as "the great place of the Western Continent, the heart, the brain, the focus, the main spring, the pinnacle, the extremity, the no more beyond of the new world."

New York's harbor gave oceangoing ships direct, protected access to Manhattan Island, and from there the Hudson River provided a navigable highway flowing 150 miles north to Albany, deep in the state's agricultural interior. No other port was so ideally situated for trade. With entrepreneurial moxie, New York City merchants established the Black Ball Line in 1817, the first line of packet ships that ran on a regular schedule for moving cargoes, passengers, and mail across the Atlantic. The city's merchants also convinced the state legislature to finance the Erie Canal, which guaranteed the ongoing commercial preeminence of the port of New York.

New York City benefited not only from the increased volume of western foodstuffs sent east across the Erie Canal and down the Hudson River for export to Europe but also from the swelling flow of finished goods shipped out of New York for sale in the West. Western families with access to the Erie Canal became increasingly specialized economically. New markets encouraged them to concentrate on cash crops, and profits were spent on finished goods. The rise in the disposable income of farmers generated a demand for the textiles, shoes, and other consumer goods that the Erie Canal brought in. These goods came out of New York, but most were not manufactured in the city. Nonetheless, the jobs created by handling these goods and the profits derived from supplying the western market solidified the city's position as the nation's most dynamic economic center.

New Yorkers plowed the profits of this commerce into local real estate—which soared in value fiftyfold between 1823 and 1836—and into financial institutions such as the New York Stock Exchange, founded in 1817. The city's banks brought together the capital that made New York the country's chief financial center. Agents for the city's mercantile and financial interests used this capital to offer advantageous terms to capture much of the southern trade and dominate commerce with South America.

Commercial rivals in other port cities launched their own canal and railroad ventures to penetrate the West, but none developed a hinterland as rich or extensive as New York's. Still, Boston, Baltimore, and Philadelphia continued to grow and at midcentury remained the nation's largest cities behind New York.

As they grew, the Atlantic ports pioneered new forms of city transportation. Omnibuses (horse-drawn coaches carrying up to twenty passengers) and steam ferries were in common use by the 1820s. The first commuter railroad, the Boston and Worcester, began service in 1838. Horse-drawn street railway lines in the 1850s moved at speeds of about 6 miles an hour, overcoming some of the limitations of the "walking cities" of the early nineteenth century. Cities began to spread outward as cheaper, faster ways of traveling to work became available.

At the same time, the first slums appeared, the most notorious of which was the Five Points district of New York City. In 1842, the English novelist Charles Dickens described this area of tenement houses, brothels, and saloons as "these narrow ways, diverging to the right and left, and reeking everywhere with dirt and filth."

Small, flimsy wooden structures, often crammed into a back alley, housed the working poor in cramped, fetid conditions. Backyard privies, supplemented by chamber pots, were the standard means of disposing of human wastes. These outhouses overflowed in heavy rain and often contaminated private wells, the source of drinking water. Garbage and animal wastes simply accumulated on streets, scavenged by roving packs of hogs.

A densely packed population in a poorly drained, garbage-strewn setting made cities unhealthy. Mortality rates were much higher than in rural areas, and the death rate in New York City was double that of London. Stagnant pools of water bred mosquitoes that carried yellow fever, and contaminated water supplies produced frequent epidemics of cholera and typhus. But the cities continued to grow.

Interior Cities

The fastest-growing cities were in the interior. Their share of the urban population quadrupled from 1800 to 1840. Rochester, New York, a village that the opening of the Erie Canal rapidly transformed into a major flour-milling center, amazed one English visitor in 1827 with its spontaneous energy. "The very streets," he observed, "seemed to be starting up of their own accord, ready-made, and looking as fresh as new, as if they had been turned out of the workmen's hands but an hour before—or that a great boxful of new houses had been sent by steam from New York, and tumbled out on the half-cleared land."

Pittsburgh, at the head of the Ohio River, was the first western city to develop a manufacturing sector to complement its exchange function. With access to extensive coalfields of western Pennsylvania, Pittsburgh had a cheap fuel that provided the high heat needs to manufacture iron and glass. It emerged as America's best-known and most polluted manufacturing city. "It is surrounded," noted the French traveler Michel Chevalier in the 1830s, "with a dense, black smoke which, bursting forth in volumes from the foundries, forges, glass-houses, and the chimneys of all the factories and houses, falls in flakes of soot upon the dwellings and persons of the inhabitants. It is, therefore, the dirtiest town in the United States."

Cincinnati, downstream on the Ohio, soon became famous for its hogs. "Porkopolis," as it was called, was the West's first meatpacking center. Industries in animal by-products, such as soap, candles, shoes, and boots, gave the city a diversified manufacturing base that kept it in the forefront of western urban growth.

By the 1840s, St. Louis and the Great Lakes ports of Buffalo, Cleveland, Detroit, Milwaukee, and Chicago were the dynamic centers of western urbanization. St. Louis, just below the merger of the Missouri and the Mississippi Rivers, serviced American trade with the trans-Mississippi West. Outfitters used St. Louis as the jumping-off point for the fur trade up the middle Missouri and through the South Pass of the Rocky Mountains to rendezvous points with trappers and Native Americans in Wyoming. The city was also the eastern end of the Santa Fe Trail, a corridor of Anglo-Mexican trade that stretched across the southern plains to Santa Fe, New Mexico. St. Louis tripled in population in the 1830s, and it continued to surge after 1840 as a result of the city's importance in receiving and distributing goods for the upper Mississippi Valley. By midcentury, St. Louis was developing rail connections that linked it to the Great Lakes cities.

The Great Lakes served as an extension of the Erie Canal, and cities on the lakes where incoming and outgoing goods had to be unloaded for transshipment benefited enormously. They attracted settlers and soon evolved into regional economic centers serving the surrounding agricultural communities. They also aggressively promoted themselves into major rail hubs and thus reaped the economic advantages of being at the juncture of both water and rail transport.

The combined populations of Cleveland, Detroit, Milwaukee, and Chicago increased twenty-five-fold between 1830 and 1850. The only other cities experiencing such phenomenal rates of growth were the new industrial towns. The densest cluster of these was in rural New England along the fall line of rivers, where the rapidly falling water provided cheap power to drive the industrial machinery of factories and machine shops. Each town was tied to a transportation network that brought in raw cotton for the textile mills from the mercantile centers of Boston and Providence and shipped out the finished goods.

Lowell, Massachusetts, was America's first large-scale, planned manufacturing city. Founded in 1822 by Boston businessmen, Lowell was built around the falls of the Merrimack River. Within a decade, rural fields had been transformed into a city of eighteen thousand people. Multistoried brick factories surrounded by detached housing for the supervisory staff and large boardinghouses for the workers dominated the landscape and defined the city's industrial functions. "Everywhere one hears the noise of hammers, of spindles, of bells calling the hands to their work or dismissing them from their tasks, of coaches and six arriving or starting off, of the blasting of rocks to make a millrace or to level a road," noted Michel Chevalier in the mid-1830s. Lowell's success became a model for others to follow, and by 1840, New England led the North in both urbanization and industrialization.

Immigration

A surge of immigrants swelled the size of the cities after the 1830s. At midcentury, most of the population in New York was foreign-born, and in all the port cities of the Northeast, immigrants dominated the manufacturing work force.

In the half-century after the Revolution, immigration to the United States was well under ten thousand newcomers per year. It then jumped in the 1830s to over fifty thousand per year and soared to 140,000 in the 1840s and 280,000 in the 1850s. Most of these immigrants were Irish and Germans who settled in the Northeast.

In the 1840s, economic and political upheavals in Europe spurred mass migration, mostly to America. Catholic peasants of Ireland, dominated by their Protestant English landlords, eked out a subsistence as tenants on tiny plots of land. A potato blight wiped out the crop in 1845 and 1846, and in the next five years, about 1 million Irish died of mal-

nutrition and disease. Another 1.5 million fled, many to America.

The Irish had no money to buy land or move west unless they joined construction gangs for canals and railroads. Without marketable skills, they had to take the worst and lowest-paying jobs: ragpickers, porters, day laborers, and unskilled factory hands. Wives and daughters became laundresses and maids for the urban middle class.

Packed into dark cellars, unventilated attics, and rank tenements, Irish mortality rates were frightful. Still, cash wages and access to food made the American city enviable, compared to the prospect of starvation in Ireland. Urging her parents to join her, Margaret McCarthy, an Irish domestic servant, wrote in 1850 that New York was a place "where no man or woman ever Hungerd or ever will and where you will not be Seen Naked . . . where you would never want or be at a loss for a good Breakfast and Dinner."

German immigrants were second in number only to the Irish by the 1850s. They came to America to escape poor harvests and political turmoil. Far more Germans than Irish had the capital to purchase land in the West and the skills to join the ranks of small businesspeople in the cities. They were also more likely than the Irish to have entered the country through Baltimore or New Orleans, southern ports engaged in the tobacco and cotton trade with continental Europe. From there they fanned out into the Mississippi and Ohio Valleys. With the Irish, they made up over half of the population of St. Louis by the 1850s and were close to a majority in the other large cities of the Midwest and Northeast. With their diversified skills, the Germans found ample economic opportunities in the fast-growing cities and a setting in which to build neighborhoods of German-speaking shops, churches, schools, and benevolent societies.

About four in five of the 4.2 million immigrants from all nations who arrived from 1840 to 1860 settled in the New England and mid-Atlantic states. Their sheer numbers transformed the size and ethnic composition of the working class, especially in the cities of the Northeast. And their cheap labor provided the final ingredient in the expansion of industrialization that began after the War of 1812.

The Industrial Revolution

Regions, as well as individuals, had an incentive to specialize in goods that they could produce most efficiently with their labor and capital. Specialization in the scale of production, the organization of work, and the utilization of labor was also occurring. When these changes were combined with power-driven machinery in the new factories, the very meaning of the word *manufacturing* changed. Whereas before the 1820s it referred to the making of things by hand, it now came to mean the production of goods by machines in factories.

The Northeast led America's industrial revolution. In 1815, this region had the largest cities, the most developed capital markets, the readiest access to the technological skills of artisans, and the greatest supply of available labor. For the next thirty years, the United States had the most rapidly developing industrial economy in the world.

Early Stages

The household and the small workshop were the sites of manufacturing in Jefferson's America. Wider markets for household manufactures began to develop in the late eighteenth century with the coming of the **putting-out system**. Local merchants furnished ("put out") raw materials to rural households and paid at a piece rate for the labor that converted those raw materials into manufactured products. The supplying merchant then marketed and sold these goods.

In the cities and larger towns, most manufacturing was done by artisans, skilled craftsmen who were also known as mechanics. Working in their own shops and with their own tools, they produced small batches of finished goods. Close to half of the population in the seaport cities, artisans and their families fed, clothed, and housed the urban population.

Each artisan had a specific skill that set him above common laborers. These skills came from hands-on experience and craft traditions that were handed down from one generation to the next.

The "mysteries of the craft" were taught by master craftsmen to the **journeymen** and **apprentices** who lived with them and worked in their shops. Journeymen had learned the skills of their craft but lacked the capital to open their own shops. Before establishing their own businesses, they saved their earnings and honed their skills while working for a wage under a master. Apprentices were adolescent boys legally sent by their fathers to live with and obey a master craftsman in return for being taught a trade. By the terms of the contract, known as an **indenture**, the master also provided for the apprentice's schooling and moral upbringing. An apprentice could reasonably expect to be promoted to journeyman in his late teens and begin advancement toward his **competency**, a secure income from an independent trade that would enable him to support a family.

Artisans controlled entry into their trades and the process of production from start to finish. They set their own work rules and were their own bosses. "The Mechanics are a class [of] men," proudly wrote "Peter Single" in the *Mechanic's Free Press* of Philadelphia, "who compose that proportion of the population of our country, on whom depends its present and future welfare; from them emanates her glory, her greatness and her power."

The factory system of production that undercut both household and artisanal manufacturing had several advantages. First, the factories could produce goods far more quickly and cheaply per worker than artisans or rural households. Factories subdivided the specialized skills of the artisan into a series of semi-skilled tasks, a process foreshadowed by the putting-out system. Second, factories put workers under systematic controls. And in the final stage of industrialization, they boosted workers' productivity through the use of power-driven machinery.

Britain pioneered the technological advances that drove early industrialization. The secrets of this technology, especially the designs for the machines that mechanized textile production, were closely guarded by the British government. Despite attempts to prohibit the emigration of artisans who knew how this machinery worked, some British mechanics got to the United States. Samuel Slater was one of them, and he took over the operation of a fledging mill in Providence, Rhode Island. With his knowledge of how to build water-powered spinning machinery, Slater converted the mill into the nation's first permanent cotton factory.

Slater's factory, and those modeled after it, manufactured yarn that was put out to rural housewives to be woven into cloth. The first factory to mechanize the operations of spinning and weaving and turn out finished cloth was incorporated in Waltham, Massachusetts in 1813 by the Boston Associates, a group of wealthy merchants. The Waltham factory was heavily capitalized, relied on the latest technology, and recruited its work force from rural farm families.

The first real spurt of factory building came with the closing off of British imports during the Embargo and the War of 1812. Hundreds of new cotton and woolen mills were established from 1808 to 1815. But the great test of American manufacturing came after 1815 when peace with Britain brought a flood of cheap British manufactured goods. If factories were to continue to grow, American manufacturers had to reach more consumers in their home

Shown here working at power looms under the supervision of a male overseer, young single women comprised the bulk of the labor force in the first textile factories of New England.

market and overcome the British advantage of lower labor costs.

Sources of Workers in Manufacturing

The economy was at a crossroads in 1815. Future growth would have to come from within as capital and resources were diverted from carrying goods to producing them. To expand significantly the factories needed abundant sources of cheap labor.

Industrial labor was more expensive in America than in England, where the high cost of land forced the peasantry into the cities to find work. In contrast, land was cheap and plentiful in the United States, and Americans preferred the independence of farm work to the dependence of factory labor. Consequently, the first mill workers were predominantly children. For example, the mills that advertised in the *Massachusetts Spy* in the 1820s called for families "of five or six children each." The owners set up the father on a plot of company-owned land, provided piecework for the mother, and put the children to work in the mills.

Although this so-called **Rhode Island system** of family employment sufficed for small mills, it was inadequate for the larger, more mechanized factories that were built in New England after the War of 1812. These mill owners recruited single, adolescent daughters of farmers from across New England as their laborers in the **Waltham system.**

Throughout the 1820s and 1830s, most mill hands in New England were young farm daughters. Jemima Sanborn explained when she went into the mills in Nashua, New Hampshire, that they left home because of "the hard times to get a living off the farm for so large a family." Although factory wages were low (a little over a dollar per week after deductions for room and board), they were more than these young women could earn doing piecework in the home or as domestics. The wages also brought a liberating degree of financial independence. "When they felt the jingle of silver in their pockets," recalled Harriet Hanson Robinson of her fellow workers at Lowell in the 1830s, "there for the first time, their heads became erect and they walked as if on air."

Based on what they had heard of conditions in British factories, most Americans associated mill towns with morally depraved, impoverished workers. To overcome parental fears of sending their daughters into such an unwholesome environment, New England manufacturers set up paternalistic moral controls. Single female workers had to live in boardinghouses owned by the company. Curfews were imposed, visitors were screened, and church attendance was mandatory.

The mill women still worked six days a week from dawn to dusk for low wages. The operatives tended clattering, fast-moving machinery in a work environment kept humid to minimize the snapping of threads in the machines. In 1834 and 1836, the female hands at Lowell "turned out" to protest wage reductions in demonstrations that were the largest strikes in American history up to that time. They insisted that "as our fathers resisted unto blood the lordly avarice of the British ministry, so we, their daughters, will never wear the yoke which has been prepared for us" (see "American Views: Proclamation of Striking Women Workers, Lowell, 1834").

After the economic downturn of the late 1830s, conditions in the mills got worse. By the mid-1840s, however, the Irish, desperate for work, sent their children into the mills at an earlier age than Yankee farm families had. These workers did not leave after two or three years of building up a small dowry for marriage, as many New Englanders did. In the mid-1830s, some 95 percent of the textile operatives in New England were native-born and mostly women; by the early 1850s, more than half were Irish women.

In the mid-Atlantic region, the farm population was more prosperous than in New England, and fewer young women were available for factory work. So as early as 1820, about half of the factory workers in the mid-Atlantic states were immigrants.

The rise in immigration after the 1820s was crucial for urban manufacturing. The port cities lacked usable water power, but by drawing on this cheap pool of immigrant labor, manufacturers could increase production while driving down the cost.

Especially in finished consumer goods, such as the clothing and leather industries, where low-paid workers could stitch cloth or sole a shoe, urban manufacturing became labor-intensive, depending more heavily on workers than on investment in machines and other capital. New York and Philadelphia, followed by Boston in the 1840s, thus built up a diversified manufacturing sector in consumer goods.

Except in New England textile factories and the smaller factories and shops in the seaboard cities, native-born males were the largest group of early manufacturing workers. As late as 1840, women, including those working at home, made up about half of the manufacturing work force and one-quarter of the factory hands. Regardless of their sex, few of these workers brought any specific skills to their jobs, and hence they had little bargaining power. Economic necessity forced them to accept low wages and harsh working conditions. The sheer increase in their numbers, as opposed to any productivity gains from technological innovations, accounted by 1850 for two-thirds of the gains in manufacturing output.

The Role of Technology

In closing the technological gap with Britain, manufacturers first relied on the trade secrets brought to America by British mechanics such as Samuel Slater for starting up the textile industry. But elsewhere the versatile, practical skills of American mechanics provided the impetus for technological innovation.

Mechanics, especially in the countryside, had an extensive range of skills. The Dominy family of Easthampton, Long Island, for example, worked with wood and iron, built grist mills, and made clocks and watches. Mechanics experimented with new designs, improved old ones, and patented inventions that found industrial applications outside their own crafts. Oliver Evans, a wagonmaker in the Delaware Valley, developed machinery for a highly automated flour mill in the 1780s.

The most famous early American invention was the cotton gin. Eli Whitney, a Massachusetts Yankee who had turned out knives and blades at a forge on his father's farm as a teenager, built the first prototype in 1793 while working as a tutor on a Georgia plantation. By cheaply and mechanically removing the seeds from cotton fibers, the cotton gin spurred the cultivation of cotton across the South.

Whitney also pushed the idea of basing production on interchangeable parts. After receiving a federal contract to manufacture muskets, he designed new milling machines and turret lathes that transformed the technology of machine tool production. The federal arsenal at Harpers Ferry, Virginia, developed machine tools that could manufacture standardized, interchangeable parts. The new techniques were first applied in 1815 to the manufacture of wooden clocks and by the 1840s to sewing machines, farm machinery, and watch parts. The **American system of manufacturing**—low-cost, standardized mass production, built around interchangeable parts stamped out by machines—was America's unique contribution to the industrial revolution.

As the pace of technological innovation accelerated after 1840, so did the growth of manufacturing. Indeed, the 1840s registered the highest rate of expansion in the manufacturing sector of the economy in the nineteenth century. The adoption of the stationary steam engine in urban manufacturing fueled much of this expansion.

American Views

PROCLAMATION OF STRIKING WOMEN WORKERS, LOWELL, 1834

In February 1834, eight hundred women operatives staged the first work stoppage at the textile mills in Lowell, Massachusetts. They were protesting a proposed cut in their wages. Part of a wave of labor unrest in the mid-1830s, the striking workers in Lowell marched, temporarily shut down the mills, and outlined their grievances and demands in a formal protest. Although the strike lasted less than a week and failed to reverse the wage cuts, it revealed that women workers were as militant as their male counterparts in their quest for economic independence and justice.

❖ How did the women link their struggle with that of the patriots in the American Revolution? Whom were they referring to when they spoke of "Tories in disguise"?

❖ How would wage cuts threaten the economic independence and social equality that these women valued?

❖ How did the strikers reject the benevolent paternalism the mill owners tried to impose on them? How did they step outside the bounds of proper "womanly" behavior?

❖ What "bondage" did these women want to avoid?

Our present object is to have union and exertion, and we remain in possession of our unquestionable rights. We circulate this paper wishing to obtain the names of all who imbibe the spirit of our Patriotic Ancestors, who preferred privilege to bondage, and parted with all that renders life desirable and even life itself to procure independence for their children. The oppressing hand of avarice would enslave us, and to gain their object, they gravely tell us of the pressure of the time, this we are already sensible of, and deplore it. If any are in want, the Ladies will be compassionate and assist them; but we prefer to have the disposing of our charities in our own hands; and as we are free, we would remain in possession of what kind Providence has bestowed upon us, and remain daughters of freemen still. . . .

Let oppression shrug her shoulders,
And a haughty tyrant frown,
And little upstart Ignorance,
In mockery look down.
Yet I value not the feeble threats
Of Tories in disguise,
While the flag of Independence
O'er our noble nation flies.

Resolved, That we will not go back into the mills to work unless our wages are continued . . . as they have been.
Resolved, That none of us will go back, unless they receive us all as one.
Resolved, That if any have not enough money to carry them home they shall be supplied.

Source: *Boston Evening Transcript, February 18, 1834, as cited in Thomas Dublin,* Women at Work: The Transformation of Work and Community in Lowell, Massachusetts, 1826–1860 (1979).

In the 1840s, high-pressure steam engines enabled power-driven industry to locate in the port cities of the Northeast. Steam power and more mechanized manufacturing also benefited the booming cities in the Great Lakes corridor of the Old Northwest. With limited access to water power, early manufacturing in the West was confined to the processing of farm goods By turning to steam power and new machine tools, western manufacturers after 1840 enlarged their region's industrial base and created a new industry, the mass production of agricultural implements. The McCormick reaper factory in Chicago was one of the world's most modern industrial facilities by the 1850s. Steam-powered conveyer belts moved parts through the factory in an assembly-line system of production. The West was the center of the farm machinery industry, and the region produced 20 percent of the nation's manufacturing output by the 1850s.

Steam power was beginning to transform the American landscape by the mid-nineteenth century. However, most of the change evident in the countryside by 1850 was the product of preindustrial technologies and the aftermath of impounding water for factory use.

About one-fifth of the original forest cover in the United States east of the Mississippi was gone by 1850. Most of this loss resulted from agricultural use. Wood that was not needed for farmhouses, fences, and fuel found a ready market in the cities and factories, where it was both the primary energy source and the basic building material.

As the land was being cleared and carved into private farms, the lakes and streams became dumping grounds for agricultural and industrial wastes. The dyes and chemical sulfates used in tanneries and in clothing and textile production were released into water supplies. By 1840, the woolens industry alone was discarding some 18,000 tons of grease into rivers and streams.

To provide their mills with a steady, reliable source of water, one that would not be affected by the whims of nature, the Boston Associates constructed a series of dams and canals that extended to the headwaters of the Merrimack River in northern New Hampshire. Inevitably, the ecology of the region under control changed. The level of lakes was altered, the flow of rivers interrupted, the upward migration of spawning fish blocked, and the foraging terrain of wild game flooded. Farmers protested when their fields and pastures were submerged, but lawyers for the Boston Associates successfully argued that water, like any other natural resource, should be treated as a commodity that could contribute to economic progress. Increasingly, the law treated nature as an economic resource to be engineered and bought and sold.

Growing Inequality and New Classes

As the economy expanded after 1815 and the industrial revolution began to take hold, per capita income doubled in the first half of the century. Living standards for most Americans improved. Houses, for those who could afford them, became larger and better furnished and heated. Food was more plentiful and varied, and factory-made consumer goods made domestic life easier and more comfortable.

There was a price to be paid, however, for the benefits of economic growth. Half of the adult white males were now propertyless. Wealth had become more concentrated, and extremes of wealth and poverty eroded the Jeffersonian ideal of a republic of independent proprietors who valued liberty because they were economically free.

The Old Rich

The gap between the rich and the poor widened considerably in the early phases of industrialization. In 1800, the richest 10 percent of Americans owned 40 to 50 percent of the national wealth. By the 1850s, that share was about 70 percent. Most of this increase occurred after 1815 when industrial development accelerated, and the most glaring discrepancies in wealth appeared in the large cities. In all American cities by the 1840s, the top 10 percent of the population owned over 80 percent of urban wealth.

Most of the urban rich at midcentury had been born wealthy, the offspring of old-money families who had married and invested wisely. To be sure, there were popular stories of a rise from rags to riches, and many of them focused on John Jacob Astor. Born poor in Germany, he amassed a fortune of $25 million in the fur trade and was the richest man in New York by 1845. But for every Astor, twenty Americans benefited from inherited wealth and family connections to stay in the ranks of the very rich.

The urban rich created their own society. As one of them noted, it was a society "characterised by a spirit of exclusiveness and persecution unknown in any other country. Its gradations not being regulated according to rank and titles, selfishness and conceit are its principal elements; and its arbitrary distinctions the more offensive, as they principally refer to fortune." The urban wealthy belonged to exclusive clubs, attended lavish balls and dinners, were waited on by a retinue of servants in their mansions, and generally recoiled from what they considered the "mob government" ushered in by the Jacksonian Democrats.

The New Middle Class

The economy was now growing three times faster than in the eighteenth century, and incomes were rising. New employment opportunities opened up, especially in nonmanual work. Most of these jobs were in northern cities and bustling market towns, where the need was greatest for office and store clerks, managerial personnel, sales agents, and independent retailers. The result by midcentury was a new middle class superimposed on the older one of independent farmers, artisans, shopkeepers, and professionals.

The apparent separation of work and home constituted the first step in an evolving sense of class consciousness. As the market revolution advanced, the workplace increasingly became a specialized location of production or selling. Middle-class fathers left for their jobs in the morning, while mothers governed households that were primarily residential units.

Homes became places of material comfort for the rising middle class. Growing quantities of consumer goods—pianos, carpets, draperies, mirrors, oil lamps, and ornate furniture—filled their homes. Stoves replaced open fireplaces as the main source of heat, and plumbing eliminated outdoor privies.

Having servants, the single largest field of employment in the cities, became a status symbol. Shunned as degrading by most native-born white women, these low-paying jobs were filled by African-American and young immigrant (especially Irish) women. Work had not left the middle-class home; instead, it was disguised as the "domestic duties' of middle-class wives who supervised servants.

Etiquette books for the middle class laid down rules for presenting oneself in public and in the home. "Don't drum with your fingers on chair, table, or window-pane. Don't hum a tune. The instinct for making noise is a survival of savagery," warned one adviser. Above all, these advise manuals stressed decorum and self-restraint.

Besides seeking guidance from etiquette manuals on achieving respectability, the middle class also tried to shape its behavior by the tenets of evangelical religion. Revivals swept northern cities in the late 1820s. Charles G. Finney led the most dramatic and successful ones in the cities along the Erie Canal

in upstate New York. Finney preached that salvation was available to those who willed it.

"A self-indulgent Christian is a contradiction," insisted Finney. Both economic and moral success depended on the virtues of sobriety, self-restraint, and hard work. Aggressiveness and ambition at work were not necessarily sinful so long as businessmen reformed their own moral lives and helped others do the same. This message was immensely reassuring to employers and entrepreneurs in the urban middle class, for it confirmed and sanctified their own pursuit of economic self-interest. It also provided them with a religious inspiration for attempting to exert moral control over their communities and employees.

Merchants, manufacturers, and professionals along with their wives and daughters, were the first to be converted by Finney's preaching. **Temperance**— the prohibition of alcoholic beverages—was the greatest of the evangelically inspired reforms, and abstinence from alcohol became the most telling evidence of middle-class respectability. (For more on reform, see Chapter 14.)

In a reversal of traditional Calvinist doctrine, the evangelical ministers of the northern middle class enshrined women as the moral superiors of men. Though considered weak and passive, women were also held to be uniquely pure and pious. Women were now responsible for converting their homes into loving, prayerful centers of domesticity. "There is a ministry that is older and deeper and more potent than ours," wrote a liberal Presbyterian clergyman; "it is the ministry that presides over the crib and impresses the first gospel influence on the infant soul."

This sanctified notion of motherhood accompanied new views of childhood. Evangelical preachers saw young children as "little immortal beings," pure and innocent, though potentially corruptible. The primary task of motherhood now became the Christian nurturing of the souls entrusted to their care. "My Children how will they get along through this World of sin and vanity?" worried Mercy Flynt Morris. "It is my duty to warn them against those vices and try to instill into their minds the importance of seeking an interest in Christ— without which they will be miserable."

These changing images of women and children reflected and reinforced shifting patterns of family life. Families became smaller as the birthrate fell by 25 percent in the first half of the nineteenth century. The decline was greatest in the urban middle class after 1820. Children were no longer an economic asset as they had been as workers on a family farm. Middle-class couples consciously limited the size of their families, and women stopped having children at a younger age.

Beginning in the 1820s, ministers and female writers elevated the family role of middle-class women into a **cult of domesticity**. This idealized conception of womanhood insisted that the biological differences of God's natural order determined separate social roles for men and women. Characterized as strong, aggressive, and ambitious, men naturally belonged in the competitive world of business and politics. Women's providential task was to preserve religion and morality in the home and family. Only they possessed the moral purity necessary for rearing virtuous children and preserving the home as a refuge from the outside world.

Parents were now able to devote more care and financial resources to child rearing. Middle-class children lived at home longer than children had in the past and received more schooling than working-class children.

Unlike the wealthy, whose riches were inherited, members of the middle class believed that their property was the product of hard work and self-denial. They also saw themselves as the industrious Americans whose moral fortitude and discipline enabled them to escape the clutches of poverty, the fate of those who were presumed to be lazy and undisciplined.

The Working Classes

The economic changes that produced a new middle class also fundamentally transformed the working class. In preindustrial America, the working class was predominantly native-born and of artisan origins. By midcentury, most urban workers were immigrants or the children of immigrants and had never been artisans in a skilled craft (see Figure 11-1).

Job skills, sex, race, and ethnicity all divided workers after 1840. Master craftsmen were the most highly skilled and best-paid members of the labor force. As industrialization proceeded, the unity of the old artisan class splintered. Ambitious master craftsmen with access to capital ignored craft traditions to rise into the ranks of small businessmen and manufacturers. They expanded output and drove down the cost of production by contracting out work at piece wages and hiring the cheapest workers they could find. The result was to transform the apprentice system into a system of exploited child labor.

By the 1830s, most journeymen were becoming a class of permanent wage earners with little prospect of opening their own shops. They denounced the new industrial relations as a "system of mental and physical slavery." To protect their liberties from what they considered a new aristocracy of manufacturers, they organized workingmen's political parties in the 1830s. At the top of these parties' list of reforms were free public education, the abolition of imprisonment for debt, and a ten-hour workday. But the depression of 1839–1843 forced mechanics to concentrate on their economic survival, and the Democrats siphoned off many of their political leaders.

Journeymen also turned to trade union activity in the 1820s and 1830s to gain better wages, shorter hours, and enhanced job security. Benefiting from a strong demand for their skills, workers in the building trades organized the first unions. They were soon followed by shoemakers, printers, and weavers, workers in trades where pressure on urban journeymen was the most intense. Locals from various trades formed the National Trades Union, the first national union, in 1834. The new labor movement launched more than 150 strikes in the mid-1830s.

Although the Panic of 1837 decimated union membership, the early labor movement did achieve two notable victories. First, by the late 1830s, it had forced employers to accept the ten-hour day as the standard for most skilled workers. Second, in a landmark decision handed down in 1842, the Massachu-

Figure 11-1   New York City Working Class, 1855
Especially in the large eastern cities, a new working class of wage laborers dominated by immigrants emerged by the 1850s.
Source: Richard B. Stott, *Workers in the Metropolis: Class, Ethnicity, and Youth in Antebellum New York City* (1990), p. 92.

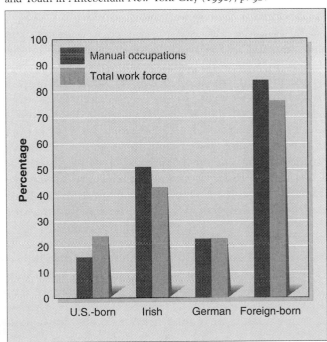

setts Supreme Court ruled in **Commonwealth** v. **Hunt** that a trade union was not necessarily subject to laws against criminal conspiracies and that a strike could be used to force employers to hire only union members.

The unions were the defenders of artisanal rights and virtues, and they ignored workers whose jobs had never had craft status. As massive immigration merged with industrialization after 1840, this basic division between workers widened. On one side was the male, Protestant, and native-born class of skilled artisans. Artisans by midcentury accounted for only 20 percent of the manual workers in the large eastern cities, and two-thirds of these artisans were foreign-born.

On the other side was the working-class majority of factory laborers and the unskilled. These workers were predominantly immigrants and women who worked for a wage as domestic or factory hands. On average, they earned less than $500 a year, about half what skilled workers earned. Their financial survival rested on a family economy in which all members contributed whatever they could earn.

Increasingly fearing these workers as a threat to their job security and Protestant values, American-born artisans joined **nativist** organizations in the 1840s that sought to curb mass immigration from Europe and limit the political rights of Catholic immigrants. Ethnic workers viewed temperance as business-class meddling in their lives, while successful native-born workers tended to embrace the evangelical, middle-class ideology of temperance and self-help. The greatest unity achieved by labor was the nearly universal insistence of whites that blacks be confined to the most menial jobs.

Gender also divided workers. Working-class men shared the dominant ideology of female dependence. They measured their own status as husbands by their ability to keep their wives and daughters from having to work. Beginning in the 1830s, male workers argued that their wages would be higher if women were barred from the work force. A report of the National Trades Union in 1836 cited women's "ruinous competition to male labor." It insisted that a woman's "efforts to sustain herself and family are actually the same as tying a stone around the neck of her natural protector, Man, and destroying him with the weight she has brought to his assistance."

With these views, male workers helped lock wage-earning women into the lowest-paying and most exploited jobs. Of the 25,000 women in 1860 working in manufacturing in New York City, two-thirds were in the clothing trades. Many were seamstresses working at home fifteen to eighteen hours a day for starva-

tion wages of less than $100 a year. Over half of them were the sole breadwinners in their households.

"If we do not come forth in our defence, what will become of us?" asked Sarah Monroe of New York City in the midst of a strike by seamstresses in 1831. Women tried to organize as workers, but the male labor movement refused to lend much support. The men tried to channel the discontent of women workers into "proper female behavior" and generally restricted their assistance to pushing for legislation that would limit the hours worked by women and children, a stand that enhanced their male image as protectors of the family.

Conclusion

In 1820, manufacturing activity was a footnote in an agricultural economy. Cheap land was still abundant, and most Americans dreaded the prospect of wage labor in a factory setting. Yet with surprising speed, transportation improvements, technological innovations, and expanding markets drove the economy on a path toward industrialization. Wealth inequality increased, old classes were reshaped, and new ones formed. These changes were sharpest in the Northeast, where capital, labor, and expanding urban markets spurred the acceleration of manufacturing.

By 1850, most of the work force in the Northeast was no longer employed in agriculture. In New York, the nation's largest city, wage laborers made up 80 percent of the working population.

Review Questions

1. Why were improvements in transportation so essential to the growth of the economy after 1815? What were the nature and scope of these improvements?

2. What factors contributed to the rapid growth of cities in the Jacksonian era, and what types of cities grew the fastest?

3. What is an industrial revolution, and how can we explain the surge in manufacturing in the United States from 1815 to 1850?

4. Why did economic growth widen the gap between the rich and the poor?

5. How did the class structure change in the first half of the nineteenth century, and how would you characterize the differences between the middle class and manufacturing wage laborers at midcentury?

Recommended Reading

Jeanne Boydston, *Home and Work: Housework, Wages, and the Ideology of Labor in the Early Republic* (1990). This provocative work shows how issues of gender shaped the emergence of a market for labor and influenced the very notion of work itself.

Thomas C. Cochran, *Frontiers of Change: Early Industrialism in America* (1981). This engagingly written narrative argues for the importance of cultural factors in the rise and scope of manufacturing in the United States before 1850.

Brooke Hindle and Steven Lubar, *Engines of Change: The American Industrial Revolution, 1790–1860* (1986). This comprehensive overview is particularly strong in explaining the role of technological innovation in the American industrial revolution.

Jack Larkin, *The Reshaping of Everyday Life, 1790–1840* (1988). This is a very readable depiction of how social and economic changes were reflected in the rhythms and customs of daily life in the first half of the nineteenth century.

Walter Licht, *Industrializing America: The Nineteenth Century* (1995). This smoothly written survey interprets industrialization as both a product and a promoter of economic and social change.

Douglass C. North, *The Economic Growth of the United States, 1780–1860* (1966). North makes an elegant case for viewing the export trade, especially in cotton, as the dynamic element driving antebellum economic growth.

George R. Taylor, *The Transportation Revolution, 1815–1860* (1951). A solid economic history, this classic study persuasively argues that improvements in transportation were the catalyst for the transformation of the nineteenth-century economy.

Where to Learn More

❖ **Baltimore Center for Urban Archaeology, Baltimore, Maryland.** Operated by Baltimore City Life Museums, the center has a large collection of artifacts depicting urban life in the eighteenth and nineteenth centuries and a working archaeological library.

❖ **Hanford Mills Museum, East Meredith, New York.** This museum preserves and interprets water-powered machinery and explains the role played by local mills in the community life of the nineteenth century.

❖ **Arabia Museum, Kansas City, Missouri.** This private museum has a fascinating exhibit of the contents of a steamboat that sank on the Missouri River in 1856. The exhibit reveals the abundance and variety of consumer goods that were being shipped to river towns in the Midwest in the 1850s.

❖ **Slater Hill Historic Site, Pawtucket, Rhode Island.** The Sylvanus Brown House of 1758, the Slaren Mill of 1793, and the Wilkinson Mill of 1810 are on the site. An extensive library and holdings provide insight into the social and economic world of the early industrial revolution.

❖ **Erie Canal Museum, Syracuse, New York.** The museum houses extensive collections on the building and maintenance of the Erie Canal, and its photo holdings visually record much of the history of the canal.

12 THE WAY WEST

KEY TOPICS

❖ Western migration spurred by economic and demographic pressures in the East after the War of 1812

❖ The development of free commercial agriculture tied to eastern markets and increased industrialization and urbanization of the Old Northwest

❖ The development of a plantation economy based on cotton and slavery in the Old Southwest

❖ Manifest Destiny and westward expansion, relegating Native Americans and Mexican-Americans to subjugated status

❖ U.S. annexation of Texas and the wresting of the Southwest and California from Mexico

"Out in Oregon, I can get me a square mile of land," exclaimed a Missourian to his wife in 1843. "I am done with this country. Winters it's frost and snow to freeze a body; summers the overflow from the Old Muddy drowns half my acres. Taxes take the yield of them that's left. What say, Maw . . . it's God's country." And so it proved to be for Peter Burnett. He moved his family to Oregon and then to California, where he became the first governor of the new state, acquired through war with Mexico.

Burnett's family was among the first of the some 300,000 Americans who traveled the Oregon Trail by 1860 and eventually made the United States a nation that spanned the continent. These overlanders, as they came to be known, were part of a restless surge of white settlement that eventually saw more than fifty thousand Americans a year migrate west of the Appalachians after the War of 1812 into the Louisiana Purchase territory and across a huge area of plains, desert, mountains, and ocean coast that had seen few American settlers before 1840.

The trans-Mississippi region had become the new American West by midcentury. The West became a meeting ground of people from diverse cultures as Anglo-Americans came into contact and conflict with Plains Indians and the Mexican-Americans of the Southwest. Convinced of the superiority of their political and cultural values,

Anglo-Americans asserted a God-given right to spread across the continent and impose their notions of liberty and democracy on peoples whose land they coveted. In the process, they defeated and subjugated those who stood in their way.

Manifest Destiny, a presumed providential right, provided a justification for the aggressively expansionist Democratic administration of James K. Polk that came to power in 1845. The most dramatic result of its policies was the Mexican War of 1846–1848, which made California and the present-day Southwest part of the American continental empire.

The Agricultural Frontier

The U.S. population ballooned from 5.3 million in 1800 to more than 23 million by 1850. Four-fifths of this extraordinary gain was from natural increase—the surplus of births over deaths. As the population expanded, it shifted westward. Fewer than one in ten Americans lived west of the Appalachians in 1800; by 1850, about half did (see Map 12-1).

Through purchase and conquest, the land area of the United States more than tripled in the first half of the nineteenth century. Here was space where Americans could raise the large families of a rural society in which, on average, six to eight children survived to adolescence.

Declining soil fertility and rising population pressure in the rural East generated the impetus behind these migrations. A common desire for greater economic opportunity, however, resulted in two distinct western societies by the 1840s. North of the Ohio River, in the Old Northwest, free labor and family farms defined the social order. South of the Ohio was the Old Southwest, a society dominated by slave labor and the plantation.

The Crowded East

Looking back at his rural youth, Omar H. Morse recalled, "My Parents were in very limited circumstances financially yet blessed with a large family of children which is a poor man's capital though capital of this kind is not considered very available in case of financial Depression." Born in 1824 in the upstate New York village of Hastings, Morse had no

prospect of inheriting land from his father and was tired of taking orders as a farm hand for temporary wages. He moved in the 1840s to Wisconsin. But he lost three farms and eventually settled in Minnesota, where he worked at odd jobs and built houses. Heading west did not guarantee economic success, but it was the best option open to land-starved easterners who dreamed of leaving a productive farm to their children.

By the early nineteenth century, land was scarce in the East, especially in New England. Most New England communities no longer had enough arable land to satisfy all the young men who wanted their own farms. Even recently opened areas such as Vermont felt the pressure of rural overpopulation.

Land was more productive and expensive farther south, in the mid-Atlantic states. Keyed to the major export crop of wheat, agriculture was more commercialized than in New England, and economic inequality was thus higher. One-third to one-half of the young men in the commercialized agricultural districts of New Jersey and Pennsylvania were landless by the end of the eighteenth century. These men and their families, many of whom were recently arrived Scots-Irish and German immigrants, led the western migration from Pennsylvania.

The pressure to move west was greatest in the slave states along the eastern seaboard. Although population density here was just two-thirds of that in New England, landholdings were more concentrated and the soil more exhausted than in the Northeast. Tenants who wanted their own land and small farmers tired of competing against slave labor were forced west across the mountains. They were joined by the sons of planters. Despite marriages arranged to keep land within the wealthy families, there was no longer enough good land left to carve out plantations for all the younger sons.

By the early 1800s, the young and the poor in the rural East had every incentive to head west, where fertile land was abundant, accessible, and, at $2 to $3 per acre, far cheaper than in the East. Land was the basis of wealth and social standing, and its ownership separated the independent from the dependent, the rooted from the rootless. "Those who labor in the earth," Jefferson wrote in 1785, "are the chosen people of God . . . whose breasts He has made his peculiar deposit for substantial and genuine virtue."

The western settler, observed a traveler on the Missouri frontier in the 1820s, wanted "to be a freeholder, to have plenty of rich land, and to be able to settle his children around him." Public policy and private aspirations merged in the belief that access to land was the key to preserving American freedom.

Map 12-1   The Westward Shift of the United States Population, 1790–1850
With a speed that was unimaginable in 1790, the United States quickly became a continental nation that stretched from the Atlantic to the Pacific by 1850. Particularly dramatic was the population growth in what became the Midwest.

CHRONOLOGY

1803–1806	Lewis and Clark travel up the Missouri River in search of a water route to the Pacific.
1816	Settlers surge into the trans-Appalachian region.
1821	Mexico gains its independence from Spain.
	Santa Fe Trail opens.
	Stephen F. Austin establishes the first American colony in Texas.
1824	Rocky Mountain Fur Company begins the rendezvous system.
1830	Congress creates the Indian Territory.
1834	Protestant missions are established in Oregon.
	Santa Anna seizes power in Mexico.
1836	Texas wins its independence from Mexico.

1837	Smallpox epidemic hits the Plains Indians.
1842	First large parties of migrants set out on the Oregon Trail.
1845	United States annexes Texas.
	Democrats embrace Manifest Destiny.
1846	Mexican War breaks out.
	United States and Britain reach an agreement on Oregon.
1847	Mormons begin settlement of Utah.
1848	Oregon Territory is organized.
	Treaty of Guadalupe Hidalgo ends the Mexican War.
1851	Fort Laramie Treaty with the Plains Indians is signed.

When Jefferson took office in 1801, the minimum price for public land was $2 per acre, and a block of 320 acres had to be purchased at one time. By the 1830s, the price of public land was down to $1.25, and the minimum purchase was only 80 acres. Congress also protected squatters, who had settled on public land before it was surveyed, from being outbid by speculators at a land sale. The Preemption Act of 1841 guaranteed the right to purchase up to 160 acres at the minimum price of $1.25 when the public auction was held.

The Old Northwest

The number of Americans who settled in the heartland of the Old Northwest—Ohio, Indiana, and Illinois—rose tenfold from 1810 to 1840. Ohio had already entered the Union in 1803; Indiana joined in 1816, Illinois in 1818. The end of the War of 1812 and the abandonment by the British of their former Indian allies opened up the region to a flood of migrants.

Two streams of migrants, one predominantly northern and the other southern, met in the lower Midwest and viewed each other as strangers. Lucy Maynard, a New Englander living in south-central Illinois, noted that her neighbors were "principally from Indiana and Kentucky, some from Virginia, all friendly but very different from our people in their manners and language and every other way."

The Old Northwest was less a melting pot in which regional cultures merged than a mosaic of settlements in which the different values and folkways of regional cultures from throughout the East took root and expanded. Belts of migration generally ran along a line from east to west as settlers sought out soil types and ecological conditions similar to those they had left behind. Thus a transplanted Yankee culture from New England and upstate New York spread over the upper Midwest—northern Ohio, Indiana, and Illinois, as well as Michigan and Wisconsin. These westerners were Whiggish in their politics, tended to be antislavery, and valued a communal sense of responsibility that regulated moral behavior and promoted self-improvement. The highland Southerners who settled the lower Midwest—southern Ohio, Indiana, and Illinois, as well as Kentucky—were Democrats: They fiercely distrusted any centralized authority, political or moral, and considered Yankees intolerant do-gooders. Holding the balance of cultural and political power were the migrants from Pennsylvania and New Jersey, who were accustomed to ethnic diversity and the politics of competing economic groups. They settled principally in central Ohio, Indiana, and Illinois. By emphasizing economic growth and downplaying the cultural politics that pitted Yankees against Southerners, they built a consensus around community development.

It took about ten years of backbreaking labor to create an 80-acre farm in heavily wooded sections. Wives and daughters helped tend the field crops, milked cows and churned butter, and produced the homespun cloth that, along with their dairy goods, found a market in the first country stores on the frontier. Charlotte Webb Jacobs, from the Sugar Creek community on the Illinois prairie, proudly recalled, "I made everything that we wore; I even made my towels and table cloths, sheets and everything in the clothing line."

Communities pooled their efforts for such tasks as raising a cabin. Groups of settlers also acted as a cooperative unit at public land auctions. Members of local **claim clubs** physically intimidated speculators who refused to step aside until local settlers had acquired the land they wanted.

Surplus goods were sold to newcomers moving into the area or bartered with local storekeepers for essentials such as salt, sugar, and metalwares. This relative self-sufficiency, however, soon gave way to a more commercially oriented agriculture when steamboats, canals, and railroads opened up vast new markets (see Chapter 11).

The first large market was in the South, down the corridor of the Ohio and Mississippi Rivers, and the major staples were corn and hogs. By the 1830s, the Erie Canal and its feeder waterways in the upper Midwest began to reorient much of the western farm trade to the Northeast.

Wheat production skyrocketed when settlers overcame their initial reluctance to farming in a treeless terrain and moved into the prairies of Indiana and Illinois in the 1840s. New plows—a cast-iron one patented by Jethro Wood in 1819 and a steel version developed by John Deere in 1837—helped break the thick prairie sod. The plows were soon followed by horse-drawn mechanical harvesters equipped with a self-rake reaper that enabled family farmers to harvest vastly more wheat by the 1840s. Using traditional harvesting methods, a scythe with a cradle frame, an experienced worker could cut no more than 2 acres a day. With the new machinery the same worker could harvest 12 acres a day. Once railroads provided direct access to eastern markets, the Midwest became the nation's breadbasket.

The commercialization of agriculture in the West also contributed to the growth of eastern manufacturing. Western farms supplied eastern manufacturers with inexpensive raw materials for processing into finished goods. Western corn and wheat not only supplied eastern workers with cheap food but also forced noncompetitive eastern farmers either to move west or to work in factories in eastern cities. In turn, the West itself became an ever-growing market for eastern factory goods. For example, nearly half of the nation's iron production in the 1830s was fashioned into farm implements. At midcentury, the Old Northwest had become part of a larger Midwest whose economy was increasingly integrated with that of the Northeast. Settlers continued to pour into the region, and three additional states—Michigan (1837), Iowa (1846), and Wisconsin (1848)—joined the Union.

The combination of favorable farm prices and steadily decreasing transportation costs generated a rise in disposable income that was spent on outside goods or invested in internal economic development. Manufacturing cities grew out of towns that were favorably situated by water or rail transport. The West north of the Ohio was now economically specialized and socially diverse.

The Old Southwest

"The *Alabama Feaver* rages here with great violence and has *carried off* vast numbers of our Citizens," wrote a North Carolina planter in 1817 about the westward migration from his state. "I am apprehensive, if it continues to spread as it has done, it will almost depopulate the country." By 1850, more than 600,000 whites born in Maryland, Virginia, and the Carolinas lived in slave states to the south and west, and many of them had brought their slaves with them. Indeed, from 1790 to 1860, more than 800,000 slaves were moved from the South Atlantic region into the old Southwest. Soaring cotton prices after the War of 1812 and the smashing of Indian confederations during the war, which opened new lands to whites, propelled the first surge of migration into western Tennessee and the Black Belt, a crescent-shaped band of rich, black loamy soil arcing westward from Georgia through central Alabama and Mississippi.

Migration surged anew in the 1830s when cotton prices were again high and the Chickasaws and Choctaws had been forced out of the incredibly fertile Delta country between the Yazoo and Mississippi Rivers (see Chapter 10). In less than thirty years, six new slave states—Mississippi (1817), Alabama (1819), Missouri (1821), Arkansas (1836), Florida (1845), and Texas (1845)—joined the Union (see the summary table "Westward Expansion and the Growth of the Union, 1815–1850").

The southwestern frontier attracted both slaveholding planters and small independent farmers. The best known, though a minority, were the planters and their sons. They had the capital or the credit to acquire the best lands and the slave labor to make those lands productive. These slaveholders were responding both to the need for fresh land and

The internal slave trade was the primary means by which the slaves of the Upper South were brought into the plantation markets of the Old Southwest. Shown below are professional slave traders driving a chained group of slaves, known as a coffle, to perspective buyers in the Lower South.

to the extraordinary demand for short-staple cotton. As one North Carolina planter put it, Alabama would be a "garden of plenty" compared to the "old-fields and empty corn-houses" of his native state.

Short-staple cotton could be grown anywhere with a minimum of 210 consecutive frost-free days. Eli Whitney's gin, which eliminated the problem of removing the sticky, green seeds from the fiber, was fifty times faster than hand separation. Meanwhile, the mechanization of the British textile industry had created a seemingly unquenchable demand for raw cotton. With new fertile land and a slave labor force, the South increased its share of world cotton production from 9 percent in 1800 to 68 percent in 1850.

More typical settlers on the southern frontier were small independent yeomen farmers, who generally owned no slaves. Many of them shared the belief of the yeoman farmer Gideon Linecum "in the pleasure of frequent change of country."

The yeomanry moved onto the frontier in two waves. The first consisted of stockmen-hunters, a restless, transient group who spread from the pine barrens in the Carolina backcountry to the coastal plain of eastern Texas. They prized unfettered independence and measured their wealth in the livestock left to roam and fatten on the sweet grasses of uncleared forests. They were quick to move on when farmers, the second wave, started to clear the land for crops.

Like the stock herders, the yeoman farmers valued self-sufficiency and the leisure to hunt and fish. They practiced a diversified agriculture aimed at feeding their families. Corn and pork were the mainstays of their diet, and both could readily be produced as long as there was room for the open-range herding of swine and growing patches of corn and small grains. The yeoman's chief source of labor was his immediate family.

Measured by per capita income, and as a direct result of the profits from slave-produced cotton on virgin soils, the Old Southwest was a wealthier society than the Old Northwest in 1850. The settlement of the Old Southwest was also more significant for national economic development. More than any other commodity, cotton paid for American imports and underpinned national credit.

The Southwest Ordinance, enacted by Congress in 1790, opened all territories south of the Ohio River to slavery. Slaves, land, and cotton were the keys to wealth on the southern frontier, and agricultural profits were continually plowed back into these assets. In contrast, prosperous farmers in the Old Northwest were much more likely to invest their earnings in promotional schemes designed to attract settlers whose presence would raise land values and increase business for local entrepreneurs. As early as the 1840s, rural communities in the Old Northwest were supporting bustling towns that offered jobs in trade and manufacturing on a scale far surpassing anything in the slave West. By the 1850s, the Midwest was almost as urbanized as the Northeast had been

SUMMARY

WESTWARD EXPANSION AND THE GROWTH OF THE UNION, 1815–1850

New Free States	New Slave States	Territories (1850)
Indiana, 1816	Mississippi, 1817	Minnesota
Illinois, 1818	Alabama, 1819	Oregon
Maine, 1820	Missouri, 1821	New Mexico
Michigan, 1837	Arkansas, 1836	Utah
Iowa, 1846	Florida, 1845	
Wisconsin, 1848	Texas, 1845	
California, 1850		

in 1830, and nearly half the labor force no longer worked on farms.

The Old Southwest remained overwhelmingly agricultural. Once the land was settled, the children of the first generation of slaveholders and yeomen moved west to the next frontier. Relatively few newcomers took their place. By the 1850s, Kentucky, Tennessee, Alabama, and Mississippi were all losing more migrants than they were gaining.

The Frontier of the Plains Indians

Few white Americans had ventured west of the Mississippi by 1840. What scanty knowledge there was of this huge inland expanse was the result of government-sponsored expeditions. Reports of explorations led by Zebulon Pike in 1806 and Stephen Long in 1819 dismissed much of the area as the Great American Desert, an arid, treeless landscape with little agricultural potential.

Beyond Texas and the boundary line drawn by the Trans-Continental Treaty of 1819 lay the northern possessions of Mexico, where horse-mounted Indian tribes dominated by the Sioux were a formidable power. Before the 1840s, only fur trappers and traders, who worked with and not against the powerful Sioux, had pushed across the Great Plains and into the Rockies. The 1840s brought a sudden change, a large migration westward that rad-

ically altered the ecology of the Great Plains. Farm families trapped in an agricultural depression and enticed by Oregon's bounty turned the trails blazed by the fur traders into ruts on the Oregon Trail, the route that led to the first large settlement of Americans on the Pacific Coast.

Tribal Lands

At least 350,000 Native Americans lived in the plains and mountains of the Trans-Mississippi West in 1840. The point where the prairies of the Midwest gave way to the higher, drier plains marked a rough division between predominantly agricultural tribes to the east and nomadic, hunting tribes to the west. The Kansas, Osages, and Omahas in what is now Kansas and Iowa and the Arikaras, Mandans, and Hidatsas along the upper Missouri River grew corn, beans, and squash and lived in semipermanent villages, much as woodland Indians had in the East. On the open plains were hunting and raiding peoples, such as the western Sioux, Crows, Cheyennes, and Arapahos.

In the 1830s, the U.S. government set aside a broad stretch of country between the Platte River to the north and the Red River to the south (most of present-day Oklahoma and eastern Kansas) exclusively for tribes resettled from the East under the Indian Removal Act of 1830 and for village-living groups native to the area. Many government officials envisioned this territory as a permanent sanctuary that would separate Indians from whites and allow them to live in peace on allotments of land granted as compensation for the territory they had ceded to the federal government. However, the pressure exerted on native peoples in the Mississippi Valley both by raiding parties of Plains Indians and by the incessant demands of whites for more land was rendering a stable Indian-white boundary meaningless.

On the eve of Indian removal in the East, the defeat of the Sauks and Foxes in what whites called Black Hawk's War of 1832 opened Iowa to white settlement and forced tribes to cede land. In 1838, Congress created the Territory of Iowa, which encompassed all the land between the Mississippi and Missouri Rivers north of the state of Missouri. The Indians were now on the verge of being pushed completely out of Iowa. Throughout the upper Mississippi Valley in the 1830s, other groups suffered a similar fate.

Farming peoples whose villages straddled the woodlands to the east and the open plains to the west were caught in a vise between the loss of their land to advancing whites and the seizure of their horses and agricultural provisions by Indian raiders from the plains. The Pawnees were among the hardest hit.

By the 1830s, the Pawnees were primarily an agricultural people who embarked on seasonal hunts for game in the Platte River Valley. In 1833, they signed a treaty with the U.S. government, agreeing to withdraw from south of the Platte in return for subsidies and military protection from the hostile Indians on the plains. Once they moved north of the Platte, the Pawnees were attacked by Sioux who seized control of the prime hunting grounds. The Pawnee agricultural villages tempted Sioux raiders seeking provisions and horses. When the desperate Pawnees filtered back south of the Platte, they were constantly harassed by whites. In vain Pawnee leaders cited the provisions of the treaty that promised them protection from the Sioux. Forced back north of the Platte by the U.S. government, the Pawnees were eventually driven out of their Nebraska homeland by the Sioux.

The Sioux were more than able to hold their own against white Americans in the first half of the nineteenth century. In the eighteenth century, the western Sioux, armed with guns they had acquired from the French, dominated the prairies east of the Missouri.

The Sioux learned to use the horse from the Plains Indians. Horses made buffalo hunting vastly more productive, they made it easier to transport bulky possessions, and they made possible an aggressive, highly mobile form of warfare. The Sioux were the most successful of all the tribes in melding two facets of the white man's culture, the gun and the horse, into an Indian culture of warrior-hunters.

Although the Sioux frequently fought other tribes, casualties from these encounters were light. The Sioux and other Plains Indians fought not to kill the greatest number of the enemy but rather to dominate hunting grounds and to win individual honor by "counting coup" (touching a live foe). When an Army officer in 1819 urged the Sioux to make peace with the Chippewas, Little Crow, a Santee Sioux, explained why war was preferable: "Why, then, should we give up such an extensive country to save the life of a man or two annually?"

When the United States acquired title to the Great Plains in the Louisiana Purchase of 1803, the western Sioux economy was based on hunting buffalo on horse in summer and trapping beaver in winter. In spring, great trading fairs were held in which the western Sioux exchanged their buffalo robes and beaver pelts for goods acquired by the Santee Sioux from European traders.

As the supply of beaver dwindled and the demand for buffalo hides from American and European traders increased in the early 1800s, the Sioux extended their buffalo hunts. Sioux war parties pushed aside or subjugated weaker tribes to the south and west of the Missouri River basin.

Epidemic diseases brought to the plains by white traders helped Sioux expansion. The nomadic Sioux were less susceptible to these epidemics than the more sedentary village peoples. The Sioux were also one of the first tribes to be vaccinated against smallpox by doctors sent by the Bureau of Indian Affairs in the early 1830s. A major smallpox epidemic in 1837 probably halved the region's Indian population. Sioux losses were relatively light and, unlike the other tribes, their population grew.

Some 25,000 strong by 1850, the western Sioux had increased in power and numbers since they first encountered American officials during the Lewis and Clark Expedition in 1804 and 1805. Even then, Jefferson had cautioned Lewis to cultivate good relations with the Sioux "because of their immense power." Lewis and Clark minced no words when they wrote of the Sioux. "These are the vilest miscreants of the savage race, and must ever remain the pirates of the Missouri, until such measures are pursued by our government as will make them feel a dependence on its will for their supply of merchandise."

Americans could vilify the Sioux, but they could not force them into dependence in the first half of the nineteenth century.

The Fur Traders

"Curiosity, a love of wild adventure, and perhaps also a hope of profit—for times *are* hard, and my best coat has a sort of sheepish hang-dog hesitation to encounter fashionable folk—combined to make me look upon the project with an eye of favour." These were the motives that induced Warren A. Ferris, a New York civil engineer, to join the American Fur Company in 1829 at the age of 19 and go west as a fur trapper and mountain man. During their golden age in the 1820s and 1830s, the trappers blazed the trails that far greater numbers of white settlers would follow in the 1840s.

Until the early 1820s, the Hudson's Bay Company, a well-capitalized British concern, dominated the trans-Mississippi fur trade. A breakthrough for American interests came in 1824 when two St. Louis businessmen, William Henry Ashley and Andrew Henry of the Rocky Mountain Fur Company, developed the rendezvous system, which, in keeping with

The annual rendezvous in Wyoming of fur trappers and traders was a multinational affair in which Anglo-Americans, French Canadians, Mexican-Americans, and Native Americans gathered to trade, drink, and swap stories.

Indian traditions of periodic intertribal meetings, brought together trappers, Indians, and traders in a grand annual fair at a designated site in the high mountain country of Wyoming. White trappers and Indians exchanged the animal skins they had gathered in the seasonal hunt for the guns, traps, tobacco, whiskey, textiles, and other trading goods that agents of the fur companies in St. Louis brought to the fair.

The trappers closest relations were with Indians, and about 40 percent of the trappers married Indian women, unions that often linked them economically and diplomatically to their bride's tribe. Living conditions in the wilderness were primitive, even brutal. Mortality rates among trappers ran as high as 80 percent a year. Death could result from an accidental gunshot wound, an encounter with a grizzly, or an Indian arrow. "Peg-Leg" Smith became a legend for amputating his own leg after it was shattered by a bullet.

For all its dangers, the life of a trapper appealed to unattached young men like Warren Ferris fleeing the confinements, as well as the comforts, of white civilization. "Fancy to yourself," Ferris asked readers of his published journals, "three thousand horses of every variety of size and colour, with trappings almost as varied as their appearance . . . ridden by a thousand souls . . . their persons fantastically ornamented. . . . Listen to the rattle of numberless lodgepoles [trailed] by packhorses. . . . Yonder see a hundred horsemen pursuing a herd of antelopes." He was describing the color, bustle, and motion at the start of a hunt with the Salish Indians of Montana in the 1830s, played out on "a beautiful

level prairie, with dark blue snow-capped mountains in the distance for the *locale.*"

Such spectacles were increasingly rare after 1840, the year of the last mountain men's rendezvous on the Green River in Wyoming. The most exploitive phase of the fur trade in the 1830s had ravaged the fur-bearing animals and accelerated the spread of smallpox among the tribes. Whiskey, the most profitable item among the white man's trading goods, had corrupted countless Indians and undermined the vitality of tribal cultures.

The main trading corridor of the fur trade—up the lower Missouri to the North Platte and across the plains to the South Pass, a wide plateau crossing the Continental Divide, and into the Wyoming basin—became the main overland route to the West that migrating farm families followed in the 1840s. The mountain men had removed the mystery of western geography, and in so doing they hastened the end of the frontier conditions that had made their unique way of life possible.

The Oregon Trail

The ruts are still there. One can follow them to the horizon in the Platte River Valley of Nebraska and the dry tablelands of Wyoming, Idaho, and Nevada. They were put there by the wheels of wagons hauled by oxen on a jolting 2,000-mile journey across plains, mountains, and deserts from Missouri to Oregon, Utah, and California (see Map 12-2). Some 150,000 Americans made this overland trek in the heyday of the **Oregon Trail** in the 1840s and early 1850s. Most of them walked alongside their wagons. They covered up to 15 miles a day on a trip that lasted close to six months.

Under an agreement reached in 1818, the Oregon Country was still jointly administered by the United States and Great Britain. Furs—whether beaver pelts or the skins of the Pacific sea otter—had attracted a few American trappers and merchants, but the British-controlled Hudson's Bay Company dominated the region. Protestant missionaries established the first permanent white settlements in the 1830s. Under the leadership of Jason Lee, they set up their missions in the fertile Willamette Valley, south of the Columbia River.

The missionaries repeatedly failed to convert the Indians to Christianity. With their numbers already thinned by the diseases brought in by the trappers, Oregon tribes such as the Cayuses refused to abandon their traditional culture based on hunting and fishing and become farm laborers for whites. Unlike the trappers, the missionaries sought to change the entire structure of Indian life and beliefs. During a measles epidemic in 1847, the Cayuses killed two of the most prominent missionaries, Marcus and Narcissa Whitman. In retaliation, white Americans, who now numbered more than five thousand, virtually exterminated the Cayuses.

The first large party of overlanders left Independence, Missouri, in 1842 for the Willamette Valley. Independence and St. Joseph in Missouri and, by the 1850s, Council Bluffs in Iowa competed to capture the lucrative trade of outfitting the migrants. Merchants profited from supplying, usually at inflated prices, wagons, mules, oxen, guns, ammunition, and staples like flour, bacon, and sugar.

Most overlanders were young farm families from the Midwest, who restlessly searched for the perfect farm that would keep them out of debt. Medorum Crawford said of one family that made the journey to Oregon with him in 1842 and then quickly left for California: "They had practically lived in the wagon for more than twenty years, only remaining in one locality long enough to make a crop, which they had done in every State and Territory in the Mississippi Valley."

Usually the male head of a household made the decision to move. Besides their usual work of minding the children and cooking and cleaning, women would now have to help drive wagons and tend livestock. Still, many women were also optimistic about the journey. "Ho—for California—at last we are on the way," exclaimed Helen Carpenter in 1857, "and with good luck may some day reach the 'promised land.'" A study of 159 women's trail diaries indicates that about one-third of the women strongly favored the move, and Margaret

Frink undoubtedly spoke for many when she recalled that she "never had occasion to regret the prolonged hardships of the toilsome journey."

In the 1840s, some five thousand of the ninety thousand men, women, and children who set out on the Oregon Trail died along the way. Few died from Indian attacks. Indians killed only 115 migrants in the 1840s, and trigger-happy whites provoked most clashes. Disease, especially cholera, was the great killer. Second to disease were accidents, especially drownings when drivers tried to force overloaded wagons across swollen rivers.

Families, not individuals, comprised the basic social unit, and they were part of networks of kin and neighbors who had banded together for the westward journey. The men often drew up a formal, written

Map 12-2   *Western Overland Trails*
The great overland trails to the West began at the Missouri River. The Oregon Trail crossed South Pass in Wyoming and then branched off to Oregon, California, or Utah. The Santa Fe Trail carried American goods and traders to the Mexican Southwest.

constitution at the start of the trip spelling out the assignments and work responsibilities of each wagon. The wagon train had to leave late enough in the spring to get good grass in Nebraska for the oxen and mules. A wagon train that departed too early risked getting bogged down in spring mud; one that left late risked the danger in the Pacific coastal ranges of being trapped in the mountain snows.

"The Oregon fever is raging in almost every part of the Union," proclaimed the *Ohio Statesman* in 1843. Before the fever has run its course, the flow of whites across the continent radically changed the economy and ecology of the Great Plains. With such pressure on plant and animal life, the land could no longer support all the tribes accustomed to living off it. Far from being separated from whites by a permanent line of division, the Plains Indians now stood astride the main path of white migration to the Pacific.

In response, officials in the Bureau of Indian Affairs organized a great gathering of the tribes in 1851 to push through the **Fort Laramie Treaty**, the first U.S. government attempt to draw boundaries within which to contain the Plains Indians. In exchange for accepting limitations on their movement and for the loss of game, the tribes were to receive annual compensation of $50,000 a year for fifty years (later reduced by the U.S. Senate to ten years). When American negotiators tried to restrict Sioux hunting to north of the Platte, the Sioux demanded and received treaty rights to lands south of the Platte as well. "These lands once belonged to the Kiowas and the Crows," argued a western Sioux, "but we whipped those nations out of them, and in this we did what the white men do when they want the lands of the Indians." The Americans conceded the point.

Two great powers—the Sioux and the U.S. government—reached a standoff at Fort Laramie in 1851. If neither yielded its claims to the Great Plains, war was inevitable.

The Mexican Borderlands

By the mid-1840s, parties of emigrant Americans were beginning to branch off the main Oregon Trail on their way to Utah and California. These areas were then part of the northern borderlands of Mexico. Mostly a semiarid and thinly populated land of high plateaus, dry basins, and desert bisected north to south by mountain ranges, the borderlands had been part of the Spanish empire in North America. Mexico inherited this territory when it won independence from Spain in 1821. Mexico's hold on this region was always weak. It lost Texas in 1837, and in

the next decade, the American penetration of Utah and California set the stage for the American seizure of most of the rest in the Mexican War.

The Peoples of the Southwest

Imperial Spain had divided the population of the Southwest into four main groupings: Indians, full-blooded Native Americans who retained their own languages and customs; **mestizos**, those of racially mixed ancestry, usually Spanish and Indian; **criollos**, American-born whites of Spanish ancestry; and Spaniards.

By far the smallest group were the Spaniards. Despite their small numbers, the Spanish, along with the criollos, monopolized economic and political power. This wealthy elite controlled the labor of the mestizos in the predominantly ranching economy of the borderlands.

The largest single group in the borderlands were the Indians, about half the population in the 1820s. Most had not come under direct Spanish or Mexican control. Those who had were part of the **mission system**. This instrument of Spanish imperial policy forced Indians to live in a fixed area, to convert to Catholicism, and to work as agricultural laborers.

Spanish missions aimed both to Christianize and "civilize" the Indians, forcing the mission Indians to abandon their native economies and culture and accept a European definition of civilization that demanded that they live in settled agricultural communities and work under the tight supervision of the friars. The Franciscans friars were accompanied by Spanish soldiers and royal officials who built military garrisons known as **presidios**.

Whether as farmers, hunters, or gatherers, most Indians in the borderlands were still free of white dominance or control in the 1820s. The largest concentration of Indians—some 300,000 when the Spanish friars arrived in the 1760s—was in California. The Paiutes in the Owens Valley perfected an intricate system for irrigating wild grasses, but only the Yumans along the Colorado River in southeastern California practiced full-scale agriculture. The Spanish marveled at their lush fields of wheat, maize, beans, tobacco, and melons. The Yumans also had an elaborate religion based on an oral tradition of dream songs. (Dream songs remain a distinctive feature of Native American culture.)

The major farming Indians east of California were the Pueblo peoples of Arizona and New Mexico. Formally a part of the Spanish mission system, they had incorporated the Catholic God and Catholic rituals into their own polytheistic religion, which stressed the harmony of all living things with the forces of nature. They continued to worship in their underground sanctuaries known as *kivas*.

Once the Pueblos made their peace with the Spaniards after their great revolt in 1680 (see Chapter 3), their major enemies were the nomadic tribes that lived by hunting and raiding. These tribes outnumbered the Pueblos four to one and controlled most of the Southwest until the 1850s. Using horses to gain enormous mobility and the means of ranging far and wide for the economic resources that sustained their transformation into societies of mounted warriors.

Other tribes in the Mexican borderlands included the Navajos, the Apaches, the Comanches, and the Kiowas. The Comanches, a branch of the mountain Shoshonis who moved to the plains when horses became available, were the most feared of the nomadic peoples. They took to the horse as few other people ever had. They were utterly fearless, confident, and masterful horsemen. Their stature as mounted warriors reached mythic proportions. For food and clothing, they relied on the immense buffalo herds of the southern plains. For guns, horses, and other trading goods, they lived off their predatory raids. When the Santa Fe Trail opened in the early 1820s, their shrewdness as traders gave them a new source of firearms that strengthened their raiding prowess.

The three focal points of white settlement in the northern borderlands of Mexico—Texas, New Mexico, and Alta California (as distinguished from Lower, or Baja, California)—were never linked by an effective network of communications or transportation. Travel was limited to tortuous journeys along Indian and Spanish trails that barely indented the dry and largely barren landscape. Each of these settlements was an isolated offshoot of Hispanic culture with a semiautonomous economy based on ranching and a mostly illegal trade with French, British, and American merchants that brought in a trickle of needed goods.

Mexico's most pressing problem in the 1820s was protecting its northern states from the Comanches. To serve as a buffer against the Comanches, the Mexican government in 1821 invited Americans into Texas. The American takeover of Texas had begun.

The Americanization of Texas

The Mexicans faced the same problems governing Texas that the Spanish had. Sparsely populated and economically struggling, Mexican Texas shared a border with the United States along the Sabine River in Louisiana and the Red River in the Arkansas Territory. As one Mexican official noted with alarm: "If we do not take the present opportunity to people Texas, day by day the strength of the United States will grow until it will annex Texas, Coahuila, Saltillo, and Nuevo León like the Goths, Visigoths, and the other tribes that assailed the Roman Empire." However, attempts to promote immigration into Texas from other parts of Mexico failed. Reasoning that the Americans were going to come in any event, and anxious to build up the population of Texas against Indian attacks, the Mexican government encouraged Americans to settle in Texas by offering huge grants of land in return for promises to accept Mexican citizenship, convert to Catholicism, and obey the authorities in Mexico City.

The first American **empresario**—the recipient of a large grant in return for a promise to bring in settlers—was Stephen F. Austin, who founded the first American colony in Texas. The Austin grant encompassed 18,000 square miles. The empresarios stood to grow wealthy by leasing out land, selling parcels to settlers, and organizing the rest into large-scale farms that produced cotton with slave labor in the bottomlands of the Sabine, Colorado, and Brazos Rivers. For the Americans who followed in their wake, Texas offered the chance to acquire good land that was so cheap it was almost free. As early as 1830, eastern and south central Texas were becoming an extension of the plantation economy of the Gulf coastal plain. More than 25,000 whites, with around a thousand slaves, had poured into the region (see "American Views: A Mexican View of the Texans in 1828").

Many settlers simply ignored Mexican laws, especially the Emancipation Proclamation of 1829 that forbade slavery in the Republic of Mexico. In 1830, the Mexican government levied the first taxes on the Americans, prohibited the further importation of slaves, and closed the international border to additional immigration. Still, another ten thousand Americans spilled in during the early 1830s, and they continued to bring in slaves.

Unlike the empresarios, many of whom became Catholic and married into elite Tejano families, these newcomers lived apart from Mexicans and rejected Mexican citizenship. Cultural tensions escalated. Most of these new arrivals sneered at the Mexicans as a mongrelized race of blacks, Indians, and Spaniards and resented having to submit to their rule. As Protestants, Americans considered Catholicism a despotic, superstitious religion and ignored legal requirements that they accept the Catholic faith.

When General Santa Anna, elected president of Mexico in 1833, overturned the liberal Mexican constitution of 1824, his dictatorial centralist rule ended any hope that Texas might become an autonomous state within a federated Mexico. Skirmishing between Mexican troops and rebellious Texans began in the fall of 1835.

American Views

A MEXICAN VIEW
OF THE TEXANS IN 1828

By the late 1820s, Mexico was reassessing its policy of encouraging American immigration to Texas. Concerned over the large numbers and uncertain loyalties of the American settlers, the government appointed a commission in 1827 ostensibly to survey the boundary between Louisiana and the province of Texas. The real purpose of the commission was to recommend policy changes that would strengthen Mexico's hold on Texas. The following excerpt is from a journal kept by José María Sánchez, the draftsman of the boundary commission.

❖ **Why was the Mexican government so ineffective in maintaining control over Texas?**

❖ **What was the appeal of Texas for Americans? How did most of them enter Texas and take up land?**

❖ **Why did Sánchez have such a low opinion of the Americans in the Austin colony? What did he think of Stephen Austin?**

❖ **Why did the Mexicans fear that they would lose Texas?**

The Americans from the north have taken possession of practically all the eastern part of Texas, in most cases without the permission of the authorities. They immigrate constantly, finding no one to prevent them, and take possession of the *sitio* [location] that best suits them without either asking leave or going through any formality other than that of building their homes. Thus the majority of inhabitants in the Department are North Americans, the Mexican population being reduced to only Bejar, Nacoghoches, and La Bahía del

Espíritu Santo, wretched settlements that between them do not number three thousand inhabitants, and the new village of Guadalupe Victoria that has scarcely more than seventy settlers. The government of the state, with its seat at Saltillo, that should watch over the preservation of its most precious and interesting department, taking measures to prevent its being stolen by foreign hands, is the one that knows the least not only about actual conditions, but even about its territory. . . . Repeated and urgent appeals have been made to the

---

At first, the Anglo-Tejano leadership sought to overthrow Santa Anna, restore the constitution of 1824, and win separate statehood for Texas within a liberal Mexican republic. When Santa Anna raised a large army to crush the uprising, he radicalized the rebellion, and pushed it to declare complete independence on March 2, 1836. Four days later, a Mexican army of four thousand annihilated the 187 defenders of the **Alamo**, an abandoned mission in San Antonio. A few weeks later at **Goliad**, another three hundred Texans were killed after they had agreed to surrender (see Map 12-3).

"Remember the Alamo!" and "Remember Goliad!" were powerful rallying cries for the belea-

guered Texans. Volunteers from the American South rushed to the aid of the main Texan army, commanded by Sam Houston. A product of the Tennessee frontier and a close friend of Andrew Jackson's, Houston's victory in April 1836 at the **Battle of San Jacinto** established the independence of Texas. Captured while trying to flee, Santa Anna signed a treaty in May 1836, recognizing Texas as an independent republic with a boundary on the south and west at the Rio Grande. However, the Nueces River to the north of the Rio Grande had been the administrative border of Texas under Mexican rule. The Mexican Congress rejected the treaty, and the boundary remained in dispute.

Supreme Government of the Federation regarding the imminent danger in which this interesting Department is of becoming the prize of the ambitious North Americans, but never has it taken any measures that may be called conclusive. . . .

[Sánchez goes on to describe the village of Austin and the American colony founded by Stephen Austin.]

Its population is nearly two hundred persons, of which only ten are Mexicans, for the balance are all Americans from the North with an occasional European. Two wretched little stores supply the inhabitants of the colony: one sells only whiskey, rum, sugar, and coffee; the other, rice, flour, lard, and cheap cloth. . . . The Americans from the North, at least the great part of those I have seen, eat only salted meat, bread made by themselves out of corn meal, coffee, and homemade cheese. To these the greater part of those who live in the village add strong liquor, for they are in general, in my opinion, lazy people of vicious character. Some of them cultivate their small farms by planting corn; but this task they usually entrust to their negro slaves, whom they treat with considerable harshness. Beyond the village in an immense stretch of land formed by rolling hills are scattered the families brought by Stephen Austin, which today number more than two thousand persons. The diplomatic policy of this empresario, evident in all his actions, has, as one may say, lulled the authorities into a sense of security, while he works diligently for his own ends. In my judgment, the spark that will start the conflagration that will deprive us of Texas, will start from this colony. All because the government does not take vigorous measures to prevent it. Perhaps it does not realize the value of what it is about to lose.

Source: *José María Sánchez, "A Trip to Texas in 1828," trans. Carlos E. Castañeda,* Southwestern Historical Quarterly, 29 (1926): 260, 261, 271

In part because Mexico refused to recognize the Texas Republic, Anglos feared Tejanos as a subversive element. Pressure mounted on them to leave, especially after Santa Anna launched a major counterattack in 1842, capturing San Antonio. Those who stayed lost much of their land and economic power as Anglos used their knowledge of American legal codes or just plain chicanery to reduce the Tejanos to second-class citizens.

More difficult to subordinate were the Comanches. By the early 1840s, Texans and Comanches were in a state of nearly permanent war. Only the force of the federal army after the Civil War ended the Comanches' long reign as the effective rulers of the high, dry plains of northern and western Texas.

The Push into California and the Southwest

Mexican rule in California was always weak. The Sonoran desert and the resistance of the Yuman Indians in southeastern California cut off Mexico from any direct land contact with Alta California. Only irregular communications were maintained over a long sea route. For **Californios**, Californians of Spanish descent, Mexico was literally *la otra banda*, "the other shore." In trying to strengthen its hold on this remote and thinly populated region, the

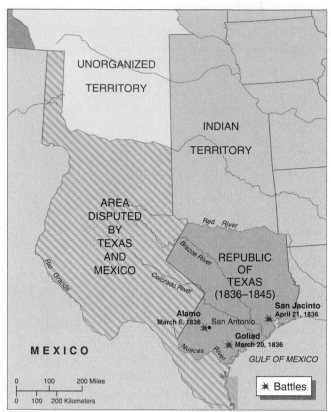

Map 12-3   Texas and Mexico after the Texas Revolt
The Battle of San Jacinto was the decisive American victory that gained the independence of Texas, but the border dispute between Texas and Mexico would not be resolved until the Mexican War a decade later.

Mexican government relied on a program of economic development. The centerpiece of the Mexican program was the secularization of the missions, opening up the landholdings of the Catholic Church to private ownership and releasing the mission Indians from paternalistic bondage. Small allotments of land were set aside for the Indians, but most returned to their homelands. Those who remained became a source of cheap labor for the rancheros who carved up the mission lands into huge cattle ranches. Thus by the 1830s, California entered its rancho era. The main beneficiaries of this process, however, were not Mexican authorities but the American traders who responded to the economic opportunities presented by the privatization of the California economy.

New England merchants shipped out hides and tallow, a trade fed by the immense cattle resources of the rancheros, for processing into shoes and candles. Ships from New England and New York sailed around Cape Horn to California ports, where they unloaded trading goods. Servicing this trade in California was a resident colony of American agents,

some three hundred strong by the mid-1840s.

Whereas Yankees dominated the American colonies in coastal California, the Americans who filtered into the inner valleys of California in the 1830s and 1840s were more representative of the Midwestern farm families who set out on the Oregon Trail. About one in ten of the overland parties ended up in the fertile Sacramento River Valley. Nearly a thousand Americans had arrived by 1846.

California belonged to Mexico in name only by the early 1840s. The program of economic development had strengthened California's ties to the outside world at the expense of Mexico. American merchants and California rancheros ran the economy, and both groups had joined separatist movements against Mexican rule.

Except for Utah, the American push into the interior of the Mexican Southwest followed the California pattern of trade preceding settlement. When Mexico liberalized the formerly restrictive trading policies of Spain, American merchants opened up the 900-mile-long **Santa Fe Trail** from Independence, Missouri, to Santa Fe, New Mexico. Starved for mercantile goods, the New Mexicans were a small but highly profitable market. They paid for their American imports with gold, silver, and furs.

Brent's Old Fort on the Arkansas River at the point where the Santa Fe Trail turned to the southwest and Taos, enabled the Brent brothers from Missouri to control a flourishing and almost monopolistic trade with Indians, trappers, caravans on the Santa Fe Trail, and the large landowners and merchants of New Mexico. This trade pulled New Mexico into the cultural and economic orbit of the United States and undermined what little sovereign power Mexico held in the region.

Ties of blood and common economic interests linked a small group of American businessmen with an influential faction of the local elite. After thwarting an 1841 Texan attempt to occupy Santa Fe, the leaders of New Mexico increasingly looked to the United States to protect their local autonomy. They quickly decided to cooperate with the American army of invasion when the Mexican War got under way. Over the opposition of the clergy and ranchers still loyal to Mexico, this group was instrumental in the American takeover of New Mexico.

At the extreme northern and inner reaches of the Mexican borderlands lay Utah. Dominated by an intermountain depression called the Great Basin, Utah was home to the Bannocks, Utes, Navajos, Hopis, and small bands of other Indians. Mexico had largely ignored this remote region. Its isolation made Utah appealing to the leaders of the Mormons, the Church of Jesus Christ of Latter-day Saints.

Founded by Joseph Smith in upstate New York in the 1820s, Mormonism grew rapidly within a communitarian framework that stressed hard work and economic cooperation under the leadership of patriarchal leaders. Harassed out of New York, Ohio, and Missouri, the Mormons thought they had found a permanent home by the late 1830s in Nauvoo, Illinois. But the murder of Joseph Smith and his brother by a mob in 1844 convinced the beleaguered Mormons that they had to leave the settled East. Under the leadership of Brigham Young, they established a new community in 1847 at the Great Salt Lake on the western slopes of the Wasatch Mountains. Ten thousand Mormons joined them.

The Mormons' intense communitarianism was ideally suited to dispensing land and organizing an irrigation system that coordinated water rights with the amount of land under production. To their dismay, however, they learned in 1848 that the United States had acquired Utah, along with the rest of the northern borderlands of Mexico, as a result of the Mexican War. (For more on the Mormons, see Chapter 14.)

Politics, Expansion, and War

In 1844, James K. Polk, the new Democratic president, fully shared the expansionist vision of his party. The greatest prize in his eyes was California. Although silent in public on California for fear of further antagonizing the Mexicans, who had never accepted the loss of Texas, Polk made the acquisition of California the cornerstone of his foreign policy. When he was stymied in his efforts to purchase California and New Mexico, he tried to force concessions from the Mexican government by ordering American troops to the mouth of the Rio Grande, far within the territory claimed by Mexico. When the virtually inevitable clash of arms occurred in late April 1846, war broke out between the United States and Mexico.

Victory resulted in the **Mexican Cession of 1848**, which added half a million square miles to the United States. Polk's administration also finalized the acquisition of Texas and reached a compromise with the British on the Oregon Territory that recognized American sovereignty in the Pacific Northwest up to the 49th parallel. The United States was now a nation that spanned a continent.

Manifest Destiny

With a phrase that soon entered the nation's vocabulary, John L. O'Sullivan, editor and Democratic politician, proclaimed in 1845 America's "manifest destiny to overspread and to possess the whole of the continent which Providence has given us for the development of the great experiment of Liberty and federated self-government entrusted to us." Central to Manifest Destiny was the assumption that white Americans were a special people, a view that dated back to the Puritans' belief that God had appointed them to establish a New Israel cleansed of the corruption of the Old World. Evangelical revivals in the early nineteenth century then added an aggressive sense of urgency to America's presumed mission to spread the benefits of Christian civilization. Protestant missionaries, as in Oregon, were often in the vanguard of American expansion.

What distinguished Manifest Destiny was its explicitly racial component. Caucasian Anglo-Saxon Americans, as the descendants of ancient Germanic tribes that purportedly brought the seeds of free institutions to England, were now said to be the foremost race in the world. This superior racial pedigree gave white Americans the natural right as a chosen people to expand westward, carrying the blessings of democracy and progress.

Advocates of Manifest Destiny were not warmongers calling for conquest. Still, the doctrine was undeniably a self-serving justification for what other peoples would see as territorial aggrandizement. Manifest Destiny and popular stereotypes lumped Indians and Mexicans together as inferior peoples. An emigrant guide of 1845 spoke of the Mexican Californians as "scarcely a visible grade in the scale of intelligence, above the barbarous tribes by whom they are surrounded." For Waddy Thompson, an American minister to Mexico in the early 1840s, the Mexicans in general were "lazy, ignorant, and, of course, vicious and dishonest." This alleged Mexican inferiority was attributed to racial intermixture with the Indians, who, it was said, were hopelessly unfit for civilization.

Manifest Destiny was closely associated with the Democratic party. For Democrats, spread-eagle expansionism would counterbalance the debilitating effects of industrialization and urbanization. As good Jeffersonians, they stressed the need for more land to realize the ideal of a democratic republic rooted in the virtues and rough equality of independent farmers. For their working-class Irish constituency, the Democrats touted the broad expanses of the West as the surest means to escape the misery of wage slavery.

Manifest Destiny captured the popular imagination when the country was still mired in a depression after the Panic of 1837. The way out of the depression, according to many Democrats, was to revive the export trade. Thomas Hart Benton, a Democratic senator from Missouri, promoted American trade with India and China, to be secured by American possession of the harbors on the Pacific Coast.

The Mexican War

Once in office, Polk was willing to compromise on Oregon because he dreaded the possibility of a two-front war against both the Mexicans and the British.

In the spring of 1846, after Polk had abrogated the agreement on the joint occupation of Oregon, the British agreed to a boundary at the 49th parallel if they were allowed to retain Vancouver Island in Puget Sound. The Senate quickly approved the offer in June 1846. British-American trade continued to flourish, Mexico lost a potential ally, and most important, Polk could now concentrate on the **Mexican War** that had erupted a month earlier.

Polk refused to budge on the American claim (inherited from the Texans, when the United States annexed Texas in 1845) that the Rio Grande was the border between Texas and Mexico. The Mexicans insisted that the Nueces River, 100 miles to the north of the Rio Grande, was the border, at it had been when Texas was part of Mexico. A boundary on the Rio Grande would more than double the size of Texas.

Polk sent 3,500 troops under General Zachary Taylor to the Nueces River in the summer of 1845. Polk also stepped up his efforts to acquire California, instructing Thomas Larkin, the American consul in Monterey, California, to inform the Californios and Americans that the United States would support them if they revolted against Mexican rule. Polk also secretly ordered the U.S. Pacific naval squadron to seize California ports if war broke out with Mexico. Polk's final effort at peaceful expansion was to send John L. Slidell to Mexico City to offer $30 million to purchase California and New Mexico and to secure the Rio Grande boundary.

When Polk learned that the Mexican government had refused to receive Slidell, he set out to draw Mexico into a war that would result in the American acquisition of California. In early 1846, Taylor blockaded the mouth of the Rio Grande (an aggressive act even if the river had been an international boundary) and built a fort on the northern bank across from the Mexican town of Matamoros. The Mexicans attacked and were repulsed on April 24 (see Map 12-4).

Even before the news reached Washington, Polk had decided on war. Informed of the clash between Mexican and American troops in early May (it took ten days for the news to reach Washington), he sent a redrafted war message to Congress on May 9 asserting that Mexico "has invaded our territory, and shed American blood on American soil." Congress declared war on May 13, 1846.

The Mexicans fought bravely, but they lacked the leadership, modern artillery, and naval capacity to check the American advances. An army sent west under Colonel Stephen W. Kearny occupied New Mexico. The conquest was relatively bloodless because most of the local elite cooperated with the American authorities. Sporadic resistance was largely confined to poorer Mexicans and the Pueblo Indians, who feared that their land would be confiscated. The largest uprising, one that was ruthlessly suppressed, was the **Taos Revolt** in January 1847, led by Jesús Trujillo and Tomasito, a Pueblo chieftain. A sympathetic observer described the rebels as "those who defend to the last their country and their homes."

Kearny's army then moved to Tucson and eventually linked up in southern California with pro-American rebels and U.S. forces sent ashore by the Pacific squadron. Despite the loss of its northern provinces, Mexico refused to concede defeat. Taylor established a secure defensive line in northeastern Mexico with a victory at Monterrey in September 1846 and repulsed a Mexican counterattack at Buena Vista in February 1847. Polk then directed General Winfield Scott to invade central Mexico. Following an amphibious assault on Vera Cruz in March 1847, Scott captured Mexico City in September.

Peace talks finally got under way and concluded in the **Treaty of Guadalupe Hidalgo**, signed on February 2, 1848. Mexico surrendered its claim to Texas north of the Rio Grande and ceded Alta California and New Mexico (including present-day Arizona, Utah, and Nevada). The United States paid $15 million, assumed over $3 million in claims of American citizens against Mexico, and agreed to grant U.S. citizenship to Mexicans resident in its new territories.

Polk had gained his strategic goals, but the cost was thirteen thousand American lives (most from diseases such as measles and dysentery), fifty thousand Mexican lives, and the poisoning of Mexican-American relations for generations. The war also, as will be seen in Chapter 15, heightened sectional tensions over slavery and weakened the political structure that was vital to preserving the Union.

Conclusion

Population pressure on overworked farms in the East impelled much of the westward migration, but by the 1840s, expansion had seemingly acquired a momentum all its own, one that increasingly rejected the claims of other peoples to the land.

Far from being a process of peaceful, evolutionary, and democratic change, as was once thought, expansion involved the spread of slavery, violent con-

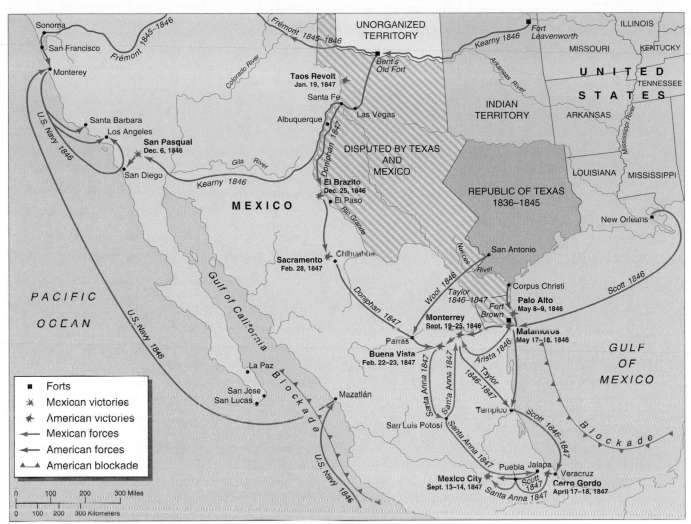

Map 12-4   The Mexican War
Victories under General Zachary Taylor in northern Mexico secured the Rio Grande as the boundary between Texas and Mexico. Colonel Stephen Kearny's expedition won control of New Mexico, and reinforcements from Kearny assured the success of American troops landed by the Pacific Squadron in gaining Alta California for the United States. The success of General Winfield Scott's amphibious invasion at Vera Cruz and his occupation of Mexico City brought the war to an end.

frontations, and the uprooting and displacement of native peoples. By 1850, the earlier notion of reserving the trans-Mississippi West as a permanent Indian country had been abandoned. The Sioux and Comanches were still feared by whites, but their final subjugation was not far off. The derogatory stereotypes of Mexican-Americans that were a staple of both popular thought and expansionist ideology showed clearly that American control after the Mexican War would relegate Spanish-speaking people to second-class status.

However misleading and false much of it was, the rhetoric of Manifest Destiny did highlight a central truth. A broad, popular base existed for expanding across the continent. As the Mexican War made clear, the United States was now unquestion-ably the dominant power in North America. The only serious threat to its dominance in the near future would come from inside, not outside, its continental domain.

Review Questions

1. What accounted for the westward movement of Americans? How did the presence or absence of slavery affect developmental patterns in the new settlements?

2. How was the West of the Plains Indians trans-formed after 1830 as peoples migrated both within the region and into it from various direc-

tions? Why were the Sioux so powerful, and how did they interact with other Native Americans and the U.S. government?

3. Who lived in the Mexican borderlands of the Southwest, and why was it so difficult for Mexican authorities to maintain effective control of the region? What role did trade play in the American penetration of the Southwest?

4. What did Americans mean by Manifest Destiny? Why was territorial expansion so identified with the Democratic party?

5. Who was responsible for the outbreak of the Mexican War? Were Mexicans the victims of American aggression?

Recommended Reading

Ray Allen Billington, *The Far Western Frontier, 1830–1860* (1956). This is still a useful survey and an excellent example of an older approach to the West from the perspective of whites entering the region with their values of freedom and individualism.

Richard Brandon, *The Last Americans: The Indian in American Culture* (1974). This beautifully written, panoramic account looks at Indian cultures and their interactions with the spread of white settlement.

Patricia Nelson Limerick, *The Legacy of Conquest: The Unbroken Past of the American West* (1987). This forcefully argued work overturns many stereotypes and places the federal government and cultural antagonisms at the center of western history.

D. W. Meinig, *The Shaping of America, Vol. 2: Continental America, 1800–1867* (1993). Meinig's comprehensive work offers a distinctive interpretation of continental expansion from the perspective of historical geography.

Frederick Merk, *Manifest Destiny and Mission in American History* (1963). This book is valuable not only for its revisionist look at the appeal of Manifest Destiny in the 1840s but also for its insights into how a sense of mission influenced American foreign policy in the future.

Clyde A. Milner II, Carol A. O'Connor, and Martha A. Sandweiss, eds., *The Oxford History of the American West* (1994). The essays in this comprehensive collection summarize much of the best work in the modern rethinking of the history of the American West.

Albert K. Weinberg, *Manifest Destiny: A Study of Nationalist Expansion in American History* (1957). This remains the most complete study of the ideas that flowed into the concept of Manifest Destiny.

Richard White, *"Its Your Misfortune and None of My Own": A History of the American West* (1991). This outstanding work draws on cultural and environmental approaches to show how complex and often unequal relationships among a host of peoples shaped the history of the West.

Where to Learn More

❖ **Indian Pueblo Cultural Center, Albuquerque, New Mexico.**   This center provides an excellent orientation to the culture, crafts, and community life of the Pueblo and Southwestern Indians. It also includes much material on archaeological findings.

❖ **Museum Association of American Frontier and Fur Trade, Chadron, Nebraska.**   The library in the museum holds archives, maps, and some photographs dealing with the western fur trade.

❖ **Indian Museum of North America, Crazy Horse, South Dakota.**   This is one of the best sources for learning of the culture of the Teton Sioux and other American and Canadian tribes on the Great Plains. Holdings include outstanding examples of Indian art and artifacts.

❖ **Living History Farms, Des Moines, Iowa.**   This site includes several working farms, operated as they were at different points in the nineteenth century, as well as a mid-twentieth-century farm. A vintage town with a general store, church, and other buildings has also been re-created.

❖ **Scotts Bluff National Monument, Gering, Nebraska.**   Scotts Bluff was a prominent landmark on the Oregon Trail, and the museum exhibits here have interpretive material on the trail and the western phase of expansion.

❖ **Conner Prairie, Noblesville, Indiana.**   The museum and historic area re-create a sense of life on the Indiana frontier during the period of the Old Northwest.

❖ **Fort Union National Monument, Watrous, New Mexico.**   Fort Union was a nineteenth-century military post, and the holdings and exhibits in the museum relate to frontier military life and the Santa Fe Trail.

13 SLAVERY AND THE OLD SOUTH, 1800–1860

CHAPTER OUTLINE

KEY TOPICS

❖ How the increasing demand for cotton made slavery highly profitable in the Lower South
❖ The decline of slavery after 1800 in the increasingly diversified economy of the Upper South
❖ Slave culture and slave resistance
❖ The divisions of free white society
❖ The southern defense of slavery in response to increasing attacks from northern abolitionists

"This morning I had a difficulty with Matt. I tied him up and gave him a gentle admonition in the shape of a good whipping. I intended to put him in jail and keep him there until I sold him, but he seemed so penitent & promised so fairly & the other negroes promising to see that he would behave himself in future that I concluded that I would try him once more." Thus did David Golightly Harris, an upcountry South Carolina farmer who owned ten slaves, casually record in his journal for January 8, 1858, his punishment of a recalcitrant slave.

Few of Harris's neighbors would have protested the "good whipping" he had laid on Matt's back. White Southerners routinely inflicted pain on slaves to control them and coerce them into productive labor. An overseer on a large plantation informed a northern visitor in the 1850s, "they'd never do any work at all if they were not afraid of being whipped."

Only the widespread presence of slaves south of Pennsylvania and the Ohio River enables us to speak of "the" South before the Civil War. For despite the region's geographical and cultural diversity, black slavery created a bond among whites and cast the South in a common mold.

Slavery was also the source of the region's immense agricultural wealth, the foundation on which planters built their fortunes, the basis for upward mobility by ambitious whites, and the means by which whites controlled the large black minority. Slavery made southern whites acutely sensitive to the need to protect their own personal liberties, not the least of which was, paradoxically, the right to enslave African-Americans. Precisely because slavery was so deeply embedded in southern life and customs, white leadership reacted to mounting attacks on slavery after 1830 with an ever more defiant defense of the institution. That defense in turn reinforced a growing sense of sectionalism among southern whites, the belief that their values divided them from their fellow citizens in the Union.

The South of 1860 was geographically much larger and more diverse than it had been in 1800, but it was also more uniformly committed to a single cash crop, cotton. Demand for cotton had exploded as the industrial revolution made the mass production of textiles possible. New England mill owners were now as dependent on slavery as southern planters were. Cotton became king, as contemporaries put it, and it provided the economic basis for southern sectionalism. During the reign of King Cotton, however, regional differences emerged between the Lower South, where the linkage between cotton and slavery was strong, and the Upper South, where slavery was relatively less important and the economy was more diversified. Though the lives of whites and African-Americans in this slave society were starkly different, southern whites also came to believe that they were different from the rest of the nation, giving rise to the proslavery defense that was to deepen sectional divisions.

The Lower South

South and west of South Carolina in 1800 stretched some of the best cotton land in the world. A long growing season, adequate rainfall, navigable rivers, and untapped fertility gave the Lower South—consisting in 1850 of South Carolina, Georgia, Florida, Alabama, Mississippi, Louisiana, and Texas—incomparable natural advantages for growing cotton. Ambitious southern whites exploited these advantages by extending slavery after 1800 to the newer cotton lands that opened up in the Lower South. Cotton production and slavery thus went hand in hand.

Cotton and Slaves

Once the cotton gin removed the technical barrier to its commercial production, upland, or short-staple, cotton could be planted far inland, and small farmers could grow it profitably because it required

no additional costs for machinery. As a result, after the 1790s, the production of short-staple cotton boomed. Moreover, like the South's other cash crops, upland cotton required fairly continuous tending throughout most of the year. Once the harvest was in—a time when northern agricultural workers were laid off—the slaves cleared land, cut wood, and made repairs. The long workyear maximized the return on capital invested in slave labor.

The cultivation of cotton left plenty of time for slaves to grow food. The major grain in the southern diet was corn, which needed little attention while cotton was being harvested and could be planted earlier or later than cotton during the long growing season. Surplus corn could be fed to hogs and converted into pork. Because almost all cotton farms and plantations also raised corn and hogs, the South virtually fed itself.

From its original base in South Carolina and Georgia, the cotton kingdom moved into the Old Southwest and then into Texas and Arkansas. As wasteful agricultural practices exhausted new lands, planters moved to the next cotton frontier farther west. Cotton output exploded from 73,000 bales (each bale weighed close to 500 pounds) in 1800 to over 2 million bales by midcentury, thanks to the fertility of virgin land and technological changes, such as improved seed varieties and steam-powered cotton gins. Slave labor accounted for more than 90 percent of cotton production.

The harvest was the busiest time on a cotton plantation. Working in gangs, and often supervised by a slave driver, the field hands were assigned a daily quota of cotton to pick.

CHRONOLOGY

1790s	Large-scale conversions of slaves to Christianity begin.
1793	Eli Whitney patents the cotton gin.
1800	Gabriel Prosser leads a rebellion in Richmond, Virginia.
1808	Congress prohibits the African slave trade.
1811	Slaves rebel in Louisiana.
1816–1819	First cotton boom in the South.
1822	Denmark Vesey's Conspiracy fails in Charleston, South Carolina.
1831	Nat Turner leads a rebellion in Southampton County, Virginia.

1831–1832	Virginia legislature debates and rejects gradual emancipation.
1832	Thomas R. Dew publishes the first full-scale defense of slavery.
1837–1845	Slavery issue divides Presbyterians, Methodists, and Baptists into separate sectional churches.
1845	Florida and Texas, the last two slave states, are admitted to the Union.
1850s	Cotton production doubles.
1857	Hinton R. Helper publishes *The Impending Crisis of the South*.

Plantations, large productive units specializing in a cash crop and employing at least twenty slaves, were the leading economic institution in the Lower South. Planters were the most prestigious social group, and, though less than 5 percent of white families were in the planter class, they controlled more than 40 percent of the slaves, cotton output, and total agricultural wealth. Most had inherited or married into their wealth, but they could stay at the top of the South's class structure only by continuing to profit from slave labor.

Planters had the best land. The ownership of twenty or more slaves enabled planters to use gangs to do both routine and specialized agricultural work. This **gang system**, a cruder version of the division of labor that was being introduced in northern factories, permitted a regimented pace of work that would have been impossible to impose on free agricultural workers. Teams of field hands, made up of women as well as men, had to work at a steady pace or else feel the lash. They were supervised by white overseers and black drivers, slaves selected for their management skills and agricultural knowledge.

"During two days' sail on the Alabama River from Mobile to Montgomery," noted a traveler in 1860, "I did not see so many houses standing together in any one spot as could be dignified with the appellation of village." The plantation districts of the Lower South stifled the growth of towns and the economic enterprise they fostered. Planters, as well as ordinary farmers, strove to be self-sufficient.

The most significant economic exchange—exporting cotton—took place in international markets and was handled by specialized commission merchants in Charleston, Mobile, and New Orleans. The Lower South had amassed great wealth, but most outsiders saw no signs of progress there.

The Profits of Slavery

The average rate of return on capital invested in a slave was about 10 percent a year, a rate that at least equaled what was available in alternative investments in the South or the North. The newer regions of the cotton kingdom in the Lower South, with the most productive land and the greatest commitment to plantation agriculture, consistently led the nation in per capita income.

The profitability of slavery ultimately rested on the enormous demand for cotton outside the South. This demand grew at about 5 percent a year in the first half of the nineteenth century. Demand was so strong that prices held steady at around 10 cents a pound in the 1850s even as southern production of cotton doubled. Textile mills in Britain were always the largest market, but demand in continental Europe and the United States grew even faster after 1840.

Prices for a male field hand rose from $250 in 1815 to $900 by 1860. The steady appreciation of prices meant that owners could sell some of their slaves and realize a profit over and above what they had already earned from the slaves' labor. Slave women of childbearing age were therefore valued nearly as much as male field hands. More than 800,000 slaves were moved between regions in the South from 1790 to 1860, and professional slave traders transported at least 60 percent of them. Drawing on lines of credit from banks, the traders paid cash for slaves, most of whom they bought from plantations in the Upper South. By selling these slaves in regional markets where demand had driven up the price, they turned a tidy profit. About half of all slave sales separated family members. Slave children born in the Upper South after 1820 stood a one-in-three chance of being sold during their lifetime.

As long as slaves employed in growing cash staples returned 10 percent a year, slave owners had little economic incentive to shift their capital resources into manufacturing or urban development. The South had one-third of the nation's population in 1860 but produced by value only 10 percent of the nation's manufacturing output. Fewer than one in ten Southerners lived in a city, compared to more than one in three Northeasterners and one in seven Midwesterners.

The Lower South had the smallest urban population and the fewest factories. Planters here were not opposed to economic innovations, but they feared social changes that might undermine the stability of slavery. Urbanization and industrialization both entailed such risks.

An editorial in the New Orleans *Crescent* charged that slaves in the city were "demoralized to a deplorable extent, all owing to the indiscriminate license and indulgence extended them by masters, mistresses, and guardians, and to the practice of *forging passes,* which has now become a regular business in New Orleans." Urban slaves, though scarcely free, enjoyed a degree of personal and economic independence that blurred the line between freedom and servitude.

Urban slaves were artisans, semiskilled laborers, and domestics, and unlike their rural counterparts, they usually lived apart from their owners. They had much more freedom than field hands to move around and interact with whites and other blacks. If they had a marketable skill, such as carpentry or tailoring, they could hire out their labor and retain some wages for themselves after reimbursing their owners. In short, the direct authority of the slave owner was less clear-cut in the town than in the country.

From 1820 to 1860 slaves decreased from 22 percent to 10 percent of the urban population. This decline reflected both doubts about the stability of slavery in an urban setting and the large profits that slave labor earned for slave owners in the rural cotton economy.

The ambivalence of planters toward urban slavery also characterized their attitudes toward industrialization itself. Many planters considered free workers potential abolitionists.

But the use of slaves as factory operatives threatened slave discipline because an efficient level of production required special incentives. "Whenever a slave is made a mechanic, he is more than half freed," complained James Hammond, a South Carolina planter. Elaborating on Hammond's fears, a Virginian noted of slaves that he had hired out for industrial work: "They were worked hard, and had too much liberty, and were acquiring bad habits. They earned money by overwork, and spent it for whisky, and got a habit of roaming about and *taking care of themselves;* because, when they were not at work in the furnace, nobody looked out for them."

The anxieties of planters over industrialization and their refusal to shift capital from plantation agriculture to finance it ensured that manufacturing played only a minor economic role in the Lower South. Planters did invest in railroads and factories, but their holdings remained concentrated in land and slaves. They augmented their income by renting slaves to manufacturers and railroad contractors but were quick to recall these slaves to work on the plantations when needed.

The Upper South

Climate and geography distinguished the Upper South from the Lower South. The eight slave states of the Upper South lay north of the best growing zones for cotton. The northernmost of these states—Delaware, Maryland, Kentucky, and Missouri—bordered on free states and were known as the Border South. The four states south of them—Virginia, North Carolina, Tennessee, and Arkansas—constituted a middle zone. Slavery was entrenched in all these states, but it was less dominant than in the cotton South.

The key difference from which others followed was the suitability of the Lower South for growing cotton with gangs of slave labor. For the most part, the Upper South lacked the fertile soil and long growing season necessary for the commercial production of cotton, rice, or sugar (see Map 13-1). Consequently, the demand for slaves was less than in the Lower South. Percentages of slave ownership and of slaves in the overall population were roughly half those in the cotton South.

While the Lower South was undergoing a cotton boom after the War of 1812, the Upper South was mired in a long economic slump from which it did not emerge until the 1850s. The improved economy of the Upper South in the late antebellum period increasingly relied on free labor, a development that many cotton planters feared would splinter southern unity in defense of slavery.

A Period of Economic Adjustment

Upper South land values fell as whites dumped their property and headed west. "Emigration is here raging with all the strength of fanaticism," wrote a Virginian in 1837, "and nothing else can be talked of but selling estates, at a great sacrifice, and '*packing off*' for the '*far west.*'"

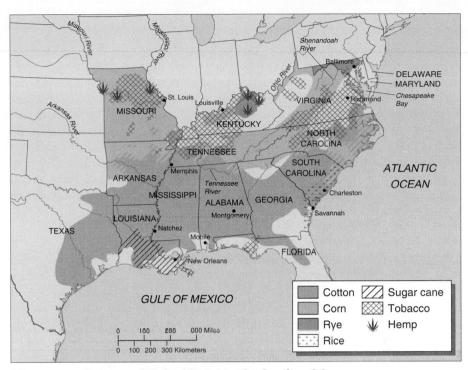

Map 13-1   *Cotton and Other Crops in the South, 1860*
Most of the Upper South was outside the cotton belt where the demand for slave labor was greatest

Agricultural reform emerged in the 1830s as one proposed solution to the economic crisis. Its leading advocate was Edmund Ruffin, a Virginia planter who tirelessly promoted the use of marl (shell deposits) to neutralize the overly acidic and worn-out soils of the Upper South. He also called for deeper plowing, systematic rotation of crops, and upgrading the breeding stock for animal husbandry.

Ruffin's efforts, and reform programs pushed in agricultural societies and fairs, met with some success but only a minority of farmers ever embraced reform. These were generally the well-educated planters who read the agricultural press and could afford to change their farming practices. The landscape of Ruffin's beloved Virginia Tidewater still provoked travelers to remark, as one did in the early 1850s, "I've heard 'em say out West that old Virginny was the mother of statesmen—reckon she must be about done, eh? This 'ere's about the *barrenest* look for a mother ever I see."

Although soil exhaustion and wasteful farming persisted, agriculture in the Upper South had revived by the 1850s. A rebound in the tobacco market accounted for part of this revival, but the growing profitability of general farming was responsible for most of it.

Particularly in the Border South, farmers and planters lessened their dependence on slave labor or on a single cash crop and practiced a thrifty, efficient agriculture geared to producing grain and livestock for urban markets. Western Maryland and the Shenandoah Valley and northern sections of Virginia grew wheat, and in the former tobacco districts of the Virginia and North Carolina Tidewater, wheat, corn, and garden vegetables became major cash crops.

Expanding urban markets and a network of internal improvements facilitated this transition to general farming. Although not far advanced by northern standards, urbanization and industrialization in the Upper South were considerably greater than in the Lower South. By 1860, the Upper South accounted for three-fourths of the South's manufacturing capital and output and nearly all of its heavy industry. Canals and railroads linked cities and countryside in a denser transportation grid than in the Lower South.

The Upper South at midcentury was gradually becoming less tied to plantation agriculture and slave labor. The rural majority increasingly prospered by growing foodstuffs for city-dwellers and factory workers. The labor market for railroad construction and manufacturing work was strong enough to attract northern immigrants and help reduce the loss of the native-born population that had migrated to other states.

The economic adjustment in the Upper South converted the labor surplus of the 1820s into a labor scarcity by the 1850s. "It is a fact," noted Edmund Ruffin in 1859, "that labor is greatly deficient in all Virginia, and especially in the rich western counties, which, for want of labor, scarcely yet yield in the proportion of one tenth of their capacity." Like many planters in the cotton states, Ruffin feared that free labor was about to replace scarce and expensive slave labor in Virginia and much of the Upper South.

The Decline of Slavery

Slavery was clearly growing weaker in the Upper South by the 1850s. The decline was most evident along the northern tier of the Upper South. By 1860, slaves in the Border South had dropped to 2 percent of the population in Delaware, 13 percent in Maryland, 19 percent in Kentucky, and 10 percent in Missouri. In Virginia from 1830 to 1860, slaves fell from 39 to 31 percent of the population.

Elsewhere in the Upper South, slavery was more or less holding its own by the 1850s. Only in Arkansas, whose alluvial lands along the Mississippi River offered a new frontier for plantation agriculture, was slavery growing rapidly. Still, slaves made up only 25 percent of the population of Arkansas in 1860 and were confined mainly to the southeastern corner of the state.

In every decade after 1820, the internal slave trade drained off about 10 percent of the slaves in the Upper South, virtually the entire natural increase. The sale of surplus slaves was a windfall for planters whose slaves had become an economic burden. This same windfall gave planters the capital to embark on agricultural reform and shift out of tobacco production. Investment capital in the Upper South was not flowing into slave property but into economic diversification that expanded urban manufacturing. Both of these structural changes increasingly put slavery at a competitive disadvantage against free labor.

The wheat, small grains, and fodder crops that replaced tobacco in much of the Upper South did not require the nearly continuous attention of a work force. As planters abandoned tobacco, they kept fewer slaves and relied on seasonal and cheap agricultural workers to meet peak labor demand.

Cheapness and flexibility was also what urban manufacturers wanted in their labor supply—workers who could be hired and fired at a moment's notice. Immigrant workers displaced slaves in most of the factories in the Border South. By 1860, slaves made up just 1 percent of the population in St. Louis and Baltimore, the South's major industrial cities.

After 1830, there were still plantation districts with large concentrations of slaves, and slave owners retained enough political power to defeat all challenges to their property interests. Nevertheless, the gradual turn to free labor was unmistakable. Agitation for emancipation had begun in the cities of the Border South. As Alfred Iveson, a Georgia planter, noted with alarm in 1860: "Those border States can get along without slavery. Their soil and climate are appropriate to white labor; they can live and flourish without African slavery; but the cotton States cannot."

Slave Life and Culture

Nearly 4 million slaves lived in the South by 1860, more than a fivefold increase since the ratification of the Constitution. Although some slaves were smuggled in after the African slave trade was banned in 1808, and excess of births over deaths accounted for nearly all of this population increase.

Almost all southern slaves were thus native-born by the mid-nineteenth century. They were not Africans but African-Americans, and they shared the common fate of bondage. In their family life and religious beliefs, slaves found the strength to sustain themselves under nearly intolerable circumstances.

Work Routines and Living Conditions

Each southern state had its own **slave codes**, laws defining the status of slaves and the rights of masters; the codes gave slave owners near-absolute power over their human property.

"The right of personal liberty in the slave is utterly inconsistent with the idea of slavery," wrote Thomas R. R. Cobb of Georgia in a legal treatise on slavery. Slaves could not own property, make contracts, possess guns or alcohol, legally marry (except in Louisiana), leave plantations without the owner's written permission, or testify against their masters or any other white person in a court of law. Many states also prohibited teaching a slave to read or write. The murder of a slave by a master was illegal, but in practice the law and community standards looked the other way if a disobedient slave was killed while being disciplined.

Whippings were the most common authorized punishment for slaves' infractions of plantation rules: twenty lashes on the bare back for leaving a plantation without a pass, one hundred lashes for writing a pass for another slave, and so on. Striking a master, committing arson, or conspiring to rebel were punishable by death.

Richmond, Virginia, was a major market for slave sales in the Upper South. Shown above are slaves at an auction as their owners wait for bids from the slave traders.

The owner, as expressed in the Alabama Slave Code of 1852, had "the right to the time, labor and services of the slave." Most masters recognized that it was good business sense to feed, clothe, and house their slaves well enough to ensure productive labor and to encourage a family life that would enable the slave population to reproduce itself. However, planters rarely provided more than the bare necessities. The slaves lived mainly on rations of cornmeal, salt pork, vegetables they grew on small garden plots, and occasional catches of game and fish. This diet was often insufficient in vitamins and nutrients. As a result, diseases such as beriberi and pellagra were common. Slaves also faced frequent outbreaks of dysentery and cholera. According to one study, the life expectancy for slaves at birth was 21 to 22 years, roughly half that for whites.

Planters furnished slaves with two sets of coarse clothing, one for summer and one for winter. Their housing, typically a 15-by-15-foot one-room cabin for five or six occupants, provided little more than basic shelter against the elements. "They were built of logs," a traveler noted of slave cabins in South Carolina, "with no windows—no opening at all, except the doorway, with a chimney of sticks and mud; with no trees about them, no porches, or shades, of any kind. Except for the chimney . . . I should have conjectured that it had been built for a powder-house, or perhaps an ice-house—never for an animal to sleep in." Large planters placed these cabins in a row, an arrangement that projected precision and undifferentiated order.

The diet and housing of most slaves may have been no worse than that of the poorest whites in both the North and the South, but their workload was undoubtedly heavier. Just over half of the slave population at midcentury was concentrated on plantation units with twenty or more slaves, and most of these slaves worked as field hands in gang labor. Overseers freely admitted that they relied on whippings to make slaves work in these gangs.

The fear of the whip on a bare back set the work pace. At daybreak, recalled Solomon Northrup of his enslavement on a Louisiana plantation, "the fears and labors of another day begin; and until its close there is no such thing as rest. [The slave] fears he will be caught lagging through the day; he fears to approach the gin-house with his basket-load of cotton at night; he fears, when he lies down, that he will oversleep himself in the morning."

Some 15 to 20 percent of plantation slaves were house servants or skilled artisans who had lighter and less regimented workloads than field hands. Some planters used the prospect of transfer to these relatively privileged positions as an incentive to field hands to work harder. Extra rations, time off on weekends, passes to visit a spouse on a nearby plantation, and the right to have a garden plot were among the other incentives planters used to keep labor productivity high.

Nearly three-fourths of the slaves worked on plantations and medium-sized farms. Most of the remainder—those in units with fewer than ten slaves—worked on small farms in close contact with the master's family. Holdings of a few slaves on small farms scattered across the countryside meant that husbands and wives often lived on different farms, and the owners of only a few slaves were more vulnerable than planters to market downturns that could force them to sell their slaves and thus further divide families.

One in ten slaves worked outside the plantations and farms at jobs that most native whites generally shunned. Extractive industries, such as mining and lumbering, relied heavily on these slaves, and every southern industry employed some slaves. The Tredegar Iron Company in Richmond, the largest iron foundry in the South, used slaves as its main work force after 1847, partly to curb strikes by its white workers. Racial tensions often flared in southern industry. When the races worked together, skilled whites typically insisted on being placed in supervisory positions over the slaves.

Compared to plantation slaves, industrial slaves had more independence off the job and greater opportunities to earn money of their own. By undertaking extra factory work, known as "overwork," industrial slaves could earn $50 or more a month, money that could be used to buy goods for their families or, in rare cases, to purchase their freedom.

Families and Religion

The core institution of slave life was the family. Despite all the obstacles arrayed against them, many slave marriages produced enduring commitments and a supportive moral code for family members. Most slave unions remained intact until death or, more likely, the sale of a spouse ended the partnership. Close to one-third of slave marriages were broken up by sales or forced removals. A slave bitterly recalled that "the separation of slaves in this way is little thought of. A few masters regard their union as sacred, but where one does, a hundred care nothing about it."

Both parents were present in about two-thirds of slave families, the same ratio as in contemporary peasant families in western Europe. Most slave fathers struggled to help feed their families by hunting and fishing, and they risked death or a terrible beating to defend their wives from sexual abuse by the overseer or master. Besides their field labor, slave mothers had all the burdens of pregnancy, caring for children, laundering, and preparing meals. After escaping from slavery, Sojourner Truth told how she placed her babies in a basket hanging from a tree while she worked in the field and had older children care for them.

No anguish under slavery was more heart-rending than that of a mother whose child was sold away from her. "Oh, my heart was too full!" recalled Charity Bowery on being told that her boy Richard was sold. "[My mistress] had sent me away on an errand, because she didn't want to be troubled with our cries. I hadn't any chance to see my poor boy. I shall never see my poor boy. I shall never see him again in this world. My heart felt as if it was under a great load."

Most parents could only teach their children the skills of survival in a world in which whites had a legal monopoly on violence. The most valuable of these skills was the art of hiding one's true feelings from whites and telling them what they wanted to hear. As a perceptive traveler noted: "When therefore a white man approaches [the slaves] with inquiries concerning their condition, they are at once put upon their guard, and either make indefinite and vague replies, or directly contradict their real sentiments."

Extensive kinship ties provided a support network for the vulnerable slave family. These networks included both blood relatives and other slaves who influenced the life of the family. Children were taught to address elders as "Aunt" and "Uncle" and fellow slaves as "sister" and "brother." If separated from a parent, a child could turn to relatives or the larger slave community for care and assistance.

The ancestors of nineteenth-century slaves brought no common religion with them when they were taken to the New World. However, beliefs common to a variety of African religions survived. In keeping with African traditions, the religion of the slaves fused the natural and spiritual worlds, accepted the power of ghosts over the living, and relied on an expressive form of worship in which the participants shouted and swayed in rhythm with the beat of drums and other instruments. Associated with reverence for ancestors, dance was sacred in Africa. Spirituals, the religious songs of the slaves, were sung in a dance known in America as the "ring shout."

Moving counterclockwise and stamping their feet to establish a beat for the music, slaves blended dance and song in a religious ceremony that helped them endure oppression and sustain their self-confidence.

By most estimates, no more than 20 percent of the slaves ever converted to Christianity. Those who did convert found in Christianity a message of deliverance rooted in the liberation of Moses's people from bondage in Egypt. The Jesus of the New Testament spoke to them as a compassionate God who had shared their burden of suffering so that all peoples could hope to find the Promised Land of love and justice. By blending biblical imagery into their spirituals, the slaves expressed their yearning for freedom: "Didn't my Lord deliver Daniel/Then why not every man?"

The initial exposure of slaves to Christianity usually came from evangelical revivalists. The evangelical message of universal spiritual equality confirmed the slaves' sense of personal worth. Less formal in both their doctrines and organization than the Presbyterians and Episcopalians, Baptist and Methodist evangelical sects allowed the slaves more leeway to choose their own preachers and engage in the physical activism and the call-and-response pattern that characterized slave religion. Perhaps because they baptized by total immersion, which evoked the purifying power of water so common in African religions, the Baptists gained the most slave converts.

Most planters favored Christianity among their slaves only if they could control it. Worried that abolitionist propaganda might attract the slaves to Christianity as a religion of secular liberation, some planters invited white ministers to their plantations to preach a gospel of passivity and obedience centered on Paul's call for servants to "obey in all things your Masters."

Slaves often feigned acceptance of the religious wishes of their masters at the special slave chapels on some plantations or in the segregated galleries of white churches on Sunday mornings. But in the evening, out of sight of the master or overseer, they held their own services in the woods and listened to their own preachers. As much as they could, the slaves hid their religious life from whites. In creating a spiritual life for themselves, many slaves experienced religion as a rebirth that gave them the inner strength to endure their bondage. As one of them recalled, "I was born a slave and lived through some hard times. If it had not been for *my God,* I don't know what I would have done."

Resistance

Open resistance to slavery was futile. The fate of Richard, Charity Bowery's boy who was sold away from her, typified that of the openly defiant slave. He resisted the efforts of his new owner in Alabama to break his will. When the owner threatened to shoot him if he did not consent to being whipped, Richard replied, "Shoot away, I won't come to be flogged." The master shot and killed him.

Although the odds of succeeding were infinitesimal, four major uprisings occurred in the nineteenth century. The first, **Gabriel Prosser's Rebellion** in 1800, involved about fifty armed slaves around

After fleeing from slavery in Maryland in 1849, Harriet "Moses" Tubman, standing on left, risked reenslavement by returning to the South on several occasions to assist other slaves in escaping. She is photographed here with some of those she helped free.

Richmond. State authorities executed Prosser and twenty-five of his followers before the rebellion got under way.

A decade later, in what seems to have been a spontaneous bid for freedom, several hundred slaves in the river parishes (counties) above New Orleans marched on the city. Poorly armed, they were no match for the U.S. Army troops and militiamen who stopped them. More than sixty slaves died, and the heads of the leading rebels were posted on poles along the Mississippi River to warn others of the fate that awaited rebellious slaves.

The most carefully planned slave revolt, *Denmark Vesey's Conspiracy*, like Prosser's, failed before it got started. Vesey, a literate carpenter and lay preacher in Charleston who had purchased his freedom with the money he had won in a lottery, planned the revolt in the summer of 1822. Vesey assigned teams of rebels specific targets, such as the municipal guardhouse and arsenal. Once Charleston was secured, the rebels apparently planned to flee to Haiti. The plot collapsed when two domestic servants betrayed it. White authorities hanged thirty-five conspirators, including Vesey, and banished thirty-seven others. After destroying the African Methodist Episcopal Church where Vesey had preached, they also passed the Negro Seamen's Act, which mandated the imprisonment of black sailors while their ships were berthed in Charleston.

Nat Turner's Rebellion in Southampton County, Virginia, did erupt before it could be suppressed. Turner was a literate field hand driven by prophetic visions of black vengeance against white oppressors, who led a small band of followers on a murderous rampage in late August 1831. The first white to be killed was Joseph Travis, Turner's owner. In the next two days, sixty other whites were also killed. An enraged posse, aided by slaves loyal to the whites, captured or killed most of Turner's party. Turner hid for two months before being apprehended. He and more than thirty other slaves were executed, and panicky whites killed more than a hundred other slaves.

Slaves well understood that the odds against a successful rebellion were insurmountable. Whites had all the guns and were also more numerous. Mounted patrols of whites were part of the police apparatus of slavery, and their surveillance limited organized rebellion by slaves to small, local affairs that were quickly suppressed.

Nor could many slaves escape to freedom. The **Underground Railroad**, a secret network of stations and safe houses organized by Quakers and other antislavery whites and blacks, provided some assistance. However, out of more than 3 million slaves in the 1850s, only about a thousand a year permanently escaped (see "American Views: A Letter from an Escaped Slave to His Former Master").

The few who made it to the North did so by running at night and hiding during the day. The most ingenious resorted to clever stratagems. Henry "Box" Brown arranged to have himself shipped in a box from Richmond to Philadelphia. Ellen Craft, a light-skinned slave who could pass as white, disguised herself as a male slaveholder accompanied by his dark-skinned servant (her husband, William). What could have been a fatal flaw in their plan as they traveled from Savannah to Philadelphia—their inability to write and hence sign their names or document their assumed identities—was overcome by having Ellen pose as a sickly, rheumatic master whose right hand had to be kept bandaged.

Running away was common, but most runaways fled no father than to nearby swamps and woods. Most voluntarily returned or were tracked down by bloodhounds within a week.

Slaves resisted complete domination by their masters by maintaining a rich oral tradition in which folktales, such as those based on Brer Rabbit, enabled them to mock powerful whites by identifying themselves with apparently defenseless animals who used wit and cunning to outsmart their stronger enemies. Slave owners routinely complained of slaves malingering at work, abusing farm animals, losing tools, stealing food, and committing arson. Subversive protests confirmed slaves' sense of their humanity and value as a people. By resisting dehumanization, slaves endured with dignity and self-respect.

Free Society

Southern cities, though small by northern standards, provided jobs for a growing class of free workers who increasingly clashed with planters over the use of slave labor. These same cities, notably in the Upper South, were also home to the nation's largest concentration of free blacks. Though restricted in their freedom, these blacks competed with whites for jobs. Pressure was mounting on them by the 1850s to leave the South or be enslaved. Overriding racism bonded most whites together to defend the prerogatives of white supremacy.

The Slaveholding Minority

The white-columned plantation estate approached from a stately avenue of shade trees and framed by

SUMMARY

STRUCTURE OF FREE SOCIETY IN THE SOUTH, C. 1860

Group	Size	Characteristics
Large planters	Less than 1 percent of white families	Owned fifty or more slaves and plantations in excess of one thousand acres; the wealthiest class in America
Planters	About 3 percent of white families	Owned twenty to forty-nine slaves and plantations in excess of one hundred acres; controlled bulk of southern wealth and provided most of the political leaders
Small slaveholders	About 20 percent of white families	Owned fewer than twenty slaves, and most often less than five; primarily farmers, though some were part of a small middle class in towns and cities
Nonslaveholding whites	About 75 percent of white families	Most were yeomen farmers who owned their own land and stressed production for family use; one in five owned neither slaves nor land and squatted on least desirable land where they planted some corn and grazed some livestock; in cities they worked as artisans or, more typically, day laborers
Free blacks	About 3 percent of all free families	Concentrated in the Upper South; hemmed in by legal and social restrictions; most were tenants or farm laborers; about one-third lived in cities and generally were limited to lowest-paying jobs

luxuriant gardens remains the most popular image of the slave South. In fact, only the wealthiest planters could live in such splendor, and they comprised less than 1 percent of southern white families in 1860. Yet displayed in their homes and grounds, their wealth and status were so imposing that they created an idealized image of grace and grandeur that has obscured the cruder realities of the slave regime.

Families of the planter class—defined as those who held a minimum of twenty slaves—constituted only around 3 percent of all southern families in 1860. Most planters lived in drab log cabins. "The planter's home is generally a rude ungainly structure, made of logs, rough hewn from the forest; rail fences and rickety gates guard its enclosures," complained a speaker to the Alabama horticultural society in 1851. "We murder our soil with wasteful culture because there is plenty of fresh land West— and we live in tents and huts when we might live in rural palaces."

Most planters were acquisitive and restless. The sheer drive and penny-pinching materialism of these planters on the make impressed Tyrone Power, an Irish actor who visited the South in the 1830s. The slaveholders he saw carving plantations out of the wilderness were "hardy, indefatigable, and enterprising to a degree; despising and condemning luxury and refinement, courting labour, and even making a pride of the privations which they, without any necessity, continue to endure with their families."

Besides raising her own children, the plantation mistress managed the household staff, oversaw the cooking and cleaning, gardened, dispensed medicine and clothing to the slaves, and often assisted in their religious instruction. When guests or relatives came for an extended visit, the wife had to make all the special arrangements that this entailed. On the occasions when the master was called off on a business or political trip, she kept the plantation accounts. In many respects, she worked harder than her husband.

Planter wives often complained in their journals and letters of their social isolation from other white women and the physical and mental toil of managing slaves. Still, they only rarely questioned the

American Views

A LETTER FROM AN ESCAPED SLAVE TO HIS FORMER MASTER

In 1859, Jackson Whitney was one of six thousand fugitive slaves living in Canada, a sanctuary of freedom beyond the reach of the Fugitive Slave Act of 1850. Like most fugitives, he was male, and he had been forced to leave his family behind in Kentucky. His letter, as well as other direct testimony by African-Americans about their experiences and feelings while enslaved, gives us information about slavery that only the slaves could provide.

❖ **How would you characterize the tone of Whitney's letter? How did he express his joy at being a free man?**

❖ **How did Whitney feel that he had been betrayed by Riley, his former owner? What did Whitney mean by the phrase "a slave talking to 'massa' "? How did he indicate that he had been hiding his true feelings as a slave?**

❖ **How did Whitney contrast his religious beliefs and those of Riley? How did he expect Riley to be punished?**

❖ **What pained Whitney about his freedom in Canada, and what did he ask of Riley?**

March 18, 1859

Mr. Wm. Riley, Springfield, Ky. —Sir: I take this opportunity to dictate a few lines to you, supposing you might be curious to know my whereabouts. I am happy to inform you that I am in Canada, in good health, and have been here several days. Perhaps, by this time, you have concluded that robbing a woman of her husband, and children of their father does not pay, at least in your case; and I thought, while lying in jail by your direction, that if you had no remorse or conscience that would make you feel for a poor, broken-hearted man, and his worse-than-murdered wife and child, . . . and could not by any entreaty or permission be induced to do as you promised you would, which was to let me go with my family for $800—but contended for $1,000, when you had promised to take the same you gave for me (which was $660.) at the time you bought me, and let me go with my dear wife and children! but instead would render me miserable, and lie to me, and to your neighbors . . . and when you was at Louisville trying to sell me!

---

institution of slavery. Their deepest anger stemmed from their humiliation by husbands who kept slave mistresses or sexually abused slave women. "Sometimes white mistresses will surmise that there is an intimacy between a slave woman & the master," recalled a former slave, "and perhaps she will make a great fuss & have her whipped, & perhaps there will be no peace until she is sold."

Generally younger than the planters, small slaveholders were a diverse lot. About 10 percent were women, and another 20 percent or so were merchants, businessmen, artisans, and urban professionals. Most were farmers trying to acquire enough land and slaves to enter the ranks of planters.

Small slaveholders enjoyed scant economic security. A deadly outbreak of disease among their slaves or a single bad crop could destroy their credit and force them to sell their slaves to clear their debts. Owners of fewer than ten slaves stood a fifty-fifty chance within a decade of dropping out of the slaveholding class. In any given area suitable for plantations, small holders were gradually pushed out as then I thought it was time for me to make my feet feel for Canada, and let your conscience feel in your pocket. —Now you cannot say but that I did all that was honorable and right while I was with you, although I was a slave. I pretended all the time that I thought you, or some one else had a better right to me than I had to myself, which you know is rather hard thinking. —You know, too, that you proved a traitor to me in the time of need, and when in the most bitter distress that the human soul is capable of experiencing; and could you have carried out your purposes there would have been no relief. But I rejoice to say that an unseen, kind spirit appeared for the oppressed, and bade me take up my bed and walk—the result of which is that I am victorious and you are defeated.

I am comfortably situated in Canada, working for George Harris [another fugitive slave from Kentucky who had bought a farm in Canada]. . . .

There is only one thing to prevent me being entirely happy here, and that is the want of my dear wife and children, and you to see us enjoying ourselves together here. I wish you could realize the contrast between Freedom and Slavery;

but it is not likely that we shall ever meet again on this earth. But if you want to go to the next world and meet a God of love, mercy, and justice, in peace; who says, "Inasmuch as you did it to the least of them my little ones, you did it unto me"— making the professions that you do, pretending to be a follower of Christ, and tormenting me and my little ones as you have done—[you] had better repair the breaches you have made among us in this world, by sending my wife and children to me; thus preparing to meet your God in peace; for, if God don't punish you for inflicting such distress on the poorest of His poor, then there is no use of *having any* God, or *talking* about one. . . .

I hope you will consider candidly, and see if the case does not justify every word I have said, and ten times as much. You must not consider that it is a slave talking to 'massa' now, but one as free as yourself.

I subscribe myself one of the *abused* of America, but one of the *justified* and *honored* of Canada.

Jackson Whitney

Source: John W. Blassingame, ed., Slave Testimony: Two Centuries of Letters, Speeches, Interviews, and Autobiographies (1977).

planters bought up land to raise livestock or more crops.

Especially in the Lower South, owning slaves was a necessary precondition for upward mobility, but it was hardly a sufficient one. As a Baptist opponent of slavery put it, "Without slaves a man's children stand but poor chance to marry in reputation." Aside from conferring status, owning a few slaves could relieve a white household of much hard domestic labor. "I wish to God every head of a family in the United States had one [slave] to take the drudgery and menial service off his family," proclaimed Andrew Johnson of Tennessee in the U.S. Senate.

The White Majority

Three-fourths of southern white families owned no slaves in 1860. Nonslaveholders predominated wherever the soil and climate were not suitable for plantation agriculture. Most of them were yeoman farmers who worked their own land with family labor.

A yeoman farmstead in New Braumfels, Texas. The yeomanry strove for self-sufficiency by growing food crops and grazing livestock.

These farmers were quick to move when times were bad and their land was used up, but once settled in an area, they formed intensely localized societies. The community extended 5 to 10 miles around the nearest country store or county courthouse. Networks of kin and friends provided labor services when needed, fellowship in evangelical churches, and staple goods that an individual farm could not produce. The yeomanry aimed to be self-sufficient and limited market involvement to the sale of livestock and an occasional cotton crop that could bring in needed cash.

Yeoman farmers prized their independence. They tried to avoid debt and wanted to limit government authority. Rather than risk financial ruin by buying slaves on credit to grow cotton, they grew food crops and depended on their sons and, when needed, their wives and daughters to work the fields. Far longer than most northern farmers, they continued to make their own clothes, shoes, soap, and other consumer items.

In areas where there were both small farms and scattered plantations, the interests of the yeomen and the planters were often complementary. Planters provided local markets for the surplus grain and livestock of nonslaveholders and, for a small fee, access to grist mills and gins for grinding corn and cleaning cotton. They lent small sums to poorer neighbors in emergencies or to pay taxes. The yeomen staffed the slave patrols and became overseers on the plantations. Both groups sought to protect property rights from outside interference and to maintain a system

of racial control in which white liberties rested on black degradation.

When yeomen and planters did clash, it was usually over economic issues. Large slaveholders needing better credit and marketing facilities gravitated toward the Whig party, which called for banks and internal improvements. Nonslaveholding farmers, especially in the Lower South, tended to be Democrats who opposed banks and state-funded economic projects. But as long as planters deferred to the egalitarian sensibilities of the yeomen by courting them at election time and promising to safeguard their liberties, the planters were able to maintain broad support for slavery across class lines.

Around 15 percent of rural white families owned neither land nor slaves. These were the so-called poor whites, stigmatized by both abolitionists and planters as lazy and shiftless. The abolitionists considered these whites a kind of underclass who proved that slavery so degraded the dignity of labor that many whites shunned all work and lapsed into a wretched poverty. Planters habitually complained that these poor whites demoralized the slaves by showing that a person could survive without steady labor.

Most landless whites were resourceful and enterprising enough to squat on a few acres of land, put up crude cabins for shelter, plant some corn, and graze livestock in the surrounding woods. Although poor by most standards, they were also defiantly self-reliant.

Nonslaveholders were a growing majority in southern cities, and their numbers were growing fastest among the working classes. These urban workers shared no agricultural interests or ties with the planters. Nor were most of them, especially in the unskilled ranks, southern-born. Northerners and immigrants dominated the urban work force.

Free workers, especially Irish and German immigrants, increasingly replaced slaves in urban labor markets. These white workers bitterly resented competition from black slaves, and their demands to exclude slaves from the urban workplace reinforced planters' belief that cities bred abolitionism.

Free Blacks

A few southern blacks—6 percent of the total in 1860—were "free persons of color" and constituted 3 percent of the free population in the South. White intimidation and special legal provisions known as **black codes** (found throughout the North as well) denied them nearly all the rights of citizenship. Because of the legal presumption in the South that all blacks were slaves, they had to carry freedom papers, official certificates of their freedom. Many occupations, especially those involved in the communication of ideas, such as the printing trades, were closed to them.

Every slave state forbade the entry of free blacks, and every municipality had its own rules and regulations that forced them to live as an inferior caste. In Charleston, for example, a free black could not smoke a cigar or carry a cane in public. Whites had the right of way, and a free black who bumped into a white on the street was likely to be flogged.

More than four-fifths of the free blacks lived in the Upper South. Most of them were the offspring of slaves freed by private manumissions between 1780 and 1800 when a slump in tobacco markets and the Revolutionary War creed of natural rights had loosened slavery in the Chesapeake region.

As in the North, legal barriers and white prejudice generally confined these free blacks to the poorest-paying and most menial work. Most rural blacks were farm laborers or tenants. The best economic opportunities came in the cities, where some blacks found factory jobs and positions in the skilled trades. The percentage of blacks in the skilled trades was generally higher in the South than in the North. Highly skilled blacks, such as Thomas Day, widely recognized as the finest cabinetmaker in North Carolina, could command a premium in wages from white employers.

Cities offered blacks not only jobs but also enough social space to found their own churches and mutual-aid associations. Especially after 1840, urban African-American churches proliferated, and they were at the center of black community life.

These churches sponsored Sunday schools and day schools that were about the only means of education open to black people. Despite white opposition to black schools, the demand for schooling persisted. A "good education," declared a black schoolmaster in Baltimore, "is the *sine qua non* as regards the elevation of our people."

Less than 2 percent of the blacks in the Lower South were free in 1860. Most of the Lower South's free blacks descended from black emigrants who fled the revolutionary unrest in Haiti in the 1790s. Able to secure a solid economic footing, their descendants inherited more wealth than any other free blacks in the United States. Free blacks in the Lower South were more likely than those in the Upper South to have a marketable skill, and two-thirds of them lived in cities.

A light skin also enhanced the social standing of free blacks among color-conscious whites in the Lower South. Nearly 70 percent of free blacks in 1860 were mulattoes, and from their ranks came nearly all of the very small number of black planters. A mulatto elite emerged in Charleston, Mobile, and New Orleans that carefully distanced itself from most blacks, slave or free. In New Orleans, where the tradition of racially mixed unions dated back to French and Spanish rule, mulattoes put on lavish "octoroon balls" attended by free women of color and white men. Even here, however, the mulatto elite remained suspended between black and white worlds that never fully accepted them.

Despite the tendency toward a three-tiered racial hierarchy in the port cities of the Lower South, whites still insisted on making a racial dichotomy between white and black the overriding social division in the South. As the racial defense of slavery intensified in the 1850s, more calls were made for laws to banish or enslave free blacks.

Despised and feared by whites as a subversive element in a slave society, free blacks across the South were daily reminded that their freedom rested on the whims of the white majority. As white attitudes turned uglier in the late antebellum period, that freedom was less secure than ever.

The Proslavery Argument

In the early nineteenth century, most Southern whites would have called slavery a necessary evil, an unfortunate legacy from earlier generations that was needed to maintain racial peace with so many blacks living in their midst.

The 1830s marked a turning point. The twin shocks of Nat Turner's Rebellion and the onset of the abolitionist crusade in the North unleashed mobs of whites who stifled any open criticism of slavery in the Lower South. Southern whites also began to reassess how they justified slavery, both to the outside world and to themselves. By the 1850s, politicians, intellectuals, and evangelical ministers were defending slavery as a positive good, an institution ordained by God as the foundation of southern prosperity, white democracy, and Christian instruction for heathen Africans. They portrayed slavery as a mild, paternalistic, and even caring institution.

Evangelical Protestantism dominated southern religious expression by the 1830s, and its ministers took the lead in combating abolitionist charges that slavery was a moral and religious abomination. Most of the southern churches had always supported slavery. This support grew more pronounced and articulate once the abolitionists stepped up their attacks on slavery in the mid-1830s. Through a selective reading of the Bible, the proslavery ideologues found abundant evidence to proclaim that slavery was fully in accord with the moral law of God.

Southern evangelicals also turned to the Bible to support their argument that patriarchal authority—the unquestioned power of the father— was the basis of all Christian communities. Slavery thus became a matter of family governance, a domestic institution in which Christian masters of slaves accepted responsibility for caring for their workers in sickness and old age. Slavery was part of God's plan to Christianize an inferior race and teach its people how to produce raw materials that benefited the world's masses.

The growing commitment of southern evangelicals to slavery clashed with the antislavery position and the generally more liberal theology of northern evangelicals. In 1837, differences over slavery and theology formally split the Presbyterians along sectional lines. In 1844, and as a direct result of the slavery issue, the Methodist Episcopal Church, the nation's largest, divided into northern and southern churches. The Baptists did the same a year later. These religious schisms foreshadowed the sectionalized political divisions of the 1850s; they also severed one of the main emotional bonds between northern and southern whites.

The religious defense of slavery was central to the slaveholding ethic of paternalism that developed after 1830. By the 1850s, planters commonly described slaves as members of an extended family who were treated better than free workers in the North. Led by Charles Colcock Jones, a minister and planter in the Georgia lowcountry, a group of evangelical masters founded religious missions to

the slaves and sought reforms, such as legal measures that would prevent the separation of slave families. Such efforts to reform slavery failed largely because most masters would accept no limits on their power to control and work their slaves as they saw fit.

More common than the biblical defense of slavery was the racial argument that blacks were unfit to live as a free people among whites. The racial defense alleged that blacks were naturally lazy and inherently inferior to whites. If freed, so went the argument, they would steal from whites and sexually assault their women.

Slavery as a necessary means of racial control was a central theme in Thomas R. Dew's *Review of the Debates in the Virginia Legislature of 1831 and 1832.*, the first major justification of slavery by a Southerner. Concerned by the efforts of nonslaveholders in Virginia to ban a program of gradual emancipation, Dew, a tidewater planter tried to unit whites behind slavery by stressing the issue of race.

The racial argument resonated powerfully among whites. The attitude of a Tennessee farmer, as recorded by a northern traveler in the 1850s, was typical: "He said he'd always wished there hadn't been any niggers here . . ., but he wouldn't like to have them free." Most whites could see no middle ground between slavery and the presumed social chaos of emancipation.

Despite its apparent success in forging white solidarity, the racial argument could be turned on its head and used to weaken slavery. Most northern whites were about as racist as their southern counterparts, but they were increasingly willing to end slavery on the grounds that the stronger white race should assist weaker blacks to improve themselves as free persons. Some southern whites challenged the economic prerogatives of slaveholders. Why, for example, should any whites, as members of the master race, be forced into economic competition against skilled slave artisans? Why should not all nonagricultural jobs be legally reserved for whites? Doctrines of black inferiority could not prevent white unity from cracking when the economic interests of nonslaveholders clashed with those of planters.

Conclusion

The spread of plantation agriculture across the Lower South after 1830 deepened the involvement of southern whites in cotton and slavery. At the same time, an abolitionist movement in the North morally attacked slavery and demanded that it be abolished. As southern interests became more enmeshed in an institution that outsiders condemned, religious and intellectual leaders portrayed slavery as a Christian institution and a positive good necessary for white democracy and harmonious race relations. Proslavery ideologues stridently described the South as separate from and superior to the rest of the nation.

The proslavery argument depicted a nearly ideal society blessed by class and racial harmony. In reality, social conditions in the slave South were far more contradictory and conflict-ridden. Slaves were not content in their bondage. They hungered for freedom and sustained that dream through their own forms of Christianity and the support of family and kin. Relations between masters and their slaves were antagonistic, not affectionate, and wherever the system of control slackened, slaves resisted their owners. The publication in 1857 of Hinton Rowan Helper's *Impending Crisis of the South,* a scathing indictment by a white North Carolinian of how slavery stunted economic opportunities for average whites, was a vivid reminder that the proslavery argument had not converted all whites.

Planters were not fooled by the public rhetoric of white unity. They knew that slavery was increasingly confined to the Lower South and that elsewhere in the South, white support for it was gradually eroding. Facing the threat of outside interference with slavery and internal white disloyalty, planters feared the double-edged challenge to their privileged positions. By the 1850s, many of them were concluding that the only way to resolve their dilemma was to make the South a separate nation.

Review Questions

1. What factors accounted for the tremendous expansion of cotton production in the South? How was this expansion linked to slavery and westward movement?

2. What differentiated the Upper South from the Lower South? What role did slavery play in each region after 1815?

3. How would you characterize the life of a plantation slave? Why were religion and family such key features of the world that slaves built for themselves? What evidence is there of resistance and rebellion among the slaves?

4. How did most nonslaveholding whites live? What values did they prize most highly? Why did most nonslaveholders accept slavery or at least not attack it directly?

5. What was the position of free blacks in southern society? How were their freedoms restricted?

6. How did southern whites attempt to defend slavery and reconcile it with Christianity?

Recommended Reading

Shearer Bowman, *Masters and Lords: Mid-19th Century U.S. Planters and Prussian Junkers* (1993). This fascinating study in comparative history portrays southern planters as agrarian capitalists.

Clement Eaton, *The Growth of Southern Civilization, 1790–1860* (1961). Although dated, this remains a useful and readable introduction to the broad themes in the development of the Old South.

William W. Freehling, *The Road to Disunion: Secessionists at Bay, 1776–1854* (1990). A fine introduction to the social diversity of the Old South, this work is especially strong in exploring the tensions over slavery between the Upper South and the Lower South.

Eugene D. Genovese, *Roll Jordan Roll: The World the Slaveholders Made* (1974). This richly textured study of slavery is an excellent source for the interaction between masters and slaves. Genovese argues that paternalistic relations of dependent rights and obligations characterized slavery.

James Oakes, *The Ruling Race* (1982). This relatively short but provocative history of the slave-owning class stresses the restless, acquisitive nature of the small slave owners, the most typical holders of slaves.

Kenneth M. Stampp, *The Peculiar Institution* (1956). This work, which has aged well, is still the best one-volume history of southern slavery and leaves no doubt that slavery was both brutal and profitable.

Charles S. Sydnor, *The Growth of Southern Sectionalism, 1819–1848* (1948). This is the most thorough account of how the South moved from its nationalist stance in the early nineteenth century toward increasing sectional self-consciousness.

Bertram Wyatt-Brown, *Southern Honor: Ethics and Behavior in the Old South* (1982). This book is valuable for its insights into the culture of the planter class and the notions of honor that structured social relations among all whites.

Where to Learn More

❖ **Appalachian Museum of Berea College, Berea, Kentucky.**   This museum is an excellent source for understanding the lifestyles and material culture of the nonslaveholding farmers in the Appalachian highlands.

❖ **Museum of African-American Culture, Columbia, South Carolina.**   This museum provides a wealth of material on the culture of nineteenth-century blacks, including the free black population in the South.

❖ **Cottonlandia Museum, Greenwood, Mississippi.**   The library and museum depict the history of cotton in the Mississippi Delta. Special collections include some Native American artifacts.

❖ **Jarrell Plantation, Juliette, Georgia.**   This state historic site consists of a fifteen-building farm complex that conveys a good sense of the physical dimensions of a nineteenth-century Georgia plantation.

❖ **Meadow Farm Museum, Richmond, Virginia.**   The archives and museum are especially strong on southern farm life in the mid-nineteenth century.

14 REFORMING ANTEBELLUM SOCIETY, 1815–1850

KEY TOPICS

❖ The rise of the reform movement after the War of 1812
❖ The spread of reform from moral to social issues in the 1820s
❖ The development of regimented institutions—penitentiaries, asylums, workhouses—for criminals, the poor, and the insane
❖ The growth of abolitionist agitation and sentiment in the North
❖ Women's crucial role in the reform movements and the rise of an organized women's rights movement

"Would to God this [Fourth of July] were truly—what it is not, though lying lips declare it to be—the JUBILEE OF FREEDOM! That Jubilee cannot come, so long as one slave is left to grind in his prison-house. It will come only when liberty is proclaimed throughout ALL the land, unto ALL the inhabitants thereof." The abolitionist William Lloyd Garrison issued this call for freeing the slaves in a speech on July 4, 1839. He had been instrumental in organizing an antislavery movement in the 1830s that branded slavery as a sin, an unconscionable blot on America as a Christian nation. The abolitionists demanded in the name of Christian morality and human rights that all Americans commit themselves to the immediate end of slavery.

Abolitionism was the most radical extension of the reform impulse after the War of 1812 that swept many Americans into organized movements for individual improvement and social betterment. This reform impulse was strongest in the North in areas where traditional social and economic relations were undergoing wrenching changes as a market revolution accelerated the spread of cities, factories, and commercialized farms. These were also the areas where the emotional fires of evangelical revivals burned the hottest.

The religious message of the Second Great Awakening provided a framework for responding to change. New within mainstream Protestantism was the belief that anyone who sought salvation could attain it, not just those whom God had predestined to be saved. Evangelicalism taught that in both the spiritual and secular realms, individuals were accountable for their own actions. Through Christian activism, individuals could strive toward moral perfectibility. Social evils, and the sinful consequences of change, could be cleansed if only good Christians would help others find the path of righteousness.

The first wave of reform after the War of 1812 focused on changing individual behavior and targeted drinking, gambling, sexual misconduct, and Sabbath-breaking. By the 1830s, a second phase of reform turned to institutional solutions for crime, poverty, and social delinquency, largely untouched by voluntary moral suasion. One group of reformers, the abolitionists, aimed to reshape the very structure of American society through their moral crusade to eliminate slavery.

Women, especially those from the evangelical middle class, were active in both these phases of reform. Abolitionism, more than any other reform movement, radicalized many women. In identifying with the plight of blacks under slavery, female abolitionists drew parallels with their own lack of power in a male-dominated society. Women reformers founded a women's rights movement in the 1840s. They organized the Seneca Falls Convention of 1848, which called for extending the full rights and privileges of citizenship to women.

Abolitionists who opposed Garrison and his support of women's rights broke away in 1840 and formed an independent political party. These anti-Garrisonian abolitionists set out to win northern voters over to the antislavery stance.

Reform and Moral Order

American society was being transformed after 1815. The growth of cities, the spread of industrialization, and the vast westward migration accelerated in the generation after the War of 1812. Religious leaders and wealthy businessmen in the East saw evidence of disorder and unchristian wickedness all around them in the more fluid, materialistic society that was emerging.

These eastern elites, aided by their wives and daughters, created a network of voluntary, church-affiliated reform organizations known collectively as the **benevolent empire**. Revivals in the 1820s and 1830s then broadened the base of reform to include the newly evangelicalized middle class in northern cities and towns. From this class emerged the temperance crusade, the largest reform movement in pre–Civil War America.

The Benevolent Empire

For the Reverend Lyman Beecher, the American condition in 1814 presented "a scene of destitution and wretchedness." From his Presbyterian pulpit in Litchfield, Connecticut, and then in Boston, he became the leader of a clerical drive to restore moral leadership to America.

The America these ministers valued was one of respectable churchgoers whose behavior conformed to Puritan and Federalist standards of freedom as defined and ordered by an educated clergy. Beecher believed that only religion, as preached by "pious, intelligent, enterprising ministers through the nation," could provide the order that would preserve the Union and place it under "the moral government of God."

Evangelical businessmen in the seaboard cities backed Beecher's call to restore moral order. Worried by the increasing number of urban poor, wealthy merchants contributed vital financial support for a network of reform associations, which grew to include the American Board of Commissioners for Foreign Missions (1810), the American Bible Society (1816), the American Sunday School Union (1824), the American Tract Society (1825), and the American Home Missionary Society (1826).

The reform societies were radical innovators in adapting the Second Great Awakening's techniques of organization and communication. The Christian reformers sent out speakers on regular schedules along prescribed routes. They developed organizations that maintained a constant pressure for reform. National and local boards of directors supervised the work of salaried managers, who inspired volunteers to combat sin among the unconverted.

When steam presses and stereotype plates halved the cost of printing and dramatically increased its speed, the American Bible Society was the first to exploit this revolution in the print media. Between 1790 and 1830, the number of religious newspapers grew from fourteen to more than six hundred. By then, religious presses were churning out more than 1 million Bibles and 6 million tracts a year. These publications were mass-distributed by traveling agents and heavily promoted in national advertising campaigns. As the *Christian Herald* editorialized in 1823, "Preaching of the gospel is a Divine

CHRONOLOGY

1817 American Colonization Society is founded.	**1836** Congress passes gag rule.
1820s Shaker colonies grow.	**1837** Horace Mann begins campaign for school reform as secretary of the Massachusetts Board of Education.
1825 Robert Owen begins his utopian experiment at New Harmony, Indiana.	Antiabolitionist mob kills Elijah P. Lovejoy.
1826 American Temperance Society launches its crusade.	**1838** Sarah Grimké publishes *Letters on the Equality of the Sexes and the Condition of Women*.
1829 David Walker publishes *Appeal to the Colored Citizens of the World*.	**1840** Abolitionists split into Garrisonian and anti-Garrisonian societies.
1830 Joseph Smith founds the Church of Jesus Christ of Latter-day Saints.	Political abolitionists launch the Liberty party.
1830–1831 Evangelical revivals are held in northern cities.	**1841** Brook Farm is established.
1831 William Lloyd Garrison begins publishing *The Liberator*.	Dorothea Dix begins her work to improve conditions for the mentally ill.
1832 New England Anti-Slavery Society is founded.	**1846–1848** Mormons migrate to the West.
1833 Slaves in the British Empire are emancipated. American Anti-Slavery Society is organized.	**1847** John Humphrey Noyes establishes the Oneida Community.
1834 New York Female Moral Reform Society is founded.	**1848** Seneca Falls Convention outlines a program for women's rights.

institution—'printing' is no less so. . . . The PULPIT AND THE PRESS are inseparably connected."

A host of local societies were more concerned with stamping out individual vices. Their purpose, as summed up by a Massachusetts group, the Andover South Parish Society for the Reformation of Morals, was "to discountenance [discourage] immorality, particularly Sabbath-breaking, intemperance, and profanity, and to promote industry, order, piety, and good morals." These goals linked social and moral discipline in a broad sweep of benevolence that appealed both to pious churchgoers concerned about godlessness and profit-oriented businessmen eager to curb their workers' unruly behavior.

With volunteers drawn largely from the teenage daughters of evangelical businessmen, Sunday interdenominational schools combined elementary education with the teaching of the Bible and Christian principles. The American Sunday School Union was both a coordinating agency for local efforts and a publishing house for books and periodicals. By 1832, nearly 10 percent of all American children aged 5 to 14 were attending one of eight thousand Sunday schools.

The boldest expression of the drive to enhance Christian power was the **Sabbatarian movement**. In 1828, evangelicals led by Lyman Beecher formed the **General Union for Promoting the Observance of the Christian Sabbath** whose immediate goal was the repeal of a law passed by Congress in 1810 directing post offices to deliver mail on Sunday. This law symbolized to Christian reformers the moral degeneracy into which the republic had fallen. Its broader mission was to enforce local statutes that shut down business and leisure activities on Sundays. The Sabbatarians considered such statutes no less "necessary to the welfare of the state" than "laws against murder and polygamy." To their opponents, such statutes were "repugnant to the rights of private property and irreconcilable with the free exercise of civil liberty."

In 1829, insisting on the separation of church and state, the Democratic Congress upheld the postal law of 1810. Businessmen, workingmen, Southern evangelicals, and religious conservatives in New England all felt that the Sabbath purists had gone too far.

The General Union disbanded in 1832, but it left an important legacy for future reform movements. On the one hand, it developed techniques that converted the reform impulse into direct political action. In raising funds, training speakers, holding rallies, disseminating literature, lobbying for local Sunday regulations, and coordinating a petition to Congress, the Sabbatarians created an organizational model for other reformers to follow in mobilizing public opinion and influencing politicians. On the other hand, the failure of the Sabbatarians revealed that heavy-handed attempts to force the "unconverted" to follow Christian standards of conduct were self-defeating. A new approach was needed that encouraged individuals to reform themselves without coercive controls. It soon emerged in the temperance movement.

The Temperance Movement

The greatest reform movement, in both immediate impact and the number of people involved, was temperance, the drive against drinking alcohol. The success of temperance rested on what Lyman Beecher called "a new moral power." Dismayed by popular resistance to the coercive moralism of the first wave of Christian reform, evangelicals like the Reverend John Chester concluded in 1821 that "you cannot coerce a free people that are jealous to fastidiousness of their rights." Therefore, reform had to rest on persuasion, and it had to begin with the voluntary decision of individuals to free themselves from sin. For these evangelicals, the self-control to renounce alcohol became the key to creating a harmonious Christian society of self-regulating citizens.

In 1826, evangelicals founded the **American Temperance Society** in Boston and took control of the movement. They were inspired by Beecher's *Six Sermons on Temperance,* a stirring call for voluntary associations dedicated to the belief that "the daily use of ardent spirits, in any form, or in any degree" was a sin. They now sought a radical change in American attitudes toward alcohol and its role in social life.

American consumption of alcohol reached an all-time high by 1830 of 7.1 gallons of pure alcohol per year for every American aged 14 and over (about three times present-day levels). Alcoholic beverages were plentiful and cheaper than tea or coffee. "Liquor at that time," recalled a carpenter, "was used as commonly as the food we ate." An English observer in 1819 was shocked to discover that "you cannot go into hardly any man's house without being asked to drink wine, or spirits, even *in the morning.*"

In pre-1830 America, taverns easily outnumbered churches as centers of community sociability. Alcohol was used to pay both common laborers and the itinerant preachers on the early Methodist circuit. Masters and journeymen shared a drink as a customary way of taking a break from work. No wedding, funeral, or meeting of friends was complete without alcohol.

For the temperance crusade to succeed, the reformers had to finance a massive propaganda campaign and link it to an organization that could mobilize and energize thousands of people. They built such a mass movement by merging temperance into the network of churches and lay volunteers that the benevolent empire had developed and by adopting the techniques of revivals to win new converts.

Evangelical reformers denounced intemperance as the greatest sin of the land. In the words of the Reverend Herman Humphrey, it deprived "its victims of the means of grace. . . . If there is any evil which hardens the heart faster, or fills the mouth with 'cursing and bitterness' sooner, or quickens hatred [of] God and man into a more rapid and frightful maturity, I know not what it is." Alcohol became the master symbol for all that was wrong in America—crime, poverty, insanity, broken families, boisterous politicking, Sabbath-breaking.

This message, with its dark overtones of damnation but bright assurances of salvation through self-discipline, was thundered from the pulpit and the public lectern. Thanks to the generous financial subsidies of such wealthy benefactors as Stephen Van Rensselaer and Edward Delavan of New York, it was also broadcast in millions of tracts printed on the latest high-speed presses. As in the revivals, temperance rallies combined emotionally charged sermons with large, tearful prayer meetings to evoke guilt among sinners, who would then seek release by taking the pledge of abstinence.

Within a decade, more than five thousand local chapters and statewide groups were affiliated with the American Temperance Society. A million members had pledged abstinence by 1833. New England and New York alone claimed 72 percent of all temperance societies in the mid-1830s. Most of the converts came from the upper and middle classes. Businessmen welcomed temperance as a model of self-discipline in their efforts to regiment factory work. Young, upwardly mobile professionals and petty entrepreneurs learned in temperance how to be thrifty, self-controlled, and more respectable and creditworthy. Many of them presumably agreed with the *Temperance Recorder* that "the enterprise of this country is so great, and competition so eager in every branch of business . . ., that profit can only result from . . . *temperance.*"

Women were indispensable to the temperance movement. Women comprised 35 to 60 percent

SUMMARY

THE REFORM IMPULSE

Type	Objects of Reform	Means	Example	Origin
Moral reform	Individual failings such as drinking, sexual misconduct, Sabbath-breaking	Mass distribution of literature, speaker tours, lobbying	American Temperance Society	1810s–1820s
Institutional reform	Crime, poverty, delinquency	Penitentiaries, asylums, almshouses, state-supported schools	Massachusetts Board of Education	1830s
Utopian societies	Selfish materialism of society	New, highly structured communities	Shakers	1820s
Abolition	Slavery	Petition and mailing campaigns	American Anti-Slavery Society	1830s
Women's rights	Legal subordination of women	Lobbying, petition campaigns	Seneca Falls Convention	1840s

of the members in local temperance societies. As the moral protectors of the family, they pressured their husbands to take the teetotaler's pledge and stick by it, raised sons to shun alcohol, and banished liquor from their homes. By the 1840s, temperance and middle-class domesticity had become synonymous.

Temperance made its first significant inroads among the working classes when the economic depression of 1839–1843 created widespread hardships in eastern cities. Joining together in what they called **Washington Temperance Societies**, small businessmen and artisans, many of them reformed drunkards, carried temperance into working-class districts. The Washingtonians gained a considerable following by insisting that workers could survive the depression only if they stopped drinking and adopted the temperance ethic of frugality and self-help. Their wives organized auxiliary societies and pledged to enforce sobriety and economic restraint at home.

Annual per capita consumption of alcohol by adults fell from over 7 gallons in 1830 to less than 2 gallons by 1845, a telling measure of the temperance movement's success. In 1851, Maine passed the first statewide prohibition law. Other northern states followed suit, but antitemperance coalitions soon overturned most of these laws outside New England.

Nonetheless, alcohol consumption remained at the low level set in the 1840s.

Backlash against Benevolence

Some of the benevolent empire's harshest critics came out of the populist revivals of the early 1800s. They considered the Christian reformers' program a conspiracy of orthodox Calvinists from old-line denominations to impose social and moral control on behalf of a religious and economic elite. The goal of the "orthodox party," warned the Universalist *Christian Intelligencer,* was the power of "governing the nation"; the societies they formed "are but so many strings . . . , the ultimate design of which is to draw them into power."

These criticisms revealed a profound mistrust of the emerging market society. In contrast to the evangelical reformers, drawn from the well-educated business and middle classes who were benefiting from economic change, most evangelical members of the grass-roots sects and followers of the itinerant preachers were unschooled, poor, and hurt by market fluctuations that they could not control. Often they were farmers forced by debt to move west or artisans and tradesmen displaced by new forms of factory production and new commercial outlets.

Socially uprooted and economically stranded, they found a sense of community in their local churches and resisted control by wealthier, better-educated outsiders. Above all, they clung to beliefs that shored up the threatened authority of the father over his household.

Middle-class evangelicalism in the Northeast was becoming feminized with the elevation of women to the status of moral guardians of the family (see Chapter 10) and agents of benevolent reform outside the household. This new social role for women was especially threatening—indeed, galling—for men who were the causalities of the more competitive economy. Raised on farms where the father had been the unquestioned lawgiver and provider, these men attacked feminized evangelicalism for undermining their paternal authority. They found in Scripture an affirmation of the patriarchal power that any man, no matter how poor or economically dependent, could exercise over his wife and children.

The **Church of Jesus Christ of Latter-day Saints** (also known as the **Mormon Church**) represented the most enduring religious backlash of economically struggling men against the aggressive efforts of reforming middle-class evangelicals. Joseph Smith and his followers were alienated not only from the new market economy but also from what they saw as the religious and social anarchy around them.

Based on Smith's divine revelations as set forth in *The Book of Mormon* (1830), their new faith offered early converts to Mormonism a sanctuary as a biblical people and a release from social and religious uncertainties. They believed that the mainstream evangelical churches had corrupted Christ's original gospel. "This generation abounds in ignorance, superstition, selfishness, and priestcraft," charged the Mormon John Whitmer; "for this generation is truly led by . . . hireling priests whose God is the substance of the world's goods."

Mormonism provided both a theology and an economic and gender organization that defended communal beliefs centered on male authority by assigning complete spiritual and secular authority to men. Unlike female-dominated evangelicalism, men led their families into Mormonism. Only through subordination and obedience to their husbands could women hope to gain salvation.

To be a Mormon was to join a large extended family that was part of a shared enterprise. Men bonded their labor in a communal economy to benefit all the faithful. A law of tithing, instituted in 1841, required Mormons to give 10 percent of their property to the church upon conversion and 10 percent of

their annual income thereafter. Driven by a strong sense of social obligation, the Mormons forged the most successful alternative vision in antebellum America to the individualistic Christian republic of the benevolent reformers. (For the Mormons' role in the westward movement, see Chapter 12.)

Institutions and Social Improvement

Although evangelical Protestantism was its mainspring, antebellum reform also had its roots in the European Enlightenment. Enlightenment thinkers, like the evangelicals inspired by religious optimism, had unbounded faith in social improvement.

Studies published in the 1820s that documented increasing urban poverty, crime, and teenage delinquency created a sense of urgency for many reformers. Guided by the Enlightenment belief that environmental conditions shaped human character, reformers created a new system of public schooling in the North. They also prodded state legislatures to fund penitentiaries for criminals, asylums for the mentally ill, reformatories for the delinquent, and almshouses for the poor.

As reformers were implementing new institutional techniques for shaping individual character after 1820, a host of utopian communities sprang up. These communities also tapped into an impulse for human betterment. They typically rejected either private property or families based on monogamous marriage and offered a communitarian life designed to help a person reach perfection. Most of these communities were short-lived.

School Reform

"An ignorant people always has been and always will be a degraded and oppressed people—they are always at the mercy of the corrupt and designing," cautioned Philadelphia school officials in their annual report for 1836. They warned that "if we fail by Education to awake—guide—confirm the moral energies of our people, we are lost!" Secular revivalists as much as they were institutional innovators, the school reformers embarked on a crusade to save America from ignorance and vice.

Before the 1820s, schooling in America was an informal, haphazard affair that nonetheless met the basic needs for reading, writing, and arithmetic skills of an overwhelmingly rural population. Private tutors and academies for the wealthy, a few charitable schools for the urban poor, and rural one-room schoolhouses open for a few months a year comprised formal education at the primary level.

The first political demands for free tax-supported schools originated with the **Workingmen's movement** in eastern cities in the 1820s. Decrying what the Philadelphia Working Men's Committee in 1830 described as "a monopoly of talent, which consigns the multitude to comparative ignorance, and secures the balance of knowledge on the side of the rich and the rulers," workers called for free public schooling. In pushing for what they called "equal republican education," they were also seeking to guarantee that all citizens, no matter how poor, could achieve meaningful liberty and equality. However, the stiff resistance of wealthier property holders who refused to be taxed to pay for the education of working-class children blocked most of their proposals.

The breakthrough in school reform came in New England. Increasing economic inequality, growing numbers of Irish Catholic immigrants, and the emergence of a mass democracy based on nearly universal white male suffrage convinced reformers of the need for state-supported schools.

In 1837, the Massachusetts legislature established the nation's first state board of education. The head of the board for the next twelve years was Horace Mann, a former Whig politician and temperance advocate who now tirelessly championed educational reform. Mann demanded that the state government assume centralized control over Massachusetts schools. All schools should have the same standards of compulsory attendance, strict discipline, common textbooks, professionally trained teachers, and graded, competitive classes of age-segregated students.

Once this system was in place, Mann promised that schools would become "the great equalizer of the conditions of men—the balance-wheel of the social machinery." Poverty would no longer threaten social disruption because the ignorant would have the knowledge to acquire property and wealth. Education, Mann stated, "does better than disarm the poor of their hostility against the rich; it prevents being poor." Trained in self-control and punctuality, youths would be able to take advantage of economic opportunities and become intelligent voters concerned with the rights of property.

Democrats in the Massachusetts legislature denounced Mann's program as "a system of centralization and of monopoly of power in a few hands, contrary in every respect, to the true spirit of our democratical institutions." The laboring poor, who depended for economic survival on the wage income that their children could contribute to the family economy, resisted compulsory attendance laws and a longer school year. Farmers fought to maintain local control over schooling and to block the higher taxes needed for a more comprehensive and professionalized system. The Catholic Church protested the thinly veiled attempts of the reformers to indoctrinate all students in the moral strictures of middle-class Protestantism. Catholics began

The sewing table on the right in this painting, Girls' Evening School, *from about 1840, indicates how notions of women's domestic sphere limited the educational opportunities available for young women in the mid-nineteenth century. Still, women trained in female academies and seminaries increasingly displaced men as teachers in public schools.*

building at great expense their own parochial schools.

Despite the cries of tyranny they provoked, Mann and his allies prevailed in most of the industrializing states. The educational reformers received strong support from the professional and business constituencies of the Whig party.

Most important for its political success, school reform appealed to the growing northern urban middle class. Opposing both the "vicious passions" of the poor and the "idle luxury" of the rich, schools would instill the moral and economic discipline that the middle class deemed essential for a progressive and ordered society. Teaching morality and national pride was central to the educational curriculum, and from the popular McGuffey Readers used as a classroom text, students learned such lessons as "God gives a great deal of money to some persons, in order that they may assist those [who] are poor."

Out of the northern middle class also came the young female teachers who increasingly staffed elementary schools. Presumed by their nature to be more nurturing than men, women now had an entry into teaching, the first profession open to them. Besides the superior moral qualities they supposedly brought to teaching young children, women could also be hired far more cheaply than men: School boards assumed that they would accept low wages while waiting to be married.

Just over 50 percent of the white children between 5 and 19 years of age in the United States were enrolled in school in 1850—the highest percentage in the world at the time. Working-class parents were quicker to pull their children out of school at an early age than higher-income middle-class parents. Planters continued to rely on private tutors or academies for their children, and southern farmers saw little need for public education. The slave states, especially in the Lower South, lagged behind the rest of the nation in providing for common schools.

Prisons, Workhouses, and Asylums

Up to this time, Americans had depended on voluntary efforts to cope with crime, poverty, and social deviance. Reformers now turned to public authorities to establish a host of new institutions—penitentiaries, workhouses, mental hospitals, orphanages, and reformatories—to deal with social problems.

Eighteenth-century Americans never thought of rehabilitating criminals. Prisons were simple structures whose only purpose was to hold criminals before they were fined, whipped, mutilated, or executed in a public ritual that drew large crowds of festive onlookers. But the institutional reformers of the Jack-

sonian era believed that criminals, as well as the poor and other deviants, could be morally redeemed.

The reformers believed that people's environments shaped their character for good or evil. The Boston Children's Friend Society was devoted to the young, "whose plastic natures may be molded into images of perfect beauty, or . . . perfect repulsiveness." Samuel Gridley Howe, a prison reformer, proclaimed: "Thousands of convicts are made so in consequence of a faulty organization of society. . . . They are thrown upon society as a sacred charge; and that society is false to its trust, if it neglects any means for their reformation." In the properly ordered environment of new institutions, discipline and moral character would be instilled in criminals and other deviants who lacked the self-control to resist the corrupting vices and temptations that pervaded society.

As two French observers noted in the early 1830s, "The penitentiary system . . . to them seems the remedy for all the evils of society." Unlike earlier prisons, the penitentiaries were huge, imposing structures that isolated the prisoners from each other and the outside world. Inmates in the New York system pioneered in the 1820s worked together in gangs during the day, but under the Pennsylvania plan, each prisoner was held in solitary confinement.

No longer were criminals to be brutally punished or thrown together under inhumane conditions that perpetuated a cycle of moral depravity. Now, cut off from all corrupting influences, forced to learn that hard work teaches moral discipline, and uplifted by religious literature, criminals would be guided toward becoming law-abiding, productive citizens.

The same philosophy of reform provided the rationale for asylums to house the poor and the insane. The number of transient poor and the size of urban slums increased as commercial capitalism uprooted farmers from the land and undercut the security of craft trades. Believing that the poor, much like criminals, had only themselves to blame, public officials and their evangelical allies prescribed a therapeutic regimen of discipline and physical labor to cure the poor of their moral defects. The structured setting for that regimen was the workhouse.

The custodians of the workhouses banished drinking, gambling, and idleness. Under the workhouse rules in New York, officers could "rightly exercise . . . a measure of moral force upon the will of these persons, to induce them to do that which their own uncultivated understanding might oppose." Officers were to administer their duties "with strictness— severity." Their prime responsibility was to supervise the inmates in a tightly scheduled daily routine built around manual labor. Once purged of their laziness and filled with self-esteem as the result of work discipline, the poor would be released to become useful members of society.

Public insane asylums offered a similar order for the mentally ill. Reformers believed that too many choices in a highly mobile, materialistic, and competitive society drove some people insane. Following the lead of New York and Massachusetts in the 1830s, twenty-eight states had established mental hospitals by 1860. These facilities set rigid rules and work assignments to teach patients how to order their lives.

In the early 1840s Dorothea Dix, a Massachusetts schoolteacher, discovered that the insane in her home state were dumped into jails and almshouses, where they suffered filthy, inhumane treatment. She found the insane "confined . . . in *cages, closets, cellars, stalls, pens! Chained, naked, beaten with rods,* and *lashed* into obedience." Horrified, Dix lobbied state legislatures across the nation for the next twenty years to improve treatment for the mentally ill.

While the reformers did provide social deviants with cleaner and safer living conditions, their penitentiaries and asylums succeeded more in classifying and segregating their inmates than in reforming them. Submission to routine turned out not to be the best builder of character. Witnessing the rigorous control of every movement of the isolated prisoners at the Eastern State Penitentiary in Philadelphia, English novelist Charles Dickens declared "this slow and daily tampering with the mysteries of the brain to be immeasurably worse than any torture of the body."

Penitentiaries, reformatories, and workhouses failed to eliminate or noticeably check poverty, crime, and vice. By midcentury, reformers were defining deviants and dependents as permanent misfits who suffered from ingrained character defects. The asylums remained, but stripped of their earlier optimism, they became little more than holding pens for the outcasts of society.

Utopian Alternatives

Unlike the reformers, who aimed to improve the existing order by guiding individuals to greater self-discipline, the utopians sought perfection by withdrawing from society and its confining institutions. A radically new social order, not an improved old one, was their goal.

Though following different religious and secular philosophies of communitarian living, all the utopians wanted to fashion a more rational and personally satisfying alternative to the competitive materialism of antebellum America. Robert Owen, a proponent of utopian **socialism**, promised to create a new order where "the degrading and pernicious practices in which we are now trained, of buying cheap and selling dear, will be rendered unnecessary" and "union and co-operation will supersede individual interest." Nearly all their communities sought to transform the organization and rewards of work, thus challenging the prevailing dogmas about private property.

The most successful utopian communities were religious sects whose reordering of both sexual and economic relations departed most sharply from middle-class norms. The **Shakers**, at their height in the 1830s, attracted some six thousand followers. Named for the convulsive dancing that was part of their religious ceremonies, the Shakers traced their origins to the teachings of Ann Lee ("Mother Ann"). An illiterate factory laborer in mid-eighteenth-century England, Lee had a revelation in 1770 that the Second Coming of Christ was about to occur and would express itself in a womanly form, that of Mother Ann. Fired by another vision in 1774, Lee led eight of her followers to America, where, after her death in 1784, her disciples established the first Shaker community in New Lebanon, New York.

Organized around a doctrine of celibate **communism**, Shaker communities held all property in common. The sexes worked and lived apart from each other. Dancing during religious worship brought men and women together and provided an emotional release from enforced sexual denial. As an early Shaker leader explained, "There is evidently no labor which so fully absorbs all the faculties of soul and body, as real spiritual devotion and energetic exercise in sacred worship." In worldly as well as spiritual terms, women enjoyed an equality in Shaker life that the outside world denied them. For this reason, twice as many women as men joined the Shakers.

The Shakers gradually dwindled. Their rule of celibacy meant, of course, that they could propagate themselves only by recruiting new members and few new converts joined the movement after 1850. Viewed as eccentric outsiders by contemporaries, the Shakers today are best remembered for the beautiful simplicity of the furniture they made in their workshops.

John Humphrey Noyes, a graduate of Dartmouth who studied for the ministry at Yale, preached that marriage, the selfish "exclusive possession of one woman to one man," was the main barrier to perfection. He proposed instead "complex marriage," the mutual love of all the saved for each other. His goal was a religious society in which cooperative arrangements between men and women regulated child care and the distribution of property.

After he had been drummed out of the ministry for his radical teachings, Noyes established the **Oneida Community** in upstate New York in 1847. He attracted over two hundred followers with his perfectionist vision of plural marriage, community nurseries, group discipline, and common ownership of property. Charged with adultery, Noyes fled to Canada in 1879, but the Oneida Community, reorganized in 1881 as a joint-stock company in the United States and committed thereafter to conventional sexual mores, survived into the twentieth century.

Secular utopians aspired to perfect social relations through the rational design of planned communities. Bitter critics of the social evils of industrialization, they tried to construct models for a social order free from poverty, unemployment, and inequality. They envisioned cooperative communities that balanced agricultural and industrial pursuits in a mixed economy that recycled earnings to the laborers who actually produced the wealth.

Despite their high expectations, nearly all the planned communities ran into financial difficulties and soon collapsed. The pattern was set by the first of the controversial socialist experiments, **New Harmony** in Indiana, the brainchild of the wealthy Scottish industrialist and philanthropist Robert Owen. Within two years of its founding in 1825, New Harmony fell victim to inadequate financing and internal bickering.

About the only secular cooperative that gained lasting fame was **Brook Farm** in West Roxbury, Massachusetts (today part of Boston). Established in 1841, Brook Farm was a showcase for the transcendentalist philosophy of Ralph Waldo Emerson. A former Unitarian minister in Boston, Emerson taught that intuition and emotion could grasp a truer ("transcendent") reality than the senses alone could. The Boston intellectuals drawn to Brook Farm in the 1840s saw it as a refuge from the pressures and coarseness of commercial society, a place where they could realize the Emersonian ideal of spontaneous creativity. Although disbanded after six years as an economic failure, Brook Farm inspired intellectuals such as Nathaniel Hawthorne, who briefly lived there. In turn, his writings and those of other writers influenced by **transcendentalism** flowed into the great renaissance of American literature in the mid-nineteenth century.

In an 1837 address at Harvard titled "The American Scholar," Emerson had called for a distinctly national literature devoted to the democratic possibilities of American life. "The literature of the poor, the feelings of the child, the philosophy of the street, the meaning of household life, are the topics of the time," he proclaimed. Writers soon responded to Emerson's call.

Walt Whitman, whose *Leaves of Grass* (1855) foreshadowed modern poetry in its use of free verse, shared Emerson's faith in the possibilities of individual fulfillment, and his poems celebrated the democratic variety of the American people. David Henry Thoreau, Emerson's friend and neighbor, embodied the transcendentalist fascination with nature and self-discovery by living in relative isolation for sixteen months at Walden Pond, near Concord, Massachusetts. His *Walden, or Life in the Woods* (1854) became an American classic. "I went to the woods," he wrote, "because I wished to . . . confront only the essential facts of life, and see if I could not learn what it had to teach, and not, when I came to die, discover that I had not lived."

Novelists Hawthorne and Herman Melville focused on the existence of evil and the human need for community. In *The Scarlet Letter* (1850) and *The House of the Seven Gables* (1851), Hawthorne probed themes of egoism and pride to reveal the underside of the human soul. Melville's *Moby Dick* (1851) depicted the consequences of a competitive individualism unchecked by a social conscience.

Much of the initial appeal of utopian communities rested on the same concerns over the splintering and selfishness of antebellum society that Hawthorne and Melville expressed. Although the works of these novelists have endured, the utopian experiments quickly collapsed. They offered economic security and social harmony to buttress a threatened sense of community, but the acquisitiveness and competitive demands of the larger society exerted a stronger pull on most Americans.

Women's Role in Reform

Women played a central role in the major reform movements. They first entered reform through benevolent and missionary societies in the early 1800s.

A second phase of women's reform by the 1830s began to question the assumptions of a male-dominated society. Those most determined to demand fundamental change came from the abolitionist crusade.

Reform and Women's Sphere

An idealized image of "true womanhood" emerged in the commercializing Northeast after 1815. Often labeled the cult of domesticity (see Chapter 11), this image limited women's social role to home and family. Ministers, male moralists, and many women writers redefined femininity to encompass the virtues of piety, purity, and submissiveness. Because of their allegedly unique virtues, women's natural place was at home, morally training and uplifting their families.

The first phase of women's reform represented an extension of this domestic ideal for women. Founded in 1797, the **Society for the Relief of Poor Widows with Small Children** in New York typified these early approaches to reform. The women in the society came from socially prominent families. Motivated by religious charity and social duty, they visited poor women and children, dispensed funds, and set up work programs. However, they limited their benevolence to the "deserving poor" and screened out all they thought to be unworthy.

The revivalist call in the 1820s for moral action inspired middle-class women to join voluntary female groups. They founded maternal associations, where they prayed and fasted for the moral strength to save the souls of their children. Other associations sponsored revivals, visited the poor, established Sunday schools, and distributed Bibles and religious tracts. These reformers widened the public role of women, but their efforts also reinforced cultural stereotypes of women as nurturing helpmates who deferred to males.

A New Militancy

Unlike their benevolent counterparts, the reformers in the 1830s challenged male prerogatives and moved beyond moral suasion. The crusade against prostitution exemplified the new militancy. Women seized leadership of the movement in 1834 with the founding of the New York Female Moral Reform Society. This exclusively female organization replaced the New York Magdalen Society, a male-dominated group forced to disband when its first report scandalized the city fathers with its exposé of "kept women and ruined servant girls." The female reformers used their society to publicize the names of the male patrons at the city's brothels. Through the society's journal, *Advocate for Moral Reform*, they identified male greed and licentiousness as the causes for the fallen state of women. They blamed male businessmen for the low wages that forced some women to resort to prostitution and denounced lustful men for engaging in "a regular crusade against [our] sex."

In 1839, this attack on the sexual double standard became a national movement with the establishment of the **American Female Moral Reform Society**. With 555 affiliates throughout the evangelical heartland of the North, female activists mounted a lobbying campaign that, unlike earlier efforts, bypassed prominent men and reached out to a mass audience for signatures. By the 1840s, women secured the first state laws criminalizing seduction and adultery.

Newer women's groups formed after 1830 that focused on poverty also developed a more radical critique of American society and its male leadership. The **Boston Seamen's Aid Society**, founded in 1833 by Sarah Josepha Hale, a widow with five children, soon rejected the benevolent tradition of distinguishing between the "respectable" and the "unworthy" poor. Hale discovered that her efforts to guide poor women toward self-sufficiency flew in the face of the low wages and substandard housing that trapped her clients in poverty. She concluded in 1838 that "it is hardly possible for the hopeless poor to avoid being vicious." Hale attacked male employers for exploiting the poor. "Combinations of selfish men are formed to beat down the price of female labor," she wrote in her 1836 annual report, "and then . . . they call the diminished rate the market price."

The Appeal of Abolitionism

The rising concern of female reformers in the 1830s over the inequities of a male-controlled power structure and the injustices inflicted on women and children found its greatest expression in abolitionism. "From the beginning," noted the Boston abolitionist Lydia Maria Child in 1838, "women, by paying their money, have become members of anti-slavery societies and conventions in various free states." As Christian wives and mothers, they could identify with the plight of the black family under slavery. The most powerful abolitionist depiction of slavery showed a chained female slave imploring, "Am I not a woman and a sister?"

Women established their own antislavery societies in the 1830s as auxiliaries to the national organizations run and dominated by men. Initially, their gender-segregated role was limited to raising funds, circulating petitions, and visiting homes to gain converts. Often operating out of local churches, women were grass-roots organizers of a massive petition campaign that the abolitionists launched in the mid-1830s. Women signed more than half of the anti-

The black artist Patrick Reason made this engraving in 1835. White female abolitionists identified strongly with his image of the chained female slave.

slavery memorials sent to Congress. "There would be but few abolition petitions if the ladies . . . would let us alone," complained a Mississippi congressman.

Some antislavery women found in abolitionism a liberating message of individualism and equality that spoke to them as oppressed members of society. For these women, abolitionism was a bridge to feminism, a bold effort to make women the political and social equals of men.

Abolitionism and Women's Rights

Abolitionism emerged from the same religious impulse that energized reform throughout the North. Like other reformers, the abolitionists came predominantly from evangelical, middle-class families, particularly those of New England stock. What distinguished the abolitionists was their insistence that slavery was *the* great national sin, mocking American ideals of liberty and Christian morality.

Under the early leadership of William Lloyd Garrison, the abolitionists uncompromisingly attacked not only slaveholders but also all others whose moral apathy helped support slavery.

After provoking a storm of protest in both North and South, the abolitionist movement split in 1840. Crucial in this division was Garrison's support of women's rights. Most abolitionists broke with him and founded their own antislavery organization.

Female abolitionists took the lead in organizing a separate women's rights movement.

Rejecting Colonization

As slavery expanded westward in the early nineteenth century, most whites were convinced that emancipation would lead either to a race war or the debasement of their superior status through racial interbreeding. This paralyzing fear of general emancipation, rooted in pervasive racism, long shielded slavery from sustained attack.

In 1817, antislavery reformers from the North and South founded the **American Colonization Society**. Slaveholding politicians from the Upper South, notably Henry Clay, James Madison, and President James Monroe, were the leading organizers of the society. Gradual emancipation followed by the removal of blacks from America to Africa was the only solution that white reformers could imagine for ridding the nation of slavery and avoiding a racial bloodbath. Their goal was to make America all free and all white.

The American Colonization Society had no real chance of success. No form of emancipation, however gradual, could appeal to slave owners who could profit from the demand for their slaves in the Lower South. Blacks already free accounted for nearly all of those the society transported to its West African colony, Liberia. At the height of its popularity in the 1820s, the society colonized only fourteen hundred blacks. During that same decade, the American slave population increased by 700,000.

Free African-Americans bitterly attacked the colonizers' central assumption that free blacks were unfit to live as free citizens in America. Typical of the colonizers' racist thinking was the claim by Henry Clay in 1827 that the "free coloured" were the "most vicious" of all Americans. "Contaminated themselves, they extend their vices to all around them, to the slaves and to the whites." The annual report of the American Colonization Society in 1824 approvingly quoted a New England minister who said of the free black: "You cannot raise him from the abyss of his degradation. You may call him free . . . but you cannot bleach him into the enjoyment of freedom."

Most American blacks were native-born, and they considered themselves Americans with every right to enjoy the blessings of republican liberty. As a black petition in 1817 stated, banishment from America "would not only be cruel, but in direct violation of the principles, which have been the boast of this republic."

Organizing through their own churches in northern cities, free blacks founded some fifty aboli-

SUMMARY

TYPES OF ANTISLAVERY REFORM

Type	Definition	Example
Gradualist	Accepts notions of black inferiority and attempts to end slavery gradually by purchasing the freedom of slaves and colonizing them in Africa	American Colonization Society
Immediatist	Calls for immediate steps to end slavery and denounces slavery and racial prejudice as moral sins	Abolitionists
Political antislavery	Recognizes slavery in states where it exists but insists on keeping slavery out of the territories	Free-Soilers

tionist societies, offered refuge to fugitive slaves, and launched the first African-American newspaper in 1827, *Freedom's Journal*. David Walker, a free black who had moved from North Carolina to Massachusetts, published his *Appeal to the Colored Citizens of the World* in 1829. Rejecting colonization, Walker insisted that "America is more our country, than it is the whites' we have enriched it with our *blood and tears*," and he warned white Americans that "wo, wo, will be to you if we have to obtain our freedom by fighting."

As if in response to his call for revolutionary resistance by the enslaved, Nat Turner's Rebellion exploded in the summer of 1831 (see Chapter 13). Both alarmed and inspired by the increased tempo of black militancy, a small group of antislavery whites abandoned all illusions about colonization and embarked on a radically new approach for eradicating slavery.

Abolitionism

The leading figure in early abolitionism was William Lloyd Garrison, a Massachusetts printer, who became coeditor of an antislavery newspaper in Baltimore in 1829. Before the year was out, Garrison was arrested and convicted of criminal libel for his editorials against a Massachusetts merchant engaged in the domestic slave trade, and he spent seven weeks in jail before a wealthy New York City philanthropist paid his $100 fine. Recognizing that his lack of freedom in jail paled against that of the slave, Garrison emerged with an unquenchable hatred for slavery. Returning to Boston, he launched his own antislavery newspaper, **The Liberator**, in 1831. A year later, he was instrumental in founding the New England Anti-Slavery Society.

As militant as the free blacks who comprised the bulk of the early subscribers to *The Liberator*, Garrison thundered, "If we would not see our land deluged in blood, we must instantly burst asunder the shackles of the slaves." He committed abolitionism to the twin goals of immediatism—an immediate moral commitment to end slavery—and racial equality. Only by striving toward these goals, he insisted, could white America ever hope to end slavery without massive violence.

The demand of the abolitionists for the legal equality of blacks was as unsettling to public opinion as their call for immediate, uncompensated emancipation. Discriminatory laws, aptly described by abolitionist Lydia Maria Child as "this legalized contempt of color," restricted the political and civil liberties of free blacks in every state. Denied the vote outside New England, segregated in all public facilities, prohibited from moving into several western states, and excluded from most jobs save menial labor, free blacks everywhere were walled off as an inferior caste unfit for equality (see "American Views: Appeal of a Female Abolitionist").

Garrison was harsh and uncompromising in denouncing slavery and advocating black rights. But without the organizational and financial resources of a national society, the message of the early Garrisonians rarely extended beyond free black communities in the North. The success of British abolitionists in 1833 when gradual, compensated emancipation was enacted for Britain's West Indian colonies, inspired white and black abolitionists to gather at Philadelphia in December 1833 and form the **American Anti-Slavery Society**.

Arthur and Lewis Tappan, two wealthy merchants from New York City, provided financial backing, and Theodore Dwight Weld, a young evangelical minister, fused abolitionism with the moral passion of religious revivalism. Weld brought abolitionism to the

American Views

APPEAL OF A FEMALE ABOLITIONIST

Lydia Maria Child's *Appeal*, published in Boston in 1833, was a landmark in abolitionist literature for both the thoroughness of its attack on slavery and its refutation of racist ideology and discrimination. This condemnation of racial prejudice was the most radical feature of abolitionist ideology. It directly challenged the deeply held beliefs and assumptions of nearly all white Americans, in the North as well as the South. Racism and slavery, as Child shows in this excerpt from her *Appeal*, fed off one another in the national curse of slavery.

❖ **How does Child argue that northern whites must bear some of the responsibility for perpetuating slavery?**

❖ **What arguments does Child make against racial discrimination in northern society?**

❖ **What did Child mean when she wrote that "the Americans are peculiarly responsible for the example they give"? Do you agree with her?**

❖ **How does Child deal with the charge that the abolitionists threatened the preservation of the Union?**

While we bestow our earnest disapprobation on the system of slavery, let us not flatter ourselves that we are in reality any better than our brethren of the South. Thanks to our soil and climate, and the early exhortations of the Quakers, the *form* of slavery does not exist among us; but the very *spirit* of the hateful and mischievous thing is here in all its strength. . . . Our prejudice against colored people is even more inveterate than it is at the South. The planter is often attached to his negroes, and lavishes caresses and kind words upon them, as he would on a favorite hound: but our cold-hearted, ignoble prejudice admits of no exception—no intermission.

The Southerners have long continued habit, apparent interest and dreaded danger, to palliate the wrong they do; but we stand without excuse. . . . If the free States wished to cherish the system of slavery forever, they could not take a more direct course than they now do. Those who are kind and liberal on all other subjects, unite with the selfish and the proud in their unrelenting efforts to keep the colored population in the lowest state of degradation; and the influence they unconsciously exert over children early infuses into their innocent minds the same strong feelings of contempt. . . .

The state of public feeling not only makes it difficult for the Africans to obtain information, but it prevents them from making profitable use of what knowledge they have. A colored man, how-

West in 1834 with the revivals he preached at Lane Theological Seminary in Cincinnati. The "Lane rebels," students gathered by Weld, fanned out as itinerant agents to seek converts for abolitionism throughout the Yankee districts of the rural North. Weld's *American Slavery as It Is: Testimony of a Thousand Witnesses*, a massively documented indictment of slavery, became a best-seller in 1839. Abolitionist women, notably Angelina Grimké, Weld's wife and the daughter of a South Carolina planter, contributed much of the research.

Revivalistic exhortations were just one of the techniques the abolitionists exploited to mobilize public opinion against slavery. They spread their message through rallies, paid lecturers, children's games and toys, and the printed word. Drawing on the experience of reformers in Bible and tract societies, the abolitionists harnessed steam printing to the cause ever intelligent, is not allowed to pursue any business more lucrative than that of a barber, a shoe-black, or waiter. These, and all other employments, are truly respectable, whenever the duties connected with them are faithfully performed; but it is unjust that a man should, on account of his complexion, be prevented from performing more elevated uses in society. Every citizen ought to have a fair chance to try his fortune in any line of business, which he thinks he has ability to transact. Why should not colored men be employed in the manufactories of various kinds? If their ignorance is an objection, let them be enlightened, as speedily as possible. If their moral character is not sufficiently pure, remove the pressure of public scorn, and thus supply them with motives for being respectable. All this can be done. It merely requires an earnest wish to overcome a prejudice, which . . . is in fact opposed to the spirit of our religion, and contrary to the instinctive good feelings of our nature. . . . When the majority heartily desire a change, it is effected, be the difficulties what they may. The Americans are peculiarly responsible for the example they give; for in no other country does the unchecked voice of the people constitute the whole of government. . . .

The strongest and best reason that can be given for our supineness on the subject of slavery, is the fear of dissolving the Union. The Constitution of the United States demands our highest reverence. . . . But we must not forget that the Constitution provides for any change that may be required for the general good. The great machine is constructed with a safety valve, by which any rapidly increasing evil may be expelled whenever the people desire it.

If the Southern politicians are determined to make a Siamese question of this also—if they insist that the Union shall not exist without slavery—it can only be said that they join two things, which have no affinity with each other, and which cannot permanently exist together. —They chain the living and vigorous to the diseased and dying; and the former will assuredly perish in the infected neighborhood.

The universal introduction of free labor is the surest way to consolidate the Union, and enable us to live together in harmony and peace. If a history is ever written entitled "The Decay and Dissolution of the North American Republic," its author will distinctly trace our downfall to the existence of slavery among us.

Source: *Lydia Maria Child*, An Appeal in Favor of That Class of Americans Called Africans, *ed. Carolyn L. Karcher (1996).*

of moral suasion. They distributed millions of anti-slavery tracts, and by the late 1830s, abolitionist sayings appeared on posters, emblems, song sheets, and even candy wrappers.

To break through that white apathy and change public opinion, the abolitionists described slavery in horrific terms of absolute moral and physical degradation. By 1840, nearly 200,000 Northerners belonged to two thousand local affiliates of the American Anti-Slavery Society. Most whites, however, remained unmoved, and some violently opposed the abolitionists.

Antiabolitionist mobs in the North went on a rampage in the mid-1830s. They disrupted antislavery meetings, beat and stoned speakers, destroyed printing presses, burned the homes of the wealthy benefactors of the movement, and vandalized free black neighborhoods in a wave of terror that drove blacks from several northern cities. Although Garrison and Weld, the most frequent targets of mob violence, escaped with their lives, Elijah P. Lovejoy, an abolitionist editor in Illinois, was killed by a mob in 1837. Local elites, especially those with profitable ties to the slave economy of the South, often incited the mobs, whose fury expressed the anxieties of semiskilled and common laborers that they might lose their jobs if freed slaves moved north.

In the South, the hostility to abolitionism took the form of burning and censoring antislavery literature, offering rewards for the capture of leading abolitionists to stand trial for inciting slave revolts, and tightening up slave codes and the surveillance of free blacks. Meanwhile, Democrats in Congress yielded to slaveholding interests in 1836 by passing a gag rule that automatically tabled antislavery petitions.

In 1838, Garrison helped found the **New England Non-Resistant Society,** dedicated to the belief that a complete moral regeneration, based on renouncing force in all human relationships, was necessary if America were ever to live up to its Christian and republican ideals. The Garrisonian nonresistants rejected all coercive authority, whether expressed in human bondage, clerical support of slavery, male dominance in the patriarchical family, the racial oppression of blacks, or the police power of government. The logic of their stand as Christian **anarchists** drove them to denounce all formal political activities and even the legitimacy of the Union, based as it was on a pact with slaveholders.

Garrison's support for the growing demand of antislavery women to be treated as equals in the movement brought the factional bickering to a head in 1840 and split the American Anti-Slavery Society. In turn, the opposition of most male abolitionists to the public activities of their female counterparts provoked a militant faction of these women into founding their own movement to achieve equality in American society.

The Women's Rights Movement

Feminism grew out of abolitionism because of the parallels many women drew between the exploited lives of the slaves and their own subordinate status in northern society. Considered biologically inferior to men, women were denied the vote, deprived of property or control of any wages after marriage, and barred from most occupations and advanced education. "In striving to cut [the slave's] irons off, we found most surely that *we* were manacled *ourselves*," argued Abby Kelley, a Quaker abolitionist.

In 1837, Angelina and Sarah Grimké, South Carolinians born into the planter aristocracy, attracted large crowds of men and women to their antislavery lectures in New England. The Grimké sisters had moved north because of their opposition to slavery and had become Quakers. But by publicly lecturing to a "promiscuous" (mixed) audience of men and women, they defied restrictions on women's proper role and enraged the Congregational clergy of Massachusetts. Harshly criticized for their unwomanly behavior, the Grimkés publicly responded with an indictment of the male patriarchy and the shocking assertion that "men and women are *created equal*! They are both moral and accountable beings and whatever is right for man to do is right for woman."

Antislavery women now demanded an equal voice in the abolitionist movement. Despite strong opposition from many of his fellow male abolitionists, Garrison helped Abby Kelley win a seat on the business committee of the American Anti-Slavery Society at its convention in 1840. The anti-Garrisonians walked out of the convention and formed a separate organization in 1840, the **American and Foreign Anti-Slavery Society.**

What was rapidly becoming known as the "woman question" also disrupted the 1840 World Anti-Slavery Convention in London. The refusal of the convention to seat the American female delegates was the final indignity that transformed the discontent of women into a self-conscious movement for women's equality. Two of the excluded delegates, Lucretia Mott and Elizabeth Cady Stanton, vowed to build an organization to "speak out for *oppressed* women."

Their work went slowly. Early feminists were dependent on the abolitionists for most of their followers. Many women sympathetic to the feminist movement held back lest they be shunned in their communities. A minister's wife in Portsmouth, New Hampshire, spoke for many of these women when she wrote to a feminist friend, "There are but few here who think of women as anything more than slave or a plaything, and they think I am different from most women."

In 1848, Stanton and Mott were finally able to call the first national convention ever devoted to women's rights at Seneca Falls, in upstate New York. The **Seneca Falls Convention** issued the **Declaration of Sentiments**, a call for full female equality. It identified male patriarchy as the source of women's oppression and demanded the vote for women as a sacred and inalienable right of republican citizenship.

The Seneca Falls agenda defined the goals of the women's movement for the rest of the century.

The call for the vote met the stiffest opposition. The feminists' few successes before the Civil War came in economic rights. By 1860, fourteen states had granted women greater control over their property and wages—most significantly under New York's Married Women's Property Act of 1860. Largely the result of the intense lobbying of Susan B. Anthony, the act established women's legal right to their own wage income and to sue fathers and husbands who tried to deprive them of their wages.

The feminist movement did not attract broad support. Most women found in the doctrine of separate spheres a reassuring feminine identity that they could express either at home or in benevolent and reform societies. Within the reform movement as a whole, women's rights were always of minor concern.

Political Antislavery

Most abolitionists who had broken with Garrison in 1840 believed that emancipation could best be achieved by moving abolitionism into the mainstream of American politics. Political abolitionism had its roots in the petition campaign of the late 1830s. Congressional efforts to suppress the discussion of slavery backfired when John Quincy Adams, the former president who had become a Massachusetts congressman, resorted to an unending series of parliamentary ploys to get around the gag rule. A failure as president, Adams became a hero to antislavery Northerners, a champion of the constitutional right to petition Congress for redress of grievances. Northern whites who had shown no interest in abolitionism as a moral crusade for blacks now began to take a stand against slavery when the issue involved the civil liberties of whites and the overwhelming political power of the South. By the hundreds of thousands, they signed abolitionist petitions in 1837 and 1838 to protest the gag rule and block the admission of Texas as a slave state.

In 1840, anti-Garrison abolitionists tried to turn this new antislavery constituency into an independent political party. They formed the **Liberty party** and ran for the presidency James G. Birney. Birney who failed to draw even 1 percent of the total popular vote, but antislavery districts elected several antislavery congressmen.

The Liberty party condemned racial discrimination in the North, as well as slavery in the South, and won the support of most black abolitionists. "To it," recalled Samuel Ward of New York, "I devoted my political activities; with it I lived my political life." In 1843, a national African-American convention in Buffalo endorsed the Liberty party.

After escaping to freedom in 1838, Frederick Douglass became a commanding figure in the abolitionist movement. His speeches denouncing slavery were fiery and eloquent.

Frederick Douglass was the black abolitionists' most dynamic spokesman. After escaping from slavery in 1838, Douglass became a spellbinding lecturer for abolitionism and in 1845 published his classic autobiography, *Narrative of the Life of Frederick Douglass, an American Slave*. Increasingly dissatisfied with Garrison's Christian pacifism and his stand against political action, Douglass broke with Garrison in 1847 and founded a black abolitionist newspaper, **The North Star**. The break became irreparable in 1851 when Douglass publicly denied the Garrisonian position that the Constitution was a proslavery document. If properly interpreted, Douglass insisted, "the Constitution is a *glorious liberty document*," and he called for a political war against slavery.

That war had started in the 1840s with the Liberty party. Although the party elected only one of its candidates to Congress (Gerrit Smith of New York), it kept slavery in the limelight of national politics. Led by Joshua R. Giddings, a small but vocal bloc of antislavery politicians began to popularize the frightening concept of "the **Slave Power**"—a vast conspiracy of planters and their northern lackeys that had seized control of the federal government and

CHRONOLOGY

1846 Wilmot Proviso is submitted to Congress but is defeated.

1848 Gold is discovered in California.

Whig party candidate Zachary Taylor defeats Democrat Lewis Cass and Free-Soiler Martin Van Buren for the presidency.

1850 California applies for statehood.

President Taylor dies; Vice President Millard Fillmore succeeds him.

Compromise of 1850 is passed.

1851 Harriet Beecher Stowe publishes *Uncle Tom's Cabin*.

1852 Democrat Franklin Pierce is elected president in a landslide over Whig candidate Winfield Scott.

Whig party disintegrates.

1853 National Black Convention called in Rochester, New York, to demand repeal of the Fugitive Slave Act.

1854 Ostend Manifesto is issued.

Kansas-Nebraska Act repeals the Missouri Compromise.

Know-Nothing and Republican parties are formed.

1855 Civil war erupts in "Bleeding Kansas."

William Walker attempts a takeover of Nicaragua.

1856 "Sack of Lawrence" occurs in Kansas; John Brown makes a retaliatory raid at Pottawatomie Creek.

Democratic congressman Preston Brooks of South Carolina canes Massachusetts senator Charles Sumner in the U.S. Senate.

Democrat James Buchanan is elected president over Republican John C. Frémont and American (Know-Nothing) candidate Millard Fillmore.

1857 Supreme Court issues *Dred Scott* decision.

Kansas territorial legislature passes the proslavery Lecompton Constitution.

Panic of 1857 begins.

Hinton Rowan Helper publishes *The Impending Crisis*.

1858 Senatorial candidates Abraham Lincoln and Stephen A. Douglas hold series of debates in Illinois.

1859 John Brown's Raid fails at Harpers Ferry, Virginia.

1860 Constitutional Union party forms.

Democratic party divides into northern and southern factions.

Republican candidate Abraham Lincoln is elected president over southern Democratic candidate John C. Breckinridge, northern Democratic candidate Stephen A. Douglas, and Constitutional Unionist candidate John Bell.

South Carolina secedes from the Union.

1861 The rest of the Lower South secedes from the Union.

Crittenden Plan and Tyler's Washington peace conference fail.

Jefferson Davis assumes presidency of the Confederate States of America.

Lincoln is inaugurated.

Fort Sumter is bombarded; Civil War begins.

Several Upper South states secede.

---

troversy, and they selected their presidential candidates accordingly. The Democrats nominated Michigan senator Lewis Cass, a veteran party stalwart whose public career stretched back to the War of 1812. Cass understood the destructive potential of the slavery issue and suggested that territorial residents, not Congress, should decide slavery's fate. This solution, **popular sovereignty**, had a do-it-yourself charm: Keep the politicians out of it and let the people decide. Cass was deliberately ambiguous, however, on *when* the people should decide. If residents could decide only when applying for statehood, slavery would be legal up to that point. The ambiguity aroused more fears than it allayed.

The Whigs were silent on the slavery issue. Reverting to their winning 1840 formula of nominating a war hero, they selected General Zachary Taylor of Mexican War fame. Taylor belonged to no party and had never voted. He was also inarticulate to the point of unintended humor. If one had to guess his views, it may have been significant that he lived in Louisiana in the Lower South, owned a one-hundred-slave plantation, and he was related by marriage to Jefferson Davis, currently Mississippi's staunch proslavery senator.

Taylor's background disturbed many antislavery northern Whigs. These **Conscience Whigs** along with remnants of the old Liberty party and a scattering of northern Democrats bolted their parties and formed the **Free-Soil party**. Its slogan—"Free soil, free speech, free labor, free men"—was a catalog of white liberties that the South had allegedly violated. The Free-Soilers nominated former president Martin Van Buren, the old New Yorker, who had little hope of winning but might cause the election to be thrown into the House of Representatives. Van Buren ran strongly enough in eleven of the fifteen northern states to deny the winning candidate in those states a majority of the votes cast, but he could not overcome Taylor's strength in the South. Taylor was elected, giving the nation its first president from the Lower South.

The Compromise of 1850

Taylor had little time to savor his victory. Gold had been discovered in California in January 1848, and in little more than a year, eighty thousand people, most of them from the North, had rushed into the territory. These **Forty-Niners**, as they were called, included free blacks as well as slaves brought into the gold fields by their southern masters. Open hostility flared between white prospectors and their black competitors. When the territory's new residents began asking for statehood and drafted a state constitution, the document contained no provision for slavery. "Free" in the context of territorial politics became a synonym for "whites only."

If Congress accepted the residents' request for statehood, California would enter the Union as a free state, tipping the balance between the fifteen free and fifteen slave states in the Senate. New Mexico (which then included most of present-day New Mexico, Arizona, small parts of Nevada, and Colorado) appeared poised to follow suit and enter the Union as the seventeenth free state. Southerners saw their political power slipping away.

When Congress confronted the issue of California statehood in December 1849, partisans on both sides began marshaling forces for what promised to be a long and bitter struggle. South Carolina senator John C. Calhoun understood that only a politically unified South could protect its interests. Calhoun and his Democratic party supporters in the South issued a call for a southern convention in Nashville for June 1850. The implication was clear: If Congress did not resolve the California statehood issue to the South's satisfaction, some southern leaders were prepared for secession.

On the other side, the supporters of the Wilmot Proviso hoped to build a northern coalition dedicated to excluding slavery from the territories and reducing southern political power. Some hoped to go further and spark a liberation movement in the South.

No one, at first, knew where Taylor stood. Later it became apparent that he favored allowing California and the other territories acquired from Mexico to decide the slavery issue for themselves. Since California already easily exceeded the population threshold for statehood, Taylor proposed bypassing the territorial stage—and congressional involvement in it—and having California and New Mexico admitted as states directly. The result would be to bring both into the Union as free states. Taylor did not oppose slavery, but he abhorred the slavery issue because it threatened his vision of a continental empire. He was thus willing to forgo the extension of slavery into the territories. "Whatever dangers may threaten [the Union] I shall stand by it and maintain it in its integrity."

Southerners resisted Taylor's plan, and Congress deadlocked on the territorial issue. Henry Clay then stepped forward with his last great compromise. To break the impasse, Clay urged that Congress should take four steps:

❖ Admit California as a free state, as its residents clearly preferred

❖ Allow the residents of the New Mexico and Utah territories to decide the slavery issue for themselves too

❖ End the slave trade in the District of Columbia

❖ Pass a new fugitive slave law to enforce the constitutional provision stating that a person "held to Service or Labor in one state . . . escaping into another . . . shall be delivered upon Claim of the party to whom such Service or Labor may be due."

Clay's proposal provoked a historic Senate debate in February 1850, featuring America's three most prominent elder statesmen—Clay, Calhoun, and Daniel Webster, all of whom would be dead in the next two years. After a tumultuous six-month debate that lasted into the summer of 1850, the Senate rejected the compromise. President Taylor, who had vowed to veto any compromise, died unexpectedly of a stomach ailment after overindulging in cherries and milk in the hot sun at a July 4 celebration in Washington. Vice President Millard Fillmore, a pro-Clay New Yorker, assumed the presidency after Taylor's death. A back-room man, quiet, at home with the cigar-and-brandy crowd, and effective with the deal, Fillmore let it be known that he favored Clay's package and would sign it if passed.

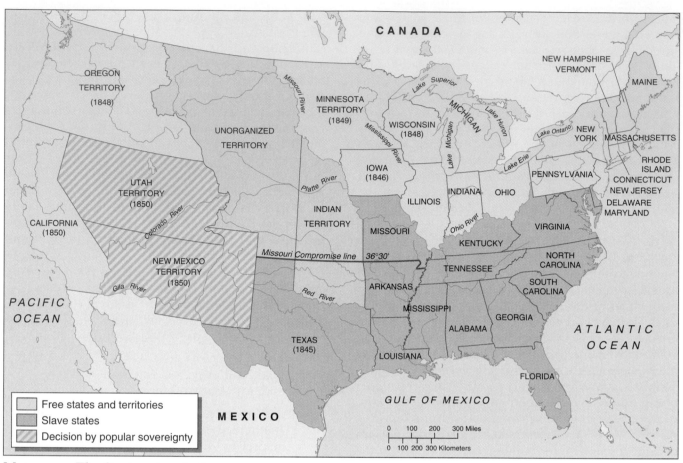

Map 15-1   The Compromise of 1850
Given the unlikely prospect that any of the western territories would opt for slavery, the compromise sealed the South's minority status in the Union.

Although the Senate had rejected the compromise, Illinois senator Stephen A. Douglas kept it alive. A small man with a large head that made him mushroomlike in appearance, Douglas epitomized the promise of American life for men of his generation. He envisioned an urban, industrial West linked to the East by a vast railroad network eventually extending to the Pacific. Like Webster, Douglas feared for the Union if the compromise failed. Realizing that it would never pass as a package, he proposed to break it up into its components and hold a separate vote on each. With a handful of senators voting for all parts, and with different sectional blocs supporting one provision or another, Douglas engineered a majority for the compromise, and Fillmore signed it (see Map 15-1).

The **Compromise of 1850** was not a compromise in the sense of opposing sides consenting to certain terms desired by the other. Southern leaders looked to the West and saw no slave territories awaiting statehood. They gained the **Fugitive Slave Act**, which reinforced their right to seize and return to bondage slaves who had fled to free territory, but it was slight consolation for few slave owners from the Lower South would bear the expense and uncertainty of chasing an escaped slave into free territory. And the North's hostile reception to the law made Southerners doubt their commitment to the compromise.

Response to the Fugitive Slave Act

The effect of the Fugitive Slave Act on public opinion, however, was to polarize North and South even further. The strongest reaction to the act was in the black communities of the urban North. Previously, black abolitionists in the North had focused on freeing slaves in the South. The Fugitive Slave Act brought the danger of slavery much closer to home. Northern blacks formed associations to protect each other and repel—violently, if necessary—any attempt to capture and reenslave fellow blacks. Boston's black leaders created the **League of Freedom**. Chicago blacks organized the **Liberty Association**, with teams assigned to "patrol the city, spying for possible slave-hunters." Similar associations appeared in Cleveland and Cincinnati. Black leader Frederick Douglass, an escaped slave himself, explained the need for such organizations: "We must be prepared . . . to see the streets . . . running with blood . . . should this law be put into operation."

During the early 1850s, blacks across the North gathered in conventions to demand the repeal of the Fugitive Slave Act. Frederick Douglass convened the **National Black Convention** in Rochester, New York, in July 1853, at which he established a national council of black leaders to address issues of political and civil rights. Although the council was short-lived, it reflected a growing militancy among northern blacks.

How much of this militancy filtered down to slaves in the South is difficult to say. Slaveholders noted an increase in black resistance during the early 1850s. A white Virginian observed in 1852 that "it is useless to disguise the fact, that a greater degree of insubordination has been manifested by the negro population within the last few months, than at any previous period in our history as a state."

Uncle Tom's Cabin

Sectional controversy over the Fugitive Slave Act was relatively modest compared to the firestorm abolitionist writer Harriet Beecher Stowe ignited with the publication of a novel about southern slavery. *Uncle Tom's Cabin*, which first appeared in serial form in 1851, moved many northern whites from the sidelines of the sectional conflict to more active participation.

Stowe was the daughter of Lyman Beecher, a prominent evangelical reformer, and an active opponent of slavery. What first drew Harriet Beecher Stowe to the subject of slavery was her concern about its impact on family life in the South. It was not until the passage of the Fugitive Slave Act that abolition became a major focus in her life. Even then, her views on blacks remained ambivalent. She did not, like William Lloyd Garrison, advocate racial equality. She supported abolition, but she also believed America should be a white person's country, and favored repatriating the blacks to Africa. Slavery was an abstract concept to most white Northerners. Stowe's challenge was to personalize it in a way that would make them see it as an institution that not just oppressed blacks but destroyed families and debased well-meaning Christian masters as well.

At the beginning of *Uncle Tom's Cabin*, a Kentucky slave owner is reluctantly forced by financial ruin to sell some of his slaves. Among them are the

Harriet Beecher Stowe, the daughter of a prominent Northern evangelist, catapulted to international fame with the publication of Uncle Tom's Cabin. *The novel helped raise the debate over slavery from a political to a moral level.*

son of two mulatto slaves, George and Eliza Harris, and an older slave, Tom. Eliza escapes across the ice-choked Ohio River, clutching her son to her breast as slavecatchers and their bloodhounds pursue them. Tom submits to sale to a New Orleans master. When that master dies, Tom is sold to Simon Legree, a Vermonter who owns a plantation on the Red River in Louisiana. Legree is vicious and sadistic—the only major slaveholding character in the book whom Stowe portrays in this manner. Tom, a devout Christian, remains loyal and obedient until Legree asks him to whip another slave. When Tom refuses, Legree beats him to death.

Stowe offered not abstractions but characters who seemed real. She aimed to evoke strong emotions in the reader. The broken family, the denial of freedom, and the Christian martyr were emotional themes. The presence of mulattoes in the book testified to widespread interracial and extramarital sex, which Northerners, then in the midst of a religious revival, viewed as an abhorrent sin destructive to family life. And the depiction of southern masters struggling unsuccessfully with their consciences focused public attention on how slavery subverted Christianity.

Uncle Tom's Cabin created a sensation in the United States and abroad. By the time of the Civil War, the book had sold an unprecedented 3 million copies in the United States and tens of thousands more in Europe. Stowe's book gave slavery a face. Northern blacks embraced Uncle Tom's Cabin. Frederick Douglass's National Black Convention resolved that the book was "a work plainly marked by the finger of God" on behalf of black people. Some blacks hoped that the popularity of Uncle Tom's Cabin would highlight the hypocrisy of northern whites who were quick to perceive evil in the South but were often blind to discrimination against African-Americans in the North. For Southerners, Uncle Tom's Cabin was a damnable lie, a political tract disguised as literature.

The Election of 1852

While the nation read and reacted to Uncle Tom's Cabin, a presidential election campaign took place. The Compromise of 1850 had divided the Whigs deeply. The Democratic party entered the campaign more united. Despite reservations, both northern and southern wings of the party announced their support for the Compromise of 1850. Southern Democrats viewed the party's nominee, Franklin Pierce of New Hampshire, as safe on the slavery issue despite his New England heritage. Pierce satisfied Northerners as a nationalist devoted to the idea of Manifest Destiny. He belonged to **Young America**, a mostly Democratic group that advocated extending American influence into Central and South America and the Caribbean with an aggressive foreign policy. His service in the Mexican War and his good looks and charm won over doubters from both sections, winning him the election.

But Pierce's landslide victory could not obscure the deep fissures in the American party system. The Whigs were ultimately finished as a national party. And the Democrats, despite their electoral success, emerged frayed from the election. In the Lower South, conflicts within the party between supporters and opponents of the Compromise of 1850 had overshadowed the contests between Democrats and Whigs.

As Franklin Pierce took office in March 1853, it seemed that the only thing holding Democrats together was the thirst for political patronage. The low voter turnout in the 1852 election—Whig participation declined by 10 percent and Democratic participation by 17 percent, mostly in the Lower South—reflected public apathy and disgust at the prevailing party system. As the slavery issue confronted the nation with the most serious challenge it had faced since its inception, American voters were losing faith in their parties' ability to govern and in each other.

Political Realignment

Franklin Pierce, only 48 when he took office, was one of the youngest presidents in American history. He hoped to duck the slavery issue by focusing on Young America's dreams of empire. Americans were still susceptible to nationalist fervor. For all their sectional, religious, ethnic, and racial differences, they shared a common language and political institutions. New technologies like the railroad and the telegraph were working to bind them together physically as well. As Florida senator Stephen R. Mallory claimed, "It is no more possible for this country to pause in its career, than for the free and untrammeled eagle to cease to soar." But President Pierce's attempts to forge national sentiment around an aggressive foreign policy failed. And his administration's inept handling of a new territorial controversy in Kansas forced him to confront the slavery debate.

No matter what policies a president pursued, Congress and the American people interpreted them in the light of their impact, real or potential, on slavery. The issue, said Missouri Senator Thomas Hart Benton, was like the plague of frogs that God had inflicted on the Egyptians to convince them to release the Hebrews from bondage. So it was with "this black question, forever on the table, on the nuptial couch, everywhere!"

Franklin Pierce lacked the skilled leadership the times demanded. Troubled by alcoholism, worried about his chronically ill wife, and grief-stricken over the death of three young sons, Pierce presided weakly over the nation and increasingly deferred to proslavery interests in his policies.

Young America's Foreign Misadventures

Pierce's first missteps occurred in pursuit of Young America's foreign ambitions. The administration turned a greedy eye toward Spanish-ruled Cuba, just 90 miles off the coast of Florida. Southerners supported an aggressive Cuba policy, seeing the island as a possible new slave state. And nationalists saw great virtue in replacing what they perceived as a despotic colonial regime with a democratic government under the guidance of the United States.

In October 1854, three American diplomats met in Ostend, Belgium, to compose a document on Cuba called the **Ostend Manifesto** that claimed that the island belonged "naturally to the great family of states of which the Union is the Providential Nursery." The implication was that if Spain wouldn't sell, the United States could wrest control of Cuba. The Ostend Manifesto caused an uproar and embarrassed the Pierce administration when it became public. In the polite world of nineteenth-century diplomacy, it was a significant breach of etiquette. It also provoked a reaction in the United States, raising suspicions in the North that the South was willing to provoke a war with Spain to expand the number of slaveholding states. The Franklin administration also suffered from the greedy and ultimately unsuccessful exploits of self-styled "General" William Walker, who invaded Mexican-owned Baja California and later temporarily gained control of Nicaragua.

Stephen Douglas's Railroad Proposal

As Pierce was fumbling in foreign policy, Senator Stephen A. Douglas of Illinois was developing another national project that promised to draw the country together—the construction of a transcontinental railroad and the settling of the land it traversed. Douglas had in mind a transcontinental route extending westward from Chicago through the Nebraska Territory. Unfortunately for his plans, Indians already occupied this region, many of them on land the U.S. government had set aside as Indian Territory and barred to white settlement. Once again, and not for the last time, the federal government responded by reneging on earlier promises and forcing Indians to move. With the Indian "obstacle" removed, Douglas sought congressional approval to establish a government for the Nebraska Territory. As he predicted, the new bill did "raise a hell of a storm."

The Kansas-Nebraska Act

Douglas's Kansas-Nebraska Bill split the Nebraska Territory into two territories, Kansas and Nebraska, with the implicit understanding that Kansas would become a slave state and Nebraska a free state. Consistent with Douglas's belief in popular sovereignty, it left the actual decision on slavery to the residents of the territories. But because it allowed Southerners to bring slaves into an area formerly closed to slavery, it repealed the Missouri Compromise.

Northerners of all parties were outraged, using language indicative of the way religious and conspiratorial imagery had infected political debate. Transforming it into a contest of good against evil, of liberty against oppression, they said it was "a gross violation of a sacred pledge," "a criminal betrayal of precious rights," and "part and parcel of an atrocious plot" to make a free territory a "dreary region of despotism, inhabited by masters and slaves." President Pierce, however, backed the bill, assuring the support of enough northern Democrats to secure it a narrow margin of victory. The **Kansas-Nebraska Act** was law, but dissatisfaction with it continued to fester.

In August 1854, shortly after Congress adjourned, Douglas left Washington for his home in Chicago, to rest and mend political fences. He did not enjoy a pleasant journey home. "I could travel," he later recalled, ". . . by the light of my own effigy on every tree we passed." Arriving in Chicago, he addressed a large, hostile crowd outside his hotel balcony. As he departed, he lost his temper and blurted, "It is now Sunday morning. I'll go to church; you can go to hell."

"Bleeding Kansas"

Because of its fertile soil, favorable climate, and location adjacent to the slave state of Missouri, Kansas was the most likely of the new territories to support slavery. As a result, both Southerners and antislavery Northerners began an intensive drive to recruit settlers and establish a majority there.

After much legislative maneuvering by both sides, a sporadic civil war erupted in Kansas in November 1855 and reached a climax in the spring of 1856. Journalists dubbed the conflict "**Bleeding Kansas**," for it was characterized by an unprecedented level of personal hatred and hostility including a proslavery attack on the town of Lawrence, which the Northern press inflated into the "**sack of Lawrence**" and a bloody retaliatory raid by antislavery agitator John Brown.

Know-Nothings and Republicans

From 1854 to 1856, Northerners moved into new political parties that altered the national political landscape and sharpened sectional conflict. Although the slavery issue was mainly responsible for party realignment in the North, other factors played a role as well. Nearly 3.5 million immigrants entered the United States between 1848 and 1860, the greatest influx in American history in proportion to the total population. Some of these newcomers, especially the Germans, were escaping failed democratic revolutions in Europe. They were predominantly middle-class Protestants who, along with fewer German Catholics and Jews, settled mostly in the cities, where they established shops and other businesses. More than 1 million of the immigrants, however, were poor Irish Roman Catholics fleeing their homeland to avoid starvation.

The Irish immigrants made their homes in northern cities, at the time in the midst of Protestant revivals and reform. They also competed for jobs with native-born Protestant workers. Because the Irish would work for lower wages, the job competition bred animosity and sometimes violence. But it was their Roman Catholic religion that most concerned some urban Protestants. Democrats wooed the Irish newcomers. The champions of individual rights against intrusive government and meddling reformers, they supported the strict separation of church and state. Evangelical Protestants, especially those who were not Democrats, took a different view.

New parties emerged from this cauldron of religious, ethnic, and sectional strife. Anti-immigrant, anti-Catholic sentiment gave rise to the **Know-Nothing party**, which began as a secret organization in July 1854. Its name derived from the reply that members gave when asked about the party: "I know nothing." In addition to their biases against Catholics and foreigners, the Know-Nothings shared a fear that the slavery issue could destroy the Union. Know-Nothing candidates fared surprisingly well in local and congressional elections during the fall of 1854, carrying 63 percent of the statewide vote in Massachusetts and making strong showings in New York and Pennsylvania. In office, Know-Nothings achieved some notable reforms. In Massachusetts, where they pursued an agenda similar to that of the Whigs in earlier years, they secured administrative reforms and supported public health and public education programs.

The Know-Nothings' anti-Catholicism, however, overshadowed their reform agenda. Ethnic and religious bigotry were weak links to hold together a national party. Southern and northern Know-Nothings soon fell to quarreling among themselves over slavery, despite their vow to avoid it, and the party split. Many northern Know-Nothings soon found a congenial home in the new **Republican party**.

The Republican party formed in the summer of 1854 from a coalition of antislavery Conscience Whigs and Democrats disgusted with the Pierce administration's Kansas policy. The Republicans supported many of the same kinds of reforms as the Know-Nothings, and like them, the Republicans also supported strong state and national governments to promote those reforms. The overriding bond among Republicans was their opposition to the extension of slavery in the territories. Unlike the Know-Nothings, the Republicans confronted the slavery issue head on.

Reflecting its opposition to slavery, the Republican party was an antisouthern sectional party. The overwhelming majority of its members were Northerners. Northern Whig merchants and entrepreneurs who joined the party were impatient with southern obstruction in Congress of federal programs for economic development, such as a transcontinental railroad, harbor and river improvements, and high tariffs to protect American industries (located mostly in the North) from foreign competition. In a bid to keep slavery out of the territories, the Republicans favored limiting homesteads in the West to 160 acres. Not incidentally, populating the territories with northern whites would ensure a western base for the new party.

The Republicans found strong backing in Horace Greeley's *New York Tribune*. Greeley, a New Englander who arrived in New York in 1831, had emerged by the mid-1840s as one of the nation's most influential journalists. He was convinced that a society founded on free white labor had made his success possible, and he attacked the South at every opportunity. New York was the nation's financial and commercial center and controlled its lines of communication.

Heightened sectional animosity laced with religious and ethnic prejudice fueled the emergence of new parties and the weakening of old political affiliations in the early 1850s and the Republican party was becoming an important political force in the North and, to Southerners, the embodiment of evil.

The Election of 1856

The presidential election of 1856 proved one of the strangest in American history. The Know-Nothings and the Republicans faced a national electorate for the first time. The Democrats were deeply divided over the Kansas issue. Rejecting both Pierce and Douglas, they turned instead to a longtime insider, James Buchanan, whose major asset was that he had been absent from the country the previous three years as ambassador to Great Britain and was thus untainted by the Kansas controversy. The Republicans passed over their most likely candidate, the New York senator and former Whig William H. Seward. Instead, they followed a tried-and-true Whig precedent and nominated a military hero, John C. Frémont, a handsome, dark-haired soldier of medium height and medium intelligence. His wife, Jessie Benton, the daughter of Missouri senator Thomas Hart Benton, was his greatest asset. In effect, she ran the campaign and wisely encouraged her husband to remain silent.

Openly reviling what they called the "Black Republican party," Southerners threatened disunion if Frémont won. Buchanan claimed to be the only national candidate on the ballot. Voters agreed, for Buchanan bested Frémont in the North and Fillmore in the South to win the presidency.

The overall result pleased Southerners, but the details left them uncomfortable. Buchanan won by carrying every southern state and the Lower North—Pennsylvania, New Jersey, Illinois, Indiana, and California. But Frémont, a political novice running on his party's first national ticket, carried eleven free states, and the rest he lost by scant margins to Buchanan. It was a remarkable showing for a two-year-old party. In the South and border states, Fillmore managed more than 40 percent of the vote and carried Maryland, despite bearing the standard of a fragmented party.

Buchanan, who brought more than a generation of political experience to the presidency, would need every bit and more. He had scarcely settled into office when two major crises confronted him: a Supreme Court decision that challenged the right of Congress to regulate slavery in the territories and renewed conflict over Kansas.

The *Dred Scott* Case

Dred Scott was a slave owned by an army surgeon based in Missouri. In the 1830s and early 1840s, he had traveled with his master to the state of Illinois and the Wisconsin Territory before returning to Missouri. In 1846, Scott sued his master's widow for freedom on the grounds that the laws of Illinois and the Wisconsin Territory barred slavery. After a series of appeals, the case reached the Supreme Court.

Chief Justice Roger Taney of Maryland, joined by five other justices of the nine-member Supreme Court (five of whom came from slave states), dismissed Scott's suit two days after Buchanan's inauguration in March 1857. Taney's opinion contained two bombshells. First, using dubious logic and failing to take into account the status of blacks in several northern states, he argued that blacks were not citizens of the United States. Because Scott was not a citizen, he could not sue. In reaching this conclusion, Taney noted that the framers of the Constitution had never intended citizenship for slaves.

Second, Taney held that even if Scott had standing in court, his residence in the Wisconsin Territory did not make him a free man. This was because the Missouri Compromise, which was still in effect in the 1840s, was, in Taney's view, unconstitutional. The compromise, the Chief Justice explained, deprived citizens of their property (slaves) without the due process of law granted by the Fifth Amendment to the U.S. Constitution. In effect, Taney ruled that Congress could not bar slavery from the territories.

Black Americans reacted bitterly to the *Dred Scott* decision. Throughout the struggle of black abo-

Dred Scott and his wife Harriet are portrayed here with their children as an average middle-class family, an image that fueled Northern opposition to the Supreme Court's 1857 decision that denied both Scott's freedom and his citizenship.

litionists to free their compatriots in the South, they had appealed to the basic American ideals of freedom, liberty, and self-determination. Now Taney was saying that these ideals did not apply to blacks. Throughout the urban North, blacks held meetings to denounce the decision.

The decision also shocked Republicans. The right of Congress to ban slavery from the territories, which Taney had apparently voided, was one of the party's central tenets. Republicans responded by ignoring the implications of the decision for the territories while promising to abide by it so far as it affected Dred Scott himself. Once in office, Republicans vowed, they would seek a reversal. This position allowed them to attack the decision without appearing to defy the law.

The *Dred Scott* decision boosted Republican fortunes in the North even as it seemed to undercut the party. Fears of a southern Slave Power conspiracy, which some had dismissed as fanciful and politically motivated, now seemed justified.

The Lecompton Constitution

Establishing a legitimate government in Kansas was the second major issue to bedevil the Buchanan administration. The president made a good start, sending Missouri resident Robert Walker, a man of integrity, to Kansas as territorial governor to oversee the election of a constitutional convention in June 1857.

But free-staters, fearing that the slavery forces planned to stuff the ballot box with fraudulent votes, announced a boycott of the June election. As a result, proslavery forces dominated the constitutional convention, which was held in Lecompton. And Walker, although a slaveholder, let it be known that he thought Kansas would never be a slave state, and thereby put himself at odds with proslavery residents.

Walker convinced the free-staters to vote in October to elect a new territorial legislature. The returns gave the proslavery forces a narrow victory, but Walker discovered irregularities. Undeterred, the proslavery forces drafted a proslavery constitution at the constitutional convention in Lecompton. Buchanan, who had promised Southerners a proslavery government in Kansas, dismissed Walker before he could rule on the **Lecompton Constitution**, and submitted the Lecompton Constitution to the Senate for approval even though it clearly sidestepped the popular sovereignty requirement of the Kansas-Nebraska Act.

As with the Kansas-Nebraska Act, many Northerners were outraged by the Lecompton Constitution. The proslavery Kansans behind the constitution had a record of fraud. Northern Democrats, among them Stephen A. Douglas, killed the constitution in Congress. Douglas knew that the *Dred Scott* decision and Buchanan's support of the Lecompton Constitution would help the Republicans and hurt him and his fellow northern Democrats in the 1858 congressional elections.

The **Panic of 1857**, a severe economic recession that lingered into 1858, also worked to the advantage of the Republicans. The Democratic administration did nothing as unemployment rose, starvation stalked the streets of Northern cities, and homeless women and children begged for food and shelter.

The panic had scarcely touched the South. Cotton seemed indeed to be king. The financial crisis in the North reinforced the southern belief that northern society was corrupt and greedy. The Republicans' proposed legislative remedies, in their view, would enrich the North and beggar the South.

Such were the issues confronting Douglas as he returned home to Illinois in the summer of 1858 to begin his reelection campaign.

The Lincoln-Douglas Debates

Douglas faced a forceful opponent. The Republicans had nominated Abraham Lincoln, a 49-year-old lawyer and former Whig congressman. The Kentucky-born Lincoln had risen from modest circumstances to become a prosperous lawyer in the Illinois state capital of Springfield. His marriage to wealthy and well-connected Mary Todd helped both his law practice and his pocketbook. Strongly opposed to the extension of slavery into the territories, Lincoln had developed a reputation as an excellent stump speaker with a homespun sense of humor, a quick wit, and a self-deprecating style that fit well with the small-town residents and farmers who composed the majority of the Illinois electorate.

But substance counted more than style with Illinois voters. Most of them opposed the extension of slavery into the territories, not out of concern for the slaves, but to keep the territories free for white people. Little known beyond the Springfield area, Lincoln also had to find a way to gain greater exposure. So in July 1858, he challenged Douglas to a series of debates across the state.

The **Lincoln-Douglas debates** were defining events in American politics that put the differences between Lincoln and Douglas, Republicans and Democrats, and North and South into sharp focus. In the debates, Lincoln asked Douglas to reconcile popular sovereignty, which Douglas had long championed, with the *Dred Scott* decision, which seemed to outlaw it by prohibiting a territorial legislature from excluding slavery before statehood. Douglas replied with what became known as the **Freeport Doctrine**. Slavery, he argued, could exist in a territory only if residents passed a law to protect it. Without such a law, no slaveholders would move in, and the territory would be free. Thus if residents did nothing, there could be no slavery in the territory.

For Douglas, slavery was not a moral issue. What mattered was what white people wanted. For Lincoln and many Republicans, slavery *was* a moral issue. As such, it was independent of what the residents of a territory wanted. In the final Lincoln-Douglas debate, Lincoln turned to his rival and explained, "The real issue in this controversy . . . is the sentiment on the part of one class that looks upon the institution of slavery *as a wrong*, and of another class that *does not* look upon it as a wrong. . . ."

Lincoln tempered his moralism with practical politics. He took care to distance himself from abolitionists, asserting that he abided by the Constitution and did not seek to interfere where slavery existed. Privately, however, he prayed for its demise. Nor did he agree, publicly at least, with abolitionist calls for racial equality. At the Springfield debate, he echoed the wishes of most white Illinoisans when he declared, "What I would most desire would be the separation of the white and black races." The Republican party was antislavery, but it did not advocate racial equality. Lincoln lost the senatorial contest but won national respect and recognition.

Despite Lincoln's defeat in Illinois, the Republicans made a strong showing in the 1858 congressional elections across the North. The increased Republican presence and the sharpening sectional divisions among Democrats portended a bitter debate over slavery in the new Congress. *Northern* and *Southern* took on meanings that expressed a great deal more than geography.

The Road to Disunion

The unsatisfying Compromise of 1850, the various misadventures in the Caribbean and Central America, the controversies over Kansas and the *Dred Scott* case, and abolitionist John Brown's failed attempt to spark a slave revolt in 1859 drove a wedge between the North and South.

The presidential election campaign of 1860 began before the uproar over Brown's raid had subsided. In the course of that contest, one of the last nationally unifying institutions, the Democratic party, broke apart. The election of Abraham Lincoln, an avowedly sectional candidate, as president in 1860 triggered a crisis that defied peaceful resolution.

Although the crisis spiraled into a civil war, this outcome did not signal the triumph of sectionalism over nationalism. Ironically, in defending their stands, both sides appealed to time-honored nationalist and democratic sentiments.

North-South Differences

Behind the ideological divide that separated North and South lay real and growing social and economic differences (see the summary table "South and North Compared in 1860"). As the North became increasingly urban and industrial, the South remained primarily rural and agricultural. The demand for farm machinery in the North reflected growing demand for manufactured products in general. The need of city-dwellers for ready-to-wear shoes and clothing, household iron products, processed foods, homes, workplaces, and public amenities boosted industrial production in the North. In contrast, in the South, the slower rate of urbanization, the lower proportion of immigrants, and the region's labor-intensive agriculture kept industrial development modest.

More subtle distinctions in culture and values between North and South became evident as well by midcentury. Southerners tended to be more violent than Northerners. Southern values stressed courtesy, honor, and courage. Southerners were more inclined to military service than Northerners. The South had a high illiteracy rate, nearly three times greater than the North—eight times greater if southern blacks are included.

Evangelical Protestantism attracted increasing numbers in both North and South, but its character differed in the two regions. The Methodist Church divided along sectional lines over slavery in 1844, and the Baptists split the following year. The Presbyterians splintered in 1837 over mainly doctrinal issues, but the rupture became complete in 1861. In the North, evangelical Protestants viewed social reform as a prerequisite for the Second Coming of Christ. As a result, they were in the forefront of most reform movements. Just as southern politics stressed individual rights, southern religion emphasized individual salvation over social reform and defended slavery. Northern churches hunted sinners outside their congregations (and often found them in Southerners); southern churches confined their preaching to their members.

Slavery accounted for many of the differences between the North and the South. Investment in land and slaves limited investment in manufacturing. The availability of a large slave labor force reduced the need for farm machinery and limited the demand for manufactured products. Slavery contributed to the South's martial tradition and its lukewarm attitude toward public education. Fully 95 percent of the nation's black population lived in the South in 1860, 90 percent of them slaves.

The South's defense of slavery and the North's attack on it fostered an array of stereotypes that exaggerated the real differences between the sections. Like all stereotypes, these reduced individuals to dehumanized categories. They encouraged the people of each section to view those of the other less as fellow Americans than as aliens in their midst.

Ironically, although slavery increasingly defined the character of the South in the 1850s, a growing majority of white Southerners did not own slaves. Slavery nonetheless implicated nonslaveholders in ways that assured their support for it. By satis-

---

SUMMARY

SOUTH AND NORTH COMPARED IN 1860

	South	North
Population	Biracial: 35 percent African-American	Overwhelmingly white: less than 2 percent African-American
Economy	Growing though relatively undiversified; 84 percent of work force in agriculture	Developing through industrialization and urbanization; 40 percent of work force in agriculture
Labor	Heavily dependent on slave labor, especially in Lower South	Free wage labor
Factories	15 percent of national total	85 percent of national total; concentrated in the Northeast
Railroads	Approximately 10,000 miles of track; primarily shorter lines, with fewer links to trunk lines	Approximately 20,000 miles of track; more effectively linked in trunk lines connecting east and west
Literacy	17 percent illiteracy rate for free population	6 percent illiteracy rate

---

fying the demand for labor on large plantations, it relieved many rural whites from serving as farm hands and enabled them to work their own land. Slaveholders also recruited nonslaveholders to suppress slave violence or rebellion. Finally, regardless of a white man's social or economic status, he shared an important feature with the largest slaveholder: As long as racial slavery existed, the color of his skin made him a member of a privileged class that could never be enslaved.

While white Southerners were more united on slavery than on other issues, their defense of slavery presented them with a major dilemma: it left them vulnerable to moral condemnation because in the end, slavery was morally indefensible.

John Brown's Raid

Ever intent on igniting a revolution among the slaves, abolitionist John Brown proposed in 1859 to attack and capture the federal arsenal at Harpers Ferry, Virginia, a small town near the Maryland border. The assault, Brown imagined, would spark a slave uprising in the area, eventually spreading to the rest of the state. With funds from his New England friends, he equipped a few dozen men and hired an English army officer to train them. When Brown outlined his scheme to Frederick Douglass,

the noted black abolitionist warned him against it. But his white New England friends were less cautious, and a group of six prominent abolitionists (the "**Secret Six**") gave Brown additional funds for his project. On the night of October 16, 1859, Brown and twenty-two followers captured the federal arsenal at Harpers Ferry and waited for the slaves to rally to his banner. Meanwhile, the townspeople alerted outside authorities. The Virginia militia and a detachment of United States Marines under the command of Colonel Robert E. Lee arrived and put a quick end to **John Brown's Raid**. They wounded Brown and killed or captured most of his force.

Brown had launched the ill-conceived operation without provisions and at a site from which escape was impossible. Although the primary goal of the attack had been to inspire a slave insurrection, no one had bothered to inform the local slaves. Was Brown crazy? As the *Boston Post* editorialized after the raid, "John Brown may be a lunatic, [but if so] then one-fourth of the people of Massachusetts are madmen."

The raid, though foolish and unsuccessful, played on Southerners' worst fears of slave rebellion, adding a new dimension: Here was an attack engineered not from within the South but from the North. Some southern whites may have dismissed the ability or even the desire of slaves to mount revolts on their own, but they less easily dismissed the potential impact of outside white agitators.

The state of Virginia tried Brown on the charge of treason to the state, and the jury sentenced him to hang. Throughout his brief imprisonment and trial, Brown maintained a quiet dignity that impressed even his jailers. The governor of Virginia spoke admirably of him as "a man of clear head, of courage, fortitude, and simple ingenuousness." Some Northerners compared Brown's execution with the death of a religious martyr. Abolitionist William Lloyd Garrison asked readers of *The Liberator* to "let the day of [Brown's] execution . . . be the occasion of such a public moral demonstration against the bloody and merciless slave system as the land has never witnessed." When the state of Virginia hanged Brown, church bells tolled across the North. Thoreau compared Brown with Jesus and called the abolitionist "an angel of light." Emerson observed that Brown would "make the gallows glorious like the cross." Condemning Brown's deed, these Northerners nevertheless embraced the cause.

The outpouring of northern grief over Brown's death convinced white Southerners that the threat to their security was not over. John Brown's Raid significantly changed southern public opinion. It was one thing to condemn slavery in the territories but another to attack it violently where it was long established. Southerners now saw in the Republican party the embodiment of John Brown's ideals and actions. So in their view, the election of a Republican president would be a death sentence for the South.

The impact of this shifting sentiment was immediately apparent in Congress when it reconvened three days after Virginia hanged Brown. Debate quickly turned tense and ugly. South Carolina senator James H. Hammond captured the mood well, remarking of his colleagues on the Senate floor that "the only persons who do not have a revolver and a knife are those who have two revolvers."

The Election of 1860

An atmosphere of mutual sectional distrust and animosity characterized the campaign for the presidential election of 1860. The Democrats disintegrated into two sectional factions united respectively behind Douglas and John C. Breckinridge. Former Whigs from the upper South who could not support southern Democrat Breckinridge and northern Whigs who had not defected to the Republicans or to Douglas formed the **Constitutional Union** party and nominated John Bell of Tennessee for president. Sensing victory, the Republicans convened in Chicago. If they could hold the states won by Frémont in 1856, add Minnesota (a new Republican-leaning state), and win Pennsylvania and one of three other Lower North states—Illinois, Indiana, or New Jersey—their candidate would win. These calculations dictated a platform and a candidate who could appeal to the four Lower North swing states where antislavery sentiment was not so strong. Along with the issue of slavery in the territories, the Republicans' now embraced a tariff plank calling for the protection of American industry.

John Brown, wounded during his raid on the federal arsenal at Harpers Ferry, lies on a cot during his trial for murder and treason in Charlestown, Virginia in 1859.

In selecting an appropriate presidential nominee, the Republicans faced a dilemma. Senator William H. Seward came to Chicago as the leading Republican candidate. But his immoderate condemnation of Southerners and slavery made moderate northern voters wary of him. Reservations about Seward benefited Abraham Lincoln. A year after his losing 1858 Senate campaign, he had embarked on a speaking tour of the East at the invitation of influential newspaper editor Horace Greeley. Lincoln's lieutenants at the convention stressed their candidate's moderation and morality, distancing him from both the abolitionists and Seward. When Seward faltered, Lincoln rose and won the Republican nomination.

The presidential campaign of 1860 actually comprised two campaigns. In the South, the contest was between Breckinridge and Bell; in the North, it was Lincoln against Douglas. Lincoln did not even appear on the ballot in most southern states.

Lincoln's strategy was to say practically nothing. He spent the entire campaign in Springfield, Illinois. When he did speak, it was to a reporter or friends but not in a public forum. He discounted southern threats of disunion if he were to become president.

States in those days held gubernatorial elections on different days, even in different months, from the national presidential election. When, in mid-October, Republicans had swept the statehouses in two crucial states, Pennsylvania and Indiana, Douglas made an extraordinary decision, but one consistent with his ardent nationalism. He abandoned his campaign and headed south at great personal peril to urge Southerners to remain in the Union now that Lincoln's election was inevitable.

Lincoln became the nation's sixteenth president with 39 percent of the popular vote (see Map 15-2). He took most northern states by significant margins and won all the region's electoral votes except three in New Jersey. This gave him a substantial majority of 180 electoral votes.

Secession Begins

The events following Lincoln's election demonstrated how wildly mistaken were those who dismissed southern threats of secession. Four days after Lincoln's victory, the South Carolina legislature called on the state's citizens to elect delegates to a convention to consider secession. Meeting on December 20, the delegates voted unanimously to leave the Union. By February 1, six other states—Mississippi, Florida, Alabama, Georgia, Louisiana, and Texas—had all held similar conventions and decided to leave the Union. Representatives from the seven seceding states met to form a separate country, the **Confeder-**

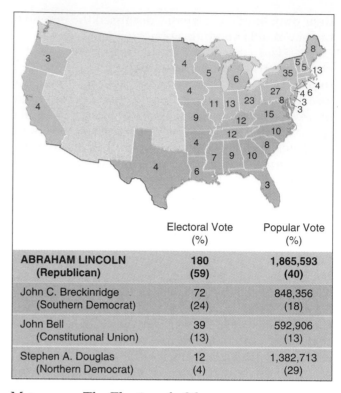

	Electoral Vote (%)	Popular Vote (%)
ABRAHAM LINCOLN (Republican)	**180 (59)**	**1,865,593 (40)**
John C. Breckinridge (Southern Democrat)	72 (24)	848,356 (18)
John Bell (Constitutional Union)	39 (13)	592,906 (13)
Stephen A. Douglas (Northern Democrat)	12 (4)	1,382,713 (29)

Map 15-2   The Election of 1860
The election returns from 1860 vividly illustrate the geography of sectionalism.

ate States of America. On February 18, Jefferson Davis was sworn in as its president.

Secessionists mounted an effective propaganda campaign, deftly using the press to convince voters to elect their delegates to the state conventions. Framing the issue as a personal challenge to every southern citizen, they argued that it would be cowardly to remain in the Union, a submission to despotism and enslavement. Southerners, they maintained, were the true heirs to the spirit of 1776. Lincoln and the Republicans were like King George III and the British—they meant to deny Southerners the right to life, liberty, and the pursuit of happiness. Unionists, in response, could only offer voters a wait-and-see strategy.

Presidential Inaction

Because Lincoln would not take office until March 4, 1861, it was the Buchanan administration that had to cope with the secession crisis during the critical months of December and January. The president's failure to work out a solution with Congress as secession fever swept the Lower South further undermined Unionist forces in the seceding states.

Thereafter, Buchanan's administration quickly fell apart. As the Lower South states left the Union, their representatives and senators left Washington, and with them went Buchanan's closest advisers and key cabinet officials. Commenting on the emotionally charged atmosphere in the Senate as prominent Southerners gave their farewells and departed, one observer wrote, "There was everywhere a feeling of suspense, as if, visibly, the pillars of the temple were being withdrawn and the great Government structure was tottering." Buchanan, a lame duck, bereft of friends and advisers, did little more than condemn secession. He hoped that waiting might bring an isolated Lower South to its senses and give efforts to mediate the sectional rift a chance to succeed.

Peace Proposals

Kentucky senator John J. Crittenden in January 1861 and later ex-President John Tyler in February proposed similar packages of constitutional amendments designed to solve the sectional crisis. The central feature of the **Crittenden Plan** was the extension of the Missouri Compromise line through the territories all the way to the state of California. The plan was of marginal interest to the South, however, because it was unlikely to result in any new slave states. Neither plan got anywhere in Congress.

Lincoln's Views on Secession

President-elect Lincoln monitored the secession of the Lower South states and the attempts to reach a compromise from his home in Springfield. Although he said nothing publicly, he made it known that he did not favor compromises like those proposed by Crittenden and Tyler. Lincoln counted on Unionist sentiment to keep the Upper South from seceding. Like Buchanan, he felt that the longer the Lower South states remained isolated, the more likely they would be to return to the fold. For a while, events seemed to bear him out. In North Carolina, the *Wilmington Herald* responded to South Carolina's secession by asking readers, "Will you suffer yourself to be spit upon in this way? Are you *submissionists* to the dictation of South Carolina . . . ?" One by one, Upper South states registered their support for the Union. A closer look, however, reveals that there were limits to the Upper South's Unionism. Most voters in the region went to the polls assuming that Congress would eventually reach a compromise based on Crittenden's or Tyler's proposals, or some other remedy. Leaders in the Upper South saw themselves as peacemakers. But it was unlikely that the Upper South would ever abide the use of federal force against its southern neighbors.

Lincoln believed that the slavery issue had to come to a crisis before the nation could solve it.

Although he said in public that he would never interfere with slavery in the slave states, the deep moral revulsion he felt toward the institution left him more ambivalent in private. As he confided to a colleague in 1860, "The tug has to come, and better now, than any time hereafter" (see "American Views: Lincoln on Slavery").

Fort Sumter: The Tug Comes

In his inaugural address on March 4, 1861, Abraham Lincoln denounced secession and vowed to uphold federal law but tempered his firmness with a conciliatory conclusion. Addressing Southerners specifically, he assured them, "We are not enemies but friends. . . . Though passion may have strained, it must not break our bonds of affection. The mystic chords of memory, stretching from every battlefield, and patriot grave, to every living heart and hearthstone, all over this broad land, will yet swell the chorus of the Union, when again touched, as surely they will be, by the better angels of our nature."

Southerners wanted concessions, not conciliation, however. The new president said nothing about slavery in the territories, nothing about constitutional amendments proposed by Crittenden and Tyler, and nothing about the release of federal property in the South to the Confederacy. Even some Northerners hoping for an olive branch were disappointed.

One day after Lincoln's inauguration, Major Robert Anderson (like Lincoln, a native Kentuckian), the commander of **Fort Sumter** in Charleston harbor, informed the administration that he had only four to six weeks' worth of provisions left. Sumter was one of three southern forts still under federal control. Anderson assumed that Lincoln would understand the hopeless military situation and order him to evacuate Fort Sumter.

News of Anderson's plight changed the mood in the North. The Slave Power, some said, was holding him and his men hostage. Frustration grew over Lincoln's silence and inaction. The Confederacy's bold resolve seemed to contrast sharply with the federal government's confusion and inertia. By the end of March, nearly a month after Anderson had informed Lincoln of the situation at Fort Sumter, the president finally made an effort to provision Major Anderson.

The president still hoped to avoid a confrontation. He did not send the troops that Anderson had requested. Instead he ordered unarmed boats to proceed to the fort, deliver the provisions, and leave. Only if the Confederates fired on them were they to force their way into the fort with the help of armed reinforcements.

American Views

LINCOLN ON SLAVERY

In the weeks after the 1860 election, northern and southern leaders sought out President-elect Abraham Lincoln for his views on slavery. Two letters, one to fellow Illinois Republican Lyman Trumbull and the other to Virginia Democrat John A. Gilmer, indicate Lincoln's firm opposition to the extension of slavery into the territories.

❖ **Lincoln's tone is considerably more conciliatory in the letter to Gilmer than in the one to Trumbull. Which one do you think better reflects his intentions?**

❖ **Despite the difference in tone, do you think both say essentially the same thing?**

Springfield, Ills. Dec. 10, 1860
Hon. L. Trumbull
My dear Sir: Let there be no compromise on the question of *extending* slavery. If there be, all our labor is lost, and ere long, must be done again. The dangerous ground—that into which some of our friends have a hankering to run—is Pop[ular] Sov[ereignty]. Have none of it. Stand firm. The tug has to come, & better now, than any time hereafter. Yours as ever,
A. Lincoln

Springfield, Ill. Dec. 15, 1860
Hon. John A. Gilmer:
My dear Sir: . . . I have no thought of recommending the abolition of slavery in the District of Columbia, nor the slave trade among the slave states . . . and if I were to make such recommendation, it is quite clear Congress would not follow it. As to the use of patronage in the slave states, where there are few or no Republicans, I do not expect to inquire for the politics of the appointee, or whether he does or not own slaves. . . . In one word, I never have been, am not now, and probably never shall be, in a mood of harassing the people, either North or South. On the territorial question, I am inflexible. . . . On that, there is a difference between you and us; and it is the only substantial difference. You think slavery is right and ought to be extended; we think it is wrong and ought to be restricted. For this, neither has any just occasion to be angry with the other.
Your obt. Servt.
A. Lincoln

Source: *John G. Nicolay and John Hay, eds.*, Works of Abraham Lincoln, *vol. 6 (1905).*

President Davis wanted to take Sumter before the provisions arrived to avoid fighting Anderson and the reinforcements at the same time. He also realized that the outbreak of fighting would compel the Upper South to join the Confederacy. But his impatience to force the issue placed the Confederacy in the position of firing, unprovoked, on the American flag.

On April 10, Davis ordered Beauregard to demand the immediate evacuation of Fort Sumter. Anderson did not yield, and before dawn on April

SUMMARY

THE EMERGING SECTIONAL CRISIS

Event	Year	Effect
Wilmot Proviso	1846	Congressman David Wilmot's proposal to ban slavery from territories acquired from Mexico touched off a bitter sectional dispute in Congress.
Compromise of 1850	1850	Law admitted California as a free state, granted the population of Utah and New Mexico Territories the right to decide on slavery, and established a new and stronger Fugitive Slave Act, all of which "solved" the territorial issue raised by the Wilmot Proviso but satisfied neither North nor South and planted the seeds of future conflict.
Election of 1852	1852	Results confirmed demise of the Whig party, initiating a period of political realignment.
Kansas-Nebraska Act	1854	Law created the Kansas and Nebraska Territories and repealed the Missouri Compromise of 1820 by leaving the question of slavery to the territories' residents. Its passage enraged many Northerners, prompting some to form the new Republican party.
"Bleeding Kansas"	1855–1856	Sometimes violent conflict between pro- and antislavery forces in Kansas further polarized the sectional debate.
Election of 1856	1856	Presidency was won by Democrat James Buchanan of Pennsylvania, but a surprisingly strong showing by the recently formed Republican party in the North set the stage for the 1860 election.
Dred Scott Case	1857	The Supreme Court ruling that slaves were not citizens and that Congress had no authority to ban slavery from the territories boosted Republican prospects in the North.
Lecompton Constitution	1857	Proslavery document, framed by a fraudulently elected convention in Kansas and supported by President Buchanan, further convinced Northerners that the South was subverting their rights.
John Brown's Raid	1859	Unsuccessful attempt to free the South's slaves, this attack on a federal arsenal in Harpers Ferry, Virginia, increased sectional tension.
Election of 1860	1860	Republican Abraham Lincoln won a four-way race for the presidency. The last major national party, the Democrats, disintegrated. Lower South states seceded.
Fort Sumter	1861	Confederate forces attacked the fort in April 1861, Lincoln called for troops, and several Upper South states seceded. The Civil War was underway.

12, 1861, the first Confederate shell whistled down on the fort. After more than a day of shelling, during which more than five thousand artillery rounds struck Fort Sumter, Anderson surrendered. Remarkably, neither side suffered any casualties, a deceptive beginning to an exceptionally bloody war.

When the verdict of Fort Sumter reached President Lincoln, he called on the southern states still in the Union to send troops to put down the rebellion. Refusing to make war on South Carolina, the Upper South states of Virginia, North Carolina, Tennessee, and Arkansas seceded, and the Confederacy expanded to eleven states.

Conclusion

When David Wilmot had submitted his amendment to ban slavery from the territories gained from Mexico, he could not have foreseen that the debate he unleashed would end in civil war just fifteen years later (see the summary table "The Emerging Sectional Crisis," p. 281). By the 1850s the slavery issue had become weighted with so much moral and political freight that it defied easy resolution. Northerners and Southerners eventually interpreted any incident or piece of legislation as an attempt by one side to gain moral and political advantage at the other's expense.

By 1861, the national political parties that had muted sectional animosities were gone, and so were national church organizations and fraternal associations. The ideals that had inspired the American Revolution remained in place, especially the importance of securing individual liberty against encroachment by government. But with each side interpreting them differently, these ideals served more to divide than to unite.

Ironically, as Americans in both sections talked of freedom and self-determination, the black men and women in their midst had little of either. Lincoln went to war to preserve the Union; Davis, to defend a new nation. Slavery was the spark that ignited the conflict, but white America seemed more comfortable embracing abstract ideals than real people. Northerners and Southerners would confront this irony during the bloodiest war in American history—but they would not resolve it.

Review Questions

1. How do you account for the great success of Harriet Beecher Stowe's *Uncle Tom's Cabin?*

2. If you were a Democratic representative from your state to the U.S. Congress in 1854, what would your position be on the Kansas-Nebraska Bill? What if you were a Whig?

3. Discuss the role of evangelical religion in sharpening the sectional conflict between North and South.

4. Between the time he was elected president in November and his inauguration in March, what options did Abraham Lincoln have for resolving the sectional crisis?

5. Northerners and Southerners appealed to the same American ideals in support of their respective positions. Could they both have been correct?

Recommended Reading

William W. Freehling, *The Road to Disunion, Vol. 1: Secessionists at Bay, 1776–1854* (1990). This is a detailed and lively treatment of events and personalities in the years leading up to passage of the Kansas-Nebraska Act.

David M. Potter, *The Impending Crisis, 1848–1861* (1976). This remains the most comprehensive analysis of the coming of the war. It is a balanced account that is especially strong on political events.

Harriet Beecher Stowe, *Uncle Tom's Cabin* (1852; reprint edition 1982, with notes by Kathryn Kish Sklar). Reading this book is essential for understanding why and how it generated so much controversy and intensified sectional antagonisms in the early 1850s.

Where to Learn More

❖ **Harpers Ferry National Historical Park, West Virginia.**   Exhibits interpret John Brown's Raid and re-create some of the atmosphere and structures of the 1850s village and the federal arsenal.

❖ **"A House Divided," mounted by the Chicago Historical Society, Chicago.**   This exhibit depicts the major events of the sectional crisis during the 1850s, the election of 1860, and the coming of the Civil War. It will continue until 2001.

❖ **Fort Sumter National Monument, Charleston, South Carolina.**   This historic site interprets the bombardment of the fort and the events that immediately preceded the Civil War.

16 BATTLE CRIES AND FREEDOM SONGS
THE CIVIL WAR, 1861–1863

CHAPTER OUTLINE

KEY TOPICS

❖ The comparative economic and human resources of the North and South
❖ Confederate and Union military strategies
❖ Changing perceptions of the nature and length of the war
❖ The course of the war through 1863 and the major battles that shifted it in the North's favor
❖ Steps leading to the Emancipation Proclamation

In October 1862, a photographic exhibit opened in New York City. The pictures were by two photographers working for Mathew Brady. Taken a month earlier near Sharpsburg, a small town in western Maryland, they featured gently rolling hills littered with bloated corpses. Until then, most Northerners had experienced the Civil War only distantly through newspaper dispatches. Now referring to Brady's photographers, a *New York Times* reviewer pointed out, "If he has not brought bodies and laid them in our door-yards and along streets, he has done something very like it."

For others, the face of war was more immediate. Kate Cumming, a nurse in a Confederate hospital in Chattanooga, once witnessed a stream of blood cascading from an operating table into a large tub that held a recently severed arm. On July 4, 1862, after a bloody weeklong battle, Confederate and Union soldiers laid down their arms to pick berries together. As a Confederate private described it, "Our boys and the Yanks . . . gathered berries . . . as if they had not been engaged for the last seven days in butchering each other." In 1862, a 70-year-old slave woman in Georgia gathered her twenty-two children and grandchildren, seized an abandoned flatboat, and drifted 40 miles down the Savannah River. When a Union vessel rescued the party, "the grandmother rose to her full height, with her youngest grandchild in her arms, and said only, 'My God! Are we free?'"

The Civil War comprised a million such stories and evoked countless emotions. Some fifty thousand books about the war have been published since it ended in 1865, an average of one a day. This outpouring attests to the country's enduring need to understand, explain, and reinterpret its bloodiest conflict. The Civil War preserved the Union, abolished slavery, and killed at least 620,000 soldiers—more than in all other wars the country fought from the Revolution to the Korean conflict.

When the war began, only a minority of Northerners linked the preservation of the Union with the abolition of slavery. By 1863, Union and freedom had become inseparable Federal objectives. The Confederacy fought for independence and the preservation of slavery. But their own ambivalence about slavery and the contempt of outside public opinion eventually led Southerners to emphasize independence.

The Confederate objectives of defending its territory and securing independence dictated a defensive military strategy; the Union objectives of putting down the rebellion and reuniting the nation dictated an offensive strategy. But during the war's early years, both sides faced similar problems—raising an army, financing the war effort, mobilizing the civilian population, and marshaling resources. The Confederacy confronted the added burden of starting a government from scratch with relatively fewer resources than the Federals.

At the end of the war's first year, the Confederacy's strong military position east of the Appalachians belied its numerical and economic inferiority. Confederate advances resulted as much from the bungling of Union commanders as from the gallant efforts of the South's own forces. By the end of 1862, Union officers had begun to expose Southern military shortcomings. Within a year, the trans-Mississippi portion of the Confederacy capitulated as dissent and despair mounted on the home front.

Mobilization, North and South

Neither side was prepared for a major war. The Confederacy lacked a national army and navy. Each southern state had a militia, but by the 1850s, these companies had become more social clubs than fighting units. The Union had a regular army of only sixteen thousand men, most of whom were stationed west of the Mississippi River.

Each government augmented these meager military reserves with thousands of new recruits and developed a bureaucracy to mount a war effort. At the same time, the administrations of Presidents Lincoln and Davis secured the loyalty of their civilian populations and devised military strategies for a war of indeterminate duration. How North and South went about these tasks reflected both the different objectives of the two sides and the distinctive personalities of their leaders, Abraham Lincoln and Jefferson Davis.

War Fever

The day after Major Robert Anderson surrendered Fort Sumter, President Lincoln moved to enlarge his small, scattered army by mobilizing state militias for ninety days. In spite of the defection of four states—Virginia, Arkansas, North Carolina, and Tennessee—and about one-third of the officer corps in the regular army, including some of the highest-ranking officers, Lincoln seemed likely to meet his target of 75,000 troops. Lincoln's modest ninety-day call-up reflected the general belief, North and South, that the war would end quickly. But not everyone thought the war would be brief. William T. Sherman, who had recently headed a Louisiana military academy and would become one of the Union's few great commanders, wrote in April 1861, "I think it is to be a long war—very long—much longer than any politician thinks."

Northerners closed ranks behind the president after the Confederacy's attack on Fort Sumter. Leading Democrat Stephen A. Douglas called on the Republican Lincoln to offer his and his party's support. "There can be no neutrals in this war," Douglas said, "*only patriots—or traitors.*" Residents of New York City, where sympathy for the South had probably been greater than anywhere else in the North, now sponsored huge public demonstrations in support of the war effort, and the city council appropriated $1 million to raise and equip Union regiments. And American flags flew everywhere. The *New York Daily Tribune*, an abolitionist paper, made the objective of this patriotic fervor clear: "We mean to conquer [the Southern people]—not merely to defeat, but to conquer, to SUBJUGATE them . . . They must find poverty at their firesides, and see privation in the anxious eyes of mothers and rags of children."

Southerners were equally eager to support their new nation. A *London Times* correspondent traveling in the South witnessed numerous renditions of "Dixie" with the high-pitched piercing sounds that would later be known as the "rebel yell." Enlistment rallies, wild send-offs at train stations, and auctions and balls to raise money for the troops were staged throughout the Confederacy during the war's early

CHRONOLOGY

1861 April: Confederates fire on Fort Sumter; Civil War begins.

1861 July: First Battle of Bull Run.

1862 February: Forts Henry and Donelson fall to Union forces.

March: Peninsula Campaign begins.

Ironclads *Monitor* and *Virginia* (*Merrimac*) do battle.

Battle of Pea Ridge, Arkansas.

Battle of Gloricta Pass, New Mexico.

April: Battle of Shiloh.

New Orleans falls to Federal forces.

May: Union captures Corinth, Mississippi.

July: Seven Days' Battles end.

Congress passes the Confiscation Act.

August: Second Battle of Bull Run.

September: Battle of Antietam.

December: Battle of Fredericksburg.

1863 January: Emancipation Proclamation takes effect.

May: Battle of Chancellorsville; Stonewall Jackson is mortally wounded.

July: Battle of Gettysburg.

Vicksburg falls to Union forces.

Black troops of the 54th Massachusetts Volunteer Infantry Regiment assault Fort Wagner outside Charleston, South Carolina.

September: Battle of Chickamauga.

November: Battle of Chattanooga.

---

months. As in the North, war fever fired hatred of the enemy. A Louisiana plantation overseer wrote:

> My prayer Sincerely to God is that Every Black Republican . . . that is opposed to negro slavery . . . shal be trubled with pestilences & calamitys of all kinds   and O God I pray the to Direct a bullet or a bayonet to pirce the art of every northern Soldier that invades southern Soil.

As war fever gripped North and South, volunteers on both sides rushed to join, quickly filling the quotas of both armies. Most soldiers were motivated by patriotism, a desire to defend their homes and loved ones, and a craving for glory and adventure. The initial enthusiasm, however, wore off quickly. After four months of war, a young Confederate soldier admitted, "I have seen quite enough of a Soldier's life to satisfy me that it is not what it is cracked up to be."

The South in particular faced a contradiction between its ideology and the demands of full-scale war. Southern leaders had been fighting for decades to defend states' rights against national authority. Now these same leaders had to forge the states of the Confederacy into a nation. By early spring 1862, the Confederate government was compelled to order the first general draft in U.S. history. The only way a recruit could get out of the army was to die or desert. But the Confederate draft law allowed several occupational exemptions. Among them was an infamous provision that allowed one white man on any plantation with more than twenty slaves to be excused from service. The reason for the exemption was to assure the security and continued productivity of large plantations, not to protect the privileged, but it led some Southerners to conclude that the struggle had become "a rich man's war but a poor man's fight."

The initial flush of enthusiasm faded in the North as well. Responding to a Federal call for additional troops, some Northern states initiated a draft during the summer of 1862. In March 1863, Congress passed the **Enrollment Act**, a draft law that, like the Confederate draft, allowed for occupational exemptions. A provision that allowed a draftee to hire a substitute aroused resentment among working-class Northerners. But the North was less dependent on conscription than the South.

The armies of both sides included men from all walks of life, from common laborers to clerks to bankers. An undetermined number of women, typically disguised as men, also served in both armies. They joined for the same reasons as men: adventure, patriotism, and glory.

The North's Advantage in Resources

The resources of the North—including its population, industrial and agricultural capacity, and transportation network—greatly exceeded those of the South (see Figure 16-1). The 2.1 million men who fought for the Union represented roughly half the men of military age in the North. The 900,000 men

Figure 16-1   A Comparison of the Union and Confederate Control of Key Resources at the Outset of the Civil War.

who fought for the Confederacy, in contrast, represented fully 90 percent of its eligible population. Nearly 200,000 blacks, most of them ex-slaves from the South, took up arms for the Union. Not until the last month of the war did the Confederacy consider arming slaves.

The Confederacy compensated somewhat for its numerical disadvantage by requiring long tours of duty, which meant that its forces tended to be more experienced than those of the Union. But the Union's greater numbers left the South vulnerable to a war of attrition. At the beginning of the war, the North controlled 90 percent of the nation's industrial capacity. It had seventeen times more cotton and woolen cloth than the South, thirty times more boots and shoes, and thirty-two times more firearms. The North had dozens of facilities for producing the tools to make war material; the South had no such factories and only one munitions plant, the Tredegar Iron Works in Richmond. The railroad system in the North was more than twice the size of the South's.

Thanks to the North's abundance of resources, no soldier in any previous army had ever been outfitted as well as the blue-uniformed Union trooper. The official color of the Confederate uniform was gray, although a dust-brown shade was more common. Most Southern soldiers, however, did not wear distinguishable uniforms, especially toward the end of the war. They also often lacked proper shoes or any footwear at all. When Confederate general Robert E. Lee invaded Maryland in 1862, he left behind several thousand barefoot soldiers because they couldn't march on gravel roads. Still, the South never lost a battle because of insufficient supplies or inadequate weaponry. New foundries opened, and manufacturing enterprises in Augusta, Georgia; Selma, Alabama; and elsewhere joined the Tredegar Iron Works to keep the Confederate armies equipped

with the weapons and other supplies they needed to keep fighting.

Unstable finances proved more of a handicap to the Confederacy than its relatively low industrial capacity. The Confederate economy—and its treasury—depended heavily on cotton exports. But a Union naval blockade and the ability of textile manufacturers in Europe to find new sources of supply restricted this crucial source of revenue. The imposition of taxes would have improved the Confederacy's finances, but Southerners resisted taxation. The government sold interest-bearing bonds to raise money, but as Confederate fortunes declined, so did bond sales. With few other options, the Confederacy financed more than 60 percent of the $1.5 billion it spent on the war with printing-press money, and inflation spiraled out of control.

The Union had more abundant financial resources than the Confederacy, and the Federal government was more successful than the Confederate government at developing innovative ways to meet the great cost of the war. Its first recourse was to borrow money by selling long-term interest-bearing bonds and shorter-term interest-bearing treasury notes. Together these bonds accounted for 66 percent of the $4 billion that the Union raised to wage the war. Like the Confederacy, the Federal government issued paper money—bills derisively known as "greenbacks"—that was not backed by gold or silver. But the Federal government also offset its expenses with the country's first income tax, which citizens could pay in greenbacks, a move that bolstered the value and credibility of the paper currency. Ruinous inflation was thereby averted in the North.

Leaders and Governments

Leadership ability, like resources, played an important role in the war. Confederate president Jefferson

Davis had to build a government from scratch during a war. Abraham Lincoln at least had the benefit of an established governmental structure, a standing army, healthy financial resources, and established diplomatic relations with the nations of Europe.

Davis and Lincoln were both born in Kentucky within a year and 100 miles of each other. Davis, like Lincoln, was born into modest circumstances. Although Davis's career qualified him for the prodigious task of running the Confederacy, aspects of his character compromised his effectiveness. He had a sharp intellect but related awkwardly to people and was not "one of the boys." Colleagues found him aloof. He was inclined to equate compromise with weakness and interpreted any opposition as a personal attack.

Southerners viewed themselves as the genuine heirs of the American Revolution and the true defenders of the United States Constitution. The Confederate Constitution differed in only minor particulars from the Federal constitution. If the South were to establish itself as a separate country, however, Southerners had to renounce their American identity and develop one of their own. But on what distinctive aspects of Southern life could the Confederacy build such an identity? Slavery was distinctively Southern, but most white Southerners, even if they believed that slavery served their interests, did not own slaves. Southerners had forcefully advanced the ideology of states' rights during the 1840s and 1850s, but with its emphasis on the primacy of state sovereignty over central authority, states' rights too was a weak foundation on which to build a national consciousness. Davis faced shifting alliances and found it difficult to build a loyal base of support.

Northerners, like Southerners, needed a convincing reason to endure the prolonged sacrifice of the Civil War. For them, the struggle was a distant one, fought mostly on Southern soil far from their homes. Lincoln and other Northern leaders secured support by convincing their compatriots of the importance of preserving the Union "not altogether for today;" but "for a vast future." The president viewed the conflict in global terms, its results affecting the hopes for democratic government around the world.

Lincoln handled disagreement better than Davis did. He defused tense situations with folksy humor, and his simple eloquence captured the imagination of ordinary people, even if it did not persuade his political enemies. Lincoln viewed himself as a man of the people and was not aloof, like Davis. But even if Jefferson Davis had been a more effective leader than Lincoln, it is unlikely that he could have overcome the odds against him. The key to Southern independence lay less with the Confederacy's president than with its forces on the battlefield.

Lincoln's Fight for the Border States

The secession of Virginia, Arkansas, North Carolina, and Tennessee left four border slave states—Maryland, Delaware, Kentucky, and Missouri—hanging in the balance. Were Maryland and Delaware to secede, the Federal capital at Washington, D.C., would be surrounded by Confederate territory. Kentucky also had special symbolic significance as the birthplace of the rival presidents, Lincoln and Davis, and Lincoln viewed it as the key to retaining the three other border states.

Early reports from the four states were troubling. The four governors displayed polite indifference or overt hostility to the Federal government. Maryland's strategic location north of Washington, D.C., rendered its loyalty to the Union vital. Although a majority of its citizens opposed secession, a mob attack on Union troops passing through Baltimore in April 1861 indicated strong pro-Southern sentiment. Lincoln dispatched Federal troops to monitor the fall elections in the state, placed its legislature under military surveillance, and arrested officials who opposed the Union cause, including the mayor of Baltimore. This show of force guaranteed the pro-Union candidate for governor an overwhelming victory and saved Maryland for the Union. Delaware, although nominally a slave state, remained staunchly for the Union.

Missourians settled their indecision by combat. The fighting culminated with a Union victory in March 1862 at the Battle of Pea Ridge, Arkansas. Pro-Confederate Missourians refused to concede defeat and waged an unsuccessful guerrilla war over the next two years.

Kentucky never seceded but attempted to remain neutral at the outset of the war. The Legislature was pro-Union, the governor pro-Southern. Both sides actively recruited soldiers in the state. In September 1861, when Confederate forces invaded Kentucky and Union forces moved to expel them, the state became one of the war's battlegrounds.

Although Virginia went with the Confederacy, some counties in the western part of the state opposed the state's secession and, as early as the summer of 1861, took steps to establish a pro-Union state. In June 1863, West Virginia became the nation's thirty-fifth state.

Strategies and Tactics

To a great extent, the political objectives of each side determined its military strategy. Southerners wanted independence; Northerners fought to preserve the Union. The North's goal required conquest. The Confederacy, for its part, did not need to conquer the North. Fighting a defensive battle in its own territory, the South had only to hang on until growing Northern opposition to the war or some decisive Northern military mistake convinced the Union to stop fighting.

But the South's strategy had two weaknesses. First, it demanded more patience than the South had shown in impulsively attacking Fort Sumter. Second, the South might not have sufficient resources to draw out the war long enough to swing Northern public opinion behind peace. The question was what would break first, Northern support for the war or Southern ability to wage it?

The Early War, 1861–1862

The North's offensive strategy dictated the course of the war for the first two years. In the West, the Federal army's objectives were to hold Missouri, Kentucky, and Tennessee for the Union, to control the Mississippi River, and eventually to detach the area west of the Appalachians from the rest of the Confederacy. In the East, Union forces sought to capture Richmond, the Confederate capital. The U.S. Navy imposed a blockade along the Confederate coast and pushed into inland waterways to capture Southern ports. The Confederates defended strategic locations throughout their territory or abandoned them when prudence required. By the end of 1862, the result remained in the balance.

First Bull Run

By July 1861, when the border states appeared more secure for the Union, President Lincoln shifted his attention southward and ordered Union general Irvin McDowell to move Federal forces into Virginia to take Richmond (see Map 16-1). Confronting McDowell 20 miles southwest of Washington at Manassas, an important junction in the railway that supplied the Confederate capital, was a Confederate army under General P. G. T. Beauregard. McDowell and Beauregard's armies clashed on July 21 at the **First Battle of Bull Run** (known to the Confederacy as the First Battle of Manassas). The Union forces seemed at first on the verge of winning. But Beauregard's forces, with General Joseph E. Johnston's reinforcements, repulsed the assault. At the height of the battle, General Barnard Bee of South Carolina in exasperation called out to Colonel Thomas J. Jackson for assistance,

Map 16-1   *From First Bull Run to Antietam: The War in the East, 1861–1862*

The early stages of the war demonstrated the strategies of both Confederate and Union forces. Federal troops stormed into Virginia hoping to capture Richmond and bring a quick end to the war. Through a combination of poor generalship and Confederate tenacity, they failed. Confederate troops hoped to defend their territory, prolong the war, and eventually win their independence as Northern patience evaporated. They proved successful initially, but, with the abandonment of the defensive strategy and the invasion of Maryland in the fall of 1862, the Confederates suffered a political and morale setback at Antietam.

shouting, "There stands Jackson—like a damned stone wall!" The rebuke became, in the curious alchemy of battlefield gossip, a shorthand for courage and steadfastness. Jackson's men henceforth called him "Stonewall."

Bull Run dispelled some illusions and reinforced others. It boosted Southerners' confidence and seemed to confirm their boast that one Confederate could whip ten Yankees, even though the opposing armies were of relatively equal strength when the fighting began. The Union rout planted the suspicion in Northern minds that perhaps the Confederates were invincible and destroyed the widespread belief in the North that the war would be over quickly.

The War in the West

While Federal forces retreated in Virginia, they advanced in the West. Two Confederate forts on the Tennessee-Kentucky border, **Fort Henry** on the Tennessee River and **Fort Donelson** on the Cumberland River, guarded the strategic waterways that linked Tennessee and Kentucky to the Mississippi Valley. The forts also defended Nashville, the Tennessee state capital (see Map 16-2). In February 1862, Union general Ulysses S. Grant coordinated a land and river campaign against the forts with Flag Officer Andrew H. Foote, who commanded a force of ironclad Union gunboats.

Grant, recently promoted to brigadier general, had resigned from the military in the 1850s after a mediocre career marked by bouts of excessive drinking. A plain-looking man with dark brown hair

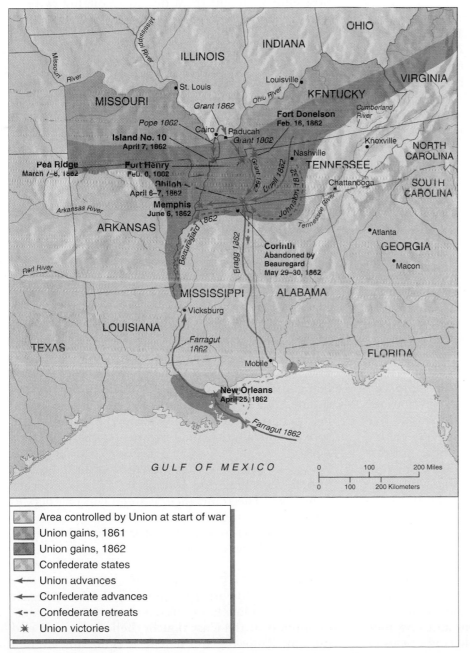

Map 16-2   The War in the West, 1861–1862

Because of the early Union emphasis on capturing Richmond, the war in the West seemed less important to Northerners. But, from a strategic standpoint, the victories at Forts Henry and Donelson, which drove a wedge into southern territory and closed the Confederacy's quickest path to the West from Virginia and the Carolinas, and the capture of New Orleans and its Mississippi River port, were crucial and set the stage for greater Federal success in the West in 1863.

and a beard streaked with gray, he often looked as if he had slept in his uniform. Behind the rumpled appearance lay a flexible military mind that would eventually grasp how the Civil War must be won. Grant appreciated the strategic importance of river systems in the conquest of the western Confederacy. Grant's combined river and land campaign caught the Southerners unprepared and outflanked. By February 16, both forts had fallen. The Union victory drove a wedge into Southern territory and closed the Confederacy's quickest path to the West from Virginia and the Carolinas. The Confederacy never recovered the strategic advantage in the West after the loss of these two forts.

Grant next moved his main army south to Pittsburg Landing on the Tennessee River to prepare for an assault on the key Mississippi River port and rail center of Vicksburg. After blunting a surprise Confederate attack at **Shiloh Church** near Pittsburg Landing, Grant pushed the Southerners back to Corinth, Mississippi. Federal forces complemented their victories at Shiloh and Corinth with a narrow success when Admiral David G. Farragut, who remained a Unionist even though born in Tennessee, blasted the Confederate river defenses protecting New Orleans and sailed a Federal fleet into the city in April 1862. The result was to open two hundred miles of the Mississippi River, the nation's most vital commercial waterway, to Union traffic. With the fall of Memphis to Union forces in June, Vicksburg remained the only major river town still in Confederate hands. The fall of New Orleans and Memphis underscored a major problem with the Confederates' defensive strategy: Their military reserves were stretched too thin to defend their vast territory.

Reassessing the War

The fierce fighting at Shiloh wrought unprecedented carnage. Each side suffered more than ten thousand casualties. By the time the smoke had cleared, the soldiers' view of the war had undergone a major transformation. The initial enthusiasm and bravado was replaced by the sober realization that death or capture was a likely outcome and that heroism, courage, and piety did not guarantee survival. A hunger for peace replaced the thirst for battle.

Kate Cumming, the nurse at the Confederate hospital in Corinth, wrote of soldiers brought from the battle "mutilated in every imaginable way." Piercing the air were the screams of men undergoing amputations, often with little or no anesthetic. Some pleaded with physicians to kill them and end their misery. Others bore the pain stoically and entrusted last words and letters to nurses, dying with the word "Mother" on their lips.

Women on both sides played a major role in caring for the wounded and sick. In the North, members of the **U.S. Sanitary Commission**, a voluntary organization, formed in 1861, attempted to upgrade hospital and medical care. But in the months after Shiloh and with the resumption of fighting in the East, the extent of casualties often overwhelmed the dedicated volunteers. And the bloodiest fighting lay ahead.

Even if a soldier escaped death on the battlefield and survived a hospital stay, he still faced the possibility of death from disease. Roughly twice as many men died from disease than on the battlefield during the Civil War. Typhoid, commonly and appropriately known as camp fever, claimed the most lives.

Many soldiers turned to religion for consolation in response to the growing carnage. The frequency of camp prayer meetings and revivals increased after Shiloh. Many a recruit carried books with titles such as *Satan's Bait* and *A Mother's Parting Words to Her Soldier Boy* in his knapsack. Soldiers often gathered with their comrades to sing hymns before retiring for the night. Stories circulated of a Bible that stopped a bullet whistling toward a soldier's heart. But veterans knew that a deck of cards did just as well, and they understood that neither Bibles nor cards offered protection against artillery.

Soldiers responded in various ways to constant danger and fear. Some talked or yelled loudly. (The Confederate rebel yell probably served to relieve some of the tension of battle as well as to frighten the enemy.) Others shook so much that they fell down, unable to control their limbs. A few soldiers could not wake up in the morning without being doused with cold water. Soldiers suffered from strained relations between officers and enlisted men, heavy chores, and boredom. Women camp followers cooked, did laundry, and provided sexual services for a price.

By 1862, the war's carnage and brutality had dispelled any lingering notions of war as a chivalrous enterprise. The reluctance of some commanders to pursue retreating armies or to initiate campaigns resulted in part from their recognition of how awful the war really was.

The War in the East

With Grant and Farragut squeezing the Confederacy in the West, Lincoln ordered a new offensive against Richmond in the East that he believed would end the war. Following the defeat at Bull Run, he had

A career army officer who resigned his commission to serve his state and new country, Confederate General Robert E. Lee's quiet courage and sense of duty inspired his men.

shaken up the Union high command and appointed General George B. McClellan to lead what was now called the Army of the Potomac. A superb organizer, McClellan would prove overly cautious on the field of battle.

In March 1862, at the outset of the **Peninsula Campaign**, McClellan moved his 112,000-man army out of Washington and maneuvered his forces by boat down the Potomac River and Chesapeake Bay to the peninsula between the York and James Rivers southeast of the Confederate capital.

Moving ponderously up the peninsula, McClellan clashed with Johnston's army inconclusively at Seven Pines in late May 1862. Johnston was badly wounded in the clash, and President Davis replaced him with General Robert E. Lee, who renamed the forces under his command the Army of Northern Virginia.

Lee was from a prominent Virginia family long accustomed to power and command. His father, "Light-Horse Harry" Lee, had been a Revolutionary War hero. Lee's reserved and aristocratic bearing

masked a gambler's disposition. Under his daring leadership, the Confederacy's defensive strategy underwent an important shift.

As McClellan had been making his way up the peninsula in May, Confederate general Stonewall Jackson had been conducting a brilliant hit-and-run campaign against confused Union troops in the Shenandoah Valley. In an offensive-defensive strategy, Jackson used selective strikes to maneuver the enemy into a vulnerable position and then deliver a decisive blow. It was this aggressive strategy, with its danger of high casualties and its promise of a knock-out victory, that Lee persuaded a reluctant President Davis to accept for the confrontation with McClellan.

Lee seized the initiative on June 25, 1862, attacking McClellan's right flank. Although inconclusive, the attack pushed the nervous McClellan into a defensive position. For a week, the armies sparred in a series of fierce engagements known collectively as the **Seven Days' Battles**. More than thirty thousand men were killed or wounded on both sides, the deadliest week of the war so far. Although McClellan prevailed in these contests, the carnage so shocked him that he withdrew down the peninsula and away from Richmond. The retreat bitterly disappointed Lincoln, who wanted McClellan to push on to the Confederate capital. The exasperated president placed John Pope at the head of the newly formed Army of Virginia to carry on the fight.

Although Lee had saved Richmond, his troops had suffered frightfully. He had lost one-fourth of his eighty thousand–man army, but he remained convinced of the wisdom of his offensive-defensive strategy. Better coordination between his staff and field commanders, he believed, would have reduced his casualties and inflicted greater damage on the enemy.

The **Second Battle of Bull Run** was as much a disaster for the Union as the first had been. Lee's generalship completely befuddled Pope and again saved Richmond. Lee and the Army of Northern Virginia were developing a reputation for invincibility.

Turning Points, 1862–1863

The impressive Confederate victories in the East masked the delicate condition of Southern fortunes. The longer the Confederacy held off Union offensives, the greater the likelihood of securing the South's independence. But the longer the war continued, the higher the probability that the Confederacy's shortcomings in men, finances, and materiel would erode its ability to keep fighting.

The waning summer months of 1862 brought other concerns to the Davis administration in Richmond. The Union was choking the South's commercial link to Europe. Davis looked to the nations of Europe for diplomatic recognition as well as for trade.

But the most important arena of the war remained the battlefield. Having stymied the Union war machine, Lee contemplated a bold move—a thrust into Northern territory to bring the conflict to the North and stoke Northerners' rising hostility to the war. President Lincoln also harbored a bold plan. Gradually during the spring and summer of 1862, the president had concluded that emancipation of the Confederacy's slaves was essential for preserving the Union. Emancipation would provide Federal forces with both a moral and strategic advantage over their foes. But Lincoln was reluctant to take this step before the Union's fortunes on the battlefield improved. As the fall of 1862 approached, both Union and Confederate governments prepared for the most significant conflicts of the war to date.

The Naval War

The Union's naval strategy was to blockade the Southern coast and capture its key seaports and river towns. The intention was to prevent arms, clothing, and food from reaching the Confederacy and keep cotton and tobacco from leaving. Destroying the South's ability to carry on trade would also prevent the Confederacy from raising money to purchase the goods it needed to wage war.

Neither side had much of a navy at the outset of the war. With more than 3,000 miles of Confederate coastline to cover, the Union blockade was weak at first. As time passed and the number of ships in the Union navy grew, the blockade tightened. The skyrocketing prices of Southern staples on world markets by 1862 attested to the effectiveness of the Union strategy.

Understandably, the Confederate naval strategy was to break the blockade and defend the South's vital rivers and seaports. They built several warships to serve as blockade runners and as privateers to attack Union merchant ships, and they did disrupt Federal operations. Historians disagree about the effectiveness of the Union naval blockade, but with limited resources and capital, the Confederacy was heavily dependent on the flow of trade. Any restriction in that flow hurt the Southern cause.

The Diplomatic War

Southerners, remembering the crucial role that timely French assistance had played in the American Revolution, thought that the recognition of their independence by overseas governments would legitimize their cause in the eyes of the world. Great Britain had several reasons to support the Confederate cause. After two wars and a succession of diplomatic wrangles, it had no great love of the United States. If the country divided, it would pose less of a threat to British economic and territorial aspirations. Also, the aristocratic pretensions of some Southerners appealed to their British counterparts. British foreign policy, however, had been antislavery for a quarter century, and the slavery issue turned many Britons against the South. The Union cause had support in high ruling circles, especially from Queen Victoria, as well as from middle-class and working-class Britons.

Emperor Napoleon III of France, who had imperial designs on Mexico, favored the Confederacy. A restored Union, he thought, would pose a greater threat to his ambitions than a divided one. But Napoleon feared antagonizing the powerful British and would not intervene unilaterally in the Confederate cause.

The Russians were probably the staunchest supporters of the Union abroad. The odd friendship between the Western world's most autocratic country and its most democratic one resulted primarily from political expediency. The Russian tsar, Alexander II, saw the United States as a counterweight to British power.

Southerners were convinced that their cotton was so important to the world economy that they could use it as a diplomatic bargaining chip. "You dare not to make war on cotton. . . . Cotton is King." So declared South Carolina senator James H. Hammond in a warning to the North in 1858. But King Cotton was no more successful at coercing the British—who had large cotton reserves and an alternate source of supply in Egypt—into granting recognition to the Confederacy than it was at stopping the North from going to war against the South.

The Davis administration did chalk up some minor diplomatic victories early in the war when Great Britain and France declared themselves neutral and allowed their merchants to sell arms and supplies to both Confederate and Union forces. This policy especially benefited the Confederacy, with its limited arsenal. But in the end, the Confederacy's hopes for diplomatic recognition depended on its ability to show that it could secure its independence on the battlefield. After Lee's victories in Virginia in the spring of 1862 and his subsequent decision to invade the North, British intervention in the war grew more likely. William Gladstone, England's future prime minister, believed that Lee would achieve his goal.

Antietam

The alarming arithmetic of the offensive-defensive strategy convinced Lee that the South could not sustain a prolonged conflict. He knew that his army must keep the pressure on Union forces and, if possible, destroy them quickly. He established camp at Frederick in September 1862, scattering his army at various sites, convinced that McClellan and the Army of the Potomac would not attack him.

At this point, luck intervened for the North. At an abandoned Confederate encampment, a Union corporal found three wrapped cigars on the ground, evidently tossed out by a careless Confederate officer. To the corporal's amazement, the wrapping was a copy of Lee's orders for the disposition of his army. But even with this information, "Little Mac" moved so cautiously that Lee had time to gather his and Jackson's regiments and retreat to defensive positions at Sharpsburg, Maryland, along Antietam Creek. There Lee's army of 50,000 men came to blows with McClellan's army of 75,000.

The **Battle of Antietam** saw the bloodiest single day of fighting in American history. About 2,100 Union soldiers and 2,700 Confederates died on the battlefield, and another 18,500, equally divided, were wounded. McClellan squandered his numerical superiority with uncoordinated and timid Union attacks. Although the armies had fought to a tactical draw, the battle was a strategic defeat for the Confederacy.

Antietam marked a major turning point in the war. It kept Lee from directly threatening Northern industry and financial institutions. It prompted Britain and France to abandon plans to grant recognition to the Confederacy. And it provided Lincoln with the victory he needed to announce the abolition of slavery.

Emancipation

President Lincoln despised slavery, but he had always maintained that preserving the Union was his primary war goal. An astute politician, Lincoln realized that he had to stress union and equivocate on slavery to keep the Northern public united in support of the war. But from the war's outset, the possibility of emancipation as a war objective was considered in the Republican Congress, within the Union army, and among citizens throughout the Northern states. Pressure grew within the Union army to declare emancipation as a way to deprive the South and the Confederate army of its labor force.

Lincoln said in his inaugural address that he had "no purpose, directly or indirectly, to interfere with the institution of slavery in the states where it exists." Despite the urging of some Republican colleagues, he stood by this pledge and revoked several emancipation edicts. By March 1862, however, his moral repugnance toward slavery and the military arguments for abolition led him to propose a resolution, which Congress adopted, supporting the compensated emancipation of slaves. The measure died, however, when Congress failed to appropriate funds for it. Pressure from Northern civilians, Union soldiers, and Congress for some form of emancipation mounted in the spring of 1862. In response, the Republican Congress prohibited slavery in the territories and abolished slavery in the District of Columbia. The act emancipating the district's slaves called for compensating slave owners and colonizing the freed slaves in black republics such as Haiti and Liberia. Then in July 1862, Congress passed the **Confiscation Act**, which ordered the seizure of land from disloyal Southerners and the emancipation of their slaves.

Although support for emancipation had grown both in the army and among civilians, Lincoln still faced political considerations that dictated against it. Emancipation was still not favored by a majority in the North, especially not in the border states. But freeing the slaves would appeal to the strong antislavery sentiment in Britain and gain support for the Union cause abroad. And it would weaken the Confederacy's ability to wage war by removing a crucial source of labor.

By mid-1862, the president had resolved to act on his moral convictions and proclaim emancipation. Taking the advice of Secretary of State Seward, however, he decided to wait for a battlefield victory so that the measure would not appear an act of desperation. Antietam gave the president his opening, narrow though it was, and on September 22, 1862, he announced his intention to issue the **Emancipation Proclamation**, to take effect January 1, 1863, in all states still in rebellion. The proclamation exempted slaves in the border states loyal to the Union and in areas under Federal occupation.

Southerners reacted to the Emancipation Proclamation with outrage, while Northerners generally approved it. But the Emancipation Proclamation represented far more than its qualified words and phrases expressed. "A mighty *act*," Massachusetts governor John Andrew called it. Lincoln had freed the slaves. He and the Union war effort were now tied to the cause of freedom. What began as a war to save the Union had became a holy war of deliverance. Freedom and Union entwined in the public consciousness of the North. Emancipation also unified the Republican party and strengthened the president's hand in conducting the war.

"Stealing" Freedom

As word of the Emancipation Proclamation raced through the slave grapevine, slaves rejoiced that their long-awaited day of jubilee had arrived.

Southern masters fought to deter their slaves by severely punishing the families of black men who fled to Union lines and employing slavecatchers to reclaim runaways. But in the end, slaveholders could not stem the tide of slaves fleeing toward the Union lines and freedom. The 1862 Confiscation Act included slaves with other Confederate property as the "contraband" of war and subject to confiscation,

a term Union general Benjamin Butler had applied to escaped slaves as early as May 1861. As they helped the Union cause, **contrabands** also sought to help fellow slaves "steal" their freedom. The former slaves who arrived at Federal camps after emancipation often encountered poor conditions but relished their freedom nonetheless. After 1863, ex-slaves served in increasing numbers in the Union army.

Black Troops in the Union Army

More than 80 percent of the roughly 180,000 black soldiers and 20,000 black sailors who fought for the Union were slaves and free blacks from the South. For the typical Southern black who joined the army, the passage from bondage to freedom came quickly. Making his escape from his master, he perhaps "stole" his family as well. He typically experienced his first days of freedom behind Union lines, where he may have learned to read and write. Finally, he put on the Federal uniform, experiencing as one Southern black volunteer commented, "the biggest thing that ever happened in my life." For blacks, the promise of freedom and redemption outweighed the dangers of combat.

Although blacks were eager to engage the enemy and fought as ably as their white comrades,

Once orders were issued allowing the recruitment of black troops, posters like this appeared throughout the North. The illustrations stressed the dignity and manhood of military service, but also showed segregated soldiers and white officers.

COME AND JOIN US BROTHERS.
PUBLISHED BY THE SUPERVISORY COMMITTEE FOR RECRUITING COLORED REGIMENTS
1210 CHESTNUT ST. PHILADELPHIA.

American Views

LEWIS DOUGLASS ON THE FIGHTING OF THE 54TH MASSACHUSETTS REGIMENT

When the Civil War began, Union officials did not permit African Americans to enlist. But northern blacks successfully pressured the Lincoln administration to reverse that policy and began fighting in all-black units as early as 1862. The excerpt here is a letter from Lewis Douglass (son of black abolitionist Frederick Douglass) of the 54th Massachusetts Regiment to his wife after the failed Union assault on Fort Wagner in South Carolina.

❖ **What motivated northern blacks, all of whom were free, to enlist by the thousands in the Union army?**

July 20 [1863]

My Dear Amelia:

I have been in two fights, and am unhurt. I am about to go in another I believe tonight. Our men fought well on both occasions. The last one was desperate. We charged that terrible battery on . . . Fort Wagner and were repulsed. . . . I escaped unhurt from amidst that perfect hail of shot and shell. It was terrible. . . . This regiment has established its reputation as a fighting regiment. Not a man flinched, though it was a trying time. Men fell all around me. . . . Our men would close up again, but it was no use. . . . How I got out of that fight alive I cannot tell, but I am here. My dear girl, I hope again to see you. I must bid you farewell should I be killed. Remember if I die, I die in a good cause. I wish we had a hundred thousand colored troops. We would put an end to this war.

Your own loving
Lewis

Source: *Carter G. Woodson, ed.*, The Mind of the Negro as Reflected in Letters Written During the Crisis 1800–1860 *(1926).*

they received lower pay than whites and performed the most menial duties in camp. Abolitionists and black leaders in the North pressured President Lincoln for more equitable treatment of African-American recruits. When Frederick Douglass complained to Lincoln about the lower pay that black troops received, the president defended the practice. Despite discrimination, blacks fought valiantly at Port Hudson, Louisiana; near Charleston; and, late in the war, at the siege of Petersburg, Virginia. The most celebrated black encounter with Confederate troops occurred in July 1863 during a futile assault by the 54th Massachusetts Regiment on **Fort Wagner** outside Charleston (see "American Views: Lewis Douglass on the Fighting of the 54th Massa-chusetts Regiment"). The Northern press, previously lukewarm toward black troops, heaped praise on the effort.

Fredericksburg and Chancellorsville

In late 1862, after Antietam, the president replaced McClellan with General Ambrose E. Burnside. The new chief of the Army of the Potomac, an imposing physical presence, sported bushy whiskers on his cheeks that came to be known as "sideburns," a transposition of the two parts of his name. Despite his commanding stature, Burnside was shy and insecure.

Moving swiftly against Lee's dispersed army in northern Virginia, Burnside reached the Rappahannock River opposite **Fredericksburg** in November 1862 (see Map 16-3). But the pontoon bridges to ford his 120,000 soldiers across the river arrived three weeks late, giving Lee an opportunity to gather his 78,000 men. On December 13, the Union forces launched a poorly coordinated and foolish frontal assault that the Confederates repelled, inflicting heavy Federal casualties. Burnside was relieved of his command, and Major General Joseph Hooker was installed in his place.

Map 16-3   From Fredericksburg to Gettysburg: The War in the East, December 1862–July 1863
By all logic, the increasingly outgunned and out-financed Confederacy should have been showing signs of faltering by 1863. But bungling by Union generals at Fredericksburg and Chancellorsville sustained Southern fortunes and encouraged Robert E. Lee to attempt another Northern invasion.

Area controlled by Union
Area controlled by Confederacy
◄— Union advances
◄— Confederate advances
◄-- Confederate retreats
✳ Union victories
✳ Confederate victories

The hard-drinking Hooker lacked Burnside's humility but not his incompetence. Between May 1 and May 4, Lee's army delivered a series of crushing attacks on Hooker's forces at **Chancellorsville**. Outnumbered two to one, Lee had pulled off another stunning victory—but at a high cost, losing some thirteen thousand men. Lee also lost Stonewall Jackson at Chancellorsville. Nervous Confederate sentries mistakenly shot and wounded him as he returned from a reconnoitering mission, and he died a few days later. Known for his lightning strikes at the enemy and his brilliant understanding of the tactics of modern warfare, Jackson had helped Lee win some of the Confederacy's most stunning victories in 1862. Lee recognized the tragedy of Jackson's loss for himself and his country.

Still, Lee appeared invincible. Chancellorsville thrust Lincoln into another bout of despair. "My God!" he exclaimed in agony, "What will the country say! What will the country say!" Meanwhile, Lee took advantage of the Confederacy's momentum and the Union's gloom, broke camp and headed north once again.

Gettysburg

President Lincoln sent the Union Army of the Potomac after Lee. But General Hooker dallied, and an infuriated Lincoln replaced Hooker with George Gordon Meade.

Lee and Meade were personal friends—they had served together during the Mexican War—and the change in command worried the Confederate general. He had counted on the bungling Hooker as his opponent. "General Meade," he commented prophetically, "will commit no blunder in my front."

Meade set out after the Confederate army, which was encamped at Cashtown, Pennsylvania, 45 miles from Harrisburg. That the greatest battle of the war erupted at nearby **Gettysburg** was pure chance (see Map 16-4). During the first day of battle, July 1, the Confederates appeared to gain the upper hand, forcing Union forces back from the town to a new position on Cemetery Hill. On the second day, they seized the initiative and took several key locations along Cemetery Ridge before Federal forces pushed them back to the previous day's positions. On July 3, the third day of the battle, Lee made a fateful error. Believing that the center of Meade's line was weak, he ordered an all-out assault against it. Meade was prepared for Lee's assault. When the Union guns suddenly went silent, the Confederates, thinking they had knocked them out, began a charge led by General George Pickett. As the Confederate infantry

Map 16-4   *The Battle of Gettysburg, July 1–3, 1863*
In a war that lasted four years, it is difficult to point to the decisive battle. But clearly the outcome during those hot July days at Gettysburg set the tone for the rest of the war. The result was unclear until the final day of battle and, even then, it might have gone either way. Winning by a whisker was enough to propel Union armies to a string of victories over the next year, and throw Confederate forces back on their defenses among an increasingly despairing population. Gettysburg marked the last major Southern invasion of the North.

marched out with battle colors flying, the Union artillery opened up again, supported by Federal riflemen. They tore apart the charging Southerners and half of Pickett's thirteen thousand–man division lay dead or wounded.

At Gettysburg, Lee had violated his own rule never to order a frontal assault. After the battle, he explained, "I believed my men were invincible." By the second day of the battle, he may have been suffering from combat fatigue. Meade allowed Lee to withdraw into Maryland and cross the Potomac to Virginia. Gettysburg was the bloodiest battle of the war. The Union suffered 23,000 casualties; the Confederacy, 28,000 (see "American Views: The Horror of Battle").

Vicksburg

On July 4, one day after Pickett's charge at Gettysburg, the city of **Vicksburg**, the last major Confederate stronghold on the Mississippi, surrendered to Ulysses S. Grant. Grant is often perceived, incorrectly, as a general who ground out victories by dint of his superior numbers, with little finesse and less concern for his troops' safety. But in his campaigns in the western Confederacy, he demonstrated an ability to use his forces creatively, swiftly, and with a minimum loss of life.

Vicksburg presented Grant with several strategic obstacles (see Map 16-5). The formidable defenses on the city's western edge, which towered over the Mississippi, had thwarted a naval assault by Union admiral David G. Farragut in May 1862. And an assault by William T. Sherman later that year had failed in the labyrinth of swamps, creeks, and woods that protected the city from the north. The only feasible approaches appeared to be from the south and east.

By March 1863, Grant had devised a brilliant plan to take Vicksburg that called for rapid maneuvering and expert coordination. Grant had his twenty thousand Union troops ferried across the Mississippi from the Louisiana side at a point south of Vicksburg. Then he marched them quickly into the interior of Mississippi. Cut off from supplies, they moved northeastward, captured the Mississippi state capital at Jackson, and turned west toward Vicksburg. On May 22, 1863, Grant settled down in front of the city, less than 600 yards from Confederate positions. Grant's tight siege and the Union navy's bombardment from the river cut the city off completely. As food stores dwindled, residents were forced to eat mules and rats to survive. Their situation hopeless, General John Pemberton and his thirty thousand–man garrison surrendered on July 4.

Chattanooga

As Grant was besieging Vicksburg in June 1863, Union general William S. Rosecrans, commanding the Army of the Cumberland, advanced on Confederate general Braxton Bragg, whose Army of Tennessee held **Chattanooga**, a "doorway" on the rail-

Map 16-5   *Vicksburg and Chattanooga: The War in the West, 1863*
Devising a brilliant strategy, Union General Ulysses S. Grant took the last major Mississippi River stronghold from Confederate hands on July 4, 1863, dealing a significant economic and morale blow to southern forces. Coupled with the defeat at Gettysburg a day earlier, the fall of Vicksburg portended a bitter finale to hopes for Southern independence. Grant completed his domination of the West by joining forces with several Union generals to capture Chattanooga and push Confederate forces into Georgia setting the stage for the capture of that key southern state by the Federals in 1864.

American Views

THE HORROR OF BATTLE

In this excerpt, Union general Carl Schurz describes a field hospital just after the battle of Gettysburg in July 1863. The horrors of the Civil War evoked countless such testimonials. The unprecedented carnage quickly dispelled notions of the romance of war on both sides.

❖ **Why would Schurz, a Republican, depict the hospital scene in such graphic terms?**

At Gettysburg the wounded—many thousands of them—were carried to the farmsteads behind our lines. The houses, the barns, the sheds, and the open barnyards were crowded with moaning and wailing human beings, and still an unceasing procession of stretchers and ambulances was coming in from all sides to augment the number of the sufferers. A heavy rain set in during the day . . . and large numbers had to remain unprotected in the open, there being no room left under roof. I saw long rows of men lying under the eaves of the buildings, the water pouring down upon their bodies in streams.

Most of the operating tables were placed in the open where the light was best, some of them partially protected against the rain by tarpaulins or blankets stretched upon poles. There stood the surgeons, their sleeves rolled up to the elbows, their bare arms as well as their linen aprons smeared with blood, their knives not seldom held between their teeth, while they were helping a patient on or off the table, or had their hands otherwise occupied; around them pools of blood and amputated arms or legs in heaps, sometimes more than man-high.

Carl Schurz

Source: *Carl Schurz*, The Reminiscences of Carl Schurz, *vol. 3 (1907–1908).*

---

road that linked Richmond to the Lower South. The capture of the city would complete the uncoupling of the West from the eastern Confederacy.

Bragg lacked confidence in his men and consistently overestimated the force and cunning of his enemy. At Rosecrans's approach, he abandoned Chattanooga and took up positions at nearby Chickamauga Creek. Recognizing the importance of the pending battle, President Davis ordered Lee to send General James Longstreet and eleven thousand troops to reinforce Bragg.

When the two armies clashed at Chickamauga on September 19, Bragg and Longstreet pushed Rosecrans back to Chattanooga. Bragg seized the railroad leading into Chattanooga and bottled up Rosecrans there much as Grant had confined Pemberton at Vicksburg. Both sides had suffered heavily.

Suddenly, the Union's careful strategy for the conquest of the western Confederacy seemed in jeopardy. President Lincoln, determined to hold Chattanooga and deal a heavy blow to the Army of Tennessee, shuffled his command, replacing Rosecrans with George Thomas and appointing Grant to head all Union operations in the West.

The Confederate position on the heights overlooking Chattanooga appeared impregnable. But the Confederate camp was plagued by dissension. Some officers openly questioned Bragg's ability. President Davis considered replacing him but had no one else available with Bragg's experience. Instead, he ordered Longstreet (along with one-third of Bragg's army) on a futile expedition against Union forces at Knoxville, Tennessee. Converging on Chattanooga with reinforcements, Union generals Grant, Sherman, and Hooker took advantage of the divided Confed-

SUMMARY

MAJOR BATTLES OF THE CIVIL WAR, 1861–1863

Battle or Campaign	Date	Outcome and Consequences
First Bull Run	July 21, 1861	Confederate victory, destroyed the widespread belief in the North that the war would end quickly, fueled Confederate sense of superiority
Forts Henry and Donelson	Feb. 6–16, 1862	Union victory, gave the North control of strategic river systems in the western Confederacy and closed an important link between the eastern and western Confederacy
Shiloh Church	Apr. 6–7, 1862	Union victory, high casualties transformed attitudes about the war on both sides
Seven Days' Battles	June 25–July 1, 1862	Standoff, halted Union General McClellan's advance on Richmond in the Peninsula Campaign
Second Bull Run	Aug. 29–30, 1862	Confederate victory, reinforced Confederate General Robert E. Lee's reputation for invincibility
Antietam	Sept. 17, 1862	Standoff, halted Lee's advance into the North, eliminated Confederacy's chance for diplomatic recognition, encouraged Lincoln to issue the Emancipation Proclamation
Fredericksburg	Dec. 13, 1862	Confederate victory, revived morale of Lee's army
Chancellorsville	May 2–6, 1863	Confederate victory, Confederate General Stonewall Jackson killed, encouraged Lee to again invade North
Gettysburg	July 1–3, 1863	Union victory, halted Confederate advance in the North, major psychological blow to Confederacy
Vicksburg	Nov. 1862–July 1863	Union victory, closed the key remaining Confederate port on the Mississippi, with Gettysburg, dealt a severe blow to Confederate cause
Chattanooga	Aug.–Nov. 1863	Union victory, solidified Union dominance in the West and cleared the way to Atlanta

erate army to break the siege. In a series of precise and coordinated maneuvers, the four generals captured Confederate positions and forced Bragg's army to retreat into Georgia. The Union now dominated most of the West and faced an open road to the East.

The War in the Trans-Mississippi West

The Confederacy's reverses at Vicksburg and Chattanooga mirrored its misfortunes farther west beyond the Mississippi River. Although a relatively minor theater of war, the territory west of the Mississippi, particularly Texas, provided supplies and strategic advantages for the Confederate West. Texas was critical to Confederate fortunes, both as a source of supply for the East and as a base for the conquest of the Far West. Texas, however, was far from secure. It suffered from internal dissent and violence on its borders. For a time, Texas maintained commercial contact with the rest of the Confederacy through Matamoros, Mexico. But by 1864, with the Union in control of the Mississippi, Texas had lost its strategic importance. The Confederacy's transcontinental aspirations died early in the war. In March 1862, a Confederate army seeking to conquer the Southwest was overwhelmed by Union forces at the **Battle of Glorieta Pass** in New Mexico. The Southwest from New Mexico to California would remain firmly in Union hands.

Conclusion

By late fall 1863, the Civil War was over in large portions of the former Confederacy. Northern forces controlled the Mississippi River and all the ports along its banks. Federal gunboats patrolled other rivers in the Confederate West, and Union troops garrisoned strategic forts along these waterways.

The Confederacy had also lost the war over slavery in many parts of the South. Tens of thousands of slaves abandoned plantations, farms, and towns to find freedom behind Union lines, depriving the South of their labor. And when many former slaves signed on to fight with Union armies, the South suffered doubly.

Not the least of Union advantages in the fall of 1863 was the ability of President Lincoln to articulate the meaning of the war for soldiers and civilians, for Americans and Europeans. In November, the president was asked to say a few words at the dedication of the federal cemetery at Gettysburg. There, surrounded by a somber scene of fresh graves, Lincoln bound the cause of the Union to that of the country's founders: "Fourscore and seven years ago our fathers brought forth upon this continent a new nation, conceived in liberty and dedicated to the proposition that all men are created equal. Now we are engaged in a great civil war, testing whether that nation, or any nation so conceived and so dedicated can long endure." Not only did the two-minute Gettysburg Address capture what Union supporters were fighting for, but it also connected their sacrifices to the noble causes of freedom and democratic government.

Without battlefield victories, similar claims by the Davis administration would ring hollow. Historians have often noted how Lincoln articulated the Union cause better than Davis did the Confederate cause. Whatever shortcomings the Southern president suffered as an orator, however, the worsening situation on the battlefield left him little to say.

The Confederacy also faced an enemy with a seemingly endless reserve of troops and supplies. The North thrived on war and victory, while the South's economy and will faltered with defeat. The outcome of the war was not yet foreordained. The South still had armies in the field, a government in Richmond, and a heart for independence. But the Confederate cause was growing desperate.

Review Question

1. How did the Union and the Confederacy compare in terms of resources, leadership, and military strategies in the period 1861–1863? What impact did these factors have on the course of the war?

2. What was the significance of the battles of Antietam and Gettysburg? In what ways were they turning points in the Civil War?

3. If you were a Confederate general, what would you have done differently at Gettysburg? At Vicksburg?

4. What effects did the Emancipation Proclamation have on both the Union and Confederate causes?

Recommended Reading

Stephen Crane, *The Red Badge of Courage* (1895; reprinted 1984). The Civil War did not inspire great American novels. But this is a notable exception that not only depicts the horrors of combat, but its impact on the soldiers who fought.

Shelby Foote, *The Civil War: A Narrative*, 3 vols. (1958–1974). For a highly readable, if weighty, narrative of the Civil War, these volumes are an excellent choice. Although the account is thin on interpretation and obviously omits recent research on blacks and women in the war, it is a balanced, comprehensive view of the conflict.

James M. McPherson, *Battle Cry of Freedom: The Civil War Era* (1982). This is probably the best account of the war in print. It is more up-to-date than the Foote volumes, and more inter-

But for the immediate future, winning the war remained paramount for the Union. As Lincoln and his generals prepared the North's final campaigns, the South hoped General Lee could produce one last miracle.

War Transforms the North

Union successes by 1863 had a profound impact on both sides. For the North, hopes of victory and reunion increased. The Federal government expanded its bureaucracy to wage war efficiently, and a Republican-dominated Congress passed legislation that broadened Federal power and furthered the war effort. The Lincoln administration faced some opposition from within Congress, the Democratic party, and from state leaders. But it successfully weathered dissent thanks to the president's political skill, the desire of the Republicans to remain in power, and the Union's improving military fortunes. Boosted by Federal economic legislation and wartime demand, the Northern economy boomed. Women entered the work force in growing numbers. But labor unrest and class and racial tensions suggest that prosperity had a price.

Wartime Legislation and Politics

Before the Civil War, the Federal government rarely affected citizens' lives directly. But raising troops, protecting territory, and mobilizing the economy for war required the kind of strong and active central government the Republican party favored. With the departure of the South from the Union, Republicans dominated all branches of the Federal administration. This left them in a position to test the constitutional limits of federal authority.

President Lincoln began almost immediately to use executive authority to suppress opposition to the war effort in the North. Within the first few weeks of the conflict, he ordered raids on telegraph offices in the North and the seizure of telegrams to intercept seditious messages to the South. In one of his most controversial actions, he also issued a temporary suspension of the writ of **habeas corpus**, the constitutional requirement that protects a defendant against illegal imprisonment. Suspending it allowed authorities to arrest suspected Confederate agents

and hold them indefinitely and was permitted by the Constitution "when in cases of Rebellion or Invasion the public Safety" require it. Explaining his extraordinary actions in a July 4, 1861, message to Congress, Lincoln stated, "It became necessary for me to choose whether I should let the government fall into ruin, or whether . . . availing myself of the broader powers conferred by the Constitution, in case of insurrection, I would make an effort to save it." The suspension became permanent in September, 1862 and was used primarily in the border states to detain those suspected of trading with the enemy, defrauding the War department, draft evasion, or other offenses.

Executive sanctions fell particularly hard on the Democratic party. "Disloyalty" was difficult to define in the midst of war. Though many Democrats opposed secession and supported the Union, they challenged the president on the conduct of the war, on emancipation, and on Lincoln's coolness toward peace initiatives. A few had ties with Confederate agents. Republicans called these dissenters "Copperheads," after the poisonous snake. It was hard to know where sympathy for the South ended and active support of the Confederacy began.

Despite the suspension of habeas corpus, Lincoln compiled a fairly good record for upholding basic American civil liberties. Although the authorities shut down a handful of newspapers temporarily, the administration made no attempt to control the news or subvert the electoral process. Two major elections were held during the war. In the first, the off-year election in 1862, Republicans retained control of Congress but lost several seats to Democrats. In the presidential election of 1864, Lincoln won reelection in a hard-fought contest.

While fellow Republicans sometimes chastised the president for violating civil liberties, mismanaging military command assignments, or moving too slowly on emancipation, they rarely threatened to disrupt the party. Lincoln also found support from Republican governors and state governments.

But there was dissent in the Republican party, and it had an effect on national policy. **Radical Republicans** hounded Lincoln from early in his administration, establishing the **Joint Committee on the Conduct of the War** to examine and monitor military policy. Some of them accused Democratic generals, including McClellan, of incompetence. They also pressed Lincoln for quicker action on emancipation. But they supported the president on most crucial matters.

Lincoln likewise supported his party on an array of initiatives in Congress. Turning to the settlement of the West, they passed the **Homestead Act** in May 1862. which granted 160 acres of land free to

CHRONOLOGY

1862 May: Congress passes Homestead Act.

1862 July: Congress passes Federal Land Grant College Act (Morrill Act).

1862 September: President Lincoln suspends the writ of habeas corpus.

1863 February: Congress passes National Banking Act.

1863 July: New York Draft Riot occurs.

1864 May: Battle of the Wilderness.

1864 June: Battle of Cold Harbor.

1864 September: Sherman captures Atlanta.

1864 November: President Lincoln is reelected. Sherman begins his march to the sea.

1865 January: Congress passes Thirteenth Amendment to the Constitution, outlawing slavery (ratified December 1865).

1865 February: Charleston surrenders.

1865 March: Confederate Congress authorizes enlistment of black soldiers.

1865 April: Federal troops enter Richmond. Lee surrenders to Grant at Appomattox Court House. Lincoln is assassinated.

---

any settler in the territories who agreed to improve the land within five years of the grant. The act was a boon for railroad companies.

Other legislation to boost the nation's economy included the **Land Grant College Act** of 1862, a protective tariff that same year, and the **National Banking Act** of 1863. The Land Grant Act awarded the proceeds from the sale of public lands to the states for the establishment of colleges offering instruction in "agriculture and mechanical arts." The tariff legislation protected Northern industry from foreign competition while raising revenue for the Union. The National Banking Act of 1863 replaced the bank notes of individual states, which were often backed by flimsy reserves and subject to wild fluctuations in value, with a uniform national currency and brought order to a chaotic monetary system.

However, the expansion of government into some quarters, such as the draft laws, was not welcomed.

Conscription and the Draft Riots

Congress passed the first national conscription law in 1863. Almost immediately, evasion, obstruction, and weak enforcement threatened to undermine it. As military authorities began arresting draft dodgers and deserters, secret societies formed to harbor draftees and instruct them on evasion. Conflicts between citizens and federal officials over the draft sometimes erupted in violence. The worst draft riot occurred in New York City in July 1863, when a mostly Irish mob protesting conscription burned the federal marshal's headquarters. Racial and class antagonisms quickly joined antidraft anger as the mob went on a rampage through the city's streets, fighting police, plundering houses of the wealthy, and crying, "Down with the rich!" It was finally quelled by army units fresh from Gettysburg, and the draft resumed a month later.

The Northern Economy

"The North," one historian has said, "was fighting the South with one hand and getting rich with the other behind its back." After an initial downturn during the uncertain months preceding the war, the Northern economy picked up quickly. High tariffs and massive federal spending soon made up for the loss of Southern markets and the closing of the Mississippi River. Profits skyrocketed for some businesses like the railroads. New industries boomed, and new inventions increased manufacturing efficiency. For example, technological advances in the sewing machine industry, which was first commercialized in the 1850s, greatly increased the output of the North's garment factories.

Despite the loss of manpower to the demands of industry and the military, the productivity of Northern agriculture grew during the war. As machines replaced men on the farm, the manufacturers of farm machinery became wealthy. Crop failures in Europe dramatically increased the demand for American grain.

Working people should have benefited from wartime prosperity, with men off to war, immigration down, and labor in short supply. Although wages increased, prices rose more. Declining real wages led to exploitation, especially of women in garment factories. The trade union movement, which suffered a serious setback in the depression of 1857, revived. Local unions of shoemakers, carpenters, and miners emerged in 1862 across the North, and so did a few national organizations. By 1865, more than 200,000 Northern workers belonged to a labor union.

Employers struck back at union organizing by hiring strikebreakers, usually blacks. Labor conflicts between striking white workers and black strikebreakers sparked riots in New York City and Cincinnati. The racial antagonism accounted in part for workers' opposition to Lincoln's Emancipation Proclamation and for the continued strength of the Democratic party in Northern cities.

The promise of enormous profits bred greed and corruption as well as exploitation. Illicit trade between North and South was inevitable when cotton could be bought at 20 cents a pound in New Orleans and sold for $1.90 a pound at Boston. Profiteers not only defied the government to trade with the enemy but also sometimes swindled the government outright, supplying defective clothing to soldier at inflated prices.

Some Northerners viewed the spending spree uneasily. They were disturbed to see older men flaunting their wealth while young men were dying on the battlefield. "The lavish profusion in which the old southern cotton aristocracy used to indulge," wrote an indignant reporter for the *New York World*, "is completely eclipsed by the dash, parade, and magnificence of the new northern shoddy aristocracy. . . . "

Exploited workers likewise resented the "shoddy aristocracy."

Comments like these hinted at the deep social and ethical problems that were emerging in Northern society and would become more pronounced in the decades after the Civil War. For the time being, the benefits of economic development for the Union cause outweighed its negative consequences. The thriving Northern economy fed, clothed, and armed the Union's soldiers and kept most civilians employed providing Northern women with unprecedented opportunities.

Northern Women and the War

More than 100,000 Northern women took jobs in factories, sewing rooms, and arsenals during the Civil War. Stepping in for their departed husbands, fathers, and sons, they often performed tasks previously reserved for men, but at lower pay.

Women also had the opportunity to serve the war effort directly in another profession previously dominated by men—nursing. Physicians and officers, however, although they tolerated women nurses as nurturing morale boosters, thought little of their ability to provide medical care. Women sometimes challenged this condescending view, braving dismissal to confront the medical-military establishment head-on. Clara Barton, among the most notable nurses of the war, treated soldiers on the battlefield at great peril to her safety and to the consternation of officers.

If the war created opportunities for many women, it also left tens of thousands widowed and devastated. In a society that assumed that men supported women, the death of a husband could be a financial and psychological disaster. Many women

Nurse Ann Bell tends a fallen Union soldier. Although medical practices were primitive and many young men died from poorly treated wounds or disease, the U.S. Sanitary Commission attempted to improve care in Union hospitals during the war. The war helped open nursing as a respectable occupation for women.

were left to survive on meager pensions with few skills they could use to support themselves.

The new economic opportunities the war created for women left Northern society more open to a broader view of women's roles. One indication of this change was the admission of women to eight previously all-male state universities after the war. Like the class and racial tensions that surfaced in Northern cities, the shifting role of women during the Civil War hinted at the promises and problems of postwar life. The changing scale and nature of the American economy, the expanded role of government, and the shift in class, racial, and gender relations are all trends that signaled what historians call the "modernization" of American society.

The Confederacy Disintegrates

Even under the best of conditions, the newly formed political and economic institutions of the Confederacy would have had difficulty maintaining control over the country's class and racial tensions. But as battlefield losses mounted, the Confederacy disintegrated. Defeat dissolves the bonds that hold a small society like the Confederacy together and exposes the large and small divisions within it. After 1863, defeat infected Confederate politics, ruined the Southern economy, and eventually invaded the hearts and minds of the Southern people. As the Davis administration tried to deal with a maddening array of dissenting or indifferent politicians, the South pinned its waning hopes on its defensive military strategy. If it could prolong the conflict a little longer, perhaps a war-weary North would replace Lincoln and the Republicans in the 1864 elections with a Democratic president and Congress inclined to make peace.

Southern Politics

Dissent plagued Southern politics before the end of the war's first year. Residents of western Virginia mounted a secession movement of their own, declaring themselves for the Union and forming the new state of West Virginia. Several counties in north Alabama, in German-speaking districts in Texas, and throughout the mountains of Tennessee and North Carolina contemplated similar action.

But as the war turned against the Confederacy, southerners increasingly turned against each other. Some joined the peace societies that emerged as early as 1861 in Arkansas and soon after in most other Southern states.

States' rights, a major principle of the seceding states, proved an obstacle to the Davis administration's efforts to exert central authority. The governors of Georgia and North Carolina gave the Richmond government particular difficulty, hoarding munitions, soldiers, supplies, food, and money. Even cooperative governors refused to allow state agents to collect taxes for the Confederacy.

Unlike Abraham Lincoln, Jefferson Davis could not appeal to party loyalty to control dissent because the Confederacy had no parties. Davis's frigid personality, his insistence on attending to minute details, and his inability to accept even constructive criticism gracefully also set him apart from Lincoln and worsened political tensions within the Confederacy.

Several parts of the South began clamoring for peace during the fateful summer of 1863. In a tour of his state that year, North Carolina political leader Jonathan Worth heard calls for the overthrow of the Davis administration and a separate peace with the North. "Every man [I] met," he concluded "was for reconstruction on the basis of the old [U.S.] constitution." By November 1864, the Confederacy suffered as much from internal disaffection as from the attacks of Union armies. Confederate authorities could not suppress civilian unrest in Virginia, North Carolina, and Tennessee, and Union spies operated openly in Mobile, Wilmington, and Richmond.

Davis and other Confederate leaders might have averted some of these political problems had they succeeded in building a strong sense of Confederate nationalism among soldiers and civilians. They tried several strategies to do so. For example, Davis tried to identify the Confederacy's fight for independence with the American Revolution of 1776. But egalitarian Revolutionary ideals quickly lost their appeal in the face of poverty, starvation, and defeat. Davis also tried to cast the Confederacy as a bastion of freedom standing up to Lincoln's despotic abuse of executive authority, but he, too, eventually invoked authority similar to Lincoln's. The diaries of Southern soldiers reveal devotion to God, state, locality, family, and friends but rarely to the Confederacy. In a devout society convinced it was fighting a holy war, some Southerners sought some moral failing to account for their mounting losses. Some identified slavery as the culprit.

The Southern Economy

Defeat came to the South, according to one historian, "not because the government failed to mobilize the South's resources" but "because there was virtually nothing left to mobilize." By 1863, the Confederacy

American Views

SOUTHERN WOMEN AGAINST THE WAR

As Confederate military fortunes deteriorated during and after 1863, food shortages, marauding Yankees and deserters, and widespread poverty plagued the home front. The documents excerpted here reflect the growing desperation of the women left to cope with these conditions, the pressures on soldiers to desert and return to their families, and the inability of public officials to boost sagging Confederate morale.

❖ **Why did some Southern women encourage their husbands to desert?**

❖ **How should Confederate officials have responded to women who wanted their men to return home?**

❖ **What do these documents reveal about their authors' attitude toward Southern independence?**

Letter of Martha Revis to her husband
Marshall, Madison County, North Carolina, July 20, 1863
Dear Husband: I seat myself to drop you a few lines to let you know that me and Sally is well as common, and I hope these few lines will come to hand and find you well and doing well. . . . The people is all turning to Union here since the Yankees has got Vicksburg [on July 4]. I want you to come home as soon as you can after you git this letter. . . . That is all I can think of, only I want you to come home the worst that I ever did. . . . The folks is leaving here, and going North as fast as they can.
Your wife, till death.

Petition from Women of Miller County, Georgia, to President Jefferson Davis
September 8, 1863
Our crops is limited and so short . . . cannot reach the first day of march next . . . our fencing is unanamosly allmost decayed . . . But little of any sort to Rescue us and our children from a unanamus starveation. . . . An allwise god ho is slow to anger and full of grace and murcy and without Respect of persons and full of love and charity that he will send down his fury and judgement in a very grate manar [on] all those our leading men and those that are in power ef thare is no more favors shone to those the mothers and wives. . . . I tell you that with out some grate and speadly alterating in the conduckting of afares in this our little nation god will frown on it and that speadly.

Source: *Paul D. Escott and David R. Goldfield, eds.,* Major Problems in the History of the American South *(1990).*

was having a difficult time feeding itself. Destruction of farms by both sides and growing Union control of waterways and rail lines restricted the distribution of food. Speculators held certain commodities off the market to drive up prices, making shortages worse. People ate rats and mules to supplement their meager diets. More than one-quarter of Alabama's population was receiving public welfare by the end of the war. "Deaths from starvation have absolutely occurred," a Confederate official in the state informed President Davis in 1864.

Southern soldiers had marched off to war in neat uniforms with shiny buttons, many leaving behind self-sustaining families. But during the winter

Wartime food shortages, skyrocketing inflation, and rumors of hoarding and price-gouging drove women in several southern cities to protest violently. Demonstrations like the 1863 food riot shown here reflected a larger rending of southern society as Confederate losses and casualties mounted on the battlefield. Some Southern women placed survival and providing for their families ahead of boosting morale and silently supporting a war effort that had taken their men away. Their defection hurt the Confederate cause.

of 1863–1864, women lined their clothes with rags and newspapers to keep warm. The predations of both Union and Confederate soldiers further threatened civilians in the South. The women and children left alone on farms and plantations were vulnerable to stragglers and deserters from both armies. Southerners also feared that slaves on isolated plantations would rise up against their masters. Most slaves, however, were more intent on escape than revenge. Some felt genuine affection for the families they served and stayed on with them even after the war.

As Confederate casualties mounted, more and more Southern women and children, like their Northern counterparts, faced the pain of grief. Funeral processions became commonplace in the cities and black the color of fashion. With little food,

worthless money, and a husband or father gone forever, the future looked bleak.

Southern Women and the War

In the early days of the Civil War, Southern white women continued to live their lives according to antebellum conventions. Magazine articles urged them to preserve themselves as models of purity for men debased by the violence of war. Women flooded newspapers and periodicals with patriotic verses and songs. A major theme of these works was the need to suppress grief and fear for the good of the men at the front.

By the time of the Civil War, such emotional concealment had become second nature to Southern white women. They had long had to endure their anguish over their husbands' nocturnal visits to the slave quarters. They were used to the condescension of men who assumed them to be intellectually inferior. And they accepted in bitter, self-sacrificing silence the contradiction between the myth of the pampered leisure they were presumed to enjoy and the hard demands their lives actually entailed.

But some Southern women chafed at their supporting role and, as Confederate manpower and materiel needs became acute, they took on new productive responsibilities. Initially, they did so within the domestic context, but soon began to fill positions vacated by men. They managed plantations. They worked in the fields alongside slaves, and if they had worked there before, they worked harder. They worked in factories to make uniforms and munitions. They taught school. A few, like Belle Boyd and Rose O'Neal Greenhow, spied for the Confederacy. And many, like their Northern counterparts, served as nurses. Eventually, battlefield reverses and economic collapse undermined all these roles, leaving women and men alike struggling simply to survive.

Not all women shared the patriotic fervor that impelled some to toil to support the war effort. As the war dragged on and the Southern economy deteriorated, even the patriots suffered from resentment and doubt. By 1864, many women were helping their deserting husbands or relatives elude Confederate authorities. A North Carolina official explained that "desertion takes place because desertion is encouraged. . . . And though the ladies may not be willing to concede the fact, they are nevertheless responsible . . . " (see "American Views: Southern Women against the War"). Some devoutly religious women concluded that it was God, not the Yankees, who had brought destruction on the South for its failure to live up to its responsibilities to women and children.

The Union Prevails, 1864–1865

Despite the Union's dominant military position after Vicksburg and Gettysburg and the Confederacy's mounting home-front problems, three obstacles to Union victory remained. Federal troops under General William T. Sherman controlled Chattanooga and the gateway to Georgia, but the Confederate Army of Tennessee, commanded by Joseph E. Johnston, was still intact, blocking Sherman's path to Atlanta. Robert E. Lee's formidable Army of Northern Virginia still protected Richmond. And the Confederacy still controlled the rich Shenandoah Valley, which fed Lee's armies and supplied his cavalry with horses. In March 1864, President Lincoln brought General Ulysses S. Grant to Washington and appointed him commander of all Union armies. Grant set about devising a strategy to overcome these obstacles.

Grant's Plan to End the War

Grant brought two innovations to the final campaign. First, he coordinated the Union war effort, directing the Union's armies in Virginia and the Lower South to attack at the same time, keeping steady pressure on all fronts. Second, Grant changed the tempo of the war, eliminating the long periods

Union General Ulysses Grant had the pews from a local church moved to a grove of trees where he and his officers planned the following day's assault on Confederate troops at Cold Harbor, Virginia. Grant appears at the left of the photograph, leaning over a bench and studying a map.

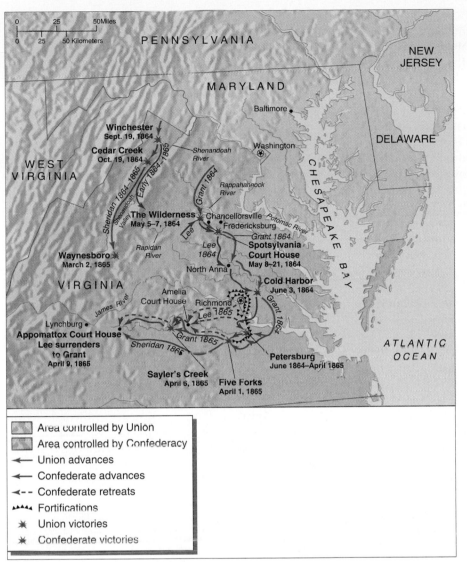

Map 17-1   *Grant and Lee in Virginia, 1864–1865*
The engagements in Virginia from May 1864 to April 1865 between the two great generals for the Union and the Confederacy proved decisive in ending the Civil War. Although General Lee fared well enough in the Wilderness, Spotsylvania, and Cold Harbor campaigns, the sheer might and relentlessness of Grant and his army wore down the Confederate forces. When Petersburg fell after a prolonged siege on April 2, 1865, Richmond, Appomattox, and dreams of Southern independence soon fell as well.

of rest that had intervened between battles and waging nonstop warfare.

Although Grant's strategy ultimately worked, several problems and miscalculations undermined its effectiveness. With Sherman advancing in Georgia, Grant's major focus was Lee's army in Virginia. But Grant underestimated Lee. The Confederate general thwarted him for almost a year and inflicted horrendous casualties on his army. Confederate forces under Jubal Early drove off Union forces from the Shenandoah Valley in June 1864, depriving Grant of troops and allowing the Confederates to maintain their supply lines. And the incompetence of General Benjamin Butler, charged with advancing up the James River to Richmond in May 1864 to relieve Lee's pressure on Grant, further eroded Grant's plan. Grant also faced administrative problems. Finally, he had to contend with disaffection in his officer corps. Many officers in the Army of the Potomac felt endur-

ing loyalty to General George McClellan, whom Lincoln had dismissed in 1862, and considered Grant a mediocrity who had triumphed in the West only because his opposition there had been third-rate.

Lee's only hope was to make Grant's campaign so costly and time-consuming that the Northern general would abandon it before the Southerners ran out of supplies and troops. But despite problems and setbacks, Grant kept relentless pressure on Lee.

From the Wilderness to Cold Harbor

Grant and General George Meade began their campaign against Lee in May 1864, crossing the Rapidan River near Fredericksburg, Virginia, and marching toward an area known as the Wilderness (see Map 17-1). Lee attacked the Army of the Potomac, which outnumbered his 118,000 to 60,000, in the **Battle of the Wilderness** on May 5 and 6 before it could reach open ground. The densely wooded terrain reduced the Union army's advantage in numbers and artillery. Much of the fighting involved fierce hand-to-hand combat. Exchanges of gunfire at close range set the dry underbrush ablaze. Wounded soldiers, trapped in the fires, begged their comrades to shoot them before they burned to death. The toll was frightful—eighteen thousand casualties on the Union side, ten thousand on the Confederate side.

In the past, Union commanders would have pulled back and rested after such an encounter. But Grant startled Lee's army by pushing on. Attacking the entrenched Confederate Army at **Spotsylvania**, his army suffered another eighteen thousand casualties to the Confederates' eleven thousand. Undeterred, Grant moved on toward **Cold Harbor**, where Lee's troops again awaited him in entrenched positions. Flinging his army against withering Confederate fire on June 3, he lost seven thousand men in eight minutes. In less than a month of fighting, the Army of the Potomac had lost 55,000 men. The slaughter undermined Grant's support in Northern public opinion and led peace advocates to renew their quest for a cease-fire.

At this point, Grant decided to change his tactics. Abandoning his march on Richmond from the north, he shifted his army south of the James River to approach the Confederate capital from the rear. Wasting no time, he crossed his army over the James and on June 17, 1864, surprised the Confederates with an attack on **Petersburg**, a critical rail junction 23 miles south of Richmond. It was a brilliant maneuver, but the hesitant actions of Union corps commanders gave Lee time to reinforce the town's defenders. Both armies dug in for a lengthy siege.

Atlanta

While Grant advanced on Lee in Virginia, Union forces under William T. Sherman in Georgia engaged in a deadly dance with the Army of Tennessee under the command of Joseph E. Johnston as they began the **Atlanta Campaign**, a scheme to take Atlanta, Georgia (see Map 17-2). Johnston shared Lee's belief that the Confederacy's best hope lay in a defensive strategy. Hoping to lure Sherman into a frontal assault, Johnston settled his forces early in May at Dalton, an important railroad junction in Georgia 25 miles south of Chattanooga and 75 miles north of Atlanta. The wily Union general declined to attack and instead made a wide swing around the Confederates, prompting Johnston to abandon Dalton, rush south, and dig in again at Resaca to prevent Sherman from cutting the railroad. Again Sherman swung around without an assault, and again Johnston rushed south to cut him off, this time at Cassville.

Map 17-2   The Atlanta Campaign and Sherman's March, 1864–1865 *Sherman, a brilliant tactician who generally refused to be goaded into a frontal assault, "danced" with Confederate General Joseph E. Johnston until an impatient Jefferson Davis replaced Johnston with John Bell Hood, and soon, Atlanta was in Federal hands. The fall of Atlanta opened the way to the rest of Georgia, a key supply state for the Confederacy. With orders not to harm the civilian population, Sherman's men took their wrath out on property as they made their way through Georgia and South Carolina.*

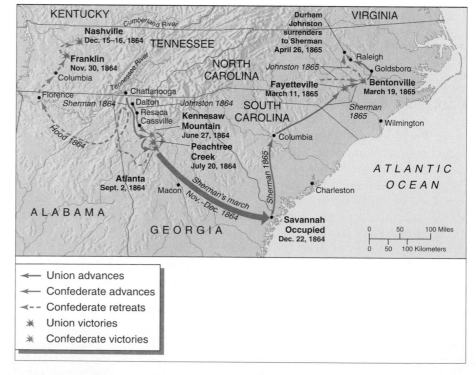

This waltz continued for two months until Johnston had retreated to a strong defensive position on Kennesaw Mountain, barely 20 miles north of Atlanta. At this point, early in July, Sherman decided to attack, with predictably disastrous consequences. Sherman would not make such a mistake again. He resumed his maneuvering and by mid-July had forced Johnston into defensive positions on Peachtree Creek just north of Atlanta. President Davis feared that Johnston would let Sherman take Atlanta without a fight. He dismissed Johnston and made the error of installing John Bell Hood of Texas in his place.

In late July, Hood began a series of attacks on Sherman, beginning at Peachtree Creek on July 20, and was thrown back each time with heavy losses. Sherman launched a series of flanking maneuvers around the city in late August that left Hood in danger of being surrounded. The Confederate general had no choice but to abandon Atlanta and save his army. On the night of September 1, Hood evacuated the city, burning everything of military value.

The loss of Atlanta was a severe blow to the Confederacy, and revived the morale of the war-weary North, helping assure Lincoln's reelection in November. The last hope of the Confederacy—that a peace candidate would replace Lincoln and end the war—was fast fading.

The Election of 1864

Before Sherman's victory at Atlanta, Northern dismay over Grant's enormous losses and his failure to take Richmond raised the prospect of a Democratic election victory. Nominating George B. McClellan, former commander of the Union's armies, as their presidential candidate, the Democrats appealed to the voters as the party of peace.

The fall of Atlanta and the Union's suddenly improved military fortunes undermined Democratic prospects. So did a further military victory under General Philip H. Sheridan in the Shenandoah Valley on October 19.

In the voting on November 8, Lincoln captured 55 percent of the popular vote, losing only New Jersey, Delaware, and Kentucky. Republicans likewise swept the congressional elections, retaining control of both the Senate and the House of Representatives.

The Republican victory reinforced the Union commitment to emancipation. A proposed constitutional amendment outlawing slavery everywhere in the United States, not just those areas still in rebellion, passed Congress and was ratified as the **Thirteenth Amendment** to the U.S. Constitution in 1865.

Sherman's March to the Sea

After Sherman took Atlanta, he proposed to break Confederate resistance once and for all by marching his army to the sea and destroying everything in its path. **Sherman's March** got under way on November 15. His force of sixty thousand men encountered little resistance, prompting North Carolina's marveling governor, Zebulon Vance, to comment, "It shows what I have always believed, that the great *popular heart* is not now and never had been in this war!" Sherman entered Savannah on December 22, 1864, and presented the city to Lincoln as a Christmas present. Just a few weeks earlier, Union forces in Tennessee had routed Hood's army at the **Battle of Franklin** and then crushed it entirely at the **Battle of Nashville**. Hood's defeat removed any threat to Sherman's rear.

Sherman resumed his march in February 1865, heading for South Carolina, the heart of the Confederacy and the state where the Civil War had begun. "The truth is," Sherman wrote "the whole army is burning with an insatiable desire to wreak vengeance on South Carolina." South Carolinians sent taunting messages promising stiff resistance, but these served only further to provoke Sherman's troops. They wreaked greater destruction in South Carolina than they had in Georgia and burned the state capitol at Columbia. Sherman sent the colonel of a black regiment to receive the surrender of Charleston and ordered black troops to be the first to take possession of the city.

Sherman ended his march in Goldsboro, North Carolina, in March 1865 after repelling a surprise Confederate attack at Bentonville led by the restored Joseph E. Johnston and the remnants of the Army of Tennessee. Behind the Union army lay a barren swath 425 miles long from Savannah to Goldsboro.

Arming the Confederacy's Slaves

In a move reflecting their desperation in March 1865 and a major policy shift, Confederate leaders revived a proposal that they had previously rejected to arm and free slaves. President Davis hoped it would gain the Confederacy not only a military benefit but also diplomatic recognition from countries that had balked because of slavery.

The issue divided Confederate leaders. Confederate general Howell Cobb argued that "if slaves will make good soldiers, our whole theory of slavery is wrong." Others thought it was preferable to aban-

SUMMARY

MAJOR BATTLES OF THE CIVIL WAR, 1864–1865

Battle or Campaign	Date	Outcome and Consequences
Wilderness and Cold Harbor	May and June 1864	Both Confederate victories that inflicted huge losses on Grant's army; turned public opinion against Grant but failed to force him to withdraw
Atlanta	May–September 1864	Union victory; Confederacy lost key rail depot and industrial center
Sherman's March	November 1864–March 1865	Nearly unopposed, Sherman's army cut a path of destruction through Georgia and South Carolina, breaking Southern morale
Battles of Franklin and Nashville	November and December 1864	Union victories in Tennessee; effectively destroyed Army of Tennessee
Siege of Petersburg	June 1864–April 1865	Long stalemate ended in Union victory; led to fall of Richmond and surrender of Lee's army at Appomattox Court House

don slavery than to lose independence. Not surprisingly, slaves themselves greeted the proposal with little enthusiasm.

On March 13, 1865, a reluctant Confederate Congress passed a bill to enlist black soldiers, but without a provision offering them freedom. President Davis and the War Office bypassed the equivocal congressional legislation ten days later, issuing a general order that promised immediate freedom to slaves who enlisted. The war ended before the order could have any effect. The irony was that in the summer of 1864, a majority of Northerners probably would have accepted reunion without emancipation had the Confederacy abandoned its fight.

The Road to Appomattox

With Sherman's triumph in Georgia and the Carolinas and Sheridan's rout of the Confederates in the Shenandoah Valley, Lee's army remained the last obstacle to Union victory. On April 1, Sheridan's cavalry seized a vital railway junction on Lee's right flank, forcing Lee to abandon Petersburg and the defense of Richmond. He tried a daring run westward toward Lynchburg, hoping to secure much-needed supplies and join Johnston's Army of Tennessee in North Carolina to continue the fight. While President Davis fled Richmond with his cabinet and headed toward North Carolina. Grant's army of 80,000 outran Lee's diminishing force of 35,000 and cut off his escape at **Appomattox Court House**, Virginia, on April 7. Convinced that further resistance was futile, the Confederate commander met Grant on April 9, 1865, at Appomattox Court House to sign the documents of surrender. The Union general offered generous terms, allowing Lee's men to go home unmolested and to take with them horses or mules "to put in a crop." Grant reported feeling "sad and depressed" at "the downfall of a foe who had fought so long and valiantly."

The fleeing Davis met Joseph E. Johnston at Greensboro, North Carolina, hoping to convince him to continue fighting. But Johnston, like Lee, saw no point in continued bloodshed and surrendered to Sherman near Durham, North Carolina, on April 26. On May 10, Union cavalry captured Davis and his companions in southern Georgia and within two weeks the Civil War came to an end.

The Death of Lincoln

Washington greeted the Confederate surrender at Appomattox with predictable and raucous rejoicing—torchlight parades, cannon salutes, and crowds spontaneously bellowing "The Star-Spangled Banner." On April 11, President Lincoln addressed a large crowd from the White House balcony and spoke briefly of his plans to reconstruct the South with the help of persons loyal to the Union, including recently freed slaves. At least one listener found the speech disappointing. Sometime actor and full-time Confederate patriot John Wilkes Booth muttered to a friend in the throng, "That means nigger citizenship. Now, by God . . . That is the last speech he will ever make."

On the evening of April 14, Good Friday, the president went to Ford's Theater in Washington to view a comedy, *Our American Cousin*. During the performance, Booth shot the president, wounding him mortally, then jumped from Lincoln's box to the stage shouting "Sic semper tyrannis" ("Thus ever to tyrants") and fled the theater. Union troops tracked him down to a barn in northern Virginia and killed him.

Southerners reacted to Lincoln's assassination with surprisingly mixed emotions. Many saw in the death of the man they had regarded as their bitterest enemy for four years some slight hope of relief for the South's otherwise bleak prospects. But General Johnston and others like him understood Lincoln's influence with the radical elements in the Republican party who were pressing for harsh terms against the South. The president's death, Johnston wrote, was "the greatest possible calamity to the South."

Conclusion

Just before the war, William Sherman had warned a friend from Virginia, "You people of the South don't know what you are doing. This country will be drenched in blood. . . . War is a terrible thing." He was right. More than 365,000 Union soldiers died during the war, 110,000 in battle, and more than 256,000 Confederate soldiers, 94,000 of them in battle. Total casualties on both sides, including wounded, were more than 1 million.

Southern armies suffered disproportionately higher casualties than Northern armies. One in four Confederate soldiers died or endured debilitating wounds, compared to one in ten Federal soldiers. During the first year after the war, Mississippi allocated one-fifth of its budget for artificial limbs. Compounding the suffering of the individuals behind these gruesome statistics was the incalculable suffering—in terms of grief, fatherless children, women who never married, families never made whole—of the people close to them.

The war devastated the South. The region lost one-fourth of its white male population between the ages of 20 and 40. It also lost two-fifths of its livestock and half its farm machinery. Union armies destroyed many of the South's railroads and shattered its industry. Between 1860 and 1870, the wealth of the South declined by 60 percent, and its share of the nation's total wealth dropped from more than 30 percent to 12 percent. The wealth of the North, in contrast, increased by half in the same period.

The Union victory did solve the constitutional question about the right of secession and seal the fate of slavery. Now when politicians intoned in Independence Day orations or campaign speeches

This photograph of Abraham Lincoln was taken four days before John Wilkes Booth assassinated him in Ford's Theater.

about the ideals of democracy and freedom, the glaring reality of human bondage would no longer mock their rhetoric.

For black Southerners, emancipation was the war's most significant achievement. Journalists sponsored by the federal government who recorded the testimony of ex-slaves in the 1930s during the Great Depression, seventy years after emancipation, found their memory of the jubilee as fresh as yesterday. Lincoln entered African-American folklore as a larger-than-life figure. At age 91, Fanny Burdock of Valdosta, Georgia, told a recorder a common tale of seeing Lincoln "coming all dusty and on foot" past her Georgia home.

We run right to the fence and had the oak bucket and the dipper. When he draw up to us, he so tall, black eyes so sad. Didn't say not one word, just looked hard at all us, every one us crying. We give him nice cool water from the dipper. Then he nodded and set off and we just stood there till he get to being dust then nothing. After, didn't our owner or nobody credit it, but me and all my kin, we knowed. I still got the dipper to prove it.

The Civil War stimulated other changes that grew more significant over time. It did not make the Union an industrial nation, but it taught the effectiveness of centralized management, new financial techniques, and the coordination of production, marketing, and distribution. Entrepreneurs would apply these lessons to create the expanding corporations of the postwar American economy.

Likewise, the war did not revolutionize gender relations in American society, but by opening new opportunities to women in fields such as nursing and teaching, it helped lay the foundation for the women's suffrage movement of the 1870s and 1880s.

For many Americans, especially black and white Southerners, the war was the most important event in their lives. It had a devastating impact on the families and friends of those who died. But it was not responsible for every postwar change in American society, and it left many features of American life intact. The experience of pulling together in a massive war effort, for example, did not soften class antagonisms. European socialist and father of communism Karl Marx hailed Lincoln as a son of the working class and predicted that "as the American War of independence initiated a new era of ascendancy for the middle class, so the American anti-slavery war will do for the working classes." But capitalism, not labor, triumphed during the war. And it was industrialists and entrepreneurs, not working people, who most benefited from the war's bonanza. Lincoln brutally suppressed strikes at defense plants and threw labor leaders into military prisons.

The war to end slavery changed some American racial attitudes, especially in the North. When Lincoln broadened the war's objectives to include the abolition of slavery, he connected the success of the Union to freedom for the slave. At the outset of the Civil War, only a small minority of Northerners considered themselves abolitionists. After the Emancipation Proclamation, every Northern soldier became a liberator. By the end of the war, perhaps a majority of Northerners supported granting freedmen the right to vote and to equal protection under the law, even if they believed (as many did) that blacks were inferior to whites. The courage of black troops and the efforts of African-American leaders to link the causes of reunion and freedom were influential in bringing about this shift.

Most white Southerners did not experience a similar enlightenment. Some were relieved by the end of slavery, but most greeted it with fear, anger, and regret. For them, the freed slaves would be living reminders of the South's defeat and the end of a way of life grounded in white supremacy.

If the Civil War resolved the sectional dispute of the 1850s by ending slavery and denying the right of the Southern states to secede, it created two new equally troubling problems: how to reunite South and North and how to deal with the legacy of slavery. At his last cabinet meeting on April 14, Lincoln gave little indication of how he intended to proceed on these problems. He seemed inclined to be conciliatory, cautioning against reprisals on Confederate leaders and noting the courage of General Lee and his officers. The president said nothing about the rights of freedmen, although earlier statements indicated that he favored suffrage, but not social equality, for African-Americans.

America's greatest crisis had closed. In its wake, former slaves tested their new freedom and the nation groped for reconciliation. The struggle to preserve the Union and abolish slavery had renewed and vindicated the nation's ideals. It was time to savor the hard-fought victories before plunging into the uncertainties of Reconstruction.

Review Questions

1. Compare and contrast the roles played by women, in the North and in the South, during the Civil War, and explain how their actions and activities

aided or hindered the war effort of their respective nations.

2. Some historians view the 1864 presidential election as one of the most important elections in American history. Why?

3. Looking back at the Confederacy's position after Gettysburg, defeat seemed inevitable. But even as late as the summer of 1864, many Southerners still believed that they had a fighting chance at independence. Why did they feel this way, and what happened between then and the end of the year to dash such hopes?

4. Given the enormity of the losses in lives and property, it is not surprising that some historians have attributed major changes in American society to the Civil War. But other historians claim that the Civil War's impact has been exaggerated. Analyze and assess what the Civil War did or did not accomplish.

Recommended Reading

Two recent biographies of major Civil War figures provide remarkable insight not only into the men who led the fight on both sides, but on the nature of the war itself, especially the final two years. See Emory M. Thomas, *Robert E. Lee: A Biography* (1995), which presents the enigmatic Confederate leader in a balanced account; and John P. Marszalek, *Sherman: A Soldier's Passion for Order* (1993), another balanced biography that dispels many myths about the mercurial Union general whose march through Georgia became a symbol for a new type of warfare.

Where to Learn More

❖ **Cyclorama, Grant Park, Atlanta, Georgia.** This exhibit vividly depicts the 1864 Battle of Atlanta, complete with "gunfire" and oozing "blood." Interpretive literature at the site helps make sense of the panoramic depiction.

❖ **Appomattox Court House, Virginia.** What historian Bruce Catton termed "a stillness at Appomattox" can be felt at the McLean House in this south central Virginia town. The house is much as it was when Confederate general Robert E. Lee surrendered his forces to Union general Ulysses S. Grant on April 9, 1865. An almost reverential solitude covers the house and the well-maintained grounds today. Other sites related to the last year of the war include Kennesaw Mountain National Battlefield Park, Petersburg National Battlefield, and Richmond National Battlefield Park.

WE THE PEOPLE

1789-1865

Self-government is a difficult business. Like a never-finished painting by an artist sensitive to new themes and ideas, a self-governing nation changes in response to the changing priorities of the people who compose it. The men who gathered in Philadelphia in 1787 began the American experiment in democracy. The Constitution they created was vague enough to satisfy contending parties yet specific enough to provide a framework for government.

Over the next eighty years, the United States experienced remarkable geographic and economic expansion that challenged its constitutional framework. The electorate expanded as states eliminated property qualifications for voting, but suffrage remained restricted to white men. Two major questions that dogged the framers remained persistently troublesome: How should power be distributed between the states and the national government? And how could minority rights be protected in a society predicated on majority rule?

Americans and their political parties often behaved in contradictory ways on these issues. Thomas Jefferson, for example, was a champion of limited government and strict adherence to the terms of the Constitution, but he acted with questionable constitutional authority to secure the Louisiana Purchase and double the country's territory. Andrew Jackson was likewise inconsistent on state versus federal power. He angrily struck down the Bank of the United States, a federal creation, and defied the Supreme Court to allow Georgia to expel the Cherokees from its borders. But he also upheld the federal government's authority against South Carolina's claim that it could nullify federal tariffs.

The rapid territorial expansion of the United States exacerbated tensions over state and federal authority and minority rights that eventually threatened the nation's existence. Bound up with expansion was the question of power over the new lands. The Indians whose land it had been were denied control of it: they were allowed to remain or forced to move at the whim of the government. Control of new land became a pressing issue for white Southerners when, after the Mexican War, the national government sought to prohibit slavery in the territories. With slavery restricted, white Southerners began to see themselves as a disadvantaged minority without power in a nation of majority rule.

That explains how the issue of states' rights and federal power became bound up with the question of minority rights. The framers believed that the Constitution offered protection to minorities. The First Amendment, for example, guaranteed the rights of religious minorities. By protecting minority rights, the Constitution encouraged freedom of thought and expression. Free thinking in turn encouraged innovation and the flourishing of the many religious and other reform movements that emerged in the antebellum period.

But as abolitionists and women's rights advocates pointed out, there was a discrepancy between the status of many Americans and the ideals expressed in the Declaration of Independence and Constitution. The protections of the Constitution did not extend to all. Slaves had no political rights, and other African-Americans, women, and Native Americans had few rights. Little wonder at the panic of white Southerners who saw themselves slipping into the ranks of a dependent minority alongside slaves, Indians, and women.

The Civil War brought to a head the merged disputes about state and federal power and minority rights. Many white Southerners questioned the legitimacy of Abraham Lincoln and his fellow Republicans when they took control of the federal government after the election of 1860. Southerners feared that a party elected by a minority of the nation would, acting in the name of the majority, deprive them of their right to property and mobility. Republicans, in turn, viewed the white overlord South as a threat to the national government and slavery as a denial of its principles.

The ensuing bloody and costly conflict ended slavery and resolved the issue of secession but left open the two major constitutional questions that had dominated the national conversation since the Philadelphia convention. If the war boosted the profile of the federal government over the states, it did not resolve the question of how far the national government could extend its power. Nor did a formula emerge for the guarantee of minority rights. African-Americans, Indians, working people, and women would struggle for such a guarantee during the late nineteenth century, with only partial success. But the struggle affirmed the value and strength of American ideals forged, however imperfectly, a century earlier. The work known as America remained in progress.

RECONSTRUCTION, 1865–1877

KEY TOPICS

❖ The clash between African-American aspirations
and southern white expectations
❖ Federal government plans to bring the South
back into the Union and secure freedom for
former slaves
❖ The efforts and results of southern Republican
governments to keep the allegiance of blacks
and win the support of whites
❖ Why and how Reconstruction ended

s Union general William T. Sherman burned
his way through Georgia and South Carolina in late 1864 and early 1865, slaves left
their plantations to work for and follow the conquering
army. In January 1865, Sherman allowed former slaves to
settle on farms abandoned by their masters along the
Atlantic coast. Tom Mansart, a former slave, seized this
opportunity to stake out a farm near Port Royal, South
Carolina. Less than a year later, the federal government
returned the land to its previous owner. Mansart found
work as a stevedore in nearby Charleston and joined a
labor union founded by free blacks before the war. By
1871, he had married and risen to prominence in his community. He was president of his eight-hundred-member
union, and his backing helped elect local Republican candidates to office.

The Mansart family's good fortune declined after
1871 as first an economic depression and then racial violence stole their dream. Tom Mansart was killed at the
door of his house during the election campaign of 1876,
the victim of one of the white mobs roaming through
South Carolina to discourage blacks from voting. The federal troops that had been sent to Charleston to maintain
an open political process instead fraternized with the city's
white leaders.

Tom Mansart's story, as told by African-American
leader W. E. B. Du Bois in *The Black Flame* (1957), exemplified both the promise of the Reconstruction era and its
eventual betrayal by northern and southern whites. The
position of African-Americans in American society was one

of the two great issues of **Reconstruction**. The other great issue was how and under what terms to readmit the former Confederate states. The Constitution was silent on the subject. As with the issue of black equality, opinions in both sections varied widely.

The formation of a national consensus on freedom and reunification began with the demands and hopes of three broad groups. Most Republicans were unwilling to accept the seceding states back in the Union without an expression of loyalty and a commitment to protecting the rights of freedmen. A second group, the more than 4 million former slaves, demanded voting rights, access to education, and the opportunity to seek economic self-sufficiency, benefits then enjoyed by very few northern blacks. The third group, southern whites, hoped to restore their shattered lives, fortunes, and dignity, keeping blacks subservient and the federal government out of southern affairs.

Between 1865 and 1867, under President Andrew Johnson's Reconstruction plan, southern whites pretty much had their way with the former slaves and with their own state governments. Congressional action between 1867 and 1870 attempted to balance black rights and home rule, with mixed results. After 1870, white Southerners gradually regained control of their states and localities, often through violence and intimidation, denying black Southerners their political gains while Republicans in Washington lost interest in policing their former enemies. By the time the last federal troops left the South in 1877, southern whites had prevailed.

Southern Whites and the Ghosts of the Confederacy, 1865

Confederate soldiers—generals and troops alike—returned to devastated homes they could scarcely recognize. Their cause lost and their society reviled, white Southerners lived through the summer and fall of 1865 surrounded by ghosts—the ghosts of lost loved ones, joyful times, bountiful harvests, self-assurance, and slavery. Defeat shook the basic tenets of their religious beliefs. But many other white Southerners refused to accept their defeat as a divine judgment. Instead, they insisted, God had spared the

South for a greater purpose. Robert E. Lee became the patron saint of this cause, his poignant nobility a contrast to the crassness of the Yankee warlords. Some white Southerners would not allow the memory of the bloody struggle to die, transforming it into a symbol of courage against great odds.

Fifteen years after the war, Mark Twain traveled the length of the East Coast. After visiting a gentlemen's club in Boston, he recalled that the conversation had covered a variety of topics, none of which included the Civil War. Northerners had relegated that conflict to history books and moved on. In the South, on the other hand, defeat and destruction demanded rationalization and remembrance.

Most white Southerners approached the great issues of freedom and reunification with unyielding views. They saw African-Americans as adversaries whose attempts at self-improvement were a direct challenge to whites' beliefs in their own racial superiority. They also saw outside assistance to blacks as another invasion.

More than Freedom: African-American Aspirations in 1865

If blacks could have peered into southern white minds, they would have been stunned. The former slaves did not initially even dream of social equality; far less did they plot the kind of vengeful murder and mayhem whites feared. They did harbor two potentially contradictory aspirations. The first was to be left alone, free of white supervision. The second was land, voting and civil rights, and education. To secure these, they needed the intervention and support of the white power structure.

The first step Congress took beyond emancipation was to establish the Bureau of Refugees, Freedmen, and Abandoned Lands in March 1865. Congress envisioned the **Freedmen's Bureau**, as it came to be called, as a multipurpose agency to provide social, educational, and economic services, advice, and protection to former slaves and destitute whites. Congress also authorized the bureau to rent confiscated and abandoned farmland to freedmen in 40-acre plots with an option to buy. This auspicious beginning to realizing African-American aspirations belied the great disappointments that lay ahead.

Education

The greatest success of the Freedmen's Bureau was in education. The bureau coordinated more than fifty

CHRONOLOGY

1863 Lincoln proposes his Ten Percent Plan.

1864 Congress proposes the Wade-Davis Bill.

1865 Sherman issues Field Order No. 15.

Freedmen's Bureau is established.

Andrew Johnson succeeds to the presidency, unveils his Reconstruction plan.

Massachusetts desegregates all public facilities.

Blacks in several southern cities organize Union Leagues.

Former Confederate states begin to pass black codes.

1866 Congress passes Southern Homestead Act, Civil Rights Act of 1866.

Ku Klux Klan is founded.

Fourteenth Amendment to the Constitution is passed (ratified in 1868).

President Johnson goes on a speaking tour.

1867 Congress passes Military Reconstruction Acts, Tenure of Office Act.

1868 President Johnson is impeached and tried in the Senate for defying the Tenure of Office Act.

Republican Ulysses S. Grant is elected president.

1869 Fifteenth Amendment passed (ratified 1870).

1870 Congress passes Enforcement Act.

Republican regimes topple in North Carolina and Georgia.

1871 Congress passes Ku Klux Klan Act.

1872 Freedmen's Bureau closes down.

Liberal Republicans emerge as a separate party.

Ulysses S. Grant is reelected.

1873 Severe depression begins.

Colfax Massacre occurs.

U.S. Supreme Court's decision in the *Slaughterhouse* cases weakens the intent of the Fourteenth Amendment.

Texas falls to the Democrats in the fall elections.

1874 White Leaguers attempt a coup against the Republican government of New Orleans.

Democrats win off-year elections across the South amid widespread fraud and violence.

1875 Congress passes Civil Rights Act of 1875.

1876 Supreme Court's decision in *United States* v. *Cruikshank* nullifies Enforcement Act of 1870.

Outcome of the presidential election between Republican Rutherford B. Hayes and Democrat Samuel J. Tilden is contested.

1877 Compromise of 1877 makes Hayes president and ends Reconstruction.

northern philanthropic and religious groups, which in turn established three thousand freedmen's schools in the South serving 150,000 men, women, and children.

Initially, single young women from the Northeast comprised much of the teaching force. One of them, a 26-year-old Quaker named Martha Schofield, came to Aiken, South Carolina, from rural Pennsylvania in 1865. The school she founded has been part of Aiken's public school system since 1953.

By the time Schofield opened her own school in 1871, blacks outnumbered whites in the teaching corps of the "colored" schools. Support for them came from black churches, especially the **African Methodist Episcopal (AME) Church**. The former slaves crowded into basements, shacks, and churches to attend school. At the end of the Civil War, roughly 90 percent of southern blacks could not read or write, compared with less than 30 percent of southern whites. Within a decade, the freedmen's schools had reduced illiteracy among the former slaves to below 70 percent.

Some blacks went on to one of the thirteen colleges established by the American Missionary Association and black and white churches. Between 1860 and 1880 more than one thousand southern blacks earned college degrees at institutions still serving students today such as Howard University in Washington, D.C., Fisk University in Nashville and Biddle Institute (now Johnson C. Smith University), in Charlotte.

Pursuing freedom of the mind involved challenges beyond those of learning to read and write. Many whites condemned efforts at "Negro improvement." They viewed the time spent on education as wasted, forcing the former slaves to catch their lessons in bits and pieces between work, often by candlelight or on Sundays. Whites also harassed white female teachers, questioning their morals and motivations and threatening people who rented rooms to them. After the Freedmen's Bureau folded in 1872, education for southern blacks became more haphazard.

This painting of a mother and daughter reading captures the enduring thirst for education that dramatically reduced illiteracy among African-Americans of the Reconstruction era.

"Forty Acres and a Mule"

Although education was important to the freed slaves in their quest for civic equality, land ownership offered them the promise of economic independence.

Even before the war's end, rumors circulated through black communities in the South that the government would provide each black family with 40 acres and a mule. These rumors were fueled by General William T. Sherman's **Field Order No. 15** in January 1865, which set aside a vast swath of abandoned land along the South Atlantic coast from the Charleston area to northern Florida for grants of up to 40 acres. The Freedmen's Bureau likewise raised expectations when it was initially authorized to rent 40-acre plots of confiscated or abandoned land to freedmen.

Early indications in various parts of the South suggested that freedmen might realize their hope of land ownership. By June 1865, about forty thousand former slaves had settled on "Sherman land" along the southeastern coast. In 1866, Congress passed the **Southern Homestead Act**, giving blacks preferential access to public lands in five southern states. By the

late 1870s, more than fourteen thousand African-American families had taken advantage of a program to finance land purchases with state-funded, long-term, low-interest loans.

Land ownership did not ensure financial success. Most black-owned farms were small and of marginal land quality. The value of these farms in 1880 was roughly half that of white-owned farms. Blacks also had trouble obtaining credit to purchase or expand their holdings. A lifetime of field work left some freedmen without the managerial skills to operate a farm.

The vast majority of former slaves, especially those in the Lower South, never fulfilled their dreams of land ownership. Rumors to the contrary, the federal government never intended to implement a land redistribution program in the South. General Sherman viewed his field order as a temporary measure to support freedmen for the remainder of the war. President Andrew Johnson nullified the order in September 1865, returning confiscated lands to their former owners. Even Republican supporters of black land ownership questioned the constitutionality of seizing privately owned real estate. They envisioned former slaves assuming the status of free laborers, not necessarily of independent landowners.

For most officials of the Freedmen's Bureau, who shared these views, reviving the southern economy was a higher priority than helping former slaves acquire farms. They wanted both to get the crop in the field and start the South on the road to a free labor system. They thus encouraged freedmen to work for their former masters under contract and postpone their quest for land.

At first, agents of the Freedmen's Bureau supervised labor contracts between former slaves and masters. But after 1867, bureau surveillance declined. Agents assumed that both blacks and whites had become accustomed to the mutual obligations of contracts. The bureau, however, underestimated the power of white landowners to coerce favorable terms or to ignore those they did not like.

Migration to Cities

While some blacks asserted their rights as workers on southern farms, others affirmed their freedom by moving to towns and cities. Even before the war, the city had offered slaves and free blacks a measure of freedom unknown in the rural South. After the war, African-Americans moved to cities to find families, seek work, escape the tedium and supervision of farm life, or simply test their right to move about. Between 1860 and 1870, the official African-American population in every major southern city rose significantly.

Once in the city, blacks faced two immediate problems: finding a place to live and securing a job. They usually settled for the cheapest accommodations in low-lying areas or on the outskirts of town where building codes did not apply. Rather than developing one large ghetto, as in many northern cities, southern blacks lived in several concentrations in and around cities.

Sometimes armed with a letter of reference from their former masters, blacks went door to door to seek employment. Many found work serving white families—as guards, laundresses, maids—for very low wages. Both skilled and unskilled laborers found work rebuilding war-torn cities like Atlanta. Most rural blacks, however, arrived in cities untrained in the kinds of skills sought in an urban work force and so worked as unskilled laborers. In both Atlanta and Nashville, blacks comprised more than 75 percent of the unskilled work force in 1870.

Faith and Freedom

Religious faith framed and inspired the efforts of African-Americans to test their freedom on the farm and in the city. Much as southern whites interpreted their destiny in religious terms, blacks found hope for the future in their Christian faith and saw emancipation as the beginning of an exodus from bondage to the promised land.

Some black churches in the postwar South originated in the slavery era, but most split from white-dominated congregations after the war. The First African Baptist Church in Richmond originated in a white Baptist congregation founded before the war. An 1846 agreement allowed blacks to hold separate services, but only with a white minister officiating. In 1866, the white pastor resigned, noting that blacks "would naturally and justly prefer a minister of their own color." The white church transferred the deed to blacks that year, and the Reverend James Henry Holmes, a former slave, became their first black pastor. The church flourished under Holmes, paid off its debt, and by the 1870s boasted the largest black congregation in the United States.

The church became a primary focus of African-American life. It gave blacks the opportunity to hone skills in self-government and administration that white-dominated society denied them. Within the supportive confines of the congregation, they could assume leadership positions, render important decisions, deal with financial matters, and engage in politics. The church also operated as an educational institution.

The church spawned other organizations that served the black community over the next cen-tury. Burial societies, Masonic lodges, temperance groups, trade unions, and drama clubs originated in churches. By the 1870s, blacks in Memphis had more than two hundred such organizations.

African-Americans took great pride in their churches, which became visible measures of their progress. In Charleston, the first building erected after the war was a black church. Blacks donated a greater proportion of their earnings to their churches than whites did. The church and the congregation were a cohesive force in black communities. They supported families under stress from discrimination and poverty. Most black churches looked inward to strengthen their members against the harsh realities of postbellum southern society. Few ministers dared to engage in or even support protest activities. Some, especially those in the Colored Methodist Episcopal Church, counseled congregants to abide by the rules of second-class citizenship and to trust in God's will to right the wrongs of racism.

Northern-based denominations, however, notably the AME Church, were more aggressive advocates of black rights. AME ministers stressed the responsibility of individual blacks to realize God's will of racial equality. Henry McNeal Turner, probably the most influential AME minister of his day, helped expand the denomination into the South from its small primarily northern base at the end of the Civil War. His church elevated him to bishop in 1880.

Turner's career and the efforts of former slaves in the classroom, on the farm, in cities, and in the churches reflect the enthusiasm and expectations with which southern blacks greeted freedom. But the majority of southern whites were unwilling to see those expectations fulfilled. For this reason, African-Americans could not secure the fruits of their emancipation without the support and protection of the federal government and the issue of freedom was therefore inextricably linked to that of the rejoining of the Confederacy to the Union, as expressed in federal Reconstruction policy.

Federal Reconstruction, 1865–1870

When the Civil War ended in 1865, no acceptable blueprint existed for reconstituting the Union. In 1863, Lincoln proposed to readmit a seceding state if 10 percent of its prewar voters took an oath of loyalty to the Union and it prohibited slavery in a new state constitution. But this **Ten Percent Plan** did not require states to grant equal civil and political rights to former

SUMMARY

CONTRASTING VIEWS OF RECONSTRUCTION: PRESIDENT AND CONGRESS

Politician or Group	Policy on Former Slaves	Policy on Readmission of Former Confederate States
President Johnson	Opposed to black suffrage Silent on protection of black civil rights Opposed to land redistribution	Maintained that rebellious states were already readmitted Granted pardons and restoration of property to all who swore allegiance to the United States
Radical Republicans	Favored black suffrage Favored protection of black civil rights Favored land redistribution	Favored treating rebellious states as territories and establishing military districts* Favored limiting franchise to blacks and loyal whites
Moderate Republicans	Favored black suffrage Favored protection of civil rights Opposed land redistribution	Favored some restrictions on white suffrage* Favored requiring states to meet various requirements before being readmitted* Split on military rule

True of most but not all members of the group.

slaves, and many Republicans in Congress thought it was not stringent enough. In 1864, a group of them responded with the **Wade-Davis Bill**, which required a *majority* of a state's prewar voters to pledge their loyalty to the Union and demanded guarantees of black equality before the law. The bill was passed, but Lincoln kept it from becoming law by refusing to sign it (an action known as a pocket veto).

The controversy over these plans reflected two obstacles to Reconstruction that would continue to plague the ruling Republicans after the war. First, neither the Constitution nor legal precedent offered any guidance on whether the president or Congress should take the lead on Reconstruction policy. Second, there was no agreement on what that policy should be.

President Andrew Johnson, some conservative Republicans, and most Democrats believed that because the Constitution made no mention of secession, the southern states never left the Union, so there was no need for a formal process to readmit them. Moderate and radical Republicans disagreed, arguing that the defeated states had forfeited their rights. Moderates and radicals parted company, however, on the

conditions necessary for readmission to the Union. No group held a majority in Congress, and legislators sometimes changed their positions (see the summary table "Contrasting Views of Reconstruction").

Presidential Reconstruction, 1865–1867

When the Civil War ended in April 1865, Congress was not in session and would not reconvene until December. Thus the responsibility for developing a Reconstruction policy initially fell on Andrew Johnson, who succeeded to the presidency upon Lincoln's assassination. Johnson seemed well suited to the difficult task. Johnson was the only southern senator to remain in the U.S. Senate after secession. This defiant Unionism won him popular acclaim in the North and credibility among Republican leaders.

Most Northerners and many Republicans approved Johnson's Reconstruction plan when he unveiled it in May 1865. Johnson extended pardons and restored property rights, except in slaves, to Southerners who swore an oath of allegiance to the Union and the Constitution. The plan had nothing to say about the voting rights and civil rights of former slaves.

Northern Democrats applauded the plan's silence on these issues and its promise of a quick restoration of the southern states to the Union. They expected the southern states to favor their party and expand its political power. White Southerners, however, were not so favorably impressed, and their response turned northern public opinion against the president. On the two great issues of freedom and reunion, white Southerners quickly demonstrated their eagerness to reverse the results of the Civil War. Although most states accepted President Johnson's modest requirements, several objected to one or more provisions. Mississippi and Texas refused to ratify the Thirteenth Amendment, which abolished slavery. South Carolina declined to nullify its secession ordinance. No southern state authorized black voting. When Johnson ordered special congressional elections in the South in the fall of 1865, the all-white electorate returned many prominent Confederate leaders to office, including Alexander Stephens, the former vice president of the Confederacy.

In late 1865, the newly elected southern state legislatures revised their antebellum slave codes. The updated and renamed **black codes** allowed local officials to arrest blacks who could not document employment and residence, or who were "disorderly," and sentence them to forced labor on farms or road construction crews. The codes also restricted blacks to certain occupations, barred them from jury duty, and forbade them to possess firearms. President Johnson did not seem perturbed about this turn of events.

The Republican-dominated Congress reconvened in December 1865 in a belligerent mood. A consensus formed among radical Republicans, who comprised nearly half of the party's strength in Congress, that to gain readmission, a state would have to extend suffrage to blacks, protect freedmen's civil rights, and have its white citizens officially acknowledge these rights. Some radicals also supported the redistribution of land to former slaves, but few pressed for social equality.

Thaddeus Stevens of Pennsylvania led the radical forces in the House of Representatives, while abolitionist veteran Charles Sumner of Massachusetts rallied radicals in the Senate. Stevens dreamed of a South populated by white and black yeoman farmers. With no large plantations and few landless farmers, the South would become an ideal republic, a boon to the rest of the nation instead of a burden. Few shared his vision, and when he died in 1868, a reporter noted that "no man was oftener outvoted."

Charles Sumner was among the foremost abolitionist politicians before the Civil War. His combative nature won him few friends, even within his own party. As fierce as Stevens in the promotion of black civil and political rights after the war, he also believed that the Reconstruction era offered a "golden moment" to remake the South into an egalitarian region. Sumner died in 1874 as his dream was fading.

But the radicals could not unite behind a program, and it fell to their moderate colleagues to take the first steps toward a Congressional Reconstruction plan. The moderates shared the radicals' desire to protect the former slaves' civil and voting rights. But they would not support land redistribution schemes or punitive measures against prominent Confederates. The **Civil Rights Act of 1866** was a direct response to the black codes. The act specified the civil rights to which all U.S. citizens were entitled. In creating a category of national citizenship with rights that superseded state laws restricting them, the act changed federal-state relations (and in the process overturned the *Dred Scott* decision). President Johnson vetoed the act, but it became law when Congress mustered a two-thirds majority to override his veto, the first time in American history that Congress passed major legislation over a president's veto.

Andrew Johnson's position reflected both his view of government and his racial attitudes. The Republican president remained a Democrat in spirit. Like most Democrats, he favored a balance between federal and state power. He also shared with many of his white southern neighbors a belief in black inferiority.

To keep freedmen's rights safe from presidential vetoes, state legislatures, and federal courts, the Republican-dominated Congress moved to incorporate some of the provisions of the 1866 Civil Rights Act into the Constitution with an amendment. The **Fourteenth Amendment**, which Congress passed in June 1866, addressed the issues of civil and voting rights and marked a fundamental shift of power from the states to the federal government. It guaranteed every citizen equality before the law. The two key sections of the amendment prohibited states from violating the civil rights of their citizens, thus outlawing the black codes, and gave states the choice of enfranchising blacks or losing representation in Congress.

The amendment disappointed advocates of woman suffrage, for the first time using the word *male* in the Constitution to define who could vote. Susan B. Anthony, who had campaigned for the abolition of slavery before the war and helped mount a petition drive that collected 400,000 signatures for the Thirteenth Amendment, formed the **American Equal Rights Association** in 1866 with her colleagues to push for woman suffrage at the state level.

The amendment had little immediate impact on the South. Although enforcement of black codes diminished, white violence against blacks increased. In the 1870s, several decisions by the U.S. Supreme Court would weaken the amendment's provisions. Eventually, however, the Fourteenth Amendment would play a major role in securing the civil rights of African-Americans when the issue reemerged in the 1950s.

President Johnson seemed to encourage white intransigence by openly denouncing the Fourteenth Amendment. The president's diatribes against the Republican Congress won him followers in those northern states with a reservoir of opposition to black suffrage. But the tone and manner of his campaign offended many as undignified. In the November elections, Republicans managed better than two-thirds majorities in both the House and Senate, sufficient to override presidential vetoes. Radical Republicans, joined by moderate colleagues buoyed by the election results and revolted by the president's and the South's intransigence, seized the initiative.

Congressional Reconstruction, 1867–1870

The radicals' first salvo in their attempt to take control over Reconstruction occurred with the passage over President Johnson's veto of the **Military Reconstruction Acts**. The measures, passed in March 1867, inaugurated a period known as **Congressional Reconstruction** or Radical Reconstruction. They generally divided the ex-Confederate states into five military districts (see Map 18-1) and provided for elections to a state constitutional convention guaranteeing **universal manhood suffrage**.

The Reconstruction Acts fulfilled the radicals' three major objectives. First, they secured the freedmen's right to vote. Second, they ensured the likelihood that southern states would be run by Republican regimes that would enforce the new constitutions, protect former slaves' rights, and maintain the Republican majority in Congress. Finally, the acts set standards for readmission that required the South to accept the consequences of defeat: the preeminence of the federal government and the end of involuntary servitude.

To limit presidential interference with their policies even further, Republicans passed the **Tenure of Office Act**, prohibiting the president from removing certain officeholders without the Senate's consent. Johnson, angered at what he believed was an unconstitutional attack on presidential authority, deliberately violated the act in February 1868. He fired Secretary of War Edwin M. Stanton, a leading radical. The House responded to this defiance of

Map 18-1 *Congressional Reconstruction, 1865–1877*
When Congress wrested control of Reconstruction policy from President Andrew Johnson, it divided the South into the five military districts depicted here. The commanding generals for each district held the authority both to hold elections and decide who could vote.

congressional authority by approving, for the only time in American history, articles of impeachment against the president. The Senate voted 35 to 19 to convict, one vote short of the two-thirds necessary to remove Johnson. The outcome weakened the radicals' clout in Congress and eased the way for moderate Republican Ulysses S. Grant to gain the party's nomination for president in 1868.

The Republicans viewed the 1868 presidential election as a referendum on Congressional Reconstruction. Grant won the election, but his margin of victory was uncomfortably narrow.

The Republicans retained a strong majority in both houses of Congress and managed to pass another major piece of Reconstruction legislation, the **Fifteenth Amendment**, in February 1869. In response to growing concerns about voter fraud and violence against freedmen, the amendment guaranteed the right of American men to vote, regardless of race. Although the amendment provided a loophole allowing states to impose restrictions on the right to vote based on literacy requirements or property qualifications and also failed to address the issue of woman suffrage, it was nonetheless a milestone. It made the right to vote perhaps the most distinguishing characteristic of American citizenship.

The Fifteenth Amendment allowed states to keep the franchise a male prerogative. Susan B. Anthony now broke with her abolitionist colleagues and opposed the amendment. Fellow abolitionist and woman suffragist Elizabeth Cady Stanton warned that "if you do not wish the lower orders of Chinese, African, Germans and Irish, with their low ideas of womanhood to make laws for you and your daughters . . . awake to the danger . . . and demand that woman, too, shall be represented in the government!" Such ethnic and racial animosity created a major rift in the nascent women's movement. Women who supported the amendment formed the New England Woman Suffrage Association, challenging Anthony's American Equal Rights Association.

Southern Republican Governments, 1867–1870

Away from Washington, the first order of business was to draft state constitutions. The documents embodied progressive principles new to the former Confederacy. They mandated the election of numerous local and state offices. Self-perpetuating local elites could no longer appoint themselves or cronies to powerful positions. The constitutions committed southern states, many for the first time, to public education. Lawmakers enacted a variety of reforms, including social welfare, penal reform, legislative reapportionment, and universal manhood suffrage.

The Republican regimes that gained control in southern states promoted vigorous state government and the protection of civil and voting rights. Three diverse Republican constituencies supported these governments. One consisted of native whites, most of them yeomen farmers. Residing mainly in the upland regions of the South and long ignored by lowland planters and merchants in state government, the conflict had left many of them devastated. They struggled to keep their land and hoped for an easing of credit and for debt-stay laws to help them escape foreclosure. They wanted public schools for their children and good roads to get their crops to market. Collectively, these native whites were called **scalawags**, a derogatory term derived from the name of the district of Scalloway, on Scotland's Shetland Islands, known for its scraggly livestock. The term was first applied in western New York before the Civil War to an idle person and then to a mischievous one. Although their opponents may have perceived them as a unified group, scalawags in fact held a variety of views.

Northern transplants, or **carpetbaggers**, as their opponents called them, constituted a second group of southern Republicans. The term also had

antebellum origins, referring to a suspicious stranger. Cartoonists depicted carpetbaggers as shoddily dressed and poorly groomed men, their worldly possessions in a ratty cloth satchel, slinking into a town and swindling the locals before departing with their ill-gotten gains. The reality was far different from the caricature. Many were Union soldiers who simply enjoyed the climate and perhaps married a local woman. Most were drawn by economic opportunity. Land was cheap and the price of cotton high. Some also hoped to aid the freedmen.

Carpetbaggers never comprised more than 2 percent of any state's population. Most white Southerners viewed them as an alien presence, instruments of a hated occupying force. They provoked resentment because they seemed to prosper while most Southerners struggled in poverty.

African-Americans constituted the Republican party's largest southern constituency. In three states—South Carolina, Mississippi, and Louisiana—they also formed the majority of eligible voters. They viewed the franchise as the key to civic equality and economic opportunity and demanded an active role in party and government affairs. In February 1865, blacks in Norfolk, Virginia, gathered to demand a say in the new government that Union supporters were forming in that portion of the state. In April, they created the Colored Monitor Union club, modeled after Republican party organizations in northern cities, called **Union Leagues**. They demanded "the right of *universal* suffrage" for "*all* loyal men, without distinction of color." Despite white threats, blacks thronged to Union League meetings in 1867, even forging interracial alliances in states such as North Carolina and Alabama. Focusing on political education and recruitment, the leagues successfully mobilized black voters.

Southern blacks were not content just to vote; they also demanded political office. The number of southern black congressmen in the U.S. House of Representatives increased from two in 1869 to seven in 1873, and more than six hundred blacks, most of them former slaves from plantation counties, were elected to southern state legislatures between 1867 and 1877.

White fears that black officeholders would enact vengeful legislation proved unfounded. African-Americans generally did not promote race-specific legislation. Rather, they supported measures such as debt relief and state funding for education that benefited all poor and working-class people, white and black alike. Like all politicians, however, black officials in southern cities sought to enact measures beneficial to their constituents.

Republicans gained support by expanding the role of state government to a degree unprecedented in the South. Southern Republican administrations appealed to hard-pressed upland whites by prohibiting foreclosure and passing stay laws that allowed farm owners extra time to repay debts. They undertook building programs that benefited both blacks and whites, erecting hospitals, schools, and orphanages. Stepping further into social policy than most northern states at the time, Republican governments in the South expanded women's property rights, enacted legislation against child abuse, and required child support from fathers of mulatto children. In South Carolina, the Republican government provided medical care for the poor; in Alabama, it provided free legal aid for needy defendants.

Despite these impressive policies, southern Republicans were unable to hold their diverse constituency together. The high costs of their activist policies further undermined the Republicans by forcing them to raise state taxes. Small property holders, already reeling from declining staple prices, found the taxes especially burdensome, despite liberal stay laws. Revenues nonetheless could not keep pace with expenditures. The expenditures and the liberal use of patronage sometimes resulted in waste and corruption.

Counter-Reconstruction, 1870–1874

Republicans might have survived battles over patronage, differences over policy, and the resentment provoked by extravagant expenditures and high taxes. But they could not overcome racism. Racism killed Republican rule in the South because it deepened divisions within the party, encouraged white violence, and eroded support in the North. Southern Democrats discovered that they could use race baiting and racial violence to create racial solidarity among whites that overrode their economic and class differences. Unity translated into election victories.

Northerners responded to the persistent violence in the South not with outrage but with a growing sense of tedium. Racism became respectable. Noted intellectuals and journalists espoused "scientific" theories that claimed to demonstrate the natural superiority of whites over blacks. These theories influenced the **Liberal Republicans**, followers of a new political movement that splintered the Republican party, further weakening its will to pursue Reconstruction policy.

By 1874, Americans were concerned with an array of domestic problems that overshadowed Re-

construction. With the rest of the nation thus distracted and weary, Southern whites reclaimed control of the South.

The Uses of Violence

Racial violence preceded Republican rule. As African-Americans moved about, attempted to vote, haggled over labor contracts, and carried arms as part of occupying Union forces, they tested the patience of southern whites.

Cities, where blacks and whites competed for jobs and where black political influence was most visible, became flashpoints for interracial violence.

White paramilitary groups flourished in the South during the Reconstruction era and were responsible for much of the violence directed against African-Americans. Probably the best known of these groups was the **Ku Klux Klan**. Founded in Tennessee by six Confederate veterans in 1866, the Klan was initially a social club that soon assumed a political purpose. Klan night riders in ghostlike disguises intimidated black communities. The Klan directed much of its violence toward subverting the electoral process. One historian has estimated that roughly 10 percent of all black delegates to the 1867 state constitutional conventions in the South became victims of political violence during the next decade. The most serious example of political violence occurred in Colfax, Louisiana in 1873 when a white Democratic mob attempted to wrest control of local government from Republicans. For three weeks, black defenders held the town against the white onslaught. When whites finally broke through, they massacred the remaining blacks, including those who had surrendered and laid down their weapons.

Racial violence and the combative reaction it provoked both among blacks and Republican administrations energized white voters. Democrats regained power in North Carolina during the election of 1870, and that same year, the Republican regime in Georgia fell as well.

The federal government responded to requests for help from southern Republican administrations with a variety of legislation. One example was the Fifteenth Amendment, ratified in 1869, which guaranteed the right to vote. Another was the **Enforcement Act of 1870**, which enabled the federal government to appoint supervisors in states that failed to protect citizens' voting rights. A more sweeping measure was the **Ku Klux Klan Act of 1871**, which permitted federal authorities, with military assistance, if necessary, to arrest and prosecute members of groups that denied a citizen's civil rights if state authorities failed to do so, and established a new precedent in federal-state relations.

The Failure of Northern Will

The success of political violence after 1871 reflected less the inadequacy of congressional legislation than the failure of will on the part of northern Republicans to follow through on commitments to southern Republican administrations. The commitment to voting rights for southern blacks, widespread among Republicans in 1865 and affirmed in the Fifteenth Amendment passed in 1869, faded as well. American politics in the 1870s seemed more corrupt and less responsible to the electorate than ever before. Scandal abounded. Democratic boss William M. Tweed and his associates transformed **Tammany Hall**, a Democratic Club, into a full-fledged political machine that robbed New York City of an astounding $100 million. Federal officials allowed private individuals to manipulate the stock market for spectacular gains. Several members of Congress and President Grant's vice president exchanged government favors for railroad stock.

Racism gained an aura of scientific respectability in the late nineteenth century. Science was held in high esteem at the time, helping assure public acceptance of the putatively scientific views of the racial theorists. According to those views, some peoples are inherently inferior to others, a natural state of affairs that no government interference can change.

Concerns about the quality of the electorate, also tinged with racism, reflected the rising stakes of public office in post–Civil War America. The urban industrial economy boomed in the five years after the war. Engineers flung railroads across the continent. Steam propelled factories to unprecedented levels of productivity and ships to new speed records. Discoveries of rich natural resources such as oil and iron presaged a new age of industrial might. Republicans promoted and benefited from the boom, and it influenced their priorities. Railroad, mining, and lumber lobbyists crowded Washington and state capitals begging for financial and land subsidies and favorable legislation. In an era before conflict-of-interest laws, leading Republicans sat on the boards of railroads, land development companies, and industrial corporations. While the federal government denied land to the freedman, it doled out millions of acres to corporations.

Not all Republicans approved the party's promotion of economic development. Some questioned the prudence of government intervention in the "natural" operation of the nation's economy. The emerging scandals of the Grant administration led to calls for reform. Republican governments, North and South, were condemned for their lavish spending and high taxes. The time had come to restore good government.

Liberal Republicans and the Election of 1872

Liberal Republicans put forward an array of suggestions to improve government and save the Republican party. They advocated civil service reform to reduce reliance on patronage and the abuses that accompanied office seeking. To limit government and reduce artificial economic stimuli, the reformers called for tariff reduction and an end to federal land grants to railroads. For the South, they recommended a general amnesty for whites and a return to "local self-government" by men of "property and enterprise."

When the Liberals failed to convince other Republicans to adopt their program, they broke with the party. Taking advantage of this split, the Democrats forged an alliance with the Liberals. Together, the Democrats and Liberals nominated journalist Horace Greeley to challenge Ulysses S. Grant for the presidency in the election of 1872. Grant won resoundingly, helped by high voter turnout among blacks in the South. The election suggested that the excesses of the Grant administration had not yet exceeded public tolerance and that the Republican experiment in the South retained some public support. But within a year, an economic depression, continued violence in the South, and the persistent corruption of the Grant administration would turn public opinion against the Republicans. With this shift, support for Reconstruction and black rights would also fade.

Redemption, 1874–1877

For southern Democrats, the Republican victory in 1872 underscored the importance of turning out larger numbers of whites and restricting the black vote. They accomplished these goals over the next four years with a surge in political violence. Preoccupied with corruption and economic crisis and increasingly indifferent, if not hostile, to African-American aspirations, most Americans looked the other way. The elections of 1876—on the local, state, and national levels—affirmed the triumph of southern whites. Reconstruction did not end; it was overthrown. Southern Democrats called their victory "Redemption," and this interpretation of the Reconstruction era would affect race relations for nearly a century.

The Democrats' Violent Resurgence

The violence between 1874 and 1876 differed in several respects from earlier attempts to restore white government by force. Attackers operated more openly and more closely identified themselves with the Democratic party. Mounted, gray-clad ex-Confederate soldiers flanked Democratic candidates

American Views

BLACK HOPES AND WHITE REPRESSION

The following two extracts frame the Reconstruction era. The first, a memorial that the Colored People's Convention of South Carolina presented to Congress in November 1865, expresses the expectations with which African-Americans greeted emancipation and their hopes for federal protection of their rights. The second is from instructions that a white paramilitary group issued to members on harassing black political meetings before the elections of 1876 in South Carolina. Its remarkable openness about the use of violence to thwart the democratic process reflects the impunity with which southern whites felt they could operate given the absence of the kinds of federal protections the first document called for.

❖ Why did South Carolina whites find the demands of the Colored People's Convention of South Carolina objectionable?

❖ Did the black petitioners demand too much?

❖ Given the open admission that the Red Shirts aimed to do violence, or at least intimidate black voters, why didn't the federal government intervene?

Colored People's Convention of South Carolina Petition to Congress, November 1865

We, the colored people of the State of South Carolina, in Convention assembled, respectfully present for your attention some prominent facts in relation to our present condition, and make a modest yet earnest appeal to your considerate judgment. . . . Conscious of the difficulties that surround our position, we would ask for no rights or privileges but such as rest upon the strong basis of justice and expediency, in view of the best interests of our entire country.

We ask first, that the strong arm of law and order be placed alike over the entire people of this State; that life and property be secured, and the laborer free to sell his labor as the merchant his goods.

We ask that a fair and impartial instruction be given to the pledges of the government to us concerning the land question.

We ask that the three great agents of civilized society—the school, the pulpit, the press—be as secure in South Carolina as in Massachusetts or Vermont.

We ask that equal suffrage be conferred upon us, in common with the white men of this State. This we ask, because "all free governments derive their just powers from the consent of the governed"; and we are largely in the majority in this State, bearing for a long period the burden of onerous taxation, without a just representation. We ask for equal suffrage as a protection for the hostility evoked by our known faithfulness to our country and flag under all circumstances.

---

at campaign rallies and "visited" black neighborhoods afterward to discourage blacks from voting. With blacks intimidated and whites already prepared to vote, election days were typically quiet (see "American Views: Black Hopes and White Repression").

Democrats swept to victory across the South in the 1874 elections. "A perfect reign of terror" redeemed Alabama for the Democrats. In Louisiana, a group of elite Democrats in New Orleans organized a military organization known as the **White League** in 1874 to challenge the state's Republican government. In September 1874, more than eight thousand White Leaguers staged a coup to overthrow the Republican government of New Orleans.

The Weak Federal Response

Unrest like that in Louisiana also plagued Mississippi and South Carolina. When South Carolina governor

We ask that colored men shall not in every instance be tried by white men; and that neither by custom nor enactment shall we be excluded from the jury box.

We protest against any code of black laws the Legislature of this State may enact, and pray to be governed by the same laws that control other men.

Thus we ever pray.
Charleston, S.C., November 24, 1865;
Zion Presbyterian Church

Instructions to South Carolina Red Shirts, 1876

1. That every Democrat in the Townships must be put upon the Roll of the Democratic Clubs. . . .
2. That a Roster must be made of every white and of every Negro in the Townships and returned immediately to the County Executive Committee.
3. That the Democratic Military Clubs are to be armed with rifles and pistols and such other arms as they may command. . . .
12. Every Democrat must feel honor bound to control the vote of at least one Negro, by intimidation, purchase, keeping him away or as each individual may determine, how he may best accomplish it.
13. We must attend every Radical [Republican] meeting that we hear of whether they meet at night or in the day time. Democrats must go in as large numbers as they can get together, and well armed, behave at first with great courtesy and assure the ignorant Negroes that you mean them no harm and so soon as their leaders or speakers begin to speak and make false statements of facts, tell them then and there to their faces that they are liars, thieves and rascals, and are only trying to mislead the ignorant Negroes. . . .
14. In speeches to Negroes you must remember that argument has no effect upon them: they can only be influenced by their fears, superstitions and cupidity. . . . Treat them so as to show them, you are the superior race, and that their natural position is that of subordination to the white man. . . .
16. Never threaten a man individually. If he deserves to be threatened, the necessities of the times require that he should die.

Sources: *Colored People's Convention:* Philip S. Foner and George E. Walker, eds., Proceedings of the Black State Conventions, 1840–1865, vol. 2 (1979); *Red Shirts:* Paul D. Escott and David Goldfield, eds., Major Problems in the History of the American South, vol. 1 (1990).

Daniel H. Chamberlain could no longer contain the violence in his state in 1876, he asked the president for help. Although President Grant acknowledged the gravity of Chamberlain's situation, the president would only offer the governor the lame hope that South Carolinians would exercise "better judgment and cooperation" and assist the governor in bringing offenders to justice "without aid from the federal Government."

Congress responded to the violence with the **Civil Rights Act of 1875**. Introduced by Charles Sumner, the bill finally passed in a watered-down version after Sumner's death. The act prohibited discrimination against blacks in public accommodations such as theaters, parks, and trains and guaranteed freedmen's rights to serve on juries. It had no provision for voting rights, which Congress presumed the Fifteenth Amendment protected. The only way to enforce the law was for individual blacks to bring grievances related to it before federal courts in the South. Congress did not concern itself with the personal and financial difficulties blacks would face in doing so.

When blacks tested the law by trying to make free use of public accommodations, they were almost always turned away. In 1883, the U.S. Supreme Court pronounced the Civil Rights Act unconstitutional, declaring that only the states, not Congress, could redress "a private wrong, or a crime of the individual."

The Election of 1876 and the Compromise of 1877

Reconstruction officially ended with the presidential election of 1876 in which Democrat Samuel J. Tilden ran against Republican Rutherford B. Hayes. When the ballots were counted, it appeared that Tilden, a conservative New Yorker respectable enough for northern voters and Democratic enough for white southerners, had won. But despite a majority in the popular vote, disputed returns in three southern states left him with 184 of the 185 electoral votes needed to win. The three states—Florida, South Carolina, and Louisiana—were the last in the South still to have Republican adminstrations.

Both camps maneuvered intensively in the months following the election to claim the disputed votes. Congress appointed a fifteen-member commission to settle the issue.

Eventually the so-called **Compromise of 1877** installed Hayes in the White House and gave Democrats control of all state governments in the South.

Southern Democrats emerged the major winners of the Compromise of 1877. President Hayes and his successors into the next century left the South alone. In practical terms, the Compromise of 1877 signaled the revocation of civil rights and voting rights for southern blacks. The Fourteenth and Fifteenth Amendments would be dead letters in the South until well into the twentieth century. On the two great issues confronting the nation at the end of the Civil War, reunion and freedom, the white South had won. It reentered the Union largely on its own terms with the freedom to pursue a racial agenda consistent with its political, economic, and social interests.

The Failure of Reconstruction

Most blacks and whites in 1877 would have agreed on one point. Reconstruction had failed.

If the demise of Reconstruction elicited a sigh of relief from most white Americans, blacks greeted it with frustration. Their dreams of land ownership faded as a new labor system relegated them to a lowly position in southern agriculture. Redemption reversed their economic and political gains and deprived them of most of the civil rights they had enjoyed under Congressional Reconstruction.

The former slaves were certainly better off in 1877 than in 1865. They were free, however limited their freedom. Some owned land; some held jobs in cities. But by 1877, the "golden moment"—an unprecedented opportunity for the nation to live up to its ideals by extending equal rights to all its citizens, black and white alike—had passed.

Sharecropping

When they lost political power, blacks also lost economic independence. As the Freedmen's Bureau retreated from supervising farm labor contracts and opportunities for blacks to possess their own land dried up, the bargaining power of black farm laborers decreased and the power of white landlords increased.

The upshot was that by the late 1870s, most former slaves in the rural South had been drawn into a subservient position in a new labor system called **sharecropping**. The premise of this system was relatively simple: The landlord furnished the sharecroppers a house, a plot of land to work, seed, some farm animals and farm implements and advanced them credit at a store the landlord typically owned. In exchange, the sharecroppers promised the landlord a share of their crop, usually one-half. The croppers kept the proceeds from the sale of the other half to pay off their debts at the store and save or spend as they and their families saw fit. In theory, a sharecropper could save enough to secure economic independence.

With whites holding the accounts at the store, blacks found that the proceeds from their share of the crop never left them very far ahead. In exchange for extending credit to sharecroppers, store owners felt justified in requiring collateral. But sharecroppers had no assets other than the cotton they grew. So southern states passed **crop lien laws**, which gave the store owner the right to the next year's crop in exchange for this year's credit. The sharecropper sank deeper into dependence.

Sharecropping represented a significant step down from tenancy. Tenants owned their own draft animals, farm implements, and seed. Once they negotiated with a land owner for a fixed rent, they kept whatever profits they earned. Eventually, they could hope to purchase some land and move into the landlord class themselves.

Historians have often depicted the sharecropping system as a compromise between white landlord and black laborer. But compromise implies a give-and-take between relatively equal negotiators. As northern and federal support for Reconstruction waned after 1870 and southern Democrats regained political control, white power over black labor increased. Blacks had no recourse to federal and state authorities or, increasingly, to the polls as a white reign of terror stripped them of their political rights.

The only difference between northern and southern employers' outlook on labor was that Southerners exercised more control over their workers. What had been a triangular debate—among northern whites, southern whites, and freedmen—had become a lopsided discourse divided along racial rather than sectional lines.

Segregation

A labor arrangement like sharecropping was not feasible in the fluid labor markets of southern cities. Whites relied instead on racial **segregation** to control urban blacks and keep them in an inferior economic and social position. Racial segregation, which had prevailed nationwide before the Civil War, restricted blacks to separate and rarely equal public facilities or excluded them entirely. After the war, and especially after 1870, it spread rapidly in southern cities. In Richmond by the early 1870s, segregation laws required blacks registering to vote to enter through separate doors and registrars to count their ballots separately. The city's prison and hospitals were segregated. So too were its horse-drawn railways, its schools, and most of its restaurants, hotels, and theaters.

Barred from juries, excluded from some public facilities, and segregated into inferior accommodations in others, blacks fell into a twilight category of citizenship with few rights and many obligations. As W. E. B. Du Bois said in 1877, "The slave went free; stood a brief moment in the sun; then moved back again toward slavery."

Modest Gains and Future Victories

Southern blacks experienced some advances in the decade after the Civil War, but these owed little to Reconstruction. Black families functioned as economic and psychological buffers against unemployment and prejudice. Black churches played crucial roles in their communities. Self-help and labor organizations offered mutual friendship and financial assistance. All of these institutions existed in the slavery era, although on a smaller scale. And some of them, such as black labor groups, schools, and social welfare associations, endured because comparable white institutions excluded blacks. Blacks also scored some modest economic successes during the Reconstruction era, mainly from their own pluck.

The Fourteenth and Fifteenth Amendments to the Constitution are among the few bright spots in Reconstruction's otherwise dismal legacy. The Fourteenth Amendment guaranteed former slaves equality before the law; the Fifteenth Amendment protected their right to vote. Both amendments elevated the federal government over the states by protecting freedmen from state attempts to deny them their rights. But the benefits of these two landmark amendments did not accrue to African-Americans until well into the twentieth century. In the **Slaughterhouse cases** (1873), the Supreme Court contradicted the intent of the Fourteenth Amendment by decreeing that most citizenship rights remained under state, not federal, control. In **United States** v. **Cruikshank** (1876), the Court overturned the convictions of some of those responsible for the Colfax Massacre, ruling that the Enforcement Act applied only to violations of black rights by states, not individuals. Within the next two decades, the Supreme Court would uphold the legality of racial segregation and black disfranchisement, in effect declaring that the Fourteenth and Fifteenth Amendments did not apply to African-Americans. The Civil War had killed secession forever, but states' rights enjoyed a remarkable revival.

As historian John Hope Franklin accurately concluded, Reconstruction "had no significant or permanent effect on the status of the black in American life. . . . [Blacks] made no meaningful steps toward economic independence or even stability."

Conclusion

Blacks had entered freedom with many hopes, among the most prominent of which was to be let alone. White southerners, after four bloody years of unwanted attention from the federal government, also longed to be left alone. But they did not include their ex-slaves as equal partners in their vision of solitude. Northerners, too, began to seek escape from the issues and consequences of the war, eventually abandoning their commitment to secure civil and voting rights for southern blacks.

White Southerners robbed blacks of their gains and sought to reduce them again to servitude and dependence, if not to slavery. But in the processs, the majority of whites lost as well. Yeoman farmers missed an opportunity to break cleanly from the Old South and establish a more equitable society. Instead, they allowed the old elites to regain power and gradually ignore their needs. They preserved the social benefit of a white skin at the cost of almost everything else. Many lost their farms and sank into tenancy, leasing land from others. Fewer had a voice in state legislatures or Congress. A new South, rid of slavery and sectional antagonism, had indeed emerged, redeemed, regenerated, and disenthralled. But the old South lingered on in the new like Spanish moss on live oaks.

As federal troops left the South to be redeployed restraining striking workers in the North and suppressing Native Americans on the Great Plains, an era of possibility for American society ended and a new era began. "The southern question is dead," a Charleston newspaper proclaimed in 1877. "The question of labor and capital, work and wages" had moved to the forefront. The chance to redeem the sacrifice of a bloody civil war with a society that fulfilled the promise of the Declaration of Independence and the Constitution for all citizens slipped away. It would take a new generation of blacks a long century later to revive it.

Review Questions

1. Given the devastation in the South after the Civil War and the loss of property, lives, and hope among many white Southerners, do you think they should have supported black aspirations for civil rights, land, and suffrage? How differently would things have turned out if they had?

2. Some historians have placed a great deal of the blame for Reconstruction's failures on the backs of southern Republicans. Is this fair? Explain your response.

3. By 1874, political violence directed at blacks and at white Republicans in the South was almost routine. Why did the federal government not respond more vigorously to suppress the violence?

4. Blacks did achieve some notable gains during Reconstruction, despite its overall failure. What were those gains?

Recommended Reading

W. E. B. Du Bois, *Black Reconstruction in America, 1860–1880* (1935). This early and long-ignored study by the foremost black scholar of his time refuted the contemporary historical wisdom that Reconstruction was a horror visited on the South by an overbearing federal government and ignorant, willful blacks.

Eric Foner, *Reconstruction: America's Unfinished Revolution, 1863-1877* (1988). The standard work on Reconstruction is notable for its emphasis on the experience and aspirations of black Southerners.

Gaines M. Foster, *Ghosts of the Confederacy: Defeat, the Lost Cause, and the Emergence of the New South, 1865 to 1913* (1987). Foster paints a fine picture of how the memory of the Civil War affected white southerners and their views on Reconstruction policy.

Leon Litwack, *Been in the Storm So Long: The Aftermath of Slavery* (1979). This is an eloquent account of the early days of freedom from the freedmen's perspective, up to 1867.

Whitelaw Reid, *After the War: A Southern Tour, May 1, 1865, to May 1, 1866* (1866). A northern journalist's critical view of southern white defiance during the early days of Reconstruction predicts future difficulties for federal policies and black aspirations.

Albion W. Tourgée, *A Fool's Errand* (1879). The author was an Ohioan who migrated to North Carolina in 1865 to take advantage of economic opportunities in the state and eventually became involved in politics. His frustrations with Reconstruction and his keen analysis of racism are important themes of this novel.

Where to Learn More

❖ **Penn Center Historic District, St. Helena Island, South Carolina.** The Penn School was a sea-island experiment in the education of free blacks established by northern missionaries Laura Towne and Ellen Murray in 1862 that they operated until their deaths in the early 1900s. The Penn School became Penn Community Services in 1948, serving as an educational institution, health clinic, and a social service agency.

❖ **Hampton University Museum, Hampton, Virginia.** Hampton University was founded by the Freedmen's Bureau in 1868 to provide "practical" training in the agricultural and mechanical fields for former slaves. In addition to a history of the institution, the museum includes one of the oldest collections of African art in the United States.

❖ **Beauvoir, Biloxi, Mississippi.** The exhibits at Beauvoir, the home of Jefferson Davis, evoke the importance of the Lost Cause for the white survivors of the Confederacy. Especially interesting is the Jefferson Davis Soldiers Home on the premises and the Confederate Veterans Cemetery. Davis spent his retirement years in Beauvoir.

❖ **Valentine Museum, Richmond, Virginia.** This urban history museum was the first to mount a comprehensive exhibit on Reconstruction in 1996. The exhibit is expected to travel to locations around the country beginning in 1997. Contact the Valentine at (804) 649–0711 for the exhibit's itinerary.

19 A NEW SOUTH, 1877–1900

KEY TOPICS

❖ Continuity and change between the Old South and the New South
❖ The origins and nature of Southern Populism
❖ Women's roles in the New South
❖ How and why segregation and disfranchisement changed race relations in the South

The members of the Holtzclaw family worked hard to supplement the meager income they earned sharecropping on an Alabama farm in the late 1870s. Little more than a decade out of slavery, they hoped to rent and eventually buy a piece of land. Ten-year-old William Holtzclaw foraged for wild nuts and fruits in the swamps around the farm. William's mother cooked for a white family. His father earned extra money hauling logs from a nearby sawmill. When the timber was all gone, he found work on a railroad that kept him away from his family three months at a time.

In 1880, the Holtzclaws bought a mule, a horse, and two oxen and rented a 40-acre farm. But then bad weather and a crippling injury suffered by the elder Holtzclaw dimmed their prospects. By 1884, they had lost their crop and farm animals to debt and were once again sharecropping.

William, a member of the first generation of southern blacks born in freedom, persevered. He graduated from Tuskegee Institute, a black college in Alabama established in 1881, and worked as a teacher and administrator of black schools. He became a prominent educator and founded a vocational college for blacks in Mississippi, the Utica Normal and Industrial Institute.

In 1876, while William Holtzclaw and his family were struggling in Alabama, a 14-year-old white youth, William Henry Belk, went to work as a store clerk in a small North Carolina town to help support his widowed mother. Over the next twelve years, he saved $750. Borrowing an additional $500, he opened his own retail store, which he called the New York Racket Store. *Racket* in those days meant "cheap," and the word fit both his prices and his merchandise. His one-price, cash-only strategy was successful in his town of 2,500 people. By 1895, he had earned enough from his modest venture to move to Charlotte and open a department store. Charlotte had excellent railroad connections to the rest of the country, so Belk could stock his store with the latest fashions from New York City and the newest household appliances and products from the industrial centers of the Northeast and Midwest. The railroad also brought people—potential Belk customers—to Charlotte. Combining brash advertising with personal attention to customers and attractive prices, Belk prospered. He expanded, opening new stores in the Carolinas. By the early 1900s, Belk owned the largest retail chain in the South.

The experience of the Holtzclaw family shows that despite rising racial hostility in the late-nineteenth-century South, blacks could aspire to land ownership, education, and a professional career. But it also shows the tenuous plight of southern farmers. Narrowing economic opportunities and growing social and political isolation made the road to recovery harder and longer for African-Americans than for white Southerners. William Belk's story shows how some Southerners, especially whites, could find opportunity in the South's burgeoning urban centers.

The Newness of the New South

While southern farmers, both black and white, faced limited prospects in a stagnant agricultural economy, other Southerners were building railroads, erecting factories, and moving to towns and cities. The factories did not dramatically alter the South's rural economy, and the towns and cities did not make it an urban region. The changes nonetheless brought political and social turmoil. By 1900, southern white leaders, urban and rural, had used the banner of white supremacy to stifle dissent. They removed blacks from political life and constricted their social and economic role.

The New South's "newness" was to be found primarily in its economy. After Reconstruction, new industries absorbed tens of thousands of first-time industrial workers from impoverished rural areas. Southern cities grew faster than those in any other region of the country. A burst of railroad construc-

tion linked these cities to one another and to the rest of the country, giving them increased commercial prominence. Growing in size and taking on new functions, cities extended their influence into the countryside with newspapers, consumer products, and new values. But this urban influence did not bring electricity, telephones, public health services, or public schools to the rural South or greatly broaden the rural economy with new jobs. And it left the countryside without the daily contact with the outside world that fostered a broader perspective.

The Democratic party dominated southern politics after 1877, significantly changing the South's political system. Through various deceits, Democrats purged most blacks and some whites from the electoral process and suppressed challenges to their leadership. The result was the emergence by 1900 of the **Solid South**, a period of white Democratic party rule that lasted into the 1950s.

Most southern women remained at home or on the farm, but some white and black middle-class women in the cities organized clubs, lobbied for various causes, and assumed regional leadership on a number of important issues. Tens of thousands of young white women from impoverished rural areas found work in textile mills, in city factories, or as servants. These new options posed a challenge to prevailing views about the role of women but ultimately did not change them.

The status of southern blacks changed significantly between 1877 and 1900. The members of the first generation born after Emancipation expected dignity and self-respect and the right to work, to vote, to go to school, and to travel freely. Whites responded with the equivalent of a second Civil War—and they won. By 1900, blacks found themselves more isolated from whites and with less political power than at any time since 1865. Despite these setbacks, they succeeded in building a rich community life and spawning a vibrant middle class.

An Industrial and Urban South

Since the 1850s, public speakers calling for economic reform in the South had been rousing audiences with the tale of the burial of a southern compatriot whose headstone, clothes, and coffin, as well as the gravediggers' tools all came from the North. The speakers urged their listeners to found industries, build railroads, and grow great cities so that the South could make its own goods and no one in the future would have to suffer the indignity of journeying to the next world accompanied by Yankee artifacts.

Certainly, Southerners manufactured very little in 1877, less than 10 percent of the national

CHRONOLOGY

1872 Texas and Pacific Railway connects Dallas to eastern markets.	**1892** The Populist party forms.
1880 First southern local of the Women's Christian Temperance Union is formed in Atlanta.	**1894** United Daughters of the Confederacy is founded. Populist and Republican fusion candidates win control of North Carolina.
1881 Booker T. Washington establishes Tuskegee Institute.	**1895** Booker T. Washington delivers his "Atlanta Compromise" address.
1882 Agricultural Wheel is formed in Arkansas.	**1896** Populists endorse the Democratic presidential candidate and fade as a national force. In *Plessy* v. *Ferguson*, the Supreme Court permits segregation by law.
1883 Laura Haygood founds the home mission movement in Atlanta.	
1884 James B. Duke automates his cigarette factory.	**1898** North Carolina Mutual Life Insurance is founded. Democrats regain control of North Carolina.
1886 Dr. John Pemberton creates Coca-Cola. Southern railroads conform to national track gauge standards.	**1903** W. E. B. Du Bois publishes *The Souls of Black Folk.*
1887 Charles W. Macune expands the Southern Farmer's Alliance from its Texas base to the rest of the South.	**1905** James B. Duke forms the Southern Power Company. Thomas Dixon publishes *The Clansman.*
1888 The Southern Farmers' Alliance initiates a successful boycott of jute manufacturers.	**1906** Bloody race riots break out in Atlanta.
1890 Mississippi becomes the first state to restrict black suffrage with literacy tests.	**1907** Pittsburgh-based U.S. Steel takes over Birmingham's largest steel producer.

total. By 1900, however, they boasted a growing iron and steel industry, textile mills that rivaled those of New England, a world-dominant tobacco industry, a timber-processing industry that helped make the South a leading furniture-manufacturing center, and a variety of regional enterprises rising to prominence, including Coca-Cola.

Birmingham, barely a scratch in the forest in 1870, exemplified one aspect of what was new about the New South. By 1889, Birmingham was preparing to challenge Pittsburgh, the nation's preeminent steelmaking city.

The southern textile industry also experienced significant growth during the 1880s. Several factors drew local investors into textile enterprises, including low farm income. The entrepreneurs located their mills mostly in rural areas, not in cities. The center of the industry was in the Carolina Piedmont, a region with good railroads, plentiful labor, and cheap energy. By 1900, the South had surpassed New England to become the nation's foremost textile-manufacturing center.

Virginia was the dominant tobacco producer, and its main product was chewing tobacco. The discovery of bright-leaf tobacco, a strain suitable for smoking in the form of cigarettes, changed Americans' tobacco habits. In 1884, James B. Duke installed the first cigarette-making machine in his Durham, North Carolina, plant. By 1900, Duke's American Tobacco Company controlled 80 percent of all tobacco manufacturing in the United States.

Atlanta pharmacist Dr. John Pemberton developed a soft drink—a mixture of oils, caffeine, coca leaves, and cola nuts—in his backyard in an effort to find a good-tasting cure for headaches. He called his concoction Coca-Cola. Pemberton, short of cash, sold the rights to it to another Atlantan, Asa Candler, in 1889. Candler tinkered with the formula to improve the taste and marketed the product heavily. By the mid-1890s, Coca-Cola enjoyed a national market.

Southern track mileage doubled between 1880 and 1890, with the greatest increases in Texas and Georgia (see Map 19-1). By 1890, nine out of

Map 19-1   *Railroads in the South, 1859 and 1899*
A postwar railroad construction boom promoted commercial agriculture and industry in the South. Unlike the railroads of the prewar South, uniform gauges and connections to major trunk lines in the North linked southerners to the rest of the nation. Northern interests, however, owned the major southern railroads in 1899, and most of the products flowing northward were raw materials to be processed by northern industry or shipped elsewhere by northern merchants.

ten Southerners lived in a county with a railroad running through it. In 1886, the southern railroads agreed to conform to a national standard for track width, firmly linking the region into a national transportation network and ensuring quick and direct access for southern products to the booming markets of the Northeast.

The railroads connected many formerly isolated small southern farmers to national and international agricultural markets and gave them access to a whole new range of products, from fertilizers to fashions.

The railroad also opened new areas of the South to settlement and economic development. In 1892, according to one guidebook, Florida was "in the main inaccessible to the ordinary tourist, and

unopened to the average settler." By 1912, there were tourist hotels as far south as Key West. Railroads also penetrated the Appalachian Mountains, expanding markets for farmers but also opening the area to outside timber and coal-mining interests.

The railroad increased the prominence of interior cities at the expense of older cities along the southern Atlantic and Gulf Coasts. Antebellum ports such as New Orleans, Charleston, and Savannah declined as commerce rode the rails more than the water. Cities such as Dallas, Atlanta, Nashville, and Charlotte, astride great railroad trunk lines, emerged to lead southern urban growth. No fewer than five major rail lines converged on Atlanta by the 1870s. As early as 1866, it had become "the radiating point for Northern and Western trade coming

Southward, and . . . the gate through which passes Southern trade and travel going northward." When the Texas and Pacific Railway linked Dallas to eastern markets in 1872, it was a small town of three thousand people. Eight years later, its population had grown to more than ten thousand, and within thirty years it had become the South's twelfth largest city. By 1920, New Orleans and Norfolk were the only coastal ports still among the ten most populous southern cities.

A town on a rail line that invested in a cotton press and a cottonseed oil mill would become a marketing hub for the surrounding countryside within a day's wagon ride away. Local merchants would stock the latest fashions from New York, canned foods, and current issues of popular magazines such as *Atlantic* or *Harper's*. The number of towns with fewer than five thousand people doubled between 1870 and 1880 and had doubled again by 1900.

The Limits of Industrial and Urban Growth

Rapid as it was, urban and industrial growth in the South barely kept pace with that of the booming North (see Chapter 20). Between 1860 and 1900, the South's share of the nation's manufacturing increased only marginally from 10.3 percent to 10.5 percent, and its share of the nation's capital declined slightly from 11.5 percent to 11 percent. About the same percentage of people worked in manufacturing in the southern states east of the Mississippi in 1900 as in 1850. Between 1860 and 1880, the per capita income of the South declined from 72 percent of the national average to 51 percent and by 1920 had recovered to only 62 percent.

Southern industrial workers earned roughly half the national average manufacturing wage during the late nineteenth century. Business leaders promoted the advantages of this cheap labor to northern investors. In 1904, a Memphis businessman boasted that his city "can save the northern manufacturer . . . who employs 400 hands, $50,000 a year on his labor bill."

Despite their attractiveness to industrialists, low wages undermined the southern economy in several ways. Poorly paid workers didn't buy much, limiting the market for southern manufactured goods. They kept tax revenue low, restricting the states' ability to fund services like public education. Birmingham, Alabama, probably spent more on public education than any other southern city, but the skilled workers in its steel mills tended to leave as soon as they could for higher-wage opportunities in north-

ern cities like Pittsburgh and Cleveland. Investment in education lagged in the South. Per-pupil expenditure in the region was at least 50 percent below that of the rest of the nation in 1900.

Low wages kept immigrants—and the skills and energy they brought with them—out of the South. With steady work available at higher wages north of the Mason-Dixon line, only a scattering of Italian farm laborers, Chinese railroad workers, and Jewish peddlers ventured below it. Between 1860 and 1900—during one of the greatest waves of immigration the United States has yet experienced—the foreign-born population of the South actually declined from about 10 percent to less than 2 percent.

Why didn't the South benefit more from the rapid expansion of the national economy in the last three decades of the nineteenth century? The simple answer is that the Civil War had wiped out the South's capital resources. Northern goods flowed into the South, but northern capital, technology, and people did not. Northern-based national banks emerged in the wake of the Civil War to fund northern economic expansion. The South, in contrast, had few banks, and those lacked sufficient capital reserves to fuel an equivalent expansion there.

Northern banks imposed higher interest rates and shorter terms on loans to Southerners than on loans to their northern customers. When southern rail lines failed during a depression in the 1870s, northern financiers purchased the companies at bargain prices. By the 1890s, northern firms owned the five major rail lines serving the South.

With limited access to other sources of capital, the South's textile industry depended on thousands of small investors in towns and cities. These investors avoided risk, shunned innovation, and remained small-scale.

The lumber industry, the South's largest, typified the shortcomings of southern economic development in the late nineteenth century. It required little capital, relied on unskilled labor, and processed its raw materials on site. After clear-cutting—felling all the trees—in one region, sawmills moved quickly to the next stand of timber, leaving behind a bare landscape, rusting machinery, and a work force no better off than before.

Birmingham's iron and steel industry also suffered from financial weakness. Mill owners relied on cheap black labor rather than investing in expensive technology. Another problem was the limited market for steel in the mostly agricultural South. Pittsburgh-based U.S. Steel took over Birmingham's largest steel producer in 1907. Thereafter, pricing policies favoring Pittsburgh plants limited Birmingham's growth.

The tobacco industry, however, avoided the problems that plagued other southern enterprises. James B. Duke's American Tobacco Company was so immensely profitable that he became, in effect, his own bank. With more than enough capital to install the latest technology in his plants, Duke bought out his competitors. He then diversified into electric power generation and endowed what became Duke University.

Southern industry fit into a narrow niche of late-nineteenth-century American industrialization. With an unskilled and uneducated work force, poor access to capital and technology, and a weak consumer base, the South processed raw agricultural products and produced cheap textiles, cheap lumber products, and cheap cigarettes. "Made in the South" became synonymous with bottom-of-the-line goods.

In the South most textile mills were typically located in the countryside, often in mill villages, where employers could easily recruit families and keep them isolated from the distractions and employment alternatives of the cities. The timber industry similarly remained a rural-based enterprise. Tobacco manufacturing helped Durham and Winston, North Carolina, grow, but they remained small compared to northern industrial cities. Duke moved his corporate headquarters to New York to be near that city's financial, advertising, and communications services.

The Impact on Southerners

If industrialization in the South was limited compared to the North, it nonetheless had an enormous impact on southern society. In the southern Piedmont, for example, failed farmers moved to textile villages to earn a living. Entire families secured employment and often a house in exchange for their labor. Widows and single young men also moved to the mills, usually the only option outside farm work in the South. Nearly one-third of the textile mill labor force by 1900 consisted of children under the age of 14 and women. They worked twelve hours a day, six days a week, although some firms allowed a half-day off on Saturday.

Southern urban growth, which also paled in comparison with that of the North, had a similarly disproportionate impact on southern society. One observer noted the changes in a North Carolina town between 1880 and 1890. The town in 1880 presented a sorry aspect: rutted roads, a shanty for a school, a few forlorn churches, and perhaps three families of prominence. Twenty years later, another railroad, bustling commerce, and textile mills had produced

a new scene: paved streets, two public schools—one for blacks, one for whites—and a cosmopolitan frame of mind among its residents. "The men have a wider range of activities and the women have more clothes." In another twenty years, the observer predicted, it will be "very like hundreds of towns in the Middle West."

By 1900, a town in the New South would boast a business district and more elegant residences than before. Its influence would extend into the countryside. Farm families visited nearby towns and cities more often. A South Carolina writer related in 1900 that "Country people who . . . went to town annually or semiannually, can now go quickly, safely, pleasantly, and cheaply several times a day." Many never returned to the farm. "Cheap coal, cheap lights, convenient water supply offer inducements; society and amusements draw the young; the chance to speculate, to make a sudden rise in fortunes, to get in the swim attracts others."

The urban South drew the region's talented and ambitious young people. White men like William Henry Belk moved to cities to open shops or take jobs as bank clerks, bookkeepers, merchants, and salesmen. White women worked as retail clerks, telephone operators, and office personnel. Black women filled the growing demand for laundresses and domestic servants. And black men also found prospects better in towns than on the farm, despite a narrow and uncertain range of occupations available to them.

To some Southerners, urbanization and the emphasis on wealth, new technology, and display represented a second Yankee conquest. Ministers warned against traffic with the urban devil, whose temptations could overcome even the most devout individual. Evangelist Sam Jones, a reformed alcoholic, chose Atlanta for his largest revivals in the 1890s, challenging its residents to keep the Sabbath holy, reject alcohol, and obey the Golden Rule.

White Southerners in town and country, who not long ago had lived similar lives, grew distant. Evelyn Scott recalled how rural folk looked to her when they visited her town, Clarksville, Tennessee, at the turn of the century:

These beings [farmers and their families] I regarded as from another planet. . . . The little girls whose petticoats were never of a length with their frocks; the little boys whose misfit "store pants" were cut of material . . . uncongenial . . . to the human form; the misses in muslin dresses of [a] diluted [pink] color; . . . already-weary mothers wearing hats on which reposed entire flimsy gardens and orchards, or else pathetically alighted, stuffed birds! [They engaged] in bouts of window-shopping in which stoical hearts and vacant imaginations were replenished.

Once the backbone of the South, small landholding white farmers and their families like those Scott thought so alien had fallen on hard times. The market that lured them into commercial agriculture threatened to take away their independence. They faced the loss of their land and livelihood. Their way of life no longer served as the standard for the South. New South spokesmen promoted cities and industries and ordered farmers to get on board the train of progress before it left the station without them. (See "American Views: Textile Workers and Farmers Comment on the New South".)

The Agrarian Revolt

Even more than before the Civil War, cotton dominated southern agriculture between 1877 and 1900. And the economics of cotton brought despair to cotton farmers. Rice and tobacco production increased, and Louisiana and Arkansas overtook South Carolina in rice production. Steady demand, however, allowed rice and tobacco growers to maintain a decent standard of living. Cotton was another matter. The size of the cotton crop continued to set annual records after 1877. The railroad opened new areas for cultivation in Mississippi and eastern Texas. But the price of cotton fell while the price of fertilizers, agricultural tools, food, and most other necessities went up. As a result, the more cotton the farmers grew, the less money they made.

Before the Civil War, the South fed itself. After the war, with railroads providing direct access to major cotton-marketing centers, the South became an importer of food. As a common lament went in 1890, "Five-cent cotton, forty-cent meat, how in the world can a poor man eat?"

Cotton and Credit

The solution to this agrarian dilemma seemed simple: Grow less cotton. But in a cash-poor economy, credit ruled. Food crops generated less income per acre than cotton, even in the worst years. Local merchants, themselves bound in a web of credit to merchants in larger cities, accepted cotton as collateral. "No cotton, no credit" became a standard refrain throughout the South after 1877.

Trapped in debt by low cotton prices, high interest rates, and **crop liens** (creditors' claims on farmers' crops), small landowning farmers lost their land in record numbers. Less than one-third of white farmers in the South were tenants or sharecroppers just after the Civil War. By the 1890s, nearly half were.

Publicists for the New South attacked one-crop agriculture—to little avail. Farmers lacked the capital, the machinery, and often the expertise to experiment with alternative farm enterprises. Furthermore, large landowners supported **fence laws**, which restricted farmers' ability to raise livestock by requiring them to keep animals penned. Hunting restrictions kept them from supplementing their diet with game.

Some areas did diversify. Good rail connections in Georgia, for example, made peach farming profitable for some farmers. Cattle ranching spread in Texas. But few crops or animals had the geographical range of cotton. Soil type, rainfall, animal parasites, and frost made alternatives unfeasible for many farmers. Cotton required no machinery or irrigation system. James Barrett, a farmer outside Augusta, Georgia, said of his experiment with diversification in 1900: "I have diversified, and I have not made any money by diversification. . . . I grow green peas and everything I know of. I have raised horses, cows, and hogs, and I have diversified it for the last three years and have not been able to make a dollar."

Farmers Organize, 1877–1892

As their circumstances deteriorated, farmers lobbied for debt-stay laws and formed farmer organizations to widen the circle of their community to include other farmers sharing their plight. They wanted to make the market fairer, to lower interest rates and ease credit, to regulate railroad freight rates, and to keep the prices of necessities in check.

These goals required legislation. But presidential administration between 1877 and 1900, Republican or Democrat, did not favor debt relief or extensive regulation of business. And the Redeemer Democrats who gained control of the southern state governments after Reconstruction represented large landowners and merchants, not poor farmers.

Redeemer governments reduced the proportion of state property taxes paid by the wealthiest landowners. They cut expenditures for public services such as education while giving huge tax breaks and land grants to railroads. And to control farm labor they passed fence laws and vagrancy acts, set tough penalties for petty crimes, and supported the convict lease system that made cheap convict labor available to large landowners.

Corrupt officials throughout the region absconded with hundreds of thousands of dollars. In

American Views

TEXTILE WORKERS AND FARMERS COMMENT ON THE NEW SOUTH

There was much that was new about the New South and much that lingered from an earlier era. One's assessment depended on one's vantage point. Urban merchants, journalists, and industrialists tended to see a prosperous, up-and-coming region in the late nineteenth century. Workers and farmers, in contrast, saw low wages and debt eroding their independence and pushing them toward poverty. The following comments are from letters written by textile mill workers and farmers to the North Carolina Bureau of Labor Statistics.

❖ **How might employers have justified the low wages and long hours the workers complained of?**

❖ **By 1900, relatively little northern capital had ventured south. Is there anything in these comments to suggest why?**

Textile Worker, 1887: The only trouble about wages is that they are not paid in cash—trade checks are issued with which employees are expected to buy what they need at the company's store, which is not right. . . . This, with the long hours required for a day's work [twelve hours], is the only cause for complaint.

Textile Worker, 1887: This long-hour system is destroying the health of all the young women who work in the mills. The employment of children in the mills at low wages keeps a great many men out of employment. Our Legislature should do something in regard the long-hour system and trade checks, and compel employers to pay cash for labor; then, you see, competition in trade would take place, and we could save some of our earnings, which would enable us to have night schools and improve our condition much in the way of education.

---

the biggest scandal, Louisiana's treasurer stole $1,777,000 in state lottery money. Such problems aroused particular bitterness among small farmers at a time when thousands were losing their land to debt.

To strengthen their authority and suppress dissent, the Redeemer Democrats portrayed themselves as having saved the South from the rule of blacks and Republicans. Insurgent farmers who challenged this leadership risked being branded as disloyal.

The Democrats nonetheless faced some opposition. In some states, like North Carolina, the Republicans retained support in mountain areas and among blacks. In addition, disaffected white farmers mounted independent political campaigns against the Redeemers in several states in the late 1870s and early 1880s to demand currency reform and the easing of credit. But the Democrats, in firm control of the election machinery throughout the South, turned back these challenges. Although Independents at one point succeeded in gaining control of the Virginia legislature, their few other victories were confined to the local level. Hard-pressed farmers began to organize on a broader scale.

After the Civil War, nearly 250,000 southern landowners joined a national organization called the National Grange of the Patrons of Husbandry or, more popularly, the **Grange** (see Chapter 22). The leaders of the Grange, however, were large landowners. Their interests were not the same as the small farmers who made up the organization's rank and file. The Grange leadership in the South, for example, favored fence laws, limited government assistance, controls on farm labor, and other policies that

Farmer, 1887: There is general depression and hard times and almost broken spirits among the tenant farmers. There are many things that contribute somewhat to this bad state of things but the one great cause is the outrageous per cent charged for supplies bought on credit; it is sapping the life of North Carolina.

Farmer, 1887: The system of buying on time and using guano [fertilizer] has broken up many farmers, and has driven so many to the towns to seek employment that wages have been greatly reduced.

Farmer, 1887: Attendance at school ought to be enforced by law; the schools are now usually taught in winter when the child of the poor man is poorly clad and hence unable to attend; in summer they must work, and so they do not attend school. This should not be so—we must get out of this condition or we shall go backward as a people and State.

Farmer, 1889: Time was in this vicinity nearly every farmer not only supported himself and family from the products of the farm, but had something to spare as well. That time has passed away, I fear, forever. Then very little cotton was raised, and the farmers looked well to grain crops, horses, cattle, hogs and sheep. There was not much opulence, but much of substantial independence. Now, instead of being a year before, they are a year, at least behind, and, toil as they may, too many of them at the close of the year, when the books are opened, find the balance-sheet against them. . . . No farmer can borrow money, or buy on crop-time, at an advance of from thirty to fifty per cent. No farmer can farm successfully without some money; the present rates offered him amounts to prohibition.

hurt small farmers. The rank-and-file members, in contrast, pushed a more radical agenda including establishing community stores, cotton gins, and warehouses to bypass the prevailing credit system.

The Grange failed to stem the reverses of small southern farmers. In 1882 a group of farmers in Arkansas formed an organization called the **Agricultural Wheel** that had attracted more than 500,000 southern farmers by 1887. Wheelers tried to purchase farm equipment directly from manufacturers, avoiding merchant middlemen. Unlike the Grange, they called for an array of federal programs to ease the credit and cash burdens of farmers, including a graduated income tax and the printing and distribution of more paper money.

The most potent agricultural reform organization, the **Southern Farmers' Alliance**, originated in Texas in the late 1870s. Alliance-sponsored farmers' **cooperatives** provided their members with discounts on supplies and credit. Members also benefited from marketing their cotton crops collectively. Although it endorsed some candidates for office, the Alliance was not a political party and did not challenge Democratic domination of the South.

The Alliance was still very much a Texas organization in 1887 when Charles W. Macune, a Wisconsin native, became its driving force. Macune sent a corps of speakers to create a network of southern cooperatives. Within two years, the Alliance had spread throughout the South and into the North and West. By 1890, it claimed more than a million members. Almost all were small farmers who owned their own land. The success of the Alliance reflected both the desperate struggle of these small farmers to keep their land and the failure of other organizations to help them.

The Alliance operated like a religious denomination. Its leaders preached a message of salvation through cooperation to as many as twenty thousand people at huge revival-like rallies. Qualifications for membership included a belief in the divinity of Christ and the literal truth of the Bible. Alliance speakers, many of them rural ministers, often held meetings in churches, combining biblical nostrums with economic policy. They urged members to visit "the homes where lacerated hearts are bleeding, to assuage the suffering of a brother or a sister, bury the dead, care for the widows and educate the orphans." The Alliance lobbied state legislatures to fund rural public schools. To increase the sense of community, the Alliance sponsored picnics, baseball games, and concerts.

The Alliance imposed strict morality on its members, prohibiting drinking, gambling, and sexual misconduct. Alliance leaders criticized many Baptist, Methodist, and Presbyterian ministers for straying from the traditional emphasis on individual salvation and for defending a status quo that benefited large planters and towns. Cyrus Thompson, North Carolina Alliance president and a prominent Methodist, declared in 1889 that "the church today stands where it has always stood, on the side of human slavery."

Some Alliance members left their churches for new religious groups. **Holiness movement** disciples advocated simple dress, avoided coffee and pork, and swore off all worldly amusements. The members of the **Church of God**, which formed in the mountains of Tennessee and North Carolina in 1886, similarly sought to cleanse themselves of secular evils. The new churches promoted a vision of an egalitarian South. They accepted women on an equal basis and occasionally blacks as well. As many as a third of Holiness preachers were women.

Women also found an active role as officers and speakers in the Alliance. As a Texas woman declared, "The Alliance has come to redeem woman from her enslaved condition. She is admitted into the organization as the equal of her brother, and the ostracism which has impeded her intellectual progress in the past is not met with."

However, the Alliance did not accept black members. Black farmers formed the first **Colored Farmers' Alliance** in Texas in 1886, which had fewer landowners and more tenants and sharecroppers in its ranks than the white organization. It concerned itself with issues relevant to this constituency, such as higher wages for cotton pickers. In 1891, the Colored

Alliance attempted a regionwide strike over farm wages but was unable to enforce it in the worsening southern economy.

The white Alliance had better results with a protest over price fixing. To protect cotton shipped to market, farmers wrapped it in a burlaplike material called jute. In 1888, jute manufacturers combined to raise the price from 7 cents to as much as 14 cents a yard. The Alliance initiated a jute boycott throughout the South, telling farmers to use cotton bagging as an alternative. The protest worked, forcing the chastened jute manufacturers to offer farmers their product at a mere 5 cents per yard.

This success encouraged Macune to propose his **subtreasury plan**. Alliance members were to store their crops in a subtreasury (a warehouse), keeping their cotton off the market until the price rose. In the meantime, the government would loan the farmers up to 80 percent of the value of the stored crops at a low interest rate of 2 percent per year. This arrangement would free farmers from merchants' high interest rates and crop liens.

Macune urged Alliance members to endorse political candidates who supported the subtreasury scheme. Many Democratic candidates for state legislatures throughout the South did endorse it and were elected with Alliance backing in 1890. Once in office, however, they failed to deliver.

The failure of the subtreasury plan combined with a steep drop in cotton prices after 1890 undermined the Alliance. Its cooperatives collapsed as crop liens cut down small landowners as though with scythes. A Georgia Allianceman wrote in 1891 that "Hundreds of farmers will be turned adrift, and thousands of acres of our best land allowed to grow up in weeds through lack of necessary capital to work them." Alliance membership declined by two-thirds in Georgia that year. Desperate Alliance leaders merged their organization with a new national political party in 1892, the People's or **Populist party**. Populists appropriated the Alliance program and challenged Democrats in the South and Republicans in the West. The merger reflected desperation more than calculation.

Southern Populists

Northern farmers, like their southern counterparts, faced growing financial pressure in the 1880s that by the early 1890s had led them too to join the Alliance. Just as southern farmers had turned to the Democratic party to redress their grievances, northern farmers turned to the dominant party in the northern farming states—the Republican party—to redress theirs. Like the Democrats, the Republicans failed to respond. Beginning in Kansas in 1890, disillusioned farmers formed the People's party, soon called the Populist party.

The Populists supported a wide range of reforms, many adopted from the Alliance, including the direct election of United States senators by popular vote rather than by state legislatures, an income tax, woman suffrage, government ownership of railroads, and various proposals to ease credit. In the South, they challenged the Democratic party, sometimes courting the votes of Republicans, including blacks.

Southern populists were ambivalent about African-Americans. On the one hand, blacks constituted a sizable portion of the southern electorate. On the other hand, appealing to blacks would expose Populists to demagogic attacks from Democrats for undermining white supremacy, frightening away potential white backers. The *Baton Rouge Daily Advocate*, for example, informed its readers in 1892 that the Populist party was "the most dangerous and insidious foe of white supremacy."

Despite the risks, in Texas, black Populist John B. Rayner, the "silver-tongued orator of the colored race," spoke to racially mixed audiences around the state. The Texas Populist platform called for "equal justice and protection under the law to all citizens without reference to race, color or nationality." In Georgia, Populist leader Tom Watson supported a biracial party organization and counseled whites to accept blacks as partners in their common crusade. "You are kept apart," Watson told Georgia blacks and whites, "that you may be separately fleeced of your earnings. You are made to hate each other because upon that hatred is rested the keystone of the arch of financial despotism which enslaves you both."

Despite Rayner's and Watson's efforts, most blacks remained loyal to the Republican party for its role in abolishing slavery and for the few patronage crumbs the party still threw their way. Blacks also suspected Populists' motives. The party appealed mainly to small, landowning farmers, not, as most blacks were, propertyless tenants and sharecroppers. And even the Texas Populists opposed black officeholding and jury service.

The Populists finished a distant third in the 1892 presidential election. In the South, their only significant inroads were in the state legislatures of Texas, Alabama, and Georgia. Even in these states, widespread voter fraud among Democrats undermined Populist strength.

Despite a deepening economic depression, the Populists had only a few additional successes in

Tom Watson, the agrarian rebel from Georgia, led the Populist movement in his state. Racism, Democratic party chicanery, and rising cotton prices soon doomed the Populists in the South.

the South after 1892. Adopting a **fusion** strategy, the Populists ran candidates on a combined ticket with Republicans in North Carolina. The fusion candidates captured the governorship and state legislature.

Higher cotton prices and returning prosperity in the late 1890s, however, undermined Populist support in North Carolina, as in the rest of the South. In 1896, the Populists assisted in their own nationwide demise by merging with the Democrats for the presidential election of 1896. In 1898, Democrats surged back into office in North Carolina on the strength of a virulent white supremacy campaign and promptly undid the work of the fusionists.

Women in the New South

Just as farm women found their voices in the Alliance movement of the 1880s, a growing group of middle-class white and black urban women entered the public realm and engaged in policy issues. In the late-nineteenth-century North, women became increasingly active in reform movements, including woman suffrage, labor legislation, social welfare, and city planning. Building on their antebellum activist traditions, northern women, sometimes acting in concert with men, sought to improve the status of women in society.

Southern women had a meager reform tradition to build on. The war also left them ambivalent about independence. With male family members dead or incapacitated, some determined never again to depend on men. Others, responding to the stress of running a farm or business, would have preferred less independence.

Southern men had been shaken by defeat. They had lost the war and placed their families in peril. Many responded with alcoholism and violence. To regain their self-esteem, they recast the war as a noble crusade and imagined southern white women as paragons of virtue and purity who required men to defend them. Even small changes in traditional gender roles would threaten this image. Southern women never mounted an extensive reform campaign like their sisters in the North.

Urban middle-class southern women found opportunities to broaden their social role and enter the public sphere in the two decades after 1880 when servants, stores, and schools freed them of many of the productive functions—like making clothing, cooking, and child care—that burdened their sisters in the country and kept them tied to the home.

Church Work and Preserving Memories

Southern women waded warily into the public arena. The movement to found **home mission societies**, for example, was led by single white women in the Methodist church to promote industrial education among the poor and help working-class women become self-sufficient. Laura Haygood, an Atlantan who had served as a missionary in China, founded a home mission in Atlanta when she returned in 1883. Lily Hammond, another Atlantan, extended the mission concept when she opened **settlement houses** in black and white city neighborhoods in Atlanta in the 1890s. Settlement houses, pioneered in New York in the 1880s, promoted middle-class values in poor neighborhoods and provided them with a permanent source of services. In the South, they were supported by the Methodist church and known as **Wesley Houses**, after John Wesley, the founder of Methodism.

Religion also prompted southern white women to join the **Women's Christian Temperance Union (WCTU)**. The first southern local formed in Lucy Haygood's church in Atlanta in 1880. WCTU members visited schools to educate children about the evils of alcohol, addressed prisoners, and blanketed men's meetings with literature. As a result, they became familiar with the South's abysmal school system and its archaic criminal justice system. They

thus began advocating education and prison reform as well as legislation against alcohol.

By the 1890s, many WCTU members realized that they couldn't achieve their goals unless women had the vote. Rebecca Latimer Felton, an Atlanta suffragist and WCTU member, reflected the frustration of her generation of southern women in an address to working women in 1892:

> But some will say—you women might be quiet—you can't vote, you can't do anything! Exactly so—we have kept quiet for nearly a hundred years hoping to see relief come to the women of this country—and it hasn't come. How long must our children be slain? If a mad dog should come into my yard, and attempt to bite my child or myself—would you think me out of my place, if I killed him with a dull meat axe? . . . [You] would call that woman a brave woman . . . and yet are we to sit by while drink ruins our homes?

WCTU rhetoric implied a veiled attack on men. Felton, for example, often referred to men who drank as "beasts." When the WCTU held its national convention in Atlanta in 1890, local Baptist and Methodist ministers launched a bitter attack against the organization, claiming that it drew women into activities contrary to the Scriptures and that its endorsement of woman suffrage subverted traditional family values.

Few women, however, had such radical objectives in mind. Rebecca Felton and her husband Dr. William H. Felton, a physician and minister, eked out a modest living teaching school and working a small farm during the Civil War and its aftermath. Four of their five children died. Seeing southern families worse off than her own, Felton threw herself into a variety of reform activities, ranging from woman suffrage to campaigns against drinking, smoking, and Coca-Cola. She fought for child care facilities, sex education, and compulsory school attendance and pushed for the admission of women to the University of Georgia. But she had no qualms about the **lynching** of black men—executing them without trial—"a thousand times a week if necessary" to preserve the purity of white women. In 1922, she became the first woman member of the U.S. Senate.

The dedication of southern women to commemorating the memory of the Confederate cause also suggested the conservative nature of middle-class women's reform in the New South. **Ladies' Memorial Associations** formed after the war to ensure the proper burial of Confederate soldiers and suitable markings for their graves. These activities reinforced white solidarity and constructed a common heritage for all white Southerners regardless of class or location. A new organization, the **United Daughters of the Confederacy (UDC)**, appeared in 1894 to preserve southern history and honor its heroes.

Women's Clubs

A broader spectrum of southern middle-class women joined women's clubs than joined church-sponsored organizations or memorial associations. By 1890, some clubs and their members had begun to discuss political issues such as child labor reform, educational improvement, and prison reform. The Lone Star (Texas) Federation scrutinized public hospitals, almshouses, and orphanages at the turn of the century. Its president asserted, "The Lone Star Federation stands for the highest and truest type of womanhood—that which lends her voice as well as her hand." Southern women's club members sought out their sisters in the North. As Georgia's federated club president, Mrs. A. O. Granger, wrote in 1906, "Women of intellectual keenness in the South could not be left out of the awakening of the women of the whole country to a realization of the responsibility which they properly had in the condition of their fellow-women and of the children."

The activities of black women's clubs paralleled those of white women's clubs. Only rarely, however—as at some meetings of the Young Women's Christian Association (YWCA) or occasional meetings in support of prohibition—did black and white club members interact.

Most white clubwomen were unwilling to sacrifice their own reform agenda to the cause of racial reconciliation. Some women suffragists in the South argued that the combined vote of white men and women would further white interests.

The primary interest of most southern white women's clubs was the plight of young white working-class and farm women. Single and adrift in the city, many worked for low wages, and some slipped into prostitution. The clubs sought to help them make the transition from rural to urban life or to improve their lives on the farm. To this end, they focused on child labor reform and on upgrading public education.

Settling the Race Issue

To counter the aspirations of blacks, white leaders enlisted the support of young white men. Blacks resisted the resulting efforts to deprive them of their remaining freedoms. Though some left the South, many more built new lives and communities within the restricted framework whites allowed them.

The Fluidity of Southern Race Relations, 1877–1890

Despite the departure of federal troops and the end of Republican rule, many blacks continued to vote and hold office. Some Democrats even courted the black electorate.

In 1885, T. McCants Stewart, a black newspaperman from New York, traveled to his native South Carolina expecting a rough reception once his train headed south from Washington, D.C. To his surprise, the conductor allowed him to remain in his seat while whites sat on baggage or stood. He provoked little reaction among whites when he entered the dining car. Some of them struck up a conversation with him. Stewart, who admitted he had begun his journey with "a chip on my shoulder . . . [daring] any man to knock it off," now observed that "the whites of the South are really less afraid to [have] contact with colored people than the whites of the North." In Columbia, South Carolina, Stewart found that he could move about with no restrictions. "I can ride in first-class cars. . . . I can go into saloons and get refreshments even as in New York. I can stop in and drink a glass of soda and be more politely waited upon than in some parts of New England."

To be sure, blacks faced discrimination in employment and voting and random retaliation for perceived violations of racial barriers. But those barriers were by no means fixed.

The White Backlash

The generation of blacks that came of age in this environment demanded full participation in American society. As the young black editor of Nashville's *Fisk Herald* proclaimed in 1889, "We are not the Negro from whom the chains of slavery fell a quarter of a century ago. . . . We are now qualified, and being the equal of whites, should be treated as such." Charles Price, an educator from North Carolina, admonished colleagues in 1890, "If we do not possess the manhood and patriotism to stand up in the defense of . . . constitutional rights and protest long, loud and unitedly against their continual infringements, we are unworthy of heritage as American citizens and deserve to have fastened on us the wrongs of which many are disposed to complain."

Many young whites, raised on the myth of the Lost Cause, were continually reminded of the heroism and sacrifice of their fathers during the Civil War. For many conditions were worse than their families had enjoyed before the war, and they resented the changed status of blacks. David Schenck, a Greensboro, North Carolina, businessman wrote in 1890 that "the breach between the races widens as the young free negroes grow up and intrude themselves on white society and nothing prevents the white people of the South from annihilating the negro race but the military power of the United States Government." Using the Darwinian language popular among educated whites at the time, Schenck concluded, "I pity the Negro, but the struggle is for the survival of the fittest race."

The South's deteriorating rural economy and the volatile politics of the late 1880s and early 1890s exacerbated the growing tensions between assertive blacks and threatened whites. In the cities, blacks and whites came in close contact, competing for jobs and jostling each other for seats on streetcars and trains. Racist rhetoric and violence against blacks accelerated in the 1890s.

Lynch Law

In 1892, three prominent black men, Tom Moss, Calvin McDowell, and William Stewart, opened a grocery on the south side of Memphis, an area with a large African-American population. The People's Grocery prospered while a white-owned store across the street struggled. The proprietor of the white-owned store, W. H. Barrett, secured an indictment against Moss, McDowell, and Stewart for maintaining a public nuisance. Outraged black community leaders called a protest meeting at the grocery during which two people made threats against Barrett. Barrett learned of the threats, notified the police, and warned the gathering at the People's Grocery that whites planned to attack and destroy the store. Nine sheriff's deputies, all white, approached the store to arrest the men who had threatened Barrett. Fearing Barrett's threatened white assault, the people in the grocery fired on the deputies, unaware who they

were, and wounded three. When the deputies identified themselves, thirty blacks surrendered, including Moss, McDowell, and Stewart, and were imprisoned. Four days later, deputies removed the three owners from jail, took them to a deserted area, and shot them dead.

The men at the People's Grocery had violated two of the unspoken rules that whites imposed on blacks to maintain racial barriers: They had prospered, and they had forcefully challenged white authority. Whites lynched nearly two thousand southern blacks between 1882 and 1903. Most lynchers were working-class whites with rural roots who were struggling in the depressed economy of the 1890s and enraged at the fluidity of urban race relations.

The substitution of lynch law for a court of law seemed a cheap price to pay for white solidarity at a time when political and economic pressures threatened entrenched white leaders. In 1893, Atlanta's Methodist bishop, Atticus G. Haygood, typically a spokesman for racial moderation, objected to the torture some whites inflicted on their victims but added, "Unless assaults by Negroes on white women and little girls come to an end, there will most probably be still further displays of vengeance that will shock the world."

Haygood's comments reflect the most common justification for lynching—the presumed threat posed by black men to the sexual virtue of white women. Sexual "crimes" could include remarks, glances, and gestures. Yet only 25 percent of the lynchings that took place in the thirty years after 1890 had some alleged sexual connection. Certainly, the men of the People's Grocery had committed no sex crime.

Ida B. Wells, who owned a black newspaper in Memphis, used her columns to publicize the

Lynchings often drew huge crowds of white onlookers, who came to see victims tortured (here with a red-hot iron to the soles of the victim's feet) and murdered.

People's Grocery lynchings. The great casualty of the lynchings, she noted, was her faith that education, wealth, and upright living guaranteed blacks the equality and justice they had long sought. The reverse was true. The more blacks succeeded, the greater was their threat to whites. She investigated other lynchings, countering the claim that they were the result of assaults on white women. When she suggested that, on the contrary, perhaps some white women were attracted to black men, she enraged Memphis whites, who destroyed her press and office. Exiled to Chicago, Wells devoted herself to the struggle for racial justice.

Segregation by Law

Southern white lawmakers sought to cement white solidarity and ensure black subservience in the 1890s by instituting segregation by law and the **disfranchisement** of black voters. States began to legislate segregation in the 1890s when urbanization, industrial development, and railroads increased the opportunities for racial contact and muddled the rules of racial interaction.

Whites objected to blacks' implied assertion of economic and social equality when they sat with them in dining cars and first-class compartments. Southern blacks, in contrast, viewed equal access to railroad facilities as a sign of respectability and acceptance. When southern state legislatures required railroads to provide segregated facilities, blacks protested.

In 1890, Homer Plessy, a Louisiana black, refused to leave the first-class car of a railroad traveling through the state. Arrested, he filed suit, arguing that his payment of the first-class fare entitled him to sit in the same first-class accommodations as whites. He claimed that under his right of citizenship guaranteed by the Fourteenth Amendment, neither the state of Louisiana nor the railroad could discriminate against him on the basis of color. The Constitution, he claimed, was colorblind.

The U.S. Supreme Court ruled on the case, ***Plessy v. Ferguson,*** in 1896. In a seven-to-one decision, the Court held that Louisiana's railroad segregation law did not violate the Constitution as long as the railroads or the state provided equal accommodations. The decision left unclear what "equal" meant. In the Court's view, "Legislation is powerless to eradicate racial instincts," meaning that segregation of the races was natural and transcended constitutional considerations. The only justice to vote against the decision was John Marshall Harlan, a Kentuckian and former slave owner. In a stinging dissent, he predicted that the decision would result in an all-out assault on black rights. "The destinies of the two races

. . . are indissolubly linked together," Harlan declared, "and the interests of both require that the common government of all shall not permit the seeds of race hate to be planted under the sanction of law."

Both northern and southern states enacted new segregation laws in the wake of *Plessy* v. *Ferguson*. In practice, the separate facilities for blacks these laws required, if provided at all, were rarely equal. By 1900, segregation by law extended to public conveyances, theaters, hotels, restaurants, parks, and schools.

The segregation statutes came to be known collectively as **Jim Crow laws**, after the blackface stage persona of Thomas Rice, a white northern minstrel show performer in the 1820s. Reflecting white stereotypes of blacks, Rice caricatured Crow as a foolish, elderly, lame slave who spoke in an exaggerated dialect.

Economic segregation followed social segregation. Before the Civil War, black men had dominated crafts such as carpentry and masonry. By the 1890s, whites were replacing them in these trades and excluding them from new trades such as plumbing and electrical work. Trade unions, composed primarily of craft workers, began systematically to exclude African-Americans. Confined increasingly to low or unskilled positions in railroad construction, the timber industry, and agriculture, blacks underwent **deskilling**—a decline in work force expertise—after 1890. With lower incomes from unskilled labor, they faced reduced opportunities for better housing and education.

Disfranchisement

Following the political instability of the late 1880s and the 1890s, white leaders determined to disfranchise blacks altogether, thereby reinforcing white solidarity and eliminating the need to consider black interests. Obstacles loomed—the Fifteenth Amendment, which guaranteed freedmen the right to vote, and a Republican-dominated Congress—but with a national consensus emerging in support of white supremacy, they proved easy to circumvent.

Support for disfranchisement was especially strong among large landowners in the South's plantation districts, where heavy concentrations of blacks threatened their political domination. Urban leaders, especially after the turmoil of the 1890s, looked on disfranchisement as a way to stabilize politics and make elections more predictable.

Democrats enacted a variety of measures to attain their objectives without violating the letter of the Fifteenth Amendment. States enacted **poll taxes**, requiring citizens to pay to vote. They adopted the secret ballot, which confused and intimidated illiterate blacks accustomed to using ballots with colors to identify parties. States set literacy and educational qualifications for voting or required prospective registrants to "interpret" a section of the state constitution. To avoid disfranchising poor, illiterate whites with these measures, states enacted **grandfather clauses** granting the vote automatically to anyone whose grandfather could have voted prior to 1867 (the year Congressional Reconstruction began). The grandfathers of most black men in the 1890s had been slaves, ineligible to vote.

Tennessee was the first state to pass disfranchising legislation. A year later, Mississippi amended its constitution to require voters to pass a literacy test and prove they "understood" the state constitution. When a journalist asked an Alabama lawmaker if Jesus Christ could pass his state's "understanding" test, the legislator replied, "That would depend entirely on which way he was going to vote."

Alarmed by the Populist uprising, Democratic leaders also used disfranchisement to gut dissenting parties. During the 1880s, minority parties in the South consistently polled an average of 40 percent of the statewide vote; by the mid-1890s, that figure had diminished to 30 percent, despite the Populist insurgency. Turnout dropped even more dramatically. In Mississippi, for example, voter turnout in gubernatorial races during the 1880s averaged 51 percent; during the 1890s, it was 21 percent. Black turnout in Mississippi, which averaged 39 percent in the 1880s, plummeted to near zero in the 1890s. Overall turnout, which averaged 64 percent during the 1880s, fell to only 30 percent by 1910.

When 160 South Carolina delegates gathered to amend the state constitution in 1895, the six blacks among them mounted a passionate but futile defense of their right to vote. Black delegate W. J. Whipper noted the irony of whites clamoring for supremacy when they already held the vast majority of the state's elected offices. Robert Smalls, the state's leading black politician, urged delegates not to turn their backs on the state's black population: "Some morning," he warned, "you may wake up to find that the bone and sinew of your country is gone. . . . If you impose too hard conditions upon the negro in this State there will be nothing else for him to do but to leave." Such pleas fell on deaf ears.

A National Consensus on Race

How could the South get away with it? How could Southerners openly segregate, disfranchise, and lynch African-Americans without a national outcry? Apparently, the majority of Americans in the 1890s subscribed to the notion that blacks were inferior to

whites and deserved to be treated as second-class citizens. Contemporary depictions of blacks show scarcely human stereotypes: black men with bulbous lips and bulging eyes, fat black women wearing turbans and smiling vacuously, and black children contentedly eating watermelon or romping with jungle animals. These images appeared on cereal boxes, in advertisements, in children's books, in newspaper cartoons, and as lawn ornaments. Among the widely read books of the era was *The Clansman,* a glorification of the rise of the Ku Klux Klan by Thomas Dixon, a North Carolinian living in New York City and an ardent white supremacist. D. W. Griffith transformed *The Clansman* into an immensely popular motion picture epic under the title *Birth of a Nation.*

So-called scientific racism purported to establish white superiority and black inferiority on biological grounds. Northern-born professional historians reinterpreted the Civil War and Reconstruction in the white South's favor. Historian William A. Dunning, the generation's leading authority on Reconstruction, wrote in 1901 that the North's "views as to the political capacity of the blacks had been irrational." The progressive journal *Outlook* hailed disfranchisement because it made it "impossible in the future for ignorant, shiftless, and corrupt negroes to misrepresent their race in political action." Harvard's Charles Francis Adams Jr. chided colleagues who disregarded the "fundamental, scientific facts" he claimed demonstrated black inferiority. The *New York Times,* summarizing this national consensus in 1903, noted that "practically the whole country" supported the "southern solution" to the race issue, since "there was no other possible settlement."

Congress and the courts upheld discriminatory legislation. As a delegate at the Alabama disfranchisement convention of 1901 noted, "The race problem is no longer confined to the States of the South, [and] we have the sympathy instead of the hostility of the North."

The Republican party, which stood to lose votes in the South if states disfranchised African-Americans, nonetheless made no effort to protect their rights after 1890 because they did not need southern votes to win presidential elections or to control Congress.

Although no northern states threatened to deny blacks the right to vote, they did increase segregation. The booming industries of the North generally did not hire blacks. Antidiscrimination laws on the books since the Civil War went unenforced. In 1904, 1906, and 1908, race riots erupted in Springfield, Ohio; Greensburg, Indiana; and Springfield,

Illinois, matching similar disturbances in Wilmington, North Carolina, and Atlanta, Georgia.

Response of the Black Community

African-Americans organized more than a dozen boycotts of streetcar systems in the urban South between 1896 and 1908 in an effort to desegregate them, but not one succeeded. The Afro-American Council, formed in 1890 to protest the deteriorating conditions of black life, accomplished little and disbanded in 1908. W. E. B. Du Bois organized an annual Conference on Negro Problems at Atlanta University beginning in 1896, but it produced no effective plan of action.

A few blacks chose to leave the South. Henry McNeal Turner of Georgia, an African Methodist Episcopal (AME) bishop, promoted migration to Liberia, but only a few hundred made the trip in the late 1870s, Turner not included, and most of those returned disappointed. Most blacks who moved in the 1890s stayed within the South.

More commonly, blacks withdrew to develop their own rich community life. Particularly in the cities of the South, they could live relatively free of white surveillance and even white contact. In 1890, fully 70 percent of urban blacks lived in the South; and between 1860 and 1900, the proportion of blacks in the cities of the South rose from one in six to more than one in three.

By the 1880s, a new black middle class had emerged in the South. Urban-based, professional, business-oriented, and serving a primarily black clientele, its members fashioned an interconnected web of churches, fraternal and self-help organizations, families, and businesses. Black Baptists, AME, and AME Zion churches led reform efforts in the black community, seeking to eliminate drinking, prostitution, and other vices in black neighborhoods.

African-American fraternal and self-help groups, led by middle-class blacks, functioned as surrogate welfare organizations for the poor. Some groups, such as the Colored Masons and the Colored Odd Fellows, paralleled white organizations. Black membership rates usually exceeded those in the white community. More than 50 percent of Nashville's black men, for example, belonged to various fraternal associations in the city. Fraternal orders also served as the seedbed for such business ventures as the **North Carolina Mutual Life Insurance Company**, founded in Durham in 1898. Within two decades, North Carolina Mutual became the largest black-owned business in the nation and helped transform Durham into the "capital of the black middle class." Most southern cities boasted active black business districts by the 1890s.

Nashville's J. C. Napier typified the activism of the African-American urban middle class in the New South era. He belonged to two of the city's prominent black churches, was active in Republican politics, played an important role in several temperance and fraternal societies, served as president of the local black YMCA chapter, and as an attorney helped his fellow African-Americans with numerous legal matters.

The African-American middle class worked especially hard to improve black education. Black students in cities had only makeshift facilities; those in the countryside had almost no facilities. To improve these conditions, black middle-class leaders solicited educational funds from northern philanthropic organizations.

Black women played an increasingly active and prominent role in African-American communities after 1877, especially in cities. Ida B. Wells moved to Memphis from Mississippi in 1884. In 1886, she attended a lecture at an interracial Knights of Labor meeting and witnessed a religious revival conducted by the nation's leading evangelist, Dwight Moody. The following year, Wells began her journalism career and soon purchased a one-third interest in a local black newspaper.

Black women's clubs supported day care facilities for working mothers and settlement houses in poor black neighborhoods modeled after those in northern cities. Atlanta's **Neighborhood Union**, founded by Lugenia Burns Hope in 1908, provided playgrounds and a health center and secured a grant from a New York foundation to improve black education in the city. Black women's clubs also established homes for single black working women to protect them from sexual exploitation, and they worked for woman suffrage "to reckon with men who place no value on her [black woman's] virtue," as Nannie H. Burroughs of the **National Association of Colored Women** argued at the turn of the century.

Anna J. Cooper, a Nashville clubwoman, wrote in 1892 that to be a member of this generation was "to have a heritage unique in the ages." Assertive black women did not arouse the same degree of white antagonism as assertive black men. They could operate in a broader public arena than men and speak out more forcefully.

The extension of black club work into rural areas of the South, where the majority of the African-American population lived, to educate families about hygiene, nutrition, and child care, anticipated similar efforts among white women after 1900. But unlike

Booker T. Washington (left) and W. E. B. Du Bois (right). The differences between these two prominent black leaders reflected in part the differences between the North and the South in the late nineteenth and early twentieth centuries. The northern-born Du Bois challenged segregation and pinned his hopes for improving the condition of African-Americans on a talented elite. The southern-born Washington counseled acquiescence to segregation, maintaining that blacks could ultimately gain the acceptance of white society through self-improvement and hard work.

their white counterparts, these middle-class black women worked with limited resources in a context of simmering racial hostility and political and economic impotence. In response, they nurtured a self-help strategy to improve the conditions of the people they sought to help. One of the most prominent African-American leaders of the late nineteenth and early twentieth centuries, Booker T. Washington, adopted a similar approach to racial uplift.

Born a slave in Virginia in 1856, Washington and his family worked in the salt and coal mines of West Virginia after the Civil War. Ambitious and flushed with the postwar enthusiasm for advancement that gripped freedmen, he worked his way through Hampton Normal and Agricultural Institute, the premier black educational institution in the South at that time. In 1881, he founded the **Tuskegee Institute** for

black students in rural Alabama. By learning industrial skills, Washington maintained, black people could secure self-respect and economic independence. Tuskegee emphasized vocational training over the liberal arts.

At an Atlanta exposition in 1895, Washington argued that African-Americans should accommodate themselves to segregation and disfranchisement until they could prove their economic worth to American society. In exchange, whites should help provide blacks with the education and job training they would need to gain their independence. This position was known as the **Atlanta Compromise**. Despite his conciliatory public stance, Washington secretly helped finance legal challenges to segregation and disfranchisement. But increasingly, blacks were shut out of the kinds of jobs for which Washington hoped to train them. Facing a depressed rural economy and growing racial violence, they had little prospect of advancement.

Another prominent African-American leader, W. E. B. Du Bois, challenged Washington's acceptance of black social inequality. Du Bois was the first African-American to earn a doctorate at Harvard. Du Bois promoted self-help, education, and black pride. A gifted teacher and writer, he taught at Atlanta University and wrote eighteen books on various aspects of black life in America. Du Bois was a cofounder, in 1910, of the **National Association for the Advancement of Colored People (NAACP)**, an interracial organization dedicated to restoring African-American political and social rights.

Despite their differences, which reflected their divergent backgrounds, Washington and Du Bois agreed on many issues. Both believed that black success in the South required some white assistance. As Du Bois wrote in *The Souls of Black Folk*, "Any movement for the elevation of the Southern Negro needs the cooperation, the sympathy, and the support of the best white people in order to succeed." But "the best white people" did not care to elevate southern blacks. In 1906, after a bloody race riot in Atlanta, Du Bois left the South, a decision millions of black Southerners would make over the next two decades.

As long as it provided the raw materials for the North's new urban industrial economy and maintained the peace, the South could count on the rest of the country not to interfere in its solution to race relations. Indeed, to the extent that most white Americans concerned themselves with race, they agreed with the southern solution.

Conclusion

In many respects, the South was more like the rest of the nation in 1900 than at any other time since 1860. Young men and women migrated to southern cities to pursue opportunities unavailable to their parents. Advances in the production and marketing of cigarettes and soft drinks would soon make southern entrepreneurs and their products household names. Southerners ordered fashions from Sears, Roebuck catalogs and enjoyed electric lights, electric trolleys, and indoor plumbing as much as other urban Americans.

Americans idealized a mythical South of rural grace and hospitality, a land of moonlight and magnolias, offering it as a counterpoint to the crowded, immigrant-infested, factory-fouled, money-grubbing North. Northern journalists offered admir-

ing portraits of southern heroes like Robert E. Lee, of whom one declared in 1906, "the nation has a hero to place beside her greatest."

White Southerners cultivated national reconciliation but remained fiercely dedicated to preserving the peculiarities of their region: a one-party political system, disfranchisement, and segregation by law. The region's urban and industrial growth, impressive from the vantage of 1865, paled before that of the North. The South remained a colonial economy characterized more by deep rural poverty than urban prosperity.

Middle-class whites in the urban South enjoyed the benefits of a national economy and a secure social position. Middle-class women enjoyed increased influence in the public realm, but not to the extent of their northern sisters. And the institutionalization of white supremacy gave even poor white farmers and factory workers a place in the social hierarchy a rung or two above the bottom.

For blacks, the New South proved a crueler ruse than Reconstruction. No one now stepped forward to support their cause and stem the erosion of their economic independence, political freedom, and civil rights. They built communities and worked as best they could to challenge restrictions on their freedom.

The New South was thus both American and southern. It shared with the rest of the country a period of rapid urban and industrial growth. But the legacy of war and slavery still lay heavily on the South, manifesting itself in rural poverty, segregation, and black disfranchisement.

Review Questions

1. In what ways did the growing activism of white middle-class women, the increasing assertiveness of young urban blacks, and the persistence of the agricultural depression affect the politics of the South in the late 1880s and early 1890s?

2. We associate segregation and disfranchisement with reactionary political and social views. Yet many whites who promoted both seriously believed them to be reforms. How could whites hold such a view?

3. What strategies did southern blacks employ in response to the narrowing of economic and political opportunities in the New South?

4. New South publicists promoted the South as an emerging urban and industrial region. How accurate were their assertions in 1900?

Recommended Reading

Edward L. Ayers, *The Promise of the New South: Life after Reconstruction* (1992). Ayers illuminates how the people of the late-nineteenth-century South accommodated the conflict between the economic and cultural legacies of the slave South and the currents of modernity such as industrialization and the creation of a national state.

Paul M. Gaston, *The New South Creed: A Study in Southern Mythmaking* (1970). Gaston provides an important assessment of how New South booster rhetoric matched up against the economic reality. The work is especially good at examining how New South spokesmen turned images of the Old South and other southern traditions to the ends of urban and industrial development.

Walter Hines Page, *The Rebuilding of Old Commonwealths* (1902). The classic argument for the New South comes from one of its most serious promoters.

Howard N. Rabinowitz, *The First New South, 1865–1920* (1992). An interpretive survey of recent research on the era, this book explores a continuity between the Old South and the New that may have limited the latter's potential.

Howard N. Rabinowitz, *Race Relations in the Urban South, 1865–1890* (1978). This is a fine survey of how African-Americans built communities in the urban South despite the worsening racial situation after Reconstruction.

Joel Williamson, *The Crucible of Race: Black-White Relations in the American South since Emancipation* (1984). This innovative work details the racial attitudes of white Southerners and reveals how elites particularly used race to further political and social objectives.

C. Vann Woodward, *Origins of the New South, 1877–1913* (1951). This classic interpretation of the New South era stresses the discontinuities between Old South and New.

Where to Learn More

❖ **Museum of the New South, Charlotte, North Carolina.**   The museum has exhibits on various New South themes. A semipermanent exhibit called "The New South: From A to Z" summarizes New South history, particularly in the southern Piedmont region.

❖ **Atlanta History Center, Atlanta, Georgia.**   The major exhibit, "Metropolitan Frontiers, 1835–2000," includes a strong segment on the New South era, including the development of separate black and white economies in Atlanta. The Herndon home, also on the grounds of the center, has an exhibit on black upper-class life in Atlanta from 1880 to 1930.

❖ **Museum of the Confederacy, Richmond, Virginia.** The museum is developing an exhibit, "Southern Women, 1860–1900," that will cover many of the themes noted in this chapter.

❖ **Sloss Furnaces National Historical Landmark, Birmingham, Alabama.**   The site recalls the time when Birmingham challenged Pittsburgh as the nation's primary steel-producing center.

20 INDUSTRY, IMMIGRANTS, AND CITIES, 1870–1900

CHAPTER OUTLINE

KEY TOPICS

❖ The technological and organizational innovations behind the emergence of large industrial corporations

❖ Changes in the American work force in the urban-industrial economy and the attempts by labor to organize to protect workers' interests

❖ The impact of the new immigration and the start of African American migration to the cities of the North

❖ The changing physical and social structure of the industrial city

❖ New patterns of residence and recreation in the consumer society

*P*hiladelphia, May 10, 1876. President Ulysses S. Grant and several hundred political and military dignitaries rise to their feet as the orchestra and chorale reach the climax of Handel's "Hallelujah Chorus." A huge American flag unfurls above a nearby building, and one hundred cannons roar a deafening salute to the start of America's second century.

This ceremony opened Philadelphia's **Centennial Exposition**, which more than 8 million people would visit over the next six months. There they witnessed the ingenuity of the world's newest industrial power. Thomas Edison explained his new automatic telegraph, and Alexander Graham Bell demonstrated his telephone to the wonder of onlookers. A giant Corliss steam engine loomed over the entrance to Machinery Hall, dwarfing the other exhibits and providing them with power. "Yes," a visitor concluded, "it is in these things of iron and steel that the national genius most freely speaks."

For many Americans, however, the fanfare of the exposition rang hollow. The country was in the midst of a depression. Most Philadelphians could not afford the exposition's 50-cent admission price. They celebrated instead at "Centennial City," a ragtag collection of cheap bars, seedy hotels, small restaurants, and circus sideshows hurriedly constructed of wood and tin along a muddy mile-long strip across the street from the exposition's sturdy halls and manicured lawns.

This small area of Philadelphia reflected the promise and failure of late-nineteenth century America, a period often called the **gilded age**, from the title of a novel by Mark Twain. The term serves as a shorthand description of the shallow worship of wealth that characterized the period, and to the veneer of respectability and prosperity underneath which lay deep economic and social divisions.

Between 1870 and 1900, the country experienced rapid industrial development that changed the nature of the work force and the workplace. Skilled craftsmen and small shops were displaced by large factories staffed by semiskilled laborers. Urbanization accelerated. Between the Civil War and 1900, the proportion of the nation's population living in cities increased from 20 percent to 40 percent. During the 1880s alone, more than 5 million immigrants came to the United States, twice as many as in any previous decade.

New opportunities opened as old opportunities disappeared. Vast new wealth was created, but poverty deepened and broadened. New technologies eased life for some but left others untouched. It would be the great dilemma of early-twentieth-century America to reconcile these contradictions and satisfy the American quest for a decent life for all within the new urban industrial order.

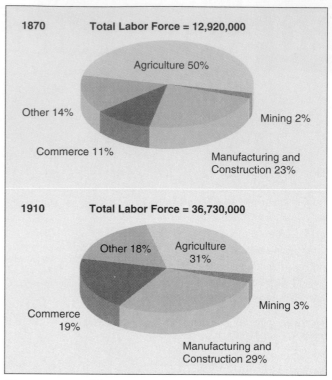

Figure 20-1   Changes in the American Labor Force, 1870–1910
The transformation of the American economy in the late nineteenth century changed the nature and type of work. By 1910 the United States was an urban, industrial nation with a matching work force that toiled in factories and for commercial establishments (including railroads), and less frequently on farms.

New Industry

Between 1870 and 1900, the United States transformed itself from an agricultural nation—a nation of farmers, merchants, and artisans—into the world's foremost industrial power, producing more than one-third of the world's manufactured goods. By the early twentieth century, factory workers made up one-fourth of the work force, and agricultural workers had dropped from a half to less than a third (see Figure 20-1). By the early twentieth century, many industries employed thousands of workers in a single plant. Some industries—petroleum, steel, and meatpacking, for example—had been unknown before the Civil War. At the same time, the number of firms in a given industry shrank. Mergers, changes in corporate management and the organization of the work force, and a compliant government left a few

companies in control of vast segments of the American economy. Workers, reformers, and eventually government challenged this concentration of economic power.

Inventing Technology

Technology transformed factory work and increased the scale of production. Steam engines and, later, electricity freed manufacturers from dependence on water power. Factories could now be built anywhere accessible to the transportation system and a concentration of labor. Technology also enabled managers to substitute machines for workers, skewing the balance of power in the workplace toward employers. By the early twentieth century, electric lights, appliances, ready-made clothing, and store-bought food eased middle-class life. Electric trolleys whisked clerks, salespeople, bureaucrats, and bankers to new urban and suburban subdivisions. Electric streetlights lit up city streets at night. As historian and novelist Henry Adams put it at the turn of the century, "In the essentials of life . . . the boy of 1854 stood nearer [to] the year one than to the year 1900."

For much of the nineteenth century, the United States was dependent on the industrial nations of Europe for technological innovation. American engineers often went to England and Germany for education and training, and the textile industry, railroads, and the early steel industry benefited from German and English inventions.

In the late nineteenth century, the United States changed from a technological borrower to a technological innovator. By 1910, a million patents had been issued in the United States, 900,000 of them after 1870. Nothing represented this shift better than Thomas A. Edison's electric light bulb and electric generating system, which transformed electricity into a new and versatile form of industrial energy. Until the late nineteenth century, advances in scientific theory usually followed technological innovation. Techniques for making steel, for example, developed before scientific theories emerged to explain how they worked. Textile machinery and railroad technology developed similarly. In contrast, a theoretical understanding of electricity preceded its practical use as a source of energy. Scientists had been experimenting with electricity for half a century before Edison unveiled his light bulb in 1879. Edison's research laboratory at Menlo Park, New Jersey, also established a model for corporate-sponsored research and development that would rapidly increase the pace of technological innovation.

In 1876, Edison established his research laboratory at Menlo Park, and turned his attention to the electric light. Scientists had already discovered that passing an electric current through a filament in a vacuum produced light. They had not yet found a filament, however, that could last for more than a few minutes. Edison tried a variety of materials, from grass

to hair from a colleague's beard, before succeeding with charred sewing thread. In 1879, he produced a bulb that burned for an astounding forty-five hours. Then he devised a circuit that provided an even flow of current through the filament. After thrilling a crowd with the spectacle of five hundred lights ablaze on New Year's Eve in 1879, Edison went on to build a power station in New York City to serve businesses and homes by 1882. The electric age had begun.

Edison's initial success touched off a wave of research and development in Germany, Austria, Great Britain, France, and the United States to improve on his light bulb and develop new applications of electricity. Whoever could light the world cheaply and efficiently held the key to an enormous fortune. Ultimately the prize fell not to Edison but to Elihu Thomson, a high school chemistry teacher in Philadelphia. Leaving teaching to devote himself to research full time, Thomson founded his own company and in 1883 moved to Connecticut. Thomson purchased Edison's General Electric Company in 1892 and established the country's first corporate research and development division. By 1914, General Electric was producing 85 percent of the world's light bulbs.

Other major American companies now established research and development laboratories. Standard Oil, U.S. Rubber, the chemical giant Du Pont, and the photographic company Kodak all became world leaders in their respective industries because of innovations their laboratories developed.

The modernization of industry that made the United States the world's foremost industrial nation after 1900 reflected organizational as well as technological innovation. As industries applied new technology and expanded their markets within and beyond national borders, their work forces expanded and their need for capital expenditures mounted.

A humorous view of Thomas Edison's laboratories in Menlo Park, New Jersey, around 1880. There was no joking, however, about the potential of Edison's incandescent bulb and his other practical adaptations of electricity for everyday use. Electricity would soon transform life for millions of people. Edison's methods set the precedent for corporate research and development that would accelerate the pace of new discoveries with practical applications.

CHRONOLOGY

1869 The Knights of Labor is founded in Philadelphia.

1870 John D. Rockefeller forms the Standard Oil Company.

Congress passes the Naturalization Act barring Asians from citizenship.

1876 The Centennial Exposition opens in Philadelphia.

1877 The "Great Uprising" railroad strike, the first nationwide work stoppage in the United States, provokes violent clashes between workers and federal troops.

1879 Thomas Edison unveils the electric light bulb.

1880 Founding of the League of American Wheelmen in 1880 helps establish bicycling as one of urban America's favorite recreational activities.

1881 Assassination of Russian Tsar Alexander II begins a series of pogroms that triggers a wave of Russian Jewish immigration to the United States.

1882 Congress passes the Chinese Exclusion Act.

First country club in the United States founded in Brookline, Massachusetts.

1883 National League merges with the American Association and opens baseball to working-class fans.

1886 The Neighborhood Guild, the nation's first settlement house, opens in New York City.

Riot in Chicago's Haymarket Square breaks the Knights of Labor.

American Federation of Labor is formed.

1887 Anti-Catholic American Protective Association is formed.

1888 Wanamaker's department store introduces a "bargain room," and competitors follow suit.

1889 Jane Addams opens Hull-House, the nation's most celebrated settlement house, in Chicago.

1890 Jacob A. Riis publishes *How the Other Half Lives.*

1891 African-American Chicago physician Daniel Hale Williams establishes Provident Hospital, the nation's first interracially staffed hospital.

1892 General Electric opens the first corporate research and development division in the United States.

Strike at Andrew Carnegie's Homestead steelworks fails.

1894 Pullman Sleeping Car Company strike fails.

Immigration Restriction League is formed.

1895 American-born Chinese in California form the Native Sons of the Golden State to counter nativism.

1897 George C. Tilyou opens Steeplechase Park on Coney Island in Brooklyn, New York.

1898 Congress passes the Erdman Act to provide for voluntary mediation of railroad labor disputes.

1901 Socialist Party of America is formed.

1905 Militant labor organization, the Industrial Workers of the World, is formed.

Coping with these changes required significant changes in corporate management.

The Corporation and Its Impact

A corporation is an association of individuals with legal rights and liabilities separate from those of its members. This form of business organization had existed since colonial times but became a significant factor in the American economy with the growth of railroad companies in the 1850s. A key feature of a corporation is the separation of ownership from management. A corporation can raise capital by selling stock—ownership shares—to shareholders who may have no direct role in running it. The shareholders benefit from dividends drawn on the profits and, if the corporation thrives, from the rising value of its stock.

The corporation had two major advantages over other forms of business organization. First, unlike a partnership, which can dissolve when a partner dies, a corporation can outlive its founders. This organizational stability permits long-term planning and is reassuring to investors. Second, corporations enjoy limited liability. That means officials and shareholders are not personally liable for a corporation's debts. If it goes bankrupt, they stand to lose only what they have invested in it. This characteristic also helped attract investors.

As large corporations emerged in major American industries, they had a ripple effect throughout the economy. Large corporations needed huge supplies of capital. They turned to the banks to help meet those needs, and the banks grew in response. The corporations stimulated technological change as they looked for ways to speed production, improve products, and lower costs. As they grew, they generated jobs throughout the economy.

By the early twentieth century, control of the workplace was shifting from well-paid, skilled partisans to managers, and semiskilled and unskilled workers were replacing skilled artisans. These new workers, often foreign-born, performed repetitive tasks for low wages.

Because the large industrial corporations usually located factories in cities, they stimulated urban growth. Large industrial districts sprawled along urban rivers and near urban rail lines, attracting thousands of workers. There were exceptions. Southern textile manufacturers tended to locate plants in villages and small towns and on the outskirts of larger cities. A few northern entrepreneurs also constructed industrial communities outside major cities to save on land costs and ensure control over labor. Nonetheless, by 1900, fully 90 percent of all manufacturing occurred in cities.

Two organizational strategies—vertical integration and horizontal integration—helped successful corporations reduce competition and gain dominance in their industries. **Vertical integration** involved the consolidation of all functions related to a particular industry, from the extraction and transport of raw materials to the manufacture of products to finished-product distribution and sales. Geographical dispersal went hand in hand with vertical integration. Different functions—a factory and its source of raw materials, for example—were likely to be in different places, a development made possible by advances in communication like the telephone. The multiplication of functions also prompted the growth of corporate bureaucracy.

A good example of vertical integration occurred in the meatpacking industry under the influence of Gustavus Swift.

Swift, a Boston native who moved to Chicago in 1875, realized that refrigerated railway cars would make it possible to ship butchered meat from western ranges to eastern markets, eliminating the need to transport live cattle. When he invented a refrigerated car, however, he could not sell it to the major railroads. They feared losing the heavy investment they had already made in cattle cars and pens. Swift had the cars built himself and convinced a Canadian railroad with only a small stake in cattle shipping to haul them to eastern markets. He established packing houses in Omaha and Kansas City, near the largest cattle markets; built refrigerated warehouses at key distribution points to store beef for transport or sale; and hired a sales force to convince eastern butchers

of the quality of his product. He now controlled the production, transportation, and distribution of his product, the essence of vertical integration. By 1881, he was shipping $200,000 worth of beef a week. His competitors soon followed his example.

Horizontal integration involved the merger of competitors in the same industry. John D. Rockefeller's Standard Oil Company pioneered horizontal integration in the 1880s. Born in western New York State, the son of a traveling patent medicine salesman, Rockefeller moved to Ohio at the age of 14 in 1853. He began investing in Cleveland oil refineries by his mid-twenties. Together with some associates, he formed Standard Oil in 1870. Using a variety of tactics—including threats, deceit, and price wars—Rockefeller rapidly acquired most of his competitors. Supported by investment bankers like J. P. Morgan, Standard Oil controlled 90 percent of the nation's oil refining by 1890. Acquiring oil fields and pipelines as well as refineries, Standard Oil achieved both vertical and horizontal integration. Rockefeller's dominant position allowed him to impose order and predictability in what had been an often chaotic industry, ensuring a continuous flow of profits. He closed inefficient refineries, opened new ones, and kept his operations up-to-date with the latest technologies.

Other entrepreneurs achieved similar dominance in other major industries and amassed similarly enormous personal fortunes. James B. Duke, who automated cigarette manufacturing, gained control of most of the tobacco industry. Andrew Carnegie consolidated much of the U.S. steel industry within his Carnegie Steel Company (later U.S. Steel). By 1900, Carnegie's company was producing one-quarter of the country's steel.

The giant corporations threatened to restrict opportunities for small entrepreneurs like the shopkeepers, farmers, and artisans who abounded at midcentury. In the words of one historian, the corporations "seemed to signal the end of an open, promising America and the beginning of a closed, unhappier society." Impersonal and governed by the profit margin, the modern corporation challenged the ideal of the self-made man and the belief that success and advancement would reward hard work.

Tabloid newspapers reinforced distrust of the corporations with exposés of the sharp business practices of corporate barons like Rockefeller and Carnegie and accounts of the sumptuous lifestyles of the corporate elite. Public concern notwithstanding, however, the giant corporations helped increase the efficiency of the American economy, raise the national standard of living, and transform the United States into a major world power. Corporate expansion generated jobs that attracted rural migrants and immigrants by the millions from Europe and Asia to American cities.

The Changing Nature of Work

The corporations provided abundant jobs, but they firmly controlled working conditions and the nature of the work done. A Pennsylvania coal miner spoke for many of his fellows in the 1890s when he remarked: "The working people of this country . . . find monopolies as strong as government itself. They find capital as rigid as absolute monarchy. They find their so-called independence a myth."

The deskilling process accelerated in the 1890s in response to new technologies, new workers, and workplace reorganization. By 1906, according to a U.S. Department of Labor report, industrial labor had been reduced to minute, low-skilled operations, making skilled artisans obsolete.

On the other hand, the birth of whole new industries—steel, automobiles, electrical equipment, cigarettes, food canning, and machine tools—created a huge demand for workers. Innovations in existing industries, like railroads, similarly spurred job growth. The number of people working for U.S. railroads increased from eighty thousand to more than 1 million between 1860 and 1910.

With massive waves of immigrants arriving from Europe and Asia between 1880 and 1920 (joined after 1910 by migrants from the American South), the supply of unskilled workers seemed limitless. The new workers, however, shared little of the wealth generated by industrial expansion. The eastern European immigrants who comprised three-quarters of U.S. Steel's work force during the first decade of the twentieth century received less than $12.50 a week, significantly less than the $15.00 a week a federal government survey in 1910 said an urban family needed to subsist.

Nor did large corporations put profits into improved working conditions. In 1881, on-the-job accidents maimed or killed thirty thousand railroad workers. At a U.S. Steel plant in Pittsburgh, injuries or death claimed one out of every four workers between 1907 and 1910. In Chicago's meat plants, workers grew careless from fatigue and long-term exposure to the extreme temperatures of the workplace. Meat cutters working rapidly with sharp knives often sliced fingers off their numb hands. Upton Sinclair wrote in his novel *The Jungle* (1906), a chronicle of the killing floors of meatpacking plants in Chicago, "It was to be counted as a wonder that there were not more men slaughtered than cattle."

Factory workers typically worked ten hours a day, six days a week in the 1880s. Steel workers put in twelve hours a day. Because the mills operated around the clock, once every two weeks, when the workers changed shifts, one group took a "long turn" and stayed on the job for twenty-four hours.

Long hours affected family life. By Sunday, most factory workers were too tired to do more than sit around home. During the week, they had time only to eat and sleep. As one machinist testified before a U.S. Senate investigative committee in 1883:

> They were pretty well played out when they come home, and the first thing they think of is having something to eat and sitting down, and resting, and then of striking a bed. Of course when a man is dragged out in that way he is naturally cranky, and he makes all around him cranky . . . and staring starvation in the face makes him feel sad, and the head of the house being sad, of course the whole family are the same, so the house looks like a dull prison.

Workers lived as close to the factory as possible to reduce the time spent going to and from work and to save transportation expenses. The environment around many factories, however, was almost as unwholesome as the conditions inside. A visitor to Pittsburgh in 1884 noticed "a drab twilight" hanging over the areas around the steel mills, where "gaslights, which are left burning at mid-day, shine out of the murkiness with a dull, reddish glare." Industrial wastes fouled streams and rivers around many plants.

In some industries, like the "needle," or garment, trade, operations remained small-scale. But salaries and working conditions in these industries were, if anything, worse than in the big factories. The garment industry was dominated by small manufacturers who contracted to assemble clothing for retailers from cloth provided by textile manufacturers. The manufacturers squeezed workers into small, cramped, poorly ventilated workplaces known accurately as **sweatshops**. The workers pieced together garments on the manufacturer's sewing machines. A government investigator in Chicago in the 1890s described one sweatshop in a three-room tenement where the workers—a family of eight—both lived and worked: "The father, mother, two daughters, and a cousin work together making trousers at seventy-five cents a dozen pairs. . . . They work seven days a week. . . . Their destitution is very great."

Child Labor

Child labor was common in the garment trade and other industries. Shocked reformers in the 1890s told of the devastating effect of factory labor on children's lives. The legs of a 7-year-old girl were paralyzed and deformed because she toiled "day after day with little legs crossed, pulling out bastings from garments."

In the gritty coal mines of Pennsylvania, breaker boys, youths who stood on ladders to pluck waste matter from coal tumbling down long chutes, breathed harmful coal dust all day. Girls under sixteen made up half the work force in the silk mills of Scranton and Wilkes-Barre, Pennsylvania. Girls with missing fingers from mill accidents were a common sight in those towns.

By 1900, Pennsylvania and a few other states had passed legislation regulating child labor, but enforcement of these laws was lax. Parents desperate for income often lied about their children's age, and authorities were often sympathetic toward mill or mine owners, who paid taxes and provided other civic benefits.

Working Women

The head of the Massachusetts Bureau of Labor Statistics observed in 1882, "A family of workers can always live well, but the man with a family of small children to support, unless his wife works also, has a small chance of living properly." Between 1870 and 1920, the number of women and children in the work force more than doubled.

Middle-class reformers worried about the impact on family life and on the women themselves. Employers paid them less than they paid men. A U.S. Department of Labor commissioner asserted that women worked only for "dress or pleasure." In one St. Louis factory in 1896, women received $4 a week for work for which men were paid $16 a week. An Iowa shoe saleswoman complained in 1886, "I don't get the salary the men clerks do, although this day I am 600 sales ahead! Call this justice? But I have to grin and bear it, because I am so unfortunate as to be a woman."

In 1900, fully 85 percent of wage-earning women were unmarried and under the age of 25. They supported siblings and contributed to their parents' income. A typical female factory worker earned $6 a week in 1900. On this wage, a married woman might help pull her family up to subsistence level. For a single woman on her own, however, it allowed little more, in writer O. Henry's words, "than marshmallows and tea."

Some working-class women turned to prostitution. The income from prostitution could exceed factory work by four or five times. "So is it any wonder," asked the Chicago Vice Commission in 1894, "that a tempted girl who receives only six dollars per week working with her hands sells her body for twenty-five dollars per week . . . ?" As much as 10

percent of New York City's female working-age population worked in the sex business in the 1890s. During depression years, the percentage was probably higher.

Victorian America condemned anyone guilty of even the most trivial moral transgression to social ostracism and treated the prostitute as a social outcast. Even those who urged understanding for women who violated convention faced exclusion. Kate Chopin, a New Orleans novelist, caused a tremendous uproar in the 1890s with stories that took a compassionate view of women involved in adultery, alcoholism, and divorce. Booksellers boycotted Theodore Dreiser's 1900 novel *Sister Carrie*, whose title character lived with a succession of men, one of them married.

Over time, more work options opened to women, but low wages and poor working conditions persisted. Women entered the needle trades after widespread introduction of the sewing machine in the 1870s. Factories gradually replaced sweatshops in the garment industry after 1900, but working conditions improved little. In 1909, twenty thousand women protesting working conditions staged a walkout from New York City's garment factories.

The introduction of the typewriter transformed clerical office work, dominated by men until the 1870s, into a female preserve. Women were alleged to have the greater dexterity and tolerance for repetition that the new technology required. But they earned only half the salary of the men they replaced. Middle-class parents saw office work as clean and honorable compared with factory or sales work. Consequently, clerical positions drew growing numbers of native-born women into the urban work force after 1890. A top-paid office worker in the 1890s earned as much as $900 a year. Teaching, another acceptable occupation for middle-class women, typically paid only $500 a year.

By the turn of the century, women were gaining increased access to higher education. Coeducational colleges were rare, but by 1900 there were many women-only institutions. By 1910, women comprised 40 percent of all American college students, compared to 20 percent in 1870. Despite these gains, many professions—including those of physician and attorney—remained closed to women. Men still accounted for more than 95 percent of all doctors in 1900. Women also were rarely permitted to pursue doctoral degrees.

Women college graduates mostly found employment in such "nurturing" professions as nursing, teaching, and library work. Between 1900 and 1910, the number of trained women nurses increased sevenfold. In response to the growing problems of

Secretaries of the Metropolitan Life Insurance Company in New York City pound away on Remington typewriters. Before the typewriter, men dominated clerical office work.

urban society, a relatively new occupation, social work, opened to women. Reflecting new theories on the nurturing role of women, school boards after 1900 turned exclusively to female teachers for the elementary grades.

Despite these gains, women's work remained segregated. Some reforms meant to improve working conditions for women reinforced this state of affairs. **Protective legislation** restricted women to "clean" occupations and limited their ability to compete with men in other jobs. As an economist explained in 1901, "The wage bargaining power of men is weakened by the competition of women and children, hence a law restricting the hours of women and children may also be looked upon as a law to protect men in their bargaining power."

Women also confronted negative stereotypes. Most Americans in 1900 believed a woman's proper role was to care for home and family. The system of "treating" on dates reinforced stories about loose salesgirls, flirtatious secretaries, and easy factory workers. Newspapers and magazines published exposés of working girls descending into prostitution. These images encouraged sexual harassment at work, which was rarely punished.

Working women faced a difficult dilemma. To justify their desire for education and training, they had to argue that it would enhance their roles as wives and mothers. To gain improved wages and working conditions, they increasingly supported protective legislation that restricted their opportunities in the workplace.

Responses to Poverty and Wealth

While industrial magnates flaunted their fabulous wealth, working men and women led hard lives on meager salaries and in crowded dwellings. In his exposé of poverty in New York, *How the Other Half Lives* (1890), Danish-born urban reformer Jacob Riis wrote that "the half that is on top cares little for the struggles, and less for the fate of those who are underneath so long as it is able to hold them there and keep its own seat."

The industrial economy strained working-class family life. Workplace accidents and deaths left many families with only one parent. Infant mortality among the working poor was nearly twice the citywide norm in 1900. Epidemic diseases, especially typhoid, an illness spread by impure water, devastated crowded working-class districts.

Inadequate housing was the most visible badge of poverty. Crammed into four- to six-story buildings on tiny lots, **tenement** apartments in urban **slums** were notorious for their lack of ventilation and light. According to Jacob Riis, a typical apartment in New York's Mulberry Bend neighborhood consisted of a parlor—a combined livingroom and kitchen—and "two pitch-dark coops called bedrooms." The furniture included three beds, "if the old boxes and heaps of foul straw can be called by that name," which gave off an appalling smell. In 90-degree July heat, temperatures inside the six-person apartment soared to 115 degrees.

Authorities did nothing to enforce laws prohibiting overcrowding for fear of leaving people homeless. The population density of New York's tenement district in 1894 was 986.4 people per acre, the highest in the world at the time. (Today, the densest areas of American cities rarely exceed 400 people per acre, and only Calcutta, India, and Lagos, Nigeria, approach the crowding of turn-of-the-century New York; today Manhattan has 84 residents per acre).

The settlement house movement, which originated in England, sought to moderate the effects of

SUMMARY

WORKERS ORGANIZE

Knights of Labor	Founded in 1869; open to all workers; declined after 1886	Disapproved of strikes; supported a broad array of labor reforms, including cooperatives; favored political involvement
American Federation of Labor	Founded in 1886; open to craft workers only, and organized by craft; hostile to blacks and women; became the major U.S. labor organization after 1880s	Opposed political involvement; supported a limited number of labor reforms; approved of strikes
Industrial Workers of the World	Founded in 1905; consisted mainly of semiskilled and unskilled immigrant workers; represented a small portion of the work force; disappeared after World War I	Highly political; supported socialist programs; approved of strikes and even violence to achieve ends

poverty through neighborhood reconstruction. New York's Neighborhood Guild, established in 1886, was the first settlement house in the country; Chicago's **Hull-House**, founded in 1889 by Jane Addams, a young Rockford (Illinois) College graduate, became the most famous.

The settlement house provided the working poor with facilities and education to help them improve their environment and, eventually, to escape it. By 1900, there were more than one hundred settlement houses throughout the country.

At Hull-House, a rambling old residence in a working-class immigrant neighborhood, Italian immigrants and their families came to settle legal disputes and formed the Young Citizens' Club to discuss municipal issues. Addams renovated an adjacent saloon and transformed it into a gym. She began a day nursery as well. When workers at a nearby knitting factory went on strike, Addams arbitrated the conflict.

Settlement house gyms like the one Addams built for Hull-House provided them with much-needed recreational space. So too did the athletic fields and playgrounds built adjacent to public schools after 1900.

According to the **Gospel of Wealth**, a theory popular among industrialists, intellectuals, and some politicians, *any* intervention on behalf of the poor was of doubtful benefit. Hard work and perseverance, in this view, led to wealth. Poverty, by implication, resulted from the flawed character of the poor. Steel tycoon Andrew Carnegie sought to soften this doctrine by stressing the responsibility of the affluent to set an example for the working class and to return some of their wealth to the communities in which they lived. Carnegie accordingly endowed libraries, cultural institutions, and schools throughout the country. Beneficial as they might be, however, these philanthropic efforts scarcely addressed the causes of poverty, and few industrialists followed Carnegie's example.

Social Darwinism, a flawed attempt to apply Charles Darwin's theory of biological evolution to human society, emerged as a more common justification than the Gospel of Wealth for the growing gap between rich and poor. According to social Darwinism, the human race evolves only through competition. The fit survive, the weak perish, and humanity moves forward. Wealth reflects fitness; poverty, weakness. For governments or private agencies to interfere with this natural process is futile. Thus Columbia University president Nicholas Murray Butler, claiming that "nature's cure for most social and political diseases is better than man's," warned against charity for the poor in 1900. Standard Oil's John D. Rockefeller concurred, asserting that the survival of the fittest is "the working out of a law of nature and a law of God."

Workers Organize

The growing power of industrial corporations and the declining power of workers generated social tensions reminiscent of the sectional crisis that triggered the Civil War. Two prolonged depressions, one beginning in 1873 and the other in 1893—threw as many as 2 million laborers out of work. Skilled workers, their security undermined by deskilling and their hopes of becoming managers or starting their own businesses disappearing, saw the nation "drifting," as a carpenter put it in 1870, "to that condition of society where a few were rich, and the many very poor." Labor reformer George McNeill, writing in 1887, called the contest between wage labor and the new industrial management an "irresistible conflict" and feared that "extremes of wealth and poverty are threatening the existence of the government."

Beginning after the depression of 1873 and continuing through World War I, workers fought their loss of independence to industrial capital by organizing and striking (see the summary table "Workers Organize"). The first episode in this conflict was the railroad strike of 1877, sometimes referred to as the **Great Uprising**. When Baltimore & Ohio Railroad workers struck in July to protest another series of pay cuts, President Rutherford B. Hayes dispatched federal troops to protect the line's property. The use of federal troops infuriated railroad workers throughout the East and Midwest, and they stopped work as well. Violence erupted in Pittsburgh when the state militia opened fire on strikers and their families, killing twenty-five, including a woman and three children. As news of the violence spread, so did the strike, as far as Galveston, Texas, and San Francisco. Over the next two weeks, police and federal troops continued to clash with strikers. By the time this first nationwide work stoppage in American history ended, more than one hundred had been killed. The wage cuts remained.

The **Knights of Labor**, a union of craft workers founded in Philadelphia in 1869, grew dramatically after the Great Uprising under the leadership of Terence V. Powderly. The Knights saw "an inevitable . . . conflict between the wage system of labor and [the] republican system of government." Remarkably inclusive for its time, the Knights welcomed blacks and women to its ranks. Victories in several small railroad strikes in 1884 and 1885 boosted its membership to nearly one million workers by 1886.

In that year, the Knights led a movement for an eight-hour workday. Ignoring the advice of the national leadership to avoid strikes in pursuit of this goal, local chapters staged more than 1,500 strikes involving more than 340,000 workers. Workers also organized boycotts against manufacturers who refused to concede the eight-hour day and ran candidates for local elections. Social reformer Henry George made a strong, though losing, effort in the New York City mayoral race, and labor candidates won several local offices in Chicago.

Employers convinced the courts to order strikers back to work and used local authorities to arrest strikers for trespassing or obstructing traffic. In early May 1886, police killed four unarmed workers during a skirmish with strikers in Chicago. A bomb exploded at a meeting to protest the slayings in the city's **Haymarket Square**, killing seven policemen and four strikers and wounding one hundred. Eight strike leaders were tried for the deaths, and despite a lack of evidence linking them to the bomb, four were executed.

The Haymarket Square incident and a series of disastrous walkouts that followed it weakened the Knights of Labor. By 1890, it had shrunk to less than 100,000 members. Thereafter, the **American Federation of Labor (AFL)**, formed in 1886, became the major organizing body for skilled workers.

The AFL, led by British immigrant Samuel Gompers, emphasized **collective bargaining**—negotiations between management and union representatives—to secure workplace concessions. The AFL also discouraged political activism among its members. With this **business unionism**, the AFL proved more effective than the Knights of Labor at meeting the needs of skilled workers, but it left out the growing numbers of unskilled workers, blacks, and women to whom the Knights had given a glimmer of hope.

The AFL organized skilled workers by craft and focused on a few basic workplace issues important to each craft. The result was greater cohesion and discipline. In 1889 and 1890, more than 60 percent of AFL-sponsored strikes were successful. A series of work stoppages in the building trades between 1888 and 1891, for example, won an eight-hour day and a national agreement with builders.

In the **Homestead strike**, against Andrew Carnegie's Homestead steel plant in Pennsylvania in 1892, unionized steelworkers suffered a major setback. Carnegie's manager, Henry Clay Frick, announced that he would negotiate only with workers individually at Homestead and not renew the union's collective bargaining contract. Frick locked the union workers out of the plant and hired three hundred armed guards to protect the nonunion ("scab") workers he planned to hire in their place. Union workers, with the help of their families and unskilled workers, seized control of Homestead's roads and utilities. In a bloody confrontation, they drove back Frick's forces. Nine strikers and seven guards died. But Pennsylvania's governor called out the state militia to open the plant and protect the nonunion workers. After four months, the union capitulated. With the defeat of the union, skilled steelworkers lost their power on the shop floor. Eventually, mechanization cost them their jobs.

In 1894, workers suffered another setback in the **Pullman strike**, against George Pullman's Palace Sleeping Car Company. When the company cut wages for workers at its plant in the "model" suburb it built outside Chicago without a corresponding cut in the rent it charged workers for their company-owned housing, the workers appealed for support to the **American Railway Union (ARU)**, led by Eugene V. Debs. The membership of the ARU, an independent union not affiliated with the AFL, had swelled to more than 150,000 workers after it won a strike earlier in 1894 against the Great Northern Railroad. Debs ordered a boycott of any trains with Pullman cars. The railroads fired workers who refused to handle trains with Pullman cars. Debs called for all ARU members to walk off the job, crippling rail travel nationwide. When Debs refused to honor a federal court injunction against the strike, President Cleveland, at the railroads' request, ordered federal troops to enforce it. Debs was arrested, and the strike and the union were broken.

The **Erdman Act** of 1898, rarely used for the next decade, provided for the voluntary mediation of railroad labor disputes. If mediation failed, the parties were to submit their differences to a board of arbitration. Growing public opposition to the use of troops, the high-handed tactics of industrialists, and the rising concerns of Americans about the power of big business sustained the unions. Workers would call more than 22,000 strikes over the next decade, the majority of them union-sponsored. Still, no more than 7 percent of the American work force was organized by 1900.

American Workers and Socialism

European workers formed powerful labor organizations and political parties in the late nineteenth and early twentieth centuries. These parties advocated a policy of **socialism**, calling for state ownership of industry and worker control of corporations. The Greenback-Labor Party and the Socialist Labor Party attracted some American workers in the 1870s. So too did the **Socialist Party of America**, formed in 1901. Immigrant German socialists and anarchists (who advocated the abolition of government) played prominent roles in the Haymarket affair, for example.

Although the influence of socialist ideas in the United States grew during the Progressive Era of the early twentieth century (see Chapter 23), several factors limited socialism's strength and appeal and that of more radical leftist movements among workers. First, American socialism was terribly fragmented. One wing supported cooperation with the Democratic party and another insisted on independent action. A third group emerged during the Progressive Era that supported the **Industrial Workers of the World (IWW)**, mostly of recent immigrants espousing a fiery class-conscious program of militant action.

Second, the diversity of the American working force limited concerted political and union activity. Skilled native-born workers, their ranks diminishing, were reluctant to associate with unskilled foreigners.

Religious differences compounded ethnic diversity. Jewish and Catholic workers demanded a different sabbath and different holidays. Jewish vestmakers quoted from the Torah to justify a strike. Slavic steelworkers in Hammond, Indiana, in 1910 voted to strike at a ceremony where "the lights of the hall were extinguished. A candle stuck into a bottle was placed on a platform along with a crucifix. One by one the men came and kissed the ivory image on the cross, kneeling before it."

Third, Americans prized individualism and saw it threatened by collective worker action as well as by corporate mergers. The press and political leaders discredited labor actions as evidence of foreign (and hence "un-American") political radicalism and social disorder. Many workers (especially the native-born) backed away from radical groups. In 1900, the Massachusetts Bureau of Labor Statistics reported that while most workers believed in unions "in the abstract," many considered them "simply vehicles for the fomentation of incipient riots and disorderly conduct."

Fourth, the existing political system and the two major political parties provided some channels for the expression and redress of labor grievances. The Republican and Democratic parties were large and diffuse enough to appeal to the diverse working force. Big-city political machines, with thousands of patronage jobs at their disposal, lured potential third-party supporters back into major-party ranks. After labor candidates won several offices in Chicago in

1886, Chicago Democrats hired more than four hundred Knights of Labor members for various city positions. Social critic Friedrich Engels, observing American labor from England, concluded in 1892 that "there is no place yet in America for a *third* party. . . . The divergence of interests even in the *same* class is so great . . . that wholly different groups and interests are represented in each of the two big parties."

Some states with large industrial work forces passed prolabor legislation as early as the 1880s. Massachusetts provided for arbitration of labor disputes, limits on the working hours of children and women, compensation for certain work-related accidents, and factory safety standards. New York passed similar measures during the 1880s. Southern states, with much fewer industrial workers, did not pass protective legislation until after 1900.

Federal labor policy between 1877 and 1894 consisted primarily of mobilizing troops to put down worker uprisings. Congress appeased the fears of native-born workers about competition from Chinese immigrants with the **Chinese Exclusion Act** in 1882. Congress also established a bureau of labor in 1884, but at the outset the bureau viewed its role strictly as a compiler of statistics. Over the next fifteen years, additional state and federal legislation removed many important issues from labor's legislative agenda.

Fifth, the success of the AFL after 1890 kept more radical labor voices from emerging. Samuel Gompers urged his followers to reject radical programs to restructure industrial capitalism: "Whatever ideas we may have as to the future state of society . . . they must remain in the background, and we must subordinate our convictions . . . to the general good that the trades-union movement brings to the laborer." Gompers continued to stress short-term advances for workers rather than long-term solutions for the problems of urban industrial society.

Perhaps another reason most American workers rejected socialism was that unskilled foreign-born labor flooded onto the shop floor. Because of adjustments required for life in a new country, labor radicalism was not a high priority for many of the newcomers. Immigrants not only transformed the workplace, but also transformed the cities where they settled and the nation many eventually adopted. In the process, they changed themselves.

New Immigrants

The late nineteenth century was a period of unprecedented worldwide population movements. The United States was not the only New World destination for the migrants of this period. Many also found their way to Brazil, Argentina, and Canada.

The scale of overseas migration to the United States after 1870 dwarfed all that preceded it. Between 1870 and 1910, the country received more than 20 million immigrants. Before the Civil War, most immigrants came from northern Europe. Most of the new immigrants, in contrast, came from southern and eastern Europe. Swelling their ranks were migrants from Mexico and Asia, as well as internal migrants moving from the countryside to American cities (see Map 20-1).

Old World Backgrounds

A growing rural population combined with unequal land distribution to create economic distress in late-nineteenth-century Europe. More and more people found themselves working ever-smaller plots as laborers rather than owners. In Poland, laborers accounted for 80 percent of the agricultural population in the 1860s. Similar conditions prevailed in the Mezzogiorno region of southern Italy, home of three out of four Italian emigrants to America.

For Russian Jews, religious persecution compounded economic hardship. In tsarist Russia, Jews could not own real estate and were barred from work in farming, teaching, the civil service, and the law. Confined to designated cities, they struggled to support themselves. After the assassination of Tsar Alexander II in 1881, which some leaders falsely blamed on Jews, the government sanctioned a series of violent attacks on Jewish settlements known as **pogroms**. At the same time, the government forced Jews into fewer towns, deepening their poverty and making them easier targets for violence.

The late nineteenth century transportation technologies permitted people to leave Europe. Railroad construction boomed in Europe during the 1870s and 1880s, and steamship companies in several European countries built giant vessels to transport passengers quickly and safely across the Atlantic. The companies sent agents into Russia, Poland, Italy, and the Austro-Hungarian empire to solicit business.

Sometime during the 1880s, an agent from the Hamburg-American Line (HAPAG), a German steamship company, visited a village in the Russian Ukraine where the great grandparents' of one of this book's authors lived. Shortly after his visit, they boarded a train to Austrian-occupied Poland and Hamburg. There they boarded a HAPAG steamer emblazoned with a large banner proclaiming "Willkommen" ("Welcome"). Just boarding that ship they felt they were entering the United States. Millions of others like them sailed on ocean liners from Ger-

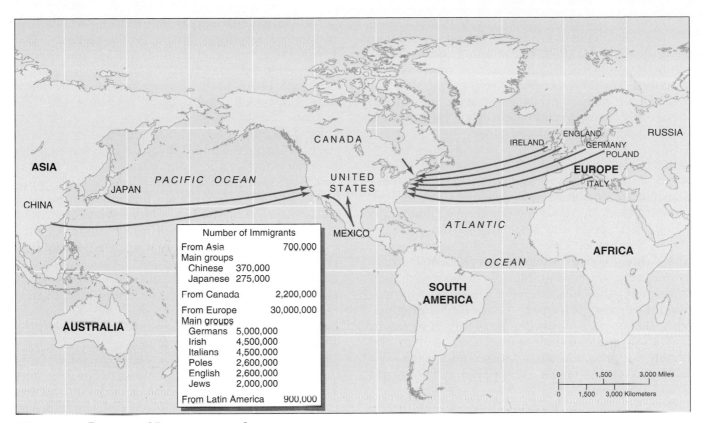

Map 20-1   Patterns of Immigration, 1820–1914
The migration to the United States was part of a world-wide transfer of population that accel-erated with the industrial revolution and the accompanying improvements in transportation.

many, Italy, and Great Britain over the next thirty years.

Chinese and Japanese immigrants also came to the United States in appreciable numbers for the first time during the late nineteenth century; the Chinese in the 1860s and 1870s and the Japanese in the 1880s and 1890s. Most Chinese immigrants came from Canton in South China and worked on railroads and in mines throughout the West and as farm laborers in California. Many eventually settled in cities such as San Francisco where they established residential enclaves referred to as Chinatowns.

The first wave of Japanese immigrants came by way of Hawaii to work on farms in California, taking the place of Chinese workers who had moved to the cities.

Most migrants intended to stay only a year or two, long enough to earn money to buy land or, more likely, to enter a business back home and improve life for themselves and their families. Roughly half of all immigrants to the United States between 1880 and World War I returned to their country of origin. Some made several round trips. As Jews were unwelcome in the lands they left, no more than 10 percent of Jewish immigrants returned to Europe, or went back home.

Most newcomers were young men. (Jews again were the exception: They tended to migrate permanently in families.) Immigrants easily found work in the large urban factories with their voracious demands for unskilled labor. Except for the Japanese, few immigrants came to work on farms after 1880.

By 1900, women began to equal men among all immigrant groups as young men who decided to stay sent for their families. The success of Francesco Barone, a Buffalo tavern owner, convinced eight thousand residents of his former village in Sicily to migrate to that city, many arriving on tickets Barone purchased, a process called **chain migration**.

Immigrants tended to live in neighborhoods among people from the same homeland and preserve key aspects of their Old World culture. For Italians from the Mezzogiorno, for example, the family was the basic institution for obtaining work and securing assistance in times of stress, death, or sickness.

The desire of the new immigrants to retain their cultural traditions led contemporary observers to doubt their ability to assimilate into American society. Even sympathetic observers, such as social workers, marveled at the utterly foreign character of immigrant districts. In 1900, Philadelphia social worker Emily Dinwiddie visited an Italian neighborhood and described "black-eyed children, rolling and tumbling together, the gaily colored dresses of the women and the crowds of street vendors, that give the neighborhood a wholly foreign appearance."

The Neighborhood

Rarely did a particular ethnic group comprise more than 50 percent of a neighborhood. Chinese were the exception, but even the borders of Chinatowns usually overlapped with other neighborhoods.

In smaller cities and in the urban South, where foreign-born populations were smaller, ethnic groups were more geographically dispersed, though occasionally they might inhabit the same neighborhood. In turn-of-the-century Memphis, for example, Irish, Italian, and Jewish immigrants lived cheek by jowl in a single immigrant district (called the "Pinch"), sharing schools and recreational space even as they led their singular institutional, religious, and family lives.

Immigrants maintained their cultural traditions through the establishment of religious and communal institutions. The church or synagogue became the focal point for immigrant neighborhood life. Much more than a place of worship, it was a school for transmitting Old World values and language to American-born children and a recreational facility and a gathering place for community leaders. Jewish associations called *landsmanshaften* arranged for burials, jobs, housing, and support for the sick, poor, and elderly.

Religious institutions played a less formal role among Chinese and Japanese neighborhoods. For them, the family functioned as the source of religious activity and communal organization. Chinatowns were organized in clans of people with the same surname. An umbrella organization called the **Chinese Consolidated Benevolent Association** emerged; it functioned like the Jewish *landsmanshaften*. Perhaps most important, the association shipped the bones of deceased members back to China for burial in ancestral cemeteries. A similar association, the **Japanese Association of America**, governed the Japanese community in the United States. This organization was sponsored by the Japanese government, which was sensitive to mistreatment of its citizens abroad and anxious that immigrants set a good example. The Japanese Association, unlike other ethnic organizations, actively encouraged assimilation and stressed the importance of Western dress and learning English.

Ethnic newspapers, theaters, and schools supplemented associational life for immigrants. The Jewish *Daily Forward*, first published in New York in 1897, reminded readers of the importance of keeping the Sabbath while admonishing them to adopt American customs.

The Job

All immigrants perceived the job as the way to independence and as a way out, either back to the Old World or into the larger American society. Immigrants typically received their first job with the help of a countryman. Italian, Chinese, Japanese, and Mexican newcomers worked with contractors who placed them in jobs. They exacted a fee, sometimes extortionate, for their services. Other immigrant groups, such as Poles and Russian Jews, often secured work through their ethnic associations or village or family connections. Family members sometimes exchanged jobs with one another (see "American Views: Immigrants and Work").

The type of work available to immigrants depended on their skills, the local economy, and local discrimination. Mexican migrants to southern California, for example, concentrated in railroad construction, replacing Chinese laborers when the the federal government excluded Chinese immigration after 1882. Mexicans built the interurban rail lines of Los Angeles in 1900 and established communities at their construction camps. Los Angeles businessmen barred Mexicans from other occupations. Similarly, Chinese immigrants were confined to work in laundries and restaurants within the boundaries of Los Angeles's Chinatown. The Japanese who came to Los Angeles around 1900 were forced into sectors of the economy native-born whites had either shunned or failed to exploit. The Japanese turned this discrimination to their benefit when they transformed the cultivation of market garden crops into a major agricultural enterprise. By 1904, Japanese farmers owned more than 50,000 acres in California. George Shima, who came to California from Japan in 1889 with a little capital, made himself the "Potato King" of the Sacramento Delta. By 1913, Shima owned 28,000 acres of farmland.

Stereotypes also channeled immigrants' work options, sometimes benefiting one group at the expense of another. Jewish textile entrepreneurs, for example, sometimes hired only Italians because they thought them less prone to unionization than Jewish workers. Pittsburgh steelmakers preferred Polish workers to the black workers who began arriving in northern cities in appreciable numbers after 1900. This began the decades-long tradition of handing down steel mill jobs through the generations in Polish families.

Jews, alone among European ethnic groups, found work almost exclusively with one another. Jews comprised three-quarters of the more than half-million workers in New York's City's garment industry in 1910. Jews were also heavily concentrated in the retail trade.

Like their native-born counterparts, few married immigrant women worked outside the home, but unlike the native-born, many Italian and Jewish women did piecework for the garment industry in their apartments. Unmarried Polish women often worked in factories or as domestic servants. Japanese women, married and single, worked with their families on farms. Until revolution in China in 1911 began to erode traditional gender roles, married Chinese immigrant women typically remained home.

The paramount goal for many immigrants was to work for themselves rather than someone else. Most new arrivals, however, had few skills and no resources beyond their wits with which to realize their dreams. Major banks at the time were unlikely to extend even a small business loan to a budding ethnic entrepreneur. Family members and small ethnic-based community banks provided the initial stake for most immigrant businesses. Many of these banks failed, but a few survived and prospered. For example, the Bank of Italy, established by Amadeo Pietro Giannini in San Francisco in 1904, eventually grew into the Bank of America, one of the nation's largest financial institutions today.

Immigrants could not fully control their own destinies in the United States any more than native-born Americans could. Hard work did not always ensure success. Almost all immigrants, however, faced the antiforeign prejudice of American **nativism**.

Nativism

Immigrants have not always received a warm reception. Ben Franklin groused about the "foreignness" of German immigrants during the colonial era. From the 1830s to 1860, nativist sentiment, directed mainly at Irish Catholic immigrants, expressed itself in occasional violence and job discrimination.

When immigration revived after the Civil War, so did antiforeign sentiment. But late-nineteenth-century nativism differed in two ways from its antebellum predecessor. First, the target was no longer Irish Catholics but the even more numerous Catholics and Jews of southern and eastern Europe, people whose language and usually darker complex-

ions set them apart from the native-born majority. Second, late-nineteenth-century nativism maintained that there was a natural hierarchy of race. At the top, with the exception of the Irish, were northern European whites, especially those of Anglo-Saxon descent. Following below them were French, Slavs, Poles, Italians, Jews, Asians, and Africans. Social Darwinism, which justified the class hierarchy, reinforced scientific racism.

When the "inferior" races arrived in the United States in significant numbers after 1880, a prominent Columbia University professor wrote in 1887 that Hungarians and Italians were "of such a character as to endanger our civilization." Nine years later, the director of the U.S. census warned that eastern and southern Europeans were "beaten men from beaten races. They have none of the ideas and aptitudes which fit men to take up readily and easily the problem of self-care and self-government." The result of unfettered migration would be "race suicide."

In the mid-1870s, a Chicago newspaper described recently arrived Bohemian immigrants (from the present-day Czech Republic) as "depraved beasts, harpies, decayed physically and spiritually, mentally and morally, thievish and licentious." A decade later, with eastern Europeans still pouring into Chicago, another newspaper suggested: "Let us whip these slavic wolves back to the European dens from which they issue, or in some way exterminate them." The *New York Times* concluded that Americans "pretty well agreed" that these foreigners were "of a kind which we are better without." *Scientific American* warned immigrants to "assimilate" quickly or "share the fate of the native Indians" and face "a quiet but sure extermination."

Such sentiments generated proposals to restrict foreign immigration. Chinese immigrants' different culture and their willingness to accept low wages in mining and railroad construction provoked resentment among native- and European-born workers. In 1870, the Republican-dominated Congress passed the **Naturalization Act**, which limited citizenship to "white persons and persons of African descent." The act was specifically intended to prevent Chinese from becoming citizens—a ban not lifted until 1943—but it affected other Asian groups also. The Chinese Exclusion Act of 1882 made the Chinese the only ethnic group in the world that could not emigrate freely to the United States. Anti-Asian violence raced through mining communities in the West for the next two years.

Labor competition also contributed to the rise of another anti-immigrant organization. A group of skilled workers and small businessmen formed the

American Views

Immigrants and Work

In 1906, a magazine called *The Independent* published a series of stories documenting immigrant work experiences, two of which are excerpted here. The first story is told by Rocco Corrersca, an Italian immigrant whose first job in the United States was as a ragpicker. The second story is told in the halting English of a young Japanese immigrant who migrated to Portland, Oregon, and worked as a domestic servant. Their jobs typified what most immigrants could expect: not glamorous, not well-paying, and probably involving hard physical labor. Although the stories are generally upbeat, they reflect some of the hardships new immigrants faced.

As Corrersca's story indicates, immigrants often received their first jobs through an agent. The agents often extracted a fee, sometimes quite high, for this service. But the system enabled employers to find staff more efficiently than they could on their own.

❖ **Did the costs of the agent system outweigh its benefits?**

❖ **Do you think it is likely that Corrersca's English was as idiomatic as it appears here? Or do you think the editors of *The Independent* corrected it for him? If so, why do you think they didn't correct it for the Japanese immigrant? Is it significant that Corrersca is named and the Japanese immigrant isn't?**

❖ **Immigrants experienced considerable job and geographical mobility. Was this good or bad?**

❖ **Were these immigrants ever exploited? What recourse did they have to counter exploitation?**

Rocco Corrersca Becomes an Entrepreneur

We came to Brooklyn, New York, to a wooden house in Adams street that was full of Italians from Naples. Bartolo had a room on the third floor and there were fifteen men in the room, all boarding with Bartolo. . . . The next morning, early, Bartolo told us to go out and pick rags and get bottles. . . . Most of the men in our room worked at digging the sewer. Bartolo got them the work and they paid him about one-quarter of their wages. Then he charged them for board and he bought the clothes for them, too. So they got little money after all. . . .

We went away one day to Newark [New Jersey] and got work on the street. . . . We paid a man five dollars each for getting us the work and we were with that boss for six months. He was Irish, but a good man and he gave us our money

---

American Protective Association (APA) in 1887 and claimed half a million members a year later. The APA sought to limit Catholic civil rights in the United States to protect the jobs of Protestant workingmen.

The **Immigration Restriction League (IRL)**, formed in 1894, proposed to require prospective immigrants to pass a literacy test that they presumed most southern and eastern Europeans would fail. The IRL vowed that its legislation would protect "the wages of our workingmen against the fatal competition of low-price labor." The IRL played an impor-

tant role in attracting native-born workers to the Republican party in the 1896 election. Republicans generally supported measures restricting immigration. The Democrats, in contrast, often appealed to the newcomers in the big cities of the Northeast and Midwest.

The IRL ultimately failed to have its literacy requirement enacted. The return of prosperity and the growing preference of industrialists for immigrant labor put an end to calls for formal restrictions on immigration for the time being.

every Saturday night. We lived much better than with Bartolo, and when the work was done we each had nearly $200 saved. Plenty of the men spoke English and they taught us, and we taught them to read and write. . . .

We went back to Brooklyn to a saloon . . . where we got a job cleaning it out and slept in a little room upstairs. There was a bootblack named Michael on the corner and when I had time I helped him and learned the business. . . . Then [Francesco and I] thought we would go into business and we got a basement and put four chairs in it. . . . Outside we had a big sign that read:

THE BEST SHINE FOR TEN CENTS

We had said that when we saved $1,000 each we would go back to Italy and buy a farm, but now that the time is coming we are so busy and making so much money that we think we will stay.

A Japanese Immigrant Becomes a Servant

The desire to see America was burning at my boyish heart. . . . My destination was Portland, Ore., where my cousin is studying. . . . I can be any use here, but become a domestic servant, as the field for Japanese very narrow and limited. . . . The place where I got work in the first time was a boarding house. My duties were to peel potatoes, wash the dishes, a few laundry work, and also I was expected to do whatever mistress, waitress and cook has told me. . . .

My real objection was that the work was indeed too hard and unpleasant for me to bear and also there were no times even to read a book. But I thought it rather impolite to say so and partly my strange pride hated to confess my weakness. . . . At the end of the second week I asked my wages, but she refused on the ground that if she does I might leave her. . . . Believing the impossibility to obtain her sanction, early in the next morning while everybody still in the bed, I hide my satchel under the bush in the back yard. . . . Leaving the note and wages behind me, I hurried back to Japanese Christian Home.

Since then I have tried a few other places with a better success at each trial and in course of time I have quite accustomed to it and gradually become indifferent as the humiliation melted down. Though I never felt proud of this vocation, in several cases I have commenced to manifest the interest of my avocation as a professor of Dust and Ashes.

Sources: The Independent, March and May 1906.

Immigrants and their communal associations fought attempts to impede free access of their countrymen to the United States. The Japanese government even hinted at violent retaliation if Congress ever enacted restrictive legislation similar to that imposed on the Chinese. But most immigrants believed that the more "American" they became, the less prejudice they would encounter.

In 1895, a group of American-born Chinese in California formed a communal association called the Native Sons of the Golden State (a deliberate response to a nativist organization that called itself the Native Sons of the Golden West). The association's constitution declared, "It is imperative that no members shall have sectional, clannish, Tong [a secret fraternal organization] or party prejudices against each other. . . . Whoever violates this provision shall be expelled." A guidebook written at the same time for immigrant Jews recommended that they "hold fast," calling that attitude "most necessary in America. Forget your past, your customs, and your ideals." Although it is doubtful whether most Jewish immigrants followed this advice whole, it nonetheless reflects the way the pressure to conform modified the cultures of all immigrant groups.

Assimilation connotes the loss of one culture in favor of another. The immigrant experience of the late nineteenth and early twentieth centuries might better be described as a process of adjustment between old ways and new, which resulted in entirely new cultural forms. The Japanese, for example, had not gone to Los Angeles to become truck farmers, but circumstances dictated otherwise. Sometimes economics and the availability of alternatives resulted in cultural modifications. In the old country, Portuguese held *festas* every Sunday honoring a patron saint. In New England towns, they confined the tradition to their churches instead of parading through the streets.

In a few cases, the New World offered greater opportunities to observe the values of the culture of origin than the Old. Young women who migrated from Italy's Abruzzi region to Rochester, New York, found that it was easier to retain their Old World moral code and marry earlier in late-nineteenth-century Rochester, where young men outnumbered them significantly. In a similar way, Sicilians who migrated to lower Manhattan discovered that ready access to work and relatively high geographical mobility permitted them to live near and among their extended families much more easily than in Sicily.

Despite native-born whites' antagonism toward recent immigrants, the greatest racial divide in America remained that between black and white. Newcomers viewed their "whiteness" as both a common bond with other European immigrant groups and a badge of acceptance into the larger society.

Roots of the Great Migration

Nearly 90 percent of African-Americans still lived in the South in 1900, most in rural areas. Between 1880 and 1900 black families began to move into the great industrial cities of the Northeast and Midwest. They were drawn by the same economic promise that attracted overseas migrants and were pushed by growing persecution in the South. They were also responding to the appeals of northern blacks. As a leading black newspaper, the *Chicago Defender* argued in the early 1900s, "To die from the bite of frost is far more glorious than at the hands of a mob. I beg you, my brother, to leave the benighted land." Job opportunities probably outweighed all other factors in motivating what became known as the **Great Migration**.

In most northern cities in 1900, blacks typically worked as common laborers or domestic servants. They competed with immigrants for jobs, and in most cases they lost. Immigrants even claimed jobs that blacks had once dominated, like barbering and service work in hotels, restaurants, and transportation. Fannie Barrier Williams, a turn-of-the-century black activist in Chicago, complained that between 1895 and 1905, "the colored people of Chicago have lost . . . nearly every occupation of which they once had almost a monopoly."

Black women had particularly few options in the northern urban labor force. The retail and clerical jobs that attracted young working-class white women remained closed to black women. As one historian concluded, advertisers and corporate executives demanded "a pleasing physical appearance (or voice)—one that conformed to a native-born white American standard of female beauty [and served] as an important consideration in hiring office receptionists, secretaries, department store clerks, and telephone operators." Addie W. Hunter, who qualified for a civil service clerical position in Boston, could not find work to match her training. She concluded in 1916, "For the way things stand at present, it is useless to have the requirements. Color . . . will always be in the way."

Migrating blacks confronted similar frustrations in their quest for a place to live. They were restricted to segregated urban **ghettos**. In 1860, four out of every five blacks in Detroit lived in a clearly defined district, for example. The black districts in northern cities were more diverse than those of southern cities. Migration brought rural Southerners, urban Southerners, and West Indians (especially in New York) together with the northern blacks already living there. People of all social classes lived in these districts.

The difficulties that black families faced to make ends meet paralleled in some ways those of immigrant working-class families. Restricted job options, however, limited the income of black families, even with black married women five times more likely to work than married white women. In black families, moreover, working teenage children were less likely to stay home and contribute their paychecks to the family income.

Popular culture reinforced the marginalization of African-Americans, belittling blacks and black characters with names like "Useless Peabody" and "Moses Abraham Highbrow." Immigrants frequented vaudeville and minstrel shows and absorbed the culture of racism from them. The new medium of film perpetuated the negative stereotypes.

An emerging middle-class leadership—including Robert Abbott, publisher of the *Chicago Defender*—sought to develop black businesses. But chronic lack

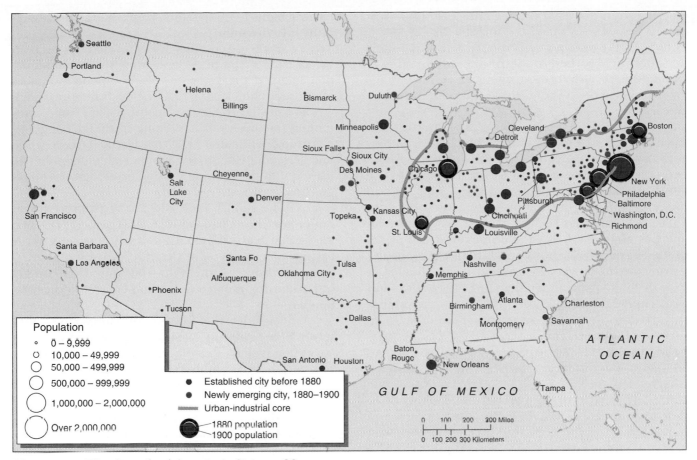

Map 20-2   The Growth of America's Cities, 1880–1900
Several significant trends stand out on this map. First is the development of an urban-industrial core stretching from New England to the Midwest where the largest cities were located. And second is the emergence of relatively new cities in the South and West, reflecting the national dimensions of innovations in industry and transportation.

of capital kept black businesses mostly small and confined to the ghetto. Black businesses failed at a high rate. Most blacks worked outside the ghetto for white employers. Economic marginalization often attracted unsavory businesses to black neighborhoods. One recently arrived migrant from the South complained that in his Cleveland neighborhood, his family was surrounded by loafers, "gamblers [and] pocket pickers; I can not raise my children here like they should be. This is one of the worst places in principle you ever looked on in your life."

Other black institutions proved more lasting than black businesses. In Chicago in 1891, black physician Daniel Hale Williams established Provident Hospital, the nation's first interracially staffed hospital, with the financial help of wealthy white Chicagoans. Although it failed as an interracial experiment, the hospital thrived, providing an important training ground for black physicians and nurses.

The organization of black branches of the Young Men's and Young Women's Christian Association provided living accommodations, social facilities, and employment information for young blacks. By 1910, black settlement houses modeled after white versions appeared in several cities.

New Cities

Despite the hardships associated with urban life for both immigrants and blacks, the American city continued to act, in the words of contemporary novelist Theodore Dreiser, as a "giant magnet." Immigration from abroad and migration from American farms to the cities resulted in an urban explosion during the late nineteenth century (see Map 20-2). The nation's population tripled between 1860 and 1920, but the urban population increased ninefold. Of the 1,700 cities listed in the 1900 census, only a handful—less than 2 percent—even existed in 1800.

In Europe, a few principal cities like Paris and Berlin absorbed most of the urban growth during this period. In the United States, in contrast, growth was more evenly distributed among many cities.

Despite the relative evenness of growth, a distinctive urban system had emerged by 1900, with New York and Chicago anchoring an urban-industrial core extending in a crescent from New England to the cities bordering the Great Lakes. This region included nine of the nation's ten largest cities in 1920. Western cities such as Denver, San Francisco, and Los Angeles emerged as dominant urban places in their respective regions but did not challenge the urban core for supremacy. Southern cities, limited in growth by low consumer demand, low wages, and weak capital formation, were drawn into the orbit of the urban core. Atlanta, an offspring of the railroad, prospered as the region's major way station for funneling wealth into the urban North. Dallas emerged as Atlanta's counterpart in the western South (see Chapter 19).

The crush of people and the emergence of new technologies expanded the city outward and upward as urban dwellers sorted themselves by social class and ethnic group. While the new infrastructure of water and sewer systems, bridges, and trolley tracks kept steel mills busy, it also fragmented the urban population by allowing settlements well beyond existing urban boundaries.

Centers and Suburbs

The centers of the country's great cities changed in scale and function in this era, achieving a prominence they would eventually lose in the twentieth century. Downtowns expanded up and out as tall buildings arose—monuments to business and finance—creating urban skylines. Residential neighborhoods were pushed out, leaving the center dominated by corporate headquarters and retail and entertainment districts.

Corporate heads administered their empires from downtown, even if their factories were located on the urban periphery or in other towns and cities. Banks and insurance companies clustered in financial centers like Atlanta's Five Points district to service the corporations. Department stores and shops clustered in retail districts in strategic locations along electric trolley lines. It was to these areas that urban residents usually referred when they talked about going "downtown." In the entertainment district,

electric lights lit up theaters, dance halls, and restaurants into the night.

As retail and office uses crowded out residential dwellings from the city center, a new phenomenon emerged: the residential neighborhood. Advances in transportation technology, first the horse-drawn railway and, by the 1890s, the electric trolley, eased commuting for office workers. Some in the growing and increasingly affluent middle class left the crowded, polluted city altogether to live in new residential suburbs, leaving it to the growing ranks of working-class immigrants and African-Americans.

The suburb emerged as the preferred residence for the urban middle class after 1870. The ideals that had promoted modest suburban growth earlier in the nineteenth century—privacy, aesthetics, and home ownership—became increasingly important for the growing numbers of middle-class families after 1880.

Consider the Russells of Short Hills, New Jersey. Short Hills lay 18 miles by railroad from New York City. William Russell; his wife, Ella Gibson Russell; and their six children moved there from Brooklyn in the late 1880s, seeking a "pleasant, cultured people whose society we could enjoy" and a cure for Russell's rheumatism. Russell owned and managed a small metal brokerage in New York and enjoyed gardening, reading, and socializing with his new neighbors. Ella Russell cared for the six children with the help of a servant and also belonged to several clubs and charities.

The design of the Russells's home reflected the principles Catharine Beecher and Harriet Beecher Stowe outlined in their suburban home Bible, *American Woman's Home* (1869). The new technology of central heating made it unnecessary to divide a house into many small rooms, each with its own fireplace or stove. Beecher and Stowe recommended that a home's ground floor have fewer but larger rooms to encourage the family to pursue their individual activities in a common space.

The entire Russell family was to be found enjoying the tennis, swimming, and skating facilities on the grounds of the Short Hills Athletic Club.

The emphasis on family togetherness also reflected the changing role of men in late-nineteenth-century society. Beecher and Stowe praised fathers who took active roles in child rearing and participated fully in the family's leisure activities. Women's roles also broadened, as Ella Russell's club work attested.

With the growth after 1890 of the electric trolley, elevated rail lines, and other relatively inexpensive forms of commuter travel, suburbs became accessible to a broader spectrum of the middle class. The social structure, architecture, and amenities of suburbs varied, depending on the rail service and distance from the city. The trolley and elevated railroads generated modest middle-class urban neighborhoods and suburbs, with densities decreasing and income increasing toward the ends of the lines. But for the working class—even skilled artisans—suburban living remained out of reach.

Residence, consumer habits, and leisure activities reflected growing social and class divisions. Yet, at the same time, the growing materialism of American society promised a common ground for its disparate ethnic, racial, and social groups.

The New Middle Class

From the colonial era, America's urban middle class had included professionals—physicians, lawyers, ministers, educators, editors—as well as merchants, shopkeepers, and skilled artisans (until they dropped from the middle class in the late nineteenth century). In the late nineteenth century, industrial technology and urban growth expanded the urban middle class to include salespeople, factory supervisors, managers, civil servants, technicians, and a broad range of "white-collar" office workers like insurance agents, bank tellers, and legal assistants. This newer middle class set national trends in residential patterns, consumption, and leisure activities and in doing so defined themselves as a key group in American society.

The more affluent members of the new middle class repaired to new subdivisions within and outside the city limits. Simple row houses sheltered the growing numbers of clerks and civil servants who remained in the city. These dwellings contrasted sharply with the crowded one- or two-room apartments that confined the working class. Rents for these apartments ran as much as $3 a week at a time when few workers made more than $9 or $10.

The new middle class was a class of consumers. In earlier times, land had been a symbol of prestige. Now it was things. And the new industries obliged with a dazzling array of goods and technologies to make life easier and allow more time for family and leisure.

By 1910, the new middle class lived in all-electric homes, with indoor plumbing and appliances that eased food preparation. The modern city-dweller worked by the clock, not by the sun. Eating patterns changed: cold, packaged cereals replaced hot meats at breakfast; fast lunches of Campbell's soup—"a

meal in itself"—or canned stews weaned Americans from the heavy lunch. In Nashville Joel Cheek ground and blended coffee beans in his store for customers' convenience. He convinced the city's Maxwell House Hotel to serve his new concoction, and in 1907, when President Theodore Roosevelt visited the hotel and drained his cup, he declared that the coffee was "good to the very last drop." A slogan and Maxwell House coffee were born.

Advertisers now told Americans what they wanted; they created demand and developed loyalty for brand-name products. In early-twentieth-century New York, a six-story-high Heinz electric sign was a sensation, especially the 40-foot-long pickle at its top.

The middle class liked anything that saved time: trolleys, trains, electric razors, vacuum cleaners. By 1900, some 1.4 million telephones were in service, and many middle-class homes had one.

The middle class liked its news in an easy-to-read form. Urban tabloids multiplied after 1880, led by Joseph Pulitzer's *New York World* and William Randolph Hearst's *New York Journal.* The newspapers organized the news into topical sections, used bold headlines and graphics to catch the eye, ran human interest stories to capture the imagination, inaugurated sports pages to attract male readers, and offered advice columns for women.

As the visual crowded out the printed in advertising, newspapers, and magazines, these materials became more accessible to a wider urban audience. The tabloid press drew urban society together with new features such as the comic strip, and heart-rending personal sagas drawn from real life. Immigrants received their initiation into the mainstream of American society through the tabloids.

Originating in the 1850s and 1860s with the construction of retail palaces such as Boston's Jordan Marsh, Philadelphia's Wanamaker & Brown, New York's Lord & Taylor, and Chicago's Marshall Field, the department store came to epitomize the bounty of the new industrial capitalism. The department store exuded limitless abundance with its extensive inventories, items for every budget, sumptuous surroundings, and efficient, trained personnel.

At first, most department store customers were middle-class married women. Industry churned out uniform, high-quality products in abundance, and middle-class salaries absorbed them. Department stores maintained consumers' interest with advertising campaigns arranged around holidays such as Easter and Christmas, the seasons, and the school calendar. Each event required new clothing and accessories, and the ready-made clothing industry changed fashions accordingly.

Soon the spectacle and merchandise of the department store attracted shoppers from all social strata, not just the middle class. "The principal cause of the stores' success," one shopper explained in 1892, "is the fact that their founders have understood the necessity of offering a new democracy whose needs and habits" are satisfied "in the cheapest possible way," providing "a taste for elegance and comfort unknown to previous generations." After 1890, department stores increasingly hired young immigrant women to cater to their growing foreign-born clientele. Jewish immigrant Mary Antin recalled how she and her teenage friends and sister would spend their Saturday nights in 1898 patrolling "a dazzlingly beautiful palace called a 'department store.'" It was there that Mary and her sister "exchanged our hateful homemade European costumes . . . for real American machine-made garments, and issued forth glorified in each other's eyes."

By 1900, department stores had added sporting goods and hardware sections and were attracting male as well as female customers from a wide social spectrum.

The expanding floor space devoted to sporting goods reflected the growth of leisure in urban society. And like other aspects of that society, leisure and recreation both separated and cut across social classes. As sports like football became important extracurricular activites at Harvard, Yale, and other elite universities, intercollegiate games became popular occasions for the upper class to congregate, renew school ties, and, not incidentally, discuss business. The first country club in the United States was founded in Brookline, Massachusetts, a Boston suburb, in 1882. Country clubs built golf courses for men and tennis courts primarily for women. The clubs offered a suburban retreat, away from the diverse middle- and working-class populations, where the elite could play in privacy.

Middle-class urban residents rode electric trollies to suburban parks and bicycle and skating clubs. Both middle-class men and women participated in these sports, especially bicycling. New bikes cost at least $50, putting them beyond the reach of the working class.

Baseball was the leading spectator sport among the middle class. Baseball epitomized the nation's transition from a rural to an urban industrial society. Reflecting industrial society, baseball had clearly defined rules and was organized into leagues. Professional leagues were profit-making enterprises, and like other enterprises of the time, they frequently merged. Initially, most professional baseball games were played on weekday afternoons, making it hard for working-class spectators to attend. After merging with the American Association (AA) in 1883, the National League adopted some of the AA's innovations to attract more fans, including beer sales, cheap admission, and, over the objections of Protestant churches, began playing Sunday games.

The tavern, or saloon, was the workingman's club. Typically an all-male preserve, the saloon provided drink, cheap food, and a place for workingmen to read a newspaper, socialize, and learn about job opportunities.

The amusement park, with its mechanical wonders, was another hallmark of the industrial city. Declining trolley fares made them accessible to the working class around 1900. Unlike taverns, they provided a place for working-class men and women to meet and date.

The most renowned of these parks was Brooklyn's Coney Island, a monument to new technology and the working class that technology helped create. In 1897, George C. Tilyou opened Steeplechase Park on Coney Island. He brought an invention by George Washington Ferris—a giant rotating vertical wheel equipped with swinging carriages—to the park from Chicago, and the Ferris Wheel quickly became a Coney Island signature. Together with such attractions as mechanical horses and 250,000 of Thomas Edison's light bulbs, Steeplechase dazzled patrons with its technological wonders. Steeplechase Park was quickly followed by Luna Park and Dreamland, and the Coney Island attractions became collectively known as "the poor man's paradise." One German immigrant opened a small café serving sausages that he named "frankfurters" after his native Frankfurt.

After 1900, the wonders of Coney Island began to lure people from all segments of an increasingly diverse city. Sightseers came from around the world. Notables such as Herman Melville, Mark Twain, and even Sigmund Freud (what did he think of Dreamland?) rubbed shoulders with factory workers, domestics, and department store clerks. Baseball was also becoming a national pastime as games attracted a disparate crowd of people who might have little in common but their devotion to the home team.

Increasing materialism had revealed great fissures in American urban society by 1900. Yet places like deparment stores, baseball parks, and amusement parks provided democratic spaces for some interaction. Newspapers and schools also indirectly offered diverse groups the opportunity to share similar experiences.

Conclusion

By 1900, the factory worker and the department store clerk were more representative of the new America than the farmer and small shopkeeper. Industry and technology had created thousands of new jobs, many that had not existed before 1870. But they also eliminated the autonomy many workers had enjoyed and limited their opportunities to advance to the managerial class.

Immigrants thronged to the United States to realize their dreams of economic and religious freedom. They found both to varying degrees but also discovered a darker side to the promise of American life. The great cities thrilled newcomers with their possibilities and their abundance of goods and activities. But the cities also bore witness to the growing divisions in American society. As the new century dawned, the prospects for urban industrial America seemed limitless, yet the stark contrasts that had appeared so vividly inside and outside the Centennial Exposition persisted and deepened.

Labor unions, ethnic organizations, government legislation, and new urban institutions promised ways to remedy the worst abuses of the new urban, industrial economy. Whether they could succeed would determine the quality of life for all Americans and test the ideals of equality and independence.

Review Questions

1. During the late nineteenth century, American industry produced an amazing array of products that improved the lives of millions of Americans. At the same time, poverty and worker exploitation increased. Were there ways to achieve the benefits of industrialization without its social costs, or did the nation's political and economic systems make that impossible?

2. Given the widespread grievances among unskilled workers in the late nineteenth and early twentieth centuries, why did so few turn to socialism?

3. When historians speak of immigrant groups adjusting rather than assimilating to American society, what do they mean?

4. American cities exploded in the late nineteenth century, in terms of both population growth and geographical expansion. The growing fragmentation of urban life reflected deep divisions in modern urban industrial society. At the same time, there were forces that tended to overcome these divisions. What were these forces, and were they sufficient to bridge the divisions?

Recommended Reading

Stuart M. Blumin, *The Emergence of the Middle Class: Social Experience in the American City, 1760–1900* (1989). The book analyzes the key factors in the emergence of the urban middle class, especially in the late nineteenth century, and the impact of that class on urban society and culture.

John Bodnar, *The Transplanted: A History of Immigrants in Urban America* (1985). This book is an excellent starting point for learning about the diverse immigrant experience in the United States that is also sensitive to conditions in the countries of origin.

Roger Daniels, *Coming to America: A History of Immigration and Ethnicity in American Life* (1990). Some people prefer this survey to Bodnar's. The book's great virtue is its coverage of all immigrant groups; the discussion of Asian immigrants is especially good.

Theodore Dreiser, *Sister Carrie* (1900). Few novels capture life in late-nineteenth-century Chicago and New York better than this one, and even fewer detail so clearly the moral and economic dilemmas newcomers faced in the fast-evolving American urban environment.

David Goldfield and Blaine A. Brownell, *Urban America: A History* (1990). This comprehensive overview of the development of American cities places particular emphasis on the interaction of social, economic, and geographical forces on urban growth.

John Higham, *Strangers in the Land: Patterns of American Nativism, 1860–1925* (1965). Despite its age, this book serves as an excellent overview of and introduction to the subject of nativism; it is especially good in setting the context of nativism in American society and politics.

Raymond A. Mohl, *A New City: Urban America in the Industrial Age, 1860–1920* (1985). This is a fine introduction to the relationship between urbanization and industrialization.

Where to Learn More

❖ **Henry Ford Museum and Greenfield Village,** Dearborn, Michigan.   With 12 acres of exhibit space, the museum houses nearly 250,000 artifacts of American industry (not merely the automobile industry). The major attraction is a long-term exhibit, "Made in America: The History of the American Industrial System."

❖ **Edison National Historic Site,** West Orange, New Jersey.   The site contains the Edison archives, including photographs, sound recordings, and industrial and scientific machinery. Its twenty historic structures dating from the 1880–1887 period include Edison's home and laboratory.

❖ **Japanese American National Museum,** Los Angeles, California.   Housed in a converted Buddhist temple, this museum includes artifacts and photographs of early Japanese immigration and settlement. The core exhibit is "Issei Pioneers: Japanese Immigration to Hawaii and the Mainland from 1885 to 1924."

❖ **Chinatown History Museum,** New York, New York. Housed in a former school erected in 1893, the museum is a treasure trove of archives, photos, and oral histories of the Chinese-American community in New York. There is also a library of two thousand works on Asian-American history and culture.

❖ **Statue of Liberty National Monument and Ellis Island,** New York, New York.   More than 12 million immigrants were processed at Ellis Island between 1892 and 1954. The exhibits provide a fine overview of American immigration history during this period. There is an ongoing oral history program as well.

❖ **Lower East Side Tenement Museum,** New York, New York.   Step inside two tenement apartments, one occupied by the Gumpertz family and the other by the Baldizzis. The museum interprets tenement life in these apartments from 1863 to 1935.

21 TRANSFORMING THE WEST, 1865–1890

CHAPTER OUTLINE

Native Americans
Tribes and Cultures
Federal Indian Policy
Warfare and Dispossession
Life on the Reservation

Exploiting the Mountains: The Mining Bonanza
Rushes and Mining Camps
Labor and Capital

Exploiting the Grass: The Cattle Kingdom
Cattle Drives and Cow Towns
Rise and Fall of Open-Range Ranching
Cowhands

Exploiting the Earth: The Expansion of Agriculture
Settling the Land
Home on the Range
Farming the Land

Conclusion

KEY TOPICS

❖ The subjugation of Native Americans in the West, their confinement to reservations, and the attempted destruction of their culture and economy through Americanization

❖ The integration of the West into the national economy through the construction of transcontinental railroads

❖ The flood of migrants from the East and South and immigrants from Europe, Mexico, and China to the West in the late nineteenth century seeking work as railroad workers, miners, cowboys, and farmers

❖ The transformation of mining, ranching, and farming in the West from individual pursuits to corporate enterprises linked into the productive, financial, and marketing structures of American capitalism

---

The celebration began with a group of workers, soldiers, and railroad company officials at Promontory Point, a desolate sagebrush basin in western Utah. Chicago staged a seven-mile-long parade, Philadelphia rang the Liberty Bell, and New York held services in its greatest churches. The triumphal occasion was the completion of the nation's first transcontinental railroad, marked by the driving of a golden spike uniting the tracks of the Union Pacific and Central Pacific Railroads on May 10, 1869. The celebrations symbolized the nation's hopes, but the transcontinental railroad itself symbolized much more. It was, as the author Robert Louis Stevenson declared, "the one typical achievement of the age." It made the West as much a part of the nation as the East or the South and set a precedent for western development.

The two railroads were huge corporate enterprises, not individual efforts, and corporations would dominate western growth as much as they did eastern industrialization. But this corporate undertaking was scarcely private enterprise, for the federal government played a crucial role in railroad construction, as it did in virtually all aspects of western development. Congress had authorized the Union Pacific and Central Pacific to build the railroad link, given them the right-of-way for their tracks, and provided financial subsidies. Construction became a race to collect the largest subsidy. The Union Pacific worked westward from Omaha, Nebraska; the Central Pacific, eastward from Sacramento, California.

The railroads' dependence on capital investment, engineering knowledge, technological innovations, and labor skills also typified western development. Their labor forces both reflected and reinforced the region's racial and ethnic diversity. Too few native-born whites and blacks were willing to build the roads, so the Union Pacific recruited European immigrants, especially Irish. The Central Pacific hired Mexicans, Irish, and Paiute Indians, both male and female, but eventually relied on Chinese recruited in California and Asia.

Laying track as quickly as possible to collect the subsidies awarded by the mile, each corporation built substandard railroads marked by improper grades, defective materials, dangerous curves, and flimsy bridges that might collapse under a locomotive's weight. Much of the work had to be redone almost immediately at the cost of millions of dollars. Wood consumption alone was tremendous. Union Pacific tie cutters stripped the Platte Valley in Nebraska of its timber, and the Central Pacific used 64 million feet of timber just to build snowsheds. Finally, perhaps as many as a thousand Chinese on the Central Pacific, and even more workers on the Union Pacific, died from accidents or exposure.

The construction of the transcontinental railroad was thus both a technological achievement that integrated the West into the rest of the nation and evidence that the development of the West, however fabled in folklore, was an integral part of the larger economic revolution that transformed America after the Civil War.

Native Americans

Despite Easterners' image of the West as an unsettled wilderness, Native Americans had long inhabited it and had developed a variety of economies and cultures. As whites pressed westward, they attempted to subjugate the Indians, displace them from their lands, and strip them of their culture. Conquest gradually forced Indians onto desolate reservations, but efforts to destroy their beliefs and transform their way of life were less successful.

Tribes and Cultures

Throughout the West, Indians had adapted to their environment. Each activity encouraged their sensitivity to the natural world, and each had social and political implications.

In the Northwest, abundant food from rich waters and dense forests gave rise to complex and stable Indian societies. During summer fishing runs, the Tillamooks, Chinooks, and other tribes caught salmon, which sustained them throughout the year. During the mild winters, they developed artistic handicrafts, elaborate social institutions, and a satisfying religious life.

The Cahuillas of the southern California desert survived only through their ability to extract food and medicines from desert plants. In the dry and barren Great Basin of Utah and Nevada, Shoshones and Paiutes ate grasshoppers and other insects to supplement their diet of rabbits, mice, and other small animals. Such harsh environments restricted the size, strength, and organizational complexity of societies.

In the Southwest, the Pueblos dwelled in permanent towns of adobe buildings and practiced intensive agriculture. Because tribal welfare depended on maintaining complex irrigation systems, the Zunis, Hopis, and other Pueblos emphasized community solidarity rather than individual ambition. Town living encouraged social stability and the development of complex civil governments, elaborate religious ceremonies, and creative arts.

The most numerous Indian groups in the West lived on the Great Plains. The largest of these tribes included the Lakotas or Sioux, who roamed from western Minnesota through the Dakotas; the Cheyennes and Arapahos, who controlled much of the central plains between the Platte and Arkansas Rivers; and the Comanches, predominant on the southern plains.

Despite their diversity, all tribes emphasized community welfare over individual interest. Their economies were based on subsistence rather than profit. They tried to live in harmony with nature to ward off sickness, injury, death, or misfortune. And they were absorbed with the need to establish proper relations with supernatural forces that linked human beings with all other living things. These connections also shaped Indians' attitude toward land, which they regarded—like air and water—as part of nature to be held and used communally.

CHRONOLOGY

1858 Gold is discovered in Colorado and Nevada.

1860 Gold is discovered in Idaho.

1862 Homestead Act is passed.

Gold is discovered in Montana.

1864 Militia slaughters Cheyennes at Sand Creek, Colorado.

1867 Cattle drives make Abilene the first cow town.

1868 Fort Laramie Treaty is signed.

1869 First transcontinental railroad is completed.

1874 Gold is discovered in the Black Hills.

Turkey Red wheat is introduced to Kansas.

Barbed wire is patented.

1876 Indians devastate U.S. troops in the Battle of the Little Bighorn.

1879 "Exodusters" migrate to Kansas.

1885 Chinese massacred at Rock Springs, Wyoming.

1887 Dawes Act is passed.

1890 Government troops kill 200 Sioux at Wounded Knee, South Dakota.

1892 Mining violence breaks out at Coeur d'Alene, Idaho.

1893 Western Federation of Miners is organized.

Disdaining Native Americans and their religion, whites condemned them as "savages" to be converted or exterminated. Rejecting the concept of communal property, most whites demanded land for the exclusive use of ambitious individuals.

Perhaps no one expressed these cultural differences better than the great Sioux leader Sitting Bull. Referring to the forces of the spirit world, he declared:

> It is through this mysterious power that we too have our being and we therefore yield to our neighbors, even our animal neighbors, the same right as ourselves, to inhabit this land. Yet, hear me, people. We have now to deal with another race. . . . Possession is a disease with them. These people have made many rules that the rich may break but the poor may not. . . . They claim this mother of ours, the earth, for their own and fence their neighbors away; they deface her with their buildings. . . . That nation is like a spring freshet that overruns its banks and destroys all who are in its path. We cannot dwell side by side.

Federal Indian Policy

The U.S. government had in the 1830s adopted the policy of separating whites and Indians. Eastern tribes were moved west of Missouri and resettled on land then scorned as "the Great American Desert," unsuitable for white habitation and development. This division collapsed in the 1840s when the United States acquired Texas, California, and Oregon. Mormons developed a trail through Indian country in 1847 and settled on Indian lands; gold and silver discoveries beginning in 1848 prompted miners to migrate across Indian lands. Rather than controlling white entry into Indian country, the federal government built forts along the overland trails and instructed the army to punish Indians who threatened travelers.

White migration devastated the Plains Indians. Livestock destroyed timber and pastures along streams in the semiarid region; trails eliminated buffalo from tribal hunting ranges. The Pawnees in particular suffered from the violation of their traditional hunting grounds. One observer reported that "their trail could be followed by the dead bodies of those who starved to death. Children, young men, and women have shared this fate." The Plains Indians also suffered from the white migrants' diseases for which Indians had no natural immunity. Cholera killed more than half of the Comanches and Kiowas, and most other tribes lost up to 40 percent of their population from the new diseases. Emigrants along the Platte River routes came across "villages of the dead."

Recognizing that the Great American Desert could support agriculture, white settlers pressed on the eastern edge of the plains and demanded the removal of the Indians. Simultaneously, railroad companies developed plans to lay tracks across the plains. The federal government decided to relocate the tribes to separate and specific reserves. In exchange for accepting such restrictions, the government would provide the tribes with annual payments of

Sitting Bull, the Sioux spiritual leader photographed here c. 1868, urged resistance to the white invasion. "If we must die we die defending our rights."

One notorious example of white aggression occurred in 1864 at Sand Creek, Colorado. When Gold was discovered on land only recently guaranteed to the Cheyennes and Arapahos, white settlers wanted to eliminate the Indian presence altogether. John Chivington, a Methodist minister, led a militia force to the Sand Creek camp of a band of Cheyennes under Black Kettle, an advocate of peace and accommodation. An American flag flew over the Indian camp. Under Chivington's orders to "kill and scalp all, big and little," the militia attacked Black Kettle's sleeping camp without warning. One white trader later described the helpless Indians: "They were scalped, their brains knocked out; the [white] men used their knives, ripped open women, clubbed little children, knocked them in the head with their guns, beat their brains out, mutilated their bodies in every sense of the word."

Many Easterners were appalled by the **Sand Creek Massacre**. The Cheyennes, protested the commissioner of Indian affairs, were "butchered in cold blood by troops in the service of the United States." A congressional investigating committee denounced Chivington for "a foul and dastardly massacre which would have disgraced the veriest savage among those who were the victims of his cruelty." Westerners, however, justified the brutality as a means to secure their own opportunities. One western newspaper demanded, "Kill all the Indians that can be killed. Complete extermination is our motto."

Other tribes were more formidable. None was more powerful than the Sioux, who valued bravery and whose military skills had been honed in conflicts with other tribes. On the Bozeman Trail, in what the Lakotas called the **Battle of One Hundred Slain**, the Sioux wiped out an army detachment led by a captain who had boasted that he would destroy the Sioux nation. General William T. Sherman, who had marched through Georgia against the Confederates, knew that the odds were different in the West. Fifty Plains Indians, he declared, could "checkmate" three thousand soldiers. General Philip Sheridan calculated that the army suffered proportionately greater losses fighting Indians than either the Union or the Confederacy had suffered in the Civil War.

Describing white actions as "uniformly unjust," a federal peace commission in 1868 negotiated the **second Treaty of Fort Laramie**, in which the United States abandoned the Bozeman Trail and other routes and military posts on Sioux territory—one of the few times Indians forced the advancing whites to retreat. The United States also guaranteed the Sioux permanent ownership of the western half of South Dakota and the right to inhabit and hunt in

livestock, clothing, and other materials. The army was charged with keeping the Indians on their assigned reservations. To implement this policy, the government negotiated treaties, extinguishing Indian rights to millions of acres.

The commissioner of Indian affairs aptly described the Indians' lot: "By alternate persuasion and force these tribes have been removed, step by step, from mountain to valley, and from river to plain, until they have been pushed halfway across the continent. They can go no further; on the ground they now occupy the crisis must be met, and their future determined."

Warfare and Dispossession

From the 1850s to the 1880s, warfare engulfed the advancing frontier. Invading Americans bore ultimate responsibility for these wars. Even the men who led the white military assault conceded as much. General Philip Sheridan, for example, declared of the Indians: "We took away their country and their means of support, broke up their mode of living, their habits of life, introduced disease and decay among them, and it was for this and against this that they made war. Could anyone expect less?"

the Powder River country in Wyoming and Montana, an area to be henceforth closed to all whites.

For several years, peace prevailed on the northern plains, but in 1872, the Northern Pacific Railroad began to build westward on a route that would violate Sioux territory. Rather than stopping the railroad, the government sent an army to protect the surveyors. Sherman regarded railroad expansion as the most important factor in defeating the Indians, for it would allow troops to travel as far in a day as they could march in weeks. Other technological developments, from the telegraph to rapid-fire weapons, also undercut the skills of the Indian warrior.

The whites' destruction of the buffalo also threatened Native Americans. From 1872 to 1874, white hunters killed approximately 4 million buffalo. Railroad construction disrupted grazing areas, and hunters working for the railroads killed hordes of buffalo, both to feed construction crews and to prevent the animals from obstructing rail traffic. Hide hunters slaughtered even more of the beasts for their skins, leaving the bodies to rot. Reporters found vast areas covered with "decaying, putrid, stinking remains" of buffalo. Federal officials encouraged the buffalo's extermination because it would destroy the Indians' basis for survival and hence their ability to resist.

The climactic provocation of the Sioux began in 1874 when Colonel George A. Custer led an invasion to survey the Black Hills for a military post and confirm the presence of gold. Thousands of white miners then illegally poured onto Sioux land. The army insisted that the Sioux leave their Powder River hunting grounds. When the Sioux refused, the army attacked. The Oglala Sioux under Crazy Horse checked one prong of this offensive at the Battle of the Rosebud in June 1876 and then joined a larger body of Sioux under Sitting Bull and their Cheyenne and Arapaho allies to overwhelm a second American column, under Custer, at the **Battle of the Little Bighorn**.

But the Indians had to divide their forces to find fresh grass for their horses and to hunt for their own food. "We have been running up and down in this country, but they follow us from one place to another," lamented Sitting Bull about the Army's pursuit. He led his followers to Canada, but the other bands capitulated in the winter of 1876–1877. The conquest of the northern plains came through attrition and the inability of the traditional Indian economy to support resistance to the technologically and numerically superior white forces.

The defeat of the Sioux nearly completed the Indian Wars. Smaller tribes, among them the Kiowas, Modocs, and Utes, had been overrun earlier. In the Northwest, the Nez Percé had outwitted and out-fought the larger forces of the U.S. Army over a 1,500-mile retreat toward Canada. The exhausted Nez Percé surrendered after being promised a return to their own land. But the government refused to honor that pledge too, and imprisoned the tribe in Oklahoma, where more than a third perished within a few years.

In the Southwest, the Navajos and the Comanches were subdued as the Sioux had been— by persistent pursuit that prevented them from obtaining food. The last to abandon resistance were the Apaches, under Geronimo. In 1886, he and thirty-six followers, facing five thousand U.S. troops, finally surrendered. Geronimo and five hundred other Apaches were sent to a military prison in Florida; the tribes were herded onto reservations. The Oglala chief Red Cloud concluded of the white invasion: "They made us many promises, more than I can remember, but they never kept but one. They promised to take our land, and they took it."

Life on the Reservation

The next objective of government policy was to require Indians to adopt white ways. This goal did not involve assimilation but merely "Americanization," an expression of cultural conquest.

The government received the assistance of many Christian denominations, which had long proposed nonviolent methods of controlling Indians. Beginning in the 1860s, they gained influence in reaction to the military's brutality. Religious groups helped staff the reservations as agents, missionaries, or civilian employees. Reformers wanted to change Indian religious and family life, train Indian children in Protestant beliefs, and force Indians to accept private ownership and market capitalism.

Isolated on reservations and dependent on government rations, Indians were a captive audience for white reformers. White administrators replaced the tribal council and hereditary chiefs as the central authority. To destroy traditional Indian government, agents imprisoned tribal leaders and prohibited tribal councils from meeting.

Protestant religious groups persuaded the Bureau of Indian Affairs to frame a criminal code prohibiting and penalizing tribal religious practices. Established in 1884, the code remained in effect until 1933. It was first invoked to ban the Sun Dance, the chief expression of Plains Indian religion. To enforce the ban, the government withheld rations and disrupted the religious ceremonies that transmitted traditional values. In 1890, the government even used machine guns to suppress the Ghost Dance religion, killing at least 200 Sioux men, women, and children at **Wounded Knee**, South Dakota.

The government and religious groups also used education to eliminate Indian values and traditions. They isolated Indian children from tribal influences at off-reservation boarding schools. Troops often seized Indian children for these schools, where they were confined until after adolescence. The schoolchildren were forced to speak English, attend Christian services, and profess white American values (see "American Views: Sitkala-Sa's View of Americanization").

Finally, government agents taught Indian men how to farm and distributed agricultural implements; Indian women were taught various household tasks. These tactics reduced the status of Indian women, whose traditional responsibility for agriculture had guaranteed them respect and authority. Nor could men farm successfully on reservation lands, which whites had already rejected as unproductive. Whites, however, believed that the real obstacle to economic prosperity for the Indians was their rejection of private property. As one Bureau of Indian Affairs official declared, Indians must be taught to be more "mercenary and ambitious to obtain riches." Congress in 1887 passed the **Dawes Act**, which divided tribal lands among individual Indians. Western settlers and developers who had no interest in the Indians supported the law because it provided that reservation lands not allocated to individual Indians should be sold to whites. Under this "reform," the amount of land held by Indians declined by more than half by 1900.

White acquisition and exploitation of Indian land seemed to be the only constant in the nation's treatment of Native Americans. Assimilation itself failed because most Indians clung to their own values and rejected as selfish, dishonorable, and obsessively materialistic those favored by whites. But if it was not yet clear what place Native Americans would have in America, it was at least clear by 1900 that they would no longer stand in the way of western development.

Exploiting the Mountains: The Mining Bonanza

White migrants to the American West exploited the region's natural resources in pursuit of wealth and success. Promoters, artists, and novelists developed images of the West as a land of adventure, opportunity, and freedom; pioneers as self-reliant individuals. All too often, however, reality differed from legend.

In the later nineteenth century, the West experienced several stages of economic development, but all of them transformed the environment, produced economic and social conflict, and integrated the region into the modern national economy. The first stage of development centered on mining, which attracted swarms of eager prospectors into the mountains and deserts in search of gold and silver. They founded vital communities, stimulated the railroad construction that brought further development, and contributed to the disorderly heritage of the frontier (see Map 21-1). But few gained the wealth they had expected.

Rushes and Mining Camps

The first important gold rush in the Rocky mountains came in Colorado in 1859. More than 100,000 prospectors arrived in Denver and the nearby mining camps. Simultaneously, the discovery of the famous Comstock Lode in Nevada produced an eastward rush of miners from California. Some 17,000 claims were made around Virginia City, Nevada, the main mining camp. Strikes in the northern Rockies followed in the 1860s. Boise City and Lewiston in Idaho and Helena in Montana became major mining centers, and other camps prospered briefly before fading into ghost towns. Later, other minerals shaped frontier development: silver in Nevada, silver and lead in Colorado and Idaho, silver and copper in Arizona, and copper in Montana.

Mining camps were often isolated by both distance and terrain. They frequently consisted of only flimsy shanties, saloons, crude stores, dance halls, and brothels, all hastily built by entrepreneurs. Such towns reflected the speculative, exploitive, and transitory character of mining itself. And yet they did contribute to permanent settlement by encouraging agriculture, industry, and transportation in the surrounding areas.

The social and economic structure was unusual. The population of mining camps was overwhelmingly male. In 1860, for example, about 2,300 men and only 30 women resided in the Nevada mining camps of Virginia City and Gold Hill. Women found far fewer economic opportunities than men did on the mining frontier. Several opened hotels. Those with less capital worked as seamstresses and cooks and took in washing. The few married women often earned more than their husbands by boarding other miners willing to pay for the trappings of family life.

But the largest source of paid employment for women in the mining camps was prostitution. Mary Josephine Welch, an entrepreneurial Irish

Map 21-1   *Economic Development of the West: Railroads, Mining, and Cattle, 1860–1900*
The spread of the railroad network across the West promoted economic development by providing access to outside markets for its resources. The discovery of precious metals often attracted the railroads, but stockraisers had to open cattle trails to reach the railheads.

immigrant, settled in Helena in 1867 and soon established the Red Light Saloon, the first of many saloons, dance halls, and brothels that she owned and operated. Most women who engaged in such activities, however, were far less successful, and they entered brothels because they already suffered from economic hardship or a broken family. But prostitution usually only aggravated their distress. By the 1890s, as men gained control of the vice trade, violence, suicide, alcoholism, disease, drug addiction, and poverty overcame most prostitutes. Public authorities showed little concern for the abuse and even murder of prostitutes, although they used the women to raise revenue by fining or taxing them. Protestant women in Denver and other cities established "rescue homes" to protect or rehabilitate prostitutes and dance hall girls from male vice and violence.

American Views

SITKALA-SA'S VIEW OF AMERICANIZATION

Sitkala-Sa, or Red Bird, was an 8-year-old Sioux girl when she was taken from her South Dakota reservation in 1884 and placed in a midwestern missionary school, where she encountered what she called the "iron routine" of the "civilizing machine." Here she recalls her first day at the school.

❖ **What lessons were the missionaries trying to teach Sitkala-Sa by their actions?**

❖ **What lessons did Sitkala-Sa learn?**

Soon we were being drawn rapidly away by the white man's horses. When I saw the lonely figure of my mother vanish in the distance, a sense of regret settled heavily upon me. . . . I no longer felt free to be myself, or to voice my own feelings. The tears trickled down my cheeks, and I buried my face in the folds of my blanket. Now the first step, parting me from my mother, was taken, and all my belated tears availed nothing. . . . Trembling with fear and distrust of the palefaces . . . I was as frightened and bewildered as the captured young of a wild creature. . . .

[At the missionary school,] the constant clash of harsh noises, with an undercurrent of many voices murmuring an unknown tongue, made a bedlam within which I was securely tied. And though my spirit tore itself in struggling for its lost freedom, all was useless. . . .

We were placed in a line of girls who were marching into the dining room. . . . A small bell was tapped, and each of the pupils drew a chair from under the table. Supposing this act meant they were to be seated, I pulled out mine and at once slipped into it from one side. But when I turned my head, I saw that I was the only one seated, and all the rest at our table remained standing. Just as I began to rise, looking shyly around to see how chairs were to be used, a second bell was sounded. All were seated at last, and I had to crawl back into my chair again. I heard a man's voice at one end of the hall, and I looked around to see him. But all others hung their heads over their plates. As I glanced at the long chain of tables, I caught the eyes of a paleface woman upon me. Immediately I dropped my eyes, wondering why I was so keenly watched by the strange woman. The man ceased his mutterings, and then a third bell was tapped. Every one picked up his knife and fork and began eating. I began crying instead, for by this time I was afraid to venture anything more.

Another consequence of the gender imbalance in the mining camps was the prevalence of saloons among local businesses. An 1879 business census of Leadville, Colorado, reported 10 dry goods stores, 4 banks, and 4 churches but 120 saloons, 19 beer halls, and 118 gambling houses. Saloons were social centers in towns where most miners lived in crowded and dirty tents and rooming houses. As Mark Twain wrote in *Roughing It* (1872), his account of Virginia City, "The cheapest and easiest way to become an influential man and be looked up to by the community at large, was to stand behind a bar, wear a cluster-diamond pin, and sell whiskey." One observer of the Montana camps reported that men, "unburdened by families, drink whenever they feel like it, whenever they have money to pay for it, and whenever there is nothing else to do. . . . Bad manners follow, profanity becomes a matter of course. . . . Excitability and nervousness brought on by rum help these tendencies along, and then to correct this state of things the pistol comes into play." Disputes over mining claims could become violent, adding to the disorder. The California mining town of Bodie experienced forty-four shootings and twenty-nine killings between 1877 and 1883. But such killings occurred only within a small group of males who were known as the Badmen of Bodie. Daily life for most people was safe.

But this eating by formula was not the hardest trial in that first day. Late in the morning, my friend Judewin gave me a terrible warning. Judewin knew a few words of English; and she had overheard the paleface woman talk about cutting our long, heavy hair. Our mothers had taught us that only unskilled warriors who were captured had their hair shingled by the enemy. Among our people, short hair was worn by mourners, and shingled hair by cowards!

. . . I remember being dragged out, though I resisted by kicking and scratching wildly. In spite of myself, I was carried downstairs and tied fast in a chair. I cried aloud, shaking my head all the while until I felt the cold blades of the scissors against my neck, and heard them gnaw off one of my thick braids. Then I lost my spirit. . . . My long hair was shingled like a coward's. In my anguish I moaned for my mother, but no one came to comfort me. Not a soul reasoned quietly with me, as my own mother used to do; for now I was only one of many little animals driven by a herder. . . .

I blamed the hard-working, well-meaning, ignorant [missionary] woman who was inculcating in our hearts her superstitious ideas. Though I was sullen in all my little troubles, as soon as I felt better I was . . . again actively testing the chains which tightly bound my individuality like a mummy for burial. . . .

Many specimens of civilized peoples visited the Indian school. The city folks with canes and eyeglasses, the countrymen with sunburnt cheeks and clumsy feet, forgot their relative social ranks in an ignorant curiosity. Both sorts of these Christian palefaces were alike astounded at seeing the children of savage warriors so docile and industrious. . . .

In this fashion many [whites] have passed idly through the Indian schools during the last decade, afterward to boast of their charity to the North American Indian. But few there are who have paused to question whether real life or long-lasting death lies beneath this semblance of civilization.

Source: Sitkala-Sa, "The School Days of an Indian Girl" (1900).

Indeed, personal and criminal violence, which remains popularly associated with the West, was less pervasive than collective violence. Whites often drove Mexicans and Chinese from their claims or refused to let them work in higher-paid occupations in the mining camps. The Chinese had originally migrated to the California gold fields and thereafter spread to the new mining areas of the Rockies and the Great Basin, where they worked in mining when possible, operated laundries and restaurants, and held menial jobs like hauling water and chopping wood. In 1870, more than a quarter of Idaho's population and nearly 10 percent of Montana's was Chinese. Where they were numerous, the Chinese built their own communities and maintained their customs.

But racism and fear of economic competition sparked hostility and violence against the Chinese almost everywhere. The worst anti-Chinese violence occurred in Rock Springs, Wyoming, in 1885 when white miners killed twenty-eight unresisting Chinese miners and drove away all seven hundred residents from the local Chinatown. Although the members of the mob were well known, the grand jury, speaking for the white majority, found no cause for legal action: "Though we have examined a large number of witnesses, no one has been able to testify to a single criminal act committed by any known white person." There was community sanction for violence against racial minorities.

Labor and Capital

New technology had dramatic consequences for both miners and the mining industry. Initially, mining was an individual enterprise in which miners used simple tools, such as picks and shovels, wash pans, and rockers to work shallow surface deposits known as placers. More expensive operations were needed to reach the precious metal buried in the earth.

Hydraulic mining, for example, required massive capital investment to build reservoirs, ditches, and troughs to power high-pressure water cannons that would pulverize hillsides and uncover the mineral deposits. Still more expensive and complex was quartz, or lode, mining, sometimes called hard rock mining. Time, money, and technology were required to sink a shaft hundreds of feet, timber underground chambers and tunnels, install pumps to remove underground water and hoists to lower men and lift out rock, and build stamp mills and smelters to treat the ore.

Such complex, expensive, and permanent mining operations necessarily came under corporate control. Often financed with eastern or British capital, new corporations integrated the mining industry into the larger economy. Hard rock mining produced more complex ores than could be treated in remote mining towns, but with the new railroad network, they were shipped to smelting plants as far away as Kansas City and St. Louis and then to refineries in Baltimore and other eastern cities. Western ores thus became part of national and international business. The mining industry's increasing development of lower-grade deposits led to greater capital investment and larger operations employing more workers and machinery.

But the new corporate mining had many disturbing effects. Hydraulic mining washed away hillsides, depositing debris in canyons and valleys to a depth of 100 feet or more, clogging rivers and causing floods, and burying thousands of acres of farmland. Such damage provoked an outcry and eventually led to government regulation.

Corporate mining also transformed prospectors into wage workers with restricted opportunities. Miners' status declined as new machinery like power drills reduced the need for skilled laborers and prompted employers to hire cheaper workers from eastern and southern Europe. Moreover, mining corporations did little to protect miners' health or safety. Miners died in cave-ins, explosions, and fires or from the great heat and poisonous gases in underground mines. Miners called the power hoists "man killers" because they frequently crushed and dismembered workers. In 1889, a Montana inspector of mines concluded that "death lurks even in the things which are designed as benefits."

To protect their interests, miners organized unions. Unions functioned as benevolent societies, using members' dues to pay benefits to injured miners or their widows and orphans. Several unions established hospitals. Union halls offered an alternative to the saloons by serving as social and educational centers. The Miners' Union Library in Virginia City, established in 1877, was the largest library in Nevada. Unions also promoted miners' interests on the job, both by striking when management cut wages and by campaigning for mine safety. They persuaded governments to adopt mine safety legislation and, beginning in the late 1880s, to establish the office of state mine inspector. The chief role of the state officials was to answer the question posed by the Colorado mining inspector: "How far should an industry be permitted to advance its material welfare at the expense of human life?"

But mining companies frequently controlled state power and used it to crush unions and their attempts to protect miners. Thus in 1892, in the Coeur d'Alene district of Idaho, mining companies locked out strikers and imported a private army, which battled miners in a bloody gunfight. Management next persuaded the governor and the president to send in the state militia and the U.S. Army. State officials then suppressed the strike and the union by confining all union members and their sympathizers in stockades. When mining companies in Utah, Colorado, and Montana pursued the same aggressive tactics, the local miners' unions in the West united for strength and self-protection. In 1893, they formed one of the nation's largest and most militant unions, the **Western Federation of Miners**.

As the law grew stronger and the owners adopted "legalized violence" as a repressive tool, miners turned to extralegal violence. In the western mines, then, both management's tactics—blacklisting union members, locking out strikers, obtaining court injunctions against unions, and using soldiers against workers—and labor's response mirrored conditions in the industrial East. Western mining, in sum, had been transformed from a small-scale prospecting enterprise characterized by individual initiative and simple tools into a large-scale corporate business characterized by impersonal management, outside capital, advanced technology, and wage labor. As such, it both reflected and was fully integrated into national industrialization.

Exploiting the Grass: The Cattle Kingdom

The so-called **Cattle Kingdom**, the development of the range cattle industry, reflected the needs of an emerging eastern urban society, the economic possibilities of the grasslands of the Great Plains, the technology of the expanding railroad network, and the requirements of corporations and capital. It also brought "cow towns" and urban development to the West.

Cattle Drives and Cow Towns

The cattle industry originated in southern Texas, where the Spanish had introduced cattle in the eighteenth century. Developed by Mexican ranchers, "Texas longhorns" proved well adapted to the plains grasslands.

Following the Civil War, industrial expansion in the East and Midwest enlarged the urban market for food and increased the potential value of Texas steers. The extension of the railroad network into the West, moreover, opened the possibility of tapping that market. The key was to establish a shipping point on the railroads west of the settled farming regions, a step first taken in 1867 by Joseph McCoy, an Illinois cattle shipper. McCoy selected Abilene, Kansas, in his words "a very small, dead place, consisting of about one dozen log huts, low, small, rude affairs." But Abilene was also the western railhead of the Kansas Pacific Railroad and was ringed by lush grasslands for cattle. McCoy bought 250 acres for a stockyard and imported lumber for stock pens, loading facilities, stables, and a hotel for cowhands. Texans opened the **Chisholm Trail** through Indian Territory to drive their cattle northward to Abilene. Within three years, a million and a half cattle arrived in Abilene, divided into herds of several thousand, each directed by a dozen cowhands on a "long drive" taking two to three months. With the arrival of the cattle trade, other entrepreneurs created a bustling town. As both railroads and settlement advanced westward, a series of other cow towns—Ellsworth, Wichita, Dodge City, Cheyenne—attracted the long drives, cattle herds, and urban development.

As with the mining camps, the cow towns' reputation for violence was exaggerated. They adopted gun control laws, prohibiting the carrying of handguns within city limits, and established police forces to maintain order. The towns taxed prostitutes and gamblers and charged high fees for liquor licenses. By collecting such "sin taxes," Wichita was able to forgo general business taxes, thereby increasing its appeal to prospective settlers.

Most cow towns, like Abilene, dwindled into small towns serving farm populations. But like mining camps, cow towns contributed to the growth of an urban frontier. Railroads often determined the location and growth of western cities, providing access to markets for local products, transporting supplies and machinery for residents, and attracting capital for commercial and industrial development. The West, in fact, had become the most urban region in the nation by 1890, with two-thirds of its population living in communities of at least 2,500 people.

Rise and Fall of Open-Range Ranching

Indian removal and the extension of the railroad network opened land for ranching in Kansas, Nebraska, Wyoming, Colorado, Montana, and the Dakotas. Cattle reaching Kansas were increasingly sold to stock these northern ranges rather than for shipment to the packing houses. Ranches soon spread across the Great Plains and into the Great Basin, the Southwest, and even eastern Oregon and Washington. Calves were cheap, and ranchers did not buy, but merely used, the grazing lands of the open range, which was public land. It sufficed to acquire title to the site for a ranch house and a water source because controlling access to water in semiarid lands gave effective control of the surrounding public domain "the same as though I owned it," as one rancher explained. Ranchers thus needed to invest only in horses, primitive corrals, and bunkhouses. Their labor costs were minimal: they paid cowboys in the spring to round up new calves for branding and in the fall to herd steers to market.

By the early 1880s, the high profits from this enterprise and an expanding market for beef attracted speculative capital and reshaped the industry. Eastern and European capital flooded the West, with British investors particularly prominent after a Scottish group reported returns of 80 percent. British and American corporations acquired, expanded, and managed huge ranches.

Large companies soon dominated the industry, just as they had gained control of mining. Some large companies illegally began to enclose the open range, building fences to exclude newcomers and minimize labor costs by reducing the number of cowboys needed to control the cattle. One Wyoming newspaper complained that "some morning we will wake up to find that a corporation has run a wire fence about the boundary lines of Wyoming, and all within the same have been notified to move." And a Coloradan wondered, "Will the government protect us if we poor unite and cut down their fences and let our stock have some of Uncle Sam's feed as well as them?"

The industry eventually collapsed in an economic and ecological disaster. Overgrazing replaced nutritious grasses with sagebrush, Russian thistle, and other plants that livestock found unpalatable. Ten times as much land was required to support a steer by the 1880s. Droughts in the mid-1880s further withered vegetation and enfeebled the animals. Millions of cattle starved or froze to death in terrible blizzards in 1886 and 1887.

The surviving ranchers reduced their operations, restricted the size of their herds, and tried to ensure adequate winter feed by growing hay. To decrease their dependence on natural vegetation even further, they introduced drought-resistant sorghum and new grasses; to reduce their dependence on rainfall, they drilled wells and installed windmills to pump water.

Cowhands

Cowboys' work was hard, dirty, seasonal, tedious, sometimes dangerous, and poorly paid. Many of the initial recruits were white Southerners unwilling or unable to return home after the Civil War. Blacks made up perhaps 25 percent of the trail-herd outfits. Mexican cowboys developed most of the tools, techniques, and trappings that characterized the cattle industry: from boots, chaps, and the "western" saddle to roundups and roping. Blacks and Mexicans were often relegated to the more lowly jobs, such as wrangler, a "dust-eater" who herded horses for others to use, but most were ordinary hands on ranch or trail. Except in the few all-black outfits, they were rarely ranch or trail bosses. As the industry expanded northward, more cowboys came from rural Kansas, Nebraska, and neighboring states.

Initially, in the frontier-ranching phase dominated by the long drive, cowboys were seasonal employees who worked closely with owners. They frequently expected to become independent stock raisers themselves and typically enjoyed the right to "maverick" cattle, or put their own brand on unmarked cattle. These informal rights provided opportunities to acquire property and move up the social ladder.

With the appearance of large, corporate enterprises, the traditional rights of cowboys disappeared. Employers now prohibited cowhands from running a brand of their own. One cowboy complained that these restrictions deprived a cowhand of his one way "to get on in the world." To increase labor efficiency, some companies prohibited their cowboys from drinking, gambling, and carrying guns.

Cowboy strikes broke out where corporate ranching was most advanced. The first such strike occurred in Texas in 1883 when the Panhandle Stock Association, representing large operators, prohibited ranch hands from owning their own cattle and imposed a standard wage. More than three hundred cowboys struck seven large ranches for higher wages—$50 rather than $30 per month—and the right to brand mavericks for themselves and to run small herds on the public domain. Ranchers evicted the cowboys, hired scabs, and brought in the Texas Rangers for assistance. The strikers were forced to leave the region.

Other strikes also failed because corporate ranches and their stock associations had the power and cowhands faced long odds in their efforts to organize. They were isolated across vast spaces and had little leverage in the industry. Members of the Northern New Mexico Cowboys Union, formed in 1886, recognized their weakness: after

Employees of the Prairie Cattle Company at the ranch headquarters in Dry Cimarron, New Mexico, in 1888. This company, a British corporation, held 8,000 square miles of land.

asking employers for "what we are worth after many years' experience," they conceded, "We are dependent on you."

The transformation of the western cattle industry and its integration into a national economy dominated by corporations thus made the cherished image of cowboy independence and rugged individualism more myth than reality. One visitor to America in the late 1880s commented: "Out in the fabled West, the life of the 'free' cowboy is as much that of a slave as is the life of his Eastern brother, the Massachusetts mill-hand. And the slave-owner is in both cases the same—the capitalist."

Exploiting the Earth: The Expansion of Agriculture

Even more than ranching and mining, agricultural growth boosted the western economy and bound it tightly to national and world markets. In this process, the government played a significant role, as did the railroads, science and technology, eastern and foreign capital, and the dreams and hard work of millions of rural settlers. The development of farming produced remarkable economic growth, but it left the dreams of many unfulfilled.

Settling the Land

To stimulate agricultural settlement, Congress passed the most famous land law, the Homestead Act of 1862 (see the summary table "Government Land Policy"; see also Chapter 17). The measure offered 160 acres of free land to anyone who would live on the plot and farm it for five years. The governor of Nebraska exclaimed, "What a blessing this wise and humane legislation will bring to many a poor but honest and industrious family. Its benefits can never be estimated in dollars and cents."

However, prospective settlers found less land open to public entry than they expected. Federal land laws did not apply in much of California and the Southwest, where Spain and Mexico had previously transferred land to private owners, or in all of Texas. Elsewhere, the government had given away millions of acres to railroads, or authorized selling millions more for educational and other purposes.

Settlers in Kansas, Nebraska, Minnesota, and the Dakotas in the late 1860s and early 1870s often found most of the best land unavailable for homesteading and much of the rest remote from transportation facilities and markets. Forty percent of the land in Kansas, for example, was closed to homesteading, which prompted the editor of the *Kansas Farmer* to complain that "the settlement of the state is retarded by land monopolists, corporate and individual." Although 375,000 farms were claimed by 1890 through the Homestead Act—a success by any measure—most settlers had to purchase land for their farms and homes.

The Homestead Act also reflected traditional eastern conceptions of the family farm, which were inappropriate in the West. Here larger-scale farming was necessary. And the law ignored the need for capital for machinery, buildings, livestock, and fencing that prospective settlers would face in developing a successful farm on the Great Plains.

Other forces stimulated and promoted settlement. Newspaper editors trumpeted the prospects of their region. Land companies, eager to sell their speculative holdings, sent agents through the Midwest and Europe to encourage migration. Steamship companies, interested in selling transatlantic tickets, advertised the opportunities in the American West across Europe. The Scandinavian Immigration Society generated both publicity and settlers for Minnesota; the Hebrew Emigrant Aid Society established Jewish agricultural colonies in Kansas and North Dakota. The Mormons organized the Perpetual Emigrating Fund Company, which helped more than 100,000 European immigrants settle in Utah and Idaho. Their agricultural communities, relying on communal cooperation under church supervision, succeeded where individual efforts often failed in developing this region.

Most important, railroad advertising and promotional campaigns attracted people to the West. In 1882 alone, the Northern Pacific distributed more than 630,000 pieces of promotional literature in English, Swedish, Dutch, Danish, and Norwegian. "The glowing accounts of the golden west sent out by the R.R. companies," one pioneer later recalled, had convinced her that "they were doing a noble work to let poor people know there was such a grand haven they could reach." Only later did she realize that not only would the railroads profit from selling their huge land reserves to settlers, but also a successful agricultural economy would produce crops to be shipped east and a demand for manufactured goods to be shipped west on their lines. The railroads therefore advanced credit to prospective farmers, provided transportation assistance, and extended technical and agricultural advice.

Migrants poured into the West, occupying and farming more acres between 1870 and 1900 than

SUMMARY

GOVERNMENT LAND POLICY

Railroad land grants (1850–1871)	Granted 181 million acres to railroads to encourage construction and development
Homestead Act (1862)	Gave 80 million acres to settlers to encourage settlement
Morrill Act (1862)	Granted 11 million acres to states to sell to fund public agricultural colleges
Other grants	Granted 129 million acres to states to sell for other educational and related purposes
Dawes Act (1887)	Allotted some reservation lands to individual Indians to promote private property and weaken tribal values among Indians and offered remaining reservation lands for sale to whites (by 1906, some 75 million acres had been acquired by whites)
Various laws	Permitted direct sales of 100 million acres by the Land Office

Americans had in the previous 250 years. Farmers settled in every region. But most streamed into the Great Plains states, from the Dakotas to Texas. Much of Oklahoma was settled in virtually a single day in 1889 when the government opened up lands previously reserved for Indians. A reporter described the wild land rush that created Oklahoma City in hours and claimed 2 million acres of land by nightfall: "With a shout and a yell the swift riders shot out, then followed the light buggies or wagons and last the lumbering prairie schooners and freighters' wagons, with here and there even a man on a bicycle and many too on foot—above all a great cloud of dust hovering."

Whites predominated in the mass migration, but African-Americans initiated one of its most dramatic episodes, a millenarian folk movement they called the Exodus, which established several black communities in Kansas and Nebraska. Many settlers came from Europe, sometimes in a chain migration of entire villages, bringing with them not only their own attitudes toward the land but also special crops, skills, settlement patterns, and agricultural practices. By 1890, the foreign-born population of North Dakota exceeded 40 percent, and nonnatives made up much of the population in California and other western states.

Migrants moved into the West in search of opportunity, which they sometimes seized at the expense of others already there. In the Southwest, Hispanics had long lived in village communities largely outside a commercial economy, farming small tracts of irrigated land and herding sheep on communal pastures. But as more Anglos, or white Americans, arrived, their political and economic influence undermined traditional Hispanic society. Congress restricted the original Hispanic land grants to only the villagers' home lots and irrigated fields, throwing open most of their common lands to newcomers. The notorious **Santa Fe Ring**, a group of lawyers and land speculators, seized millions of acres through fraud and legal chicanery.

Spanish Americans resisted these losses, in court or through violence. **Las Gorras Blancas** (the White Caps) staged night raids to cut fences erected by Anglo ranchers and farmers and to attack the property of railroads, the symbol of the encroaching new order. "Our purpose," they announced, "is to protect the rights of the people in general and especially those of the helpless classes." Such resistance, however, had little success.

As their landholdings shrank, Hispanic villagers could not maintain their pastoral economy. Many became seasonal wage laborers in the Anglo-dominated economy, sometimes working as stoop labor in the commercial sugar beet fields that emerged in the 1890s, sometimes working on the railroads or in the mines. Women also participated in this new labor market. Previously crucial to the subsistence village economy, they now sought wage labor as cooks and domestic servants in railroad towns and mining camps. Hispanics retained some cultural autonomy, but they had little influence over the larger processes of settlement and development.

Home on the Range

Farmers and their families encountered many difficulties, especially on the Great Plains, where they had to adapt to a radically new environment. The scarcity of trees on the plains meant that there was little wood for housing, fuel, and fencing. Until they had reaped several harvests and could afford to import lumber, pioneer families lived in dark and dirty sod houses. One Nebraska homesteader recalled that her first sight of a sod house "sickened me."

For fuel, settlers often had to rely on buffalo or cattle "chips"—dried dung. One farmer reported in 1879 that "it was comical to see how gingerly our wives handled these chips at first. They commenced by picking them up between two sticks, or with a poker. Soon they used a rag, and then a corner of their apron. Finally, growing hardened, a wash after handling them was sufficient. And now? Now it is out of the bread, into the chips and back again—and not even a dust of the hands!"

Women's domestic labor was also complicated by the scarcity of water. They often transported water over long distances, pulling barrels on "water sleds" or carrying pails on neck yokes. Where possible, they also helped dig wells by hand.

Some women farmed the land themselves. Single women could claim land under the Homestead Act, and in some areas, women claimants made up 18 percent of the total and succeeded more frequently than men in gaining final title. At times, married women operated the family farm while their husbands worked elsewhere to earn money. In the 1870s, one Dakota woman recounted the demands women faced: "I had lived on a homestead long enough to learn some fundamental things: that while a woman had more independence here than in any other part of the world, she was expected to contribute as much as a man—that people who fought the frontier had to be prepared to meet any emergency; that the person who wasn't willing to try anything once wasn't equipped to be a settler."

Women especially suffered from isolation and loneliness on the plains because they frequently had less contact with others than the farm men. One farm woman complained that "being cut off from everybody is almost too much for me." Luna Kellie recalled that from her Nebraska farm "there were no houses in sight and it seemed like the end of the world." To break the silence, to provide some music and color, many homesteading families kept canaries among their few belongings.

Farming the Land

Pioneer settlers had to make daunting adjustments to develop the agricultural potential of their new land. Advances in science, technology, and industry made such adjustments possible. The changes would not only reshape the agricultural economy but also bring their own great challenges to traditional rural values and expectations.

Fencing was an immediate problem on the treeless plains. Barbed wire, developed in the mid-1870s, solved the problem. By 1900, farmers were importing nearly 300 million pounds of barbed wire each year from eastern and midwestern factories.

The aridity of most of the West also posed difficulties. In California, Colorado, and a few other areas, settlers used streams fed by mountain snowpacks to irrigate land. Elsewhere, enterprising farmers developed variants of the "dry farming" practices that the Mormons had introduced in Utah, attempting to preserve and maximize the limited rainfall. Some farmers erected windmills to pump underground water. The scarce rainfall also encouraged farmers to specialize in a single cash crop for market. Many plains farmers turned from corn to wheat, especially the drought-resistant Turkey Red variety of hard winter wheat that German Mennonites had introduced into Kansas from Russia. Related technological advancements included grain elevators that would store grain for shipment and load it into rail cars mechanically and mills that used corrugated, chilled-iron rollers rather than millstones to process the new varieties of wheat.

In semiarid regions, farmers required special plows to break the tough sod, new harrows to prepare the soil for cultivation, grain drills to plant the crop, and harvesting and threshing machines to bring it in. Thanks to more and better machines, agricultural efficiency and productivity shot up. By the 1890s, machinery permitted the farmer to produce eighteen times more wheat than hand methods had.

These developments reflected both the expansion of agriculture and its increasing dependence on the larger society. The rail network provided essential transportation for crops; the nation's industrial sector produced necessary agricultural machinery. Banks and loan companies extended the credit and capital that allowed farmers to take advantage of mechanization and other new advances; and many other businesses graded, stored, processed, and sold their crops. In short, because of its market orientation, mechanization, and specialization, western agriculture relied on other people or impersonal forces as it was incorporated into the national and international economy.

When conditions were favorable—good weather, good crops, and good prices—western farmers prospered. Too often, however, they faced adversity. In the late 1880s, drought coincided with a slump in crop prices. Expanding production in Argentina, Canada, Australia, and Russia helped create a world surplus of grain that drove prices steadily downward. Prices for other farm commodities also declined.

Each of the four Chrisman sisters claimed a homestead and built a sodhouse near Goheen, Nebraska. Farming on the Great Plains was typically a family operation, with all members of the family having important tasks.

Squeezed between high costs for credit, transportation, and manufactured goods and falling agricultural prices, western farmers faced disaster. They responded by lashing back at their points of contact with the new system. They especially condemned the railroads. Luna Kellie complained, "The minute you crossed the Missouri River your fate both soul and body was in their hands. What you should eat and drink, what you should wear, everything was in their hands and they robbed us of all we produced except enough to keep body and soul together and many many times not that."

Farmers censured the grain elevators in the local buying centers that were often owned by eastern corporations, including the railroads themselves. A Minnesota state investigation found systematic fraud by elevators, which collectively cost the state's farmers a massive sum.

Farmers also denounced the many eastern bankers and mortgage lenders who had provided the credit for them to acquire land, equipment, and machinery. With failing crops and falling prices, many western farms were foreclosed.

Stunned and bitter, western farmers concluded that their problems arose because they had been incorporated into the new system, an integrated economy directed by forces beyond their control. And it was a system that did not work well. "There is," one of them charged, "something radically wrong in our industrial system. There is a screw loose."

Conclusion

With determination, ingenuity, and hard work millions of people had settled vast areas, made farms and ranches, built villages and cities, brought forth mineral wealth, and imposed their values on the land. These achievements were tempered by a shameful treatment of Indians and an often destructive exploitation of natural resources. But if most Westerners took pride in their accomplishments, and a few enjoyed wealth and power, many also grew discontented with the new conditions they encountered as the "Wild" West receded.

Railroad expansion, population movements, eastern investment, corporate control, technological innovations, and government policies had incorporated the region fully into the larger society. Indians experienced this incorporation most thoroughly and most tragically, losing their lands, their traditions, and often their lives; the survivors were dependent on the decisions and actions of interlopers. Cowboys and miners also learned that the frontier merely marked the cutting edge of eastern industrial society; neither could escape integration into the national economy by managerial decisions, transportation links, and market forces. Most settlers in the West were farmers, but they too learned that their distinctive environment did not insulate them from assimilation into larger productive, financial, and marketing structures.

Review Questions

1. What factors were most influential in the subjugation of American Indians?

2. What were the major goals of federal Indian policy, and how did they change?

3. How did railroads shape the settlement and development of the West?

4. How did technological developments affect Indians, miners, and farmers in the West?

5. How did the federal government help transform the West?

Recommended Reading

Robert R. Dykstra, *The Cattle Towns* (1968). This classic analysis of town building and social conflict in Kansas cattle towns is both fascinating and fun to read.

Gilbert C. Fite, *The Farmers' Frontier, 1865–1900* (1966). Fite has produced a comprehensive account of agricultural settlement in all areas of the West.

Richard E. Lingenfelter, *The Hardrock Miners: A History of the Mining Labor Movement in the American West, 1863–1893* (1974). This is an important analysis of the relationship between the labor movement and the industrialization of the western mines.

Rodman W. Paul, *The Far West and the Great Plains in Transition* (1988). This valuable survey of regional development devotes particular attention to mining.

Glenda Riley, *The Female Frontier: A Comparative View of Women on the Prairie and the Plains* (1988). Riley's is a useful guide to women's experiences in the West.

Robert M. Utley, *The Indian Frontier of the American West, 1846–1890* (1984). This is a balanced survey of United States–Indian relations in the late nineteenth century.

Philip Weeks, *Farewell, My Nation: The American Indian and the United States, 1820–1890* (1990). Modern discussions of Indian policy provide insights into the perspectives of the Indians.

Richard White, *"It's Your Misfortune and None of My Own": A New History of the American West* (1991). White's important and original analysis of the development of the West highlights environmental, ethnic, labor, and social history.

Mark Wyman, *Hard Rock Epic: Western Miners and the Industrial Revolution, 1860–1910* (1979). Miners experience the dual frontiers of the West and the industrial revolution.

Where to Learn More

❖ **National Agricultural Hall of Fame, Bonner Springs, Kansas.** This expansive museum preserves and documents agricultural machinery, including the innovations that made possible the settlement and development of the Great Plains.

❖ **Fort Larned National Historic Site, Larned, Kansas.** With nine surviving buildings and a reconstructed blockhouse, Fort Larned is one of the best-preserved frontier Army posts. A visitor center with audio-visual programs, a museum, park rangers, and living-history demonstrations help explain the Fort's role as a base for military campaigns and as an agency for the Indian Bureau.

❖ **Peabody Museum, Harvard University, Cambridge, Massachusetts.** The Hall of the North American Indian showcases the Peabody Museum's vast collection of artifacts of North American Indians. Several exhibitions focus on different regions of the American West and stress the ways in which Native Americans often creatively adapted to major disruptions in their lives produced by contact with the expanding white society.

❖ **Little Bighorn Battlefield National Monument, Crow Agency, Montana.** The site of Custer's crushing defeat includes a monument to the Seventh Cavalry atop Last Stand Hill. A new authorized Indian Memorial will include sacred texts, artifacts, and pictographs to immerse visitors in the culture of the Plains Indians.

❖ **American Historical Society of Germans from Russia Museum, Lincoln, Nebraska.** This unique museum, consisting of a complex of restored homes, exhibitions, and archives, preserves the history and culture of Germans who emigrated to Russia and then to the American Great Plains, where they contributed importantly to the development of a multicultural society and an agricultural economy.

❖ **National Cowboy Hall of Fame, Oklahoma City, Oklahoma.** This large institution contains an outstanding collection of Western Art, displays of cowboy and Indian artifacts, and both kitschy exhibitions of the mythic, Hollywood West and serious galleries depicting the often hard realities of the cattle industry. Its many public programs also successfully combine fun with learning.

22 POLITICS AND GOVERNMENT, 1877–1900

KEY TOPICS

❖ The exuberant partisan politics and the close balance between the Republican and Democratic parties in the late nineteenth century
❖ The inability and unwillingness of a weak federal government to address problems of America's industrializing economy
❖ The pressure for civil service reform
❖ The tariff issue
❖ Monetary policy and the call for free silver
❖ Agricultural protest and the emergence of the Populist party
❖ The end of political stalemate after the election of 1896

incinnati throbbed with excitement as the October 1884 congressional election approached. Republicans and Democrats staged mammoth campaign parades, each with more than twenty thousand torch-bearing marchers organized into uniformed companies, brigades, and divisions and accompanied by resplendent brass bands. Orators stirred the huge crowds with patriotic, religious, and cultural bombast. Partisans of the Anti-Monopoly party explained the dangers of corporate and money monopolies, but most voters ignored such complex issues amid the stirring spectacles presented by the major parties.

On October 14, in the dead of night, just hours before the polls opened, Cincinnati's partisan police, representing the Democratic-controlled city government, arrested hundreds of African-American men, and hurried them to jail. Those who promised to vote the Democratic ticket in exchange for 60 cents were escorted to the polls; those who remained steadfastly Republican were jailed until the polls closed and then released without charges. A thousand newly appointed Democratic deputies joined the police in attacking blacks who tried to vote elsewhere in the city and arresting several hundred more Republicans at the polls.

Simultaneously, the U.S. marshal, a Republican, appointed nearly two thousand deputies. These deputies, "'roustabouts' and 'roughs,' men of no character or bad character," sought to incite violence among the Democratic voters in the city's Irish wards to keep them from the polls. They too made mass arrests, often of Kentucky Democrats who had crossed the Ohio River to "colonize" Cincinnati's election. Local Republican leader William Howard Taft, later a U.S. president, wrote his mother about witnessing a Democrat "shot & killed about fifteen feet from me at our polling place. . . . He drew a pistol on a Deputy Marshal but the Deputy was too quick for him." Although he considered the marshal's violence justified, Taft thought it risky for Republicans "to furnish revolvers to men who are close to or belong to the criminal class."

At the end of the day, according to the *Cincinnati Enquirer*, the "reign of terror" had left eight dead (including one federal deputy and one deputy sheriff), another two dozen with knife or bullet wounds, and "hundreds of cases of clubbing, sandbagging, and brass-knuckle exercise." All in all, the newspaper concluded, it was a quiet election reflecting a "reasonably happy state of affairs."

As the *Enquirer*'s report suggests, this Cincinnati election, though more riotous than some, was in many ways typical of late nineteenth-century American politics. From the military-style campaign to the act of voting, elections were a masculine business. Marked by pageantry and hoopla, campaigns attracted mass participation but often avoided substantive policy issues. Third parties regularly challenged but rarely threatened the Democratic and Republican parties. The two major political parties shaped campaigns and controlled elections, which were usually tumultuous if not always violent. Partisan divisions overlapped with ethnic and racial divisions. The lack of a common national election day, which allowed Kentuckians to vote in Cincinnati's October election without missing their own in November, reflected **localism**—the belief that local concerns took precedence over national concerns. One newspaper even denied the legitimacy of federal involvement in the city's elections, declaring that federal deputies "can all be kicked and cuffed about like ordinary citizens, and will be compelled to take their chances with common people on election day."

These features of late-nineteenth-century politics would eventually be transformed in significant ways. But while they endured, they shaped not only campaigns and elections but the form and role of government as well.

The Structure and Style of Politics

Political parties dominated political life. They organized campaigns, controlled balloting, and held the unswerving loyalty of most of the electorate. While the major parties worked to maintain a sense of unity and tradition among their followers, third parties sought the support of those the major parties left unserved. Other Americans looked outside the electoral arena to fulfill their political goals.

Campaigns and Elections

In the late nineteenth century, campaign pageantry absorbed communities large and small. The town of Emporia, Kansas, once witnessed a campaign rally of twenty thousand people, several times its population. A parade of wagons stretched 5 miles, reported the proud local newspaper. "When the head of the procession was under the equator the tail was coming around the north pole."

The excitement of political contests prompted the wife of Chief Justice Morrison Waite to write longingly on election day, 1876, "I should want to vote all day." But women could not vote at all. Justice Waite himself had just a year earlier written the unanimous opinion of the Supreme Court (in *Minor* v. *Happersett*) that the Constitution did not confer suffrage on women.

But turnout among male voters was remarkably high, averaging nearly 80 percent in presidential elections between 1876 and 1900, a figure far greater than ever achieved thereafter. In many states, even immigrants not yet citizens were eligible to vote and flocked to the polls. African-Americans voted regularly in the North and irregularly in the South before being disfranchised at the end of the century.

Political parties kept detailed records of voters, transported them to the polls, saw that they were registered where necessary, and sometimes even paid their poll taxes or naturalization fees to make them eligible. With legal regulations and public machinery for elections negligible, parties dominated the campaigns and elections. Election clerks and judges were not public officials but partisans chosen by the political parties. Until the 1890s, most states had no laws to ensure secrecy in voting, and ballots were printed by the parties. Because they had only the names of the candidates of the party issuing them and often varied in size and color, ballots revealed the voters' party alliance.

When California officials sought to make the state's ballots uniform, party managers developed the translucent "isinglass ticket," which kept the voter's choice public. Paid party workers known as peddlers or hawkers stationed themselves near the polls, each trying to force his ticket on prospective voters. Fighting and intimidation were so commonplace at the polls that one state supreme court ruled in 1887 that they were "acceptable" features of elections.

As the court recognized, the open and partisan aspects of the electoral process did not necessarily lead to election fraud, however much they shaped the nature of political participation.

Partisan Politics

Democrats and Republicans had virtually the same level of electoral support, one reason they worked so hard to get out the vote (see Map 22-1). Rarely did either party control both the presidency and Congress at once. The party balance also gave great influence to New York, New Jersey, Ohio, and Indiana, whose evenly divided voters controlled electoral votes that could swing an election either way. Both parties concentrated campaign funds and strategy on the swing states. Thus Republican presidential candidate James Garfield of Ohio com-

Map 22-1   The Two-Party Stalemate of the Late Nineteenth Century
Strong parties, staunch loyalties, and an evenly divided electorate made for exciting politics but often stalemated government in the late nineteenth century. Most states voted consistently for one of the major parties, leaving the few swing states like New York and Indiana the scenes of fierce partisan battles.

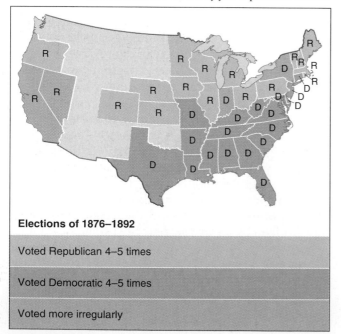

Elections of 1876–1892

Voted Republican 4–5 times

Voted Democratic 4–5 times

Voted more irregularly

mented during the election campaign in 1880: "Nothing is wanting except an immediate and liberal supply of money for campaign expenses to make Indiana certain. With a victory there, the rest is easy." Garfield narrowly carried Indiana by six thousand votes and the nation by nine thousand out of 9.2 million cast.

Interrelated regional, ethnic, religious, and local factors determined the party affiliations of most Americans. Economic issues generally did not decide party ties. Like religious belief and ethnic identity, partisan loyalty was largely a cultural trait passed from father to son, which helps explain the electoral stability of most communities.

Republicans were strongest in the North and Midwest, where they benefited from their party's role as the defender of the Union in the Civil War. The Republican party appealed primarily to old-stock Americans and other Protestants, including those of German and Scandinavian descent. African-Americans, loyal to the party that had emancipated and enfranchised the slaves of the South, also supported the Grand Old Party, or GOP, where they could vote. Democrats were strongest in the South, where they stood as the defender of the traditions of the region's white population. But Democrats also drew support in the urban Northeast, especially from Catholics and recent immigrants.

Each major party thus consisted of a complex coalition of groups with differing traditions and interests. One observer of the Democratic party in California described it as "a sort of Democratic happy family, like we see in the prairie-dog villages, where owls, rattlesnakes, prairie dogs, and lizards all live in the same hole."

Republicans identified their party with nationalism and national unity and attacked the Democrats as an "alliance between the embittered South and the slums of the Northern cities." They combined a "bloody shirt" appeal to the memories of the Civil War with campaigns for immigration restriction and cultural uniformity. Republican legislatures in several eastern and midwestern states in the 1880s and 1890s enacted laws regulating parochial schools, the use of foreign languages, and alcohol consumption.

Democrats portrayed themselves as the party of limited government and "personal liberties," a theme that appealed both to the racism of white Southerners and the resentment Irish, German, and other immigrants felt about the nativist meddling the Republicans favored. The Democrats' commitment to personal liberties had limits. They supported the disfranchisement of African-Americans, the exclusion

CHRONOLOGY

1867 Patrons of Husbandry (the Grange) is founded.

1869 Massachusetts establishes the first state regulatory commission.

1873 Silver is demonetized in the "Crime of '73."

1874 Woman's Christian Temperance Union is organized.

1875 U.S. Supreme Court, in *Minor* v. *Happersett*, upholds denial of suffrage to women.

1876 Greenback party runs presidential candidate.

1877 Rutherford B. Hayes becomes president after disputed election.

Farmers' Alliance is founded.

Supreme Court, in *Munn* v. *Illinois*, upholds state regulatory authority over private property.

1878 Bland-Allison Act obliges the government to buy silver.

1880 James A. Garfield is elected president.

1881 Garfield is assassinated; Chester A. Arthur becomes president.

1883 Pendleton Civil Service Act is passed.

1884 Grover Cleveland is elected president.

1886 Supreme Court, in *Wabash* v. *Illinois*, rules that only the federal government, not the states, can regulate interstate commerce.

1887 Interstate Commerce Act is passed.

1888 Benjamin Harrison is elected president.

1890 Sherman Antitrust Act is passed.

McKinley Tariff Act is passed.

Sherman Silver Purchase Act is passed.

National American Woman Suffrage Association is organized.

Wyoming enters the Union as the first state with woman suffrage.

1892 People's party is organized.

Cleveland is elected to his second term as president.

1893 Depression begins.

Sherman Silver Purchase Act is repealed.

1894 Coxey's Army marches to Washington.

Pullman strike ends in violence.

1895 Supreme Court, in *Pollock* v. *Farmers' Loan and Trust Company*, invalidates the federal income tax.

Supreme Court, in *United States* v. *E. C. Knight Company*, limits the Sherman Antitrust law to commerce, excluding industrial monopolies.

1896 William Jennings Bryan is nominated for president by Democrats and Populists.

William McKinley is elected president.

1900 Currency Act puts U.S. currency on the gold standard.

---

of Chinese immigrants, and the dispossession of American Indians from their lands. Nevertheless, their emphasis on traditional individualism and localism proved popular.

To its genteel critics, the partisan politics of both major parties climaxed in party machines, especially at the local level. Led by powerful bosses like Democrat Richard Croker of New York or Republican George Cox of Cincinnati, these machines not only controlled city politics but municipal government. Working-class voters were mobilized by party activists operating well-organized ward clubs and rewarded by municipal jobs and baskets of food or coal doled out by the machine. Such assistance was often necessary given the lack of public welfare systems, but to buy votes the machine also sold favors. Public contracts and franchises were peddled to businesses whose high bids covered kickbacks to the machine.

Third parties organized around specific issues or groups. The **Prohibition party** persistently championed the abolition of alcohol but also introduced many important reform ideas into American politics. Some farmers and workers formed larger but shorter-lived third parties, charging that Republicans and Democrats had failed to respond to economic problems caused by industrialization or, worse still, had deliberately promoted powerful business interests at the expense of ordinary Americans. The **Greenback party** of the 1870s denounced "the infamous financial legislation which takes all from the many to enrich the few." Its policies of labor reform and currency inflation (to stimulate and democratize the economy) attracted supporters from Maine to

Texas. The most significant third party was the **People's** or **Populist party** of the 1890s.

Associational Politics

Associations of like-minded citizens, operating outside the electoral arena, worked to achieve public policies beneficial to their members. Farmers organized the Patrons of Husbandry, known familiarly as the Grange (see Chapter 19). Its campaign for public regulation to control the rates charged by railroads and grain elevators helped convince midwestern states to pass the so-called **Granger laws**. The Grange also sought reforms in the nation's financial system.

To the Grangers' dismay, industrialists also formed pressure groups. Organizations such as the American Iron and Steel Association and the American Protective Tariff League lobbied Congress for high tariff laws and made campaign contributions to friendly politicians of both parties. A small group of conservative reformers known derisively as **Mugwumps** (the term derives from the Algonquian word for *chief*) devoted most of their efforts to campaigning for honest and efficient government through civil service reform. They organized the National Civil Service Reform League to publicize their plans, lobby Congress and state legislatures, and endorse sympathetic candidates.

Women were also active in associational politics. Susan B. Anthony and others formed groups to lobby Congress and state legislatures for constitutional amendments extending the right to vote to women. The leading organizations merged in 1890 as the **National American Woman Suffrage Association**. Despite the opposition of male politicians of both major parties, suffragists had succeeded by the mid-1890s in gaining full woman suffrage in four western states—Wyoming, Colorado, Idaho, and Utah—and partial suffrage (the right to vote in school elections) in several other states, east and west.

With petition campaigns, demonstrations, and lobbying, women's social service organizations sought to remedy poverty and disease, improve education and recreation, and provide day nurseries for the children of workingwomen. The Illinois Woman's Alliance, organized in 1888 by suffragists, women assemblies of the Knights of Labor, and middle-class women's clubs, investigated the conditions of women and children in workshops and factories and campaigned for protective labor legislation and compulsory school attendance laws.

The Woman's Christian Temperance Union (WCTU) gained a massive membership campaigning for restrictive liquor laws. Under the leadership of Frances Willard, however, it inserted domestic issues into the political sphere with a campaign for social and economic reforms far beyond temperance. It particularly sought to strengthen and enforce laws against rape. Willard bitterly noted that twenty states fixed the age of consent at 10 and that "in Massachusetts and Vermont it is a greater crime to steal a cow" than to rape a woman. The WCTU also pushed for improved health conditions and workplace and housing reforms.

The Limits of Government

Despite enthusiasm for politics and the activity of associations, government in the late nineteenth century was neither active nor productive by present standards. The receding government activism of the Civil War and Reconstruction years coincided with a resurgent belief in localism and laissez-faire policies. In addition, a Congress and presidency divided between the two major parties, a small and inefficient bureaucracy, and judicial restraints joined powerful private interests to limit the size and objectives of the federal government.

The Weak Presidency

The presidency was a weak and restricted institution. The impeachment of President Johnson at the outset of Reconstruction had undermined the office. Then President Grant left it clearly subordinate to the legislative branch by deferring to Congress on appointments and legislation. And the men who filled the office between 1877 and 1897—Republicans Rutherford B. Hayes (1877–1881), James A. Garfield (1881), and Chester A. Arthur (1881–1885), Democrat Grover Cleveland (1885–1889 and 1893–1897), and Republican Benjamin Harrison (1889–1893)—were all conservatives with a narrow view of the presidency and proposed few initiatives. The most aggressive of them, Cleveland, vetoed two-thirds of all the bills Congress passed, more than all his predecessors combined. Vetoing a relief measure for drought-stricken Texas farmers, Cleveland stated, "though the people support the Government, the Government should not support the people."

Presidents of the post-Reconstruction era made little effort to reach out to the public or to exert legislative leadership. In 1885, Woodrow Wilson, at the time a professor of history and government, described "the business of the president" as "not much above routine" and concluded that the office might "not inconveniently" be made purely administrative, its occupant a sort of tenured civil servant. (Wilson took a very different view when he became president himself in 1913.) Benjamin Harrison devoted as many as six hours a day to dealing with office seekers, and Garfield lamented, "My day is frittered away by the personal seeking of people, when it ought to be given to the great problems which concern the whole country."

The presidency was also hampered by its limited control over bureaus and departments and by its small staff, which consisted of no more than half a dozen secretaries, clerks, and telegraphers. As Cleveland complained, "If the President has any great policy in mind or on hand he has no one to help him work it out."

The Inefficient Congress

Congress exercised authority over the federal budget, oversaw the cabinet, debated public issues, and controlled legislation. Its members, as one senator conceded, "tolerated no intrusion from the President or from anybody else."

But Congress was scarcely efficient. Its chambers were noisy and chaotic, and members rarely devoted their attention to the business at hand. Instead they played cards, read newspapers, or sent a page to get fruit or tobacco from the vendors who lined the hallways of the capitol. The repeated shifts in party control of Congress also impeded effective action. So too did the loss of experienced legislators to rapid turnover. In some Congresses, a majority of members were first-termers.

Procedural rules often kept Congress from acting. The most notorious rule required that a quorum be not only present but voting. When the House was narrowly divided along party lines, the minority could block all business simply by refusing to answer when the roll was called.

But as a nationalizing economy required more national legislation, business before Congress grew relentlessly (see Figure 22-1). The expanding scale of congressional work prompted a gradual reform of procedures and the centralization of power in the speaker of the House and the leading committees. These changes did not, however, create a coherent program for government action.

The Federal Bureaucracy and the Spoils System

The federal bureaucracy remained small and limited in the late nineteenth century. There were little more than fifty thousand government employees in 1871, and three-fourths of them were local post-

Figure 22-1   *Increase in Congressional Business, 1871–1901*
Industrialization, urbanization, and western expansion brought increased demands for government action, but the party stalemate, laissez-faire attitudes, and inefficient public institutions often blocked effective responses.

masters scattered across the nation. Only six thousand, from President Grant to janitors, worked in Washington.

Most federal employees were selected under the so-called spoils system. Its basic principle was that victorious politicians awarded government jobs to party workers, with little regard for qualifications, and ousted the previous employees. Appointees then typically promised part of their salary and time to the political interests of their patron or party. The spoils system enabled party leaders to strengthen their organizations, reward loyal party service, and attract the political workers that parties needed to mobilize the electorate.

Critics charged that the system was riddled with corruption, abuse, and inefficiency. Rapid turnover bred instability; political favoritism bred incompetence. One secretary of the navy, appointed at the behest of Indiana's Republican machine, was said to have exclaimed during his first official inspection of a ship: "Why, the thing's hollow!" Certainly the spoils system was ineffective for filling positions that required special skills. More serious, the spoils system also absorbed the president and Congress in unproductive conflicts over patronage.

Inconsistent State Government

Considered closer and more responsible to the people, state governments had long exercised police power and regulatory authority. They collected taxes for education and public works, and they promoted private enterprise and public health. Still, they did little by today's standards. Few people thought it appropriate for government at any level to offer direct help to particular social groups, and state constitutions often restricted the scope of public authority.

But state governments gradually expanded their role in response to the stresses produced by industrialization. Following the lead of Massachusetts in 1869, a majority of states had by the turn of the century created commissions to investigate and regulate industry. One observer complained in 1887 that state governments enacted many laws and established numerous state agencies in "utter disregard of the *laissez-faire* principle." In Minnesota, for example, the state helped dairy farmers by establishing a dairy commission, prohibiting the manufacture or sale of margarine, creating a bureau of animal industry, and employing state veterinarians. Other laws regulated railroads, telegraphs, and dangerous occupations, prohibited racial discrimination in inns, and otherwise protected the public welfare.

Not all such agencies and laws were effective. Southern states especially lagged, and one Midwesterner complained that his legislature merely "meets in ignorance, sits in corruption, and dissolves in disgrace every two years." Still, the widening scope of state action represented a growing acceptance of public responsibility for social welfare and economic life.

Public Policies and National Elections

Several great issues dominated the national political arena in the late nineteenth century, including civil service reform, tariffs, and business and financial regulation. Rarely, however, did these issues clearly and consistently separate the major political parties. Instead they divided each party into factions along regional, interest, and economic lines. As a consequence, these leading issues often played only a small role in determining elections and were seldom resolved by government action.

Civil Service Reform

Reform of the spoils system emerged as a prominent issue during the Hayes administration. Reformers like the Mugwumps wanted a professional civil service based on merit and divorced from politics. They wanted officeholders to be selected on the basis of competitive written examinations and protected from removal on political grounds. They expected such a system to promote efficiency, economy, and honesty

in government. But they also expected it to increase their own influence and minimize that of "mere politicians." As one Baltimore Mugwump said, civil service reform would replace ignorant and corrupt officeholders with "gentlemen . . . who need nothing and want nothing from government except the satisfaction of using their talents."

President Hayes favored civil service reform. He struck a blow for change when he fired Chester A. Arthur from his post as New York customs house collector after an investigation pronounced Arthur's patronage system to be "unsound in principle, dangerous in practice, . . . and calculated to encourage and perpetuate the official ignorance, inefficiency, and corruption which, perverting the powers of Government to personal and party ends, have burdened the country."

The weakness of the civil service reformers was dramatically underscored in 1880 when the Republicans, to improve their chances of carrying the crucial state of New York, nominated Arthur for vice president on a presidential slate headed by James A. Garfield of Ohio. They won, and Garfield immediately found himself enmeshed in the demands of the unreformed spoils system. He once complained to his wife, "I had hardly arrived before the door-bell began to ring and the old stream of office-seekers began to pour in. They had scented my coming and were lying in wait for me like vultures for a wounded bison. All day long it has been a steeple chase, I fleeing and they pursuing." Within a few months of his inauguration in 1881, Garfield was assassinated by a disappointed and crazed office seeker, and Arthur became president.

Public dismay over this tragedy finally spurred changes in the spoils system. Arthur himself urged Congress to act on the problem. In 1883, it passed the **Pendleton Civil Service Act**, which prohibited federal employees from soliciting or receiving political contributions from government workers and created the Civil Service Commission to administer competitive examinations to applicants for government jobs. A professional civil service free from partisan politics gradually emerged, strengthening the executive branch's ability to handle its increasing administrative responsibilities.

The new emphasis on merit and skill rather than party ties opened new opportunities to women. By the early 1890s, women held a third of the clerical positions in the executive departments in Washington. Their work in public life challenged the conventional belief that a woman's ability and personality limited her to the domestic sphere. Julia Henderson described her work as an examiner of accounts in

SUMMARY

ARGUMENTS IN THE TARIFF DEBATES

Area Affected	High-Tariff Advocates	Low-Tariff Advocates
Industry	Tariffs promote industrial growth.	Tariffs inflate corporate profits.
Employment	Tariffs stimulate job growth.	Tariffs restrict competition.
Wages and prices	Tariffs permit higher wages.	Tariffs increase consumer prices.
Government	Tariffs provide government revenue.	Tariffs violate the principle of laissez-faire and produce revenues that tempt the government to activism.
Trade	Tariffs protect the domestic market.	Tariffs restrict foreign trade.

the Interior Department in 1893 as "brain work of a character that requires a knowledge not only of the rulings of this Department, but also those of the Treasury, Second Auditor, Second Comptroller, and Revised Statutes; demanding the closest and most critical attention, together with a great deal of legal and business knowledge."

The Political Life of the Tariff

Tariffs on imported goods provided revenue for the federal government and protected American industry from European competition. They promoted industrial growth but often allowed favored industries to garner high profits. By the 1880s, separate tariffs covered more than four thousand items and generated more revenue than the government needed to carry on its limited operations.

Reflecting its commitment to industry, the Republican party vigorously championed protective tariffs. Party leaders also claimed that American labor benefited from tariff protection. "Reduce the tariff, and labor is the first to suffer," declared William McKinley of Ohio. Most Democrats, by contrast, favored tariff reduction. They argued that lower tariffs would encourage foreign trade and, by reducing the treasury surplus, minimize the temptation for the government to pursue activist policies. (See the summary table "Arguments in the Tariff Debates".)

Regardless of party position, congressmen of both parties voted for tariffs that would benefit their districts. California Democrats called for protective duties on wool and raisins, products produced in California; Massachusetts Republicans, to aid their state's shoe manufacturers, supported tariffs on shoes but opposed tariffs on leather. A Democratic senator from Indiana, elected on a campaign pledge to reduce tariffs, summed up the prevailing rule succinctly: "I am a protectionist for every interest which I am sent here by my constituents to protect."

In the 1884 campaign, Republican presidential candidate James G. Blaine maintained that prosperity and high employment depended on high duties. The Democrats' platform endorsed a lowered tariff, but their candidate, Grover Cleveland, generally ignored the issue, and both parties turned to scandalmongering. The Democrats exploited Blaine's image as a beneficiary of the spoils system. Republicans responded by exposing Cleveland as the father of an illegitimate child.

Cleveland continued to avoid the tariff issue for three years after his election, until the growing treasury surplus and rising popular pressure for tariff reduction prompted him to act. He devoted his entire 1887 annual message to attacking the "vicious, inequitable, and illogical" tariff, apparently making it the dominant issue of his 1888 reelection campaign. However, Cleveland then proposed a Democratic platform that ignored his recent message and did not even use the word *tariff*. When the party convention adopted a tariff reduction plank, Cleveland named high-tariff advocates to manage his campaign. "What a predicament the party is placed in," lamented one Texas Democrat, with tariff reform "for its battle cry and with a known protectionist . . . as our chairman." Cleveland won slightly more popular votes than his Republican opponent, Benjamin Harrison of Indiana, but Harrison carried the electoral college, indicating the decisive importance of strategic campaigning, local issues, and large campaign funds over great national issues.

The triumphant Republicans raised tariffs to unprecedented levels with the **McKinley Tariff Act** of 1890. The law provoked a popular backlash that helped return the Democrats to power. Still, the Democrats made little effort to push tariff reform. The *Atlanta Constitution* mused about such tariff politics in a bit of doggerel:

It's funny 'bout this tariff—how they've lost it or forgot;
They were rushing it to Congress once; their collars were so hot
They could hardly wait to fix it 'till we harvested a crop;
Was it such a burnin' question that they had to let it drop?

The Beginnings of Federal Regulation

Popular pressure compelled Congress to take the first steps toward the regulation of business with the passage of the **Interstate Commerce Act** in 1887 and the **Sherman Antitrust Act** in 1890.

Farmers condemned the power of corporations over transportation facilities and their monopolization of agriculture-related industries ranging from those that manufactured agricultural machinery to those that ran flour mills. Small business owners condemned the power of corporations to drive them out of business. Workers suffered from low wages and poor working conditions. Consumers felt victimized by high prices. The result was a growing clamor to rein the corporations in.

The first target of this concern was the nation's railroads, the preeminent symbol of big business. Farm groups like the Grange and business shippers complained of the discriminatory rates, lower for big shippers and higher for small shippers. They and other consumers also condemned the railroads' use of pooling arrangements to suppress competition and raise rates. The resulting pressure was responsible for the Granger laws enacted in several midwestern states in the 1870s to regulate railroad freight and storage rates.

In 1886, the Supreme Court ruled in *Wabash, St. Louis, and Pacific Railway Company* v. *Illinois* that only the federal government could regulate interstate commerce. This decision effectively ended state regulation of railroads but simultaneously increased popular pressure for congressional action. "Upon no public question are the people so nearly unanimous as upon the proposition that Congress should undertake in some way the regulation of interstate business," concluded a Senate committee. With the support of both major parties, Congress in 1887 passed the Interstate Commerce Act.

The act prohibited rebates, discriminatory rates, and pooling and established the **Interstate Commerce Commission (ICC)** to investigate and prosecute violations. The ICC was the first federal regulatory agency. But its powers were too limited to be effective. Senator Nelson Aldrich of Rhode Island, a leading spokesman for business interests, described the law as an "empty menace to great interests, made to answer the clamor of the ignorant." The railroads continued their objectionable practices. In its first fifteen years, only one court case was decided in favor of the ICC. Not surprisingly, then, popular dissatisfaction with the railroads continued into the twentieth century.

As with railroad regulation, the first antitrust laws—laws intended to break up or regulate corporate monopolies—were passed by states. Exposés of the monopolistic practices of such corporations as Standard Oil forced both major parties to endorse national antitrust legislation. In 1890, Congress enacted the Sherman Antitrust Act with only a single vote in opposition. Although it emphatically prohibited any combination in restraint of trade, any attempt to restrict competition, it was otherwise vaguely written and hence weak in its ability to prevent abuses. The courts further weakened it, and presidents of both parties made little effort to enforce it. Large corporations remained an ominous threat in the eyes of many Americans.

The Money Question

Persistent wrangling over questions of currency and coinage made monetary policy the most divisive political issue in the late nineteenth century. President Garfield hinted at the complexities of this subject when he wryly suggested that a member of Congress had been committed to an asylum after "he devoted himself almost exclusively to the study of the currency, became fully entangled with the theories of the subject, and became insane."

Creditors, especially bankers, as well as conservative economists and many business leaders favored limiting the money supply. They called this a **sound money** policy and insisted that it would ensure economic stability, maintain property values, and retain investor confidence. Farmers and other debtors feared this would depress already low crop prices, drive debtors further into debt, and restrict economic opportunities. They favored expanding the money supply to match the country's growing population and economy. They expected this inflationary policy to raise prices, stimulate the economy, reduce debt burdens, and increase opportunities.

The conservative leadership of both major parties supported the sound money policy, but their rank-and-file membership, especially in the West and the South, included many inflationists. As a result, the parties avoided confronting each other on the money issue.

The conflict between advocates of sound money and inflation centered on the use of paper money—"greenbacks"—and silver coinage. To meet its expenses during the Civil War, the federal government issued $450 million in greenbacks—paper money backed only by the credit of the United States, not by gold or silver, the traditional basis of currency. After the war, creditors demanded that these greenbacks be withdrawn from circulation. Debtors and other Americans caught up in a postwar depression favored retaining the greenbacks and even expanding their use.

In 1874, Congress passed a bill to increase the supply of greenbacks, but President Grant vetoed it. The following year, sound money advocates enacted a deflationary law that withdrew some greenbacks from circulation and required that the remainder be convertible into gold after 1878. Outraged inflationists organized the Greenback party. The Greenbackers polled more than a million votes in 1878 and elected fourteen members of Congress, nearly gaining the balance of power in the House. As the depression faded, however, so did interest in the greenback issue, and the party soon withered.

Inflationists then turned their attention to the silver issue, which would prove more enduring and disruptive. Historically, the United States had used both gold and silver as the basis of its currency. But in 1873, Congress passed a law "demonetizing" silver, making gold the only standard for American currency. Gold standard supporters hoped the law would promote international trade by aligning U.S. financial policy with that of Great Britain, which insisted on gold-based currency. But they also wanted to prevent new silver discoveries in the American West from expanding the money supply.

Indeed, silver production soon boomed, flooding the commercial market and dropping the value of the metal. Dismayed miners wanted the Treasury Department to purchase their surplus silver on the old terms and demanded a return to the bimetallic system. More important, the rural debtor groups seeking currency inflation joined in this demand. Many passionately denounced the "Crime of '73" as a conspiracy of eastern bankers and foreign interests to control the money system to the detriment of ordinary Americans.

Eastern conservatives of both parties denounced silver; Southerners and Westerners demanded **free silver**, which meant unlimited silver coinage. By 1878, a bipartisan coalition succeeded in passing the **Bland-Allison Act**. This compromise measure required the government to buy at least $2 million of silver a month. However, the government never exceeded the minimum, and the law had little inflationary effect.

As hard times hit rural regions in the late 1880s, inflationists secured the passage of the **Sherman Silver Purchase Act** of 1890. The Treasury now had to buy more silver and pay for it with Treasury notes redeemable in either gold or silver. But this too produced little inflation because the government did not coin the silver it purchased, redeemed the notes only with gold, and, as western silver production increased further, had to spend less and less to buy the stipulated amount of silver. Debtors of both parties remained convinced that the government favored the "classes rather than the masses." Gold standard advocates (again of both parties) were even less happy with the law and planned to repeal it at their first opportunity.

The Crisis of the 1890s

In the 1890s, a third-party political challenge generated by agricultural discontent disrupted traditional party politics. A devastating depression spawned social misery and labor violence. Changing public attitudes led to new demands on the government and a realignment of parties and voters.

Agricultural Protest

In the late 1880s, falling crop prices and rising debt overwhelmed many people already exhausted from overwork and alarmed by the new corporate order. "At the age of 52 years, after a long life of toil, economy, and self-denial, I find myself and family virtual paupers," lamented one Kansan. Their farm, rather than being "a house of refuge for our declining years, by a few turns of the monopolistic crank has been rendered valueless." To a large extent, the farmers' plight was the result of bad weather and an international overproduction of farm products. Looking for remedies, however, the farmers focused on the inequities of railroad discrimination, tariff favoritism, a restrictive financial system, and apparently indifferent political parties.

Disgruntled farmers particularly singled out the systems of money and credit that worked so completely against agricultural interests. Government rules for national banks directed credit into the urbanized areas of the North and East at the expense of the rural South and West and prohibited banks from making loans on farm property and real estate. In the West, farmers borrowed money from mortgage companies to buy land and machinery. In hard times, mortgage foreclosures crushed the hopes of many farmers. In the South, the credit shortage interacted with the practices of cotton marketing and retail trade to create the sharecropping system, which trapped more and more farmers, black and white, in a vicious pattern of exploitation. The government's policies of monetary deflation then worsened the debt burden under which all such farmers struggled.

Farmers also protested railroad freight rates that were two or three times higher in the West and South than in the North and East. The near-monopolistic control of grain elevators and cotton brokerages left farmers feeling exploited. Protective tariff rates on agricultural machinery and other manufactured goods further raised their costs. The failure of the government to correct these inequities capped their anger.

In response, farmers turned to the Farmers' Alliance, the era's greatest popular movement of protest and reform. Originating in Texas, the Southern Farmers' Alliance spread throughout the South and across the Great Plains to the Pacific coast. By 1890, it had 1.2 million members. African-American farmers organized the Colored Farmers' Alliance. The Northwestern Farmers' Alliance spread westward and northward from Illinois to Nebraska and Minnesota. In combination, these groups constituted a massive grass-roots movement committed to an agenda of economic and ultimately political reform.

The Farmers' Alliance restricted its membership to men and women of the "producing class" and urged them to stand "against the encroachments of monopolies and in opposition to the growing corruption of wealth and power." The Alliance attempted to establish farmers' cooperatives to market crops and purchase supplies. It also developed ingenious proposals to remedy rural credit and currency problems. In the South, the Alliance pushed the subtreasury system, which called on the government to warehouse farmers' cotton and advance them credit based on the cotton's value (see Chapter 19). In the West, the Alliance proposed a system of federal loans to farmers using land as security. These proposals were immensely popular among farmers, but the major parties and Congress rejected them. The Alliance also took up earlier calls for free silver, government control of railroads, and banking reform, again to no avail. William A. Peffer, the influential editor of the Alliance newspaper the *Kansas Farmer*, declared that the "time has come for action. The people will not consent to wait longer. . . . The future is full of retribution for delinquents."

The People's Party

In the West, discontented agrarians organized independent third parties, which eventually adopted the labels "People's" or "Populist." The founders of the Kansas People's Party, including members of the Farmers' Alliance, the Knights of Labor, the Grange, and the old Greenback party, launched a campaign, marked by grim determination and fierce rhetoric. These people, women as well as men, were earnest organizers and powerful orators. One was *Kansas Farmer* editor Peffer. Others included "Sockless Jerry" Simpson, Annie Diggs, and Mary E. Lease. When hostile business and political leaders attacked the Populist plans as socialistic, Lease retorted, "You may call me an anarchist, a socialist, or a communist. I care not, but I hold to the theory that if one man has not enough to eat three times a day and another has $25,000,000, that last man has something that belongs to the first." Lease spoke as clearly against the colonial status experienced by the South and West: "The great common people of this country are slaves, and monopoly is the master. The West and South are bound and prostrate before the manufacturing East."

The Populist parties gained control of the legislatures of Kansas and Nebraska and won congressional elections in Kansas, Nebraska, and Minnesota. Their victories contributed to a massive defeat of the GOP in the 1890 midterm elections after the passage of the McKinley Tariff and the Sherman Silver Purchase Act. Thereafter, Populists gained further victories throughout the West. In the mountain states, where their support came more from miners than farmers, they won governorships in Colorado and Montana. On the Pacific coast, angry farmers found allies among urban workers and the Populists elected a governor in Washington, congressmen in California, and legislators in both states.

In Oklahoma, the Populist party drew support from homesteaders and tenant farmers; in Arizona, from miners and railroad workers. In New Mexico, the Southern Alliance established itself among small ranchers who felt threatened by corporate ranchers and land companies. The fear of corporate expansion even united usually antagonistic Anglo New Mexicans and poor Hispanics. One Alliance paper wrote of the need to defend Hispanics from the "mighty land monopoly which is surely grinding their bones into flour that it may make its bread." In the 1890 election, Populists gained the balance of power in the New Mexico legislature.

In the South, the Alliance did not initially form third parties but instead swept "Alliance Democrats" into office, electing four governors, several dozen members of Congress, and a majority of legislators in eight states.

With their new political power, farmers enacted reform legislation in many western states. New laws regulated banks and railroads and protected poor debtors by capping interest rates and restricting mortgage foreclosures. Others protected unions and mandated improved workplace conditions. Populists were also instrumental in winning woman suffrage in Colorado and Idaho, although the united opposition of Democrats and Republicans blocked their efforts to win it in other states. In the South, however, the Democratic party frustrated reform, and most Alliance Democrats abandoned their promise to support Alliance goals in favor of loyalty to their party and its traditional opposition to governmental activism.

Populists met in Omaha, Nebraska, on July 4, 1892, to organize a national party and nominated former Greenbacker James B. Weaver for president. The party platform, known as the **Omaha Platform**, rejected the laissez-faire policies of the old parties and declared: "We believe that the powers of government—in other words, of the people, should be expanded . . . to the end that oppression, injustice, and poverty shall eventually cease in the land." The platform demanded government ownership of the railroads and the telegraph and telephone systems, a national currency issued by the government rather than private banks, the subtreasury system, free and unlimited silver coinage, a graduated income tax, and the redistribution to settlers of land held by railroads and speculative corporations. Accompanying resolutions endorsed the direct popular election of senators, the secret ballot, and other electoral reforms to make government more democratic and responsive to popular wishes. When the platform was adopted, "cheers and yells," one reporter wrote, "rose like a tornado from four thousand throats and raged without cessation for 34 minutes, during which women shrieked and wept, men embraced and kissed their neighbors . . . in the ecstasy of their delirium" (see "American Views: The Populist View of America").

The Populists left Omaha to begin an energetic campaign. Southern Democrats, however, used violence and fraud to intimidate Populist voters and cheat Populist candidates out of office. Some local Populist leaders were murdered. One Democrat confessed that Alabama's Populist gubernatorial candidate "carried the state, but was swindled out of his victory . . . with unblushing trickery and corruption." Southern Democrats also appealed effectively to white supremacy, which undermined the Populist effort to build a biracial reform coalition.

Midwestern farmers unfamiliar with Alliance ideas and organization ignored Populist appeals and stood by their traditional political allegiances. So did most eastern working-class voters, who learned little of the Populist program beyond its demand for inflation, which they feared would hurt them.

The Populists lost the election but got more than a million votes (one out of every twelve votes cast). Populist leaders began immediately working to expand their support, to the alarm of both southern Democrats and northern Republicans.

The Challenge of the Depression

A harsh and lengthy depression began in 1893, cruelly worsening conditions not only for farmers but for most other Americans as well. Labor unrest and violence engulfed the nation, reflecting workers' distress but frightening more comfortable Americans. The persistent failure of the major parties to respond to serious problems contributed mightily to growing popular discontent.

Although the Populists had not triumphed in 1892, the election nonetheless reflected the nation's spreading dissatisfaction. President Harrison and his fellow Republicans in Congress had been decisively defeated; Democrat Grover Cleveland had been returned to the White House. Almost oblivious to the mounting demand for reform, Cleveland delivered an inaugural address championing the doctrine of laissez-faire and rejecting government action to solve social or economic problems.

The economy collapsed in the spring of 1893. Railroad overexpansion, a weak banking system, tight credit, and plunging agricultural prices all contributed to the disaster. A depression in Europe reduced American export markets and prompted British investors to sell their American investments for gold. Hundreds of banks closed, and thousands of businesses, including the nation's major railroads, went bankrupt. By winter, 20 percent of the labor force was unemployed, and the jobless scavenged for food in a country that had no public unemployment or welfare programs. "Never within memory," said

American Views

THE POPULIST VIEW OF AMERICA

Meeting in Omaha, Nebraska, on July 4, 1892, the Populists organized a protest party representing the aggrieved farmers of the West and South. They adopted a platform indicting the economic and political conditions of their time. The following is from the preamble of the Omaha Platform.

❖ **In what ways did the Populists believe that the course of industrialization and the distribution of political power threatened traditional American values?**

❖ **How would Populists respond to an argument about the necessity for laissez-faire?**

❖ **Why did the Populists think a third party was necessary?**

Assembled upon the 116th anniversary of the Declaration of Independence, the People's Party of America, in their first national convention, invoking upon their action the blessing of Almighty God, puts forth, in the name and on behalf of the people of this country, the following preamble and declaration of principles:

The conditions which surround us best justify our cooperation: we meet in the midst of a nation brought to the verge of moral, political, and material ruin. Corruption dominates the ballot-box, the legislatures, the Congress, and touches even the ermine of the bench. The people are demoralized; most of the states have been compelled to isolate the voters at the polling-places to prevent universal intimidation or bribery. The newspapers are largely subsidized or muzzled; public opinion silenced; business prostrated; our homes covered with mortgages; labor impoverished; and the land concentrating in the hands of the capitalists. The urban workmen are denied the right of organization for self-protection; imported pauperized labor beats down their wages; a hireling standing army, unrecognized by our laws, is established to shoot them down, and they are rapidly degenerating into European conditions. The fruits of the toil of millions are boldly stolen to build up colossal fortunes for a few, unprece-

---

one New York minister, "have so many people literally starved to death as in the past few months."

Most state governments offered little relief beyond encouraging private charity to the homeless. In Kansas, however, the Populist governor insisted that traditional laissez-faire policies were inappropriate in industrialized America: "It is the duty of government to protect the weak, because the strong are able to protect themselves." Cleveland disagreed. The functions of the government, he said in 1893, "do not include the support of the people."

Jacob Coxey, a Populist businessman from Ohio, proposed a government public works program for the unemployed to be financed with paper money. This plan would improve the nation's infrastructure, create jobs for the unemployed, and provide an infla-tionary stimulus to counteract the depression's deflationary effects. In short, Coxey was advocating positive government action to combat the depression.

Coxey organized a march of the unemployed to Washington as "a petition with boots on" to support his ideas. **Coxey's Army** of the unemployed, as the excited press dubbed it, marched through the industrial towns of Ohio and Pennsylvania and into Maryland, attracting attention and support. Other armies formed in eastern cities from Boston to Baltimore and set out for the capital. Some of the largest armies organized in the western cities of Denver, San Francisco, and Seattle. Three hundred men in an army from Oakland elected as their commander Anna Smith, who promised to "land my men on the steps of the Capitol at Washington." "I am a San dented in the history of mankind; and the possessors of these, in turn, despise the Republic and endanger liberty. From the same prolific womb of governmental injustice we breed two great classes—tramps and millionaires.

. . . We have witnessed for more than a quarter of a century the struggles of the two great political parties for power and plunder, while grievous wrongs have been inflicted upon the suffering people. We charge that the controlling influences dominating both these parties have permitted the existing dreadful conditions to develop without serious effort to prevent or restrain them. Neither do they now promise us any substantial reform. They have agreed together to ignore in the coming campaign every issue but one. They propose to drown the outcries of a plundered people with the uproar of a sham battle over the tariff, so that capitalists, corpora-

tions, national banks, rings, trusts, watered stock, the demonetization of silver, and the oppressions of the usurers may all be lost sight of. They propose to sacrifice our homes, lives, and children on the altar of mammon; to destroy the multitude in order to secure corruption funds from the millionaires. . . .

We pledge ourselves, if given power, we will labor to correct these evils by wise and reasonable legislation, in accordance with the terms of our platform. We believe that the powers of government—in other words, of the people—should be expanded (as in the case of the postal service) as rapidly and as far as the good sense of an intelligent people and the teachings of experience shall justify, to the end that oppression, injustice, and poverty shall eventually cease in the land.

Source: *Edward McPherson, A Handbook of Politics for 1892 (1892).*

Francisco woman, a woman who has been brought up on this coast, and I'm not afraid of anything," Smith explained. "I have a woman's heart and a woman's sympathy, and these lead me to do what I have done for these men, even though it may not be just what a woman is expected to do."

Despite public sympathy for Coxey, the government acted to suppress him. When he reached Washington with 600 marchers, police and soldiers arrested him and his aides, beat sympathetic bystanders in a crowd of twenty thousand, and herded the marchers into detention camps. Unlike the lobbyists for business and finance, Coxey was not permitted to reach Congress to deliver his statement, urging the government to assist "the poor and oppressed."

The depression also provoked labor turmoil. There were some 1,400 industrial strikes involving nearly 700,000 workers in 1894. One result was the government's violent suppression of the Pullman strike (see Chapter 20).

In a series of decisions in 1895, the Supreme Court strengthened the bonds between business and government. First, it upheld the use of a court-ordered injunction to break the Pullman strike. As a result, injunctions became a major weapon for courts and corporations against labor unions until Congress finally limited their use in 1932. In *United States* v. *E. C. Knight Company*, the Court gutted the Sherman Antitrust Act by ruling that manufacturing, as opposed to commerce, was beyond the reach of federal regulation. The American Sugar Refining Com-

Jacob Coxey's "Army" of the unemployed marches to Washington, D.C., in 1894. Many such "industrial armies" were organized during the depressed 1890s, revealing dissatisfaction with traditional politics and limited government.

pany, a trust controlling 90 percent of the nation's sugar, was allowed to retain its great power. Finally, the court invalidated an income tax that agrarian Democrats and Populists had maneuvered through Congress as an "assault upon capital." Not until 1913, and then only with an amendment to the Constitution, would it be possible to adopt an equitable system of taxation.

Cleveland's financial policies stirred further discontent. Cleveland blamed the economic collapse on the Sherman Silver Purchase Act, which he regarded as detrimental to business confidence and a threat to the nation's gold reserve. He persuaded Congress in 1893 to repeal the law but thereby enraged southern and western members of his own party, including William Jennings Bryan of Nebraska, who saw the silver issue in the context of a struggle between "the corporate interests of the United States, the moneyed interests, aggregated wealth and capital, imperious, arrogant, compassionless" and "an unnumbered throng . . . work-worn and dust-begrimed."

By 1894, the Treasury had begun borrowing money from Wall Street to bolster the gold reserve. These transactions benefited a syndicate of bankers headed by J. P. Morgan. It seemed to critics that an indifferent Cleveland was helping rich bankers profit from the nation's economic agony. "A set of vampires headed by a financial trust has control of our

destiny," cried one rural newspaper.

The Battle of the Standards and the Election of 1896

These unpopular actions, coupled with the unrelenting depression, alienated workers and farmers from the Cleveland administration and the Democratic party. In the off-year elections of 1894, the Democrats suffered the greatest loss of congressional seats in American history. Populists increased their vote by 42 percent, making especially significant gains in the South, but the real beneficiaries of Cleveland's unpopularity were the Republicans, who gained solid control of Congress as well as state governments across the North and West. All three parties began to plan for the presidential election of 1896.

The silver issue came to overshadow all others. Populist Weaver declared the silver issue "the line upon which the battle should be fought. It is the line of least resistance and we should hurl our forces against it at every point." Both to undercut the Populists and to distance themselves and their party from the despised Cleveland, leading Democrats began using the silver issue to reorganize their party.

William McKinley, governor of Ohio and author of the McKinley Tariff Act of 1890, emerged as the leader of a crowd of hopeful Republican presidential candidates. His candidacy benefited particularly from the financial backing and political management of Marcus A. Hanna, a wealthy Ohio industrialist. Hanna thought McKinley's passion for high tariffs as the key to revived prosperity would appeal to workers as well as industry and business. Republicans nominated McKinley on the first ballot at their 1896 convention. Their platform called for high tariffs but also endorsed the gold standard, placating eastern delegates but prompting several western Silver Republicans to withdraw from the party.

The Democratic convention met shortly thereafter. With a fervor that conservatives likened to "scenes of the French Revolution," the Silver Democrats revolutionized their party. They adopted a platform that repudiated the Cleveland administration and its policies and endorsed free silver, the income tax, and tighter regulation of trusts and railroads. A magnificent speech supporting this platform by William Jennings Bryan helped convince the delegates to nominate him for president.

Holding their convention last, the Populists now faced a terrible dilemma. The Democratic nomination of Bryan on a silver platform undercut their hopes of attracting into their own ranks disappointed reformers from the major parties. Some Populists urged the party to endorse Bryan rather than split the silver vote and ensure the victory of McKinley and the gold standard. Others argued that fusing—joining with the Democrats—would cost the Populists their separate identity and subordinate their larger political principles to the issue of free silver. After anguished discussion, the Populists nominated Bryan.

The campaign was intense and dramatic, with each side demonizing the other. Eastern financial and business interests contributed millions of dollars to Hanna's campaign for McKinley. Standard Oil alone provided $250,000, about the same amount as the Democrats' total national expenses. Hanna used these funds to organize an unprecedented campaign. Republicans issued 250 million campaign documents, printed in a dozen languages. Many newspapers not only shaped their editorials but distorted their news stories to Bryan's disadvantage.

The Democrats relied on Bryan's superb voice, oratorical virtuosity, and youthful energy. Bryan was the first presidential candidate to campaign systematically for election, speaking hundreds of times to millions of voters. McKinley stayed home in Canton, Ohio, where he conducted a "front porch" campaign. Explaining his refusal to campaign outside Canton, McKinley said, "I might just as well put up a trapeze . . . and compete with some professional athlete as go out speaking against Bryan." But Hanna brought groups of Republicans from all over the country to visit McKinley every day, and McKinley reiterated his simple promise to restore prosperity.

In the depression, that appeal proved enough. As the Democratic candidate, Bryan was ironically burdened with the legacy of the hated Cleveland administration. The intense campaign brought a record voter turnout. McKinley won decisively by capturing the East and Midwest as well as Oregon and California (see Map 22-2). Bryan carried the traditionally Democratic South and the mountain and plains states where Populists and silverites dominated. He failed to gain support in either the Granger states of the Midwest or the cities

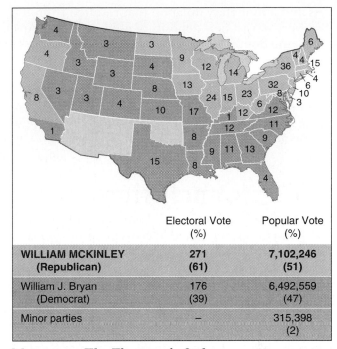

	Electoral Vote (%)	Popular Vote (%)
WILLIAM MCKINLEY **(Republican)**	**271** **(61)**	**7,102,246** **(51)**
William J. Bryan (Democrat)	176 (39)	6,492,559 (47)
Minor parties	–	315,398 (2)

Map 22-2   The Election of 1896
William Jennings Bryan carried most of the rural South and West, but his free silver campaign had little appeal to more urban and industrial regions, which swung strongly to Republican candidate William McKinley.

of the East. His silver campaign had little appeal to industrial workers. Hanna realized that Bryan was making a mistake in subordinating other popular grievances to silver: "He's talking silver all the time, and that's where we've got him."

The elections of 1894 and 1896 ended the close balance between the major parties. Cleveland's failures, coupled with an economic recovery in the wake of the election of 1896, gained the Republicans a reputation as the party of prosperity and industrial progress, firmly establishing them in power for years to come. By contrast, the Democratic party receded into an ineffectual sectional minority dominated by southern conservatives, despite Bryan's liberal views. The People's party simply dissolved.

McKinley plunged into his presidency. Unlike his predecessors, he had a definite, if limited, program, consisting of tariff protection, sound money, and overseas expansion. He worked actively to see it through Congress and to shape public opinion, thereby helping establish the model of the modern presidency. He had promised prosperity, and it returned, although not because of the record high tariff his party enacted in 1897 or the Currency Act of 1900, which firmly established the gold standard. Prosperity returned instead because of reviving markets and a monetary inflation that resulted from the discovery of vast new deposits of gold in Alaska, Australia, and South Africa. This inflation, ironically, was greater than would have resulted from free silver. An expanding industrial economy, as the silverites recognized, required an expanding money supply. With the return of prosperity and the decline of social tensions, McKinley easily won reelection in 1900, defeating Bryan a second time.

Conclusion

In late-nineteenth-century America, politics and government often seemed at cross-purposes. Closely balanced political parties commanded the zealous support of their constituents and wielded power and influence. The institutions of government, by contrast, were limited in size, scope, and responsibility. A weakened presidency and an inefficient Congress, hampered by a restrictive judiciary, were often unable to resolve the very issues that were so dramatically raised in the political arena. The issue that most reflected this impasse was civil service reform. The patronage system provided the lifeblood of politics but also disrupted government business.

The localism, laissez-faire, and other traditional principles that shaped both politics and government were becoming increasingly inappropriate for America's industrializing society. The national nature of the railroad network, for example, finally brought the federal government into the regulatory arena, however imperfectly, with the Interstate Commerce Act of 1887. Both the depression of the 1890s and the popular discontent underscored the need for change and discredited the limited government of the Cleveland administration.

By the end of the decade, the Republicans had emerged as the dominant party, ending the two-party stalemate of previous decades. Campaign hoopla in local communities had given way to information-based campaigns directed by and through national organizations. A new, activist presidency was emerging. And the disruptive currency issue faded with the hard times that had brought it forth.

Review Questions

1. What were the social and institutional factors that shaped the disorderly nature of elections in the late nineteenth century?

2. What social and institutional factors determined the role of government? How and why did the role of government change during this period?

3. What factors determined the party affiliation of American voters? Why did so many third parties develop during this era?

4. How might the planks of the Omaha Platform have helped solve farmers' troubles?

5. What factors shaped the conduct and outcome of the election of 1896? How did that contest differ from earlier elections?

Recommended Reading

Sean Dennis Cashman, *America in the Gilded Age: From the Death of Lincoln to the Rise of Theodore Roosevelt* (1984). This useful synthesis is written for a general audience.

Paul Glad, *McKinley, Bryan, and the People* (1964). Glad provides an excellent brief analysis of the issues and personalities in the 1896 election.

Morton Keller, *Affairs of State: Public Life in Late Nineteenth Century America* (1977). This is a detailed and fascinating account of the changing dimensions of government and politics.

Robert C. McMath Jr., *American Populism: A Social History, 1877–1898* (1993). This, the best modern history of Populism, is balanced and readable.

R. Hal Williams, *Years of Decision: American Politics in the 1890s* (1978). Scholarship on the political complexities of the 1890s is given a brief and valuable synthesis.

Where to Learn More

❖ **Rest Cottage, Evanston, Illinois.** Frances Willard's home, from which she directed the Woman's Christian Temperance Union, is carefully preserved as a museum. The Willard Memorial Library contains more memorabilia and papers of Willard and the WCTU.

❖ **President Benjamin Harrison Home, Indianapolis, Indiana.** President Harrison's brick Italianate mansion, completed in 1875, has been completely restored with the family's furniture and keepsakes. The former third-floor ballroom serves as a museum with exhibits of many artifacts of the Harrisons' public and private lives.

❖ **Fairview, Lincoln, Nebraska.** A National Historic Landmark, Fairview was the home of William Jennings Bryan, who described it as "the Monticello of the West." Faithfully restored to depict the Bryan family's life in the early 1900s, it includes a museum and interpretive center.

❖ **Rutherford B. Hayes Presidential Center, Fremont, Ohio.** This complex contains President Hayes's home, office, and extensive grounds together with an excellent library and museum holding valuable collections of manuscripts, artifacts, and photographs illustrating his personal interests and political career.

❖ **James A. Garfield Home, Mentor, Ohio.** Operated by the Western Reserve Historical Society as a museum, Garfield's home is the site of his successful 1880 front-porch campaign for president.

23 THE PROGRESSIVE ERA, 1900–1917

KEY TOPICS

❖ The reform movement known as progressivism
❖ Women and progressivism
❖ Accommodation of some aspects of
    progressivism to the antidemocratic strands
    in American society
❖ Strengthening of the executive under the
    moderately progressive Theodore Roosevelt
❖ Climax of progressivism under Woodrow Wilson

omorrow Woodrow Wilson would be inaugurated as the nation's president. But today, March 3, 1913, Washington, D.C., belonged to America's women. Women had poured into the capital from across the country. They came to participate in a great protest parade demanding **woman suffrage**—the right of women to vote—a reform that Woodrow Wilson declined to endorse. Before half a million spectators, the women set out down Pennsylvania Avenue. Behind a banner reading "Women of the World, Unite!" rolled elaborate floats representing countries where women already had the vote. Another column of floats portrayed working women: farmers, wage earners, homemakers, government employees, and professionals, including nurses, teachers, and social workers. Large groups of women paraded with each float. Two hundred striking garment workers fresh from their picket lines in Baltimore marched with a float depicting a sweatshop. In the education division, black women in caps and gowns from Howard University walked with students from Bryn Mawr, Goucher, and other colleges. Nine-month-old Mei Ching Wu, her mother a student at George Washington University, was the parade's youngest member. Bringing up the rear were members of the National Men's League for Woman Suffrage.

Many spectators cheered, but others insulted the suffragists, broke into their ranks, attacked their floats, and blocked their passage. The embattled women fought their way "foot by foot up Pennsylvania Avenue through two walls of antagonistic humanity," reported an astonished observer. They finally gained some help when male supporters counterattacked their assailants. Even so, the parade could not be completed until troops restored order. Hundreds were hospitalized. "No inauguration has ever produced such scenes," noted one reporter, "which in many instances amounted to nothing less than riots."

In the **Progressive Era**, important movements challenged traditional relationships and attitudes—here involving women's role in American life—and often met strong resistance. "Progressives" seeking reforms organized their supporters across lines of class, education, occupation, geography, gender, and, at times, race and ethnicity—as the variety of groups in the suffrage parade demonstrated. Reformers adopted new political techniques, including lobbying and demonstrating, as nonpartisan pressure groups. Reform work begun at the local and state levels—where the suffrage movement had already met some success—inexorably moved to the national level as the federal government expanded its authority and became the focus of political interest. This suffrage demonstration also reveals the exceptional diversity of the progressive movement, for the women marched, in part, against Woodrow Wilson, who had campaigned for the presidency as a progressive.

Progressivism represented the coalescing of different and sometimes even contradictory movements that sought changes in the nation's social, economic, and political life. But reformers did share the beliefs that industrialization and urbanization had produced serious social disorders, from city slums to corporate abuses, and that new ideas and methods were required to correct these problems. In particular, they rejected the ideology of individualism in favor of broader concepts of social responsibility, and they sought to achieve social order through organization and efficiency. Finally, most progressives believed that government itself, as the organized agent of public responsibility, should address social and economic problems. Their achievements, and their failures, profoundly shaped America.

The Ferment of Reform

The diversity of progressivism reflected the diverse impulses of reform. Clergy and professors provided new ideas to guide remedial action. Journalists exposed corporate excesses and government corruption and stirred public demand for reform. Business leaders sought to curtail disorder through efficiency and regulation, while industrial workers struggled to improve the horrible conditions in which they worked and lived. Women organized to protect their families and homes from new threats and even to push beyond such domestic issues. Nearly every movement for change encountered fierce opposition, while also helping America grapple with the problems of industrial society. (See the summary table "Major Progressive Organizations and Groups.")

The Context of Reform: Industrial and Urban Tensions

The origins of progressivism lay in the crises of the new urban-industrial order that emerged in the late nineteenth century. The severe depression and consequent mass suffering of the 1890s, the labor violence and industrial armies, the political challenges of Populism and an ineffective government shattered the complacency many middle-class Americans had felt about their nation and made them aware of social and economic inequities that rural and working-class families had long recognized.

By 1900, a returning prosperity had eased the threat of major social violence (widely feared in the 1890s), but the underlying problems intensified. Big business, which had disrupted traditional economic relationships in the late nineteenth century, suddenly became bigger in a series of mergers between 1897 and 1903. Giant corporations threatened to squeeze opportunities for small firms and workers, dominate markets, and raise social tensions. They also inspired calls for public control.

Most workers still toiled nine to ten hours a day; steelworkers and textile employees usually worked twelve-hour shifts. Wages were minimal; an economist in 1905 calculated that 60 percent of all adult male breadwinners made less than a living wage. Family survival, then, often required women and children to work, often in the lowest-paid, most exploited positions. Southern cotton mills employed children as young as 7; coal mines paid 12-year-old slate pickers 39 cents for a ten-hour day. Dangerous work environments and an absence of safety programs threatened not only workers' health but their lives as well. In 1911 a fire killed 146 workers, most of them young women, trapped inside the factory of the **Triangle Shirtwaist Company** in New York, because management had locked the exits. The fire chief found "skeletons bending over sewing machines." The United States had the highest rate of industrial accidents in the world. Half a million workers were injured and thirty thousand killed at

SUMMARY

MAJOR PROGRESSIVE ORGANIZATIONS AND GROUPS

Group	Activity
Social Gospel movement	Urged churches and individuals to apply Christian ethics to social and economic problems
Muckrakers	Exposed business abuses, public corruption, and social evils through investigative journalism
Settlement House movement	Attempted through social work and public advocacy to improve living and working conditions in urban immigrant communities
National Consumers' League (1898)	Monitored businesses to ensure decent working conditions and safe consumer products
Women's Trade Union League (1903)	United workingwomen and their middle-class "allies" to promote unionization and social reform
National Child Labor Committee (1904)	Campaigned against child labor
Country Life movement	Attempted to modernize rural social and economic conditions according to urban-industrial standards
National American Woman Suffrage Association	Led the movement to give women the right to vote
Municipal reformers	Sought to change the activities and structure of urban government to promote efficiency and control
Conservationists	Favored efficient management and regulation of natural resources rather than uncontrolled development or preservation

work each year. These terrible conditions cried out for reform.

Other Americans saw additional social problems in the continuing flood of immigrants who were transforming America's cities. From 1900 to 1917, more than 14 million immigrants entered the United States, and most became urban dwellers. By 1910, immigrants and their children comprised more than 70 percent of the population of New York, Chicago, Buffalo, Milwaukee, and other cities. Most of the arrivals were so-called **new immigrants** from southern and eastern Europe, rather than the British, Irish, Germans, and Scandinavians who had arrived earlier. Crowding into urban slums, immigrants overwhelmed municipal sanitation, education, and fire protection services. One Russian described his new life as "all filth and sadness."

Ethnic prejudices abounded. Woodrow Wilson, then president of Princeton University, declared in 1902: "The immigrant newcomers of recent years are men of the lowest class from the South of Italy, and men of the meaner sort out of Hungary and Poland, men out of the ranks where there was neither skill nor energy, nor any initiative or quick intelligence." Americans of the **Old Stock** often considered the predominantly Catholic and Jewish newcomers a threat to social stability and cultural identity and so demanded programs to reform either the urban environment or the immigrants themselves.

Church and Campus

Many groups, drawing from different traditions and inspirations, responded to such economic and social issues. Reform-minded Protestant ministers created the **Social Gospel movement**, which sought to introduce religious ethics into industrial relations and appealed to churches to meet their social responsibilities. Washington Gladden, a Congregational minister in Columbus, Ohio, was shocked in 1884 by a

CHRONOLOGY

1893–1898	Depression grips the nation.
1898	South Dakota adopts initiative and referendum.
	National Consumers' League is organized.
1900	Robert La Follette is elected governor of Wisconsin.
1901	United States Steel Corporation is formed, the world's largest business at the time.
	President William McKinley is assassinated; Theodore Roosevelt becomes president.
	Socialist Party of America is organized.
	Galveston, Texas, initiates the city commission plan.
1902	Antitrust suit is filed against Northern Securities Company.
	Mississippi enacts the first direct primary law.
	National Reclamation Act is passed.
	Roosevelt intervenes in coal strike.
1903	Women's Trade Union League is organized.
1904	National Child Labor Committee is formed.
	Roosevelt is elected president.
1905	Industrial Workers of the World is organized.
1906	Hepburn Act strengthens the Interstate Commerce Commission.

	Meat Inspection Act extends government regulation.
	Pure Food and Drug Act is passed.
1908	*Muller* v. *Oregon* upholds maximum workday for women.
	William Howard Taft is elected president.
1909	National Association for the Advancement of Colored People is organized.
1910	Ballinger-Pinchot controversy erupts.
1912	Children's Bureau is established.
	Progressive Party organizes and nominates Roosevelt.
	Woodrow Wilson is elected president.
1913	Sixteenth and Seventeenth Amendments are ratified.
	Underwood-Simmons Tariff Act establishes an income tax.
	Federal Reserve Act creates the Federal Reserve System.
1914	Federal Trade Commission is established.
	Harrison Act criminalizes narcotics.
1915	National Birth Control League is formed.
1916	Keating-Owen Act prohibits child labor.
1917	Congress enacts literacy test for immigrants.
1920	Nineteenth Amendment is ratified.

bloody strike crushed by wealthy members of his own congregation. Gladden began a ministry to working-class neighborhoods that most churches ignored. He endorsed unions and workers' rights and proposed replacing a cruelly competitive wage system with profit sharing.

Social Gospeler Walter Rauschenbusch, a Baptist minister, argued in his book *Christianity and the Social Crisis* (1907) that Christians should support social reform to alleviate poverty, slums, and labor exploitation. He attacked low wages for transforming workers "into lean, sallow, hopeless, stupid, and vicious young people, simply to enable some group of stockholders to earn 10 percent."

The Social Gospel movement flowered mainly among certain Protestant denominations, especially Episcopalians, Congregationalists, and Methodists. It climaxed in 1908 in the formation of the Federal Council of Churches of Christ in America. The council, representing thirty-three religious groups, adopted a program that endorsed welfare and regulatory legislation to achieve social justice. By linking reform with religion (as "applied Christianity," in the words of Washington Gladden), the Social Gospel movement gave progressivism a powerful moral drive that affected much of American life.

The Social Gospel movement provided an ethical justification for government intervention to improve the social order. Scholars in the social sciences such as Lester Ward also called for social progress through rational planning and government intervention rather than through unrestrained and unpredictable competition. Economists rejected laissez-faire principles in favor of state action to accomplish social evolution. Industrialization, declared economist Richard T. Ely, "has brought to the front a vast number of social problems whose solution is impossible without the united efforts of church, state, and science."

Muckrakers

Journalists also spread reform ideas by developing a new form of investigative reporting known as **muckraking**. Samuel S. McClure sent his reporters to uncover political and corporate corruption for *McClure's Magazine*. Sensational exposés sold magazines, and soon *Cosmopolitan, Everybody's,* and other journals began publishing investigations of business abuses, dangerous working conditions, and the miseries of slum life.

Muckraking articles aroused indignant public demands for reform. Lincoln Steffens detailed the corrupt links between "respectable" businessmen and crooked urban politicians in a series of articles called "The Shame of the Cities." Ida Tarbell revealed John D. Rockefeller's sordid construction of Standard Oil. Muckraking novels also appeared. *The Octopus* (1901) by Frank Norris dramatized the Southern Pacific Railroad's stranglehold on California's farmers, and *The Jungle* (1906) by Upton Sinclair exposed nauseating conditions in Chicago's meatpacking industry.

The Gospel of Efficiency

Many progressive leaders believed that efficiency and expertise could control or resolve the disorder of industrial society. President Theodore Roosevelt (1901–1909) praised the "gospel of efficiency." Like many other progressives, he admired corporations' success in applying management techniques to guide economic growth. Drawing from science and technology as well as from the model of the corporation, many progressives attempted to manage or direct change efficiently. They used scientific methods to collect extensive data and relied on experts for analysis and recommendations. "Scientific management" seemed the key to eliminating waste and inefficiency in government, society, and industry. Rural reformers thought that "scientific agriculture" could bring prosperity to the impoverished southern countryside; urban reformers believed that improvements in medical science and the professionalization of physicians through uniform licensing standards could eradicate the cities' wretched public health problems.

Industrialists were drawn to the ideas of Frederick Taylor, a proponent of scientific management. Taylor proposed to increase worker efficiency through imposed work routines, speedups, and mechanization. Workers, Taylor insisted, should "do what they are told promptly and without asking questions. . . . It is absolutely necessary for every man in our organization to become one of a train of gear wheels." By assigning workers simple and repetitive tasks on machines, Taylorization made their skills expendable and enabled managers to control the production, pace of work, and hiring and firing of personnel. When labor complained, one business leader declared that unions failed "to appreciate the progressivism of the age."

Sophisticated managers of big business combinations favored government regulations that could bring about safer and more stable conditions in society and the economy. Government regulations, they reasoned, could reassure potential consumers, open markets, mandate working conditions that smaller competitors could not provide, or impose systematic procedures that competitive pressures would otherwise undercut.

Labor's Demand for Rights

Industrial workers with different objectives also hastened the ferment of reform. Workers resisted the new rules of efficiency experts and called for improved wages and working conditions and reduced work hours. They and their middle-class sympathizers sought to achieve some of these goals through state intervention, demanding laws to compensate workers injured on the job, curb child labor, and regulate the employment of women. After the Triangle Shirtwaist fire, for example, urban politicians with working-class constituencies created the New York State Factory Commission and enacted dozens of laws dealing with fire hazards, machine safety, and wages and hours for women.

Workers also organized unions to improve their lot. The American Federation of Labor (AFL) claimed 4 million members by 1920. But it recruited mainly skilled workers, particularly native-born white males. New unions organized the factories and sweatshops where most immigrants and women worked. Despite strong employer resistance, the International Ladies Garment Workers Union (1900) and the Amalgamated Clothing Workers (1914) organized the garment trades, developed programs for social and economic reforms, and led their members—mostly young Jewish and Italian women—in spectacular strikes. The "Uprising of the 20,000," a 1909 strike in New York City, included months of massive rallies, determined picketing, and police repression. One observer marveled at the women strikers' "emotional endurance, fearlessness, and entire willingness to face danger and suffering."

A still more radical union tried to organize miners, lumberjacks, and Mexican and Japanese farm workers in the West, black dockworkers in the South, and immigrant factory hands in New England. Founded in 1905, the Industrial Workers of the World (IWW), whose members were known as "**Wobblies**," used sit-down strikes, sit-ins, and mass rallies, tactics adopted by other industrial unions in the 1930s and the civil rights movement in the 1960s. "Respectable people" considered the Wobblies violent revolutionaries, but most of the violence was committed against them.

Extending the Woman's Sphere

Women reformers and their organizations played a key role in progressivism. By the early twentieth century, more women than before were working outside the home—in the factories, mills, and sweatshops of the industrial economy and as clerks in stores and offices. In 1910, more than a fourth of all workers were women, increasing numbers of them married. Their importance in the work force and participation in unions and strikes challenged assumptions that woman's "natural" role was to be a submissive housewife.

Often founded for cultural purposes, women's clubs soon began adopting programs for social reform and gave their members a route to public influence. In 1914, an officer of the General Federation of Women's Clubs proudly declared that she could not find a cause for social reform that "has not received a helpful hand from the clubwomen."

Women also joined or created other organizations that pushed beyond the limits of traditional domesticity. By threatening healthy and happy homes, urban problems required that women become "social housekeepers" in the community. The National Congress of Mothers, organized in 1897, worried about crime and disease and championed kindergartens, foster-home programs, juvenile courts, and compulsory school attendance. Led by the crusading Florence Kelley, the National Consumers' League tried to protect both women wage earners and middle-class housewives by monitoring stores and factories to ensure decent working conditions and safe products. The Women's Trade Union League, or WTUL, united working women and their self-styled middle-class "allies" to unionize women workers and eliminate sweatshop conditions. Its greatest success came in the 1909 garment workers' strike when the allies—dubbed by one worker the "mink brigade"—assisted strikers with relief funds, bail money, food supplies, and public relations campaign.

While most progressive women stressed women's special duties and responsibilities as social housekeepers, others began to demand women's equal rights. In 1914, for example, critics of New York's policy of dismissing women teachers who married formed a group called the Feminist Alliance and demanded "the removal of all social, political, economic and other discriminations which are based upon sex, and the award of all rights and duties in all fields on the basis of individual capacity alone."

Socialism

Another force promoting the spirit of progressivism was the growing influence of socialist ideas. Socialists never attracted a large following, even among workers (see Chapter 20), but their criticism of the industrial economy gained increasing attention in the early twentieth century. American socialists condemned social and economic inequities, criticized limited government, and demanded public ownership of railroads, utilities, and communications. They also campaigned for tax reforms, better housing, factory inspections, and recreational facilities for all. Muckrakers like Lincoln Steffens and Upton Sinclair were committed socialists, as were some Social Gospel ministers and labor leaders, but the most prominent socialist was Eugene Debs. In 1901, Debs helped organize the Socialist Party of America. In the next decade, the party won many local elections, especially in Wisconsin and New York, where it drew support from German and Russian immigrants, and in Oklahoma, among poor tenant farmers. Socialism was also promoted by newspapers and magazines, including the *Appeal to Reason* in Girard, Kansas, which had a circulation of 500,000 by 1906.

Most progressives considered socialist ideas too drastic. Nevertheless, socialists contributed importantly to the reform ferment, not only by providing support for reform initiatives but often also by prompting progressives to push for some changes to undercut increasingly attractive radical alternatives.

Opponents of Reform

Not all Americans supported progressive reforms, and many people regarded as progressives on some issues opposed change in other areas. Social Gospeler Rauschenbusch, for instance, opposed expanding women's rights. More typically, opponents of reform held consistently traditional attitudes.

Social Gospelers themselves faced opposition. Particularly strong among evangelical denominations with rural roots, Protestant **fundamentalists** stressed personal salvation rather than social reform. "To attempt reform in the black depths of the great city," said one, "would be as useless as trying to purify the ocean by pouring into it a few gallons of spring water." The most famous evangelist was Billy Sunday, who scorned all reforms but prohibition and denounced labor unions, women's rights, and business regulation as interfering with traditional values. Declaring that the Christian mission was solely to save individual souls, he condemned the Social Gospel as "godless social service nonsense" and attacked its advocates as "infidels and atheists."

Business interests angered by exposés of corporate abuse and corruption attacked muckrakers. Major corporations like Standard Oil created public relations bureaus to improve their image and to identify business, not its critics, with the public interest. Advertising boycotts discouraged magazines from running critical stories, and credit restrictions forced some muckraking journals to suspend publication. By 1910, the heyday of muckraking was over.

Labor unions likewise encountered resistance. Led by the National Association of Manufacturers, employer associations denounced unions as corrupt and radical, hired thugs to disrupt them, organized strikebreaking agencies, and used blacklists to eliminate union activists. The antiunion campaign peaked in Ludlow, Colorado, in 1914. John D. Rockefeller's Colorado Fuel and Iron Company used the state militia to shoot striking workers and their families. The courts aided employers by issuing injunctions against strikes and prohibited unions from using boycotts, one of their most effective weapons.

Progressives campaigning for government intervention and regulation also met stiff resistance. Many Americans objected to what they considered unwarranted interference in private economic matters. Their political representatives were called the "Old Guard," implying their opposition to political and economic change. The courts often supported these attitudes. In *Lochner* v. *New York* (1905), the Supreme Court overturned a maximum-hours law on the grounds that it deprived employers and employees of their "freedom of contract." Progressives constantly had to struggle with such opponents, and progressive achievements were limited by the persistence and influence of their adversaries.

Reforming Society

With their varied motives and objectives, progressives worked to transform society by improving living conditions, educational opportunities, family life, and social and industrial relations. They sought what they called "social justice," but their plans for social reform sometimes also smacked of social control—coercive efforts to impose uniform standards on a diverse population.

Settlement Houses and Urban Reform

The spearheads for social reform were settlement houses, community centers in urban immigrant neighborhoods. Reformers created four hundred settlement houses, largely modeled after Hull House in Chicago, founded in 1889 by Jane Addams.

Most settlements were led and staffed primarily by middle-class young women. Settlement work did not immediately violate prescribed gender roles because it initially focused on the "woman's sphere": family, education, domestic skills, and cultural "uplift." Thus settlement workers organized kindergartens and nurseries; taught classes in English, cooking, and personal hygiene; held musical performances and poetry readings; and sponsored recreation.

However, settlement workers soon saw that the root problem for immigrants was widespread poverty that required more than changes in individual behavior. Unlike earlier reformers, they regarded many of the evils of poverty as products of the social environment rather than of moral weakness. Slum-dwellers, Addams sadly noted, suffered from "poisonous sewage, contaminated water, infant mortality, adulterated food, smoke-laden air, juvenile crime, and unwholesome crowding." Thus settlement workers campaigned for stricter building codes to improve slums, better urban sanitation systems to enhance public health, public parks to revive the urban environment, and laws to protect women and children.

Lawrence Veiller played the leading role in the crusade for housing reform. His work at the University Settlement in New York City convinced him that "the improvement of the homes of the people was the starting point for everything." Veiller relied on settlement workers to help investigate housing conditions, prepare public exhibits depicting rampant disease in congested slums, and agitate for improvements. Based on their findings, Veiller drafted a new housing code limiting the size of tenements and requiring toilet facilities, ventilation, and fire protection. In 1901, the New York Tenement House Law became a model for other cities. To promote uniform building codes throughout the nation, the tireless Veiller founded the National Housing Association in 1910.

SUMMARY

MAJOR LAWS AND CONSTITUTIONAL AMENDMENTS OF THE PROGRESSIVE ERA

Legislation	Effect
New York Tenement House Law (1901)	Established a model housing code for safety and sanitation
Newlands Act (1902)	Provided for federal irrigation projects
Hepburn Act (1906)	Strengthened authority of the Interstate Commerce Commission
Pure Food and Drug Act (1906)	Regulated the production and sale of food and drug products
Meat Inspection Act (1906)	Authorized federal inspection of meat products
Sixteenth Amendment (1913)	Authorized a federal income tax
Seventeenth Amendment (1913)	Mandated the direct popular election of senators
Underwood-Simmons Tariff Act (1913)	Lowered tariff rates and levied the first regular federal income tax
Federal Reserve Act (1913)	Established the Federal Reserve System to supervise banking and provide a national currency
Federal Trade Commission Act (1914)	Established the FTC to oversee business activities
Harrison Act (1914)	Regulated the distribution and use of narcotics
Smith-Lever Act (1914)	Institutionalized the county agent system
Keating-Owen Act (1916)	Indirectly prohibited child labor
Eighteenth Amendment (1919)	Instituted prohibition
Nineteenth Amendment (1920)	Established woman suffrage

Protective Legislation for Women and Children

Settlement workers eventually concluded that only government power could achieve social justice and demanded that state and federal governments protect the weak or disadvantaged. As Veiller insisted, it was "unquestionably the duty of the state" to enforce justice in the face of "greed on the part of those who desire to secure for themselves an undue profit."

As they learned of children maimed or killed in industrial accidents or exhausted from factory work, it was "inevitable," Addams said, "that efforts to secure a child labor law should be our first venture into the field of state legislation." The National Child Labor Committee, organized in 1904, led the campaign. Reformers met stiff resistance from manufac-

American Views

MOTHER JONES AND THE MEANING OF CHILD LABOR IN AMERICA

Born in Ireland in 1830, the legendary Mother Jones (Mary Harris Jones) became one of America's greatest social activists, organizing workers, participating in strikes, and protesting social and industrial conditions from the 1870s through the 1920s. Here she recounts one of her efforts to end child labor, one of the most persistent reform goals of the Progressive Era. Using the techniques of exposure and publicity characteristic of the period and adroitly employing patriotic symbols and references, Jones skillfully raised troubling questions about the concepts of social and economic opportunity that many Americans associated with national development and identity.

❖ **How did Mother Jones direct public attention to child labor?**

❖ **How did she invoke the treasured American concept of opportunity to gain support for her goal?**

❖ **What did she argue was the relationship between child labor and the privileged status of other Americans?**

❖ **How successful was her crusade against child labor?**

In the spring of 1903 I went to Kensington, Pennsylvania, where 75,000 textile workers were on strike. Of this number at least 10,000 were little children. The workers were striking for more pay and shorter hours. Every day little children came into Union Headquarters, some with their hands off, some with the thumb missing, some with their fingers off at the knuckle. They were stooped little things, round shouldered and skinny. Many of them were not over ten years of age. . . .

We assembled a number of boys and girls one morning in Independence Park and from there we arranged to parade with banners to the court house where we would hold a meeting.

A great crowd gathered in the public square in front of the city hall. I put the little boys with their fingers off and hands crushed and maimed on a platform. I held up their mutilated hands and showed them to the crowd and made the statement that Philadelphia's mansions were built on the broken bones, the quivering hearts, and drooping heads of these children. . . .

I called upon the millionaire manufacturers to cease their moral murders, and I cried to the officials in the open windows opposite, "Some day the workers will take possession of your city hall, and when we do, no child will be sacrificed on the altar of profit."

The reporters quoted my statement that Philadelphia mansions were built on the broken bones and quivering hearts of children. The Philadelphia papers and the New York papers got

turers who used child labor, conservatives who opposed government action as an intrusion into family life, and some poor parents who needed their children's income. Child labor reformers documented the problem with extensive investigations and also benefited from the public outrage stirred by socialist John Spargo's muckraking book *The Bitter Cry of the Children* (1906). By 1914, every state but one had a minimum working age law. Effective regulation, however, required national action, for many state laws were weak or poorly enforced (see "American Views: Mother Jones and the Meaning of Child Labor in America").

Social reformers also lobbied for laws regulating the wages, hours, and working conditions of women and succeeded in having states from New York into a squabble with each other over the question. The universities discussed it. Preachers began talking. That was what I wanted. Public attention on the subject of child labor.

The matter quieted down for a while and I concluded the people needed stirring up again. . . . I decided to go with the children to see President Roosevelt to ask him to have Congress pass a law prohibiting the exploitation of childhood. I thought that President Roosevelt might see these mill children and compare them with his own little ones who were spending the summer at the seashore at Oyster Bay. . . .

Everywhere we had meetings, showing up with living children, the horrors of child labor. . . . [In New Jersey] I called on the mayor of Princeton and asked for permission to speak opposite the campus of the University. I said I wanted to speak on higher education. The mayor gave me permission. A great crowd gathered, professors and students and the people; and I told them that the rich robbed these little children of any education of the lowest order that they might send their sons and daughters to places of higher education. . . . And I showed those professors children in our army who could scarcely read or write because

they were working ten hours a day in the silk mills of Pennsylvania. . . .

[In New York] I told an immense crowd of the horrors of child labor in the mills around the anthracite region and . . . I showed them Gussie Rangnew, a little girl from whom all the childhood had gone. Her face was like an old woman's. Gussie packed stockings in a factory, eleven hours a day for a few cents a day. . . . "Fifty years ago there was a cry against slavery and men gave up their lives to stop the selling of black children on the block. Today the white child is sold for two dollars a week to the manufacturers."

. . . We marched down to Oyster Bay but the president refused to see us and he would not answer my letters. But our march had done its work. We had drawn the attention of the nation to the crime of child labor. And while the strike of the textile workers in Kensington was lost and the children driven back to work, not long afterward the Pennsylvania legislature passed a child labor law that sent thousands of children home from the mills, and kept thousands of others from entering the factory until they were fourteen years of age.

Source: *The Autobiography of Mother Jones*, 3rd ed. (1977).

to Oregon pass maximum-hours legislation. After the Supreme Court upheld such laws in ***Muller*** v. ***Oregon*** (1908), thirty-nine states enacted new or stronger laws on women's maximum hours between 1909 and 1917. Fewer states established minimum wages for women.

Protective legislation for women posed a troubling issue for reformers. In California, for example, middle-class clubwomen favored protective leg-

islation on grounds of women's presumed weakness. More radical progressives, as in the socialist-led Women's Trade Union League of Los Angeles, supported legislation to help secure economic independence and equality in the labor market for women, increase the economic strength of the working class, and serve as a precedent for laws improving conditions for all workers.

Progressive Era lawmakers limited protective legislation to measures reflecting the belief that women needed paternalist protection, even by excluding them from certain occupations. Laws establishing a minimum wage for women, moreover, usually set a wage level below what state commissions reported as subsistence rates. Protective legislation thus assured women not economic independence but continued dependence on husbands or fathers.

Social justice reformers forged the beginnings of the welfare state, as many states began in 1910 to provide "mothers' pensions" to indigent widows with dependent children. Twenty-one states, led by Wisconsin in 1911, enacted workers' compensation programs.

Compared to social insurance programs in western Europe, however, these were feeble responses to the social consequences of industrialization. Proposals for health insurance and old-age pension programs went nowhere. Business groups and other conservative interests curbed the movement toward state responsibility for social welfare.

Reshaping Public Education

Concerns about child labor overlapped with increasing attention to public schools. In 1900, for example, women's clubs in North Carolina launched a program to improve school buildings, increase teachers' salaries, and broaden the curriculum. Claiming efficiency and expertise, school administrators also pushed for changes, both to upgrade their own profession and to expand their public influence. And some intellectuals predicted that schools themselves could promote social progress and reform. Philosopher John Dewey sketched his plans for such progressive education in *The School and Society* (1899).

Between 1880 and 1920, compulsory school attendance laws, kindergartens, age-graded elementary schools, professional training for teachers, vocational education, parent-teacher associations, and school nurses became standard elements in American education. School reformers believed in both the educational soundness of these measures and their importance for countering slum environments. As Jacob Riis contended, the kindergartner would "rediscover . . . the natural feelings that the tenement had smothered."

Public education in the South lagged behind the North. After 1900, per capita expenditures for education doubled, school terms were extended, and thousands of new schoolhouses were erected across the region. But the South frittered away its limited resources on a segregated educational system that shortchanged both races. South Carolina spent twelve times as much per white pupil as per black pupil. Booker T. Washington complained in 1906 that the educational reforms meant "almost nothing so far as the Negro schools are concerned." As a northern critic observed, "To devise a school system which shall save the whites and not the blacks is a task of such delicacy that a few surviving reactionaries are willing to let both perish together."

Challenging Gender Restrictions

Most progressives held fairly conservative, moralistic views about sexuality and gender roles. Margaret Sanger, however, radically challenged conventional ideas of the social role of women. A public health nurse and an IWW organizer, she soon made the struggle for reproductive rights her personal crusade. Sanger saw in New York's immigrant neighborhoods the plight of poor women worn out from repeated pregnancies or injured or dead from self-induced knitting-needle abortions. Despite federal and state laws against contraceptives, Sanger began promoting birth control as a way to avert such tragedies. In 1914, Sanger published a magazine, *Woman Rebel*, in which she argued that "a woman's body belongs to herself alone. It does not belong to the United States of America or any other government on the face of the earth." Prohibiting contraceptives meant "enforced motherhood," Sanger declared. "Women cannot be on an equal footing with men until they have full and complete control over their reproductive function."

Sanger's crusade infuriated those who regarded birth control as a threat to the family and morality. Indicted for distributing information about contraception, Sanger fled to Europe. Other women took up the cause, forming the National Birth Control League in 1915 to campaign for the repeal of laws restricting access to contraceptive information and devices.

Reforming Country Life

Although most progressives focused on the city, others sought to reform rural life. They worked to improve rural health and sanitation, to replace inefficient one-room schools with modern consolidated ones under professional control, and to extend new roads and communication services into the countryside. To further these goals, President Theodore Roosevelt created the Country Life Commission in 1908 to investigate rural problems.

Agricultural scientists, government officials, and many business interests also sought to promote efficient, scientific, and commercial agriculture. A key innovation was the county agent system: the U.S. Department of Agriculture and business groups placed an agent in each county to teach farmers new techniques and encourage changes in the rural social values that had spawned the Populist radicalism that most progressives decried. The Smith-Lever Act (1914) provided federal subsidies for county agents throughout the country. Its purpose, claimed Woodrow Wilson, was to produce "an efficient and contented population" in rural America.

Few farmers, however, welcomed these efforts. As one Illinois county agent said in 1915, "Farmers, as a whole, resent exceedingly those forces which are at work with missionary intent trying to uplift them." School consolidation meant the loss of community control of education; good roads would raise taxes and chiefly benefit urban business interests. Besides, most farmers believed that their problems stemmed not from rural life but from industrial society.

Even so, government agencies, agricultural colleges, and railroads and banks steadily tied farmers to urban markets. Telephones and rural free delivery of mail, permanently established in 1902, lessened countryside isolation but quickened the spread of city values. Improved roads and the coming of the automobile eliminated many rural villages and linked farm families directly with towns and cities. Consolidated schools wiped out the social center of rural neighborhoods and carried children out of their communities, many never to return.

Social Control and Moral Crusades

The tendency toward social control evident in the movements to pass protective legislation and transform country life also marked other less attractive progressive efforts. These efforts, moreover, often meshed with the restrictive attitudes that conservative Americans held about race, religion, immigration, and morality. The result was widespread attempts to restrict certain groups and control behavior.

Many Americans wanted to limit immigration for racist reasons. Nativist agitation in California prompted the federal government to restrict Japanese immigration in 1907. Californians, including local progressives, also hoped to curtail the migration of Mexicans. A Stanford University researcher condemned Mexicans as an "undesirable class" compared to "the more progressive races."

Nationally, public debate focused on restricting the flow of new immigrants from southern and eastern Europe. Many backed their prejudice with a distorted interpretation of Darwinism, labeling the Slavic and Mediterranean peoples "inferior races." As early as 1894, nativists had organized the Immigration Restriction League, which favored a literacy test for admission, sure that it would "bear most heavily upon the Italians, Russians, Poles, Hungarians, Greeks, and Asiatics, and very lightly or not at all upon English-speaking immigrants or Germans, Scandinavians, and French." Congress enacted a literacy law in 1917.

Other nativists demanded the "Americanization" of immigrants already in the country. The Daughters of the American Revolution sought to inculcate loyalty, patriotism, and conservative values. Settlement workers and Social Gospelers also attempted to transfer their own values to the newcomers. The most prominent advocate of Americanization was a stereotypical progressive, Frances Kellor. She studied social work at the University of Chicago, worked in New York settlement houses, wrote a muckraking exposé of employment agencies that exploited women, and became director of the New York Bureau of Immigration. In 1915, she helped organize the National Americanization Committee and increasingly emphasized destroying immigrants' old-country ties and imposing an American culture.

Closely linked to progressives' worries about immigrants was their campaign for **prohibition**. Social workers saw liquor as a cause of crime, poverty, and family violence; employers blamed it for causing industrial accidents and inefficiency; Social Gospel ministers condemned the "spirit born of hell" because it impaired moral judgment and behavior. But also important was native-born Americans' fear of new immigrants. Many immigrants, in fact, viewed liquor and the neighborhood saloon as vital parts of daily life, and so prohibition became a focus of nativist hostilities, cultural conflict, and Americanization pressures.

Protestant fundamentalists also stoutly supported prohibition, working through the Anti-Saloon League, founded in 1893. Their nativism and antiurban bias surfaced in demands for prohibition to prevent the nation's cities from lapsing into "raging mania, disorder, and anarchy." With most urban Catholics and Jews opposing prohibition, the Anti-Saloon League justified imposing its reform on city populations against their will: "Our nation can only be saved by turning the pure stream of country sentiment . . . to flush out the cesspools of cities and so save civilization from pollution."

With these varied motivations, prohibitionists campaigned for local and state laws against the manufacture and sale of alcohol. Eventually, Congress approved the Eighteenth Amendment, which made prohibition the law of the land by 1920.

A meeting of the Niagara Movement in Boston in 1907. W.E.B. Du Bois is seated on the left. Half of the delegates were women, indicating the important role that black women played in the struggle for racial justice.

California provided other examples of progressives' interest in social control and moral reform. The state assembly, described by the *San Francisco Chronicle* as "a legislature of progressive cranks," prohibited "wagering or pool selling or bookmaking in any way, shape, form, or place," draw poker, and prizefighting. Los Angeles banned premarital sex and introduced artistic censorship. One critic in 1913 complained of the reformers' "frenzy of virtue" that made "Puritanism . . . the inflexible doctrine of Los Angeles."

For Whites Only?

Racism permeated the Progressive Era. In the South, progressivism was built on black disfranchisement and segregation. Like most white Southerners, progressives believed that racial control was necessary for social order. Governors Hoke Smith of Georgia and James Vardaman, "the White Chief," of Mississippi supported progressive reforms, but they also viciously attacked black rights. Their racist demagogy incited violence against blacks throughout the South. Antiblack race riots, like that produced in Atlanta by Smith's election in 1906, and lynching—defended on the floor of the U.S. Senate by a southern progressive—were part of the system of racial control that made the era a terrible time for African-Americans.

Even in the North, where relatively few blacks lived, race relations deteriorated. A reporter in Pennsylvania found "this disposition to discriminate against Negroes has greatly increased within the past decade." Antiblack race riots exploded in New York in 1900 and in Springfield, Illinois—Lincoln's hometown—in 1908.

But blacks' own progressive activism was growing. Even in the South, some African-Americans struggled to improve conditions. In Atlanta, for example, black women created progressive organizations and established settlement houses, kindergartens, and day care centers. The women of the Neighborhood Union, organized in 1908, even challenged the discriminatory policies of Atlanta's board of education, demanding equal facilities and appropriations for the city's black schools. They had only limited success, but their efforts demonstrated a persisting commitment to reforming society.

In the North, blacks more openly criticized discrimination. Ida Wells-Barnett, the crusading journalist who had fled the South for Chicago, became nationally prominent for her militant protests. She fought fiercely against racial injustices, especially school segregation, agitated for woman suffrage, and organized kindergartens and settlement houses for Chicago's black migrants.

Still more important was W. E. B. Du Bois, who campaigned tirelessly against all forms of racial discrimination. In 1905, Du Bois and other black activists met in Niagara Falls, Canada, to make plans to promote political and economic equality. In 1910, this **Niagara Movement** joined with a small group of white reformers, including Jane Addams, to organize the National Association for the Advancement of Colored People. The NAACP sought to overthrow segregation and establish equal justice and educational opportunities. As its director of publicity and research, Du Bois launched the influential magazine *The Crisis* to shape public opinion. "Agitate," he counseled, "protest, reveal the truth, and refuse to be silenced." By 1918, the NAACP had 44,000 members in 165 branches.

Reforming Politics and Government

Progressives of all kinds clamored for the reform of politics and government. But their political activism was motivated by different concerns, and they sometimes pursued competing objectives. Many wanted to change procedures and institutions to promote greater democracy and responsibility. Others hoped to improve the efficiency of government, to eliminate corruption, or to increase their own influence. All justified their objectives as necessary to adapt the political system to the nation's new needs.

Woman Suffrage

The woman suffrage movement had begun in the mid-nineteenth century, but suffragists had been frustrated by the prevailing belief that women's "proper sphere" was the home and the family. Woman suffrage, particularly when championed as a step toward women's equality, seemed to challenge the natural order of society, and it generated much opposition among traditionalist-minded men and women.

In the early twentieth century, under a new generation of leaders like Carrie Chapman Catt, suffragists adopted activist tactics, including parades, mass meetings, and "suffrage tours" by automobile. They also organized by political districts and attracted workingwomen and labor unions. By 1917, the National American Woman Suffrage Association had over 2 million members.

But some suffrage leaders shifted arguments to gain more support. Rather than insisting on the "justice" of woman suffrage or emphasizing equal rights, they spoke of the special moral and maternal instincts women could bring to politics if allowed to vote. The suffrage movement now appeared less a radical, disruptive force than a vehicle for extending traditional female benevolence and service to society. The new image of the movement increased public support by appealing to conventional views of women. Noted one Nebraska undergraduate, women students no longer feared "antagonizing the men or losing invitations to parties by being suffragists."

Gradually, the suffrage movement began to prevail. In 1910, Washington became the first state to approve woman suffrage since the mid-1890s, followed by California in 1911 and Arizona, Kansas, and Oregon in 1912. Suffragists also mounted national action, such as the dramatic inaugural parade in March 1913 described at the beginning of this chapter. By 1919, thirty-nine states had established full or partial woman suffrage, and Congress finally approved an amendment. Ratified by the states in 1920, the **Nineteenth Amendment** marked a critical advance in political democracy.

Electoral Reform

Other Progressive Era reforms changed the election process and the meaning of political participation. The so-called **Australian ballot** adopted by most states during the 1890s provided for secret voting and replaced the individual party tickets with an official ballot listing all candidates and distributed by public officials. The Australian ballot led to quiet, orderly elections. One Cincinnati editor, who recalled the "howling mobs" and chaos at the polls in previous elections, declared: "The political bummer and thug has been relegated to the background . . . while good citizenship . . . has come to the front."

Public regulation of other parts of the electoral process previously controlled by parties soon followed. Beginning with Mississippi in 1902, nearly every state provided for direct primaries to remove nominations from the boss-ridden caucus and convention system. Many states also reformed campaign practices.

The decreasing ability of parties to mobilize voters was reflected in a steady decline in voter participation, from 79 percent in 1896 to 49 percent in 1920. As parties contracted, the influence of nonpartisan organizations and pressure groups grew, promoting narrower objectives. Thus the National Association of Manufacturers (1895) and the United States Chamber of Commerce (1912) lobbied for business interests; the National Farmers Union (1902), for commercial agriculture; the American Federation of Teachers (1916), for professional educators. The organized lobbying of special-interest groups would give them greater influence over government in the future and contribute to the declining popular belief in the value of voting or participation in politics.

Disfranchisement more obviously undermined American democracy. In the South, Democrats—progressive and conservative alike—eliminated not only blacks but many poor whites from the electorate through poll taxes, literacy tests, and other restrictions. Republicans in the North adopted educational or literacy tests in ten states, enacted strict registration laws, and gradually abolished the right of aliens to vote once they declared their intention to become citizens. These restrictions reflected both the progressives' anti-immigrant prejudices and their obsessions with social control and with purifying politics and "improving" the electorate. Such electoral reforms reduced the political power of ethnic and working-class Americans, often stripping them of their political rights and means of influence.

Municipal Reform

Muckrakers had exposed crooked alliances between city bosses and business leaders that resulted in wasteful or inadequate municipal services. In some cities, urban reformers attempted to break these alliances and improve conditions for those suffering most from municipal misrule. For example, in Toledo, Ohio, Samuel "Golden Rule" Jones won enough working-class votes to be elected mayor four times despite the hostility of both major parties. Serving from 1897 to 1904, Jones opened public playgrounds and kindergartens, established the eight-hour day for city workers, and improved public services. Influenced by the Social Gospel, he also provided free lodging for the homeless and gave his own salary to the poor. Other reforming mayors also fought municipal corruption, limited the political influence of corporations, and championed public ownership of utilities.

More elitist progressives attempted to change the structure of urban government. Middle-class reformers worked to replace ward elections with city-wide elections which required greater resources and therefore helped swell middle-class influence at the expense of working-class wards. So did nonpartisan elections, which reformers introduced to weaken party loyalties.

Urban reformers developed two other structural innovations: the city commission and the city manager. Both attempted to institutionalize efficient, businesslike government staffed by professional administrators. By 1920, hundreds of cities had adopted one of the new plans.

Business groups often promoted these reforms. In Des Moines, for example, the president of the Commercial Club declared that "the professional politician must be ousted and in his place capable businessmen chosen to conduct the affairs of the city." Again, then, reform in municipal government often shifted political power from ethnic and working-class voters, represented however imperfectly by partisan elections, to smaller groups with greater resources.

Progressive State Government

Progressives also reshaped state government. Some tried to democratize the legislative process, regarding the legislature—the most important branch of state government in the nineteenth century—as ineffective and even corrupt, dominated by party bosses and corporate influences. The Missouri legislature reportedly "enacted such laws as the corporations paid for, and such others as were necessary to fool the people." Populists had first raised such charges in the 1890s and proposed novel solutions adopted by many states in the early twentieth century. The **initiative** enabled reformers themselves to propose legislation directly to the electorate, bypassing an unresponsive legislature; the **referendum** permitted voters to approve or reject legislative measures.

Other reforms also expanded the popular role in state government. The **Seventeenth Amendment**, ratified in 1913, provided for the election of U.S. senators directly by popular vote instead of by

state legislatures. Beginning with Oregon in 1908, ten states adopted the **recall**, enabling voters to remove unsatisfactory public officials from office before their terms expired.

As state legislatures and party machines were curbed, dynamic governors like Robert La Follette pushed progressive programs into law. Elected in 1900, "Fighting Bob" La Follette turned Wisconsin into "the laboratory of democracy." "His words bite like coals of fire," wrote one observer. "He never wearies and he will not allow his audience to weary." Overcoming fierce opposition from "stalwart" Republicans, La Follette established direct primaries, railroad regulation, the first state income tax, workers' compensation, and other important measures before being elected to the U.S. Senate in 1906.

La Follette also stressed efficiency and expertise. The Legislative Reference Bureau that he created was staffed by university professors to advise on public policy. He used regulatory commissions to oversee railroads, banks, and other interests. Most states followed suit, and expert commissions became an important feature of state government, gradually gaining authority at the expense of local officials.

"Experts" were presumed to be disinterested and therefore committed to the general welfare. In practice, however, regulators were subject to pressures from competing interest groups, and some commissions became captives of the very industries they were supposed to control. This irony was matched by the contradiction between the expansion of democracy through the initiative and referendum and the increasing reliance on nonelected professional experts to set and implement public policy.

Theodore Roosevelt and the Progressive Presidency

When a crazed anarchist assassinated William McKinley in 1901, Theodore Roosevelt entered the White House, and the progressive movement gained its most prominent national leader. The son of a wealthy New York family, Roosevelt had been a New York legislator, U.S. civil service commissioner, and assistant secretary of the navy. After his exploits in the Spanish-American War, he was elected governor of New York in 1898 and vice president in 1900. His remarkable public life was matched by an active private life in which he both wrote works of history and obsessively pursued what he called the "strenuous life": boxing, wrestling, hunting, rowing, even ranching and chasing rustlers in Dakota Territory. His own son observed that Roosevelt "always wanted to be the bride at every wedding and the corpse at every funeral."

Mark Twain fretted that "Mr. Roosevelt is the Tom Sawyer of the political world of the twentieth century; always showing off; always hunting for a chance to show off; in his frenzied imagination the Great Republic is a vast Barnum circus with him for a clown and the whole world for audience." But Roosevelt's flamboyance and ambitions made him the most popular politician of the time and enabled him to dramatize the issues of progressivism and to become the first modern president.

TR and the Modern Presidency

Roosevelt believed that the president could do anything to meet national needs that the Constitution did not specifically prohibit. "Under this interpretation of executive power," he later recalled, "I did and caused to be done many things not previously done. . . . I did not usurp power, but I did greatly broaden the use of executive power." Indeed, the expansion of government power and its consolidation in the executive branch were among his most significant accomplishments.

Roosevelt spelled out his policy goals in more than four hundred messages to Congress, sent drafts of bills to Capitol Hill, and intervened to win passage of "his" measures. Some members of Congress resented such "executive arrogance" and "dictatorship." Roosevelt generally avoided direct challenges to the conservative Old Guard Republicans who controlled Congress, but his activities helped shift the balance of power within the national government.

Roosevelt also reorganized the executive branch. He believed in efficiency and expertise. To promote rational policymaking and public management, he staffed the expanding federal bureaucracy with able professionals. The president, complained one Republican, was "trying to concentrate all power in Washington . . . and to govern the people by commissions and bureaus."

Finally, Roosevelt exploited and skillfully handled the mass media, which made him a celebrity, "TR" or "Teddy" (a nickname he hated but one that stuck). The publicity not only kept TR in the spotlight but also enabled him to mold public opinion.

Roosevelt and Labor

One sign of TR's vigorous new approach to the presidency was his handling of a coal strike in 1902.

Members of the United Mine Workers Union walked off their jobs, demanding higher wages, an eight-hour day, and recognition of their union. The mine owners closed the mines and waited for the union to collapse. But led by John Mitchell, the strikers held their ranks. Management's stubborn arrogance contrasted with the workers' orderly conduct and willingness to negotiate and hardened public opinion against the owners. TR's legal advisers told him that the government had no constitutional authority to intervene.

As public pressure mounted, however, Roosevelt decided to act. He invited both the owners and the union leaders to a White House conference. He declared that the national interest made government action necessary. Mitchell agreed to negotiate. The owners, however, refused even to speak to the miners and demanded that Roosevelt use the army to break the union, as Cleveland had done in the Pullman strike in 1894.

Roosevelt was not a champion of labor. But furious with the owners' "arrogant stupidity" and "insulting" attitude toward the presidency, Roosevelt announced that he would use the army to seize and operate the mines, not to crush the union. Questioned about the constitutionality of such an action, Roosevelt bellowed: "To hell with the Constitution when the people want coal." Reluctantly, the owners accepted the arbitration commission they had previously rejected. The commission gave the miners a 10 percent wage increase and a nine-hour day, but not union recognition, and permitted the owners to raise coal prices by 10 percent. Roosevelt described his intervention as simply giving both labor and management a "square deal." It also set important precedents for an active government role in labor disputes and a strong president acting as a steward of the public.

Managing Natural Resources

Federal land policy had helped create farms and develop transportation, but it had also ceded to speculators and business interests much of the nation's forests, mineral deposits, waterpower sites, and grazing lands. A new generation believed in the **conservation** of natural resources through efficient and scientific management. Conservationists achieved early victories in the Forest Reserve Act (1891) and the Forest Management Act (1897), which authorized the federal government to withdraw timberlands from development and to regulate grazing, lumbering, and hydroelectric sites in the forests (see Map 23-1).

Roosevelt and his friend Gifford Pinchot made conservation a major focus of his presidency.

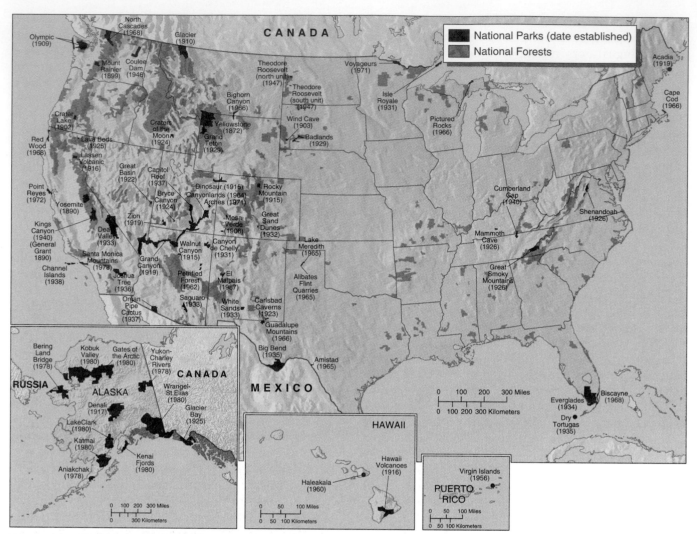

Map 23-1   *The growth of National Forests and National Parks.*
Rapid exploitation of the West prompted demands to preserve its spectacular scenery and protect its remaining forests. In 1872 Yellowstone became the first National Park, and the National Forest system began in the 1890s. Conservation became increasingly important during the Progressive Era but often provoked western hostility.

Appointed in 1898 to head the new Division of Forestry (renamed the Forest Service in 1905), Pinchot brought rational management and regulation to resource development. With his advice, TR used presidential authority to triple the size of the forest reserves to 150 million acres, set aside another 80 million acres valuable for minerals and petroleum, and establish dozens of wildlife refuges. In 1908, Roosevelt held a White House conference of state and federal officials that led to the creation of the National Conservation Commission, forty-one state conservation commissions, and widespread public support for the conservation movement.

Some interests opposed conservation. Many Westerners resented having Easterners make key decisions about western growth and saw conservation as a perpetuation of this colonial subservience. Many ranchers refused to pay grazing fees to the Forest Service. Colorado arsonists set forest fires to protest the creation of forest reserves.

But Westerners were happy to take federal money for expensive irrigation projects that private capital would not undertake. They favored the 1902 Newlands (National Reclamation) Act, named after its sponsor, Francis Newlands of Nevada, which established the **Bureau of Reclamation**. Its engineers were to construct dams, reservoirs, and irrigation canals, and the government was to sell the irrigated lands in tracts no larger than 160 acres. With massive dams and networks of irrigation canals, it reclaimed fertile valleys from the desert. Unfortunately, the bureau did not enforce the 160-acre limitation and thus helped create powerful corporate farms in the West.

Corporate Regulation

Nothing symbolized Roosevelt's active presidency better than his popular reputation as a "trust buster." TR regarded the formation of large business combinations favorably. But he was, he said, "exceedingly alarmed at the growth of popular unrest and popular distrust" of big business and knew he could not ignore it. Business leaders and Old Guard conservatives opposed any government intervention in the large trusts, but Roosevelt knew better. "You have no conception of the revolt that would be caused if I did nothing," he said privately. TR proposed to "develop an orderly system, and such a system can only come through the gradually exercised right of efficient government control." Rather than invoking "the foolish antitrust law," he favored government regulation to prevent corporate abuses and defend the public interest. But he did sue some "bad trusts."

In 1902, the Roosevelt administration filed its most famous antitrust suit, against the Northern Securities Company, a holding company organized by J. P. Morgan to control the railroad network of the Northwest. For TR, this popular action was an assertion of government power that reassured a worried public and made corporate responsibility more likely. In 1904, the Supreme Court ordered the dissolution of the Northern Securities Company.

Elected president in his own right in 1904 over the colorless and conservative Democratic candidate, Judge Alton B. Parker, Roosevelt responded to the growing popular demand for reform by pushing further toward a regulatory government. He proposed legislation "to work out methods of controlling the big corporations without paralyzing the energies of the business community."

The Hepburn Act, passed in 1906, authorized the Interstate Commerce Commission to set maximum railroad rates and extended its jurisdiction. It was a weaker law than many progressives had wanted, but it marked the first time the federal government gained the power to set rules in a private enterprise.

In the same year, Congress passed the Pure Food and Drug Act and the Meat Inspection Act. In part, this legislation reflected public demand, but many business leaders also supported government regulation of food and drugs, convinced that it would expand their markets by certifying the quality of their products and drive their smaller competitors out of business. The meat and food and drug acts thus did extend government regulation over business to protect the public health and safety, but they also served some corporate purposes.

Despite the compromises and weaknesses in the three laws, TR contended that, "taken together," they marked "a noteworthy advance in the policy of securing federal supervision and control over corporations." In 1907 and 1908, he pushed for an eight-hour workday, stock market regulation, and inheritance and income taxes. Republican conservatives in Congress blocked such reforms. Old Guard Republicans thought Roosevelt had extended government powers dangerously, but in fact his accomplishments had been relatively modest. As La Follette noted, Roosevelt's "cannonading filled the air with noise and smoke, which confused and obscured the line of action, but, when the battle cloud drifted by and the quiet was restored, it was always a matter of surprise that so little had really been accomplished."

Taft and the Insurgents

TR handpicked his successor as president: a loyal lieutenant, William Howard Taft. Member of a prominent Ohio political family, Taft had been a federal judge, governor-general of the Philippines, and TR's secretary of war. Later he would serve as chief justice of the United States. But Taft's election as president in 1908, over Democrat William Jennings Bryan in his third presidential campaign, led to a Republican political disaster.

Taft did preside over a more active and successful antitrust program than Roosevelt's. He supported the Mann-Elkins Act (1910), which extended the ICC's jurisdiction to telephone and telegraph companies. Taft set aside more public forest lands and oil reserves than Roosevelt had. He also supported a constitutional amendment authorizing an income tax, which went into effect in 1913 under the **Sixteenth Amendment.** One of the most important accomplishments of the Progressive Era, the income tax would provide the means for the government to expand its activities and responsibilities.

Nevertheless, Taft soon alienated progressives and floundered into a political morass. His problems were twofold. First, midwestern reform Republicans, led by La Follette, clashed with more conservative Republicans led by Senator Nelson Aldrich of Rhode Island. Second, Taft was politically inept. He was unable to mediate between these two groups, and the party split apart.

Reformers wanted to restrict the power of the speaker of the House, "Uncle Joe" Cannon, a reactionary who blocked reform. After seeming to promise support, Taft backed down when conservatives threatened to defeat important legislation. The insurgents in Congress never forgave what they saw as Taft's betrayal. The tariff also alienated progressives from Taft. He had campaigned in 1908 for a lower tariff to curb inflation, and midwestern Republicans favored tariff reduction to trim the power of big business. But when they introduced tariff reform legislation, the president failed to support them. Aldrich's Senate committee added 847 amendments, many of which raised tariff rates. Taft justified his inaction as avoiding presidential interference with congressional business, but progressives concluded that Taft had sided with the Old Guard.

That perception solidified when Taft stumbled into a controversy over conservation. When Pinchot challenged secretary of the interior Richard Ballinger's role in a questionable sale of public coal lands in Alaska to a J. P. Morgan syndicate, Taft upheld Ballinger and fired Pinchot. Progressives concluded that Taft had repudiated Roosevelt's conservation policies.

In 1911, reformers formed the National Progressive League to champion La Follette for the Republican nomination in 1912. They appealed to TR for support, but Roosevelt's own position was closer to Taft's than to what he called "the La Follette type of fool radicalism." But condemning Taft as "disloyal to our past friendship . . . [and] to every canon of ordinary decency," TR began to campaign for the Republican nomination himself. In thirteen state primaries, TR won 278 delegates to only 46 for Taft. But most states did not then have primaries; that allowed Taft to dominate the Republican convention and win renomination. Roosevelt's forces formed a third party—the Progressive party—and nominated the former president. The Republican split almost guaranteed victory for the Democratic nominee, Woodrow Wilson.

Woodrow Wilson and Progressive Reform

Elected president in 1912 and 1916, Woodrow Wilson mediated among differing progressive views to achieve a strong reform program, enlarge the power of the executive branch, and make the White House the center of national politics.

The Election of 1912

In Congress, Southern Democrats more consistently supported reform measures than Republicans did, and Democratic leader William Jennings Bryan surpassed Roosevelt as a persistent advocate of significant political and economic reform. As the Democrats pushed progressive remedies and the Republicans quarreled during Taft's administration, Democrats achieved major victories in the state and congressional elections of 1910. To improve the party's chances in 1912, Bryan announced he would step aside. The Democratic spotlight shifted to the governor of New Jersey, Woodrow Wilson.

Born in Virginia as the son and grandson of Presbyterian ministers, Wilson combined public eloquence with a cold personality; he balanced a self-righteousness that led to stubborn inflexibility with an intense ambition that permitted the most expedient compromises. Wilson first entered public life as a conservative. In 1910, while he was president of Princeton University, New Jersey's Democratic bosses selected him for governor to head off the progressives. But once in office, Wilson championed popular reforms and immediately began to campaign as a progressive for the party's 1912 presidential nomination.

Wilson's progressivism differed from that of Roosevelt. TR emphasized a strong government that would promote economic and social order. He defended big business as inevitable and healthy provided that government control ensured that it would benefit the entire nation. Roosevelt called this program the **New Nationalism**, reflecting his belief in a powerful state and a national interest. He also supported demands for social welfare, including workers' compensation and the abolition of child labor.

Wilson was horrified by Roosevelt's vision. His **New Freedom** program rejected what he called TR's "regulated monopoly." Wilson wanted "regulated competition," with the government's role limited to breaking up monopolies through antitrust action and preventing artificial barriers like tariffs from blocking free enterprise. Wilson opposed social welfare legislation as "paternalistic."

Unable to add progressive Democrats to the Republicans who followed him into the Progressive party, TR could not win despite his personal popularity. Other reform voters embraced the Socialist candidate, Eugene V. Debs, who captured 900,000 votes—6 percent of the total. Taft played little role in the campaign. "I might as well give up as far as being a candidate," he lamented. "There are so many people in the country who don't like me."

Wilson won an easy electoral college victory, though he received only 42 percent of the popular vote (see Map 23-2). Roosevelt came in second, Taft

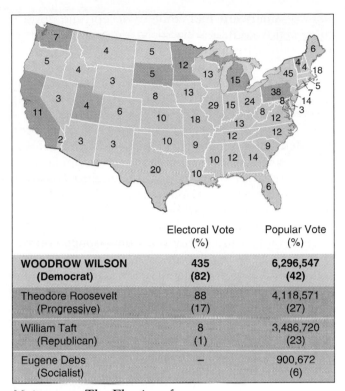

	Electoral Vote (%)	Popular Vote (%)
WOODROW WILSON (Democrat)	**435** (82)	**6,296,547** (42)
Theodore Roosevelt (Progressive)	88 (17)	4,118,571 (27)
William Taft (Republican)	8 (1)	3,486,720 (23)
Eugene Debs (Socialist)	–	900,672 (6)

Map 23-2   *The Election of 1912.*
The split within the Republican party enabled Woodrow Wilson to carry most states and become president even though he won only a minority of the popular vote.

third. The Democrats also gained control of Congress, giving Wilson the opportunity to enact his New Freedom program.

Implementing the New Freedom

Wilson built on Roosevelt's precedent to strengthen executive authority. He summoned Congress into special session in 1913 and delivered his message in person, the first president to do so since John Adams. Wilson proposed a full legislative program and worked forcefully to secure its approval. He held regular conferences with Democratic leaders and had a private telephone line installed between the Capitol and the White House to keep tabs on congressional actions. When necessary, he appealed to the public for support or doled out patronage and compromised with conservatives.

Wilson turned first to the traditional Democratic goal of reducing the high protective tariff. "The object of the tariff duties," Wilson announced, "must be effective competition." He forced through the **Underwood-Simmons Tariff Act** of 1913, the first substantial reduction in duties since before the Civil War. The act also levied the first income tax under the recently ratified Sixteenth Amendment.

Wilson next reformed the nation's banking and currency system, which was inadequate for a modernizing economy. He skillfully maneuvered a compromise measure through Congress, balancing the demands of agrarian progressives for government control with the bankers' desires for private control. The **Federal Reserve Act** of 1913 created twelve regional Federal Reserve banks that, although privately controlled, were to be supervised by the Federal Reserve Board, appointed by the president. The law also provided for a flexible national currency and improved access to credit. Serious problems remained, but the new system promoted the progressive goals of order and efficiency and fulfilled Wilson's New Freedom principle of introducing limited government regulation while preserving private business control.

Wilson's third objective was new legislation to break up monopolies. To this end, he initially supported the Clayton antitrust bill, which prohibited unfair trade practices and restricted holding companies. But when business leaders and other progressives strenuously objected, Wilson reversed himself. Opting for continuous federal regulation rather than for the dissolution of trusts, Wilson endorsed the creation of the **Federal Trade Commission (FTC)** to oversee business activity and prevent illegal restrictions on competition.

The Federal Trade Commission Act of 1914 embraced the New Nationalism's emphasis on positive regulation. Wilson now accepted what he had earlier denounced as a partnership between trusts and the government that the trusts would dominate. Indeed, Wilson's conservative appointments to the FTC ensured that the agency would not seriously interfere with business.

Wilson now announced that no further reforms were necessary. He refused to support woman suffrage and helped kill legislation abolishing child labor and expanding credits to farmers. Race relations provided a flagrant instance of Wilson's indifference to social justice issues. Raised in the South, he believed in segregation and backed the Southern Democrats in his cabinet when they introduced formal segregation within the government itself. Government offices, shops, restrooms, and restaurants were all segregated; employees who complained were fired.

The Expansion of Reform

Wilson had won in 1912 only because the Republicans had split. By 1916, Roosevelt had returned to the GOP, and Wilson realized that he had to attract some of TR's former followers. Wilson therefore promoted measures he had previously condemned as paternalistic. He also now recognized that some problems could be resolved only by positive federal action. "Old political formulas," he said, "do not fit the present."

In 1916, Wilson convinced Congress to pass the Federal Farm Loan Act, which provided farmers with federally financed, long-term agricultural credits. The Warehouse Act of 1916 improved short-term agricultural credit. The Highway Act of 1916 provided funds to construct and improve rural roads.

Wilson and the Democratic Congress also reached out to labor. Wilson signed the Keating-Owen Act prohibiting the interstate shipment of products made by child labor. In 1902, Wilson had denounced Roosevelt's intervention in the coal strike, but in 1916, he broke a labor-management impasse and averted a railroad strike by helping pass the Adamson Act establishing an eight-hour day for railway workers. Wilson pushed the Kern-McGillicuddy Act, which achieved the progressive goal of a workers' compensation system for federal employees.

Wilson also promoted activist government when he nominated Louis Brandeis to the Supreme Court. Known as the "people's lawyer," Brandeis had successfully defended protective labor legislation before the conservative judiciary. Brandeis was the first Jew nominated to the court, and anti-Semitism motivated some of his opponents. Wilson overcame a vicious campaign against Brandeis and secured his confirmation.

By these actions, Wilson brought progressivism to a culmination of sorts and consolidated reformers behind him for a second term. Less than a decade earlier, Wilson the private citizen had assailed government regulation and social legislation; by 1916, he had guided an unprecedented expansion of federal power.

Conclusion

Progressive reformers responded to the tensions of industrial and urban development by moving to change society and government. Programs and laws to protect women, children, and injured workers testified to their compassion; the creation of new agencies and political techniques indicated their interest in order and efficiency; campaigns to end corruption, whether perceived in urban political machines, corporate influence, drunkenness, or "inferior" immigrants, illustrated their self-assured vision of the public good.

Americans had come to accept that government action could resolve social and economic problems, and the role and power of government expanded accordingly. The emergence of an activist presidency, capable of developing programs, mobilizing public opinion, directing Congress, and taking forceful action, epitomized this key development.

Progressivism had its ironies and paradoxes. It called for democratic reforms—and did achieve woman suffrage, direct legislation, and popular election of senators—but helped disfranchise southern blacks and northern immigrants. It advocated social justice but often enforced social control. It demanded responsive government but helped create bureaucracies largely removed from popular control. It endorsed the regulation of business in the public interest but forged regulatory laws and commissions that tended to aid business. Some of these seeming contradictions reflected the persistence of traditional attitudes and the necessity to accommodate conservative opponents; others revealed the progressives' own limitations in vision, concern, or nerve.

Review Questions

1. How and why did the presidency change during the Progressive Era?

2. How did the progressive concern for efficiency affect social reform efforts, public education, government administration, and rural life?

3. How and why did the relationship between business and government change during this time?

4. Why did social reform and social control often intermingle in the Progressive Era? Can such objectives be separate?

5. What factors, old and new, stimulated the reform movements of progressivism?

6. How did the role of women change during the Progressive Era? How did that affect progressivism itself?

Recommended Reading

Jane Addams, *Twenty Years at Hull House* (1910). This is Jane Addams's own classic story of settlement work.

Kendrick A. Clements, *The Presidency of Woodrow Wilson* (1992). This excellent book provides important new information on both Wilson and the presidency.

William Deverell and Tom Sitton, *California Progressivism Revisited* (1994). This valuable collection of essays examines the complex motivations underlying progressivism in California.

Lewis L. Gould, *The Presidency of Theodore Roosevelt* (1991). Gould gives a balanced and comprehensive account of TR's presidency.

Arthur S. Link and Richard L. McCormick, *Progressivism* (1983). This work provides a superb brief analysis of the complexities and scholarly interpretations of progressivism.

Upton Sinclair, *The Jungle* (1906). The famous muckraking novel still fascinates.

Robert Wiebe, *The Search for Order, 1877–1920.* (1967). This masterful essay emphasizes the organizational thrust of middle-class progressives.

Where to Learn More

❖ **National Museum of American History, Smithsonian Institution, Washington, D.C.** A permanent exhibition, "Parlor to Politics: Women and Reform, 1890–1925," uses design, artifacts, and recent scholarship to vividly illustrate the changing role of women in the Progressive Era. It effectively emphasizes their work in settlement houses and their growing politicization and demonstrates the importance of the work of black women's organizations.

❖ **Hull House, Chicago, Illinois.** This pioneering settlement house is now a museum on the campus of the University of Illinois, Chicago.

❖ **Lowell National Historic Park, Lowell, Massachusetts.** "The Working People," a permanent exhibition, uses artifacts and photographs to chart the activities of immigrant workers at different times in the past, particularly during the Progressive Era.

❖ **Lower East Side Tenement Museum, New York City, New York.** A six-story tenement building containing 22 apartments, this museum vividly illustrates the congested and unhealthy living conditions of urban immigrants from the 1870s to the early twentieth century.

❖ **Sagamore Hill, Oyster Bay, New York.** Theodore Roosevelt's home is now a National Historic Site and open to the public.

❖ **Staunton, Virginia.** The birthplace and childhood home of Woodrow Wilson, restored with period furnishings, reveals many of the influences that shaped Wilson's career.

SUMMARY

RATIONALES FOR IMPERIALISM

Category	Beliefs
Racism and social Darwinism	Convictions that "Anglo-Saxons" were racially superior and should dominate other peoples, either to ensure national success, establish international stability, or benefit the "inferior" races by imposing American ideas and institutions on them
Righteousness	The conviction that Christianity, and a supporting American culture, should be aggressively spread among the benighted peoples of other lands
Mahanism	The conviction, following the ideas advanced by Alfred Thayer Mahan, that U.S. security required a strong navy and economic and territorial expansion
Economics	A variety of arguments holding that American prosperity depended on acquiring access to foreign markets, raw materials, and investment opportunities

included politicians like Lodge and Theodore Roosevelt, journalists like Whitelaw Reid of the *New York Tribune* and Albert Shaw of the *Review of Reviews*, and diplomats and lawyers like John Hay and Elihu Root.

Such men favored imperial expansion, as Shaw wrote, "for the sake of our destiny, our dignity, our influence, and our usefulness." Roosevelt promoted Mahan's ideas when he became assistant secretary of the navy in 1897, but he was even more militaristic. Praising "the most valuable of all qualities, the soldierly virtues," Roosevelt declared in 1897: "No triumph of peace is quite so great as the supreme triumphs of war." One British observer concluded that Mahan's influence had transformed the American spirit, serving "as oil to the flame of 'colonial expansion' everywhere leaping into life."

The large navy policy popular among imperialists began in 1881, when Congress established the Naval Advisory Board. An extensive program to replace the navy's obsolete wooden ships with modern cruisers and battleships was well under way by 1890 when the first volume of Mahan's book appeared. The United States soon possessed a formidable navy, which in turn, demanded strategic bases and coaling stations. One writer indicated the circular nature of this development by noting in 1893 that Manifest Destiny now meant "the acquisition of such territory, far and near," that would secure "to our navy facilities desirable for the operations of a great naval power."

Economic Designs

Nearly all Americans favored economic expansion through foreign trade. Such a policy promised national prosperity: larger markets for manufacturers and farmers, greater profits for merchants and bankers, more jobs for workers. Far fewer favored the acquisition of colonies that was characteristic of European imperialism. One diplomat declared in 1890 that the nation was more interested in the "annexation of trade" than in the annexation of territory.

As early as 1844, the United States had negotiated a trade treaty with China, and ten years later, a squadron under Commodore Matthew Perry had forced the Japanese to open their ports to American products. In the late nineteenth century, the dramatic expansion of the economy caused many Americans to favor more government action to open foreign markets to American exports. Alabama Senator John Morgan had the cotton and textiles produced in the New South in mind when he warned in 1882: "Our home market is not equal to the demands of our producing and manufacturing classes and to the capital which is seeking employment. . . . We must either enlarge the field of our traffic, or stop the business of manufacturing just where it is." More ominous, a naval officer trying to open Korea to U.S. products declared in 1878, "We must *export* these products or *deport* the people who are creating them."

Exports, particularly of manufactured goods, which grew ninefold between 1865 and 1900, did increase greatly in the late nineteenth century. Still, periodic depressions fed these fears of overproduction and the massive unemployment and social unrest that accompanied these economic crises also

CHRONOLOGY

1861–1869	Seward serves as secretary of state.
1867	U.S. purchases Alaska from Russia.
1870	Annexation of the Dominican Republic is rejected.
1881	Naval Advisory Board is created.
1887	U.S. gains naval rights to Pearl Harbor.
1889	First Pan-American Conference is held.
1890	Alfred Thayer Mahan publishes *The Influence of Sea Power upon History*.
1893	Harrison signs but Cleveland rejects a treaty for the annexation of Hawaii.
1893–1897	Depression increases interest in economic expansion abroad.
1894–1895	Sino-Japanese War is fought.
1895	U.S. intervenes in Great Britain–Venezuelan boundary dispute.
	Cuban insurrection against Spain begins.
1896	William McKinley is elected president on an imperialist platform.
1898	Spanish-American War is fought.
	Hawaii is annexed.
	Anti-Imperialist League is organized.
	Treaty of Paris is signed.
1899–1902	Filipino-American War is fought.
1899	Open Door note is issued.
1901	Theodore Roosevelt becomes president.
1903	Platt Amendment restricts Cuban autonomy.
	Panama "revolution" is abetted by the United States.
1904	United States acquires the Panama Canal Zone.
	Roosevelt Corollary is announced.
1904–1905	Russo-Japanese War is fought.
1905	Treaty of Portsmouth ends the Russo-Japanese War through U.S. mediation.
1906–1909	United States occupies Cuba.
1907–1908	Gentlemen's Agreement restricts Japanese immigration.
1909	United States intervenes in Nicaragua.
1912–1933	United States occupies Nicaragua.
1914	Panama Canal opens.
1914–1917	United States intervenes in Mexico.
1915–1934	United States occupies Haiti.
1916–1924	United States occupies the Dominican Republic.
1917	Puerto Ricans are granted U.S. citizenship.
1917–1922	United States occupies Cuba.

provided social and political arguments for economic relief through foreign trade.

In the depression of the 1890s, this interest in foreign trade became obsessive. More systematic government efforts to promote trade seemed necessary, a conclusion strengthened by new threats to existing American markets, including higher European tariffs. Moreover, Japan and the European imperial powers began to restrict commercial opportunities in the areas of China that they controlled.

First Steps

Before the mid-1890s, the government did not pursue a policy of **isolationism** from international affairs, for the nation maintained normal diplomatic and trade ties and at times vigorously intervened in Latin America and East Asia. But in general the government deferred to the initiative of private interests, reacted haphazardly to outside events, and did little to create a professional foreign service. In a few bold if inconsistent steps, however, the United States moved toward expanding its influence.

Seward and Blaine

Two secretaries of state, William H. Seward, secretary under Presidents Lincoln and Andrew Johnson (1861–1869), and James G. Blaine, secretary under Presidents Garfield and Harrison (1881, 1889–1892), laid the foundation for a larger and more aggressive American role in world affairs. Seward possessed an elaborate imperial vision, based on his understanding

American Views

OUR COUNTRY, RACISM, AND AMERICAN IMPERIALISM

In 1885, the American Home Missionary Society published a small volume by Josiah Strong that would prove phenomenally popular and be reprinted repeatedly. Its very title, *Our Country*, consciously raised the question of America's national identity and purpose. In the selection featured here, Strong, the minister of Cincinnati's Central Congregational Church, sketches his view that America would achieve its proper role in the world by spreading the influence of white Anglo-Saxon Protestants.

❖ **What developments in American life did Strong regard as demonstrating the superiority of "Anglo-Saxons"?**

❖ **How did the era's preoccupation with geographical influences shape his views?**

❖ **How would Strong be likely to view the Filipino independence movement?**

❖ **What do you think he thought about immigration and race relations?**

It seems to me that God, with infinite wisdom and skill, is training the Anglo-Saxon race for an hour sure to come in the world's future. Heretofore there has always been in the history of the world a comparatively unoccupied land westward, into which the crowded countries of the East have poured their surplus populations. But the widening waves of migration, which millenniums ago rolled east and west from the valley of the Euphrates, meet today on our Pacific coast. There are no more new worlds. The unoccupied arable lands of the earth are limited, and will soon be taken. . . . Then will the world enter upon a new stage of its history—*the final competition of races, for which the Anglo-Saxon is being schooled.* . . . The mighty centrifugal tendency, inherent in this stock and strengthened in the United States, will assert itself. Then this race of unequaled energy, with all the majesty of numbers and the might of wealth behind it—the representative, let us hope, of the

---

of commercial opportunities, strategic necessities, and national destiny. Seward purchased Alaska from Russia in 1867, approved the navy's occupation of the Midway Islands in the Pacific, pushed American trade on a reluctant Japan, and repeatedly tried to acquire Caribbean naval bases (see Map 24-1). But his policy of expansion, as one observer noted, "went somewhat too far and too fast for the public," and many of his plans fizzled. Congressional opposition frustrated his efforts to obtain Haiti and the Dominican Republic and to purchase the Danish West Indies; Colombia blocked his attempt to gain construction rights for a canal across the isthmus of Panama.

Blaine was an equally vigorous advocate of expansion. He worked to extend what he called America's "commercial empire" in the Pacific. And he sought to ensure U.S. sovereignty over any canal in Panama, insisting that it be "a purely American waterway to be treated as part of our own coastline." In an effort to induce the nations of Latin America to import manufactured products from the United States rather than Europe, Blaine proposed a conference among the nations of the Western Hemisphere in 1881. The First International American Conference finally met in 1889. There Blaine called for the establishment of a customs union to reduce trade barriers among the nations of the Americas. He expected this union to strengthen U.S. control of hemispheric markets. The nations of Latin America, however, wary of ecolargest liberty, the purest Christianity, the highest civilization—having developed peculiarly aggressive traits calculated to impress its institutions upon mankind, will spread itself over the earth. If I read not amiss, this powerful race will move down upon Mexico, down upon Central and South America, out upon the islands of the sea, over upon Africa and beyond. And can anyone doubt that the result of this competition of races will be the "survival of the fittest"? . . .

To this result no war of extermination is needful; the contest is not one of arms, but of vitality and civilization. "At the present day," says Mr. Darwin, "civilized nations are everywhere supplanting barbarous nations, excepting where the climate opposes a deadly barrier; and they succeed mainly, though not exclusively, through their arts, which are products of the intellect." Thus the Finns were supplanted by the Aryan races in Europe and Asia, the Tartars by the Russians, and thus the aborigines of North America, Australia, and New Zealand are now disappearing before the all-conquering Anglo-Saxons. It seems as if these inferior tribes were only precursors of a superior race, voices in the wilderness crying: "Prepare ye the way of the Lord!" . . .

Whether the extinction of inferior races before the advancing Anglo-Saxon seems to the reader sad or otherwise, it certainly appears probable. . . . Is there room for reasonable doubt that this race, unless devitalized by alcohol and tobacco, is destined to dispossess many weaker races, assimilate others, and mold the remainder, until, in a very true and important sense, it has Anglo-Saxonized mankind? . . . In my own mind, there is no doubt that the Anglo-Saxon is to exercise the commanding influence in the world's future. . . or that the United States is to be the home of this race, the principal seat of his power, the great center of his influence.

Source: Josiah Strong, *Our Country: Its Possible Future and Its Present Crisis*, rev. ed. (1891).

nomic subordination to the colossus of the north, rejected Blaine's plan.

Hawaii

Blaine regarded Hawaii as "indispensably" part of "the American system." As early as 1842, the United States had announced its opposition to European control of Hawaii, a key way station in the China trade where New England missionaries and whalers were active. Although the islands remained under native monarchs, American influence grew, particularly as other Americans arrived to establish sugar plantations and eventually dominate the economy.

Treaties in 1875 and 1887 integrated the islands into the American economy and gave the United States control over Pearl Harbor on the island of Oahu. In 1887, the United States rejected a proposal from Britain and France for a joint guarantee of Hawaii's independence and endorsed a new Hawaiian constitution that gave political power to wealthy white residents. The obvious next step was U.S. annexation, which Blaine endorsed in 1891.

American planters soon bid for annexation. The McKinley Tariff Act of 1890 effectively closed the U.S. market to Hawaiian sugar producers, facing them with economic ruin. At the same time, Queen Liliuokalani moved to restore native control of Hawaiian affairs. To ensure market access and protect their political authority, the American planters decided to seek annexation to the United States. In

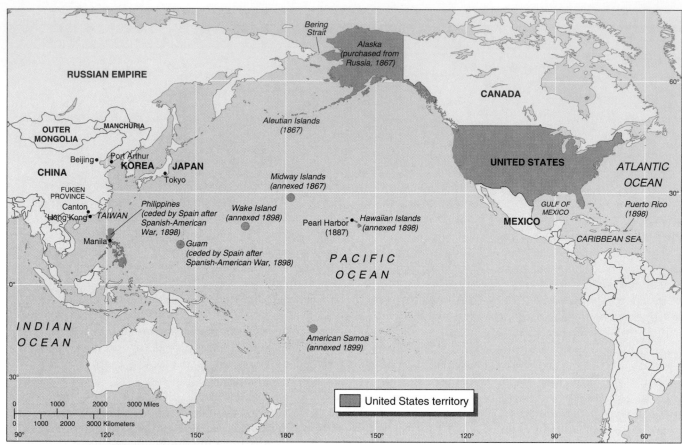

Map 24-1   United States Expansion in the Pacific, 1867-1899
Pursuing visions of a commercial empire in the Pacific, the United States steadily expanded its territorial possessions as well as its influence there in the late nineteenth century.

1893, they overthrew the queen. John Stevens, the American minister, ordered U.S. Marines to help the rebels. He then declared an American protectorate over the new Hawaii government and wired Washington: "The Hawaiian pear is now fully ripe, and this is the golden hour for the United States to pluck it." A delegation from the new provisional government, containing no native Hawaiians, went to Washington to draft a treaty for annexation. President Harrison signed the pact but could not get Senate approval before the new Cleveland administration took office.

Cleveland immediately called for an investigation of the whole affair. Soon convinced that "the undoubted sentiment of the people is for the Queen, against the provisional Government, and against annexation," Cleveland apologized to the queen for the "flagrant wrong" done her by the "reprehensible conduct of the American minister and the unauthorized presence on land of a military force of the United States." But the American-dominated provisional government refused to step down, and Cleveland's rejection of annexation set off a noisy debate.

Many Republicans strongly supported annexation. One eastern Republican manufacturer called for the annexation of Hawaii as the first step toward making the Pacific "an American ocean, dominated by American commercial enterprise for all time." On the West Coast, where California business interests had close ties with the islands, the commercial and strategic value of Hawaii seemed obvious. The *San Francisco Examiner* declared, "Hoist the Stars and Stripes. It is a case of manifest destiny."

Arguments for annexation also reflected racial imperialism. Annexation, so it was said, would both fittingly reward the enterprising white residents of Hawaii and provide an opportunity to civilize native Hawaiians.

Democrats generally opposed annexation. They doubted, as Missouri Senator George Vest declared, whether the United States should desert its traditional principles and "venture upon the great colonial system of the European powers."

The Hawaiian episode of 1893 thus foreshadowed the arguments over imperialism at the end of the century and emphasized the policy differences between Democrats and the increasingly expansionist Republicans.

Chile and Venezuela

American reactions to developments in other countries in the 1890s also reflected an increasingly assertive national policy and excitable public opinion. In 1891, American sailors on shore leave in Chile became involved in a drunken brawl that left two of them dead, seventeen injured, and dozens in jail. Encouraged by a combative navy, President Harrison threatened military retaliation against Chile, provoking an outburst of bellicose nationalism in the United States. Harrison relented only when Chile apologized and paid an indemnity.

A few years later, the United States again threatened war over a minor issue, but against a more formidable opponent. In 1895, President Cleveland intervened in a boundary dispute between Great Britain and Venezuela over British Guiana. Cleveland was motivated not only by the long-standing U.S. goal of challenging Britain for Latin American markets but also by ever more expansive notions of the **Monroe Doctrine** and the authority of the United States. Secretary of State Richard Olney sent Britain a blunt note (a "twenty-inch gun," Cleveland called it) demanding arbitration of the disputed territory and stoutly asserting American supremacy in the Western Hemisphere.

Cleveland urged Congress to establish a commission to determine the boundary and enforce its decision by war if necessary. As war fever swept the United States, Britain agreed to arbitration, recognizing the limited nature of the issue that so convulsed Anglo-American relations.

The United States' assertion of hemispheric dominance angered Latin Americans, and their fears deepened when it decided arbitration terms with Britain without consulting Venezuela, which protested before bowing to American pressure. The further significance of the Venezuelan crisis, as Captain Mahan noted, lay in its "awakening of our countrymen to the fact that we must come out of our isolation . . . and take our share in the turmoil of the world."

The Spanish-American War

The forces pushing the United States toward imperialism and international power came to a head in the Spanish-American War. Cuba's quest for independence from the oppressive colonial control of Spain activated Americans' long-standing interest in the island. But few foresaw that the war that finally erupted in 1898 would dramatically change America's relationships with the rest of the world and give it a colonial empire.

The Cuban Revolution

Cuba was the last major European colony in Latin America, with an economic potential that attracted American business interests and a strategic significance for any Central American canal. In the 1880s, Spanish control became increasingly harsh, and in 1895 the Cubans launched a revolt.

The rebellion was a classic guerrilla war in which the rebels controlled the countryside and the Spanish army the towns and cities. American economic interests were seriously affected, for both Cubans and Spaniards destroyed American property and disrupted American trade. But the brutality with which Spain attempted to suppress the revolt promoted American sympathy for the Cuban insurgents. Determined to cut the rebels off from their peasant supporters, the Spaniards herded most civilians into "reconcentration camps," where tens of thousands died of starvation and disease.

Americans' sympathy was further aroused by the sensationalist **yellow press**. To attract readers and boost advertising revenues, the popular press of the day adopted bold headlines, fevered editorials, and real or exaggerated stories of violence, sex, and corruption. A circulation war between William Randolph Hearst's *New York Journal* and Joseph Pulitzer's *New York World* helped stimulate interest in Cuban war. "Blood on the roadsides, blood on the fields, blood on the doorsteps, blood, blood, blood! The old, the young, the weak, the crippled—all are butchered without mercy," the *World* feverishly reported of Cuba. "Is there no nation wise enough, brave enough to aid this blood-smitten land?" The nation's religious press, partly because it reflected the prejudice many Protestants held against Catholic Spain, also advocated American intervention.

As the Cuban rebellion dragged on, more and more Americans advocated intervention to stop the carnage, protect U.S. investments, or uphold various principles. Expansionists like Roosevelt and Lodge clamored for intervention, but so did their opponents. Populists, for example, sympathized with a people seeking independence from colonial rule and petitioned Congress to support the crusade for Cuban freedom. In the election of 1896, both major parties endorsed Cuban independence.

Growing Tensions

President William McKinley's administration soon focused on Cuba. McKinley's principal complaint was that chronic disorder in Cuba disrupted America's investments and agitated public opinion. Personally opposed to military intervention, McKinley first used diplomacy to press Spain to adopt reforms that would settle the rebellion. Following his instructions, the U.S. minister to Spain warned the Spanish government that if it did not quickly establish peace, the United States would take whatever steps it "should deem necessary to procure this result." In late 1897, Spain modified its brutal military tactics and offered limited autonomy to Cuba. But Cubans insisted on complete independence, which Spain refused to grant.

Relations between the United States and Spain deteriorated. On February 15, 1898, the U.S. battleship *Maine* blew up in Havana harbor, killing 260 men. The Spaniards were not responsible for the tragedy, which a modern naval inquiry has attributed to an internal accident. But many Americans agreed with Theodore Roosevelt, the assistant secretary of the navy, who called it "an act of dirty treachery on the part of the Spaniards" and told McKinley that only war was "compatible with our national honor."

Other pressures soon began to build on the president. Senator Lodge reported a consensus "that this situation must end. We cannot go on indefinitely with this strain, this suspense, and this uncertainty, this tottering upon the verge of war. It is killing to business." McKinley also feared that a moderate policy would endanger congressional candidates. Again Senator Lodge, although hesitant to suggest "war for political reasons," nevertheless advised McKinley, "If the war in Cuba drags on through the summer with nothing done, we shall go down in the greatest [election] defeat ever known."

At the end of March 1898, McKinley sent Spain an ultimatum. He demanded an armistice in Cuba, an end to the reconcentration policy, and the acceptance of American arbitration, which implied Cuban independence. Desperately, Spain made concessions, abolishing reconcentration and declaring a unilateral armistice. But McKinley had already begun war preparations. He submitted a war message to Congress on April 11, asking for authority to use force against Spain "in the name of humanity, in the name of civilization, in behalf of endangered American interests." Congress declared war on Spain on April 25, 1898.

Most interventionists were not imperialists, and Congress added the **Teller Amendment** to the war resolution, disclaiming any intention of annexing Cuba and promising that Cubans would govern themselves. Congress also refused to approve either a canal bill or the annexation of Hawaii. Neverthe-

less, the Spanish-American War did turn the nation toward imperialism.

War and Empire

The decisive engagement of the war took place not in Cuba but in another Spanish colony, the Philippines, and it involved the favored tool of the expansionists, the new navy (see Map 24-2). Once war was declared, Commodore George Dewey led the U.S. Asiatic squadron into Manila Bay and destroyed the weaker Spanish fleet on May 1, 1898. The navy had long coveted Manila Bay as a strategic harbor, but other Americans, casting an eye on commercial opportunities in China, saw a greater significance in the victory. With Dewey's triumph, exulted one expansionist, "We are taking our proper rank among the nations of the world. We are after markets, the greatest markets now existing in the world." To expand this foothold in Asia, McKinley ordered troops to the Philippines, postponing the military expedition to Cuba itself.

Dewey's victory also precipitated the annexation of Hawaii, which had seemed hopeless only weeks before. Annexationists now pointed to the islands' strategic importance as steppingstones to Manila. "To maintain our flag in the Philippines, we must raise our flag in Hawaii," the *New York Sun* contended. McKinley himself privately declared, "We need Hawaii just as much and a good deal more than we did California. It is Manifest Destiny." In July, Congress approved annexation, a decision welcomed by Hawaii's white minority. Natives solemnly protested this step taken "without reference to the consent of the people of the Hawaiian Islands." Filipinos would soon face the same American imperial impulse.

Military victory also came swiftly in Cuba, once the U.S. Army finally landed in late June. Victory depended largely on Spanish ineptitude, for the American troops had to fight with antiquated weapons and wear wool uniforms in the sweltering tropics. They were issued rotting and poisoned food by a corrupt and inefficient War Department. More than five thousand Americans died of diseases and accidents brought on by such mismanagement; only 379 were killed in battle. State militias supplemented the small regular army, as did volunteer units, such as the famous Rough Riders, a cavalry unit of cowboys and eastern dandies assembled by Theodore Roosevelt.

U.S. naval power again proved decisive. In a lopsided battle on July 3, the obsolete Spanish squadron in Cuba was destroyed, isolating the Spanish army and guaranteeing its defeat. U.S. forces occupied the nearby Spanish colony of Puerto Rico

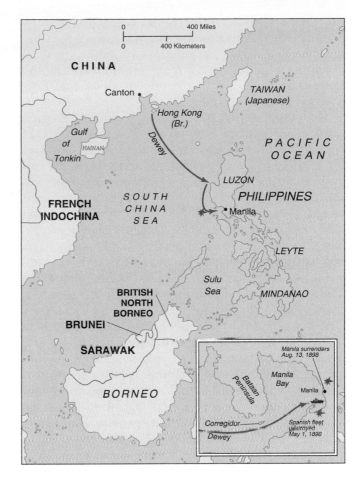

Map 24-2   The Spanish-American War
The United States gained quick victories in both theaters of the Spanish-American War. Its naval power proved decisive, with Commodore Dewey destroying one enemy fleet in the Philippines and a second U.S. naval force cutting off the Spanish in Cuba.

without serious opposition. Humbled, Spain signed an armistice ending the war on August 12.

Americans were delighted with their military achievements, but the *Philadelphia Inquirer* cautioned, "With peace will come new responsibilities, which must be met. We have colonies to look after and develop."

The Treaty of Paris

The armistice required Spain to accept Cuban independence, cede Puerto Rico and Guam (a Pacific island between Hawaii and the Philippines), and allow the Americans to occupy Manila pending the final disposition of the Philippines at a formal peace conference. The acquisition of Puerto Rico and Guam indicated the expansionist nature the conflict had assumed for the United States. So did the postponement of the Philippine issue. McKinley knew that delay would permit the advocates of expansion to build public support for annexation.

But he was motivated to acquire the Philippines primarily by a determination to use the islands to strengthen America's political and commercial position in East Asia. Moreover, he believed the Filipinos poorly suited to self-rule, and he feared that Germany or Japan might seize the Philippines if the United States did not. Meeting in Paris in December, American and Spanish negotiators settled the final terms for peace. Spain agreed—despite Filipino demands for independence—to cede the Philippines to the United States.

The decision to acquire the Philippines sparked a dramatic debate over the ratification of the Treaty of Paris. The *United States Investor* spoke for business leaders, for example, in demanding the Philippines as "a base of operations in the East" to protect American interests in China; other economic expansionists argued that the Philippines themselves had valuable resources and were a market for American goods or warned that "our commercial rivals in the Orient" would grab the islands if the United States did not. The *Presbyterian Banner* spoke for what it termed a nearly unanimous religious press in affirming "the desirability of America's retaining the Philippines as a duty in the interest of human freedom and Christian progress."

Opponents of the treaty included such prominent figures as the civil service reformer Carl Schurz, steel baron Andrew Carnegie, social reformer Jane Addams, labor leader Samuel Gompers, and author Mark Twain. Their organizational base was the **Anti-Imperialist League**, which campaigned against the treaty, distributing pamphlets, petitioning Congress, and holding rallies. League members' criticisms reflected a conviction that imperialism was a repudiation of America's moral and political traditions embodied in the Declaration of Independence. The acquisition of overseas colonies, they argued, conflicted with the nation's commitment to liberty and its claim to moral superiority. They regarded as loathsome and hypocritical the transformation of a war to free Cuba into a campaign for imperial conquest and subjugation. Some African-Americans derided the rhetoric of Anglo-Saxon superiority that underlay imperialism and even organized the Black Man's Burden Association to promote Philippine independence.

But other arguments were less high-minded. Many anti-imperialists objected to expansion on the racist grounds that Filipinos were inferior and unassimilable. Gompers feared that cheap Asian labor would undercut the wages and living standards of American workers. The *San Francisco Call*, representing California-Hawaiian sugar interests, also wanted no competition from the Philippines.

Finally, on February 6, 1899, the Senate narrowly ratified the treaty. Then, by a single vote, the Republicans defeated a Democratic proposal for Philippine independence once a stable government had been established; the United States would keep the islands.

William Jennings Bryan attempted to make the election of 1900 a referendum on "the paramount issue" of imperialism, promising to free the Philippines if the Democrats won. But some of the most ardent anti-imperialists were conservatives who remained loyal to McKinley because they could not tolerate Bryan's economic policies. Republicans also played on the nationalist emotions evoked by the war, especially by nominating Theodore Roosevelt for vice president. "If you choose to vote for America, if you choose to vote for the flag for which we fought," Roosevelt said, "then you will vote to sustain the administration of President McKinley." Bryan lost again, as

in 1896, and under Republican leadership, the United States became an imperial nation.

Imperial Ambitions: The United States and East Asia, 1899–1917

In 1899, as the United States occupied its new empire, Assistant Secretary of State John Bassett Moore observed that the nation had become "a world power. . . . Where formerly we had only commercial interests, we now have territorial and political interests as well." American policies to promote those expanded interests focused first on East Asia and Latin America, where the Spanish-American War had provided the United States with both opportunities and challenges. In Asia, the first issue concerned the fate of the Philippines, but looming beyond it were American ambitions in China, where other imperial nations had their own goals.

The Filipino-American War

Filipino nationalists, like Cuban insurgents, were already fighting Spain for their independence before the sudden American intervention. The Filipino leader, Emilio Aguinaldo, welcomed Dewey's naval victory as the sign of a de facto alliance with the United States; he then issued a declaration of independence and proclaimed the Philippine Republic. But the Filipinos' optimism declined as American officials acted in an increasingly imperious manner toward them, first refusing to meet with the "savages," then insisting that Filipino forces withdraw from Manila or face "forcible action," and finally dismissing the claims of Aguinaldo and "his so-called government." When the Treaty of Paris provided for U.S. ownership rather than independence, Filipinos felt betrayed. Mounting tensions erupted in a battle between American and Filipino troops outside Manila on February 4, 1899, sparking a long and brutal war.

Ultimately, the United States used nearly four times as many soldiers to suppress the Filipinos as to defeat Spain in Cuba and, in a tragic irony, employed many of the same brutal methods for which it had condemned Spain. Americans often made little effort to distinguish between soldiers and noncombatants, viewing all Filipinos with racial antagonism. Before the military imposed censorship on war news, reporters confirmed U.S. atrocities; one wrote that "American troops have been relentless, have killed to exterminate men, women, and children, prisoners

Roosevelt's well-advertised exploits in the Spanish-American War propelled his political career. After being elected governor of New York in 1898, he received the Republican nomination for vice president in 1900 and often seemed to overshadow President McKinley.

and captives, active insurgents and suspected people, from lads of 10 and up." A California newspaper defended such actions with remarkable candor: "Let us all be frank. WE DO NOT WANT THE FILIPINOS. WE DO WANT THE PHILIPPINES. . . . The more of them killed the better. It seems harsh. But they must yield before the superior race."

The overt racism of the war repelled African-Americans. John Mitchell, a Virginia editor, condemned all the talk of "white man's burden" as deceptive rhetoric for brutal acts that could not be "defended either in moral or international law."

The Anti-Imperialist League revived, citing the war as proof of the corrosive influence of imperialism on the nation's morals and principles. Professors addressed antiwar rallies on college campuses. "Alas, what a fall," one University of Michigan professor told his audience. "Within the circuit of a single year to have declined from the moral leadership of mankind into the common brigandage of the robber nations of the world."

By 1902, however, the American military had largely suppressed the rebellion, and the United

States had established a colonial government. Compared to the Americans' brutal war policies, U. S. colonial rule was relatively benign, though paternalistic. William Howard Taft, the first governor general, launched a program that brought the islands new schools and roads, a public health system, and an economy tied closely to both the United States and a small Filipino elite.

China and the Open Door

America's determined involvement in the Philippines reflected its preoccupation with China. By the mid-1890s, other powers threatened prospects for American commercial expansion in China. Japan, after defeating China in 1895, annexed Taiwan and secured economic privileges in the mainland province of Fukien (Fujian); the major European powers then competed aggressively to claim other areas of China as their own **spheres of influence**. In Manchuria, Russia won control of Port Arthur (Lüshun) and the right to construct a railway. Germany secured a ninety-nine year lease on another Chinese port and mining and railroad privileges on the Shandong Peninsula. The British wrung special concessions in Kowloon, opposite Hong Kong, as well as a port facing the Russians in Manchuria. France gained a lease on ports and exclusive commercial privileges in southern China.

These developments alarmed the American business community. It was confident that given an equal opportunity, the United States would prevail in international trade because of its efficient production and marketing systems. But the creation of exclusive spheres of influence would limit the opportunity to compete. In early 1898, business leaders organized the Committee on American Interests in China to lobby Washington to promote American trade in the shrinking Chinese market. The committee persuaded the nation's chambers of commerce to petition the McKinley administration to act. And the State Department soon reported that, given overproduction for the home market, "the United States has important interests at stake in the partition of commercial facilities in regions which are likely to offer developing markets for its goods. Nowhere is this consideration of more interest than in its relation to the Chinese Empire."

In 1899, Secretary of State John Hay asked the imperial powers to maintain an **Open Door** for the commercial and financial activities of all nations within their Chinese spheres of influence. Privately, Hay had already approved a plan to seize a Chinese port for the United States if necessary to join in the partition of China, but equal opportunity for trade and investment would serve American interests far better. It would avoid the expense of military occupation, avert further domestic criticism of U.S. imperialism, and guarantee a wider sphere for American business.

The other nations replied evasively, except for Russia, which rejected the Open Door concept. In 1900, an antiforeign Chinese nationalist movement known as the Boxers laid seige to the diplomatic quarters in Beijing. The defeat of the Boxer Rebellion by a multinational military force, to which the United States contributed troops, again raised the prospect of a division of China among colonial powers. Hay sent a second Open Door note, reaffirming "the principle of equal and impartial trade" and respect for China's territorial integrity.

The Open Door became a cardinal doctrine of American foreign policy in the twentieth century. The United States promoted an informal or economic empire, as opposed to the traditional territorial colonial empire that Americans preferred to identify with European powers. Henceforth, American economic interests expected the U.S. government to oppose any developments that threatened to close other nations' economies to American penetration and to advance "private enterprise" abroad.

Rivalry with Japan and Russia

At the turn of the twentieth century, both the Japanese and the Russians were more deeply involved in East Asia than the United States was. They expressed little support for the Open Door, which they correctly saw as favoring American interests over their own. But in pursuing their ambitions in China, the two came into conflict with each other. Japan in 1904 attacked the Russian fleet at Port Arthur and defeated the Russians in Manchuria.

In this Russo-Japanese war, American sympathies lay with Japan, for the Russians were attempting to close Manchuria to foreign trade. President Theodore Roosevelt thus welcomed the Japanese attack in the belief that "Japan is playing our game." But he soon feared that an overwhelming Japanese victory could threaten American interests as much as Russian expansionism did, so he skillfully mediated an end to the war. In the Treaty of Portsmouth in 1905, Japan won control of Russia's sphere of influence in Manchuria, half the Russian island of Sakhalin, and recognition of its domination of Korea.

This treaty marked Japan's emergence as a great power, but ironically, it worsened relations with the United States. Anti-American riots broke out in Tokyo. The Japanese people blamed Roosevelt for

obstructing further Japanese gains. Tensions were then aggravated by San Francisco's decision in 1906 to segregate Asian schoolchildren to avoid affecting the "youthful impressions" of white children. Japan regarded this as a racist insult, and Roosevelt worried that "the infernal fools in California" would provoke war. Finally he got the school board to rescind its order in exchange for his limiting Japanese immigration. Under the **Gentlemen's Agreement**, Japan agreed not to issue passports to workers coming to the United States, and the United States promised not to prohibit Japanese immigration overtly or completely.

To calm their mutual suspicions in East Asia, the United States and Japan adopted other agreements but failed to halt the deteriorating relationship. Increasingly, Japan began to exclude American trade from its territories in East Asia and to press for further control over China. Elihu Root, Roosevelt's secretary of state, insisted that the Open Door and American access be maintained but asserted also that the United States did not want to be "a protagonist in a controversy in China with Russia and Japan or with either of them." This paradox would plague American foreign policy in Asia for decades.

Imperial Power: The United States and Latin America, 1899–1917

In Latin America, where no major powers directly challenged American objectives, the United States was more successful in exercising imperial power (see Map 24-3). In the two decades after the Spanish-American War, the United States intervened militarily in Latin America no fewer than twenty times to promote its own strategic and economic interests (see the summary table "U.S. Interventions in Latin America, 1891–1933"). Policymakers believed that these goals required restricting the influence of European nations in the region, building an isthmian canal under American control, and establishing the order thought necessary for American trade and investments to expand. Intervention at times achieved these goals, but it often ignored the wishes and interests of Latin Americans, provoked resistance and disorder, and created lasting ill will.

U.S. Rule in Puerto Rico

Well before 1898, expansionists like James G. Blaine had advocated acquiring Puerto Rico because of its strategic location in the Caribbean. During the Span-

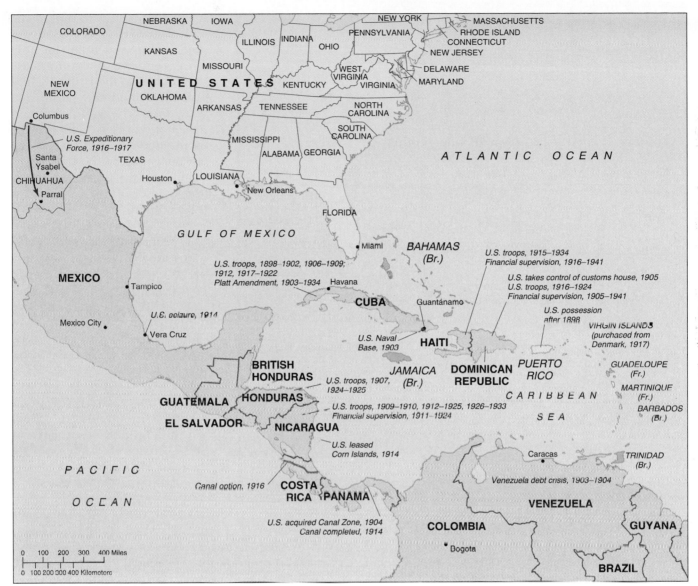

Map 24-3 The United States in the Caribbean
*For strategic and economic reasons, the United States repeatedly intervened in the Caribbean
in the first three decades of the twentieth century. Such interventions protected the U.S. claim
to dominance but often provoked great hostility among Latin Americans.*

ish-American War, Roosevelt urged Washington, "Do not make peace until we get" Puerto Rico. Military invasion and the Treaty of Paris soon brought the island under American rule.

In 1900, the United States established a civil government, but it was under U.S. control, and popular participation was even less than under Spain. In the so-called *Insular Cases* (1901), the Supreme Court upheld Congress's authority to establish an inferior status for Puerto Rico, as an "unincorporated territory" without promise of statehood. Disappointed Puerto Ricans pressed to end this colonial status. In 1917, the United States granted

citizenship and greater political rights to Puerto Ricans, but their island remained an unincorporated territory under an American governor appointed by the president.

Economic development also disappointed most islanders, for American investors quickly gained control of the best land and pursued large-scale sugar production for the U.S. market. By 1929, the new governor—ironically, Theodore Roosevelt Jr.—found that under the domination of American capital, "poverty was widespread and hunger, almost to the verge of starvation, common." A subsequent investigation concluded that while "the influx of capital has

SUMMARY

U.S. INTERVENTIONS IN LATIN AMERICA, 1891–1933

Country	Type of Intervention	Year
Chile	Ultimatum	1892
Colombia	Military intervention	1903
Cuba	Occupation	1898–1902, 1906–1909, 1912, 1917–1922
Dominican Republic	Military and administrative intervention	1905–1907
	Occupation	1916–1924
Haiti	Occupation	1915–1934
Mexico	Military intervention	1914, 1916–1917
Nicaragua	Occupation	1912–1925, 1927–1933
Panama	Acquisition of Canal Zone	1904
Puerto Rico	Military invasion and territorial acquisition	1898

increased the efficiency of production and promoted general economic development," the benefits had gone largely to Americans not ordinary Puerto Ricans, whose conditions were "deplorable." Increasingly, they left their homes to seek work in the United States.

Cuba as a U.S. Protectorate

Despite the Teller Amendment, the Spanish-American War did not leave Cuba independent. McKinley opposed independence and a U.S. military government was established in the island. Only in 1900, when the Democrats made an issue of imperialism, did McKinley summon a Cuban convention to draft a constitution under the direction of the American military governor, General Leonard Wood. This constitution restricted suffrage on the basis of property and education, leaving few Cubans with the right to vote.

The United States made troop withdrawal contingent on Cuba's adding to its constitution the provisions of the **Platt Amendment**, which restricted

Cuba's autonomy in diplomatic relations with other countries and in internal financial policies, required Cuba to lease naval bases to the United States, and most important, authorized U.S. intervention to maintain order and preserve Cuban independence. As General Wood correctly observed, "There is, of course, little or no independence left Cuba under the Platt Amendment."

Cubans quickly learned that when the United States prevented Cuba from signing a treaty extending the same trade privileges to the British that U.S. merchants enjoyed. The Open Door would not apply in the Caribbean, which was to be an American sphere of influence. To preserve that influence, the United States sent troops into Cuba three times between 1906 and 1917 (Roosevelt admitted his recurrent itch to "wipe its people off the face of the earth"). The last occupation lasted six years.

During their occupations of Cuba, the Americans modernized its financial system, built roads and public schools, and developed a public health and sanitation program that eradicated the deadly disease of yellow fever. But most Cubans thought these material benefits did not compensate for their loss of political and economic independence.

The Panama Canal

The Spanish-American War intensified the long American interest in a canal through Central America to eliminate the lengthy and dangerous ocean route around South America. Its commercial value seemed obvious, but the war emphasized its strategic importance. McKinley declared that a canal was now "demanded by the annexation of the Hawaiian Islands and the prospective expansion of our influence and commerce in the Pacific."

Theodore Roosevelt moved quickly to implement McKinley's commitment to a canal after becoming president in 1901. His canal diplomacy helped establish the assertive presidency that has characterized U.S. foreign policy in the twentieth century.

Possible canal sites included Nicaragua and Panama, then part of Colombia. A canal through Panama would require an elaborate system of locks. But the French-owned Panama Canal Company had been unsuccessfully trying to build a canal in Panama and was now eager to sell its rights to the project before they expired in 1904.

In 1902, Congress directed Roosevelt to purchase the French company's claims for $40 million and build the canal in Panama if Colombia ceded a strip of land across the isthmus on reasonable terms. Otherwise, Roosevelt was to negotiate with Nicaragua for the alternate route. In 1903, Roosevelt pressed Colombia to sell a canal zone to the United States for $10 million and an annual payment of $250,000. Colombia, however, rejected the proposal, fearing the loss of its sovereignty in Panama and hoping for more money. After all, when the Panama Canal Company's rights expired, Colombia could then legitimately collect the $40 million so generously offered the company.

Roosevelt warned "those contemptible little creatures" in Colombia that they were "imperiling their own future." Instead of using direct force Roosevelt worked with Philippe Bunau-Varilla, a French official of the Panama Canal Company, to exploit long-smoldering Panamanian discontent with Colombia. Roosevelt's purpose was to get the canal zone, Bunau-Varilla's to get the American money. Roosevelt ordered U.S. naval forces to Panama; from New York, Bunau-Varilla coordinated a revolt against Colombian authority directed by officials of the Panama Railroad, owned by Bunau-Varilla's canal company. The bloodless "revolution" succeeded when U.S. forces prevented Colombian troops from landing in Panama, although the United States was bound by treaty to maintain Colombian sovereignty. Bunau-Varilla promptly signed a treaty accepting Roosevelt's original terms for a canal zone and making Panama a U.S. protectorate. Panamanians themselves denounced the treaty for surrendering sovereignty in the zone to the United States, which took formal control of the canal zone in 1904 and completed construction of the Panama Canal in 1914.

Many Americans were appalled by what the *Chicago American* called Roosevelt's "rough-riding assault upon another republic over the shattered wreckage of international law and diplomatic usage." But others, as *Public Opinion* reported, wanted a "canal above all things" and were willing to overlook moral questions and approve the acquisition of the canal zone as simply "a business question." Roosevelt himself boasted, "I took the Canal Zone and let Congress debate," but his unnecessary and arrogant actions generated resentment among Latin Americans that rankled for decades.

The Roosevelt Corollary

To protect the security of the canal, the United States increased its authority in the Caribbean. The objective was to establish conditions there that would both eliminate any pretext for European intervention and promote American control over trade and investment. "If we intend to say hands off to the powers of Europe," Roosevelt concluded, "then sooner or later we must keep order ourselves."

In his 1904 annual message to Congress, Roosevelt announced a new policy, the so-called **Roosevelt Corollary** to the Monroe Doctrine. "Chronic wrongdoing," he declared, would cause the United States to exercise "an international police power" in Latin America. The Monroe Doctrine had expressed American hostility to European intervention in Latin America; the Roosevelt Corollary attempted to justify U.S. intervention and authority in the region. Roosevelt invoked his corollary immediately, imposing American management of the debts and customs duties of the Dominican Republic in 1905. Financial insolvency was averted, popular revolution prevented, and possible European intervention forestalled.

Latin Americans vigorously resented the United States' unilateral claims to authority. By 1907, the so-called Drago Doctrine (named after Argentina's foreign minister) was incorporated into international law, prohibiting armed intervention to collect debts. Still, the United States would continue to invoke the Roosevelt Corollary to advance its interests in the hemisphere. As Secretary of State Elihu Root asserted, "The inevitable effect of our building the Canal must be to require us to police the surrounding premises." He then added, "In the nature of things, trade and control, and the obligation to keep order which go with them, must come our way."

Dollar Diplomacy

Roosevelt's successor as president, William Howard Taft, hoped to promote U.S. interests without such combative rhetoric and naked force. He described his plan as one of "substituting dollars for bullets"—using government action to encourage private American investments in Latin America to supplant European interests, promote development and stability, and gain profits for American bankers. Under this **dollar diplomacy**, American investments in the Caribbean increased dramatically during Taft's presidency from 1909 to 1913, and the State Department helped arrange for American bankers to establish financial control over Haiti and Honduras.

But Taft employed military force more frequently than Roosevelt had, with Nicaragua a major target. In 1909, Taft sent U.S. troops there to aid a revolution fomented by an American mining corporation and to seize the Nicaraguan customs houses. Under the new government, American bankers then gained control of Nicaragua's national bank, railroad, and customs service. To protect these arrangements, U.S. troops were again dispatched in 1912. To control popular opposition to the American client government, the marines remained in Nicaragua for two decades. Military power, not the social and economic improvement promised by dollar diplomacy, kept Nicaragua's minority government stable and subordinate to the United States.

Dollar diplomacy increased American power and influence in the Caribbean and tied underdeveloped countries to the United States economically and strategically. But this policy failed to improve conditions for most Latin Americans. U.S. officials remained primarily concerned with promoting American control and extracting American profits from the region, not with the well-being of its population. Not surprisingly, dollar diplomacy proved unpopular in Latin America.

Wilsonian Interventions

Taking office in 1913, the Democrat Woodrow Wilson promised that the United States would "never again seek one additional foot of territory by conquest" but would instead work to promote "human rights, national integrity, and opportunity" in Latin America. Wilson also named as his secretary of state the Democratic symbol of anti-imperialism, William Jennings Bryan. Their generous intentions were apparent when Bryan signed a treaty with Colombia apologizing for Roosevelt's seizure of the Panama Canal Zone in 1903.

Nonetheless, Wilson believed that the United States had to expand its exports and investments abroad and that U.S. dominance of the Caribbean was strategically necessary. He also shared the racist belief that Latin Americans were inferior and needed paternalistic guidance from the United States, through military force if necessary. His self-righteousness and determination to transform other peoples' behavior led his policies to be dubbed "missionary diplomacy," but they also contained elements of Roosevelt's commitment to military force and Taft's reliance on economic power.

In 1915, Wilson ordered U.S. Marines to Haiti. The U.S. Navy selected a new Haitian president, but real authority rested with the American military, which controlled Haiti until 1934, protecting the small elite who cooperated with foreign interests

and exploited their own people. As usual, American military rule improved the country's transportation, sanitation, and educational systems, but the forced-labor program that the U.S. adopted to build such public works provoked widespread resentment. In 1919, marines suppressed a revolt against American domination, killing more than three thousand Haitians.

Wilson also intervened elsewhere in the Caribbean. In 1916, when the Dominican Republic refused to cede control of its finances to U.S. bankers, Wilson ordered the marines to occupy the country. The marines ousted Dominican officials, installed a military government to rule "on behalf of the Dominican government," and ran the nation until 1924. In 1917, the United States intervened in Cuba, which remained under American control until 1922.

Wilson also involved himself in the internal affairs of Mexico. In 1913, General Victoriano Huerta seized control of the country from revolutionaries who had recently overthrown dictator Porfirio Diaz. Wilson was appalled by the violence of Huerta's power grab and was aware that opponents had organized to reestablish constitutional government.

Wilson hoped to bring the Constitutionalists to power and "to secure Mexico a better government under which all contracts and business and concessions will be safer than they have been." He authorized arms sales to their forces, led by Venustiano Carranza; pressured Britain and other nations to deprive Huerta of foreign support; and blockaded the Mexican port of Vera Cruz. In April 1914 Wilson exploited a minor incident to have the marines attack and occupy Vera Cruz. Even Carranza and the Constitutionalists denounced the American occupation as unwarranted aggression. By August, Carranza had toppled Huerta, and Wilson shifted his support to Francisco ("Pancho") Villa. But Carranza's growing popular support in Mexico and Wilson's preoccupation with World War I in Europe finally led the United States to grant de facto recognition to the Carranza government in October 1915.

Villa then began terrorizing New Mexico and Texas, hoping to provoke an American intervention that would undermine Carranza. In 1916, Wilson ordered troops under General John J. Pershing to pursue Villa into Mexico, leading Carranza to fear a permanent U.S. occupation of northern Mexico. Soon the American soldiers were fighting the Mexican army rather than Villa's bandits. On the brink of full-fledged war, Wilson finally ordered U.S. troops to withdraw in January 1917 and extended full recognition to the Carranza government. His aggressive tactics had not merely failed but also embittered relations with Mexico.

Conclusion

By the time of Woodrow Wilson's presidency, the United States had been expanding its involvement in world affairs for half a century. Several themes had emerged from this activity: increasing American domination of the Caribbean, continuing interest in East Asia, the creation of an overseas empire, and the evolution of the United States into a major world power. Underlying these developments were an uneasy mixture of ideas and objectives. The American involvement in the world reflected a traditional, if often misguided, sense of national rectitude and mission. Generous humanitarian impulses vied with ugly racist prejudices as Americans sought both to help other peoples and to direct them toward U.S. concepts of religion, sanitation, capitalist development, and public institutions. American motives ranged from ensuring national security and competing with European colonial powers to the conviction that the United States had to expand its economic interests abroad. But if imperialism, both informal and at times colonial, brought Americans greater wealth and power, it also increased tensions in Asia and contributed to anti-American hostility and revolutionary ferment in Latin America. It also entangled the United States in the Great Power rivalries that would ultimately result in two world wars.

Review Questions

1. What factors, old and new, shaped American foreign policy in the late nineteenth century? How were they interrelated?

2. How were individual politicians and diplomats able to affect America's foreign policy? How were they constrained by government institutions, private groups, and public opinion?

3. To what extent was the United States' emergence as an imperial power a break from, as opposed to a culmination of, its earlier policies and national development?

4. How effective were U.S. interventions in Latin America? What were the objectives and consequences?

Recommended Reading

Robert L. Beisner, *From the Old Diplomacy to the New, 1865–1900*, 2d ed. (1986). Beisner conducts an excellent analysis of historiographical issues.

Charles S. Campbell, *The Transformation of American Foreign Relations, 1865–1900* (1976). This comprehensive and cautious survey provides many insights in U.S. foreign policy.

David F. Healy, *Drive to Hegemony: The United States in the Caribbean, 1898–1917* (1988). Healy's valuable account highlights a key area of American foreign policy.

Walter LaFeber, *The American Search for Opportunity, 1865–1913* (1993). This fascinating study documents the disruptive international consequences of America's rise to world power.

Walter LaFeber, *The New Empire: An Interpretation of American Expansion, 1860–1898* (1963). This influential study emphasizes economic factors on American foreign policy.

H. Wayne Morgan, *America's Road to Empire: The War with Spain and Overseas Expansion* (1965). Morgan's is a good general survey that is especially strong on the Cuban revolution and internal politics.

John L. Offner, *An Unwanted War: The Diplomacy of the United States and Spain over Cuba, 1895–1898* (1992). This revisionist account maintains that conflict over Cuba was inevitable.

Where to Learn More

❖ **Mission Houses, Honolulu, Hawaii.** Built between 1821 and 1841, these buildings were homes and shops of missionaries sent to Hawaii by the American Board of Commissioners for Foreign Missions. Their exhibits include furnishings and memorabilia of a group important in developing American ties with Hawaii.

❖ **Funston Memorial Home, Iola, Kansas.** Operated as a museum by the Kansas State Historical Society, this is the boyhood home of General Frederick Funston, prominent in the Spanish-American War and the Filipino-American War.

❖ **James G. Blaine House, Augusta, Maine.** The Executive Mansion of Maine's governor since 1919, this house was formerly Blaine's home and still contains his study and furnishings from the time he served as secretary of state and U.S. senator.

❖ **Seward House, Auburn, New York.** The home of William H. Seward contains furniture and momentos from his career as secretary of state.

25 AMERICA AND THE GREAT WAR, 1914–1920

CHAPTER OUTLINE

On the evening of April 2, 1917, Woodrow Wilson, escorted by cavalry, drove through a misty rain down Pennsylvania Avenue to Capitol Hill, which was eerily illuminated by searchlights. All day, the antiwar Emergency Peace Federation had lobbied Congress; Senator Henry Cabot Lodge of Massachusetts had even punched one pacifist. Now mounted police with drawn sabers held back silent crowds as the president strode into the house chamber and asked Congress to declare war on Germany, a war that many Americans opposed and that Wilson conceded would sow death, misery, and reaction among them. He threatened "the firm hand of repression" against disloyalty. But he promised that the war would make the world "safe for democracy." Waving small American flags, many members of Congress broke into cheers, and Senator Lodge congratulated Wilson. The Senate passed a resolution for war on April 4, the House on April 6.

On July 10, 1919, Wilson made the same journey down Pennsylvania Avenue to Capitol Hill. This time he rode in brilliant sunshine through cheering crowds and flag-decorated streets. He asked the Senate to ratify a peace treaty that most Americans favored and that Wilson declared would prevent future wars. But many senators received Wilson's address in silence. Several refused even to stand when he entered the chamber. Senator Lodge concealed neither his hatred of the president nor his opposition to the treaty. During the fierce political struggle over the treaty that followed, the president suffered a stroke that left him crippled. The Senate ultimately rejected the treaty and Wilson's peace.

Between these two presidential appearances, Americans experienced the horrors of the Great War, confronting and overcoming challenges but also sacrificing some of their national ideals and aspirations. Not only was the war the United States' first major military conflict on foreign soil, but it also changed American life. With economic management and social control considered essential to the war effort, government authority increased sharply. Too often the war also diverted reform energies into new channels, subordinated generous impulses to those that were more coercive, and encouraged reactionary developments. The results contributed to a postwar mood that not only curtailed further reform but also helped defeat the peace treaty.

Waging Neutrality

With near unanimity, Americans supported neutrality when the Great War erupted in Europe in 1914. But American attitudes, decisions, and actions, both public and private, undercut neutrality, and the policies of governments in Berlin, London, and Washington drew the United States into the war.

The Origins of Conflict

Since the 1870s, the competing imperial ambitions of the great European powers had led to economic rivalries, military expansion, diplomatic maneuvering, and international tensions. In central Europe, the expansionist Germany of Kaiser Wilhelm II allied itself with the multinational Austro-Hungarian Empire. Confronting them, Great Britain and France formed alliances with Tsarist Russia. Observing this precarious balance of power in May 1914, an American diplomat reported anxiously, "There is too much hatred, too many jealousies." He predicted "an awful cataclysm."

On June 28, a Serbian terrorist assassinated Archduke Franz Ferdinand, the heir to the Austro-

Hungarian throne. With Germany's support, Austria declared war on Serbia on July 28. Russia then mobilized its army against Austria to aid Serbia, its Slavic client state. To assist Austria, Germany declared war on Russia and then on Russia's ally France. Hoping for a quick victory, Germany struck at France through neutral Belgium; in response, Britain declared war on Germany on August 4. Soon Turkey and Bulgaria joined Germany and Austria to form the **Central Powers**. The **Allies**—Britain, France, and Russia—were joined by Italy and Japan. Britain drew on its empire for resources, using troops from India, Canada, Australia, New Zealand, and South Africa. The war had become a global conflict, waged not only in Europe but also in Africa, the Middle East, and East Asia.

Mass slaughter enveloped Europe as huge armies battled to a stalemate. The British and French faced the Germans along a line of trenches stretching across France and Belgium from the English Channel to Switzerland. The British once suffered 300,000 casualties in an offensive that gained only a few square miles before being pushed back. Machine gunners went into shock at the carnage they inflicted. In the trenches, soldiers suffered in the cold and mud, surrounded by decaying bodies and human waste, enduring lice, rats, and nightmares, and dying from disease and exhaustion. The Great War, said one German soldier, had become "the grave of nations."

American Attitudes

Few Americans had expected this calamity. As one North Carolina congressman said, "This dreadful conflict of the nations came to most of us as lightning out of a clear sky." Most people believed that the United States had no vital interest in the war and would not become involved. "Our isolated position and freedom from entangling alliances," noted the *Literary Digest,* "inspire our press with the cheering assurance that we are in no peril of being drawn into the European quarrel." President Wilson issued a proclamation of neutrality and urged Americans to be "neutral in fact as well as in name . . . impartial in thought as well as in action."

However, ethnic, cultural, and economic ties bound most Americans to the British and French. Politically, too, most Americans felt a greater affinity for the democratic Western Allies. And whereas Britain and the United States had enjoyed a rapprochement since 1895, Germany had repeatedly appeared as a potential rival.

Wilson himself ardently admired Britain's culture and government and distrusted Germany's

President Woodrow Wilson reads his war message to Congress, April 2, 1917. He predicted "many months of fiery trial and sacrifice ahead of us."

imperial ambitions. Like other influential Americans, Wilson believed that a German victory would threaten America's economic, political, and perhaps even strategic interests. "England is fighting our fight," he said privately. Secretary of State William Jennings Bryan was genuinely neutral, but most officials favored the Allies. Early in the war, Colonel Edward House, Wilson's closest adviser on foreign affairs, wrote: "I cannot see how there can be any serious trouble between England and America, with all of us feeling as we do."

British writers, artists, and lecturers depicted the Allies as fighting for civilization against a brutal Germany that mutilated nuns and babies, shaping America's view of the conflict. Britain also cut the only German cable to the United States and censored war news to suit itself. German propaganda directed at American opinion proved ineffectual.

Sympathy for the Allies, however, did not mean that Americans favored intervention. The British ambassador complained that it was "useless" to expect any "practical" advantage from the Americans' sympathy, for they had no intention of joining the conflict. Wilson was determined to pursue peace as long as his view of national interests allowed.

The Economy of War

International law permitted neutral nations to sell or ship war material to all belligerents, and with the economy mired in a recession when the war began, many Americans looked to war orders to spur economic recovery. But the British navy prevented trade with the Central Powers. Only the Allies could buy American goods. Their orders for steel, explosives, uniforms, wheat, and other products, however, pulled the country out of the recession. One journalist rejoiced that "war, for Europe, is meaning devastation and death; for America a bumper crop of new millionaires and a hectic hastening of prosperity revival."

Other Americans worried that this one-sided war trade undermined genuine neutrality. Congress even considered embargoing munitions. But few Americans supported that idea. One financial journal declared of the Allied war trade: "We need it for the profits which it yields." The German ambassador noted that American industry was "actually delivering goods only to the enemies of Germany."

A second economic issue complicated matters. To finance their war purchases, the Allies borrowed from American bankers. Initially, Secretary of State Bryan persuaded Wilson to prohibit loans to the belligerents as "inconsistent with the true spirit of neutrality." But Wilson soon ended the ban. Secretary of the Treasury William McAdoo argued that it would be "disastrous" *not* to finance the Allies' purchases, on which "our prosperity is dependent." By April 1917, American loans to the Allies exceeded $2 billion, nearly one hundred times the amount lent to Germany. These financial ties, like the war trade they underwrote, linked the United States to the Allies and convinced Germany that American neutrality was only a formality.

The Diplomacy of Neutrality

This same imbalance characterized American diplomacy. Wilson acquiesced in British violations of American neutral rights while sternly refusing to yield on German actions. Wilson argued that while British violations of international law cost Americans property, markets, and time, German violations cost lives. As the *Boston Globe* noted, the British were "a gang of thieves" and the Germans "a gang of murderers. On the whole, we prefer the thieves, but only as the lesser of two evils."

When the war began, the United States asked belligerents to respect the 1909 **Declaration of London** on neutral rights. Germany agreed to do so; the British refused. Instead, Britain instituted a blockade of Germany, mined the North Sea, and forced neutral ships into British ports to search their cargoes and confiscate material deemed useful to the German war effort. Wilson branded Britain's blockade illegal and unwarranted, but by October he had conceded many of America's neutral rights to avoid conflict with Britain.

The British then prohibited food and other products that Germany had imported during peacetime, thereby interfering further with neutral shipping. One American official complained privately: "England is playing a . . . high game, violating international law every day." But when the Wilson administration finally protested, it undermined its own position by noting that "imperative necessity" might justify a violation of international law. In January 1915, Wilson yielded further by observing that "no very important questions of principle" were involved in the Anglo-American quarrels over ship seizures and that they could be resolved after the war.

This policy tied the United States to the British war effort and provoked a German response. Germany decided in February 1915 to use its submarines against Allied shipping in a war zone around the British Isles. Germany maintained that Britain's blockade and the acquiescence of neutral countries in British violations of international law made submarine warfare necessary.

Submarines could not readily follow traditional rules of naval warfare. Small and fragile, they depended on surprise attacks. They could not surface to identify themselves, as the rules mandated, without risking disaster from the deck guns of Britain's armed merchant ships, and they were too small to rescue victims of their sinkings. Yet Wilson refused to see the "imperative necessity" in German tactics that he found in British tactics, and he warned that he would hold Germany responsible for any loss of American lives or property.

In May 1915, a German submarine sank a British passenger liner, the *Lusitania*. Unknown to the public, it had been carrying arms. The German embassy had warned Americans against traveling on the ship, but the loss of life—1,198 people, including 128 Americans—caused Americans to condemn Germany. "To speak of technicalities and the rules of war, in the face of such wholesale murder on the high seas, is a waste of time," trumpeted one magazine. Wilson saw he had to "carry out the double wish of our people, to maintain a firm front in respect of what we demand of Germany and yet do nothing that might by any possibility involve us in the war."

Wilson demanded that Germany abandon its submarine campaign. But his language was so harsh that Bryan resigned, warning that by requiring more of Germany than of Britain, the president violated neutrality and threatened to draw the nation into war. Bryan proposed prohibiting Americans from traveling on belligerent ships. His proposal gained support in the South and West, and Senator Thomas Gore of Oklahoma and Representative Jeff McLemore of Texas introduced it in congressional resolutions in February 1916.

Wilson moved to defeat the Gore-McLemore resolutions, insisting that they impinged on presidential control of foreign policy and on America's neutral rights. In truth, the resolutions abandoned no vital national interest while offering to prevent another provocative incident. Moreover, neither law nor tradition gave Americans the right to travel safely on belligerent ships. Of the nation's "double wish," then, Wilson placed more priority on confronting what he saw as the German threat than on meeting the popular desire for peace.

In April 1916, a German submarine torpedoed the French ship *Sussex*, injuring four Americans. Wilson threatened to break diplomatic relations if Germany did not abandon unrestricted submarine warfare against all merchant vessels. This implied war. Germany promised not to sink merchant ships without warning but made its *Sussex* **Pledge** contingent on the United States' requiring Britain also to adhere to "the rules of international law universally recognized before the war." Wilson's diplomatic victory, then, was hollow. Peace for America would depend on the British adopting a course they rejected. As Wilson saw it, however, "any little German lieutenant can put us into the war at any time by some calculated outrage." Wilson's diplomacy had left the nation's future at the mercy of others.

The Battle over Preparedness

The threat of war sparked a debate over military policy. Since the outbreak of the war, Theodore Roosevelt and a handful of other politicians, mostly northeastern Republicans convinced that Allied victory was in the national interest, had advocated what they called **preparedness**, a program to expand the armed forces and establish universal military training. Conservative business groups also joined the agitation, combining demands for preparedness with attacks on progressive reforms.

But most Americans opposed expensive military preparations. Leading feminists like Jane

Addams, Charlotte Perkins Gilman, and Carrie Chapman Catt formed the Woman's Peace Party in 1915, and other organizations like the American League to Limit Armaments also campaigned against preparedness. William Jennings Bryan denounced the militarism of Roosevelt as a "philosophy [that] can rot a soul" and condemned preparedness as a program for turning the nation into "a vast armory with skull and crossbones above the door."

Wilson also opposed preparedness initially, but he reversed his position when the submarine crisis with Germany intensified. In early 1916, an election year, he made a speaking tour to generate public support for expanding the armed forces. Congress soon passed the National Defense Act and the Naval Construction Act, increasing the strength of the army and authorizing a naval construction plan.

The Election of 1916

Wilson's preparedness plans stripped the Republicans of one issue in 1916, and his renewed support of progressive reforms (see Chapter 23) helped hold Bryan Democrats in line. The slogan "He Kept Us Out of War" appealed to the popular desire for peace, and the Democratic campaign became one long peace rally. Wilson disliked the peace emphasis but exploited its political appeal. He warned, "The certain prospect of the success of the Republican party is that we shall be drawn, in one form or another, into the embroilments of the European war."

The Republicans had hoped to regain the support of their progressive members after Roosevelt urged the Progressive party to follow him back into the GOP. But many joined the Democratic camp instead. The GOP nominated Charles Evans Hughes, a Supreme Court justice and former New York governor. The platform denounced Wilson's "shifty expedients" in foreign policy and promised "strict and honest neutrality." Unfortunately for Hughes, Roosevelt's attacks on Wilson for not pursuing a war policy persuaded many voters that the GOP was a war party. "If Hughes is defeated," wrote one observer, "he has Roosevelt to thank for it."

The election was the closest in decades (see Map 25-1). When California narrowly went for Wilson, it decided the contest. The desire for peace, all observers concluded, had determined the election.

Descent into War

Still, Wilson knew that war loomed, and he made a last effort to avert it. In January 1917, he sketched out the terms of what he called a "peace without victory." Anything else, he warned, would only lead to

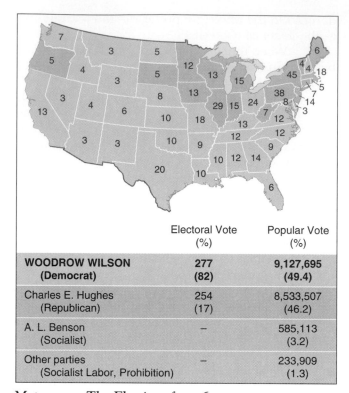

	Electoral Vote (%)	Popular Vote (%)
WOODROW WILSON (Democrat)	**277** (82)	**9,127,695** (49.4)
Charles E. Hughes (Republican)	254 (17)	8,533,507 (46.2)
A. L. Benson (Socialist)	–	585,113 (3.2)
Other parties (Socialist Labor, Prohibition)	–	233,909 (1.3)

Map 25-1   The Election of 1916
Woodrow Wilson won reelection in 1916 despite a reunified Republican party by sweeping the South and West on campaign appeals to peace and progressive reform.

another war. The new world order should be based on national equality and **self-determination**, arms reductions, freedom of the seas, and an international organization to ensure peace. It was a distinctly American vision.

But both the Allies and the Central Powers had sacrificed too much to settle for anything short of outright victory. Germany wanted to annex territory in eastern Europe, Belgium, and France and to take over Belgian and French colonies in Africa; Austria sought Balkan territory. The Allies wanted to destroy German military and commercial power, weaken the Austro-Hungarian empire, take Germany's colonies in Africa, and supplant Turkish influence in the Middle East. One British leader denounced Wilson as "the quintessence of a prig" for suggesting that after three years of "this terrible effort," the two sides should accept American principles rather than their own national objectives.

Germany now moved to win the war by cutting the Allies off from U.S. supplies. On January 31, Germany unleashed its submarines in a broad war zone.

Wilson was now virtually committed to a war many Americans opposed. He broke diplomatic relations with Germany and asked Congress to arm American merchant vessels. When the Senate refused, Wilson invoked an antipiracy law of 1819 and armed the ships anyway. Although no American ships had yet been sunk, he also ordered the naval gun crews to shoot submarines on sight. Wilson's own secretary of the navy warned that these actions violated recognized international law and were a step toward war. Huge rallies across America demanded peace.

On March 1, Wilson released an intercepted message from the German foreign minister, Arthur Zimmermann, to the German minister in Mexico. It proposed that in the event of war between the United States and Germany, Mexico should ally itself with Germany; in exchange, Mexico would recover its "lost territory in Texas, New Mexico, and Arizona." The Zimmermann note produced a wave of hostility toward Germany and increased support for intervention in the war, especially in the Southwest, which had opposed involvement.

Meanwhile a revolution in Russia overthrew the tsarist regime and established a provisional government, making Russia "a fit partner" for the United States, said Wilson. When submarines sank four American freighters in mid-March, anti-German feeling broadened.

On April 2, 1917, Wilson delivered his war message, declaring that neutrality was no longer possible, given Germany's submarine "warfare against mankind." To build support for joining a war that most people had long regarded with revulsion and as alien to American interests, Wilson set forth the nation's war goals as simple and noble. The United States would not fight for conquest or domination but for "the ultimate peace of the world and for the liberation of its peoples. . . . The world must be made safe for democracy."

After vigorous debate, the Senate passed the war resolution 82 to 6 and the House 373 to 50. On April 6, 1917, the United States officially entered the Great War, what Representative Claude Kitchin of North Carolina predicted would be "one vast drama of horrors and blood, one boundless stage upon which will play all the evil spirits of earth and hell."

SUMMARY

MAJOR GOVERNMENT WARTIME AGENCIES

Agency	Purpose
War Industries Board	Reorganized industry to maximize wartime production
Railway Administration	Modernized and operated the nation's railroads
Food Administration	Increased agricultural production, supervised food distribution and farm labor
National War Labor Board	Resolved labor-management disputes, improved labor conditions, and recognized union rights as means to promote production and efficiency
Committee on Public Information	Managed propaganda to build public support for the war effort

Waging War in America

Mobilizing for military intervention was a massive undertaking. "It is not an army that we must shape and train for war," announced President Wilson; "it is a Nation." The government reorganized the economy to emphasize centralized management, developed policies to control public opinion and suppress dissent, and transformed the role of government itself. Mobilization often built on progressives' moralism and sense of mission. In other respects, however, the war experience withered the spirits of reformers. In many different ways, people on the home front—like soldiers in Europe—would participate in the Great War; all would find their lives changed.

Managing the War Economy

Federal and state governments developed a complex structure of agencies and controls for every sector of the economy (see the summary table "Major Government Wartime Agencies"). Supervised by the **Council of National Defense**, these agencies shifted resources to war-related enterprise, increased production of goods and services, and improved transportation and distribution.

The most important agency was the **War Industries Board (WIB)**. Led by financier Bernard Baruch, the WIB exercised unprecedented powers over industry by setting prices, allocating scarce materials, and standardizing products and procedures to boost efficiency. Yet Baruch was not an industrial dictator; he aimed at business-government integration. The WIB promoted major business interests, helped suspend antitrust laws, and guaranteed huge corporate profits. So many business leaders became involved in the WIB that there was a popular outcry against business infiltration of the government, and one corporate executive admitted, "We are all making more money out of this war than the average human being ought to." Some progressives began to see the dangers, and business leaders the advantages, of government economic intervention.

Under William McAdoo, the **Railway Administration** operated the nation's railroads as a unified system to move supplies and troops efficiently. Centralized management eliminated competition, permitted improvements in equipment, and brought great profits to the owners but higher prices to the general public.

Equally effective and far more popular was the **Food Administration**, headed by Herbert Hoover. Hoover persuaded millions of Americans to accept meatless and wheatless days so that the Food Administration could feed military and foreign consumers. Half a million women went door to door to secure food conservation pledges from housewives. City residents planted victory gardens in parks and vacant lots.

Hoover also worked closely with agricultural processors and distributors. Farmers profited from the war, too. To encourage production, he established high prices for farm commodities, and agricultural income rose 30 percent. The Food Administration organized the Woman's Land Army to recruit women to work in the fields, providing sufficient farm labor despite the military draft. Most states formed units of the Boys' Working Reserve for agricultural labor. Agribusinesses in the Southwest persuaded the federal government to permit them to import Mexicans to work under government supervision and be housed in special camps.

In exchange for labor's cooperation, the **National War Labor Board** guaranteed the rights of unions to organize and bargain collectively. With such support, labor unions sharply increased their membership. The labor board also encouraged improved working conditions, higher wages, and shorter hours. These improvements limited labor disputes during the war, and Secretary of War Newton Baker praised labor as "more willing to keep in step than capital." But when unions like the Industrial Workers of the World did not keep in step, the government suppressed them.

These and other government regulatory agencies reinforced many long-standing trends in the American economy, from the consolidation of business to the commercialization of agriculture and the organization of labor. They also set a precedent for governmental activism that would prove valuable during the crises of the 1930s and 1940s.

New Opportunities, Old Issues

The reorganization of the economy also had significant social consequences, especially for women and African-Americans. In response to labor shortages, women took jobs previously closed to them. Besides farm work, they built airplanes, produced guns and ammunition, manufactured tents and cartridge belts, and worked in a wide variety of other heavy and light industries. "One of the lessons from the war," said one manufacturer, "has been to show that women can do exacting work." Harriot Stanton Blatch, a suffragist active in the Food Administration, estimated that a million women had replaced men in industry, where "their drudgery is for the first time paid for."

Many working women simply shifted to other jobs where their existing skills earned better wages and benefits. The reshuffling of jobs among white women opened new vacancies for black women in domestic, clerical, and industrial employment. As black women replaced white women in the garment and textile industries, social reformers spoke of "a new day for the colored woman worker." But racial as well as gender segregation continued to mark employment, and wartime improvements were temporary.

The war helped middle-class women reformers achieve two long-sought objectives: woman suffrage and prohibition. Emphasizing the national cooperation needed to wage the war, one magazine noted that "arbitrarily to draw the line at voting, at a time when every man and woman must share in this effort, becomes an absurd anomaly." Even Woodrow Wilson finally endorsed the reform, terming it "vital to the winning of the war." Congress approved the suffrage amendment, which was ratified in 1920. Convinced that abstaining from alcohol would save grain and make workers and soldiers more efficient, Congress also passed the prohibition amendment, which was ratified in 1919.

The demand for industrial labor caused a huge migration of blacks from the rural South, where they had had little opportunity, few rights, and no hope. Half a million African-Americans moved north during the war, doubling and tripling the black population of Chicago, Detroit, and other industrial cities.

Unfortunately, fearful and resentful whites started race riots in northern cities. In East St. Louis, Illinois, where thousands of southern blacks sought defense work, a white mob in July 1917 murdered at least thirty-nine blacks. The *Literary Digest* noted, "Race-riots in East St. Louis afford a lurid background to our efforts to carry justice and idealism to Europe." And Wilson was told privately that the riot was "worse than anything the Germans did in Belgium."

Financing the War

To finance the war, the government borrowed money and raised taxes. Business interests favored the first course, but southern and western progressives argued that taxation was more efficient and equitable and would minimize war profiteering. California Senator Hiram Johnson noted, "Our endeavours to impose heavy war profit taxes . . . have brought into sharp relief the skin-deep dollar patriotism of some of those who have been loudest in declamations on war and in their demands for blood." Nevertheless, the tax laws of 1917 and 1918 established a graduated tax structure with increased taxes on large incomes, corporate profits, and wealthy estates.

The government raised two-thirds of the war costs by borrowing. Most of the loans came from banks and wealthy investors, but the government also campaigned to sell **Liberty Bonds** to the general public. Celebrities went to schools, churches, and rallies to persuade Americans to buy bonds as their patriotic duty. "Every person who refuses to subscribe," Secretary of the Trea-

sury McAdoo told a California audience, "is a friend of Germany."

Conquering Minds

The government also tried to promote a war spirit among the American people by establishing propa-

"Beat Back the Hun," a poster to induce Americans to buy Liberty Bonds, demonizes the enemy in a raw, emotional appeal. Liberty bond drives raised the immense sum of $23 billion.

ganda agencies and enacting legislation to control social attitudes and behavior. This program drew from the restrictive side of progressivism but also reflected the interests of more conservative forces. The Wilson administration adopted this program of social mobilization because many Americans opposed the war, including German-Americans with ethnic ties to the Central Powers, Irish Catholics and Russian Jews who condemned the Allies for persecution and repression, Scandinavian immigrants averse to military service, pacifists, radicals who denounced the war as capitalist and imperialist, and many others.

To rally Americans behind the war effort, Wilson established the **Committee on Public Information (CPI)** under George Creel. Despite its title, the CPI sought to manipulate, not inform, public opinion. Creel described his goal as winning "the fight for the *minds* of men, for the 'conquest of their convictions.'" The CPI flooded the country with press releases, advertisements, cartoons, and canned editorials. It made newsreels and war movies to capture public attention. It hired artists to draw posters, professors to write pamphlets in twenty-three languages, and poets to compose war poems for children.

Other government agencies launched similar campaigns. The Woman's Committee of the Council of National Defense established the Department of Educational Propaganda and Patriotic Education. This agency worked to win over women who opposed the war.

Government propaganda had three themes: national unity, the loathsome character of the enemy, and the war as a grand crusade for liberty and democracy. Germans were depicted as brutal, even subhuman, rapists and murderers. The campaign suggested that any dissent was unpatriotic, if not treasonous, and dangerous to national survival. This emphasis on unreasoning conformity helped prompt hysterical attacks on German-Americans, radicals, and pacifists.

Suppressing Dissent

The government also suppressed dissent, now officially branded disloyalty. For reasons of their own, private interests helped shape a reactionary repression that tarnished the nation's professed idealistic war goals.

Congress rushed to stifle antiwar sentiment. The **Espionage Act** provided heavy fines and up to twenty years in prison for obstructing the war effort, a vague phrase but one "omnipotently comprehensive," warned one Idaho senator who opposed the law. "No man can foresee what it might be in its consequences." In fact, the Espionage Act became a

weapon to crush dissent and criticism. In 1918, Congress passed the still more sweeping **Sedition Act**. Based on state laws in the West designed to suppress labor radicals, the Sedition Act provided severe penalties for speaking or writing against the draft, bond sales, or war production or for criticizing government personnel or policies. Senator Hiram Johnson lamented: "It is war. But, good God, . . . when did it become war upon the American people?"

Postmaster General Albert Burleson banned antiwar or radical newspapers and magazines from the mail. A notorious bigot, Burleson suppressed literature so indiscriminately that one observer said he "didn't know socialism from rheumatism." The reactionary attorney general, Thomas Gregory, made little distinction between traitors and pacifists, war critics, and radicals. Eugene Debs was sentenced to ten years in prison for a "treasonous" speech in which he declared it "extremely dangerous to exercise the right of free speech in a country fighting to make democracy safe in the world." By war's end, a third of the Socialist party's national leadership was in prison, leaving the party in shambles.

Gregory also enlisted the help of private vigilantes, including several hundred thousand members of the reactionary **American Protective League**, which sought to purge radicals and reformers from the nation's economic and political life. They wiretapped telephones, intercepted private mail, burglarized union offices, broke up German-language newspapers, harassed immigrants, and staged mass raids, seizing thousands of people they claimed were not doing enough for the war effort.

State and local authorities established 184,000 investigating and enforcement agencies known as councils of defense or public safety committees. They encouraged Americans to spy on one another, required people to buy Liberty Bonds, and prohibited teaching German in schools or using the language in religious services and telephone conversations (see "American Views: Mobilizing America for Liberty"). When Oklahoma abolished German in its schools, a newspaper crowed: "German Deader than Latin Now." In Tulsa, a member of the county council of defense shot and killed someone for making allegedly pro-German remarks. The council declared its approval, and community leaders applauded the killer's patriotism.

Members of the business community exploited the hysteria to promote their own interests at the expense of farmers, workers, and reformers. As one Wisconsin farmer complained, businessmen "now under the guise of patriotism are trying to ram down the farmers' throats things they hardly dared before." On the Great Plains from Texas to North Dakota, the business target was the **Nonpartisan League**, a radical farm group demanding state control or ownership of banks, grain elevators, and flour mills. Although the League supported the war, oversubscribed bond drives, and had George Creel affirm its loyalty, conservatives depicted it as seditious to block its advocacy of political and economic reforms. Minnesota's public safety commission proposed a "firing squad working overtime" to deal with League members. Public officials and self-styled patriots broke up the League's meetings and whipped and jailed its leaders.

In the West, business interests targeted labor organizations, especially the Industrial Workers of the World. In Arizona, for example, the Phelps-Dodge Company armed and paid a vigilante mob to seize twelve hundred striking miners, many of them Wobblies and one-third of them Mexican-Americans, and herd them into the desert without food or water. Federal investigators found that the company and its thugs had been inspired not by "considerations of patriotism" but by "ordinary strike-breaking motives." Corporate management was merely "raising the false cry of 'disloyalty'" to suppress workers' complaints.

Nonetheless, the government itself used the army to break loggers' support for the IWW in the Pacific Northwest, and it raided IWW halls across the country in September 1917. The conviction of nearly two hundred Wobblies on charges of sedition in three mass trials in Illinois, California, and Kansas crippled the nation's largest industrial union.

The government was primarily responsible for the war hysteria. It encouraged suspicion and conflict by its own inflammatory propaganda, repressive laws, and violation of basic civil rights, by supporting extremists who used the war for their own purposes, and by not opposing mob violence against German-Americans.

Waging War and Peace Abroad

While mobilizing the home front, the Wilson administration undertook an impressive military effort to help the Allies defeat the Central Powers. Wilson also struggled to secure international acceptance for his plans for a just and permanent peace.

The War to End All Wars

When the United States entered the war, the Allied military position was dire. The losses from three years of trench warfare had sapped military strength and civilian morale. French soldiers mutinied after 120,000 casualties in five days; the German submarine campaign was devastating the British. On the eastern front, the Russian army collapsed, and the Russian government gradually disintegrated.

What the Allies needed, said French Marshal Joseph Joffre in April 1917, was simple: "We want men, men, men." In May, Congress passed the **Selective Service Act**, establishing conscription. More than 24 million men eventually registered for the draft, and nearly 3 million entered the army when their numbers were drawn in a national lottery. Almost 2 million more men volunteered, as did more than ten thousand women who served in the navy. Nearly one-fifth of America's soldiers were foreign-born (Europeans spoke of the "American Foreign Legion"); 367,000 were black.

Civilians were transformed into soldiers in hastily organized training camps, which operated according to progressive principles. Prohibition prevailed in the camps' immediate vicinity; the poorly educated and largely working-class recruits were taught personal hygiene; worries about sin and inefficiency produced campaigns against venereal disease; and immigrants were taught English and American history. Some units were ethnically segregated: At Camp Gordon, Georgia, Italians and Slavs had separate units with their own officers. Racial segregation was more rigid. The navy assigned blacks to menial positions; in the army, they were primarily gravediggers and laborers. But one black combat division was created, and four black regiments fought under French command. France decorated three of these units with its highest citations for valor.

The first American troops landed in France in June 1917. This **American Expeditionary Force (AEF)** was commanded by General John J. Pershing. Full-scale American intervention did not begin until the late spring of 1918 (see Map 25-2). The influx of American troops in June and July tipped the balance toward Allied victory. By July 18, the German chancellor later acknowledged, "even the most optimistic among us knew that all was lost."

In July, Wilson also agreed to commit fifteen thousand American troops to intervene in Russia. Russia's provisional government had collapsed when the **Bolsheviks**, or Communists, had seized power in November 1917. Under V. I. Lenin, the Bolsheviks had then signed an armistice with Germany in early 1918, which freed German troops for the summer offensive in France. The Allies' interventions were designed to reopen the eastern front and help overthrow the Bolshevik government. Lenin's call for the

American Views

MOBILIZING AMERICA FOR LIBERTY

The war years witnessed official and popular efforts to repress dissent and diversity. Much of this repression was aimed at America's immigrant groups and sought to create national unity through coercive Americanization that trampled on the rights and values that the nation claimed to be defending. The following is an official proclamation of Governor W. L. Harding of Iowa, issued May 23, 1918.

❖ **What is the rationale for the governor's proclamation? What do you think of his interpretation of the constitutional guarantees of individual rights?**

❖ **What other "inconvenience or sacrifice" might the proclamation impose on minorities?**

❖ **How might the proclamation incite vigilantism?**

The official language of the United States and the State of Iowa is the English language. Freedom of speech is guaranteed by federal and State Constitutions, but this is not a guaranty of the right to use a language other than the language of this country—the English language. Both federal and State Constitutions also provide that "no laws shall be made respecting an establishment of religion or prohibiting the free exercise thereof." Each person is guaranteed freedom to worship God according to the dictates of his own conscience, but this guaranty does not protect him in the use of a foreign language when he can as well express his thought in English, nor entitle the person who cannot speak or understand the English language to employ a foreign language, when to do so tends in time of national peril, to create discord among neighbors and citizens, or to disturb the peace and quiet of the community.

Every person should appreciate and observe his duty to refrain from all acts or conversation which may excite suspicion or produce strife among the people, but in his relation to the public should so demean himself that every word

---

destruction of capitalism and imperialism alarmed the Allied leaders. One Wilson adviser urged the "eradication" of the Russian government. Soon American and British troops were fighting Russians in an effort to influence Russia's internal affairs. U.S. forces remained in Russia until 1920, but these military interventions failed.

On the western front, the Allies launched their own advance. In late September an American army over 1 million strong attacked German trenches in the Argonne Forest. Some soldiers had been drafted only in July and had spent more time traveling than training. One officer worried, "With their unfamiliarity with weapons, a gun was about as much use as a broom in their hands." Nevertheless, the Americans advanced steadily, despite attacks with poison gas and heavy artillery. Lieutenant Maury Maverick (later a Texas congressman) described the shelling: "We were simply in a big black spot with streaks of screaming red and yellow, with roaring giants in the sky tearing and whirling and roaring." An exploding shell terrified him: "There is a great swishing scream, a smash-bang, and it seems to tear everything loose from you. The intensity of it simply enters your heart and brain, and tears every nerve to pieces."

The battle for the Argonne raged for weeks. One German general reported that his exhausted soldiers faced Americans who "were fresh, eager for fighting, and brave." But he found their sheer numbers most impressive. Despite severe casualties, the AEF helped the British and French defeat the enemy. Soon thereafter, Germany asked for peace. On November 11, 1918, an armistice ended the Great and act will manifest his loyalty to his country and his solemn purpose to aid in achieving victory for our army and navy and the permanent peace of the world. . . .

The great aim and object of all should be unity of purpose and a solidarity of all the people under the flag for victory. This much we owe to ourselves, to posterity, to our country, and to the world.

Therefore, the following rules should obtain in Iowa during the war:

First. English should and must be the only medium of instruction in public, private, denominational, or other similar schools.

Second. Conversation in public places, on trains, and over the telephone should be in the English language.

Third. All public addresses should be in the English language.

Fourth. Let those who cannot speak or understand the English language conduct their religious worship in their homes.

This course carried out in the spirit of patriotism, though inconvenient to some, will not interfere with their guaranteed constitutional rights and will result in peace and tranquility at home and greatly strengthen the country in battle. The blessings of the United States are so great that any inconvenience or sacrifice should willingly be made for their perpetuity.

Therefore, by virtue of authority in me vested, I, W. L. Harding, Governor of the State of Iowa, commend the spirit of tolerance and urge that henceforth the within outlined rules be adhered to by all, that petty differences be avoided and forgotten, and that, united as one people with one purpose and one language, we fight shoulder to shoulder for the good of mankind.

Source: B. F. Shambaugh, ed., *Iowa and War* (1919).

War. More than 115,000 Americans were among the 8 million soldiers and 7 million civilians dead.

The Fourteen Points

The armistice was only a step toward final peace. President Wilson had already enunciated American war objectives on January 8, 1918, in a speech outlining what became known as the Fourteen Points. In his 1917 war message, Wilson had advocated a more democratic world system, and this new speech spelled out how to achieve it. But Wilson also had a political purpose. The Bolsheviks had published the secret treaties the Allies had signed dividing up the economic and territorial spoils of war. Lenin called for an immediate peace based on the liberation of all colonies, self-determination for all peoples, and the rejection of annexations and punitive indemnities.

Wilson's Fourteen Points reassured the American and Allied peoples that they were fighting for more than imperialist gains and offered an alternative to what he called Lenin's "crude formula" for peace.

Eight of Wilson's points proposed creating new nations, shifting old borders, or assuring self-determination for peoples previously subject to the Austrian, German, or Russian empires. The point about Russia called on all nations to evacuate Russian territory and permit Russia "an unhampered and unembarrassed opportunity for the independent determination of her own political development" under "institutions of her own choosing." Another five points invoked principles to guide international relations: freedom of the seas, open diplomacy instead of secret treaties, reduction of armaments, free trade, and the fair settlement of colonial claims.

Map 25-2   The Western Front, 1918
*After three years of trench warfare, the arrival of large numbers of American troops in 1918
enabled the Allies to launch an offensive that drove back the Germans and forced an
armistice.*

Wilson's fourteenth and most important point proposed a league of nations to carry out these ideals and ensure international stability.

Wilson and the German government had these principles in mind when negotiating the armistice. The Allies, however, had never explicitly accepted the Fourteen Points. While Wilson favored a settlement that would promote international stability and economic expansion, he recognized (as he told one confidant) that the Allies sought "to get everything out of Germany that they can."

Convinced of the righteousness of his cause, Wilson decided to attend the peace conference in Paris himself. But Wilson weakened his position before he even set sail. First, he urged voters to support Democratic candidates in the November 1918 elections to indicate approval of his peace plans. But the electorate, responding primarily to domestic problems like inflation, gave the Republicans control of both houses of Congress. This meant that a treaty would have to be approved by Senate Republicans

angry that Wilson had tried to use war and peace for partisan purposes. Second, Wilson refused to consult with Senate Republicans on plans for the peace conference and failed to name important Republicans to the Paris delegation. It would be Wilson's treaty, but Republicans would feel no responsibility to approve it.

The Paris Peace Conference

The peace conference opened on January 18, 1919. Meeting at the Palace of Versailles, the delegations were dominated by the principal Allied leaders themselves: Wilson of the United States, David Lloyd George of Britain, Georges Clemenceau of France, and Vittorio Orlando of Italy. The Central Powers and Bolshevik Russia were excluded. Clemenceau remarked, "God gave us the Ten Commandments and we broke them. Mr. Wilson has given us the Fourteen Points. We shall see."

Wilson himself had broken two of the Fourteen Points before the conference began. He had acquiesced in Britain's rejection of freedom of the seas. And he had sent U.S. troops to intervene in Russia in violation of its right to self-determination.

For months, the conference debated Wilson's other goals and the Allies' demands for compensation and security. Lloyd George later commented, with reference to the self-righteous Wilson and the assertive Clemenceau, "I think I did as well as might be expected, seated as I was between Jesus Christ and Napoleon Bonaparte." Under protest, Germany signed the **Treaty of Versailles** on June 28, 1919. Its terms were far more severe than Wilson had proposed or Germany had anticipated. Germany had to accept sole responsibility for starting the war; to pay huge reparations to the Allies; to give up land to France, Poland, Belgium, and Denmark; to cede its colonies; to limit its army and navy; and to promise not to manufacture or purchase armaments.

Wilson gained some acceptance of self-determination. As the German, Austro-Hungarian, Turkish, and Russian empires had collapsed at the end of the war, nationalist groups had proclaimed their independence. On one hand, the peace settlement formally recognized these new nation-states in Eastern Europe. On the other hand, France, Italy, Romania, and Japan all annexed territory regardless of the wishes of the inhabitants. Germans were placed under Polish control in Silesia and Czech control in Bohemia. Austrians were not allowed to merge with Germany. And the conference sanctioned colonialism by establishing a trusteeship system that enabled France, Britain, and Japan to take over German colonies and Turkish territory.

Moreover, the Allied leaders endorsed the changes in eastern Europe in part because the new states there were anticommunist. Western leaders soon called these countries the *cordon sanitaire,* a barrier against Bolshevism. Indeed, the Allies at Versailles were preoccupied with Bolshevik Russia, which one of Wilson's aides called the "black cloud of the east, threatening to overwhelm and swallow up the world." The Allies hoped to isolate and weaken Bolshevik Russia. This hostility to Russia, like the punitive terms for Germany and the concessions to imperial interests, boded ill for a stable and just postwar order.

But Wilson hoped that the final section of the Versailles treaty would resolve the flaws of the agreement by establishing his great international organization to preserve peace: the **League of Nations**. The Covenant, or constitution, of the League was built into the treaty. Its crucial feature, Article Ten, bound the member nations to guarantee each other's independence, which was Wilson's concept of collective security. Sailing home, he mused:

"Well, it is finished, and, as no one is satisfied, it makes me hope we have made a just peace; but it is all on the lap of the gods."

Waging Peace at Home

Wilson was determined to defeat opposition to the peace treaty. But many Americans were engaged in their own struggles with the new conditions of a nation suddenly at peace but riven by economic, social, and political conflict shaped by the war experience. Wilson's battle for the League of Nations would fail tragically. The other conflicts would rage until the election of 1920 restored a normalcy of sorts.

Battle over the League

Most Americans favored the Versailles treaty. A survey of fourteen hundred newspapers found fewer than two hundred opposed. Thirty-three governors and thirty-two state legislatures approved of the League of Nations. But when Wilson called for the Senate to accept "the moral leadership . . . and confidence of the world" by ratifying the treaty, he met resistance. Republican opponents of the treaty raised serious questions. Nearly all Democrats favored the treaty, but they were a minority; some Republicans had to be converted for the treaty to be approved.

Progressive Republican senators, such as Robert La Follette and Hiram Johnson, led one group of opponents. Called the **Irreconcilables**, they opposed participation in the League of Nations, which they saw as designed to perpetuate the power of imperialist countries. Article Ten, they feared, would require the United States to help suppress rebellions in Ireland against British rule or to enforce disputed European borders. Most of the Irreconcilables gave priority to restoring civil liberties and progressive reform at home.

A larger group of opponents, the **Reservationists**, were led by Senator Henry Cabot Lodge, the chair of the Senate Foreign Relations Committee. They regarded Article Ten as eroding congressional authority to declare war. They also fretted that the League might interfere with domestic questions, such as immigration laws. Lodge held public hearings on the treaty to rouse and focus opposition. German-Americans resented the war guilt clause; Italian- and Polish-Americans complained that the treaty did not satisfy the territorial ambitions of Italy and Poland; Irish-Americans condemned the treaty's failure to give self-determination to Ireland. Many progressives also criticized the treaty's compromises on self-determination, reparations, and colonies.

When Lodge proposed reservations or amendments to the treaty, Wilson opened "a direct frontal attack" on his opponents. If they wanted war, he declared, he would "give them a belly full." In early September 1919, Wilson set out across the country to win popular support for the League. In three weeks, he traveled 8,000 miles and delivered thirty-seven speeches. He collapsed in Pueblo, Colorado. Confused and in tears, Wilson mumbled, "I seem to have gone to pieces." Taken back to Washington, Wilson on October 2 suffered a massive stroke that paralyzed his left side and left him psychologically unstable and temporarily blind. Wilson's physician and his wife, Edith Galt Wilson, kept the nature of his illness secret from the public, Congress, and even the vice president and cabinet. The administration was immobilized.

By February 1920, Wilson had partially recovered, but he remained suspicious and quarrelsome. He still refused to compromise to win Senate approval of the treaty. On March 19, 1920, the Senate killed the treaty.

Economic Readjustment and Social Conflict

The League was not the only casualty of the struggle to conclude the war. Grave problems shook the United States in 1919 and early 1920. An influenza epidemic had erupted in Europe in 1918 among the massed armies. It now hit the United States, killing perhaps 700,000 Americans, far more than had died in combat.

Meanwhile, the Wilson administration had no plans for an orderly reconversion of the wartime economy. The secretary of the Council of National Defense later reported, "the mobilization that had taken many months was succeeded by an instantaneous demobilization." The government canceled war contracts and dissolved the regulatory agencies. Noting that "the war spirit of cooperation and sacrifice" had disappeared with the Armistice, Bernard Baruch decided to "turn industry absolutely free" and abolished the War Industries Board as of January 1, 1919. Other agencies followed in such haste that turmoil engulfed the economy.

The army discharged 600,000 soldiers still in training camps; the navy brought AEF soldiers home from France. With no planning or assistance, troops were hustled back into civilian life. There they competed for scarce jobs with workers recently discharged from the war industries.

As unemployment mounted, the removal of wartime price controls brought runaway inflation. The cost of food, clothing, and other necessities more than doubled over prewar rates. The return of the soldiers caused a serious housing shortage, and rents skyrocketed. Farmers also suffered from economic readjustments. Net farm income declined by 65 percent between 1919 and 1921. Farmers who had borrowed money for machinery and land to expand production for the war effort were left impoverished and embittered.

Women also lost their wartime economic advances. Returning soldiers took away their jobs. Male trade unionists insisted that women go back to being housewives. One New York union maintained that "the same patriotism which induced women to enter industry during the war should induce them to vacate their positions after the war." At times, male workers struck to force employers to fire women. "During the war they called us heroines," one woman complained, "but they throw us on the scrapheap now." By 1920, women constituted a smaller proportion of the work force than they had in 1910.

African-Americans were also disappointed by the postwar readjustments. During the war, they had agreed with W. E. B. Du Bois to "forget our special grievances and close our ranks shoulder to shoulder with our own white fellow citizens." They had contributed to the fighting and home fronts. Now, housing shortages and job competition interacted with racism in 1919 to produce race riots in twenty-six towns and cities, resulting in at least 120 deaths. In Chicago, thirty-eight people were killed and more than five hundred injured in a five-day riot that began when white thugs stoned to death a black youth swimming too near "their" beach. Whites then fired a machine gun from a truck hurtling through black neighborhoods. But blacks fought back, no longer willing, the *Chicago Defender* reported, "to move along the line of least resistance as did their sires." Racial conflict was part of a postwar battle between Americans hoping to preserve the new social relations fostered by the war effort and those wanting to restore prewar patterns of power and control.

Even more pervasive discontents roiled as America adjusted to the postwar world. More than 4 million angry workers launched a wave of 3,600 strikes in 1919. They were reacting not only to the soaring cost of living, which undermined the value of their wages, but also to employers' efforts to reassert their authority and destroy the legitimacy labor had won by its participation in the war effort. The abolition of government controls on industry enabled employers not only to raise prices but also to rescind their recognition of unions and reimpose objectionable working conditions. In response, strikers demanded higher wages, better conditions, and recognition of unions and the right of collective bargaining.

The greatest strike involved the American Federation of Labor's attempt to organize steelworkers, who endured dangerous conditions and twelve-hour shifts. When the steel companies refused to recognize the union or even discuss issues, 365,000 workers went out on strike in September 1919. Strikers in Pennsylvania pointed out that they had worked "cheerfully, without strikes or trouble of any kind" during the war to "make the world safe for democracy" and that they now sought "industrial democracy." Employers hired thugs to beat the strikers, used strikebreakers to take their jobs, and exploited ethnic and racial divisions among them. Management also portrayed the strikers as disruptive radicals influenced by Bolshevism. After four months, the strike failed.

Employers used the same tactic to defeat striking coal miners. Coal operators claimed that Russian Bolsheviks financed the strike to destroy the American economy. The public turned against the miners. Attorney General Mitchell Palmer secured an injunction against the strike under the authority of wartime legislation. Since the government no longer controlled coal prices or enforced protective labor rules, miners complained bitterly that the war had ended for corporations but not for workers.

Two municipal strikes in 1919 also alarmed the public when their opponents depicted them as revolutionary attacks on the social order. In Seattle in February, the Central Labor Council called a general strike to support 35,000 shipyard workers striking for higher wages and shorter hours. When 60,000 more workers from 110 local unions also walked out, the city ground to a halt. Seattle's mayor, business leaders, and newspapers attacked the strikers as Bolsheviks and anarchists. Threatened with military intervention, the labor council called off the strike. In Boston, the police commissioner fired police officers for trying to organize a union to improve their inadequate pay. In response, the police went on strike. As in Seattle, Boston newspapers, politicians, and business leaders attributed the strike to Bolshevism. Governor Calvin Coolidge mobilized the National Guard and gained nationwide acclaim when he stated, "There is no right to strike against the public safety by anybody, anywhere, anytime." The police were all fired; many of their replacements were war veterans.

Red Scare

The strikes contributed to an anti-Bolshevik hysteria that swept the country in 1919. This **Red Scare**

Postwar labor unrest met determined suppression. Here mounted police attack striking steelworkers in Pittsburgh in 1919. The strikers were seeking union recognition and an end to twelve-hour days.

reflected fears that the Bolshevik revolution in Russia might spread to the United States. Steeped in the antiradical propaganda of the war years, many Americans were appalled by Russian Bolshevism, described by the *Saturday Evening Post* as a "compound of slaughter, confiscation, anarchy, and universal disorder." Their alarm grew in 1919 when Russia established the **Third International** to foster revolution abroad, and a few American socialists formed the American Communist Party. But the Red Scare also reflected the willingness of antiunion employers, ambitious politicians, sensational journalists, zealous veterans, and racists to exploit the panic to advance their own purposes.

The Red Scare reached panic levels by mid-1919. Bombs mailed anonymously to several prominent people on May Day seemed proof enough that a Bolshevik conspiracy threatened America. The Justice Department, Congress, and patriotic organizations like the American Legion joined with business groups to suppress radicalism, real and imagined. The government continued to enforce the repressive laws against Wobblies, socialists, and other dissenters. Indeed, Wilson and Attorney General Palmer called for more stringent laws. State governments harassed and arrested hundreds.

Palmer created a new agency, headed by J. Edgar Hoover, to suppress radicals and impose conformity. Its war on radicalism became the chief focus of the Justice Department. Hoover collected files on labor leaders and other "radical agitators" from Senator La Follette to Jane Addams, issued misleading reports on Communist influence in labor strikes and race riots, and contacted all major newspapers "to acquaint people like you with the real menace of evil-thinking, which is the foundation of the Red Movement." Indeed, the Justice Department itself promoted the Red Scare hysteria, which Palmer hoped would lead to his presidential nomination and Hoover hoped would enhance his own power and that of his bureau.

In November 1919, Palmer and Hoover began raiding groups suspected of subversion. A month later, they deported 249 alien radicals, including the anarchist Emma Goldman, to Russia. Rabid patriots endorsed such actions. One minister favored deporting radicals "in ships of stone with sails of lead, with the wrath of God for a breeze and with hell for their first port."

In January 1920, Palmer and Hoover rounded up more than four thousand suspected radicals in thirty-three cities. Without warrants, they broke into union halls, club rooms, and private homes, assaulting and arresting everyone in sight. People were jailed without access to lawyers; some were beaten into signing false confessions. In Lynn, Massachusetts, thirty-nine people meeting to organize a bakery were arrested for holding a revolutionary caucus. The *Washington Post* clamored, "There is no time to waste on hairsplitting over infringement of liberty."

Other Americans began to recoil from the excesses and illegal acts. Assistant Secretary of Labor Louis Post stopped further deportations by demonstrating that most of the arrested were "working men of good character, who are not anarchists or revolutionists, nor politically or otherwise dangerous in any sense." When Palmer's predictions of a violent attempt to overthrow the government on May 1,

1920, came to naught, most Americans agreed with the *Rocky Mountain News*: "We can never get to work if we keep jumping sideways in fear of the bewhiskered Bolshevik." Even one conservative Republican concluded that "too much has been said about Bolshevism in America." But if the Red Scare faded in mid-1920, the hostility to immigrants, organized labor, and dissent it reflected endured.

The Election of 1920

The Democratic coalition that Wilson had cobbled together on the issues of progressivism and peace came apart after the war. Workers resented the administration's hostility to the postwar strikes. Ethnic groups brutalized by the Americanization of the war years blamed Wilson for the war or condemned his peace settlement. Farmers grumbled about wartime price controls and postwar falling prices. Wartime taxes and the social and economic turmoil of 1919–1920 alienated the middle class. In the words of Kansas journalist William Allen White, Americans were "tired of issues, sick at heart of ideals, and weary of being noble." They yearned for what Republican presidential candidate Warren Harding of Ohio called "normalcy."

The Republican ticket in 1920 symbolized the reassurance of simpler times. Harding was a genial, Old Guard conservative. His running mate, Calvin Coolidge, governor of Massachusetts, owed his nomination to his handling of the Boston police strike.

Wilson called the election of 1920 "a great and solemn referendum" on the League of Nations, but the League was not a decisive issue in the campaign.

Harding defeated Democratic nominee James Cox, former governor of Ohio, in a landslide. "The Democrats are inconceivably unpopular," wrote Walter Lippmann, a prominent journalist. Harding received 16 million popular votes to Cox's 9 million. Running for president from his prison cell, Socialist Eugene Debs polled nearly a million votes. Not even his closest backers considered Harding qualified for the White House, but as Lippmann said, the nation's "public spirit was exhausted" after the war years. The election of 1920 was "the final twitch" of America's "war mind."

Conclusion

The Great War disrupted the United States and much of the rest of the world. The initial American policy of neutrality yielded to sentimental and substantive links with the Allies and the pressure of German submarine warfare. Despite popular opposition, America joined the conflict when its leaders concluded that national interests demanded it. Using both military and diplomatic power, Woodrow Wilson sought to secure a more stable and prosperous world order, with an expanded role for the United States. But the Treaty of Versailles only partly fulfilled his hopes, and the Senate refused to ratify the treaty and its League of Nations. The postwar world order would be unstable and dangerous.

Participation in the war, moreover, had changed the American government, economy, and society. Some of these changes, including the centralization of the economy and an expansion of the regulatory role of the federal government, were already under way; some offered opportunities to implement progressive principles or reforms. Woman suffrage and prohibition gained decisive support because of the war spirit. But other consequences of the war betrayed both progressive impulses and the democratic principles the war was allegedly fought to promote. The suppression of civil liberties, manipulation of human emotions, repression of radicals and minorities, and exploitation of national crises by narrow interests helped disillusion the public. The repercussions of the Great War would linger for years, at home and abroad.

Review Questions

1. What were the major arguments for and against U.S. entry into the Great War? What position do you find most persuasive? Why?

2. How and why did the United States shape public opinion in World War I? What were the consequences, positive and negative, of the propaganda of the Committee on Public Information, Food Administration, and other government agencies?

3. How did other groups exploit the war crisis and the government's propaganda and repression?

4. Evaluate the role of Woodrow Wilson at the Paris Peace Conference. What obstacles did he face? How successful was he in shaping the settlement?

5. Discuss the arguments for and against American ratification of the Treaty of Versailles.

Recommended Reading

Kendrick A. Clements, *The Presidency of Woodrow Wilson* (1992). This remains the best single volume on the Wilson presidency.

Edward M. Coffman, *The War to End All Wars* (1968). This valuable study provides details of the U.S. military role in World War I.

Robert H. Ferrell, *Woodrow Wilson and World War I, 1917–1921* (1985). Ferrell's useful synthesis emphasizes diplomatic issues.

David M. Kennedy, *Over Here: The First World War and American Society* (1980). Discussion of the impact of World War I on American society is thorough and illuminating.

Robert K. Murray, *The Red Scare: A Study in National Hysteria, 1919–1920* (1955). Murray's important early study retains much value.

Ronald Schaffer, *America in the Great War: The Rise of the War Welfare State* (1991). This effective and provocative summary illuminates the expanding role of government.

Where to Learn More

❖ **Fort George G. Meade Museum, Fort Meade, Maryland.**   This museum contains unparalelled exhibits depicting U.S. military life during World War I, including artifacts, photographs, and French and American tanks designed for trench warfare.

❖ **General John J. Pershing Boyhood Home, Laclede, Missouri.**   Maintained by the Missouri State Park Board, Pershing's restored nineteenth-century home exhibits some of his personal belongings and papers.

❖ **Wisconsin Veterans Museum, Madison, Wisconsin.**   The most stunning museum of its size in the United States, this large building combines impressive collections of artifacts ranging from uniforms to tanks, with substantive exhibits and video programs based on remarkable historical research. It both documents and explains the participation of Wisconsin soldiers in the nation's wars, including the Spanish-American War and World War I.

WE THE PEOPLE
1865–1920

*B*etween Reconstruction and World War I, the United States experienced great change. Industrialization, urbanization, and mass immigration provoked unprecedented conflict over the fundamental issues—citizenship, individual rights, social equity, economic freedom, political liberty, and democratic authority—that define what it means to be an American.

After a long struggle over their role in society, women gained the right to vote with the ratification of the Nineteenth Amendment in 1920. Opponents of woman suffrage had maintained that society's "natural order" required women to avoid public life and serve a domestic role centered on the family. Now, rejoiced suffrage leader Carrie Chapman Catt, American women would cease to be "wards" of the nation and become "free and equal citizens." But to overcome their determined opponents, many suffragists had themselves downplayed the connection between voting and equality. As the 1920s would soon show, Catt's assessment was wildly optimistic. It would require continued struggle in the decades to come for women to approach full civil and political equality, to say nothing of social and economic equality.

As women gained some rights, African-Americans had theirs restricted. The Fourteenth and Fifteenth Amendments, adopted during Reconstruction, had extended both citizenship and suffrage to African-Americans, but the subsequent spread of racial segregation and disfranchisement limited blacks' social and economic freedoms and political power. Some African-Americans organized to oppose these exclusionist trends, and some hoped that their military service in World War I would secure their rights and status as full-fledged Americans. But those hopes soon faded. The war years, as black author James Weldon Johnson sadly observed in 1919, brought instead "an increased hatred of race" and a murderous racial climate.

Native Americans did experience one gain in the aftermath of World War I: citizenship. Indian veterans were made citizens in 1919, a status extended to all Indians five years later. But as the oldest Americans thus became the newest Americans, they benefited little. Many states still prohibited Indians from voting and denied them other basic rights of citizenship. Since the last independent Native American peoples had been subdued in the late nineteenth century and confined to reservations, their economic and social conditions had steadily deteriorated. Forced acculturation had nearly obliterated their cultural identity. By 1920, the Indian death rate exceeded the birthrate. Not surprisingly, one newspaper found Native Americans cynical about receiving "their new citizenship" from those who had "robbed them of a continent, and . . . . deprived them of freedom of action, freedom of social custom, and freedom of worship."

Similar tensions characterized the nation's treatment of immigrants. In the Progressive Era, many groups adopted programs to "Americanize" the newcomers, some by practical efforts to promote education and improve social conditions, others by more coercive measures to secure cultural conformity and social order. The Great War and the Red Scare shifted the balance to the repressive approach. Nativists demanding "100 percent Americanism" forcibly suppressed ethnic traditions, languages, and cultures. By 1919, one Italian-American concluded gloomily that "Americanization is an ugly word." In this new social climate, those seeking to restrict immigration gained the upper hand. A law enacted in 1917 required immigrants to pass a literacy test. More restrictive and discriminatory laws, based on overt racism, would follow in the 1920s. Nativist crusades and cultural conflict would plague postwar political life as Americans continued to struggle over competing definitions of Americanism.

Indeed, such tensions were inherent in a nation that professed the ideals of democracy and equality yet often enforced the rules of order and hierarchy. In the decades to come, the struggle to realize the nation's ideals would wax and wane, manifesting itself in industrial conflict and civil rights marches, in political campaigns and public laws, in women's organizations and consumer groups, in peace rallies and veterans' protests, in lawsuits and civil disobedience. By appealing to the national ideals to achieve their goals, the participants in these struggles testified to their enduring power.

TOWARD A MODERN AMERICA:
THE 1920S

KEY TOPICS

❖ The technological and managerial reorganization of the American economy in the 1920s
❖ The cult of business
❖ Republican efforts to limit government's role to helping U.S. business
❖ Economic change and social dislocation
❖ Materialism, consumerism, and the new mass culture
❖ The exclusion of farmers, African-Americans, new immigrants, Hispanics, and others from the prosperity of the 1920s

"*M*achinery," proclaimed Henry Ford, "is the new Messiah." Others in the 1920s thought Ford too deserved homage. "Just as in Rome one goes to the Vatican and endeavours to get audience of the Pope," noted one British observer, "so in Detroit one goes to the Ford Works and endeavours to see Henry Ford." Ford had introduced the moving assembly line at his automobile factory on the eve of World War I, and by 1925, it was turning out a Model T every ten seconds. Mass production was becoming a reality; in fact, the term originated in Henry Ford's 1926 description of the system of flow production techniques popularly called "Fordism." The system symbolized the nation's booming economy: In the 1920s, Europeans used the word *Fordize* as a synonym for *Americanize*. Ford coupled machines and technology with managerial innovations. He established the "five-dollar day," twice the prevailing wage in Detroit's auto industry, and slashed the workweek from forty-eight to forty hours, hoping to reduce the costs of labor turnover and boost consumer purchasing power, leading to further profits from mass production.

The assembly line, however, alienated workers. Fordism meant that skills, experience, and creativity were no longer necessary, that "upward mobility" was a meaningless phrase; all Ford wanted, said one observer, were machine tenders who "will simply do what they are told to do, over and over again from bell-time to bell-time." Even

Ford conceded the repetitive operations of the assembly line and tried to adapt his mostly immigrant workers to these conditions through an Americanization program. His "Education Department" taught classes in English, sobriety, obedience, and industrial efficiency to the unskilled laborers entering the factory. After the course, they participated in a symbolic pageant: They climbed into a huge "melting pot," 15 feet across and 7 feet deep. After Ford managers stirred the pot with 10-foot ladles, the workers emerged wearing new clothes and waving American flags—new Americans made for the factory. As one Ford leader said, "As we adapt the machinery in the shop to turning out the kind of automobile we have in mind, so we have constructed our educational system with a view to producing the human product in mind."

When the labor market became more favorable to management in the early 1920s, Ford abolished the Education Department and relied on discipline to control workers. To ensure efficiency, he prohibited talking, whistling, sitting, or smoking on the job. Wearing fixed expressions—"Fordization of the face"—workers could communicate only without moving their lips in the "Ford whisper." "Ford employees are not really alive," noted one labor leader; "they are half dead."

Fordism, like the 1920s, had an even darker side. Henry Ford was an anti-Semite. His diatribes against Jews were reprinted by the Nazis in the 1930s. Ford also joined in the assault on labor unions that marked the 1920s. He declared that Jews organized unions to control industry. He banned unions and used spies and informants to prevent union activity, hiring an underworld thug to enforce a discipline that even involved searches of workers' homes.

Fordism thus reflected the complexity of the 1920s, a time of economic growth and technological innovation as well as social conflict as traditions were destroyed and values displaced. Industrial production and national wealth soared, buoyed by new techniques and markets for consumer goods. Business values pervaded society and dominated government. City factories like the Ford Works attracted workers from the countryside, increasing urbanization; rapid suburbanization opened other horizons. Leisure activities flourished, and new mass media promoted modern ideas and stylish products. But not all Americans prospered. Many workers saw their wages stagnant or falling. Farmers endured grim conditions and worse prospects. Social change brought pleasure to some and deep concern to others. Some Americans sought reassurance by imposing their cultural or religious values on everyone around them. And

Ford so dominated the age that when college students were asked to rank the greatest people of all time, Ford came in third—behind Christ and Napoleon.

The Economy that Roared

Following a severe postwar depression in 1920 and 1921, the American economy boomed through the remainder of the decade. Gross domestic product soared nearly 40 percent; output per worker-hour, or productivity, rose 72 percent in manufacturing; average per capita income increased by a third. Although the prosperity was not evenly distributed and some sectors of the economy were deeply troubled, most Americans welcomed the industrial expansion and business principles of the "New Era."

Boom Industries

Many factors spurred the economic expansion of the 1920s. The huge wartime and postwar profits provided investment capital that enabled business to mechanize. Mass production spread quickly in American industry; machine-made standardized parts and the moving assembly line increased efficiency and production. Businesses steadily adopted the scientific management principles of Frederick W. Taylor (see Chapter 23). These highly touted systems, though often involving little more than an assembly-line "speed-up," also boosted efficiency. In factories, electric motors cut costs and improved manufacturing; in homes, electricity spurred demand for new products. Henry Ford was right: Mass production and consumption went hand in hand. Although not one in ten farm families had access to electric power, most other families did by 1929, and many bought electric sewing machines, vacuum cleaners, washing machines, and other labor-saving appliances.

The automobile industry drove the economy. Its productivity increased constantly, and sales rose from about 1.9 million vehicles in 1920 to nearly 5 million by 1929. The automobile industry also employed one of every fourteen manufacturing workers and stimulated other industries from steel to rubber and glass. It created a huge new market for the petroleum industry and fostered oil drilling in Oklahoma, Texas, and Louisiana. It also encouraged

Ford Motor Company's first moving assembly line in Highland Park, Michigan, in 1913. The increasing mechanization of work, linked to managerial and marketing innovations, boosted productivity in the 1920s and brought consumer goods within the reach of far more Americans than before.

the construction industry, a mainstay of the 1920s economy.

New industries also sprang up. The aviation industry grew rapidly during the 1920s, with government support. The U.S. Post Office subsidized commercial air service by providing air mail contracts to private carriers. Congress then authorized commercial passenger service over the mail routes, with regular traffic opening in 1927 between Boston and New York. By 1930, more than one hundred airlines crisscrossed America.

The Great War also stimulated the chemicals industry. The government confiscated chemical patents from German firms that had dominated the field and transferred them to U.S. companies like Du Pont. With this advantage, Du Pont in the 1920s became one of the nation's largest industrial firms, a chemical empire producing plastics, finishes, dyes, and organic chemicals, which it developed into enamel for household appliances and automobile finishes, rayon for women's clothing, and cellophane to package consumer goods.

The new radio and motion picture industries also flourished in the 1920s. Commercial broadcasting began with a single station in 1920. By 1927,

there were 732 stations (58 in Chicago alone), and Congress created what became the Federal Communications Commission to prevent wave band interference. Corporations quickly dominated the new industry. Westinghouse, RCA, and General Electric began opening strings of stations in the early 1920s.

The motion picture industry became one of the nation's five largest businesses, with some twenty thousand movie theaters selling 100 million tickets a week. Hollywood studios were huge factories, producing films on an assembly-line basis. While Americans watched Charlie Chaplin showcase his comedic genius in films like *The Gold Rush* (1925), corporations like Paramount were integrating production with distribution and exhibition to maximize control and profit and eliminate independent producers and theaters.

Corporate Consolidation

A wave of corporate mergers, rivaling that at the turn of the century, swept over the 1920s economy. Great corporations swallowed up thousands of small firms. Particularly significant was the spread of oligopoly—the control of an entire industry by a few giant firms. Three companies—Ford, General Motors, and

CHRONOLOGY

1915 Ku Klux Klan is founded anew.

1919 Volstead Act is passed.

1920 Urban population exceeds rural population for the first time.

Warren Harding is elected president.

Prohibition takes effect.

First commercial radio show is broadcast.

Sinclair Lewis publishes *Main Street.*

1921 Sheppard-Towner Maternity and Infancy Act is passed.

Washington Naval Conference limits naval armaments.

1922 Fordney-McCumber Act raises tariff rates.

Sinclair Lewis publishes *Babbitt*

Country Club Plaza in Kansas City opens.

1923 Harding dies; Calvin Coolidge becomes president.

1924 National Origins Act sharply curtails immigration.

Coolidge is elected president.

1925 Scopes trial is held in Dayton, Tennessee.

F. Scott Fitzgerald publishes *The Great Gatsby.*

1927 Charles A. Lindbergh flies solo across the Atlantic.

1928 Kellogg-Briand Pact is signed.

Herbert Hoover is elected president.

1929 Ernest Hemingway publishes *A Farewell to Arms*

Chrysler—produced 83 percent of the nation's cars. Their large-scale, integrated operations eliminated competition from small firms. In the electric light and power industry, nearly four thousand local utility companies were merged into a dozen holding companies. By 1929, the nation's two hundred largest corporations controlled nearly half of all nonbanking corporate wealth.

Oligopolies also dominated finance and marketing. By 1929, a mere 1 percent of the nation's banks controlled half of its banking resources. In marketing, national chain stores like A&P and Woolworth's displaced local retailers.

The corporate consolidation of the 1920s provoked little public opposition. Americans mostly accepted that size brought efficiency and productivity.

Open Shops and Welfare Capitalism

Business also launched a vigorous assault on labor. In 1921, the National Association of Manufacturers organized an **open shop** campaign to break union shop contracts, which required all employees to be union members. Denouncing collective bargaining as un-American, businesses described the open shop, in which union membership was not required and usually prohibited, as the "American plan." They forced workers to sign so-called **yellow dog contracts** that bound them to reject unions to keep their jobs. Business also used boycotts to force employers into a uniform antiunion front. Bethlehem Steel, for

example, refused to sell steel to companies employing union labor. Where unions existed, corporations tried to crush them, using spies or hiring strikebreakers.

Some companies advocated a paternalistic system called **welfare capitalism** as an alternative to unions. Eastman Kodak, General Motors, U.S. Steel, and other firms provided medical services, insurance programs, pension plans, and vacations for their workers to undercut labor unions and persuade workers to rely on the corporation. Welfare capitalism, however, covered scarcely 5 percent of the work force and often benefited only skilled workers who were already tied to the company through seniority. Moreover, it was directed primarily at men.

Corporations in the 1920s also promoted company unions, management-sponsored substitutes for labor unions. Company unions were usually forbidden to handle wage and hour issues. Their function was to implement company policies and undermine real unionism.

Partly because of these pressures, membership in labor unions fell from 5.1 million in 1920 to 3.6 million in 1929. But unions also contributed to their own decline. Conservative union leaders neglected ethnic and black workers in mass production industries. Nor did they try to organize women, nearly one-fourth of all workers by 1930. The growing numbers of white-collar workers regarded themselves as middle-class and beyond the scope of union action.

With increasing mechanization and weak labor unions, workers suffered from job insecurity and stagnant wages. The promise of business to pay high wages proved hollow. Real wages (purchasing power) did improve, but most of the improvement came before 1923 and reflected falling prices more than rising wages. After 1923, American wages stabilized. Henry Ford made no general wage hike after 1919, although his workers would have needed an increase of 65 percent to recover the buying power they had enjoyed in 1914. Indeed, in 1928, Ford lowered wage rates. U.S. Steel also reduced weekly wages, even while its profits almost doubled between 1923 and 1929. The failure to raise wages when productivity was increasing threatened the nation's long-term prosperity. In short, rising national income largely reflected salaries and dividends, not wages.

Overall, the gap between rich and poor widened during the decade. By 1929, fully 71 percent of American families earned less than what the U.S. Bureau of Labor Statistics regarded as necessary for a decent living standard. The maldistribution of income meant that eventually Americans would be unable to purchase the products they made.

The expansion of consumer credit, rare before the 1920s, offered temporary relief by permitting consumers to buy goods over time. General Motors introduced consumer credit on a national basis to create a mass market for expensive automobiles. By 1927, two-thirds of automobiles were purchased on the installment plan. Nevertheless, installment loans did not in the long run raise the purchasing power of an income; they simply added interest charges to the price of products.

Sick Industries

Despite the general appearance of prosperity, several "sick" industries dragged on the economy. Coal mining, textile and garment manufacturing, and railroads suffered from excess capacity (too many mines and factories), shrinking demand, low returns, and management-labor conflicts. Unemployment in the coal industry approached 30 percent; by 1928, a reporter found "thousands of women and children literally starving to death" in Appalachia and the remaining miners held in "industrial slavery." The textile industry coped with overcapacity and declining demand by shifting operations from New England to the cheap-labor South, employing girls and young women for fifty-six-hour weeks at 18 cents an hour. Despite substandard

wages and repressive policies, textile companies remained barely profitable.

American agriculture never recovered from the 1921 depression. In 1919, gross farm income amounted to 16 percent of the national income; by 1929, it had dropped to half that. Agricultural surpluses and shrinking demand forced down prices. After the war, foreign markets dried up, and domestic demand for cotton slackened. Moreover, farmers' wartime expansion left them heavily mortgaged in the 1920s. Small farmers, unable to compete with larger, better-capitalized farmers, suffered most. Many lost their land and became tenants or farm hands. By 1930, only 57 percent of American farmers owned the land they worked, the lowest percentage ever.

By the end of the 1920s, the average per capita income for people on the nation's farms was only one-fourth that of Americans off the farm; in the South, farm families had per capita income of less than $200 a year. "Widespread agricultural disaster," warned one Iowa newspaper, was producing "a highly dangerous situation." Like textile workers in New England and the Piedmont and coal miners in Appalachia, rural Americans suffered in the 1920s.

The Business of Government

The Republican surge in national politics also shaped the economy. In the 1920 election, the Republican slogan was "Less government in business, more business in government." Under such direction, the federal government advanced business interests at the expense of other objectives (see "American Views: The Cult of Business").

Republican Ascendancy

Republicans in 1920 had retained control of Congress and put Warren Harding in the White House. Harding was neither capable nor bright. One critic described a Harding speech as "an army of pompous phrases moving over the landscape in search of an idea." But he had a genial touch that contrasted favorably with Wilson. He pardoned Eugene Debs, whom Wilson had refused to release from prison, and he spoke out against racial violence. He also helped shape the modern presidency by supporting the Budget and Accounting Act of 1921, which gave the president authority over the budget and created the Budget Bureau and the General Accounting Office. Moreover, some of his cabinet appointees were highly accomplished, and two of them, Secretary of Commerce Herbert Hoover and Secretary of the Treasury Andrew Mellon, shaped economic policy throughout the 1920s.

A self-described progressive, dedicated to efficiency, Hoover made the Commerce Department the government's most dynamic office. He cemented its ties with the leading sectors of the economy, expanded its collection and distribution of industrial information, pushed to exploit foreign resources and markets, and encouraged innovation. Hoover's goal was to expand prosperity by making business efficient, responsive, and profitable. Andrew Mellon had a narrower goal. A wealthy banker and industrialist, he pressed Congress to reduce taxes on businesses and the rich. Despite the opposition of progressives in Congress, Mellon succeeded in lowering maximum tax rates and eliminating wartime excess-profits taxes in 1921.

The Harding administration promoted business interests in other ways, too. The tariff of 1922 raised import rates to protect industry from foreign competition. Attorney General Harry Daugherty aided the business campaign for the open shop. And the Republicans also curtailed government regulation. By appointing advocates of big business to the Federal Trade Commission, the Federal Reserve Board, and other regulatory agencies established earlier by the progressives, Harding made government the collaborator rather than the regulator of business. Progressive Republican Senator George Norris of Nebraska angrily asked, "If trusts, combinations, and big business are to run the government, why not permit them to do it directly rather than through this expensive machinery which was originally honestly established for the protection of the people of the country against monopoly?"

Finally, Harding reshaped the Supreme Court between 1921 and 1923 into a still more aggressive champion of business. He named the conservative William Howard Taft as chief justice and matched him with three other justices who were, as one of them proclaimed, sympathetic to business leaders "beset and bedeviled with vexatious statutes, prying commissions, and government intermeddling of all sorts." The Court struck down much of the government economic regulation adopted during the Progressive Era, invalidated restraints on child labor and a minimum wage law for women, and approved restrictions on labor unions.

Government Corruption

The green light that Harding Republicans extended to private interests led to corruption and scandals. Harding appointed many friends and cronies who saw public service as an opportunity for graft. The head of the Veterans Bureau went to prison for cheating disabled veterans of $200 million dollars. Albert Fall, the secretary of the interior, leased the petroleum reserves set aside by progressive conservationists to oil companies in exchange for cash, bonds, and cattle for his New Mexico ranch. Exposed for his role in the **Teapot Dome scandal**, named after a Wyoming oil reserve, Fall became the first cabinet officer in history to go to jail. Attorney General Daugherty escaped a similar fate by destroying records and invoking the Fifth Amendment.

Harding was appalled as the scandals began to unfold. He died shortly thereafter, probably of a heart attack.

Coolidge Prosperity

On August 3, 1923, Vice President Calvin Coolidge was sworn in as president by his father while visiting his birthplace in rural Vermont, thereby reaffirming his association with traditional values. This image reassured Americans troubled by the Harding scandals.

Coolidge supported business with ideological conviction. He opposed the activist presidency of the Progressive Era, cultivating instead a deliberate inactivity calculated to lower expectations of government. He endorsed Secretary of the Treasury Mellon's ongoing efforts to reverse the progressive tax policies of the Wilson years and backed Secretary of Commerce Hoover's persistent efforts on behalf of the business community (although he privately sneered at Hoover as the "Wonder Boy"). Coolidge continued, like Harding, to install business supporters in the regulatory agencies. To chair the Federal Trade Commission he appointed an attorney who had condemned the agency as "an instrument of oppression and disturbance and injury instead of help to business." The *Wall Street Journal* soon crowed, "Never before, here or anywhere else, has a government been so completely fused with business."

"Coolidge prosperity" determined the 1924 election. The Democrats, hopelessly divided, took 103 ballots to nominate the colorless, conservative Wall Street lawyer John W. Davis. A more interesting opponent for Coolidge was Robert La Follette, nominated by discontented farm and labor organizations that formed a new Progressive party. La Follette campaigned against "the power of private monopoly over the political and economic life of the American people." The Republicans, backed by immense contributions from business, denounced La Follette as an agent of Bolshevism. The choice, Republicans insisted, was "Coolidge or Chaos." Thus instructed,

American Views

THE CULT OF BUSINESS

During the 1920s, publicists and politicians joined manufacturers and merchants in proclaiming that business promoted not only material but also social and even spiritual well-being. In his best-seller *The Man Nobody Knows* (1924), advertising executive Bruce Barton portrayed Jesus Christ as the founder of modern business. The following excerpt from an article by Edward E. Purinton, a popular lecturer on business values and efficiency, makes even more extensive claims for business.

❖ **How accurate are Purinton's claims of great opportunity in the corporate world of the 1920s? Of occupational mobility in the factory economy?**

❖ **What does this view of business imply about the role of government in American life?**

❖ **How do you think Protestant fundamentalists might have viewed the cult of business?**

Among the nations of the earth today America stands for one idea: *Business*. National opprobrium? National opportunity. For in this fact lies, potentially, the salvation of the world.

Through business, properly conceived, managed, and conducted, the human race is finally to be redeemed. How and why a man works foretells what he will do, think, have, give, and be. And real salvation is in doing, thinking, having, giving, and being—not in sermonizing and theorizing. . . .

What is the finest game? Business. The soundest science? Business. The truest art? Business. The fullest education? Business. The fairest opportunity? Business. The cleanest philanthropy? Business. The sanest religion? Business.

You may not agree. That is because you judge business by the crude, mean, stupid, false imitation of business that happens to be located near you.

The finest game is business. The rewards are for everybody, and all can win. There are no favorites—Providence always crowns the career of the man who is worthy. And in this game there is no "luck"—you have the fun of taking chances but the sobriety of guaranteeing certainties. The speed and size of your winnings are for you alone to determine. . . .

The soundest science is business. All investigation is reduced to action, and by action proved or disproved. The idealistic motive animates the materialistic method. . . . Capital is furnished for

---

Americans chose Coolidge, though barely half the electorate bothered to vote.

The Fate of Reform

Progressive reform was not completely dead, but the fate of women's groups illustrated the difficulties reformers faced in the 1920s. At first, the adoption of woman suffrage prompted politicians to champion women's reform issues. In 1920, both major parties endorsed many of the goals of the new **League of Women Voters**. Within a year, many states had granted women the right to serve on juries, several

enacted equal pay laws, and Wisconsin adopted an equal rights law. Congress passed the **Sheppard-Towner Maternity and Infancy Act**, the first federal social welfare law, in 1921. It provided federal funds for infant and maternity care, precisely the type of protective legislation that the suffragists had described as women's special interest.

But thereafter, women reformers gained little. As it became clear that women did not vote as a bloc but according to their varying social and economic backgrounds, Congress lost interest in "women's issues." In 1929, Congress killed the Sheppard-Towner the researches of "pure science"; yet pure science is not regarded pure until practical. Competent scientists are suitably rewarded—as they are not in the scientific schools. . . .

The fullest education is business. A proper blend of study, work and life is essential to advancement. The whole man is educated. Human nature itself is the open book that all business men study; and the mastery of a page of this educates you more than the memorizing of a dusty tome from a library shelf. In the school of business, moreover, you teach yourself and learn most from your own mistakes. What you learn here you live out, the only real test.

The fairest opportunity is business. You can find more, better, quicker chances to get ahead in a large business house than anywhere else on earth. . . . Recognition of better work, of keener and quicker thought, of deeper and finer feeling, is gladly offered by the men higher up, with early promotion the rule for the man who justifies it. There is, and can be, no such thing as buried talent in a modern business organization. . . .

The sanest religion is business. Any relationship that forces a man to follow the Golden Rule rightfully belongs amid the ceremonials of the church. A great business enterprise includes and presupposes this relationship. I have seen more Christianity to the square inch as a regular part of the office equipment of famous corporation presidents than may ordinarily be found on Sunday in a verbalized but not vitalized church congregation. . . . You can fool your preacher with a sickly sprout or a wormy semblance of character, but you can't fool your employer. I would make every business house a consultation bureau for the guidance of the church whose members were employees of the house. . . .

The future work of the businessman is to teach the teacher, preach to the preacher, admonish the parent, advise the doctor, justify the lawyer, superintend the statesman, fructify the farmer, stabilize the banker, harness the dreamer, and reform the reformer.

Source: Edward E. Purinton, "Big Ideas from Big Business," *Independent*, April 16, 1921.

Act. Nor could reformers gain ratification of a child labor amendment after the Supreme Court invalidated laws regulating child labor. Conservatives attacked women reformers as "Bolsheviks."

Disagreements among women reformers and shifting interests also limited their success. Led by the **National Woman's Party**, some feminists campaigned for an **Equal Rights Amendment**. But other women reformers feared that such an amendment would nullify the progressive laws that protected working women. Reform organizations like the Consumers' League lost their energy and focus, and

many younger women rejected the public concerns of progressive feminists for what the president of the Women's Trade Union League called "cheap hopes and cheaper materialism."

Cities and Suburbs

The 1920 census reported that for the first time, more Americans lived in urban than in rural areas. The trend toward urbanization accelerated in the 1920s as millions of Americans fled the depressed countryside for the booming cities. This massive population movement interacted with technological innovations to reshape cities, build suburbs, and transform urban life (see Map 26-1).

Expanding Cities

Urbanization affected all regions of the country. In absolute terms, the older industrial cities of the Northeast and Upper Midwest grew the most, attracting migrants from the rural South and distressed Appalachia. New York remained the nation's foremost metropolis. All other major cities expanded—none more spectacularly than Detroit, which grew to 1.6 million people. The "Motor City" thrived on the booming automobile industry and related industries like glass manufacturing.

Rural Southerners also headed for southern cities. In fact, the South was the nation's most rapidly urbanizing region. Migrants from the countryside poured into Atlanta, Birmingham, Memphis, and Houston. Little more than jungle before 1914, Miami became the fastest-growing city in the United States during the 1920s—"the Magic City." In the West, Denver, Portland, and Seattle (each a regional economic hub) and several California cities grew rapidly. Los Angeles grew by 115 percent and by 1930 was the nation's fifth-largest city, with over 1.2 million people.

The population surge transformed the urban landscape. As land values soared, developers built skyscrapers. By the end of the decade, American cities had nearly four hundred skyscrapers taller than twenty stories. The tallest, New York's 102-story Empire State Building, symbolized the urban boom.

The Great Black Migration

A significant feature of the rural-to-urban movement was the **Great Migration** of African-Americans from the South in search of job opportunities. Prosperity created jobs, and with the decline in European immigration, blacks filled the positions previously given to

Map 26-1   Population Shifts, 1920–1930

Rural Americans fled to the cities during the 1920s, escaping a declining agricultural economy to search for new opportunities. African-Americans in particular left the rural South for Eastern and Midwestern cities, but the urban population also jumped in the West and in the South itself.

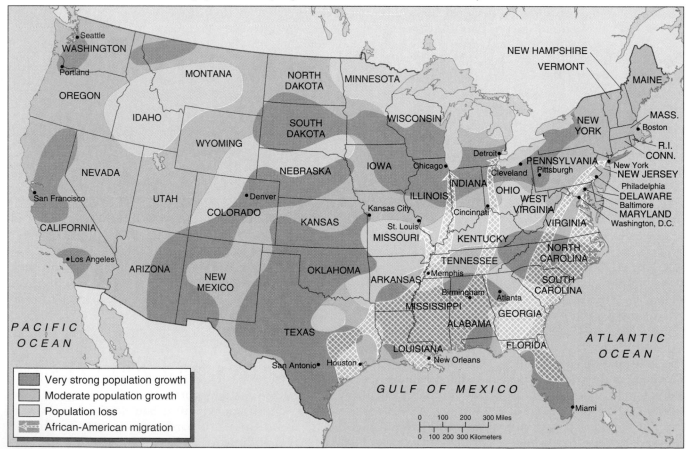

new immigrants. Though generally the lowest-paid and least secure jobs, they were better than share-cropping in the rural South. Black men worked as unskilled or semiskilled laborers; black women became domestics in white homes. More than a million and a half African-Americans moved to northern cities in the 1920s.

Black ghettos developed in most northern cities, more because of prejudice than the wishes of the migrants. With thousands of newcomers limited to certain neighborhoods by racist restrictions, housing shortages developed. Rapacious landlords charged ever-increasing rents for ever-declining housing. High rents and low wages forced black families to share inferior and unsanitary housing that threatened their health and safety. In Pittsburgh, only 20 percent of black houses had bathtubs and only 50 percent had indoor toilets.

However, the Great Migration also increased blacks' racial consciousness, autonomy, and power. In 1928, for instance, the black population of Chicago, using the ballot denied to African-Americans in the South, elected the first black to Congress since the turn of the century. Mutual aid societies and fraternal orders proliferated. Churches were particularly influential.

Another organization also sought to appeal to poor blacks in the ghettos. The **Universal Negro Improvement Association (UNIA)**, organized by Marcus Garvey, a Jamaican immigrant to New York, rejected the NAACP's goal of integration. A black nationalist espousing racial pride, Garvey exhorted blacks to migrate to Africa to build a "free, redeemed, and mighty nation." UNIA organized many enterprises, including groceries, restaurants, laundries, a printing plant, and the Black Star Steamship Line, intended as a commercial link between the United States, the West Indies, and Africa. UNIA attracted half a million members, the first black mass movement in American history. When Garvey was convicted of mail fraud and deported, however, the movement collapsed.

Racial pride also found expression in the **Harlem Renaissance**, an outpouring of literature, painting, sculpture, and music. Inspired by African-American culture and black urban life, writers and artists created works of power and poignancy. The poetry of Langston Hughes reflected the rhythm and mood of jazz and the blues.

Barrios

Hispanic migrants also entered the nation's cities in the 1920s, creating their own communities, or barrios. Fifty thousand Puerto Ricans settled in New York, mostly in East ("Spanish") Harlem, where they found low-paying jobs. Far more migrants arrived from Mexico, usually settling in western and southwestern cities. The barrios, with their own businesses, churches, and cultural organizations, created a sense of permanency.

These communities enabled the newcomers to preserve their cultural values and build social institutions like *mutualistas* (mutual aid societies) that helped them get credit, housing, and health care. But the barrios also reflected the hostility that Hispanics encountered in American cities, for racism often restricted them to such districts. The number of Mexicans in Los Angeles tripled during the 1920s to nearly 100,000, but segregation confined them to East Los Angeles. Other areas of the city, like El Segundo or Lynwood, boasted of being "restricted to the white race" and having "no Negroes or Mexicans." Los Angeles maintained separate schools for Mexicans, and a social worker reported that "America has repulsed the Mexican immigrant in every step he has taken" toward integration.

Some Hispanics fought discrimination. *La Orden de Hijos de America* (The Order of the Sons of America), organized in San Antonio in 1921, campaigned against inequities in schools and the jury system. In 1929, it helped launch the larger **League of United Latin American Citizens (LULAC)**, which would help advance civil rights for all Americans.

The Road to Suburbia

As fast as the cities mushroomed in the 1920s, the suburbs grew twice as fast. Park Ridge outside Chicago, Inglewood outside Los Angeles, Shaker Heights outside Cleveland, and many others expanded by 400 percent. Automobiles created the modern suburb. The new developments were sprawling and dispersed, for thanks to the automobile, people could now live in formerly remote areas. A single-family house surrounded by a lawn became the social ideal, a pastoral escape from the overcrowded and dangerous city. Many suburbs excluded African-Americans, Hispanics, Jews, and working-class people.

Suburbanization and the automobile brought other changes. In 1922, J. C. Nichols opened the Country Club Plaza, the first suburban shopping center, in Kansas City; it provided free, off-street parking. Department stores and other large retailers began leaving the urban cores for the suburbs, where both parking and more affluent customers were waiting. Drive-in restaurants began with Royce Hailey's Pig Stand in Dallas in 1921. Later in the decade, the first fast-food franchise chain, White Tower, appeared, with its standardized menu and building.

To serve the automobile, governments spent more on road construction and maintenance. By 1930, road construction was the largest single item in the national budget.

Mass Culture in the Jazz Age

The White Tower chain symbolized a new society and culture. Urbanization and the automobile joined with new systems of distributing, marketing, and communications to mold a mass culture of standardized experiences and interests. Not all Americans participated equally in the new culture, however, and some attacked it.

Advertising the Consumer Society

Advertising and its focus on increasing consumption shaped the new society. President Coolidge considered advertising "the most potent influence in adopting and changing the habits and modes of life, affecting what we eat, what we wear, and the work and play of the whole nation." Advertisers exhorted consumers via newspapers, billboards, streetcar signs, junk mail, radio, movies, and even skywriting. They sought to create a single market where everyone, regardless of region and ethnicity, consumed brand-name products. Advertisers attempted to stimulate new wants by ridiculing previous models or tastes as obsolete, acclaiming the convenience of a new brand, or linking the latest fashion with status or sex appeal.

The home became a focus of consumerism. Middle- and upper-class women purchased mass-produced household appliances, such as electric irons, toasters, vacuum cleaners, washing machines, and refrigerators. Working-class women bought packaged food, ready-made clothing, and other consumer goods to lighten their workload. Advertisers attempted to redefine the housewife's role as primarily that of a consumer, purchasing goods for her family.

A shifting labor market also promoted mass consumption. The increasing number of white-collar workers had more time and money for leisure and consumption. Women clerical workers, the fastest-growing occupational group, found in the purchase of clothes and cosmetics a sign of social status and an antidote to workplace monotony. "People are seeking to escape from themselves," insisted a writer in *Advertising and Selling* in 1926. "They want to live in a more exciting world."

Under the stimulus of advertising, consumption increasingly displaced the traditional virtues of

Advertisements for brand-name products, like this 1929 ad for Campbell's tomato soup, often tried to link simple consumption with larger issues of personal success and achievement.

thrift, prudence, and avoidance of debt. Installment buying became common. By 1928, fully 85 percent of furniture, 80 percent of radios, and 75 percent of washing machines were bought on credit. But with personal debt rising more than twice as fast as incomes, even aggressive advertising and the extension of credit could not indefinitely prolong the illusion of a healthy economy.

Leisure and Entertainment

During the 1920s, Americans also spent more on recreation and leisure, important features of the new mass society. Millions of people packed into movie theaters whose ornate style symbolized their social importance. Movies helped spread common values and set national trends in dress, language, and behavior. Whether or not they qualified as art, movies were always produced to make a profit. Studios made films to attract the largest audiences and fit prevailing stereotypes. Cecil B. De Mille titillated audiences while reinforcing conventional standards with religious epics, like *The Ten Commandments* (1923) or *The King of Kings* (1927).

Radio also helped mold national popular culture. In 1926, the Radio Corporation of America (RCA) helped form the National Broadcasting Company (NBC), the first radio network. Soon it was charging $10,000 to broadcast commercials to a national market. Networks provided standardized entertainment, personalities, and news to Americans across the nation. Radio incorporated listeners into a national society. Rural residents, in particular, welcomed the "talking furniture" for giving them access to the speeches, sermons, and business information available to city-dwellers.

The phonograph, another popular source of entertainment, allowed families to listen to music of their choice in their own homes. Record companies promoted dance crazes, such as the Charleston, and developed regional markets for country, or "hillbilly," music in the South and West as well as a "race market" for blues and jazz among the growing urban population, black and white. The popularity of the trumpet player Louis Armstrong and other jazz greats gave the decade its nickname, the **Jazz Age**.

Jazz derived from African-American musical traditions. The Great Migration spread it from New Orleans and Kansas City to cities throughout the nation. Its improvisational and rhythmic characteristics differed sharply from older and more formal music and were often condemned by people who feared that jazz would undermine conventional restraints on behavior. But conductor Leopold Stokowski defended jazz as the music of modern America: "Jazz has come to stay because it is an expression of the times, of the breathless, energetic, superactive times in which we are living; it is useless to fight against it."

Professional sports also flourished and became more commercialized. Millions of Americans, attracted by the popularity of such celebrities as Babe Ruth of the New York Yankees, crowded into baseball parks to follow major league teams. Ruth treated himself as a commercial commodity, hiring an agent, endorsing Cadillacs and alligator shoes, and defending a salary in 1932 that dwarfed that of President Hoover by declaring, "I had a better year than he did."

Another celebrity who captured popular fascination was the aviator Charles Lindbergh, who flew alone across the Atlantic in 1927. In the *Spirit of St. Louis,* a tiny airplane built on a shoestring budget and nearly outweighed by the massive amount of fuel it had to carry, Lindbergh fought bad weather and fatigue for thirty-four hours before landing to a hero's welcome in Paris. Named its first "Man of the Year" by

Time, one of the new mass-circulation magazines, Lindbergh won adulation and awards from Americans who still valued the image of individualism.

The New Morality

The promotion of consumption and immediate gratification weakened traditional self-restraint and fed a desire for personal fulfillment. The failure of wartime sacrifices to achieve promised glories deepened Americans' growing disenchantment with traditional values. The social dislocations of the war years and growing urbanization accelerated moral and social change. Sexual pleasure became an increasingly open objective, as the growing availability of birth control information enabled women to enjoy sex with less fear of pregnancy and movie stars like Clara Bow, known as "the It Girl," and Rudolph Valentino flaunted sexuality to mass audiences. Traditionalists worried as divorce rates, cigarette consumption, and hemlines went up while respect for parents, elders, and clergy went down.

Young people seemed to embody the new morality. Rejecting conventional standards, they embraced the era's frenzied dances, bootleg liquor, smoking, more revealing clothing, and sexual experimentation. They welcomed the freedom from parental control that the automobile afforded. The "flapper"—a frivolous young woman with short hair and a skimpy skirt who danced, smoked, and drank in oblivious self-absorption—was a major obsession in countless articles, bearing such titles as "These Wild Young People" and "The Uprising of the Young." Few people were more alarmed than the president of the University of Florida, "The low-cut gowns, the rolled hose and short skirts are born of the Devil," he cried, "and are carrying the present and future generations to chaos and destruction."

But the new morality was neither as new nor as widespread as its advocates and critics believed. Signs of change had appeared before the war in the popularity of new clothing fashions, social values, and public amusements among working-class and ethnic groups. And if it now became fashionable for the middle class to adopt such attitudes and practices, most Americans still adhered to traditional beliefs and values. Moreover, the new morality offered only a limited freedom. It certainly did not promote social equality for women, who remained subject to traditional double standards, with marriage and divorce laws, property rights, and employment opportunities biased against them.

The Searching Twenties

Many writers rejected what they considered the materialism, conformity, and provincialism of the emerging mass culture. Their criticism made the postwar decade one of the most creative periods in American literature. The brutality and hypocrisy of the war stimulated their disillusionment and alienation. What Gertrude Stein called the **Lost Generation** considered, in the words of F. Scott Fitzgerald, "all Gods dead, all wars fought, all faiths in man shaken." Ernest Hemingway, wounded as a Red Cross volunteer during the war, rejected idealism in his novel *A Farewell to Arms* (1929), declaring that he no longer saw any meaning in "the words *sacred, glorious,* and *sacrifice.*"

Novelists also turned their attention to American society. In *The Great Gatsby* (1925), Fitzgerald traced the self-deceptions of the wealthy. Sinclair Lewis ridiculed middle-class society and its narrow business culture in *Babbitt* (1922), whose title character provided a new word applied to the smug and shallow. In 1930, Lewis became the first American to win the Nobel Prize in literature.

Culture Wars

Despite the blossoming of mass culture and society in the 1920s, conflicts divided social groups. Some of these struggles involved reactions against the new currents in American life, including technological and scientific innovations, urban growth, and materialism. But movements to restrict immigration, enforce prohibition, prohibit the teaching of evolution, and even sustain the Ku Klux Klan did not have simple origins, motives, or consequences. The forces underlying the culture wars of the 1920s would surface repeatedly in the future (see the summary table "Issues in the Culture Wars of the 1920s").

Nativism and Immigration Restriction

For years, many Americans, from racists to reformers, had campaigned to restrict immigration. In 1917, Congress required immigrants to pass a literacy test. But renewed immigration after the war revived the anti-immigration movement, and the propaganda of the war and Red Scare years generated public support for more restriction. Depicting immigrants as radicals, racial inferiors, religious subversives, or criminals, nativists clamored for congressional action.

Congress passed the Emergency Quota Act in 1921, reducing immigration by about two-thirds and establishing quotas for nationalities on the basis of their numbers in the United States in 1910. Coolidge himself urged that America "be kept American," by which he meant white, Anglo-Saxon, and

Protestant. Congress adopted this racist rationale in the **National Origins Act** of 1924, which proclaimed its objective to be the maintenance of the "racial preponderance" of "the basic strain of our population." This law restricted immigration quotas to 2 percent of the foreign-born population of each nationality as recorded in the 1890 census, which was taken before the mass immigration from southern and eastern Europe. Another provision completely excluded Japanese immigrants.

In Japan, the law provoked anti-American demonstrations. California, Oregon, Washington, Arizona, and other western states had recently prohibited Japanese residents from owning or leasing land, and in 1922, the Supreme Court had ruled that, as nonwhites, they could never become naturalized citizens. A Japanese newspaper in Los Angeles criticized such actions as betraying America's own ideals. Dispirited by the prejudice of the decade, Japanese residents hoped for fulfillment through their children, the **Nisei**, who were American citizens by birth.

Ironically, as a U.S. territory, the Philippines was not subject to the National Origins Act, and Filipino immigration increased ninefold during the 1920s. Similarly, because the law did not apply to immigrants from the Western Hemisphere, Mexican immigration also grew. Nativists lobbied to exclude Mexicans, but agribusiness interests in the Southwest blocked any restrictions on low-cost migrant labor.

The Ku Klux Klan

Nativism was also reflected in the popularity of the revived Ku Klux Klan, the goal of which, according to its leader, was to protect "the interest of those whose forefathers established the nation." Although founded in Georgia in 1915 and modeled on its Reconstruction predecessor, the new Klan was a national, not a southern, movement and claimed several million members by the mid-1920s. Admitting only native-born white Protestants, the Klan embodied the fears of a traditional culture threatened by social change. Ironically, its rapid spread owed much to modern business and promotional techniques as hundreds of professional recruiters raked in hefty commissions selling Klan memberships to those hoping to defend their way of life.

In part the Klan was a fraternal order, providing entertainment, assistance, and community for its members. Its picnics, parades, charity drives, and other social and family-oriented activities—perhaps a half million women joined the Women of the Ku Klux Klan—sharply distinguished the organization from both the small, secretive Klan of the nineteenth

SUMMARY

ISSUES IN THE CULTURE WARS OF THE 1920S

Issue	Proponent view	Opponent view
The new morality	Promotes greater personal freedom and opportunities for fulfillment	Promotes moral collapse
Evolutionism	A scientific advance linked to notions of progress	A threat to religious belief
Jazz	Modern and vital	Unsettling, irregular, vulgar, and primitive
Immigration	A source of national strength from ethnic and racial diversity	A threat to the status and authority of old-stock white Protestants
Great Migration	A chance for African-Americans to find new economic opportunities and gain autonomy and pride	A threat to traditional white privilege, control, and status
Prohibition	Promotes social and family stability and reduces crime	Restricts personal liberty and increases crime
Fundamentalism	An admirable adherence to traditional religious faith and biblical injunctions	A superstitious creed given to intolerant interference in social and political affairs
Ku Klux Klan	An organization promoting community responsibility, patriotism, and traditional social, moral, and religious values	A group of religious and racial bigots given to violent vigilantism and fostering moral and public corruption
Mass culture	Increases popular participation in national culture; provides entertainment and relaxation	Promotes conformity, materialism, mediocrity, and spectacle
Consumerism	Promotes material progress and higher living standards	Promotes waste, sterility, and self-indulgence

century and the still smaller, extremist Klan of the later twentieth century.

But the Klan also exploited racial, ethnic, and religious prejudices, attacking blacks in the South, Mexicans in Texas, Japanese in California, and Catholics and Jews everywhere. A twisted religious impulse ran through much of the Klan's organization and activities. It hired itinerant Protestant ministers to spread its message, erected altars and flaming crosses at its meetings, and sang Klan lyrics to the tunes of well-known hymns. The Klan also resorted to violence. In 1921, for example, a Methodist minister who belonged to the Klan murdered a Catholic priest on his own doorstep, and other Klansmen burned down Catholic churches.

The Klan also ventured into politics, with some success. But eventually it encountered resistance. In the North, Catholic workers disrupted Klan parades. In the South, too, Klan excesses provoked a backlash. After the Klan in Dallas flogged sixty-eight people in a "whipping meadow" along the Trinity River in 1922, respect turned to outrage. Newspapers demanded that the Klan disband and district attorneys began to prosecute Klan thugs. Elsewhere the Klan was stung by revelations of criminal behavior and corruption by Klan leaders who had been making fortunes pocketing membership fees and selling regalia to followers. The Klan crusade to purify society had bred corruption and conflict everywhere. By 1930, the Klan had nearly collapsed.

"The Awakening," a stage presentation by Ku Klux Klan members in Port Arthur, Texas—men, women, and children—indicates the social role the organization sometimes played. But promoting group cohesion for members also took the form of violent attacks on outsiders—those who were not white, native-born Protestants.

Prohibition and Crime

Like the Klan, prohibition both reflected and provoked social tensions in the 1920s. Prohibitionists rejoiced in 1920 when the Eighteenth Amendment, prohibiting the manufacture, sale, or transportation of alcoholic beverages, took effect. Congress then passed the **Volstead Act**, which defined the forbidden liquors and established the Prohibition Bureau to enforce the law. But many social groups, especially among urban ethnic communities, opposed prohibition, and the government could not enforce the law where public opinion did not endorse it.

Evasion was easy. By permitting alcohol for medicinal, sacramental, and industrial purposes, the Volstead Act gave doctors, priests, and druggists a huge loophole through which to satisfy their friends' needs. City-dwellers made "bathtub gin," and rural people distilled "moonshine." The limited resources of the Prohibition Bureau often allowed bootleggers to operate openly. Dozens met publicly in a Seattle hotel in 1922 and adopted "fair prices" for liquor and a code of ethics "to keep liquor runners within the limits of approved business methods."

The huge profits encouraged organized crime—which had previously concentrated on gambling and prostitution—to develop elaborate liquor distribution networks. Operating outside the law, crime "families" used violence to enforce contracts, suppress competition, and attack rivals. In Chicago, Al Capone's army of nearly a thousand gangsters killed hundreds.

Gradually, even many "drys"—people who had initially favored prohibition—dropped their support, horrified by the boost it gave organized crime and worried about a general disrespect for law that it promoted. A 1926 poll found that four-fifths of Americans wanted to repeal or modify prohibition. And in 1933, thirty-six states ratified an amendment repealing what Herbert Hoover had called a "noble experiment."

Old-Time Religion and the Scopes Trial

Religion provided another fulcrum for traditionalists attempting to stem cultural change. Protestant fundamentalism, which emphasized the infallibility of the Bible, including the Genesis story of Adam and Eve, emerged at the turn of the century as a conservative reaction to religious modernism and the social changes brought by the mass immigration of Catholics and Jews, the growing influence of science and technology, and the secularization of public education. But the fundamentalist crusade to reshape America became formidable only in the 1920s.

Fundamentalist groups, colleges, and publications sprang up throughout the nation, especially in the South. The anti-Catholic sentiment exploited by the Klan was but one consequence of fundamentalism's insistence on strict biblical Christianity. A second was the assault on Darwin's theory of evolution, which contradicted literal interpretations of biblical Creation. Fundamentalist legislators tried to prevent teaching evolution in public schools in at least twenty states. In 1925, Tennessee forbade teaching any idea contrary to the biblical account of human origins.

Social or political conservatism, however, was not an inherent part of old-time religion. The most prominent antievolution politician, William Jennings Bryan, feared that Darwinism promoted political and economic conservatism. The survival of the fittest, he complained, elevated force and brutality, ignored spiritual values and democracy, and discouraged altruism and reform. How could a person fight for social justice "unless he believes in the triumph of right?"

The controversy over evolution came to a head when the **American Civil Liberties Union (ACLU)** responded to Tennessee's violation of the constitutional separation of church and state by offering to defend any teacher who tested the antievolution law. John Scopes, a high school biology teacher in Dayton, Tennessee, did so and was arrested. Scopes's trial riveted national attention after Bryan agreed to assist the prosecution and Clarence Darrow, a famous Chicago lawyer and prominent atheist, volunteered to defend Scopes.

Millions of Americans tuned their radios to hear the first trial ever broadcast. Though the local jury took only eight minutes to convict Scopes, fundamentalists suffered public ridicule from reporters like H. L. Mencken, who sneered at the "hillbillies" and "yokels" of Dayton. But fundamentalism retained religious influence and would again challenge science and modernism in American life.

A New Era in the World?

Abroad, as at home, Americans in the 1920s sought peace and economic order. Rejection of the Treaty of Versailles and the League of Nations did not foreshadow isolationism. Indeed, in the 1920s, the United States became more deeply involved in international matters than ever before in peacetime.

War Debts and Economic Expansion

The United States was the world's dominant economic power in the 1920s, changed by the Great War from a debtor to a creditor nation. The loans that the United States had made to its allies during the war troubled the nation's relations with Europe throughout the decade. American insistence on repayment angered Europeans, who saw the money as a U.S. contribution to the joint war effort against Germany. Moreover, high American tariffs blocked Europeans from exporting goods to the United States and earning dollars to repay their debts. Eventually, the United States readjusted the terms for repayment, and American bankers extended large loans to Germany, which used the money to pay reparations to Britain and France, whose governments then used the same money to repay the United States. This unstable system depended on a constant flow of money from the United States.

America's global economic role expanded in other ways as well. By 1929, the United States was the world's largest exporter, responsible for one-sixth of all exports. American investment abroad more than doubled between 1919 and 1930. To expand their markets and avoid foreign tariffs, many U.S. companies became **multinational corporations**, establishing branches or subsidiaries abroad. Ford built assembly plants in England, Japan, Turkey, and Canada. American oil companies invested in foreign oil fields, especially in Latin America, where they controlled more than half of Venezuelan production. The United Fruit Company developed such huge operations in Central America that it often dominated national economies. In Costa Rica, the company had a larger budget than the national government.

Europeans and Latin Americans alike worried about this economic invasion; even Secretary of Commerce Hoover expressed concerns. Multinationals, he warned, might eventually take markets from American manufacturers and jobs from American workers.

These concerns did not prevent him from promoting economic expansion abroad. The government worked to open doors for American businesses in foreign countries, helping them secure access to trade, investment opportunities, and raw materials. Hoover's Bureau of Foreign Commerce opened fifty offices around the world to boost American business. Secretary of State Charles Evans Hughes negotiated access to Iraqi oil fields for U.S. oil companies. The government also authorized bankers and manufacturers to form combinations, exempt from antitrust laws, to exploit foreign markets.

Rejecting War

Although government officials cooperated with business leaders to promote American strategic and economic interests, they had little desire to use force in the process. Popular reaction against the Great War, strengthened by a strong peace movement, constrained policymakers. Indeed, the State Department sought to restrict the buildup of armaments among nations.

At the invitation of President Harding, delegations from nine nations met in Washington at the Washington Naval Conference in 1921 to discuss disarmament. The conference drafted a treaty to reduce battleship tonnage and suspend the building of new ships for a decade. The terms virtually froze the existing balance of naval power, with the first rank assigned to Britain and the United States, followed by Japan and then France and Italy. The U.S. Senate ratified the treaty with only one dissenting vote, and the 1924 Republican platform hailed it as "the greatest peace document ever drawn." The United States made a more dramatic gesture in 1928 when it helped draft the **Kellogg-Briand Pact.** Signed by sixty-four nations, the treaty renounced aggression and outlawed war. Without provisions for enforcement, however, it was little more than symbolic.

Managing the Hemisphere

The United States continued to dominate Latin America to promote its own interests. It exerted its influence through investments, control of the Panama Canal, invocation of the Monroe Doctrine, and, when necessary, military intervention.

In response to American public opinion, the peace movement, and Latin American nationalism, the United States did retreat from the extreme gunboat diplomacy of the Progressive Era, withdrawing troops from the Dominican Republic and Nicaragua. But Haiti remained under U.S. occupation throughout the decade, American troops stayed in Cuba and Panama, and the United States directed the financial policies of other Latin American countries. Moreover, it sent the marines into Honduras in 1924 and back to Nicaragua in 1926. Such interventions could establish only temporary stability while provoking further Latin American hostility. "We are hated and despised," said one American businessman in Nicaragua. "This feeling has been created by employing American marines to hunt down and kill Nicaraguans in their own country."

The anger of Latin Americans prompted the State Department to draft the Clark Memorandum. This document, not published until 1930, receded from the Roosevelt Corollary and helped prepare the way for the so-called Good Neighbor Policy toward Latin America. Still, the United States retained the means, both military and economic, to dominate the hemisphere.

Herbert Hoover and the Final Triumph of the New Era

As the national economy steamed ahead in 1928, the Republicans chose as their presidential candidate Herbert Hoover, a man who symbolized the policies of prosperity and the New Era. Hoover was not a politician—he had never been elected to office—but a successful administrator who championed rational and efficient economic development. Hoover's stiff managerial image was softened by his humanitarian record and his roots in rural Iowa.

The Democrats, in contrast, chose a candidate who evoked the cultural conflicts of the 1920s.

Alfred E. Smith, four-term governor of New York, was a Catholic, an opponent of prohibition, and a Tammany politician tied to the immigrant constituency of New York City. His nomination plunged the nation into cultural strife. Rural fundamentalism, anti-Catholicism, prohibition, and nativism were crucial factors in the campaign. The fundamentalist assault was unrelenting. A Baptist minister in Oklahoma City warned his congregation: "If you vote for Al Smith, you're voting against Christ and you'll all be damned."

But Hoover was in fact the more progressive candidate. Sympathetic to labor, sensitive to women's issues, hostile to racial segregation, and favorable to the League of Nations, Hoover had always distanced himself from what he called "the reactionary group in the Republican party." By contrast, despite supporting state welfare legislation to benefit his urban working-class constituents, Smith was essentially conservative and opposed an active government. Moreover, he was as parochial as his most rural adversaries and never attempted to reach out to them. He responded to a question about the needs of the states west of the Mississippi by asking, "What states *are* west of the Mississippi?" With the nation still enjoying the economic prosperity so closely associated with Hoover and the Republicans, the Democrats were routed (see Map 26-2).

In his campaign, Hoover boasted that Republican policies could bring America to "the final triumph over poverty." But 1928 would be the Republicans' final triumph for a long time. The vaunted prosperity of the 1920s was ending, and the country faced a future dark with poverty.

Conclusion

The New Era of the 1920s changed America. Technological and managerial innovations produced giant leaps in productivity, new patterns of labor, a growing concentration of corporate power, and high corporate profits. Government policies from protective tariffs and regressive taxation to a relaxation of regulatory laws reflected and reinforced the triumphs of a business elite over traditional cautions and concerns.

The decade's economic developments in turn stimulated social change, drawing millions of Americans from the countryside to the cities, creating an urban nation, and fostering a new ethic of materialism, consumerism, and leisure and a new mass culture based on the automobile, radio, the movies, and advertising. This social transformation swept up many Americans but left others unsettled

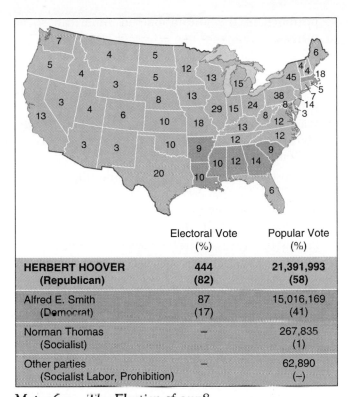

	Electoral Vote (%)	Popular Vote (%)
HERBERT HOOVER (Republican)	**444** **(82)**	**21,391,993** **(58)**
Alfred E. Smith (Democrat)	87 (17)	15,016,169 (41)
Norman Thomas (Socialist)	–	267,835 (1)
Other parties (Socialist Labor, Prohibition)	–	62,890 (–)

Map 26-2   The Election of 1928
The cultural conflicts of the 1920s shaped the 1928 election. Al Smith carried the largest cities, but Herbert Hoover swept most of the rest of the nation, even attracting much of the usually Democratic South.

by the erosion of traditional practices and values. The concerns of traditionalists found expression in campaigns for prohibition and against immigration, the revival of the Ku Klux Klan, and the rise of religious fundamentalism. Intellectuals denounced the materialism and conformity they saw in the new social order and fashioned new artistic and literary trends.

But the impact of the decade's trends was uneven. Mechanization increased the productivity of some workers but cost others their jobs; people poured into the cities while others left for the suburbs; prohibition, intended to stabilize society, instead produced conflict, crime, and corruption; government policies advanced some economic interests but injured others. Even the notion of a "mass" culture obscured the degree to which millions of Americans were left out of the New Era. With no disposable income and little access to electricity, rural Americans scarcely participated in the joys of consumerism; racial and ethnic minorities often were isolated in ghettos and barrios; and many workers faced declining opportunities. Most ominous was the uneven prosperity undergirding the New Era. Although

living standards rose for many Americans and the rich expanded their share of national wealth, more than 40 percent of the population earned less than $1,500 a year and fell below the established poverty level. The unequal distribution of wealth and income made the economy unstable and vulnerable to a disastrous collapse.

Review Questions

1. How did the automobile industry affect the nation's economy and society in the 1920s?

2. What factors characterized the "boom industries" of the 1920s? The "sick industries"? How accurate is it to label the 1920s the "decade of prosperity"?

3. What were the underlying issues in the election of 1924? Of 1928? What role did politics play in the public life of the 1920s?

4. What were the chief points of conflict in the "culture wars" of the 1920s? What were the underlying issues in these clashes? Why were they so hard to compromise?

5. In what ways did the World War I experience shape developments in the 1920s?

6. What were the chief features of American involvement in world affairs in the 1920s? To what extent did that involvement constitute a new role for the United States?

Recommended Reading

John Braeman, Robert Bremner, and David Brody, eds., *Change and Continuity in Twentieth Century America: The 1920s* (1968). Stimulating essays cover important features of economic, social, and political history.

Warren I. Cohen, *Empire without Tears: America's Foreign Relations, 1921–1933* (1987). Cohen provides splendid brief analysis of diplomatic and economic policy.

James J. Flink, *The Car Culture* (1975). The history of the automobile and its social impact remains fascinating.

Ellis W. Hawley, *The Great War and the Search for a Modern Order* (1979). Hawley focuses on economics.

Sinclair Lewis, *Babbitt* (1922). This important novel of the 1920s ridicules the empty business values of the booster society.

Where to Learn More

❖ **Smithsonian Institution, Washington, D.C.** "From Farm to Factory," a permanent exhibition at the National Museum of American History, splendidly portrays the human side of the Great Migration.

❖ **Herbert Hoover National Historic Site, West Branch, Iowa.** Visitors may tour Hoover's birthplace cottage, presidential library, and museum.

❖ **Henry Ford Museum and Greenfield Village, Dearborn, Michigan.** Among many fascinating exhibits, "The Automobile in American Life" particularly and superbly demonstrates the importance of the automobile in American social history.

❖ **George Norris Home, McCook, Nebraska.** This museum, operated by the Nebraska State Historical Society, is dedicated to a leading progressive Republican of the 1920s.

❖ **Warren G. Harding House, Marion, Ohio.** Harding's home from 1891 to 1921 is now a museum with period furnishings.

❖ **Calvin Coolidge Homestead, Plymouth, Vermont.** Operated by the Vermont Division of Historic Sites, the homestead preserves the exact interiors and furnishings from when Coolidge took the presidential oath of office there in 1923.

27 THE GREAT DEPRESSION AND THE NEW DEAL, 1929-1939

KEY TOPICS

❖ The Great Depression
❖ Hoover's reliance on voluntary remedies
❖ FDR's New Deal provides relief
❖ The New Deal and organized labor, minorities, women, and farmers
❖ FDR's Democratic coalition of reformers, labor, urban ethnic groups, white Southerners, Westerners, and African-Americans
❖ The faltering of the New Deal

In the summer of 1933, the signs were everywhere in the coal regions—on posters and billboards, in store windows: "The President wants you to join the union." In the 1920s, coal had been a sick industry, and its health had deteriorated with the onset of the **Great Depression** in 1929. Mounting unemployment and plummeting wages joined the industry's dangerous working conditions, arbitrary rules, and company domination. Membership in the United Mine Workers (UMW) had dropped from 400,000 in 1926 to barely 100,000 by 1933. Misery and hopelessness traveled in tandem. Yet now UMW officials spread the word that President Franklin Roosevelt favored the right to organize unions and bargain collectively.

The effect was electric. A UMW organizer in Pennsylvania found "a different feeling among the miners everywhere—they seem to feel that they are once more free men." In Kentucky, one organizer formed nine locals in a day, marveling that "the people have been so starved out that they are flocking into the Union by the thousands." The astonished governor of Pennsylvania told Roosevelt, "These people believe in you. . . . They trust you and all believe that you are working to get them recognition of the United Mine Workers of America."

The coal operators vainly told their workers, "President Roosevelt is not an organizer for the United Mine Workers." But attitudes were changing. One organizer reported that whereas police had once chased union representatives out of Raton, New Mexico, "now the Mayor of the town gives us the city park for our meeting." Within two months, UMW membership numbered half a million.

Once organized, locals struck for union contracts and improved conditions. Some operators resisted, employing police repression. When miners were shot, riots broke out. As one newspaper reported, "Miners' wives fought alongside their husbands, and sons joined with their fathers in battles with deputies." By September, the operators gave up, signing a contract that recognized the union, established the eight-hour day, and improved wages and working conditions. As the *New Yorker* noted, "The defeated mine-owners agreed to all the things that deputy sheriffs usually shoot people for demanding."

The union victory was not final, but these developments illustrated the forces that changed America in the 1930s. Responding to a crippling depression, the federal government—personalized by President Roosevelt—adopted an activist role in the economy and society. And federal activism restored hope and confidence for many Americans, often encouraging them to act for themselves.

The legislation that had spurred the miners' union drive was part of a massive and not always consistent program to promote economic recovery that in the process often promoted reform as well. The **New Deal**, as Roosevelt called his plan, achieved neither full recovery nor systematic reform, and its benefits were distributed unevenly. But the Great Depression, Roosevelt's New Deal, and the behavior of the American people shaped the institutions and policies that would mark the nation for decades.

Hard Times in Hooverville

The prosperity of the 1920s ended in a stock market crash that revealed the flaws honeycombing the economy. As the nation slid into a catastrophic depression, factories closed, employment and incomes tumbled, and millions lost their homes, hopes, and dignity. Some protested and took direct action; others looked to the government for relief.

Crash!

The buoyant prosperity of the New Era collapsed in October of 1929 when the stock market crashed.

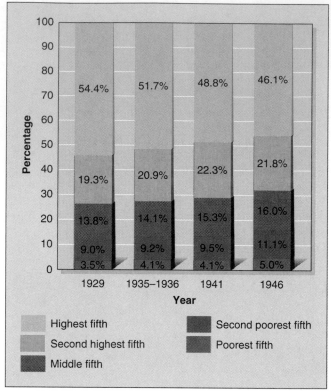

Figure 27-1   Distribution of Income in the United States, 1929–1946
An unequal distribution of income contributed to the Great Depression by limiting purchasing power. Only slight changes occurred until after World War II, but other factors gradually stabilized the national economy.

Source: *U.S. Bureau of the Census.*

After peaking in September, the market suffered several sharp checks, and on October 29, "Black Tuesday," panicked investors dumped their stocks at any price. The slide continued for months, and then years. It hit bottom in July 1932. By then, the stock of U.S. Steel had plunged from 262 to 22, Montgomery Ward from 138 to 4.

The Wall Street crash marked the beginning of the Great Depression, but it did not cause it. The depression stemmed from weaknesses in the New Era economy. Most damaging was the unequal distribution of wealth and income. By 1929, the richest 0.1 percent of American families had as much total income as the bottom 42 percent (see Figure 27-1). With more than half the nation's people living at or below the subsistence level, there was not enough purchasing power to maintain the economy.

A second factor was that oligopolies dominated American industries. Their power led to "administered prices," prices kept artificially high and rigid rather than determined by supply and

CHRONOLOGY

1929 Stock market crashes.

1932 Farmers' Holiday Association organizes rural protests in the Midwest.

Reconstruction Finance Corporation is created to assist financial institutions.

Bonus Army is routed in Washington, D.C.

Franklin D. Roosevelt is elected president.

1933 Emergency Banking Act is passed.

Agricultural Adjustment Administration (AAA) is created to regulate farm production.

National Recovery Administration (NRA) is created to promote industrial cooperation and recovery.

Federal Emergency Relief Act provides federal assistance to the unemployed.

Civilian Conservation Corps (CCC) is established to provide work relief in conservation projects.

Public Works Administration (PWA) is created to provide work relief on large public construction projects.

Civil Works Administration (CWA) provides emergency winter relief jobs.

Tennessee Valley Authority (TVA) is created to coordinate regional development.

1934 Securities and Exchange Commission (SEC) is established.

Indian Reorganization Act reforms Indian policy.

Huey Long organizes the Share-Our-Wealth Society.

Democrats win midterm elections.

1935 Supreme Court declares NRA unconstitutional.

National Labor Relations Act (Wagner Act) guarantees workers' rights to organize and bargain collectively.

Social Security Act establishes a federal social insurance system.

Banking Act strengthens the Federal Reserve.

Public Utility Holding Company Act extends federal regulatory authority over utility companies.

Revenue Act establishes a more progressive tax system.

Resettlement Administration is created to aid dispossessed farmers.

Rural Electrification Administration (REA) is created to help provide electric power to rural areas.

Soil Conservation Service is established.

Emergency Relief Appropriation Act authorizes public relief projects for the unemployed.

Works Progress Administration (WPA) is created.

Huey Long is assassinated.

1936 Supreme Court declares AAA unconstitutional.

Roosevelt is reelected president.

Sit-down strikes begin.

1937 Chicago police kill workers in Memorial Day Massacre.

FDR tries but fails to expand the Supreme Court.

Farm Security Administration (FSA) is created to lend money to small farmers to buy and rehabilitate farms.

National Housing Act is passed to promote public housing projects.

"Roosevelt Recession" begins.

1938 Congress of Industrial Organizations (CIO) is founded.

Fair Labor Standards Act establishes minimum wage and maximum hours rules for labor.

Roosevelt fails to "purge" the Democratic party.

Republicans make gains in midterm elections.

---

demand. By not responding to purchasing power, this system not only helped bring on economic collapse but also dimmed prospects for recovery.

Weaknesses in specific industries had further unbalanced the economy. Agriculture suffered from overproduction, declining prices, and heavy debt; so did the coal and textile industries. Poorly managed and regulated, banks had contributed to the instability of prosperity; they now threatened to spread the panic and depression.

International economic difficulties also contributed to the depression. Shut out from U.S. markets by high tariffs, Europeans had depended on American investments to manage their debts and reparation payments from the Great War. The stock market crash dried up the flow of American dollars to Europe, causing financial panics and industrial collapse and making the Great Depression global. In turn, European nations curtailed their imports of American goods and defaulted on their debts, further debilitating the U.S. economy. American exports fell by 70 percent from 1929 to 1932. As foreign markets shrank, so did hopes for economic recovery.

Government policies also bore some responsibility for the crash and depression. Failure to enforce antitrust laws had encouraged oligopolies and high prices; failure to regulate banking or the stock market had permitted financial recklessness. Reducing tax rates on the wealthy had also encouraged speculation and contributed to the maldistribution of income. Opposition to labor unions and collective bargaining helped keep workers' wages and purchasing power low. The absence of an effective agricultural policy and the high tariffs that inhibited foreign trade and reduced markets for agricultural products hurt farmers in the same way. In short, the same government policies that shaped the booming 1920s economy also pointed to economic disaster.

The Depression Spreads

By early 1930, factories had shut down or cut back, and industrial production plummeted; by 1932, it was scarcely 50 percent of its 1929 level. Steel mills operated at 12 percent of capacity, auto factories at 20 percent. Unemployment skyrocketed, as an average of 100,000 workers a week were fired in the first three years after the crash. By 1932, one-fourth of the labor force was out of work. Personal income dropped by more than half between 1929 and 1932; by 1933, industrial workers had average weekly wages of only $16.73. Moreover, the depression began to feed on itself in a vicious circle: Shrinking wages and employment cut into purchasing power, causing business to slash production again and lay off workers, thereby further reducing purchasing power.

Farmers were particularly battered by the depression. Commodity prices fell by 55 percent between 1929 and 1932, stifling farm income. Unable to pay their mortgages, many farm families lost their homes and fields. "We have no security left," cried one South Dakota farm woman. "Foreclosures and evictions at the point of sheriff's guns are increasing daily."

Urban families were also evicted when they could not pay their rent. Some moved in with relatives; others lived in **Hoovervilles**—the name reflects the bitterness directed at the president—shacks where people shivered, suffered, and starved. Oklahoma City's vast Hooverville covered 100 square miles; one witness described its hapless residents as squatting in "old, rusted-out car bodies," orange crates, and holes in the ground.

Soup kitchens became standard features of the urban landscape, but charities and local communities could not meet the massive needs, and nei-

ther state nor federal governments had welfare or unemployment compensation programs. To survive, people planted gardens in vacant lots and back alleys and tore apart empty houses or tapped gas lines for fuel. In immigrant neighborhoods, social workers found a "primitive communism" in which people shared food, clothing, and fuel.

"Women's Jobs" and "Men's Jobs"

Gender segregation had concentrated women in low-paid service, sales, and clerical jobs that shrank less than the heavy industries where men predominated. But traditional attitudes also provoked opposition to female employment itself, especially that of married women. As one Chicago civic organization complained, "They are holding jobs that rightfully belong to the God-intended providers of the household." The city council of Akron, Ohio, resolved that public agencies and private employers should stop employing wives. Three-fourths of the nation's school systems refused to hire married women as teachers, and two-thirds dismissed female teachers who married. Many private employers, especially banks and insurance companies, also fired married women.

Few men sought positions in the fields associated with women, so firing women simply aggravated the suffering of families already reeling from the depression. Despite hostility, the proportion of married women in the work force increased in the 1930s as women took jobs to help their families survive.

Families in the Depression

"I have watched fear grip the people in our neighborhood around Hull House," wrote Jane Addams as the depression deepened in 1931 and family survival itself seemed threatened. Divorce declined because it was expensive, but desertion increased, and marriages were postponed. Birthrates fell. Husbands and fathers, the traditional breadwinners, were often humiliated and despondent when laid off from work. One social worker observed in 1931: "Like searing irons, the degradation, the sheer terror and panic which loss of job brings, the deprivation and the bitterness have eaten into men's souls."

The number of female-headed households increased. Not only did some women become wage earners, but to make ends meet, many women sewed their own clothing and raised and canned vegetables. Some also took on extra work at home. In San Antonio, one in every ten families had boarders, and in Alabama, housewives took in laundry at 10 cents a week.

Some parents sacrificed their own well-being to protect their children. One witness described "the uncontrolled trembling of parents who have starved themselves for weeks so that their children might not go hungry." In New York City, 139 people, most of them children, died of starvation and malnutrition in 1933. Many teenagers who left home so that younger children would have more to eat suffered from starvation, exposure, illness, and accidents. The California Unemployment Commission concluded that the depression had left the American family "morally shattered. There is no security, no foothold, no future."

"Last Hired, First Fired"

With fewer resources and opportunities, racial minorities were less able than other groups to absorb the economic pain. African-Americans, reported a sociologist at Howard University in 1932, were "the last to be hired and the first to be fired." Black unemployment rates were more than twice as high as the rate for whites. Jobless whites now sought the menial jobs traditionally reserved for blacks, such as street cleaning and domestic service. Religious and charitable organizations often refused to care for blacks. Local and state governments set higher requirements for blacks than for whites to receive relief and provided them with less aid. The Urban League reported, "at no time in the history of the Negro since slavery has his economic and social outlook seemed so discouraging." African-Americans were "hanging on by the barest thread."

Hispanic Americans also suffered. As mostly unskilled workers, they faced increasing competition for decreasing jobs paying declining wages. They were displaced even in the California agricultural labor force, which they had dominated. Other jobs were lost by 1931 when Arizona, California, and Texas barred Mexicans from public works and highway construction jobs. Vigilantes threatened employers who hired Mexicans rather than white Americans. Economic woes and racism drove nearly half a million Mexican immigrants and their American-born children from the United States in the 1930s. Local authorities in the Southwest encouraged the federal government to deport Mexicans and offered free transportation to Mexico.

Protest

Bewildered and discouraged, most Americans responded to the depression with resignation. But others engaged in protests, ranging from small desperate gestures like stealing food and coal to more dramatic deeds. In Louisiana, women seized a train to call attention to the needs of their families; in New Jersey, in the "bloodless battle of Pleasantville," one hundred women held the city council hostage to demand assistance.

Communists organized the jobless into "unemployment councils" that staged hunger marches, demonstrated for relief, and blocked evictions. Mothers facing eviction in Chicago told their children: "Run quick and find the Reds." Socialists built similar organizations, including Baltimore's People's Unemployment League. However, local authorities often suppressed their protests. In 1932, police fired on the Detroit Unemployment Council as it marched to demand food and jobs from the Ford Motor Company, killing four marchers and wounding many more.

There were also rural protests. In the Midwest, the Farmers' Holiday Association stopped the shipment of produce to urban markets, hoping to drive up prices. A guerrilla war broke out as farmers blocked roads and halted freight trains, dumped milk in ditches, and fought bloody battles with deputy sheriffs. In Iowa, farmers beat sheriffs and mortgage agents and nearly lynched a lawyer conducting foreclosure proceedings.

Herbert Hoover and the Depression

The Great Depression challenged the optimism, policies, and philosophy of Herbert Hoover. The president took unprecedented steps to resolve the crisis but shrank back from the interventionist policies activists urged. His failures, personal as well as political and economic, led to his repudiation and opened the way to a new deal.

The Limits of Voluntarism

Hoover fought economic depression more vigorously than any previous president, but he believed that voluntary, private action was preferable to federal intervention. In promoting voluntarism, Hoover first secured business leaders' pledges to maintain employment and wage levels. But most corporations soon repudiated these pledges, slashed wages, and laid off workers. Hoover complained, "You know, the only trouble with capitalism is capitalists; they're too damn greedy." Still, he refused to interfere with business.

Hoover created the President's Organization for Unemployment Relief to encourage voluntary relief agencies and raise private funds. Charities and local authorities, he believed, should help the unemployed; direct federal relief would expand government power and undermine the recipients' character. He vetoed congressional attempts to aid the unemployed. "The American way of relieving distress," said Hoover, was through "the voluntary agencies of self help in the community."

But private programs to aid the unemployed scarcely existed. Private charitable groups like the Salvation Army, church associations, and ethnic societies quickly exhausted their resources. Nor could local governments cope. New York City provided relief payments of $2.39 a week for an entire family, and other cities much less. By 1932, more than one hundred cities made no relief appropriations at all, and the commissioner of charity in Salt Lake City reported that people were sliding toward starvation. Only eight state governments provided even token assistance. (See "American Views: An Ohio Mayor on Unemployment and Relief.")

Hoover blundered not in first relying on charities and local governments for relief but in refusing to admit that they were inadequate. As the depression worsened, Hoover adopted more activist policies. He persuaded Congress to cut taxes to boost consumers' buying power, and he increased the public works budget. The **Reconstruction Finance Corporation (RFC)**, established in January 1932, lent federal funds to banks, insurance companies, and railroads so that their recovery could "trickle down" to ordinary Americans.

But these programs satisfied few Americans. "While children starve," cried Pennsylvania's governor, Hoover "intends to let us have just as little relief as possible after the longest delay possible." Hoover's ideological limitations infuriated Americans who saw him as indifferent to their suffering and a reactionary protector of privileged business interests.

Repudiating Hoover: The 1932 Election

Hoover's treatment of the **Bonus Army** symbolized his unpopularity and set the stage for the 1932 election. In 1932, unemployed veterans of World War I gathered in Washington, demanding payment of service bonuses not due until 1945. Hoover refused to meet with them, and Congress rejected their plan. But ten thousand veterans erected a shantytown at the edge of Washington and camped in vacant public buildings. General Douglas MacArthur disobeyed Hoover's cautious orders and on July 28 led cavalry, infantry, and tanks against the ragged Bonus Marchers. The troops cleared the buildings and assaulted the shantytown, dispersing the veterans and their families and setting their camp on fire.

"What a pitiful spectacle is that of the great American Government, mightiest in the world, chasing unarmed men, women, and children with army tanks," commented the *Washington News*. The administration tried to brand the Bonus Marchers as Com-

munists and criminals, but official investigations refuted such claims. The incident confirmed Hoover's public image as harsh and insensitive.

In the summer of 1932, with no prospects for victory, Republicans renominated Hoover. Confident Democrats selected Governor Franklin D. Roosevelt of New York, who pledged "a new deal for the American people." Born into a wealthy family in 1882, FDR had been educated at Harvard, trained in the law, and schooled in politics, as a state legislator, assistant secretary of the navy, and the Democratic vice presidential nominee in 1920. In 1921, Roosevelt contracted polio, which paralyzed him from the waist down, leaving him dependent on braces or crutches. His continued involvement in politics owed much to his wife, Eleanor. A social reformer, she became a Democratic activist, organizing women's groups and campaigning across New York. In a remarkable political comeback, FDR was elected governor in 1928 and reelected in 1930.

The 1932 Democratic platform differed little from that of the Republicans, and Roosevelt spoke in vague or general terms. He knew that the election would be a repudiation of Hoover more than an endorsement of himself. Indeed, FDR carried every state south and west of Pennsylvania (see Map 27-1).

Map 27-1   The Election of 1932

In the midst of the Great Depression, only the most rock-ribbed Republican states failed to turn to Franklin D. Roosevelt and the Democrats for relief. The election of 1932 was a landslide.

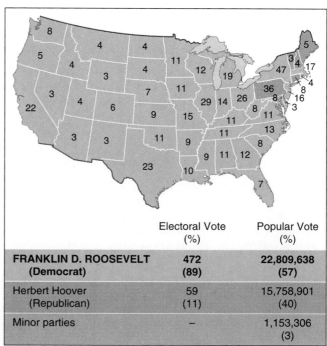

	Electoral Vote (%)	Popular Vote (%)
FRANKLIN D. ROOSEVELT (Democrat)	**472** **(89)**	**22,809,638** **(57)**
Herbert Hoover (Republican)	59 (11)	15,758,901 (40)
Minor parties	–	1,153,306 (3)

In the months before his inauguration, the depression worsened, with rising unemployment, plunging farm prices, and spreading misery. When teachers in Chicago, unpaid for months, fainted in their classrooms from hunger, it symbolized the imminent collapse of the nation itself. The final blow came in February 1933 when desperate Americans rushed to withdraw their funds from the tottering bank system. State governments shut the banks to prevent their failure. Hoover concluded, "We are at the end of our string."

Launching the New Deal

In the midst of national anxiety, Franklin D. Roosevelt pushed forward an unprecedented program to resolve the crises of a collapsing financial system, crippling unemployment, and agricultural and industrial breakdown and to promote reform. The early New Deal achieved successes and attracted support, but it also had limitations and generated criticism that suggested the need for still greater innovations.

Action Now!

On March 4, 1933, Franklin Delano Roosevelt became president and immediately reassured the American people. He insisted that "the only thing we have to fear is fear itself—nameless, unreasoning, unjustified terror, which paralyzes needed efforts to convert retreat into advance." And he promised "action, and action now!" In the first three months of his administration, the famous Hundred Days of the New Deal, the Democratic Congress passed fifteen major laws (see the summary table "Major Laws of the Hundred Days").

Roosevelt's program reflected a mix of ideas, some from FDR himself, some from a diverse group of advisers, including academic experts dubbed the "brain trust," politicians, and social workers. It also incorporated principles from the progressive movement, precedents from the Great War mobilization, and even plans from the Hoover administration. FDR had set its tone in his campaign when he declared, "The country needs, and, unless I mistake its temper, the country demands bold, persistent experimentation. . . . Above all, try something."

On March 5, FDR proclaimed a national bank holiday, closing all remaining banks. Congress then passed his **Emergency Banking Act**, a conservative measure that extended government assistance to sound banks and reorganized the weak ones. Prompt government action, coupled with a reassuring **fireside chat** over the radio by the president, restored popular confidence in the banks. When they reopened on March 13, deposits exceeded withdrawals. "Capitalism," said Raymond Moley of the brain trust, "was saved in eight days." In June, Congress created the **Federal Deposit Insurance Corporation (FDIC)** to guarantee bank deposits up to $2,500.

The financial industry was also reformed. The **Glass-Steagall Act** separated investment and commercial banking to curtail risky speculation. The Securities Act reformed the sale of stocks to prevent the insider abuses that had characterized Wall Street, and in 1934, the **Securities and Exchange Commission (SEC)** was created to regulate the stock market. Two other financial measures in 1933 created the **Home Owners Loan Corporation** and the **Farm Credit Administration**, which enabled millions to refinance their mortgages.

Relief

Roosevelt also provided relief for the unemployed. The **Federal Emergency Relief Administration (FERA)** furnished funds to state and local agencies. Directed by Harry Hopkins, FERA spent over $3 billion before it ended in 1935, and by then Hopkins and FDR had developed new programs that provided work relief to preserve both the skills and the morale of recipients. The **Civil Works Administration (CWA)** hired laborers to build roads, teachers to staff adult education programs, and singers to give public performances. The **Public Works Administration (PWA)** provided work relief and stimulated the economy by building schools, hospitals, courthouses, airports, dams, and bridges. One of FDR's personal ideas, the **Civilian Conservation Corps (CCC)** employed 2.5 million young men to work on reforestation and flood control projects, build roads and bridges in national forests and parks, restore Civil War battlefields, and fight forest fires.

Helping Some Farmers

In May 1933, Congress established the **Agricultural Adjustment Administration (AAA)** to combat the depression in agriculture caused by crop surpluses and low prices. The AAA subsidized farmers who agreed to restrict production. The objective was to boost farm prices to parity, a level that would restore farmers' purchasing power to its 1914 level. In the summer of 1933, the AAA paid southern farmers to plow up 10 million acres of cotton and midwestern farmers to bury 9 million pounds of pork. Restricting production in hard times caused public outrage.

American Views

AN OHIO MAYOR ON UNEMPLOYMENT AND RELIEF

Joesph Heffernan was the mayor of Youngstown, Ohio, when the nation sank into the Great Depression. Like other industrial cities, Youngstown soon confronted widespread unemployment and distress. In this document, written in 1932, Heffernan describes the obstacles he faced in responding to the suffering in Youngstown.

❖ **What would Heffernan think of President Hoover's belief that private charities and local authorities would provide unemployment relief?**

❖ **What did Heffernan see as obstacles to a public response to the depression?**

❖ **What did he fear would be the consequences of the failure to devise a rational and humane system of relief?**

[In 1930] I asked for a bond issue of $1,000,000 for unemployment relief. Many leading business men went out of their way to show their disapproval. One of them . . . said to me: "You make a bad mistake in talking about the unemployed. *Don't* emphasize hard times and everything will be all right." An influential newspaper chastised me for "borrowing trouble"; the depression would be over, the editor maintained, before relief would be needed. . . . The gravity of the situation was so deliberately misrepresented by the entire business community that when the bond issue finally came to a ballot, in November 1930, it was voted down.

Thus we passed into the early days of 1931—fourteen months after the first collapse— with no relief in sight except that which was provided by the orthodox charities. Not a single move had been made looking toward action by a united community.

Strange as it may seem, there was no way in which the city government could embark upon a program of its own. We had no funds available for emergency relief, and without specific authorization from the people we could not issue bonds. . . .

As time went on, business conditions showed no improvement. Every night hundreds of homeless men crowded into the municipal incinerator, where they found warmth even though they had to sleep on heaps of garbage. In January 1931, I obtained the cooperation of the City Council to convert an abandoned police station into a "flop house." The first night it was filled, and it has remained filled ever since. I made a point of paying frequent visits to this establishment so that I could see for myself what kind of men these down-and-outers were, and I heartily wish that those folk who have made themselves comfortable by ignoring and denying the suffering of their less

But agricultural conditions improved. Farm prices rose from 52 percent of parity in 1932 to 88 percent in 1935, and gross farm income rose by 50 percent. Not until 1941, however, would income exceed the level of 1929, a poor year for farmers. Moreover, some of the decreased production and increased prices stemmed from devastating droughts

and dust storms on the Great Plains. The AAA itself harmed poor farmers while aiding larger commercial growers. As southern planters restricted their acreage, they dismissed tenants and sharecroppers, and with AAA payments, they bought new farm machinery, reducing their need for farm labor. Thus while big producers moved toward prosperity, many fortunate neighbors could see some of the sights I saw. There were old men gnarled by heavy labor, young mechanics tasting the first bitterness of defeat, clerks and white-collar workers learning the equality of misery, derelicts who fared no worse in bad times than in good, Negroes who only a short time before had come from Southern cotton fields, now glad to find any shelter from the cold, immigrants who had been lured to Van Dyke's "land of youth and freedom"—each one a personal tragedy, and all together an overwhelming catastrophe for the nation. . . .

This descent from respectability, frequent enough in the best of times, has been hastened immeasurably by two years of business paralysis, and the people who have been affected in this manner must be numbered in millions. This is what we have accomplished with our bread lines and soup kitchens. I know, because I have seen thousands of these defeated, discouraged, hopeless men and women, cringing and fawning as they come to ask for public aid. It is a spectacle of national degeneration. That is the fundamental tragedy for America. If every mill and factory in the land should begin to hum with prosperity tomorrow morning, the destructive effect of our haphazard relief measures would not work itself out of the nation's blood until the sons of our sons had expiated the sins of our neglect.

Even now there are signs of rebellion against a system so out of joint that it can only offer charity to honest men who want to work. Sometimes it takes the form of social agitation, but again it may show itself in a revolt that is absolute and final. Such an instance was reported in a Youngstown newspaper on the day I wrote these lines:—

"FATHER OF TEN DROWNS SELF . . . Out of work two years, Charles Wayne, aged 57, father of ten children, stood on the Spring Common bridge this morning. . . . He took off his coat, folded it carefully, and jumped into the swirling Mahoning River. Wayne was born in Youngstown and was employed by the Republic Iron and Steel Company for twenty-seven years as a hot mill worker. 'We were about to lose our home,' sobbed Mrs. Wayne. 'And the gas and electric companies had threatened to shut off the service.'"

Source: Joseph L. Heffernan, "The Hungry City: A Mayor's Experience with Unemployment," *Atlantic Monthly*, May 1932, pp. 538–540, 546.

small farmers were forced into a pool of rural labor for which there was decreasing need or into the cities, where there were no jobs.

The Supreme Court declared the AAA unconstitutional in 1936, but new laws established the farm subsidy program for decades to come. Increasing mechanization and scientific agriculture kept production high and farmers dependent on government intervention.

The Flight of the Blue Eagle

The New Deal attempted to revive American industry with the **National Industrial Recovery Act (NIRA)**, which created the **National Recovery**

SUMMARY

MAJOR LAWS OF THE HUNDRED DAYS

Law	Objective
Emergency Banking Act	Stabilized the private banking system
Agricultural Adjustment Act	Established a farm recovery program based on production controls and price supports
Emergency Farm Mortgage Act	Provided for the refinancing of farm mortgages
National Industrial Recovery Act	Established a national recovery program and authorized a public works program
Federal Emergency Relief Act	Established a national system of relief
Home Owners Loan Act	Protected homeowners from mortgage foreclosure by refinancing home loans
Glass-Steagall Act	Separated commercial and investment banking and guaranteed bank deposits
Tennessee Valley Authority Act	Established the TVA and provided for the planned development of the Tennessee River Valley
Civilian Conservation Corps Act	Established the CCC to provide work relief on reforestation and conservation projects
Farm Credit Act	Expanded agricultural credits and established the Farm Credit Administration
Emergency Railroad Transportation Act	Promoted efficiency and cooperation among railroad companies
Economy Act	Reduced government spending by cutting salaries and veterans' pensions
Beer Tax Act	Authorized production and sale of beer and light wine in anticipation of the repeal of Prohibition
Securities Act	Required full disclosure from stock exchanges
Wagner-Peyser Act	Created a U.S. Employment Service and encouraged states to create local public employment offices

Administration (NRA). The NRA sought to halt the slide in prices, wages, and employment by suspending antitrust laws and authorizing industrial and trade associations to draft codes setting production quotas, price policies, wages and working conditions, and other business practices. The codes promoted the interests of business generally and big business in particular, but Section 7a of the NIRA guaranteed workers the rights to organize unions and bargain collectively.

Hugh Johnson became director of the NRA and persuaded business leaders to cooperate in drafting codes and the public to patronize participating companies. However, corporate leaders used the NRA to advance their own goals and discriminate against small producers, consumers, and labor. Employers also violated Section 7a, even using violence to smother independent unions. The NRA did little to enforce Section 7a, and Johnson—strongly probusiness—denounced all strikes. Workers felt betrayed.

Roosevelt tried to reorganize the NRA, but it remained controversial until the Supreme Court declared it unconstitutional in 1935.

Critics Right and Left

Though the early New Deal had not ended the depression, its efforts to grapple with problems, its successes in reducing suffering and fear, and Roosevelt's own skills carried the Democratic party to victory in the 1934 elections. But New Deal policies also provoked criticism.

Conservatives complained that the expansion of government activity and its regulatory role weakened the autonomy of American business. They also condemned the efforts to aid nonbusiness groups as socialistic, particularly the "excessive" spending on unemployment relief and the "instigation" of labor organizing. By 1934, as *Time* magazine reported, "Private fulminations and public carpings against the New Deal have become almost a routine of the business day." These critics attracted little popular support, however.

More realistic criticism came from the left. In 1932, FDR had campaigned for "the forgotten man at the bottom of the economic pyramid," and some radicals argued that the early New Deal had forgotten the forgotten man. In Arkansas and Tennessee, socialists in 1934 helped organize sharecroppers into the Southern Tenant Farmers Union protesting the "Raw Deal" they had received from the AAA. A broader labor militancy in 1934 also pressed Roosevelt. Workers acted as much against the failure of the NRA to enforce Section 7a as against recalcitrant corporations. The number of workers participating in strikes leaped from 325,000 in 1932 (about the annual average since 1925) to 1.5 million in 1934. From dockworkers in Seattle and copper miners in Butte to streetcar drivers in Milwaukee and shoemakers in Boston, workers demanded their rights.

Employers moved to crush the strikes, often using complaisant police and private strikebreakers. In Minneapolis, police shot sixty-seven teamsters, almost all in the back as they fled an ambush arranged by employers; in Toledo, company police and National Guardsmen attacked autoworkers with tear gas, bayonets, and rifle fire. At times, the workers held their ground. But against such powerful opponents, they needed help to achieve their rights.

Popular discontent was also mobilized by four prominent individuals demanding government action to assist groups neglected by the New Deal.

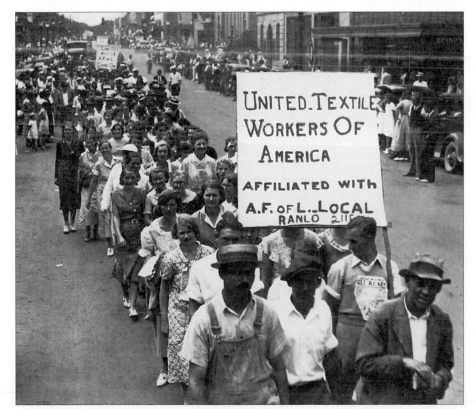

Textile workers parade in Gastonia, North Carolina, in their massive 1934 strike. Such labor activism influenced New Deal policy.

Representative William Lemke of North Dakota, an agrarian radical leader of the Nonpartisan League, objected to the New Deal's limited response to farmers crushed by the depression. The AAA's strategy of simply restricting production, he thundered, was an "insane policy in the midst of hunger, misery, want, and rags." He sought government financial aid for farmers and policies favoring inflation, a traditional rural demand.

Francis Townsend, a California physician, called for a government pension to all Americans over the age of 60, provided they retire from work and spend their entire pension. This promised to extend relief to the many destitute elderly, open jobs for the unemployed, and stimulate economic recovery. Over five thousand Townsend Clubs lobbied for government action to help the elderly poor.

Father Charles Coughlin, a Catholic priest in the Detroit suburb of Royal Oak, threatened to mobilize another large constituency against the limitations of the early New Deal. Thirty million Americans listened eagerly to his weekly radio broadcasts mixing religion with anti-Semitism and demands for social justice and financial reform. After concluding that FDR's policies favored "the virile viciousness of business and finance," Coughlin organized the National Union for Social Justice to lobby for his goals. With support among lower-middle-class, heavily Catholic, urban ethnic groups, Coughlin posed a real challenge to Roosevelt's Democratic party.

Senator Huey P. Long of Louisiana wanted more comprehensive social welfare policies, but he also wanted to be president. In 1934, he organized the Share-Our-Wealth Society. His plan to end poverty and unemployment called for confiscatory taxes on the rich to provide every family with a decent income, health coverage, education, and old-age pensions. Within months, Long's organization claimed more than 27,000 clubs and 7 million members.

These dissident movements raised complex issues and simple fears. They built on concerns about the New Deal, with programs often ill-defined or impractical. Nevertheless, their popularity warned Roosevelt that government action was needed to satisfy reform demands and assure his reelection in 1936.

Consolidating the New Deal

In 1935, Roosevelt undertook economic and social reforms that some observers have called the **Second New Deal**. The new measures shifted the relative weights accorded to the constant objectives of recovery, relief, and reform. This new phase reflected the persisting depression, growing political pressures, and the progressive inclinations of key New Dealers, including FDR himself.

Lifting and Weeding

"In spite of our efforts and in spite of our talk," Roosevelt told the new Congress in 1935, "we have not weeded out the overprivileged and we have not effectively lifted up the underprivileged." To do so, he developed "must" legislation, to which his allies in Congress added. One of the new laws protected labor's rights to organize and bargain collectively. Drafted by Senator Robert Wagner of New York to replace Section 7a, the **Wagner National Labor Relations Act**, dubbed "Labor's Magna Carta," guaranteed workers' rights to organize unions and forbade employers to adopt unfair labor practices, such as firing union activists or forming company unions. The law also set up the **National Labor Relations Board (NLRB)** to enforce these provisions, protect workers from coercion, and supervise union elections.

Of greater long-range importance was the **Social Security Act**. It provided unemployment compensation, old-age pensions, and aid for dependent mothers and children and the blind. The conservative nature of the law appeared in its stingy benefit payments, its lack of health insurance, and its exclusion of more than a fourth of all workers, including many in desperate need of protection, such as farm laborers and domestic servants. Moreover, unlike in other nations, the old-age pensions were financed through a regressive payroll tax on both employees and employers rather than through general tax revenues. Thus the new system was more like a compulsory insurance program. Despite its weaknesses, however, the Social Security Act was one of the most important laws in American history. It provided, Roosevelt pointed out, "at least some measure of protection to the average citizen and to his family against the loss of a job and against poverty-ridden old age."

Among other reform measures, the **Banking Act of 1935** increased the authority of the Federal Reserve Board over the nation's currency and credit system and decreased the power of the private bankers whose irresponsible behavior had contributed to the depression and the appeal of Father Coughlin. The **Public Utility Holding Company Act** expanded federal authority over public utilities, which had exploited consumers and frustrated government regulation. The **Revenue Act of 1935** provided for graduated income taxes and increased estate and corporate taxes. Opponents called it the

Map 27-2   The Dust Bowl

Years of overcultivation, drought, and high winds created the Dust Bowl, which most severely affected the southern Great Plains. Federal relief and conservation programs provided assistance, but many residents fled the area, often migrating to California.

Soak the Rich Tax, but with its many loopholes, it was scarcely that. Nevertheless, it set a precedent for progressive taxation and attracted popular support.

The Second New Deal also responded belatedly to the environmental catastrophe that had turned much of the Great Plains into a "Dust Bowl" (see Map 27-2). Since World War I, farmers had stripped marginal land of its native grasses to plant wheat. When drought and high winds hit the plains in 1932, crops failed, and nothing held the soil. Dust storms blew away millions of tons of topsoil, despoiling the land and darkening the sky 1,000 miles away. Families abandoned their farms in droves.

In 1935, Roosevelt established the **Resettlement Administration** to focus on land reform and help poor farmers. Under Rexford Tugwell, this agency initiated soil erosion projects and attempted to resettle impoverished farmers on better land, but the problem exceeded its resources. Congress moved to save the land, if not its people, by creating the **Soil Conservation Service** in 1935.

Expanding Relief

Relief remained critical in the Second New Deal. With millions still unemployed, Roosevelt pushed through Congress in April 1935 the **Emergency Relief Appropriation Act**, authorizing $5 billion—at the time the largest single appropriation in history—for emergency public employment. Roosevelt created the **Works Progress Administration (WPA)** under Hopkins, who set up work relief programs to assist the unemployed and boost the economy. Before its end in 1943, the WPA gave jobs to 9 million people (more than a fifth of the labor force) and spent nearly $12 billion. Three-fourths of its expenditures went on construction projects that could employ manual labor: the WPA built 125,000 schools, post offices, and hospitals; 8,000 parks; nearly 100,000 bridges; and enough roads and sewer systems to circle the earth thirty times. From New York City's La Guardia Airport to Atlanta's sewer system to irrigation ditches in the Far West, the WPA laid much of the nation's basic infrastructure on which it still relies.

The WPA also developed work projects for unemployed writers, artists, musicians, and actors. "Why not?" said FDR. "They are human beings. They have to live." These WPA programs allowed people to use their talents while surviving the depression, increased popular access to cultural performances, and established a precedent for federal support of the arts.

The National Youth Administration (NYA), another WPA agency, gave part-time jobs to students, enabling 2 million high school and college students to stay in school, learn skills, and do productive work. Law student Richard M. Nixon earned 35 cents an hour doing research in the library. Lyndon Johnson, a Texas NYA official, believed that "if the Roosevelt administration had never done another thing, it would have been justified by the work of this great institution for salvaging youth."

The Roosevelt Coalition and the Election of 1936

The 1936 election gave Americans an opportunity to judge FDR and the New Deal. Conservatives alarmed at the expansion of government, businesspeople angered by regulation and labor legislation, and well-to-do Americans furious with tax reform decried the New Deal. But they were a minority. Even the presidential candidate they supported, Republican Governor Alf Landon of Kansas, endorsed much of the New Deal, criticizing merely the inefficiency and cost of some of its programs. The reforms of 1935 had undercut the arguments of critics on the left, and the assassination of Huey Long in the same year had removed their ablest politician. They formed the Union party and nominated William Lemke for the presidency, but they were no longer a threat.

The programs and politicians of the New Deal had created an invincible coalition behind Roosevelt. The New Deal's agricultural programs reinforced the traditional Democratic allegiance of white Southerners while attracting many western farmers. Labor legislation clinched the active support of the nation's workers. Middle-class voters, whose homes had been saved and whose hopes had been raised, also joined the Roosevelt coalition.

So did urban ethnic groups, who had benefited from welfare programs and received unprecedented recognition. FDR named the first Italian-American to the federal judiciary, for example, and appointed five times as many Catholics and Jews to government positions as the three Republican presidents had during the 1920s. African-Americans voted overwhelmingly Democratic for the first time. Women, too, were an important part of the Roosevelt coalition. As one campaigner said to a roaring crowd in 1936, "Many women in this country when they vote for Franklin D. Roosevelt will also be thinking with a choke in the throat of Eleanor Roosevelt!"

This political realignment produced a landslide. Roosevelt polled 61 percent of the popular vote and the largest electoral vote margin ever recorded, 523 to 8. Landon even lost Kansas, his own state, and Lemke received fewer than 900,000 votes. Democrats also won huge majorities in Congress.

The New Deal and American Life

The landslide of 1936 reflected the impact the New Deal had on Americans. Government programs changed daily life, and ordinary people often helped shape the new policies.

Labor on the March

The labor revival in the 1930s reflected both workers' determination and government support. Workers wanted not merely to improve their wages and benefits but also to gain union recognition and union contracts to limit arbitrary managerial authority and achieve some control over the workplace. The Wagner Act sparked a wave of labor activism. But if the government ultimately protected union rights, the unions themselves had to form locals, recruit members, and demonstrate influence in the workplace.

At first, the American Federation of Labor (AFL), with its reliance on craft-based unions and its reluctance to organize immigrant, black, and women workers, was unprepared for the rush of industrial workers seeking unionization. More progressive labor leaders formed the Committee for Industrial Organization (CIO) within the AFL. They campaigned to unionize workers in the steel, auto, and rubber industries, all notoriously hostile to unions. AFL leaders insisted that the CIO disband and then in 1937 expelled its unions. The militants reorganized as the separate **Congress of Industrial Organizations**.

The split roused the AFL to increase its own organizing activities, but it was primarily the new CIO that put labor on the march. It inspired workers previously neglected. The CIO's interracial union campaign in the Birmingham steel mills, said one organizer, was "like a second coming of Christ" for black workers, who welcomed the union as a chance for social recognition as well as economic opportunity. The CIO also employed new and aggressive tactics, particularly the sit-down strike, in which workers, rather than picketing outside the factory, simply sat inside the plant, thereby blocking both production and the use of strikebreakers. Upton Sinclair said, "For seventy-five years big business has been sitting down on the American people, and now I am delighted to see the process reversed."

Sit-down strikes paralyzed General Motors in 1937 after it refused to recognize the United Auto Workers. GM tried to force the strikers out of its Flint, Michigan, plants by turning off the heat, using police and tear gas, and threatening strikers' families. The strikers held out, and after six weeks GM signed a contract with the UAW. Chrysler soon followed suit. Ford refused to recognize the union until 1941, often recruiting thugs directly from prison to disrupt organizing efforts.

Steel companies also used violence against unionization. In the **Memorial Day Massacre** in Chicago in 1937, police guarding a plant of the Republic Steel Company fired on strikers and their families, killing ten people as they tried to flee. Scores more were wounded and beaten. A Senate investigation found that Republic and other companies "dominate their employees, deny them their constitutional rights, promote disorder and disharmony, and even set at naught the powers of the government itself." Federal court orders finally forced the companies to bargain collectively.

New Deal labor legislation, government investigations and court orders, and the federal refusal to use force against strikes helped the labor movement secure basic rights for American workers. Union membership leaped from under 3 million in 1932 to 9 million by 1939, and workers won higher wages, better working conditions, and more economic democracy.

Women and the New Deal

As federal programs proliferated in 1933, a Baltimore women's group urged the administration to "come out for a square and new deal for women." Although women did gain increased attention and influence, government and society remained largely bound by traditional values.

New Deal relief programs had a mixed impact on workingwomen. Formal government policy required "equal consideration" for women and men, but local officials so flouted this requirement that Eleanor Roosevelt urged Harry Hopkins to "impress on state administrators that the women's programs are as important as the men's. They are so apt to forget us!" Women on relief were restricted to "women's work"—more than half worked on sewing projects, regardless of their skills—and were paid scarcely half what men received. And although women constituted nearly a fourth of the labor force, they obtained only 19 percent of the jobs created by the WPA, 12 percent by the FERA, and 7 percent by the CWA. The CCC excluded women altogether. But relief agencies still provided crucial assistance to women in the depression.

Other New Deal programs also had mixed benefits for women. Many NRA codes mandated lower wage scales for women than for men, which officials justified as reflecting "long-established customs." But by raising minimum wages, the NRA brought relatively greater improvements to women, who were concentrated in the lowest-paid occupations, than to male workers. The Social Security Act did not cover domestic servants, waitresses, and women who worked in the home but did help mothers with dependent children.

Women also gained political influence under the New Deal. Molly Dewson, the director of the Women's Division of the Democratic party, exercised considerable political power and helped shape the party's campaigns. Around Dewson revolved a network of women, linked by friendships and experiences in the National Consumers' League, Women's Trade Union League, and other progressive reform organizations. Appointed to positions in the Roosevelt administration, they helped develop and implement New Deal social legislation. Secretary of Labor Frances Perkins was the first woman cabinet member and a key member of the network; other women were in the Treasury Department, the Children's Bureau, and relief and cultural programs.

Eleanor Roosevelt roared across the social and political landscape of the 1930s, pushing for women's rights, demanding reforms, traveling across the country, writing newspaper columns and speaking over the radio, developing plans to help unemployed miners and abolish slums. FDR rebuffed her critics with a jaunty, "Well, that is my wife; I can't do anything about her." Indeed, Eleanor Roosevelt had become a symbol of the growing importance of women in public life.

Minorities and the New Deal

Although Roosevelt deplored racial abuses, he never pushed for civil rights legislation, fearing to antagonize the influential Southern Democrats in Congress whose support he needed. For similar reasons, many New Deal programs discriminated against blacks. The CCC segregated them; NRA codes so often specified lower wages and benefits for blacks relative to whites or even excluded blacks from jobs that the black press claimed NRA stood for "Negro Run Around" or "Negroes Ruined Again."

However, blacks did benefit from the New Deal's welfare and economic programs. W. E. B. Du Bois asserted that "large numbers of colored people in the United States would have starved to death if it had not been for the Roosevelt policies." And key New Dealers campaigned against racial discrimination. Eleanor Roosevelt, whose friends included such black leaders as Walter White of the NAACP and Mary McLeod Bethune of the National Council of Negro Women, prodded FDR to appoint blacks, wrote articles supporting racial equality, and flouted segregationist laws. Attacked by white racists, she was popular in the black community. As black votes in northern cities became important, more pragmatic New Dealers also began to pay more attention to black welfare.

Blacks themselves pressed for reforms, and FDR took more interest in their economic and social problems. He prohibited discrimination in the WPA in 1935, and the NYA adopted enlightened racial policies. Roosevelt also appointed blacks to important positions, including the first black federal judge. Many of these officials began meeting regularly at the home of Mary McLeod Bethune. Dubbed the Black Cabinet, they worked with civil rights organizations, fought discrimination in government, influenced patronage, and stimulated black interest in politics.

Under the New Deal, black illiteracy dropped because of federal education projects, and the number of black college students and graduates more than doubled, in part because the NYA provided student aid to black colleges. New Deal relief and public health programs reduced black infant mortality rates and raised life expectancy rates. Conditions for blacks continued to lag behind those for whites, and discrimination persisted, but the black switch to the Roosevelt coalition reflected the New Deal's benefits.

Native Americans also benefited from the New Deal. The CCC particularly appealed to their interests and skills. More than eighty thousand Indians received training in agriculture, forestry, and animal husbandry, along with basic academic subjects. CCC projects, together with those undertaken by the PWA and the WPA, built schools, hospitals, roads, and irrigation systems on reservations.

New Deal officials also refocused government Indian policy, which had undermined tribal authority and promoted assimilation by reducing Indian landholding and attacking Indian culture. Appointed commissioner of Indian affairs in 1933, John Collier prohibited interference with Indian religious or cultural life, directed the Bureau of Indian Affairs to employ more Indians, and prevented Indian schools from suppressing native languages and traditions. The **Indian Reorganization Act** of 1934, often called the Indians' New Deal, guaranteed religious freedom, reestablished tribal self-government, and halted the sale of tribal lands. It also provided funds to expand Indian landholdings, support Indian students, and establish tribal businesses.

Hispanic Americans received less assistance from the New Deal. Its relief programs aided many Hispanics in California and the Southwest but ignored those who were not citizens. And by excluding agricultural workers, neither the Social Security Act nor the Wagner Act gave Mexican-Americans much protection or hope. Farm workers remained largely unorganized, exploited, and at the mercy of agribusinesses.

The New Deal for the South and West

The New Deal ironically offered special benefits to the South, traditionally averse to government activism, and to the West, which considered itself the land of rugged individualism.

The New Deal's agricultural program boosted farm prices and income more in the South than any other region. By controlling cotton production, it also promoted diversification; its subsidies financed mechanization. The resulting modernization helped replace an archaic sharecropping system with an emergent agribusiness. The rural poor were displaced, but the South's agricultural economy advanced.

The New Deal also improved southern cities. FERA and WPA built urban sewer systems, airports, bridges, schools, roads, and harbor facilities. Whereas northern cities had already constructed such facilities themselves—and were still paying off their debts—the federal government largely paid for such modernization in the South, giving its cities an economic advantage.

While southern politicians welcomed New Deal funds—"I'm gonna grab all I can for the state of Texas," said Governor Lee O'Daniel—they refused to contribute their share of the costs. Nationally, the federal proportion of FERA expenditures was 62 percent; in the South, it was usually 90 percent and never lower than 73 percent. Some southern cities and counties refused to contribute anything to relief.

Federal money enabled southern communities to balance their own budgets, preach fiscal orthodoxy, and maintain traditional claims of limited government. Federal officials complained of the South's "parasitic" behavior in accepting aid but not responsibility, and even Southerners acknowledged the hypocrisy of the region's invocation of state's rights. "We recognize state boundaries when called on to give," noted the *Houston Press*, "but forget them when Uncle Sam is doing the giving."

The federal government had a particularly powerful impact on the South with the **Tennessee Valley Authority (TVA)**, launched in 1933 (see Map 27-3). Coordinating activities across seven states, the TVA built dams to control floods and generate hydroelectric power, produced fertilizer, fostered agricultural and forestry development, encouraged conservation, improved navigation, and modernized school and health systems. Over a vast area of the South, it provided electricity for the first time.

The New Deal further expanded access to electricity by establishing the **Rural Electrification Administration (REA)** in 1935. Private companies had refused to extend power lines into the countryside because it was not profitable, consigning 90 percent of the nation's farms to drudgery and darkness. The REA revolutionized farm life by sponsoring rural nonprofit electric cooperatives. By providing electric power to light and heat homes and barns, pump water, and run refrigerators, washing machines, and radios, one Arkansas newspaper concluded, the REA had made "a reality" of what had been only a "utopian dream."

The New Deal also changed the West. Westerners received the most federal money per capita in welfare, relief projects, and loans. Like Southerners, they accepted federal aid and clamored for more. Utah, which received the most federal relief funds per capita, was the nation's "prize 'gimme state,'" said one FERA official. Western farmers and cattle raisers were saved by federal payments, and even refugees from the Dust Bowl depended on relief assistance and medical care in federal camps.

Map 27-3   *The Tennessee Valley Authority*
*By building dams and hydroelectric power plants, the TVA controlled flooding and soil erosion
and generated electricity that did much to modernize a large region of the Upper South.*

The **Bureau of Reclamation** built huge dams to control the western river systems and promote large-scale development. The Hoover Dam on the Colorado River between Nevada and Arizona, completed in 1935; the Grand Coulee Dam on the Columbia River in Washington, finished in 1941; and other giant projects prevented flooding, produced cheap hydroelectric power, and created reservoirs and canal systems to bring water to farms and cities. By furnishing capital and expertise, the government subsidized and stimulated western economic development, particularly the growth of agribusiness.

The New Deal and Public Activism

Despite Hoover's fear that government responsibility would discourage local initiative, New Deal programs, in fact, often encouraged or empowered groups to shape public policy and social and economic behavior. Moreover, because the administration worried about centralization, some federal agencies fostered what New Dealers called "grass-roots democracy." The AAA set up committees totaling more than 100,000 people to implement agricultural policy and held referendums on crop controls; local advisory committees guided the various federal arts projects; federal management of the West's public grasslands mandated cooperation with associations of livestock raisers.

At times, federal programs allowed previously unrepresented groups to contest traditionally dominant interests. Often seeing greater opportunities for participation and influence in federal programs than in city and state governments, community groups even campaigned to expand federal authority. In short, depression conditions and New Deal programs actually increased citizen involvement in public affairs.

Ebbing of the New Deal

After his victory in 1936, Roosevelt committed himself to further reforms. "The test of our progress," he declared in his second inaugural address, "is not whether we add more to the abundance of those who have much; it is whether we provide enough for those who have too little." But determined opponents, continuing economic problems, and the president's own misjudgments blocked his reforms and deadlocked the New Deal.

Challenging the Court

During Roosevelt's first term, the Supreme Court had declared unconstitutional several important measures, including the NIRA and much of his agricultural program. FDR complained that the justices held "horse-and-buggy" ideas about government that prevented the president and Congress from responding to changes. He decided to restructure the federal judiciary and, in early 1937, proposed legislation authorizing a new judge for each one serving past the age of 70. Additional judges, he said, would increase judicial efficiency. But his real goal was to appoint new judges more sympathetic to the New Deal.

His court plan led to a divisive struggle. The proposal was perfectly legal, but Republicans and conservative Democrats attacked the plan as a scheme to "pack" the Court and subvert the separation of powers among the three branches of government. Even many liberals expressed reservations. The Court itself undercut support for FDR's proposal by upholding the Social Security and Wagner Acts. Congress rejected Roosevelt's plan.

Roosevelt's challenge to the Court hurt the New Deal. It worried the public, split the Democratic party, and revived conservatives. Opponents promptly attacked other New Deal policies, from support for unions to progressive taxation. Henceforth, a conservative coalition of Republicans and Southern Democrats in Congress blocked FDR's reforms.

More Hard Times

A sharp recession beginning in August 1937 added to Roosevelt's problems. As the economy improved in 1936, Roosevelt decided to cut federal expenditures and balance the budget. But private investment and employment remained stagnant, and the economy plunged. A record decline in industrial production canceled the gains of the previous two years, and unemployment leaped from 7 million to 11 million. Republicans delighted in attacking the "Roosevelt recession," although it stemmed from retrenchment policies they themselves advocated.

In 1938, Roosevelt reluctantly increased spending, based on the principles of British economist John Maynard Keynes. As Marriner Eccles, governor of the Federal Reserve Board, explained, the federal government had to serve as the "compensatory agent" in the economy: It should use deficit spending to increase demand and production when private investment declined and raise taxes to pay its debt and cool the economy when business activity became excessive. New appropriations for the PWA and other government programs revived the faltering economy, but only the vast expenditures for World War II would bring full recovery.

Political Stalemate

The recession interrupted the momentum of the New Deal and strengthened its opponents. In late 1937, their leaders in Congress issued a "conservative manifesto" decrying New Deal fiscal, labor, and regulatory policies. Holding seniority in a Congress malapportioned in their favor, they blocked most of Roosevelt's reforms. None of his "must" legislation passed a special session of Congress in December. In 1938, Congress rejected tax reforms and reduced corporate taxes. The few measures that passed were heavily amended. The Fair Labor Standards Act established maximum hours and minimum wages for workers but authorized so many exemptions that one New Dealer asked "whether anyone is subject to this bill."

To protect the New Deal, Roosevelt turned again to the public, with whom he remained immensely popular. In the 1938 Democratic primaries, he campaigned against the New Deal's conservative opponents. But FDR could not transfer his personal popularity to the political newcomers he supported. What his foes attacked as a "purge" failed. Roosevelt lost further political leverage when the Republicans gained seventy-five seats in the House and seven in the Senate and thirteen governorships.

The Democrats retained majorities in both houses of Congress, but the Republican revival and the survival of the conservative Southern Democrats guaranteed that the New Deal had gone as far as it ever would. With Roosevelt in the White House and his opponents controlling Congress, the New Deal ended in political stalemate.

Conclusion

The Great Depression and the New Deal mark a major divide in American history. The depression cast doubt on the traditional practices, policies, and attitudes that underlay not only the nation's economy but its social and political institutions and relationships as well. The New Deal failed to restore prosperity, but it did bring partial economic recovery. Moreover, its economic policies, from banking and securities regulation to unemployment compensation, farm price supports, and minimum wages, created barriers against another depression. The gradual adoption of compensatory spending policies also expanded the government's role in the economy. Responding to the failures of both private organizations and state and local governments, the federal government also assumed the obligation to provide social welfare. "Better the occasional faults of a Government that lives in a spirit of charity," Roosevelt warned, "than the constant omission of a Government frozen in the ice of its own indifference."

The New Deal brought political changes, too. The role of the presidency expanded; the federal government, rather than state or local governments, became the focus of public interest and expectations; and the Roosevelt coalition made the Democrats the dominant national party for years to come. Political constraints limited some New Deal efforts, particularly to curtail racial discrimination or protect the rural and urban poor, but the New Deal did change American life. By 1939, as international relations deteriorated, FDR was already considering a shift, as he later said, from Dr. New Deal to Dr. Win-the-War.

Review Questions

1. Why did President Hoover's emphasis on voluntarism fail to resolve the problems of the Great Depression?

2. Describe the relief programs of the New Deal. What were they designed to accomplish? What were their achievements and their limitations?

3. What were the major criticisms of the early New Deal? How accurate were those charges?

4. How did the policies of the New Deal shape the constituency and the prospects of the Democratic party in the 1930s?

5. Describe the conflict between management and labor in the 1930s. What were the major issues and motivations involved? How did the two sides differ in resources and tactics, and how and why did these factors change over time?

6. How did the role of the federal government change in the 1930s? What factors were responsible for those changes?

Recommended Reading

Paul Conkin, *The New Deal*, 2nd ed. (1975). Conkin provides a brief and insightful critique of FDR's programs.

Steve Fraser and Gary Gerstle, eds., *The Rise and Fall of the New Deal Order, 1930–1980* (1989). This valuable collection of essays surveys the New Deal and explores its legacy.

Frank Freidel, *Franklin D. Roosevelt: A Rendezvous with Destiny* (1990). Here is the best one-volume biography of FDR.

William Leuchtenburg, *Franklin D. Roosevelt and the New Deal, 1932–1940* (1963). This is the best single-volume study of FDR's policies during his first two terms as president.

Harvard Sitkoff, ed., *Fifty Years Later: The New Deal Evaluated* (1985). The New Deal is analyzed in an excellent selection of essays.

John Steinbeck, *The Grapes of Wrath* (1939). The classic novel of Dust Bowl migrants still makes gripping reading.

Where to Learn More

❖ **Center for New Deal Studies, Roosevelt University, Chicago, Illinois.** The center contains political memorabilia, photographs, papers, and taped interviews dealing with Franklin D. Roosevelt and the New Deal; it also sponsors an annual lecture series about the Roosevelt legacy.

❖ **Herbert Hoover National Historic Site, West Branch, Iowa.** This 186-acre site contains the birthplace cottage and grave of Herbert Hoover as well as his presidential library and museum, which contains a reconstruction of Hoover's White House office.

❖ **Franklin D. Roosevelt Home and Presidential Library, Hyde Park, New York.** The Roosevelt home, furnished with family heirlooms, and the spacious grounds, where FDR is buried, personalize the president and provide insights into his career. The nearby library has displays and exhibitions about Roosevelt's presidency, and the Eleanor Roosevelt Wing is dedicated to the career of ER.

❖ **Eleanor Roosevelt National Historic Site, Hyde Park, New York.** These two cottages, where Eleanor Roosevelt worked and, after 1945, lived, contain her furniture and memorabilia. Visitors can also watch a film biography of ER and tour the grounds of this retreat where she entertained personal friends and world leaders.

❖ **Bethune Museum and Archives National Historic Site, Washington, D.C.** This four-story townhouse was the home of Mary McLeod Bethune, a friend of Eleanor Roosevelt and the director of the New Deal's Division of Negro Affairs, and the headquarters of the National Council of Negro Women, which Bethune founded in 1935. Exhibits feature the contributions of black activist women and activities of the civil rights movement.

28 WORLD WAR II, 1939–1945

CHAPTER OUTLINE

KEY TOPICS

❖ The reluctance of most Americans to get involved in World War II
❖ FDR's efforts to support Britain and put pressure on Japan despite isolationism
❖ The nation's strategy for a two-front war against Germany and Japan
❖ The social and economic transformation of the United States in response to war mobilization
❖ The beginning of the Cold War and the emergence of the United States as the richest and most powerful nation in the world in the wake of World War II

*L*aura and Enrico Fermi arrived in the United States in 1939 as refugees from repression in **Fascist** Italy. In 1938, Enrico had earned a Nobel Prize in physics. By 1942, he was leading the efforts to develop an atomic bomb as the United States mobilized for World War II. The next year, the Fermis joined other atomic scientists, engineers, and their families at Los Alamos, a science city built hurriedly on a high plateau in northern New Mexico, where isolation was supposed to ensure secrecy.

The instant city was a cross between an army camp and a cheap subdivision. Scientists spent their days designing a bomb that would change world politics and returned to dinners cooked on wood-burning stoves. Laura Fermi and other residents remembered the sense of community. "I was in Los Alamos only a year and a half," she later wrote, "and still it seems such a big portion of my life . . . it was such intense living."

Britons and Canadians worked alongside U.S. scientists. So did Danes and Hungarians who had fled **Nazi**-dominated Europe. Workers from nearby Hispanic villages and Indian pueblos stoked the furnaces and swept the floors. Absent were scientists from the Soviet Union, carefully excluded from the secret of the A-bomb.

The internationalism of Los Alamos mirrored the larger war effort. Japan's attack on Hawaii in December 1941 thrust the United States into a war that spanned the globe. U.S. allies against Japan in the Pacific and East Asia included Great Britain, Australia, and China. In Europe, its allies against Nazi Germany and Fascist Italy included Great Britain, the Soviet Union, and more than twenty other nations.

The **Axis Powers**—Germany, Italy, and Japan—had piled one conquest on another since the late 1930s, and they continued to seize new territories in 1942. Allied defeat in a few key battles could have resulted in standoff or Axis victory. Not until 1944 did American economic power allow the United States and its allies to feel confident of victory. A new weapon might end the war more quickly or make the difference between victory and defeat.

The war highlighted racial inequalities, gave women new opportunities, and fostered growth in the South and West. By devastating the nation's commercial rivals, retraining workers, and modernizing factories, World War II left the United States dominant in the world economy. It also increased the scope of the federal government and built an alliance among the armed forces, big business, and science that helped shape postwar America.

The Dilemmas of Neutrality

Opinion polls in the fall of 1941 showed that most voters still hoped to avoid war. President Roosevelt's challenge was to lead the United States toward rearmament and support for Great Britain and China without alarming a reluctant public.

The Roots of War

The countdown to World War II started in 1931 when Japan invaded and soon conquered the northern Chinese province of Manchuria. A full-scale invasion of China followed in 1937. Japan took many of the key cities and killed tens of thousands of civilians in the "rape of Nanking," but failed to dislodge the government of Jiang Jieshi (Chiang Kai-shek) and settled into a war of attrition.

Internal Japanese propaganda in the 1930s stressed the need to rebuild Japan's greatness. Japanese nationalists believed that the United States, Britain, and France after World War I had treated Japan unfairly, despite its participation against Ger-

many. They believed that Japan should expel the French, British, Dutch, and Americans from Asia and reorganize its economy into a **Greater East Asia Co-Prosperity Sphere**.

In Germany, Adolf Hitler came to power by constitutional means in 1933 as head of the Nazi party, and quickly consolidated his grip on the country. Proclaiming the start of a thousand-year *Reich* (empire), he combined the historic German interest in eastward expansion with a long tradition of racialist thought about German superiority. Special targets of Nazi hatred were Jews, who were prominent in German business and professional life but who soon faced persecution aimed at driving them from the country.

Germany's direct challenge to Europe began in 1936, when Hitler sent troops into the Rhineland, Germany's border region with France. The *Reich* absorbed German-speaking Austria in 1938. Hitler's next target was a German-speaking border district of Czechoslovakia known as the Sudetenland. In September 1938, French premier Edouard Daladier and British prime minister Neville Chamberlain flew to Munich to meet with Hitler. Chamberlain, claiming to have secured "peace in our time," agreed to German annexation of the Sudetenland in return for Hitler's pledge to make no more territorial claims. Germany occupied the rest of Czechoslovakia six months later.

Benito Mussolini, Italy's leader since 1922, invaded and conquered Ethiopia in 1935–1936. To extend Italian influence in the Mediterranean, he sent arms and troops to General Francisco Franco's right-wing rebels when a civil war erupted in Spain in 1936. In April 1939, Italy absorbed Albania, across the Adriatic Sea.

Germany and Italy formed the Rome-Berlin Axis in 1936 and the **Tripartite Pact** with Japan in 1940. Political dissidents in all three nations had already been suppressed. Most repressive was Germany. The Nazi **concentration camp** was a device for political terrorism. Hitler decreed that opponents should disappear into "night and fog." By 1939, concentration camps held 25,000 people—mostly socialists, homosexuals, and beggars—who were overworked, starved, and abused.

Hitler's War in Europe

After annexing Austria and Czechoslovakia through diplomatic bullying and uncontested coups, Germany invaded Poland on September 1, 1939. Western journalists covering the three-week conquest of Poland coined the term **Blitzkrieg**, or "lightning war," to describe the German tactics. Armored divisions with tanks and motorized infantry punched quick

The raspy-voiced Adolf Hitler had a remarkable ability to stir the German people. He and his inner circle made skillful use of propaganda, exploiting German resentment over the country's defeat in World War I and, with carefully staged mass rallies, such as this event in 1938, inspiring an emotional conviction of national greatness.

holes in defensive positions and raced forward 30 or 40 miles per day.

Striking from a central position against scattered enemies, Hitler chose the targets and timing of each new front: east to smash Poland in September 1939; north to capture Denmark and Norway in April and May 1940; west to defeat the Netherlands, Belgium, and France in May and June 1940; south into the Balkans, enlisting Hungary, Romania, and Bulgaria as allies and conquering Yugoslavia and Greece in April and May 1941. He also launched the **Battle of Britain** in the second half of 1940, sending bombers in an unsuccessful effort to pound Britain into submission.

In June 1941, having failed to knock Britain out of the war, Hitler invaded the Soviet Union (officially the Union of Soviet Socialist Republics, or USSR). The attack caught the Red Army off guard, because the Nazis and Soviets had signed a nonaggression pact in 1939, and the USSR had helped dismember Poland. Nevertheless, from June until December 1941, more than 3 million Germans, Italians, and Romanians pushed eastward, encircling and capturing entire Soviet armies. Before desperate Soviet counterattacks and a bitter winter stopped the German tanks, they had reached the outskirts of Moscow and expected to finish the job in the spring.

Trying to Keep Out

"We Must Keep Out!" shouted the September 7, 1939, *Chicago Daily News*. Most Americans wanted to avoid foreign quarrels. Much of the emotional appeal of neutrality came from disillusionment with the

American crusade in World War I, which had failed to make the world safe for democracy. Charles A. Lindbergh and editor Robert McCormick of the *Chicago Tribune* argued that the best way to assure the safety of the United States was to conserve resources to defend the Western Hemisphere.

Congressional hearings on munitions manufacturers and financiers had strengthened antiwar leanings in 1934–1936. *Fortune* magazine and *Reader's Digest* published an exposé that blamed wars on arms manufacturers. *Merchants of Death* was a bestseller on the same theme. American society in the mid-1930s was shocked by profits from international arms sales.

The country's ethnic variety complicated U.S. responses to European conflict. Nazi aggression ravaged the homelands of Americans of Polish, Czech, Greek, and Norwegian ancestry. In contrast, Irish-Americans applauded defeats that undermined Britain's empire. German-Americans remembered the rabid anti-German sentiment of World War I and dreaded a second fight with Germany. Many Italian-Americans admired Mussolini.

American opinion seemed solid for nonintervention. The *Denver Post* argued in January 1940 that "the smallest domestic problem is more important to the American people than the most momentous European crisis."

Edging toward Intervention

Roosevelt's appeals to democratic values gained support in 1939 and 1940. Nazi persecution of minorities and Japanese atrocities in China did strike most Americans as worse than British or French imperial-

CHRONOLOGY

1931 Japan invades Manchuria.

1933 Hitler takes power in Germany.

1934 Nye Committee opens hearings on international arms trade.

1935 Congress passes first of three Neutrality acts. Italy invades Ethiopia.

1936 Germany and Italy form the Rome-Berlin Axis. Civil war erupts in Spain.

1937 Japan invades China.

1938 Germany absorbs Austria. Munich agreement promises "peace in our time."

1939 Germany and the Soviet Union sign a nonaggression pact.

Germany absorbs Czechoslovakia. Germany invades Poland; Great Britain and France declare war on Germany.

1940 Germany conquers Denmark, Norway, Belgium, the Netherlands, and France. Japan, Germany, and Italy sign the Tripartite Pact.

The United States begins to draft men into the armed forces. Franklin Roosevelt wins an unprecedented third term.

1941 The United States begins a lend-lease program to make military equipment available to Great Britain and later the USSR.

The Fair Employment Practices Committee is established.

Germany invades the Soviet Union.

Roosevelt and Churchill issue the Atlantic Charter.

Japan attacks U.S. military bases in Hawaii

1942 American forces in the Philippines surrender to Japan.

President Roosevelt authorizes the removal and internment of Japanese-Americans living in four western states.

Naval battles in the Coral Sea and off the island of Midway blunt Japanese expansion.

U.S. forces land in North Africa.

Soviet forces encircle a German army at Stalingrad.

The first sustained and controlled nuclear chain reaction takes place at the University of Chicago.

1943 U.S. and British forces invade Italy, which makes terms with the Allies.

Race conflict erupts in riots in Detroit, New York, and Los Angeles.

The landing of Marines on Tarawa initiates the island-hopping strategy.

U.S. war production peaks.

Roosevelt, Churchill, and Stalin confer at Tehran.

1944 Allied forces land in Normandy.

The U.S. Navy destroys Japanese sea power in the battles of the Philippine Sea and Leyte Gulf.

The Battle of the Bulge is the last tactical setback for the Allies.

1945 Roosevelt, Stalin, and Churchill meet at Yalta to plan the postwar world.

The United States takes the Pacific islands of Iwo Jima and Okinawa.

Franklin Roosevelt dies; Harry S Truman becomes president.

Germany surrenders to the United States, Great Britain, and the USSR.

The United Nations is organized at an international meeting in San Francisco.

Japan surrenders after the detonation of atomic bombs over Hiroshima and Nagasaki.

ism. Edward R. Murrow's radio broadcasts from England describing London under German bombing heightened the sense of imperiled freedom. And as Roosevelt pointed out, "Freedom to trade is essential to our economic life. We do not eat all the food we produce; we do not burn all the oil we can pump; we do not use all the goods we can manufacture." U.S. business leaders had little doubt that Axis victories would bring economic instability and require crushing defense budgets to protect a Fortress America.

Because 85 percent of the American people agreed that the nation should fight only if directly attacked, Roosevelt had to chip away at neutrality. In October 1939, lawmakers reluctantly passed the Neutrality Act of 1939 allowing arms sales to belligerent nations on a "cash and carry" basis, thus avoiding the unpaid debts that followed World War I. In control of the Atlantic, France and Britain were the only expected customers.

Isolationism helps explain why the United States accepted only a few thousand Jewish refugees. Unthinking anti-Semitism at the State Department also contributed to tight enforcement of immigration quotas. In 1939, officials turned the passenger ship

St. Louis away from Miami and forced its 950 German-Jewish refugees back to Europe. FDR made small gestures, such as allowing fifteen thousand German and Austrian refugees, including many scientists and artists, to remain in the United States on visitor permits, but polls showed that a whopping 83 percent of the public supported restricted immigration.

The collapse of France in June 1940 scared Americans into rearming. In the summer of 1940, Congress voted to expand the army to 2 million men, build 19,000 new war planes, and add 150 ships to the navy. September brought the nation's first peacetime draft.

In the same month, the United States concluded a "destroyer deal" with Britain, trading fifty old destroyers for the use of bases on British territories in the Caribbean, Bermuda, and Newfoundland.

In the presidential election of 1940, the big campaign issue was therefore whether FDR's unprecedented try for a third term represented arrogance or legitimate concern for continuity in a time of peril. The voters gave Roosevelt 55 percent of their votes to defeat his Republican opponent, Wendell Wilkie. The president pledged that no Americans would fight in a foreign war. But if the United States were attacked, he said privately, the war would no longer be "foreign."

The Brink of War

In January 1941, Roosevelt proposed the "lend-lease" program, which allowed Britain to "borrow" military equipment for the duration of the war. Roosevelt compared the program to lending a garden hose to a neighbor whose house had caught fire. Senator Robert Taft of Ohio countered that it was more like lending chewing gum—you wouldn't want it back after it was used. Behind the scheme was Britain's inability to go on paying for American goods.

The **Committee to Defend America by Aiding the Allies** argued the administration's position. In opposition, the **America First Committee** claimed that lend-lease would allow the president to declare anything a "defense article." Congress finally passed the measure in March 1941, giving Great Britain an unlimited line of credit.

FDR soon began an undeclared war in the North Atlantic. The United States established bases in Greenland in April and landed four thousand marines in Iceland in July. Roosevelt also instructed the navy to report sightings of German submarines to the British. In September, the U.S. destroyer *Greer* clashed with a German submarine. Roosevelt proclaimed a "shoot on sight" policy for German subs and escorted British convoys to within 400 miles of

Britain. In reply, German submarines torpedoed and damaged the destroyer *Kearny* on October 17 and sank the destroyer *Reuben James* with the loss of more than 100 lives on October 30. The United States was approaching outright naval war with Germany.

The **Atlantic Charter** of August 1941 provided a political umbrella for American involvement. Meeting off Newfoundland, Roosevelt and British prime minister Winston Churchill agreed that the first priority was to defeat Germany; Japan was secondary. Echoing Woodrow Wilson, Roosevelt also insisted on a commitment to oppose territorial change by conquest, to support self-government, and promote freedom of the seas.

Some historians think that Roosevelt's goal in the North Atlantic was to support Britain short of war. Others believe that he accepted the inevitability of war but hesitated to outpace public opinion. In this second interpretation, FDR wanted to eliminate Hitler without going to war if possible, with war if necessary. "I am waiting to be pushed into the situation," he told his secretary of the treasury.

That final shove came in the Pacific rather than the Atlantic. In 1940, as part of its rearmament program, the United States decided to build a "two-ocean navy." This decision antagonized Japan. Japan had achieved roughly 70 percent of U.S. naval strength by late 1941. However, America's buildup promised to reduce that ratio to only 30 percent by 1944. Furthermore, the United States was gradually restricting Japan's vital imports of steel, iron ore, and aluminum. In July 1941, after Japan occupied French Indochina, Roosevelt froze Japanese assets in the United States, blocked petroleum shipments, and began to build up U.S. forces in the Philippines. Both militarily and economically, it looked in Tokyo as if 1942 was Japan's last chance for victory.

Japanese war planners never seriously considered an actual invasion of the United States or expected a decisive victory. They hoped that attacks on American Pacific bases would shock the United States into letting Japan have its way in Asia or at least win time to create impenetrable defenses in the central Pacific.

December 7, 1941

It now seems that Roosevelt wanted to restrain the Japanese with bluff and intimidation so that the United States could focus on Germany. FDR also recognized the possibility of a two-front war—at least a 20 percent chance, he told military advisers in January 1941. Because the United States cracked Japanese codes, it knew by November that Japanese military

In August 1941, Winston Churchill (seated right) and Franklin Roosevelt (seated left) met on a British warship off the coast of Newfoundland to coordinate American assistance to Britain. Out of the meeting came the Atlantic Charter, a broad statement of goals for a democratic future after the defeat of Germany. Churchill reluctantly agreed to the Atlantic Charter to satisfy FDR, despite its implicit criticism of the British Empire.

shall run wild for the first six months or a year, but I have utterly no confidence for the second or third year." The admiral was right. As it turned out, Japan's conquests reached their limit after six months, but in early 1942, it was far from clear that that would be so. In Europe, Allied fortunes went from bad to worse in the first half of 1942. Decisive turning points did not come until November 1942, a year after the United States had entered the war.

Stopping Germany

In December 1941, the United States plunged into a truly global war that was being fought on six distinct fronts. In North Africa, the British battled Italian and German armies that were trying to seize the Suez Canal. On the **Eastern Front**, Soviet armies held defensive positions. In the North Atlantic, merchant ships dodged German submarines. In China, Japan controlled the most productive provinces but could not crush Chinese resistance, which was supported by supplies airlifted from British India. In Southeast Asia, Japanese troops attacked the Philippines, the Dutch East Indies, New Guinea, Malaya, and Burma. In the central Pacific, the Japanese fleet faced the U.S. Navy.

Despite the popular desire for revenge against Japan, the United States decided to defeat Germany first, as Germany was far stronger than Japan. Defeat of Japan would not assure the defeat of Germany, especially if it crushed the Soviet Union or starved Britain into submission. In contrast, a strategy that helped the Soviets and British survive and then destroyed German military power would doom Japan.

The strategy recognized that the Eastern Front held the key to Allied hopes. In 1941, Germany had seized control of 45 percent of the Soviet population, 47 percent of its grain production, and more than 60 percent of its coal, steel, and aluminum industries. Hitler next sought to destroy Soviet capacity to wage war. He targeted southern Russia, an area rich in grain and oil. The German thrust was also designed to eliminate the British from the Middle East.

action was imminent but expected the blow to come in Southeast Asia.

Instead, the Japanese fleet sailed a 4,000-mile loop through the empty North Pacific, avoiding merchant shipping and American patrols. Before dawn on December 7, six Japanese aircraft carriers launched 351 planes in two unopposed bombing strikes on **Pearl Harbor**, Hawaii.

Americans counted their losses: eight battleships, eleven other warships, and nearly all military aircraft damaged or destroyed; and 2403 people killed. Fortunately, dockyards, drydocks, and oil storage tanks remained intact because the Japanese admiral had refused to order a third attack. And the American carriers, at sea on patrol, were unharmed.

Speaking to Congress the following day, Roosevelt proclaimed December 7, 1941, "a date which will live in infamy." He asked for—and got—a declaration of war against the Japanese. Hitler and Mussolini declared war on the United States on December 11.

Holding the Line

In 1940, Admiral Isoroku Yamamoto, the chief of Japan's Combined Fleet, weighed the chances of victory against the United States and Great Britain: "If I am told to fight regardless of the consequences, I

The German offensive opened with stunning success. Every day's advance, however, stretched supply lines. Tanks ran out of fuel and spare parts. The horses that pulled German supply wagons died for lack of food.

Disaster came at **Stalingrad** (present-day Volgograd), an industrial center on the western bank of the Volga River. In September and October, 1942, German, Italian, and Romanian soldiers fought their way house by house into the city.

The Red Army delivered a counterstroke on November 18 that cut off 330,000 Axis soldiers. Airlifts kept the Germans fighting for two more months, but they surrendered in February 1943. Russians call the hills around Stalingrad "white fields" because human bones still turn up after spring thaws.

The Survival of Britain

In 1940 and 1941, from bases in France, German submarines (greatly improved since World War I) intercepted shipments of oil from Nigeria, beef from Argentina, minerals from Brazil, grain from Canada, and weapons from the United States. Through the end of 1941, German "tonnage warfare" sank British, Allied, and neutral merchant vessels faster than they could be replaced.

The **Battle of the Atlantic** forced the British to reduce their reliance on the Atlantic supply lines. Between 1939 and 1944, planning and rationing cut Britain's need for imports in half. The British also organized protected convoys. Grouping the merchant ships into convoys with armed escorts "hardened" the targets and made them more difficult to find in the wide ocean. Roosevelt's destroyer deal of 1940 and U.S. naval escorts in the western Atlantic in 1941 thus contributed directly to Britain's survival.

Nevertheless, German submarines (known as U-boats from Unterseeboot) operated as far as the Caribbean and the Carolinas in 1942. In June, U-boats sank 144 ships; drowned sailors washed up on Carolina beaches. Only the extension of the convoy system to American waters forced the subs back toward Britain. Meanwhile, allied aircraft began to track submarines with radar, spot them with searchlights as they maneuvered on the surface, and attack them with depth charges. New sonar systems allowed escort ships to measure submarines' speed and depth. By the spring of 1943, American shipyards were also launching ships faster than the Germans could sink them.

British ground fighting in 1942 centered in North Africa. By October 1942, Field Marshal Erwin Rommel's German and Italian forces were within striking distance of the Suez Canal. At **El Alamein** between October 23 and November 5, 1942, however,

General Bernard Montgomery, with twice Rommel's manpower and tanks, forced the enemy to retreat and lifted the danger to the Middle East.

Retreat and Stabilization in the Pacific

Striking the Philippines a few hours after Hawaii, the Japanese gained another tactical surprise (see Map 28-1) destroying most American air power on the ground and isolating U.S. forces. Between February 27 and March 1, Japan brushed aside a combined American, British, Dutch, and Australian fleet in the Battle of the Java Sea, and a numerically inferior Japanese force had seized Singapore.

In the spring Japan pushed the British out of Burma, and overwhelmed Filipino and U.S. defensive positions on the Bataan peninsula. On May 6, the last American bastion, the island fortress of Corregidor in Manila Bay, surrendered.

The first check to Japanese expansion came on May 7–8, 1942, in the **Battle of the Coral Sea**, where U.S. aircraft carriers halted a Japanese advance toward Australia. In June, the Japanese struck at the island of Midway, 1,500 miles northwest of Honolulu. Their goal was to destroy American carrier forces. Having cracked Japanese radio codes, U.S. forces were aware of the plan for a diversionary invasion of the Aleutian Islands. On the morning of June 4, U.S. Navy dive bombers found the Japanese fleet and sank or crippled three aircraft carriers in five minutes; another Japanese carrier sank later in the day. The **Battle of Midway** ended Japanese efforts to expand in the Pacific.

Mobilizing the Home Front

News of the Japanese attack on Pearl Harbor shattered a bright Sunday afternoon. Twelve-year-old Jean Bartlett's family was headed to the movies when news of the attack came over the car radio. Elliott Johnson and his friends were eating in a Chinese restaurant in Portland, Oregon, when the proprietor burst from the kitchen with a portable radio; the line was two blocks long by the time they got to the marine recruiting office.

In the next four years, some 350,000 women and more than 16 million men served in the armed forces; 292,000 died in battle, 100,000 survived prisoner-of-war camps, and 671,000 returned wounded. More worked in defense industries. Youngsters saved tin foil, collected scrap metal, and followed the freedom-fighting stories of Wonder Woman in the comics. College science students

Map 28·1   World War II in the Pacific, from Pearl Harbor to Midway
The first six months after the Japanese attack on Pearl Harbor brought a string of Japanese victories and conquests in the Pacific, the islands southeast of Asia, and the British colonies of Malaya and Burma. Japan's advance was halted by a standoff battle in the Coral Sea, a decisive U.S. naval victory at Midway, and the length and vulnerability of Japanese supply lines to its most distant conquests.

might be recruited to work at scientific espionage against the Nazis.

Warriors and Families

By 1945, 8.3 million men and women were on active duty in the army and army air forces and 3.4 million in the navy and Marine Corps, totals exceeded only by the Soviet Union. The military establishment was four times larger than in World War I.

Many Americans put their lives on fast forward. Men and women often decided to beat the clock with instant matrimony before the war forced

their separation. Couples who had postponed marriage because of the depression could afford to marry as the economy picked up. War intensified casual romances and heightened the appeal of marriage as an anchor in troubled times. Altogether the war years brought 1.2 million "extra" marriages compared to the rate in 1920–1939.

The federal government tried to keep civilians of all ages committed to the war. It encouraged scrap drives and backyard victory gardens. The government also managed news about the fighting. Early in the war, it blocked publication of most photographs of war casualties. Worried about flagging commitment, censors later authorized photographs of enemy atrocities to incite the public.

Government officials had a harder time controlling Hollywood. The Office of War Information told movie directors to tone down car chases because screeching tires implied wasted rubber. War films revealed the nation's racial attitudes, often drawing distinctions between "good" and "bad" Germans but uniformly portraying Japanese as subhuman and repulsive. The most successful films dramatized the courage of the Allies.

Industry Gears Up

Industry had reluctantly begun to convert from consumer goods to defense production in 1940 and 1941. The last passenger car for the duration of the war rolled off the assembly line in February 1942. Existing factories retooled to make war equipment, and huge new facilities turned out thousands of planes and ships. Baltimore, Atlanta, Fort Worth, Los Angeles, and Seattle became centers for aircraft production. New Orleans, Portland, and the San Francisco Bay area were shipbuilding centers. Henry J. Kaiser, who had helped build vast projects like the Grand Coulee Dam, turned out cargo ships by the thousands.

One historian estimates that 40 percent of the world's military production was coming from the United States by 1944. Equally impressive is the 30 percent increase in the productivity of U.S. workers between 1939 and 1945. Surging farm income pulled agriculture out of its long slump. The rich certainly got richer, but the poorest quarter of Americans also made up some of the ground lost during the Great Depression.

Behind the scenes were new federal agencies. The **War Manpower Commission** allocated workers among vital industries and the military. The **War Production Board** invested $17 billion for new factories and managed $181 billion in war supply contracts. The **Office of Price Administration (OPA)** fought inflation with price controls and rationing of automobile tires, sugar, coffee, meat, butter, gasoline, and shoes. "Use it up, wear it out, make it do or do without" was the OPA's slogan. By slowing price increases, the OPA helped convince Americans to buy the war bonds that financed half the war spending.

The Enlistment of Science

"There wasn't a physicist able to breathe who wasn't doing war work," remembered Professor Philip Morrison. At the center of the scientific enterprise was Vannevar Bush, former dean at the Massachusetts Institute of Technology. As head of the newly established **Office of Scientific Research and Development**, Bush guided spending on research and development that dwarfed previous scientific work and set the pattern of massive federal support for science that continued after the war.

The biggest scientific effort was the drive to produce an atomic bomb. As early as 1939, Albert Einstein had written FDR about the possibility of such a weapon and the danger of falling behind the Germans. In late 1941, Roosevelt established what became known as the **Manhattan Project**. On December 2, 1942, scientists manipulated graphite rods inserted in a stack of uranium ingots until they were certain they could trigger and control a self-sustaining nuclear reaction.

The Manhattan Project moved from theory to practice in 1943. Physicist J. Robert Oppenheimer directed the young scientists at Los Alamos in designing a nuclear fission bomb. Engineers in other new science cities tried two approaches to producing the fissionable material. Richland, Washington, burgeoned into a sprawling metropolis that supported the creation of plutonium at the Hanford Engineer Works. Oak Ridge, Tennessee, near Knoxville, was built around gaseous diffusion plants.

Plutonium from Hanford fueled the first bomb tested at the Trinity site, 100 miles from Alamogordo, New Mexico, on July 16, 1945. The explosion astonished even the physicists; Oppenheimer quoted from Hindu scriptures as he tried to comprehend the results: "Now I am become death, destroyer of worlds."

Boom Times

The war marked the takeoff of what Americans would later call the **Sunbelt**. Albuquerque, New Mexico more than doubled in population during the 1940s. Wartime booms accelerated the growth of larger metropolitan areas like San Diego (up 92 percent in the decade), Phoenix (up 78 percent), and Mobile (up 68 percent).

In war boom cities, factories operated three shifts, movies ran around the clock, and workers filled the streets after midnight. Most of the new industrial workers in 1941 and 1942 were unattached males—young men waiting for their draft call and older men separated from their families.

The hordes of war workers found housing scarce. Workers in Seattle's shipyards and Boeing plants scrounged for living space in offices, tents, chicken coops, and rooming houses where "hot beds" rented in shifts. When the Ford Motor Company began to build B-24 bombers at its new Willow

Run plant in Michigan, the first of 42,000 workers made do with barns, garages, rented rooms, and trailers parked in thick mud.

Women in the War Effort

As draft calls took men off the assembly line, the war gave women new job opportunities. Women made up one-quarter of West Coast shipyard workers at the peak of employment and nearly half of Dallas and Seattle aircraft workers. Most women in the shipyards were clerks and general helpers. The acute shortage of welders and other skilled workers however, opened thousands of journeyman positions to them as well.

By July 1944, fully 19 million women held paid jobs, up 6 million in four years. Women's share of government jobs increased from 19 to 38 percent and their share of manufacturing jobs from 22 to 33 percent. Mirroring the sequence in which the military draft took men, employers recruited single women before turning to married women in 1943 and 1944. The federal government assisted female entry into the labor force by funding day care programs that served 600,000 children. One of the workers recalled of herself and a friend, "We both had to work, we both had children, so we became welders, and if I might say so, damn good ones" (see "American Views: A Woman Shipyard Worker Recalls Her Experience").

While the country needed women's labor, many worried that their employment would undermine families. Men and women commonly assumed that women would want to return to the home after victory; they were to work when the nation needed them and quit when the need was past.

The nation had the same mixed reaction to the women who joined the armed forces as army and navy nurses and as members of the WACS (Women's Army Corps), WAVES (Navy), SPARS (Coast Guard), and Marine Corps Women's Reserve. The armed services tried not to change established gender roles. Most of the women hammered at typewriters, worked switchboards, inventoried supplies, and tended the ill and injured. WAC officers battled the tendency of the popular press to call females in the service "girls" rather than "women" or "soldiers" yet emphasized that military service promoted "poise and charm."

Unequal Opportunity

Not all Americans had the same chance to benefit from the economic boom. On February 19, 1942, President Roosevelt issued **Executive Order 9066**, which authorized the secretary of war to define

restricted areas and remove civilian residents who were threats to national security. The targets were 110,000 Japanese-Americans whom the army expelled from parts of Washington, Oregon, California, and Arizona in the spring of 1942. Those who had not moved voluntarily were sent to relocation camps in the West and Southwest. Most evacuees left businesses and property that they were powerless to protect. Although the U.S. Supreme Court sanctioned the removals in *Korematsu* v. *United States* (1944), the nation officially recognized its liability with the Japanese Claims Act of 1948 and its broader moral responsibility in 1988, when Congress approved redress payments to each of the sixty thousand surviving evacuees.

In contrast, less than 1 percent of Hawaii's Japanese-American population of 160,000 was interned. Hawaii's long history as a multiethnic society made residents disinclined to look for a racial scapegoat. The remainder responded as patriotic Americans. Japanese-Americans from the detention camps also demonstrated their loyalty by joining in the 442nd Regimental Combat Team, the most decorated American unit in the European war.

The experience of African-Americans was also mixed. As it had since the Civil War, the army organized black soldiers in segregated units. At some southern bases, German prisoners of war watched movies from the first rows along with white GIs while African-American soldiers watched from the back. Private Charles Wilson wrote President Roosevelt that Davis-Monthan Army Air Force Base in Tucson was color-coded: Barracks for African-Americans were coated with black tar paper, and those for whites glistened with white paint. Military courts were quick to judge and harsh to punish when blacks were the accused. Despite the obstacles, all-black units such as the 761st Tank Battalion and the 99th Pursuit Squadron earned distinguished records.

Early in the mobilization, labor leader A. Philip Randolph of the Brotherhood of Sleeping Car Porters worked with Walter White of the NAACP to plan a "Negro March on Washington" to protest racial discrimination by the federal government. To head off a major embarrassment, Roosevelt issued **Executive Order 8802** in June 1941, barring racial discrimination in defense contracts and creating the **Fair Employment Practices Committee (FEPC)**; the order coined a phrase that reverberated powerfully through the coming decades: "no discrimination on grounds of race, color, creed, or national origin."

The FEPC's small staff resolved less than half of the employment discrimination complaints. White

American Views

A WOMAN SHIPYARD WORKER RECALLS HER EXPERIENCE

World War II industry gave new opportunities to millions of women. Patricia Cain Koehler later recalled her work as a teenage electrician who helped build escort aircraft carriers in Vancouver, Washington from 1943 to 1945.

❖ **How did Koehler's experience challenge expectations about "women's work"?**

❖ **What impression does she give about the spirit with which Americans organized to win the war?**

❖ **How did the war change the patterns of everyday life?**

We girls wore leather jackets, plaid flannel shirts, and jeans we bought in the boys department of Meier & Frank. It was 1943, we were eighteen years old, our first year of college was over. My girlfriend and her mother had moved in with my mother and me for the duration of the war. Housing was tight because of the influx of war industry workers. Our fathers were overseas.

Three local shipyards were recruiting workers from the East Coast and the South. They advertised in Portland, too: HELP WANTED: WOMEN SHIPBUILDERS. Cartoons asked, "What are you doing to help the war?" They showed women sipping tea, playing cards, and relaxing.

"THIS?" And then a smiling woman worker with lunch box, her hair tied up in a scarf, a large ship in the background, "Or THIS?" . . .

Together my girlfriend and I applied to be electrician helpers at the Kaiser Vancouver Shipyards. . . . Twenty thousand workers labored around the clock to build ships—fast. At nights the yards were lit up as bright as day. . . . It was a world of strangers. . . . Coming from outside the Northwest, as most of them did, they spoke in accents we had never heard before. It became a game with us to listen and ask point of origin. Soon we could distinguish between a Brooklyn accent and one from New Jersey. . . .

---

resistance to black coworkers remained strong. In Mobile, New Orleans, and Jacksonville, agreements between shipyards and segregated unions blocked skilled black workers from high-wage jobs. When the Alabama Dry Dock Company integrated its work force in May 1943, white workers rioted. Transportation workers in Philadelphia struck the next year to protest upgrading of jobs held by blacks. Nevertheless, African-American membership in labor unions doubled, and wartime prosperity raised the average black income from 41 percent of the white average in 1939 to 61 percent by 1950.

Twenty-five thousand Indians served in the armed forces. Some were members of radio combat-communication teams, known as "code-talkers," who transmitted vital information in Navajo and other Indian languages. Forty thousand other Native Americans moved to off-reservation jobs. The average cash income of Indian households tripled during the war.

Clashing Cultures

Many African-Americans in search of defense jobs headed out of the South for well-established black neighborhoods in northern cities. And Southern whites and northern blacks with different ideas of racial etiquette found themselves side by side in West Coast shipyards. In the Midwest, southern blacks and Appalachian whites crowded into cities such as Cincinnati and Chicago, competing for the same high-wage jobs and scarce apartments.

The day came . . . when we graduated to journeyman-electrician at $1.20 per hour. We celebrated by applying for jobs on the hookup crews, which worked aboard ships at the outfitting dock. I was assigned to fire control. That meant guns! My leadman had never had a female working for him, and he was skeptical. Like a shadow, I followed his every move, anticipating what tool he needed next and handing it to him before he could ask. After a few days of this he relaxed and began teaching me the ropes—or, rather, the wires. . . .

We had watched some of the carriers launched, with wartime ceremony, gold braid, and ribbons. There was no glamour for us, though, as we slipped on the cluttered decks, dodged cables over our heads, and risked death crossing the tracks of the giant cranes. . . .

My first solo assignment was hooking up the forty-millimeter gun directors on the starboard side. . . . Occasionally I looked down into the swift current of the Columbia River and noticed small boats dragging for a worker who had fallen in. . . . Once when climbing down a ladder clogged with welding leads (large rubber hoses), I slammed a steel-toed boot against one of them and broke a toe. The doctor taped it to its neighbor and I went on working. On another occasion I broke my elbow in a fall, lost a day getting it set, and learned to work left-handed. . . .

Since every night we fell into bed exhausted, our hands chapped and our hair smelling of paint, there was really no time to spend our money. So we invested most of our earnings in war bonds to be cashed in for college.

Source: *Patricia Cain Koehler,* "Reminiscence: Pat Koehler on The Women Shipbuilders of World War II." *Oregon Historical Quarterly,* Fall 1990, pp. 285–291.

Tensions between blacks and whites exploded in at least fifty cities in 1943 alone. New York's Harlem erupted in a riot after rumors of attacks on black servicemen. In Detroit, the issue was the boundary between white and black territories. In June 1943, an argument over use of Detroit's Belle Isle Park set off three days of violence.

Tensions were simultaneously rising between Mexican-Americans and Anglos. In July 1942, the United States admitted hundreds of thousands of *braceros,* or temporary workers, from Mexico to fill labor needs in the Southwest. As the Mexican community in Los Angeles swelled to an estimated 400,000, newspapers published anti-Mexican articles. On June 6, 1943, off-duty sailors and soldiers attacked Latinos on downtown streets and invaded Mexican-American neighborhoods. The main targets were so-called *pachucos*—young Chicanos who wore flamboyant "zoot suits" with long, wide-shouldered jackets and pleated, narrow-cuffed trousers.

The End of the New Deal

Roosevelt's New Deal had run out of steam in 1938. The war had reinvigorated his political fortunes by focusing national energies on foreign policy, over which presidents have the greatest power. After the 1942 election left Congress in the hands of Republicans, conservative lawmakers ignored proposals that war emergency housing be used to improve the nation's permanent housing stock, abolished the

National Resources Planning Board, curtailed rural electrification, and crippled the Farm Security Administration.

For the presidential election of 1944, the Republicans nominated Governor Thomas Dewey of New York, who had made his reputation as a crime-fighting district attorney. The Democrats renominated Roosevelt for a fourth term. Missouri Senator Harry S Truman, a tough investigator of American military preparedness, replaced liberal New Dealer Henry Wallace as Roosevelt's running mate, which appeased Southern Democrats.

Roosevelt supporters argued that the nation could not afford to switch leaders in the middle of a war, but Dewey's vigor and relative youth (he was twenty years younger than FDR) pointed up the president's failing health and energy. Voters gave Roosevelt 432 electoral votes to 99, but the narrowing gap in the popular vote—54 percent for Roosevelt and 46 percent for Dewey—made the Republicans eager for 1948.

War and Peace

In January 1943, the U.S. War Department completed the world's largest office building, the Pentagon. The building housed 23,000 workers along 17.5 miles of corridors. The gray walls of the Pentagon symbolized an American government that was outgrowing its prewar roots.

Gathering Allied Strength

American and British landings in North Africa in 1942 and Italy in 1943 satisfied the British desire to secure western influence in the Mediterranean and Middle East but they pleased neither American policymakers nor the Soviet Union. U.S. leaders wanted to justify massive mobilization with a war-winning campaign and to strike across Europe to occupy the heart of Germany. Stalin needed a full-scale invasion of western Europe to divert German forces from the Eastern Front.

In fact, 1943 was the year in which the Allies gained the edge in quality of equipment, capacity for war production, and military sophistication. The United States poured men and equipment into Britain. The Soviets recruited, rearmed, and upgraded new armies, despite enormous losses in 1941 and 1942 and rebuilt munitions factories beyond German reach. As Soviet soldiers reconquered western Russia and the Ukraine, they

marched in 13 million pairs of American-made boots and traveled in 51,000 jeeps and 375,000 Dodge trucks made available from U.S. lend-lease assistance.

Meeting in Casablanca in January 1943, Roosevelt and Churchill demanded the "unconditional surrender" of Italy, Germany, and Japan; the phrase meant no deals that kept the enemy governments or leaders in power. Ten months later, the Allied leaders huddled again. Roosevelt and Churchill met with China's Jiang in Cairo and then flew on to meet Stalin in Tehran. At Tehran, the U.S. and Britain promised to invade France within six months. "We leave here," said the three leaders, "friends in fact, in spirit, in purpose."

The superficial harmony barely survived the end of the war. Stalin and his generals scoffed at the small scale of early U.S. efforts. Roosevelt's ideal of self-determination for all peoples seemed naive to Churchill, who wanted the major powers to carve out realistic spheres of influence in Europe. It was irrelevant to Stalin, who wanted control of eastern Europe.

Turning the Tide in Europe

The United States had entered the ground war in Europe with **Operation TORCH**. Against little opposition, British and American troops under General Dwight Eisenhower landed in French Morocco and Algeria on November 8, 1942 (see Map 28-2). The puppet French government in place there, which had collaborated with the Nazis now switched sides, giving the Allies footholds in North Africa.

German tanks in February 1943 counterattacked U.S. divisions at **Kasserine Pass** in the Atlas Mountains of Tunisia. Learning quickly from this tactical defeat, Allied troops forced the Axis in Africa to surrender in May. Eisenhower had already demonstrated his ability to handle the politics of military leadership, skills he perfected commanding a multinational army for the next two and a half years.

The central Mediterranean remained the focus of U.S. and British action for the next year. The British proposed strikes in southern Europe. U.S. Army Chief of Staff George Marshall and President Roosevelt agreed first to the action in North Africa and then to invade Italy in 1943. In July and August, Allied forces led by Montgomery and Patton overran Sicily. As Sicily fell, the Italian king and army forced Mussolini from power and began to negotiate peace with Britain and America (but not the Soviet Union). In September, the Allies announced an armistice with Italy, and Eisenhower's troops landed south of Naples. Germany responded by occupying the rest of Italy.

Map 28-2   World War II in Europe, 1942–1945
Nazi Germany had to defend its conquests on three fronts. Around the Mediterranean, American and British forces pushed the Germans out of Africa and Southern Italy, while guerrillas in Yugoslavia pinned down many German troops. On the eastern front, Soviet armies advanced hundreds of miles to drive the German army out of the Soviet Union and eastern Europe. In June 1944, U.S. and British landings opened the western front in northern France for a decisive strike at the heart of Germany.

As American military planners had feared, the Italian campaign soaked up Allied resources. Week after week, the experience of GIs on the line was the same: "You wake up in the mud and your cigarettes are all wet and you have an ache in your joints and a rattle in your chest." Despite months of bitter fighting, the Allies controlled only two-thirds of Italy when the war there ended on May 1, 1945.

On the Eastern Front, the climactic battle of the German-Soviet war had erupted on July 5, 1943. The Germans sent three thousand tanks against the **Kursk Salient**. Soviet generals had prepared a defense in depth with three thousand tanks of their own. When the attack finally stalled, it marked the last great German offensive until December 1944.

Operation OVERLORD

On **D-Day**—June 6, 1944—the western Allies landed on the coast of Normandy in northwestern France. Six divisions went ashore from hundreds of attack transports carrying four thousand landing craft. Dozens of warships and twelve thousand aircraft provided support. One British and two American airborne divisions dropped behind German positions with parachutes and gliders. When the sun set on the "longest day," the Allies had a tenuous toehold in France.

The Allies secured their beachheads and landed 500,000 men and 100,000 vehicles within two weeks. However, the German defenders kept the Allies along a narrow coastal strip. **Operation OVERLORD**, the code name for the entire campaign across northern France, met renewed success in late July and August. U.S. troops finally broke through German lines around the town of St.-Lô and then drew a ring around the Germans that slowly closed on the town of Falaise. The Germans lost a quarter of a million troops. The German command chose to regroup closer to Germany rather than fight in France. The Allies liberated Paris on August 25.

On the Eastern Front, by the end of 1944, the Red Army had entered the Balkans and reached central Poland. With the end in sight, the Soviets had suffered nearly 20 million casualties and sustained the heaviest burden in turning back Nazi tyranny (see Table 28-1).

Victory and Tragedy in Europe

In the last months of 1944, massive air strikes finally reduced German war production. The new American P-51 escort fighter helped B-17 bombers overfly Germany in relative safety after mid-1944. Thousand-bomber raids on railroads and oil facilities began to cripple the German economy. The raids also forced

TABLE 28.1	MILITARY AND CIVILIAN DEATHS IN WORLD WAR II
Nation	**Victims (millions)**
USSR	18–20
China	10–20
Germany and Austria	6
Poland	5
Japan	2.7
Yugoslavia	1.7
Romania	0.7
France	0.6
Great Britain	0.5
Hungary	0.5
Italy	0.4
Czechoslovakia	0.4
United States	0.3

Germany to devote 2.5 million workers to air defense and damage repair. Politics rather than military need governed the final great action of the European air war. British and U.S. bombers in February 1945 staged a terror raid on the nonindustrial city of Dresden, packed with refugees, filled with great art, and undefended by the Germans; a firestorm fueled by incendiary bombs and rubble from blasted buildings killed tens of thousands of civilians without military justification.

Hitler struck a last blow on December 16, 1944. Stripping the Eastern Front of armored units, he launched twenty-five divisions against thinly held U.S. positions in the Ardennes Forest of Belgium. He hoped to split U.S. and British forces by capturing the Belgian port of Antwerp. Taking advantage of snow and fog that grounded Allied aircraft, the Germans drove a 50-mile bulge into U.S. lines. But the German thrust literally ran out of gas beyond the town of Bastogne. The **Battle of the Bulge** never seriously threatened the outcome of the war.

The Nazi empire collapsed in the spring of 1945. American and British divisions crossed the Rhine in March and enveloped Germany's industrial core. The Soviets drove through eastern Germany

Map 28-3   World War II in the Pacific, 1942–1945
The Allied strategy against Japan was to cut off Japan's southern conquests by retaking the central Pacific islands, the Philippines, and Burma and then to strike at the Japanese home islands. Submarine warfare and massive air attacks from November 1944 to August 1945 crippled Japan's capacity to wage war. The detonation of atomic bombs over Hiroshima and Nagasaki then forced surrender on August 15, 1945.

toward Berlin. On April 25, American and Red Army troops met on the Elbe River. Hitler committed suicide on April 30 in his concrete bunker deep under devastated Berlin, which surrendered to the Soviets on May 2. The Nazi state formally capitulated on May 8.

The defeat of Germany revealed appalling evidence of the evil at the heart of the Nazi ideology of racial superiority. The "final solution" to what Hitler thought of as the "Jewish problem" went far beyond slave labor. The elite SS, Hitler's personal

army within the Nazi party, in 1942 set out to eliminate all of Europe's Jews. The evidence of genocide—systematic racial murder—is irrefutable. At Auschwitz and Treblinka, the SS organized the extermination of up to 6 million Jews and 1 million Poles, Gypsies, and others who failed to fit the Nazi vision of the German master race. Prisoners arrived by forced marches and cattle trains. Those who were not worked or starved to death were herded into gas chambers and then incinerated in huge crematoriums. Soviet troops could scarcely believe what they

Hiroshima in the aftermath of the atomic bomb. The bomb, dropped first on Hiroshima, and a few days later on Nagasaki in August 1945, instantly destroyed much of both cities. Now one airplane with one bomb could wreak the kind of devastation massive fire bombing raids had inflicted on cities such as Hamburg, Dresden, and Tokyo, adding new terror to the idea of total war.

saw as they overran the death camps and freed the few survivors of what we now call the **Holocaust**.

The Pacific War

Washington divided responsibilities in the Pacific theater. General Douglas MacArthur, who never admitted a mistake, operated in the islands that stretched between Australia and the Philippines. Admiral Chester Nimitz commanded in the central Pacific. The Allies planned to isolate Japan from its southern conquests. The British moved from India to retake Burma. The Americans advanced along the islands of the southern Pacific to retake the Philippines. With Japan's army still tied down in China, the Americans then planned to bomb Japan into submission.

The Pacific campaigns of 1944, often called **island hopping**, were the American naval version of the *Blitzkrieg*. Planes from American carriers controlled the air, allowing the navy and land forces to isolate and capture the most strategically located Japanese-held islands while bypassing the rest (see Map 28-3, p. 529).

Racial hatred animated both sides in the Pacific war and fueled a "war without mercy." Americans often characterized Japanese soldiers as animals or vermin. In turn, the Japanese viewed Americans as racial mongrels and called them demons.

MacArthur used a version of the bypass strategy in the Solomon Islands and New Guinea, leapfrogging over Japanese strong points. The invasion of the Philippines repeated the approach by landing on Leyte, in the middle of the island chain. The Philippine campaign also destroyed the offensive capacity of the Japanese fleet. In the **Battle of Leyte Gulf**, the U.S. military sank four Japanese battleships, four carriers, and ten cruisers. The Japanese home islands were left with no defensive screen against an expected invasion.

During 1943 and 1944, submarines choked off food, oil, and raw materials bound for Japan and island bases. By 1945, imports to Japan were one-eighth of the 1940 level. Heavy bombing of Japan began in early 1944. A firebomb raid on Tokyo on the night of March 9, 1945, killed 124,000 people and left 1 million homeless. Overall, conventional bombing destroyed 42 percent of Japan's industrial capacity. By the time the United States captured the islands of Iwo Jima and Okinawa in fierce fighting (April–June 1945) and neared the Japanese home islands, Japan's position was hopeless.

Searching for Peace

At the beginning of 1945, the Allies sensed victory. Conferring from February 4 to 11 in the Ukrainian town of Yalta, Roosevelt, Stalin, and Churchill debated plans for the postwar world. The most important American goal was to enlist the USSR in finishing off the Pacific war. Americans hoped that a Soviet attack on Manchuria would tie down enough Japanese troops to reduce U.S. casualties in invading Japan. Stalin repeated his intent to declare war on Japan within three months of victory in Europe, in return for a free hand in Manchuria.

The most that Roosevelt could coax from Stalin were vague pledges to allow participation of non-Communists in coalition governments in eastern Europe. Stalin also agreed to join a new international organization, the **United Nations**.

Conservative critics later charged that the western powers "gave away" eastern Europe at the

SUMMARY

THE DECISION TO USE THE ATOMIC BOMB

Americans have long argued whether the use of atomic bombs on the Japanese cities of Hiroshima and Nagasaki was necessary to end the war. Several factors probably influenced President Truman's decision to use the new weapon.

Military necessity	Truman later argued that the use of atomic bombs was necessary to avoid an invasion of Japan that would have cost hundreds of thousand of lives. Military planners expected Japanese soldiers to put up the same kind of suicidal resistance in defense of the home islands as they had to American landings at the Philippines, Iwo Jima, and Okinawa. More recently, historians have argued that the Japanese military was near collapse and that an invasion would have met far less resistance than feared.
Atomic diplomacy	Some historians believe that Truman used atomic weapons to overawe the Soviet Union and induce it to move cautiously in expanding its influence in Europe and East Asia. Truman and his advisers were certainly aware of how the bomb might influence the Soviet leadership.
Domestic politics	President Roosevelt and his chief military advisers had spent billions on the secret atomic bomb project without the knowledge of Congress or the American public. The managers of the Manhattan Project may have believed that only proof of its military value would quiet critics and justify the huge cost.
Momentum of war	The United States and Britain had already adopted wholesale destruction of German and Japanese cities as a military tactic. Use of the atomic bomb looked like a variation on fire bombing, not the start of a new era of potential mass destruction. In this context, some historians argue, President Truman's choice was natural and expected.

Yalta Conference. In fact, the Soviet Union gained little that it did not already control. In East Asia as well, the Soviets could seize the territories that the agreements granted them.

On April 12, two months after Yalta, Roosevelt died of a cerebral hemorrhage. Harry Truman, the new president, was a shrewd politician, but his experience was limited; Roosevelt had not even told him about the Manhattan Project. Deeply distrustful of the Soviets, Truman first ventured into personal international diplomacy in July 1945 at a British-Soviet-American conference at Potsdam, near Berlin. Most of the sessions debated the future of Germany. The leaders endorsed the expulsion of ethnic Germans from eastern Europe and moved the borders of Poland 100 miles west into historically German territory. Truman also made it clear that the United States expected to dominate the occupation of Japan. Its goal was to democratize the Japanese political system and reintroduce Japan into the international community—a policy that succeeded. The **Potsdam Declaration** on July 26 summarized U.S. policy and gave Japan an opening for surrender. However, the declaration failed to guarantee that Emperor Hirohito would not be tried as a war criminal. The Japanese response was so cautious that Americans read it as rejection.

Secretary of State James Byrnes now urged Truman to use the new atomic bomb, tested just weeks earlier. Japan's ferocious defense of Okinawa had confirmed American fears that the Japanese would fight to the death. In contrast, the bomb offered a quick end to the conflict, and it might intimidate Stalin (see the summary table "The Decision to Use the Atomic Bomb").

In early August, the United States dropped two of three available nuclear bombs on Japan. On August 6 at Hiroshima the first bomb killed at least eighty thousand people and poisoned thousands more with radiation. A second bomb three days later at Nagasaki took another forty thousand lives. Japan ceased hostilities on August 14 and surrendered formally on September 2. The world has wondered ever since if the United States might have defeated Japan without resorting to atomic bombs. In the summer of 1945, however, Truman never seriously considered the alternatives.

Conclusion

World War II made and unmade families. It gave millions of women new responsibilities and then sent them back to the kitchen. It put money in pockets that had been emptied by the Great Depression and turned struggling business owners into tycoons.

Most of the 16 million men and women in uniform served in support jobs that keep the war machine going.

World War II adventure movies in which Americans always win leave the impression that triumph was necessary, inevitable, and not terribly dirty or gruesome. In fact, victory was the hard-fought result of public leadership and military effort. Under other leadership, for example, the United States might have stood aside until it was too late to reverse the Axis conquest of Europe and East Asia.

The war unified the nation in new ways while confirming old divisions. People of all backgrounds shared a common cause.

But nothing broke the barriers that separated white and black Americans. Unequal treatment in a war for democracy outraged black soldiers, who returned to fight for civil rights. The uprooting of Japanese-Americans was another reminder of racial prejudice.

The lessons of World War II influenced the thinking of presidents from Eisenhower in the 1950s to Bush in the 1990s. Even though the United States ended 1945 with the world's mightiest navy, biggest air force, and only atomic bomb, the instability that had followed World War I made Western leaders nervous about the shape of world politics.

One result in the postwar era was conflict between the United States and the Soviet Union, which became the Cold War. At home, international tensions fed pressure for social and political conformity. Fifteen years of economic depression and sacrifice made the postwar generation sensitive to perceived threats to steady jobs and stable families. For the next generation, the unresolved business of World War II would haunt American life.

Review Questions

1. What motivated German, Italian, and Japanese aggression in the 1930s? How did Great Britain, the USSR, and other nations respond to the growing conflict?

2. What arguments did Americans make against involvement in the war in Europe? Why did President Roosevelt and many others believe it necessary to block German and Japanese expansion? What steps did Roosevelt take to increase U.S. involvement short of war?

3. What was the military balance in early 1942? What were the chief threats to the United States and its allies? Why did the fortunes of war turn in late 1942?

4. Assess how mobilization for World War II altered life in the United States. How did the war affect families? How did it shift the regional balance of the economy? What opportunities did it open for women?

5. Did World War II help or hinder progress toward racial equality in the United States? How did the experiences of Japanese-Americans, African-Americans, and Mexican-Americans challenge American ideals?

6. What factors were decisive in the defeat of Germany? How important were Soviet efforts on the Eastern Front, the bomber war, and the British-American landings in France?

7. What was the U.S. strategy against Japan, and how well did it work? What lay behind President Truman's decision to use atomic bombs against Japanese cities?

Recommended Reading

John Hersey, *Hiroshima* (1946). Hersey recounts the atomic bombing through the eyes of victims and survivors.

John Keegan, *The Second World War* (1990). This comprehensive and readable account gives a strong sense of the relative importance of the various fronts.

William L. O'Neill, *A Democracy at War: America's Fight at Home and Abroad in World War II* (1993). This insightful summary explores the choices that the United States made in mobilizing and conducting the war.

Martin J. Sherwin, *A World Destroyed: The Atomic Bomb and the Grand Alliance* (1975). Sherwin explains why American leaders never seriously considered alternatives to the atomic bomb.

Studs Terkel, *The Good War: An Oral History of World War II* (1984). Terkel has compiled eloquent testimony about the effects of the war on both ordinary and extraordinary Americans.

Where to Learn More

❖ **USS *Arizona* Memorial and Submarine Memorial Park, Pearl Harbor, Hawaii.** The memorial commemorates the men who died in the Japanese attack of December 7, 1941, and recounts the events of the day.

❖ **Air Force Museum, Dayton, Ohio.** Visitors can walk among World War II fighter planes and bombers including the B-29 that dropped the atomic bomb on Nagasaki, and learn about the role of aviation in the war.

❖ **Japanese-American Historical Plaza, Portland, Oregon.** The plaza uses landscaping and *haiku* (Japanese-style poems) to convey the meaning of internment for Japanese-Americans.

❖ **Los Alamos County Historical Museum** and **Bradbury Science Museum, Los Alamos, New Mexico.** The museum traces the origins of atomic energy for military and civilian uses. Nearby is the Los Alamos County Historical Museum, which gives the feel of everyday life in the atomic town.

❖ **United States Holocaust Memorial Museum, Washington, D.C.** The Holocaust Museum gives visitors a deeply moving depiction of the deadly impacts of Nazi ideas in the 1930s and 1940s.

29 THE COLD WAR AT HOME AND ABROAD, 1946–1952

KEY TOPICS

❖ Shortages and the massive exit of women from the work force at the end of World War II
❖ The beginning of a twenty-five-year economic boom
❖ The beginning of the postwar civil rights movement
❖ The origins of the Cold War
❖ The reelection of Harry Truman and the desire to maintain the gains of the New Deal while avoiding new activist initiatives
❖ The Korean War and the nuclear arms race
❖ McCarthyism and the Second Red Scare

In 1947, *The Best Years of Our Lives* won seven Oscars, including best picture, best director, and best actor. The immensely popular movie follows three veterans as they try to readjust to civilian life. The plot cuts between the personal problems of reconnecting with wives and sweethearts and the social challenge of finding meaningful work.

The film reminded audiences of their own difficulties with postwar inflation, shortages, and strikes and their fears of another economic depression. The end, however, is upbeat. One of the veterans relives the nightmare of bombing runs over Germany but ends up with a job recycling the planes into building materials for new houses. He will now be able to marry his girlfriend and grab a share of the American dream.

Most Americans in 1946 defined American ideals in terms of economic opportunity and the chance to finally enjoy national prosperity after years of sacrifice. Even President Truman replaced the model gun on his White House desk with a model plow.

Americans watched as congressional conservatives and President Truman fought over the fate of New Deal programs. More worrisome was the confrontation with the Soviet Union that was soon being called the **Cold War**. Triggered by the Soviet Union's imposition of Communist regimes throughout eastern Europe, the Cold War grew into a global contest in which the United States tried to counter Soviet influence around the world. By the time real war broke out in Korea in 1950, many Americans were venting their frustration by blaming international setbacks on internal subversion.

The Cold War began in the late 1940s, but it would shape the United States and the world for another generation. Massive rearmament allowed U.S. presidents to act as international policemen in the name of democratic values—a vast change from earlier American foreign relations. Defense spending also reshaped American industry and helped stimulate twenty-five years of economic growth. The Cold War narrowed the range of political discussion, making many of the left-wing ideas of the 1930s taboo by the 1950s.

Launching the Great Boom

When World War II ended, Americans feared that demobilization would bring a rerun of the inflation and unemployment that had followed World War I. In the first eighteen months of peace, rising prices, labor-management strife, and shortages of everything from meat to automobiles confirmed their anxiety. In 1947 and 1948, however, an economic expansion began that lasted for a quarter century. That prosperity would finance a military buildup and an activist foreign policy.

Reconversion Chaos

Japan's sudden surrender took U.S. officials by surprise. They had planned on taking two years to phase out military spending and reintroduce veterans to the domestic economy. Now their plans were obsolete. The Pentagon, already scaling back defense spending, canceled $15 billion in war contracts in the first forty-eight hours after the victory over Japan. Public pressure demanded that the military release the nation's 12 million servicemen and servicewomen as rapidly as possible. GIs in Europe and the South Pacific waited impatiently for their discharge determined by length of time in uniform, service overseas, combat decorations, and number of children.

Veterans came home to shortages of both food in the grocery stores and consumer goods in the department stores. Automobiles were especially

scarce; the number of vehicles registered in the United States had declined by 4 million during the war. For the privilege of spending a few hundred dollars on a junker, consumers sometimes had to pay used-car dealers for so-called accessories like $150 batteries and $100 lap robes.

Inflation squeezed unionized factory workers, who had accepted wage controls during the war effort. Since 1941, prices had risen twice as fast as base wages. In the fall of 1945, more and more workers went on strike to redress the balance. By January 1946, some 1.3 million auto, steel, electrical, and packinghouse workers were off the job. Strikes in these basic industries shut other factories down for lack of supplies. Presidential committees finally crafted settlements that allowed steel and auto workers to make up ground lost during the war, but they also allowed corporations to pass on higher costs to consumers. One Republican senator complained of "unionists who fatten themselves at the expense of the rest of us." Bill Nation, who inspected window moldings at GM's Fisher Body plant in Detroit, wondered who the senator was talking about. The strike gave him an hourly raise of 18 cents, pushing his weekly income to $59. After paying for food, housing, and utilities, that left $13.44 for Bill, his wife, and their five children to spend on clothes, comic books, and doctor bills.

Economic Policy

The **Employment Act of 1946** and the **Taft-Hartley Act** of 1947 represented contradictory liberal and conservative approaches to the peacetime economy.

The Employment Act was an effort by congressional liberals to ward off economic crisis by fine-tuning government taxation and spending. It started as a proposal to ensure everyone's "right to a useful and remunerative job." Watered down in the face of business opposition, it still defined economic growth and high employment as national goals to be fostered by the federal government. It also established the **Council of Economic Advisers** to assist the president.

In fact, more than 2 million women provided some slack by leaving the labor force outright, so that unemployment rates were far lower than economists had predicted. Federal agencies hastened their departure by publishing pamphlets asking *men* the pointed question, "Do you want your wife to work after the war?" In addition, consumer spending from a savings pool of $140 billion in bank accounts and war bonds created a huge demand for workers to fill. Total employment rose rather than fell with the end of the war.

CHRONOLOGY

1944 Servicemen's Readjustment Act (GI Bill) is passed.

1945 United Nations is established.

1946 Employment Act creates Council of Economic Advisers.

George Kennan sends his "long telegram."

Winston Churchill delivers his "iron curtain" speech.

1947 Truman Doctrine is announced.

Truman establishes a federal employee loyalty program.

Kennan explains containment policy in an anonymous article in *Foreign Affairs*.

Marshall Plan begins providing economic aid to Europe.

HUAC holds hearings in Hollywood.

Taft-Hartley Act rolls back gains of organized labor.

National Security Act creates the National Security Council and the Central Intelligence Agency.

1948 Communists stage coup in Czechoslovakia.

Berlin airlift overcomes Soviet blockade.

Truman orders desegregation of the armed forces.

Selective Service is reestablished.

Truman wins reelection.

1949 North Atlantic Treaty Organization is formed.

Communist Chinese defeat Nationalists.

Soviet Union tests an atomic bomb.

Department of Defense is established.

1950 Senator McCarthy begins his Red hunt.

Alger Hiss is convicted of perjury.

NSC-68 is drafted and accepted as U.S. policy.

Korean War begins.

1951 Senate Internal Security Subcommittee begins hearings.

Truman relieves MacArthur of his command.

Julius and Ethel Rosenberg are convicted of conspiring to commit espionage.

Truce talks begin in Korea.

1952 United States tests the hydrogen bomb.

Eisenhower is elected president.

From the other end of the political spectrum, the Taft-Hartley Act climaxed a ten-year effort by conservatives to reverse the gains made by organized labor in the 1930s. The act passed in 1947 because of anger about continuing strikes. For many Americans, the chief culprit was John L. Lewis, head of the United Mine Workers. The burly, bushy-browed, and combative Lewis was instantly recognizable—loved by his workers and hated by nearly everyone else. In April 1946, a forty-day coal strike cut into industrial production. The coal settlement was only days old when the nation faced an even more crippling walkout by railroad workers. Many middle-class Americans were convinced that organized labor needed to be curbed.

In November 1946, Republicans capitalized on the problems of reconversion chaos, labor unrest, and dissatisfaction with Truman. Their election slogan was simple: "Had enough?" The GOP won control of Congress for the first time since the election of 1928.

Adopted by the now firmly conservative Congress, the Taft-Hartley Act was a serious counterattack by big business on the power of large unions. It barred the closed shop (the requirement that all workers hired in a particular company or plant be union members) and blocked secondary boycotts (strikes against suppliers or customers of a targeted business). The federal government could postpone a strike by imposing a "cooling-off period," which gave companies time to stockpile their output. Officers of national unions had to swear they were not Communists or Communist sympathizers, even though corporate executives had no similar obligation. The bill passed over Truman's veto.

The GI Bill

Another landmark law for the postwar era passed Congress without controversy. Popularly known as the **GI Bill of Rights**, the Servicemen's Readjustment Act of 1944 was designed to ease veterans back into the civilian mainstream. Rather than pay cash bonuses to veterans, as after previous wars, Congress tied benefits to specific public goals. The GI Bill guaranteed loans for buying a house or farm or starting a business. The program encouraged veterans to attend college with money for tuition and books plus monthly stipends.

The GI Bill made college degrees accessible to men with working-class backgrounds. In the peak year of 1947, veterans made up half of all college students. "We're all trying to get where we would have been if there hadn't been a war," one vet attending Indiana University told *Time* magazine. Veterans helped convert the college degree—once available primarily to the socially privileged—into a basic business and professional credential.

An unfortunate side effect of the GI tide was to crowd women out of classrooms, although sixty thousand servicewomen did take advantage of educational benefits. Women's share of bachelor's degrees dropped from 40 percent in 1940 to 25 percent in 1950. Them most common female presence on many campuses was working wives trying to make up the gap between Veterans Administration (VA) checks and the expenses of new families.

Assembly-Line Neighborhoods

Americans faced a housing shortage after the war. College students were crowded into tiny apartments or found space in flimsy housing projects left over from the war. And in 1947, fully 3 million married couples were unable to set up their own household. Most doubled up with relatives while they waited for the construction industry to respond. Hunger for housing was fierce. Eager buyers lined up for hours and paid admission fees to tour model homes or to put their names in drawings for the opportunity to buy.

The solution started with the federal government and its VA mortgage program. By guaranteeing repayment, the VA allowed veterans to get home purchase loans from private lenders without a down payment. Eyeing the mass market created by the federal programs, William Levitt, a New York builder who had developed defense housing projects, built two thousand rental houses for veterans on suburban Long Island in 1947. His basic house had 800 square feet of living space in two bedrooms, living room, kitchen, bath, and unfinished attic waiting for the weekend handyman. It gave new families a place to start. There were six thousand **Levittown** houses by the end of 1948 and more than seventeen thousand by 1951.

Other successful builders bought hundreds of acres of land, put in utilities for the entire tract, purchased materials by the carload, and kept specialized workers busy on scores of identical houses. Floor plans were square, simple, and easy for semi-skilled workers to construct. For the first time, kitchens across America were designed for pre-assembled cabinets and appliances in standard sizes. "On-site fabrication" was mass production without an assembly line. Work crews at the Los Angeles suburb of Lakewood started a hundred houses a day as they moved down one side of the street and back up the other.

From 1946 through 1950, the federal government backed $20 billion in VA and New Deal era Federal Housing Administration (FHA) loans, approximately 40 percent of all home mortgage debt. Housing starts neared 2 million in the peak year of 1950. By the end of the 1940s, 55 percent of American households owned their homes. The suburban population grew much faster than the population of central cities, and the population outside the growing reach of metropolitan areas actually declined.

Unfortunately, the suburban solution to housing shortages also had costs. Vast new housing tracts tended to isolate women and children and did little to help African-Americans. Discrimination excluded black workers and their families from new housing. Federal housing agencies and private industry worsened the problem by **redlining** older neighborhoods, which involved withholding home purchase loans and insurance coverage from inner-city areas.

Public and private actions kept blacks in deteriorating inner-city ghettos. When severe flooding in 1948 drove thousands of African-Americans from wartime temporary housing in Portland, Oregon, for example, their only choice was to crowd into the city's small black neighborhood. Chicago landlords squeezed an estimated 27,000 black migrants per year into run-down buildings, subdividing larger apartments into one-room "kitchenette" units with sinks and hot plates but no private bathrooms. Families that tried to find new homes in white neighborhoods on the edge of black ghettos often met violence—rocks through windows, fire bombs, milling mobs of angry whites.

Steps toward Civil Rights

A new generation of black leaders began working to reduce the gap between America's ideal of equality and its performance. At the same time, a wave of lynchings and racist violence surged across the South after the war; special targets were black veterans who tried to register to vote. However, many whites felt uneasy about the contradiction between a crusade for freedom abroad and racial discrimination at home.

Caught between pressure from black leaders and the fear of alienating Southern Democrats, President Truman in 1946 appointed the Committee on

Civil Rights, whose report developed an agenda for racial justice that would take two decades to put into effect. The Justice Department began to support anti-segregation lawsuits filed by the NAACP.

The president also ordered "equality of treatment and opportunity" in the armed services in July 1948. The army in particular dragged its feet, hoping to limit blacks to 10 percent of enlistees. Manpower needs and the fighting record of integrated units in Korea from 1950 to 1953 persuaded the reluctant generals. Over the next generation, African-Americans would find the military an important avenue for career opportunities.

More Americans were interested in the lowering of racial barriers in professional team sports. Individual black champions already included heavyweight boxer Joe Louis and sprinter Jesse Owens. Jack Roosevelt (Jackie) Robinson, a proud and gifted African-American athlete, opened the 1947 baseball season as a member of the Brooklyn Dodgers. Robinson was the first African-American to play for the modern major leagues. In the segregated society of the 1940s, Robinson also found himself a powerful symbol of racial change.

Consumer Boom and Baby Boom

Americans celebrated the end of the war with weddings; the marriage rate in 1946 surpassed even its wartime high. By 1950, the median age at which women married would be just over 20 years—lower than at any previous time in the twentieth century. The United States ended the 1940s with 7 million more married couples than at the decade's start.

New marriages jump-started the "baby boom," as did already married couples who decided to catch up after postponing childbearing during the war. In the early 1940s, an average of 2.9 million children per year were born in the United States; in 1946–1950, the average was 3.6 million. Those 3.5 million "extra" babies needed diapers, swing sets, lunch boxes, bicycles, and school rooms. Fast-growing families also needed to stock up on household goods. Out of an average household income of roughly $4,000 in 1946 and 1947, a family of four had $300 to $400 a year for the furnishings and appliances that manufacturers were beginning to produce in growing volume.

From new radios to new homes to new jobs, the economic gains of the postwar years propelled Americans toward the political center. After fifteen years of economic crisis and world war, they wanted to enjoy prosperity. They wanted to keep the gains of the New Deal—but without risking new experiments. William Levitt tried to humorously capture the American satisfaction with the fruits of free enterprise when

he said in 1948 that "no man who owns his house and lot can be a Communist; he has too much to do."

Confronting the Soviet Union

In 1945, the United States and the Soviet Union were allies, victorious against Germany and planning the defeat of Japan. By 1947, they were engaged in a diplomatic and economic confrontation and soon came close to war over the city of Berlin.

Over the next forty years, the United States and the USSR contested for economic, political, and military influence around the globe in a Cold War. The heart of Soviet policy was control of eastern Europe as a buffer zone against Germany and as an economic colony. The centerpiece of American policy was to link the United States, western Europe, and Japan into an alliance of overwhelming economic power. Both sides spent vast sums on conventional military forces and atomic weapons that held the world in a balance of terror. They also competed for political advantage in Asia and Africa as newly independent nations replaced European colonial empires.

Americans and Soviets frequently interpreted each other's actions in the most threatening terms, turning miscalculations and misunderstandings into crises. At home, a U.S. public that had suffered through nearly two decades of economic depression and war reacted to international problems with frustration and anger.

The End of the Grand Alliance

The Yalta Conference of February 1945 had recognized military realities by marking out rough spheres of influence. The Soviet defeat of Germany on the Eastern Front had made the USSR the only military power in eastern Europe. The American and British attacks through Italy and France had made the Western allies dominant in western Europe and the Mediterranean. The Soviets, Americans, British, and French shared control of defeated Germany, each with its own occupation zone of the country and its own sector of Berlin. The Western allies had the better of the bargain. Defeated Italy and Japan, whose reconstruction was firmly in Western hands, had far greater economic potential than Soviet-controlled Bulgaria, Romania, or Hungary.

The victorious powers argued bitterly about Germany and eastern Europe. For Poland, Truman and his advisers claimed that Yalta had assumed open elections on the American model. The Soviet Union saw Poland as the historic invasion route from the west; it claimed that Yalta had ensured that any Polish government would be friendly to Soviet interests and acted to guarantee that this would be so.

The United States tried to involve the USSR and eastern Europe in new international organizations, such as the United Nations (UN). The Washington-based **International Monetary Fund (IMF)** and the **World Bank** were designed to revive international trade. The IMF stabilized national currencies against the short-term pressures of international trade. The World Bank drew on the resources of member nations to make economic development loans to governments for such projects as new dams or agricultural modernization. These organizations ensured that a reviving world economy would revolve around the industrial and technological power of the United States.

In 1946, the United States also presented a plan in the United Nations to control atomic energy. Bernard Baruch suggested that an international agency should oversee all uranium production and research on atomic explosives. But this plan was unacceptable to the Soviets, who did not want to open their atomic energy program to outside control or inspection. On-site inspection and verification would remain problems in arms control negotiations for the next half-century.

American leaders were also becoming convinced of Soviet aggressiveness. In February 1946, George Kennan, a senior American diplomat in Moscow, sent a "long telegram" to the State Department. In eight thousand words he depicted a USSR driven by expansionist Communist ideology. The Soviets, he argued, would constantly probe for weaknesses in the capitalist world. The best response was firm resistance to protect the western heartlands.

Lacking the strength to shape Europe on its own, Great Britain repeatedly nudged the United States into blocking Soviet influence. Speaking at Westminster College in Missouri in March 1946, Winston Churchill warned that the USSR had dropped an "iron curtain" across the middle of Europe and urged a firm Western response.

Truman's foreign policy advisers shared the belief in an aggressive Soviet Union. Administration leaders did not fear an immediate Soviet military threat to the United States itself, for they knew that World War II had exhausted the USSR. But they also knew that the Soviets were strong enough to brush aside the U.S. occupation forces in Germany. Added to military apprehension were worries about political and economic competition. Communist parties in war-ravaged Europe and Japan were exploiting discontent. In Asia and Africa, the allegiance of nationalists who were fighting for independence from France, Great Britain, and the Netherlands remained in doubt. America's leaders worried that much of the Eastern Hemisphere might fall under Soviet control and turn its back on North America.

Truman and the "wise men" who made up his foreign policy circle ignored examples of Soviet caution and conciliation. The Soviets withdrew troops from Manchuria in northern China and acquiesced in America's control of defeated Japan. They allowed a democratic government in Finland and technically free elections in Hungary and Czechoslovakia (although it was clear that Communists would do well there). They demobilized much of their huge army and reduced their forces in eastern Europe.

However, the Soviet regime also did more than enough to justify American fears. The USSR pressured Turkey to give it partial control of the exit from the Black Sea. It retained troops in northern Iran until warned out by the United States. The Soviets were ruthless in support of Communist control in Bulgaria, Romania, and Poland. U.S. policymakers read these Soviet actions as a rerun of Nazi aggression and determined not to let a new totalitarian threat undermine Western power.

The Truman Doctrine and the Marshall Plan

Early in 1947, Truman and his advisers decided on decisive action. The British could no longer afford to back the Greek government that was fighting Communist rebels, and U.S. officials feared that a Communist takeover in Greece would threaten the stability of Italy, France, and the Middle East. On March 12, he told Congress that the United States faced a "fateful hour." Taking the advice of Senator Arthur Vandenberg to "scare the hell out of the country," he said that only the appropriation of $400 million to fight Communism in Greece and Turkey could secure the free world. Congress agreed, and the United States became the dominant power in the eastern Mediterranean.

In a sweeping declaration that became known as the **Truman Doctrine**, the president pledged that "It must be the policy of the United States to support free peoples who are resisting attempted subjugation by armed minorities or by outside pressures. . . . I believe that our help should be primarily through economic and financial aid, which is essential to economic stability and orderly political processes."

Meanwhile, Europe was sliding toward chaos. Germany was close to famine after the bitter winter of 1946–1947. Western European nations were bankrupt and unable to import raw materials for their factories. Overstressed medical systems could no longer control diseases such as tuberculosis. Communist parties had gained in Italy, France, and Germany.

Secretary of State George C. Marshall announced the European Recovery Plan on June 5, 1947. What the press quickly dubbed the **Marshall Plan** committed the United States to help rebuild Europe. The United States invited Soviet and eastern European participation, but the Soviets refused, instead organizing their eastern European satellites in their own association for Mutual Economic Assistance, or **Comecon**, in 1949. In western Europe, the aid from the Marshall Plan totaled $13.5 billion over four years. It met many of Europe's economic needs and quieted class conflict. Because Europeans spent much of the aid on U.S. goods and machinery and because economic recovery promised markets for U.S. products, business and labor both supported it. In effect, the Marshall Plan created an "empire by invitation" in which America oversaw European recovery.

U.S. policy in Japan followed the pattern set in Europe. As supreme commander of the Allied Powers, General Douglas MacArthur acted as Japan's postwar dictator. He tried to change the values of the old war-prone Japan through social reform, democratization, and demilitarization. At the end of 1947, however, policymakers were fearful of economic collapse and political chaos, just as in Europe. The "reverse course" in occupation policy aimed to make Japan an economic magnet for other nations in East Asia, pulling them toward the American orbit and away from the Soviet Union. MacArthur reluctantly accepted the new policy of "economic crank-up" by preserving Japan's corporate giants and encouraging American investment. At American insistence, the new Japan accepted American bases and created its own "self-defense force" (with no capacity for overseas aggression).

George Kennan summed up the new American policies in the magazine *Foreign Affairs* in July 1947. Writing anonymously as "X," Kennan warned that the emerging Cold War would be a long conflict with no quick fixes.

Soviet Reactions

The bold American moves in the first half of 1947 put the USSR on the defensive. East of the iron curtain, Hungarian Communists expelled non-Communists from a coalition government. Bulgarian Communists shot opposition leaders. Romania, Bulgaria, and Hungary signed defense pacts with the Soviet Union.

In early 1948, the Soviets targeted Czechoslovakia. For three years, a neutral coalition govern-

Berlin in 1948 was still a devastated city of gutted buildings and heaps of rubble. When the Soviet Union shut off ground access to Berlin's British, French, and American occupation zones, the city also became a symbol of the West's Cold War resolve. Allied aircraft lifted in food, fuel, and other essentials for West Berliners for nearly a year until the Soviets ended the blockade.

ment there based on the model of Finland had balanced trade with the West with a foreign policy friendly to the USSR. In February 1948, while Russian forces assembled on the Czech borders, local communists pushed aside Czechoslovakia's democratic leadership and turned the nation into a dictatorship and Soviet satellite within a week.

The climax of the Soviet reaction came on June 24, 1948, when Soviet troops blockaded surface traffic into Berlin, cutting off the U.S., British, and French sectors. The immediate Soviet aim was to block Western plans to merge their three occupation zones into an independent federal republic (West Germany). Rather than abandon 2.5 million Berliners or shoot their way through, the Western nations responded to the **Berlin blockade** by airlifting supplies to the city. Planes landed every two minutes at Berlin's Tempelhof Airport. Stalin decided not to intercept the flights. After eleven months, the Soviets abandoned the blockade, making the Berlin airlift a triumph of American resolve.

American Rearmament

The coup in Czechoslovakia and the Berlin blockade shocked American leaders. Congress responded in 1948 by reinstating the military draft and increasing defense spending by 30 percent.

The United States had already begun to modernize and centralize its national security apparatus. The National Security Act of July 1947 created the **Central Intelligence Agency (CIA)** and the **National Security Council (NSC)**. The CIA handled intelligence gathering and covert operations. The NSC assembled top diplomatic and military advisers in one committee. In 1949, legislation also created the Department of Defense to oversee the army, navy, and air force (independent from the army since 1947).

In April 1949, ten European nations, the United States, and Canada signed the North Atlantic Treaty as a mutual defense pact. American commitments to the **North Atlantic Treaty Organization (NATO)** included military aid and the deployment of U.S. troops in western Europe. As Republican Senator Robert Taft warned in the ratification debate, NATO was the sort of "entangling alliance" that the United States had avoided for 160 years. It was also the insurance policy that western Europeans required if they were to accept the dangers as well as the benefits of a revived Germany, which was economically and militarily necessary for a strong Europe.

Two years later, the United States signed similar but less comprehensive agreements in the western Pacific: the ANZUS Pact with Australia and New Zealand and a new treaty with the Philippines. The alliances reassured Pacific allies who were nervously watching the United States negotiate a unilateral peace treaty with Japan (ignoring the Soviet Union). Taken together, peacetime rearmament and mutual defense pacts amounted to a revolution in American foreign policy.

Truman, Republicans, and the Fair Deal

Harry Truman's vigorous response to the USSR in 1947 and 1948 went hand in hand with his efforts to preserve and extend the New Deal. In the short term, they were more successful with foreign policy, creating a bi-partisan coalition to block Soviet influence in western Europe. In the longer term, they defended the core of the New Deal's social and economic agenda.

This political package is known as the strategy of the "vital center," after the title of a 1949 book by Arthur Schlesinger Jr. The book linked anti-Communism in foreign policy with efforts to enact inclusive social and economic policies—to extend freedom abroad and at home at the same time. The vital center reflected the political reality of the Cold War years, when Democrats had to prove that they were tough on Communism before they could enact domestic reforms.

Truman's Opposition

In his campaign for a full term as president in 1948, Truman faced not only the Republicans but also new fringe parties on the far right and far left that allowed him to position himself in the moderate center. The blunt, no-nonsense Missourian entered the campaign an underdog; he soon looked like the country's best option for steering a steady course.

Truman's formal opponents represented the American Progressive party (an amalgam of left-leaning political groups), the **Dixiecrats** (officially the States' Rights Democrats), and the Republicans. The president also ran against the Republican-controlled "do-nothing 80th Congress," which he used as a punching bag at every opportunity.

Progressive candidate Henry Wallace cast himself as the prophet for "the century of the common man." His background as a plant geneticist and farm journalist prepared him to deal with domestic policy but not world affairs. After Truman fired him from the cabinet in 1946 for advocating a conciliatory stance toward the Soviets, Wallace went to Europe to praise the USSR and denounced U.S. foreign policy. On his return, most liberal Democrats ran the other way when Wallace organized the Progressive party, leaving the Communist party to supply many of his campaign workers.

Wallace argued that the United States was forcing the Cold War on the Soviet Union and undermining American ideals by diverting attention from poverty and racism at home. He wanted to repeal the draft and destroy atomic weapons. His arguments had merit, for the United States was becoming a militarized society, but Wallace was the wrong person to change American minds. With his shy personality, disheveled appearance, and fanaticism about health food, he struck most voters as a kook rather than a statesman.

At the other political extreme were the Southerners who walked out when the 1948 Democratic National Convention called for full civil rights for African-Americans. Mayor Hubert Humphrey of Minneapolis challenged the Democratic party "to get out of the shadow of states' rights and walk forthrightly into the bright sunshine of human rights."

When the angry Southerners met to nominate their own candidate, however, the South's important politicians stayed away. Major southern newspapers called the revolt futile and narrow-minded.

Tom Dewey, Truman's strongest opponent, had been an effective governor of New York and represented the moderate eastern establishment within the Republican party. Fortunately for Truman, Dewey lacked the common touch. Smooth on the outside, he alienated people who should have been his closest supporters. He was an arrogant campaigner, refusing to interrupt his morning schedule to talk to voters. He acted like a snob and dressed like the groom on a wedding cake.

Dewey was also saddled with the results of the 80th Congress (1947–1948). Truman used confrontation with Congress to rally voters who had supported the New Deal. Vote for me, Truman argued, to protect the New Deal, or vote Republican to bring back the days of Herbert Hoover. After his nomination in July 1948, Truman called Congress back into session and dared Republicans to enact all the measures for which *their* party claimed to stand. Congress did nothing, and Truman had more proof that the Republicans were all talk and no show.

Whistle-Stopping across America

In the 1948 presidential campaign, a major candidate crisscrossed the nation by rail for the last time and made hundreds of speeches from the rear platforms of trains. For the first time, national television broadcast the two party conventions. The Republican campaign issued a printed T-shirt that read "Dew-It With Dewey"—the earliest advertising T-shirt in the collections of the Smithsonian Institution.

Truman was a widely read and intelligent man who cultivated the image of a backslapper. "I'll mow 'em down . . . and I'll give 'em hell," he told his vice presidential running mate, Senator Alben Barkley of Kentucky. Crowds across the country greeted him with "Give 'em hell, Harry!" He covered 31,700 miles in his campaign train and gave ten speeches a day.

On the advice of political strategist Clark Clifford, Truman tied Dewey to inflation, housing shortages, and fears about the future of Social Security. In industrial cities, he hammered at the Taft-Hartley Act. In the West, he pointed out that Democratic administrations had built dams and helped turn natural resources into jobs. He called the Republicans the party of privilege and arrogance. The Democrats, he said, offered opportunity for farmers, factory workers, and small business owners.

Truman got a huge boost from Dewey's unwillingness to fight. Going into the fall with a huge

lead in the public opinion polls, Dewey neither countered Truman's attacks nor conveyed his own vision of the national future. He packed his speeches with platitudes: "Our streams abound with fish." "You know that your future is still ahead of you." "Peace is a blessing that we all share." The results astounded the poll takers, who had stopped sampling opinion in mid-October—just as a swing to Truman gathered strength. Wallace and Thurmond each took just under 1.2 million votes. Dewey received nearly 22 million popular votes and 189 electoral votes, but Truman won more than 24 million popular votes and 303 electoral votes (see Map 29-1).

Truman's Fair Deal

Truman hoped to build on the gains of the New Deal. In his State of the Union address in January 1949, he called for a **Fair Deal** for all Americans. He promised to extend the New Deal and ensure "greater economic opportunity for the mass of the people."

Map 29-1   The Election of 1948

Harry Truman won a narrow victory in the presidential election of 1948 by holding many of the traditionally Democratic states of the South and West and winning key industrial states in the Middle West. His success depended on the coalition of rural and urban interests that Franklin Roosevelt had pulled together in the 1930s.

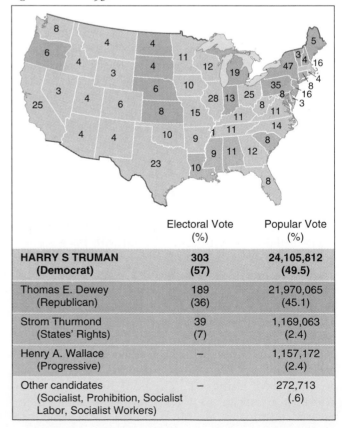

	Electoral Vote (%)	Popular Vote (%)
HARRY S TRUMAN (Democrat)	**303 (57)**	**24,105,812 (49.5)**
Thomas E. Dewey (Republican)	189 (36)	21,970,065 (45.1)
Strom Thurmond (States' Rights)	39 (7)	1,169,063 (2.4)
Henry A. Wallace (Progressive)	–	1,157,172 (2.4)
Other candidates (Socialist, Prohibition, Socialist Labor, Socialist Workers)	–	272,713 (.6)

In the Housing Act of 1949, the federal government reaffirmed its concern about families who had been priced out of the private market. Passed with the backing of conservative Senator Robert Taft—"Mr. Republican" to his admirers—the act provided money for local housing agencies to buy, level, and resell land for housing. The intent was to level slums and replace them with affordable modern apartments. The program never worked as intended because of scanty appropriations and poor design of the replacement housing, but it established the goal of decent housing for all Americans.

In 1950, Congress revitalized the weak Social Security program. Benefits went up by an average of 80 percent, and 10.5 million additional people received old-age and survivors' insurance. Most of the new coverage went to rural and small-town people.

Congress rejected other Fair Deal proposals that would remain on the national agenda for decades. A plan to alter the farm subsidy system to favor small farmers rather than agribusiness went nowhere. A Senate filibuster killed a permanent Fair Employment Practices Commission to fight racial discrimination in hiring. The medical establishment blocked a proposal for national health insurance as "socialistic." The overall message from Truman's second term was clear: Americans liked what the New Deal had given them but were hesitant about new initiatives.

Cold War and Hot War

The first phase of the Cold War reached a crisis in the autumn of 1949. The two previous years had seen an uneasy equilibrium in which American success in southern and western Europe and the standoff over Berlin (the blockade and airlift ended in May 1949) balanced the consolidation of Soviet power in eastern Europe. Now, suddenly, two key events seemed to tilt the world balance against the United States and its allies. In September, Truman announced that the Soviet Union had tested its own atomic bomb. A month later, the Chinese Communists under Mao Zedong (Mao Tse-tung) took power in China. The following summer, civil war in Korea sucked the United States into a fierce war with communist North Korea and China. The United States government accelerated a forty-year arms race with the Soviet Union.

The Nuclear Shadow

Experts in Washington had known that the Soviets were working on an A-bomb, but the news shocked the average citizen. In 1946, advocates of civilian control had won a small victory when Congress shifted control of atomic energy from the Manhattan Project to the new **Atomic Energy Commission (AEC)**. The AEC tried to balance research on atomic power with continued testing of new weapons. Now Truman told the AEC to double the output of fissionable uranium and plutonium for "conventional" nuclear weapons.

A more momentous decision soon followed. Truman decided in January 1950 to authorize work on the "super" bomb—the thermonuclear fusion weapon that would become the hydrogen bomb (H-bomb). As would be true in future nuclear defense debates, the underlying question was how much capacity for nuclear destruction was enough (see "American Views: Deciding on a Nuclear Arms Race").

Nuclear weapons proliferated in the early 1950s. The United States exploded the first hydrogen bomb in the South Pacific in November 1952. Releasing one hundred times the energy of the Hiroshima bomb, the detonation tore a mile-long chasm in the ocean floor. Great Britain became the third nuclear power in the same year. The Soviet Union tested its own hydrogen bomb only nine months after the U.S. test.

Under the guidance of the Federal Civil Defense Administration, Americans learned that they should always keep a battery-powered radio and tune to 640 or 1240 on the AM dial for emergency information when they heard air raid sirens. Schoolchildren learned to hide under their desks if they saw the blinding flash of a nuclear detonation.

Soldiers were exposed to post-test radiation with minimal protection. Nuclear tests in the South Pacific dusted fishing boats with radioactivity and forced islanders to abandon contaminated homes. Radioactive fallout from Nevada testing contaminated large sections of the West and increased cancer rates among "downwinders" in Utah. Weapons production and atomic experiments contaminated vast tracts in Nevada, Washington, and Colorado and left huge environmental costs for later generations.

The Cold War in Asia

Communist victory in China's civil war was as predictable as the Soviet nuclear bomb but no less controversial. American military and diplomatic missions in the late 1940s pointed out that the collapse of Jiang Jieshi's Nationalist regime was nearly inevitable, given its corruption and narrow support. But advocates for Jiang, mostly conservative Republicans from the Midwest and West, were certain that

American Views

DECIDING ON A NUCLEAR ARMS RACE

In 1950, the United States began work on a hydrogen (thermonuclear) bomb. The decision locked the United States and the Soviet Union into a nuclear arms race that lasted another forty years. In the first document reprinted here, an excerpt from a letter to President Truman written on November 25, 1949, Lewis Strauss, chairman of the Atomic Energy Commision, urged work on the H-bomb. In the second, scientist Edward Teller agreed. A refugee from Nazi-dominated Europe who had worked at Los Alamos, Teller remained an advocate of massive defense spending through the 1980s.

❖ **How did memories of World War II affect this Cold War decision?**

❖ **How did U.S. policymakers evaluate the intentions of the Soviet Union?**

Lewis Strauss, November 1949

Dear Mr. President:

As you know, the thermonuclear (super) bomb was suggested by scientists working at Los Alamos during the war. . . . I believe that the United States must be as completely armed as any possible enemy. From this, it follows that I believe it unwise to renounce, unilaterally, any weapon which an enemy can reasonably be expected to possess. I recommend that the President direct the Atomic Energy Commission to proceed with the development of the thermonuclear bomb, at highest priority. . . .

Obviously the current atomic bomb as well as the proposed thermonuclear weapon are horrible to contemplate. All war is horrible. Until, however, some means is found of eliminating war, I cannot agree with those of my colleagues who feel that an announcement should be made by the President to the effect that the development of the thermonuclear weapon will not be undertaken by the United States at this time. This is because I do not think the state-ment will be credited in the Kremlin . . . and because primarily until disarmament is universal, our arsenal must be not less well equipped than with the most potent weapons that our technology can devise.

Edward Teller, March 1950

President Truman has announced that we are going to make a hydrogen bomb. . . . The scientist is not responsible for the law of nature. It is his job to find out how these laws operate. . . . However, it is not the scientist's job to determine whether a hydrogen bomb should be constructed, whether it should be used, or how it should be used. This responsibility rests with the American people and their chosen representatives. Personally, as a citizen, I do not know in what other way President Truman could have acted. . . . To my mind we are in a situation no less dangerous than the one we were facing in 1939, and it is of the greatest importance that we realize it. We must realize . . . that democracy will not be saved by ideals alone.

Source: *Lewis L. Strauss*, Men and Decisions (*1962*).

Truman's administration had done too little. "China asked for a sword," complained one senator, "and we gave her a dull paring knife." Critics looked for scapegoats. Foreign service officers who had honestly analyzed the weakness of the Nationalists were accused of Communist sympathies and hounded from their jobs. The results were damage to the State Department and tragedy for those unfairly branded as traitors.

NSC-68 and Aggressive Containment

The turmoil of 1949 led to a comprehensive statement of American strategic goals. In April 1950, the State Department prepared a sweeping report known as **National Security Council Paper 68 (NSC-68)**. The document described a world divided between the forces of "slavery" and "freedom" and assumed that the Soviet Union was actively and broadly aggressive, motivated by greed for territory and a "fanatic faith" in Communism. To defend civilization itself, said the experts, the United States should use as much force as needed to resist Communist expansion anywhere and everywhere.

Truman and his advisers in 1947 and 1948 had hoped to contain the Soviets by diplomacy and by integrating the economies of Europe and Japan with that of the United States. Now that the Soviets had the atomic bomb, NSC-68 argued that the United States needed to press friendly nations to rearm and to make its former enemies into military allies. It also argued the need for the nation to acquire expensive conventional forces to defend Europe. NSC-68 thus advocated nearly open-ended increases in the defense budget (which in fact tripled between 1950 and 1954).

Although it was not a public document, NSC-68's portrait of an implacable Communist conspiracy would have made sense to most Americans; it certainly did to Harry Truman. The outbreak of war in Korea at the end of June 1950 seemed to confirm that Communism was a military threat. The thinking behind the report led the United States to approach the Cold War as a military competition and to view political changes in Africa and Asia as parts of a Soviet plan.

War in Korea

The success of Mao and the Chinese Communists forced the Truman administration to define national interests in East Asia and the western Pacific. The most important U.S. interest was Japan, still an industrial power despite its devastating defeat. The United States had shaped a more democratic Japan that would be a strong and friendly trading partner. Protected by American armed forces, Japan would be part of a crescent of offshore strong points that included Alaska, the Philippines, Australia, and New Zealand.

Two questions remained unresolved at the start of 1950 (and were still troublesome in the 1990s). One was the future of Taiwan and the remnants of Jiang's regime. The other question was Korea, whose own civil war would soon bring the world to the brink of World War III.

The Korean peninsula is the closest point on the Asian mainland to Japan. With three powerful neighbors—China, Russia, and Japan—Korea had always had to fight for its independence. As World War II ended, Soviet troops hamd moved down the peninsula from the north and American forces had landed in the south, creating a situation similar to that in Germany. The 38th parallel, which Russians and Americans set as the dividing line between their zones of occupation, became a de facto border. The United States in 1948 recognized an independent South Korea, with its capital at Seoul, under a conservative government led by Syngman Rhee. Rhee's support came from large landowners and a police force trained by the Japanese colonialists between 1910 and 1945. The Soviets recognized a separate North Korea, whose leader, Kim Il Sung, advocated radical social and political change. Both leaders hoped to unify all Koreans under their own rule, and each crushed political dissent and tried to undermine the other with economic pressure and commando raids.

United States military planners assumed that U.S. air power in Japan could neutralize unfriendly forces on the Korean peninsula. But Korea remained politically important as the only point of direct confrontation with the Soviet Union in Asia.

On June 25, 1950, North Korea, helped by Soviet equipment and Chinese training, attacked South Korea (see Map 29-2). Truman and Secretary of State Dean Acheson believed that Moscow lay behind the invasion. The outbreak of what Americans refer to as the **Korean War** is best understood as an intensification of an ongoing civil war that Stalin was willing to exploit.

As the South Korean army collapsed, Truman committed American ground troops from Japan on June 30. The United States also had the diplomatic good fortune of securing an endorsement from the United Nations. Because the USSR was boycotting the UN, the Korean conflict remained officially a United Nations action, although U.S. Generals Douglas

Map 29-2   *The Korean War*
After rapid reversals of fortune in 1950 and early 1951, the war in Korea settled into stalemate. Most Americans agreed with the need to contain Communist expansion but found it deeply frustrating to fight for limited objectives rather than total victory.

MacArthur, Matthew Ridgway, and Mark Clark ran the show as the successive heads of the UN command.

The Politics of War

The first U.S. combat troops were outnumbered, outgunned, and poorly trained. They could not stop the North Koreans. By early August, the Americans clung to a narrow toehold around the port of Pusan on the tip of the Korean peninsula. As reinforcements arrived from the United States, however, MacArthur transformed the war with a daring amphibious counterattack at Inchon, 150 miles behind North Korean lines. The North Korean army

was already overextended and exhausted. It collapsed and fled north.

MacArthur and Washington officials disregarded warnings by China that it would enter the war if the United States tried to reunite Korea by force. U.S. and South Korean troops rolled north, drawing closer and closer to the boundary between North Korea and China.

Chinese forces attacked MacArthur's command in late October but then disappeared. MacArthur dismissed the attacks as a token gesture. But on November 26, the Chinese struck the overextended American columns. They had massed 300,000 troops without detection by American aviation. Their assault drove the UN forces into a two-month retreat that again abandoned Seoul.

In March 1951, with the UN forces again pushing north, Truman prepared to offer a cease-fire that would have preserved the separate nations of South and North Korea. MacArthur tried to preempt the president by demanding that China admit defeat or suffer the consequences. He then published a direct attack on the administration's policy of limiting the Asian war to ensure the security of Europe.

To protect civilian control of the armed forces, he was forced to relieve MacArthur of his commands on April 11, 1951. The general returned to parades and a hero's welcome when he addressed a joint session of Congress. He quoted a line from an old barracks song: "Old soldiers never die; they just fade away." But Truman remained in charge of the war.

In Korea itself, U.S. and South Korean forces stabilized a strong defensive line that cut diagonally across the 38th parallel. For two years, UN and Communist armies faced boredom that alternated with fierce inch-by-inch battles for territory with names like Heartbreak Ridge and Pork Chop Hill. In the air, the arrival of new F-86 Saberjets in 1952 allowed American pilots to clear the skies of Chinese aviators in Russian-made MIG 15s.

After 1950, the Chinese were careful to keep their war planes north of the ground combat zone, the Russians had stayed out of the war, and the United States was willing to accept a divided Korea.

Truce negotiations stalled over the political decision to turn free choice for Chinese POWs into a symbol of resistance to Communism. Nearly half of the 140,000 U.S. casualties came after the truce talks started. The war was a decisive factor behind the Republican victory in the November 1952 elections and dragged on until June 1953, when an armistice returned the peninsula roughly to its prewar political division.

The blindly ambitious attack into North Korea was one of the great failures of intelligence and strategic leadership in American military history. Nearly everyone in Washington shared the blame for letting the excitement of battlefield victories obscure limited war aims. Civilian leaders couldn't resist the desire to go beyond containment and roll back Communism. Truman hoped for a striking victory before the 1950 congressional elections. The Joint Chiefs of Staff failed to question a general with MacArthur's heroic reputation. MacArthur himself allowed ambition and wishful thinking to jeopardize his army.

American leaders found themselves propping up an undemocratic regime to defend democracy. Both North Koreans and South Koreans engaged in savage political reprisals as the battlefront shifted back and forth. American emphasis on the massive application of firepower led U.S. forces to demolish entire villages to kill single snipers. General Curtis Le May estimated that Air Force bombings killed a million Koreans.

The Korean War helped to legitimize the United Nations. In Washington, it confirmed the ideas behind NSC-68, with its call for the United States to lead an anti-communist alliance. Two days after the North Korean invasion, President Truman ordered the Seventh Fleet to protect the Nationalist Chinese on Taiwan, a decision that guaranteed twenty years of hostility between the United States and the People's Republic of China. In the same month, the United States began to aid France's struggle to retain control over its colony of Indochina, which included Laos, Cambodia, and Vietnam.

In Europe, the United States pushed to rearm West Germany as part of a militarized NATO and sent troops to Europe as a permanent defense force. It increased military aid to European governments and secured a unified command for the national forces allocated for NATO. The unified command made West German rearmament acceptable to France and the smaller nations of western Europe because it meant that the West German military would be subordinate to NATO.

The Second Red Scare

The Korean War reinforced the second Red Scare, an assault on civil liberties that stretched from the mid-1940s to the mid-1950s and dwarfed the Red Scare of 1919–1920. Legitimate concerns about espionage mixed with suspicions that Communist sympathizers in high places were helping Stalin and Mao (see the summary table "The Second Red Scare").

Efforts to root out suspected **subversives** operated on three tracks. National and state governments established loyalty programs to identify and fire suspect employees. The courts punished members of suspect organizations. Congressional and state legislative investigations followed the whims of committee chairs. Anti-communist crusaders often relied on dubious evidence and eagerly believed the worst. They also threatened basic civil liberties.

The Communist Party and the Loyalty Program

The Communist party in the United States was actually in rapid decline after World War II. Many intellectuals had left the party over the Nazi-Soviet Pact in 1939. And the postwar years brought a series of failures. In 1946, Walter Reuther defeated a Communist for the presidency of the huge United Auto Workers union, and other large CIO unions froze Communists out of leadership positions.

Nevertheless, Republicans used **red-baiting** as a campaign technique in 1944 and 1946, setting the stage for a national loyalty program. Republicans in 1944 tried to frighten voters about "commydemocrats" by linking FDR, CIO labor unions, and Communism. Democrats slung their own mud by trying to convince voters that Hitler preferred the Republicans. Two years later, Republican campaigners told the public that the basic choice was "between Communism and Republicanism." The argument helped dozens of Republicans win congressional seats.

The Temporary Commission on Employee Loyalty devised a loyalty program for federal employees, which Truman initiated in March 1947 with **Executive Order 9835**. Order 9835 authorized the attorney general to prepare a list of "totalitarian, Fascist, Communist, or subversive" organizations and made membership or even "sympathetic association" with such groups grounds for dismissal. The loyalty program applied to approximately 8 million Americans working for the federal government or defense contractors; similar state laws affected another 5 million.

Many accusations were just malicious gossip, but allegations stayed in a worker's file even if refuted. Many New Dealers and people associated with presumably liberal East Coast institutions were targets. An Interior Department official boasted that he had been especially effective in squeezing out graduates of Harvard and Columbia.

Federal employees worked under a cloud of fear. Loyalty boards asked about religion, racial equality, and a taste for foreign films; they also tried to identify homosexuals, who were thought to be tar-

SUMMARY

THE SECOND RED SCARE

Type of Anti-Communist Effort	Key Tools	Results
Employee loyalty programs	U.S. attorney general's list of subversive organizations	Thousands of federal and state workers fired, careers damaged
Congressional investigations	HUAC McCarren Committee Army-McCarthy hearings	Employee blacklists, harassment of writers and intellectuals
Criminal prosecutions	Trials for espionage and conspiracy to advocate violent overthrow of the U.S. government	Convictions of Communist party leaders (1949), Rosenbergs (1951)

gets for blackmail by foreign agents. The loyalty program resulted in 1,210 firings and 6,000 resignations under Truman and comparable numbers during Dwight Eisenhower's first term from 1953 to 1956.

Naming Names to Congress

The congressional hunt for subversives had its roots in 1938, when Congressman Martin Dies, a Texas Democrat, created the Special Committee on Un-American Activities. Originally intended to ferret out pro-Fascists, the Dies Committee evolved into the permanent **House Committee on Un-American Activities (HUAC)** in 1945. It investigated "un-American propaganda" that attacked constitutional government.

One of HUAC's juiciest targets was Hollywood. In 1946, Americans bought an average of 90 million tickets every *week*. But Hollywood's reputation for loose morals, high living, foreign-born directors, Jewish producers, and left-leaning writers aroused the suspicions of many congressmen. HUAC sought to make sure that no un-American messages were being peddled through America's most popular entertainment.

When the hearings opened in October 1947, studio executives assured HUAC of their anti-Communism. So did popular actors Gary Cooper and Ronald Reagan. In contrast, eight screenwriters and two directors—the Hollywood Ten—refused to discuss their past political associations, citing the free speech protections of the First Amendment to the Constitution. HUAC countered with citations for contempt of Congress. The First Amendment defense failed when it reached the Supreme Court, and the Ten went to jail in 1950.

HUAC changed the politics of Hollywood. Before 1947, it had been fashionable to lean toward the left. After the hearings, it was imperative to tilt the other way. The government refused to let British-born Charlie Chaplin reenter the United States in 1952 because of his left-wing views. Other actors, writers, and directors found themselves on the Hollywood blacklist, banned from jobs where they might insert Communist propaganda into American movies.

At the start of 1951, the new Senate Internal Security Subcommittee joined the sometimes bumbling HUAC. The **McCarran Committee,** named for the Nevada senator who chaired it, targeted diplomats, labor union leaders, professors, and schoolteachers. The real point of the investigations was not to force personal confessions from witnesses but to badger them into identifying friends and associates who might have been involved in suspect activities.

The only sure way to avoid "naming names" was to respond to every question by citing the Fifth Amendment to the Constitution, which protects Americans from testifying against themselves. Many Americans wrongly assumed that citing the amendment was a sure sign of guilt, not a matter of principle, and talked about Fifth Amendment Communists.

State legislatures imitated Congress by searching for "Reducators" among college faculty in such states as Oklahoma, Washington, and California. College presidents frequently fired faculty who took the Fifth Amendment. The experience of an economics professor fired from the University of Kansas City after testimony before the McCarran Committee was typical. He found it hard to keep any job once his name had been in the papers. A local dairy fired him because it thought its customers might be uneasy having a radical handle their milk bottles.

Subversion Trials

In 1948, the Justice Department indicted the leaders of the American Communist party under the Alien Registration Act of 1940. Eleven men and women went on trial in 1949, charged with conspiring to advocate the violent overthrow of the United States government through their speech and publications. The prosecution convinced the judge and jury that their writings promoted revolution. Some of the testimony came from Herbert Philbrick, an advertising manager and FBI informer who had posed as a party member. Philbrick parlayed his appearance into a bestseller titled *I Led Three Lives* and then into a popular television series on which the FBI foiled Communist spies every Friday night.

Then, in 1948, former Communist Whittaker Chambers named Alger Hiss as a Communist with whom he had associated in the 1930s. Hiss, who had held important posts in the State Department, sued Chambers for slander. As proof, Chambers gave Congressman Richard Nixon microfilms that he had hidden inside a pumpkin on his Maryland farm. Tests seemed to show that the "pumpkin papers" were State Department documents that had been copied on a typewriter that Hiss had once owned. The Justice Department indicted Hiss for perjury—lying under oath. A first perjury trial ended in deadlock, but a second jury convicted Hiss in January 1950.

The essence of the Hiss case has been a matter of faith, not facts. Even his enemies agreed that any documents he might have stolen were of limited importance. His smugness as a member of the East Coast establishment enraged them. To his opponents, Hiss stood for every wrong turn that the nation had taken since 1932. Many supporters believed that he had been framed. Their belief gained support in 1992 when a Russian official reported that Soviet KGB archives had no record of Hiss as a Russian spy.

In 1950, the British arrested nuclear physicist Klaus Fuchs, who confessed to passing atomic secrets to the Soviets when he worked at Los Alamos in 1944 and 1945. The "Fuchs spy ring" soon implicated Julius and Ethel Rosenberg, New York radicals of strong beliefs but limited sophistication. Convicted in 1951 of the vague charge of conspiring to commit espionage, they were sent to the electric chair in 1953 after refusing to buy a reprieve by naming other spies.

As in the case of Alger Hiss, the government had a plausible but not airtight case against the Rosenbergs. There is no doubt that Julius Rosenberg was a convinced Communist, and he may well have been a minor figure in an atomic spy net, but it is likely that Ethel Rosenberg was charged to pressure her husband into confessing.

Senator McCarthy on Stage

The best-remembered participant in the second Red Scare was Senator Joseph McCarthy of Wisconsin. He burst into national prominence on February 9, 1950.

Senator Joe McCarthy (seated), shown here with his aide Roy Cohn (left) and J. David Schine (right), used press releases and congressional committee hearings to attack suspected communists. By 1954 he was reaching to more and more extreme accusations to keep his name before the public.

In a rambling speech in Wheeling, West Virginia, he supposedly stated: "I have here in my hand a list of 205 that were known to the Secretary of State as being members of the Communist Party and who, nevertheless, are still working and shaping the policy of the State Department." McCarthy's rise to fame climaxed with an incoherent six-hour speech to the Senate. He tried to document the charges by mixing previously exposed spies and security risks with people who no longer worked for the government or who never had worked for it. Over the next several years, his speeches were full of multiple untruths. He threw out so many accusations that the facts could never catch up.

Senators treated McCarthy as a crude outsider in their exclusive club, but voters in 1950 turned against his most prominent opponents. In 1951, McCarthy even called George Marshall, now serving as secretary of defense, an agent of Communism. The idea was ludicrous. Marshall was one of the most upright Americans of his generation, the architect of victory in World War II and a key contributor to the stabilization of Europe. Nevertheless, McCarthy was so popular that the Republicans featured him at their 1952 convention. That fall, the Republicans' presidential candidate, Dwight Eisenhower, appeared on the same campaign platform with McCarthy and conspicuously failed to defend George Marshall—who was chiefly responsible for Eisenhower's fast-track career.

McCarthy's personal crudeness made him a media star but eventually undermined him. Given control of the Senate Committee on Government Operations in 1953, one of his investigations targeted the U.S. Army's promotion of an army dentist with a supposedly subversive background. Two months of televised hearings revealed the emptiness of the charges. The cameras also put McCarthy's style on trial. "Have you no decency?" asked the army's lawyer Joseph Welch at one point.

The end came quickly. McCarthy's "favorable" rating in the polls plummeted. The comic strip *Pogo* began to feature a foolishly menacing figure with McCarthy's face named Simple J. Malarkey. The U.S. Senate finally voted 67 to 22 in December 1954 to condemn McCarthy for conduct "unbecoming a Member of the Senate." When he died from alchoholism in 1957, he was repudiated by the Senate and ignored by the media.

Understanding McCarthyism

The antisubversive campaign now called **McCarthyism**, however, died a slower death. Legislation, such as the Internal Security Act (1950) and the Immi-

gration and Nationality Act (1952), remained as tools of political repression. HUAC continued to mount investigations as late as the 1960s.

Fear of Communist subversion reached deep into American society. In the early 1950s, Cincinnati's National League baseball team tried out a new name. Harking back to its origins as the Red Stockings, the team was now the "Redlegs," not the "Reds," to avoid associations with communism. Cities and states required loyalty oaths from their employees; Ohio even required oaths from recipients of unemployment compensation.

In retrospect, at least four factors made Americans afraid of Communist subversion. One was a legitimate but exaggerated concern about atomic spies. A second was an undercurrent of anti-Semitism and nativism, for many labor organizers and Communist party members (like the Rosenbergs) had Jewish and eastern European backgrounds. Third was southern and western resentment of the nation's Ivy League elite. Most general, finally, was that it was basically reassuring if Soviet and Chinese Communist successes were the result of American traitors rather than Communist strengths.

Partisan politics mobilized the fears and resentments into a political force. From 1946 through 1952, the conservative wing of the Republican party used the Red Scare to attack New Dealers and liberal Democrats. The Republican elite used McCarthy until they won control of the presidency and Congress in 1952 and then abandoned him.

Conclusion

The Cold War stayed cool because each side achieved its essential goals. The Soviet Union controlled eastern Europe, while the United States built increasingly strong ties with the NATO nations and Japan. Though the result was a stalemate that would last through the 1980s, it nevertheless absorbed huge shares of Soviet and American resources and conditioned the thinking of an entire generation.

The shift from prewar isolationism to postwar internationalism was one of the most important changes in the nation's history. To many of its advocates, internationalism represented a commitment to spread political democracy to other nations. As the 1950s and 1960s would show, the results often contradicted the ideal when the United States forcibly imposed its will on other peoples. However, the new internationalism highlighted and helped change domestic racial attitudes.

The Truman years brought increasing stability. The economic chaos of 1946 faded quickly. By identifying liberalism at home with anti-Communism abroad, Truman's efforts to define a vital center helped protect the New Deal. If the Republicans had won in 1948, they might have dismantled the New Deal. By 1952, both presidential candidates affirmed the consensus that placed economic opportunity at the center of the national agenda. The suburban housing boom seemed to turn the dream of prosperity into reality for millions of families.

The United States emerged from the Truman years remarkably prosperous. It was also more secure from international threats than many nervous Americans appreciated. The years from 1946 to 1952 set the themes for a generation that believed that the United States could do whatever it set its mind to. As the world moved slowly toward greater stability in the 1950s, Americans were ready for a decade of confidence.

Review Questions

1. What were the key differences between Harry Truman and congressional Republicans about the legacy of the New Deal? Why did regulating labor unions become a central domestic issue in the late 1940s? Why did Truman manage to win the presidential election of 1948 despite starting as an underdog?

2. How did the postwar years expand opportunity for veterans and members of the working class? How did they limit opportunities for women? How did they begin to challenge racial inequities in American society? How did the postwar readjustment create a suburban society?

3. What foreign policy priorities did the United States set after 1945? To what extent did the United States achieve its most basic objectives? How did mutual mistrust fuel the origins and deepen the Cold War?

4. How did the Cold War change character in 1949 and 1950? What were key actions by the Soviet Union and China, and how did the United States respond? What was the effect of the chaotic fighting in Korea on U.S. domestic politics and diplomacy?

5. What factors motivated an increasingly frantic fear of domestic subversion in the late 1940s and early 1950s? Who were the key actors in the second Red Scare? What was its long-term impact on American society?

Recommended Reading

Paul Boyer, *By the Bomb's Early Light: American Thought and Culture at the Dawn of the Atomic Age* (1985). Boyer examines the mixture of hopes and fears with which Americans greeted the arrival of the atomic age, giving detailed attention to popular culture as well as national policy.

Joseph C. Goulden, *The Best Years, 1945–1950* (1976). Here is a very readable portrayal of the ways in which Americans adjusted to the postwar years, drawing heavily on contemporary magazine accounts.

Melvyn Leffler, *A Preponderance of Power: National Security, the Truman Administration, and the Cold War* (1992). Leffler provides a balanced interpretation of responsibility for the Cold War in this detailed but readable account of American policy.

Samuel Lubell, *The Future of American Politics* (1952). Lubell's incisive analysis of the social forces that shaped the American political scene in the 1940s gives insights that are still telling after more than four decades.

David McCullough, *Truman* (1992). McCullough has produced a readable and sympathetic biography of the thirty-third president.

Where to Learn More

❖ **Harry S Truman National Historic Site, Library and Museum, Independence, Missouri.** The museum has exhibits and materials on Truman's political career and American history during his administration. Also in Independence is the Harry S Truman Courtroom and Office, with exhibits focusing on his early career.

❖ **General Douglas MacArthur Memorial, Norfolk, Virginia.** The MacArthur Memorial in downtown Norfolk commemorates the career of a key figure in the shaping of the postwar world.

❖ **United Nations Headquarters, New York, New York.** A tour of the United Nations complex in New York is a reminder of the new organizations for international cooperation and coordination that emerged from World War II.

THE CONFIDENT YEARS, 1953–1964

CHAPTER OUTLINE

KEY TOPICS

❖ Affluence and conformity in the American middle class during the 1950s
❖ The Cold War confrontation with the USSR during the Eisenhower and Kennedy administrations
❖ The struggle for African-American civil rights from *Brown* v. *Board of Education of Topeka* to the Civil Rights Act of 1964 and the Voting Rights Act of 1965
❖ Lyndon Johnson and the Great Society

The United States gained a new hero on April 12, 1955, when Dr. Jonas Salk announced an effective vaccine for polio. In the confident mid-1950s, the polio vaccine seemed another proof of American ability to improve the world.

Poliomyelitis, or infantile paralysis, can paralyze the legs or kill by short-circuiting muscles in the throat and chest. The virus sometimes struck adults—it cost Franklin Roosevelt the use of his legs when he was in his thirties—but most victims were children.

Most Americans knew at least one child who hobbled through life on crutches and metal leg braces. Hospitals filled with new cases every summer—58,000 in 1952 alone. Many children clung to life inside iron lungs, metal cylinders that pumped air in and out of a hole in the throat.

Polio season peaked in July and August. Worried parents kept their children out of movie theaters and swimming pools, but the disease struck even the most careful families. "Polio?" one girl remembered from the 1950s. "That was the big fear when I was young."

Salk's announcement was welcome news. Hundreds of thousands of children had participated in vaccine field trials, and millions of Americans had funded the research with contributions to the March of Dimes. A generation later, President Ronald Reagan would list the polio vaccine with the steam engine and silicon chip as one of the great modern discoveries.

Salk's triumph affirmed American faith in the future. The prosperous years from 1953 to 1964 spread the economic promise of the 1940s across American society. Young couples could afford large families and new houses. Labor unions grew conservative because cooperation with big business offered immediate gains for their members.

The Cold War consensus that paired strength at home with strength abroad guided U.S. foreign policy. Few leaders questioned the rightness or necessity of fighting the Cold War—or America's ultimate triumph. The consensus gave U.S. policy an overarching goal of containment but also narrowed its options by casting every issue in terms of U.S.-Soviet rivalry.

Social dissenters argued that the United States was misusing its wealth. They criticized fifties society for ignoring the talents of women. They pointed to persistent poverty and racial inequities. Critics also spoke for a civil rights movement that sprang from deep roots in southern black communities.

A Decade of Affluence

Americans in the 1950s believed in the basic strength of the United States. Examples of self-assurance were everywhere. Television's *General Electric Theater* was third in the ratings in 1956–1957. Every week, its host, Ronald Reagan, a popular Hollywood lead from the late 1930s, stated, "At General Electric, progress is our most important product." Large, technologically sophisticated corporations were introducing new marvels: Orlon sweaters and Saran Wrap, long-playing records and Polaroid cameras.

Social and intellectual conformity assured a united front. National leaders argued that strong families were bulwarks against Communism and that churchgoing inoculated people against subversive ideas. Under the lingering cloud of McCarthyism, the range of political ideas that influenced government policy was narrower than in the 1930s and 1940s. Nevertheless, disaffected critics began to voice the discontents that exploded in the 1960s and 1970s.

What's Good for General Motors

Dwight Eisenhower presided over the prosperity of the 1950s. Both Democrats and Republicans had courted him as a presidential candidate in 1948. Four years later, he picked the Republicans and easily defeated Democrat Adlai Stevenson, the moderately liberal governor of Illinois.

Publicists tried a variety of labels for Eisenhower's domestic views: "progressive moderation," "**New Republicanism**," "dynamic conservatism." Satisfied with postwar America, Eisenhower accepted much of the New Deal but saw little need for further reform. In a 1959 poll, liberals considered him a fellow liberal and conservatives thought him a conservative.

Eisenhower's first secretary of defense, "Engine Charlie" Wilson, had headed General Motors. At his Senate confirmation hearing, he proclaimed, "For years, I thought what was good for the country was good for General Motors and vice versa." Wilson's statement captured a central theme of the 1950s.

The economy in the 1950s gave Americans much to like. Between 1950 and 1964, the American economy grew by a solid 3.2 percent per year. Automobile production, on which dozens of other industries depended, neared 8 million vehicles per year in the mid-1950s; less than 1 percent of new car sales were imports.

The U.S. accounted for approximately 35 percent of global production in the mid-1950s. Nevertheless, Americans still worried about the Soviet Union. Although the Soviet economy was less than half the size of the American, it was growing more rapidly. When Soviet leader Nikita Khrushchev told the West, "We will bury you," he was talking about the supposed superiority of Communism as an economic system.

In the 1950s American workers' productivity, or output per worker, increased steadily. Average wages rose faster than consumer prices in nine of eleven years between 1953 and 1964. The steel and auto industries gave their workers a middle-class way of life. In turn, labor leaders lost interest in radical changes in American society. In 1955, the older and politically more conservative American Federation of Labor absorbed the younger Congress of Industrial Organizations. The new AFL-CIO positioned itself as a partner in prosperity and foe of Communism at home and abroad.

Industrial cities offered members of minority groups factory jobs at wages that could support a family. Blacks worked through the Urban League, the National Association of Colored Women, and other race-oriented groups to secure fair employment laws and jobs with large corporations. Many Puerto Rican migrants to New York found steady work in the Brooklyn Navy Yard. Mexican-American families in San Antonio benefited from maintenance jobs at the city's military bases.

CHRONOLOGY

1953 CIA-backed coup returns the Shah to power in Iran.

USSR detonates hydrogen bomb.

1954 Vietnamese defeat the French.

Geneva conference divides Vietnam.

United States and allies form SEATO.

Supreme Court decides *Brown* v. *Board of Education of Topeka*.

CIA overthrows the government of Guatemala.

China provokes a crisis over Quemoy and Matsu.

1955 Salk polio vaccine is announced.

Blacks boycott Montgomery, Alabama, bus system.

USSR forms the Warsaw Pact.

AFL and CIO merge.

1956 Interstate Highway Act is passed.

Soviets repress Hungarian revolt.

Israel, France, and Britain invade Egypt.

1957 U.S. Army maintains law and order in Little Rock.

Soviet Union launches *Sputnik*.

1958 U.S. and USSR voluntarily suspend nuclear tests.

1959 Fidel Castro takes power in Cuba.

Nikita Khrushchev visits the United States.

1960 U-2 shot down over Russia.

Sit-in movement begins in Greensboro, North Carolina.

1961 Bay of Pigs invasion fails.

Kennedy establishes the Peace Corps.

Vienna summit fails.

Freedom rides are held in the Deep South.

Berlin crisis leads to construction of the Berlin Wall.

1962 John Glenn orbits the earth.

Cuban missile crisis brings the world to the brink.

Michael Harrington publishes *The Other America*.

1963 Civil rights demonstrations rend Birmingham.

Civil rights activists march in Washington.

Betty Friedan publishes *The Feminine Mystique*.

Limited Test Ban Treaty is signed.

Ngo Dinh Diem is assassinated in South Vietnam.

President Kennedy is assassinated.

1964 Civil Rights Act is passed.

Freedom Summer is organized in Mississippi.

Office of Economic Opportunity is created.

Gulf of Tonkin Resolution is passed.

Wilderness Act launches the modern environmental movement.

1965 Medical Care Act establishes Medicare and Medicaid.

Elementary and Secondary Education Act extends direct federal aid to local schools.

Selma-Montgomery march climaxes era of nonviolent civil rights demonstrations.

Voting Rights Act suspends literacy tests.

However, there were never enough family-wage jobs for all of the African-American and Latino workers who continued to move to northern and western cities. Many Mexican-Americans were still migrant farm laborers and workers in nonunionized sweatshops. Minority workers were usually the first to suffer from the erosion of industrial jobs that began in the 1960s.

To cut costs and accelerate Native American assimilation, Congress pushed the policy of **termination** between 1954 and 1962. The government sold tribal land and assets, distributed the proceeds among tribal members, and terminated its treaty relationship with the tribe. Termination cut thousands of Indians adrift from the security of tribal organizations. The Bureau of Indian Affairs also encouraged Indians to move to large cities, but jobs were often unavailable.

Reshaping Urban America

If Eisenhower's administration opted for the status quo on many issues, it nevertheless reshaped American cities around an agenda of economic development. In 1954, Congress transformed the public housing program into **urban renewal**. Cities used federal funds to replace low-rent businesses and run-down housing on the fringes of their downtowns with new hospitals, civic centers, sports arenas, office towers, and luxury apartments.

Los Angeles demolished the seedy Victorian mansions of Bunker Hill, just northwest of downtown, for a music center and bank towers. A mile to the north was Chavez Ravine, whose Mexican-American population lived in substandard housing but maintained a lively community. When conservative opposition blocked plans for public housing, the residents were evicted, and Dodger Stadium was built. Here as elsewhere, urban showplaces rose at the expense of minority groups.

The Eisenhower administration also revolutionized American transportation. The **Federal Highway Act of 1956** created a national system of Interstate and Defense Highways. The legislation wrapped a program to build 41,000 miles of freeways in the language of the Cold War. The roads would be wide and strong enough for trucks hauling military hardware; they were also supposed to make it easy to evacuate cities in case of a Soviet attack.

Interstates halved the time of city-to-city travel. They were good for General Motors, the steel industry, and the concrete industry, requiring the construction equivalent of sixty Panama Canals. The highways promoted long-distance trucking at the expense of railroads. As with urban renewal, the bulldozers and road graders most often plowed through African-American or Latino neighborhoods.

The beltways or perimeter highways that began to ring most large cities made it easier and more profitable to develop new subdivisions and factory sites than to reinvest in city centers. Federal grants for sewers and other basic facilities further cut suburban costs. Continuing the pattern of the late 1940s, suburban growth added a million new single-family houses per year.

Comfort on Credit

The 1930s had taught Americans to avoid debt. The 1950s taught them to buy on credit. Families financed their new houses with 90 percent FHA mortgages and 100 percent VA mortgages. They filled the rooms by signing installment contracts at furniture and appliance stores and charging the drapes and carpeting on department store credit cards. The value of consumer debt, excluding home mortgages, tripled from 1952 to 1964.

New forms of marketing facilitated credit-based consumerism. The first large-scale suburban shopping center was Northgate in Seattle, which assembled all the pieces of the full-grown mall. By the end of the decade, developers were building malls with 1 million square feet of shopping floor. At the start of the 1970s, the universal credit card (Visa, MasterCard) made shopping even easier.

Where cities of the early twentieth century had been built around the public transportation of streetcars and subways, the 1950s depended on private automobiles. Interstate highways sucked retail business from small-town main streets to interchanges on the edge of town. Nationally franchised motels and fast-food restaurants sprang up along suburban shopping strips, pioneered by Holiday Inn (1952) and McDonald's (nationally franchised in 1955).

More extreme than the mall were entirely new environments for high-intensity consumption and entertainment that appeared in the Southwest, such as Las Vegas with its hotel-casinos. Opening in Orange County, California, in 1955, Disneyland was safe and artificial—a never-ending state fair without the smells and dust.

The New Fifties Family

Family life in the Eisenhower years departed from historic patterns. Prosperity allowed children to finish school and young adults to marry right after high school. Young women faced strong social pressure to pursue husbands rather than careers. The proportion of single adults reached its twentieth-century low in 1960. At all social levels, young people married quickly and had an average of three children spaced closely together. Family activities replaced the street corner for kids and the neighborhood tavern for men. Strong families, said experts, defended against Communism by teaching American values.

Television was made to order for the family-centered fifties. By 1960, fully 87 percent of households had sets (see Figure 30-1). Popular entertain-

Television sets were major pieces of living room furniture in the 1950s. This 1951 Motorola ad from Woman's Home Companion emphasizes television as a source of family togetherness, a popular theme in the 1950s.

ment was now enjoyed in the privacy of the home, rather than in a crowd. Situation comedies were the most popular programs. Successful shows depicted families who had northern European names and lived in single-family houses with friendly neighbors representing the 1950s ideal of American success.

Television programming helped limit women's roles by power of example. Women in the fifties had a smaller share of new college degrees and professional jobs. Despite millions of new electric appliances, the time spent on housework *increased.* Magazines proclaimed that proper families maintained distinct roles for dad and mom, who was urged to find fulfillment in a well-scrubbed house and children.

But in reality the number of employed women reached new highs. By 1960, nearly 35 percent of all women held jobs, including 7.5 million mothers with children under 17.

Teenagers in the 1950s joined adults as consumers of movies, clothes, and automobiles. Advertisers tapped and expanded the growing youth market by promoting a distinct "youth culture," an idea that became omnipresent in the 1960s and 1970s. While psychologists pontificated on the special problems of adolescence, many cities matched their high schools to the social status of their students: college-prep curricula for middle-class neighborhoods, vocational and technical schools for future factory workers, and separate schools or tracks for African-Americans and Latinos.

All teenagers shared rock-and-roll, a new music of the mid-1950s that adapted the rhythm-and-blues of urban blacks for a white mass market. Rock music drew vitality from poor southern whites (Buddy Holly, Elvis Presley), Hispanics (Richie Valens), and, in the 1960s, the British working class (the Beatles). Record producers played up the association between rock music and youthful rebellion.

Turning to Religion

Leaders from Dwight Eisenhower to FBI Director J. Edgar Hoover advocated churchgoing as an antidote for Communism. Regular church attendance grew from 48 percent of the population in 1940 to 63 percent in 1960. Congress created new connections between religion and government when it added "under God" to the Pledge of Allegiance in 1954 and required currency to bear the phrase "In God We Trust" in 1955.

Radio and television preachers added a new dimension to religious life. Bishop Fulton J. Sheen brought vigorous anti-Communism and Catholic doctrine to millions of TV viewers who would never have entered a Catholic church. Norman Vincent Peale

blended popular psychology with Protestantism. His book *The Power of Positive Thinking* (1952) told readers to "stop worrying and start living" and sold millions of copies.

Another strand in the religious revival was revitalized evangelical and fundamentalist churches. During the 1950s, the theologically and socially conservative Southern Baptists became the largest Protestant denomination. Evangelist Billy Graham continued the grand American tradition of the mass revival meeting. Graham was a pioneer in the resurgence of evangelical Christianity that stressed an individual approach to belief and social issues. "Before we can solve the economic, philosophical, and political problems in the world," he said, "pride, greed, lust, and sin are going to have to be erased."

African-American churches were community institutions as well as religious organizations. Black congregations in northern cities swelled in the postwar years and often supported extensive social service programs. In southern cities, churches were centers for community pride and training grounds for the emerging civil rights movement.

Boundaries between many Protestant denominations blurred as church leaders emphasized national unity. Supreme Court decisions sowed the seeds for later political activism among evangelical Christians. In *Engel* v. *Vitale* (1962), the Court said that public schools could not require children to start the school day with group prayer. *Abington Township* v. *Schempp* (1963) prohibited devotional Bible reading in the schools. Such decisions alarmed many evangelicals.

The Gospel of Prosperity

Writers and intellectuals often marveled at the prosperity of Eisenhower's America. William H. Whyte Jr. searched American corporations for the changing character of the United States in *The Organization Man* (1956). Historian David Potter brilliantly analyzed Americans in *People of Plenty* (1954), contending that their national character had been shaped by the abundance of natural resources. In *The Affluent Society* (1958), economist John Kenneth Galbraith predicted that the challenge of the future would be to ensure the fair distribution of national wealth.

Officially, the American message was that abundance was a natural by-product of a free society. In fact, it was easy to present prosperity as a goal in itself, as Vice President Richard Nixon did when he represented the United States at a technology exposition in Moscow in 1959. The American exhibit included a complete six-room ranch house. In its "miracle kitchen," Nixon engaged Soviet Communist party chairman Nikita Khrushchev in the "kitchen debate." The vice president claimed that the "most important thing" for Americans was "the right to choose": "We have so many different manufacturers and many different kinds of washing machines so that the housewives have a choice."

The Underside of Affluence

The most basic criticism of the ideology of prosperity was the simplest—that affluence concealed vast inequalities. Michael Harrington wrote *The Other America* (1962) to remind Americans about the "underdeveloped nation" of 40 to 50 million poor people who had missed the last two decades of prosperity.

C. Wright Mills found dangers in the way that the Cold War distorted American society at the top. *The Power Elite* (1956) described an interlocking alliance of big government, big business, and the military. The losers in a permanent war economy, said Mills, were economic and political democracy.

Other critics targeted the alienating effects of consumerism and the conformity of homogeneous suburbs. Sociologist David Riesman saw suburbia as the home of "other-directed" individuals who lacked inner convictions.

There was far greater substance to increasing dissatisfaction among women. In 1963, Betty Friedan's book *The Feminine Mystique* followed numerous articles in *McCall's*, *Redbook*, and the *Ladies' Home Journal* about the unhappiness of college-educated women who were expected to find total satisfaction in kids and cooking. What Friedan called "the problem that has no name" was a sense of personal emptiness. "I got up one morning," remembered Geraldine Bean, "and I got my kids off to school. I went in to comb my hair and wash my face, and I stood in front of the bathroom mirror crying . . . because at eight-thirty in the morning I had my children off to school. I had my housework done. There was absolutely nothing for me to do the rest of the day." She went on to earn a Ph.D. and win election to the board of regents of the University of Colorado.

Eventually, the critical analyses of Harrington, Mills, and Friedan would fuel radical politics.

Facing Off with the Soviet Union

Americans got a reassuring new face in the White House in 1953, but not new policies toward the world. The United States pushed ahead in an arms race with the Soviet Union, stood guard on the borders of China and the Soviet empire, and judged political changes in Latin America, Africa, and Asia for their effect on the global balance of power.

Why We Liked Ike

In the late twentieth century, few leaders can master both domestic policy and foreign affairs. Some recent presidents, such as Lyndon Johnson, were more adept at social problems than diplomacy. In contrast, Richard Nixon and George Bush were more interested in the world outside the United States.

Dwight Eisenhower was one of these "foreign policy presidents." Most of his experience was military and diplomatic. He had helped hold together the alliance that defeated Nazi Germany and built NATO into an effective force in 1951–1952. He then sought the Republican nomination, he said, to ensure that the United States kept its international commitments. He sealed his victory in 1952 by emphasizing foreign policy expertise, telling a Detroit campaign audience that "to bring the Korean war to an early and honorable end . . . requires a personal trip to Korea. I shall make that trip . . . I shall go to Korea."

Many of Eisenhower administration's accomplishments were things that didn't happen. Eisenhower refused to dismantle the social programs of the New Deal. He exerted American political and military power around the globe but avoided war.

It helped Eisenhower's political agenda if Americans thought of him as a smiling grandfather. The "Ike" who gave rambling, incoherent answers at White House press conferences was controlling information and keeping the opposition guessing. When his press secretary advised him to duck questions at one press conference, Ike replied, "Don't worry, I'll just confuse them." He was easily reelected in 1956.

A Balance of Terror

The backdrop for U.S. foreign policy was the growing capacity for mutual nuclear annihilation. The old balance of power had become a balance of terror.

The Eisenhower administration's doctrine of massive retaliation was a grand strategy that economized on military spending. Eisenhower compared uncontrolled military spending to crucifying humankind on a "cross of iron." "Every gun that is fired," he warned, "every warship launched, every rocket fired signifies . . . a theft from those who hunger and are not fed, those who are cold and not clothed." The administration concentrated military spending where the nation already had the greatest advantage—on atomic weapons, instead of attempting to match the land armies of the Soviet Union and China. In response to any serious attack, the United States would direct maximum force against the homeland of the aggressor. The National Security Council in 1953 made reliance on "massive retaliatory damage" by nuclear weapons official policy to offset the larger Communist armies in eastern Europe.

The doctrine grew even more fearful as the Soviet Union developed its own hydrogen bombs. The chairman of the Atomic Energy Commission terrified the American people by mentioning casually that the Soviets could now obliterate New York City. Signs for air raid shelters posted on downtown buildings, air raid drills in schools, and appearance of radioactivity in milk supplies in the form of the isotope strontium 90 carried by fallout made the atomic threat very immediate.

The USSR added to worries about atomic war by launching the world's first artificial satellite. On the first Sunday of October 1957, Americans discovered that *Sputnik*—Russian for "satellite"—was orbiting the earth. The Soviets soon lifted a dog into orbit while U.S. rockets fizzled on the pad. Soviet propagandists claimed that their technological "first" showed the superiority of Communism, and Americans wondered if the United States had lost its edge. The new **National Aeronautics and Space Administration (NASA)** took over the satellite program in 1958.

The crisis was more apparent than real. The combination of Soviet rocketry and nuclear capacity created alarm about a missile gap. The USSR was said to be building hundreds of intercontinental ballistic missiles (ICBMs) to overwhelm American air defenses designed to intercept piloted bombers. Although there was no such gap, Eisenhower was unwilling to reveal secret information that might have allayed public anxiety.

Containment in Action

Someone who heard only the campaign speeches in 1952 might have expected sharp foreign policy changes under Eisenhower, but there was more continuity than change. John Foster Dulles, Eisenhower's secretary of state, had attacked the Democrats as defeatists and appeasers. He demanded that the United States liberate eastern Europe from Soviet control and encourage Jiang Jieshi to attack Communist China. In 1956, Dulles proudly claimed that tough-minded diplomacy had repeatedly brought the United States to the verge of war: "We walked to the brink and looked it in the face. We took strong action."

In fact, Eisenhower viewed the Cold War in the same terms as Truman. Caution replaced campaign rhetoric about "rolling back" Communism.

Around the periphery of the Communist nations, from eastern Asia to the Middle East to Europe, the United States accepted the existing sphere of Communist influence but attempted to block its growth, a policy most Americans accepted.

The American worldview assumed both the right and the need to intervene in the affairs of other nations, especially in Latin America, Asia, and Africa. Policymakers saw these nations as markets for U.S. products and sources of vital raw materials. When political disturbances arose in these states, the United States blamed Soviet meddling to justify U.S. intervention. If Communism could not be rolled back in eastern Europe, the CIA could still undermine anti-American governments in the **third world**. The Soviets themselves took advantage of local revolutions even when they did not instigate them.

Twice during Eisenhower's first term, the CIA subverted democratically elected governments that seemed to threaten U.S. interests. In Iran, which had nationalized British and U.S. oil companies in an effort to break the hold of western corporations, the CIA in 1953 backed a coup that toppled the government and helped the young Shah, or monarch, gain control. The Shah then cooperated with the United States until his overthrow in 1979. In Guatemala, the leftist government was upsetting the United Fruit Company. When the Guatemalans accepted weapons from the Communist bloc in 1954, the CIA imposed a regime friendly to U.S. business (see Map 30-1).

For most Americans in 1953, democracy in Iran was far less important than ending the war in Korea and stabilizing relations with China. Soviet and Chinese interest in improving relations with the United States after the death of Joseph Stalin in March 1953 set the stage. Eisenhower declined to escalate the Korean War by blockading China and sending more U.S. ground forces. Instead he shifted atomic bombs to Okinawa, only 400 miles from China. The nuclear threat, along with the continued cost of the war on both sides, brought the Chinese to a truce that left Korea divided into two nations.

In Vietnam, on China's southern border, France was fighting to maintain its colonial rule against rebels who combined Communist ideology with fervor for national independence under the leadership of Ho Chi Minh. The United States picked up three-quarters of the costs, but the French military position collapsed in 1954. The French had had enough, and Eisenhower was unwilling to join another Asian war. A Geneva peace conference in 1954 "temporarily" divided Vietnam into a Communist north and a non-Communist

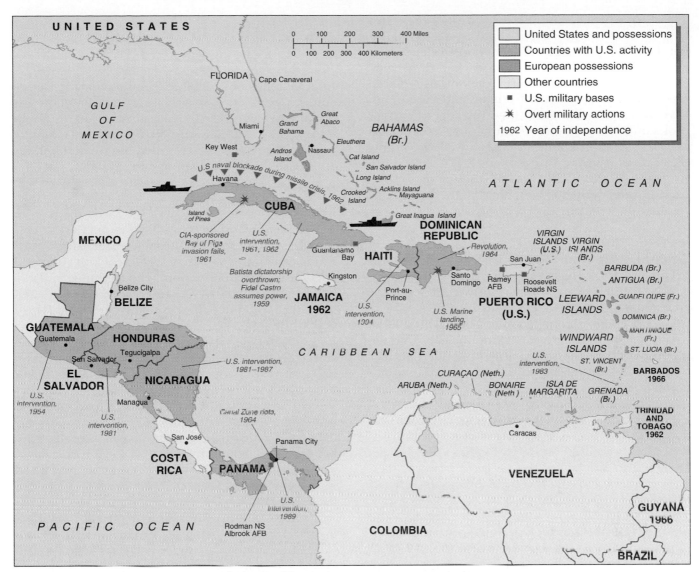

Map 30-1   *U.S. Intervention around the Caribbean since 1954*
The United States has long kept a careful eye on the politics of neighboring nations to its
south. In the second half of the twentieth century, the United States has frequently used military assistance or force to influence or intervene in Caribbean and Central American nations.
The most common purpose has been to counter or undermine left-leaning governments; some
interventions, as in Haiti, have been intended to stabilize democratic regimes.

south and scheduled elections for a single Vietnamese government.

The United States then replaced France as
the supporter of pro-Western Vietnamese in the
south. Washington's client was Ngo Dinh Diem, an
anti-Communist from South Vietnam's Roman
Catholic elite. U.S. officials encouraged Diem to put
off the elections and backed his efforts to construct
an authoritarian South Vietnam. Ho meanwhile consolidated the northern half as a Communist state that
claimed to be the legitimate government for all Vietnam. The United States further reinforced contain-

ment in Asia by creating the **Southeast Asia Treaty
Organization (SEATO)** in 1954.

Halfway around the world, there was a new
crisis when three American friends—France, Britain,
and Israel—ganged up on Egypt, each for its own
reasons. On October 29, 1956, Israel attacked Egypt.
A week later, British and French forces attempted to
seize the canal. The United States forced a quick
cease-fire, partly to maintain its standing with oil-producing Arab nations. The war left Britain and France
dependent on American oil that Eisenhower would
not provide until they left Egypt.

In Europe, Eisenhower accepted the status quo because conflicts there could result in nuclear war. In 1956, challenges to Communist rule arose in East Germany, Poland, and Hungary and threatened to break up the Soviet empire. The Soviets replaced liberal Communists in East Germany and Poland with hard-liners. In Hungary, however, open warfare broke out. Hungarian freedom fighters in Budapest used rocks and fire bombs against Soviet tanks while pleading in vain for Western aid. NATO would not risk war with the USSR. Tens of thousands of Hungarians died and 200,000 fled when the Soviets crushed the resistance.

Global Standoff

As documents from both sides of the Cold War become available, historians have realized what dangerously different meanings the two sides gave to confrontations between 1953 and 1964.

A good example was the U-2 affair of 1960, which derailed progress toward nuclear disarmament. Both countries voluntarily suspended nuclear tests in 1958 and prepared for a June 1960 summit meeting in Paris, where Eisenhower intended to negotiate a test ban treaty.

But on May 1, 1960, Soviet air defenses shot down an American U-2 spy plane over the heart of Russia and captured the pilot, Francis Gary Powers. Designed to soar above the range of Soviet antiaircraft missiles, U-2s had assured American officials that there was no missile gap.

When Moscow trumpeted the news of the downing, Eisenhower took personal responsibility in hopes that Khrushchev would accept the U-2 as an unpleasant reality of international espionage. Unfortunately, the planes meant something very different to the Soviets, touching their festering sense of inferiority. They had stopped protesting the flights in 1957 because complaints were demeaning. The Americans thought that silence signaled acceptance. When Eisenhower refused to apologize in Paris, Khrushchev stalked out. Disarmament was set back for years.

The most important aspect of Eisenhower's foreign policy was continuity. The administration pursued containment as defined under Truman. The Cold War consensus, however, prevented the United States from seeing the nations of the developing world on their own terms. By viewing every independence movement and social revolution as part of the competition with Communism, American leaders created unnecessary problems (see "American Views: Two Presidents Assess the Implications of the Cold War").

John F. Kennedy and the Cold War

John Kennedy was a man of contradictions. A Democrat, he presided over policies whose direction was set under Eisenhower. Despite stirring rhetoric about leading the nation toward a **New Frontier** of scientific and social progress, he recorded his greatest failures and successes in the continuing Cold War.

The Kennedy Mystique

Kennedy won the presidency over Richard Nixon in a cliffhanging 1960 election that was more about personality and style than substance (see Map 30-2). Both candidates were determined not to yield another inch to Communism. The charming and eloquent Kennedy narrowly skirted scandal in his personal life. Well publicized as a war hero from World War II, he tempered ruthless ambition with respect for public service. His forthright campaigning allayed voter concern about his Roman Catholicism. Nixon had wider experience and was a shrewd tactician, but he was also self-righteous and awkward.

Television was crucial to the outcome. The campaign featured the first televised presidential debates. In the first session, Nixon actually gave better replies, but his nervousness and a bad makeup job turned off millions of viewers who admired Kennedy's energy. Nixon never overcame the setback. Kennedy's televised inauguration was the perfect setting for his impassioned plea for national unity: "My fellow Americans," he challenged, "ask not what your country can do for you—ask what you can do for your country."

Kennedy brought dash to the White House. His beautiful and refined wife, Jackie, outshined previous first ladies. Kennedy's staff and large family played touch football, not golf. No president had shown such verve since Teddy Roosevelt. People began to talk about Kennedy's "charisma," his ability to lead by sheer force of personality.

Kennedy's Mistakes

Talking tough to satisfy more militant countrymen, Kennedy and Khrushchev pushed each other into corners, continuing the problems of mutual misunderstanding. When Khrushchev promised in January 1961 to support "wars of national liberation," he was really fending off Chinese criticism. But Kennedy overreacted in his first State of the Union address by asking for more military spending.

Three months later, Kennedy fed Soviet fears of American aggressiveness by sponsoring an inva-

American Views

TWO PRESIDENTS ASSESS THE IMPLICATIONS OF THE COLD WAR

In speeches two days apart in January 1961, outgoing President Dwight Eisenhower and incoming President John Kennedy offered contrasting interpretations of America's Cold War crusade. Eisenhower spoke with concern about the effects of defense spending on American society. Kennedy promised an unlimited commitment of resources to achieve national goals.

❖ **Why did Kennedy define the American mission to the world so broadly?**

❖ **What changes in the 1950s led Eisenhower to warn about the dangers of pursuing that mission?**

❖ **Do the selections show basic agreement or disagreement about the goals of national policy?**

Dwight D. Eisenhower, Farewell Address, January 18, 1961

Our military organization today bears little relation to that known by any of my predecessors in peacetime. . . .

This conjunction of an immense military establishment and a large arms industry is new in the American experience. The total influence—economic, political, even spiritual—is felt in every city, every State house, every office of the federal government. We recognize the imperative need for this development. Yet we must not fail to comprehend its grave implications. . . .

In the councils of government, we must guard against the acquisition of unwarranted influence, whether sought or unsought, by the military-industrial complex. The potential for the disastrous rise of misplaced power exists and will persist.

We must never let the weight of this combination endanger our liberties or democratic processes. We should take nothing for granted. Only an alert and knowledgeable citizenry can compel the proper meshing of the huge industrial and military machinery of defense with our peaceful methods and goals.

John F. Kennedy, Inaugural Address, January 20, 1961

Let the word go forth from this time and place, to friend and foe alike, that the torch has been passed to a new generation of Americans—born in this century, tempered by war, disciplined by a hard and bitter peace, proud of our ancient heritage—and unwilling to witness or permit the slow undoing of those human rights to which this nation has always been committed, and to which we are committed today at home and around the world.

Let every nation know, whether it wishes us well or ill, that we shall pay any price, bear any burden, meet any hardship, support any friends, oppose any foe to assure the survival and the success of liberty.

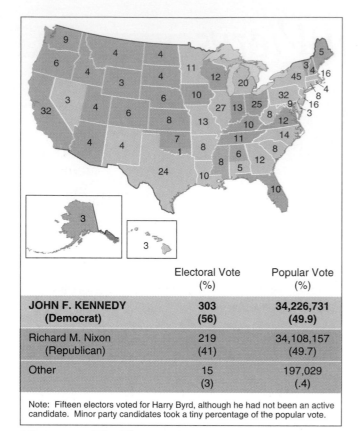

	Electoral Vote (%)	Popular Vote (%)
JOHN F. KENNEDY (Democrat)	303 (56)	34,226,731 (49.9)
Richard M. Nixon (Republican)	219 (41)	34,108,157 (49.7)
Other	15 (3)	197,029 (.4)

Note: Fifteen electors voted for Harry Byrd, although he had not been an active candidate. Minor party candidates took a tiny percentage of the popular vote.

Map 30-2   The Election of 1960
The presidential election of 1960 was one of the closest in American history. John Kennedy's victory depended on his appeal in northern industrial states with large Roman Catholic populations and his ability to hold much of the traditionally Democratic South. Texas, the home state of his vice-presidential running mate Lyndon Johnson, was vital to the success of the ticket.

sion of Cuba. At the start of 1959, Fidel Castro replaced another Cuban dictator, Fulgencio Batista.

When fourteen hundred anti-Castro Cubans landed at Cuba's **Bay of Pigs** on April 17, 1961, they were following a plan from the Eisenhower administration. The CIA had trained and armed the invaders and convinced Kennedy that the landing would trigger spontaneous uprisings. But when Kennedy refused to commit American armed forces to support them, Cuban forces captured the attackers.

Kennedy followed the Bay of Pigs debacle with a hasty and ill-prepared summit meeting with Khrushchev in Vienna in June, that left the Soviets with the impression that the president was weak. To exploit Kennedy's perceived vulnerability, the USSR renewed tension over Berlin, deep within East Germany. The divided city served as an escape route from Communism for hundreds of thousands of East Germans. Khrushchev now threatened to transfer the Soviet sector in Berlin to East Germany, which had

no treaty obligations to France, Britain, or the United States. If the West had to deal directly with East Germany for access to Berlin, it would have to recognize a permanently divided Germany. Kennedy sounded the alarm; he doubled draft calls, called up reservists, and warned families to build fallout shelters. Boise, Idaho, families paid $100 for a share in a community shelter with its own power plant and hospital.

Rather than confront the United States directly, however, the Soviets and East Germans on August 13, 1961, built the **Berlin Wall** around the western sectors of Berlin while leaving the access route to West Germany open. In private, Kennedy accepted the wall as a clever way to stabilize a dangerous situation: "A wall," he said, "is a hell of a lot better than a war."

Another indirect consequence of the Vienna summit was growing American involvement in South Vietnam. Kennedy saw South Vietnam as a promising arena for containment. The anti-Communist Diem controlled the cities with the help of a large army and a Vietnamese elite that had worked with the French. In the countryside, Communist insurgents known as the **Viet Cong** were gaining strength. The United States stepped up its supply of weapons and sent advisers, including members of one of Kennedy's military innovations, the Army Special Forces Group (Green Berets).

U.S. aid did not work. Diem's government by 1963 was losing the loyalty—"hearts and minds"—of many South Vietnamese. North Vietnamese support for the Viet Cong canceled the effect of U.S. assistance. Kennedy's administration tacitly approved a coup on November 1 that killed Diem and his brother and installed an ineffective military junta.

Missile Crisis: A Line Drawn in the Waves

On October 15, 1962 reconnaissance photos revealed construction work on Cuban launching sites from which Soviet-operated nuclear missiles could hit the United States. Top officials met as the Executive Committee for National Security. Doing nothing meant political disaster. Full-scale invasion of Cuba was infeasible on short notice, and "surgical" air strikes were technically impossible. Secretary of Defense Robert McNamara suggested demanding removal of the missiles and declaring a naval "quarantine" against the arrival of further offensive weapons. A blockade would buy time for diplomacy.

Kennedy imposed the blockade in a terrifying speech on Monday, October 22. He emphasized the "deceptive" deployment of the Soviet missiles and raised the specter of nuclear war. Americans would have been even more afraid had they known that some of the missiles were operational and that Soviets in Cuba were authorized to use them in self-defense. On Friday, Khrushchev offered to withdraw the missiles in return for an American pledge not to invade Cuba. On Saturday, a second communication raised a new complaint about American missiles on the territory of NATO allies. The letter was the result of pressure by Kremlin hard-liners and Khrushchev's own wavering. Kennedy decided to accept the first letter and ignore the second. The United States pledged not to invade Cuba and secretly promised to remove obsolete Jupiter missiles from Turkey.

Why did Khrushchev risk the Cuban gamble? One reason was to protect Castro as a symbol of Soviet commitment to anti-Western regimes in the developing world. Kennedy had tried to preempt Castroism in 1961 by launching the **Alliance for Progress**, an economic development program for Latin America that tied aid to social reform. However, the United States had also orchestrated the Bay of Pigs invasion and funded "Operation Mongoose," a CIA campaign to sabotage Cuba and assassinate its leaders. Castro and Khrushchev had reason to fear the worst.

Khrushchev also hoped to redress the strategic balance. Intermediate-range rockets gave the USSR a nuclear club over western Europe, but in October 1962, the USSR had fewer than fifty ICBMs to aim at the United States and China. The United States was creating a defensive triad of a thousand land-based Minuteman missiles, five hundred long-range bombers, and six hundred Polaris missiles on nuclear submarines targeted on the USSR. The strategic imbalance had sustained NATO during the Berlin confrontation, but forty launchers in Cuba with two warheads each would have doubled the Soviet capacity to strike at the United States.

Soviet missiles in Cuba thus flouted the Monroe Doctrine and posed a real military threat. In the end, both sides were cautious. Khrushchev backed down rather than fight. Kennedy fended off hawkish advisers who wanted to destroy Castro. The world had trembled, but neither nation wanted war over "the missiles of October." In the long run, the crisis accelerated the global arms race. Never again, Soviet leaders vowed, would they submit to American nuclear superiority.

Science and Foreign Affairs

When Kennedy took office, the United States was still playing catch-up in space technology. A Russian, Yuri Gagarin, was the first human to orbit the earth, on April 12, 1961. American John Glenn did not match Gagarin's feat until February 1962. Kennedy committed the United States to placing an American astronaut on the moon by 1970. The decision nar-

rowed a multi-faceted scientific and military program to a massive engineering project that favored the economic capacity of the United States.

After the three-year moratorium, both resumed nuclear weapons tests in 1961–1962. In July 1963, the United States, Britain, and the USSR signed the **Limited Test Ban Treaty**, which outlawed nuclear testing in the atmosphere, in outer space, and under water, and invited other nations to join in. A more comprehensive treaty was impossible because the Soviet Union refused the on-site inspections. France and China, the other nuclear powers, refused to sign, and the treaty did not halt weapons development, but it was the most positive achievement of Kennedy's foreign policy and a step toward later disarmament treaties.

Righteousness like a Mighty Stream: The Struggle for Civil Rights

Linda Brown of Topeka, Kansas, was a third-grader whose parents were fed up with sending her past an all-white public school to attend an all-black school a mile away. The Browns volunteered to help the NAACP challenge Topeka's school segregation by trying to enroll Linda in their neighborhood school, beginning a legal challenge that reached the Supreme Court. Three years later, on May 17, 1954, in *Brown v. Board of Education of Topeka*, the justices reversed the 1896 case of *Plessy v. Ferguson* by ruling that sending black children to "separate but equal" schools denied them equal treatment under the Constitution.

Getting to the Supreme Court

The *Brown* decision climaxed a twenty-five-year campaign to reenlist the federal courts on the side of equal rights *(see the Summary table "Civil Rights in the South: The Struggle for Racial Equality")*. The work began in the 1930s when Charles Hamilton Houston, dean of Howard University's law school, trained a corps of civil rights lawyers. Working on behalf of the NAACP, he hoped to erode *Plessy* by suits focused on interstate travel and professional graduate schools (the least defensible segregated institutions because states seldom provided alternatives). In 1938, Houston's student Thurgood Marshall, a future Supreme Court justice, took over the NAACP job.

The *Brown* case combined lawsuits from Delaware, Virginia, South Carolina, the District of Columbia, and Kansas. In each instance, students and families braved community pressure to demand

SUMMARY

CIVIL RIGHTS IN THE SOUTH: THE STRUGGLE FOR RACIAL EQUALITY

Area of Concern	Key Actions	Results
Public school integration	Federal court cases	*Brown* v. *Board of Education of Topeka* (1954) Enforcement by presidential action, Little Rock (1957) Follow-up court decisions, including mandatory busing programs
Equal access to public facilities	Montgomery bus boycott (1955) Lunch counter sit-ins (1960) Freedom rides (1961) Birmingham demonstrations (1963) March on Washington (1963)	Civil Rights Act of 1964
Equitable voter registration	Voter registration drives, including Mississippi Summer Project (1964) Demonstrations and marches, including Selma to Montgomery march (1965)	Voting Rights Act of 1965

equal access to a basic public service. Viewing public education as central for the equal opportunity that lay at the heart of American values, the Court weighed the *consequences* of segregated school systems and concluded that separate meant unequal.

Brown also built on efforts by Mexican-Americans in the Southwest to assert their rights of citizenship. In 1946, the federal courts had prohibited segregation of Mexican-American children in California schools. Eight years later, the Supreme Court forbade Texas from excluding Mexican-Americans from juries.

Deliberate Speed

Racial segregation by law was largely a southern problem, the legacy of Jim Crow laws from early in the century. At first, Americans elsewhere thought of racial injustice as a regional issue.

Southern responses to *Brown* emphasized regional differences. Few southern communities desegregated schools voluntarily. Their reluctance was bolstered in 1955 when the Supreme Court allowed segregated states to carry out the 1954 decision "with all deliberate speed" rather than immediately. The following year, 101 southern congressmen and senators reinforced southern denial by issuing the **Southern Manifesto**, which asserted that the Court decision was unconstitutional. President Eisenhower privately deplored the desegregation decision, which violated his sense of states' rights and upset Republican attempts to gain southern votes.

The first crisis came in Little Rock, Arkansas, in September 1957. The city school board admitted nine African-Americans to Central High, only to be upstaged by Governor Orval Faubus. Claiming to fear violence, he surrounded Central with the National

Guard and turned the new students away. Meanwhile, segregationists stirred up white fears. Under intense national pressure, Faubus withdrew the Guard, and a howling crowd surrounded the school. When the black students entered anyway, the mob threatened to storm the building. The police had to sneak them out after two hours. Fuming at the governor's defiance of federal authority, which bordered on insurrection, Eisenhower reluctantly nationalized the National Guard and sent in the 101st Airborne Division to keep order. Eight of the students endured a year of harassment in the hallways of Central.

The breakthrough in school integration did not come until the end of the 1960s, when the courts rejected further delays and federal authorities threatened to cut off education funds. As late as 1968, only 6 percent of African-American children in the South attended integrated schools. By 1973, the figure was 90 percent.

Public Accommodations

Most southern states separated the races in bus terminals and movie theaters. They required black riders to take rear seats on buses. They labeled separate restrooms and drinking fountains for "colored" users. Hotels denied rooms to blacks, and restaurants refused them service.

The struggle to end segregated facilities started in Montgomery, Alabama. On December 1, 1955, Rosa Parks, a seamstress who worked at a downtown department store, refused to give up her bus seat to a white passenger and was arrested. Parks acted spontaneously, but she was part of a network of civil rights activists who wanted to challenge segregated buses and was the secretary of the Montgomery NAACP. As news of her action spread, the Women's Political Council, a group of college-trained black women, initiated a mass boycott of the privately owned bus company. Martin Luther King Jr., a twenty-six-year-old pastor, galvanized a mass meeting with a speech that quoted the biblical prophet Amos: "We are determined here in Montgomery to work and fight until justice runs down like water, and righteousness like a mighty stream."

A car pool substituted for the buses despite police harassment. As the boycott survived months of pressure, the national media began to pay attention. After nearly a year, the Supreme Court agreed that the bus segregation law was unconstitutional.

Victory in Montgomery depended on the steadfastness of African-American involvement. Participants cut across the class lines that had divided black Southerners. Success also revealed the discrepancy between white attitudes in the Deep South and national opinion. For white Southerners, segregation was a local concern best defined as a legal or constitutional matter. For other Americans, it was increasingly an issue of the South's deviation from national moral norms.

The Montgomery boycott won a local victory and made King famous. King formed the **Southern Christian Leadership Conference (SCLC)**. But four African-American college students in Greensboro, North Carolina, started the next phase of the struggle. On February 1, 1960, they sat down at the segregated lunch counter in Woolworth's, waiting through the day without being served. Their patient courage brought more demonstrators; within two days, eighty-five students packed the store. Nonviolent sit-ins spread throughout the South.

In a comparatively sophisticated border city like Nashville, Tennessee, sit-ins integrated lunch counters. Elsewhere they precipitated white violence and mass arrests. Like soldiers on a battlefield, nervous participants in sit-ins and demonstrations drew strength from one another. "If you don't have courage," said one young woman in Albany, Georgia, "you can borrow it." SCLC leader Ella Baker helped the students form a new organization, the **Student Nonviolent Coordinating Committee (SNCC)**.

The year 1961 brought "freedom rides" to test the segregation of interstate bus terminals. The idea came from James Farmer of the Congress of Racial Equality (CORE). Two buses carrying black and white passengers met only minor problems in Virginia, the Carolinas, and Georgia, but Alabamians burned one of the buses and attacked the riders in Birmingham, where they beat demonstrators senseless and clubbed a Justice Department observer. The governor and police refused to protect the freedom riders, bringing the SCLC and SNCC into the protest. The riders traveled into Mississippi under National Guard protection but were arrested at the Jackson bus terminal. Freedom rides continued through the summer.

March on Washington, 1963

John Kennedy was a tepid supporter of the civil rights movement and entered office with no civil rights agenda. He appointed segregationist judges to mollify southern congressmen and would have preferred that blacks stop disturbing the fragile Democratic party coalition.

In the face of slow federal response, the SCLC concentrated for 1963 on rigidly segregated Birmingham. April began with sit-ins and marches that aimed to integrate lunch counters, restrooms, and stores and secure open hiring for some clerical jobs. Birmingham's commissioner of public safety, Bull Connor, used fire hoses to blast demonstrators against buildings and roll children down the streets. When demonstrators fought back, his men chased them with dogs. Continued marches brought the arrest of hundreds of children. King's own "Letter from Birmingham City Jail" stated the case for protest: "We have not made a single gain in civil rights without determined legal and nonviolent pressure. . . . Freedom is never voluntarily given by the oppressor; it must be demanded by the oppressed."

The events in Alabama had forced President Kennedy to board the freedom train with an eloquent June 11 speech and to send a civil rights bill to Congress. "Are we to say . . . that this is the land of the free, except for Negroes, that we have no second-class citizens, except Negroes . . . ? Now the time has come for the nation to fulfill its promise."

On August 28, 1963, a quarter of a million blacks and whites marched to the Lincoln Memorial. The day gave Martin Luther King Jr. a national pulpit. His call for progress toward Christian and American goals had immense appeal. Television cut away from afternoon programs for his "I Have a Dream" speech. The March on Washington demonstrated the mass appeal of civil rights and its identification with national values.

"Let Us Continue"

The optimism of the March on Washington shattered with the assassination of John Kennedy in November 1963. In 1964 and 1965, however, President Lyndon Johnson pushed through Kennedy's legislative agenda and much more.

Dallas, 1963

In November 1963, President Kennedy visited Texas to patch up feuds among Texas Democrats. On November 22, the president's motorcade took him near the Texas School Book Depository building in Dallas, where Lee Harvey Oswald had stationed himself at a window on the sixth floor. When Kennedy's open car swung into the sights of his rifle, Oswald fired three shots that wounded Texas Governor John Connally and killed the president. As doctors vainly treated the president in a hospital emergency room, Dallas police arrested Oswald. Vice President Lyndon Johnson took the oath of office as president in the plane on the way back to Washington while the blood-spattered Jacqueline Kennedy looked on. Two days later, as Oswald was being led to a courtroom, Texas nightclub owner Jack Ruby killed Oswald with a handgun, in full view of TV cameras.

Lee Oswald was a twenty-four-year old misfit. He had served in the Marines and worked maintaining U-2 spy planes before defecting to the Soviet Union. He returned to the United States after three years with a fervent commitment to Fidel Castro's Cuban revolution. He visited the Soviet and Cuban embassies in Mexico City in September trying to drum up a job, but neither country thought him worth hiring.

Some Americans believe there is more to the story. Why? One possibility is that Oswald seems too insignificant to be responsible on his own for the murder of a charismatic president. The sketchy job done by the Warren Commission, appointed to investigate the assassination, calmed fears in the short run but left loose ends that have fueled conspiracy theories.

All of the theories remain unproved. Logic holds that the simplest explanation for cutting through a mass of information is usually the best. Oswald was a social misfit with a grievance against American society. Ruby was an impulsive man who told his brother on his deathbed that he thought he was doing the country a favor.

War on Poverty

Five days after the assassination, Lyndon Johnson claimed Kennedy's progressive aura for his new administration. "Let us continue," he told the nation, promising to implement Kennedy's policies. Lyndon Johnson was a professional politician who had reached the top through Texas politics and congressional infighting. Johnson's presence on the ticket in 1960 had helped elect Kennedy by attracting southern voters, but he lacked Kennedy's polish and easy relations with the eastern elite. He had entered public life with the New Deal in the 1930s and believed in its principles. Johnson, not Kennedy, was the true heir of Franklin Roosevelt.

Johnson inherited a domestic agenda that the Kennedy administration had defined but not enacted. Initiatives in education, medical insurance, tax reform, and urban affairs had stalled or been gutted by conservatives in Congress.

When Michael Harrington's study *The Other America* became an unexpected bestseller, Kennedy had taken notice. As poverty captured public attention, Kennedy's economic advisers devised a community action program that emphasized education and job training, a national service corps, and a youth conservation corps.

Johnson made Kennedy's antipoverty package his own. Adopting Cold War rhetoric, he declared "unconditional war on poverty." The core of Johnson's program was the **Office of Economic Opportunity**

(OEO). Established under the direction of Kennedy's brother-in-law R. Sargent Shriver in 1964, the OEO operated the **Job Corps** for school dropouts, the **Neighborhood Youth Corps** for unemployed teenagers, the **Head Start** program to prepare poor children for school, and **VISTA** (Volunteers in Service to America), a domestic Peace Corps. OEO's biggest effort went to **Community Action Agencies**. By 1968, more than five hundred such agencies provided health and educational services. Despite flaws, the War on Poverty improved life for millions of Americans.

Civil Rights, 1964–1965

In Johnson's view, segregation not only deprived African-Americans of access to opportunity but also distracted southern whites from their own poverty and underdevelopment.

One solution was the **Civil Rights Act of 1964**, which Kennedy had introduced but Johnson got enacted. The law prohibited segregation in public accommodations, such as hotels, restaurants, gas stations, theaters, and parks, and outlawed employment discrimination on federally assisted projects. It also created the **Equal Employment Opportunity Commission (EEOC)** and included gender in a list of categories protected against discrimination, a provision whose consequences were scarcely suspected in 1964.

Even as Congress was debating the 1964 law, **Freedom Summer** moved political power to the top of the civil rights agenda. Organized by SNCC, the Mississippi Summer Freedom Project was a voter registration drive that sent white and black volunteers to the small towns and back roads of Mississippi. The target was a southern political system that used rigged literacy tests and intimidation to keep blacks from voting. In Mississippi in 1964, only 7 percent of eligible blacks were registered voters. Freedom Summer gained sixteen hundred new voters and taught two thousand children in SNCC-run Freedom Schools at the cost of beatings, bombings, church arson, and the murder of three project workers.

Another outgrowth of the SNCC effort was the Mississippi Freedom Democratic Party (MFDP), a biracial coalition that bypassed Mississippi's all-white Democratic party, followed state party rules, and sent its own delegates to the 1964 Democratic convention. To preserve party harmony, President Johnson refused to expel the "regular" Mississippi Democrats and offered instead to seat two MFDP delegates and enforce party rules for 1968. The MFDP walked out. Fannie Lou Hamer, a MFDP delegate, remembered, "We learned the hard way that even though we had all the law and all the righteousness on our side—that white man is not going to give up his power to us. We have to build our own power."

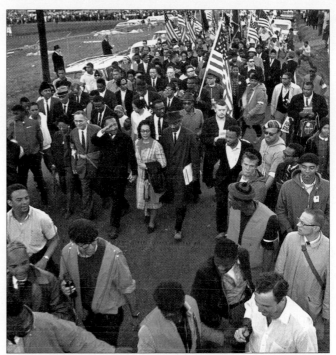

After being attacked and dispersed by Alabama state police as they attempted a 53-mile march from Selma to Montgomery, Alabama, civil rights demonstrators regrouped. Under the glare of national press coverage, Alabama authorities let the march proceed. Here the leaders—including Martin Luther King, Jr., Coretta Scott King, Hosea Williams, Bayard Rustin, and Ralph Bunche—enter Montgomery.

Lyndon Johnson and Martin Luther King Jr. agreed on the need for federal voting legislation when King visited the president in December 1964 after winning the Nobel Peace Prize. For King, power at the ballot box would help black Southerners take control of their own communities. For Johnson, voting reform would fulfill the promise of American democracy. It would also benefit the Democratic party by replacing with black voters the southern whites who were drifting toward anti-integration Republicans.

The target for King and the SCLC was Dallas County, Alabama, where only 2 percent of eligible blacks were registered, compared with 70 percent of whites. Peaceful demonstrations started in January 1965. By early February, jails in the county seat of Selma held 2,600 blacks whose offense was marching to the courthouse to demand the vote. The campaign climaxed with a march from Selma to the state capital of Montgomery. SNCC leader John Lewis remembered, "I don't know what we expected. I think maybe we thought we'd be arrested and jailed, or maybe they wouldn't do anything to us. I had a little knapsack on my shoulder with an apple, a toothbrush, toothpaste, and two books in it: a history of America and a book by [Christian theologian] Thomas Merton."

On Sunday, March 7, five hundred marchers crossed the bridge over the Alabama River to meet a sea of state troopers. The troopers gave them two minutes to disperse and then attacked on foot and horseback "as if they were mowing a big field." The attack drove the demonstrators back in bloody confusion while television cameras rolled.

As violence continued, Johnson addressed a joint session of Congress to demand a voting rights law: "Our mission is at once the oldest and the most basic of this country: to right wrong, to do justice, to serve man." He ended with the refrain of the civil rights movement: "We shall overcome."

Johnson signed the **Voting Rights Act** on August 6, 1965. The law outlawed literacy tests and provided for federal voting registrars in states where registration or turnout in 1964 was less than 50 percent of eligible population. It applied initially in seven southern states. Black registration in these states jumped from 27 percent to 55 percent within the first year. In 1975, Congress extended coverage to Hispanic voters in the Southwest. By the end of 1992, Virginia had elected a black governor and nearly every southern state had sent blacks to Congress. Less obvious but just as revolutionary were the thousands of blacks and Latinos who won local offices and the new moderation of white leaders who had to satisfy black voters.

War, Peace, and the Landslide of 1964

Johnson had maintained Kennedy's commitment to South Vietnam. On the advice of Kennedy holdovers like Defense Secretary Robert McNamara, he stepped up commando raids and naval shelling of North Vietnam. On August 2, North Vietnamese torpedo boats attacked the U.S. destroyer *Maddox* in the Gulf of Tonkin while it was eavesdropping on North Vietnamese military signals. Two days later, the *Maddox* and the *C. Turner Joy* reported another torpedo attack (probably false sonar readings). Johnson ordered a bombing raid and asked Congress to authorize "all necessary measures" to protect American forces and stop further aggression. Congress passed the **Gulf of Tonkin Resolution** with only two nay votes.

Johnson's Republican opponent, Senator Barry Goldwater of Arizona, a former Air Force pilot, wanted aggressive confrontation with Communism. Campaign literature declared that "extremism in the defense of liberty is no vice," raising visions of vigilantes and mobs. Goldwater's campaign made Johnson look moderate. Johnson pledged not "to send American boys nine or ten thousand miles from home to do what Asian boys ought to be doing for themselves" while Goldwater proposed an all-out war.

Johnson's 61 percent of the popular vote was the greatest margin ever recorded in a presidential election. Democrats racked up two-to-one majorities in Congress. For the first time in decades, liberal Democrats could enact their domestic program without begging votes from conservative Southerners or Republicans, and Johnson could achieve his goal of a **Great Society** based on freedom and opportunity for all.

The result in 1965 was a series of measures that Johnson rushed through Congress before his political standing began to erode and Vietnam distracted national attention. The **National Endowment for the Humanities**, **National Endowment for the Arts**, and highway beautification were part of the Great Society for the middle class. The **Wilderness Act** (1964), an early success of the modern environmental movement, preserved 9.1 million acres from all development.

More central to Johnson's vision were efforts to increase opportunity for all. As he told a July 1965 news conference, "When I was young, poverty was so common that we didn't know it had a name. An education was something that you had to fight for. . . . It is now my opportunity to help every child get an education, to have every family get a decent home, and to help bring healing to the sick and dignity to the old." The **Elementary and Secondary Education Act** was the first general federal aid program for public schools, allocating $1.3 billion for textbooks and special education. The **Higher Education Act** funded low-interest student loans and university research facilities. The Medical Care Act created federally funded health insurance for the elderly (**Medicare**) and helped states offer medical care to the poor (**Medicaid**). The Appalachian Regional Development Act funded economic development in the depressed mountain counties of twelve states from Georgia to New York and proved a long-run success.

The United States came closer to winning the war on poverty than the war in Vietnam. New or expanded social insurance and income support programs, such as Medicare, Medicaid, Social Security, and food stamps, cut the proportion of poor people from 22 percent of the American population in 1960 to 13 percent in 1970. Infant mortality dropped by a third because of improved nutrition and better access to health care for mothers and children. Taken together, the political results of the 1964 landslide moved the United States far toward Lyndon Johnson's vision of an end to poverty and racial injustice.

Conclusion

From 1953 to 1964, consistent goals guided American foreign policy including vigilant anti-Communism and the confidence to intervene in trouble spots around the globe. At home, the Supreme Court's *Brown* decision introduced a decade-long civil rights revolution. However, many patterns of personal behavior and social relations remained unchanged. Women faced similar expectations from the early fifties to the early sixties. Churches showed more continuity than change.

In retrospect, it is remarkable how widely and deeply the Cold War shaped U.S. society. Fundamental social institutions, such as marriage and religion, got extra credit for their contributions to anti-Communism. The nation's long tradition of home-grown radicalism was virtually silent in the face of the Cold War consensus. Even economically meritorious programs like more money for science and better roads went down more easily if linked to national defense.

Review Questions

1. What were the sources of prosperity in the 1950s and 1960s? How did prosperity shape cities, family life, and religion? What opportunities did it create for women and for young people? How did it affect the American role in the world? Why did an affluent nation still need a war on poverty in the 1960s?

2. What assumptions about the Soviet Union shaped U.S. foreign policy? What assumptions about the United States shaped Soviet policy? What did American leaders think was at stake in Vietnam, Berlin, and Cuba?

3. Who initiated and led the African-American struggle for civil rights? What role did the federal government play? What were the goals of the civil rights movement? Where did it succeed, and in what ways did it fall short?

4. How did the growth of nuclear arsenals affect international relations? How did the nuclear shadow affect American politics and society?

5. In what new directions did Lyndon Johnson take the United States? Were there differences in the goals of the New Frontier and the Great Society?

Recommended Reading

Michael Beschloss, *May-Day: Eisenhower, Khrushchev, and the U-2 Affair* (1986). The U-2 affair is used to interpret the meaning of the Cold War for the United States and the Soviet Union.

Michael Harrington, *The Other America* (1962). Published early in the Kennedy years, Harrington's impassioned study reminded Americans of continuing economic inequality and helped launch the War on Poverty.

Gerald Posner, *Case Closed* (1993). This is as close as we are likely to get to a definitive analysis of John Kennedy's death. *Case Closed* convincingly refutes the most popular conspiracy theories.

Theodore White, *The Making of the President, 1960* (1961). White's is a vivid account of the issues and personalities of the 1960 campaign.

Juan Williams, *Eyes on the Prize: America's Civil Rights Years, 1954–1965* (1988). This graphic and fast-moving account of the civil rights movement accompanied a PBS television series.

Where to Learn More

❖ **National Air and Space Museum, Washington, D.C.** Part of the Smithsonian Institution's complex of museums in Washington, the Air and Space Museum is the richest source for artifacts and discussion of the American space program.

❖ **Sixth Floor Museum, Dallas, Texas.** Occupying the sixth floor of the former Texas School Book Depository building, exhibits examine the life, death, and legacy of John F. Kennedy.

❖ **Birmingham Civil Rights Institute, Birmingham, Alabama.** This museum and archive deal with the background of southern racial segregation, civil rights activism, and the 1963 demonstrations in Birmingham.

❖ **Martin Luther King Jr., National Historic Site, Atlanta, Georgia.** The birthplace and grave of Reverend King are the nucleus of a park set in the historic black neighborhood of Auburn.

❖ **National Civil Rights Museum, Memphis, Tennessee.** Located in the Lorraine Motel, where Martin Luther King Jr. was killed, the museum traces the participants, background, and effects of key events in the civil rights movement.

❖ **National Afro-American Museum and Cultural Center, Wilberforce, Ohio.** The exhibit, "From Victory to Freedom: Afro-American Life in the Fifties," looks at home, family, music, and religion as well as politics and civil rights.

❖ **New Museum at the John F. Kennedy Library, Boston, Massachusetts.** Exhibits offer a sympathetic view of Kennedy's life and achievements.

31 SHAKEN TO THE ROOTS, 1965–1980

KEY TOPICS

❖ Vietnam, civil rights, and the unraveling of the national consensus
❖ The prolonged military struggle that resulted from Lyndon Johnson's decision to commit American forces to direct combat in Vietnam
❖ Growing opposition to the Vietnam War from 1965 to 1972
❖ The unraveling of the New Deal coalition beginning with the election of 1968
❖ Nixon's presidency and the Watergate scandal
❖ The growing militance of the struggle for civil rights among African-Americans, Hispanic Americans, and Native Americans

At 2 A.M. on February 7, the Viet Cong attacked the U.S. base in Pleiku, 240 miles north of Saigon (now Ho Chi Minh City), killing eight Americans, wounding a hundred, and destroying ten planes and helicopters. National security advisor McGeorge Bundy, in Saigon on a fact-finding visit, Ambassador Maxwell Taylor, and military commander General William Westmoreland quickly recommended a retaliatory air strike against North Vietnam. President Johnson concurred, and navy bombers roared off aircraft carriers in Operation FLAMING DART. A month later, Johnson ordered a full-scale air offensive code-named ROLLING THUNDER.

The official reason for the bombing was to pressure North Vietnam to negotiate an end to the war. As the South Vietnamese government lost control of the countryside, air strikes on North Vietnam looked like an easy way to shore up South Vietnamese morale.

The air strikes pushed the United States over the line from propping up the South Vietnamese government to leading the war effort. A president who desperately wanted a way out of Southeast Asia kept adding American forces. The war in Vietnam hovered like a shadow over the next two presidents, set back progress toward global stability, and divided the American people.

The war eroded the nation's confidence. Most Americans had agreed about the goals of the Cold War, the benefits of economic growth, and the value of equal opportunity. Stalemate in Vietnam, an oil supply crisis, and political changes in other nations outside the framework of the Cold War challenged U.S. influence in the world. Frustrated with slow progress toward racial equality, many minority Americans advocated separation rather than integration. Political scandals undercut faith in government. Fifteen years of turmoil forced a grudging recognition of limits to American military power, economic capacity, and even the ideal of a single American dream.

The End of Consensus

Nineteen sixty-five brought triumphal progress for the goals of the Great Society with such measures as the Voting Rights Act and Medicare. But in the same year, the Viet Cong gained strength in the villages and hills of Vietnam. African-Americans rioted in Los Angeles. Well-educated and articulate young people pursued goals outside the mainstream. The cumulative effect was to unravel the national consensus of the 1950s and early 1960s.

Deeper into Vietnam

Advisers persuaded Lyndon Johnson that controlled military escalation—a middle course between withdrawal and all-out war—could secure Vietnam (see **Map 31-1**). They failed to understand the extent of popular opposition to the official government in Saigon, the depth of Viet Cong organization, and the willingness of North Vietnam to sacrifice to achieve national unity.

ROLLING THUNDER required ground troops to protect bases in South Vietnam. Marines landed on March 8. More bombs, a pause, an offer of massive U.S. aid—nothing brought North Vietnam to the negotiating table. Johnson dribbled in new forces and expanded their mission from base security to combat. On July 28, he finally gave Westmoreland doubled draft calls and an increase in U.S. combat troops from 75,000 to 275,000 by 1966.

Secretary of Defense McNamara was clear about the change: "We have relied on South Vietnam to carry the brunt. Now we would be responsible for

a satisfactory military outcome." At the end of 1967, American forces in South Vietnam totaled 485,000; they reached their maximum of 543,000 in August 1969. In all, more than 2 million Americans served in Vietnam.

The U.S. strategy on the ground was **search and destroy**. As originally conceived by Westmoreland, it used sophisticated surveillance and heavily armed patrols to locate enemy detachments, which could then be destroyed by air strikes, artillery, and reinforcements carried in by helicopter.

However, most opponents were South Vietnamese guerrillas forcing the United States to make repeated sweeps through farms and villages. The enemy was hard to find and impossible for Americans to recognize among farmers and workers, making South Vietnamese society itself the target. The American penchant for massive firepower killed thousands of Vietnamese and made millions refugees.

Pilots dropped tons of bombs on the "Ho Chi Minh Trail," a network of supply routes from North Vietnam to South Vietnam through the mountains of neighboring Laos. Despite the bombing, thousands of workers converted rough paths into roads that were repaired as soon as they were damaged. Air assault on North Vietnam itself remained "diplomatic," intended to force North Vietnam to stop intervening in the South Vietnamese civil war. Since Ho Chi Minh considered North and South to be one country, the American goal was unacceptable. Attacking North Vietnam's poorly developed economy, the United States soon ran out of targets.

At home, protest against the war mounted (see "American Views: An Antiwar Protester Describes the Generation Gap"). In the 1950s, dissenters on the left had been too intimidated by McCarthyism to protest overcommitment to the Cold War. Now the first national antiwar march took place in Washington on April 17. Twenty-five thousand people picketed the White House, assembled at the Washington Monument, and walked up the Mall to the Capitol.

Over the next two years, antiwar activity changed to direct confrontations. Much of the anger was directed at the military draft administered by the **Selective Service System**. Draft deferral criteria helped make Vietnam a working-class war. Full-time college enrollment was good for a deferment; so was graduate school until 1967. Draftees and enlistees tended to be small-town and working-class youth who had few opportunities outside the military. They were also young. The average GI in World War II had been in his mid-twenties;

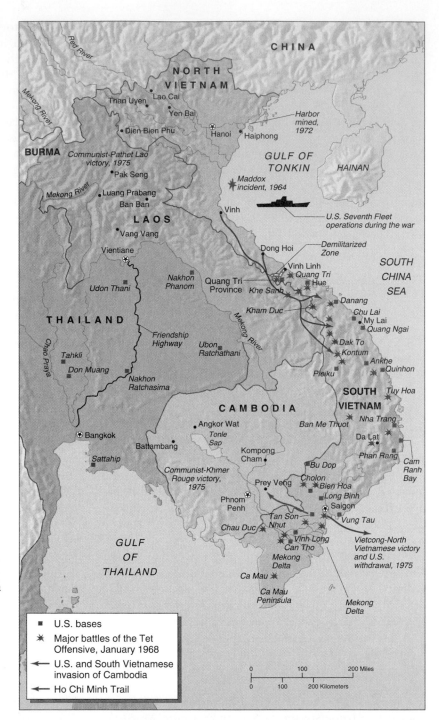

Map 31-1   *The War in Vietnam*
The United States attacked North Vietnam with air strikes but confined large-scale ground operations to South Vietnam and Cambodia. In South Vietnam, U.S. forces faced both North Vietnamese army units and Viet Cong rebels, all of whom received supplies by way of the so-called Ho Chi Minh Trail, named for the leader of North Vietnam. The coordinated attacks on cities and towns throughout South Vietnam during the Tet Offensive in 1968 surprised the United States.

the typical soldier in Vietnam was 19 or 20. Women who served as military nurses tended to come from the same backgrounds.

In 1965, blacks made up 11 percent of the nation's population but 24 percent of its war dead, figures that forced the Defense Department to revise its combat assignments. Martin Luther King Jr. joined the protest in 1967. King called the war a moral disaster whose costs weighed most heavily on the poor

and a new form of white colonialism that was destroying Vietnamese society.

Community Activism

The antiwar movement took much of its tone from the university-based **Students for a Democratic Society (SDS)**. Its **Port Huron Statement**, adopted in 1962, called for grass-roots action and "participatory democracy." SDS tried to harness youthful disillu-

CHRONOLOGY

1962 Rachel Carson publishes *Silent Spring*.

Port Huron Statement launches Students for a Democratic Society.

1965 Congress approves Wilderness Act.

Malcolm X is assassinated.

Residents of Watts neighborhood in Los Angeles riot.

1967 African-Americans riot in Detroit and Newark.

1968 Viet Cong launches Tet Offensive.

James Earl Ray kills Martin Luther King Jr.

Lyndon Johnson declines to run for reelection.

SDS disrupts Columbia University.

Sirhan Sirhan kills Robert Kennedy.

Peace talks start between the United States and North Vietnam.

Police riot against antiwar protesters during the Democratic National Convention in Chicago.

Richard Nixon is elected president.

1969 Neil Armstrong walks on the moon.

1970 United States invades Cambodia.

National Guard units kill students at Kent State and Jackson State Universities.

Earth Day is celebrated.

Environmental Protection Agency is created.

1971 *New York Times* publishes the secret "Pentagon Papers."

President Nixon freezes wages and prices.

"Plumbers" unit is established in the White House.

1972 Nixon visits China.

United States and Soviet Union adopt SALT I.

Operatives for Nixon's reelection campaign break into Democratic headquarters in the Watergate complex in Washington, D.C.

1973 Paris accords end direct U.S. involvement in South Vietnamese war.

United States moves to all-volunteer armed forces.

Watergate burglars are convicted.

Senate Watergate hearings reveal the existence of taped White House conversations.

Spiro Agnew resigns as vice president, is replaced by Gerald Ford.

Arab states impose an oil embargo after the third Arab-Israeli War.

1974 Nixon resigns as president, is succeeded by Gerald Ford.

1975 Communists triumph in South Vietnam.

United States, USSR, and European nations sign the Helsinki Accords.

1976 Jimmy Carter defeats Gerald Ford for the presidency.

1978 Carter brings the leaders of Egypt and Israel to Camp David for peace talks.

1979 SALT II agreement is signed but not ratified.

OPEC raises oil prices.

Three Mile Island nuclear plant comes close to disaster.

Iranian militants take U.S. embassy hostages.

1980 Iranian hostage rescue fails.

Soviet troops enter Afghanistan.

Ronald Reagan defeats Jimmy Carter for the presidency.

---

sionment about consumerism, racism, and imperialism and thought of itself as a "new left" that was free from doctrinal squabbles that marked the old left of the 1930s and 1940s.

The civil rights movement influenced both SDS leaders and Mario Savio, founder of the **Free Speech Movement (FSM)** at the University of California at Berkeley. Savio hoped to build a multi-issue "community of protest" around the idea of "a free university in a free society." FSM protests climaxed with a December sit-in that led to 773 arrests and stirred protest on other campuses.

The federal **Model Cities Program** (1966), another form of a community action organization, invited residents of poor neighborhoods to write their own plans for improving local housing, education, health services, and job opportunities. Model Cities assemblies challenged the racial bias in programs like urban renewal and helped train community leaders.

The lessons of grass-roots reform strengthened democracy from the bottom up. Activists staffed food cooperatives, free clinics, women's health groups, and drug counseling centers across the country. Community-based organization was a key element

American Views

AN ANTIWAR PROTESTER DESCRIBES THE GENERATION GAP

Robert S. McNamara was one of the architects of the war in Vietnam as secretary of defense for John Kennedy and Lyndon Johnson from 1961 to 1968. Like thousands of other parents, including many Washington officials, McNamara found opposition to the war within his own family. Here his son, Craig McNamara, describes his actions as an antiwar demonstrator and his decision to drop out of mainstream society (he eventually became a farmer in northern California). In 1995, Robert McNamara revealed that he had serious but silent doubts about the wisdom of the war long before he left the Defense Department.

❖ **What do Craig McNamara's recollections tell us about the "generation gap" of the 1960s?**

❖ **What do they suggest about the connection between political dissent and decisions to drop out of mainstream culture?**

You know, things were so split in the Sixties. You were either for the war or against it, and I was definitely against it. My father knew where I stood, but we didn't discuss it. . . . It just wasn't possible during those years for us to talk about the issues of the war. . . .

    Not long after I got to Stanford, I began taking part in antiwar demonstrations. . . . I participated in a major event at the San Francisco airport. A group of students had got together to read

a list of the California men who had been killed in Vietnam. We just stood in one of the main terminal buildings on a marble floor, with thirty-foot ceilings above and all the traffic of people going back and forth. It became very clear to us immediately that we were antagonizing a lot of people. . . . It was amazing to realize how threatening one person reading a list of the war dead in Vietnam could be to other people. And it was a tremendous list. . . . Each of us would read for two or three

---

in self-help efforts by African-Americans, Asian-Americans, and Latinos.

Youth Culture and Counterculture

Millions of young people in the second half of the 1960s expressed their alienation from American society by sampling drugs or chasing the rainbow of a youth culture. Some just smoked marijuana, grew long hair, and listened to psychedelic rock. Others plunged into ways of life that scorned their middle-class backgrounds. The middle-aged and middle-class ignored the differences and dubbed the rebellious young **hippies**. A high point of the youth culture was the 1969 Woodstock rock festival in New York State, a weekend of "sex, drugs, and rock-and-roll" for 400,000 young people.

    Within the broad youth culture known as the **Woodstock Generation** was a smaller and more

intense **counterculture** that added Eastern religion, social radicalism, and evangelistic belief in the drug LSD. Harvard professor Timothy Leary and writer Aldous Huxley claimed that hallucinogenic or psychedelic drugs, such as mescaline and LSD, would swing open the "doors of perception."

    The cultural rebels of the late 1950s and early 1960s had been trying to combine personal freedom with new social arrangements. Many hippies were more interested in altering their minds with drugs than with politics or poetry. Serious exploration of societal alternatives was left for a minority who devoted themselves to communal living, women's liberation, gay liberation, and other movements.

Racial Rioting

Prominent black writers, such as James Baldwin in *The Fire Next Time* (1963), had warned of mount-hours at a time, and then the next person would take over.

I remember a variety of men coming up to me at various times during those hours, men in their mid-fifties saying, "You son of a bitch!" or "We're going to kick your knees in!" or "You haven't been there. What do you know?" I just remember taking a deep breath and keeping on reading and feeling sad, tremendously sad. . . . I think that is the feeling that we probably all share now about Vietnam: what sadness, what tremendous sadness.

[After being physically disqualified from military service], I left for South America. Two friends and I went on motorcycles down to Texas with our shoulder-length hair and ponytails and leather pants. Nobody stopped us. We just kept

going until we got into Mexico, and started the long journey to the south. When we got to Bogotá [Colombia], my two friends decided they'd gone far enough. They were going to stay, and I was on my own. I decided to send my motorcycle home. To me it represented imperialism. I set out myself, into the unknown, and traveled for the next few months on trucks, buses, trains, hitchhiking. . . .

While I was in Santiago [Chile], my father came down to a big United Nations conference on trade. He was head of the World Bank at that time. I was staying probably a mile away from where he was, but we didn't see each other. I think it was probably a decision on both our parts, that we were in different worlds and those worlds couldn't seem to come together.

Source: *Joan Morrison and Robert K. Morrison,* From Camelot to Kent State: The Sixties Experience in the Words of Those Who Lived It (1987).

---

ing African-American anger, but few people listened. Suddenly the fires were real. Riots in Rochester, Harlem, and Brooklyn in July 1964 opened four years of racial violence. Before they subsided, the riots scarred most big cities and killed two hundred people, most of them African-Americans.

Trouble started in the Watts neighborhood in Los Angeles on August 11, 1965, when a white highway patrol officer arrested a young African-American for drunken driving. Loud complaints drew a crowd, and the arrival of Los Angeles police turned the bystanders into an angry mob that attacked passing cars. Rioting, looting, and arson spread through Watts for two days until the National Guard cordoned off the trouble spots and occupied the neighborhood on August 14 and 15.

After Watts, Americans expected "long hot summers" and got them. In 1966, Puerto Ricans in Chicago rioted over the same problems blacks faced. The following year, the worst violence was in Newark, New Jersey, and in Detroit, where forty-three deaths and blocks of blazing buildings stunned television viewers.

Politicians' impulse was to blame riffraff and outside agitators—"lawbreakers and mad dogs," to quote California Governor Ronald Reagan. But almost all participants were neighborhood residents with serious grievances. Their violence came from the frustration of rising expectations. Despite the political gains of the civil rights movement, unemployment remained high, ghetto merchants continued to sell shoddy goods at high prices, and the police still treated all blacks as potential criminals. The riots were protests about ghetto life. "What are these people rioting about?" asked one resident. "They want recognition, and the only way they're going to get it is to riot."

Minority Separatism

Minority separatists challenged the central goal of the civil rights movement, which sought full participation in American life. The phrase "**Black Power**" summed up the new alternative. The term came from frustrated SNCC leader Stokely Carmichael in 1966: "We've been saying freedom for six years—and we ain't got nothing. What we're going to start saying now is 'Black Power'!"

Black power translated many ways—control of one's own community through the voting machine, celebration of African-American heritage, creation of a parallel society that shunned white institutions. It propelled the successful political campaigns of Richard Hatcher in Gary, Indiana, and Carl Stokes in Cleveland, the first African-Americans elected mayors of large northern cities.

Black Power also meant increased interest in the Nation of Islam, or **Black Muslims**. Organized in 1931 by Elijah Muhammad, the Black Muslims combined a version of Islam with radical separatism. They called for self-discipline, support of black institutions and businesses, and total rejection of whites.

In the early 1960s, Malcolm X emerged as a leading Black Muslim. Growing up as Malcolm Little, he was a streetwise criminal until he converted to the Nation of Islam in prison. After his release, Malcolm preached that blacks should stop letting whites set the terms by which they judged their appearance, communities, and accomplishments. He emphasized the African cultural heritage and economic self-help and proclaimed himself an extremist for black rights. In the last year of his life, however, he returned from a pilgrimage to Mecca willing to consider limited acceptance of whites. Rivals within the movement assassinated him in February 1965, but his ideas lived on in *The Autobiography of Malcolm X*.

Bobby Seale and Huey Newton grew up in the Oakland, California, area and saw African-American ghettos as internal colonies in need of self-determination. They created the **Black Panthers** in 1966, began to carry firearms, and recruited an ex-convict named Eldridge Cleaver as chief publicist.

The Panthers shadowed police patrols to prevent mistreatment of African-Americans and carried weapons into the California State Legislature in May 1967 to protest gun control. As Seale recalled, the goal was "to read a message to the world" and use the press to "blast it across the country." The Panthers also promoted community-based self-help

efforts, such as a free breakfast program and medical clinics, and ran political candidates. In contrast to the rioters in Watts, the Panthers had a political program. The movement was shaken when Newton was convicted of manslaughter for killing a police officer, Cleaver fled to Algeria, and an unjustified police raid killed Chicago Panther leader Fred Hampton. Nevertheless, the Panthers survived as a political party into the 1970s.

Led by Reies López Tijerina, Hispanics in rural New Mexico demanded "brown power" and the return of lands that had been lost to Anglo-Americans despite the guarantees of the Treaty of Guadalupe Hidalgo in 1848. Tijerina's "Letter from the Santa Fe Jail" denounced the "rich people from outside the state with their summer homes and ranches" and "all those who have robbed the people of their land and culture for 120 years." Mexican-Americans in the 1970s organized for political power in southern Texas communities where they were a majority. In Denver, Rodolfo Gonzales established the Crusade for Justice. His "Plan for the Barrio" emphasized Hispanic cultural traditions, community control of schools, and economic development. Best known among the Latino activists was César Chávez, who organized the multiracial United Farm Workers in California (see chapter 32).

Native Americans also fought both for equal access to American society and to preserve cultural traditions through tribal institutions. Congress in 1968 restored the authority of tribal laws on reservations. A few years later, it granted native Alaskans 40 million acres to settle claims for their ancestral lands. Larger tribes established their own colleges, such as Navajo Community College (1969), which stated in its catalog, that it "exists to fulfill many needs of the Navajo people. . . . It provides a place where Navajo history and culture can be studied and learned; it provides training in the skills necessary for many jobs on the reservation which today are held by non-Navajos."

In new media-oriented protests, Chippewas in Minneapolis created the **American Indian Movement (AIM)** which dramatized the needs of Native Americans by seizing the abandoned Alcatraz Island as a cultural and educational center (1969–1971) and leading the cross-country Broken Treaties Caravan, which occupied the Bureau of Indian Affairs in Washington (1972). In the early 1970s, AIM allied with Sioux traditionalists on the Pine Ridge Reservation in South Dakota against the tribe's elected government. In 1973, they took over the village of Wounded Knee, where the U.S. Army in 1890 had massacred three hundred Indians. They held out for seventy days before leaving peacefully.

The American Indian Movement (AIM) drew its strength from young Indians in the cities. In 1972 AIM led a march of Indians along the "Trail of Broken Treaties" to Washington, D.C., where members occupied the offices of the Bureau of Indian Affairs. The occupation ended after a week but succeeded in publicizing Native American grievances.

The Black Power, Brown Power, and Red Power movements were all efforts by minorities to define themselves through their own heritage and backgrounds, not simply by looking in the mirror of white society. They thus questioned the American assumption that everyone wanted to be part of the same homogeneous society.

The Year of the Gun, 1968

In 1968, mainstream Americans turned against the war in Vietnam, student protest and youth counterculture turned ugly, and political consensus shattered.

The Tet Offensive

The longer the Vietnam War continued and the less interest that China or the Soviet Union showed in it, the less valid the conflict seemed to the American people. It looked more and more like a war for pride, not national security.

At the end of 1967, U.S. officials predicted victory in the coming year. They also fell for a North Vietnamese feint by committing U.S. forces to the defense of Khe Sanh, a strongpoint near the North-South border. The defense was a tactical success for the United States but thinned its forces elsewhere in South Vietnam. Then, at the beginning of Tet, the Vietnamese New Year on January 30, 1968, the Viet Cong attacked thirty-six of forty-four provincial capitals, the historic city of Hue, and the capital, Saigon. They hit the U.S. embassy and reached the runways of Tan Son Nhut air base. U.S. and South Vietnamese troops repulsed the attacks and cleared the cities. But the offensive was a psychological blow that convinced the American public that the war was an endless quagmire.

Images from Vietnam went direct to the evening television news; it was a "living room war." Viewers could hear cigarette lighters clicking open to set villages in flames. A handful of images stayed in people's memories—a Buddhist monk burning himself to death in protest; a child with flesh peeled off by napalm; a South Vietnamese official executing a captive on the streets of Saigon.

In the wake of the Tet crisis, General Westmoreland's request for 200,000 more troops forced a political and military reevaluation. Clark Clifford, a dedicated Cold Warrior, and the new secretary of defense, as well as twenty "wise men"—the big names of the Cold War—told the president that the war was unwinnable. The best option, the wise men told LBJ, was disengagement. "He could hardly believe his ears," Clifford remembered.

LBJ's Exit

Minnesota's liberal Senator Eugene McCarthy had decided to challenge Johnson in the presidential primaries. Because he controlled the party organizations in two-thirds of the states, Johnson didn't need the primary states for renomination and ignored the first primary in New Hampshire. Enthusiastic college students staffed McCarthy's campaign. McCarthy won a startling 42 percent of the popular vote and twenty of twenty-four delegates in the March 16 election. The vote proved that the political middle ground would no longer hold.

By showing Johnson's vulnerability, New Hampshire also drew Robert Kennedy into the race. Younger brother of the former president, Kennedy inspired both fervent loyalty and strong distaste. In the 1950s, he had worked for Senator Joe McCarthy and had been a reluctant supporter of civil rights during his brother's administration. More than other mainstream politicians of the 1960s, however, he touched the hearts of Hispanic and African-American voters as well as the white working class.

Facing political challenges and an unraveling war, on March 31, 1968, Johnson announced a halt to most bombing of North Vietnam, opening the door for negotiations. He then astounded the country by withdrawing from the presidential race. As he told an aide, the war made him feel like a hitchhiker in a hailstorm: "I can't run, I can't hide, and I can't make it stop." Hoping to save his domestic program, he served out his term with few friends and little credit for his accomplishments.

Red Spring

In the months that followed the Tet crisis grass-roots rebellion shook the Soviet grip on eastern Europe. University students in Poland protested the stifling of political discussion. Alexander Dubček, the new leader of the Czech Communist party, brought together students and the middle class around reforms that caused people to talk about "Prague Spring"—a blossoming of democracy inside the iron curtain. In August, the Soviets sent in their tanks to crush the reforms and bring Czechoslovakia back into line.

Students rioted in Italy and Berlin. Workers and students protested against the Franco regime in Spain. In Paris, student demonstrations against the Vietnam War turned into attacks on the university system and the French government. Students fought police in the Paris streets in the first days of May. Radical industrial workers called a general strike. The government nearly toppled.

At Columbia University in New York African-American students and its SDS chapter had several grievances. One was the university's cooperation with the Pentagon-funded Institute for Defense Analysis. Another was its plan to build a gymnasium on park land that might better serve the residents of Harlem. Some students wanted changes in university policy, others a confrontation that would recruit new radicals. They occupied five university buildings, including the library and the president's office, for a week in April until police evicted them. The "battle of Morningside Heights" (the location of Columbia) gave Americans a glimpse of the gap that divided radicalized students from national institutions.

Violence and Politics

On April 4, 1968, ex-convict James Earl Ray shot and killed Martin Luther King Jr. as he stood on the balcony of a Memphis motel. King's death triggered a climactic round of violence in black ghettos. Fires devastated the West Side of Chicago and downtown Washington, D.C. The army guarded the steps of the Capitol, ready to protect Congress from its fellow citizens.

The shock of King's death was still fresh when another political assassination stunned the nation. On June 5, Robert Kennedy won California's primary election. He was still behind Vice-President Hubert Humphrey in the delegate count but coming on strong. As Kennedy walked out of the ballroom at his headquarters in the Ambassador Hotel in Los Angeles, a Jordanian immigrant named Sirhan Sirhan put a bullet in his brain.

Kennedy's death ensured the Democratic nomination for Humphrey, a liberal who had loyally supported Johnson's war policy. After his nomination, Humphrey faced Republican Richard Nixon and Independent George Wallace. Nixon positioned himself as the candidate of the political middle and claimed he had a secret plan for winning the war. Wallace appealed to southern whites and working-class Northerners who feared black militancy and hated "the ivory-tower folks with pointed heads."

Both got great help from the Democratic Convention, held in Chicago on August 26–29. While Democrats feuded among themselves, Chicago Mayor Richard Daley and his police department monitored antiwar protesters. Leaders of the National Mobilization Committee to End the War in Vietnam were experienced peace activists—people who had long fought against nuclear weapons in the 1950s and the Vietnam War. They wanted to embarrass the Johnson-Humphrey administration by marching to the convention hall on nomination night. Mixed in were the **Yippies**. The term supposedly stood for Youth International Party. The Yippies planned to attract young people to Chicago with a promise of street theater, media events, and confrontation that would puncture the pretensions of the power structure.

On August 28, the same night that Democratic delegates were nominating Humphrey, protesters and Yippies had congregated in Grant Park, across Michigan Avenue from downtown hotels. Undisciplined police waded into the crowds with clubs and tear gas. Young people fought back with rocks and bottles. Television caught the hours of violence that ended when the National Guard separated police from demonstrators. On the convention floor, Senator Abraham Ribicoff of Connecticut decried "Gestapo tactics" on the streets of Chicago. Mayor Daley shouted back obscenities. For Humphrey, the convention was a catastrophe, alienating liberal Democrats.

Election day gave Wallace 13.5 percent of the popular vote, Humphrey 42.7 percent of the popular vote and 191 electoral votes, and Nixon 43.4 percent of the popular vote and 301 electoral votes. The national media saw Wallace in terms of bigotry and backlash against civil rights. But many of Wallace's northern backers were unhappy with both parties.

Nixon and Watergate

The new president was an unlikely politician. After losing a 1962 race for governor of California, he announced that he was quitting politics and that the press would no longer have Dick Nixon "to kick around." In 1968, he skillfully sold a "new Nixon" to the media. Seven years later, the press was his undoing as it uncovered the Watergate scandal.

Getting Out of Vietnam, 1969–1973

Nixon had no secret plan to end the war. Protests culminated in 1969 with the Vietnam Moratorium on October 15, when 2 million protesters joined rallies across the country. A month later, at least 500,000 demonstrators gathered in Washington.

Disaffection also mounted in Vietnam. Nurses found their idealism strained as they treated young men maimed in thousands of nasty skirmishes in the jungles and mountains. Racial tensions sapped morale on the front lines. Troops lost discipline, took drugs, and hunkered down waiting for their tours of duty to end. Soldiers "fragged" (killed) their own gung-ho or racist officers, and the high command had to adapt its code of justice to keep an army on the job.

Nixon and Vice President Spiro Agnew responded by trying to isolate the antiwar opposition, but Nixon also reduced the role of U.S. ground forces. He claimed that his policies represented "the great silent majority of my fellow Americans." Agnew blamed bad morale on journalists and intellectuals—on "nattering nabobs of negativism" and "an effete corps of impudent snobs."

The New Left had already collapsed into factions. About a hundred angry SDS members declared themselves the **Weather Underground** in 1969, taking their name from a Bob Dylan lyric. They tried to disrupt Chicago and Washington with window-smashing "days of rage." They also placed bombs in draft induction centers and ROTC build-

ings. Three Weatherpeople blew themselves up with a homemade bomb in New York in 1970. Others bombed a University of Wisconsin building and killed a student.

Nixon's secretary of defense, Melvin Laird, responded to the antiwar sentiment with "Vietnamization," withdrawing U.S. troops as fast as possible without undermining the South Vietnamese government. In July 1969, the president announced the "Nixon Doctrine." The policy substituted weapons and money for men. Americans rearmed and expanded the South Vietnamese army and secretly bombed Communist bases in neutral Cambodia.

The secret war against Cambodia culminated on April 30, 1970 with an invasion. Americans who had hoped that the war was fading away were outraged. Students shut down hundreds of colleges. At Kent State University in Ohio, the National Guard was called in to maintain order. On May 4, one unit unexpectedly fired on a group of non-threatening students and killed four of them. At Jackson State University in Mississippi, two unsuspecting students were also killed when troops fired on their dormitory.

The Cambodian "incursion" extended the military stalemate in Vietnam to United States policy. In December 1970, Congress repealed the Gulf of Tonkin Resolution and prohibited use of U.S. ground troops outside South Vietnam. Cambodia, however, was already devastated. The U.S. invasion had destabilized its government and opened the way for the bloodthirsty Khmer Rouge, who killed millions of Cambodians in the name of working-class revolution. Only ninety thousand U.S. ground troops were still in Vietnam by early 1972. A final air offensive in December smashed Hanoi into rubble and helped force four and a half years of peace talks to a conclusion.

The cease-fire began on January 27, 1973. The United States promised not to increase its military aid to South Vietnam. Immediately after coming to terms with North Vietnam, Nixon suspended the draft in favor of an all-volunteer military.

Nixon and the Wider World

To his credit, Richard Nixon took American foreign policy in new directions even while he was struggling to escape from Vietnam and Cambodia. He hoped to distract the American people from frustration in Southeast Asia with more important accomplishments elsewhere.

Nixon's first foreign policy success was a gift from Kennedy and Johnson. NASA had been working since 1961 to meet Kennedy's goal of a manned trip to the moon before the end of the decade. On July 20, 1969 the lunar lander *Eagle* detached from the command module circling the moon and landed on the level plain known as the Sea of Tranquillity. Six hours later, Armstrong was the first human to walk on the moon.

For Nixon and Henry Kissinger, his national security adviser (and later secretary of state), foreign policy was about the balance of world economic and military power and securing the most advantageous agreements, alliances, and military positions. In particular, they hoped to trade improved relations with China and the USSR for help in settling the Vietnam War.

China was increasingly isolated within the Communist world. In 1969, it almost went to war with the USSR. Nixon was eager to take advantage of Chinese-Soviet tension. In April 1971

The shootings at Kent State University in May 1970 reflected the deep divisions in American society created by the Vietnam War, including those between anti-war college students and those serving in the armed forces.

secret talks led to an easing of the American trade embargo begun in 1950 and a tour of China by a U.S. table tennis team. Kissinger then arranged for Nixon's startling visit to Mao Zedong in Beijing in February 1972.

Playing the "China card" helped improve relations with the Soviet Union. The Soviets needed increased trade with the United States and a counterweight to China, the United States was looking for help in getting out of Vietnam, and both countries wanted to limit nuclear armaments. Protracted negotiations led to arms agreements known as **SALT**—the Strategic Arms Limitation Treaty—that Nixon signed in Moscow in May 1972. The agreements blocked creation of extensive antiballistic missiles (ABM) systems but failed to limit bombers, cruise missiles, or multiple independently targeted warheads on single missiles.

Diplomats used the French word *détente*, meaning easing of tension, to describe the new U.S. relations with China and the Soviet Union. It facilitated travel between the United States and China. It allowed U.S. farmers to sell wheat to the Soviets. More broadly, détente implied that the United States and China recognized mutual interests in Asia and

that the United States acknowledged the Soviet Union as an equal in world affairs.

Courting Middle America

Nixon designed domestic policy to help him win reelection. His goal was to solidify his "Middle American" support; the strategy targeted the suburbs and the South. The Nixon White House preferred not to deal with troubled big cities. Spokesmen announced that the "urban crisis" was over and then dismantled the urban initiatives of Johnson's Great Society. Instead, Nixon tilted federal assistance to the suburbs. The centerpiece of his **New Federalism** was General Revenue Sharing (1972). By 1980, it had transferred more than $18 billion from the federal treasury to the states and more than $36 billion to local governments. Revenue sharing grants supplemented the general funds of every full-service government, whether a city of 2 million or a suburban town of five hundred.

Nixon pursued the southern strategy through Supreme Court nominations of southerns Clement Haynsworth of Florida and G. Harrold Carswell of Alabama. Although the Senate rejected both as unqualified, the nominations nonetheless gave

Nixon a reputation as a champion of the white South. He hoped to move cautiously in enforcing school desegregation, but a task force led by Secretary of Labor George Shultz crafted an approach that allowed substantial desegregation.

More troublesome was inflation, one of Lyndon Johnson's unpleasant legacies. One of the causes was LBJ's decision to fight in Vietnam without tax increases until 1968. An income tax cut in 1969, supported by both parties, made the situation worse. Inflation eroded the value of savings and pensions. It also made U.S. goods too expensive for foreign buyers and generated a trade deficit.

A price and wage freeze in August 1971 was a public relations gesture that was full of loopholes and contradicted explicit public avowals that the administration would never take such action. Nixon then undermined the freeze by speeding up federal spending to create an economic boom before the presidential election year; the Defense Department claimed to have bought a two-year supply of toilet paper.

After the election, inflation came roaring back. The main cause was sharp increases in the cost of energy. Angry at American support for Israel in the Arab-Israeli War of October 1973, Arab nations imposed an embargo on oil exports that lasted from October 1973 to March 1974. Gasoline and heating oil became scarce and expensive. The shortages eased when the embargo ended, but the **Organization of Petroleum Exporting Countries (OPEC)** had challenged the ability of the industrial nations to dictate world economic policy.

Americans switched off unused lights, turned down thermostats, and put on sweaters. Congress required states to enforce a highway speed limit of 55 miles per hour to get federal highway funds and enacted the first fuel economy standards for automobiles. More efficient imports captured a third of the U.S. car market by 1980.

After thirty years at the top, the United States could no longer dominate the world economy by itself. Germany and Japan now had economies as modern as that of the United States. In 1971, **stagflation** was the new term to describe the painful combination of inflation, high unemployment, and flat economic growth that matched no one's economic theory but everyone's daily experience.

Americans as Environmentalists

In the turbulent 1970s, resource conservation grew into a multifaceted environmental movement. Environmentalism dealt with serious problems. It was broad enough for both scientific experts and activists, for both Republican Richard Nixon and Democrat Jimmy Carter.

After the booming 1950s, Americans had started to pay attention to the damage that advanced technologies and industrial production did to natural systems. Rachel Carson's *Silent Spring* in 1962 described the side effects of DDT and other pesticides on animal life. In her imagined future, spring was silent because all the birds had died of pesticide poisoning. Meanwhile, an offshore oil well polluted the beaches of Santa Barbara, California, in 1969. Fire danced across the Cuyahoga River in Cleveland when industrial discharges ignited.

On April 22, children in ten thousand schools and 20 million other people took part in Earth Day, an occasion first conceived by Wisconsin Senator Gaylord Nelson. Earth Day gained a grassroots following in towns and cities across the country.

The mainstream media discovered the ravaged planet; so did a politically savvy president. Nixon had already signed the National Environmental Policy Act on January 1, 1970, and later in the year created the **Environmental Protection Agency (EPA)** to enforce environmental laws. The rest of the Nixon years brought legislation on clean air, clear water, pesticides, hazardous chemicals, and endangered species that made environmental management and protection part of governmental routine.

Americans began to realize that low-income and minority communities had more than their share of environmental problems. Residents near the Love Canal in Buffalo discovered in 1978 that an entire neighborhood was built on land contaminated by decades of chemical dumping. Activists sought to understand the health effects and force compensation, paving the way for the **Superfund** cleanup legislation. African-Americans often lived downstream and downwind of heavily polluting industries. Landfills and waste disposal sites were frequently located near minority neighborhoods. Efforts to fight environmental racism became important in many minority communities.

From Dirty Tricks to Watergate

Subordinates learned during his first administration that Richard Nixon would condone dishonest actions—"dirty tricks"—if they stood to improve his political position. In 1972 and 1973, dirty tricks grew from a scandal into a constitutional crisis when Nixon abused the power of his office to cover up wrongdoing and hinder criminal investigations.

The chain of events that undermined Nixon's presidency started with the **Pentagon Papers**. In his last year as secretary of defense, Robert McNamara had commissioned a report on America's road to Vietnam. The documents showed that the country's leaders had planned to expand the war even while they claimed to be looking for a way out. In June 1971, one of the contributors to the report, Daniel Ellsberg, leaked it to the *New York Times*. Its publication infuriated Nixon.

In response, the White House compiled a list of journalists and politicians who opposed Nixon. As White House staffer John Dean put it, the president's men could then "use the available federal machinery [Internal Revenue Service, FBI] to screw our political enemies." Former CIA employees E. Howard Hunt and G. Gordon Liddy became the chief "plumbers," as the group was known because its job was to prevent leaks of information. The plumbers cooked up schemes to embarrass political opponents and ransacked the office of Ellsberg's psychiatrist.

Early in 1972, Hunt went to work for CREEP—the Committee to Re-Elect the President—while Liddy took another position on the presidential staff. CREEP had already raised millions from corporations and was hatching plans to undermine Democrats with rumors and pranks. Then, on June 17, 1972, five inept burglars hired with CREEP funds were caught breaking into the Democratic National Committee office in Washington's Watergate apartment building. Nixon initiated a coverup. On June 23, he ordered his assistant H. R. Haldeman to warn the FBI off the case with the excuse that national security was involved. Nixon compounded this obstruction of justice by arranging a $400,000 bribe to keep the burglars quiet. The coverup worked in the short run.

Nixon's opponent in the 1972 election was South Dakota Senator George McGovern, an impassioned opponent of the Vietnam War. McGovern was honest, intelligent, and well to the left on issues like the defense budget and legalization of marijuana. He did not appeal to the white Southerners and blue-collar Northerners. An assassination attempt that took George Wallace out of national politics also helped Nixon win in a landslide. McGovern carried only the District of Columbia and Massachusetts.

The coverup began to come apart with the trial of the Watergate burglars in January 1973. Federal Judge John Sirica used the threat of heavy sentences to pressure one burglar into a statement that implied that higher-ups had been involved. Meanwhile, the *Washington Post* was linking Nixon's people to dirty tricks and illegal campaign contributions. The White House scrambled to find a defensible story. Nixon now began to coach people on what they should tell investigators, claimed his staff had lied to him, and tried to set up John Dean to take the fall.

In the late spring and early summer, attention shifted to the televised hearings of the Senate's Select Committee on Presidential Campaign Activities. Its chair was Sam Ervin of North Carolina. A parade of White House and party officials described their own pieces in the affair, often accusing each other and revealing the plumbers and the enemies list. The real questions, it became obvious, were what the president knew and when he knew it. It seemed to be John Dean's word against Richard Nixon's.

A bombshell turned the scandal into a constitutional crisis. A mid-level staffer told the committee that Nixon made tape recordings of his White House conversations. Both the Senate and the Watergate special prosecutor, Archibald Cox, subpoenaed the tapes. Nixon refused to give them up. In late October, after he failed to cut a satisfactory deal, he fired his attorney general and the special prosecutor. Many Americans thought that these actions proved that Nixon had something to hide. In April 1974, he finally issued *edited* transcripts of the tapes, with foul language deleted and key passages missing. Finally, on July 24, 1974, the U.S. Supreme Court ruled unanimously that Nixon had to deliver sixty-four tapes to the new special prosecutor.

In Congress, Republicans joined Democrats in voting three articles of impeachment: for hindering the criminal investigation of the Watergate break-in, for abusing the power of the presidency by using federal agencies to deprive citizens of their rights, and for ignoring the committee's subpoena for the tapes. Before the full House could vote on the articles of impeachment, Nixon delivered the tapes containing direct evidence that he had participated in the coverup on June 23, 1972, and had been lying ever since. On August 8 he announced his resignation, effective the next day.

Watergate was two separate but related stories. On one level, it was about individuals, Nixon and his cronies who wanted to win so badly they repeatedly broke the law. Nixon paid for his overreaching ambition with the end of his political career; more than twenty others paid with jail terms.

On another level, the crisis was a lesson about the Constitution. The separation of powers allowed Congress and the courts to rein in a president who had spun out of control.

The Ford Footnote

Gerald Ford was the first president who had been elected neither president nor vice president. Ford was Nixon's appointee to replace Spiro Agnew, who resigned and pleaded no contest to charges of bribery and income tax evasion in 1973. On September 8, Ford pardoned Richard Nixon for "any and all crimes" committed while president. Since Nixon had not yet been indicted, the pardon saved him from future prosecution. He also offered clemency to thousands of draft resisters.

In 1975, South Vietnam collapsed. Only the American presence had kept its political, ethnic, and religious factions together. In the spring of 1975, North Vietnam opened an offensive. South Vietnamese resistance crumbled so rapidly that the United States had to evacuate its embassy in Saigon by helicopter while frantic Vietnamese tried to join the flight.

Elsewhere in the world, détente continued. American diplomats joined the Soviet Union and thirty other European nations in the capital of Finland to sign the **Helsinki Accords**, which called for increased commerce between the Eastern and Western blocs and human rights guarantees. They also legitimized the national boundaries that had been set in eastern Europe in 1945.

At home during Ford's two and a half years in office, the economy slid into recession; unemployment climbed above 10 percent; inflation diminished the value of savings and wages.

Ford was the Republican presidential candidate in the 1976 election. His Democratic opponent was a political enigma. James Earl Carter Jr. had been a navy officer, a farmer, and governor of Georgia. Carter and other new style Southern politicians left race-baiting behind to talk like modern New Dealers. He appealed to Democrats as someone who could reassemble LBJ's political coalition and return the South to the Democratic party. In his successful campaign, Carter presented himself as an alternative to party hacks and Washington insiders.

Jimmy Carter: Idealism and Frustration in the White House

As an outsider in Washington's political establishment, Carter had one great advantage: freedom from the narrow mind-set of experts who talk only to each other. However, he lacked both the knowledge of key political players and the experience to resolve legislative gridlock.

Carter, Energy, and the Economy

Carter was refreshingly low-key. After his inauguration, he walked from the Capitol to the White House as Jefferson had. He signed official documents "Jimmy." He tended to tell the public what he thought rather than what pollsters said the people wanted to hear.

Carter's approach to politics reflected his training as an engineer. He was analytical, logical, and given to breaking a problem into its component parts. He filled his cabinet with experts rather than political operators. He didn't seem to understand the basic rules of Washington politics. For example, he and his cabinet officers developed policies and made appointments without consulting key congressional committee chairs.

The biggest domestic problem remained the economy, which slid into another recession in 1978. Unemployment grew. Another jump in petroleum prices helped make 1979 and 1980 the worst years for inflation in the postwar era. Carter himself was a fiscal conservative whose impulse was to cut federal spending. This worsened unemployment and alienated liberal Democrats, who wanted to revive the Great Society.

Carter simultaneously proposed a comprehensive energy policy. He asked Americans to make energy conservation the moral equivalent of war—to accept individual sacrifices for the common good. Congress created the Department of Energy but refused to raise taxes on oil and natural gas to reduce consumption. However, the Energy Policy and Conservation Act (1978) did encourage alternative energy sources to replace foreign petroleum. Big oil companies poured billions of dollars into western Colorado to squeeze a petroleum substitute from shale. Solar energy research prospered. Breezy western hillsides sprouted "wind farms" to wring electricity out of the air.

However, antinuclear activism blocked one obvious alternative to fossil fuels. In the late 1970s, activists staged sit-ins at the construction sites of nuclear plants. A near-meltdown at the Three Mile Island nuclear plant in Pennsylvania in March 1979 stalemated efforts to expand nuclear power capacity.

When the OPEC price hikes undermined the inflation-fighting effort in the summer of 1979, Carter proposed new steps to solve the energy crisis. A cabinet reshuffle a few days later was supposed to show that he was firmly in charge, but instead conveyed the message that he was erratic. By 1979, opinion leaders had decided that Carter was not capable of leading the nation and then interpreted every action as confirming that belief.

Building a Cooperative World

Despite troubles on the home front, Carter's first two years brought foreign policy success that reflected a new vision of a multilateral world. He appointed Andrew Young—a fellow Georgian with long experience in the civil rights movement—as ambassador to the United Nations, where he worked effectively to build bridges to third-world nations.

Carter's moral convictions were responsible for a new concern with human rights around the globe. He criticized the Soviet Union for preventing free speech and denying its citizens the right to emigrate, angering Soviet leaders, who didn't expect the human rights clauses of the Helsinki Accords to be taken seriously. Carter also withheld economic aid from South Africa, Guatemala, Chile, and Nicaragua, which had long records of human rights abuses. In Nicaragua, the change in policy helped left-wing Sandinista rebels topple the Somoza dictatorship.

The triumph of the new foreign policy was the **Camp David Agreement** between Egypt and Israel. Carter risked his reputation and credibility in September 1978 to bring Egyptian President Anwar el-Sadat and Israeli Prime Minister Menachem Begin together at Camp David, the presidential retreat. A formal treaty signed in Washington on March 26, 1979 normalized relations between Israel and its most powerful neighbor and led to Israeli withdrawal from the Sinai Peninsula.

Return of the Cold War

The Soviets ignored the human rights provisions of the Helsinki Accords. Soviet advisers or Cuban troops intervened in African civil wars. At home, Cold Warriors who had never accepted détente found it easier to attack Carter than Nixon.

Carter inherited negotiations for SALT II—a strategic arms limitation treaty that would have reduced both the American and Soviet nuclear arsenals—from the Ford administration. SALT II met stiff resistance in the Senate. Opponents claimed it would create a "window of vulnerability" in the 1980s that would invite the Soviets to launch a nuclear first strike. Carter tried to counter criticism by stepping up defense spending, starting a buildup that would accelerate under Ronald Reagan.

Hopes for SALT II vanished on January 3, 1980, when Soviet troops entered Afghanistan. Muslim tribespeople unhappy with modernization had attacked Afghanistan's pro-Communist government, which invited Soviet intervention. The situation resembled the American involvement in South Vietnam. In the end, it took the Soviets a decade to extract themselves from this quicksand.

The final blow to Carter's foreign policy came in Iran. Since 1953, the United States had strongly backed Iran's monarch, the Shah. The Shah modernized Iran's economy but jailed political opponents. U.S. aid and oil revenues helped him build a vast army, but the Iranian middle class despised his authoritarianism, and Muslim fundamentalists opposed modernization. Revolution toppled the Shah at the start of 1979.

The upheaval installed a nominally democratic government, but the Ayatollah Ruhollah Khomeini, a Muslim cleric who hated the United States, exercised real power. Throughout 1979, Iran grew increasingly anti-American. After the United States allowed the exiled Shah to seek medical treatment in New York, a mob stormed the U.S. embassy in Tehran on November 4, 1979, and took more than sixty Americans hostage. They demanded that Carter surrender the Shah.

Television brought pictures of blindfolded hostages and anti-American mobs burning effigies of Uncle Sam and wrapping American flags around garbage. The administration tried economic pressure and diplomacy, but Khomeini had no desire for accommodation. When Iran announced in April 1980 that the hostages would remain in the hands of the militants rather than be transferred to the government, Carter ordered an airborne rescue. The attempt misfired when three of eight helicopters malfunctioned and one crashed in the Iranian desert. The fiasco added to the national embarrassment. The United States and Iran finally reached agreement on the eve of the 1980 election. The hostages gained their freedom after 444 days at the moment Ronald Reagan took office as the new president.

The hostage crisis consumed Jimmy Carter the way that Vietnam had consumed Lyndon Johnson. It gripped the public and stalemated other issues. For weeks, Carter's tragedy was that "his" Iranian crisis was the fruit of policies hatched by the Eisenhower administration and pursued by every president since then, all of whom overlooked the Shah's despotic government because of his firm anti-Communism.

After thirty years in which the United States had viewed the entire world as a Cold War battlefield, Carter was willing to accept the developing world on its own terms. His human rights efforts showed that evangelical religious convictions could be tied to progressive aims. Iranian rage at past policies of the sort Carter hoped to change destroyed his ability to direct a new course.

Conclusion

A period of remarkable prosperity ended in 1974. Long lines at gas stations suggested that prosperity was fragile. Cities and regions began to feel the costs of obsolete industries. Environmental damage caused many Americans to reconsider the goal of economic expansion.

American withdrawal from Vietnam in 1973 and the collapse of the South Vietnamese government in 1975 were defeats; the United States ended up with little to show for a long and painful war. SALT I stabilized the arms race, but it also recognized that the Soviet Union was an equal. The American nuclear arsenal might help deter a third world war, but it could not prevent the seizure of hostages in Iran.

The nation finished the 1970s more egalitarian than it had been in the early 1960s but also more divided. More citizens had the opportunity to advance economically and to seek political power, but there were deepening fissures between social liberals and cultural conservatives, old and new views about roles for women, rich and poor, whites and blacks.

Review Questions

1. Why did the United States fail to achieve its objectives in Vietnam? What factors limited President Johnson's freedom of action there? How did the Tet Offensive affect U.S. policy? How did antiwar protests in the United States influence national policy?

2. How did racial relations change between 1965 and 1970? What were the relationships between the civil rights movement and minority separatism? What were the similarities and differences among African-American, Latino, and Native American activism?

3. In what ways was 1968 a pivotal year for American politics and society?

4. What were the implications of détente? Why did the Cold War reappear in the late 1970s? How and why did U.S. influence over the rest of the world change during the 1970s?

5. How did Richard Nixon's political strategy respond to the growth of the South and West? How did it respond to the shift of population from central cities to suburbs?

6. How did the backgrounds of Presidents Johnson, Nixon, and Carter shape their successes and failures as national leaders?

7. What political and constitutional issues were at stake in the Watergate scandal? How did it change American politics?

Recommended Reading

Tom Bates, *Rads: The 1970 Bombing of the Army Math Research Center at the University of Wisconsin and*

Its Aftermath (1992). Bates attempts to use a specific episode to understand the collapse of the New Left.

David Caute, *Year of the Barricades* (1988). Tour the events of 1968 on both sides of the Atlantic.

Gloria Emerson, *Winners and Losers* (1976). The impact of the war in Vietnam on American society is told through the stories of individuals changed by the war.

David Farber, *Chicago '68* (1988); *Medium Cool* (1969), directed by Haskell Wexler. Farber's book contrasts the perspectives and language of city officials and protesters. Wexler's film captures the tension of Chicago in the hot summer through the eyes of a reporter.

David Halberstam, *October 1964* (1994). Halberstam uses the baseball season of 1964 and the World Series between the St. Louis Cardinals and New York Yankees to encapsulate the impacts of changing racial relations on American society.

Stanley Karnow, *Vietnam: A History* (1983). This comprehensive history of American involvement in Vietnam details the collapse of French rule and early U.S. relations with Vietnam.

Lynda Van Devanter, *Home before Morning* (1984). This interesting book recounts the experiences of an army nurse in Vietnam and beyond.

Where to Learn More

❖ **Lyndon B. Johnson National Historical Park, Johnson City, Texas.**   Johnson's ranch, southwest of Austin, gives visitors a feeling for the open landscape in which Johnson spent his early years.

❖ **Vietnam Veterans Memorial, Washington, D.C.** A simple wall engraved with the names of the nation's Vietnam War dead is testimony to one of the nation's most divisive wars.

❖ **Richard Nixon Library and Birthplace, Yorba Linda, California.**   Exhibits trace Nixon's political career and related world events with a sympathetic interpretation.

❖ **Titan Missile Museum, Green Valley, Arizona.** The Green Valley complex near Tucson held eighteen Titan missiles. They were deactivated after SALT I, and the complex is now open to visitors.

32 SHAPING A NEW AMERICA, 1965–1995

KEY TOPICS

❖ Changes in immigration policy and the resulting new wave of immigration from Latin America, the Caribbean, and Asia after 1965
❖ The effect of global competition on the U.S. economy
❖ The shift from the Rustbelt to the Sunbelt
❖ The changing role of women
❖ The culture wars

In June 1992, Hiroshi Yamauchi paid $100 million for a controlling interest in the Seattle Mariners baseball team, using a fortune acquired as head of American-based but Japanese-owned Nintendo America. The purchase of the M's demonstrated the growing international dimension of American society. So did other aspects of professional baseball, such as the prominence of players from Latin America and the 1993 World Series victory of Canada's Toronto Blue Jays.

Starting in 1958, when the New York Giants moved to San Francisco and the Brooklyn Dodgers to Los Angeles, the big leagues followed population and business southward and westward, adding teams in cities such as San Diego, Atlanta, and Miami. In 1994–1995, a long players' strike mirrored new labor-management battles in other industries. Baltimore, Cleveland, and Denver joined the national shift from manufacturing to service employment by leveling old warehouses and factories to build downtown stadiums that could boost tourism and convention business.

Baseball's new look was part of a broad transformation of American society after 1965. Just as the nation entered a decade of political turmoil, Americans reopened basic questions about their personal lives and communities. Who constituted the American people? What were the best ways to earn a living and the preferred places to live? Where could individuals find a sense of reassurance in troubled times? The answers were different by the 1980s and 1990s than they had been in the 1950s.

A globalizing economy was one powerful engine of change. As leader of the Western nations, the United

States opened itself to a world developing beyond American control. Immigration reshaped and revitalized cities. Foreign competition accelerated the transition from old industries to new. One effect was to *decentralize* the United States: Central cities declined relative to their suburbs; the Northeast declined relative to the South and West; mass-production manufacturing declined relative to competitors in Asia and Latin America.

Americans also explored new ways to find their identity as individuals and members of groups. The outcome of such profound questioning was *decentering*—an erosion of the unspoken assumption that tight, white, middle-class families were the national norm. Growing immigration made the benefits and perils of a multicultural society a topic of concern. Millions of Americans followed old or new avenues to spiritual assurance and a sense of community, generating conflicts over cultural values that entered the political arena as battles over affirmative action, abortion, or religion in the schools.

A Globalized America

Since 1965, the United States has followed the global political reach of the Cold War with new international connections at every level from the corporate to the personal. Foreign tourism became big business, exploding from a few hundred thousand annual visitors from outside North America in the 1950s to 20 million a year in the mid-1990s. Foreign involvement in the U.S. economy benefits New York and San Francisco but also such unexpected places as Greenville and Spartanburg, South Carolina, deeply American communities where the chamber of commerce rolls out the red carpet for German executives and forty thousand residents work for European corporations.

New Americans

The **Immigration and Nationality Act of 1965** initiated a change in the composition of the American people by abolishing the national quota system in effect since 1924. Quotas had favored immigrants from western Europe and limited those from other parts of the world. The old law's racial bias contradicted the self-proclaimed role of the United States as a defender of freedom. The new law gave prefer-

ence to family reunification and set overall limits of 170,000 immigrants per year from the Eastern Hemisphere (with no more than 20,000 from any one country) and 120,000 from the Western Hemisphere. The United States also welcomed refugees from Communism outside the annual limits.

Immigration reform opened the doors to Mediterranean Europe, Latin America, and Asia. Legal migration to the United States surged from 1.1 million in 1960–1964 to nearly 4 million in 1990–1994. Nonlegal immigrants may have doubled the total number of newcomers in the 1970s and early 1980s. Meanwhile, over 2 million nonlegal immigrants had taken advantage of the **Immigration Reform and Control Act of 1986** to legalize their presence in the United States.

Immigration changed the nation's ethnic mix. Members of officially defined ethnic and racial minorities accounted for one out of every four Americans in 1990. Asians and Hispanics were the fastest-growing groups (see Table 32-1).

New immigrant groups did not distribute themselves evenly across American states and regions. Most Mexican immigrants moved to the states adjacent to Mexico. The East Coast has meanwhile welcomed migrants from the West Indies and Central America. Many Puerto Ricans, who hold U.S. citizenship, came to Philadelphia and New York in the 1950s and 1960s. Other countries sending large numbers of immigrants include Haiti, the Dominican Republic, Guatemala, Honduras, Nicaragua, El Salvador, and Jamaica.

In contrast to Puerto Ricans and Mexicans, who can easily travel back and forth between their old and new homes, Cubans have been one-way migrants. Fidel Castro's Cuban revolution pushed 250,000 Cuban businessmen, white-collar workers, and their families to the United States. Virtually all Cubans settled in Florida or in major cities, such as New York and Chicago.

Another great immigration has occurred eastward across the Pacific. Chinese, Filipinos, Koreans, Samoans, and other Asians and Pacific Islanders constituted only 6 percent of newcomers to the United States in 1965 but nearly half of all arrivals in 1990.

The numbers of ethnic Chinese in the United States jumped from a quarter of a million in 1965 to 1,645,000 in 1990. Immigrants from Taiwan, Hong Kong, and the People's Republic created new Chinatowns in Houston and San Diego and crowded into the historic Chinatowns of New York and San Francisco. Social and economic divisions appeared between upwardly mobile and assimilat-

TABLE 32.1	MAJOR RACIAL AND ETHNIC MINORITIES IN THE UNITED STATES (IN MILLIONS)			
	1960	% of total	1990	% of total
American Indians	.5	0.3%	2.0	0.8%
Asians & Pacific Islanders	1.1	0.6%	7.3	2.9%
Blacks	18.9	10.5%	30.0	12.1%
Hispanics	(not available)		22.4	9.0%

ing students and professionals, Chinatown businessmen, and isolated immigrant workers in sweatshops and service jobs.

The most publicized Asian immigrants were refugees from Indochina after Communist victories in 1975. Many settled on the West Coast. The San Francisco Bay Area, for example, had fifteen Vietnamese-language newspapers, magazines, and cable television programs in the late 1980s.

The United States has provided economic opportunity for millions of newcomers. More than half the Cuban households in Miami are homeowners. The 130,000 Vietnamese immigrants of 1975 now have an average adjusted income above the national average. Asians in the early 1980s constituted 20 percent of the students in California's public universities and were moving into the professions. Many West Indian blacks, Asians, and second-generation Mexicans are now comfortable members of the middle class in scores of cities (see "American Views: Growing Up Mexican-American").

Many newcomers have opened groceries, restaurants, and other businesses that serve their own group before expanding into larger markets. Juan Fernandez found it easier to set up a successful car repair shop in Gary, Indiana, than in Guadalajara, Mexico, because his fellow immigrants prefer a Spanish-speaking mechanic. Asian-born business owners have filled retail vacuums in central city neighborhoods abandoned by chain stores.

In the World Market

Expanding foreign commerce became a deliberate goal of national policy with the **General Agreement on Tariffs and Trade (GATT)** in 1947. GATT regularized international commerce after World War II and helped ensure that world markets remained open to American industry. The Trade Expansion Act in 1962 authorized President Kennedy to make reciprocal trade agreements to cut tariffs by up to 50 per-

cent to keep American companies competitive in the new European Common Market. Although both measures were aimed at trade with Europe, they also helped expand American commerce across the Pacific.

The value of American imports and exports more than doubled from 7 percent of the gross domestic product in 1965 to 16 percent in 1990—the largest percentage since World War I. Americans in the 1970s began to worry about a "colonial" status in which the United States exported food, lumber, and minerals and imported automobiles and television sets. By the 1980s, foreign economic competitiveness and trade deficits, especially with Japan, became issues of national concern.

Recent steps to expand the global reach of the American economy were the **North American Free Trade Agreement (NAFTA)** in 1993 and a new worldwide GATT approved in 1994. Negotiated by Republican George Bush and pushed through Congress in 1993 by Democratic Bill Clinton, NAFTA combined 25 million Canadians, 90 million Mexicans, and 250 million U.S. consumers in a single "common market" similar to that of western Europe. GATT cut tariffs among 100 nations.

NAFTA revived the old debate between free traders and protectionists. Support was strongest from professional businesses and industries that sought foreign customers, including agriculture and electronics. Opponents included organized labor, communities already hit by industrial shutdowns, and environmentalists worried about lax regulations in Mexico. Evidence from the first two years favored NAFTA supporters, indicating that few manufacturing jobs relocated to Mexico.

Old Gateways and New

The globalization of the United States had its most striking effects in coastal and border cities. New York again became the great mixing bowl of the American population. Between 1965 and 1980, it received a million legally recorded immigrants and between 500,000 and 750,000 illegal newcomers. Journalist Andy Logan described the new immigrants' impact by the early 1970s: "A third of the children now in the city's public schools are said to be the children of parents who were born in other countries. . . . Whole areas of the city, such as Washington Heights, in Manhattan, and Elmhurst, in Queens, would be half

CHRONOLOGY

1960 Birth control pill is marketed.

1962 *Baker* v. *Carr* establishes the principle of "one person, one vote" for creating state legislative districts.

1963 Betty Friedan publishes *The Feminine Mystique*.

1964 Beatles make first visit to the United States.

1965 Immigration reform eases immigration for Asians and Latin Americans.

1966 National Organization for Women is founded.

1969 Stonewall Inn riot opens era of gay militancy.

1971 Twenty-Sixth Amendment lowers the voting age to eighteen.

     U.S. Supreme Court, in *Swann* v. *Charlotte-Mecklenburg Board of Education*, approves busing for racial integration of public schools.

     Walt Disney World opens near Orlando, Florida.

1972 Equal Rights Amendment is sent to the states for ratification.

1973 *Roe* v. *Wade* decision expands abortion rights.

1975 Busing plan is implemented to integrate Boston public schools.

1978 People's Temple adherents commit mass suicide at Jonestown, Guyana.

1981 AIDS is recognized as new disease.

1982 Equal Rights Amendment fails to achieve ratification.

1986 Immigration Reform and Control Act regularizes illegal immigration.

1993 North American Free Trade Agreement is ratified.

     Branch Davidian followers die in flames at Waco, Texas.

1996 *Romer* v. *Evans* overturns a Colorado constitutional amendment limiting the legal recourse of homosexuals against discrimination.

---

empty without the new arrivals." ZIP code 11373 in North Queens was reportedly the most diverse neighborhood in the world.

Southern and western cities became gateways for immigrants from Latin America and Asia. Los Angeles emerged as "the new Ellis Island." As *Time* magazine put it in 1983, the arrival of more than 2 million immigrants in greater Los Angeles altered "the collective beat and bop of L.A." In 1960, a mere 1 percent of the Los Angeles County population was Asian and 11 percent was Hispanic. By 1990, the figures for a population of 8.8 million were 11 percent Asian and 37 percent Hispanic. Many other ethnic communities appeared in Los Angeles suburbs. A hundred languages are spoken among students entering Los Angeles schools.

Smaller international cities dot the southern border of the United States. Latin American connections have altered the character of Miami, where Hispanics now constitute nearly half of the metropolitan-area population. Access to the Caribbean and South America make Miami an international banking and commercial center with hundreds of offices for corporations engaged in U.S.–Latin American trade.

Cross-border communities in the Southwest, such as El Paso, Texas, and Juarez, Mexico, or San Diego, California, and Tijuana, Mexico, are "Siamese twins joined at the cash register." Employees with work permits commute from Mexico to the United States. American popular culture flows southward. Bargain hunters and tourists pass in both directions.

Both nations have promoted the cross-border economy. The Mexican government in the mid-1960s began to encourage a "platform economy" by allowing companies on the Mexican side of the border to import components and inputs duty-free as long as 80 percent of the items were reexported and 90 percent of the workers were Mexicans. Such factories can employ lower-wage workers and avoid strict antipollution laws (leading to serious threats to public health on both sides of the border). From the Gulf of Mexico to the Pacific Ocean, eighteen hundred *maquiladora* plants employed half a million workers. North of the border, U.S. factories supplied components under laws that meshed with the Mexican regulations.

Ethnic Identity and Conflict

Despite its positive economic contributions, the new immigration revived old American racisms and created new racial tensions.

Some of the deepest conflicts arose between old and new minorities. African-Americans have resented special services for political refugees and

American Views

GROWING UP MEXICAN-AMERICAN

Three Americans of Mexican heritage—Richard Rodriguez, Dolores Huerta, and Ana Caballero—recall experiences during their school years that have shaped their identification with American culture and their sense of ethnic identity. Rodriguez grew up in Sacramento, the son of immigrants from Mexico who had found steady jobs. He entered school with limited English; his family spoke Spanish at home. He would become a professional writer and scholar. Huerta's family has lived in the United States for many generations. She grew up in Stockton, California, in the 1950s, became a Chicano activist in college, and served as vice president of the United Farm Workers. Here she recalls two formative experiences from her teens. Caballero's grandparents moved to El Paso in 1958; her father, César, became a successful professional as a library director at the University of Texas–El Paso. She was 16 when the family was interviewed in the late 1980s.

❖ How do the psychological pressures on new immigrants differ from those that affect Mexican-American families long established in the United States?

❖ Do differences between the stories of Dolores Huerta in the 1950s and Ana Caballero in the 1980s result from their different economic positions or from changes in American society?

❖ How does the ability to speak a second language, either English or Spanish, affect each person's sense of identity?

❖ What does "being Mexican" mean to each individual?

Richard Rodriguez

When I first entered a classroom, [I was] able to understand some fifty stray English words. . . . Half a year passed. Unsmiling, ever watchful, my teachers noted my silence. They began to connect my behavior with the difficult progress my older brother and sister were having. Until one Saturday morning three nuns arrived at the house to talk to our parents. Stiffly, they sat on the blue living room sofa. . . . I overheard one voice gently wondering, "Do your children speak only Spanish at home, Mrs. Rodriguez? . . . Is it possible for you and your husband to encourage your children to practice their English when they are home?" Of course my parents complied. What would they not do for their children's well-being?

Again and again in the days following, increasingly angry, I was obliged to hear my mother and father: "Speak to us *en ingles*" . . . Only then did I determine to learn classroom English. Weeks after, it happened: One day in school I raised my hand to volunteer an answer. I spoke out in a loud voice. And I did not think it remarkable when the entire class understood. . . . At last, seven years old, I came to believe what had been technically true since my birth: I was an American citizen.

ambitious immigrants who seem to be shoving their way to the head of the line for economic and political influence. In Miami, Cubans asserted political leverage at the perceived expense of African-Americans. Blacks in every major city have resented Asian immigrant storekeepers who run convenience stores and markets in ghettos.

Whites in the 1980s expressed their own discomfort with the new immigration by moving. In the 1950s, whites had fled the growing African-American populations of large cities for segregated suburbs. A generation later, they seemed to be fleeing concentrations of Asians and Hispanics by moving to whiter states. Between 1985 and 1990, a net of 1 million

Dolores Huerta

When I got to high school, then it was really segregated. There was the real rich and the real poor. We were poor too, and I got hit with a lot of racial discrimination. . . . I got straight A's in all of my compositions. . . . But the teacher told me at the end of the year she couldn't give me an A because she knew that somebody else was writing my papers for me. That really discouraged me, because I used to stay up all night and think, and try to make every paper different, and try to put words in there that I thought were nice. Well, it just kind of crushed me. . . .

I was the only Chicano at Stockton Junior College. . . . I was frustrated . . . because I seemed to be out of step with everybody and everything. You're trying to go to school and yet you see all of these injustices. . . .

Then my mother took me to Mexico City when I was about seventeen. She had never been there either. It was our first trip. But that opened my eyes to the fact that there was nothing wrong with Chicanos.

Ana Caballero and her father, César

Ana: Most of the kids in my high school are Anglo. I'm the only Mexican-American girl on my cheerleading team. I'm the only cheerleader with black hair. . . . There's a lot of competition within the school, but other kids accept me for who I am rather than for my background or nationality.

César: Busing had a lot to do with that. Ana was involved in one of the last phases of court-ordered integration of the schools. . . . There was some tension. But as time moved on, busing has worked really well. . . ."

Ana: When I moved to this neighborhood, I felt strange getting started. My first day in fifth grade in the new school, it seemed so different. Not only because they were new kids, but the way they talked. There were so many blondes! Then, when I began to get used to everyone, I was bused to a new school. There were a lot of blondes there, too. But they were the children of doctors and the rich. The way they looked down on certain styles was very upsetting for me. After seventh grade, I started to fit in with them. I became more relaxed. There are a few kids who come from Mexico, so I get to speak some Spanish. . . . I don't speak Spanish as fluently as I should. I'm studying Spanish in school now, because I don't write it well. I was born here, but I'll always feel part Mexican. . . . I think I'll always have a little of both cultures.

Sources: *Richard Rodriguez,* Hunger of Memory: The Education of Richard Rodriguez *(1982); Joan M. Jensen, ed.,* With These Hands: Women Working on the Land *(1981); Al Santoli,* New Americans, An Oral History: Immigrants and Refugees in the U.S. Today *(1988).*

whites left the high-immigrant states of New York, Illinois, and Texas. Hundreds of thousands of others left California for "whiter" states, such as Utah, Oregon, and Nevada.

A second reaction against the new immigration has been discrimination against Latinos. The Immigration Reform and Control Act requires employers to verify the citizenship or immigration status of their workers. Some employers stopped hiring anyone who looked or sounded Hispanic as a way to avoid illegal immigrants. The Immigration and Naturalization Service (INS) under the Reagan and Bush administrations (1981–1993) denied political asylum and deported refugees from civil war in El Salvador and murderous dictatorships in Guatemala and Haiti. Officials were more likely to grant legal entry to similarly motivated white immigrants from the Soviet Union.

The INS acted while Americans were arguing over the economic impact of illegal immigration. Advocates of tight borders assert that illegal immigrants take jobs away from legal residents and eat up public assistance. Many studies, however, find that illegal immigrants fill jobs that nobody else wants. High employment among all immigrants means that their tax contributions through sales taxes and Social Security and payroll deductions more than pay for their use of welfare, food stamps, and unemployment benefits (which illegal immigrants are often afraid to claim for fear of calling attention to themselves).

In struggling for their place in American society, immigrants have added new panethnic identities to their national identities. In the nineteenth century, English-speaking Americans looked at European immigrants from widely separated regions and backgrounds and saw "Italians" or "Jews." In turn, newcomers found economic and political strength by making common cause across their differences, molding identities as ethnic groups within the U.S. context. Similarly, Hispanic activists revived the term *Chicano* to bridge the gap between recent Mexican immigrants and Latinos whose families had settled in the Southwest before American conquest in 1848. Great gaps of experience and culture separate Chinese, Koreans, Filipinos, and Vietnamese, but they gain political recognition and influence if they deal with other Americans as "Asians."

Some native-born Americans applauded the creative stimulus of increased cultural diversity; others feared that the United States needed to work even harder to maintain an American identity. The social challenge of new peoples blended with the challenge of establishing new patterns of production and trade within the world economy just as the domestic economy was changing.

Making a Living

The American economy after 1965 told two stories. Fast-growing "sunrise industries" shouldered aside declining industries making obsolete products.

Communities divided between white-collar and working-class worlds. Teenagers in Hamilton, Ohio, recognized the social chasm. One young woman described the country club set: "The girls act like they don't know you if you're not one of them.

You don't have their clothes, you're not in their college prep classes, and you better not go out with their brothers. . . . Not one of my ten best friends is going to college."

The winners and losers among industries and the class division between workers and managers were tied to the U.S. role in the world. The need to project an American military presence around the world fueled a prosperous defense economy. Foreign competitors undercut established industries, but markets abroad helped high-end service industries, such as engineering and professional consulting.

The Defense Economy

The Vietnam buildup and reinvestment in the military during the Carter (1977–1981) and Reagan (1981–1989) administrations made the defense budget one of the most direct paths to prosperity. Over the forty years from the Korean conflict to the **Persian Gulf War**, the United States made itself the mightiest military power ever known. Military bases and defense contractors remolded the economic landscape, as mild winters and clear skies for training and operations helped the South and West attract more than 75 percent of military payrolls.

Defense dependent places included big cities and small. Southern California thrived on 500,000 jobs in the aircraft industry (the 1967 figure). Visitors to Colorado Springs could drive past sprawling Fort Carson and visit the new Air Force Academy, opened in 1958. Sunk deep from view was the North American Air Defense command post beneath Cheyenne Mountain. Malmstrom Air Force Base transformed Great Falls, Montana, into a coordinating center for Minuteman missiles targeted at Moscow and Beijing. Dark blue Air Force vans carried crews from Great Falls to missile sites dotted over a swath of rolling plains as vast as Maryland.

Defense spending underwrote the expansion of American science and technology. Large universities, such as MIT, Michigan, Cal Tech, and Stanford, were leading defense contractors. The modern electronics business started in Boston and the San Francisco Bay Area with research and development for military uses. The space component of the aerospace industry was equally reliant on the defense economy, with NASA spending justified by competition with the USSR. NASA's centers of operation were scattered across the South.

Deindustrialization

Here's how novelist John Updike described the fictional city of Brewer, Pennsylvania, at the start of the 1970s:

Railroads and coal made Brewer. Everywhere in this city, once the fourth largest in Pennsylvania but now slipped to seventh, structures speak of expended energy. Great shapely stacks that have not issued smoke for half a century. . . . The old textile plants given over to discount clothing outlets teeming with a gimcrack cheer of banners FACTORY FAIR and slogans *Where a Dollar Is Still a Dollar.* . . . All this had been cast up in the last century by what now seem giants, in an explosion of iron and brick still preserved intact in this city where the sole new buildings are funeral parlors and government offices.

Industrial decay stalked "gritty cities" like Allentown, Pennsylvania; Trenton, New Jersey; and Gary, Indiana. Communities whose businesses and workers had made products in high volume for mass markets found that technological revolutions made them obsolete. When radial tires replaced bias-ply tires, Akron rubber workers paid the price. Asian steelmakers undercut the aging mills of Pittsburgh and Birmingham. Critics renamed the old manufacturing region of the Northeast and Middle West the **Rustbelt** in honor of its abandoned factories.

Stories of industrial decline were similar in small cities like Springfield, Ohio, and large cities like Cleveland. Springfield lost ten thousand manufacturing jobs and four thousand people during the 1970s, suffered unemployment of 17 percent, and needed $30 million in public subsidies to keep its largest factory going in 1982. Cleveland had built a century of prosperity on oil refining, steel, and metalworking; the metropolitan area had grown from 1.3 million in 1940 to 2.1 million in 1970. In the 1970s, however, it lost 165,000 people. As high-paying jobs in unionized industries disappeared, sagging income undermined small businesses and neighborhoods. Falling tax revenue brought the city to the verge of bankruptcy in 1978; bankers forced public service cuts and tax increases, which meant further job losses.

Plant closures were only one facet of nationwide efforts to increase productivity by substituting machinery for employees. Between 1947 and 1977, American steelmakers doubled output while cutting their work force from 600,000 to 400,000. Lumber companies automated mills, retaining only a fraction of their workers. White-collar industries like insurance computerized operations and farmed out routine work to part-time employees.

Parallel to the decline of heavy industry was the continuing transformation of American agriculture from small, family enterprises to corporate "agribusinesses." The number of farms slid from 4 million in 1960 to just over 2 million in 1994. Fewer than 2 percent of all American workers made their living from farming by 1994, down from 8 percent in 1960. Farm bankruptcies in Iowa reached levels unseen since the 1930s. Some family farmers found that they had to farm more acreage to stay competitive. Other farmers kept their land by working full time in factories and raising crops and livestock on the side.

Big farms were also the greatest beneficiaries of federal farm subsidy programs. The downside of corporate investment was excessive irrigation and massive use of pesticides and fertilizers. Wildlife was destroyed, ground-water was contaminated, underground water supplies were exhausted, and flowing streams, such as the lower Colorado River, were polluted with chemical-laden agricultural runoff.

Some older industries and their workers did find new competitive capacities in the sink-or-swim environment of technological and international competition. Buffalo, New York, lost much of its steel industry but retained smaller and more flexible factories making diverse products. The auto industry went through a similar cycle of crisis and response. Booming imports of well-made Toyotas and Hondas and customer demand for smaller cars destroyed auto-industry complacency in the fuel-short 1970s. In response, Ford, Chrysler, and finally General Motors remade themselves on the Japanese model as lean and flexible manufacturers. They cast off old plants, workers, and executives, started over, often in new locations, and forced Japanese companies to shift production to U.S. localities and workers.

Sunrise Industries and Service Jobs

With its fierce competition, the capitalist economy involves what is sometimes called "creative destruction," in which new enterprises push aside inefficient and outmoded industries. After 1965, the pressures for change included both foreign competition and technological breakthroughs that opened new opportunities even while they undermined old industries.

The epitome of the "sunrise" economy was electronics. Employment in computer manufacturing rose in the mid-1960s. California's **Silicon Valley**, north of San Jose, took off with corporate spinoffs and civilian applications of military technologies. Invention of the microprocessor in 1971 kicked the industry into high gear. In 1950, Santa Clara County had eight hundred factory workers. In 1980, it had 264,000 manufacturing workers and three thousand electronics firms. Related hardware and microchip factories spread the industry through the entire West.

As fewer Americans drove tractors and toiled on assembly lines, more became service workers. The service sector includes everyone not directly involved in producing and processing physical products. Service workers range from lawyers to hairstylists, from police officers to theater employees. In 1965, services already accounted for more than half of American jobs. By 1990, their share had risen to 70 percent.

At the bottom of the service scale were minimum wage jobs—cleaning people, child care workers, hospital orderlies, and fast-food workers. These positions offered little in terms of advancement, job security, or benefits. In contrast, many of the best new jobs were in information industries. Teaching, research, government, advertising, mass communications, and professional consulting depend on producing and manipulating information.

The information economy flourishes in large cities with libraries, universities, research hospitals, advertising agencies, and corporate headquarters. New York's bankers and stockbrokers made Manhattan an island of prosperity in the 1980s. Pittsburgh, with major universities and corporate headquarters, made the transition to the information economy even while its steel industry failed.

Rapid expansion of jobs in state and local government triggered popular revolts against state taxes that started in 1978 with passage of California's Proposition 13, which limited property taxes, and continued into the 1990s. Another growth industry was health care. Spending on medical and health services amounted to 12 percent of the gross domestic product in 1990, up from 5 percent in 1960. The need to share this huge expense fairly was the motivation for Medicare and Medicaid in the 1960s and the search for a national health insurance program in the 1990s.

Crisis for Organized Labor

Organized labor counted a million fewer members in 1989 than in 1964, even though the number of employed Americans had nearly doubled.

Corporations seized the opportunity for "union busting." They often demanded wage rollbacks and concessions on working conditions as trade-offs for continued employment, squeezing workers in one plant and then using the settlement to pressure another. The wave of corporate consolidations and mergers in the 1980s had especially damaging effects on the workplace. One 16-year-old described the changes in the grocery chain where her father worked for twenty-six years: "They're letting people go with no feelings for how long they've worked there, just lay 'em off. It's sad. He should be

getting benefits after all these years and all the sacrifices he's made. Now they're almost ready to lay him off without a word."

Immigration, both legal and illegal, added to the numbers of nonunion workers. In the Southwest, for example, low-paid immigrants filled the work forces of the electronics and garment industries. People in Silicon Valley knew the electronics company Hewlett-Packard as "Little Vietnam" in the mid-1980s and Advanced Micro Devices as "Little Manila." By one estimate, two-thirds of the workers in the Los Angeles garment trade were undocumented immigrants.

Another cause for shrinking union membership was the overall decline of blue-collar jobs—from 36 percent of the American work force in 1960 to 27 percent in 1990. Unions were most successful recruiting government workers, such as police officers, teachers, and bus drivers. In the private sector, however, many white-collar jobs were in small firms and offices that were difficult to organize. In the 1990s, microcomputers and electronic communication allowed companies to create even greater barriers to unionization by turning many of their employees into part-timers or home-based workers paid by output rather than hours.

The union effort that partly renewed the labor movement was the United Farm Workers, led by César Chávez. Committed to nonviolent action for social justice and to the labor movement, Chávez organized the UFW among Mexican-American farm workers in California in 1965. Their demands included better wages and safer working conditions, such as less exposure to pesticides. Chávez supplemented work stoppages with national boycotts against table grapes, lettuce, and certain brands of wine, making *la huelga* ("the strike") into *la causa* for urban liberals. Rival organizing by the Teamsters Union and the short attention span of the national public gradually undermined the UFW's initial success. Nevertheless, Chávez's dogged toughness and self-sacrifice gave the country a new hero. His work also gave a generation of Chicano men and women the confidence to fight for social and political rights.

The Rise of the Sunbelt

In contrast to troubled industrial cities in the Northeast and Midwest, journalists and scholars found headlong prosperity in cities like Orlando, Atlanta, Dallas, and Phoenix. Houston's sprawling and unplanned growth epitomized the booming metropolitan areas of the South and West. It was, said one reporter in 1976, "the place that scholars flock to for the purpose of seeing what modern civilization has wrought."

Kevin Phillips's *The Emerging Republican Majority*, published in 1969, popularized the term "Sunbelt." He described a region of conservative voting habits where Republicans might solidify their status as a majority party (a process that continued in the 1990s).

The Sunbelt benefited from each of the leading economic trends of the years since 1965: Asian and Latin American immigration, defense spending, high-tech industries, and recreation and retirement spending that supported service employment. The South and Southwest also gained from industrial flight from the Northeast. Corporations that wanted to escape union contracts liked the business climate of the Sunbelt, which promised weak unions and low taxes.

California, Texas, and Florida anchored the Sunbelt. The common definition sets the regional boundary at the line of state borders that runs along the northern edges of North Carolina, Tennessee, Arkansas, Oklahoma, New Mexico, and Arizona with an extension to include greater Los Angeles. However, at least three other areas have shared the underlying patterns of economic change and metropolitan growth: the Pacific coast from Monterey, California, north to Seattle; the central Rocky Mountains of Colorado and Utah; and the Chesapeake Bay region. These areas enjoy at least two of the three big *S*'s—sun, sea, and skiing.

However, economic shadows cooled parts of the Sunbelt in the 1980s and 1990s. Oil-producing Texas, Oklahoma, and the Rocky Mountain states felt severe recession from declining oil prices in the 1980s. California suffered from defense cutbacks. Poverty in the rural South remained as bad as in northern slums.

Driven in part by new industries, Pacific trade, and non-Atlantic migrations, the rise of the Sunbelt helped open an insular nation to a wider world and to broaden the cultural range subsumed by the word *American*. Sections of the South and West, historically controlled from the northeastern industrial core, developed as independent centers of economic change. Income per capita in the South neared the national average in the mid-1990s, ending several generations when it was the poor cousin among American regions.

Cities and Suburbs

Between 1965 and 1990, the proportion of Americans living in metropolitan areas (large cities and their suburbs) rose from 66 percent to just under 80 percent. Despite social problems, urban areas remained the centers of commerce and job creation in the fast-changing economy. New businesses benefited from cities' specialized manufacturers and wholesalers. Corporate executives, bankers, and attorneys depended on easy access to each other's expertise. The diverse urban labor force, including millions of immigrants, met the employment needs of new and old businesses.

Urban growth itself stimulated the economy. As city officials rebuilt urban centers and new suburbs sprawled over surrounding farmland, the United States had to provide freeways, schools, shopping centers, fast-food outlets, and housing for 66 million new metropolitan residents. It was the equivalent of building an entire new Paris every three and a half years, a new Singapore every thirteen months.

Most of the new development decentralized metropolitan areas and pushed the suburban frontier further into open countryside, spreading people and their daily environments more and more thinly over the landscape.

Urban Crisis

The nation entered the 1960s with the assumption that urban problems were growing pains. Politicians viewed the difficulties of central cities as by-products of exuberant suburban growth, which left outmoded downtowns in need of physical redevelopment. In mid-decade, however, TV networks and newsmagazines began to run stories of the "Battlefield, USA" and "Crisis in the Cities" type. The public heard that American cities were sinking under racial violence, crime, unemployment, and obsolete industries.

Central cities had the double responsibility of helping immigrants adjust to a new country and caring for the domestic poor. Baltimore had 27 percent of the Maryland population in 1970 but 66 percent of the state's welfare recipients. Boston had 14 percent of the Massachusetts population but 32 percent of the welfare clients. Impoverished and often fragmented families needed schools that would serve as social work agencies as well as educational institutions. Poor people with no other access to health care treated city hospital emergency rooms as the family doctor.

At the start of World War II, black Americans had been much more rural than white Americans. By 1970, they were more urban. Fully one-third of all African-Americans lived in the twelve largest cities, crowding into ghetto neighborhoods dating from World War I. Postwar black migrants found systems of race relations that limited their access to decent housing, to the best schools, and to many unionized jobs. Many families also arrived just in time to face the consequences of industrial layoffs and plant clo-

The movie Taxi Driver (1976), in which Jodie Foster played a young prostitute, showed a New York in which isolated individuals lived out desperate lives within failing communities. It reflected the pessimism with which many Americans regarded not only their cities but their larger society in the 1970s.

sures in the 1970s and 1980s. Already unneeded in the South because of the mechanization of agriculture, the migrants found themselves equally unwanted in the industrial North, caught in decaying neighborhoods and victimized by crime.

Because ghettos grew block by block, middle-class black families had to pioneer as intruders into white neighborhoods and then see ghetto problems crowd in behind them. Their children faced the seductions of the street, which became increasingly violent with the spread of handguns and trade in illegal drugs. Successful African-American families began to flee to suburbs when fair housing laws slowly opened the real estate market, leaving ghettos with fewer middle-class leaders.

Closure of the elevated West Side Highway along the Hudson River in Manhattan after huge chunks fell out of the roadway symbolized a spreading urban problem. Decay of the urban infrastructure of utility and transportation systems was a by-product of market forces and public policy. Private developers often borrowed money saved through northeastern bank accounts, insurance policies, and pension funds to finance new construction in the Sunbelt. The defense budget pumped tax dollars from the old industrial cities into the South and West.

High local taxes in older cities were one result, for the American system of local government demands that cities—and the poor—help themselves. By the early 1970s, the average resident of a central city paid roughly twice the state and local taxes per $1,000 of income as the average suburbanite. As Mayor Moon Landrieu of New Orleans commented, "We've taxed everything that moves and everything that stands still; and if anything moves again, we tax that, too."

In part because of their need to increase the value of the real estate on which they collected property taxes, big-city leaders fought back by emphasizing the renewal of downtowns. Office construction booms in the late 1970s and again in the mid-1980s created new office buildings to house the executives and consultants in the growing national and international information economy.

From 1930 to 1960, Boston's historic core had attracted virtually no private investment. One banker stated in 1957 that "no one can buy land within the city of Boston, put up an office building, and make money." In the 1960s, the city used urban renewal to level run-down blocks for a new city hall and office buildings. In the 1970s, redevelopment extended to the waterfront, where investors converted nineteenth-century wharves and huge granite warehouses into condominiums and restaurants. The historic Faneuil Hall market reopened in 1976 as an upscale "festival market." A private building boom doubled downtown office space. Downtown Boston by 1980 was a diverse and lively mixture of old and new buildings, districts, and people.

Obvious beneficiaries of urban renewal were downtown property owners, retailers, metropolitan newspapers, and utilities with huge investments in facilities serving older parts of cities. Revitalization also favored managers and professionals who could enjoy the attractions and convenience of strong downtowns and recycled neighborhoods near business districts. But with fewer unskilled and semi-skilled jobs available in manufacturing and construction, undereducated city people either tended the wants of the elite or did nothing. At its worst, the redeveloped city was a community of dangerous extremes, where enormous wealth contrasted with hopeless poverty. In New York, the real incomes of people on the lower third of the economic ladder declined during the 1980s, while those of the top 10 percent rose by 40 percent.

Suburban America

Downtown revitalization ran against the tide of metropolitan decentralization. Just after World War II, most new suburbs had been bedroom communities that depended on the jobs, services, and shopping of central cities. By the late 1960s, suburbs were evolving into "outer cities" whose inhabitants had little need for the central city.

One key to the changing character of the suburbs was a shift in their sources of population. In the first decades after the war, "white flight" described the hundreds of thousands of young families who left old walk-up apartments and row houses for bright new tract houses, distancing themselves from minority and racially changing neighborhoods. After the mid-1960s, however, new residents in a suburban ring typically moved from other suburbs and felt no personal connection to or responsibility for old city neighborhoods.

In the fifteen largest metropolitan areas, the number of central city jobs fell by 800,000 in the 1960s, while the number of suburban jobs rose by 3.2 million. The shift from rail to air for business travel accentuated suburban job growth. Sales representatives and executives could arrive at airports on the edge of town rather than railroad stations at the center and transact business without ever going downtown.

Suburban rings gained a growing share of public facilities intended to serve the entire metropolitan area. As pioneered in California, community colleges as well as many of the new four-year schools that state university systems added in the 1960s and early 1970s were built for suburbanites. New sports complexes in the 1980s were as likely to be suburban as urban. The California Angels in baseball and New York Islanders in hockey gave suburban regions their own major league sports franchises.

In the 1980s and 1990s, suburban retailing, employment, and services fused into so-called **edge cities**. Huge complexes of shopping malls, high-rise hotels, and glass-sided office buildings have as much space as old business districts in cities. But in edge cities, however, population remained more scattered than in older city neighborhoods. "I live in Garden Grove," one southern Californian reported, "work in Irvine, shop in Santa Ana, go to the dentist in Anaheim, . . . and used to be president of the League of Women Voters in Fullerton."

Suburbs and Politics

Suburban political power grew along with economic clout. In 1962, the Supreme Court handed down a landmark decision in the case of **Baker** v. **Carr**. Overturning laws that treated counties or other political subdivisions as the units to be represented in state legislatures, *Baker* required that legislative seats be apportioned on the basis of population. This principle of "one person, one vote" broke the stranglehold of rural counties on state governments, but the big beneficiaries were not older cities but fast-growing suburbs.

In **Swann** v. **Charlotte-Mecklenburg Board of Education** (1971), the U.S. Supreme Court held that crosstown busing was an acceptable solution to de facto segregation that resulted from residential patterns within a single school district. When school officials failed to achieve racial balance, federal judges ordered their own busing plans. For many Americans, the image of busing for racial integration was fixed in 1975 when whites in Boston reacted with violence against black students who were bused to largely white high schools in the South Boston and Charlestown neighborhoods. The goal of equal opportunity clashed with equally strong values of neighborhood, community, and ethnic solidarity. White students rioted in the halls of Charlestown High.

Busing was self-defeating, for it caused whites to move out of the integrating school district or to place their children in private academies, as happened frequently in the South. Busing also caused suburbanites to defend their political independence fiercely.

Zoning was another powerful tool of suburban self-defense. Restrictive building codes, requirements for large lots, and expensive subdivision fees could price all but the rich out of the local housing market. Many suburbs refused to zone land for apartments. As one Connecticut suburbanite put it, for a moderate-income family to hope to move into one of the state's most exclusive suburbs was "like going into Tiffany and demanding a ring for $12.50. Tiffany doesn't have any rings for $12.50."

However, as continued decentralization pushed the suburban share of the U.S. population toward 50 percent in the 1990s, most suburban rings displayed the full range of American society with the same economic, traffic, and pollution problems as the central cities.

New Meanings for American Families

The political and social changes of the 1960s altered the patterns and meaning of family life. Americans began to rethink ideas about families and to emphasize personal identities in addition to traditional family roles. Women redefined themselves as individuals and workers as well as wives and mothers. Gays and lesbians asserted that their sexual orientations were not aberrations from "normal" family patterns but were valid in their own right. As average life spans lengthened, older Americans found personal satisfaction and political influence as members of their own communities and interest groups.

If one result of changing family patterns was new political groupings and new policies, another was deep confusion. In 1992, Vice President Dan Quayle earned headlines, and some derision, by criticizing the television comedy *Murphy Brown* for a positive and unrealistic portrayal of its lead character as a single mother. In the same year, however, 98 percent of Americans agreed that the label "family" applied to a married couple living with their children and 81 percent also applied "family" to the *Murphy Brown* scenario of an unwed mother living with her child. More than a quarter were even comfortable using "family" for two lesbian women or two gay men living together and raising children.

The Feminist Critique

The growing dissatisfaction of many women with the domestic role expected of them in the 1950s helped set the stage for a revived feminism. Important steps in this revival included the Presidential Commission on the status of women in 1961; the addition of gender as one of the categories protected by the Civil Rights Act of 1964 (see Chapter 30); and creation of the **National Organization for Women (NOW)** in 1966.

Throughout the 1970s, activists battled to open one job category after another to women who proved that they could indeed use tools, run computers, or pick stocks on Wall Street. They also battled for equal pay for everyone with equal qualifications and responsibilities.

Changes in sexual behavior paralleled efforts to equalize treatment in the workplace. More reliable methods of contraception, especially birth control pills introduced in the early 1960s, gave women greater control over child-bearing. In some ways a replay of ideas from the 1920s, a new sexual revolution eroded the double standard that expected chastity of women but tolerated promiscuity among men. One consequence was a singles culture that accepted sexual activity between unmarried men and women.

Feminist radicals caught the attention of the national media with a demonstration against the 1968 Miss America pageant. Protesters crowned a sheep as Miss America and set out barrels for women who wanted to make a statement by tossing their bras and makeup in the trash.

Women's liberation took off as a social and political movement in 1970 and 1971. Within a few years, millions of women had recognized events and patterns in their lives as discrimination based on gender.

Women's Rights and Public Policy

Congress wrote key goals of the feminist movement into law in the early 1970s. Title IX of the Educational Amendments (1972) to the Civil Rights Act prohibited discrimination by sex in any educational program receiving federal aid. In the same year, Congress sent the **Equal Rights Amendment (ERA)** to the states for ratification. The amendment read, "Equal rights under the law shall not be denied or abridged by the United States or by any state on account of sex." More than twenty states ratified quickly in the first few months and another dozen after increasingly tough battles in state legislatures. The ERA then stalled, three states short, when the time limit for ratification expired in 1982.

In January 1973, the U.S. Supreme Court expanded the debate about women's rights with the case of **Roe** v. **Wade**. Voting 7 to 2, the Court struck down state laws forbidding abortion in the first three months of pregnancy and set guidelines for abortion during the remaining months. Drawing on the earlier decision of *Griswold* v. *Connecticut,* which dealt with access to information about birth control, the justices held that the Fourteenth Amendment includes a right to privacy that blocks states from interfering with a woman's right to terminate a pregnancy.

The feminist movement and specific policy measures related to it put equal rights and the fight against sexism (a word no one knew before 1965) on the national agenda and gradually changed how Americans thought about the relationships between men and women. Feminists focused attention on rape as a crime of violence, calling attention to the burdens the legal system placed on rape victims. In the 1980s and 1990s, they also challenged sexual harassment in the workplace, gradually refining the boundaries between acceptable and unacceptable behavior.

These changes came in the context of increasingly sharp conflict over the feminist agenda. Both the ERA and *Roe* stirred impassioned support and equally passionate opposition. Opponents of the ERA worried about unisex restrooms (not a problem on commercial airliners) and women in the military (not a problem in the Persian Gulf War). Also fueling the debate was a deep split between the main-

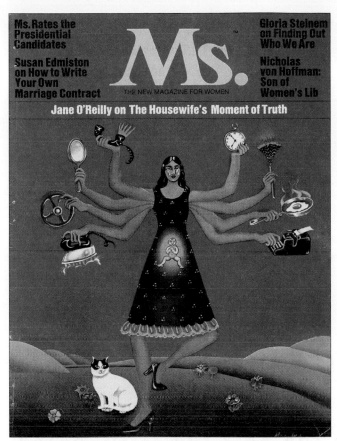

Ms. magazine published its first issue in 1972. Edited by Gloria Steinem, the magazine attempted to bring a radical feminist message to a wide audience. Ms. emphasized the need for women to have equal access with men to education, health care, and employment and tried to help Americans rethink traditional gender roles.

stream feminist view of women as fully equal individuals and the contrary belief that women had a special role as anchors of families, an updating of the nineteenth-century idea of separate spheres.

Women in the Labor Force, Women in Poverty

The most sweeping change in the lives of American women did not come from federal legislation or court cases but from the growing likelihood that a married woman would work outside the home. In 1960, some 32 percent of married women were in the labor force; thirty years later, 58 percent were working or looking for work (along with 67 percent of single women). Federal and state governments slowly responded to the changing demands of work and family with new policies such as a federal child care tax credit.

One reason for more working women was inflation in the 1970s and declining wages in the

1980s, both of which eroded the ability of families to live comfortably on one income. Between 1979 and 1986, fully 80 percent of married households saw the husband's income fall in constant dollars. The result, headlined the *Wall Street Journal* in 1994: "More Women Take Low-Wage Jobs Just So Their Families Can Get By." One young woman juggled community college courses and full-time work as an insurance company clerk, earning more than her husband brought home as a heavy equipment operator. Another worked at the drive-up window of a shopping center bank and cleaned offices on Saturdays to help pay the mortgage on a house purchased before her husband's employer imposed pay cuts.

A second reason for the increase in working women from 29 million in 1970 to 60 million in 1994 was increasing need for "women's jobs" like data entry clerks, reservation agents, and nurses. Indeed, the American economy still divides job categories by sex. Despite some movement toward gender-neutral hiring in the 1970s job types were more segregated by sex than by race in the early 1990s.

Nor could most women, even those working full time and year round, expect to earn as much as men. In the 1960s and 1970s, the average workingwoman earned just 60 percent of the earnings of the average man. The gap narrowed in the 1980s, with women's earnings rising to 74 percent of men's by 1994. About half of the change was the result of bad news, namely, a decline of earnings among men as high-wage factory jobs disappeared. The other half was the positive result of better-educated younger women finding better jobs. Indeed, women took more than half of the four-year college degrees awarded in the late 1980s (up from 38 percent in 1960) and 35 percent of first professional degrees (up from 3 percent).

But low earning capacity of women with limited educations meant that women were far more likely than men to be poor. Women constituted nearly two-thirds of poor adults at the end of the 1980s. The feminization of poverty and American reliance on private support for child rearing also meant that children had a higher chance of living in poverty than adults and that poor American children were worse off than their peers in other advanced nations.

Coming Out

New militancy among gay men and lesbians drew on several of the social changes of the late 1960s. Willingness to talk about nonstandard sexual behavior was part of a change in public values. Tactics of political pressure came from the antiwar and civil rights movements. The timing, with a series of key events from 1969 to 1974, coincided with that of women's liberation.

When police raided Manhattan's Stonewall Inn, a gay bar, in June 1969 patrons fought back in a weekend of disorder. The "Stonewall rebellion" was a catalyst for homosexuals to assert themselves as a political force. San Francisco also became a center of gay life. By the late 1970s, the city had more than three hundred business and social gathering places identified as gay and lesbian.

With New Yorkers and San Franciscans as examples, more and more gay men and lesbians "came out" or went public about their sexual orientation. In 1974, the American Psychiatric Association eliminated homosexuality from its official list of mental disorders.

The character of life in gay communities took an abrupt turn in the 1980s when the worldwide **AIDS** epidemic began to impact the United States. Scientists first identified a new disease pattern, **acquired immune deficiency syndrome**, in 1981. The name described the symptoms resulting from the human immunodeficiency virus (HIV), which destroys the body's ability to resist disease. HIV is transferred through blood and semen. In the 1980s, the most frequent American victims were gay men or intravenous drug users, although infected blood transfusions claimed many others. By the end of 1993, AIDS had been responsible for 200,000 deaths in the United States, and transmission to heterosexual women was increasing.

AIDS triggered many of the same intense emotions as polio. By the early 1990s, it was the leading cause of death for men aged 25 to 44. Since many gay men were estranged from their families, death from AIDS was often preceded by social isolation. The spread of the epidemic gave new ammunition to people opposed to homosexuality. And it inspired intense anger among gays who believed that straight society and government agencies were indifferent to their plight and had failed to fund sufficient research on vaccines and treatment. Spending rose substantially in the late 1980s and 1990s.

The Graying of America

Between 1965 and 1990, the number of Americans aged 65 and over jumped from 18.2 million to 31.3 million. For the first time, most Americans could expect to survive into old age.

Older Americans have become a powerful voice in public affairs. They tend to vote against local taxes but fight efforts to slow the growth of Social Security, even though growing numbers of the elderly are being supported by a relatively smaller proportion of working men and women.

Retired Americans changed the social geography of the United States, moving steadily to attractive Sunbelt communities. Much growth in the South and Southwest has been financed by money earned in the Northeast and Midwest and transferred by retirees.

Sunbelt developers invented age-segregated new towns in the 1960s as full-service environments for people aged 50 or older. The first Sun City opened south of Tampa and another near Phoenix in 1960. Close behind were several Leisure World communities in California. Sun City's physical characteristics and national advertising helped define retirement as a distinct stage of life offering "an unending treasure of perfect days, filled with interesting activities." These unprecedented developments substitute organized services and voluntary association with other older people for traditional reliance on care within families.

The Search for Spiritual Grounding

Between 1980 and 1984, efforts to develop oil shale resources turned Grand Junction, Colorado, into a boom town. Newcomers searched for family stability and a sense of community by joining established religious congregations and organizing new churches. The telephone book in 1985 listed twenty-eight mainstream Protestant and Catholic churches, twenty-four Baptist churches (reflecting the Oklahoma and Texas roots of many oil workers), five more liberal churches (such as Unitarians and Bahais), and more than fifty Pentecostal, Bible, and Evangelical churches. Nearly a dozen Christian schools supplemented the public schools.

Grand Junction was typical of the United States. In the mid-1970s, 56 percent of Americans said that religion was "very important" to them, compared to only 27 percent of Europeans. Spiritual searches have followed both the well-marked routes of established denominations and new paths through avant-garde philosophies and feel-good therapies.

Communes and Cults

Self-isolating communes and cults represent a long heritage of American utopian communities. Thousands of Americans in the late 1960s and 1970s formed "intentional communities" or "communes." Their members usually tried to combine individual freedom and spontaneity with cooperative living. Upper New England and the Southwest were commune country. Rural communes usually located on marginal land too poor to support commercial farming.

A few communes followed coherent social theories, but most were free-form. Journalist Sara Davidson described one California commune in 1970:

> Women in long skirts and shawls, men in lace-up boots, coveralls, and patched jeans tied with pieces of rope, sitting on the grass playing banjos, guitars, lyres, wood flutes, dulcimers, and an accordion. . . . Nine-year-old Michelle is prancing around in a pink shawl and a floppy hat warbling "It's time for the feast." Nancy says, "The pickin's are sort of spare, because tomorrow is welfare day and everybody's broke." She carries from the outdoor wood stove pots of brown rice.

As the description implies, communes were artificial families, financed by inheritances, food stamps, and handicraft sales, and suffered from the same inequality between men and women that was fueling the feminist revolt. Like natural families, they were emotional hothouses; most collapsed because their members had incompatible goals.

Similar to communes but far more organized were exotic religious communities. One of the most successful has been the Holy Spirit Association for the Unification of World Christianity (Unification Church), which Sun Myung Moon brought from Korea to the United States in 1973. Converts ("Moonies") have never numbered more than a few tens of thousands, but Moon amassed a huge fortune and dabbled in conservative politics.

Americans usually hear about cults only if they clash with authorities or end in disaster. Most tragic was the case of Jim Jones, founder of the People's Temple, who moved nearly a thousand followers to Guyana in South America and violently resisted authorities' efforts to penetrate his walls of secrecy. A congressional investigation of abuses within the colony led to the murder of Congressman Leo Ryan and mass suicide by nine hundred of Jones's followers, who drank cyanide-laced punch on November 18, 1978.

Personal Religion

"The sixties" opened Americans to new spiritual experiences. Many young people in their twenties and thirties had left conventional Christian churches but had not lost their spiritual hunger. Some turned to Sufis, Zen Buddhists, Hare Khrishnas, and others who adapted Eastern religious traditions for modern Americans. The counterculture softened and blended into human potential movements of the 1970s and **New Age** movements of the 1980s. For understanding American culture, the particular answers are less important than the strength of the search for greater wholeness, meaning, self-realization, and spiritual revitalization.

One important change in national religious life has been the continuing "Americanization" of the Roman Catholic church following the second Vatican Council in 1965, in which church leaders sought to respond to postwar industrial society. Church practice lost some of its distinctiveness; celebrating Mass in English rather than Latin was symbolic of numerous changes that split the church between reformers and traditionalists.

The mainline Protestant denominations that traditionally defined the center of American belief struggled after 1960. The United Methodist Church, the Presbyterian Church U.S.A., the United Church of Christ, and the Episcopal Church battled internally over the morality of U.S. foreign policy, the role of women in the ministry, and the reception of gay and lesbian members. Liberal Protestantism has also historically been strongest in the slow-growing Northeast and Midwest.

In contrast, evangelical churches have benefited from the direct appeal of their message and from strong roots in the booming Sunbelt. Members of evangelical churches (25 percent of white Americans) now outnumber the members of mainline Protestant churches (20 percent). Major evangelical denominations include Baptists, the Church of the Nazarene, and the Assemblies of God.

Outsiders know evangelical Christianity through "televangelists." Spending on religious television programming rose from $50 to $600 million in the 1970s. The "electronic church" built on the radio preaching and professional revivalism of the 1950s. By the 1970s, it reached 20 percent of American households. Video evangelism has been especially popular in southern communities with high membership in evangelical denominations, northern Appalachia, and small markets in the Midwest (Fort Wayne, Indiana, but not Detroit, for example).

Behind the glitz and hype of the television pulpit, evangelical churches emphasized religion as an individual experience focused on personal salvation. The conservative nature of their theology and social teaching in a changing society offered

SUMMARY

RELIGION AND POLITICS

Americans in the 1980s and 1990s battled over abortion, the teaching of evolution, limits to artistic expression, and other social values. Much of the conflict in social expectations and political goals stems from opposing tendencies in religious belief: the traditional impulse versus the progressive impulse.

	The Traditional Impulse	The Progressive Impulse
Religious basis	Orthodox theology that relies on unchanging truths and moral traditions	Theology that reconciles belief with findings of science and respects multiple ways to know the divine
Subscribers	Evangelical and fundamentalist Protestants, Orthodox Jews, conservative Roman Catholics	Mainline and liberal Protestants, Conservative and Reform Jews, Roman Catholics influenced by changes introduced by of the Second Vatican Council
Social assumption	Traditional family as the basic social unit	Acceptance of diverse groups and treatment of individuals as equal before God as basis for a just society
Moral imperative	Responsibility to order one's personal life in accord with religious teaching	Responsibility to heed scriptural calls to end inequality and social injustice
Political goals	Protection of opportunities for religious expression (such as prayer in schools); protection of rights of individual economic initiative; support for nuclear families	Strict separation of church and state; protection of individual freedom of expression and belief; assistance for the poor at home and abroad
Political technique	Grass-roots organizing and campaigning	Legislative lobbying

certainty that was especially attractive to many younger families.

Values in Conflict

Americans who are undogmatic in religion are often liberal in politics as well, hoping to lessen economic inequities and strengthen individual social freedom. Religious and political conservatism also tend to go together. To some degree, this cultural division runs all the way through American society, dividing liberal North from conservative South, cities from small towns, and college professors from Kiwanis Club members (see the summary table "Religion and Politics").

The "conservative" emphasis on personal salvation and the literal truth of the Bible also expresses itself in a desire to restore "traditional" social patterns. Conservatives worry that social disorder occurs when people follow personal impulses and pleasures. In contrast, the "liberal" or "modern" emphasis on the universality of the Christian message restates the Social Gospel with its call to build the Kingdom of God through social justice and may recognize divergent pathways toward truth. Liberals worry that rampaging greed in the unregulated marketplace creates disorder and injustice.

The cultural conflict transcends the historic three-way division of Americans among Protestants,

Catholics, and Jews. Instead, the conservative-liberal division now cuts through each group. For example, conservative Catholics, fundamentalist Protestants, and Orthodox Jews may find themselves in agreement on issues of cultural values despite theologies that are worlds apart. The same may be true of Catholic reformers, liberal Protestants, and Conservative and Reform Jews.

Conservatives have initiated the culture wars, trying to stabilize what they fear is an American society spinning out of control because of personal sexual indulgence. In fact, growing numbers of teenagers reported being sexually active in the 1970s, but the rate of increase tapered off in the 1980s. The divorce rate began to drop after 1980 as births to teenagers dropped after 1990. Most adults remained staid and monogamous, according to a survey published in 1994, but sexual self-help and advice books proliferated.

The explosion of explicit attention to sexual behavior set the stage for religiously rooted battles over two sets of issues. One cluster revolves around so-called "family values," questioning the morality of access to abortion, the acceptability of homosexuality, and the roles and rights of women. A second set of concerns has focused on the supposed role of public schools in undermining morality through sex education, unrestricted reading matter, nonbiblical science, and the absence of prayer. Opinion polls show clear differences among religious denominations on issues such as censorship of library books, acceptability of racially segregated neighborhoods, freedom of choice in terminating pregnancy, and homosexuality.

A culturally conservative issue with great popular appeal in the early 1990s was an effort to prevent states and localities from protecting homosexuals against discrimination. Using the slogan "No special rights," antigay measures passed in Cincinnati, Colorado, and communities in Oregon in 1993 and 1994, only to have the Supreme Court overturn the Colorado law in **Romer** v. **Evans** (1996).

On the national level, President Ronald Reagan gave respectability to what critics called a "politics of nostalgia," but the movement's strength came from outside the political establishment. For example, Jerry Falwell was an outsider to politics before he founded the Moral Majority in 1979 and influenced the 1980 election. Television appeals and direct-mail fund-raising became powerful tools for both sides in the 1980s—for the liberal People for the American Way and the American Civil Liberties Union as well as for the Moral Majority.

A good occasion for observing the full spectrum of religiously based politics came in 1988, when two different preachers sought a presidential nomination. Pat Robertson's campaign for the Republican nomination tapped deep discontent with social change. He used the mailing list from his 700 Club program to mobilize evangelical and charismatic Christians and pushed the Republican party further to the right on family and social issues. Jesse Jackson's grass-roots campaign had the opposite goal of moving the Democratic party to the left on social and economic policy. He assembled a "rainbow coalition" that included militant labor unionists, feminists, and others whom Robertson's followers feared. Both Jackson and Robertson used their powerful personalities and religious convictions to inspire support from local churches and churchgoers, but the sharp divergence of their goals is a reminder about the continuing variety of American religious beliefs.

Conclusion

After twenty years of consensus, Americans since the mid-1960s have revisited basic questions about our character as a nation and people.

In the face of economic and cultural dislocation, some Americans moved to self-contained suburbs or constructed entirely new communities. Others turned to a wide range of religious organizations. Groups as different as feminists, gays, and evangelicals forged grass roots political movements to place their own concerns on the national agenda.

Even as Americans rallied around conflicting visions of the good society, the clamor of new voices and new concerns demonstrated the strength of American democracy. What remained to be tested was the continuing viability of the political process— the nation's capacity to recognize the values of diverse groups while enlisting them around a common vision of the public good.

Review Questions

1. Describe how the United States has become more international since 1965. What policy changes have promoted globalization? How have increased foreign trade and immigration affected American cities and states? What political conflicts stem from the nation's growing international connections?

2. How did the changing economy affect the various regions of the United State? How does an economy based on information and services differ from the earlier manufacturing economy? Have recent

economic changes helped or hurt organized labor?

3. Why did Americans in the 1960s come to believe that larger cities were in crisis? What have been the major trends in suburban growth since the 1960s? How has this growth affected prominent political issues and the balance of political power?

4. Describe key changes in American family patterns since the 1960s. To what extent are these changes the result of economic forces? Of changing social values? How is an aging population likely to affect national politics in the twenty-first century?

5. Describe the variety of ways in which recent Americans have searched for spiritual connection and community. How does the social and political role of religion in the United States differ from that in other industrialized nations? What key issues have brought religious groups into the political arena? What positions do different groups take on these issues?

Recommended Reading

Elijah Anderson, *Streetwise: Race, Class, and Change in an Urban Community* (1990). This is a deeply troubling portrait of the culture of the streets in the Philadelphia ghetto.

Stephanie Coontz, *The Way We Never Were* (1992). Coontz places modern family patterns in accurate historical context, puncturing a series of myths and preconceptions about family decline.

Peter Davis, *Hometown: A Contemporary American Chronicle* (1982). Davis profiles the small city of Hamilton, Ohio, in the late 1970s.

Francis Fitzgerald, *Cities on a Hill* (1986). Here are incisive portraits of new American communities in the 1980s, including retirees' Sun City, Florida; gay San Francisco; and the religious commune of Rajneeshpuram.

Joel Garreau, *Edge City: Life on the New Frontier* (1991). A journalist argues that suburban rings are developing their own "downtowns."

Milton Rogovin and Michael Frisch, *Portraits in Steel* (1993). The transformation of an American industrial city (Buffalo) is told through photographs and interviews.

Wade Clark Roof, *A Generation of Seekers: The Spiritual Journeys of the Baby Boom Generation* (1993). Roof examines the range of religious and spiritual experiences of contemporary Americans.

Where to Learn More

❖ **Museum of Broadcast Communication, Chicago, Illinois.** Exhibits on the rise of broadcasting plus a library of television and radio programs and commercials offer a window into American popular culture.

❖ **Downtown Baltimore, Maryland.** A visit to the Harborplace festival market, the revitalized waterfront, the old Lexington Market food market, and the new Camden Yards baseball stadium is a quick way to see the sort of "new downtown" that cities tried to build after 1975.

❖ **Youngstown Historical Center of Industry and Labor, Youngstown, Ohio.** A permanent exhibit, "Forging the Steel Valley," focuses on the daily lives of steelworkers and the decline of the industry.

33 SEARCHING FOR STABILITY IN A CHANGING WORLD, SINCE 1980

KEY TOPICS

❖ Economic and social change during the Reagan Revolution
❖ The collapse of the USSR and the end of the Cold War
❖ Concern for the economy, the desire for stability, and the election and reelection of Bill Clinton

On June 1, 1980, CNN—Cable News Network—gave television viewers their first chance to watch news coverage twenty-four-hours a day. Newscasters Bernard Shaw and Mary Alice Williams brought instant information to an initial audience of 1.7 million subscribers; a decade later, CNN had hundreds of millions of viewers in more than seventy-five countries.

Fourteen months after CNN came another new cable channel with immediate impact—MTV: Music Television, round-the-clock programming of music videos which created a new form of popular art and advertising.

Before 1980, ordinary Americans had few choices for learning about their nation and world—virtually identical newscasts on NBC, CBS, and ABC and similar stories in *Time* and *Newsweek*. Fifteen years later, they had learned to surf through dozens of cable channels in search of specialized programs. Hundreds of magazines for niche markets had replaced the general-circulation periodicals of the postwar generation. Vast quantities of information were more easily available, but much of it was packaged for a subdivided marketplace of specialized consumers.

The new cable channels are also reminders of the powerful connections between the United States and the rest of the world. MTV by 1990 had spawned MTV Europe, MTV Australia, MTV Japan, and MTV Latin America. CNN made a global reputation with live reporting on the student revolt in Beijing in 1989. When American bombs began to fall on Baghdad in January 1991, White House officials watched CNN to find out how their war was going.

New rules governed foreign affairs and the national economy in the 1980s and 1990s. Even as the world grew safer with the breakup of the Soviet Union, it also grew more complicated. Americans had to learn new principles for understanding diplomatic relations when nations no longer had to choose sides in the Cold War. At home, Americans decided to halt and then reverse the growth of federal government responsibilities that had marked both Republican and Democratic administrations since the 1930s. By the mid-1990s, the center of U.S. politics had shifted substantially to the right.

The Reagan Revolution

Political change began in 1980, when Ronald Reagan rode the tide of American discontent to a narrow but decisively important victory in the presidential election (see Map 33-1). He built on a conservative critique of American policies and on issues that Jimmy Carter had placed on the national agenda. Reagan was a "Teflon president" who managed to take credit for successes but avoid blame for problems and rolled to a landslide reelection in 1984. The consequences of his two terms were startling. They included an altered role for government, powerful but selective economic growth, and a shift of domestic politics away from bread-and-butter issues toward moral or lifestyle concerns.

Reagan's Majority

A CBS News–*New York Times* poll after the election found that only 11 percent of Reagan's supporters voted for him because of his conservative platform. Fully 38 percent pulled the Reagan lever simply because he was not Jimmy Carter.

Some of Reagan's most articulate support came from anti-Communist conservatives of both parties who feared that the United States was losing influence in the world. Despite Carter's tough actions in 1979 and 1980 and increases in defense spending, his inability to free the hostages in Iran grated. The Panama Canal and SALT II treaties seemed to give away American power. The Soviet military buildup, charged the critics, was creating a "window of vulnerability."

Christian conservatives worried that liberal social activists were using the federal courts to alter traditional values to the detriment of American society. Wealthy entrepreneurs from the Sunbelt states believed that Nixon-era federal offices like the Environmental Protection Agency and the Occupational

Safety and Health Administration were choking their businesses in red tape.

Foreign policy activists and antiestablishment crusaders would have been unable to elect Reagan without disaffected blue collar and middle-class voters who deserted the Democrats. Reagan's campaign hammered on the question: "Are you better off than you were four years ago?" Many white working-class voters believed that minorities were getting an unfair edge in hiring and social services. The same voters worried about inflation, which had essentially halted growth in the average family's spending power since 1973, and blamed their difficulties on runaway government spending.

In *The Unheavenly City* (1968), Edward Banfield questioned the basic idea of public solutions for social problems. He argued that liberal programs failed because inequality is based on human character and rooted in the basic structure of society; government action can solve only the problems that required better engineering, such as pollution control, better highways, or the delivery of explosives to military targets.

Map 33-1   Election of 1980
Ronald Reagan won in a landslide in 1980. Independent candidate John Anderson took more votes from Jimmy Carter than from Reagan, but Reagan's personal magnetism was a powerful political force. His victory confirmed the shift of the South to the Republican party.

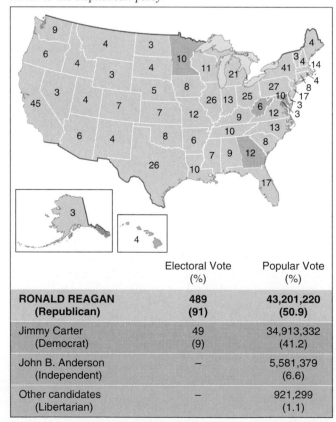

	Electoral Vote (%)	Popular Vote (%)
RONALD REAGAN (Republican)	**489 (91)**	**43,201,220 (50.9)**
Jimmy Carter (Democrat)	49 (9)	34,913,332 (41.2)
John B. Anderson (Independent)	–	5,581,379 (6.6)
Other candidates (Libertarian)	–	921,299 (1.1)

CHRONOLOGY

1980   Ronald Reagan is elected president.

CNN begins cable broadcasting.

Reagan breaks strike by air traffic controllers.

1982   Nuclear freeze movement peaks.

United States begins to finance Contra rebels against the Sandinista government in Nicaragua.

1983   241 Marines are killed by a terrorist bomb in Beirut, Lebanon.

1984   Reagan wins reelection.

1985   Mikhail Gorbachev initiates reforms in the USSR.

1986   Economic Recovery Tax Act is adopted.

1987   Congress holds hearings on the Iran-Contra scandal.

Reagan and Gorbachev sign the Intermediate Nuclear Force treaty.

1988   George Bush is elected president.

1989   Communist regimes in eastern Europe collapse; Germans tear down Berlin Wall.

Financial crisis forces federal bailout of many savings and loans.

United States invades Panama to capture General Manuel Noriega.

1990   Iraq invades Kuwait; and United States sends forces to the Persian Gulf.

West Germany and East Germany reunite.

1991   Operation Desert Storm drives the Iraqis from Kuwait.

Soviet Union dissolves into independent nations.

Strategic Arms Reduction Treaty (START) is signed.

Clarence Thomas is seated on the Supreme Court.

1992   Acquital of officers accused of beating Rodney King triggers Los Angeles riots.

Bill Clinton defeats George Bush for the presidency.

1993   Congress approves the North American Free Trade Agreement.

1994   Republicans sweep to control of Congress.

Federal government temporarily shuts down for lack of money.

1995   United States sends troops to Bosnia.

1996   Clinton wins a second term as president.

By the late 1970s and early 1980s, others were elaborating Banfield's **neoconservative** thesis. Some were academics, such as Irving Kristol, editor of the magazine *The Public Interest*. Others were journalists, such as Charles Murray, who attacked the welfare system in the book *Losing Ground*. Still others were political activists, such as Reagan's secretary of Education, William Bennett.

The common themes were simple: Free markets work better than government programs; government intervention does more harm than good; government assistance may be acceptable for property owners, but it saps the initiative of the poor; anyway, the chief beneficiaries of government programs are special interests and the bureaucratic elites who serve them. The critics built an intellectual justification for gut-level antiestablishment feelings. In 1964, three-quarters of Americans had trusted Washington "to do what is right." By 1980, three-quarters were convinced that the federal government wasted tax money. The neoconservatives agreed and offered the details to support Reagan's own summary: "Government is not the solution to our problems; government is the problem."

The president's Hollywood background made it easy for him to use films to make his points. He once threatened to veto unwanted legislation by challenging Congress with Clint Eastwood's "Make my day." In fact, many blockbuster movies reinforced two of Reagan's messages. One was the importance of direct confrontation with the bad guys: Communists (*Rambo*), global terrorists (*Die Hard*), drug dealers (*Lethal Weapon*). The second was the incompetence or dishonesty of government bureaucracies from the CIA to local police, whose elitist mistakes could only be set right by average but tough individuals like "Dirty Harry Callahan" and "John Rambo."

Taxes, Deficits, and Deregulation

The heart of the 1980s revolution was the **Economic Recovery and Tax Act of 1981 (ERTA)**, which reduced personal income tax rates by 25 percent over three years. The explicit goal was to stimulate business activity by lowering taxes overall and slashing rates for the rich. Cutting the government's total income by $747 billion over five years, ERTA meant less money for federal programs and more money in the hands of consumers and investors to stimulate economic growth.

Reagan's first budget director, David Stockman, later revealed a second goal. Because defense spending and Social Security were politically untouchable, Congress would find it impossible to create and fund new programs without cutting old ones. The first year's tax reductions were accompanied by cuts of $40 billion in federal aid to mass transit, school lunches, and similar programs. If Americans still wanted social programs, they could enact them at the local or state level.

The second part of the economic agenda was to free eager capitalists from government regulations to increase business initiative, innovation, and efficiency. The **deregulation** revolution built on a head start from the 1970s. A federal antitrust case had split the unified Bell System of AT&T and its subsidiaries into seven regional telephone companies and opened long-distance service to competition. Congress also deregulated air travel in 1978. The result has been cheaper and more frequent air service for major hubs and poorer and more expensive service for small cities. The transformation of telecommunications similarly meant more choices for sophisticated consumers but higher prices for basic phone service.

Corporate America used the Reagan administration to attack environmental legislation as "strangulation by regulation." Vice President George Bush headed the White House Task Force on Regulatory Relief, which delayed or blocked regulations on hazardous wastes, automobile emissions, and exposure of workers to chemicals on the job.

Most attention, however, went to the instantly controversial appointment of Colorado lawyer James Watt as Secretary of the Interior. He was sympathetic to a western movement known as the **Sagebrush Rebellion**, which wanted the vast federal land holdings in the West transferred to the states for more rapid economic use. He once blamed air pollution on natural emissions from trees and in another speech compared environmentalists to both Nazis and Bolsheviks. Federal resource agencies sold trees to timber companies at a loss to the Treasury, expanded offshore oil drilling, and expedited exploration for minerals.

The early 1980s also transformed American financial markets. **Individual Retirement Accounts (IRAs),** a creation of the 1981 tax act, made millions of households into new investors. Dollars poured from savings accounts into higher-paying money market funds. Savings and loans had traditionally been conservative and limited financial institutions that funneled individual savings into safe home mort-

gages. Under rules changed by deregulation, they began to compete for deposits by offering high interest rates and reinvested the money in much riskier commercial real estate. By 1990, the result would be a financial crisis in which bad loans destroyed hundreds of S&Ls, especially in the Southwest.

Corporate raiders snapped up "cash cows," profitable and cash-rich companies that could be milked of profits and assets. Dealmakers brought together often mismatched companies into huge conglomerates. They raised money with "junk bonds," high-interest, high-risk securities that could be paid off only in favorable conditions. The merger mania channeled capital into paper transactions rather than investments in new equipment and products. Another effect was to damage the economies of small and middle-sized communities by transferring control of local companies to outside managers.

The flip side of corporate consolidation was another round in the Republican offensive against labor unions. President Reagan set the tone when he fired more than eleven thousand members of PATCO—the Professional Air Traffic Controllers Organization. Reagan claimed to be enforcing the letter of the law, citing a no-strike clause in their hiring agreements with the FAA. But the message to organized labor was clear. Over the next eight years, the National Labor Relations Board and other federal agencies weakened the power of collective bargaining.

The Election of 1984

An unresolved question is whether Ronald Reagan directed an economic revolution, or simply presided over changes initiated by others. Most memoirs by White House insiders suggest the latter; so do journalists who titled books about the Reagan administration *Sleepwalking through History, The Acting President,* and *The Role of a Lifetime.* But if Americans had voted against Carter in 1980, they voted for Reagan in 1984.

A sharp recession in 1981–1982 had helped the Democrats slow the progress of Reagan's initiatives in Congress, but the national Democratic party continued to have a problem. The Democrats' challenge was to hold key voting groups, such as labor unions and African-Americans, without being labeled the party of "special interests."

Democrats faced a special dilemma with the deepening tension between working-class whites and blacks. In one set of focused interviews, pollsters read white Detroiters a statement from Robert Kennedy that called on Americans to recognize special obligations to black citizens who had endured racial discrimination. The responses were vehement: "I can't go along with that." "That's bull!" "No wonder they killed him."

A further Democratic challenge was Ronald Reagan's personal popularity. The president won over many Americans by surviving a 1981 assassination attempt in fine spirits. Polls in the mid-1980s consistently showed that roughly two-thirds of people in their twenties and early thirties were choosing the Republicans as the party of energy and new ideas.

Democrats sealed their fate in 1984 by nominating Walter Mondale, who had been vice president under Carter. Mondale assumed that Americans cared enough about the exploding federal deficit to accept an across-the-board tax increase. With the economy growing and inflation in check, most voters didn't want Mondale to remind them of long-range financial realities. Reagan took 59 percent of the popular vote and 98 percent of the electoral votes.

Progress and Poverty

In the mid-1980s, deregulated credit and massive deficit spending fueled exuberant economic growth. The decade as a whole brought nearly 20 million new jobs. Inflation dipped to 3 percent per year. The Dow Jones average of blue-chip industrial stock prices more than tripled from August 1982 to August 1987.

However, federal tax and budget changes contributed to the widest income gap since World War II between the richest fifth and the poorest fifth of the American population. The 1981 tax cuts came with sharp increases in the Social Security tax, which hit lower-income workers the hardest. The tax changes meant that the average annual income of households in the bottom 40 percent declined and that many actually paid higher taxes. In contrast, Americans at the upper end of the economic scale increased their share of after-tax income at the expense of everyone else.

Cities and their residents absorbed approximately two-thirds of the cuts in the 1981–1982 federal budget. The new administration's National Urban Policy Report in 1982 took direct aim at older urban centers. Provisions for accelerated depreciation (tax write-offs) of factories and equipment in the 1981 tax act encouraged the abandonment of center-city factories in favor of new facilities in the suburbs.

In contrast to the treatment of central cities, federal aid recognized both the economic independence and political power of America's suburbs. By 1975, suburbanites held the largest block of seats in the House of Representatives—131 suburban districts, 130 rural, 102 central-city, and 72 mixed. Reap-

portionment in 1982, based on the 1980 census, produced a House that was even more heavily suburban.

Federal tax and spending policies made life even harder for middle-class families who were caught by industrial restructuring. By 1992, more than half of younger married women, aged 18 to 33, contributed between 30 and 70 percent of total household income. Even with two incomes, many families found it hard to buy a house because of skyrocketing prices in urban markets and sky-high interest rates. The national home ownership rate actually fell for the first time in almost fifty years, from 66 to 64 percent of American households.

At the lower end of the economic ladder, the proportion of Americans living in poverty increased from a low of 11.1 percent in 1973, to the 13 to 15 percent range. Conservative critics began to talk about an **"underclass"** of Americans permanently outside the mainstream economy because of poor education, drug abuse, or sheer laziness. In fact, most of the nation's 40 million poor people lived in households with employed adults. In 1992, fully 18 percent of all full-time jobs did not pay enough ($13,091 in 1992 dollars) to lift a family of four out of poverty (see the summary table "Why Are 40 Million Americans Poor?").

Falling below even the working poor were growing numbers of homeless Americans. In the 1980s, a new approach to the treatment of the mentally ill reduced the population of mental hospitals from 540,000 in 1960 to only 140,000 in 1980. Deinstitutionalized patients were supposed to receive community-based treatment, but many ended up on the streets and in overnight shelters. New forms of self-destructive drug abuse, such as crack addiction, joined alcoholism. A boom in downtown real estate destroyed old skid row districts with their bars, employment offices, missions, flophouses, and dollar-a-night hotels.

These factors tripled the number of permanently homeless people during the early and middle 1980s, from 200,000 to somewhere between 500,000 to 700,000. For every person in a shelter on a given night, two people were sleeping on sidewalks, in parks, in cars, and in abandoned buildings.

The Second (Short) Cold War

Ronald Reagan considered the Soviet Union not a coequal nation with legitimate world interests but an "evil empire," like something from the *Star Wars* movies. After the era of détente, global tensions had

SUMMARY

WHY ARE 40 MILLION AMERICANS POOR?

	Culture of Poverty Theory	Malfunctioning Economy Theory
Explanation of poverty	Poverty is the result of learned behaviors that are transmitted through families and communities. Individuals learn to scorn education and saving, expect instant gratification and fall into laziness.	The economy is not structured to generate decent-paying jobs for all Americans who want to work. Economic and social changes have repeatedly yanked opportunity away from African-American families.
Focus of Attention	Individual behavior, poor neighborhoods	Location and availability of family wage jobs, effects of discrimination on employment chances
Political Bias	Conservative	Progressive
Policy Suggestions	Reduce welfare, food stamps, and other public assistance to encourage individuals to behave responsibly.	Ensure equal access to the job market; make the tax system more family-friendly; adequately fund public education and job training.
Buzzwords	"welfare queen," "underclass"	"blaming the victim," "housing-jobs mismatch"

started to mount in the late 1970s. They were soon higher than they had been since the 1960s.

Confronting the USSR

Who renewed the Cold War after Nixon's diplomacy of détente and Carter's early efforts at negotiation? The Soviets had pursued military expansion in the 1970s, and in 1980 were supporting Marxist regimes in civil wars in Angola, Ethiopia, Nicaragua, and especially Afghanistan. Given the aging Soviet leadership and the economic weaknesses revealed in the late 1980s, it makes more sense to see the Soviets as muddling along rather than executing a well-planned global strategy.

The new Reagan administration reemphasized central Europe as the focus of superpower rivalry. To counter improved Soviet armaments, the United States began to place cruise missiles and midrange Pershing II missiles in Europe in 1983. NATO

governments approved the action, but it frightened millions of their citizens.

The controversy over the new missile systems was part of new thinking about nuclear weaponry. Multiple warheads on U.S. missiles already allowed Washington to target 25,000 separate places in the Soviet Union. National Security Directive D-13 (1981) stated that a nuclear war might be winnable, despite its enormous costs. All Americans needed for survival, said one administration official, were "enough shovels" to dig fallout shelters.

The **nuclear freeze** campaign caught the imagination of many Americans in 1981 and 1982. It sought to halt the manufacture and deployment of new atomic weapons by the great powers. The movement gained urgency when a group of distinguished scientists argued that the smoke and dust thrown up by an atomic war would devastate the ecology of the entire globe by triggering "nuclear winter." Nearly a million people turned out for a nuclear freeze rally in New York in 1982.

In response, Reagan announced the **Strategic Defense Initiative (SDI)** or "Star Wars" program in March 1983. SDI would deploy new defenses that could intercept and destroy ballistic missiles as they rose from the ground and arced through space. Ideas included superlasers, killer satellites, and clouds of projectiles to rip missiles to shreds before they neared their targets. Few scientists thought that SDI could work. Nevertheless, President Reagan found SDI appealing, for it offered a way around the balance of terror. By presenting the United States as following a defensive and preventive program, it also had the political advantage of countering the nuclear freeze movement.

Risky Business: Foreign Policy Adventures

Reagan kept the United States out of a major war and backed off in the face of serious trouble. Foreign interventions were designed to achieve symbolic victories rather than the global balance of power. The exception was the Caribbean and Central America.

Lebanon was the model for Reagan's small-scale military interventions. Israel invaded Lebanon in 1982 to clear Palestinian guerrillas from its borders and set up a friendly Lebanese government. The Israeli army found itself bogged down in civil war. Reagan sent U.S. Marines to preserve the semblance of a Lebanese state and provide a face-saving exit for Israel. But the Marines were on an ill-defined "presence mission" that angered Arabs. In October 1983, a car bomb killed 241 Marines. The remainder were soon gone, confirming the Syrian observation that Americans were "short of breath" when it came to Middle East politics.

The administration had already found an easier target. On October 25, 1983, only days after the disaster in Beirut, U.S. troops invaded the small independent Caribbean island of Grenada. A left-leaning government had invited Cuban help in building an airfield, which the U.S. feared would turn into a Cuban military base. Two thousand American troops overcame Cuban soldiers who were thinly disguised as construction workers, "rescued" American medical students, and put a more sympathetic and locally popular government in power.

The Caribbean was also the focus of a secret foreign policy operated by the CIA and then by National Security Council staff. The target was Nicaragua, the Central American country where leftist Sandinista rebels had overthrown the Somoza dictatorship in 1979. Reagan and his people were determined to prevent Nicaragua from becoming "another Cuba," especially when Sandinistas helped left-wing insurgents in neighboring El Salvador. The CIA organized perhaps ten thousand "Contras" from remnants of Somoza's national guard. From bases in Honduras, they harassed the Sandinistas with sabotage and raids. Reagan called the Contras "freedom fighters."

Constitutional trouble started when an unsympathetic Congress blocked U.S. funding for the Contras. Under the direction of CIA director William Casey, Lieutenant Colonel Oliver North flouted the law by organizing aid from private donors while serving on the staff of the National Security Council. The arms pipeline operated until a supply plane was shot down in 1986.

Even shadier were the administration's arms-for-hostages negotiations with Iran. Using questionable Middle Eastern arms dealers as go-betweens, the United States in 1985 joined Israel in selling five hundred antitank missiles to Iran. The deal followed stern public pronouncements that the United States would never negotiate with terrorists, and it violated this nation's official trade embargo against Iran. Iran helped in securing the release of several Americans held hostage in Lebanon by pro-Iranian radicals; they were released, but other hostages were soon taken. Colonel North funneled proceeds from the arms sales to the Contras, in a double evasion of the law.

Like Watergate, the Iran-Contra affair was a two-sided scandal. First was the blatant misjudgment of operating a secret and bumbling foreign policy that depended on international arms dealers and ousted Nicaraguan military officers. Second was a concerted effort to cover up the actions. North shredded relevant documents and lied to Congress. In his final report in 1994, Special Prosecutor Lawrence Walsh found that President Reagan and Vice President Bush participated in efforts to withhold information and mislead Congress.

American policy in Asia was a refreshing contrast with Central America and the Middle East. In the Philippines, American diplomats helped push corrupt President Ferdinand Marcos out and opened the way for a popular uprising to put Corazon Aquino in office. Secretary of State George Shultz made sure that the United States supported popular democracy while reassuring the Philippine military. In South Korea, the United States similarly helped ease out an unpopular dictator by firmly supporting democratic elections that brought in a more popular but still pro-U.S. government.

Embracing Perestroika

Thaw in the Cold War started in Moscow. Mikhail Gorbachev became general secretary of the Communist party in 1985. Gorbachev was the picture of vigor compared to his three sick or elderly predecessors, Leonid Brezhnev, Yuri Andropov, and Constantin Chernenko. He was a master of public relations who charmed western Europe's leaders and public. Gorbachev startled Soviet citizens by urging *glasnost*, or political openness and free discussion of issues. He followed by setting the goal of *perestroika*, or restructuring of the painfully bureaucratic Soviet economy.

Gorbachev also decided that he needed to reduce the crushing burden of Soviet defense spending if the USSR was to have any chance of modernizing. During Reagan's second term, the Soviets offered one concession after another in a relentless drive for arms control.

Reagan cast off decades of belief in the dangers of Soviet Communism and took Gorbachev seriously. He was willing to forget his own rhetoric and abandon many of his most fervent supporters. He frightened his own staff when he met Gorbachev in Iceland in the summer of 1986 and accepted the principle of deep cuts in strategic forces. Reagan explained that when he railed against the "evil empire," he had been talking about Brezhnev and the bad old days; Gorbachev and *glasnost* were different.

In the end, Reagan negotiated the **Intermediate Nuclear Force (INF)** agreement over the strong objections of the CIA and the Defense Department but with the support of Secretary of State Shultz. Previous treaties had only slowed the growth of nuclear weapons. The new pact matched Soviet SS-20s with American cruise missiles as an entire class of weapons that would be destroyed, with on-site inspections for verification.

Government by Gestures

George Bush, Reagan's vice president and successor as president, loved to run the world by Rolodex and telephone. He upgraded the hot line to Moscow from a teletype machine to a modern communications system. When a crisis threatened world peace, his reaction was to pick up the phone and start chatting with presidents and prime ministers.

This view of national and world politics reflected a background in which personal connections counted. He was raised as part of the New England elite, built his own oil business in Texas, and then held a series of high-level federal appointments that produced a résumé with little impact on American politics. The result was a caretaker administration at home and abroad until forced to act by the pressure of events in the Soviet Union and the Middle East.

George Bush, Willie Horton, and Manuel Noriega

Michael Dukakis, the Democratic nominee in 1988, was a dry by-the-numbers manager who offered the American people "competence." Campaign Director Lee Atwater looked for Reagan's "hot button" issues to discredit Dukakis. He found that Dukakis as governor of Massachusetts had delayed cleanup of Massachusetts Bay, favored gun control, and had vetoed a bill requiring schoolchildren to recite the Pledge of Allegiance (arguing correctly that it would be overturned in the courts). Even more damaging was that Massachusetts officials had allowed a murderer named Willie Horton a weekend furlough from prison, during which he had committed a brutal rape.

The Republican campaign exploited all of these issues. Pro-Bush advertisements tapped real worries among the voters—fear of crime, racial tension (Willie Horton was black), worry about eroding social values. Dukakis had no effective reply.

The ads also locked Bush into a rhetorical war on crime and drugs that was his major domestic policy. Americans had good cause to be worried about public safety, but most were generally unaware that the victimization rate—the likelihood of becoming the target of a violent crime—had leveled off and that crime was far worse in minority communities than elsewhere.

The Bush administration stepped up the fight against illegal drugs. The federal drug control budget tripled. The United States tried to stop the flow of cocaine by blockading its borders with airplanes, sea patrols, and sniffer dogs at airport customs lines. Casual and middle-class use of cocaine and marijuana began to decline in the mid-1980s. Drug use and drug sales were increasingly a problem of poor and minority neighborhoods.

Bush also parlayed the war on drugs into war on Panama. General Manuel Noriega, the Panamanian strongman, had once been on the CIA payroll. He had since turned to international drug sales in defiance of United States antismuggling efforts. On December 20, 1989, American troops invaded Panama, hunted down Noriega, and brought him back to stand trial in the United States on drug-trafficking charges. A handful of Americans and thousands of Panamanians died, many of them civilians caught in cross-fire.

Otherwise, George Bush had little domestic policy. He ignored a flood of new ideas from entrepreneurial conservatives, such as HUD Secretary Jack

Kemp and "drug tsar" William Bennett. He used dozens of vetoes to block congressional initiatives and to court favor with special interests, such as antiabortionists and big business.

Major legislation from the Bush years featured a reauthorized and strengthened the **Clean Air Act**. Congress also passed a transportation bill that shifted federal priorities from highway building toward mass transit. The **Americans with Disabilities Act** (1990) was to prevent discrimination against people with physical handicaps. In the areas of crime and health care, however, Bush's lack of leadership left festering problems.

The administration expected private individuals to take up the slack. Bush's often ridiculed but sincere vision was of a "kinder and gentler America" in which personal acts of social responsibility would shine like a "thousand points of light." If individuals failed to respond, however, Bush did not think that government should step in.

The national debt had amounted to 50 percent of personal savings in 1980 but swelled to 125 percent by 1990. The massive budget deficits of the 1980s combined with growing trade deficits to turn the United States from an international creditor to a debtor nation. When Reagan took office, foreigners owed the United States and its citizens the equivalent of $2,500 for every American family. When Bush took office, the United States had used up its foreign assets and become the world's biggest debtor, with liabilities that averaged $7,000 per family. After pledging "no new taxes" in his campaign, Bush backed into a tax increase in 1990. Voters found it hard to forget not the taxes themselves, which a strong leader might have justified to the nation, but the president's waffling and trying to downplay the importance of his decision.

Crisis and Democracy in Eastern Europe

As a believer in personal diplomacy, George Bush based much of his foreign policy on his changing attitudes toward Mikhail Gorbachev. He started lukewarm, talking tough to please the Republican right wing. Before 1989 was over, however, the president had decided that Gorbachev was OK. For the next two years, the United States pushed reform in Europe while being careful not to gloat in public or damage Gorbachev's position at home.

The people of eastern Europe overcame both American and Soviet caution. Gorbachev had urged his eastern European allies to emulate *perestroika*. Poland and Hungary were the first satellite nations to eject their Communist leadership in favor of democracy in mid-1989. When East Germans began to flee westward through Hungary, the East German regime bowed to mounting pressure and opened the Berlin Wall on November 9. By the end of 1989, there were new governments in Czechoslovakia, Romania, Bulgaria, and East Germany. These largely peaceful revolutions destroyed the military and economic agreements that had harnessed the satellites to the Soviet economy. The USSR swallowed hard, accepted the loss of its satellites, and slowly withdrew its army from eastern Europe.

Events in eastern Europe left German reunification as a point of possible conflict. West German Chancellor Helmut Kohl removed one obstacle when he reassured Poland and Russia that Germany would seek no changes in the boundaries drawn after World War II. By July 1990, the United States and USSR had agreed that a reunited Germany would belong to NATO. The decision satisfied France and Britain that a stronger Germany would still be under the influence of the Western allies. In October, the two Germanies completed their political unification, although it would be years before their mismatched economies functioned as one.

Throughout these events, the Bush administration proceeded cautiously. Asked whether the United States had a new foe after the end of the Cold War, Bush answered without hesitation: "The enemy is unpredictability. The enemy is instability." He tried not to push the Soviet Union too hard and infuriate Russian hard-liners. "I don't want to do something that would inadvertently set back the progress," Bush said.

The same desire not to create "big problems" affected U.S. policy as the Soviet Union itself began to break up. The USSR had absorbed the small Baltic republics of Estonia, Lithuania, and Latvia during World War II. In 1990, they reasserted their independence. When Gorbachev refused to recognize the action, Bush said little. In August 1991, Bush visited the USSR and disappointed an independence-minded crowd in the Ukrainian capital of Kiev by warning against "suicidal nationalism based on ethnic hatred."

The Persian Gulf War

On August 2, 1990, President Saddam Hussein of Iraq seized the small neighboring country of Kuwait. The conquest gave Iraq control of 20 percent of the world's oil production and reserves. Bush demanded unconditional withdrawal, enlisted European and Arab allies in an anti-Iraq coalition, and persuaded Saudi Arabia to accept substantial U.S. forces for its protection against Iraqi invasion. Within weeks, the Saudis were host to Operation **Desert Shield**—tens of thousands of U.S. soldiers and hundreds of aircraft under the command of General Norman Schwarzkopf.

Iraq was a dictatorship that had just emerged from an immensely costly eight-year war with Iran. Saddam Hussein had depended on help from the United States and Arab nations in this war, but Iraq was now economically exhausted. Kuwait itself was a small, rich nation whose ruling dynasty enjoyed few friends but plenty of oil royalties. The U.S. State Department had signaled earlier in 1990 that it might support some concessions by Kuwait in the disputes. Saddam Hussein read the signal as an open invitation to do what he wanted.

The Iraqis gave George Bush a golden opportunity to assert America's world influence. The importance of Middle Eastern oil helped enlist France and Britain as military allies and secure billions of dollars from Germany and Japan. A short-term oil glut also meant that the industrial nations could boycott Iraqi production. The collapse of Soviet power and Gorbachev's interest in cooperating with the United States meant that the Soviets would not interfere with U.S. plans.

President Bush and his advisers offered a series of justifications for American actions. First and most basic were the desire to punish armed aggression and the presumed need to protect Iraq's other neighbors. In fact, there was scant evidence of Iraqi preparations against Saudi Arabia. Sanctions and diplomatic pressure might also have brought withdrawal from most or all of Kuwait. However, additional American objectives—to destroy Iraq's capacity to create atomic weapons and to topple Saddam's regime—would require direct military action.

The Persian Gulf itself offered an equally golden opportunity to the American and allied armed forces. The terrain was open and nearly uninhabited. Indeed, the U.S. could try out the tactics of armored maneuver and close land-air cooperation that the Pentagon had devised to protect Germany against Soviet invasion.

In October, Bush decided to increase the number of American troops in Saudi Arabia to 580,000. The United States stepped up diplomatic pressure by securing a series of increasingly tough United Nations resolutions that culminated in November 1990 with Security Council Resolution 678, authorizing "all necessary means" to liberate Kuwait. The president convinced Congress to agree to military action under the umbrella of the UN.

War began one day after the UN's January 15 deadline for Iraqi withdrawal from Kuwait. **Desert Storm** opened with massive air attacks on command centers, transportation facilities, and Iraqi forward positions. The allies lost few planes. The air war destroyed 40 to 50 percent of Iraqi tanks and artillery

by late February. The attacks also seriously hurt Iraqi civilians by disrupting utilities and food supplies.

Americans watched CNN's live transmission of Baghdad under bombardment and stared in fascination at pictures of Patriot missiles presumably intercepting Iraqi Scud missiles. They read about Stealth fighter bombers that were invisible to radar and precision-guided missiles that could home in on specified targets (although most of the damage came from traditional bombing and low-tech A-10 antitank aircraft).

The forty-day rain of bombs was the prelude to a ground attack (see Map 33-2). Despite Saddam Hussein's threats that the coalition faced the "mother of all battles," the Iraqi military made the land war easy. They concentrated their forces near the Persian Gulf in Kuwait. Instead, the allies moved 235,000 U.S., French, and British soldiers far into the interior. On February 24, 1991, these forces swept into Iraq in a great arc. Americans, Saudis, Syrians, and Egyptians advanced directly to liberate Kuwait. A cease-fire came one hundred hours after the start of the ground war. Allied forces suffered only 240 deaths in action, compared to perhaps 100,000 for the Iraqis.

Bush and Schwartzkopf fought Desert Storm with the "Vietnam syndrome" in mind. They believed

Map 33-2 Persian Gulf War
Ground operations against Iraq in the Persian Gulf War followed six weeks of aerial bombardment. The ground attack, which met quick success, was a multinational effort by the United States, Britain, France, Saudi Arabia, and other Arab nations threatened by an aggressive Iraq. The war freed Kuwait from Iraqi occupation but stopped before forcing a change in Iraq's government.

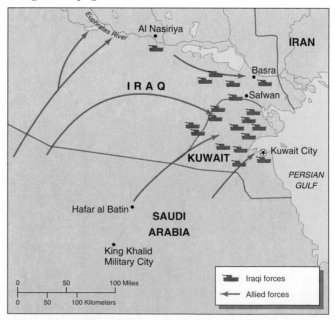

that Americans were willing to accept war only if it involved overwhelming U.S. force and ended quickly. Militarily, overwhelming the Iraqis turned out to be easy.

The United States hoped to replace Saddam Hussein without disrupting Iraqi society. Instead, the hundred-hour war incited armed rebellions against Saddam by Shi'ite Muslims in southern Iraq and by ethnically distinct Kurds in the north. Since Bush and his advisers were unwilling to get embroiled in a civil war, they stood by while Saddam crushed the uprisings. Saddam Hussein became a hero to many in the Islamic world simply by remaining in power. But Bush had accomplished exactly what he wanted—the restoration of the status quo.

A New World Order?

There was no such status quo in the Soviet Union. The final act in the transformation of the USSR began with an attempted coup against Mikhail Gorbachev in August, 1991. Old-line Communist bureaucrats arrested Gorbachev in his vacation house and tried to take over the government apparatus in Moscow. They turned out to be bumblers and drunks who hadn't secured military support and even failed to take over radio and television stations. Boris Yeltsin, president of the Russian Republic, organized the resistance. Within three days, the plotters themselves were under arrest.

Before the month was out, the Soviet parliament banned the Communist party. By December, Gorbachev had resigned and all of the fifteen component republics of the Soviet Union had declared their independence. Eleven of them formed the weak Commonwealth of Independent States; the superpower Union of Soviet Socialist Republics ceased to exist. Russia remained the largest and strongest of the new states. Ukraine and Kazakhstan were both substantial in size and inherited parts of the Soviet atomic arsenal. A challenge for the 1990s was how to implement the destruction of nuclear weapons called for in the **Strategic Arms Reduction Treaty (START)** of July 1991, one of the last accomplishments of more than thirty years of U.S.-Soviet arms negotiations.

Analysts agree that the relentless pressure of American defense spending helped bankrupt and undermine the USSR. It is an open question whether this same American defense spending also weakened the United States' economy and its ability to compete in the world marketplace. Some scholars see the demise of the Soviet empire as ultimate justification for forty years of Cold War. Dissenters argue the opposite—that the collapse of European Communism shows that American leaders had magnified its threat.

Since the 1940s, diplomats and politicians had judged every choice in terms of the great standoff between the United States and the USSR. Now they had to understand the complex interactions of not only the United States and Russia but also a reunified Germany, Japan, the European Union, and rising economies like China, Brazil, and Mexico.

President Bush saw a new world order in which the United States would be a global police force. In his 1991 State of the Union speech, Bush talked about the necessity for the United States to "bear a major share of leadership" in keeping the world orderly, for only the United States had "both the moral standing and the means" to do so.

The debate about foreign policy influenced another debate about the future of American armed forces. In the 1990s, the Pentagon closed dozens of military bases and facilities, disrupting local economies and reducing the military establishment. Military and civilian employment directly related to defense dropped from 7.2 million in 1987 to 4.5 million in 1997. In this context, it is important to remember that public excitement about Desert Storm did not solve the problem of how to intervene and retain the initiative in civil wars.

Searching for the Center

In Bill Clinton's race for president in 1992, the "war room" was the decision center where Clinton and his staff planned tactics and countered Republican attacks. On the wall was a sign with a simple message: "It's the economy, stupid." The short sentence was a reminder that victory lay in emphasizing everyday problems that George Bush neglected.

The message also revealed an insight into the character of the United States in the 1990s. What mattered most were down-to-earth issues, not the distant problems of foreign policy.

Political Generations

Every fifteen to twenty years, a new group of voters and leaders comes to power, driven by the desire to fix the mess that the previous generation left behind. The leaders who dominated the 1980s believed that the answer was to turn the nation's social and economic problems over to the market while asserting America's influence and power around the world.

In the mid-1990s the members of "Generation X" came of voting age with deep worries about the foreclosing of opportunities. They worried that previous administrations had neglected social prob-

American Views

THE RELIGIOUS IMPERATIVE IN POLITICS

The strong religious faith of many Americans frequently drives them to different stands on political issues. The first of these two documents, a letter by Jerry Falwell to potential supporters of the Moral Majority, reflects the politically conservative outlook of many evangelical Christians. Falwell is pastor of the Thomas Road Baptist Church in Lynchburg, Virginia. He founded the Moral Majority, a conservative religious lobbying and educational organization, in 1979 and served as its president until 1987, the year he wrote the letter reprinted here. The second document, from an open letter issued by the Southside United Presbyterian Church in Tucson in 1982, expresses the conviction of other believers that God may sometimes require civil disobedience to oppose oppressive government actions. The letter explains the Church's reasons for violating immigration law to offer sanctuary to refugees from repressive Central American regimes supported by the United States.

❖ **How do Falwell and the Southside Presbyterian Church define the problems that demand a religious response?**

❖ **Are there any points of agreement?**

❖ **How does each statement balance the claims of God and government?**

From the Reverend Jerry Falwell

I believe that the overwhelming majority of Americans are sick and tired of the way that amoral liberals are trying to corrupt our nation from its commitment to freedom, democracy, traditional morality, and the free enterprise system.

And I believe that the majority of Americans agree on the basic moral values which this nation was founded upon over 200 years ago.

Today we face four burning crises as we continue in this Decade of Destiny—the 1980s—loss of our freedom by giving in to the Commu-

nists; the destruction of the family unit; the deterioration of the free enterprise system; and the crumbling of basic moral principles which has resulted in the legalizing of abortion, wide-spread pornography, and a drug problem of epidemic proportions.

That is why I went to Washington, D.C., in June of 1979, and started a new organization—The Moral Majority

Right now you may be wondering: "But I thought Jerry Falwell was the preacher on the Old-Time Gospel Hour television program?"

---

lems and let the competitive position of the United States deteriorate.

Young and successful but not widely known as governor of Arkansas, Democrat Bill Clinton's campaign for the 1992 nomination overcame minimal name recognition, accusations of womanizing, and his use of a student deferment to avoid military service in Vietnam. Clinton made sure that the Democrats fielded a full baby boomer (and southern) ticket by choosing the equally youthful Tennessean Albert Gore Jr. as his running mate.

Bush won renomination by beating back archconservative Patrick Buchanan. The party platform conformed to the beliefs of the Christian right. At the Republican National convention in Houston, Pat Buchanan called for right-thinking Americans to crusade against unbelievers. Buchanan's startling speech was a reminder of the multiple ways that religious belief was reshaping American politics (see "American Views: The Religious Imperative in Politics").

The wild card was Texas billionaire Ross Perot, whose independent campaign started with an

You are right. For over twenty-four years I have been calling the nation back to God from the pulpit on radio and television.

But in recent months I have been led to do more than just preach—I have been compelled to take action.

I have made the commitment to go right into the halls of Congress and fight for laws that will save America. . . .

I will still be preaching every Sunday on the Old-Time Gospel Hour—and I still must be a husband and father to my precious family in Lynchburg, Virginia.

But as God gives me the strength, I must do more. I must go into the halls of Congress and fight for laws that will protect the grand old flag . . . for the sake of our children and grandchildren."

From Southside United Presbyterian Church

We are writing to inform you that Southside Presbyterian Church will publicly violate the Immigration and Nationality Act, Section 274 (A). . . .

We take this action because we believe the current policy and practice of the United States Government with regard to Central American refugees is illegal and immoral. We believe our government is in violation of the 1980 Refugee Act and international law by continuing to arrest, detain, and forcibly return refugees to the terror, persecution, and murder in El Salvador and Guatemala.

We believe that justice and mercy require the people of conscience actively assert our God-given right to aid anyone fleeing from persecution and murder. . . .

We beg of you, in the name of God, to do justice and love mercy in the administration of your office. We ask that "extended voluntary departure" be granted to refugees from Central America and that current deportation proceedings against these victims be stopped.

Until such time, we will not cease to extend the sanctuary of the church. . . . Obedience to God requires this of us all.

Sources: Gary E. McCuen, ed., *The Religious Right* (1989); Ann Crittenden, *Sanctuary* (1988).

---

appearance on a television talk show. Perot also tried to claim the political center, appealing to the middle of the middle-class—to small business owners, middle managers, and professionals who had approved of Reagan's antigovernment rhetoric but distrusted his corporate cronies. In May, Perot outscored both Bush and Clinton in opinion polls, but his behavior became increasingly erratic.

Bush campaigned as a foreign policy expert. He expected voters to reward him for the end of the Cold War, but he ignored anxieties about the nation's direction at home. In fact, voters in November ranked the economy first as an issue, the deficit second, health care third, and foreign policy eighth. Clinton hammered away at economic concerns and the need for change from the Reagan-Bush years. He presented himself as the leader of new, pragmatic, and livelier Democrats. His campaign theme song came from Fleetwood Mac, one of the favorite rock groups of thirty-something Americans: "Don't stop thinking about tomorrow. . . . Yesterday's gone. Yesterday's gone."

Election day gave the Clinton-Gore ticket 43 percent of the popular vote, Bush 38 percent, and Perot 19 percent. Millions who voted for Perot were casting a protest vote for "none of the above" and against "politics as usual" rather than hoping for an actual Perot victory. Clinton ran best among voters over 65, who remembered FDR and Harry Truman, and voters under 30.

Minorities at the Ballot Box

Clinton's first cabinet, in which four minority men and three women balanced seven white men, marked the maturing of minorities and women as distinct political constituencies. In both cases, their new prominence in the national government followed years of growing success in cities and states.

After the racial violence of the 1960s, many blacks had turned to local politics to gain control of their own communities. The first black mayors of major twentieth-century cities included Carl Stokes in Cleveland and Richard Hatcher in Gary, Indiana in 1967, Tom Bradley in Los Angeles in 1973, Maynard Jackson in Atlanta, and Coleman Young in Detroit. By 1983, three of the nation's four largest cities had black mayors. In 1989, Virginia made Douglas Wilder the first black governor in any of the United States since Reconstruction.

Most midsized cities had stopped electing city councils by wards or districts during the first half of the twentieth century. In the 1970s, minority leaders and community activists realized that a return to district voting could convert neighborhood segregation from a liability to a political resource. As amended in 1975, the federal Voting Rights Act allowed minorities to use the federal courts to challenge at-large voting systems that diluted the impact of their votes. Blacks and Mexican-Americans used the act to reestablish city council districts in the late 1970s and early 1980s in city after city across the South and Southwest. By the 1980s and 1990s, younger Latino and African-American mayors, such as Henry Cisneros in San Antonio, Andrew Young in Atlanta, and Dennis Archer in Detroit, won election on positive platforms of growth and equity; they mended fences with local business leaders and promised newly empowered minorities a fair share of an expanding economic pie.

At the national level, minorities gradually increased their representation in Congress. Ben Nighthorse Campbell of Colorado, a Cheyenne, brought a Native American voice to the U.S. Senate in 1992. The number of African-Americans in the House of Representatives topped forty after 1992 with the help of districts drawn to concentrate black voters. Even after a series of Supreme Court cases invalidated districts drawn with race as the "predominant factor," however, African-Americans and Latinos held their gains in 1996.

Women from the Grass Roots to Congress

A second quiet political change was the increasing prominence of women and family issues in national politics. The period opened with two actions that were both symbolic and substantive. In 1981, President Reagan appointed Arizona judge Sandra Day O'Connor to be the first woman on the United States Supreme Court. In 1984, Walter Mondale chose New York Congresswoman Geraldine Ferraro as his vice presidential candidate.

The spreading suburbs of postwar America were "frontiers" that required concerted action to solve immediate needs. Postwar metropolitan areas offered numerous opportunities for women to engage in volunteer civic work, learn political skills, and run for local office. Moreover, new cities and suburbs had fewer established political institutions, such as political machines and strong parties; their politics were open to energetic women.

Important support and training grounds for women's entry into politics were the League of Women Voters, which did nonpartisan studies of basic issues, and the **National Women's Political Caucus**, designed to support women candidates of both parties.

In 1991, the nomination of Judge Clarence Thomas to the U.S. Supreme Court ensured that everyone knew that the terms of American politics were changing. Thomas, an African-American, was controversial because of his conservative positions on social and civil rights issues. Controversy deepened when law professor Anita Hill accused Thomas of harassing her sexually while she had served on his staff at the U.S. Civil Rights Commission. Critics tried to discredit Hill with vicious attacks on her character but failed to discredit her story. Thomas presented himself as the victim of false accusations and a media lynching. The Senate confirmed Thomas to the Supreme Court.

Whatever the merits of her charges, Hill's badgering by skeptical senators angered millions of women. In the shadow of the hearings, women made impressive gains in the 1992 election, when the number of women in the U.S. Senate jumped from two to six (and grew further to six Democrats and three Republicans after November 1996). The 1992 election pushed women's share of seats in the fifty state legislatures above 20 percent. Bill Clinton appointed women to 37 percent of the five hundred or so high-level jobs in the White House and federal departments, far higher than Jimmy Carter's 15 percent or Lyndon Johnson's 4 percent.

Since the 1980s, voting patterns have shown a widening gender gap. Women now identify with the Democratic party and vote for its candidates at a markedly higher rate than men. In the 1990s, the gender gap has helped keep Democrats competitive and dampened the nation's conservative swing.

Clinton's First Term

Bill Clinton's first term and his reelection in 1996 show the attraction of the political center. In his first inaugural address in January 1993, Clinton pledged "an end to the era of deadlock and drift—and a new season of American renewal." What he found in his first four years in office was an equilibrium that resulted in narrow, bipartisan victories and defeats. In 1996, voters showed that they liked the nation's break from an activist government by keeping the balance of a Democratic White House and Republican Congress.

In foreign affairs, Clinton inherited Bush's New World Order and the expectation that the United States could keep the world on an even keel and counter ethnic hatred. During the administration's first years, U.S. diplomats helped broker an Israel-PLO accord that gave Palestinians self-government in Gaza and the West Bank, only to watch extremists on both sides undermine the accords. The United States in 1994 used firm diplomatic pressure to persuade North Korea to stop building nuclear weapons, calming a potentially explosive trouble spot.

Elsewhere in the world, Clinton responded far more effectively than critics expected. He withdrew American forces from Somalia when their humanitarian mission of guarding food relief to starving Somalis was overshadowed by the need to take sides in civil war. Clinton intervened decisively in Haiti to restore an elected president. He reluctantly committed the United States to a multinational effort to end bloody civil war in ethnically and religiously divided Bosnia (in southeastern Europe), where U.S. troops monitored a brittle peace agreement. The United States, its European allies, and a reluctant Russia agreed in 1997 that NATO could add several former Soviet satellites, extending western military commitments deep into Eastern Europe.

The heart of Clinton's agenda was efforts to make the United States economy more equitable domestically and more competitive internationally; these goals marked Clinton as a **neoliberal** who envisioned a partnership between a leaner government and a dynamic private sector. Federal employment

dropped below Reagan administration levels. A new tax bill reversed some of the inequities of the 1980s by increasing taxes on the well-off who had benefited from Reagan's policies (the top 1.2 percent of households). At the other end of the income scale was expansion of the Earned Income Tax Credit, a Nixon-era program that helps lift working Americans out of poverty. An improved college student aid program spread benefits to more students by allowing direct federal loans. The **National and Community Service Trust Act** created a pilot program for a domestic Peace Corps, although it was hampered by its small size.

The administration's most important victory was the approval of the treaty creating a North American Free Trade Area (NAFTA) (see Chapter 31). Clinton lobbied reluctant Representatives, and Al Gore took a political risk and convincingly defended NAFTA against treaty opponent Ross Perot in a debate on CNN. In November 1993, NAFTA finally passed.

The administration's record in pursuing a broad set of liberal civil rights goals was mixed in its first two years. The administration lifted a ban on abortion counseling in federally assisted family planning clinics. It backpedaled on the issue of gays in the military, but Congress and the Pentagon accepted a policy that made engaging in homosexual acts, but not sexual orientation itself, grounds for discharge.

The administration's biggest setback was the failure of comprehensive health care legislation. The goals seemed simple at first: containment of health care cost and extension of basic medical insurance from 83 percent of Americans under age 65 to 100 percent. In the abstract, voters agreed with the 25-year-old photographer's assistant who found herself facing cancer surgery without savings or health insurance: "I work full-time, and because it's a very small business, we don't get any benefits. . . . It just devastated everybody financially. And that shouldn't happen. That's the American dream that's lost."

Unfortunately, the plan that emerged from the White House ran to 1,342 pages of complex regulations with something for everyone to dislike. Senior citizens worried about limits on Medicare spending. Insurance companies didn't want more regulations. Businesses didn't want the costs of insuring their workers. Taxpayers liked the idea of wider medical insurance coverage but not the idea of paying for it through higher taxes or rationing of medical services.

Perhaps because he sometimes started with absolute statements and positions, what might look in another leader like a willingness to compromise looked like waffling in Clinton. Both the president and his wife attracted extreme and bitter hatred from the far right. Indeed, Hillary Rodham Clinton became a symbol of discomfiting changes in American families. Adding to the Clinton's problems was a protracted but inconclusive investigation of possible wrongdoing associated with the Whitewater real estate development in Arkansas.

In an extraordinary off-year election in 1994, voters defeated dozens of incumbents and gave Republicans control of both House and Senate. For most of 1995, the new speaker of the House, Newt Gingrich of Georgia, dominated political headlines as he pushed the **Contract with America**, the official Republican campaign platform for the 1994 elections, which called for a revolutionary reduction of federal responsibilities.

Clinton laid low and let the new Congress attack environmental protections, propose cuts in federal benefits for the elderly, and push a cut in the capital gains tax to help the rich. As Congress and president battled over the budget, congressional Republicans refused to authorize interim spending and forced the federal government to shut down for more than three weeks between November 1995 and January 1996. Gingrich was the clear loser in public opinion, both for the shutdowns and his ideas. Democrats painted Gingrich and his congressional allies as a radical fringe who wanted to gut Medicare and Medicaid, undermine education, punish legal immigrants, and sell off the national parks—core values and programs that most Americans wanted to protect.

After the budget confrontations, 1996 brought a series of measures to reward work. The minimum wage increased. Congress made pension programs easier for employers to create and made health insurance portable when workers changed jobs. A welfare reform bill that emphasized work as a condition for public assistance shifted responsibilities to the states.

Clinton's reelection in 1996 was a virtual replay of 1992. His opponent, Robert Dole, represented an earlier political generation. The Republican party tried to paper over its uneasy mix of traditional country club Republicans (probusiness and socially moderate), radical proponents of unregulated markets, and religious conservatives affiliated with the Christian Coalition. The Republicans thus displayed many of the internal fractures that characterized American society as a whole.

Clinton's campaign again stressed the economy, but this time it emphasized positive accom-

plishments. Unemployment had dropped from 7.2 percent to 5.5 percent since 1992 as American businesses created 10 million new jobs. Tight federal spending and the 1993 tax increase had cut the annual federal deficit in half, allowing interest rates to fall and the stock market to soar.

The Clinton-Gore ticket took 70 percent of the electoral votes and 49 percent of the popular vote (versus 41 percent for Dole and 9 percent for a recycled Ross Perot).

Beyond the legislative battles and elections, the big stories of the mid-1990s were prosperity, the widening of American pluralism with greater roles for women and minorities, and the revitalization of the pragmatic center in the Democratic party (allowing Clinton to sound like Dwight Eisenhower). Voters liked the constriction of the federal role in domestic affairs that began in the 1980s. An example was the 1997 budget deal between Clinton and Congress to balance the budget with a combination of tax cuts and spending changes.

Conclusion

Americans entered the 1980s searching for stability. The 1970s had brought unexpected and uncomfortable change. Soviet actions in Asia and Africa seemed to be destabilizing the world. The memory of defeat in Vietnam left a bitter taste, and hostages in Tehran seemed to signal the end to America's global postwar dominance. Deep economic problems undermined confidence in the future. Traditional values seemed under siege. Ronald Reagan's presidential campaign played to these insecurities by promising to revitalize the older ways of life and restore the United States to its former influence.

The political liberalization and then the astonishing collapse of the Soviet Union ended forty years of Cold War. New political leadership in Washington reversed the fifty-year expansion of federal government programs to deal with economic and social inequities. Prosperity alternated with recessions that shifted the balance between regions. The stock market rode a roller coaster, familiar corporate names vanished, and the national media made temporary heroes of business tycoons. Middle-class Latinos and African-Americans made substantial gains while many other minority Americans sank deeper into poverty.

In the mid-1990s, the United States found itself with uncontested political and miliary influence in the world. It had one of the world's most broadly educated populations and the greatest concentration of scientific and technical capacity. After struggling in the 1980s, its highly flexible economy was outperforming most rivals.

Left unsolved were two challenges to basic American values. One was the challenge of equality. Americans struggled to reconcile their belief in equal opportunity with the realities of long-term poverty and racial discrimination. While most Americans believed in giving everyone a fair chance, they disagreed about how to define and assure that chance.

The second task was to strengthen the nation's civic life. Here, too, Americans disagreed. Was the solution to social problems for individuals to be more upright or for communities to take more responsibility for common needs? Many Americans in the mid-1990s distrusted government but were still willing to attack problems through grass-roots organizations. The job for citizens and leaders was to revive faith in public institutions and in the belief that Americans of all backgrounds could work together to achieve common national goals.

Review Questions

1. Is it accurate to talk about a Reagan Revolution in American politics? Did Reagan's presidency change the economic environment for workers and business corporations? How did economic changes in the 1980s affect the prospects of the richest and poorest Americans?

2. What caused the break up of the Soviet Union and the end of the Cold War? Did U.S. foreign policy under Reagan and Bush contribute significantly to the withdrawal of Soviet power from eastern Europe? Did the collapse of the USSR show the strength of the United States and its allies or the weakness of Soviet Communism?

3. Was the American political system more polarized and divided in 1996 than in 1980? How did religiously conservative Americans understand issues of foreign relations and economic policy? How did religiously liberal Americans understand these same issues? What was the gender gap in national politics in the 1990s? Why were Republicans unable to appeal to most black and Hispanic voters in 1992 and 1996?

4. What were Bill Clinton's major policy accomplishments? Do these represent "liberal," "moderate,"

or "conservative" positions? What was the Contract with America? What are other examples of a conservative political trend in the 1990s?

Recommended Reading

Michael Beschloss and Strobe Talbott, *At the Highest Levels* (1993). This dramatic narrative of the last years of the Cold War is based on detailed interviews with American and Soviet participants.

Elliot Liebow, *Tell Them Who I Am: The Lives of Homeless Women* (1993). In Liebow's sensitive depiction, "street people" and "bag ladies" appear as complex individuals coping with personal problems and economic crisis.

Kevin Phillips, *Boiling Point: Democrats, Republicans, and the Decline of Middle-Class Prosperity* (1992). Phillips believes that the economic policies of the Reagan and Bush administrations systematically damaged working- and middle-class families.

Lillian Rubin, *Families on the Fault Line: American's Working Class Speaks about the Family, the Economy, Race, and Ethnicity* (1994). Rubin interviews American families about their efforts to cope with economic and social change.

Garry Wills, *Reagan's America: Innocents at Home* (1987). This biography is critical of Reagan's ideas but insightful about his personality.

Where to Learn More

❖ **Ronald Reagan Boyhood Home, Dixon, Illinois.** The home where Reagan lived from 1920 to 1923 tells relatively little about Reagan himself but a great deal about the small-town context that shaped his ideas.

❖ **State Humanities Councils.** Every state has a council or committee for the humanities that is affiliated with the National Endowment for the Humanities. They sponsor a wide variety of events and publications that often link historical perspectives to current social issues of importance in each state.

❖ **C-SPAN.** The Cable Satellite Public Affairs Network allows cable television viewers to observe the public workings of the national government in ways previously available only to Washington insiders.

WE THE PEOPLE
1865–1920

*B*etween Reconstruction and World War I, the United States experienced great change. Industrialization, urbanization, and mass immigration provoked unprecedented conflict over the fundamental issues—citizenship, individual rights, social equity, economic freedom, political liberty, and democratic authority—that define what it means to be an American.

After a long struggle over their role in society, women gained the right to vote with the ratification of the Nineteenth Amendment in 1920. Opponents of woman suffrage had maintained that society's "natural order" required women to avoid public life and serve a domestic role centered on the family. Now, rejoiced suffrage leader Carrie Chapman Catt, American women would cease to be "wards" of the nation and become "free and equal citizens." But to overcome their determined opponents, many suffragists had themselves downplayed the connection between voting and equality. As the 1920s would soon show, Catt's assessment was wildly optimistic. It would require continued struggle in the decades to come for women to approach full civil and political equality, to say nothing of social and economic equality.

As women gained some rights, African-Americans had theirs restricted. The Fourteenth and Fifteenth Amendments, adopted during Reconstruction, had extended both citizenship and suffrage to African-Americans, but the subsequent spread of racial segregation and disfranchisement limited blacks' social and economic freedoms and political power. Some African-Americans organized to oppose these exclusionist trends, and some hoped that their military service in World War I would secure their rights and status as full-fledged Americans. But those hopes soon faded. The war years, as black author James Weldon Johnson sadly observed in 1919, brought instead "an increased hatred of race" and a murderous racial climate.

Native Americans did experience one gain in the aftermath of World War I: citizenship. Indian veterans were made citizens in 1919, a status extended to all Indians five years later. But as the oldest Americans thus became the newest Americans, they benefited little. Many states still prohibited Indians from voting and denied them other basic rights of citizenship. Since the last independent Native American peoples had been subdued in the late nineteenth century and confined to reservations, their economic and social conditions had steadily deteriorated. Forced acculturation had nearly obliterated their cultural identity. By 1920, the Indian death rate exceeded the birthrate. Not surprisingly, one newspaper found Native Americans cynical about receiving "their new citizenship" from those who had "robbed them of a continent, and . . . deprived them of freedom of action, freedom of social custom, and freedom of worship."

Similar tensions characterized the nation's treatment of immigrants. In the Progressive Era, many groups adopted programs to "Americanize" the newcomers, some by practical efforts to promote education and improve social conditions, others by more coercive measures to secure cultural conformity and social order. The Great War and the Red Scare shifted the balance to the repressive approach. Nativists demanding "100 percent Americanism" forcibly suppressed ethnic traditions, languages, and cultures. By 1919, one Italian-American concluded gloomily that "Americanization is an ugly word." In this new social climate, those seeking to restrict immigration gained the upper hand. A law enacted in 1917 required immigrants to pass a literacy test. More restrictive and discriminatory laws, based on overt racism, would follow in the 1920s. Nativist crusades and cultural conflict would plague postwar political life as Americans continued to struggle over competing definitions of Americanism.

Indeed, such tensions were inherent in a nation that professed the ideals of democracy and equality yet often enforced the rules of order and hierarchy. In the decades to come, the struggle to realize the nation's ideals would wax and wane, manifesting itself in industrial conflict and civil rights marches, in political campaigns and public laws, in women's organizations and consumer groups, in peace rallies and veterans' protests, in lawsuits and civil disobedience. By appealing to the national ideals to achieve their goals, the participants in these struggles testified to their enduring power.

APPENDIX

THE DECLARATION OF INDEPENDENCE

When in the course of human events it becomes necessary for one people to dissolve the political bands which have connected them with another and to assume, among the powers of the earth, the separate and equal station to which the laws of nature and of nature's God entitle them, a decent respect to the opinions of mankind requires that they should declare the causes which impel them to the separation.

We hold these truths to be self-evident, that all men are created equal; that they are endowed by their Creator with certain unalienable rights; that among these are life, liberty, and the pursuit of happiness. That, to secure these rights, governments are instituted among men, deriving their just powers from the consent of the governed; that, whenever any form of government becomes destructive of these ends, it is the right of the people to alter or to abolish it, and to institute a new government, laying its foundation on such principles, and organizing its powers in such form, as to them shall seem most likely to effect their safety and happiness. Prudence, indeed, will dictate that governments long established should not be changed for light and transient causes; and, accordingly, all experience hath shown that mankind are more disposed to suffer, while evils are sufferable, than to right themselves by abolishing the forms to which they are accustomed. But when a long train of abuses and usurpations, pursuing invariably the same object, evinces a design to reduce them under absolute despotism, it is their right, it is their duty, to throw off such government and to provide new guards for their future security. Such has been the patient sufferance of these colonies, and such is now the necessity which constrains them to alter their former systems of government. The history of the present King of Great Britain is a history of repeated injuries and usurpations, all having, in direct object, the establishment of an absolute tyranny over these States. To prove this, let facts be submitted to a candid world:

He has refused his assent to laws the most wholesome and necessary for the public good.

He has forbidden his governors to pass laws of immediate and pressing importance, unless suspended in their operation till his assent should be obtained; and, when so suspended, he has utterly neglected to attend to them.

He has refused to pass other laws for the accommodation of large districts of people, unless those people would relinquish the right of representation in the legislature, a right inestimable to them and formidable to tyrants only.

He has called together legislative bodies at places unusual, uncomfortable, and distant from the depository of their public records, for the sole purpose of fatiguing them into compliance with his measures.

He has dissolved representative houses, repeatedly for opposing, with manly firmness, his invasions on the rights of the people.

He has refused, for a long time after such dissolutions, to cause others to be elected; whereby the legislative powers, incapable of annihilation, have returned to the people at large for their exercise; the state remaining, in the meantime, exposed to all the danger of invasion from without and convulsions within.

He has endeavored to prevent the population of these States; for that purpose, obstructing the laws for naturalization of foreigners, refusing to pass others to encourage their migration hither, and raising the conditions of new appropriations of lands.

He has obstructed the administration of justice by refusing his assent to laws for establishing judiciary powers.

He has made judges dependent on his will alone for the tenure of their offices and the amount and payment of their salaries.

He has erected a multitude of new offices and sent hither swarms of officers to harass our people and eat out their substance.

He has kept among us, in time of peace, standing armies, without the consent of our legislatures.

He has affected to render the military independent of, and superior to, the civil power.

He has combined with others to subject us to a jurisdiction foreign to our Constitution and unacknowledged by our laws, giving his assent to their acts of pretended legislation—

For quartering large bodies of armed troops among us;

For protecting them, by mock trial, from punishment for any murders which they should commit on the inhabitants of these States;

For cutting off our trade with all parts of the world;

For imposing taxes on us without our consent;

For depriving us, in many cases, of the benefit of trial by jury;

For transporting us beyond seas to be tried for pretended offences;

For abolishing the free system of English laws in a neighboring province, establishing therein an arbitrary government, and enlarging its boundaries, so as to render it at once an example and fit instrument for introducing the same absolute rule into these colonies;

For taking away our charters, abolishing our most valuable laws, and altering, fundamentally, the powers of our governments.

For suspending our own legislatures and declaring themselves invested with power to legislate for us in all cases whatsoever.

He has abdicated government here by declaring us out of his protection and waging war against us.

He has plundered our seas, ravaged our coasts, burnt our towns, and destroyed the lives of our people.

He is, at this time, transporting large armies of foreign mercenaries to complete the works of death, desolation, and tyranny already begun with circumstances of cruelty and perfidy scarcely paralleled in the most barbarous ages, and totally unworthy the head of a civilized nation.

He has constrained our fellow citizens, taken captive on the high seas, to bear arms against their country, to become the executioners of their friends and brethren, or to fall themselves by their hands.

He has excited domestic insurrections amongst us and has endeavored to bring on the inhabitants of our frontiers, the merciless Indian savages, whose known rule of warfare is an undistinguished destruction of all ages, sexes, and conditions.

In every stage of these oppressions, we have petitioned for redress in the most humble terms; our repeated petitions have been answered only by repeated injury. A prince whose character is thus marked by every act which may define a tyrant is unfit to be the ruler of a free people.

Nor have we been wanting in attention to our British brethren. We have warned them, from time to time, of attempts made by their legislature to extend an unwarrantable jurisdiction over us. We have reminded them of the circumstances of our emigration and settlement here. We have appealed to their native justice and magnanimity, and we have conjured them, by the ties of our common kindred, to disavow these usurpations, which would inevitably interrupt our connections and correspondence. They, too, have been deaf to the voice of justice and consanguinity. We must, therefore, acquiesce in the necessity which denounces our separation, and hold them, as we hold the rest of mankind, enemies in war, in peace, friends.

We, therefore, the representatives of the United States of America, in general Congress assembled, appealing to the Supreme Judge of the world for the rectitude of our intentions, do, in the name and by the authority of the good people of these colonies, solemnly publish and declare, that these united colonies are, and of right ought to be, free and independent states: that they are absolved from all allegiance to the British Crown, and that all political connection between them and the state of Great Britain is, and ought to be, totally dissolved; and that, as free and independent states, they have full power to levy war, conclude peace, contract alliances, establish commerce, and to do all other acts and things which independent states may of right do. And, for the support of this declaration, with a firm reliance on the protection of Divine Providence, we mutually pledge to each other our lives, our fortunes, and our sacred honor.

THE CONSTITUTION OF THE UNITED STATES OF AMERICA

We the people of the United States, in order to form a more perfect union, establish justice, insure domestic tranquillity, provide for the common defense, promote the general welfare, and secure the blessings of liberty to ourselves and our posterity, do ordain and establish this Constitution for the United States of America.

Article I

SECTION 1. All legislative powers herein granted shall be vested in a Congress of the United States, which shall consist of a Senate and House of Representatives.

SECTION 2. 1. The House of Representatives shall be composed of members chosen every second year by the people of the several States, and the electors in each State shall have the qualifications requisite for electors of the most numerous branch of the State legislature.

2. No person shall be a representative who shall not have attained to the age of twenty-five years,

and been seven years a citizen of the United States, and who shall not, when elected, be an inhabitant of that State in which he shall be chosen.

3. Representatives and direct taxes[1] shall be apportioned among the several States which may be included within this Union, according to their respective numbers, which shall be determined by adding to the whole number of free persons, including those bound to service for a term of years, and excluding Indians not taxed, three fifths of all other persons.[2] The actual enumeration shall be made within three years after the first meeting of the Congress of the United States, and within every subsequent term of ten years, in such manner as they shall be law direct. The number of representatives shall not exceed one for every thirty thousand, but each State shall have at least one representative; and until such enumeration shall be made, the State of New Hampshire shall be entitled to choose three, Massachusetts eight, Rhode Island and Providence Plantations one, Connecticut five, New York six, New Jersey four, Pennsylvania eight, Delaware one, Maryland six, Virginia ten, North Carolina five, South Carolina five, and Georgia three.

4. When vacancies happen in the representation from any State, the executive authority thereof shall issue writs of election to fill such vacancies.

5. The House of Representatives shall choose their speaker and other officers; and shall have the sole power of impeachment.

SECTION 3. 1. The Senate of the United States shall be composed of two senators from each State, chosen by the legislature thereof,[3] for six years; and each senator shall have one vote.

2. Immediately after they shall be assembled in consequence of the first election, they shall be divided as equally as may be into three classes. The seats of the senators of the first class shall be vacated at the expiration of the second year, of the second class at the expiration of the fourth year, and of the third class at the expiration of the sixth year, so that one third may be chosen every second year; and if vacancies happen by resignation, or otherwise, during the recess of the legislature of any State, the executive thereof may make temporary appointments until the next meeting of the legislature, which shall then fill such vacancies.[4]

3. No person shall be a senator who shall not have attained to the age of thirty years, and been

nine years a citizen of the United States, and who shall not, when elected, be an inhabitant of that State for which he shall be chosen.

4. The Vice President of the United States shall be President of the Senate, but shall have no vote, unless they be equally divided.

5. The Senate shall choose their other officers, and also a president pro tempore, in the absence of the Vice President, or when he shall exercise the office of the President of the United States.

6. The Senate shall have the sole power to try all impeachments. When sitting for that purpose, they shall be on oath or affirmation. When the president of the United States is tried, the chief justice shall preside: and no person shall be convicted without the concurrence of two thirds of the members present.

7. Judgment in cases of impeachment shall not extend further than to removal from office, and disqualification to hold and enjoy any office of honor, trust or profit under the United States: but the party convicted shall nevertheless be liable and subject to indictment, trial, judgment and punishment, according to law.

SECTION 4. 1. The times, places, and manner of holding elections for senators and representatives, shall be prescribed in each State by the legislature thereof; but the Congress may at any time by law make or alter such regulations, except as to the places of choosing senators.

2. The Congress shall assemble at least once in every year, and such meeting shall be on the first Monday in December, unless they shall by law appoint a different day.

SECTION 5. 1. Each House shall be the judge of the elections, returns and qualifications of its own members, and a majority of each shall constitute a quorum to do business; but a smaller number may adjourn from day to day, and may be authorized to compel the attendance of absent members, in such manner, and under such penalties as each House may provide.

2. Each House may determine the rules of its proceedings, punish its members for disorderly behavior, and, with the concurrence of two thirds, expel a member.

3. Each House shall keep a journal of its proceedings, and from time to time publish the same, excepting such parts as may in their judgment require secrecy; and the yeas and nays of the members of either house on any question shall, at the desire of one fifth of those present, be entered on the journal.

---

[1]See the Sixteenth Amendment.
[2]See the Fourteenth Amendment.
[3]See the Seventeenth Amendment.
[4]See the Seventeenth Amendment.

4. Neither House, during the session of Congress, shall, without the consent of the other, adjourn for more than three days, nor to any other place than that in which the two Houses shall be sitting.

SECTION 6. 1. The senators and representatives shall receive a compensation for their services, to be ascertained by law, and paid out of the Treasury of the United States. They shall in all cases, except treason, felony, and breach of the peace, be privileged from arrest during their attendance at the session of their respective Houses, and in going to and returning from the same; and for any speech or debate in either House, they shall not be questioned in any other place.

2. No senator or representative shall, during the time for which he was elected, be appointed to any civil office under the authority of the United States, which shall have been created, or the emoluments whereof shall have been increased, during such time; and no person holding any office under the United States shall be a member of either House during his continuance in office.

SECTION 7. 1. All bills for raising revenue shall originate in the House of Representatives; but the Senate may purpose or concur with amendments as on other bills.

2. Every bill which shall have passed the House of Representatives and the Senate, shall, before it become a law, be presented to the President of the United States; if he approves he shall sign it, but if not he shall return it, with his objections, to that House in which it shall have originated, who shall enter the objections at large on their journal, and proceed to reconsider it. If after such reconsideration two thirds of that House shall agree to pass the bill, it shall be sent, together with the objections, to the other House, by which it shall likewise be reconsidered, and if approved by two thirds of that House, it shall become a law. But in all such cases the votes of both Houses shall be determined by yeas and nays, and the names of the persons voting for and against the bill shall be entered on the journal of each House respectively. If any bill shall not be returned by the President within ten days (Sundays excepted) after it shall have been presented to him, the same shall be a law, in like manner as if he had signed it, unless the Congress by their adjournment prevent its return, in which case it shall not be a law.

3. Every order, resolution, or vote to which the concurrence of the Senate and the House of Representatives may be necessary (except on a question of adjournment) shall be presented to the President of the United States; and before the same shall take effect, shall be approved by him, or being disapproved by him, shall be repassed by two thirds of the Senate and House of Representatives, according to the rules and limitations prescribed in the case of a bill.

SECTION 8. The Congress shall have the power

1. To lay and collect taxes, duties, imposts, and excises, to pay the debts and provide for the common defense and general welfare of the United States; but all duties, imposts, and excises shall be uniform throughout the United States.

2. To borrow money on the credit of the United States;

3. To regulate commerce with foreign nations, and among the several States, and with the Indian tribes;

4. To establish a uniform rule of naturalization, and uniform laws on the subject of bankruptcies throughout the United States;

5. To coin money, regulate the value thereof, and of foreign coin, and fix the standard of weights and measures;

6. To provide for the punishment of counterfeiting the securities and current coin of the United States;

7. To establish post offices and post roads;

8. To promote the progress of science and useful arts, by securing for limited times to authors and inventors the exclusive right to their respective writings and discoveries;

9. To constitute tribunals inferior to the Supreme Court;

10. To define and punish piracies and felonies committed on the high seas, and offenses against the law of nations;

11. To declare war, grant letters of marque and reprisal, and make rules concerning captures on land and water;

12. To raise and support armies, but no appropriation of money to that use shall be for a longer term than two years;

13. To provide and maintain a navy;

14. To make rules for the government and regulation of the land and naval forces;

15. To provide for calling forth the militia to execute the laws of the Union, suppress insurrections and repel invasions;

16. To provide for organizing, arming, and disciplining the militia, and for governing such part of them as may be employed in the service of the United States, reserving to the States respectively, the appointment of the officers, and the authority of training the militia according to the discipline prescribed by Congress;

17. To exercise exclusive legislation in all cases whatsoever, over such district (not exceeding ten miles square) as may, by cession of particular States, and the acceptance of Congress, become the seat of the government of the United States, and to exercise like authority over all places purchased by the consent of the legislature of the State in which the same shall be, for the erection of forts, magazines, arsenals, dockyards, and other needful buildings; and

18. To make all laws which shall be necessary and proper for carrying into execution the foregoing powers, and all other powers vested by this Constitution in the government of the United States, or any department or officer thereof.

SECTION 9. 1. The migration or importation of such persons as any of the States now existing shall think proper to admit, shall not be prohibited by the Congress prior to the year one thousand eight hundred and eight, but a tax or duty may be imposed on such importation, not exceeding ten dollars for each person.

2. The privilege of the writ of habeas corpus shall not be suspended, unless when in cases of rebellion or invasion the public safety may require it.

3. No bill of attainder or ex post facto law shall be passed.

4. No capitation, or other direct, tax shall be laid, unless in proportion to the census or enumeration herein before directed to be taken.[5]

5. No tax or duty shall be laid on articles exported from any State.

6. No preference shall be given by any regulation of commerce or revenue to the ports of one State over those of another: nor shall vessels bound to, or from, one State be obliged to enter, clear, or pay duties in another.

7. No money shall be drawn from the treasury, but in consequence of appropriations made by law; and a regular statement and account of the receipts and expenditures of all public money shall be published from time to time.

8. No title of nobility shall be granted by the United States: and no person holding any office of profit or trust under them, shall, without the consent of the Congress, accept of any present, emolument, office, or title, of any kind whatever, from any king, prince, or foreign State.

SECTION 10. 1. No State shall enter into any treaty, alliance, or confederation; grant letters of marque and reprisal; coin money; emit bills of credit; make any thing but gold and silver coin a tender in payment of debts; pass any bill of attainder, ex post facto law, or law impairing the obligation of contracts, or grant, any title of nobility.

2. No State shall, without the consent of the Congress, lay any imposts or duties on imports or exports, except what may be absolutely necessary for executing its inspection laws: and the net produce of all duties and imposts laid by any State on imports or exports, shall be for the use of the treasury of the United States; and all such laws shall be subject to the revision and control of the Congress.

3. No State shall, without the consent of the Congress, lay any duty of tonnage, keep troops, or ships of war in time of peace, enter into any agreement or compact with another State, or with a foreign power, or engage in war, unless actually invaded, or in such imminent danger as will not admit of delay.

Article II

SECTION 1. 1. The executive power shall be vested in a President of the United States of America. He shall hold his office during the term of four years, and, together with the Vice President, chosen for the same term, be elected, as follows:

2. Each State shall appoint, in such manner as the legislature thereof may direct, a number of electors, equal to the whole number of senators and representatives to which the State may be entitled in the Congress: but no senator or representative, or person holding any office of trust or profit under the United States, shall be appointed an elector.

The electors shall meet in their respective States, and vote by ballot for two persons, of whom one at least shall not be an inhabitant of the same State with themselves. And they shall make a list of all the persons voted for, and of the number of votes for each; which list they shall sign and certify, and transmit sealed to the seat of the government of the United States, directed to the president of the Senate. The president of the Senate shall, in the presence of the Senate and House of Representatives, open all the certificates, and the votes shall then be counted. The person having the greatest number of votes shall be the President, if such number be a majority of the whole number of electors appointed; and if there be more than one who have such majority, and have an equal number of votes, then the House of Representatives shall immediately choose by ballot one of them for President; and if no person have a majority, then from the five highest on the list the said House shall in like manner choose the President. But in choosing the President, the

---

[5]See the Sixteenth Amendment.

votes shall be taken by States, the representation from each State having one vote; a quorum for this purpose shall consist of a member or members from two thirds of the States, and a majority of all the States shall be necessary to a choice. In every case after the choice of the President, the person having the greatest number of votes of the electors shall be the Vice President. But if there should remain two or more who have equal votes, the Senate shall chose from them by ballot the Vice President.[6]

3. The Congress may determine the time of choosing the electors, and the day on which they shall give their votes; which day shall be the same throughout the United States.

4. No person except a natural born citizen, or a citizen of the United States, at the time of the adoption of this Constitution, shall be eligible to the office of President; neither shall any person be eligible to the office who shall not have attained to the age of thirty-five years, and been fourteen years a resident within the United States.

5. In case of the removal of the President from office, or of his death, resignation, or inability to discharge the powers and duties of the said office, the same shall devolve on the Vice President, and the Congress may by law provide for the case of removal, death, resignation or inability, both of the President and Vice President, declaring what officer shall then act as President, and such officer shall act accordingly until the disability be removed, or a President shall be elected.

6. The President shall, at stated times, receive for his services a compensation which shall neither be increased nor diminished during the period for which he shall have been elected, and he shall not receive within that period any other emolument from the United States, or any of them.

7. Before he enter on the execution of his office, he shall take the following oath or affirmation:—"I do solemnly swear (or affirm) that I will faithfully execute the office of president of the United States, and will to the best of my ability, preserve, protect and defend the Constitution of the United States."

SECTION 2. 1. The President shall be commander in chief of the army and navy of the United States, and of the militia of the several States, when called into the actual service of the United States; he may require the opinion in writing, of the principal officer in each of the executive departments, upon any subject relating to the duties of their respective offices, and he shall have power to grant reprieves and pardons for offenses against the United States, except in cases of impeachment.

2. He shall have power, by and with the advice and consent of the Senate, to make treaties, provided two thirds of the senators present concur; and he shall nominate, and by and with the advice and consent of the Senate, shall appoint ambassadors, other public ministers and consuls, judges of the Supreme Court, and all other officers of the United States, whose appointments are not herein otherwise provided for, and which shall be established by law; but the Congress may by law vest the appointment of such inferior officers, as they think proper, in the President alone, in the courts of laws, or in the heads of departments.

3. The President shall have power to fill up all vacancies that may happen during the recess of the Senate, by granting commissions which shall expire at the end of their next session.

SECTION 3. He shall from time to time give to the Congress information of the state of the Union, and recommend to their consideration such measures as he shall judge necessary and expedient; he may, on extraordinary occasions, convene both houses, or either of them, and in case of disagreement between them with respect to the time of adjournment, he may adjourn them to such time as he shall think proper; he shall receive ambassadors and other public ministers; he shall take care that the laws be faithfully executed, and shall commission all the officers of the United States.

SECTION 4. The President, Vice President, and all civil officers of the United States, shall be removed from office on impeachment for, and conviction of, treason, bribery, or other high crimes and misdemeanors.

Article III
SECTION 1. The judicial power of the United States shall be vested in one Supreme Court, and in such inferior courts as the Congress may from time to time ordain and establish. The judges, both of the Supreme and inferior courts, shall hold their offices during good behavior, and shall, at stated times, receive for their services, a compensation, which shall not be diminished during their continuance in office.

SECTION 2. 1. The judicial power shall extend to all cases, in law and equity, arising under this Constitution, the laws of the United States, and treaties made, or which shall be made, under their authority;—to all cases of admiralty and maritime jurisdiction;—to controversies to which the United

[6]Superseded by the Twelfth Amendment.

States shall be a party;[7]—to controversies between two or more States;—between a State and citizens of another State;—between citizens of different States;—between citizens of the same State claiming lands under grants of different States, and between a State, or the citizens thereof, and foreign States, citizens or subjects.

2. In all cases affecting ambassadors, other public ministers and consuls, and those in which a State shall be party, the Supreme Court shall have original jurisdiction. In all the other cases before mentioned, the Supreme Court shall have appellate jurisdiction, both as to law and fact, with such exceptions, and under such regulations as the Congress shall make.

3. The trial of all crimes, except in cases of impeachment, shall be by jury; and such trial shall be held in the State where the said crimes shall have been committed; but when not committed within any State, the trial shall be such place or places as the Congress may by law have directed.

SECTION 3. 1. Treason against the United States shall consist only in levying war against them, or in adhering to their enemies, giving them aid and comfort. No person shall be convicted of treason unless on the testimony of two witnesses to the same overt act, or on confession in open court.

2. The Congress shall have power to declare the punishment of treason, but no attainder of treason shall work corruption of blood, or forfeiture except during the life of the person attained.

Article IV

SECTION 1. Full faith and credit shall be given in each State to the public acts, records, and judicial proceedings of every other State. And the Congress may by general laws prescribe the manner in which such acts, records and proceedings shall be proved, and the effect thereof.

SECTION 2. 1. The citizens of each State shall be entitled to all privileges and immunities of citizens in the several States.[8]

2. A person charged in any State with treason, felony, or other crime, who shall flee from justice, and be found in another State, shall on demand of the executive authority of the State from which he fled, be delivered up to be removed to the State having jurisdiction of the crime.

3. No person held to service or labor in one State under the laws thereof, escaping into another, shall, in consequence of any law or regulation therein, be discharged from such service or labor, but shall be delivered up on claim of the party to whom such service or labor may be due.[9]

SECTION 3. 1. New States may be admitted by the Congress into this Union; but no new State shall be formed or erected within the jurisdiction of any other State, nor any State be formed by the junction of two or more States, or parts of States, without the consent of the legislatures of the States concerned as well as of the Congress.

2. The Congress shall have power to dispose of and make all needful rules and regulations respecting the territory or other property belonging to the United States; and nothing in this Constitution shall be so construed as to prejudice any claims of the United States, or of any particular State.

SECTION 4. The United States shall guarantee to every State in this Union a republican form of government, and shall protect each of them against invasion; and on application of the legislature, or of the executive (when the legislature cannot be convened) against domestic violence.

Article V

The Congress, whenever two thirds of both Houses shall deem it necessary, shall propose amendments to this Constitution, or, on the application of the legislatures of two thirds of the several States, shall call a convention for proposing amendments, which in either case shall be valid to all intents and purposes, as part of this Constitution, when ratified by the legislatures of three fourths of the several States, or by conventions in three fourths thereof, as the one or the other mode of ratification may be proposed by the Congress; Provided that no amendment which may be made prior to the year one thousand eight hundred and eight shall in any manner affect the first and fourth clauses in the ninth section of the first article; and that no State, without its consent, shall be deprived of its equal suffrage in the Senate.

Article VI

1. All debts contracted and engagements entered into, before the adoption of this Constitution, shall be as valid against the United States under this Constitution, as under the Confederation.[10]

2. This Constitution, and the laws of the United States which shall be made in pursuance

---

[7]See the Eleventh Amendment.
[8]See the Fourteenth Amendment, Sec. 1.

[9]See the Thirteenth Amendment.
[10]See the Fourteenth Amendment, Sec. 4.

thereof; and all treaties made, or which shall be made, under the authority of the United States, shall be the supreme law of the land; and the judges in every State shall be bound thereby, any thing in the Constitution or laws of any State to the contrary notwithstanding.

3. The senators and representatives before mentioned, and the members of the several State legislatures, and all executive and judicial officers, both of the United States and of the several States, shall be bound by oath or affirmation to support this Constitution; but no religious test shall ever be required as a qualification to any office or public trust under the United States.

Article VII

The ratification of the conventions of nine States shall be sufficient for the establishment of this Constitution between the States so ratifying the same.

Done in Convention by the unanimous consent of the States present the seventeenth day of September in the year of our Lord one thousand seven hundred and eighty-seven, and of the independence of the United States of America the twelfth. In witness whereof we have hereunto subscribed our names.

Articles in addition to, and amendment of, the Constitution of the United States of America, proposed by Congress, and ratified by the legislatures of the several States, pursuant to the fifth article of the original Constitution.

Amendment I

[First ten amendments ratified December 15, 1791] Congress shall make no law respecting an establishment of religion, or prohibiting the free exercise thereof; or abridging the freedom of speech, or of the press; or the right of the people peaceably to assemble, and to petition the government for a redress of grievances.

Amendment II

A well regulated militia, being necessary to the security of a free State, the right of the people to keep and bear arms, shall not be infringed.

Amendment III

No soldier shall, in time of peace be quartered in any house, without the consent of the owner, nor in time of war, but in a manner to be prescribed by law.

Amendment IV

The right of the people to be secure in their persons, houses, papers, and effects, against unreasonable searches and seizures, shall not be violated, and no warrants shall issue, but upon probable cause, supported by oath or affirmation, and particularly describing the place to be searched, and the persons or things to be seized.

Amendment V

No person shall be held to answer for a capital or otherwise infamous crime, unless on a presentment or indictment of a grand jury, except in cases arising in the land or naval forces, or in the militia, when in actual service in time of war or public danger; nor shall any person be subject for the same offense to be twice put in jeopardy of life or limb; nor shall be compelled in any criminal case to be a witness against himself, nor be deprived of life, liberty, or property, without due process of law; nor shall private property be taken for public use, without just compensation.

Amendment VI

In all criminal prosecutions, the accused shall enjoy the right to a speedy and public trial, by an impartial jury of the State and district wherein the crime shall have been committed, which district shall have been previously ascertained by law, and to be informed of the nature and cause of the accusation; to be confronted with the witnesses against him; to have compulsory process for obtaining witnesses in his favor, and to have the assistance of counsel for his defense.

Amendment VII

In suits at common law, where the value in controversy shall exceed twenty dollars, the right of trial by jury shall be preserved, and no fact tried by a jury shall be otherwise reexamined in any court of the United States, than according to the rules of the common law.

Amendment VIII

Excessive bail shall not be required, nor excessive fines imposed, nor cruel and unusual punishments inflicted.

Amendment IX

The enumeration in the Constitution of certain rights shall not be construed to deny or disparage others retained by the people.

Amendment X

The powers not delegated to the United States by the Constitution, nor prohibited by it to the States, are reserved to the States respectively, or to the people.

Amendment XI [January 8, 1798]

The judicial power of the United States shall not be construed to extend to any suit in law or equity, commended or prosecuted against one of the United States by citizens of another State, or by citizens or subjects of any foreign State.

Amendment XII [September 25, 1804]

The electors shall meet in their respective States, and vote by ballot for President and Vice President, one of whom, at least, shall not be an inhabitant of the same

State with themselves; they shall name in their ballots the person voted for as President, and in distinct ballots, the person voted for as Vice President, and they shall make distinct lists of all persons voted for as President and of all persons voted for as Vice President, and of the number of votes for each, which lists they shall sign and certify, and transmit sealed to the seat of the government of the United States, directed to the President of the Senate;—The President of the Senate shall, in the presence of the Senate and House of Representatives, open all the certificates and the votes shall then be counted;—The person having the greatest number of votes for President, shall be the President, if such number be a majority of the whole number of electors appointed; and if no person have such majority, then from the persons having the highest numbers not exceeding three on the list of those voted for as President, the House of Representatives shall choose immediately, by ballot, the President. But in choosing the President, the votes shall be taken by States, the representation from each State having one vote; a quorum for this purpose shall consist of a member or members from two thirds of the States, and a majority of all the States shall be necessary to a choice. And if the House of Representatives shall not choose a President whenever the right of choice shall devolve upon them, before the fourth day of March next following, then the Vice President shall act as President, as in the case of the death or other constitutional disability of the President. The person having the greatest number of votes as Vice President shall be the Vice President, if such number be a majority of the whole number of electors appointed, and if no person have a majority, then from the two highest numbers on the list, the Senate shall choose the Vice President; a quorum for the purpose shall consist of two thirds of the whole number of Senators, and a majority of the whole number shall be necessary to a choice. But no person constitutionally ineligible to the office of president shall be eligible to that of Vice President of the United States.

Amendment XIII [December 18, 1865]

SECTION 1. Neither slavery nor involuntary servitude, except as punishment for crime whereof the party shall have been duly convicted, shall exist within the United States, or any place subject to their jurisdiction.

SECTION 2. Congress shall have power to enforce this article by appropriate legislation.

Amendment XIV [July 28, 1868]

SECTION 1. All persons born or naturalized in the United States, and subject to the jurisdiction thereof, are citizens of the United States and of the State wherein they reside. No State shall make or enforce any law which shall abridge the privileges or immunities of citizens of the United States; nor shall any State deprive any person of life, liberty, or property, without due process of law; nor deny to any person within its jurisdiction the equal protection of the laws.

SECTION 2. Representatives shall be apportioned among the several States according to their respective numbers, counting the whole number of persons in each State, excluding Indians not taxed. But when the right to vote at any election for the choice of electors for President and Vice President of the United States, representatives in Congress, the executive and judicial officers of a State, or the members of the legislature thereof, is denied to any of the male inhabitants of such State, being twenty-one years of age, and citizens of the United States, or in any way abridged, except for participating in rebellion, or other crime, the basis of representation there shall be reduced in the proportion which the number of such male citizens shall bear to the whole number of male citizens twenty-one years of age in such State.

SECTION 3. No person shall be a senator or representative in Congress, or elector of President and Vice President, or hold any office, civil or military, under the United States, or under any State, who having previously taken an oath, as a member of Congress, or as an officer of the United States, or as a member of any State legislature, or as an executive or judicial officer of any State, to support the Constitution of the United States, shall have engaged in insurrection or rebellion against the same, or given aid or comfort to the enemies thereof. But Congress may by a vote of two thirds of each House, remove such disability.

SECTION 4. The validity of the public debt of the United States, authorized by law, including debts incurred for payment of pensions and bounties for services in suppressing insurrection or rebellion; shall not be questioned. But neither the United States nor any State shall assume or pay any debt or obligation incurred in aid of insurrection or rebellion against the United States, or any claim for the loss or emancipation of any slave; but all such debts, obligations, and claims shall be held illegal and void.

SECTION 5. The Congress shall have the power to enforce, by appropriate legislation, the provisions of this article.

Amendment XV [March 30, 1870]

SECTION 1. The right of citizens of the United States to vote shall not be denied or abridged by the United States or by any State on account of race, color, or previous condition of servitude.

SECTION 2. The Congress shall have power to enforce this article by appropriate legislation.

Amendment XVI [February 25, 1913]

The Congress shall have power to lay and collect taxes on incomes, from whatever source derived, without apportionment among the several States, and without regard to any census or enumeration.

Amendment XVII [May 31, 1913]

The Senate of the United States shall be composed of two senators from each State, elected by the people thereof, for six years; and each senator shall have one vote. The electors in each State shall have the qualifications requisite for electors of the most numerous branch of the State legislature.

When vacancies happen in the representation of any State in the Senate, the executive authority of such State shall issue writs of election to fill such vacancies: *Provided,* That the legislature of any State may empower the executive thereof to make temporary appointments until the people fill the vacancies by election as the legislature may direct.

This amendment shall not be so construed as to affect the election or term of any senator chosen before it becomes valid as part of the Constitution.

Amendment XVIII[11] [January 29, 1919]

After one year from the ratification of this article, the manufacture, sale, or transportation of intoxicating liquors within, the importation thereof into, or the exportation thereof from the United States and all territory subject to the jurisdiction thereof for beverage purposes is thereby prohibited.

The Congress and the several States shall have concurrent power to enforce this article by appropriate legislation.

This article shall be inoperative unless it shall have been ratified as an amendment to the Constitution by the legislatures of the several States, as provided in the Constitution, within seven years from the date of the submission hereof to the States by Congress.

Amendment XIX [August 26, 1920]

The right of citizens of the United States to vote shall not be denied or abridged by the United States or by any State on account of sex.

Congress shall have the power to enforce this article by appropriate legislation.

Amendment XX [January 23, 1933]

SECTION 1. The terms of the President and Vice President shall end at noon on the 20th day of January and the terms of Senators and Representatives at noon on the 3d day of January, of the years in which such terms would have ended if this article had not been ratified; and the terms of their successors shall then begin.

SECTION 2. The Congress shall assemble at least once in every year, and such meeting shall begin at noon on the 3d day of January, unless they shall by law appoint a different day.

SECTION 3. If, at the time fixed for the beginning of the term of president, the President-elect shall have died, the Vice President-elect shall become President. If a President shall not have been chosen before the time fixed for the beginning of his term, or if the President-elect shall have failed to qualify, then the Vice President-elect shall act as president until a President shall have qualified; and the Congress may by law provide for the case wherein neither a President-elect nor a Vice President-elect shall have qualified, declaring who shall then act as President, or the manner in which one who is to act shall be selected, and such person shall act accordingly until a President or Vice President shall have qualified.

SECTION 4. The Congress may by law provide for the case of the death of any of the persons from whom, the House of Representatives may choose a President whenever the right of choice shall have devolved upon them, and for the case of the death of any of the persons from whom the Senate may choose a Vice President whenever the right of choice shall have devolved upon them.

SECTION 5. Sections 1 and 2 shall take effect on the 15th day of October following the ratification of this article.

SECTION 6. This article shall be inoperative unless it shall have been ratified as an amendment to the Constitution by the legislatures of three-fourths of the several States within seven years from the date of its submission.

Amendment XXI [December 5, 1933]

SECTION 1. The Eighteenth Article of amendment to the Constitution of the United States is hereby repealed.

SECTION 2. The transportation or importation into any State, Territory, or possession of the United States for delivery or use therein of intoxicating liquors in violation of the laws thereof, is hereby prohibited.

SECTION 3. This article shall be inoperative unless it shall have been ratified as an amendment to the Constitution by conventions in the several States, as provided in the Consitution, within seven years from the date of the submission thereof to the States by the Congress.

---

[11]Repealed by the Twenty-first Amendment.

Amendment XXII [March 1, 1951]

No person shall be elected to the office of the President more than twice, and no person who has held the office of President, or acted as President, for more than two years of a term to which some other person was elected President shall be elected to the office of the President more than once.

But this article shall not apply to any person holding the office of President when this article was proposed by the Congress, and shall not prevent any person who may be holding the office of President, or acting as President, during the term within which this article becomes operative from holding the office of President or acting as President during the remainder of such term.

This article shall be inoperative unless it shall have been ratified as an amendment to the Constitution by the legislatures of three-fourths of the several States within seven years from the date of its submission to the States by the Congress

Amendment XXIII [March 29, 1961]

SECTION 1. The District constituting the seat of Government of the United States shall appoint in such manner as the Congress may direct.

A number of electors of President and Vice President equal to the whole number of Senators and Representatives in Congress to which the District would be entitled if it were a State, but in no event more than the least populous State; they shall be in addition to those appointed by the States, but they shall be considered, for the purposes of the election of President and Vice Presient, to be electors appointed by a State; and they shall meet in the District and perform such duties as provided by the twelfth article of amendment.

SECTION 2. The Congress shall have power to enforce this article by appropriate legislation.

Amendment XXIV [January 23, 1964]

SECTION 1. The right of citizens of the United States to vote in any primary or other election for President or Vice President, for electors for President or Vice President, or for Senator or Representative in Congress, shall not be denied or abridged by the United States or any State by reason of failure to pay any poll tax or other tax.

SECTION 2. The Congress shall have power to enforce this article by appropriate legislation.

Amendment XXV [February 10, 1967]

SECTION 1. In case of the removal of the President from office or of his death or resignation, the Vice President shall become President.

SECTION 2. Whenever there is a vacancy in the office of the Vice president, the President shall nominate a Vice President who shall take office upon confirmation by a majority of both Houses of Congress.

SECTION 3. Whenever the President transmits to the President pro tempore of the Senate and the Speaker of the House of Representatives his written declaration that he is unable to discharge the powers and duties of his office, and until he transmits to them a written declaration to the contrary, such powers and duties shall be discharged by the Vice President as Acting President.

SECTION 4. Whenever the Vice president and a majority of either the principal officers of the executive departments or of such other body as Congress may by law provide, transmit to the President pro tempore of the Senate and the Speaker of the House of Representatives their written declaration that the President is unable to discharge the powers and duties of his office, the Vice President shall immediately assume the powers and duties of the office as Acting President.

Thereafter, when the President transmits to the President pro tempore of the Senate and the Speaker of the house of Representatives his written declaration that no inability exists, he shall resume the powers and duties of his office unless the Vice President and a majority of either the principal officers of the executive departments or of such other body as Congress may by law provide, transmit within four days to the President pro tempore of the Senate and the Speaker of the House of Representatives their written declaration that the President is unable to discharge the powers and duties of his office. Thereupon Congress shall decide the issue, assembling within forty-eight hours for that purpose if not in session. If the Congress, within twenty-one days after receipt of the latter written declaration, or, if Congress is not in session, within twenty-one days after Congress is required to assemble, determines by two-thirds vote of both houses that the President is unable to discharge the powers and duties of his office, the Vice President shall continue to discharge the same as Acting President; otherwise, the President shall resume the powers and duties of his office.

Amendment XXVI [June 30, 1971]

SECTION 1. The right of citizens of the United States who are eighteen years of age or older to vote shall not be denied or abridged by the United States or by any State on account of age.

SECTION 2. The Congress shall have power to enforce this article by appropriate legislation.

PRESIDENTS AND VICE PRESIDENTS

1. George Washington (1789)
   John Adams (1789)

2. John Adams (1797)
   Thomas Jefferson (1797)

3. Thomas Jefferson (1801)
   Aaron Burr (1801)
   George Clinton (1805)

4. James Madison (1809)
   George Clinton (1809)
   Elbridge Gerry (1813)

5. James Monroe (1817)
   Daniel D. Thompkins (1817)

6. John Quincy Adams (1825)
   John C. Calhoun (1825)

7. Andrew Jackson (1829)
   John C. Calhoun (1829)
   Martin Van Buren (1833)

8. Martin Van Buren (1837)
   Richard M. Johnson (1837)

9. William H. Harrison (1841)
   John Tyler (1841)

10. John Tyler (1841)

11. James K. Polk (1845)
    George M. Dallas (1845)

12. Zachary Taylor (1849)
    Millard Fillmore (1849)

13. Millard Fillmore (1850)

14. Franklin Pierce (1853)
    William R. King (1853)

15. James Buchanan (1857)
    John C. Breckinridge (1857)

16. Abraham Lincoln (1861)
    Hannibal Hamlin (1861)
    Andrew Johnson (1865)

17. Andrew Johnson (1865)

18. Ulysses S. Grant (1869)
    Schuyler Colfax (1869)
    Henry Wilson (1873)

19. Rutherford B. Hayes (1877)
    William A. Wheeler (1877)

20. James A. Garfield (1881)
    Chester A. Arthur (1881)

21. Chester A. Arthur (1881)

22. Grover Cleveland (1885)
    T. A. Hendricks (1885)

23. Benjamin Harrison (1889)
    Levi P. Morgan (1889)

24. Grover Cleveland (1893)
    Adlai E. Stevenson (1893)

25. William McKinley (1897)
    Garret A. Hobart (1897)
    Theodore Roosevelt (1901)

26. Theodore Roosevelt (1901)
    Charles Fairbanks (1905)

27. William H. Taft (1909)
    James S. Sherman (1909)

28. Woodrow Wilson (1913)
    Thomas R. Marshall (1913)

29. Warren G. Harding (1921)
    Calvin Coolidge (1921)

30. Calvin Coolidge (1923)
    Charles G. Dawes (1925)

31. Herbert C. Hoover (1929)
    Charles Curtis (1929)

32. Franklin D. Roosevelt (1933)
    John Nance Garner (1933)
    Henry A. Wallace (1941)
    Harry S. Truman (1945)

33. Harry S. Truman (1945)
    Alben W. Barkley (1949)

34. Dwight D. Eisenhower (1953)
    Richard M. Nixon (1953)

35. John F. Kennedy (1961)
    Lyndon B. Johnson (1961)

36. Lyndon B. Johnson (1963)
    Hubert H. Humphrey (1965)

37. Richard M. Nixon (1969)
    Spiro T. Agnew (1969)
    Gerald R. Ford (1973)

38. Gerald R. Ford (1974)
    Nelson A. Rockefeller (1974)

39. James E. Carter Jr. (1977)
    Walter F. Mondale (1977)

40. Ronald W. Reagan (1981)
    George H. Bush (1981)

41. George H. Bush (1989)
    James D. Quayle III (1989)

42. William J. B. Clinton (1993)
    Albert Gore (1993)

PRESIDENTIAL ELECTIONS

Year	Number of States	Candidates	Party	Popular Vote*	Electoral Vote†	Percentage of Popular Vote
1789	11	GEORGE WASHINGTON	No party designations		69	
		John Adams			34	
		Other Candidates			35	
1792	15	GEORGE WASHINGTON	No party designations		132	
		John Adams			77	
		George Clinton			50	
		Other Candidates			5	
1796	16	JOHN ADAMS	Federalist		71	
		Thomas Jefferson	Democratic-Republican		68	
		Thomas Pinckney	Federalist		59	
		Aaron Burr	Democratic-Republican		30	
		Other Candidates			48	
1800	16	THOMAS JEFFERSON	Democratic-Republican		73	
		Aaron Burr	Democratic-Republican		73	
		John Adams	Federalist		65	
		Charles C. Pinckney	Federalist		64	
		John Jay	Federalist		1	
1804	17	THOMAS JEFFERSON	Democratic-Republican		162	
		Charles C. Pinckney	Federalist		14	
1808	17	JAMES MADISON	Democratic-Republican		122	
		Charles C. Pinckney	Federalist		47	
		George Clinton	Democratic-Republican		6	
1812	18	JAMES MADISON	Democratic-Republican		128	
		DeWitt Clinton	Federalist		89	
1816	19	JAMES MONROE	Democratic-Republican		183	
		Rufus King	Federalist		34	
1820	24	JAMES MONROE	Democratic-Republican		231	
		John Quincy Adams	Independent Republican		1	
1824	24	JOHN QUINCY ADAMS		108,740	84	30.5
		Andrew Jackson		153,544	99	43.1
		William H. Crawford		46,618	41	13.1
		Henry Clay		47,136	37	13.2
1828	24	ANDREW JACKSON	Democrat	647,286	178	56.0
		John Quincy Adams	National Republican	508,064	83	44.0
1832	24	ANDREW JACKSON	Democrat	687,502	219	55.0
		Henry Clay	National Republican	530,189	49	42.4
		William Wirt	Anti-Masonic	33,108	7	2.6
		John Floyd	National Republican		11	

*Percentage of popular vote given for any election year may not total 100 percent because candidates receiving less than 1 percent of the popular vote have been omitted.

†Prior to the passage of the Twelfth Amendment in 1904, the electoral college voted for two presidential candidates; the runner-up became Vice-President. Data from Historical Statistics of the United States, Colonial Times to 1957 (1961), pp. 682–683, and The World Almanac.

PRESIDENTIAL ELECTIONS
(continued)

Year	Number of States	Candidates	Party	Popular Vote	Electoral Vote	Percentage of Popular Vote
1836	26	MARTIN VAN BUREN	Democrat	765,483	170	50.9
		William H. Harrison	Whig		73	
		Hugh L. White	Whig		26	
		Daniel Webster	Whig	739,795	14	49.1
		W. P. Mangum	Whig		11	
1840	26	WILLIAM H. HARRISON	Whig	1,274,624	234	53.1
		Martin Van Buren	Democrat	1,127,781	60	46.9
1844	26	JAMES K. POLK	Democrat	1,338,464	170	49.6
		Henry Clay	Whig	1,300,097	105	48.1
		James G. Birney	Liberty	62,300		2.3
1848	30	ZACHARY TAYLOR	Whig	1,360,967	163	47.4
		Lewis Cass	Democrat	1,222,342	127	42.5
		Martin Van Buren	Free Soil	291,263		10.1
1852	31	FRANKLIN PIERCE	Democrat	1,601,117	254	50.9
		Winfield Scott	Whig	1,385,453	42	44.1
		John P. Hale	Free Soil	155,825		5.0
1856	31	JAMES BUCHANAN	Democrat	1,832,955	174	45.3
		John C. Frémont	Republican	1,339,932	114	33.1
		Millard Fillmore	American ("Know Nothing")	871,731	8	21.6
1860	33	ABRAHAM LINCOLN	Republican	1,865,593	180	39.8
		Stephen A. Douglas	Democrat	1,382,713	12	29.5
		John C. Breckinridge	Democrat	848,356	72	18.1
		John Bell	Constitutional Union	592,906	39	12.6
1864	36	ABRAHAM LINCOLN	Republican	2,206,938	212	55.0
		George B. McClellan	Democrat	1,803,787	21	45.0
1868	37	ULYSSES S. GRANT	Republican	3,013,421	214	52.7
		Horatio Seymour	Democrat	2,706,829	80	47.3
1872	37	ULYSSES S. GRANT	Republican	3,596,745	286	55.6
		Horace Greeley	Democrat	2,843,446	*	43.9
1876	38	RUTHERFORD B. HAYES	Republican	4,036,572	185	48.0
		Samuel J. Tilden	Democrat	4,284,020	184	51.0
1880	38	JAMES A. GARFIELD	Republican	4,453,295	214	48.5
		Winfield S. Hancock	Democrat	4,414,082	155	48.1
		James B. Weaver	Greenback-Labor	308,578		3.4
1884	38	GROVER CLEVELAND	Democrat	4,879,507	219	48.5
		James G. Blaine	Republican	4,850,293	182	48.2
		Benjamin F. Butler	Greenback-Labor	175,370		1.8
		John P. St. John	Prohibition	150,369		1.5
1888	38	BENJAMIN HARRISON	Republican	5,447,129	233	47.9
		Grover Cleveland	Democrat	5,537,857	168	48.6
		Clinton B. Fisk	Prohibition	249,506		2.2
		Anson J. Streeter	Union Labor	146,935		1.3

Because of the death of Greeley, Democratic electors scattered their votes.

PRESIDENTIAL ELECTIONS
(continued)

Year	Number of States	Candidates	Party	Popular Vote	Electoral Vote	Percentage of Popular Vote
1892	44	GROVER CLEVELAND	Democrat	5,555,426	277	46.1
		Benjamin Harrison	Republican	5,182,690	145	43.0
		James B. Weaver	People's	1,029,846	22	8.5
		John Bidwell	Prohibition	264,133		2.2
1896	45	WILLIAM MCKINLEY	Republican	7,102,246	271	51.1
		William J. Bryan	Democrat	6,492,559	176	47.7
1900	45	WILLIAM MCKINLEY	Republican	7,218,491	292	51.7
		William J. Bryan	Democrat, Populist	6,356,734	155	45.5
		John C. Woolley	Prohibition	208,914		1.5
1904	45	THEODORE ROOSEVELT	Republican	7,628,461	336	57.4
		Alton B. Parker	Democrat	5,084,223	140	37.6
		Eugene V. Debs	Socialist	402,283		3.0
		Silas C. Swallow	Prohibition	258,536		1.9
1908	46	WILLIAM H. TAFT	Republican	7,675,320	321	51.6
		William J. Bryan	Democrat	6,412,294	162	43.1
		Eugene V. Debs	Socialist	420,793		2.8
		Eugene W. Chafin	Prohibition	253,840		1.7
1912	48	WOODROW WILSON	Democrat	6,296,547	435	41.9
		Theodore Roosevelt	Progressive	4,118,571	88	27.4
		William H. Taft	Republican	3,486,720	8	23.2
		Eugene V. Debs	Socialist	900,672		6.0
		Eugene W. Chafin	Prohibition	206,275		1.4
1916	48	WOODROW WILSON	Democrat	9,127,695	277	49.4
		Charles E. Hughes	Republican	8,533,507	254	46.2
		A. L. Benson	Socialist	585,113		3.2
		J. Frank Hanly	Prohibition	220,506		1.2
1920	48	WARREN G. HARDING	Republican	16,143,407	404	60.4
		James M. Cox	Democrat	9,130,328	127	34.2
		Eugene V. Debs	Socialist	919,799		3.4
		P. P. Christensen	Farmer-Labor	265,411		1.0
1924	48	CALVIN COOLIDGE	Republican	15,718,211	382	54.0
		John W. Davis	Democrat	8,385,283	136	28.8
		Robert M. La Follette	Progressive	4,831,289	13	16.6
1928	48	HERBERT C. HOOVER	Republican	21,391,993	444	58.2
		Alfred E. Smith	Democrat	15,016,169	87	40.9
1932	48	FRANKLIN D. ROOSEVELT	Democrat	22,809,638	472	57.4
		Herbert C. Hoover	Republican	15,758,901	59	39.7
		Norman Thomas	Socialist	881,951		2.2
1936	48	FRANKLIN D. ROOSEVELT	Democrat	27,752,869	523	60.8
		Alfred M. Landon	Republican	16,674,665	8	36.5
		William Lemke	Union	882,479		1.9
1940	48	FRANKLIN D. ROOSEVELT	Democrat	27,307,819	449	54.8
		Wendell L. Willkie	Republican	22,321,018	82	44.8
1944	48	FRANKLIN D. ROOSEVELT	Democrat	25,606,585	432	53.5
		Thomas E. Dewey	Republican	22,014,745	99	46.0

PRESIDENTIAL ELECTIONS
(continued)

Year	Number of States	Candidates	Party	Popular Vote	Electoral Vote	Percentage of Popular Vote
1948	48	HARRY S. TRUMAN	Democrat	24,105,812	303	49.5
		Thomas E. Dewey	Republican	21,970,065	189	45.1
		J. Strom Thurmond	States' Rights	1,169,063	39	2.4
		Henry A. Wallace	Progressive	1,157,172		2.4
1952	48	DWIGHT D. EISENHOWER	Republican	33,936,234	442	55.1
		Adlai E. Stevenson	Democrat	27,314,992	89	44.4
1956	48	DWIGHT D. EISENHOWER	Republican	35,590,472	457*	57.6
		Adlai E. Stevenson	Democrat	26,022,752	73	42.1
1960	50	JOHN F. KENNEDY	Democrat	34,227,096	303†	49.9
		Richard M. Nixon	Republican	34,108,546	219	49.6
1964	50	LYNDON B. JOHNSON	Democrat	42,676,220	486	61.3
		Barry M. Goldwater	Republican	26,860,314	52	38.5
1968	50	RICHARD M. NIXON	Republican	31,785,480	301	43.4
		Hubert H. Humphrey	Democrat	31,275,165	191	42.7
		George C. Wallace	American Independent	9,906,473	46	13.5
1972	50	RICHARD M. NIXON ‡	Republican	47,165,234	520	60.6
		George S. McGovern	Democrat	29,168,110	17	37.5
1976	50	JIMMY CARTER	Democrat	40,828,929	297	50.1
		Gerald R. Ford	Republican	39,148,940	240	47.9
		Eugene McCarthy	Independent	739,256		
1980	50	RONALD REAGAN	Republican	43,201,220	489	50.9
		Jimmy Carter	Democrat	34,913,332	49	41.2
		John B. Anderson	Independent	5,581,379		
1984	50	RONALD REAGAN	Republican	53,428,357	525	59.0
		Walter F. Mondale	Democrat	36,930,923	13	41.0
1988	50	GEORGE BUSH	Republican	48,901,046	426	53.4
		Michael Dukakis	Democrat	41,809,030	111	45.6
1992	50	BILL CLINTON	Democrat	43,728,275	370	43.2
		George Bush	Republican	38,167,416	168	37.7
		H. Ross Perot	United We Stand, America	19,237,247		19.0
1996	50	BILL CLINTON	Democrat	45,590,703	379	49.0
		Bob Dole	Republican	37,816,307	159	41.0
		H. Ross Perot	Reform	7,866,284		8.0

*Walter B. Jones received 1 electoral vote.

†Harry F. Byrd received 15 electoral votes.

‡Resigned August 9, 1974: Vice President Gerald R. Ford became President.

ADMISSION OF STATES INTO THE UNION

State	Date of Admission	State	Date of Admission
1. Delaware	December 7, 1787	26. Michigan	January 26, 1837
2. Pennsylvania	December 12, 1787	27. Florida	March 3, 1845
3. New Jersey	December 18, 1787	28. Texas	December 29, 1845
4. Georgia	January 2, 1788	29. Iowa	December 28, 1846
5. Connecticut	January 9, 1788	30. Wisconsin	May 29, 1848
6. Massachusetts	February 6, 1788	31. California	September 9, 1850
7. Maryland	April 28, 1788	32. Minnesota	May 11, 1858
8. South Carolina	May 23, 1788	33. Oregon	February 14, 1859
9. New Hampshire	June 21, 1788	34. Kansas	January 29, 1861
10. Virginia	June 25, 1788	35. West Virginia	June 20, 1863
11. New York	July 26, 1788	36. Nevada	October 31, 1864
12. North Carolina	November 21, 1789	37. Nebraska	March 1, 1867
13. Rhode Island	May 29, 1790	38. Colorado	August 1, 1876
14. Vermont	March 4, 1791	39. North Dakota	November 2, 1889
15. Kentucky	June 1, 1792	40. South Dakota	November 2, 1889
16. Tennessee	June 1, 1796	41. Montana	November 8, 1889
17. Ohio	March 1, 1803	42. Washington	November 11, 1889
18. Louisiana	April 30, 1812	43. Idaho	July 3, 1890
19. Indiana	December 11, 1816	44. Wyoming	July 10, 1890
20. Mississippi	December 10, 1817	45. Utah	January 4, 1896
21. Illinois	December 3, 1818	46. Oklahoma	November 16, 1907
22. Alabama	December 14, 1819	47. New Mexico	January 6, 1912
23. Maine	March 15, 1820	48. Arizona	February 14, 1912
24. Missouri	August 10, 1821	49. Alaska	January 3, 1959
25. Arkansas	June 15, 1836	50. Hawaii	August 21, 1959

DEMOGRAPHICS OF THE UNITED STATES

POPULATION GROWTH

Year	Population	Percent Increase
1630	4,600	
1640	26,600	478.3
1650	50,400	90.8
1660	75,100	49.0
1670	111,900	49.0
1680	151,500	35.4
1690	210,400	38.9
1700	250,900	19.2
1710	331,700	32.2
1720	466,200	40.5
1730	629,400	35.0
1740	905,600	43.9
1750	1,170,800	29.3
1760	1,593,600	36.1
1770	2,148,100	34.8
1780	2,780,400	29.4
1790	3,929,214	41.3
1800	5,308,483	35.1
1810	7,239,881	36.4
1820	9,638,453	33.1
1830	12,866,020	33.5
1840	17,069,453	32.7
1850	23,191,876	35.9
1860	31,443,321	35.6
1870	39,818,449	26.6
1880	50,155,783	26.0
1890	62,947,714	25.5
1900	75,994,575	20.7
1910	91,972,266	21.0
1920	105,710,620	14.9
1930	122,775,046	16.1
1940	131,669,275	7.2
1950	150,697,361	14.5
1960	179,323,175	19.0
1970	203,235,298	13.3
1980	226,545,805	11.5
1990	248,709,873	9.8

Source: *Historical Statistics of the United States* (1975); *Statistical Abstract by the United States* (1991).
Note: Figures for 1630–1780 include British colonies within limits of present United States only; Native American population included only in 1930 and thereafter.

IMMIGRATION, BY ORIGIN
(in thousands)

Period	Europe	Americas	Asia
1820–30	106	12	—
1831–40	496	33	—
1841–50	1,597	62	—
1851–60	2,453	75	42
1861–70	2,065	167	65
1871–80	2,272	404	70
1881–90	4,735	427	70
1891–1900	3,555	39	75
1901–10	8,065	362	324
1911–20	4,322	1,144	247
1921–30	2,463	1,517	112
1931–40	348	160	16
1941–50	621	355	32
1951–60	1,326	997	150
1961–70	1,123	1,716	590
1971–80	800	1,983	1,588
1981–90	762	3,616	2,738

Source: *Historical Statistics of the United States* (1975); *Statistical Abstract of the United States* (1991).

WORK FORCE

Year	Total Number Workers (1000s)	Farmers as % of Total	Women as % of Total	% Workers in Unions
1810	2,330	84	(NA)	(NA)
1840	5,660	75	(NA)	(NA)
1860	11,110	53	(NA)	(NA)
1870	12,506	53	15	(NA)
1880	17,392	52	15	(NA)
1890	23,318	43	17	(NA)
1900	29,073	40	18	3
1910	38,167	31	21	6
1920	41,614	26	21	12
1930	48,830	22	22	7
1940	53,011	17	24	27
1950	59,643	12	28	25
1960	69,877	8	32	26
1970	82,049	4	37	25
1980	108,544	3	42	23
1990	117,914	3	45	16
1995	124,900	3	46	15

Source: *Historical Statistics of the United States* (1975); *Statistical Abstract of the United States* (1991 and 1996).

RACIAL COMPOSITION OF THE POPULATION
(in thousands)

Year	White	Black	Indian	Hispanic	Asian
1790	3,172	757	(NA)	(NA)	(NA)
1800	4,306	1,002	(NA)	(NA)	(NA)
1820	7,867	1,772	(NA)	(NA)	(NA)
1840	14,196	2,874	(NA)	(NA)	(NA)
1860	26,923	4,442	(NA)	(NA)	(NA)
1880	43,403	6,581	(NA)	(NA)	(NA)
1900	66,809	8,834	(NA)	(NA)	(NA)
1910	81,732	9,828	(NA)	(NA)	(NA)
1920	94,821	10,463	(NA)	(NA)	(NA)
1930	110,287	11,891	(NA)	(NA)	(NA)
1940	118,215	12,866	(NA)	(NA)	(NA)
1950	134,942	15,042	(NA)	(NA)	(NA)
1960	158,832	18,872	(NA)	(NA)	(NA)
1970	178,098	22,581	(NA)	(NA)	(NA)
1980	194,713	26,683	1,420	14,609	3,729
1990	208,704	30,483	2,065	22,354	7,458

Source: U.S. Bureau of the Census, U.S. Census of Population: 1940, vol. II, part 1, and vol. IV, part 1; 1950, vol. II, part 1; 1960, vol. I, part 1; 1970, vol. I, part B; and Current Population Reports, P25-1095 and P25-1104; and unpublished data.

THE ECONOMY AND FEDERAL SPENDING

Year	Gross National Product (GNP) (in billions)	Foreign Trade (in millions) Exports	Imports	Balance of Trade	Federal Budget (in billions)	Federal Surplus/Deficit (in billions)	Federal Debt (in billions)
1790	(NA)	$ 20	$ 23	$ −3	$ 0.004	$+0.00015	$ 0.076
1800	(NA)	71	91	−20	0.011	+0.0006	0.083
1810	(NA)	67	85	−18	0.008	+0.0012	0.053
1820	(NA)	70	74	−4	0.018	−0.0004	0.091
1830	(NA)	74	71	+3	0.015	+0.100	0.049
1840	(NA)	132	107	+25	0.024	−0.005	0.004
1850	(NA)	152	178	−26	0.040	+0.004	0.064
1860	(NA)	400	362	−38	0.063	−0.01	0.065
1870	$ 7.4	451	462	−11	0.310	+0.10	2.4
1880	11.2	853	761	+92	0.268	+0.07	2.1
1890	13.1	910	823	+87	0.318	+0.09	1.2
1900	18.7	1,499	930	+569	0.521	+0.05	1.2
1910	35.3	1,919	1,646	+273	0.694	−0.02	1.1
1920	91.5	8,664	5,784	+2,880	6.357	+0.3	24.3
1930	90.7	4,013	3,500	+513	3.320	+0.7	16.3
1940	100.0	4,030	7,433	−3,403	9.6	−2.7	43.0
1950	286.5	10,816	9,125	+1,691	43.1	−2.2	257.4
1960	506.5	19,600	15,046	+4,556	92.2	+0.3	286.3
1970	992.7	42,700	40,189	+2,511	195.6	−2.8	371.0
1980	2,631.7	220,783	244,871	+24,088	590.9	−73.8	907.7
1990	5,524.5	394,030	494,042	−101,012	1,251.8	−220.5	3,233.3
1995	7,237.5	786,529	891,593	−105,064	1,519.1	−163.9	6,207.0

Source: U.S. Office of Management and Budget, Budget of the United States Government, annual; Statistical Abstract of the United States, 1996.

GLOSSARY

Acquired immune deficiency syndrome (AIDS) A complex of deadly pathologies resulting from infection with the human immunodeficiency virus (HIV).

Act for Religious Toleration The first law in America to call for freedom of worship for all Christians. It was enacted in Maryland in 1649 to quell disputes between Catholics and Protestants, but it failed to bring peace.

Actual representation The practice whereby elected representatives normally reside in their districts and are directly responsive to local interests.

Administration of Justice Act One of the **Coercive** or **Intolerable Acts** passed by Parliament in 1774 in response to the **Boston Tea Party**. It provided that British officials accused of capital crimes could be tried in England.

African Methodist Episcopal (AME) Church Religious body founded by blacks for blacks in the North during the early nineteenth century that gained adherents among former slaves in the South after the Civil War.

Age of Enlightenment Major intellectual movement occurring in western Europe in the late seventeenth and early eighteenth centuries. Inspired by recent scientific advances, thinkers emphasized the role of human reason in understanding the world and directing its events. Their ideas placed less emphasis on God's role in ordering worldly affairs.

Agricultural Adjustment Administration (AAA) **New Deal** agency that attempted to regulate agricultural production through farm subsidies.

Agricultural Wheel One of several farmer organizations that emerged in the South during the 1880s. It sought federal legislation to deal with credit and currency issues.

Alamo Franciscan mission at San Antonio, Texas, that was the site in 1836 of a siege and massacre of Texans by Mexican troops.

Albany Congress Intercolonial congress called in 1754 in Albany, New York, to deal with Iroquois grievances against the English. At the congress, prominent colonists proposed the **Albany Plan of Union**.

Albany Plan of Union Plan put forward in 1754 by Massachusetts Governor William Shirley, Benjamin Franklin, and other colonial leaders, calling for an intercolonial union to manage defense and Indian affairs. The plan was rejected by participants at the **Albany Congress**.

Albany Regency Popular name after 1820 for the state political machine in New York headed by Martin Van Buren.

Alien and Sedition Acts Collective name given to four acts passed by Congress in 1798 that curtailed freedom of speech and the liberty of foreigners resident in the United States.

Alien Enemies Act Law passed by Congress in 1798 authorizing the president in the event of war to deport aliens suspected of endangering the public peace; one of the **Alien and Sedition Acts**.

Alien Friends Act Law passed by Congress in 1798 authorizing the president during peacetime to expel aliens suspected of subversive activities; one of the **Alien and Sedition Acts**.

Alliance for Progress Program of economic aid to Latin America during the Kennedy administration.

Allies Britain, France, Russia, Italy, and other belligerent nations fighting against the **Central Powers** in World War I but not including the United States.

America First Committee Officially the Committee to Defend America First, organized in 1940 to promote the policy of building and defending "Fortress America."

American and Foreign Anti-Slavery Society Antislavery organization formed in 1840 when a group of moderate abolitionists split off from the **American Anti-Slavery Society** in protest of the radicalism of William Lloyd Garrison and his support of women's rights.

American Anti-Slavery Society The first national organization of abolitionists, founded in 1833. *See also* **American and Foreign Anti-Slavery Society**.

American Civil Liberties Union (ACLU) Organization formed in 1920 to guard the constitutional rights of Americans against government infringement.

American Colonization Society Organization, founded in 1817 by antislavery reformers, that called for gradual emancipation and the removal of freed blacks to Africa.

American Equal Rights Association Association formed by women's rights activists in 1866 to advocate universal **suffrage** at the state level after the **Fourteenth Amendment** failed to provide federal guarantees for women's voting rights.

American Expeditionary Force (AEF) The American army that fought with but was independent of the Allied armies in World War I.

American Federation of Labor (AFL) Union formed in 1886 that organized skilled workers along craft lines and emphasized a few workplace issues rather than a broad social program.

American Female Moral Reform Society Organization founded in 1839 by female reformers that established homes of refuge for prostitutes and petitioned for state laws that would criminalize adultery and the seduction of women.

American Indian Movement (AIM) Group of Native American political activists who used confrontations with the federal government to publicize their case for Indian rights.

American Liberty League Business group organized to sway popular opinion against the **New Deal**.

American Protective Association (APA) Association formed in 1893 by skilled workers and small businessmen in response to increasing immigration from eastern and southern Europe; sought to limit Catholic civil rights and save jobs for Protestant workers.

American Protective League One of the leading vigilante organizations that suppressed dissent while promoting reactionary causes during World War I.

American Railway Union (ARU) Union led by Eugene V. Debs; supported the **Pullman strike**.

American Revenue Act Commonly known as the **Sugar Act**, law passed in 1764 to raise revenue in the American colonies. It lowered the duty from 6 pence to 3 pence per gallon on foreign molasses imported into the colonies and increased the restrictions on colonial commerce.

American System   The program of government subsidies favored by Henry Clay and his followers to promote American economic growth and protect domestic manufacturers from foreign competition.

American system of manufacturing   A technique of production pioneered in the United States in the first half of the nineteenth century that relied on precision manufacturing with the use of interchangeable parts.

American Temperance Society   National organization established in 1826 by evangelical Protestants that campaigned for total abstinence from alcohol and was successful in sharply lowering per capita consumption of alcohol.

Americans with Disabilities Act   Legislation in 1992 that banned discrimination against physically handicapped persons in employment, transportation, and public accommodations.

Anarchist   A person who believes that all government interferes with individual liberty and should be abolished by whatever means.

Anglican   Of or belonging to the Church of England, a Protestant denomination.

Anglo-American Accords   Series of agreements reached in the British-American Convention of 1818 that fixed the western boundary between the United States and Canada at the 49th parallel, allowed for the joint occupation of the Oregon Country, and restored to Americans fishing rights off Newfoundland.

Anglo-Saxon   Broadly, a person of English descent.

Annapolis Convention   Conference of state delegates at Annapolis, Maryland, that issued a call in September 1786 for a convention to meet at Philadelphia in May 1787 to consider fundamental changes to the **Articles of Confederation**.

Anti-Imperialist League   Organization, established in 1898, that opposed the annexation of the Philippines and the ratification of the **Treaty of Paris**.

Anti-Masons   Third party formed in 1827 in opposition to the presumed power and influence of the Masonic order.

Antietam, Battle of   Narrow strategic Union victory in the Civil War in September 1862 that turned back the first Confederate invasion of the North and enabled President Lincoln to issue the **Emancipation Proclamation**.

Antifederalist   An opponent of the **Constitution** in the debate over its ratification.

Antinomian   A person who believes that salvation comes through faith alone and that individuals who are saved obey the spirit within them rather than the moral law.

Appeal to the Colored Citizens of the World   Pamphlet published in 1829 by David Walker, a Boston free black, calling for slaves to rise up in rebellion.

Appomattox   Town in south-central Virginia where Confederate general Robert E. Lee surrendered to Union general Ulysses S. Grant on April 9, 1865, ending the Civil War.

Apprentice   A person, usually a young male, bound by a legal agreement to serve an employer for a specified amount of time in return for training in a craft, trade, or business.

Archaic   The period roughly between 8000 and 1500 B.C., during which time Native Americans adapted to a changed continental climate, developed larger communities, and, in several regions, adopted agriculture.

Articles of Confederation   Written document setting up the loose confederation of states that comprised the first national government of the United States from 1781 to 1788.

Atlanta Campaign   Decisive Civil War campaign in 1864 in which Union general William T. Sherman maneuvered past Confederate general Joseph E. Johnson from northwestern Georgia toward Atlanta until President Davis replaced Johnson with General John B. Hood, who promptly engaged Sherman and lost this vital rail junction to the Union.

Atlanta Compromise   Booker T. Washington's policy accepting segregation and **disfranchisement** for African-Americans in exchange for white assistance in education and job training.

Atlantic Charter   Statement of common principles and war aims developed by President Franklin Roosevelt and British Prime Minister Winston Churchill at a meeting in August 1941.

Atlantic, Battle of the   A struggle for control of the North Atlantic (1940–1943) between German submarines and British and American naval and air forces.

Atomic Energy Commission (AEC)   Civilian agency created in 1946 to develop and control military and civilian uses of atomic energy; its functions were transferred to the Nuclear Regulatory Commission in 1975.

Australian ballot   Secret voting and the use of official ballots rather than party tickets.

Axis Powers   The opponents of the United States and its allies in World War II. The Rome-Berlin Axis was formed between Germany and Italy in 1936 and included Japan after 1940.

Backcountry   The western edges of settlement in colonies from Pennsylvania south to the Carolinas. Colonists first began moving to this region in the eighteenth century, developing a society that was at first somewhat cruder than longer-settled eastern communities.

Bacon's Rebellion   Violent conflict in Virginia (1675–1676), beginning with settler attacks on Indians but culminating in a rebellion led by Nathaniel Bacon against Virginia's government.

Baker* v. *Carr   U.S. Supreme Court decision in 1962 that allowed federal courts to review the apportionment of state legislative districts and established the principle that such districts should have roughly equal populations ("one person, one vote").

Bank War   The political struggle between President Andrew Jackson and the supporters of the **Second Bank of the United States**.

Banking Act of 1935   Law that strengthened the authority of the Federal Reserve Board over the nation's currency and credit system.

Bay of Pigs   Site in Cuba of an unsuccessful landing by fifteen hundred anti-Castro Cuban refugees in April 1961.

Beats   Nonconformists in the late 1950s who came together in large cities to reject conventional dress and sexual standards and cultivate poetry, jazz, and folk music; also known as *beatniks*.

Beaver Wars   Series of bloody conflicts, occurring between 1640s and 1680s, during which the Iroquois fought the French and their Indian allies for control of the fur trade in eastern North America and the Great Lakes region.

Benevolent empire   Network of reform associations affiliated with Protestant churches in the early nineteenth century dedicated to the restoration of moral order.

Berlin blockade   Three-hundred-day Soviet blockade of land access to United States, British, and French occupation zones in Berlin, 1948–1949.

Berlin Wall   Wall erected by East Germany in 1961 and torn down in 1989 that isolated West Berlin from the surrounding areas in Communist-controlled East Berlin and East Germany.

Bicameral legislature   A legislative body composed of two houses.

Bill of rights A written summary of inalienable rights and liberties.

Black codes Laws passed by states and municipalities denying many rights of citizenship to free blacks. Also, during **Reconstruction**, laws passed by newly elected southern state legislatures to control black labor, mobility, and employment.

Black Death Outbreak of the pneumonic form of bubonic plague in Europe between 1347 and 1351 that killed perhaps a third of Europe's population.

Black Hawk's War Short 1832 war in which federal troops and Illinois militia units defeated the Sauk and Fox Indians led by Black Hawk.

Black Muslims Common name for the Nation of Islam, a religious movement among black Americans that emphasizes self-sufficiency, self-help, and separation from white society.

Black Panthers Political and social movement among black Americans, founded in Oakland, California, in 1966 and emphasizing black economic and political power.

Black Power Philosophy emerging after 1965 that real economic and political gains for African-Americans could come only through self-help, **self-determination**, and organizing for direct political influence. Latinos and Native Americans developed their own versions as Brown Power and Red Power, respectively.

Bland-Allison Act A 1978 compromise currency law that provided for limited silver coinage.

"Bleeding Kansas" Violence between pro- and antislavery forces in Kansas Territory after the passage of the **Kansas-Nebraska Act** in 1854.

Blitzkrieg German war tactic in World War II ("lightning war") involving the concentration of air and armored firepower to punch and exploit holes in opposing defensive lines.

Board of Indian Commissioners A nonpartisan board established in 1869 as an advisory agency to eliminate politics and corruption from the government bureaucracy dealing with Indian affairs.

Board of Trade Committee set up by King William in 1696 that replaced the Lords of Trade as overseers of colonial affairs. The board gathered information about the colonies and recommended policy changes but had no executive authority.

Bolshevik Member of the Communist movement in Russia that established the Soviet government after the 1917 Russian Revolution; hence, by extension, any radical or disruptive person or movement seeking to transform economic and political relationships.

Bonus Army A group of unemployed veterans who demonstrated in Washington for the payment of service bonuses, only to be violently dispersed by the U.S. Army in 1932.

Boston Massacre Incident that occurred in Boston on March 5, 1770, in which British soldiers fired on a crowd that had been harassing them. Five civilians were killed.

Boston Port Act One of the **Coercive Acts** passed by Parliament in 1774 in response to the **Boston Tea Party**. It closed the port of Boston until townspeople paid for the tea and the duties on it.

Boston Seamen's Aid Society Female reform organization founded in 1833 to assist widows and orphans of sailors.

Boston Tea Party Incident that occurred on December 16, 1773, in which Bostonians, disguised as Indians, destroyed £9,000 worth of tea belonging to the British East India Company in order to prevent payment of the duty on it.

Brandywine Creek, Battle of Revolutionary War engagement on September 11, 1777, in southeastern Pennsylvania in which British forces under Sir William Howe defeated Americans under General George Washington, thereby clearing the way for the British occupation of Philadelphia.

Britain, Battle of Series of air engagements in 1940 during World War II that pitted British interceptor fighter planes against German bombers attacking British cities and industry.

British Constitution The principles, procedures, and precedents that governed the operation of the British government. These could be found in no single written document; Parliament and the king made the Constitution by their actions.

Broad constructionist Person who favors reading implied powers into the **Constitution**.

Brook Farm A utopian community and experimental farm established in 1841 near Boston.

Brooklyn Heights, Battle of Revolutionary War battle fought on August 27, 1776, when Sir William Howe landed a large British force on Long Island, New York, outflanked the American defenders, and attacked their rear. Although the Americans suffered heavy casualties, General George Washington was later able under cover of darkness to withdraw his forces to Manhattan Island.

Brown v. Board of Education of Topeka Supreme Court decision in 1954 that declared that "separate but equal" schools for children of different races violated the **Constitution**.

Bulge, Battle of the German counteroffensive in December 1944 during World War II that slowed the Allied advance on Germany.

Bull Run, First Battle of The first major battle of the Civil War in July 1861; a disaster for Federal forces.

Bull Run, Second Battle of Federal Civil War defeat in August 1862 one year after a similar loss at the same place.

Bunker Hill, Battle of Revolutionary War battle actually fought on nearby Breed's Hill, overlooking Boston Harbor, on June 17, 1775. It was a costly engagement for the British, who suffered more than a thousand casualties.

Bureau of Indian Affairs Government agency, within the U.S. Department of the Interior, responsible for carrying out official Indian policy.

Bureau of Reclamation Federal agency established in 1902 providing public funds for irrigation projects in arid regions; played a major role in the development of the West by constructing dams, reservoirs, and irrigation systems, especially beginning in the 1930s.

Business unionism The **American Federation of Labor** stance that members should avoid political activism and concentrate on basic workplace issues.

Cabinet The body of secretaries appointed by the president to head executive departments and serve as advisers.

Californio A person of Spanish descent in California.

Camden, Battle of Decisive British victory at Camden, South Carolina, on August 16, 1780, with more than one thousand Americans killed or wounded and many captured. A second battle near Camden on April 25, 1781, was more nearly a draw.

Camp David Agreement Agreement to reduce points of conflict between Israel and Egypt, hammered out in 1977 with the help of U.S. President Jimmy Carter.

Carpetbaggers Northerners who came to the post–Civil War South, initially for economic reasons, and then became involved in Republican politics; a disparaging term.

Cattle Kingdom The open-range cattle industry that stretched from Texas into Montana in the 1870s and 1880s.

Centennial Exposition Fair held in Philadelphia in 1876 to celebrate the hundredth anniversary of the United States and to showcase American industry and technology.

Central Intelligence Agency (CIA) Agency that coordinates the gathering and evaluation of military and economic information on other nations, established in 1947.

Central Powers Germany and its World War I allies Austria, Turkey, and Bulgaria.

Chain migration Process common to many immigrant groups whereby one family member brings over other family members, who in turn bring other relatives and friends and occasionally entire villages.

Chancellorsville Battle ending in a Confederate victory in Virginia in May 1863 during which General Thomas "Stonewall" Jackson was mortally wounded.

Charles River Bridge* v. *Warren Supreme Court decision of 1837 that promoted economic competition by ruling that the broader rights of the community took precedence over any presumed right of monopoly granted in a corporate charter.

Charleston, Battle of Revolutionary War engagement that began on February 11, 1780, when Sir Henry Clinton, leading eight thousand British troops from New York, encircled and laid siege to Charleston, South Carolina. On May 12, of that year, 5,400 American defenders under Benjamin Lincoln surrendered in the costliest American defeat of the Revolutionary War.

Chattanooga Site of a series of Civil War campaigns culminating in a smashing Union victory in November 1863 as federal troops broke a Confederate siege of the city and opened the road to Georgia.

Cherokee War Conflict (1759–1761) on the southern frontier between the Cherokee Indians and colonists from Virginia southward. It caused South Carolina to request the aid of British troops and resulted in the surrender of more Indian land to whites.

Cherry Valley Site of a Revolutionary War incident that occurred on November 11, 1778, when Joseph Brant of the Mohawks and Captain Walter Butler led seven hundred Indians and **Tories** on a raid of a New York valley that left as many as fifty **Whig** settlers dead.

***Chesapeake* Incident** Attack in 1807 by the British ship *Leopard* on the American ship *Chesapeake* in American territorial waters that nearly provoked an Anglo-American war.

Chicago Defender A major black newspaper that encouraged black migration from the South to the urban North.

Children's Bureau Federal agency established in 1912 to investigate and report on matters pertaining to the welfare of children.

Chinese Consolidated Benevolent Association Umbrella social service organization for Chinese immigrants that pooled their resources to assist in such activities as job hunting, housing, support for the sick or poor, and burial.

Chinese Exclusion Act Law passed by Congress in 1882 prohibiting Chinese immigration to the United States; overturned in 1943.

Chisholm Trail The route followed by Texas cattle raisers driving their herds north to markets at Kansas railheads.

Church of God A religious movement that emerged from the mountains of Tennessee and North Carolina in 1886 as part of the **Holiness movement**. It accepted women, and sometimes blacks, on an equal basis with white men.

Civil Rights Act of 1866 Law that defined national citizenship and specified the civil rights to which all national citizens were entitled.

Civil Rights Act of 1875 Law that prohibited racial discrimination in jury selection, public transportation, and public accommodations; declared unconstitutional by the U.S. Supreme Court in 1883.

Civil Rights Act of 1964 Federal legislation that outlawed discrimination in public accommodations and employment on the basis of race, skin color, sex, religion, or national origin.

Civil Works Administration (CWA) Government agency under Harry Hopkins that created 4 million relief jobs for the unemployed during the winter of 1933–1934.

Civilian Conservation Corps (CCC) Popular **New Deal** program that provided young men with relief jobs working on reforestation, flood control, and other **conservation** projects.

Claims club A group of local settlers on the nineteenth-century frontier who banded together to prevent the price of their land claims from being bid up by outsiders at public land auctions.

Clean Air Act Legislation in 1970 that set federal standards for air quality.

Coercive Acts Legislation passed by Parliament in 1774; included the **Boston Port Act**, the **Massachusetts Government Act**, the **Administration of Justice Act**, and the **Quartering Act** of 1774.

Cold Harbor Crossroads 10 miles northeast of Richmond where in June 1864, General Ulysses S. Grant launched a disastrous assault on Confederate positions during the Civil War.

Cold War The political and economic confrontation between the Soviet Union and the United States that dominated world affairs from 1946 to 1980.

Collective bargaining Representatives of a union negotiating with management on behalf of all members.

Colored Farmers' Alliance An organization of southern black farmers formed in Texas in 1886 in response to the **Southern Farmers' Alliance**, which did not accept blacks as members.

Columbian exchange The transatlantic exchange of plants, animals, and diseases that occurred after the first European contact with the Americas.

Comecon The Council for Mutual Economic Assistance, established in 1949 by the Soviet Union and its eastern European satellites.

Committee of Safety Any of the extralegal committees that directed the Revolutionary movement and carried on the functions of government at the local level in the period between the breakdown of royal authority and the establishment of regular governments under the new state constitutions. Some Committees of Safety continued to function throughout the Revolutionary War.

Committee on Public Information (CPI) Government agency during World War I that sought to shape public opinion in support of the war effort through newspapers, pamphlets, speeches, films, and other media.

Committees of Correspondence Committees formed in Massachusetts and other colonies in the pre-Revolutionary period to keep Americans informed about British measures that would affect the colonies.

Committee to Defend America by Aiding the Allies Group organized to support Franklin Roosevelt's policy of resisting Nazi Germany by actively aiding the British war effort.

Common Sense Influential pamphlet by Thomas Paine. Published in Philadelphia in January 1776, it convinced many Americans that common sense dictated that the colonies should be independent of Great Britain.

Commonwealth* v. *Hunt Case in which the Massachusetts Supreme Court in 1842 ruled that labor unions were not inherently criminal conspiracies guilty of restraining trade.

Communism A social structure based on the common ownership of property.

Community Action Agencies Locally based antipoverty organizations created under federal legislation in 1964 and intended to allow poor people to help plan programs and services.

Competency In colonial New England, the possession of enough property to maintain a family's independent economic existence.

Compromise of 1850 Congressional solution to the controversy over California's admission to the Union as a free state; it granted the populations of other territories the right to decide on slavery (**popular sovereignty**) and established the **Fugitive Slave Act**.

Compromise of 1877 A deal that settled the contested presidential election of 1876 by installing Republican Rutherford B. Hayes in the White House and returning home rule to the South. It formally ended **Reconstruction** and left the fate of the freedmen in the hands of southern whites.

Concentration camp A prison camp for political dissenters and social undesirables, used extensively in **Nazi** Germany.

Conciliatory Proposition Plan proposed by Lord North and adopted by the House of Commons in February 1775 whereby Parliament would "forbear" taxation of Americans in colonies whose assemblies imposed taxes considered satisfactory by the British government. The Continental Congress rejected this plan on July 31, 1775.

Confederate States of America Nation proclaimed in Montgomery, Alabama, in February 1861 after the seven states of the Lower South seceded from the United States.

Confiscation Act of 1862 Second confiscation law passed by Congress, ordering the seizure of land from disloyal Southerners and the emancipation of their slaves.

Congress of Industrial Organizations An alliance of industrial unions that spurred the 1930s organizational drive among the mass-production industries.

Congress on Racial Equality (CORE) Civil rights group formed in 1942 and committed to nonviolent civil disobedience, such as the 1961 "freedom rides."

Congressional Reconstruction Name given to the period 1867–1870 when the Republican-dominated Congress controlled **Reconstruction** policy. It is sometimes known as Radical Reconstruction, after the radical faction in the **Republican party**.

Conquistador Spanish for "conqueror," applied to a Spanish soldier who participated in the conquest and colonization of America.

Conscience Whigs Primarily northern members of the **Whig party** who opposed the extension of slavery in the territories. When the party disintegrated after 1852, many of these Whigs eventually joined the **Republican party**.

Conservation The efficient management and use of natural resources, such as forests, grasslands, and rivers, as opposed to **preservation** or uncontrolled exploitation.

Constitutional Convention Convention that met in Philadelphia in 1787 and drafted the **Constitution of the United States**.

Constitutional Union party National party formed in 1860, mainly by former **Whigs**, that emphasized allegiance to the Union and strict enforcement of all national legislation.

Constitution of the United States The written document providing for a new central government of the United States drawn up at the **Constitutional Convention** in 1787 and ratified by the states in 1788.

Continental Army The regular or professional army authorized by the Second Continental Congress and commanded by General George Washington during the Revolutionary War. Better training and longer service distinguished its soldiers from the state militiamen.

Continental Association Agreement, adopted by the **First Continental Congress** in 1774 in response to the **Coercive Acts**, to cut off trade with Britain until the objectionable measures were repealed. Local committees were established to enforce the provisions of the association.

Continental dollars Paper money issued by the Continental Congress to finance the Revolution. Lacking tax revenues to back it up, this money depreciated rapidly. By mid-1781, it was literally worthless, but it had served its purpose by helping Congress conduct the war for six years.

Contrabands Slaves who escaped from their masters to Union lines during the Civil War.

Contract theory of government The belief that government is established by human beings to protect certain rights—such as life, liberty, and property—that are theirs by natural, divinely sanctioned law and that when government protects these rights, people are obligated to obey it. But when government violates its part of the bargain (or contract) between the rulers and the ruled, the people are no longer required to obey it and may establish a new government that will do a better job of protecting them. Elements of this theory date back to the ancient Greeks; John Locke used it in his *Second Treatise on Government* (1682), and Thomas Jefferson gave it memorable expression in the Declaration of Independence, where it provides the rationale for renouncing allegiance to King George III.

Contract with America Platform on which many Republican candidates ran for Congress in 1994. Associated with House Speaker Newt Gingrich, it proposed a sweeping reduction in the role and activities of the federal government.

Cooperative An organization that allowed a group of farmers to buy tools, seed, livestock, and other farm-related products at discounted prices in bulk.

Copperhead A term Republicans applied to Northern war dissenters and those suspected of aiding the Confederate cause during the Civil War.

Coral Sea, Battle of the Battle between U.S. and Japanese aircraft carriers that halted the Japanese advance toward Australia in May 1942 during World War II.

Cordon sanitaire The belt of anti-Communist eastern European nations that separated western Europe from the Soviet Union after World War I.

Council of Economic Advisers Board of three professional economists established in 1946 to advise the president on economic policy.

Council of National Defense The government body, consisting of **cabinet** officials and economic leaders, that oversaw the wartime agencies controlling the nation's economy during World War I.

Counterculture Various alternatives to mainstream values and behaviors that became popular in the 1960s, including experimentation with psychedelic drugs, communal living, a return to the land, Asian religions, and experimental art.

Country (Real Whig) ideology Strain of thought first appearing in England in the late seventeenth century in response to the growth of governmental power and a national debt. Main ideas stressed the threat to personal liberty posed by a standing army and high taxes and emphasized the need for property holders to retain the right to consent to taxation.

Coureur de bois French for "woods runner," an independent fur trader in New France.

Covenant A formal agreement or contract. The idea of a covenant became an important organizing principle in early New England. Settlers believed that they made a covenant with the Lord to create a godly society, and in their towns and churches, settlers made covenants whereby they agreed to live and worship in harmony.

Cowpens, Battle of January 17, 1781, engagement in upstate South Carolina during the Revolutionary War involving approximately one thousand men on each side, in which Americans won a resounding victory over the British under Banastre Tarleton, thereby compromising his reputation for invincibility and boosting American morale.

Coxey's Army A protest march of unemployed workers, led by Populist businessman Jacob Coxey, demanding inflation and a public works program during the depression of the 1890s.

Creole A slave of African descent born in the colonies.

Criollo A person of Spanish descent born in the Americas or the West Indies.

Crittenden Plan Series of measures submitted to Congress in January 1861 by John Crittenden of Kentucky to permit slavery below the **Missouri Compromise** line.

Crop lien A claim against all or a portion of a farmer's crop as security against a debt.

Crop lien laws In the Reconstruction and post-Reconstruction South, laws that gave merchants the right to sharecroppers' future cotton crop in exchange for credit.

Cult of domesticity The belief that women, by virtue of their sex, should stay home as the moral guardians of family life.

Culture area A geographical region inhabited by peoples who share similar basic patterns of subsistence and social organization.

Currency Act Law passed by Parliament in 1764 to prevent the colonies from issuing **legal tender** paper money, which often depreciated.

Dartmouth College **v.** *Woodward* Supreme Court decision of 1819 that prohibited states from interfering with the privileges granted to a private corporation.

Dawes Act An 1887 law terminating tribal ownership of land and allotting some parcels of land to individual Indians with the remainder opened for white settlement.

D-Day June 6, 1944, the day of the first paratroop drops and amphibious landings on the coast of Normandy, France, in the first stage of **Operation OVERLORD** during World War II.

Declaration of Independence The document by which the Second Continental Congress announced and justified its decision (reached July 2, 1776) to renounce the colonies' allegiance to the British government. Drafted mainly by Thomas Jefferson and adopted by Congress on July 4, the declaration's indictment of the king provides a remarkably full catalog of the colonists' grievances, and Jefferson's eloquent and inspiring statement of the **contract theory of government** makes the document one of the world's great state papers.

Declaration of London Statement drafted by an international conference in 1909 to clarify international law and specify the rights of neutral nations.

Declaration of Rights and Grievances Resolves, adopted by the **Stamp Act Congress** at New York in 1765, asserting that the **Stamp Act** and other taxes imposed on the colonists without their consent, given through their colonial legislatures, were unconstitutional.

Declaration of Sentiments The resolutions passed at the **Seneca Falls Convention** in 1848 calling for full female equality, including the right to vote.

Declaration of the Causes and Necessity of Taking Up Arms Document, written mainly by John Dickinson of Pennsylvania and adopted on July 6, 1775, by which the Second Continental Congress justified its armed resistance against British measures.

Declaratory Act Law passed in 1766 to accompany repeal of the **Stamp Act** that stated that Parliament had the authority to legislate for the colonies "in all cases whatsoever." Whether "legislate" meant tax was not clear to Americans.

Deism Religious orientation that rejects divine revelation and holds that the workings of nature alone reveal God's design for the universe.

Democratic party Political party formed in the 1820s under the leadership of Andrew Jackson; favored states' rights and a limited role for the federal government, especially in economic affairs.

Denmark Vesey's Conspiracy The most carefully devised slave revolt, named after its leader, a free black in Charleston. The rebels planned to seize control of Charleston in 1822 and escape to freedom in Haiti, a free black republic, but they were betrayed by other slaves, and seventy-five conspirators were executed.

Deregulation Reduction or removal of government regulations and encouragement of direct competition in many important industries and economic sectors.

Desert Shield The U.S. and Allied military operation to protect Saudi Arabia from possible attack after Iraq's invasion of Kuwait in 1990; set the stage for the military offensive in 1991 code-named **Desert Storm**.

Desert Storm Code name for the successful offensive against Iraq by the United States and its allies in the Persian Gulf War (1991).

Deskilling A decline in work force skills due to discrimination, as for southern blacks in the late nineteenth century, or to mechanization, as for white industrial workers in the same period.

Détente A lessening of tension, applied to improved American relations with the Soviet Union and China in the mid-1970s.

Direct Tax of 1798 A national tax levied on land, slaves, and dwellings.

Disfranchisement The use of legal means to bar individuals or groups from voting.

Dixiecrats Southern Democrats who broke from the party in 1948 over the issue of civil rights and ran a presidential ticket as the States' Rights Democrats.

Dollar diplomacy The U.S. policy of using private investment in other nations to promote American diplomatic goals and business interests.

Dominion of New England James II's failed plan of 1686 to combine eight northern colonies into a single large province, to be governed by a royal appointee (Sir Edmund Andros) with an appointed council but no elective assembly. The plan ended with James's ouster from the English throne and rebellion in Massachusetts against Andros's rule.

Dred Scott **decision** Supreme Court ruling, in a lawsuit brought by Dred Scott, a slave demanding his freedom based on his residence in a free state and a free territory with this master, that slaves could not be U.S. citizens and that Congress had no jurisdiction over slavery in the territories.

Dutch West India Company Trading enterprise that established and governed the Dutch colony of New Netherlands from its first permanent settlement at Fort Orange in 1624 until it was seized by the English in 1664.

Eastern Front The area of military operations in World War II located east of Germany in eastern Europe and the Soviet Union.

Economic Recovery and Tax Act of 1981 (ERTA) A major revision of the federal income tax system.

Edge city A suburban district that has developed as a center for employment, retailing, and services comparable to a traditional downtown.

El Alamein, Battle of British victory during World War II that checked the advance of the German army into Egypt in June 1942.

Elementary and Secondary Education Act Federal legislation in 1965 that provided the first large-scale federal aid for needy public school districts.

Emancipation Proclamation Decree announced by President Abraham Lincoln in September 1862 and formally issued on January 1, 1863, freeing slaves in all Confederate states still in rebellion.

Embargo Act of 1807 Act passed by Congress in 1807 prohibiting American ships from leaving for any foreign port.

Emergency Banking Act of 1933 A law that stabilized the banking system through government aid and supervision.

Emergency Relief Appropriation Act of 1935 Law authorizing a massive program of public work relief projects for the unemployed.

Employment Act of 1946 Federal legislation that committed the United States to the goal of "maximum employment, production and purchasing power."

Empresario An agent who received a land grant from the Spanish or Mexican government in return for organizing settlements.

Encomienda In the Spanish colonies, the grant to a Spanish settler of a certain number of Indian subjects, who would pay him tribute in goods and labor.

Enforcement Act of 1870 Largely ineffectual law passed in response to growing political violence in the South, enabling the federal government to appoint supervisors where states failed to protect citizens' voting rights.

Engel v. *Vitale* Supreme Court decision in 1962 that found that reading a nondenominational prayer in public schools violated the First Amendment to the Constitution.

Enrollment Act A law passed by the U.S. Congress in 1863 during the Civil War subjecting all able-bodied men between the ages of twenty and forty-five to the draft. Its unpopularity contributed to the **New York Draft Riot** later that year.

Enumerated products Items produced in the colonies and enumerated in acts of Parliament that could be legally shipped from the colony of origin only to specified locations, usually England and other destinations within the British empire.

Environmental Protection Agency (EPA) Federal agency created in 1970 to oversee environmental monitoring and cleanup programs.

Equal Employment Opportunity Commission (EEOC) Federal commission established by the **Civil Rights Act of 1964** to monitor and enforce nondiscrimination in employment.

Equal Rights Amendment (ERA) A proposed but never adopted amendment to the **Constitution** to prevent abridgment of rights on account of a person's sex.

Era of Good Feelings The period from 1817 to 1823 in which the disappearance of the **Federalists** enabled the **Republicans** to govern in a spirit of seemingly nonpartisan harmony.

Erdman Act Law providing for the voluntary mediation of railroad labor disputes and recourse to a board of arbitration; passed by Congress in 1898 in response to growing public opposition to the use of federal troops to put down strikes.

Espionage Act of 1917 Law whose vague prohibition against obstructing the nation's war effort was used to crush dissent and criticism during World War I.

Established church A church supported in part by public taxes.

Executive Order 8802 Presidential order in 1943 that required racial nondiscrimination clauses in war contracts and subcontracts.

Executive Order 9066 Presidential order in February 1942 that authorized the forcible relocation of Japanese-Americans from portions of four western states.

Executive Order 9835 Presidential order implemeting a loyalty program for federal employees.

Fair Deal Program for expanded economic opportunity and civil rights proposed by President Truman in 1949.

Fair Employment Practice Committee (FEPC) Federal agency established in 1941 to curb racial discrimination in war production jobs and government employment.

Fallen Timbers, Battle of Battle fought in northern Ohio in August 1794, in which an American army led by General Anthony Wayne decisively defeated an Indian confederation.

Farm Credit Administration Government agency established in 1933 to refinance farm mortgages, thereby saving farms and protecting banks.

Farmers' Alliance A broad mass movement in the rural South and West during the late nineteenth century, encompassing several organizations and demanding economic and political reforms; helped create the **Populist party**.

Fascist Subscribing to a philosophy of governmental dictatorship that merges the interests of the state, armed forces, and big business; associated with the dictatorship of Italian leader Benito Mussolini between 1922 and 1943 and also often applied to **Nazi** Germany.

Federal Communications Commission (FCC) Government agency established in 1934 with authority to regulate radio and television.

Federal Deposit Insurance Corporation (FDIC) Government agency that guarantees bank deposits, thereby protecting both depositors and banks.

Federal Emergency Relief Administration (FERA) Agency set up to provide direct federal grants to the states for assisting the unemployed in the **Great Depression**.

Federal Highway Act of 1956 Measure that provided federal funding to build a nationwide system of interstate and defense highways.

Federal Reserve Act The 1913 law that revised banking and currency by extending limited government regulation through the creation of the Federal Reserve System.

Federal Trade Commission (FTC) Government agency established in 1914 to provide regulatory oversight of business activity.

Federalism The sharing of powers between the national government and the states.

Federalist A supporter of the **Constitution** who favored its ratification.

Federalist, The A series of eighty-five essays, written anonymously and individually by Alexander Hamilton, James Madison, and John Jay, published in New York in 1787 and 1788 to rally support for the ratification of the **Constitution**.

Federalist party Political party organized within the Washington administration by supporters of Alexander Hamilton who favored a strong national government, commercial development, and a pro-British stance in foreign policy.

Fence laws Legislation that required the penning of animals so that they would not disturb crops.

Field Order No. 15   Order by General William T. Sherman in January 1865 to set aside abandoned land along the southern Atlantic coast for 40-acre grants to freedmen; rescinded by President Andrew Johnson later that year.

Fifteenth Amendment   Reconstruction amendment passed by Congress in February 1869 guaranteeing the right of all American male citizens to vote regardless of race.

Fireside chats   Speeches broadcast nationally over the radio in which President Franklin Roosevelt explained complex issues and programs in plain language, as though his listeners were gathered around the fireside with him.

First Continental Congress   Meeting of delegates from most of the colonies held in 1774 in response to the **Coercive Acts**. The Congress endorsed the **Suffolk Resolves**, adopted the **Declaration of Rights and Grievances**, and agreed to establish the **Continental Association** to put economic pressure on Britain to repeal its objectionable measures. The Congress also wrote addresses to the king, the people of Britain, and the American people.

Fletcher v. Peck   Supreme Court decision of 1810 that overturned a state law by ruling that it violated a legal contract.

Food Administration   The agency that sought to increase agricultural production and food conservation to supply the U.S. military and the **Allies** during World War I.

Fort Donelson   With **Fort Henry**, one of two strategic forts on the Tennessee and Cumberland Rivers; site of a January 1862 Union victory during the Civil War.

Fort Henry   With **Fort Donelson**, one of two strategic forts on the Tennessee and Cumberland Rivers; site of a January 1862 Union victory during the Civil War.

Fort Laramie Treaty   Treaty of 1851 in which the United States attempted to establish definite boundaries for each of the major Indian tribes on the Central Plains.

Fort Sumter   Begun in the late 1820s to protect Charleston, South Carolina, it became the center of national attention in April 1861 when President Lincoln attempted to provision federal troops at the fort, triggering a hostile response from on-shore Confederate forces, opening the Civil War.

Fort Ticonderoga   Strategically important fort between Lake George and Lake Champlain in New York State. Benedict Arnold and Ethan Allen, leading forces from Massachusetts and Vermont, respectively, captured the fort, its fifty defenders, and its military stores on May 10, 1775, at the outset of the Revolutionary War.

Fort Wagner   Confederate installation guarding the entrance to Charleston harbor during the Civil War and site of a failed Federal assault in July 1863 during which a black Union regiment, the 54th Massachusetts, distinguished itself.

Forty Niners   Miners who rushed to California after the discovery of gold in the northern part of the territory in 1848.

Fourierist communities   Short-live utopian communities in the 1840s based on the ideas of economic cooperation and self-sufficiency popularized by the Frenchman Charles Fourier.

Fourteenth Amendment   Constitutional amendment passed by Congress in April 1866 incorporating some of the features of the **Civil Rights Act of 1866**. It prohibited states from violating the civil rights of its citizens and offered states the choice of allowing blacks to vote or losing representation in Congress.

Frame of Government   William Penn's 1682 plan for the government of Pennsylvania, which created a relatively weak legislature and a strong executive. It also contained a provision for religious freedom.

Franco-American Accord of 1800   Settlement reached with France that brought an end to the **Quasi-War** and released the United States from its 1778 alliance with France.

Franklin, Battle of   Confederate general John B. Hood's disastrous frontal assault on well-entrenched Union positions south of Nashville in November 1864 during the Civil War.

Fredericksburg   Site of a Union setback in late 1862 that ended another Federal attempt to march on Richmond during the Civil War.

Freedmen's Bureau   Agency established by Congress in March 1865 to provide social, educational, and economic services, advice, and protection to former slaves and destitute whites; lasted seven years.

Freedom Summer   Voter registration effort in rural Mississippi organized by black and white civil rights workers in 1964.

Freedom's Journal   The first African-American newspaper, founded in 1827 by John Russwurm and Samuel Cornish.

Freeport Doctrine   Illinois Senator Stephen A. Douglas's statement during the 1858 **Lincoln-Douglas debates** that slavery could exist in a territory only if residents passed a law to protect it and that if residents did not pass such a law, there would be no slavery.

Free silver   Philosophy that the government should expand the money supply by purchasing and coining all the silver offered to it.

Free Soil party   Anti-Southern party centered on keeping slavery out of the territories.

Free Speech Movement (FSM)   Student movement at the University of California, Berkeley, formed in 1964 to protest limitations on political activities on campus.

French and Indian War   The last of the Anglo-French colonial wars (1754–1763) and the first in which fighting began in North America. The war (which merged with the European conflict known as the **Seven Years' War**) ended with France's defeat and loss of its North American empire.

Fries's Rebellion   An armed attempt to block enforcement of the **Direct Tax of 1798** in the eastern counties of Pennsylvania, named for an auctioneer who played a prominent role.

Fugitive Slave Act   Law, part of the **Compromise of 1850**, that required that authorities in the North assist southern slavecatchers and return runaway slaves to their owners.

Fundamental Constitutions of Carolina   A complex plan for organizing the colony of Carolina, drafted in 1669 by Anthony Ashley Cooper and John Locke. Its provisions included a scheme for creating a hierarchy of nobles who would own vast amounts of land and wield political power; below them would be a class of freedmen and slaves. The provisions were never implemented by the Carolina colonists.

Fundamentalists   Religious conservatives who believe in the literal accuracy and divine inspiration of the Bible; the name derives from an influential series of pamphlets, *The Fundamentals* (1909–1914).

Fundamental Orders   Design for Connecticut government, adopted in 1639, that was modeled on that of Massachusetts Bay, except that voters did not have to be church members.

Funded debt   Means by which governments allocate a portion of tax revenues to guarantee payment of interest on loans from private investors. England used this process to begin paying debts incurred during the first two Anglo-French wars, thereby harnessing private capital to serve the nation's military needs.

Fusion   Political strategy adopted by Populists and Republicans in North Carolina during their successful 1894 election campaign.

Gabriel Prosser's Rebellion   Slave revolt that failed when Gabriel Prosser, a slave preacher and blacksmith, organized a thousand slaves for an attack on Richmond, Virginia, in 1800. A thunderstorm upset the timing of the attack, and a slave informer alerted the whites. Prosser and twenty-five of his followers were executed.

Gag rule   Procedural rule passed in the House of Representatives that prevented discussion of antislavery proposals from 1836 to 1844.

Gang system   The organization and supervision of slave field hands into working teams on southern plantations.

Gaspee   British revenue schooner burned in Narragansett Bay by Rhode Islanders in 1772. The incident led to the appointment of a British commission of inquiry whose powers prompted Americans to establish **committees of correspondence**.

General Agreement on Tariffs and Trade (GATT)   International agreement aimed at lowering barriers to international trade, first signed in 1947 and updated periodically.

General Court   The legislature of the colony of Massachusetts.

General Union for Promoting the Observance of the Christian Sabbath   Reform organization founded in 1828 by Congregationalist and Presbyterian ministers that lobbied for an end to the delivery of mail on Sundays and other Sabbath violations.

Gentlemen's Agreement   A diplomatic agreement in 1907 between Japan and the United States curtailing but not abolishing Japanese immigration.

Gettysburg   Town in Pennsylvania; site of a pivotal Union victory in July 1863 during the Civil War.

Ghent, Treaty of   Treaty signed in December 1814 between the United States and Britain that ended the **War of 1812**.

Ghetto   A neighborhood or district in which members of a particular racial or ethnic group are forced to live by law or as a result of economics or social discrimination.

GI   World War II slang for a U.S. soldier, derived from the words *government issue* stamped on equipment and supplies.

GI Bill of Rights   Legislation in June 1944 that eased the return of veterans into American society by providing educational and employment benefits.

Gibbons* v. *Ogden   Supreme Court decision of 1824 involving coastal commerce that overturned a steamboat monopoly granted by the state of New York on the grounds that only Congress had the authority to regulate interstate commerce.

Gilded Age   Term applied to late-nineteenth-century America that refers to the shallow display and worship of wealth characteristic of the period.

Glasnost   Russian for "openness," applied to Mikhail Gorbachev's encouragement of new ideas and easing of political repression in the Soviet Union.

Glass-Steagall Act of 1933   Law that separated investment from commercial banking to limit speculation by bankers and created the **Federal Deposit Insurance Corporation**.

Glorieta Pass   Mountain pass in New Mexico; site of an important Civil War battle in April 1862 that maintained the Southwest under Union control.

Glorious Revolution   Bloodless revolt that occurred in England in 1688 when parliamentary leaders invited William of Orange, a Protestant, to assume the English throne and James II fled to France. James's ouster was prompted by fears that the birth of his son would establish a Catholic dynasty in England.

Goliad   Town in Texas where Mexican troops put to death over three hundred American prisoners on March 27, 1836, during the Texas War for Independence.

Gospel of Wealth   Thesis that hard work and perseverance lead to wealth, implying that poverty is a character flaw.

Grand Settlement of 1701   Separate peace treaties negotiated by Iroquois diplomats at Montreal and Albany that marked the beginning of Iroquois neutrality in conflicts between the French and the British in North America.

Grandfather clause   Rule that required potential voters to demonstrate that their grandfathers had been eligible to vote; used in some southern states after 1890 to limit the black electorate, as most black men's grandfathers had been slaves.

Grange   The National Grange of the Patrons of Husbandry, a national organization of farm owners formed after the Civil War.

Granger laws   State laws enacted in the Midwest in the 1870s that regulated rates charged by railroads, grain elevator operators, and other middlemen.

Great Awakening   Tremendous religious revival in colonial America. Sparked by the tour of the English evangelical minister George Whitefield, the Awakening struck first in the Middle Colonies and New England in the 1740s and eventually spread to the southern colonies by the 1760s.

Great Bridge   Causeway near Norfolk, Virginia, that on December 9, 1775, was the site of a Revolutionary War battle between Americans and a British force composed mostly of African-Americans and other **Loyalists** who had joined the governor of Virginia, Lord Dunmore. Victory by the Americans enabled them to occupy Norfolk shortly thereafter.

Great Compromise   Plan proposed by Roger Sherman of Connecticut at the 1787 **Constitutional Convention** for creating a national **bicameral legislature** in which all states would be equally represented in the Senate and proportionally represented in the House.

Great Depression   The nation's worst economic crisis, extending throughout the 1930s, producing unprecedented bank failures, unemployment, and industrial and agricultural collapse and prompting an expanded role for the federal government.

Greater East Asia Co-Prosperity Sphere   Japanese goal of an East Asian economy controlled by Japan and serving the needs of Japanese industry.

Great Migration   The mass movement of Afrian-Americans from the rural South to the urban North, spurred especially by new job opportunities during World War I and the 1920s.

Great Society   Theme of Lyndon Johnson's administration, focusing on poverty, education, and civil rights.

Great Uprising   Unsuccessful railroad strike of 1877 to protest wage cuts and the use of federal troops against strikers; the first nationwide work stoppage in American history.

Greenback party   A third party of the 1870s and 1880s that garnered temporary support by advocating currency inflation to expand the economy and assist debtors.

Greenville, Treaty of   Treaty of 1795 in which Indians in the Old Northwest were forced to cede most of the present state of Ohio to the United States.

Guadalupe Hidalgo, Treaty of   Treaty signed in 1848 that ended the **Mexican War**; Mexico surrendered its claim to Texas above the Rio Grande and, in the **Mexican Cession of 1848**, ceded New Mexico and Alta California to the United States in return for a payment of $15 million.

Guilford Court House, Battle of   A fiercely fought Revolutionary War engagement that occurred on March 15, 1781, near modern Greensboro, North Carolina, in which British forces under Lord

Cornwallis and Americans commanded by General Nathanael Greene both sustained heavy losses. The British technically won but were forced to withdraw to Wilmington, North Carolina.

Gulf of Tonkin Resolution   Congressional resolution in August 1964 that authorized the president to take all necessary steps to protect South Vietnam, adopted after reports of North Vietnamese attacks on U.S. ships in the Gulf of Tonkin off North Vietnam.

Habeas corpus   Writ that requires arresting authorities to explain the grounds for a person's imprisonment or detention before a court of law.

Halfway Covenant   Plan adopted in 1662 by New England clergy to deal with the problem of declining church membership. It allowed adults who had been baptized because their parents were church members but who had not yet experienced conversion to have their own children baptized. Without the Halfway Covenant, these third-generation children would remain unbaptized until their parents experienced conversion.

Harlem Renaissance   A new African-American cultural awareness that flourished in literature, art, and music in the 1920s.

Harrison Act   The 1914 law that prohibited the dispensing and use of narcotics for other than medicinal purposes.

Hartford Convention   A meeting of New England **Federalists** in late 1814 in which they protested the **War of 1812** and demanded constitutional changes to protect the commercial interests of New England.

Haymarket Square   Location in Chicago where workers gathered in May 1886 to protest the slayings of colleagues who had struck for an eight-hour workday; a bomb exploded, throwing the gathering into chaos and resulting in the arrest and execution of strike leaders and the decline of the **Knights of Labor**.

Headright system   Adopted first in Virginia and later in Maryland, a system of land distribution during the early colonial era that granted settlers 50 acres for themselves and another 50 for each "head" (or person) they brought with them to the colony.

Head Start   Federal program that since 1965 has helped prepare children from disadvantaged backgrounds for success in school.

Helsinki Accords   Agreement in 1975 among **NATO** and **Warsaw Pact** members that recognized European national boundaries as set after World War II and included guarantees of human rights.

Higher Education Act   Federal legislation in 1965 that provided federal financial aid for college students.

High Federalists   Followers of Alexander Hamilton who wanted President John Adams to declare war against France in 1798 and stamp out political dissent within the United States.

Hippie   A person who dropped out of mainstream society or adopted some of the styles associated with the **counterculture** of the 1960s and early 1970s.

Holiness movement   Religious movement originating in the antebellum North and revived among Texas farmers in the 1880s that stressed simplicity in lifestyle and appealed especially to the poor.

Holocaust   The systematic murder of millions of European Jews and others deemed undesirable by **Nazi** Germany.

Holy Roman Empire   The loose confederation of German and Italian territories under the authority of an emperor that existed from the ninth or tenth century until 1806.

Home mission societies   Organizations founded by white Methodist Church women in the South during the 1870s to promote industrial education among the southern poor and help working-class women become self-sufficient.

Home Owners Loan Corporation   Federal agency that rescued individual homeowners from foreclosure by refinancing mortgage loans.

Homestead Act   Law passed by Congress in May 1862 providing homesteaders (mainly in the West) with 160 acres of free land in exchange for improving the land (as by cultivating it and erecting a house) within five years of the grant.

Homestead strike   A bloody, lengthy, and ultimately unsuccessful strike against Andrew Carnegie's Homestead, Pennsylvania, steelworks in 1892.

Hooverville   Shantytown, sarcastically named after President Hoover, in which unemployed and homeless people lived in makeshift shacks, tents, and boxes. Hoovervilles cropped up in many cities in 1930 and 1931.

Horizontal integration   The merger of competitors in the same industry.

House Committee on Un-American Activities (HUAC)   Congressional committee (1938–1975) that investigated suspected **Nazi** and Communist sympathizers.

House of Burgesses   The legislature of colonial Virginia. First organized in 1619, it was the first institution of representative government in the English colonies.

House of Commons   The lower house of the British Parliament, which included representatives elected by England's propertied class.

House of Lords   The upper house of the British Parliament, where members of the aristocracy were represented.

Hull House   Chicago **settlement house** that became part of a broader neighborhood revitalization project led by Jane Addams.

Immigrant Restriction League (IRL)   New England–based organization formed in 1894 to restrict immigration from southern and eastern Europe by mandating a literacy test for every immigrant.

Immigration and Nationality Act of 1965   Federal legislation that replaced the national quota system for immigration with overall limits of 170,000 immigrants per year from the Eastern Hemisphere and 120,000 per year from the Western Hemisphere.

Immigration Reform and Control Act of 1986   Legislation that granted legal status to 2,650,000 undocumented immigrants and established penalties for employers who knowingly hire illegal immigrants.

Impeachment   The formal charging of a public official with improper conduct.

Imperialism   The policy and practice of exploiting nations and peoples for the benefit of an imperial power either directly through military occupation and colonial rule or indirectly through economic domination of resources and markets.

Indenture   A contract binding a person to the legal service of another for a specified period.

Indentured servant   An individual—usually male but occasionally female—who contracted to serve a master for a period of four to seven years in return for payment of the servant's passage to America. Indentured servitude was the primary labor system in the Chesapeake colonies for most of the seventeenth century.

Independent Treasury System   Fiscal arrangement first instituted by President Martin Van Buren in which the federal government kept its money in regional vaults ("pet banks") and transacted its business entirely in hard money.

Indian Removal Act   Legislation passed by Congress in 1830 that provided funds for removing and resettling eastern Indians in the West. It granted the president the authority to use force if necessary.

Indian Reorganization Act of 1934   Law that reversed previous Indian policy by guaranteeing religious freedom and tribal self-government and providing economic assistance.

Individual Retirement Accounts (IRAs)   Personal saving and investment accounts that allow workers and their spouses to accumulate retirement savings on a tax-deferred basis.

Industrial Workers of the World (IWW)   Militant labor organization founded in 1905 that attracted mostly recent immigrants and espoused a class-conscious program and ideology. Its members were known as **Wobblies**.

Initiative   Procedure by which citizens can introduce a subject for legislation, usually through a petition signed by a specific number of voters.

Intendant   A royally appointed government official in New France.

Intermediate Nuclear Force Agreement (INF)   Disarmament agreement between the United States and the Soviet Union under which an entire class of missiles would be removed and destroyed and on-site inspections would be permitted for verification.

International Monetary Fund (IMF)   International organization established in 1945 to assist nations in maintaining stable currencies.

Interstate Commerce Act   The 1887 law that expanded federal power over business by prohibiting pooling and discriminatory rates by railroads and establishing the first federal regulatory agency, the **Interstate Commerce Commission**.

Interstate Commerce Commission (ICC)   The first federal regulatory agency, established in 1887 to oversee railroad practices.

Intolerable Acts   American term for the **Coercive Acts** and the **Quebec Act**.

Iroquois League   The union of five Indian nations (Mohawks, Oneidas, Onondagas, Cayugas, and Senecas) formed around 1450, also known as the League of Five Nations. Essentially a religious organization, its purpose was to maintain peace among the five nations and unite them to fight against other enemies. After the Tuscarora War (1713–1715), the Tuscaroras joined the league, thereafter known as the League of Six Nations.

Irreconcilables   Group of U.S. senators adamantly opposed to ratification of the **Treaty of Versailles** after World War I.

Island hopping   In the Pacific theater during World War II, the strategy in which U.S. land and amphibious forces seized selected Japanese-held islands while bypassing and isolating other islands held by Japan.

Isolationism   The belief that the United States should not involve itself in international (especially European) political and military developments.

Jacksonian Democrats   See **Democratic party**.

Japanese Association of America   Social service organization for Japanese immigrants that stressed assimilation.

Jay's Treaty   Treaty with Britain negotiated in 1794 in which the United States made major concessions to avert a war over the British seizure of American ships.

Jazz Age   The 1920s, so called for the popular music of the day as a symbol of the many changes taking place in the mass culture.

Jeffersonian Republicans   See **Republican party**.

Jim Crow laws   **Segregation** laws that became widespread in the South during the 1890s, named for a minstrel show character portrayed satirically by white actors in blackface.

Jobs Corps   Antipoverty program created in 1964 that has provided job training and public service work for young people aged 16 to 21 in residential centers.

John Brown's Raid   New England abolitionist John Brown's ill-fated attempt to free Virginia's slaves with a raid on the federal arsenal at Harpers Ferry, Virginia, in 1859.

Joint Committee on the Conduct of the War   Committee created by the Republican-dominated Congress in December 1861 to examine and monitor Civil War military policy, although it ultimately devoted itself more to harassing Democratic officers and promoting the political agenda of **Radical Republican** congressmen.

Joint-stock company   Business enterprise in which a group of stockholders pooled their money to engage in trade or to fund colonizing expeditions. Joint-stock companies participated in the founding of the Virginia, Plymouth, and Massachusetts Bay colonies.

Journeyman   A person who has completed an apprenticeship in a trade or craft and is now a qualified worker in another person's employ.

Judicial review   A power implied in the **Constitution** that gives federal courts the right to review and determine the constitutionality of acts passed by Congress and state legislatures.

Judiciary Act of 1789   Act of Congress that implemented the judiciary clause of the **Constitution** by establishing the Supreme Court and a system of lower federal courts.

Judiciary Act of 1801   Law passed by a **Federalist**-dominated Congress that created new judgeships and judicial offices that outgoing President John Adams filled with prominent **Federalists**.

Kansas-Nebraska Act   Law passed in 1854 creating the Kansas and Nebraska Territories but leaving the question of slavery open to residents, thereby repealing the **Missouri Compromise**.

Kaskaskia   Illinois town on the Mississippi River occupied on July 4, 1778, during the Revolutionary War, by George Rogers Clark, commanding troops from Virginia; Cahokia, Illinois, and Vincennes, Indiana, soon capitulated, though the British later reoccupied Vincennes before Clark recaptured it on February 23, 1779. Clark's operations strengthened American claims to the areas at the end of the war.

Kasserine Pass   Site of the first large-scale World War II encounter between U.S. and German ground forces, in February 1942 in North Africa.

Kellogg-Briand Pact   International treaty negotiated in 1928 to outlaw war but containing no enforcement provisions.

Kettle Creek, Battle of   Revolutionary War engagement in upstate Georgia on February 14, 1779, in which Americans under General Andrew Pickens defeated a band of about seven hundred **Tories** from North and South Carolina. This victory boosted American morale and intimidated **Tories** in the area.

King George's War   The third Anglo-French war in North America (1744–1748), part of the European conflict known as the **War of the Austrian Succession**. During the North American fighting, New Englanders captured the French fortress of Louisbourg, only to have it returned to France after the peace negotiations.

King Philip's War   Conflict in New England (1675–1676) between Wampanoags, Narragansetts, and other Indian peoples against English settlers; sparked by English encroachments on native lands.

Kings Mountain, Battle of   Decisive American Revolutionary War victory in northwestern South Carolina on October 7, 1780, when nine hundred American militia from Virginia, the western Carolinas, and eastern Tennessee annihilated or captured over one thousand **Loyalists**, an important turning point in the southern campaign.

King William's War   The first Anglo-French conflict in North America (1689–1697), the American phase of Europe's **War of the League of Augsburg**. Ended in negotiated peace that reestablished the balance of power.

Kiva   A Pueblo Indian ceremonial structure, usually circular and underground.

Knights of Labor   Labor union that included skilled and unskilled workers irrespective of race or gender; founded in 1869, peaked in the 1880s, and declined when its advocacy of the eight-hour workday led to violent strikes in 1886.

Know-Nothing party   Anti-immigrant party formed from the wreckage of the **Whig party** and some disaffected northern Democrats in 1854.

Korean War   War between North Korea and South Korea (1950–1953) in which the People's Republic of China fought on the side of North Korea and the United States and other nations fought on the side of South Korea under the auspices of the **United Nations**.

Ku Klux Klan   Perhaps the most prominent of the vigilante groups that terrorized blacks in the South during **Reconstruction**, founded by Confederate veterans in 1866.

Ku Klux Klan Act of 1871   Law that held the perpetrators responsible for denying a citizen's civil rights and allowed the federal government to prosecute and send military assistance if states failed to act.

Kursk Salient   Site of the largest tank battle in World War II (July 1943), when Germans failed to throw back Soviet forces that had pushed a huge bulge or salient into German lines.

Ladies' Memorial Associations   Women's organizations formed in the South after the Civil War to commemorate Confederate soldiers.

Lancaster, Treaty of   Negotiation in 1744 whereby Iroquois chiefs sold Virginia land speculators the right to trade at the Forks of the Ohio. Although the Iroquois had not intended this to include the right to settle in the Ohio Country, the Virginians assumed that it did. Ohio Valley Indians considered this treaty a great grievance against both the English and the Iroquois.

Land Grant College Act   Law passed by Congress in July 1862 awarding proceeds from the sale of public lands to the states for the establishment of agricultural and mechanical (later engineering) colleges. Also known as the Morrill Act, after its sponsor, Congressman Justin Morrill of Vermont.

Land Ordinance of 1785   Act passed by Congress under the **Articles of Confederation** that created the grid system of surveys by which all subsequent public land was made available for sale.

Landsmanshaften   Jewish associations that provided social and economic services for their members.

Las Gorras Blancas   Hispanic villagers ("the White Caps") in New Mexico who disguised themselves and employed violent tactics to resist Anglo capitalist disruptions of their traditional life.

Lawes Divine, Morall and Martiall   A harsh code of laws in force in Virginia between 1609 and 1621, intended to use military discipline to bring order to the struggling colony.

League of Armed Neutrality   Association of European powers (Russia, Denmark, Sweden, Austria, Netherlands, Portugal, Prussia, and Sicily), formed between 1780 and 1782 to protect their rights as neutral traders against British attempts to impose a blockade on its enemies. Britain declared war on the Dutch on December 20, 1780, in an effort to cut off their trade with the United States.

League of Freedom   African-American organization formed in Boston in 1851 to protect blacks against the **Fugitive Slave Act**.

League of Nations   International organization created by the **Versailles Treaty** after World War I to ensure world stability.

League of United Latin American Citizens (LULAC)   Organization for Hispanic Americans formed in 1928 to fight segregation and promote equal rights and opportunities.

League of Women Voters   Group formed in 1920 from the **National American Woman Suffrage Association** to encourage informed voting and social reforms.

Lecompton Constitution   Proslavery draft written in 1857 by Kansas territorial delegates elected under questionable circumstances; it was rejected by two governors, supported by President Buchanan, and decisively defeated by Congress.

Legal tender   An attribute of money that results from legislation declaring it to be, as in the case of modern United States currency, "legal tender for all debts public and private." Creditors must therefore accept it at face value.

Levittown   Large post–World War II housing developments built by William Levitt and Sons outside New York and Philadelphia.

Lexington and Concord, Battles of   First skirmishes of the Revolutionary War, April 19, 1775. British forces, determined to destroy American supplies, fired on American militia at Lexington, then pushed on to Concord, where they themselves came under attack. On the long retreat back to Boston, the British suffered 273 dead, wounded, or missing, inflicted by some four thousand American militiamen.

Leyte Gulf, Battle of   World War II naval engagement in October 1944 in which the Japanese navy tried to disrupt U.S. landings in the Philippines and suffered a decisive defeat.

Liberal Republicans   Members of a reform movement within the **Republican party** in 1872 that promoted measures to reduce government influence in the economy and restore control of southern governments to local white elites.

Liberator, The   The best-known and most influential abolitionist newspaper; founded in 1831 by William Lloyd Garrison.

Liberty Association   African-American organization formed in Chicago in 1851 that patrolled the city to spot slavecatchers.

Liberty Bonds   Interest-bearing certificates sold by the U.S. government to finance the American World War I effort.

Liberty party   The first antislavery political party, formed in 1840.

Limited Test Ban Treaty   Agreement in 1963 between the United States, Britain, and the Soviet Union to halt atmospheric and underwater tests of nuclear weapons.

Lincoln-Douglas debates   Series of debates in the 1858 Illinois senatorial campaign during which Democrat Stephen A. Douglas and Republican Abraham Lincoln staked out their differing opinions on the issue of slavery in the territories.

Little Big Horn, Battle of the   Battle in which Colonel George A. Custer and the Seventh Cavalry were defeated by the Sioux and Cheyennes under Sitting Bull and Crazy Horse in Montana in 1876.

Localism   The belief prevalent during much of the nineteenth century that local concerns took precedence over national concerns and that people and institutions should generally resolve issues without the involvement of the national government.

Lords of Trade   A standing committee of the Privy Council, appointed to oversee colonial affairs; created by Charles II in 1675.

Lost Cause   The phrase many white Southerners applied to their Civil War defeat. They viewed the war as a noble cause but only a temporary setback in the South's ultimate vindication.

Lost Generation   The intellectuals of the 1920s, disillusioned by the brutality of World War I and alienated by the materialism and conformity of the new mass culture.

Louisiana Purchase   The U.S. purchase from France in 1803 of a huge tract of land between the Mississippi River and the Rocky Mountains.

Loyalist An American supporter of the British crown during the Revolution. *See also* **Tories**.

Lynching Execution, usually by a mob, without trial.

Macon's Bill No. 2 Act passed by Congress in 1810 that reopened American trade with Britain and France but stipulated that if either nation lifted its restrictions on American shipping, trading sanctions would be reimposed on the other.

Mahanism The ideas advanced by Alfred Thayer Mahan, stressing U.S. naval, economic, and territorial expansion.

Manhattan Project The effort, using the code name Manhattan Engineer District, to develop an atomic bomb under the management of the U.S. Army Corps of Engineers during World War II.

Manifest Destiny Doctrine, first expressed in 1845, that the expansion of white Americans across the continent was inevitable and ordained by God.

Marbury v. Madison Supreme Court decision of 1803 that created the precedent of judicial review by ruling as unconstitutional part of the **Judiciary Act of 1789**.

Marshall Plan The European Recovery Program (1949), which provided U.S. economic assistance to European nations; named for Secretary of State George Marshall.

Massachusetts Government Act Law passed in 1774 in response to the **Boston Tea Party** and directed at Massachusetts; one of the **Coercive** or **Intolerable Acts**. It provided for an appointed rather than an elected upper house of the legislature and restricted the number and kind of town meetings that a community might hold.

Matrilineal Descriptive of societies in which family descent is traced through the mother's line.

Mayflower Compact Document creating a civil government for Plymouth Colony. The compact was signed by all adult males before their ship, the *Mayflower*, landed in 1620.

McCarran Committee The Senate Internal Security Subcommittee, chaired by Senator Pat McCarran and charged to investigate potentially subversive activities.

McCarthyism Anti-Communist attitudes and actions associated with Senator Joe McCarthy in the early 1950s, including smear tactics and innuendo.

McCulloch v. Maryland Supreme Court decision of 1819 that established the supremacy of federal over state authority by declaring that states could not tax federal institutions.

McKinley Tariff Act A Republican enactment of 1890 that sharply raised tariff rates to protect American manufacturers but thereby provoked a political backlash against the GOP.

Medicaid Supplementary medical insurance for the poor, financed through the federal government; program created in 1965.

Medicare Basic medical insurance for the elderly, financed through the federal government; program created in 1965.

Memorial Day Massacre A murderous attack on striking steelworkers and their families by Chicago police in 1937.

Mercantilism Economic system whereby the government intervenes in the economy for the purpose of increasing national wealth. Mercantilists advocated possession of colonies as places where the mother country could acquire raw materials not available at home.

Mestizo A person of mixed Spanish and Indian ancestry.

Mexican Cession of 1848 The ceding of New Mexico and Alta California to the United States by Mexico as a result of the U.S. victory in the **Mexican War**. *See also* **Treaty of Guadalupe Hidalgo**.

Mexican War War fought between the United States and Mexico from May 1846 to February 1848. *See also* **Treaty of Guadalupe Hidalgo; Mexican Cession of 1848**.

Middle Passage The voyage between West Africa and the New World slave colonies.

Midway, Battle of World War II naval and air battle in which the United States turned back a Japanese effort to seize Midway Island in June 1942 and inflicted severe damage on the Japanese navy.

Military Reconstruction Acts The first major legislation in the period known as **Congressional Reconstruction**. Passed in March 1867 over President Johnson's veto, these laws divided the ten remaining ex-Confederate states into five military districts each headed by a general who was charged to conduct voter registration drives among blacks and bar whites who had held office before the Civil War and who had supported the Confederacy. The remaining voters would elect a constitutional convention to write a new state constitution that guaranteed **universal manhood suffrage**. If a majority of voters ratified both the new constitution and the **Fourteenth Amendment**, their state would be readmitted into the Union.

Minute Men Special companies of militia formed in Massachusetts and elsewhere beginning in late 1744. These units were composed of men who were to be ready to assemble with their arms at a minute's notice.

Mission system Chain of missions established by Franciscan monks in the Spanish Southwest and California that forced Indians to convert to Catholicism and work as agricultural laborers.

Missouri Compromise Sectional compromise in Congress in 1820 that admitted Missouri to the Union as a slave state and Maine as a free state and prohibited slavery in the **Louisiana Purchase** territory above 36°30′ north latitude.

Model Cities Program Effort to target federal funds to upgrade public services and economic opportunity in specifically defined urban neighborhoods between 1966 and 1974.

Molasses Act Law passed by Parliament in 1733 that taxed sugar products from foreign sources in order to encourage British colonists to buy sugar and molasses only from the British West Indies.

Monmouth Court House, Battle of Last major Revolutionary War engagement between the main British and American forces in the North; occurred on June 28, 1778, in central New Jersey as the British withdrew from Philadelphia toward their headquarters at New York City. The Americans under General George Washington and the British under Sir Henry Clinton each suffered about 350 casualties.

Monroe Doctrine Declaration by President James Monroe in 1823 that the Western Hemisphere was to be closed off to further European colonization and that the United States would not interfere in the internal affairs of European nations.

Moore's Creek Bridge, Battle of Revolutionary War engagement that occurred on February 27, 1776, near Wilmington, North Carolina, when an American force of approximately one thousand militia clashed with about eighteen hundred **Loyalists**, most of them Highland Scots. The smashing American victory disrupted British plans for the **Loyalists** to link up with a large British expedition that sailed from Ireland to North Carolina during the winter of 1775–1776.

Mormon Church (Church of Jesus Christ of Latter-day Saints) Church founded in 1830 by Joseph Smith and based on the revelations in a sacred book he called the Book of Mormon.

Muckraking Journalism exposing economic, social, and political evils, so named by Theodore Roosevelt for its "raking the muck" of American society.

Mugwumps   Elitist and conservative reformers who favored **sound money** and limited government and opposed tariffs and the **spoils system**.

Muller* v. *Oregon   Supreme Court decision (1908) upholding a maximum-hour law for women workers; opened the way to an expansion of state regulation.

Multinational corporation   Firm with direct investments, branches, factories, and offices in a number of countries.

Nashville, Battle of   Union general George H. Thomas's destruction of the Confederacy's Army of Tennessee in December 1864 during the Civil War.

National Aeronautics and Space Administration (NASA)   Federal agency created in 1958 to manage American manned and unmanned space flights and exploration.

National American Woman Suffrage Association   The organization, formed in 1890, that coordinated the ultimately successful campaign to achieve women's right to vote.

National and Community Service Trust Act   Legislation in 1994 creating a pilot program for a domestic Peace Corps for young Americans.

National Association for the Advancement of Colored People (NAACP)   National interracial organization founded in 1910 and dedicated to restoring African-American political and social rights.

National Association of Colored Women   Group founded in 1896 as an umbrella organization for black women's clubs that worked to improve the lives of black women, especially in the rural South.

National Banking Act   Law passed in 1863 authorizing certain banks to issue bank notes backed by U.S. bonds and guaranteed by Washington. It brought order to a chaotic monetary system and raised the creditworthiness of the federal government.

National Black Convention   A prominent gathering of northern black leaders in 1853, called to protest the **Fugitive Slave Act**.

National Endowment for the Arts   Federal agency created in 1965 to fund research, public programs, and museum exhibits dealing with the performing arts, visual arts, and design arts.

National Endowment for the Humanities   Federal agency created in 1965 to fund research, publications, and museum exhibits dealing with history, literature, and related fields.

National Industrial Recovery Act (NIRA)   A 1933 law that created the National Recovery Administration and, in Section 7a, guaranteed workers the rights to organize unions and bargain collectively.

Nationalists   Group of leaders in the 1780s who spearheaded the drive to replace the **Articles of Confederation** with a stronger central government.

National Labor Relations Board (NLRB)   Federal board established in 1935 to enforce workers' rights to organize, supervise union elections, and oversee **collective bargaining**.

National Organization for Women (NOW)   Group organized in 1966 to expand civil rights for women.

National Origins Act   A 1924 law sharply restricting immigration on the basis of immigrants' national origins and discriminating against southern and eastern Europeans and Asians.

National Recovery Administration (NRA)   Federal agency established in 1933 to promote economic recovery by promulgating codes to control production, prices, and wages.

National Republican party   Short-lived political party opposed to Andrew Jackson that unsuccessfully ran John Quincy Adams for the presidency in 1828 and Henry Clay in 1832.

National Security Council (NSC)   The formal policymaking body for national defense and foreign relations, created in 1947 and consisting of the president, the secretary of defense, the secretary of state, and others appointed by the president.

National Security Council Paper 68 (NSC-68)   Policy statement that committed the United States to a military approach to the **Cold War**.

National War Labor Board   Government agency that supervised labor relations during World War I, guaranteeing union rights in exchange for industrial stability.

National Women's Party   Political organization formed in 1916 that campaigned aggressively first for **woman suffrage** and thereafter for the **Equal Rights Amendment**.

National Women's Political Caucus   Political organization formed in 1971 to help elect women to local, state, and federal offices.

Nativist   Favoring the interests and culture of native-born inhabitants over those of immigrants.

Nat Turner slave revolt   Uprising of slaves in Southampton County, Virginia, in the summer of 1831 led by Nat Turner that resulted in the death of fifty-five whites.

Naturalization Act of 1798   Law passed by Congress in 1798 that extended the residency requirement of alien residents for U.S. citizenship from five to fourteen years. One of the **Alien and Sedition Acts**.

Naturalization Act of 1870   Law passed by Congress in 1870 that limited citizenship to "white persons and persons of African descent."

Natural rights   Political philosophy that maintains that individuals have an inherent right, found in nature and preceding any government or written law, to life and liberty.

Navigation Act of 1651   First piece of mercantilist legislation passed to regulate colonial commerce; called for imperial trade to be conducted using English or colonial ships with mainly English crews.

Navigation Act of 1696   Law that closed loopholes in earlier mercantilist legislation and also created **vice-admiralty courts** in the colonies.

Nazi   Truncated form of the name of the National Socialist German Workers' party, led by Adolf Hitler, which ruled Germany from 1933 to 1945.

Neighborhood Union   Organization founded by Lugenia Burns Hope, a middle-class black woman in Atlanta in 1908 and modeled on similar efforts in the urban North, that provided playgrounds, a health center, and education for young urban blacks.

Neighborhood Youth Corps   Antipoverty program that recruited young people from low-income areas for community projects.

Neoconservative   Advocate of or participant in the revitalized conservative politics of the 1980s and 1990s, calling for a strong government role in defense and foreign policy and a limited role in social and economic policy.

Neoliberal   Advocate of or participant in the effort to reshape the **Democratic party** for the 1990s around a policy emphasizing economic growth and competitiveness in the world economy.

New Age   Term applied to a wide range of ideas and practices that seek to enhance individual potential and spiritual well-being outside the boundaries of traditional religion.

New Deal   The economic and political policies of the Roosevelt administration in the 1930s.

New England Non-Resistant Society   Pacifist organization founded by Garrisonian abolitionists in 1838 that was opposed to all authority resting on force.

New Federalism   President Richard Nixon's policy to shift responsibilities for government programs from the federal level to the states.

New Freedom   Woodrow Wilson's 1912 program for limited government intervention in the economy to restore competition by curtailing the restrictive influences of trusts and protective tariffs, thereby providing opportunities for individual achievement.

New Frontier   John F. Kennedy's domestic and foreign policy initiatives, designed to reinvigorate a sense of national purpose and energy.

New Harmony   Short-lived utopian community established in Indiana in 1825, based on the socialist ideas of Robert Owen, a wealthy Scottish manufacturer.

New immigrants   Immigrants from southern and eastern Europe, predominantly Catholic and Jewish and often unskilled and poorly educated, who entered the United States in increasing numbers after the 1880s.

New Jersey Plan   Proposal of the New Jersey delegation at the 1787 **Constitutional Convention** for a strengthened national government in which all states would have equal representation in a **unicameral legislature**.

New Lights   People who experienced conversion during the revivals of the **Great Awakening**.

New Nationalism   Theodore Roosevelt's 1912 program calling for a strong national government to foster, regulate, and protect business, industry, workers, and consumers.

New Orleans, Battle of   Decisive American **War of 1812** victory over British troops in January 1815 that ended any British hopes of gaining control of the lower Mississippi River Valley.

New Republicanism   Dwight Eisenhower's vision of the Republicans as a relatively moderate party of the political center.

New York Draft Riot   A mostly Irish-immigrant protest against conscription in New York City in July 1863 that escalated into class and racial warfare that had to be quelled by federal troops.

Niagara Movement   African-American group organized in 1905 to promote racial integration, civil and political rights, and equal access to economic opportunity.

Nineteenth Amendment   Constitutional revision that in 1920 established women citizens' right to vote.

Nisei   U.S. citizens born of immigrant Japanese parents.

Nonimportation   A tactical means of putting economic pressure on Britain by refusing to buy its exports to the colonies. Initiated in response to the taxes imposed by the **Sugar** and **Stamp Acts**, it was used again against the **Townshend duties** and the **Coercive Acts**. The nonimportation movement popularized resistance to British measures and deepened the commitment of many ordinary people to a larger American community.

Nonintercourse Act   Law passed by Congress in 1809 that prohibited American trade with Britain and France.

Nonpartisan League   A radical farmers' movement in the Great Plains states after 1915 that sought to restrain railroads, banks, elevators, and other major corporations.

North American Free Trade Agreement (NAFTA)   Agreement reached in 1993 by Canada, Mexico, and the United States to substantially reduce barriers to trade.

North Atlantic Treaty Organization (NATO)   Military alliance of the United States, Canada, and western European nations created in 1949 to protect Europe against possible Soviet aggression.

North Carolina Mutual Life Insurance Company   Insurance company founded in Durham, North Carolina, in 1898 that eventually became the largest black-owned business in the nation.

North Star, The   Antislavery newspaper established by Frederick Douglass in Rochester, New York, in 1847.

Northwest Ordinance of 1787   Legislation passed by Congress under the **Articles of Confederation** that prohibited slavery in the Northwest Territories and provided the model for the incorporation of future territories into the Union as coequal states.

Nuclear freeze   Proposal that the United States and the Soviet Union should stop further production and deployment of nuclear weapons.

Nullification   A constitutional doctrine holding that a state has a legal right to declare a national law null and void within its borders.

Nullification crisis   Sectional crisis in the early 1830s in which a **states' rights** party in South Carolina attempted to nullify federal law.

Office of Economic Opportunity (OEO)   Federal agency that coordinated many programs of the **War on Poverty** between 1964 and 1975.

Office of Price Administration (OPA)   Federal agency during World War II that fixed price ceilings on all commodities, controlled rents in defense areas, and rationed scare goods such as sugar, fuel, and automobile tires.

Office of Scientific Research and Development   Federal agency established in 1941 to mobilize American science on behalf of national defense.

Old Stock   European ethnic groups prominent in the eighteenth-century United States, especially English, Dutch, German, and Scots-Irish.

Olive Branch Petition   Petition, written largely by John Dickinson and adopted by the Second Continental Congress on July 5, 1775, as a last effort of peace that avowed America's loyalty to George III and requested that he protect them from further aggressions. Congress continued military preparations, and the king never responded to the petition.

Omaha Platform   The 1892 platform of the **Populist party** repudiating laissez-faire and demanding economic and political reforms to aid distressed farmers and workers.

One Hundred Slain, Battle of   An 1866 Sioux defeat of the U.S. Army on the Bozeman Trail that whites call the Fetterman Massacre.

Oneida Community   Utopian community established in upstate New York in 1848 by John Humphrey Noyes and his followers.

Open Door   American policy of seeking equal trade and investment opportunities in foreign nations or regions.

Open shop   Factory or business employing workers whether or not they are union members; in practice, such a business usually refuses to hire union members and follows antiunion policies.

Operation OVERLORD   U.S. and British invasion of France in June 1944 during World War II.

Operation TORCH   U.S. and British landings in French North Africa in November 1942 during World War II.

Order of the Heroes of America   Loosely knit group of pro-Unionists in the Piedmont and mountain sections of North Carolina who demonstrated for peace and sometimes violently opposed Confederate authorities during the Civil War.

Orders in Council   Decrees of the British ministry setting up a naval blockade of Europe and controls over neutral shipping during the Napoleonic Wars.

Ordinance of 1784   Act passed but never put into effect by the Congress under the **Articles of Confederation** that embodied the proposals of Thomas Jefferson for dividing the public domain into states and immediately granting settlers the right of self-government.

Oregon Trail Overland trail of more than 2,000 miles that carried American settlers from the Midwest to new settlements in Oregon, California, and Utah.

Organization of Petroleum Exporting Countries (OPEC) Cartel of oil-producing nations in Asia, Africa, and Latin America that gained substantial power over the world economy in the mid- to late 1970s by controlling the production and price of oil.

Ostend Manifesto Message sent by U.S. envoys to President Franklin Pierce from Ostend, Belgium, in 1854, stating that the United States had a "divine right" to wrest Cuba from Spain.

Paleo-Indians The first human inhabitants of the Americas, who crossed the land bridge from Asia perhaps as long as fifty thousand years ago and survived by hunting large mammals.

Pan American Union International organization originally established as the Commercial Bureau of American Republics by Secretary of State James Blaine's first Pan-American Conference in 1889 to promote cooperation among nations of the Western Hemisphere through commercial and diplomatic negotiations.

Pan-Indian resistance movement Movement calling for the political and cultural unification of Indian tribes in the late eighteenth and early nineteenth centuries.

Panic of 1819 A severe tightening of credit set off by a fall in cotton prices and more restrictive financial policies by the **Second Bank of the United States**.

Panic of 1837 A sharp contraction in credit and currency triggered by a fall in cotton prices.

Panic of 1857 Banking crisis that caused a credit crunch in the North; it was less severe in the South, where high cotton prices spurred a quick recovery.

Paris, Treaty of The 1898 treaty that ended the **Spanish-American War** and transferred the Spanish colonies of Puerto Rico, Guam, and the Philippines to the United States while recognizing the independence of Cuba.

Paris, Treaty of Treaty concluded in 1763 to end the **French and Indian War (Seven Years' War)**. Its principal feature was France's loss of nearly all of its North American empire, retaining only its West Indian possessions.

Parson's Cause Series of developments (1758–1763) that began when the Virginia legislature modified the salaries of Anglican clergymen, who complained to the crown and sued to recover damages. British authorities responded by imposing additional restrictions on the legislature. Virginians, who saw this as a threat, reacted by strongly reasserting local autonomy.

Party caucus A meeting of party leaders to decide questions of policy or to select candidates running for office.

Patent medicines Trademarked concoctions, often of little medical value, available for purchase without a physician's prescription.

Patriarchal Descriptive of societies in which fathers are the heads of clans or families, women and children are legally dependent on husbands and fathers, and family descent and inheritance follow the male line.

Patrilineal Descriptive of societies in which family descent is traced through the father's line.

Patriot Term usually used to refer to Americans during the Revolutionary period whose resistance to British measures included a willingness to resort to arms and, ultimately, a commitment to American independence. However, many **Loyalists** were also patriotic in their allegiance to Great Britain.

Patronage The power to appoint individuals to governmental positions.

Patroonship The grant of a vast estate of land in New Netherlands, offered by Dutch authorities as a way to attract settlers. Very few patroonships were actually created.

Paxton Boys Frontiersmen from Paxton township (near modern Harrisburg, Pennsylvania) who responded in 1763 to **Pontiac's Rebellion** by massacring nearby Indians; later they marched toward Philadelphia to demand greater military protection for the frontiers.

Peace of Paris Treaties signed in 1783 by Great Britain, the United States, France, Spain, and the Netherlands that ended the Revolutionary War. First in a preliminary agreement and then in the final treaty with the United States, Britain recognized the independence of the United States, agreed that the Mississippi River would be its western boundary, and permitted it to fish in some Canadian waters. Prewar debts owed by the inhabitants of one country to those of the other were to remain collectible, and Congress was to urge the states to return property confiscated from **Loyalists**. British troops were to evacuate United States territory without removing slaves or other property. In a separate agreement, Britain relinquished its claim to East and West Florida to Spain.

Pearl Harbor Site of a United States naval base in Hawaii attacked from Japanese aircraft carriers on December 7, 1941, during World War II.

Pendleton Civil Service Act A law of 1883 that reformed the **spoils system** by prohibiting government workers from making political contributions and creating the Civil Service Commission to oversee their appointment on the basis of merit rather than politics.

Peninsula Campaign Civil War campaign launched by Union general George B. McClellan in the spring of 1862 with Richmond as its objective; it failed despite superior numbers of Federal troops.

Pentagon Papers Classified Defense Department documents on the history of the United States' involvement in Vietnam, prepared in 1968 and leaked to the press in 1971.

People's party See **Populist party**.

Pequot War Conflict between English settlers (who had Narragansett and Mohegan allies) and Pequot Indians over control of land and trade in eastern Connecticut. The Pequots were nearly destroyed in a set of bloody confrontations, including a deadly English attack on a Mystic River village in May 1637.

Perestroika Russian for "restructuring," applied to Mikhail Gorbachev's efforts to make the Soviet economic and political systems more modern, flexible, and innovative.

Petersburg During the Civil War, a key Confederate rail and supply center that guarded the Confederate capital of Richmond 30 miles to the north; besieged by Union forces from June 1864 to March 1865.

Pietists Protestants who stress a religion of the heart and the spirit of Christian living.

Pilgrims Settlers of Plymouth Colony, who viewed themselves as spiritual wanderers.

Pinckney's Treaty Treaty with Spain in 1795 in which Spain recognized the 31st parallel as the boundary between the United States and Spanish Florida and opened the Mississippi River through the port of New Orleans to American shipping.

Platt Amendment A stipulation the United States had inserted into the Cuban constitution in 1901 restricting Cuban autonomy and authorizing U.S. intervention and naval bases.

Plattsburg, Battle of American naval victory on Lake Champlain in September 1814 in the **War of 1812** that thwarted a British invasion from Canada.

Plessy* v. *Ferguson The 1896 case in which the U.S. Supreme Court ruled that providing "separate but equal" facilities for whites and blacks did not violate the **Constitution**.

Plymouth Company One of two **joint-stock companies** chartered in 1606 to establish English colonies in America. Composed of merchants from England's western ports, the company organized the founding of Plymouth Colony in 1620.

Pogroms Government-directed attacks against Jewish citizens, property, and villages in tsarist Russia beginning in the 1880s; a primary reason for Russian Jewish migration to the United States.

Poll tax A tax imposed on voters as a requirement for voting. Most southern states imposed poll taxes after 1900 as a way to disfranchise blacks; the measures also restricted the white vote.

Pontiac's Rebellion Indian uprising (1763–1766) led by Pontiac of the Ottawas and Neolin of the Delawares. Fearful of their fate at the hands of the British after the French had been driven out of North America, the Indian nations of the Ohio River Valley and the Great Lakes area united to oust the British from the Ohio-Mississippi Valley. They failed and were forced to make peace in 1766.

Popular sovereignty The notion that territorial residents should have the right to decide whether they wanted slavery.

Populist party A major third party of the 1890s, also known as the **People's party**. Formed on the basis of the **Southern Farmers' Alliance** and other reform organizations, it mounted electoral challenges against the Democrats in the South and the Republicans in the West.

Port Huron Statement Founding document of **Students for a Democratic Society**, proclaiming an idealistic vision of grass-roots democracy.

Potsdam Declaration Statement issued by the United States during a meeting of U.S. President Harry Truman, British Prime Minister Winston Churchill, and Soviet Premier Joseph Stalin held at Potsdam, near Berlin, in July 1945 to plan the defeat of Japan and the future of eastern Europe and Germany. In it, the United States declared its intention to democratize the Japanese political system and reintroduce Japan into the international community and gave Japan an opening for surrender.

Praying towns Villages established in Massachusetts for Indian converts to Christianity. The inhabitants were expected to follow an English way of life as well as the **Puritan** religion.

Predestination The belief that God decided at the moment of Creation which humans would achieve salvation.

Preparedness Military buildup in preparation for possible U.S. participation in World War I.

Preservation Protecting forests, land, and other features of the natural environment from development or destruction, often for aesthetic appreciation.

Presidio A military post established by the Spanish in the Southwest.

Princeton, Battle of Revolutionary War battle fought on January 3, 1777. Eluding the main British forces under Cornwallis, General Washington attacked a British column near Princeton, New Jersey, inflicting heavy losses before withdrawing into winter quarters not far away at Morristown. The battles of **Trenton** and Princeton greatly improved **Patriot** morale.

Proclamation Line Boundary, decreed as part of the **Proclamation of 1763**, that limited British settlements to the eastern side of the Appalachian Mountains, thereby threatening colonial expansionists and causing resentment. It proved unenforceable.

Proclamation of 1763 Royal proclamation setting the boundary known as the **Proclamation Line**.

Progressive Era The period of the twentieth century before World War I when many groups sought to reshape the nation's government and society in response to the pressures of industrialization and urbanization.

Prohibition A ban on the production, sale, and consumption of liquor, achieved temporarily through state laws and the Eighteenth Amendment.

Prohibition party A venerable third party still in existence that has persistently campaigned for the abolition of alcohol but has also introduced many important reform ideas into American politics.

Proprietary colony A colony created when the English monarch granted a huge tract of land to an individual or group of individuals, who became "lords proprietor." Many lords proprietor had distinct social visions for their colonies, but these plans were hardly ever implemented. Examples of proprietary colonies are Maryland, Carolina, New York (after it was seized from the Dutch), and Pennsylvania.

Protective legislation Measures designed to protect women from labor exploitation that also served to narrow their employment opportunities.

Protective tariff A tax on imported goods specifically intended to raise their price high enough to protect domestic producers of those goods from foreign competition.

Provincial congress An extralegal, Revolutionary representative body that conducted government and waged the Revolution at the state level in the period between the breakdown of royal authority and the establishment of regular legislatures under new state constitutions. Many members of these congresses had been members of the old colonial assemblies; the Massachusetts **General Court** and the Virginia **House of Burgesses**, in fact, transformed themselves into provincial congresses or conventions. (The terms were used interchangeably at first.)

Public Utility Holding Company Act of 1935 Law giving the **Securities and Exchange Commission** extensive regulatory powers over public utility companies.

Public Works Administration (PWA) Federal agency under Harold Ickes that provided work relief by building schools, hospitals, roads, and other valuable projects during the 1930s.

Pueblo Revolt Rebellion in 1680 of Pueblo Indians in New Mexico against their Spanish overlords, sparked by religious conflict and excessive Spanish demands for tribute.

Pullman strike Violent 1894 worker protest against wage cuts at the Pullman Palace Sleeping Car Company outside Chicago.

Puritan An individual who believed that Queen Elizabeth's reforms of the Church of England had not gone far enough in improving the church, particularly in ensuring that church members were among the saved. Puritans led the settlement of Massachusetts Bay Colony.

Put-in-Bay, Battle of American naval victory on Lake Erie in September 1813 in the **War of 1812** that denied the British strategic control over the Great Lakes.

Putting-out system System of manufacturing in which merchants furnished households with raw materials for processing by family members.

Quakers Members of the Society of Friends, a radical religious group that arose in the mid-seventeenth century. Quakers rejected formal theology and an educated ministry, focusing instead on the importance of the "Inner Light," or Holy Spirit that dwelt within them. Quakers were important in the founding of Pennsylvania.

Quartering Acts   Acts of Parliament requiring colonial legislatures to provide supplies and quarters for the troops stationed in America. Americans considered this taxation in disguise and objected. None of these acts passed during the pre-Revolutionary controversy required that soldiers be quartered in an occupied house without the owner's consent.

Quasi-War   Undeclared naval war of 1797 to 1800 between the United States and France.

Quebec Act   Law passed by Parliament in 1774 that provided an appointed government for Canada, enlarged the boundaries of Quebec southward to the Ohio River, and confirmed the privileges of the Catholic Church. Alarmed Americans termed this act and the **Coercive Acts** the **Intolerable Acts**.

Quebec, Siege of   An attempt during the Revolutionary War by American forces under Richard Montgomery and Benedict Arnold to capture Quebec City during the winter of 1775–1776. In an abortive attack on the city on December 31, 1775, Arnold was wounded and Montgomery killed. The siege failed, and Canada remained in British hands, serving as a base for later British expeditions down the Hudson River Valley.

Queen Anne's War   American phase (1702–1713) of Europe's **War of the Spanish Succession**. At its conclusion, England gained Nova Scotia.

Queenston Height, Battle of   Major defeat in October 1812 for an American army attempting to invade Canada along the Niagara frontier during the **War of 1812**.

Quiet Period   The apparently calm years (1770–1773) between Britain's repeal of most of the **Townshend duties** and the **Boston Tea Party**. No general grievances against Britain united Americans during this period, though many localized disputes continued.

Radical Republicans   A shifting group of Republican congressmen, usually a substantial minority, who favored the abolition of slavery from the beginning of the Civil War and later advocated harsh treatment of the defeated South.

Railroad Administration   Federal agency that operated and modernized the nation's railways to improve transportation related to the World War I war effort.

Real Whig ideology   *See* **Country (Real Whig) ideology**.

Recall   The process of removing an official from office by popular vote, usually after using petitions to call for such a vote.

Reconquista   The long struggle (ending in 1492) during which Spanish Christians reconquered the Iberian peninsula from Muslim occupiers, who first invaded in the eighth century.

Reconstruction   The era (1865–1877) when the resolution of two major issues—the status of the former slaves and the terms of the Confederate states' readmission into the Union—dominated political debate.

Reconstruction Finance Corporation (RFC)   Federal agency established in 1932 to provide funds to financial institutions to save them from bankruptcy.

Red Scare   Post–World War I public hysteria over **Bolshevik** influence in the United States directed against labor activism, radical dissenters, and some ethnic groups.

Red-baiting   Accusing a political opponent of sympathizing with or being "soft on" Communism.

Redeemers   Southern Democrats who wrested control of governments in the former Confederacy, often through electoral fraud and violence, from Republicans beginning in 1870.

Redemptioners   Similar to **indentured servants**, except that redemptioners signed labor contracts in America rather than in Europe, as

indentured servants did. Shipmasters sold redemptioners into servitude to recoup the cost of their passage if they could not pay the fare upon their arrival.

Redlining   Refusing mortgage loans and insurance to properties in designated inner-city neighborhoods.

Referendum   Submission of a law, proposed or already in effect, to a direct popular vote for approval or rejection.

Reformation   Sixteenth-century movement to reform the Catholic Church that began with Martin Luther's critique of church practices in 1517. The Reformation ultimately led to the founding of a number of new Protestant Christian religious groups.

Regulators   Vigilante groups active in the 1760s and 1770s in the western parts of North and South Carolina. The South Carolina Regulators attempted to rid the area of outlaws; the North Carolina Regulators sought to protect themselves against excessively high taxes and court costs. In both cases, westerners lacked sufficient representation in the legislature to obtain immediate redress of their grievances. The South Carolina government eventually made concessions; the North Carolina government suppressed its Regulator movement by force.

Renaissance   Major cultural movement in Europe during the fifteenth and sixteenth centuries that began in the city-states of Italy and spread to other parts of the continent. Sharing a "rebirth" of interest in the classical civilizations of ancient Greece and Rome, many artists of the period produced notable works in painting, sculpture, architecture, writing, and music.

Repartimiento   In the Spanish colonies, the assignment of Indian workers to labor on public works projects.

Republicanism   A complex, changing body of ideas, values, and assumptions, closely related to **country ideology**, that influenced American political behavior during the eighteenth and nineteenth centuries. Derived from the political ideas of classical antiquity, **Renaissance** Europe, and early modern England, republicanism held that self-government by the citizens of a country, or their representatives, provided a more reliable foundation for the good society and individual freedom than rule by kings. The benefits of monarchy depended on the variable abilities of monarchs; the character of republican government depended on the virtue of the people. Republicanism therefore helped give the American Revolution a moral dimension. But the nature of republican virtue and the conditions favorable to it became sources of debate that influenced the writing of the state and federal constitutions as well as the development of political parties.

Republican party   Party that emerged in the 1850s in the aftermath of the bitter controversy over the **Kansas-Nebraska Act**, consisting of former **Whigs**, some northern Democrats, and many **Know-Nothings**.

Republican party (Jeffersonian)   Party headed by Thomas Jefferson that formed in opposition to the financial and diplomatic policies of the **Federalist party**; favored limiting the powers of the national government and placing the interests of farmers and planters over those of financial and commercial groups; supported the cause of the French Revolution.

Rescate   Procedure by which Spanish colonists would pay ransom to free Indians captured by rival natives. The rescued Indians then became workers in Spanish households.

Reservationists   Group of U.S. senators favoring approval of the **Treaty of Versailles**, the peace agreement after World War I, after amending it to incorporate their reservations.

Resettlement Administration   Federal agency established in 1935 to provide financial assistance and social services to displaced tenants and farm workers.

Revenue Act of 1935   Law establishing a more progressive tax system by setting graduated taxes on corporate income and increasing the top tax rates on personal income.

Rhode Island system   During the industrialization of the early nineteenth century, the recruitment of entire families for employment in a factory.

Roe v. Wade   U.S. Supreme Court decision in 1973 that disallowed state laws prohibiting abortion during the first three months (trimester) of pregnancy and established guidelines for abortion in the second and third trimesters.

Romer v. Evans   U.S. Supreme Court decision in 1996 that overturned an antigay measure adopted in Colorado.

Roosevelt Corollary   President Theodore Roosevelt's policy asserting U.S. authority to intervene in the affairs of Latin American nations; an expansion of the **Monroe Doctrine**.

Rural Electrification Administration (REA)   Federal agency that transformed American rural life by making electricity available in areas that private companies had refused to service.

Rural free delivery (RFD)   Government delivery of mail directly to farmsteads rather than merely to village post offices to which rural residents would then have to travel to retrieve their mail.

Rush-Bagot Agreement   Treaty of 1817 between the United States and Britain that effectively demilitarized the Great Lakes by sharply limiting the number of ships each power could station on them.

Rustbelt   The states of the Midwest and Northeast affected adversely by the decline of manufacturing in the 1970s and 1980s, named for the image of machinery rusting in abandoned factories.

Sabbatarian movement   *See* **General Union for Promoting the Observance of the Christian Sabbath**.

"Sack of Lawrence"   Vandalism and arson committed by a group of proslavery men in Lawrence, the free-state capital of Kansas Territory.

Sagebrush Rebellion   Political movement in the western states in the early 1980s that called for easing of regulations on the economic use of federal lands and the transfer of some or all of those lands to state ownership.

Saint   A **Puritan** who had experienced religious conversion and had been admitted to membership in a **Puritan** church.

SALT   Strategic Arms Limitation Treaty signed in 1972 by the United States and the Soviet Union to slow the nuclear arms race.

San Jacinto, Battle of   Battle fought in eastern Texas on April 21, 1836, in which Texas troops under General Sam Houston overwhelmed a Mexican army and forced its commander, General Antonio López de Santa Anna, to recognize the independence of Texas.

San Lorenzo, Treaty of   *See* **Pinckney's Treaty**.

Sand Creek Massacre   The near annihilation in 1864 of Black Kettle's Cheyenne band by Colorado troops under Colonel John Chivington's orders to "kill and scalp all, big and little."

Santa Fe Ring   A group of lawyers and land speculators who dominated New Mexico Territory in the late nineteenth century and amassed great wealth through political corruption and financial chicanery.

Santa Fe Trail   Overland trail across the Southern Plains from St. Louis to New Mexico that funneled American traders and goods to Spanish-speaking settlements in the Southwest.

Saratoga, Battle of   Two engagements (September 19 and October 7, 1777) during the Revolutionary War in the vicinity of Saratoga, New York, that resulted in the surrender on October 17 of 5,700 troops commanded by General John Burgoyne to American forces under General Horatio Gates. This stunning American victory contributed to the French decision to sign an alliance with the United States on February 6, 1778.

Savannah, Battles of   Series of Revolutionary War encounters that began when British forces routed American militia and occupied Savannah on December 29, 1778. A French fleet under the Comte d'Estaing and American forces under General Benjamin Lincoln then tried to recapture the city by siege, beginning on September 3, 1779, but an assault on October 9 failed, with heavy casualties. D'Estaing, wounded, departed with this fleet on October 28, leaving the way open for the British attack on **Charleston**, South Carolina.

Scalawags   Southern whites, mainly small landowning farmers and well-off merchants and planters, who supported the southern **Republican party** during **Reconstruction** for diverse reasons; a disparaging term.

Search and destroy   U.S. military tactic in South Vietnam, using small detachments to locate enemy units and then massive air, artillery, and ground forces to destroy them.

Second Bank of the United States   A national bank chartered by Congress in 1816 with extensive regulatory powers over currency and credit. *See also* **First Bank of the United States**.

Second Great Awakening   Series of religious revivals in the first half of the nineteenth century characterized by great emotionalism in large public meetings.

Second New Deal   The policies adopted by the Roosevelt administration from 1935 to 1937 that emphasized social and economic reform.

Second party system   The national two-party competition between **Democrats** and **Whigs** from the 1830s through the early 1850s.

Second Treaty of Fort Laramie   The treaty acknowledging U.S. defeat in the Great Sioux War in 1868 and supposedly guaranteeing the Sioux perpetual land and hunting rights in South Dakota, Wyoming, and Montana.

Second Vatican Council   A 1965 meeting of the leadership of the Roman Catholic Church that liberalized many church practices.

Secret Six   Group of prominent New England abolitionists who financially supported John Brown's scheme to attack the federal arsenal at Harpers Ferry, Virginia, and foment a slave rebellion in the South.

Securities and Exchange Commission (SEC)   Federal agency with authority to regulate trading practices in stocks and bonds.

Sedition Act   Law passed by Congress in 1798 that provided fines and imprisonment for anyone found guilty of saying or writing anything false or malicious about the government or one of its officers. One of the **Alien and Sedition Acts**.

Sedition Act of 1918   Broad law restricting criticism of America's involvement in World War I or its government, flag, military, taxes, or officials.

Segregation   A system of racial control that separated the races, initially by custom but increasingly by law during and after **Reconstruction**.

Selective Service Act of 1917   The law establishing the military draft for World War I.

Selective Service System   Federal agency that coordinated military conscription before and during the Vietnam War.

Selectmen   Group of men (usually seven) selected annually to run local affairs in a New England town.

Self-determination   The right of a people or nation to decide on its own political allegiance or form of government without external influence.

Seneca Falls Convention   The first convention for women's equality in legal rights, held in upstate New York in 1848. *See also* **Declaration of Sentiments**.

Separatist   Member of an offshoot branch of Puritanism. Separatists believed that the Church of England was too corrupt to be reformed and hence were convinced that they must "separate" from it to save their souls. Separatists helped found Plymouth Colony.

Settlement house   A multipurpose structure in a poor neighborhood that offered social welfare, educational, and homemaking services to the poor or immigrants; usually under private auspices and directed by middle-class women.

Seven Days' Battles   Weeklong series of fierce engagements in June and July 1862 along Virginia's peninsula that resulted in a Federal retreat during the Civil War.

Seven Years' War   Conflict (1756–1763) that pitted France, Austria, and Russia against England and Prussia; in 1762, Spain entered the war on France's side. Often called the first "world war" because fighting occurred in Europe, India, the Philippines, and North America. The American phase was known as the **French and Indian War**.

Seventeenth Amendment   Constitutional change that in 1913 established the direct popular election of U.S. senators.

Shakers   The followers of Mother Ann Lee, who preached a religion of strict celibacy and communal living.

Sharecropping   Labor system that evolved during and after **Reconstruction** whereby landowners furnished laborers with a house, farm animals, and tools and advanced credit in exchange for a share of the laborers' crop.

Shays's Rebellion   An armed movement of debt-ridden farmers in western Massachusetts in the winter of 1786–1787. The rebellion shut down courts and created a crisis atmosphere, strengthening the case of **nationalists** that a stronger central government was needed to maintain civil order in the states.

Sheppard-Towner Maternity and Infancy Act of 1921   The first federal social welfare law; funded infant and maternity health care programs in local hospitals.

Sherman Antitrust Act   The first federal antitrust measure, passed in 1890; sought to promote economic competition by prohibiting business combinations in restraint of trade or commerce.

Sherman Silver Purchase Act   An 1890 law that required the government to increase silver purchases sharply, but other provisions restricted its inflationary effect; its repeal in 1894 caused a political uproar.

Sherman's March   Three-month army march during the Civil War in late 1864 led by Union general William T. Sherman from Atlanta to Savannah and the sea, destroying property as well as the morale of Georgians.

Shiloh Church   Site of a Union victory along the Tennessee-Mississippi border in April 1862 that enabled Federal forces to capture Corinth, Mississippi, an important rail junction, during the Civil War.

Silicon Valley   The region of California between San Jose and San Francisco that holds the nation's greatest concentration of electronics firms.

Sixteenth Amendment   Constitutional revision that in 1913 authorized a federal income tax.

Slaughterhouse **cases**   Group of cases resulting in one sweeping decision by the U.S. Supreme Court in 1873 that contradicted the intent of the **Fourteenth Amendment** by decreeing that most citizenship rights remained under state, not federal, control.

Slave codes   Sometimes known as "black codes." A series of laws passed mainly in the southern colonies in the late seventeenth and early eighteenth centuries to define the status of slaves and codify the denial of basic civil rights to them. Also, after American independence and before the Civil War, state laws in the South defining slaves as property and specifying the legal powers of masters over slaves.

Slave Power   A key concept in abolitionist and northern antislavery propaganda that depicted southern slaveholders as the driving force in a political conspiracy to promote slavery at the expense of white liberties.

Slum   A poor neighborhood with many dwellings in bad repair.

Social Darwinism   The application of Charles Darwin's theory of biological evolution to society, holding that the fittest and the wealthiest survive, the weak and the poor perish, and government action is unable to alter this "natural" and beneficial process.

Social Gospel movement   An effort by leading Protestants to apply religious ethics to industrial conditions and thereby alleviate poverty, **slums**, and labor exploitation.

Socialism   A social order based on government ownership of industry and worker control over corporations as a way to prevent worker exploitation.

Socialist Party of America   Political party formed in 1901 with a strong representation from immigrants; provided a political outlet for worker grievances but fared poorly beyond a few local elections in industrial areas.

Social Security Act   A 1935 law that initiated a federal social insurance system with unemployment compensation, old-age pensions, and aid for dependent mothers and children and the blind.

Society for the Relief of Poor Widows with Small Children   Female benevolent organization founded in New York City in 1797 to assist widows and orphans.

Soil Conservation Service   A branch of the Department of Agriculture created in 1935 to undertake **conservation** projects on individual farms as well as on a broader national basis.

Solid South   The one-party (Democratic) political system that dominated the South from the 1890s to the 1950s.

Sons of Liberty   Secret organizations in the colonies formed to oppose the **Stamp Act**. From 1765 until independence, they spoke, wrote, and demonstrated against British measures. Their actions often intimidated stamp distributors and British supporters in the colonies.

Sound money   Misleading slogan that referred to a conservative policy of restricting the money supply and adhering to the gold standard.

Southeast Asia Treaty Organization (SEATO)   Mutual defense alliance signed in 1954 by the United States, Britain, France, Thailand, Pakistan, the Philippines, Australia, and New Zealand.

Southern Christian Leadership Conference (SCLC)   Black civil rights organization founded in 1957 by Martin Luther King Jr. and other clergy.

Southern Farmers' Alliance   The largest of several organizations that formed in the post-Reconstruction South to advance the interests of beleaguered small farmers.

Southern Homestead Act   Largely unsuccessful law passed in 1866 that gave blacks preferential access to public lands in five southern states.

Southern Manifesto   A document signed by 101 members of Congress from southern states in 1956 that argued that the Supreme Court's decision in *Brown* v. *Board of Education of Topeka* itself contradicted the **Constitution**.

Southwest Ordinance of 1790   Legislation passed by Congress that set up a government with no prohibition on slavery in U.S. territory south of the Ohio River.

Spanish-American War   Brief 1898 conflict in which the United States defeated Spanish forces in Cuba and the Philippines and forced Spain to relinquish control over Cuba and cede the Philippines, Puerto Rico, and other territories to the United States.

Specie Circular   Proclamation issued by President Andrew Jackson in 1836 stipulating that only gold or silver could be used as payment for public land.

Sphere of influence   A region dominated and controlled by an outside power.

Spoils system   The awarding of government jobs to party loyalists.

Spotsylvania, Battle of   Another in a series of dogged attacks in Virginia by Union general Ulysses S. Grant and entrenched Confederate positions during May 1864. Despite high casualties and mounting public criticism, Grant continued to push on until the disaster at **Cold Harbor** later in the month caused him to reconsider his tactics.

Squatters   Settlers who moved onto public land before it had been surveyed for sale.

Stagflation   Economic condition of the 1970s in which price inflation accompanied slow economic growth.

Stalingrad, Battle of   World War II battle of attrition between German and Soviet armies in Stalingrad, on the Volga River, August 1942–February 1943, ending with the surrender of the encircled German army.

Stamp Act   Law passed by Parliament in 1765 to raise revenue in America by requiring taxed, stamped paper for legal documents, publications, and playing cards. Americans opposed it as "taxation without representation" and prevented its enforcement. Parliament repealed it a year after its enactment.

Stamp Act Congress   October 1765 meeting of delegates sent by nine colonies, held in New York City, that adopted the **Declaration of Rights and Grievances** and petitioned against the **Stamp Act**.

States' rights   Favoring the rights of individual states over rights claimed by the national government.

Stono Rebellion   Uprising in 1739 of South Carolina slaves against whites; inspired in part by Spanish officials' promise of freedom for American slaves who escaped to Florida.

Strategic Arms Reduction Treaty (START)   Agreement between the United States and the Soviet Union in 1991 to substantially reduce the number of long-range nuclear weapons held by each side.

Strategic Defense Initiative (SDI)   President Reagan's program, announced in 1983, to defend the United States against nuclear missile attack with untested weapons systems and sophisticated technologies; also known as "Star Wars."

Strict constructionist   Person who holds that the national government has only those powers specifically delegated to it in the **Constitution**.

Student Nonviolent Coordinating Committee (SNCC)   Black civil rights organization founded in 1960 and drawing heavily on younger activists and college students.

Students for a Democratic Society (SDS)   The leading student organization of the New Left of the early and mid-1960s.

Subtreasury plan   A program promoted by the **Southern Farmers' Alliance** in response to low cotton prices and tight credit. Farmers would store their crop in a warehouse (or "subtreasury") until prices

rose, in the meantime borrowing up to 80 percent of the value of the stored crops from the government at a low interest rate.

Suffolk Resolves   Militant resolves adopted in September 1774 in response to the **Coercive Acts** by representatives from the towns in Suffolk County, Massachusetts, including Boston. They termed the **Coercive Acts** unconstitutional, advised the people to arm, and called for economic sanctions against Britain. The **First Continental Congress** endorsed these resolves.

Suffrage   The right to vote in a political election.

Sugar Act   *See* **American Revenue Act**.

Sunbelt   The states of the American South and Southwest.

Superfund   Federal fund devoted to the cleanup of the nation's most severely contaminated industrial and toxic waste sites.

***Sussex* Pledge**   Germany's pledge during World War I not to sink merchant ships without warning, on the condition that Britain also observe recognized rules of international law.

Swann* v. *Charlotte-Mecklenburg Board of Education   U.S. Supreme Court decision in 1971 that upheld cross-city busing to achieve the racial integration of public schools.

Sweatshops   Small, poorly ventilated shops or apartments crammed with workers, often family members, who pieced together garments.

Taft-Hartley Act   Federal legislation of 1947 that substantially limited the tools available to labor unions in labor-management disputes.

Tallmadge Amendment   Proposed amendment to the Missouri statehood bill in 1819 that mandated the gradual end of slavery in Missouri.

Tammany Hall   New York City's **Democratic party** organization, dating from well before the Civil War, that evolved into a powerful political machine after 1860, using **patronage** and bribes to maintain control of the city administration.

Taos Revolt   Uprising of Pueblo Indians in New Mexico that broke out in January 1847 over the imposition of American rule during the **Mexican War**; the revolt was crushed within a few weeks.

Tariff Act of 1798   Law placing a duty of 5 percent on most imported goods, designed primarily to generate revenue and not to protect American goods from foreign competition.

Tariff of 1816   The first openly protective tariff passed by Congress.

Tea Act of 1773   Act of Parliament that permitted the East India Company to sell tea through agents in America without paying the duty customarily collected in Britain, thus reducing the retail price. Americans, who saw the act as an attempt to induce them to pay the Townshend duty still imposed in the colonies, resisted this act through the **Boston Tea Party** and other measures.

Teapot Dome scandal   A scandal of the 1920s that sent the secretary of the interior to prison for taking bribes to lease naval oil reserves to private companies.

Tejano   A person of Spanish or Mexican descent born in Texas.

Teller Amendment   A congressional resolution adopted in 1898 renouncing any American intention to annex Cuba.

Temperance   Reform movement originating in the 1820s that sought to eliminate the consumption of alcohol.

Ten Percent Plan   Plan devised by President Lincoln in 1863 as a method for readmitting the seceding states to the Union; required 10 percent of a state's prewar voters to swear allegiance to the Union and a new state constitution that banned slavery. Many congressional Republicans considered this standard too thin to support a general reconstruction of the Union and responded with the **Wade-Davis Bill**.

Tenement Four- to six-story residential dwelling, once common in New York and certain other cities, built on a tiny lot without regard to providing ventilation or light.

Tennessee Valley Authority (TVA) Federal regional planning agency established to promote **conservation**, produce electric power, and encourage economic development in seven southern states.

Tenure of Office Act Law Congress passed in 1867 prohibiting the president from removing certain officeholders without the Senate's consent; President Andrew Johnson's defiance of the act led to an **impeachment** trial in the Senate that narrowly failed to remove him from office.

Termination Federal policy of withdrawing official recognition from American Indian tribes and dividing tribal assets among the tribe's members.

Thames, Battle of the American victory in October 1813 over combined British and Indian forces in southern Ontario during the **War of 1812.**

Third International International organization of Communist parties created in 1919 under **Bolshevik** control.

Third world Nations that were aligned with neither the Communist bloc (the "second world") nor the West (the "first world").

Thirteenth Amendment Constitutional amendment ratified in 1865 that freed all slaves throughout the United States.

Tippecanoe, Battle of American victory in November 1811 over Shawnee Indians at Prophetstown in the Indiana Territory that provoked Indians into warfare along the western frontier.

Tonnage Act of 1789 Duty levied on the tonnage of incoming ships to U.S. ports; tax was higher on foreign-owned ships to favor American shippers.

Tordesillas, Treaty of Treaty negotiated by the pope in 1494 to resolve the territorial claims of Spain and Portugal. It drew a north-south line approximately 1,100 miles west of the Cape Verde Islands, granting all lands west of the line to Spain and all lands east of the line to Portugal. This limited Portugal's New World empire to Brazil but confirmed its claims in Africa and Asia.

Tories A derisive term applied to **Loyalists** in America who supported the king and Parliament just before and during the American Revolution. The term derived from late-seventeenth-century English politics when the Tory party supported the Duke of York's succession to the throne as James II. Later the Tory party favored the Church of England and the crown over dissenting denominations and Parliament.

Townshend Duty Act Act of Parliament, passed in 1767, imposing duties on colonial tea, lead, paint, paper, and glass. Designed to take advantage of the supposed American distinction between internal and external taxes, the Townshend duties were to help support government in America. The act prompted a successful colonial **nonimportation** movement.

Trail of Tears The forced march in 1838 of the Cherokee Indians from their homelands in Georgia to the Indian Territory in the West; thousands of Cherokees died along the way.

Transcendentalism A philosophical and literary movement centered on an idealistic belief in the divinity of individuals and nature.

Trans-Continental Treaty of 1819 Treaty between the United States and Spain in which Spain ceded Florida to the United States, surrendered all claims to the Pacific Northwest, and agreed to a boundary between the **Louisiana Purchase** territory and the Spanish Southwest.

Transportation revolution Dramatic improvements in transportation that stimulated economic growth after 1815 by expanding the range of travel and reducing the time and cost of moving goods and people.

Trenton, Battle of Revolutionary War clash that occurred on December 26, 1776, when General George Washington, who had withdrawn his forces into Pennsylvania, recrossed the Delaware River and surprised approximately fourteen hundred Hessians at Trenton, New Jersey, capturing or killing nearly one thousand.

Triangle Shirtwaist Company Clothing manufacturer whose New York factory burned in 1911, prompting outrage over unsafe working conditions and the passage of remedial legislation.

Tripartite Pact An alliance of Germany, Italy, and Japan signed in September 1941 in which each nation agreed to help the others in the event of an attack by the United States.

Truman Doctrine President Harry Truman's statement in 1947 that the United States should assist other nations that were facing external pressure or internal revolution; an important step in the escalation of the **Cold War.**

Tuskegee Institute Educational institution founded by Booker T. Washington in 1881 in rural Alabama to train blacks in agricultural and industrial skills.

Uncle Tom's Cabin Novel about slave life in the South by Harriet Beecher Stowe.

Underground Railroad Support system set up by antislavery groups in the Upper South and the North to assist fugitive slaves in escaping the South.

Underwood-Simmons Tariff Act The 1913 reform law that lowered tariff rates and levied the first regular federal income tax.

Unicameral legislature A legislative body composed of a single house.

Union League A **Republican party** organization in northern cities that became an important organizing device among freedmen in southern cities after 1865.

United Daughters of the Confederacy (UDC) Organization founded in 1892 to preserve southern history and honor its heroes; it reflected the growing role of middle class white women in public affairs.

United Nations During World War II, the name adopted by the United States, Britain, and their allies against Germany and Italy; after 1945, an international organization joined by nearly all nations.

United States v. *Cruikshank* The 1876 case in which the U.S. Supreme Court nullified the **Enforcement Act of 1870**, overturning the convictions of whites accused of violence against blacks in Louisiana and declaring that the **Fifteenth Amendment** did not sanction federal interference in matters that were clearly reserved for the states.

Universal manhood suffrage The right of all male U.S. citizens to vote; a key element of **Radical Republican** policy in the South after 1867.

Universal Negro Improvement Association (UNIA) A black nationalist movement organized by Marcus Garvey to promote black pride, unity, and economic **self-determination.**

U.S. Sanitary Commission Private, voluntary medical organization founded in May 1861 and dedicated to tending Union wounded and improving soldier comfort and morale during the Civil War.

Valley Forge Area of Pennsylvania approximately 20 miles northwest of Philadelphia where General George Washington's continental troops were quartered from December 1777 to June 1778 while British forces occupied Philadelphia during the Revolutionary War. Approximately 2,500 men, about a quarter of those encamped there, died of hardship and disease.

Versailles, Treaty of   The treaty ending World War I and creating the **League of Nations**.

Vertical integration   The consolidation of numerous production functions, from the extraction of the raw materials to the distribution and marketing of the finished products, under the direction of one firm.

Vice-admiralty courts   Royal courts established in the colonies to handle maritime cases and enforce the Acts of Trade. The enlarged role of these bodies, which operated without juries, was considered a grievance.

Vicksburg   Key Mississippi River port and rail junction that fell in July 1863 to a brilliant Union campaign by Ulysses S. Grant, commander of the Army of Tennessee, during the Civil War.

Viet Cong   Communist rebels in South Vietnam who fought the pro-American government established in South Vietnam in 1954.

Vincennes, Treaty of   Treaty of 1804 in which Americans claimed that Indian leaders ceded most of southern Indiana to the United States.

Virginia Company   One of two **joint-stock companies** chartered in 1606 to establish English colonies in America. Also known as the London Company, it organized the founding of the Virginia Colony. The company went bankrupt in 1624, and a year later Virginia became a royal colony.

Virginia Plan   Proposal of the Virginia delegation at the 1787 **Constitution Convention** calling for a national legislature in which the states would be represented according to population. The national legislature would have the explicit power to veto or overrule laws passed by state legislatures.

Virtual representation   The notion, current in eighteenth-century England, that parliamentary members represented the interests of the nation as a whole, not those of the particular district that elected them.

VISTA   Volunteers in Service to America, the "domestic Peace Corps" of the 1960s that gave individuals an opportunity to work on behalf of low-income communities in the United States.

Volstead Act   The 1920 law defining the liquor forbidden under the Eighteenth Amendment and giving enforcement responsibilities to the Prohibition Bureau of the Department of the Treasury.

Voting Rights Act   Legislation in 1965 that overturned a variety of practices by which states systematically denied voter registration to minorities.

Wade-Davis Bill   Congressional alternative to Lincoln's **Ten Percent Plan**, passed in 1864; required 50 percent of prewar voters to pledge their loyalty and demanded guarantees for black equality. The president exercised a pocket veto, and it never became law.

Wagner National Labor Relations Act   The 1935 law guaranteeing workers' rights to organize unions and establishing the **National Labor Relations Board**.

Waltham system   During the industrialization of the early nineteenth century, the recruitment of unmarried young women for employment in factories.

War Hawks   Members of Congress, predominantly from the South and West, who aggressively pushed for a war against Britain after their election in 1810.

War Industries Board (WIB)   The federal agency that reorganized industry for maximum efficiency and productivity during World War I.

War Manpower Commission   Federal agency established in 1942 to allocate workers among the armed services, defense industries, and essential civilian industries.

War of 1812   War fought between the United States and Britain from June 1812 to January 1815 largely over British restrictions on American shipping.

War of the Austrian Succession   A small conflict between Britain and Spain that began in 1739 and widened into a larger European war in 1740 (lasting until 1748) when the king of Prussia attacked lands claimed by Austria's ruling family. Known in America as **King George's War**.

War of the League of Augsburg   Conflict in Europe (1688–1697) that pitted France against Spain, Sweden, the Holy Roman Empire, the Dutch republic, various German principalities, and, in 1689, England. The principal aim was to halt the growing power of France's Louis XIV. In America, this was known as **King William's War**.

War of the Spanish Succession   European conflict (1702–1713) that began in a struggle between the king of France and the Holy Roman emperor over claims to the Spanish throne. England, Holland, and the Holy Roman Empire fought France and Spain in a war known in America as **Queen Anne's War**.

War on Poverty   Set of programs introduced by Lyndon Johnson between 1963 and 1966 designed to break the cycle of poverty by providing funds for job training, community development, nutrition, and supplementary education.

War Production Board   Federal agency established in 1942 to coordinate defense production and allocate scarce resources to serve the war effort.

Warsaw Pact   Military alliance of the Soviet Union and Communist nations in eastern Europe from 1955 to 1989.

Washington Temperance Societies   **Temperance** associations dominated by mechanics and laborers that first formed in Baltimore in 1840.

Watergate   A complex scandal involving attempts to cover up illegal actions taken by administration officials and leading to the resignation of President Richard Nixon in 1974.

Weather Underground   Fringe group of former members of **Students for a Democratic Society**, 1969–1970, who emphasized confrontation and violence.

Webster-Ashburton Treaty   Treaty signed by the United States and Britain in 1842 that settled a boundary dispute between Maine and Canada and provided for closer cooperation in suppressing the African slave trade.

Welfare capitalism   A paternalistic system of labor relations emphasizing management responsibility for employee well-being. While providing some limited benefits, its function was primarily to forestall the formation of unions or public intervention.

Wesley Houses   Organizations modeled after the **settlement houses** of the North that began appearing in southern cities under the auspices of the Methodist Church in the 1890s to serve working-class neighborhoods.

Western Federation of Miners   A large and radical union of western miners formed in Butte, Montana, in 1893 to coordinate local unions' resistance to corporate threats to workers' wages, working conditions, and health.

Whig party   Political party formed in the mid-1830s in opposition to the **Jacksonian Democrats** that favored a strong role for the national government in promoting economic growth.

Whigs   The name used by advocates of colonial resistance to British measures during the 1760s and 1770s. The Whig party in England unsuccessfully attempted to exclude the Catholic Duke of York from succession to the throne as James II; victorious in the **Glorious**

Revolution, the Whigs later stood for religious toleration and the supremacy of Parliament over the crown.

Whiskey Rebellion   Armed uprising in 1794 by farmers in western Pennsylvania who attempted to prevent the collection of the excise tax on whiskey.

White League   One of several military organizations operating openly and in concert with the **Democratic party** in the South to thwart black voting rights during **Reconstruction**.

White Plains, Battle of   Revolutionary War engagement that took place on October 28, 1776, between General George Washington's troops, evacuating New York City, and British forces under Sir William Howe. Washington sustained more than three hundred casualties before withdrawing his troops.

Wide Awakes   Group of red-shirted, black-caped young men who paraded through city streets in the North extolling the virtues of the **Republican party** during the 1860 presidential election campaign.

Wilderness Act   Law, the Wilderness Areas Act, that in 1964 designated certain federal lands as parts of the National Wilderness Preservation System, consisting originally of 9.1 million acres.

Wilderness, Battle of the   Civil War clash between Confederate and Union forces near Chancellorsville in May 1864 marked by fierce hand-to-hand combat in dense woods.

Wilmot Proviso   Never-approved amendment to a **Mexican War** appropriations bill that would ban slavery from any territory acquired from Mexico, submitted to Congress by Pennsylvania Democrat David Wilmot.

Wobblies   Popular name for the members of the **Industrial Workers of the World (IWW)**.

Woman suffrage   The right of women to vote, achieved in the **Nineteenth Amendment**.

Women's Christian Temperance Union (WCTU)   National organization formed after the Civil War dedicated to prohibiting the sale and distribution of alcohol.

Woodstock Generation   Members of the late 1960s **counterculture**, named for a rock festival held in New York State in August 1969.

Workingmen's movement   Associations of urban workers who began campaigning in the 1820s for free public education and a ten-hour workday.

Works Progress Administration (WPA)   Key **New Deal** agency that provided work relief for the unemployed.

World Bank   Officially the International Bank for Reconstruction and Development, an international organization established in 1945 that assists governments around the world in economic development efforts.

Wounded Knee Massacre   The U.S. Army's brutal winter massacre in 1890 of 150 Sioux men, women, and children as part of the government's assault on the tribe's Ghost Dance religion.

Writs of assistance   Documents issued by a court of law that gave British officials in America the power to search for smuggled goods wherever they wished. The legality of these writs became an important cause of controversy in Massachusetts in 1761 and 1762.

Wyoming Valley   Pennsylvania site where, in June and July 1778, a force comprised of Iroquois Indians and **Tories** under colonel John Butler routed **Patriot** defenders and laid waste to settlements during the Revolutionary War.

XYZ Affair   Diplomatic incident in 1798 in which Americans were outraged by the demand of the French for a bribe as a condition for negotiating with American diplomats.

Yalta Conference   Meeting of U.S. President Franklin Roosevelt, British Prime Minister Winston Churchill, and Soviet Premier Joseph Stalin held in February 1945 to plan the final stages of World War II and postwar arrangements.

Yellow-dog contracts   Employment agreements binding workers not to join a union.

Yellow press   A deliberately sensational journalism of scandal and exposure designed to attract an urban mass audience and increase advertising revenues.

Yippies   Fringe group of radical activists, 1968–1972, who emphasized media events.

Yorktown, Siege of   Final major decisive engagement of the Revolutionary War in which American and French forces under Generals Washington and Rochambeau laid siege to British forces under Lord Cornwallis at Yorktown, Virginia, from August 30 to October 19, 1781. The surrender of approximately eight thousand British troops on October 19 led to the British government's decision to end the war.

Young America   Mid-nineteenth-century movement that espoused strong nationalistic views and the desire to expand American influence overseas.

INDEX